Fishes of the Gulf of Mexico

Volume 1

Fishes of the Gulf of Mexico

John D. McEachran and Janice D. Fechhelm

Volume 1: Myxiniformes to Gasterosteiformes

University of Texas Press, Austin

Requests for permission to reproduce material from
this work should be sent to Permissions, University of
Texas Press, P.O. Box 7819, Austin, TX 78713-7819.

⊚ The paper used in this publication meets the mini-
mum requirements of American National Standard for
Information Sciences—Permanence of Paper for
Printed Library Materials, ANSI Z39.48-1984.

Library of Congress Cataloging-in-Publication Data

McEachran, John D.
    Fishes of the Gulf of Mexico / John D. McEachran
and Janice D. Fechhelm. — 1st ed.
        p.   cm.
    Includes bibliographical references and index.
    ISBN 0-292-75206-7 (cl : alk. paper : v. 1)
    1. Fishes—Mexico, Gulf of.   2. Fishes—Mexico,
Gulf of—Identification.   I. Fechhelm, Janice D.
II. Title.   2005
    QL621.56.M383   ~~1998~~ v. 1
    597.177'364—dc21   98-4605

CONTENTS

ACKNOWLEDGMENTS

This book had a serendipitous beginning and a rather chaotic evolution. Amy Broussard, feature editor for the Texas A&M University Sea Grant Office, approached us about revising Edward O. Murdy's *Saltwater Fishes of Texas*. Initially we decided to expand the coverage to the continental shelf fishes of the northern Gulf of Mexico to serve as an update of H. Dickson Hoese and Richard H. Moore's *Fishes of the Gulf of Mexico: Texas, Louisiana and Adjacent Waters*. Within a short time the project grew into a treatment of the fish fauna of the entire Gulf of Mexico. Despite the expanded scope, both Amy Broussard and the Director of the Texas A&M University Sea Grant Office, Dr. Thomas Bright, were supportive. Amy was also instrumental in soliciting support from the Gulf Coast Conservation Association (GCCA) and Exxon Company, USA. The financial support from the Texas A&M University Sea Grant Office, the GCCA, and the Exxon Company over a five-year period provided the impetus needed to obtain a Survey and Inventory Grant from the National Science Foundation (NSF). The NSF grant provided the funds to complete the first volume and to make significant progress on the second volume of the treatise.

A large number of systematic ichthyologists and curators of natural history museums have made major contributions to this work, and their inputs are gratefully acknowledged. Steven G. Branstetter critically read the shark accounts in the chondrichthyan section and offered numerous suggestions. George H. Burgess provided several new records of shark species from the Gulf of Mexico. Raymond R. Wilson, Jr., read and commented on the clupeiform section. David G. Smith critically reviewed the anguilliform section and offered many valuable suggestions. Douglas F. Markle read the alepocephalid and platytroctid accounts in the osmeriform section. Tracey Sutton provided a long list of new records of stomiiform species in the Gulf, and critically read the stomiiform section and contributed life history information for the species accounts. Kenneth J. Sulak provided valuable suggestions on the aulopiform section. John V. Gartner provided suggestions for the key to species and life history information for the species accounts of the myctophiform section. Daniel M. Cohen and C. Richard Robins critically reviewed the ophidiiform section. Jørgen Nielsen provided new records and descriptive data on species of ophidiiform fishes. Tomio Iwamoto read and improved the macrourid account of the gadiform section. Bruce B. Collette read the batrachoidiform and beloniform sections, and provided suggestions and data for the species accounts. Theodore W. Pietsch read and commented on the lophiiform section. John R. Paxton provided valuable comments on the stephanoberyciform section. Richard E. Matheson read and offered suggestions on the atheriniform and cyprinodontiform chapters. William N. Eschmeyer provided information on the correct spelling of generic and specific names and on authors and dates of publications of species. John W. Tunnell, Jr., provided a preliminary checklist of fishes inhabiting the coral reefs of the southwestern Gulf of Mexico that he, Mary E. Vega, and John E. Gourley prepared. Reznat Darnell gave considerable information on the ecology and distribution of fishes in the Gulf of Mexico. Kasten Hartel provided a listing of the species of fishes from the Gulf of Mexico housed at the Museum of Comparative Zoology, Cambridge, Massachusetts. Jeffrey T. Williams provided computer records of the species of fishes of the Gulf of Mexico residing at the National Museum of Natural History, Washington, D.C. The following curators are thanked for their hospitality during our visits to their collections and for loaning us specimens: Kasten Hartel, Susan Jewett, Jeffrey T. Williams, George H. Burgess, Richard E. Matheson and Mark Lieby, Stuart G. Poss, Barry Chrenoff, and Hank Bart. The following students of John D. McEachran are thanked for various contributions made during the course of this project: Jeffrey N. Childes, Johanna C. Craig, Sabrina Criscome, Katherine A. Dunn, Michael J. Grose, Thomas Henley, and Hera Konstantinou. Hera Konstantinou was especially helpful in adapting figures to accompany the keys to the orders of fishes and species of fishes.

The following institutions granted permission to reproduce copyrighted figures: Species Identification and Data Center of the Fisheries, Food, and Agriculture Organization of the United Nations; Harvard University Museums of Natural History; Bingham Laboratories of Yale University; and the National Museum of Natural History, Smithsonian Institution.

Financial support was provided by the National Science Foundation, Long Term Programs in Environmental Biology (Grant No. DEB-9400842); Texas A&M University Sea Grant Program; Gulf Coast Conservation Association; and Exxon Company, USA. Part of the research was carried out in the Center for Biosystematics and Biodiversity, a facility funded, in part, by the National Science Foundation (Grant No. DIR-8907006), and this work represents Contribution Number 56 to the Center for Biosystematics and Biodiversity at Texas A & M University.

Special thanks is given to our family members—Carolyn and Zachary, and Bob, Lauren, and Kristen—for their support during the extended life of this project.

INTRODUCTION

Scope of the Book

This book is an attempt to provide a single reference to the identification and description of the fishes that occur in the Gulf of Mexico. Although much has been written on fishes of the Gulf of Mexico, the literature is scattered among a larger number of revisionary studies of higher taxa of fishes, many regional faunal studies of other areas, and countless short papers and notes in the primary literature. The proposed audience of the book is the scientists, students, and fishers with interests in the fishes of this region.

A key is provided for the 44 orders of fishes known to occur in the Gulf of Mexico. The orders and families are arranged phylogenetically, and keys are provided for all families within each order known to occur in the Gulf. Families within each order are described and distinguished from the other families of the order. Following the family accounts, keys are provided for all species within the family that are known from the Gulf. Each of these species is arranged alphabetically, described, and distinguished from the other species within the family, and most are illustrated. Information is provided on the distribution of the fishes, both within the Gulf and worldwide. Life history information is also provided for each species, but this information is greatly condensed because of the large number of species included. However, references are provided at the end of each species account for those interested in further information.

In some respects, the family accounts and especially the species accounts are redundant in that the same characters are covered for all families within an order and for all species within a family. Thus, as a result of our attempt to make the descriptions self-contained and as consistent as possible, portions of these descriptions may be very similar. Another approach would be to present a full description for the first family of each order and first species of each family within each order, and to simply discuss the distinctions of the remaining taxa of the order or family. This approach was judged to be too subjective, and it would make the descriptive material less available to the reader, who would have to turn to the account of the first family or species of the taxon to get a complete description of the family or species of interest. Alternatively, keys to and descriptions of the genera within each family could be provided. Many of the species descriptions would then occur once in the generic description. This approach would have shortened the book slightly by reducing the redundancy of the species descriptions. However, many of the genera that occur in the Gulf are widespread to worldwide, with numerous species outside the area covered by this book, and in many cases the morphological variation and total number of species within these genera are not well established. Thus descriptions of many of these genera would be vague or inaccurate. On the other hand, morphological variation within the families that occur in the Gulf is readily available (Nelson 1994). The value of the approach adapted for this book is that a reader can use the key to identify specimens at hand and then turn to the family or species account for a full description.

In keeping with the philosophy of making the descriptions as complete and as objective as possible, the family and species accounts are not comparative; that is, the taxon under discussion is not compared with related taxa. Such comparisons tend to be subjective and often are of little value in distinguishing between taxa.

The phylogenetic ranking and sequencing largely follow Nelson (1994), with several exceptions. Sphyrnidae are considered a family separate from Carcharhinidae despite the fact that carcharhinids are not monophyletic without inclusion of sphyrnids (Nelson 1994). The reason for maintaining this more traditional albeit nonmonophyletic classification is that the interrelationships within carcharhinids are poorly known and the sister group of the sphyrnids is not entirely clear. Squaliformes are classified into three families according to Compagno (1984), rather than into the four families recognized by Nelson, following the sequencing of Shirai (1992). Shirai divided Squalidae (*sensu lato*) into six families; however, some of these families are nearly as morphologically diverse as the entire order. Accepting Shirai's classification would cause problems in constructing keys and in defining the families, and his classification has not been rigorously tested. The electric rays (Narcinidae and Torpedinidae), the sawfishes (Pristidae), the guitarfishes and skates (Rhinobatidae and Rajidae), and the stingrays (Dasyatidae, Gymnuridae, Mobulidae, Myliobatidae, Rhinopteridae, and Urolophidae) are placed in separate orders rather than classified in the same order (Rajiformes) because they form natural groups (are monophyletic), and with the exception of the electric rays, they date back to the Jurassic or Cretaceous in the fossil record. These orders (Torpediniformes, Pristiformes, Rajiformes, and Myliobatiformes) are placed after the Hexanchiformes, Squaliformes, and Squatiniformes because the three orders of sharks plus the Pristiophoriformes and the four orders of rays are considered to constitute a monophyletic group (Shirai 1992). Halosauridae and Notacanthidae are placed in their own order (Notacanthiformes) rather than in the order

Albuliformes with Albulidae. The two orders are thought to form a monophyletic group, but they are treated separately because of their distinctive body forms. Nelson follows Fink (1985) in lumping six of the families of Stomiiformes—Astronesthidae, Chauliodontidae, Idiacanthidae, Malacosteidae, Melanostomiidae, and Stomiidae—into a single family (Stomiidae). According to Fink, all six families constitute a monophyletic group, but some of the families, as traditionally recognized, are not monophyletic (do not share a common ancestor). To avoid further confusion by reallocating genera among the six families, Fink proposed lumping all of the genera within the six families into a single family (Stomiidae). The traditional view of the order is accepted herein because Fink's study has not been rigorously tested nor extensively used in the literature.

The information on the species composition of the Gulf of Mexico came from an extensive review of the literature and unpublished species lists, and from a survey of the natural history museums in the United States and Mexico. The following institutions all have extensive collections of fishes from the Gulf of Mexico: American Museum of Natural History (AMNH), New York, NY; Field Museum of Natural History (FMNH), Chicago, IL; Florida Museum of Natural History (FM), Gainesville, FL; Gulf Coast Research Laboratory (GCRL), Gulf Port, MS; Museum of Comparative Zoology (MCZ), Cambridge, MA; National Museum of Natural History (USNM), Washington, D.C.; Texas Cooperative Wildlife Collection (TCWC), College Station, TX; Tulane University Museum of Natural History (TU), New Orleans, LA; and Universidad Nacional Autónoma de México (UNAM), Mexico City. Considerable time was spent at these institutions developing lists of species previously unrecorded from the Gulf and using specimens to write descriptions and to prepare illustrations. When possible, illustrations were prepared partially or totally from museum specimens, but if specimens were unavailable or if available specimens were unrepresentative of the species, illustrations were adapted from those in the literature. In the latter case, when possible, the adapted illustrations were compared with museum specimens.

Because of the large number of species of fishes in the Gulf of Mexico, this book is divided into two volumes. This first volume treats the first 40 orders arranged in ascending phylogenetic sequence. The second volume, which will be published at a later date, will cover the remaining 4 orders.

Physical and Biological Description of the Gulf of Mexico

Overview

The Gulf of Mexico is a partially isolated body of water bordering the southeastern section of North America and straddling the Tropic of Cancer (Fig. A). With a surface area of 1,138,980 km² and 4,000 km of coastline, it is the ninth largest body of water in the world. The maximum depth of the Gulf is 3,750 m in the Sigsbee Deep off Mexico. Its eastern border, and connection with the Atlantic Ocean and the Caribbean Sea, is a line from Key West to Cape Catoche. Thus its eastern border is west of both the Florida Keys and the coast of Cuba. The northern border of the Gulf of Mexico is formed by the shoreline of the U.S. states of Florida, Alabama, Mississippi, Louisiana, and Texas, and the southern border is formed by the shoreline of the Mexican states of Tamaulipas, Veracruz, Tabasco, Campeche, and Yucatán.

The Gulf of Mexico is both a warm temperate and a tropical body of water. The northern section, from Cape Romano, Florida, in the east to Cabo Rojo, Veracruz, in the west, is part of the Carolinian Warm Temperate Provence, and is separated from the remainder of the Carolinian Provence by the tropical, southern portion of the Florida peninsula (Briggs 1974). The southern section, south of the two capes, is tropical and contiguous with the tropical western Atlantic.

FIG A

Low sandy banks or marshlands characterize the northern and southern shores of the Gulf, with extensive barrier beaches, dunes, salt marshes, and mangroves, depending on local conditions (Britton and Morton 1989). The coastline and continental shelves of the Gulf of Mexico are largely the result of three geological phenomena: alluvial deposits, biogenic limestone deposits, and orogenic volcanic deposits (Price 1954). Coasts and continental shelves of alluvial origin extend along the northern Gulf from Tamaulipas to the Florida Panhandle, and along the southern Gulf from Veracruz to western Campeche. Alluvial sediments have produced broad continental shelves (up to 210 km wide), with smooth shorelines of sandy beaches or barrier islands and rather smooth gradation of sediments, from sand inshore to mud, silt, or clay offshore. The coasts are often interrupted by river deltas, which are most extensive along the northern Gulf. Biogenic limestone, which formed in shallow marine areas during much of the life of the Gulf, dominates the coasts of Florida and Yucatán and has built continental shelves up to 160 km wide. In areas where land-derived sediments are scarce, the limestone platforms have become biogenic environments, supporting coral, mollusc, and other reef-building biota. Such communities thrive off the west coasts of Florida and Yucatán and on a variety of hard structures around the Gulf. Orogenic activity along the western Gulf of Mexico has resulted in a very narrow continental shelf, with the mountains' structural folds and faults paralleling the coastline.

The coastline is punctuated by a number of barrier islands and drowned river mouths that form estuaries. The barrier islands result from longshore transport of coastal sediments. When these islands form in front of river mouths, they give rise to primary bays with reduced exchange with the open Gulf through narrow tidal passes. Salinity of these bays is related to the magnitude of the freshwater source. Along the northern and southern coasts of the Gulf the salinities of the bays are brackish to hyposaline, while in the western Gulf, where river flow is minimal, the salinities are often hypersaline.

The sediments of the Gulf are a result of past geological events and present sediment patterns. The area east of DeSoto Canyon, southward along the Florida coast and along the west coast of Yucatán, is thickly covered with carbonate sediments, and the area west of this region is covered with thick terriginous sediments (Pequegnat et al. 1990). The northeastern Gulf is a carbonate bank that has been subsiding since the Cretaceous. The shelf off south Florida is a mosaic of soft sand and hard carbonate bottom covered with a thin veneer of sand (Antoine 1972). Rocky outcroppings are rare off south Florida except for the Florida Middle Grounds, which consist of steep-profile limestone escarpments and knolls rising 10 to 15 m above the sand and shell bottom. The Yucatán platform and Campeche Bank are very similar to the south Florida platform. In the northern Gulf, terriginous sediments increase westward of DeSoto Canyon. The shelf off the Florida Panhandle and Alabama is transitional, grading from sandy and shelly in the east to finer, terriginous sediments in the west. The northwestern Gulf is a geosyncline sinking under the weight of the terriginous sediments that have been deposited here over much of the life of the Gulf. The sediment pattern in this region has been altered by salt diapirism, or movement of salt upward through the overlying sediments. The salt was deposited early in the Gulf's history, when the Gulf was an evaporative basin, and prior to the tectonic forces that formed the deep-sea basin. The salt is rising through the sediments because it is less dense. The southern Gulf is similar to the northwestern Gulf in sediments and salt diapirism. Organic sediments, primarily from terrestrial sources, have also been trapped by the sediment load in the northern Gulf and have produced both petroleum and natural gas deposits. On the continental slope off Louisiana and east Texas there are over 40 locations of petroleum and natural gas seeps (Pequegnat et al. 1990). These areas possess rich, unique assemblages of invertebrate organisms. Chemo-autotrophic bacteria are the primary producers of these communities (Childress et al. 1986).

Although terriginous sediments predominate in the northern Gulf, these sediments are punctuated by topographic features of diverse origins (Rezak et al. 1990). These features are present at various depths, but they serve as hard-bottom substrates for biota of the Gulf. The Flower Gardens Reef off Louisiana and east Texas is built on two salt-dome formations and is the most northern coral reef in the western Atlantic. Smaller reefs occur along the outer continental shelf off Alabama, and near shore off southern Texas, Tamaulipas, and Veracruz.

Geological History of the Gulf of Mexico

Recent plate tectonic studies suggest that the Gulf of Mexico has had a long and stable history. It formed as a result of the breakup of the supercontinent Pangaea that existed during much of the late Paleozoic and early Mesozoic eras, and in the subsequent breakup of Gondwanaland, the southern half of Pangaea, during the late Mesozoic and early Cenozoic (Pindell and Dewey 1982; Pindell 1985). In the Late Triassic (200 million years ago [Ma]), the Gulf region was occupied by continental blocks that were to become Yucatán, Florida, and the western Bahamas. About 165 Ma, northwestern Africa and South America began to separate from North America, and this rift resulted in sea-floor spreading north of the Blake Plateau and continental stretching in the area of the Blake Plateau and the Straits of Florida. These events caused the Yucatán block to separate from the area now occupied by Texas and Louisiana, and a chain of continental blocks, now comprising Mexico and northern Central America, to move southeastward into the area previously occupied by South America. The Mexican blocks previously abutted against the northwestern section of South America. As the Yucatán block moved away from Texas and Louisiana it rotated counterclockwise, and the area that it previously occupied became a ma-

rine basin, the Proto-Caribbean. The stretching of the continental crust in the Gulf region caused it to subside and dip below sea level. Subsequent breaching of the western land barrier led to the intrusion of sea water, and the Gulf region became a shallow evaporation basin forming the Louann-Campeche salt deposit. In the late Jurassic (150 Ma), sea-floor spreading began in the Gulf region, leading to a deep central basin and open circulation with the Proto-Atlantic Ocean between Florida and the Yucatán blocks. The open circulation and deepening brought an end to the salt deposition. During this period the blocks representing Mexico and northern Central America continued their southeastern rotation, and the Yucatán block continued to rotate counterclockwise until about 140 Ma, in the early Cretaceous, when the tip of the Mexican blocks and the Yucatán blocks became juxtaposed (joined). The uniting of the Mexican and the Yucatán blocks brought to a close the horizontal plate motions associated with the opening of the Gulf of Mexico, and the Gulf of Mexico was formed.

Since its formation, the Gulf of Mexico has been rather tectonically stable. Its present physiography is largely due to marine carbonate deposition beginning in the Cretaceous, terriginous deposition in the west and central Gulf from the Late Cretaceous to the Eocene, severe sedimentary deposition and migration of salt upward along the northern and western Gulf that continues to the present time, and major changes in sea level that began in the Miocene.

One relatively recent tectonic event—closure of the trans-America sea passage at the end of the Miocene (5 Ma)—has had important effects on the Gulf of Mexico. Its closure forced the North Equatorial Current northward and thus formed or greatly strengthened the Gulf Stream. The latter swings into the Gulf of Mexico through the Yucatán Straits, between Cape Catoche, Yucatán, and Cuba, then moves westward to form the Loop Current that regularly penetrates to the mouth of the Mississippi River before turning eastward and exiting the

Gulf through the Florida Straits. The Loop Current periodically gives off warm-core rings that spin off the Loop Current and move into the western Gulf. Both the Loop Current and the warm-core rings affect circulation and climate in the Gulf.

Currents and Tides in the Gulf of Mexico

The Gulf of Mexico is affected by three types of currents: currents related to the density of sea water, currents produced by the stress of winds, and tidal currents. In the eastern Gulf the pattern of sea-surface circulation is largely controlled by the influx of water from the tropical Caribbean Sea through the Yucatán Channel (176 km wide). Much of this water forms an S-shaped swirl that moves northwesterly, forming the Loop Current that flows southeasterly through the Straits of Florida (144 km wide) to form the Gulf Stream (Leipper 1954b, 1970). The northward and westward extensions of the Loop Current vary both seasonally and yearly but are known to intrude upon the continental shelf of the northern Gulf of Mexico to just east of the Mississippi River (Darnell and Defenbaugh 1990).

The western Gulf of Mexico is dominated by a cyclonic circulatory pattern in Campeche Bay, an anticyclonic pattern north of Campeche Bay, and a variable cyclonic pattern in the northwestern Gulf (Merrill and Morrison 1981). The southern cyclonic circulation is generated by wind stress. The anticyclonic circulation is fed by anticyclonic rings that are pinched off the Loop Current and migrate into the western Gulf (Elliot 1982; Kirwan et al. 1984), and by wind-generated currents (Sturges and Biaha 1976; Sturges 1993). The relative importance of the anticyclonic gyres and the curl of wind stress is a matter of debate (Sturges 1993). The cyclonic circulation in the northwestern Gulf is the result of a low-pressure trough formed when the Loop Current is fully extended into the eastern Gulf. When this occurs, a well-defined cyclonic cold-water gyre is formed from the trough, and it migrates westward to lie north of the anti-

cyclonic gyre. The two-ring system causes eastward flow of surface water at about 24°30′N in the western Gulf. The northern cyclonic circulatory pattern is the most variable of the three systems in the western Gulf because a defined cyclonic gyre is only formed when the Loop Current is fully extended, and the Loop Current is not fully extended into the Gulf on a yearly basis (Merrill and Morrison 1981).

In winter the currents in the western Gulf are affected by northern winds, or "northers," that may cause fragmentation of westerly currents and reverse the direction of longshore drift of sediments.

The tides of the Gulf of Mexico are of rather low magnitude, ranging from 0.4 to 0.7 m in amplitude, and vary from diurnal (one high and one low tide per day) to mixed (varying between one high and one low per day to two lows and two highs per day) (Marmer 1954; Britton and Morton 1989). Despite the relatively small tidal amplitude, the extensive area of the continental shelves and the large number of shallow-water estuaries and lagoons can lead to significant tidal effects.

Freshwater Input and Sediment Patterns

The Gulf receives about 10.6×10^{11} m³ per year of freshwater, with about 85% of this coming from 44 major U.S. rivers. About 65% of the total is contributed by the Mississippi system alone (Darnell and Defenbaugh 1990). The Rio Grande has contributed little freshwater and sediments since the Miocene. The major Mexican freshwater sources—the Tonalá, Seco, Grijalva, Teapao, Usumacinta, San Pedro y San Pablo, and Palizada Rivers—enter the southern Gulf of Mexico.

These freshwater sources are also the major sources of terriginous sediments of the Gulf of Mexico, which dominate in the northern and southern Gulf. The Mississippi River is the dominant source of sediments, contributing about 4.1×10^{10} metric tons of sediment per year (Darnell and Defenbaugh 1990). Most of the sediment is deposited on the slope and the deep Gulf, but a significant amount is deposited on the shelves of Louisiana and east Texas (Darnell and Defenbaugh 1990).

Meteorology

The surface temperatures in the Gulf of Mexico during the summer are largely isothermal, about 29°C, but surface temperatures increase from north to south in the Gulf during the winter months, averaging 18.3°C in the north and 23.9°C in the south (Leipper 1954a). The temperature gradient is greater in the east than in the west. The annual range of sea-surface temperature varies from about 5.6°C to 8.3°C in the north and about 5.6°C in the central and southern areas of the Gulf.

During the spring and summer the weather in the Gulf of Mexico is dominated by the Bermuda High. Air temperatures are high and uniform. Winds blow predominately from the southeast but are slightly more southerly in the northern Gulf and slightly more easterly in the southern Gulf. The higher water temperatures of the Gulf compared to those of the western Atlantic and eastern Pacific cause an increase in moisture content of the air over the Gulf and thus affect precipitation during the warmer months of the year. During the winter the winds blow more easterly, with occasional winds from the south and from the north. The southeasterly winds bring warm moist air from lower latitudes and transport it from the warmer waters of the southern Gulf to the colder waters of the northern Gulf. This circulation pattern leads to precipitation and fog in the northern Gulf.

During the winter the northern Gulf is subjected to 15 to 20 one- to three-day periods of north winds. These winds have speeds of about 20 knots and are capable of rapidly decreasing the land and inshore water temperatures along the northern coast, and the decrease often leads to spectacular fish kills.

The Gulf is subjected to hurricanes during the late summer and early fall, and about 80% of these form in the warm waters of the tropical Atlantic and enter the Gulf through the Straits of Yucatán. An average of nine hurricanes per year develop in the Atlantic, and many of these enter the Gulf. These storms are destructive to the biotas of the Gulf, especially to those living in bays and lagoons and over the shallow areas of the continental shelf, and to the humans living along the shoreline and coastal plain.

Biological Assemblages

Although soft sand to silty sediments are widespread, the habitats of the Gulf of Mexico are extremely diverse; in fact, the richness of habitats may rival those anywhere in North America (Britton and Morton 1989). The assemblages are demarcated by salinity, temperature, depth, and substratum.

The inshore waters vary from brackish to hypersaline, from warm temperate to tropical, and from silty mud to igneous rock or limestone reefs, and the biota vary with these habitat parameters. Estuaries are common habitats along the northern, eastern, and to a lesser extent, southern shores of the Gulf. They formed as a result of the drowning of river mouths after the last glacial period and by the formation of barrier islands. These habitats vary in salinity with the amount of freshwater flow and have soft, level floors of mud and silt. Estuaries are bordered by marsh grasses (*Spartina* species) in the northern Gulf and by mangroves in south Florida and in the southern Gulf. Despite high levels of sediment input, estuaries have stands of submergent vegetation such as *Thalassia testudinum, Halodule wrightii, Ruppia maritima,* and *Syringodium filiforme,* and oyster reefs, *Crassostrea virginica.* The grass beds and oyster reefs support distinct faunal assemblages, including a number of fish species. In general the fishes that inhabit estuaries are salt-tolerant (euryhaline) marine fishes. Euryhaline freshwater fishes have been less successful in occupying estuaries than their marine equivalents. Freshwater fishes occupy the more brackish areas in the estuaries and include sturgeons (Acipenseridae), gars (Lepisosteidae), killifishes (Cyprinodontidae), and livebearers (Poeciliidae). Estuaries serve as nursery grounds for a large number of marine fishes that live on the inner continental shelves, such as the anchovies (Engraulidae), herrings (Clupeidae), mojarras (Gerreidae), and drums (Sciaenidae). The fish faunal composition does not change with increase in salinity among estuaries except that species diversity declines with increase in salinity.

Mangrove habitats, which grow along tropical shorelines and estuaries protected from waves and high currents, provide a habitat for a variety of organisms. The dominant vegetation is the red mangrove *Rhizophora mangle* and the black mangrove *Avicennia germinans* that largely define the habitat of the coastline along southern Florida and much of Mexico. Fish fauna is similar to that found in the warm temperate estuaries of the northern Gulf except that diversity is higher because of the structured habitats provided by the mangrove roots. This substratum attracts gobies (Gobiidae), blennies (Blenniidae), and puffers (Tetraodontidae), in addition to sciaenids, grunts (Pomadasyidae), and gerreids. The mangrove habitats also serve as nursery grounds for a number of fishes that spend their adult life on coral reefs.

Along the seaside of barrier islands and coastlines devoid of estuaries, sandy beaches predominate. These habitats are rigorous environments for both animals and plants because of the surf and lack of cover. The fauna is dominated by burrowing bivalves and pelagic fauna. Fishes found along the sandy beaches include ladyfish (Elopidae), clupeids, engraulids, and juveniles of a variety of spiny-rayed fishes.

Natural rocky shorelines are uncommon in the Gulf, except for Veracruz, but artificial jetties and groins are now of common occurrence. These structures support fishes common on coral reefs that feed on attached algae and sessile invertebrates. Fishes frequenting this habitat include damselfishes (Pomacentridae), spadefishes (Ephippidae), wrasses (Labridae), puffers (Tetraodontidae), and filefishes and triggerfishes (Balistidae).

The continental shelf, a gently sloping plain extending to about 183 m in depth, extends outward from the shoreline. This habitat is rather extensive in the Gulf and supports several assemblages of fishes. From the shoreline to about 20 m the fish fauna is dominated by sea catfishes (Ariidae), lizardfishes (Synodontidae), and sciaenids. These fishes are heavily dependent on the estuaries as nursery grounds and are associated with the white shrimp *Penaeus setiferus*, and for that reason the assemblage is referred to as the white-shrimp assemblage (Chittenden and McEachran 1976). Seaward of the white-shrimp community to a depth of about 40 to 50 m, on muddy bottoms, the fish fauna is dominated by pogies (Sparidae), batfishes (Ogcocephalidae), searobins (Triglidae), sea basses (Serranidae), and left-eyed flounders (Bothidae). These fishes are largely independent of the estuaries as nursery grounds and are associated with the brown shrimp *Penaeus aztecus*. Thus this assemblage is referred to as the brown-shrimp assemblage (Chittenden and McEachran 1976). At the same depth, but on shelly or hard bottoms, is a slightly different assemblage dominated by snappers (Lutjanidae) and other spiny-rayed fishes with a preference for hard substrata.

The outer continental shelf is less affected by seasonal temperature cycles and has a soft mud to silty bottom. Fishes dominating this habitat include hake (Phycidae), scorpionfishes (Scorpaenidae), and ogcocephalids.

The Gulf also has extensive areas of hard substrata that support coral-reef assemblages. The west coasts of Florida and Yucatán possess the majority of these habitats, but a large-scale reef complex also occurs off western Louisiana and eastern Texas, the East and West Flower Gardens Reefs (Bright and Cashman 1974), and in several areas off the east coast of Mexico. These habitats support diverse fish assemblages dominated by morays (Muraenidae), serranids, butterflyfishes (Chaetodontidae), angelfishes (Pomacanthidae), wrasses (Labridae), and gobies (Gobiidae).

The continental slope extends from the edge of the shelf to about 2,000 m. This region has little sunlight; cold temperatures (4°C to 12°C); and soft, silty bottoms. Cutthroat eels (Synaphobranchidae), macrourids (Macrouridae), and cusk-eels (Ophidiidae) dominate this habitat. The continental rise extends from the slope to the bottom of the Gulf. Eels of various families as well as synaphobranchids, macrourids, viviparous brotulas (Bythitidae), and ophidiids are the abundant fishes in this habitat.

The pelagic waters are traditionally divided into three subdivisions: the epipelagic realm, from the surface to 200 m; the mesopelagic realm, from 200 to 1,000 m; and the bathypelagic realm, below 1,000 m. The epipelagic zone is subdivided into the area that overlies the continental shelf (neritic zone) and that seaward of the continental shelf (oceanic zone). The neritic zone has two main assemblages, one associated with flotsam and Sargassum weed and one associated with the open water. The former includes fishes generally associated with the bottom over the continental shelf, such as the Sargassum fish (Antennariidae), Sargassum pipefish and dwarf seahorse (Syngnathidae), and many postlarvae and juveniles of species of spiny-rayed fishes. The open-water assemblage is dominated by requiem sharks (Carcharhinidae), clupeids, engraulids, flying fishes (Exocoetidae), mullets (Mugilidae), jacks (Carangidae), and some mackerels (Scombridae). The oceanic zone has mako sharks (Lamnidae), manta rays (Mobulidae), tunas (Scombridae), billfishes (Xiphiidae and Istiophoridae), and ocean sunfishes (Molidae). The lower section of the epipelagic zone in many respects has a distinct fauna, consisting of the poorly known oarfishes and relatives (Lampridiformes), in addition to fishes with great depth ranges (Lamnidae, Scombridae, and Xiphiidae). The mesopelagic realm is below the photic zone and in the permanent thermocline. The bristlemouths (Gonostomatidae) and lanternfishes (Myctophidae) dominate this realm, and many of these undergo daily vertical migration into the epipelagic zone. The bathypelagic zone receives very little to no sunlight, and temperatures range from 4°C to 10°C. Deep-sea anglerfishes (Ceratioidei) dominate this realm in most seas, but they are poorly known from the Gulf of Mexico. Numerous species of gonostcmatids and scaleless black dragonfishes (Melanostomiidae) are found in the bathypelagic zone in the Gulf.

History of Biological Exploration in the Gulf of Mexico

Compared with the fish assemblages of the eastern and western coasts of North America, the fish assemblages of the Gulf of Mexico are poorly known. The reason for this is a combination of the relatively recent development of major fishery industries and the lack of long-established oceanographic and marine biology institutions and laboratories in the Gulf of Mexico.

The earliest surveys were land based and relied on seining and hook-and-line fishing or on obtaining samples from commercial fishermen with access to small fishing vessels. Spencer F. Baird and Charles Girard (1854) and Girard (1858, 1859) reported on fishes from Brazos Santiago, mouth of the Rio Grande; Saint Joseph's Island; Indianola and Galveston, Texas, collected on the United States–Mexican Boundary Survey. G. Brown Goode and T. H. Bean (1878, 1879, 1880, 1882a,b), and later David S. Jordan and Charles H. Gilbert (1882, 1884, 1885), published on the fishes from the Florida Gulf coast provided for them in part by Mr. Silas Stearns. Mr. Stearns worked for the Pensacola Ice Company and later for Warren and Company, wholesale fish dealers. Both companies dealt with the red snapper fishermen that worked the "snapper banks" between Pensacola and Tampa Bay. Stearns obtained rare and unusual fishes caught on the bank and also fishes disgorged by the red snappers that were the mainstay of the fishery. For over a decade Mr. Stearns collected specimens of these fishes and shipped them on ice or in spirits to Goode and Bean at the U.S. National Museum in Washington, D.C., or to Jordan and Gilbert at Indiana University in Bloomington, Indiana. Jordan and his students also traveled to Pensacola to assist Mr. Stearns with the collections and to collect fishes along the shoreline with seines.

Goode and Bean (1882a) published a list of nearly 300 species of fishes representing 80 families reported from the Gulf of Mexico, and Barton W. Evermann and William C. Kendall (1900) wrote a checklist of the fishes of Florida, including about 300 marine species from the Gulf coast of Florida. They also included an annotated bibliography of previous studies on Florida fishes.

During the 1880s Jordan and associates also collected fishes at Key West and Cedar Key, Florida; New Orleans, Louisiana; and Galveston, Texas, for the U.S. National Museum. He and Gilbert also made a large collection of fishes from Veracruz and Tampico, Mexico, from fish markets in Mexico City and from seining along the coasts. These fishes were reported on by Jordan and Dickerson (1908). Barton W. Evermann and William C. Kendall (1894) made extensive inshore fish surveys at Galveston and Corpus Christi. The early records of fishes of the Gulf were summarized in "Fishes of North and Middle America" (Jordan and Evermann, 1896–1900).

The first surveys aboard research vessels were conducted by United States Coast Survey steamer *Blake* in 1872 and between 1877 and 1880 (Galtsoff 1954). The expeditions, especially those from 1877 and 1880, obtained a wealth of benthic, mostly invertebrate specimens. The 1,000-ton U.S. Fish Commission steamer *Albatross* first visited the Gulf of Mexico in 1884 and explored the waters around the west coast of Cuba. The following year the ship returned to make more detailed explorations around Cozumel Island on the eastern edge of Campeche Bank, the red snapper banks of Cape San Blas in the northeastern Gulf, and the west coast of Florida to Key West (Collins 1887). Fishes collected during these surveys were described by Goode and Bean (1896).

From 1895 to 1913 the U.S. Commission of Fish and Fisheries steamer *Fish Hawk* explored the oyster and sponge grounds and made hydrographic observations along the northern Gulf of Mexico from the west coast of Florida to Matagorda Bay, Texas. Some of the fishes collected during these surveys were reported on

by Evermann and Kendall (1898). In 1917 the U.S. Bureau of Fisheries research ship *Grampus* studied shrimp and fishery grounds from Key West, Florida, to Aransas Pass, Texas, and many of these species were reported on by John T. Nichols and Charles M. Breder (1922, 1924).

Extensive biological surveys, however, did not begin until 1950 when the Fish and Wildlife Service initiated a comprehensive research program in oceanography and fisheries resources of the Gulf of Mexico. The surveys were conducted aboard the USS *Alaska* and USS *Oregon*, with the *Oregon* mainly responsible for exploration of fishing grounds. Fish specimens resulting from these surveys were deposited at the National Museum of Natural History, the Museum of Comparative Zoology at Harvard University, and the Field Museum of Natural History in Chicago, and served as the material for numerous species descriptions. The stations occupied and fishes collected between 1950 and 1955 are listed in Springer and Bullis (1956). Later surveys between 1956 and 1960, by the succeeding vessels *Oregon II* and *Silver Bay*, were reported by Bullis and Thompson (1965).

The Gulf Biologic Station was one of the first marine biological stations in the Gulf. Located at Calcaseau Pass in Cameron, Louisiana, it was mainly concerned with oyster and other bivalve research and was operational from 1902 to 1910. Weymouth (1911) described a collection of fishes made by a Mr. Milo Spaulding of the Biologic Laboratory. The Carnegie Institution of Washington, D.C., established a marine laboratory at Loggerhead Key, Dry Tortugas, in 1904. Over his 25-year tenure at the lab, William H. Longley gathered data on the local fishes. His notes and manuscripts were published after his death by Samuel F. Hildebrand (Longley and Hildebrand 1940, 1941). These works are still important references on the fishes of the Florida Keys and the eastern Gulf of Mexico.

Louisiana State University maintained a small laboratory on Grande Isle from the late 1920s to the early 1950s that was mainly concerned with teaching. The Marine Laboratory of the University of Miami (now the Rosenstiel School of Marine and Atmospheric Science) was opened in 1942 in Coral Gables, Florida, for research and the teaching of oceanography and marine biology. Although the lab is located outside the Gulf of Mexico, it has greatly contributed to our knowledge of fishes of the Gulf. Students trained at the lab have made significant contributions to ichthyology, both of the Gulf and elsewhere. The state of Mississippi opened its Gulf Coast Research Laboratory at Ocean Springs, Mississippi, in 1947. Researchers at this lab have made major contributions to our knowledge of fishes of the northern Gulf of Mexico and have built a fine collection of fishes from the Gulf of Mexico and the Caribbean Sea. The Institute of Marine Science of the University of Texas in Port Aransas, Texas, was established in 1948 and has contributed to our knowledge of fishes of the northwestern Gulf of Mexico. Texas A & M University established the Department of Oceanography in 1949, and later acquired a marine lab and maintained a series of oceanographic vessels in Galveston. The vessel *Alaminos* of the University, under the direction of Willis Pequegnat, made large and important collections of slope and abyssal fishes of the Gulf of Mexico and the Caribbean Sea in the 1960s and early 1970s. Researchers in the Oceanography Department at Texas A & M University were the first to thoroughly investigate the fauna of the Flower Gardens Reefs (Bright and Cashman 1974; Bright et al. 1974). The Texas Game, Fish and Oyster Commission opened a marine laboratory in 1949 at Rockport, Texas, that contributed papers on fishes of Texas in the 1950s and 1960s. The Oceanographic Institute of Florida State University established a laboratory at Alligator Harbor in 1949, primarily for teaching, and has produced a large number of ichthyologists concerned with the Gulf of Mexico. The Fish and Wildlife Service opened a laboratory in Sarasota, Florida, and a laboratory in Galveston in 1950 for oceanographic and biological studies of the Gulf. The Alabama Marine Resources Labora-

tory established a laboratory on Dauphin Island in the 1960s, and this lab has trained a number of ichthyologists that published on the fishes of the northeastern Gulf of Mexico.

From the 1930s to the present our knowledge of the fishes of the Gulf and the number of investigators of this fauna have greatly increased. Some of the more significant, but by no means all, of these contributors are briefly mentioned below. Gordon Gunter was employed by the Institute of Marine Science of the University of Texas and later by the Gulf Coast Research Laboratory, and he published on fishes of the northern Gulf coast from the 1930s to the 1950s. J. L. Baughman worked at the Texas Game, Fish and Oyster Commission at Rockport and published a number of studies on the fishes of the Texas coast. Stewart Springer published extensively on the sharks of the Gulf and the Caribbean Sea while employed with the Fish and Wildlife Service from the late 1940s to the 1960s. Henry B. Bigelow and William C. Schroeder described many species of sharks and rays from the Gulf of Mexico and the Caribbean Sea, largely based on specimens caught by the USS *Oregon*, RV *Oregon II,* and RV *Silver Bay.* Isaac Ginsburg of the U.S. National Museum published a number of papers on fishes of the Gulf of Mexico and was one of the first to report on the subtle differences between fishes from the northern Gulf of Mexico and the southeastern coast of the United States. In the 1950s Henry Hildebrand (1954, 1955) contributed two seminal papers on fishes associated with the shrimp grounds of the Gulf of Mexico. G. K. Reid (1954) described the ecology of fishes in the northeastern Gulf of Mexico. Marion Grey, an ichthyologist at the Field Museum, wrote extensively on the deep-sea fishes of the Gulf of Mexico, mainly based on specimens captured by the *Oregon*. Giles W. Mead published several papers on Gulf of Mexico fishes and prepared an unpublished annotated list of fishes from the Gulf of Mexico while employed with the Fish and Wildlife Service. He listed over 800 species of bony fishes from the Gulf. Ralph W. Yerger contributed to our knowledge of the fishes of the Gulf of Mexico through his teaching and research during his tenure at Florida State University. Chuck E. Dawson wrote extensively on the systematics of fishes of the Gulf of Mexico and the Caribbean Sea during his tenure at the Gulf Coast Research Laboratory. John C. Briggs (1958) compiled a list of Florida fishes and discussed the biogeography of fishes in the Gulf of Mexico, in addition to writing a number of papers on fishes of the Gulf and the Caribbean Sea. G. B. Smith, H. M. Austin, S. A. Bortone, R. W. Hastings, and L. H. Ogren (1975) and G. B. Smith (1976) described the distribution and ecology of reef fishes in the eastern Gulf of Mexico. J. G. Walls (1975) published a book entitled *Fishes of the Northern Gulf of Mexico*. F. Sonnier, H. D. Hoese, and J. Teerling (1976) published observations on fishes associated with offshore reefs and platforms off Louisiana. H. Dickson Hoese (1958) prepared a checklist of marine fishes of Texas, and in collaboration with Richard H. Moore (1977), prepared a book on the marine fishes of Texas, Louisiana, and adjacent waters that dealt with 497 species. E. O. Murdy (1983) wrote *Saltwater Fishes of Texas* and recorded 540 species of fishes on the continental shelf of Texas. Victor Springer published a number of manuscripts on sharks, blennies, and gobies, and a classical study on the fishes of Tampa Bay, with K. D. Woodburn (1960), while employed with the Fish and Wildlife Service. Royal Suttkus, a professor at Tulane University from the 1950s through the 1980s, published a number of papers on fishes but is best known as a collector. During his tenure at Tulane he singlehandedly built one of the largest collections of fishes in the world. C. Richard Robins of the Rosenstiel School of Marine and Atmospheric Science published extensively on the fishes of the Gulf of Mexico and the Caribbean Sea, built a large collection of fishes, partially from the Gulf, and trained a large number of ichthyologists who in turn have contributed to our knowledge of fishes of the Gulf of Mexico. He and G. Carleton Ray wrote, and John Douglass and Rudolf Freund illustrated *A Field Guide to Atlantic Coast Fishes of North America* (1986), which includes shore and continental fishes from the northern one-half of the Gulf of Mexico. José Luis Castro-Aguirre (1978) published a systematic list of the marine fishes of the east and west coasts of Mexico and with Alba Márquez-Espinoza (1981) published an annotated list of the fishes of the Isla de Lobos and adjacent areas of Veracruz. Robert L. Shipp, a professor at the University of Alabama, published on the fish fauna of the northeastern Gulf of Mexico, including an identification guide (1988). R. M. Darnell et al. (1983) and Darnell and Kleypas (1987) published distributional atlases of the more common shorefishes and penaeid shrimps of the northwestern and northeastern Gulf of Mexico. Edward Houde, while at the Rosenstiel School of Marine and Atmospheric Science, conducted extensive studies of fish larvae distribution in the northeastern Gulf of Mexico.

These scientists and many others have set the stage for a comprehensive survey of the fishes of the Gulf of Mexico. Although additional species may be discovered and additional records may be recorded, the Gulf of Mexico has been thoroughly surveyed for fishes, and most of this information is available, although scattered, in the literature. It is hoped that organizing and consolidating this information will stimulate more comprehensive studies of fishes and other marine biota of the Gulf and contiguous areas.

How to Identify Fishes

Names of Fishes

Fishes and other organisms are classified into inclusive hierarchical systems that, as close as possible, reflect their evolutionary or genealogical relationships. Species are grouped into a genus with other species that are thought to share a common ancestral species. Genera are grouped into a family with other genera, families are grouped into an order, and orders are grouped into a class using the same criteria. The studies of the diversity and the evolutionary relationships of organisms are called systematics and phylogenetics, respectively, and one of the goals of these disciplines is to classify organisms into natural (monophyletic) groups (higher taxa). We can never be sure that our classifications totally reflect evolution because evolution is ancient history and humans were not around to directly observe it.

The basis of the study of organismic evolution is the species, which is defined as "groups of interbreeding natural populations that are reproductively isolated from other such groups" (Mayr 1969) or, alternatively, as "a single lineage of ancestor-descendant populations which maintains its identity from other such lineages and which has its own evolutionary tendencies and historical fate" (Wiley 1978). Obviously neither of these definitions is easy to use because it is difficult, if not impossible, to determine whether or not two or more groups of organisms are reproductively isolated or form a single lineage. It can only be inferred that two or more populations will or will not interbreed if they are geographically isolated from each other. Also, populations that are geographically separated at the present time may not be isolated in the future, thus it can only be inferred that they either will or will not maintain their identity if their ranges should overlap at some time in the future. It is also becoming apparent that distinct species do interbreed occasionally. In most cases the decision to consider a population a distinct species, rather than a population of a more inclusive species, is arrived at by indirect means. The distinctions are usually based on differences in morphology, counts of repetitive characters (e.g., fin rays, gill rakers, vertebrae, etc.), coloration, or behavior between or among populations. More recently scientists have been relying on electrophoretic studies of proteins, chromosome numbers and shapes, and base sequences of mitochondrial or nuclear DNA. Populations that exhibit no overlap in any of these characteristics are usually considered distinct species, based on the assumption that the differences are the result of genetic differences either between or among the populations. However, not even the DNA data can provide, in all

cases, a definitive answer to the species question. Thus the status of some species, even well-studied species, is controversial.

The formal or scientific name of a fish (a species) is binomial, consisting of a generic and a species name (epithet), followed by the describer and the date of the description. When the author's name is in parentheses, the generic name has been changed since description of the species. The generic name begins with a capital letter and the species name with a lowercase letter. Both names are based on Latin, as a result of its use by early scientists as the language of science, and are italicized to designate their formal status. A genus name can be used only once in zoology, and a species name can be used only once per genus, thus the species binomial is a unique combination accepted by scientists regardless of their native (vernacular) language. In zoology this binomial system dates back to the tenth edition of Carl Linnaeus's *Systema Naturae,* January 1, 1758. Linnaeus's system ended much confusion in biology by establishing a stable nomenclature. Today we recognize rules regarding the priority and codes for naming species and higher taxa.

Despite this system of nomenclature that has served the zoological community for nearly two and one-half centuries, there are moves afoot to establish formal vernacular names to be used in parallel with the scientific names. Obviously, separate vernacular names will be needed for each language, and scientists and interested lay people speaking different languages will have trouble with the vernacular names even if these names are well stabilized. One might ask why ichthyologists (those who study fishes) are spending time and energy to complicate a system that has worked for so long.

In addition to the potential confusion of the vernacular usage, there are other reasons for suppressing the use of common names, including loss of information, improper grammatical construction, the nonsensical nature of some of the proposed names, and disregard for the describer's intentions. A binomial name offers considerable information regarding the species. The generic name is applied to species that putatively share a common origin, and thus the generic name furnishes information regarding the species. Species that are included in the same genus, in most cases, will share a number of attributes related to appearance, habitat preferences, and other niche parameters. Common names generally offer no such information. Species in the same genus often have common names that do not reflect their affinities. For instance, according to the *Common and Scientific Names of Fishes from the United States and Canada,* 5th edition (Robins et al. 1991), the common name of *Haemulon album* is the margate, *H. aurolineatum* is the tomtate, and *H. carbonarium* is the caesar grunt. The vernacular names offer no information as to the genus of these three congeners, and it is debatable whether they will be any easier to remember than the scientific names. Occasionally the common names join together several nouns as adjectives, and these often include the names of other animals! For instance, the ophichthid eel *Myrichthys maculosus* is the tiger snake eel. The nettastomid eel *Facciolella gilberti* is the dogface witch-eel. The stomiid *Stomias boa* is the boa dragonfish. The scorpaenid fish *Scorpaena bergi* is the goosehead scorpionfish. At face value these names may be regarded as nonsensical. In some cases, common names may not be nonsensical but anthropomorphic, as in the common name of the ophichthid eel *Lethogaleos andersoni,* which is the forgetful snake eel, and the name of the balistid *Aluterus heudeloti,* which is the dotterel filefish. Finally, authors carefully choose names for new taxa, and these names often provide information regarding the appearance, life history, or locality of the taxon. Or an author may name the taxon for the collector or for a person that has made important scientific contributions. Often the common name selected by committee does not honor the author's original intent. For many of these species for which common names have been provided, only scientists will encounter them, because it is doubtful that many will enter the aquarium trade or will find their way into fish markets. Scientists supposedly rely on the scientific

names of fishes, so why has the scientific committee spent the energy proposing common names?

In this book, the accepted common name of the species will be given if available, but no common names will be proposed for those species that currently lack them. The above discussion is presented as a plea to avoid another "Tower of Babble," or an unavoidable reduction of the informational content in the science of ichthyology.

Structural Anatomy of Fishes

Most fishes are bilaterally symmetrical, with the head flowing smoothly into the trunk, and the body bearing three or four vertical fins and two sets of paired fins (Fig. B). One or two dorsal fins occur along the midline of the back, usually behind the head. The caudal fin is located at the posterior end, and an anal fin occurs on the midventral surface between the origin of the caudal fin and the vent or cloaca. The paired pectoral fins are located behind the head, and the paired pelvic fins are variously located near the ventral midline from under the head to just anterior to the vent or cloaca, and occasionally on the midflank. One or more of these fins may be lacking in certain fish taxa. In fact none of these fins are universally present in fishes. The fins consist of fin rays and membranes uniting the fin rays, and the structure of both varies among phylogenetic assemblages of fishes.

The head of fishes varies in shape and relative size, but it bears most of the sense organs in all fishes. The mouth varies in position, from on top of the head (superior), to in front of the head (terminal), to under the head (inferior), and is variously endowed with lips, barbels, cirri, or fimbriae. The nasal openings (nares) are usually paired and located on the sides or on top of the head anterior to the eyes. Small pits or canals occur in various patterns on the head and these serve as openings for the lateral line system. This sensory system is concerned with the perception of the displacement of water (near field sound) in the vicinity of the fish.

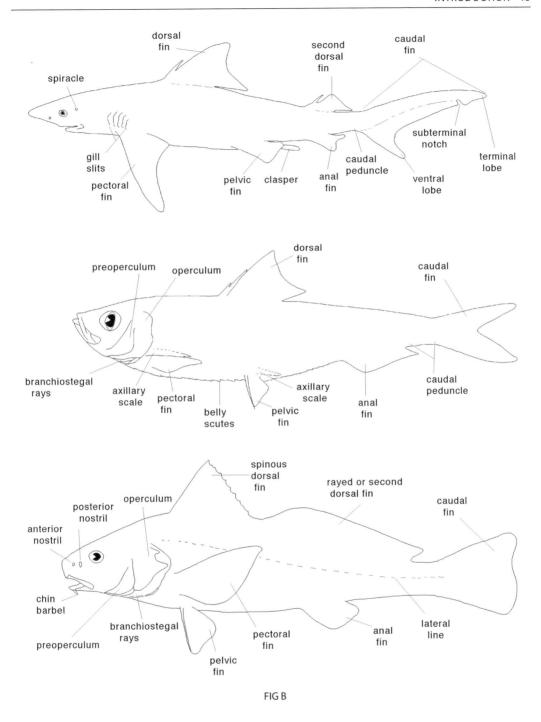

FIG B

The eyes vary in size and orientation but are usually located on the upper sides of the head. Eyes may be reduced or totally absent in fishes that live in the deep sea or other lightless environments. The gills are usually located behind the cranium but are considered part of the head. They open separately to the outside in most jawless fishes and elasmobranchs but are covered with a bony plate (opercular bones) in bony fishes. The body and, in some cases, parts of the head are covered with scales, and the structure, shape, and distribution of scales vary among the various assemblages of fishes. Chondrichthyans have placoid scales that have the same structure as teeth. The primitive bony fishes are covered with bony scutes or ganoid scales. The remainder of the bony fishes have thin cycloid or ctenoid scales. However, some bony fishes lack a scaly covering, while others are covered with a bony armor.

Teeth of fishes vary in shape, structure, and location. In the chondrichthyans the teeth are restricted to the jaws, are imbedded in the gums, and are continuously replaced. In bony fishes teeth are associated with a number of bones and are usually embedded in the bone, and replacement is less regular than in the cartilaginous fishes. Teeth occur along the margins of the mouth, which include the premaxilla and maxilla in the upper jaw and dentary bone in the lower jaw in primitive bony fishes but only the premaxilla and dentary in derived bony fishes. Teeth can also occur in the roof of the mouth in the medial vomer and parasphenoid, in the lateral palatine and pterygoid bones, and in the floor of the mouth in the tongue (basihyal bone). Additional teeth can occur in the branchial bones that support the gills, especially on the pharyngobranchs and the basibranchs. The branchial bones also bear one or two series of gill rakers on the anterior aspects of the epibranch and the ceratobranch that aid in straining food items from the water that passes over the gills.

Variations in these basic structures will be presented in the family descriptions that follow.

Measurements and Counts

The methods of making the measurements utilized in the species descriptions are illustrated in Figure B. All measurements are made from point to point by means of dial calipers or dividers. Care must be taken when using non-rigid devices such as tape measures because these can overestimate linear distances. Length of fishes is expressed in terms of total length (TL), which is the distance from the tip of the snout to the distal extension of the caudal fin, or in terms of standard length (SL), which is

the distance from the tip of the snout to the base of the caudal fin, at the end of the bony plate (hypural plate) supporting the fin rays. Standard length is the preferred length in systematics because it limits the variation caused by wear and damage to the caudal fin. Head length is measured from the tip of the snout to the distal margin of the operculum, and body depth is measured as the maximum depth of the specimen. The other measurements specific to particular fish taxa are described at appropriate sections of the text.

A number of counts are important in the description and identification of fishes. The fin ray counts follow those recommended by Hubbs and Lagler (1958). Fin spines are unpaired and unsegmented, and fin rays are segmented, bilaterally paired, and often branched. In many of the bony fishes, the last ray of the dorsal fin and the anal fin is separated to the base; in these cases the split ray is counted as one. Transverse scale row numbers and lateral line scale numbers are often included in descriptions. The former count includes all of the scale rows between the opercular flap and the base of the caudal fin. The latter count includes the number of pored scales between the opercular flap and the base of the caudal fin. Other counts, specific to particular taxa, are introduced at the appropriate sections of the text. Gill rakers are usually counted on the first arch only. These are reported as the total number on the epibranch and ceratobranch or separately for the epibranch and the ceratobranch. One or two gill rakers occasionally occur in the corner between the ceratobranch and epibranch, and these may be included in the total count or listed separately. In some taxa, gill rakers occur on the hypobranch, and if so, they are listed.

Literature Cited

Antoine, J. W. 1972. Structure of the Gulf of Mexico. *In:* Contributions on the geological and geographical oceanography of the Gulf of Mexico, ed. R. Rezak and V. J. Henry. Texas A & M University Oceanographic Studies, no. 3. Houston: Gulf Publ. Co.

Baird, S. F., and C. Girard. 1854. Descriptions of new species of fishes collected by John H. Clark on the U.S. and Mexican Survey, and in Texas by Captain Stuart Vliet, USA. Proc. Acad. Nat. Sci. Philadelphia 7: 24–29.

Briggs, J. C. 1958. A list of Florida fishes and their distribution. Bull. Fla. State Mus. 2: 223–319.

Briggs, J. C. 1974. Marine zoogeography. New York: McGraw-Hill, 475 pp.

Bright, T. J., and C. W. Cashman. 1974. Fishes. *In:* Biota of the West Flower Garden Bank, ed. T. J. Bright and L. H. Pequegnat. Houston: Gulf Publ. Co., pp. 340–409.

Bright, T. J., J. W. Tunnel, L. H. Pequegnat, T. E. Burke, C. W. Cashman, D. A. Cropper, J. P. Ray, R. C. Tresslar, J. Teerling, and J. B. Wills. 1974. Biotic zonation on the West Flower Garden Bank. *In:* Biota of the West Flower Garden Bank, ed. T. J. Bright and L. H. Pequegnat. Houston: Gulf Publ. Co., pp. 3–63.

Britton, J. C., and B. Morton. 1989. Shore ecology of the Gulf of Mexico. Austin: Univ. of Texas Press, 387 pp.

Bullis, H. R., and J. R. Thompson. 1965. Collections by the exploratory fishing vessels *Oregon, Silver Bay, Combat,* and *Pelican* made during 1956 to 1960 in southwestern North Atlantic. U.S. Fish Wildl. Serv. Spec. Sci. Rep. Fish. (510): 1–130.

Castro-Aguirre, J. L. 1978. Catálogo sistemático de los peces marinos que penetran a las aguas continentales de México, con aspectos zoogeográficos y ecológicos. Mexico: Depto. de Pesca, Dirección General del Instituto Nacional de Pesca, Serie Cientif. No. 19: 1–298.

Castro-Aguirre, J. L., and A. Márquez-Espinoza. 1981. Contribución al conocimiento de la ictiofauna de la Isla de Lobos y zonas adyacentes, Veracruz, México. Mexico: Depto. de Pesca, Dirección General del Instituto Nacional de Pesca, Serie Científ. No. 22: 1–85.

Childress, J. J., C. R. Fisher, J. M. Brooks, M. C. Kennicutt, R. Bidigare, and A. Anderson. 1986. A methanotrophic marine molluscan (Bivalvia, Mytilidae) symbiosis: mussel fueled by gas. Science 233: 1306–1308.

Chittenden, M. E., and J. D. McEachran. 1976. Composition, ecology, and dynamics of demersal fish communities on the northwestern Gulf of Mexico continental shelf, with a similar synopsis for the entire gulf. Texas A & M University Sea Grant Publication 76–206, 104 pp.

Collins, J. W. 1887. XVI. Report on the discovery and investigation of fishing grounds, made by the Fish Commission Steamer *Albatross* during a cruise along the Atlantic coast and in the Gulf of Mexico; with notes on the Gulf fisheries. U.S. Fish. Comm. Rep. Comm. 1885 (pt. 13, Apend. A): 227–311.

Compagno, L. J. V. 1984. FAO species catalogue. Vol. 4. Sharks of the world. An annotated and illustrated catalogue of shark species known to date. Part 1. Hexanchiformes to Lamniformes. FAO Fish. Synop. (125) Vol. 4 (pt. 1): 1–249.

Darnell, R. M., and R. E. Defenbaugh. 1990. Gulf of Mexico: Environmental overview and history of environmental research. Amer. Zool. 30: 3–6.

Darnell, R. M., R. E. Defenbaugh, and D. Moore. 1983. Northwestern Gulf shelf bio-atlas: A study of the distribution of demersal fishes and penaeid shrimp of soft bottoms of the continental shelf from the Rio Grande to the Mississippi River Delta. Metairie, LA: Minerals Management Service, Gulf of Mexico OCS Regional Office, U.S. Dept. Interior. OCS Study MMS 82–04, 438 pp.

Darnell, R. M., and J. A. Kleypas. 1987. Eastern Gulf shelf bio-atlas: A study of the distribution of demersal fishes and penaeid shrimp of soft bottoms of the continental shelf from the Mississippi River Delta to the Florida Keys. New Orleans, LA: Minerals Management Service, U.S. Dept. Interior. OCS Study MMS 86–0041, 548 pp.

Elliot, B. A. 1982. Anticyclonic rings in the Gulf of Mexico. J. Physical Oceanogr. 12: 1292–1309.

Evermann, B. W., and W. C. Kendall. 1894. The fishes of Texas and the Rio Grande Basin, considered chiefly with reference to their geographic distribution. Bull. U.S. Fish. Comm. 12 (1892): 57–126.

Evermann, B. W., and W. C. Kendall. 1898. Description of new or little-known genera and species of fishes from the United States. Bull. U.S. Fish. Comm. 17: 125–133.

Evermann, B. W., and W. C. Kendall. 1900. Check-list of the fishes of Florida. Rep. U.S. Fish. Comm. 25 (1899): 35–103.

Fink, W. L. 1985. Phylogenetic interrelationships of the stomiid fishes (Teleostei: Stomiiformes). Misc. Publ. Mus. Zool. Univ. Mich. 171: 1–127.

Galtsoff, P. S. 1954. Historical sketch of the exploration in the Gulf of Mexico. *In:* Gulf of Mexico, its origin, waters, and marine life. Fish and Wildl. Ser., Fish. Bull. 55(89): 3–36.

Girard, C. 1858. Notes upon various new genera and new species of fishes in the Museum of the Smithsonian Institution, and collected in connection with the United States and Mexican Boundary Survey, Major William Emory, Commissioner. Proc. Acad. Nat. Sci. Philadelphia 10: 167–171.

Girard, C. 1859. United States and Mexican Boundary Survey under order of Lt. Col. W. H. Emory, Major First Cavalry, and the United States Commissioner. Ichthyology of the Boundary Survey. *In:* Report of the U.S. and Mexican Boundary Survey 1: 1–77.

Goode, G. B., and T. H. Bean. 1878. Descriptions of *Caulolatilus microps,* a new species of fish from the Gulf coast of Florida. Proc. U.S. Nat. Mus. 1: 42–43.

Goode, G. B., and T. H. Bean. 1879. Catalogue of a collection of fishes sent from Pensacola, Florida and vicinity by Mr. Silus Stearns. Proc. U.S. Nat. Mus. 2: 121–156.

Goode, G. B., and T. H. Bean. 1880. Catalogue of a collection of fishes attained in the Gulf of Mexico by Dr. J. W. Velie, with descriptions of seven new species. Proc. U.S. Nat. Mus. 2: 333–345.

Goode, G. B., and T. H. Bean. 1882a. A list of the species of fishes recorded as occurring in the Gulf of Mexico. Proc. U.S. Nat. Mus. 5: 234–240.

Goode, G. B., and T. H. Bean. 1882b. Descriptions of twenty-five new species from the southern United States, and three new genera. Proc. U.S. Nat. Mus. 5: 412–437.

Goode, G. B., and T. H. Bean. 1896. Oceanic ichthyology: Deep-sea and pelagic fishes of the world. Spec. Bull. U.S. Nat. Mus. 2: 1–533.

Hildebrand, H. H. 1954. A study of the fauna of the brown shrimp (*Penaeus aztecus* Ives) grounds in the western Gulf of Mexico. Publ. Inst. Mar. Sci. 3: 233–366.

Hildebrand, H. H. 1955. A study of the fauna of the pink shrimp (*Penaeus duorarum* Burkenroad) grounds in the Gulf of Campeche. Publ. Inst. Mar. Sci. 4: 169–232.

Hoese, H. D. 1958. A partially annotated checklist of the marine fishes of Texas. Publ. Inst. Mar. Sci. 5: 312–352.

Hoese, H. D., and R. H. Moore. 1977. Fishes of the Gulf of Mexico: Texas, Louisiana and adjacent waters. College Station: Texas A & M Univ. Press, 327 pp.

Hubbs, C. L., and K. F. Lagler. 1958. Fishes of the Great Lakes region. Ann Arbor: Univ. of Mich. Press, 213 pp.

Jordan, D. S., and M. C. Dickerson. 1908. Notes on a collection of fishes from the Gulf of Mexico at Vera Cruz and Tampico. Proc. U.S. Nat. Mus. 34: 11–22.

Jordan, D. S., and B. W. Evermann. 1896–1900. The fishes of North and Middle America. Bull. U.S. Nat. Mus. 47: 1–3313; Pt. 1, 1–1240.

Jordan, D. S., and C. H. Gilbert. 1882. Notes on fishes observed about Pensacola, Florida, and Galveston, Texas, with descriptions of new species. Proc. U.S. Nat. Mus. 5: 241–307.

Jordan, D. S., and C. H. Gilbert. 1884. Description of two new species of fishes (*Aprion ariommus* and *Ophidion beani*) from Pensacola, Florida. Proc. U.S. Nat. Mus. 6: 142–144.

Jordan, D. S., and C. H. Gilbert. 1885. Notes

on fishes collected by David S. Jordan at Cedar Key, Florida. Proc. U.S. Nat. Mus. 7: 230–237.

Kirwan, A. D., Jr., W. J. Merrell, Jr., J. K. Lewis, and R. E. Whitaker. 1984. Lagrangian observations of an anticyclonic ring in the western Gulf of Mexico. J. Geophys. Res. 89: 3417–3424.

Leipper, D. F. 1954a. Marine meteorology of the Gulf of Mexico. *In:* Gulf of Mexico, its origin, waters and marine life, ed. P. S. Galtsoff. U.S. Fish and Wildl. Serv. Fish. Bull. 55(89): 89–98.

Leipper, D. F. 1954b. Physical oceanography of the Gulf of Mexico. *In:* Gulf of Mexico, its origin, waters and marine life, ed. P. S. Galtsoff. U.S. Fish and Wildl. Serv. Fish. Bull. 55(89): 119–137.

Leipper, D. F. 1970. A sequence of current patterns in the Gulf of Mexico. J. Geophys. Res. 75: 637–657.

Longley, W. H., and S. F. Hildebrand. 1940. New genera and species of fishes from Tortugas, Florida. Carnegie Inst. Wash. Publ. 517: 223–285.

Longley, W. H., and S. F. Hildebrand. 1941. Systematic catalogue of the fishes of Tortugas, Florida, with observations on color, habits, and local distribution. Pap. Tortugas Lab., Carnegie Inst. 34: 1–331.

Lynch, S. A. 1954. Geology of the Gulf of Mexico. *In:* Gulf of Mexico, its origin, waters, and marine life, ed. P. S. Galtsoff. U.S. Fish and Wildl. Serv. Fish. Bull. 55(89): 67–86.

Marmer, H. A. 1954. Tides and sea level in the Gulf of Mexico. *In:* Gulf of Mexico, its origin, waters, and marine life, ed. P. S. Galtsoff. U.S. Fish and Wildl. Serv. Fish. Bull. 55(69): 101–141.

Mayr, E. 1969. Principles of systematic zoology. New York: McGraw-Hill Book Co., 428 pp.

Merrill, W. J., Jr., and J. M. Morrison. 1981. On the circulation of the western Gulf of Mexico, with observations from April 1978. J. Geophys. Res. 86(5C): 4181–4185.

Murdy, E. O. 1983. Saltwater fishes of Texas. College Station: Texas A & M University Sea Grant College Program, 220 pp.

Nelson, J. S. 1994. Fishes of the world. 3rd edition. New York: John Wiley & Sons, 600 pp.

Nichols, J. T., and C. M. Breder, Jr. 1922. *Ophidium welshi*, a new cusk eel, with notes on two other species from the Gulf of Mexico. Proc. Biol. Soc. Wash. 35: 13–15.

Nichols, J. T., and C. M. Breder, Jr. 1924. New Gulf records of a Pacific *Scorpaena* and *Prionotus*, with notes on other Gulf of Mexico fishes. Proc. Biol. Soc. Wash. 37: 21–23.

Pequegnat, W., B. J. Gallaway, and L. H. Pequegnat. 1990. Aspects of the ecology of the deep-water fauna of the Gulf of Mexico. Amer. Zool. 30: 45–64.

Pindell, J. L. 1985. Alleghenian reconstruction and subsequent evolution of the Gulf of Mexico, Bahamas, and Proto-Caribbean. Tectonics 4: 1–39.

Pindell, J. L., and J. F. Dewey. 1982. Permo-Triassic reconstruction of western Pangea and the evolution of the Gulf of Mexico/Caribbean region. Tectonics 1: 179–211.

Price, W. A. 1954. Geology. *In:* Gulf of Mexico, its origin, waters, and marine life, ed. P. S. Galtsoff. U.S. Fish and Wildl. Serv. Fish. Bull. 55(89): 39–86.

Reid, G. K. 1954. An ecological study of the Gulf of Mexico fishes in the vicinity of Cedar Key, Florida. Bull. Mar. Sci. Gulf Carib. 4: 1–94.

Rezak, R., S. R. Gittings, and T. J. Bright. 1990. Biotic assemblages and ecological controls on reefs and banks of the northwest Gulf of Mexico. Amer. Zool. 30: 23–35.

Robins, C. R., R. M. Bailey, C. E. Bond, J. R. Brooker, E. A Lachner, R. N. Lea, and W. B. Scott. 1991. Common and scientific names of fishes from the United States and Canada. Amer. Fish. Soc., Spec. Publ. 29, 5th ed., Bethesda, 183 pp.

Robins, C. R., G. C. Ray, J. Douglass, and R. Freund. 1986. A field guide to Atlantic coast fishes of North America. Boston: Houghton Mufflin Co., 354 pp.

Shipp, R. L. 1988. Dr. Bob's guide to fishes of the Gulf of Mexico. Dauphin Island, 256 pp.

Shirai, S. 1992. Squalean phylogeny, a new framework of "squaloid" sharks and related taxa. Sapporo: Hokkaido Univ. Press, 151 pp., 58 pls.

Smith, G. B. 1976. Ecology and distribution of eastern Gulf of Mexico reef fishes. Fla. Dept. Nat. Resour. Mar. Res. Publ. 19: 1–78.

Smith, G. B., H. M. Austin, S. A. Bortone, R. W. Hastings, and L. H. Ogren. 1975. Fishes of the Florida Middle Ground with comments on ecology and zoogeography. Fla. Dept. Nat. Resour. Mar. Res. Publ. 9: 1–14.

Sonnier, F., H. D. Hoese, and J. Teerling. 1976. Observations on the offshore reef and platform fish fauna of Louisiana. Copeia: 105–111.

Springer, S., and H. T. Bullis. 1956. Collections of the Oregon in the Gulf of Mexico. U.S. Fish and Wildl. Serv. Spec. Sci. Rep. Fish. (196): 1–134.

Springer, V. G., and K. D. Woodburn. 1960. An ecological study of the fishes of the Tampa Bay area. Fla. State Bd. Conserv. Mar. La., Prof. Pap., Ser. 1: 1–104.

Sturges, W. 1993. The annual cycle of the Western Boundary Current in the Gulf of Mexico. J. Geophys. Res. 98(C10): 18,053–18,068.

Sturges, W., and J. P. Biaha. 1976. A western boundary current in the Gulf of Mexico. Science 192: 367–369.

Walls, J. G. 1975. Fishes of the northern Gulf of Mexico. Neptune City: T.F.H. Publ., 432 pp.

Weymouth, F. W. 1911. Notes on a collection of fishes from Cameron, Louisiana. Proc. U.S. Nat. Mus. 38: 135–145.

Wiley, E. O. 1978. Phylogenetics, the theory and practice of phylogenetic systematics. New York: Wiley-Interscience Publ., John Wiley and Sons, 439 pp.

Key to the Orders of Fishes of the Gulf of Mexico

Many of the characters that distinguish the orders of fishes are rather obscure and technical, and not available without dissecting, radiographing, or clearing and staining fish specimens. Also many of the orders are morphologically variable, and some may prove to be nonmonophyletic groups. For these reasons, additional information on morphological variation within orders is provided in brackets following the dichotomous key characters, and line drawings of body shapes of families within the order are provided to aid with identification of the orders of fishes in the Gulf. In some cases the couplet defining an order may represent only that subsection of the order that occurs in the Gulf, and thus this key may not apply to areas outside of the Gulf of Mexico. The orders Scorpaeniformes, Perciformes, Pleuronectiformes, and Tetraodontiformes are not included in this volume. They will be treated in volume 2.

1a. Mouth without upper and lower jaws; gills located on inner surface of gill arches 2

1b. Mouth with upper and lower jaws; gills located on outer surface of gill arches. 3

2a. Dorsal fin(s) absent; barbel present around mouth; teeth on tongue only [body eel shaped; caudal fin extends onto posterior aspect of dorsal surface and is continuous with anal fin; paired fins absent] . . . . Myxiniformes p. 30

2b. Dorsal fin(s) present; barbel absent around mouth; teeth present on oral disc and tongue [body eel shaped; caudal fin limited to distal end of body, separated from dorsal fin; anal fin absent] . . . . Petromyzontiformes p. 35

3a. Skeleton consists of cartilage, which is often calcified but not ossified; teeth not fused to jaws; fin rays (ceratotrichia) not bilaterally paired or segmented 4

3b. Skeleton consists, at least in part, of bone (except in Acipenseriformes); teeth are usually fused to jaw; fin rays (lepidotrichia) are bilaterally paired and segmented 14

4a. Upper jaw not fused to neurocranium; five to seven gill slits opening separately to outside; gill arches posterior to neurocranium. 5

4b. Upper jaw fused to neurocranium; four gill slits covered by flap of skin supported by cartilages; gill arches ventral to neurocranium [head rather large; body tapering posteriorly; two dorsal fins, first short and preceded by erectile spine, and second low and with long base] . . . . Chimaeriformes p. 37

5a. Gill slits laterally located behind head; anterior margin of pectoral fin not attached to head 6

5b. Gill slits ventrally located behind head; anterior margin of pectoral fin attached to side of head 11

6a. Anal fin absent 7

6b. Anal fin present 8

7a. Mouth terminal; body flattened; anterior margin of pectoral fin adjacent gill slits [body raylike, with margins of head, pectoral fin, and pelvic fin contiguous and forming expanded surface] . . . . Squatiniformes p. 127

7b. Mouth subterminal; body oval in cross section; anterior margin of pectoral fin behind gill slits [two dorsal fins, often preceded by spine; body slender to rather robust] . . . . Squaliformes p. 102

8a. Six or seven gill slits; single dorsal fin [spiracle present; teeth with elongate, serrated cusps; gill slits very long] . . . . Hexanchiformes p. 97

8b. Five gill slits; two dorsal fins. 9

9a. Mouth small, not reaching to front of eye; nostril connected to mouth by groove; barbel present on inner side of nostril [body fusiform and large (up to 15 m) or rather depressed and small to moderate in size; mouth and terminal broad or rather narrow and subterminal; gill slits very broad or rather narrow] . . . . Orectolobiformes p. 43

9b. Mouth large, extending to behind front of eye; no groove connecting nostril to mouth; no barbel on inner side of nostril. 10

10a. Eye with nictitating lid originating on lower anterior corner [body rather small and elongate to large and fusiform; caudal fin low with short ventral lobe to high with well-developed ventral lobe] . . . . Carcharhiniformes p. 60

10b. Eye without nictitating lid on lower anterior corner [body
rather flaccid and thick to firm and fusiform; caudal fin
low with short ventral lobe to very high and almost symmetrical; occasionally caudal fin almost as long as remainder of body] . . . . Lamniformes p. 48

11a. Snout elongated into rostrum bearing teeth along lateral margins [body sharklike, only slightly depressed;
dorsal fins and caudal fin well developed]
. . . . Pristiformes p. 135

11b. Snout not elongated into rostrum. 12
12a. Surface area of trunk lateral and posterior to eye with
honeycomb texture resulting from electric organs [body
greatly flattened but rather thick to edges of disc]
. . . . Torpediniformes p. 129

12b. Surface area of trunk lateral and posterior to eye without
honeycomb texture, trunk lacks electric organs 13
13a. Generally two dorsal fins located on posterior one-half
of tail; tail lacks serrated spine; spiracle with trace of
gill fold [body moderately to greatly flattened and thin
along outer sections of disc; snout generally projects
beyond anterior extension of pectoral fin]
. . . . Rajiformes p. 138

13b. Either one or no dorsal fin; if present, dorsal fin located
at base of tail; generally tail with one or several serrated
spines; spiracle without trace of gill fold [body greatly
flattened and thin along outer sections of disc; snout not
projecting beyond anterior extension of pectoral fin]
. . . . Myliobatiformes p. 171

14a. Caudal fin heterocercal; body covered with five rows of
bony scutes [snout projects beyond mouth; four barbels in
front of mouth; dorsal and anal fins posteriorly located]
. . . . Acipenseriformes p. 197

14b. Caudal fin abbreviate heterocercal or homocercal; body
lacks bony scutes 15
15a. Caudal fin abbreviate heterocercal; body covered with
thick, rhombic, ganoid scales [mouth elongate and narrow,
with needlelike teeth; body elongate; dorsal and anal fins
posteriorly located] . . . . Semionotiformes p. 199

15b. Caudal fin homocercal when present; body covered
with thin cycloid or ctenoid scales, bony plates, or naked
. . . . 16

16a. Gular plate (median bone under chin) present; leptocephalous larvae (transparent, ribbonlike larvae, with
forked tail) 17

16b. Gular plate absent; leptocephalous larvae present or
absent, but when present, without forked caudal fin . . . 18

17a. Gular plate well developed; branchiostegal rays 23 to 35;
upper jaw extending past eye [body compressed and moderately elongate; mouth terminal to slightly superior; single
dorsal fin at about midlength; pelvic fin abdominal; caudal
fin deeply forked] . . . . Elopiformes p. 204

17b. Gular plate reduced to thin splint; branchiostegal rays
6 to 16; upper jaw not reaching anterior margin of eye
[body compressed and moderately elongate; mouth subterminal; single dorsal fin at about midlength; pelvic fin
abdominal; caudal fin deeply forked]
. . . . Albuliformes p. 208

18a. Body eel-like; pelvic fin abdominal, with 8 to 10 rays; posteriorly directed spine on dorsal edge of rear of maxilla;
leptocephalous larvae without normal caudal fin [dorsal fin
short, often consisting of isolated spinous rays; anal fin
long and continuous with reduced caudal fin]
. . . . Notacanthiformes p. 210

18b. Character combinations not as above (18a) 19

19a. Body eel-like; pelvic fin absent; premaxilla, vomer, and
ethmoid bones joined into single bone; gill slits small, narrow, and located on sides of head; leptocephalous larvae
with rounded or pointed tail [body generally oval in cross
section; gill cavity very large; dorsal and anal fins very
long, generally continuous with caudal fin, and fins without spines] . . . . Anguilliformes p. 219

19b. Character combinations not as above (19a) 20

20a. No lateral line on trunk; recessus lateralis present (combined infraorbital and preopercular canals within chamber
of neurocranium); anterior extensions of swim bladder
enter back of cranium to abut against utriculus of inner
ear; 19 principal caudal fin rays [body fusiform and moderately compressed to compressed; single dorsal fin located
over midbody; pelvic fin abdominal; caudal fin forked]
. . . . Clupeiformes p. 328

20b. Character combinations not as above (20a) 21

21a. Pectoral fin preceded by strong, serrated spine; maxilla not part of gape of mouth but reduced and supporting barbels; anterior vertebrae modified to form Weberian apparatus (bony connection between swim bladder and inner ear) [body usually depressed anteriorly and compressed posteriorly; barbels variably located around mouth; dorsal fin often preceded by serrated spine; adipose fin usually present; pelvic fin abdominal; body naked or covered with bony plates] . . . . Siluriformes p. 359

21b. Character combinations not as above (21a) 22

22a. Gill rakers of fourth gill arch forming crumenal or epibranchial organ; mouth generally small, not extending beyond anterior margin of eye; jaw teeth poorly developed or absent [body elongate to moderately elongate and slightly compressed; single dorsal fin located at midlength or posterior to midlength; adipose fin present or absent; pelvic fin located under or in front of dorsal fin] . . . . Osmeriformes (Argentinoidei) p. 364

22b. Character combinations not as above (22a) 23

23a. Photophores generally present on body and head 24

23b. Photophores generally absent on body and head 25

24a. Premaxilla and maxilla included in gape of mouth and bearing teeth [body generally elongate and moderately compressed, but deep bodied and compressed in some taxa; mouth large, extending beyond orbit; pectoral fin low on flank; adipose fin generally present; pelvic fin located on abdomen when present; photophores generally present in several series on trunk] . . . . Stomiiformes p. 408

24b. Only premaxilla included in gape of mouth and bearing teeth [body moderately elongate and compressed; mouth large and terminal; single dorsal fin located at about midlength; dorsal adipose fin present; pelvic fin located under or anterior to dorsal fin; photophores on lower, and often on upper, flank and on head] . . . . Myctophiformes p. 615

25a. Caudal fin reduced and united with long anal fin; pelvic fin thoracic and consists of single ray in adults; single, short dorsal fin above pectoral fin base [snout is bulbous; mouth subterminal; body tapers behind head] . . . . Ateleopodiformes p. 545

25b. Character combinations not as above (25a) 26

26a. Dorsal adipose fin usually present (absent in Giganturidae and in one genus of Chlorophthalmidae); only premaxilla included in gape of mouth and bearing teeth; pelvic fin abdominal (thoracic in Aulopidae and absent in Giganturidae) [head depressed to slightly compressed; body moderately elongate to elongate; mouth moderately large to very large and bearing large carniform teeth; tail moderately to deeply forked] . . . . Aulopiformes p. 548

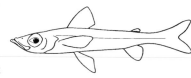

26b. Character combinations not as above (26a) 27

27a. Pelvic girdle not attached to cleithrum of shoulder girdle; no true fin spines; maxilla moves with premaxilla during jaw protrusion [generally mesopelagic to bathypelagic fishes of diverse shape; some oval shaped and compressed, with long dorsal and anal fins, and forked caudal fins; some very elongate, thin, and ribbonlike, with long dorsal fin, either short or no anal fin, and pelvic fin absent or subthoracic; others moderately to greatly elongate and covered with hairlike pile or with extremely long caudal fin] . . . . Lampridiformes p. 680

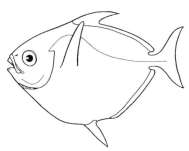

27b. Character combinations not as above (27a) 28

28a. Pair of hyoid barbels extending below jaws [body moderately elongate and compressed; dorsal fin long, consisting of several spines and numerous rays; pelvic fin subthoracic, with one spine and six rays; anal fin about one-half length of dorsal fin, with several spines and numerous rays] . . . . Polymixiiformes p. 692

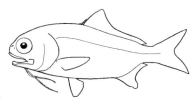

28b. Character combinations not as above (28a) 29

29a. Posterior aspect of premaxilla notched [body elongate; mouth large and subterminal to terminal; dorsal fin(s) long based; pelvic fin thoracic or jugular, rarely behind pectoral fin; fins lack true spines (except for two dorsal spines in Macrouridae)]. . . . . Gadiformes p. 749

29b. Posterior aspect of premaxilla not notched. 30

30a. Pelvic fins jugular and close together, with one spine and one or two rays or absent; when present, located at level of preoperculum or more anteriorly; head slightly to moderately depressed [body moderately elongate to elongate, compressed posteriorly; mouth large and terminal to subterminal; dorsal and anal fins long and usually continuous with caudal fin; fin spines absent except one pelvic spine may be present] . . . . Ophidiiformes p. 695

30b. Character combinations not as above (30a) 31

31a. Pelvic fins jugular and widely separated, with one spine
and two or three rays; head greatly depressed; both premaxilla and maxilla in gape of mouth; three gill arches
[body elongate and depressed; mouth large and terminal;
short, spiny dorsal fin and long, rayed dorsal fin and
scales cycloid, imbedded, or lacking]
. . . . Batrachoidiformes p. 808

31b. Character combinations not as above (31a) 32

32a. Gill openings located either behind or below pectoral fin
base; pelvic fin, if present, jugular, with one spine and
five branched rays; first dorsal spine modified into illicium
and esca [body either greatly depressed or compressed;
mouth terminal to superior and generally large to very
large; dorsal and anal fins generally posteriorly located
and similar in shape and position; pectoral fin limblike]
. . . . Lophiiformes p. 814

32b. Character combinations not as above (32a) 33

33a. Two dorsal fins widely separated, first with four spines;
pelvic girdle not attached to pectoral girdle, pelvic fin
subthoracic; branchial bones and gill rakers modified
to form filtering apparatus [body is moderately elongate and subcylindrical in cross section; mouth is
small and terminal; pectoral fin is high on flank; lateral line is poorly developed or absent]
. . . . Mugiliformes p. 872

33b. Character combinations not as above (33a) 34

34a. Rostral cartilage on snout not attached to premaxilla;
eggs large, demersal, and with many oil droplets and
adhesive filaments; third, fourth, and fifth infraorbital
bones lacking; fourth pharyngobranchial bones lacking
[surface-swimming fishes in fresh, brackish, and marine
waters; body moderately slender to slender and slightly
compressed; opercular and preopercular margins without spines or serrations; scales generally cycloid and fin
spines rare]. 35

34b. Character combinations not as above (34a) 37

35a. Generally two dorsal fins, first short and with flexible
spines; lateral line weak or absent; nostrils paired; anal
fin generally preceded by spine [body slender and slightly
compressed to moderately slender and compressed; mouth
terminal; pelvic fin abdominal, subabdominal, or thoracic
. . . . Atheriniformes p. 881

35b. Single dorsal fin; fin spines generally lacking; lateral line present or absent; nostrils single or paired 36

36a. Lateral line present on trunk; nostrils single; lower jaw elongate in some stage of development [body elongate, slender, and slightly compressed to compressed; pectoral fin high on flank; dorsal and anal fins on posterior part of body and similar in shape and position; pelvic fin abdominal; lateral line on lower flank] . . . . . Beloniformes p. 931

36b. Lateral line absent; nostrils paired; jaws not elongate during any stage of development [body moderately elongate and slightly compressed; mouth terminal to superior; pectoral fin on mid- to lower flank; pelvic fin abdominal to subthoracic or absent] . . . . Cyprinodontiformes p. 890

37a. Head bones usually very thin; orbitosphenoid bone generally absent; suborbital shelf absent; supramaxilla absent [body roundish in cross section but morphologically diverse, rather robust with large head, to moderately compressed, to elongate with small head; mouth terminal and of moderate size to extremely large; teeth absent in palatines; single dorsal fin originating at about midlength or posterior to midbody; anal fin usually originating below dorsal fin and similar in shape, occasionally anal fin posterior to and smaller than dorsal fin; lateral line in large tube or consists of series of vertical papillae in three families] . . . . Stephanoberyciformes p. 964

37b. Character combinations not as above (37a) 38

38a. Mucous cavities on head generally well developed; orbital and opercular bones usually spiny; orbitosphenoid bone present; premaxilla protractile; one or two supramaxillae; suborbital shelf well developed; dorsal, pelvic, and anal fins with spines (except *Anoplogaster* lacks spines, and *Diretmus* lacks dorsal and anal spines); pelvic fin has one spine and 6 or 7 rays (except one spine and 10 to 12 rays in *Beryx*, and one spine and 5 or 6 rays in Trachichthyidae) [body oblong or ovate and compressed; head large; mouth large and oblique; eye large; caudal peduncle slender and body covered with ctenoid scales] . . . . Beryciformes p. 997

38b. Character combinations not as above (38a) 39

39a. Caudal fin with 11 to 13 branched rays; dorsal, anal, and pectoral fin rays unbranched [body thin and deep; mouth large; upper jaw usually extremely protrusible; dorsal fin long and partially divided into anterior spinous and posterior rayed sections; pelvic fin subthoracic to thoracic] . . . . Zeiformes p. 1024

39b. Character combinations not as above (39a) 40

40a. Snout distinctly elongate, in form of tube, with small
mouth at end; pelvic fin, if present, abdominal and without
spines [mouth not protrusible; jaw teeth small or absent;
body shape diverse, from elongate and slender to oval
shaped and compressed] . . . . Syngathiformes p. 1038

40b. Character combinations not as above (40a) 41

41a. Bony stay consisting of posterior extension of third suborbital bone extending across cheek to preoperculum
[body shape diverse, ranging from stout and deep bodied
to slender and elongate, and moderately depressed to moderately compressed; pectoral fin generally large, rounded,
with membranes incised between lower fin rays; head and
body generally spiny or covered with bony plates]
. . . . Scorpaeniformes

41b. Character combinations not as above (41a) 42

42a. Head asymmetrical, both eyes on same side of head [body
greatly compressed, somewhat rounded on eyed side and
flat on blind side; dorsal and anal fins very long]
. . . . Pleuronectiformes

42b. Head symmetrical, single eye on each side of head 43

43a. Branchiostegal region covered with thick layer of scaleless
or scaled skin; gill opening restricted to small slit below
pectoral fin base; anal fin spines lacking
. . . . Tetraodontiformes

43b. Character combinations not as above (43a) . . . Perciformes

MYXINIFORMES

Myxiniformes are the most primitive of the fishes and the sister group of all other fishes and vertebrates. The single family in this order occurs in the Gulf of Mexico.

MYXINIDAE Hagfishes

Hagfishes are elongate, slightly compressed, and eel-like, with barbels on sides of head and a continuous fin running posteriorly from mid-dorsal to midventral surface. They are distinguished from the other fishes by the following combination of characters. Single nostril is located dorsal to mouth at front of head, and it communicates with pharynx. Nostril is flanked by two pairs of barbels, and mouth is flanked by one or two pairs of barbels. Mouth lacks true jaws but has eversible tonguelike structure (lingual tooth plate) bearing four rows of keratinized, rasplike teeth. Eye is rudimentary, lacks lens and iris, and is not visible externally. Gill pouches vary from 5 to 16 and open independently or by means of common aperture to outside. Paired fins are lacking. Single median fin extends along midline of posterior part of body but possesses fin rays only in tail region. Body lacks scales but possesses mucous pores and is capable of producing large quantities of mucus.

Hagfishes probably occur worldwide. They are generally restricted to the outer continental shelf and slope, and are more restricted to deep water at tropical latitudes. Food consists of soft-bodied invertebrates and carrion. Embryonic development is oviparous and direct, with no larval stage. Eggs are large and are deposited in leathery capsules with hooks at one end.

There are about 43 species in 6 genera, and 3 species in 2 genera occur in the Gulf of Mexico.

Key to the Species in the Gulf of Mexico
(Adapted from Fernholm and Hubbs 1981)

1a. One gill aperture on each side. . . *Myxine mcmillanae* p. 34
1b. Five or six gill apertures on each side 2
2a. Three anterior teeth of outer row and two anterior teeth of inner row on lingual tooth plate fused at bases (Fig. 1); slime pores range from 84 to 92
 . . . . *Eptatretus springeri* p. 33
2b. Three anterior teeth of outer row and three anterior teeth of inner row on lingual tooth plate fused at bases; slime pores range from 74 to 82 . . . . *Eptatretus minor* p. 32

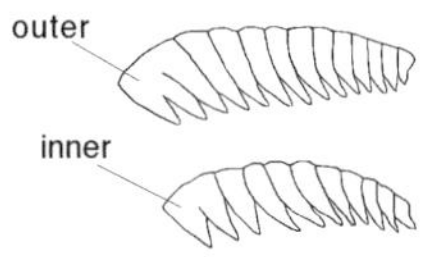

outer

inner

FIG 1

Eptatretus minor   Fernholm and Hubbs 1981

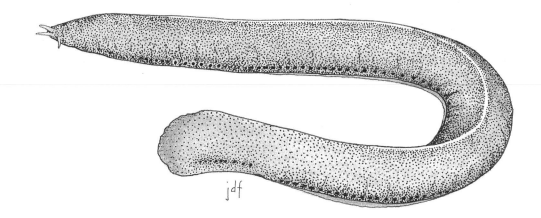

Eptatretus minor is relatively short and stout, with several gill apertures on each side of trunk. It is distinguished from the other species of the family by the following combination of characters. Nasal barbels and single barbel lateral to mouth are relatively long. Total tooth cusps on lingual plate range from 46 to 52, with 11 to 14 in outer row and 11 to 13 in inner row. Three anterior teeth of outer row and three anterior teeth of inner row are fused at bases. Gill apertures range from five (rare) to six. Total slime pores range from 74 to 82, with prebranchial pores numbering 15 to 18, branchial pores numbering 4 to 6, trunk pores numbering 41 to 48, and tail pores numbering 11 to 14. Ventral fin is poorly developed, originates posterior to last gill aperture, and extends to cloaca. Color is pale grayish brown with a thin mid-dorsal white stripe.

This species occurs in the western North Atlantic in the northern Gulf of Mexico. It has been captured from 300 to 472 m. Maximum known size is 395 mm TL; males mature at 223 mm TL, and females mature at 310 mm TL.

REFERENCE: Fernholm and Hubbs 1981.

Eptatretus springeri   (Bigelow and Schroeder 1952)

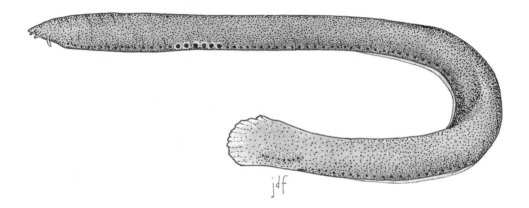

Eptatretus springeri is relatively long and slender, with several gill apertures on each side of trunk. It is distinguished from the other species of the family by the following combination of characters. Nasal barbels and single barbel lateral to mouth are of moderate length. Total tooth cusps on lingual plate range from 48 to 52, with 13 or 14 in outer row and 11 to 13 in inner row. Three anterior teeth of outer row and two anterior teeth of inner row are fused at bases. Gill apertures range from six to seven (rarely). Slime pores range from 84 to 92, with prebranchial pores numbering 16 to 19, branchial pores numbering 2 to 5, trunk pores numbering 52 to 57, and tail pores numbering 9 to 13. Ventral fin originates at about midlength and extends to cloaca. Color is dark brownish purple to light brown.

This species occurs in the western North Atlantic in the Gulf of Mexico. It has been captured from 410 to 768 m. Maximum known size is 590 mm TL, and females mature at 500 mm TL.

REFERENCES: Bigelow and Schroeder 1952; Fernholm and Hubbs 1981.

Myxine mcmillanae Hensley 1991

Myxine mcmillanae is long and slender, with a single gill aperture on each side. It is distinguished from the other species of the family by the following combination of characters. Nasal barbels and single barbel lateral to mouth are of moderate length. Total tooth cusps range from 42 to 48, with 10 to 12 in each outer row and in each inner row. Two anterior teeth of both inner and outer rows are fused at base. Gill pouches number six. Total slime pores range from 101 to 119, with prebranchial pores numbering 26 to 35, branchial pores numbering 0 to 2, trunk pores numbering 60 to 76, and tail pores numbering 9 to 12. Ventral fin is well developed and originates at about anterior 15% of trunk, and caudal fin fold originates at posterior margin of cloaca, is continuous around tail, and terminates at about posterior 15% of trunk length. Color is dark bluish gray except head anterior to first slime pore, slime pores, pharyngo-cutaneous duct, gill aperture, and fin fold are whitish.

This species occurs in the western Atlantic off Puerto Rico, the U.S. Virgin Islands, and in the northeastern Gulf of Mexico between 700 and 1,500 m. Maximum known size is 473 mm TL, and females mature at 455 mm TL.

REFERENCE: Hensley 1991.

PETROMYZONTIFORMES

Petromyzontiformes share a number of primitive characters with Myxiniformes and a number of derived characters with the jawed vertebrates (Gnathostomata), and thus they are considered to be the sister group of Gnathostomata. The single family in this order occurs in the Gulf of Mexico.

PETROMYZONTIDAE Lampreys

Lampreys are elongate and compressed posteriorly, with a funnel-shaped mouth surrounded by a circular lip bearing numerous horny teeth and with seven pairs of gill pouches. They are distinguished from other fishes by the following combination of characters. Snout lacks barbel. Single nostril is located on dorsal side of head and lacks connection with mouth. Mouth lacks jaws but has tongue bearing horny teeth. Eye is well developed. Gill pouches open separately to exterior and open into respiratory tube internally. Respiratory tube ends blindly posteriorly and opens into mouth anteriorly. Pharynx connects esophagus to mouth and is located dorsal to respiratory tube. Paired fins are lacking. One or two dorsal fins are present on posterior one-half of body. Anal fin is generally lacking. All fins are supported by fin rays. Body lacks scales and prominent rows of mucous pores.

Lampreys are anadromous or limited to freshwater in the temperate regions of the Northern and Southern Hemispheres. All species undergo a pronounced metamorphosis between their larval (ammocoete) and adult stages. Ammocoetes are wormlike in appearance and are deposit or filter feeders. The ammocoetes have a broad hood in place of the oral disc, lack teeth and eyes, and have a direct connection between the gill sacs and the pharynx. During metamorphosis the oral disc replaces the hood, eyes develop, and the separate respiratory tube develops ventral to the pharynx. There are 41 species in 6 genera, and 1 species occurs in the Gulf of Mexico.

Petromyzon marinus   Linnaeus 1758
Sea lamprey

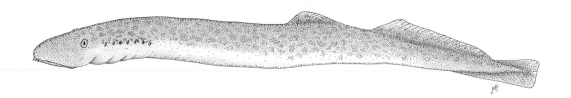

Petromyzon marinus is elongate and posteriorly compressed, with teeth on oral disc arranged in curvilinear rows and with two dorsal fins. It is distinguished from the other species of the family by the following combination of characters. Inner series of teeth on oral disc are largest. Oral plate above mouth is small and has two teeth, and oral plate below mouth is broad and has seven to nine conical teeth. Tongue has three denticulated plates, with margin of anterior plate deeply indented along midline and with tooth margins concave on each side. Nostril is surrounded by circular rim and is opposite anterior margin of eye. Gill openings are round to slightly oval, about one-half diameter of eye, and evenly spaced. Distance from mouth to last gill opening is about 20% of TL. Origin of first dorsal fin is slightly posterior to mid-length of trunk, and base length is about equal to one-half head length. Second dorsal fin is separated from first by distance equal to one-third or less length of first dorsal fin, and second dorsal fin is about 2 times length of first dorsal fin. Second dorsal fin is distinguished from caudal fin by deep notch, although fins are continuous. Color is olive-brown, yellow-brown, green, red, or blue, and generally mottled with darker shades of ground color dorsally, and whitish, gray, or a lighter shade of dorsal color ventrally. Small, recently metamorphosed specimens are blackish blue or lead colored dorsally and white ventrally.

This species occurs in the temperate waters of the North Atlantic, and in the western Atlantic it occurs from the Gulf of St. Lawrence to northern Florida and in the eastern Gulf of Mexico. It has been reported only once from the Gulf of Mexico, from a tidal pond near Cape San Blas, Florida. The sea lamprey is anadromous and leaves freshwater upon undergoing metamorphosis. Metamorphosed individuals feed on the blood of other fishes. They attach to the side of their host by means of their sucking disc and rasp through scales and skin with their tooth-bearing tongues. After sucking the fluids from a host the lamprey will seek a new host. Upon reaching maturity the lamprey migrates to freshwater to spawn. Maximum known size is about 880 mm TL, and size at metamorphosis is between 100 and 200 mm TL.

REFERENCES: Bigelow and Schroeder 1948a, 1953b; Vladykov and Kott 1980; C. R. Robins et al. 1986.

CHIMAERIFORMES

The Chimaeriformes and the Elasmobranchii make up the Chondrichthyes, the so-called cartilaginous fishes. The Chondrichthyes
are the sister group of the Teleostomi, the so-called bony fishes.
This order contains three families, and two of these occur in the
Gulf of Mexico.

Key to the Families in the Gulf of Mexico

1a. Snout relatively short and rounded or conical; clasper
      bilobed or trilobed. . . . . Chimaeridae p. 37
1b. Snout relatively long and pointed; clasper rodlike
      . . . . Rhinochimaeridae p. 41

CHIMAERIDAE Ratfishes

Ratfishes have a large, conical to rounded snout and a moderately compressed trunk tapering into a very slender tail. They are distinguished from the other families of the order by the following combination of characters. Lower surface of head has groove in front of nostril running from side to side. Nostril is large, located in front of mouth, and connected to mouth by groove covered by lateral lobes of upper lip. Mouth is subterminal. Lips are thick and fleshy. Roof of mouth lacks transverse curtain. Floor of mouth has fleshy tongue. Teeth consist of dental plates with radial ridges around their margins. Upper jaw has two pairs of plates, and lower jaw has single pair. Eye is large and located on side of head. Spiracle is absent. Gill chamber is covered by opercular fold of skin and cartilaginous supports. Pectoral and pelvic fins are broad and winglike. First dorsal fin is triangular and preceded by sharp-pointed bony spine. Spine can be raised and lowered. Second dorsal fin is lower and longer than first and is separated from first by short distance. Caudal fin is narrow and straight (diphycercal). Males possess bilobed or trilobed clasper, prepelvic clasper, and frontal clasper on head. Body is naked.

Ratfishes occur nearly worldwide in tropical to temperate seas. Most species are limited to the outer continental shelf and slope. Embryonic development is oviparous, with fertilized eggs deposited in a horny egg capsule. There are about 21 species in 2 genera, and 2 species in a single genus occur in the Gulf of Mexico.

Key to the Species in the Gulf of Mexico

1a. Second dorsal fin with concave dorsal margin, height at midlength about one-half height at anterior end
. . . . *Hydrolagus mirabilis* p. 40

1b. Second dorsal fin with straight or weakly concave dorsal margin, height at midlength about equal to height at anterior end . . . . *Hydrolagus alberti* p. 39

Hydrolagus alberti   Bigelow and Schroeder 1951

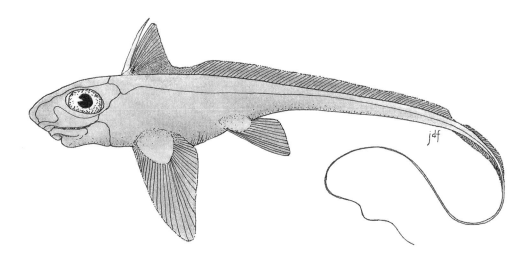

Hydrolagus alberti has a conical snout and a strongly compressed trunk tapering into a very slender, long tail. It is distinguished from the other species of the family by the following combination of characters. Head is about 21% of distance from tip of snout to origin of dorsal lobe of caudal fin. Eye is oval and large, horizontal diameter is about 40% of head length. Pectoral fin is about one-third as long as distance from tip of snout to posterior margin of second dorsal fin. Dorsal spine is largely free of anterior margin of first dorsal fin, is as long as distance from tip of snout to posterior margin of pupil, and is slightly higher than first dorsal fin. Posterior margin of dorsal spine bears two rows of thorns. First dorsal fin has acute tip and straight posterior margin. Distance between dorsal fins is about 40% of length of an-terior margin of dorsal fin. Second dorsal fin has nearly straight dorsal margin; its height at midlength is nearly as great as at anterior end. Anal fin is continuous with ventral caudal lobe. Caudal fin is prolonged as filament, about 80% as long as distance from tip of snout to posterior margin of second dorsal fin. Color is uniform dark brown.

This species occurs in the western North Atlantic from the Gulf of Mexico and the south-eastern coast of Florida. It has been captured from 348 to 823 m. Maximum known size is 275 mm long from tip of snout to origin of dorsal caudal lobe.

REFERENCES: Bigelow and Schroeder 1951b, 1953a; Grey 1959.

Hydrolagus mirabilis   (Collett 1904)
Large-eyed ratfish

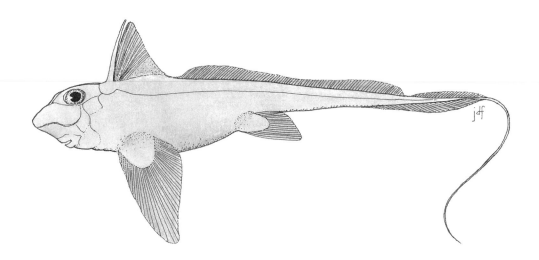

Hydrolagus mirabilis has a conical head and a greatly compressed trunk tapering to a long, very slender tail. It is distinguished from the other species of the family by the following combination of characters. Head is about 23% of distance from tip of snout to origin of dorsal lobe of caudal fin. Eye is oval shaped and moderately large; horizontal diameter is about 35% of head length. Pectoral fin is about one-third of distance from tip of snout to posterior margin of second dorsal fin. Dorsal spine is largely free of anterior margin of first dorsal fin, slightly shorter than distance from tip of snout to posterior margin of pupil, and slightly higher than first dorsal fin. Posterior margin of dorsal spine bears two rows of thorns. First dorsal fin has acute tip and slightly convex posterior margin. Distance between dorsal fins is about equal to length of anterior margin of first dorsal fin. Second dorsal fin has concave dorsal margin; its height at midlength is about one-half that at anterior end. Anal fin is continuous with ventral caudal lobe. Caudal fin is prolonged as filament that is about 73% of distance from tip of snout to posterior margin of second dorsal fin. Color is uniform dark brown, except fins are slightly darker and caudal filament is light.

This species occurs in the temperate North Atlantic. In the western North Atlantic it occurs from the Gulf of Mexico. It has been captured from 622 to 1,097 m in the Gulf of Mexico. Food consists of invertebrates and small fishes. Maximum known size is 80 cm TL, including filament.

REFERENCES: Grey 1959; Stehmann and Bürkel 1984b.

RHINOCHIMAERIDAE Longnosed ratfishes

Longnosed ratfishes have a long, pointed snout and a moderately compressed trunk tapering to a very slender tail. They are distinguished from the other families of the order by the following combination of characters. Lower surface of head lacks transverse groove in front of nostril. Nostril is large, located in front of mouth, and connected to mouth by groove covered by lateral lobe of upper lip. Mouth is subterminal. Lips are thick and fleshy. Roof of mouth lacks transverse curtain. Floor of mouth has fleshy tongue bearing small papillae. Teeth consist of dental plates that either have or lack transverse ridges. Upper jaw has two pairs of plates, and lower jaw has single pair. Eye is large and located on side of head. Spiracle is absent. Gill chamber is covered by opercular fold of skin and cartilaginous supports. Pectoral and pelvic fins are broad and winglike. First dorsal fin is triangular and preceded by sharp-pointed bony spine. Spine can be raised and lowered. Second dorsal fin is lower and longer than first dorsal fin. Tail is straight (diphycercal). Ventral lobe of caudal fin is broader than dorsal lobe in adults; lobes are about of equal breadth in juveniles. Clasper of males is rodlike.

Longnosed ratfishes occur worldwide at temperate latitudes. Species are apparently limited to the continental slope. Embryonic development is oviparous, with fertilized eggs deposited in horny egg capsules. There are about six species in three genera, and one species occurs in the Gulf of Mexico.

Rhinochimaera atlantica   Holt and Byrne 1909

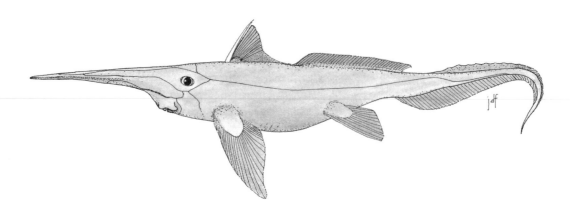

Rhinochimaera atlantica has a very long, slender, pointed snout and a moderately compressed trunk tapering into a very slender tail. It is distinguished from the other species of the family by the following combination of characters. Head is about 50% of distance from tip of snout to origin of dorsal lobe of caudal fin. Eye is broad-oval shaped; horizontal diameter is about 7% of head length. Pectoral fin is one-fourth of distance from tip of snout to posterior margin of second dorsal fin. Dorsal spine is largely connected to anterior margin of first dorsal fin, is about one-fifth as long as distance from tip of snout to posterior margin of pupil, and is slightly higher than first dorsal fin. Posterior margin of dorsal spine is smooth. First dorsal fin has acute tip and concave distal margin. Distance between dorsal fins is about 55% of length of anterior margin of first dorsal fin. Second dorsal fin has nearly straight dorsal margin; its height at midlength is nearly as great as at anterior end. Anal fin is continuous with ventral lobe of caudal fin. Dorsal lobe of caudal fin is very low and possesses a crest of sharp-pointed denticles. Caudal fin is prolonged as short filament, about 3% of distance from tip of snout to posterior margin of second dorsal fin. Color is light brown to whitish, except fins are slightly darker.

This species occurs in the temperate North Atlantic. In the western North Atlantic it occurs off Nova Scotia and New England and in the eastern Gulf of Mexico. It has been captured from 530 to 1,000 m in the western North Atlantic. Maximum known size is 140 cm TL.

REFERENCES: Bigelow and Schroeder 1954b; Schroeder 1955; Stehmann and Bürkel 1984c; Scott and Scott 1988; Compagno et al. 1990.

ORECTOLOBIFORMES

The Orectolobiformes, Heterodontiformes (absent from the Gulf), Lamniformes, and Carcharhiniformes make up the Galeomorphi, one of the two major taxa of Neoselachii (modern sharks and rays). Heterodontiformes are considered to be the sister group to the remainder of the orders, and Orectolobiformes are considered to be the sister group of Lamniformes and Carcharhiniformes, although these relationships need to be studied further. Orectolobiformes comprise seven families, and two of these occur in the Gulf of Mexico.

Key to the Families in the Gulf of Mexico
(Adapted from Castro 1983; Compagno 1984)

1a. Mouth very large and nearly terminal; external gill slits very large; internal gill slits with filter screens; caudal peduncle with well-developed keel
. . . . Rhincodontidae p. 46
1b. Mouth relatively small and subterminal; external gill slits relatively small; internal gill slits without filter screens; caudal peduncle without keel . . . . . Ginglymostomatidae p. 43

GINGLYMOSTOMATIDAE   Nurse sharks

The nurse sharks are moderately slender to stout, and cylindrical to slightly depressed in cross section, with a very short, blunt snout and a long, low tail. They are distinguished from the other sharks of the order by the following combination of characters. Head is broad and flattened and lacks skin flaps. Snout is broadly rounded. Mouth is small, transverse, and subterminal, and lacks symphyseal groove on chin. Nostril bears short to long, pointed barbel, and nostril is connected to mouth by nasoral groove. Teeth are small and similarly shaped in both jaws, with a median cusp and lateral cusplets. Eye is on dorsolateral or lateral side of head. Spiracle is located posterior to eye and is smaller than eye. Gill slits are small, and fifth nearly overlaps fourth. Pectoral fin is of moderate size, either broad and rounded or narrow and falcate. Dorsal fins are of similar size, or first is slightly larger than second. Second dorsal fin is located slightly anterior to origin of anal fin. Pelvic fin is slightly larger to slightly smaller than dorsal fins and anal fin. Anal fin is about same size as second dorsal fin.

Caudal fin is less than one-half total length, with upper lobe set at small angle above body axis.

Nurse sharks occur worldwide in tropical and subtropical seas. They live on or near the bottom from near shore to 70 m, on rocky or coral reefs, sandy bottoms, and mangrove areas. Food consists of squids, octopods, sea urchins, crabs, shrimps, lobsters, and bony fishes. Development is ovoviviparous or viviparous. There are three recognized species, and one of these occurs in the Gulf of Mexico.

Ginglymostoma cirratum (Bonnaterre 1788)
Nurse shark

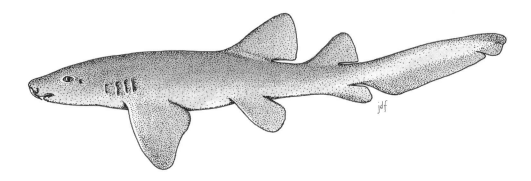

Ginglymostoma cirratum is moderately slender to moderately stout, with a very short, rounded snout and a moderately long, low tail. It is distinguished from the other species of the family by the following combination of characters. Nasal barbels extend to mouth. Teeth are conical and rather broad, with a small, short median cusp and several large lateral cusplets. Spiracle is minute. Pectoral, dorsal, and anal fins have rounded tips. Pectoral fin is broad. First dorsal fin is considerably larger than second dorsal fin and anal fin. Caudal fin is greater than one-fourth total length. Color is yellowish brown to grayish brown and is either patterned with dark spots and obscure saddle markings on dorsal surface or lacks these markings. Markings are most distinct in small specimens.

This species occurs in the tropical to warm temperate waters of the Atlantic and eastern Pacific. In the western Atlantic it occurs from Rhode Island to southern Brazil, including the Gulf of Mexico, between the shoreline and 12 m. It has been captured on or near the bottom from near the surface to 12 m. Food consists of benthic invertebrates such as sea urchins, bivalves, gastropods, squids, octopods, crabs, spiny lobsters, stingrays, and bony fishes. Development is ovoviviparous, and litters range from 21 to 28 young. Maximum known size is about 430 cm TL; males mature at about 225 cm TL, females at about 230 to 240 mm TL, and young are about 27 to 28 cm TL at birth.

REFERENCES: Bigelow and Schroeder 1948a; S. Springer 1963; Clark and von Schmidt 1965; Hoese and Moore 1977; Applegate et al. 1979; Castro 1983; Compagno 1984; Quéro 1984e; C. R. Robins et al. 1986; Bonfil et al. 1990.

RHINCODONTIDAE   Whale shark

The family contains a single species.

Rhincodon typus Smith 1828

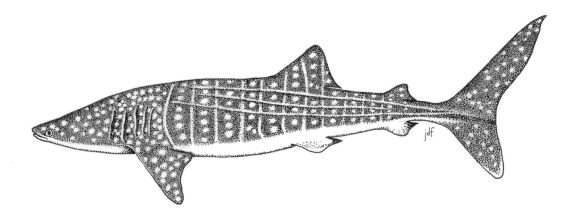

Rhincodon typus is rather fusiform, and cylindrical to slightly depressed in cross section, with a broad, depressed snout, prominent ridges on sides, and a large, high, falcate caudal fin. It is distinguished from the other species of the order by the following combination of characters. Mouth is very broad, nearly terminal, and lacks symphyseal groove on chin. Teeth are similarly shaped in both jaws and very numerous, with median cusp but no cusplets. Nasal barbels are rudimentary. Nostril lacks groove along outer edge. Head lacks lateral flaps of skin. Eye is on side of head. Spiracle is smaller than eye. Gill slits are very large, and fifth is distinctly separated from fourth. Internal gill slits possess filter screens of transverse lamellae with branching processes on inner surfaces. Pectoral fin is large, narrow, and falcate. First dorsal fin is distinctly larger than second and originates anterior to origin of pelvic fin. Pelvic fin is slightly larger than second dorsal fin and anal fin. Caudal peduncle has well-developed lateral keel and upper precaudal pit. Caudal fin is less than one-third total length, with upper lobe set at high angle above body axis and well-developed lower lobe.

Color is dark gray, reddish, or greenish gray with white to yellow spots and transverse stripes dorsally and white to yellow ventrally.

This species occurs worldwide in tropical to warm temperate coastal and oceanic waters. In the western Atlantic it occurs from New York to central Brazil, including the entire Gulf of Mexico. Large numbers frequently occur near the Flower Gardens Reefs off eastern Texas. It feeds on planktonic and nektonic crustaceans, squids, and fishes that are filtered from the water flowing into the mouth by its gill filter screens. Development is ovoviviparous, with females containing up to 300 embryos in individual capsules. The embryos hatch from the egg capsules prior to parturition. Maximum known size is about 18 m TL, but specimens are rare at lengths greater than 12 m TL.

REFERENCES: Gudger 1941; Bigelow and Schroeder 1948a; Baughman 1955; Hoese and Moore 1977; Applegate et al. 1979; Hoffman et al. 1981; Castro 1983; Wolfson 1983, 1986; Compagno 1984 as (*Rhiniodon typus*); C. R. Robins et al. 1986; Joung et al. 1996.

LAMNIFORMES

Lamniformes consist of six or seven families, and four of these oc-cur in the Gulf of Mexico. The phylogenetic interrelationships have not been worked out for the families of the order.

Key to the Families in the Gulf of Mexico
(Adapted from Compagno 1984)

1a. Caudal fin about one-half total length; fourth and fifth gill slits above pectoral fin base . . . . Alopiidae p. 48

1b. Caudal fin considerably less than one-half total length; fourth and fifth gill slits anterior to pectoral fin 2

2a. Caudal fin asymmetrical, ventral lobe much shorter than dorsal lobe; caudal peduncle without lateral keel . . . . Odontaspididae p. 57

2b. Caudal fin nearly symmetrical (lunate), ventral lobe nearly as long as dorsal lobe; caudal peduncle with well-developed lateral keel 3

3a. Teeth enlarged and bladelike; fewer than 40 tooth rows in each jaw; gill slits not extending onto dorsal side of head; internal gill slits without gill rakers . . . . . . Lamnidae p. 53

3b. Teeth very small and hooked rather than bladelike; over 150 tooth rows in each jaw; gill openings extend onto dor-sal aspect of head; internal gill slits with gill rakers . . . . Cetorhinidae p. 52

ALOPIIDAE   Thresher sharks

The thresher sharks are fusiform and cylindrical in cross section, with a moderately long, conical snout and an extremely long, asymmetrical caudal fin. They are distinguished from the other families of the order by the following combination of characters. Head is short and snout is relatively long and pointed. Mouth is small and arcuate. Teeth are small to moderate in size, single cus-pid, smooth, compressed, and bladelike, with fewer than 60 rows in each jaw. Eye is of moderate size to extremely large. Gill slits are of moderate size and do not extend to dorsal aspect of head. Fourth and fifth gill slits are located above pectoral fin base. In-ternal gill slits lack gill rakers. Pectoral fin is narrow and longer than head length in adults. First dorsal fin originates posterior to pectoral fin base and is high, erect, and angular. Second dorsal fin and anal fin are very small; second dorsal fin is anterior to anal fin base. Caudal peduncle is slightly compressed and has precaudal pit but lacks lateral keel. Caudal fin has greatly elongated dorsal lobe that equals about one-half total length.

Thresher sharks occur worldwide in tropical to temperate seas. They are strong swimmers that range from coastal to oceanic waters. Food consists of moderate-sized schooling squids and bony fishes. The elongated tail is apparently used to separate individual fish from schools and/or to stun individual prey. This behavior often results in thresher sharks being snagged by the tail on longline gear. Development is aplacental-viviparous, and young apparently feed on less-developed embryos and eggs in the uterus (ovophagous). There are three species in a single genus, and two of these occur in the Gulf of Mexico.

Key to the Species in the Gulf of Mexico
(Adapted from Compagno 1984)

1a. Head nearly flat between eyes; eye very large, extending to dorsal side of head; base of first dorsal fin closer to pelvic fin base than to pectoral fin base
. . . . *Alopias superciliosus* p. 50
1b. Head strongly convex between eyes; eye of moderate size, not extending to dorsal side of head; base of first dorsal fin about midway between pelvic fin base and pectoral fin base
. . . . *Alopias vulpinus* p. 51

Alopias superciliosus (Lowe 1841)
Bigeye thresher

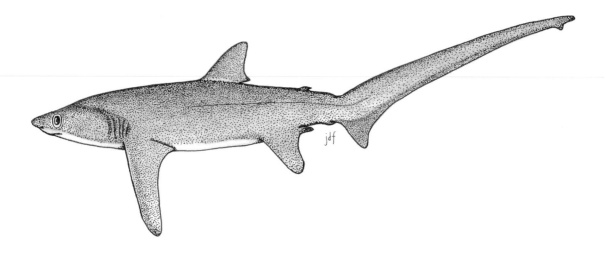

Alopias superciliosus is fusiform, with a moderately long, bulbous snout and a very long caudal fin with a well-developed subterminal notch. It is distinguished from the other species of the family by the following combination of characters. Eye is very large and extends to dorsal side of head. Dorsal profile of head is slightly convex anterior to eye and concave behind posterior margin of eye. Head has deep horizontal groove on either side, meeting just posterior to orbit and extending to level of gill slits. Labial furrows are absent. Teeth are of moderate size, with slightly curved cusps. Each jaw has fewer than 25 tooth rows. Pectoral fin is falcate, with a moderately broad tip. Base of dorsal fin is closer to pelvic fin base than to pectoral fin base. Caudal fin has relatively well-developed subterminal notch. Color is dark purplish brown with metallic hues dorsally and lighter ventrally. Light color of abdomen does not extend onto base of pectoral fin.

This species occurs worldwide in tropical to warm temperate seas. In the western Atlantic it occurs from New York to Florida, in the northwestern Gulf of Mexico, and off the Bahamas, Cuba, Venezuela, and southern Brazil. It ranges from coastal to oceanic waters and has been captured from the surface to 500 m. Food consists of squids and pelagic and demersal fishes. Litters usually consist of two young, although four young have been reported. Maximum known size is 461 cm TL; males mature at 270 cm TL and reach 400 cm TL, females mature at 355 cm TL and reach 461 cm TL, and young range from 64 to 106 cm TL at birth.

REFERENCES: Bigelow and Schroeder 1948a; Stillwell and Casey 1976; Castro 1983; Gilmore 1983; Gruber and Compagno 1983; Compagno 1984; Quéro 1984d; C. R. Robins et al. 1986.

Alopias vulpinus   (Bonnaterre 1788)
Thresher shark

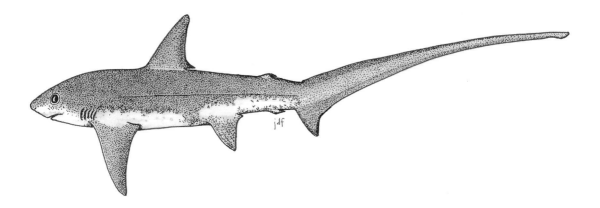

Alopias vulpinus is fusiform, with a moderately long, conical snout and a very long caudal fin with a moderately developed subterminal notch. It is distinguished from the other species of the family by the following combination of characters. Eye is of moderate size and does not extend to dorsal side of head. Dorsal profile of head is convex and lacks horizontal grooves. Labial furrows are present. Teeth are relatively small and possess slightly curved cusps. Each jaw has more than 58 tooth rows. Pectoral fin is falcate, with acutely pointed tip. Base of first dorsal fin is about midway between pelvic fin base and pectoral fin base. Caudal fin has moderately large subterminal notch. Color is brown to black with metallic hues dorsally and white ventrally. White color of belly extends onto base of pectoral fin as a broad band.

This species occurs worldwide in tropical to temperate waters. In the western Atlantic it occurs from Newfoundland to Florida, off Cuba, in the Gulf of Mexico, and from Venezuela to Argentina. It ranges from coastal to oceanic waters from the surface to 366 m. Food consists of squids, octopods, pelagic crustaceans, and pelagic bony fishes. Litters consist of two young, although four young have occasionally been reported. Maximum known size is 549 cm TL; males mature at 319 to 420 cm TL, females mature at 376 to 549 cm TL, and young range from 114 to 150 cm TL at birth.

REFERENCES: Bigelow and Schroeder 1948a; Hoese and Moore 1977; Applegate et al. 1979; Castro 1983; Compagno 1984; Quéro 1984d; C. R. Robins et al. 1986.

CETORHINIDAE   Basking shark

The family contains a single species.

Cetorhinus maximus   (Gunner 1765)

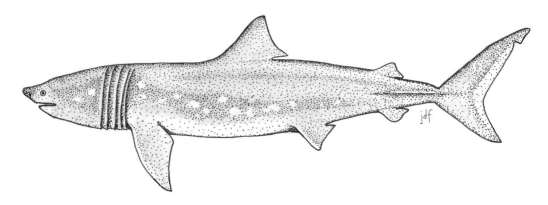

Cetorhinus maximus is moderately stout and conical in cross section, with a moderately long, conical snout and a lunate caudal fin. It is distinguished from the other species of the order by the following combination of characters. Head is of moderate length, and snout is moderately long and pointed. Mouth is large and arcuate. Teeth are very small and hooklike. Each jaw has over 200 tooth rows. Eye is small and is located on side of head. Gill slits are large, extending to dorsal and ventral sides of head. All gill slits are anterior to the pectoral fin base. Internal gill slits possess rakers that consist of hairlike dermal denticles. Pectoral fin is moderately long, but shorter than head, and moderately broad. First dorsal fin is high, erect, and angular. Second dorsal fin and anal fin are about one-half size of first dorsal fin. Caudal peduncle is depressed and possesses precaudal pit and distinct lateral keel. Caudal fin is lunate, with dorsal lobe about one-fourth total length and lower lobe nearly as long as upper lobe. Color is grayish brown to black dorsally, with or without irregular light patches, and pale grayish brown to gray ventrally, with or without white patches on snout and mouth.

This species occurs worldwide in temperate waters. In the western Atlantic it occurs from Newfoundland to Florida, from southern Brazil to southern Argentina, and in the northern Gulf of Mexico. However, it is rare in the Gulf of Mexico. The basking shark ranges from coastal to oceanic waters from the surface to an unknown depth. Food consists of planktonic crustaceans, which are captured by the shark swimming slowly through the water with its mouth open while the plankton are filtered from the water by the gill rakers. Development is thought to be ovoviviparous. Pregnant females are unknown in recent times. Maximum known size is at least 980 cm TL; males mature at about 400 to 500 cm TL and reach about 900 cm TL, females mature at about 810 to 980 cm TL, and young are about 165 cm TL at birth.

REFERENCES: Bigelow and Schroeder 1948a; Springer and Gilbert 1976; Castro 1983; Compagno 1984; Quéro 1984c; C. R. Robins et al. 1986.

LAMNIDAE Mackerel sharks

The mackerel sharks are fusiform, with a conical snout and a lunate caudal fin. They are distinguished from the other families of the order by the following combination of characters. Head is moderately long, and snout is relatively long and pointed. Mouth is large and arcuate. Teeth are large, bladelike, and moderately to greatly depressed. Each jaw has fewer than 85 tooth rows. Gill slits are large, extending to dorsal side of head, and all are located anterior to base of pectoral fin. Internal gill slits lack gill rakers. Pectoral fin is long and narrow. First dorsal fin is high, erect, and angular. Second dorsal fin and anal fin are very small. Caudal peduncle is strongly depressed and possesses well-developed lateral keel. Caudal fin is moderately long, but less than one-third total length, with lower lobe nearly as long as upper lobe.

The mackerel sharks occur worldwide in tropical to temperate seas. They are strong swimmers that range from pelagic coastal to oceanic waters. Although generally considered to be epipelagic (inhabiting the upper 200 m), they have been reported to 1,280 m. Food consists of crustaceans, squids, elasmobranchs, bony fishes, marine reptiles, birds, and mammals. Because of a specialized circulatory system, they maintain their body temperature above that of the surrounding water. Development is aplacental-viviparous, and the young feed on less-developed embryos and eggs in the uterus (oophagy). There are five species in three genera, and three species in two genera occur in the Gulf of Mexico.

Key to the Species in the Gulf of Mexico
(Adapted from Compagno 1984)

1a. Teeth broadly triangular with serrated edges (Fig. 2)
. . . . *Carcharodon carcharias* p. 54

FIG 2

1b. Teeth rather narrow, not greatly compressed, and without serrations (Fig. 3) 2
2a. Pectoral fin shorter than head length; ventral side of snout and mouth white . . . . *Isurus oxyrinchus* p. 55
2b. Pectoral fin as long as head length; ventral side of snout and mouth dusky . . . . *Isurus paucus* p. 56

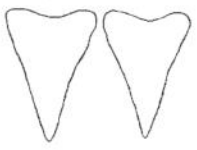

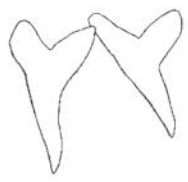

FIG 3

Carcharodon carcharias (Linnaeus 1758)
White shark

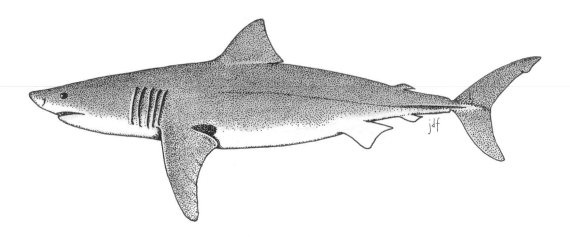

Carcharodon carcharias is fusiform and relatively stout, with a relatively short, bluntly conical snout and a lunate caudal fin. It is distinguished from the other species of the family by the following combination of characters. Nostril is located on side of rather short snout. Mouth is broadly arched. Teeth are very large, compressed, triangular, serrated, and without secondary cusps (except in very small juveniles). Upper and lower jaws have 22 to 24 tooth rows. Pectoral fin is moderately broad proximally, narrow distally, and shorter than head length. First dorsal fin is large and originates over inner margin of pectoral fin. Second dorsal fin and anal fin are very small, with anal fin originating posterior to base of second dorsal fin. Color varies from grayish white to slate brown dorsally and dusky white ventrally.

This species occurs worldwide in tropical to temperate seas but is apparently rare in tropical waters. It generally is found over continental and insular shelves in the upper 200 m but has occasionally been captured to 1,280 m. In the western Atlantic it occurs from Newfoundland to Florida, off the Bahamas and Cuba, in the northern Gulf of Mexico, and from Brazil to Argentina. However, in the northern Atlantic Ocean it occurs south of North Carolina only during the winter. Food consists of crustaceans, gastropods, squids, chondrichthyans, bony fishes, sea turtles, marine birds, and marine mammals such as sea otters, porpoises, dolphins, pinnipeds, and baleen and toothed whales. Small individuals feed mostly on fishes, and large individuals feed mostly on mammals. Litters range up to nine young. Maximum known size is 640 cm TL, possibly to 800 cm TL; males mature at 240 cm TL, females mature at 400 to 430 cm TL, and young are 120 cm TL or more at birth.

REFERENCES: Bigelow and Schroeder 1948a, 1953b; Hoese and Moore 1977; Applegate et al. 1979; Pratt et al. 1982; Castro 1983; Compagno 1984; Quéro 1984b; C. R. Robins et al. 1986; Scott and Scott 1988.

Isurus oxyrinchus   Rafinesque 1810
Shortfin mako

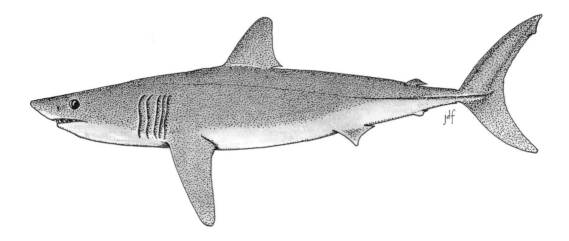

Isurus oxyrinchus is relatively slender and fusiform, with a long, slender, conical snout and a lunate caudal fin. It is distinguished from the other species of the family by the following combination of characters. Mouth is strongly arched. Teeth are large, narrow, not greatly compressed, and lack serrations and secondary cusps. Anterior teeth in both jaws are recurved lingually. Upper and lower jaws have from 24 to 26 tooth rows. Pectoral fin is narrow based, narrow tipped to acutely pointed, and shorter than head length. First dorsal fin is large and originates over or posterior to free tip of pectoral fin. Second dorsal fin is minute and originates slightly anterior to origin of anal fin. Secondary keel is lacking on caudal fin base. Color is dark metallic blue dorsally and white ventrally.

This species occurs worldwide in tropical to temperate seas from the surface to 152 m. In the western Atlantic it occurs from the Gulf of Maine to Argentina, including the Gulf of Mexico and the Caribbean Sea. Food consists almost extensively of elasmobranch and bony fishes but to a lesser degree includes squids, salps, sea turtles, and porpoises. Litters range from 8 to 10 young. Maximum known size is 394 cm TL; males mature at 195 cm TL and reach 284 cm TL, females mature at 280 cm TL, and young are 60 to 67 cm TL at birth.

REFERENCES: Bigelow and Schroeder 1948a; Hoese and Moore 1977; Applegate et al. 1979; Castro 1983; Pratt and Casey 1983; Compagno 1984; Quéro 1984b; C. R. Robins et al. 1986.

Isurus paucus   Guitart Manday 1966
Longfin mako

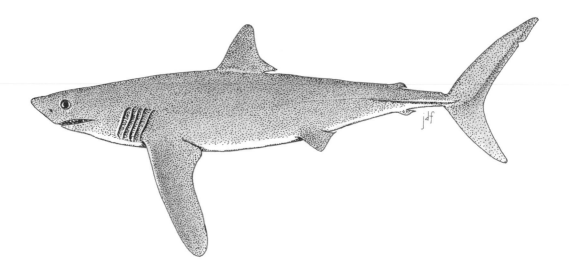

Isurus paucus is relatively fusiform, with a long, conical snout and a lunate tail. It is distinguished from the other species of the family by the following combination of characters. Mouth is strongly arched. Teeth are large, rather narrow, not greatly compressed, and lack serrations and secondary cusps. Anterior teeth of each jaw are rather straight, not recurved lingually. Upper jaw has 24 to 26 tooth rows, and lower jaw has 22 to 26. Pectoral fin is narrow based but broadly tipped and as long as head length. First dorsal fin is large and originates posterior to free tip of pectoral fin. Second dorsal fin is minute and originates anterior to base of anal fin. Short secondary keel occurs on caudal fin base. Color is dark blue to bluish black dorsally and bluish gray to dusky ventrally.

This species occurs worldwide in tropical to warm temperate seas. It has been captured from the surface to 220 m. In the western Atlantic it occurs from Georges Bank to Cuba and the Gulf of Mexico. Food consists of pelagic cephalopods and schooling fishes. Litters consist of two young. Maximum known size is at least 417 cm TL; males mature at 245 cm TL, females mature at 245 to 417 cm TL, and young are 97 cm TL at birth.

REFERENCES: Guitart Manday 1966, 1975; Dodrill and Gilmore 1979; Castro 1983; Gilmore 1983; Compagno 1984; Quéro 1984b; C. R. Robins et al. 1986.

ODONTASPIDIDAE   Sand tiger sharks

The sand tigers are moderately stout bodied to stout bodied, with a pointed snout and a moderately long, low caudal fin. They are distinguished from the other families of the order by the following combination of characters. Snout is conical to slightly depressed. Mouth is large and extends beyond eye. Teeth are large but not bladelike, with slender cusps and cusplets. Eye is small to moderately large and is located on side of head. Gill slits are moderately large but do not extend to dorsal side of head and are located anterior to origin of pectoral fin. Dorsal fins and anal fin are large, and pectoral fin is relatively small. Caudal peduncle is compressed, lacks caudal keel, but has upper precaudal pit. Caudal fin is shorter than one-fourth total length and is not lunate, with dorsal lobe considerably longer than ventral lobe.

Sand tigers occur worldwide in tropical to temperate seas. They are active swimmers in littoral and epibenthic waters and range from the shoreline to 1,600 m. Food consists of crustaceans, squids, skates, rays, sharks, and bony fishes. Development is aplacental-viviparous. Apparently embryos feed on other less well developed embryos and on fertilized and unfertilized eggs in the uterus (oophagy). There are four species in two genera, and two species in separate genera occur in the Gulf of Mexico.

Key to the Species of the Gulf of Mexico
(Adapted from Compagno 1984)

1a.   Snout relatively long and conical; two rows of relatively large teeth on either side of symphysis of upper jaw (Fig. 4); first dorsal fin larger than second dorsal fin and located closer to base of pectoral fin than to base of pelvic fin
. . . . *Odontaspis noronhai* p. 59

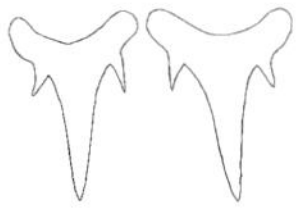

FIG 4

1b.   Snout relatively short and flattened; three rows of relatively large teeth on either side of symphysis of upper jaw (Fig. 5); first dorsal fin about same size as second dorsal fin and located closer to base of pelvic fin than to base of pectoral fin . . . . *Carcharias taurus* p. 58

FIG 5

Carcharias taurus Rafinesque 1810
Sand tiger

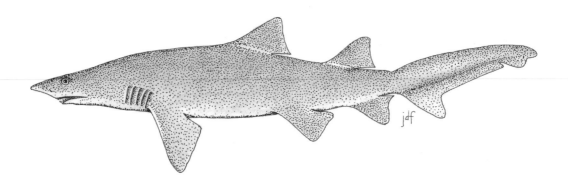

Carcharias taurus is rather stout bodied, with a relatively short, pointed, flattened snout and a relatively long, low caudal fin. It is distinguished from the other species of the family by the following combination of characters. Snout is narrowly rounded to acute. Lower jaw has well-developed labial furrows. Teeth have prominent, narrow cusp and lateral cusp on each side. Three relatively large tooth rows occur on either side of symphysis of upper jaw, and these are separated from large lateral teeth by small tooth. Eye is relatively small. Two dorsal fins and anal fin are about equal in size. First dorsal fin is located closer to pelvic fin base than to pectoral fin base. Origin of second dorsal fin is posterior to base of pelvic fin. Caudal fin has well-developed ventral lobe. Color is light brown to greenish gray dorsally and grayish white ventrally, with yellowish brown to reddish spots dorsally.

This species occurs in the western Atlantic, eastern Atlantic, southwestern Indian, and western Pacific Oceans from tropical to temperate seas and from the shoreline to 191 m. In the western Atlantic it occurs from the Gulf of Maine to southern Brazil, including Bermuda, the Gulf of Mexico, and the Bahamas. Food consists of benthic crustaceans, squids, sharks, skates, rays, and a large variety of bony fishes. Embryonic development is ovophagous, and a single embryo develops in each uterus. Maximum known size is 310 cm TL; males mature at 220 to 257 cm TL, females mature at 220 to 300 cm TL, and young are 95 to 105 cm TL at birth.

REFERENCES: Bigelow and Schroeder 1948a, 1953b; Springer 1948; Hoese and Moore 1977; Castro 1983; Gilmore et al. 1983 (all above as *Odontaspis taurus*); Compagno 1984 (as *Eugomphotus taurus*); Quéro 1984a; C. R. Robins et al. 1986 (as *Odontaspis taurus*).

Odontaspis noronhai (Maul 1955)
Bigeye sand tiger

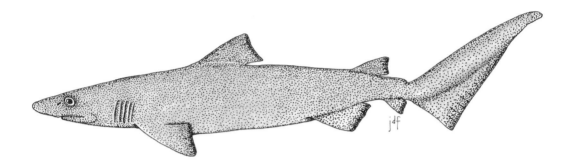

Odontaspis noronhai is rather stout bodied, with a relatively long, conical snout and a relatively long, low caudal fin. It is distinguished from the other species of the family by the following combination of characters. Snout is narrowly rounded. Lower jaw has labial furrows. Teeth have prominent, narrow cusp and lateral cusp on each side. Two relatively large tooth rows occur on either side of symphysis, and these are separated from large lateral teeth by small tooth. Eye is relatively large. First dorsal fin is distinctly larger than second dorsal fin and is located closer to pectoral fin base than to pelvic fin base. Origin of second dorsal fin is over midbase to near end of base of pelvic fin.

Caudal fin has well-developed ventral lobe. Color is gray to chocolate brown dorsally and ventrally.

This species occurs in the Atlantic and Indo-Pacific Oceans between 600 and 1,000 m. A single specimen is known from the Gulf of Mexico, off Brownsville, Texas, in 100 m of water. Several specimens were reported off southern Brazil. Maximum known size is 360 cm TL; males mature at 326 to 342 cm TL, and females mature at 326 cm TL.

REFERENCES: Maul 1955; Compagno 1984; Quéro 1984a; Sadowsky et al. 1984; Branstetter and McEachran 1986a.

CARCHARHINIFORMES

The order contains seven or eight families, and four of these occur in the Gulf of Mexico. Scyliorhinidae is considered to be the sister group of the remaining families. Triakidae is considered to be the sister group of three families, including Carcharhinidae and Sphyrnidae. Recent evidence suggests that a genus within Carcharhinidae are the sister group of Sphyrnidae, and if this view is substantiated, Sphyrnidae would have to be classified within Carcharhinidae. Sphyrnidae are considered to be a separate family pending further study of their relationships.

Key to the Families in the Gulf of Mexico

1a. Head greatly flattened, with bladelike lateral extremities
. . . . Sphyrnidae p. 91
1b. Head not flattened, without bladelike lateral extremities
. . . . 2
2a. First dorsal fin posteriorly located, over or posterior to base of pelvic fin . . . . Scyliorhinidae p. 60
2b. First dorsal fin anterior to base of pelvic fin 3
3a. Caudal peduncle without dorsal precaudal pit (Fig. 6); dorsal lobe of caudal fin without lateral undulations; ventral lobe of caudal fin poorly developed . . . . . . Triakidae p. 68
3b. Caudal peduncle with dorsal precaudal pit (Fig. 7); dorsal lobe of caudal fin with lateral undulations; ventral lobe of caudal fin strongly developed . . . . . . Carcharhinidae p. 71

FIG 6

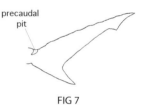

precaudal pit

FIG 7

SCYLIORHINIDAE   Catsharks

Catsharks are elongate, moderately depressed, with short to long snouts and short to moderately long and low caudal fins. They are distinguished from the other families of the order by the following combination of characters. Snout is short to moderate in length, and depressed. Anterior nasal flap is variable in shape but does not form barbel. Mouth is arched and long, extending beyond anterior margin of eye. Labial furrows are well developed to absent. Eye is elongate and oval to slitlike. Nictitating eyelid is rudimentary. Spiracle is moderately developed. First dorsal fin is small and originates above or posterior to base of pelvic fin. Anal fin is well developed. Caudal peduncle lacks dorsal precaudal pit. Dorsal lobe of caudal fin lacks lateral undulations. Ventral lobe of caudal fin is poorly developed or absent.

The catsharks occur worldwide from tropical to Arctic seas. They are benthic in habitat and range from the intertidal zone to greater than 2,000 m. Food consists of invertebrates and small fishes. Development is generally oviparous, with the fertilized egg deposited in a horny egg capsule that is laid by the female on the substratum. Some species are ovoviviparous. There are about 96 recognized species in 15 genera, and 6 species in 4 genera occur in the Gulf of Mexico.

Key to the Species of the Gulf of Mexico
(Adapted from Compagno 1984)

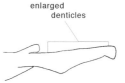

enlarged denticles

FIG 8

FIG 9

1a. Dorsal margin of caudal fin with crest of enlarged denticles (Fig. 8) 2
1b. Dorsal margin of caudal fin without crest of enlarged denticles (Fig. 9). 3
2a. Width of posterior margin of pectoral fin greater than mouth width; body with color pattern
. . . . *Galeus arae* p. 65
2b. Width of posterior margin of pectoral fin less than mouth width; body plain colored
. . . . *Parmaturus campechiensis* p. 66
3a. Labial furrows on lower jaw only (Fig. 10); anal fin separated from caudal fin by distance equal to one-half or more of anal fin base. . . . . *Scyliorhinus retifer* p. 67
3b. Labial furrows well developed on both jaws (Fig. 11); anal fin separated from caudal fin by notch 4
4a. First dorsal fin nearly as large as second, from two-thirds area to same area as second; origin of first dorsal fin over midbase of pelvic fin base . . . . *Apristurus laurussonii* p. 62
4b. First dorsal fin distinctly smaller than second, about one-half area or less than second; origin of first dorsal fin slightly anterior to or posterior to pelvic fin base 5
5a. Origin of first dorsal fin over or anterior to base of pelvic fin . . . . *Apristurus riveri* p. 64
5b. Origin of first dorsal fin posterior to pelvic fin base
. . . . *Apristurus parvipinnis* p. 63

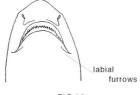

labial furrows

FIG 10

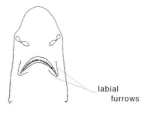

labial furrows

FIG 11

Apristurus laurussonii   (Saemundsson 1922)
Iceland catshark

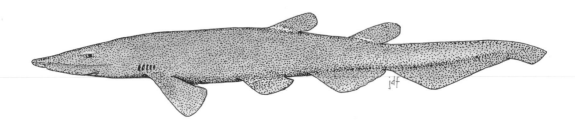

Apristurus laurussonii is relatively slender, with a moderately long, broad snout and head, and a long, low caudal fin. It is distinguished from the other species of the family by the following combination of characters. Preoral snout length is 7% to 8% of TL. Nostril is enlarged and has poorly developed anterior lobe. Distance between nostrils is about 1.4 times nostril width. Mouth is long and broadly arched. Labial furrows are well developed in both jaws. Eye length is less than 4% of TL. Gill slits are not covered with pleats or grooves. First dorsal fin is equal in size to second dorsal fin. Origin of first dorsal fin is slightly anterior to midbase of pelvic fin. Distance between dorsal fins is less than distance from snout to spiracle but greater than length of base of first dorsal fin. Anal fin is separated from caudal fin by notch. Upper lobe of caudal fin lacks crest of enlarged denticles. Color is grayish brown dorsally and ventrally.

This species occurs in the temperate North Atlantic. In the western Atlantic it occurs off Massachusetts and Delaware and in the northern Gulf of Mexico between 560 and 1,462 m. Development is thought to be oviparous. Maximum known size is 68 cm TL.

REFERENCES: Bigelow et al. 1953; Springer 1966, 1979; Castro 1983; Compagno 1984; Quéro 1984f; C. R. Robins et al. 1986.

Apristurus parvipinnis   Springer and Heemstra 1979
Smallfin catshark

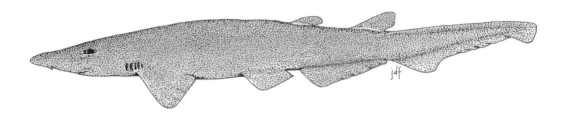

Apristurus parvipinnis is relatively slender, with a moderately long, broad snout and a low caudal fin. It is distinguished from the other species of the family by the following combination of characters. Preoral snout length is 9% to 10% of TL. Distance between nostrils is 1.2 times nostril length. Labial furrows are well developed in both jaws. Eye length is about 3% of TL. First dorsal fin is about one-half size of second dorsal fin. Origin of first dorsal fin is posterior to pelvic fin base. Distance between dorsal fins is about twice length of first dorsal fin and slightly less than preorbital snout length. Anal fin is separated from caudal fin by notch. Upper caudal lobe lacks crest of enlarged denticles. Color is uniform black.

This species occurs in the western Atlantic from the northeastern Gulf of Mexico off Florida to the Gulf of Campeche, Panama, Colombia, and French Guiana. It has been captured from 636 to 1,115 m. Maximum known size is 52 cm TL for females and 48 cm TL for males.

REFERENCES: Springer 1966, 1979; Castro 1983; Compagno 1984.

Apristurus riveri   Bigelow and Schroeder 1944
Broadgill catshark

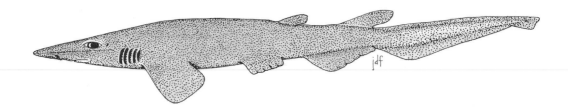

Apristurus riveri is relatively slender, with a moderately long, narrow snout and a relatively narrow, low caudal fin. It is distinguished from the other species of the family by the following combination of characters. Preoral snout length is 7% to 10% of TL. Distance between nostrils is 1.4 to 1.7 times nostril length. Labial furrows are well developed in both jaws. Gill slits are from two-thirds to slightly greater than eye length. Eye length is from 3% to 4% of TL. First dorsal fin is about one-half size of second dorsal fin. Origin of first dorsal fin is over posterior one-half of pelvic fin base. Distance between dorsal fin bases is about equal to twice length of first dorsal fin base and equal to about one-half to two-thirds of preorbital snout length. Anal fin is separated from caudal fin by notch. Upper caudal fin lobe lacks crest of enlarged denticles. Color is uniform dark brown.

This species occurs in the western North Atlantic from Cuba, the northern Gulf of Mexico, and Panama. Embryonic development is oviparous. Maximum known size is 46 cm TL; males mature at 43 to 46 cm TL, and females mature at 40 to 41 cm TL.

REFERENCES: Bigelow and Schroeder 1944, 1948a; Springer 1966, 1979; Castro 1983; Compagno 1984.

Galeus arae (Nichols 1927)
Marbled catshark

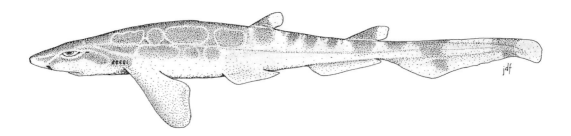

Galeus arae is relatively slender, with a moderately long, pointed snout and a relatively narrow, low caudal fin. It is distinguished from the other species of the family by the following combination of characters. Preoral snout length is 5% to 7% of TL. Prenasal snout length is equal to eye length. Labial furrows are well developed in both jaws and extend beyond corners of mouth. Mouth is broadly arched. Pelvic fin is small and angular. Distance between pelvic fin and anal fin base is less than anal fin base. Dorsal lobe of caudal fin has crest of enlarged denticles, but crest of denticles is lacking from preventral caudal margin. Color is yellowish brown, with darker spots and saddlelike blotches in bilaterally symmetrical arrangement on dorsal and lateral surfaces. These markings range from distinct and outlined with white to obscure. Smaller specimens usually have only saddle blotches.

Ventral surface is pale. Lining of mouth is black.

This species occurs in the western North Atlantic from South Carolina to the Florida Keys, in the northeastern Gulf of Mexico, off the northern coast of Cuba, and from Belize to Costa Rica. It has been captured from 292 to 732 m. Populations of this species from Hispaniola, Puerto Rico, and the Lesser Antilles, and from Panama, are now considered separate species (Hera Konstantinou, pers. com., July 2, 1996). Food consists of shrimps. Development is oviparous. Maximum known size is 43 cm TL; males mature at 27 to 36 cm TL, and females mature at 26 to 43 cm TL.

REFERENCES: Bigelow and Schroeder 1948a; Springer 1966, 1979; Bullis 1967; Castro 1983; Compagno 1984; Parsons and Candelini 1986; C. R. Robins et al. 1986.

Parmaturus campechiensis   Springer 1979
Campeche catshark

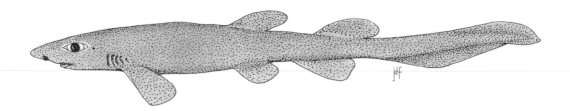

Parmaturus campechiensis is relatively slender, with a relatively short, rounded snout and a long, moderately broad, low caudal fin. It is distinguished from the other species of the family by the following combination of characters. Preoral length is 5.7% of TL. Nasal flap is poorly developed. Eye length is greater than 50% of preoral length. Distance between nostrils is less than nostril length. Labial furrows are well developed on both jaws. Pectoral fin is relatively narrow; maximum width is less than mouth width. First dorsal fin is smaller than second dorsal fin and originates above or slightly anterior to pelvic fin origin. Dorsal lobe of caudal fin has crest of enlarged denticles. Color is light to dark gray without pattern.

This species occurs in the western North Atlantic from the southern Gulf of Mexico. Only a single specimen has been captured, at 1,097 m.

REFERENCES: Springer 1979; Compagno 1984.

Scyliorhinus retifer (Garman 1881)
Chain dogfish

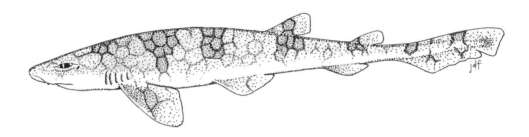

Scyliorhinus retifer is relatively slender, with a relatively short, wedge-shaped snout and a relatively narrow, low caudal fin. It is distinguished from the other species of the family by the following combination of characters. Preoral snout length is 5% to 6% of TL and slightly greater than eye length. Labial furrows are present in lower jaws only. Anterior nasal flap is not greatly expanded and fails to reach mouth. Origin of first dorsal fin is slightly posterior to pelvic fin base. Caudal fin lacks crest of enlarged dermal denticles. Color is reddish brown dorsally and yellowish ventrally, with black and brown lines on body forming chain-like pattern. There are no light or dark spots.

This species occurs in the western North Atlantic from Cape Cod to Florida and from the northern Gulf of Mexico to Nicaragua. It has been captured on or near the bottom from 73 to 550 m. Food consists of crustaceans and small bony fishes. Development is oviparous. Maximum known size is 47 cm TL; males mature at 37 to 41 cm TL, females mature at 35 to 47 cm TL, and young hatch from egg capsules at 10 cm TL.

REFERENCES: Bigelow and Schroeder 1948a; Springer 1966, 1979; Springer and Sadowsky 1970; Castro 1983; Compagno 1984; C. R. Robins et al. 1986.

TRIAKIDAE   Smoothhound sharks

The smoothhound sharks are slender, with a moderately short to long snout and a moderately low to moderately high caudal fin. They are distinguished from the other families of the order by the following combination of characters. Head and snout are moderately depressed. Eye is elongate and oval to slitlike in shape. Nictitating eyelid is variably developed. Spiracle is small to large. Labial furrows are moderately to well developed. First dorsal fin is moderate to large in size, located anterior to pelvic fin base, and generally closer to pectoral fin base. Anal fin is generally smaller than second dorsal fin. Caudal peduncle lacks keel and precaudal pit. Dorsal lobe of caudal fin lacks lateral undulations. Ventral lobe of caudal fin is absent to well developed.

The smoothhound sharks occur worldwide in tropical to temperate seas. They are, for the most part, benthic and are found from near shore to the outer continental shelf and occasionally to 2,000 m. Food consists of cephalopods, crustaceans, and bony fishes. Development is ovoviviparous or viviparous. There are 39 nominal species in 9 genera, and 2 species in a single genus occur in the Gulf of Mexico.

Key to the Species in the Gulf of Mexico
(Adapted from Compagno 1984)

1a.   Distance between nostrils 2.7% to 3.6% of TL; upper labial furrows longer than lower labial furrows (Fig. 12); caudal fin with a rounded ventral lobe
. . . . *Mustelus canis* p. 69

1b.   Distance between nostrils 1.2% to 2.4% of TL; upper labial furrows equal to or shorter than lower labial furrows (Fig. 13); caudal fin with a pointed ventral lobe
. . . . *Mustelus norrisi* p. 70

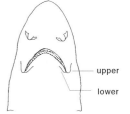

upper
lower

FIG 12

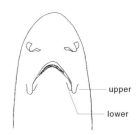

upper
lower

FIG 13

Mustelus canis (Mitchill 1815)
Smooth dogfish

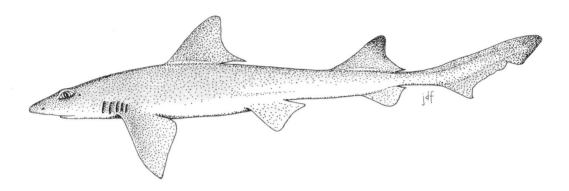

Mustelus canis is fairly slender, with a moderately long, subtriangular snout and a moderately elevated caudal fin with a distinct ventral lobe. It is distinguished from the other species of the family by the following combination of characters. Anterior nasal flap is of moderate size and does not form barbel. Distance between nostrils is 1 to 2 times nostril width. Upper labial furrow is slightly longer than lower. Teeth are broad, blunt, not strongly compressed, and possess single cusp reduced to low point. Interorbital distance is 3.6% to 4.6% of TL. Base of first dorsal fin is shorter than caudal fin and is located above or posterior to inner margin of pectoral fin. Second dorsal fin is nearly as large as first dorsal fin. Ventral caudal lobe is moderately developed but not falcate in adults. Crown of lateral trunk denticles is lanceolate. Color is olive gray to brown dorsally and yellowish or grayish ventrally. White or black spots and bars are lacking.

This species occurs in the western Atlantic from the Bay of Fundy to the northern Gulf of Mexico and the Bahamas, and from the Greater and Lesser Antilles, Venezuela, and southern Brazil. It has been captured from near shore to 200 m, and occasionally to 579 m. Food consists of polychaetes, gastropods, bivalves, crustaceans, and small bony fishes. Development is viviparous with a yolk sac placenta. Litters range from 4 to 20 young. Maximum known size is 150 cm TL; males mature at 82 cm TL, females mature at 90 cm TL, and young are 34 to 39 cm TL at birth.

REFERENCES: Springer 1939; Bigelow and Schroeder 1940, 1948a; Hoese and Moore 1977; Applegate et al. 1979; Casterlin and Reynolds 1979; Castro 1983; Compagno 1984; C. R. Robins et al. 1986; Bonfil et al. 1990.

Mustelus norrisi   Springer 1939
Florida dogfish

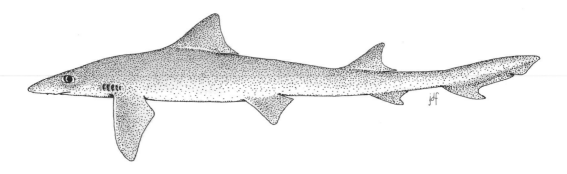

Mustelus norrisi is fairly slender, with a moderately long, subangular snout and a moderately elevated caudal fin with a distinct ventral lobe. It is distinguished from the other species of the family by the following combination of characters. Anterior nasal flap is of moderate size but does not form barbel. Distance between nostrils is 1 to 2 times nostril width. Upper labial furrow is slightly shorter than lower. Teeth are broad and blunt, not strongly compressed, with single cusp reduced to narrow point, and with asymmetrical crown. Interorbital distance is 3.3% to 4.2% of TL. Base of first dorsal fin is shorter than caudal fin and located above or posterior to inner margin of pectoral fin. Second dorsal fin is nearly as large as first dorsal fin. Ventral caudal lobe is moderately developed and strongly falcate in adults. Crown of lateral trunk denticles is lanceolate. Color is gray dorsally and paler or dirty white ventrally. White and dark spots or bars are absent.

This species occurs in the western Atlantic from Florida and the northeastern Gulf of Mexico to Venezuela, and from southern Brazil. It has been captured from near shore to 80 m. Food consists of crabs, shrimps, and small bony fishes. Embryonic development is viviparous with a yolk sac placenta. Litters range from 7 to 14 young. Maximum known size is 100 cm TL; males mature at 58 cm TL, females mature at 65 cm TL, and young are 30 cm TL at birth.

REFERENCES: Springer 1939; Bigelow and Schroeder 1948a; Clark and von Schmidt 1965; Cervigón 1966; Hoese and Moore 1977; Castro 1983; Compagno 1984; C. R. Robins et al. 1986; Bonfil et al. 1990.

CARCHARHINIDAE Requiem sharks

The requiem sharks are moderately slender to rather stout, with snouts ranging from long and slender to short and conical, and caudal fins ranging from moderately low to high and falcate. They are distinguished from the other families of the order by the following combination of characters. Head is not flattened and laterally expanded. Eye is circular to oval, and nictitating membrane is well developed. Spiracle is usually absent. Anterior nasal flap is variably developed but is not developed into barbel. Labial furrows vary from long to short. First dorsal fin is moderate in size to very large and is located anterior to pelvic fin base. Anal fin is present. Caudal peduncle possesses precaudal pit. Dorsal lobe of caudal fin has lateral undulations along its margin. Ventral lobe of caudal fin is well developed.

The requiem sharks occur worldwide from tropical to temperate seas. They are found from near shore, even in freshwater, to oceanic water, from near the bottom to the water surface. Some species swim constantly, while others remain on the bottom for extended periods. Food consists of bivalves, cuttlefishes, squids, octopods, crustaceans, elasmobranchs, bony fishes, sea turtles, sea snakes, sea birds, and marine mammals. Development is generally viviparous with a yolk sac placenta and rarely is ovoviviparous. There are about 50 species in 12 genera, and 15 to 17 species in 4 or 5 genera occur in the Gulf of Mexico.

Key to the Species in the Gulf of Mexico
(Adapted from Castro 1983; Compagno 1984)

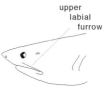

upper labial furrow

FIG 14

1a. Upper labial furrows long, extending to level of eye (Fig. 14); spiracle present and relatively large; caudal peduncle with lateral keel . . . . *Galeocerdo cuvier* p. 87
1b. Upper labial furrows long to short but not extending to eye; spiracle generally absent, if present, very small; caudal peduncle usually without lateral keel 2
2a. Second dorsal fin nearly as large as first dorsal fin; height of second dorsal fin about three-fourths height of first dorsal fin . . . . *Negaprion brevirostris* p. 88
2b. Second dorsal fin considerably smaller than first dorsal fin; height of second dorsal fin less than one-half height of first dorsal fin 3
3a. Second dorsal fin origin posterior to anal fin origin, usually nearer to end of anal fin base than to origin; preanal ridge well developed, length about equal to length of anal fin base . . . . *Rhizoprionodon terraenovae* p. 90
3b. Second dorsal fin origin usually near anal fin origin, usu-

ally distinctly anterior to end of anal fin base; preanal ridge
less than one-half length of anal fin base 4

4a. Midpoint of dorsal fin base closer to pelvic fin origin than
to pectoral axil; caudal peduncle with weak lateral keel
. . . . *Prionace glauca* p. 89

4b. Midpoint of dorsal fin base closer to pectoral axil than to
pelvic fin origin; caudal peduncle without lateral keel . . . 5

5a. Pectoral fin and first dorsal fin very slightly tapering
toward their tips, distally very broad and bluntly rounded;
fin tips mottled white in adults; fins black tipped, with
black dorsal saddle marks on caudal peduncle in juveniles
. . . .*Carcharhinus longimanus* p. 81

5b. Pectoral fin and first dorsal fin tapering distally, distally
narrow and acutely rounded; fin tips not mottled white in
adults; fins often black tipped but without black dorsal
saddle marks on caudal peduncle in juveniles. 6

6a. Ridge between dorsal fin bases present. 7

6b. Ridge between dorsal fin bases absent 12

7a. Snout very long, narrow, and acute; preoral snout length
1.7 to 1.9 times distance between nostrils
. . . . *Carcharhinus signatus* p. 86

7b. Snout long to rather short, narrow to broadly rounded;
preoral snout length less than 1.6 times distance between
nostrils. 8

8a. First dorsal fin origin posterior to free tip of pectoral fin;
inner margin of free rear tip of second dorsal fin twice as
long as height of fin . . . . . . *Carcharhinus falciformis* p. 77

8b. First dorsal fin origin over or anterior to free tip of pectoral fin; inner margin of free rear tip of second dorsal fin
less than twice as long as height of fin 9

9a. Teeth located in anterolateral section of upper jaw with
narrow cusps that are well delimited from bases (Fig. 15);
13 or fewer tooth rows on each side of upper jaw and 13
or more tooth rows on each side of lower jaw
. . . . *Carcharhinus perezi* p. 83

9b. Teeth located in anterolateral section of upper jaw with
broad cusps that are not well delimited from bases
(Fig. 16); usually 14 or more tooth rows on each side of
upper jaw and 13 or more tooth rows on each side of
lower jaw. 10

10a. First dorsal fin origin closer to axil of pectoral fin than to
pectoral free rear tip and usually over or anterior to pectoral fin base 11

10b. First dorsal fin origin closer to pectoral fin rear tip than to
axil of pectoral fin and usually on a vertical with or slightly
anterior to pectoral rear tip
. . . .*Carcharhinus obscurus* p. 82

11a. Anterior nasal flap poorly developed; mouth width more

FIG 15

FIG 16

than 2.4 times distance between nostril and mouth; usually 14 tooth rows on each side of upper jaw; height of first dorsal fin about one-half distance from snout to origin of first dorsal fin. . . . . *Carcharhinus plumbeus* p. 84

11b. Anterior nasal flap well developed and triangular; mouth width less than 2.4 times distance between nostril and mouth; usually 15 tooth rows on each side of upper jaw; height of first dorsal fin less than one-half distance from snout to origin of first dorsal fin
. . . .*Carcharhinus altimus* p. 75

12a. Snout very short and broadly rounded; teeth located in anterolateral section of upper jaw with very broad, triangular cusps and straight to concave distal margins (Fig. 17)
. . . .*Carcharhinus leucus* p. 79

FIG 17

12b. Snout moderately long to long, evenly rounded to pointed; teeth located in anterolateral section of upper jaw with narrow cusps and strongly notched distal margins (Fig. 18)
. . . . 13

13a. Origin of second dorsal fin posterior to origin of anal fin
. . . .*Carcharhinus porosus* p. 85

13b. Origin of second dorsal fin about on a vertical with origin of anal fin. 14

FIG 18

14a. Each side of upper jaw with 12 tooth rows; teeth located in anterolateral section of upper jaw with oblique cusps (Fig. 19); tip of snout with a dusky blotch
. . . .*Carcharhinus acronotus* p. 74

14b. Each side of upper jaw with 14 or more tooth rows; teeth located in anterolateral section of upper jaw with more or less erect cusps (Fig. 20); tip of snout without dusky blotch
. . . . 15

FIG 19

15a. Upper labial furrows elongated and prominent; usually 16 tooth rows on each side of upper jaw; distance between dorsal fins over 2.2 times height of first dorsal fin; origin of first dorsal fin above or slightly posterior to pectoral rear tip. . . . . *Carcharhinus brevipinna* p. 76

15b. Upper labial furrows short and obscure; usually 15 or fewer tooth rows on each side of upper jaw; distance between dorsal fins equal to or less than 2.2 times height of first dorsal fin; origin of first dorsal fin above or slightly posterior to pectoral fin base 16

FIG 20

16a. Teeth of young with smooth edges in both jaws, those of adults weakly serrated; longest gill openings equal to one-half length of first dorsal fin base; fins without black tips
. . . .*Carcharhinus isodon* p. 78

16b. Teeth with serrated edges in both jaws; longest gill openings less than one-half length of first dorsal fin base; fins usually with black tips . . . . . . *Carcharhinus limbatus* p. 80

Carcharhinus acronotus   (Poey 1860)
Blacknose shark

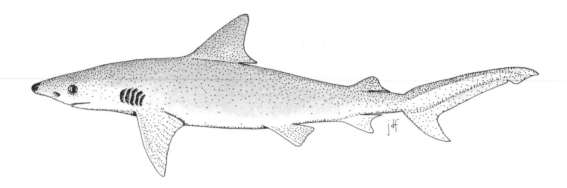

Carcharhinus acronotus is relatively slender, with a moderately long, rounded snout and a relatively low caudal fin with a moderately developed ventral lobe. It is distinguished from the other species of the family by the following combination of characters. Preoral snout length is 1.4 to 1.7 times internasal distance. Upper labial furrows are short and inconspicuous. Anterior nasal flap is relatively well developed and narrow based. Upper jaw has 12 to 13 tooth rows on each side, and lower jaw has 11 to 12. Teeth located in anterolateral section of upper jaw have moderately narrow, strongly serrated, and distinctly oblique cusps. Gill openings are short; longest (third) is 2.7% to 3.2% of TL and less than one-third of first dorsal fin base. Pectoral fin and first dorsal fin taper distally, forming narrowly rounded apical tips. Origin of first dorsal fin is over free tip of pectoral fin. Second dorsal fin is of moderate size but less than one-half height of first dorsal fin and is over or posterior to anal fin origin. Ridge between dorsal fin bases is lacking, and caudal peduncle lacks keel. Color is yellowish to greenish gray, yellowish brown, or bronze dorsally and white to pale yellow ventrally. Tip of snout has distinct dusky blotch, and tip of second dorsal fin is dusky to black.

This species occurs in the western Atlantic from North Carolina to Florida, the Bahamas, the Greater and Lesser Antilles, and the Gulf of Mexico to southern Brazil. It is common over continental and insular shelves during the summer and fall in the Gulf of Mexico. Food consists of small bony fishes. Development is viviparous with a yolk sac placenta. Litters range from three to six young. Maximum known size is 165 cm TL; males mature at 97 to 106 cm TL, females mature at 103 cm TL, and young are 38 to 50 cm TL at birth.

REFERENCES: Bigelow and Schroeder 1948a; Clark and von Schmidt 1965; Hoese and Moore 1977; Applegate et al. 1979; Branstetter 1981; Garrick 1982; Castro 1983; Compagno 1984; C. R. Robins et al. 1986; Bonfil et al. 1990.

Carcharhinus altimus   (Springer 1950)
Bignose shark

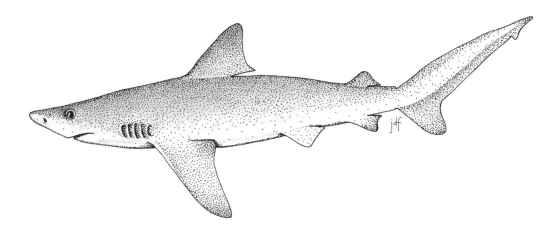

Carcharhinus altimus is relatively slender, with a moderately long, bluntly rounded snout and a moderately high caudal fin with a well-developed ventral lobe. It is distinguished from the other species of the family by the following combination of characters. Preoral snout length is 1.3 to 1.4 times internasal distance. Upper labial furrows are short and inconspicuous. Anterior nasal flap is relatively well developed and broad. Upper jaw has 14 to 16 tooth rows on each side, and lower jaw has 14 to 15. Teeth located in anterolateral section of upper jaw have broad, strongly serrated, and erect to slightly oblique cusps. Gill slits are moderately long; longest (third) is 3.1% to 3.9% of TL and about one-third of first dorsal fin base. Pectoral fin is broad, and pectoral fin and first dorsal fin taper distally, forming bluntly pointed apical tips. Origin of first dorsal fin is above or slightly posterior to axil of pectoral fin. Second dorsal fin is relatively large but less than one-half height of first dorsal fin and originates slightly anterior to origin of anal fin. Ridge extends between dorsal fin bases. Caudal peduncle lacks keel. Dorsal lobe of tail has distinct bump at base. Color is gray to bronze dorsally and white ventrally. Fin tips, except pelvic fin, are dusky.

This species occurs worldwide in tropical and warm temperate seas, generally between 90 and 430 m. In the western Atlantic it occurs from Florida, the Bahamas, Cuba, Nicaragua, Costa Rica, and Venezuela. There is one unconfirmed report of this species from DeSoto Canyon in the Gulf of Mexico. Food consists of cuttlefishes, elasmobranchs, and bony fishes. Development is viviparous. Litters range from 3 to 15 young. Maximum known size is 282 cm TL; males mature at 216 to 267 cm TL, females mature at 226 cm TL, and young range from 70 to 90 cm TL at birth.

REFERENCES: Springer 1950a; Applegate et al. 1979; Garrick 1982; Castro 1983; Compagno 1984; C. R. Robins et al. 1986; Bonfil et al. 1990.

Carcharhinus brevipinna   (Müller and Henle 1839)
Spinner shark

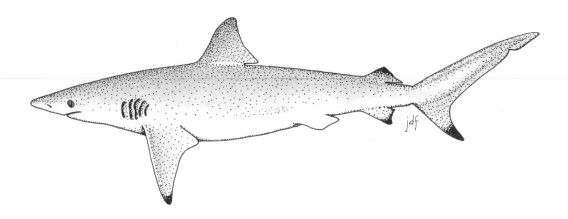

Carcharhinus brevipinna is moderately slender, with a relatively long, narrow, pointed snout and a moderately high caudal fin with a well-developed ventral lobe. It is distinguished from the other species of the family by the following combination of characters. Preoral snout length is 1.5 to 1.8 times internasal distance. Upper labial furrows are long and conspicuous. Anterior nasal flap is poorly developed. Upper jaw has 15 to 18 tooth rows on each side, and lower jaw has 14 to 17. Teeth located in anterolateral section of upper jaw have narrow, finely serrated, and erect to slightly oblique cusps. Gill slits are long; longest (third) is 3.7% to 5.5% of TL and greater than one-third of first dorsal fin base. Pectoral fin is falcate, and pectoral fin and first dorsal fin taper distally, forming narrowly rounded apical tips. Origin of first dorsal fin is above or slightly posterior to free tip of pectoral fin. Second dorsal fin is small, less than one-half height of first dorsal fin, and originates over or slightly posterior to anal fin origin. Ridge between dorsal fin bases is lacking, and caudal peduncle lacks keel. Color is gray to bronze dorsally and white ventrally. Band of dorsal coloration extends ventrally from level of pectoral fin to pelvic fin. Specimens larger than 70 cm TL have black-tipped anal, pectoral, and second dorsal fins. First dorsal fin and pelvic fins may or may not be black tipped. Specimens less than 70 cm TL lack black-tipped fins.

This species occurs worldwide in tropical to warm temperate seas in coastal waters to 75 m, except it is absent in the eastern Pacific. In the western Atlantic it occurs from North Carolina to Florida, the Bahamas, Cuba, the Gulf of Mexico, British Guiana, and southern Brazil. Food consists of cuttlefishes, squids, octopods, elasmobranchs, and a large variety of bony fishes. Development is viviparous with a yolk sac placenta. Litters range from 3 to 15 young. Maximum known size is 278 cm TL; males mature at 159 to 203 cm TL, females mature at 170 to 200 cm TL, and young are 60 to 75 cm TL at birth.

REFERENCES: Bigelow and Schroeder 1948a; Springer 1960; Clark and von Schmidt 1965; Bass et al. 1973; Hoese and Moore 1977 (as *C. maculipinnis*); Applegate et al. 1979; Branstetter 1981, 1982, 1984; Garrick 1982; Castro 1983; Compagno 1984; C. R. Robins et al. 1986; Bonfil et al. 1990.

Carcharhinus falciformis (Müller and Henle 1839)
Silky shark

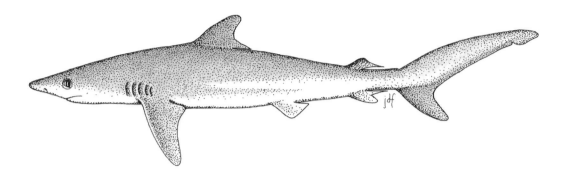

Carcharhinus falciformis is slender, with a moderately long, rounded snout and a moderately high caudal fin with a well-developed ventral lobe. It is distinguished from the other species of the family by the following combination of characters. Preoral snout length is 1.2 to 1.6 times internasal distance. Upper labial furrows are short and inconspicuous. Anterior nasal flap is poorly developed. Upper jaw has 14 to 16 tooth rows on each side, and lower jaw has 13 to 17. Teeth located in anterolateral section of upper jaw have moderately narrow, strongly serrated, and erect to moderately oblique cusps. Gill slits are of moderate size; largest (third) is 2.9% to 3.6% of TL and less than two-fifths of first dorsal fin base. Pectoral fin and first dorsal fin taper distally. Origin of first dorsal fin is posterior to free tip of pectoral fin. Second dorsal fin is small, less than one-half height of first dorsal fin, and with free tip twice as long as height of fin. Ridge extends between dorsal fin bases. Caudal peduncle lacks keel. Color is brown to bronze dorsally and white ventrally. Tips of fins are dusky.

This species occurs worldwide in tropical to warm temperate seas from the surface to 500 m. In the western Atlantic it occurs from Massachusetts to southern Brazil, including the Gulf of Mexico and the Caribbean Sea. It is most abundant on the edge of continental and insular shelves, and in epipelagic oceanic waters, although it occasionally occurs over the inner continental shelf. Food consists of squids, paper nautiluses, pelagic crabs, and a variety of pelagic bony fishes. Development is viviparous with a yolk sac placenta. Litters range from 2 to 14 young. Maximum known size is about 330 cm TL; males mature at 187 to 217 cm TL, females mature at 213 to 230 cm TL, and young range from 70 to 87 cm TL at birth.

REFERENCES: Bigelow and Schroeder 1948a; Springer 1960; Garrick et al. 1964; Garrick 1967, 1982; Bass et al. 1973; Guitart Manday 1975; Hoese and Moore 1977; Applegate et al. 1979; Castro 1983; Branstetter 1984, 1987b; Compagno 1984; Branstetter and McEachran 1986b; C. R. Robins et al. 1986; Bonfil et al. 1990.

Carcharhinus isodon   (Müller and Henle 1839)
Finetooth shark

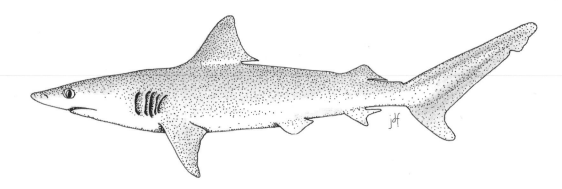

Carcharhinus isodon is rather slender, with a fairly long, moderately pointed snout and a relatively high caudal fin with a well-developed ventral lobe. It is distinguished from the other species of the family by the following combination of characters. Preoral snout length is 1.3 times internasal distance. Upper labial furrows are short and inconspicuous. Anterior nasal flap is poorly developed. Upper jaw has 12 to 15 tooth rows on each side, and lower jaw has 13 to 14. Teeth located in antero-lateral section of upper jaw have very narrow, smooth to weakly serrated, and erect to slightly oblique cusps. Gill openings are very long; longest (third) is 4.8% to 5.7% of TL and about one-half of first dorsal fin base. Pectoral fin and first dorsal fin taper distally. Origin of first dorsal fin is above or slightly posterior to axil of pectoral fin. Second dorsal fin is relatively large but less than one-half height of first dorsal fin and originates above or slightly posterior to anal fin origin. Ridge between dorsal fin bases is lacking, and caudal peduncle lacks keel. Color is bluish gray to bronze dorsally and white ventrally. Band of dorsal coloration extends ventrally from level of pectoral fin to pelvic fin.

This species occurs in the western Atlantic from New York (rarely) to Florida, Cuba, and the Gulf of Mexico, and off southern Brazil. It occurs close to shore over its entire range. Food consists of cephalopods and small bony fishes. Development is viviparous. Litters range from one to six young. Maximum known size is about 189 cm TL; males mature at about 115 cm TL, females mature at about 130 to 140 cm TL, and young are about 50 cm TL at birth.

REFERENCES: Bigelow and Schroeder 1948a; Baughman and Springer 1950; Clark and von Schmidt 1965; Applegate et al. 1979; Branstetter and Shipp 1980; Branstetter 1981, 1984; Castro 1983; Compagno 1984; C. R. Robins et al. 1986; Castro 1993a,b.

Carcharhinus leucus   (Müller and Henle 1839)
Bull shark

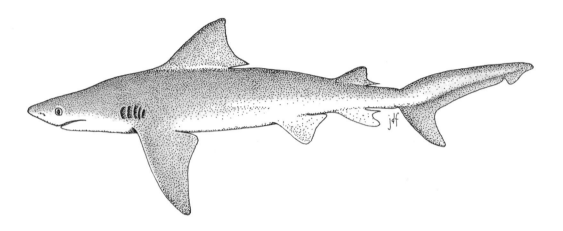

Carcharhinus leucus is rather stout, with a short, blunt snout and a rather low caudal fin with a well-developed ventral lobe. It is distinguished from the other species of the family by the following combination of characters. Preoral snout length is 0.7 to 1 times internasal width. Upper labial furrows are short and inconspicuous. Anterior nasal flap is broad and triangular shaped. Upper jaw has 12 to 14 tooth rows on each side, and lower jaw has 12 to 13. Teeth located in anterolateral section of upper jaw have very broad, triangular, strongly serrated, and erect to slightly oblique cusps. Gill openings are of moderate length; longest (third) is 3.1% to 4.1% of TL and less than one-third of first dorsal fin base. Pectoral fin and first dorsal fin taper distally. Origin of first dorsal fin is above or slightly posterior to axil of pectoral fin. Second dorsal fin is relatively large but less than one-half height of first dorsal fin and originates anterior to origin of anal fin. Ridge between dorsal fin bases is absent, and caudal peduncle lacks keel. Color is pale to dark gray dorsally and white ventrally.

This species occurs worldwide in tropical to warm temperate seas, and generally near shore. It is found in freshwater with access to the sea in the tropics. In the western Atlantic it occurs from Massachusetts to southern Brazil, including the Gulf of Mexico, the Bahamas, and the Caribbean Sea. This species has been reported from the Mississippi River, Atchafalaya River, Lake Nicaragua, San Juan River, Lake Ysabel, Palula River, Panama Canal, and the Amazon River. Food consists of crustaceans, mollusks, elasmobranchs, bony fishes, sea turtles, sea birds, and marine mammals. Development is viviparous with a yolk sac placenta. Litters range from 1 to 15 young. Maximum known size is 310 cm TL; males mature at about 157 to 226 cm TL, females mature at 180 to 230 cm TL, and young are 56 to 81 cm TL at birth.

REFERENCES: Bigelow and Schroeder 1948a; Springer 1960, 1963; Garrick and Schultz 1963; Clark and von Schmidt 1965; Thorson 1971, 1976; Hoese and Moore 1977; Applegate et al. 1979; Castro 1983; Branstetter 1984; Compagno 1984; Snelson et al. 1984; C. R. Robins et al. 1986; Branstetter and Stiles 1987; Bonfil et al. 1990; Castro 1993a.

Carcharhinus limbatus   (Müller and Henle 1839)
Blacktip shark

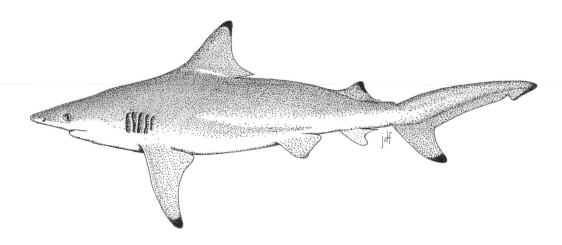

Carcharhinus limbatus is moderately stout, with an acute, moderately long, rounded snout and a moderately low caudal fin with a well-developed ventral lobe. It is distinguished from the other species of the family by the following combination of characters. Preoral snout length is 1.3 to 1.7 times internasal width. Upper labial furrows are short and inconspicuous. Anterior nasal flap is poorly developed. Upper jaw has 14 to 15 tooth rows on each side, and lower jaw has 13 to 15. Teeth located in anterolateral section of upper jaw have narrow, strongly serrated, and erect to slightly oblique cusps. Gill slits are long; longest (third) is 3.8% to 4.9% of TL, but less than one-half length of first dorsal fin base. Pectoral fin and first dorsal fin taper distally. Origin of first dorsal fin is above or slightly posterior to axil of pectoral fin. Second dorsal fin is large but less than one-half height of first dorsal fin and originates slightly anterior to or over origin of anal fin. Ridge between dorsal fin bases is absent, and caudal peduncle lacks keel. Color is dark gray, bluish gray, or dusky bronze dorsally and white to yellowish ventrally. Band of dorsal coloration extends ventrally from level of pectoral fin to pelvic fin. Dorsal fins, pectoral fins, and ventral lobe of caudal fin are black tipped.

This species occurs worldwide in tropical to warm temperate seas over continental and insular shelves, and generally in less than 30 m. In the western Atlantic it occurs from Massachusetts to southern Brazil, including the Gulf of Mexico, the Bahamas, and the Caribbean Sea. Food consists of crustaceans, cephalopods, elasmobranchs, and a wide variety of bony fishes. Development is viviparous. Litters range from 1 to 10 young. Maximum known size is about 225 cm TL; males mature at 135 to 180 cm TL, females mature at 120 to 190 cm TL, and young range from 38 to 72 cm TL at birth.

REFERENCES: Bigelow and Schroeder 1948a; Springer 1960, 1963; Garrick and Schultz 1963; Clark and von Schmidt 1965; Garrick 1967, 1982; Bass et al. 1973; Hoese and Moore 1977; Applegate et al. 1979; Branstetter 1981, 1982, 1984, 1987a; Castro 1983; Compagno 1984; Branstetter and McEachran 1986b; C. R. Robins et al. 1986; Bonfil et al. 1990.

Carcharhinus longimanus (Poey 1861)
Oceanic whitetip shark

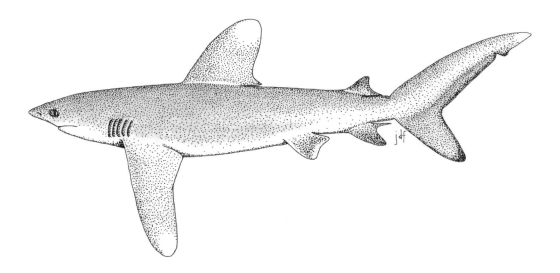

Carcharhinus longimanus is relatively stout, with a short, blunt snout and a relatively high caudal fin with a well-developed ventral lobe. It is distinguished from the other species of the family by the following combination of characters. Preoral snout length is 1 to 1.1 times internasal width. Anterior nasal flap is poorly developed. Upper labial furrows are short and inconspicuous. Upper and lower jaws have 13 to 15 tooth rows on each side. Teeth located in anterolateral section of upper jaw have broad, triangular, strongly serrated, and erect to slightly oblique cusps. Gill slits are relatively long; longest (third) is 3.1% to 4.1% of TL but less than one-third of first dorsal fin base. Pectoral fin and first dorsal fin are very slightly tapered toward tips, and are broadly and bluntly rounded. Origin of first dorsal fin is anterior to posterior free tip of pectoral fin. Second dorsal fin is large but less than one-half height of first dorsal fin and originates over or slightly anterior to origin of anal fin. Ridge extends between dorsal fin bases. Caudal peduncle lacks keel. Color is olive gray to brown dorsally and white to yellow ventrally. Pectoral, first dorsal, pelvic, and caudal fins are mottled with white in larger specimens. Smaller specimens have black blotches on tips of fins and black saddle marks on caudal peduncle.

This species occurs worldwide in tropical to warm temperate seas near the edge of continental and insular shelves, and in oceanic waters. Occasionally it occurs in water as shallow as 37 m. In the western Atlantic it occurs from Maine to Argentina, including the Gulf of Mexico and the Caribbean Sea. Food consists of gastropods, cephalopods, crustaceans, oceanic bony fishes, sea turtles, sea birds, and marine mammals. Development is viviparous with a yolk sac placenta. Litters range from 1 to 15 young. Maximum known size is 350 to 395 cm TL; males mature at 175 to 198 cm TL, females mature at 180 to 200 cm TL, and young range from 60 to 65 cm TL at birth.

REFERENCES: Bigelow and Schroeder 1948a; Springer 1950; Backus et al. 1956; Garrick and Schultz 1963; Bass et al. 1973; Applegate et al. 1979; Castro 1983; Branstetter 1984; Compagno 1984; C. R. Robins et al. 1986.

Carcharhinus obscurus   (Lesueur 1818)
Dusky shark

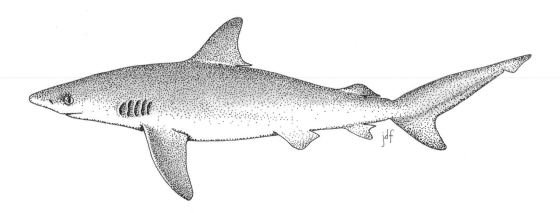

Carcharhinus obscurus is relatively slender, with a moderately short snout and a moderately high caudal fin with a well-developed ventral lobe. It is distinguished from the other species of the family by the following combination of characters. Preoral snout length is 1 to 1.4 times internasal width. Anterior nasal flap is poorly developed. Upper labial furrows are short and inconspicuous. Upper jaw has 14 to 15 tooth rows on each side, and lower jaw has 13 to 15. Teeth located in anterolateral section of upper jaw have broad, triangular, strongly serrated, and erect to slightly oblique cusps. Gill slits are moderately long; longest (third) is 2.7% to 4% of TL but less than one-third length of first dorsal fin base. Pectoral fin and first dorsal fin taper distally. Origin of first dorsal fin is above or slightly anterior to rear tip of pectoral fin. Second dorsal fin is small and originates above anal fin origin. Ridge extends between dorsal fin bases. Caudal peduncle lacks keel. Color is gray to charcoal or bronze dorsally and white ventrally. Tips of fins are dusky.

This species occurs worldwide in tropical to warm temperate seas over continental and insular shelves from the surface to 400 m. In the western Atlantic it occurs from southern Massachusetts to Florida, Cuba, the Bahamas, the northern Gulf of Mexico, Nicaragua, and southern Brazil. Food consists of barnacles, bryozoans, crustaceans, mollusks, elasmobranchs, a variety of bony fishes, and carrion of marine mammals. Development is viviparous with a yolk sac placenta. Litters range from 3 to 14 young. Maximum known size is about 400 cm TL; males mature at about 280 to 340 cm TL, females mature at about 257 to 300 cm TL, and young range from 67 to 100 cm TL at birth.

REFERENCES: Bigelow and Schroeder 1948a; Springer 1960, 1963; Clark and von Schmidt 1965; Hoese and Moore 1977; Applegate et al. 1979; Garrick 1982; Castro 1983; Branstetter 1984; Compagno 1984; Bonfil et al. 1990.

Carcharhinus perezi (Poey 1876)
Caribbean reef shark

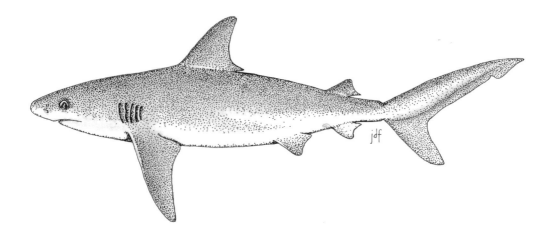

Carcharhinus perezi is relatively stout, with a short, bluntly rounded snout and a moderately high caudal fin with a well-developed ventral lobe. It is distinguished from the other species of the family by the following combination of characters. Preoral snout length is 1 to 1.1 times internasal width. Anterior nasal flap is poorly developed. Upper labial furrows are short and inconspicuous. Upper jaw has 12 to 13 tooth rows on each side, and lower jaw has 11 to 12. Teeth located in anterolateral section of upper jaw have narrow, strongly serrated, and erect to slightly oblique cusps. Gill slits are moderately long; longest (third) is 2.8% to 4% of TL but less than one-half length of first dorsal fin base. Pectoral fin and first dorsal fin taper distally. Origin of first dorsal fin base is above or slightly anterior to free rear tip of pectoral fin. Second dorsal fin is relatively large and originates above or slightly anterior to anal fin base. Ridge extends between dorsal fin bases. Caudal peduncle lacks keel. Color is grayish brown to olive gray dorsally and white to yellow ventrally. Fins are not prominently marked.

This species occurs in the western Atlantic from Florida, Bermuda, the Gulf of Mexico, the Bahamas, the Greater and Lesser Antilles, Yucatán, Venezuela, and southern Brazil. It is apparently rare in the northern Gulf of Mexico, with exception of the Flower Gardens Reefs. It is the most abundant coral reef shark in the Caribbean, where it is commonly found over continental and insular shelves in less than 30 m. Food consists of bony fishes. Development is viviparous. Litters range from four to six young. Maximum known size is 295 cm TL; males mature at 152 to 168 cm TL, females mature at 200 to 295 cm TL, and young are born at less than 73 cm TL.

REFERENCES: Bigelow and Schroeder 1948a; Springer 1960; Böhlke and Chaplin 1968; Castro 1983; Compagno 1984; Bonfil et al. 1990.

Carcharhinus plumbeus (Nardo 1827)
Sandbar shark

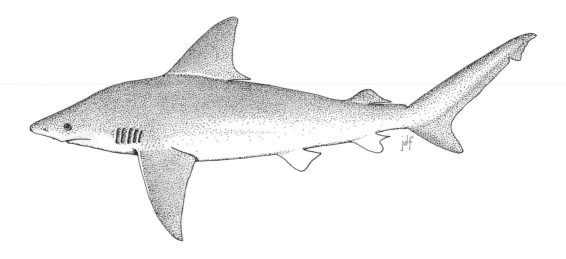

Carcharhinus plumbeus is fairly stout, with a short, rounded snout and a moderately high caudal fin with a well-developed ventral lobe. It is distinguished from the other species of the family by the following combination of characters. Preoral snout length is 1 to 1.1 times internasal width. Anterior nasal flap is poorly developed. Upper labial furrow is short and inconspicuous. Upper jaw has 14 to 15 tooth rows on each side, and lower jaw has 12 to 15. Teeth located in anterolateral section of upper jaw have broad, triangular, strongly serrated, and slightly oblique cusps. Gill openings are short; longest (third) is 2.4% to 3.6% of TL and less than one-third first dorsal fin base. Pectoral fin and first dorsal fin taper distally. First dorsal fin is large—height is equal to or greater than distance from snout to first gill slit—and originates above or slightly anterior to axil of pectoral fin. Second dorsal fin is less than one-half height of first dorsal fin, and its origin is above or slightly anterior to origin of anal fin. Ridge extends between dorsal fin bases. Caudal peduncle lacks keel. Color is bluish gray, brownish gray, bronze, or brown dorsally and paler to whitish ventrally.

This species occurs worldwide in tropical to warm temperate seas in coastal areas. In the western Atlantic it occurs from southern Massachusetts to Florida, the Gulf of Mexico, the Bahamas, and Cuba, and off Nicaragua, Costa Rica, Venezuela, and southern Brazil. Food consists of mollusks, crustaceans, elasmobranchs, and a large variety of bony fishes. Development is viviparous with a yolk sac placenta. Litters range from 1 to 14. Maximum known size is 239 to 300 cm TL; males mature at 131 to 178 cm TL, females mature at 144 to 183 cm TL, and young range from 56 to 75 cm TL at birth.

REFERENCES: Bigelow and Schroeder 1948a; Springer 1960, 1963, 1967; Clark and von Schmidt 1965; Hoese and Moore 1977; Applegate et al. 1979 (all above as *C. milberti*); Branstetter 1981, 1984, 1987a; Medved and Marshall 1981, 1983; Garrick 1982; Castro 1983; Compagno 1984; C. R. Robins et al. 1986; Bonfil et al. 1990.

Carcharhinus porosus (Ranzani 1840)
Smalltail shark

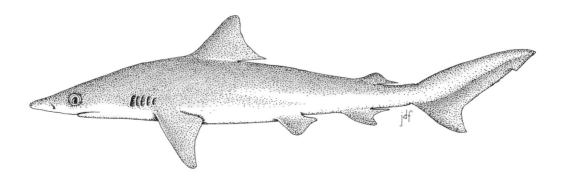

Carcharhinus porosus is relatively slender, with a moderately long, pointed snout and a moderately high caudal fin with a moderately well-developed ventral lobe. It is distinguished from the other species of the family by the following combination of characters. Preoral snout length is 1.2 to 1.8 times internasal width. Anterior nasal flap is a slender, pointed lobe. Upper labial furrows are short and inconspicuous. Upper jaw and lower jaw have 13 to 15 tooth rows on each side. Teeth located in anterolateral section of upper jaw have narrow, strongly serrated, and slightly oblique to oblique cusps. Gill slits are short; longest (third) is 2.8% to 3.4% of TL, and less than one-third first dorsal fin length. Pectoral fin and first dorsal fin taper distally. Origin of first dorsal fin is above inner margin of pectoral fin. Second dorsal fin origin is above or slightly posterior to midbase of anal fin. Ridge between dorsal fin bases is absent, and caudal peduncle lacks keel. Color is bluish gray to gray dorsally and lighter ventrally.

This species occurs in the tropical to warm temperate western Atlantic and eastern Pacific Oceans over inner continental shelves to about 36 m. In the western Atlantic it occurs from the western Gulf of Mexico, from about Corpus Christi southward, to southern Brazil, but is reported to be absent from the Bahamas and the Greater and Lesser Antilles, although it is common off Trinidad and Tobago. Food consists of shrimps, small elasmobranchs, and a large variety of bony fishes. Development is viviparous with a yolk sac placenta. Litters range from two to seven young. Maximum known size is 150 cm TL; males mature at 75 to 78 cm TL, females mature at 84 cm TL, and young range from 31 to 40 cm TL at birth.

REFERENCES: Baughman 1943b (as *C. cerdale*); Bigelow and Schroeder 1948a; Hoese and Moore 1977; Applegate et al. 1979; Garrick 1982; Castro 1983; Compagno 1984; C. R. Robins et al. 1986; Bonfil et al. 1990.

Carcharhinus signatus   (Poey 1868)
Night shark

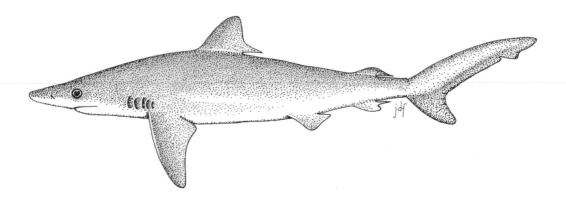

Carcharhinus signatus is slender, with a long, slender snout, large green eyes with irregular pupils, and a moderately high caudal fin with a well-developed ventral lobe. It is distinguished from the other species of the family by the following combination of characters. Preoral snout length is 1.7 to 1.9 times internasal width. Anterior nasal flap is moderately developed. Upper labial furrows are short and inconspicuous. Upper and lower jaws usually have 15 tooth rows on each side. Teeth in anterolateral section of upper jaw have narrow, smooth to irregularly serrated, and oblique cusps. Gill slits are relatively short; longest (third) is 2.5% of TL, and less than one-third first dorsal fin base. Pectoral fin and first dorsal fin taper distally. Origin of first dorsal fin is above free tip of pectoral fin. Second dorsal fin is less than one-half height of first dorsal fin, and origin is above or slightly posterior to origin of anal fin. Ridge extends between dorsal fin bases. Caudal peduncle lacks keel. Color is grayish blue with scattered black spots dorsally and grayish white ventrally.

This species occurs in the tropical to warm temperate Atlantic and possibly in the eastern Pacific Oceans, generally near the edge of continental and insular shelves at depths of 100 to 600 m. In the western Atlantic it occurs from Delaware to Florida, the Gulf of Mexico, the Bahamas, and Cuba, and off southern Brazil and Argentina. Food consists of squids and epipelagic bony fishes. Development is viviparous with a yolk sac placenta. Litters range from 4 to 12 young. Maximum known size is 280 cm TL, and young are 60 cm TL at birth.

REFERENCES: Bigelow and Schroeder 1948a; Springer and Thompson 1957 (all above as *Hypoprion bigelowi*); Applegate et al. 1979; Raschi et al. 1982; Castro 1983; Branstetter 1984; Compagno 1984; Branstetter and McEachran 1986b; C. R. Robins et al. 1986; Bonfil et al. 1990.

Galeocerdo cuvier (Peron and Lesueur 1822)
Tiger shark

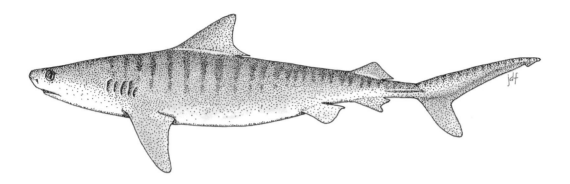

Galeocerdo cuvier is stout, with a short, blunt snout and a moderately high caudal fin with a well-developed ventral lobe. It is distinguished from the other species of the family by the following combination of characters. Preoral snout length is equal to internasal width. Anterior nasal flap is poorly developed. Upper labial furrows are very long and nearly reach anterior margin of eye. Upper jaw has 18 to 26 tooth rows, and lower jaw has 18 to 25. Teeth in both jaws have broad, curved, heavily serrated cusps with deep notch along lateral margin. Gill slits are relatively large. Pectoral fin and first dorsal fin taper distally. Origin of first dorsal fin is above or slightly anterior to axil of pectoral fin. Second dorsal fin is about two-fifths height of first dorsal fin, and its origin is slightly anterior to origin of anal fin. Prominent ridge extends between dorsal fins, and low keel occurs on caudal peduncle. Color is bluish or greenish gray to black dorsally and yellow or white ventrally. Dorsal surface of specimens less than 200 cm is covered with dark spots on a lighter background. In larger specimens, spots fuse into vertical bars. In largest specimens, bars are faded.

This species occurs worldwide in tropical to temperate seas from inshore to the edge of the continental and insular shelves. In the western Atlantic it occurs from Massachusetts to Uruguay, including the Gulf of Mexico, the Bahamas, and the Greater and Lesser Antilles. Food consists of a large variety of marine life, including jellyfishes, tunicates, mollusks, crustaceans, a large variety of elasmobranchs and bony fishes, sea snakes, sea turtles, marine iguanas, sea birds, and marine mammals. Development is ovoviviparous. Litters range from 10 to 82 young. Maximum known size is 7.4 m TL, although more questionable records range up to 9.1 m TL; males mature at 226 to 290 cm TL, females mature at 300 to 350 cm TL, and young range from 51 to 76 cm TL at birth.

REFERENCES: Bigelow and Schroeder 1948a; Baughman and Springer 1950; Springer 1960, 1963; Clark and von Schmidt 1965; Hoese and Moore 1977; Applegate et al. 1979; Castro 1983; Branstetter 1984; Compagno 1984; Branstetter and McEachran 1986b; Branstetter et al. 1987; Bonfil et al. 1990.

Negaprion brevirostris   (Poey 1868)
Lemon shark

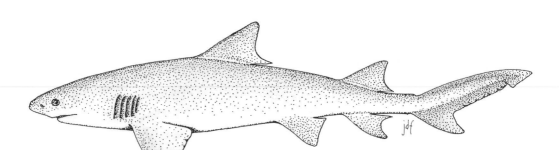

Negaprion brevirostris is stout, with a short, blunt snout and a relatively low caudal fin with a well-developed ventral lobe. It is distinguished from the other species of the family by the following combination of characters. Internasal width is greater than preoral snout length. Anterior nasal flap is broad and triangular. Upper labial furrows are very short and confined to corners of mouth. Upper jaw has 31 to 33 tooth rows, and lower jaw has 29 to 31. Teeth located in anterolateral section of upper jaw have narrow, smooth, and slightly oblique cusps and serrated bases. Gill slits are moderately long. Pectoral fin and first dorsal fin taper distally. Origin of first dorsal fin is above or slightly posterior to posterior free tip of pectoral fin. Second dorsal fin is about four-fifths height of first dorsal fin and originates above or slightly anterior to origin of anal fin. Ridge between dorsal fin bases is absent, and caudal peduncle lacks keel. Color is yellowish brown or olive gray dorsally and yellowish ventrally.

This species occurs in the tropical to warm temperate Atlantic and eastern Pacific Oceans from near shore to 92 m, and occasionally from freshwater. In the western Atlantic it occurs from New Jersey to Brazil, including the Gulf of Mexico, the Bahamas, and the Caribbean. Food consists of mollusks, crustaceans, elasmobranchs, a large variety of bony fishes, and sea birds. Development is viviparous with a yolk sac placenta. Litters range from 4 to 17 young. Maximum known length is 340 cm TL; males mature at 224 cm TL, females mature at 239 cm TL, and young are 60 to 65 cm TL at birth.

REFERENCES: Springer 1938, 1950b, 1960, 1963; Bigelow and Schroeder 1948a; Clark and von Schmidt 1965; Hoese and Moore 1977; Applegate et al. 1979; Castro 1983; Branstetter 1984; Compagno 1984; C. R. Robins et al. 1986; Bonfil et al. 1990.

Prionace glauca (Linnaeus 1758)
Blue shark

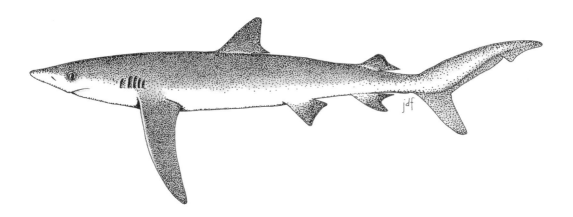

Prionace glauca is slender, with a long, slender snout and a moderately high caudal fin with a well-developed ventral lobe. It is distinguished from the other species of the family by the following combination of characters. Preoral snout length is 2 times internasal width. Anterior nasal flap is broad and triangular. Upper labial furrows are very short and inconspicuous. Upper jaw has 24 to 31 tooth rows, and lower jaw has 25 to 34. Teeth in the upper jaw have broad, triangular, curved, and serrated cusps. Gill slits are of moderate size, with papillose gill rakers on their inner openings. Pectoral fin and first dorsal fin taper distally. Origin of first dorsal fin is behind posterior rear tip of pectoral fin. Second dorsal fin is small, about one-half height of first dorsal fin, and originates slightly posterior to anal fin origin. Ridge between dorsal fin bases is absent. Caudal peduncle has low keel. Color is dark indigo blue dorsally and white ventrally. Fins lack distinct markings.

This species occurs worldwide in tropical to temperate oceanic and occasionally coastal waters. In the western Atlantic it occurs from Newfoundland to Argentina, but it is rarely recorded in the Gulf of Mexico. Food consists of a large variety of squids, elasmobranchs, and bony fishes, and occasionally sea birds and mammal carrion. Most prey are epipelagic. Development is viviparous with a yolk sac placenta. Litters range from 41 to 135 young. Maximum known size is at least 383 cm TL; males mature at 182 to 281 cm TL, females mature at 221 to 323 cm TL, and young range from 35 to 44 cm TL at birth.

REFERENCES: Bigelow and Schroeder 1948a; Clarke and Stevens 1974; Pratt 1979; Tricas 1979; Castro 1983; Branstetter 1984; Compagno 1984; C. R. Robins et al. 1986.

Rhizoprionodon terraenovae (Richardson 1836)
Atlantic sharpnose shark

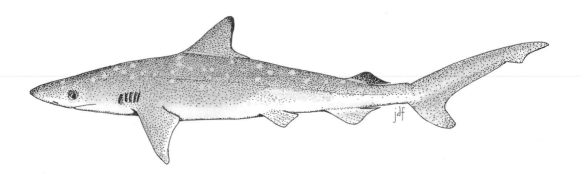

Rhizoprionodon terraenovae is moderately slender, with a long, acute snout and a moderately high caudal fin with a well-developed ventral lobe. It is distinguished from the other species of the family by the following combination of characters. Internasal width is less than preoral length. Anterior nasal flap is very short, narrow, and triangular. Upper labial furrows are long, 1.6% to 2.2% of TL. Upper jaw usually has 25 tooth rows, and lower jaw usually has 24. Teeth are similar in both jaws, and have slender, oblique, and weakly serrated cusps (in adults). Gill slits are short. Pectoral fin and first dorsal fin taper distally. Origin of first dorsal fin is above or slightly anterior to rear tip of pectoral fin. Second dorsal fin is small—height is about one-third height of first dorsal fin—and its origin is about at midbase of anal fin origin. Ridge between dorsal fin bases is absent or only weakly developed. Caudal peduncle lacks keel. Color is brownish, olive gray, or bluish gray dorsally and white ventrally. Adults have white spots dorsally and white margins on their pectoral fins.

This species occurs in the western North Atlantic from New Brunswick to Florida and the Gulf of Mexico. It is most abundant over the inner continental shelf but ranges from near shore to about 280 m, and occasionally is found in low-salinity estuaries. Food consists of polychaetes, mollusks, crustaceans, and a large variety of bony fishes. Development is viviparous with a yolk sac placenta. Litters range from one to seven young. Maximum known size is 110 cm TL; males mature at 65 to 80 cm TL, females mature at 85 to 90 cm TL, and young range from 29 to 37 cm TL at birth.

REFERENCES: Bigelow and Schroeder 1948a; Baughman and Springer 1950; V. G. Springer 1964; Clark and von Schmidt 1965; Applegate et al. 1979; Branstetter 1981, 1987a; Castro 1983; Parsons 1983; Compagno 1984; Branstetter and McEachran 1986b; C. R. Robins et al. 1986; Bonfil et al. 1990; Castro 1993b.

SPHYRNIDAE Hammerhead sharks

The hammerhead sharks are moderately slender, with short heads laterally expanded into blades, and moderately high caudal fins with well-developed ventral lobes. They are distinguished from the other families of the order by the following combination of characters. Head is greatly flattened and laterally expanded, with eye and nostril displaced to lateral extreme or near lateral extreme of head. Eye is circular, with well-developed nictitating eyelid. Spiracle is absent. Anterior nasal flap is short and triangular. Labial furrows are vestigial or absent. First dorsal fin is moderate to very large in size, shorter than caudal fin, and located anterior to pelvic fin base. Midpoint of first dorsal fin base is located anterior to pelvic fin origin. Caudal peduncle has precaudal pit. Dorsal lobe of caudal fin has lateral undulations along margin.

The hammerhead sharks occur worldwide in tropical to warm temperate seas. They are found from near shore to the edge of continental and insular shelves, from the surface to 275 m. Food consists of cephalopods, crustaceans, elasmobranchs, and a large variety of bony fishes. Development is viviparous with a yolk sac placenta. There are eight species in two genera, and three or four species in a single genus occur in the Gulf of Mexico.

Key to the Species of the Gulf of Mexico
(Adapted from Castro 1983; Compagno 1984)

1a. Head shovel shaped and relatively narrow, width less than 22% of TL; anterior margin of head not notched (Fig. 21) . . . . *Sphyrna tiburo* p. 95

FIG 21

1b. Head hammer shaped and relatively broad, width over 22% of TL; anterior margin of head notched 2

2a. Posterior margin of lateral extension of head nearly transverse (Fig. 22); free rear tip of first dorsal fin above or posterior to pelvic fin origin; posterior margin of anal fin straight to concave, not deeply notched . . . . *Sphyrna tudes* p. 96

FIG 22

2b. Posterior margin of lateral extension of head arched posterolaterally (except adults of *S. mokarran*); free rear tip of first dorsal fin anterior to pelvic fin origin; posterior margin of anal fin usually deeply notched. 3

3a. Anterior margin of head nearly straight in adults (Fig. 23); prenarial groove absent or poorly developed; teeth strongly serrated; pelvic fin and first dorsal fin falcate; second dorsal fin high, with short inner margin and deeply concave posterior margin . . . . *Sphyrna mokarran* p. 94

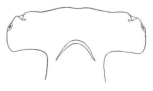

FIG 23

3b. Anterior margin of head moderately convex in adults
(Fig. 24), strongly convex in juveniles; prenarial groove
well developed; teeth without serrations in young and with
weak serrations in adults; pelvic fin not falcate, first dorsal
fin slightly falcate; second dorsal fin low, with long inner
margin and almost straight posterior margin
. . . . *Sphyrna lewini* p. 93

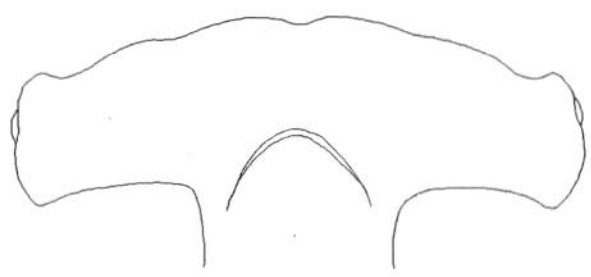

FIG 24

Sphyrna lewini (Griffith and Smith 1834)
Scalloped hammerhead shark

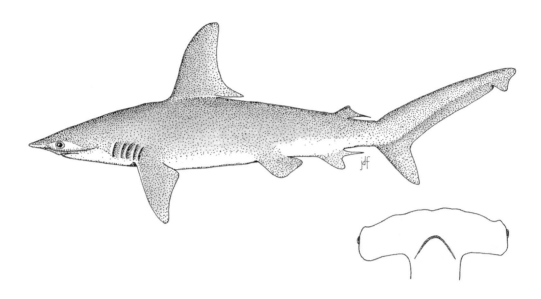

Sphyrna lewini is moderately slender, with a broad, narrow, bladelike head and a moderately high caudal fin with a well-developed ventral lobe. It is distinguished from the other species of the family by the following combination of characters. Expanded section of head is very broad and relatively narrow, width of blade is 24% to 30% of TL. Anterior margin of head is broadly arched, with medial and two lateral indentations. Posterior margin of head is angled posterolaterally. Prenarial groove, located anteromedial to nostrils, is well developed. Upper and lower jaws have 15 to 16 tooth rows on each side. Teeth are similarly shaped in both jaws, with medial teeth possessing triangular, smooth to weakly serrated, and erect cusps. First dorsal fin is slightly falcate, and its origin is above or slightly posterior to axil of pectoral fin. Second dorsal fin is low, shorter than anal fin, and has concave posterior margin and inner margin length about twice fin height. Pelvic fin has straight to slightly concave posterior margin. Color is olive to brownish gray dorsally and white ventrally. Ventral tip of pectoral fin is dark gray to black.

This species occurs worldwide in tropical to warm temperate seas over continental and insular shelves, and ranges from the surface to 275 m. It occasionally enters estuaries and bays. In the western Atlantic it occurs from New Jersey to Brazil, including the Gulf of Mexico and the Caribbean Sea. Food consists of crustaceans, cephalopods, elasmobranchs, and a large variety of bony fishes. Litters range from 15 to 31 young. Maximum known size is 370 to 420 cm TL; males mature at 140 to 165 cm TL, females mature at 212 cm TL, and young are 42 to 55 cm TL at birth.

REFERENCES: Bigelow and Schroeder 1948a; Gilbert 1967; Clarke 1971; Hoese and Moore 1977; Applegate et al. 1979; Branstetter 1981, 1987b; Castro 1983; Compagno 1984; Quéro 1984g; C. R. Robins et al. 1986; McEachran and Seret 1987; Bonfil et al. 1990.

Sphyrna mokarran (Rüppell 1837)
Great hammerhead shark

Sphyrna mokarran is moderately slender, with a broad, narrow, bladelike head and a moderately high caudal fin with a well-developed ventral lobe. It is distinguished from the other species of the family by the following combination of characters. Expanded section of head is very broad and narrow, width equals 23% to 27% of TL. Anterior margin of head is broadly arched in juveniles but is almost straight in adults. Anterior margin has medial and one lateral indentation. Prenarial groove, located anteromedial to nostrils, is either absent or poorly developed. Upper jaw has 19 to 20 tooth rows on each side, and lower jaw has 17 to 20. Teeth are similar in both jaws. Anterior teeth have slightly oblique and serrated cusps. First dorsal fin is very large and strongly falcate and originates above or slightly posterior to axil of pectoral fin. Second dorsal fin is equal in height to anal fin, and has strongly concave posterior margin and inner margin equal in height to fin height. Pelvic fin has strongly concave posterior margin. Color is grayish brown dorsally and light ventrally.

This species occurs worldwide in tropical to warm temperate seas from near shore to the edge of continental and insular shelves, from the surface to 80 m. In the western Atlantic it occurs from North Carolina to Brazil, including the Gulf of Mexico and the Caribbean Sea. Food consists of squids, crabs, other sharks and rays, and a wide variety of bony fishes. Litters range from 13 to 42 young. Maximum known size is 550 to 610 cm TL; males mature at 234 to 269 cm TL, females mature at 250 to 300 cm TL, and young are 50 to 70 cm TL at birth.

REFERENCES: Bigelow and Schroeder 1948a; S. Springer 1963; Clark and von Schmidt 1965; Gilbert 1967; Hoese and Moore 1977; Applegate et al. 1979; Castro 1983; Compagno 1984; Quéro 1986g; C. R. Robins et al. 1986; Bonfil et al. 1990.

Sphyrna tiburo (Linnaeus 1758)
Bonnethead shark

Sphyrna tiburo is moderately slender, with a relatively narrow and broad bladelike head and a moderately high caudal fin with a moderately developed ventral lobe. It is distinguished from the other species of the family by the following combination of characters. Expanded section of head is strongly convex, width equals 18% to 25% of TL. Anterior margin of head is broadly arched and lacks indentations. Prenarial groove is absent. Posterior margin of head is short and either transverse or slightly angled. Upper and lower jaws have 12 to 14 tooth rows on each side. Teeth are similarly shaped in both jaws. Anterior teeth have erect, smooth cusps. First dorsal fin is moderately falcate and originates above inner margin of pectoral fin. Second dorsal fin is about equal in height to anal fin, and has strongly concave posterior margin and inner margin equal to height of fin. Color is gray to greenish gray dorsally and pale ventrally.

This species occurs in tropical and warm temperate waters of the western Atlantic and eastern Pacific Oceans along the inner parts of continental and insular shelves to depths of 25 to 80 m. In the western Atlantic it occurs from Rhode Island to southern Brazil, including the Gulf of Mexico. Food consists of a large variety of crustaceans, and to a lesser extent, bivalves, octopods, and small bony fishes. Litters range from 4 to 16. Maximum known size is 150 cm TL; males mature at 52 to 75 cm TL, females mature at 84 cm TL, and young are 35 to 40 cm TL at birth.

REFERENCES: Bigelow and Schroeder 1948a; Baughman and Springer 1950; Hoese and Moore 1958; Clark and von Schmidt 1965; Gilbert 1967; Myrberg and Gruber 1974; Hoese and Moore 1977; Applegate et al. 1979; Castro 1983; Compagno 1984; C. R. Robins et al. 1986; Bonfil et al. 1990.

Sphyrna tudes   (Valenciennes 1822)
Smalleye hammerhead

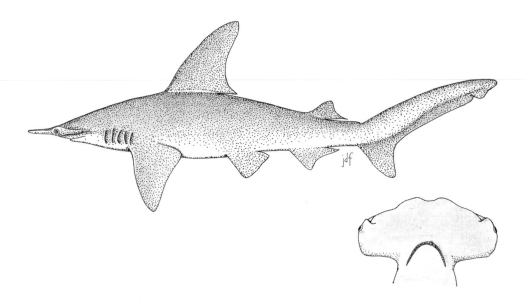

Sphyrna tudes is moderately slender, with a broad, moderately narrow, bladelike head and a moderately high caudal fin with a well-developed ventral lobe. It is distinguished from the other species of the family by the following combination of characters. Expanded section of head is very broad and moderately long, width equals 28% to 32% of TL. Anterior margin of head is broadly arched and has medial and two lateral indentations. Prenarial groove, anteromedial to nostrils, is well developed. Upper jaw has 15 to 16 tooth rows on each side, and lower jaw has 15 to 17. Teeth of upper jaw have oblique, smooth-edged cusps, and teeth of lower jaw have erect, smooth-edged cusps. First dorsal fin is slightly falcate and originates slightly posterior to axil of pectoral fin. Second dorsal fin is shorter than anal fin, and has slightly concave posterior margin and inner margin shorter than twice fin height. Pelvic fin has straight or slightly concave posterior mar-

gin. Color is gray to grayish brown dorsally and pale ventrally.

This species occurs in the tropical to warm temperate Atlantic. In the western Atlantic it has been reported from the northern Gulf of Mexico and from Venezuela to Uruguay between the shoreline and about 12 m. However, records from the Gulf of Mexico may refer to another species of *Sphyrna*. Food consists of shrimps, crabs, squids, other sharks, and bony fishes. Litters range from six to nine young. Maximum known size is about 150 cm TL; males mature at about 110 to 134 cm TL, females mature at about 120 to 148 cm TL, and young are about 30 cm TL at birth.

REFERENCES: Bigelow and Schroeder 1948a; Gilbert 1967; Castro 1983; Compagno 1984; C. R. Robins et al. 1986; McEachran and Seret 1987.

HEXANCHIFORMES

This order and the Squaliformes, Squatiniformes, Pristiophoriformes (absent from the Gulf), Torpediniformes, Pristiformes, Rajiformes, and Myliobatiformes constitute the Squalea, the second major taxon of Neoselachii. Hexanchiformes are considered to be the sister group of the remaining Squalea and consist of two families, one of which occurs in the Gulf of Mexico.

HEXANCHIDAE   Sixgill and sevengill sharks

The sixgill and sevengill sharks are moderately slender to stout, with a short to moderately long snout and a moderately long, low heterocercal caudal fin. They are distinguished from the other family in the order by the following combination of characters. Nostril is separated from mouth, and anterior nasal flap is short. Mouth is subterminal, arched, and extends beyond eye. Labial furrow is reduced or absent. Teeth of upper jaw are narrow, with a large main cusp and often small lateral cusplets. Teeth of lower jaw are broad and sawlike, with short to long cusps and series of large cusplets. Spiracle is small and located well posterior to eye. Gill slits number six or seven, and first is not continuous across throat. Anal fin is smaller than single dorsal fin. Caudal fin has long dorsal lobe with subterminal notch and little or no ventral lobe.

The sixgill and sevengill sharks occur worldwide in boreal to tropical seas over the outer continental shelf to the upper slope, and occasionally occur inshore. They range in depth from near the surface to 1,875 m. Food consists of crustaceans, other sharks, rays, bony fishes, and carrion. Development is ovoviviparous. There are four recognized species in three genera, and three species in two genera occur in the Gulf of Mexico.

Key to the Species of the Gulf of Mexico

(Adapted from Compagno 1984)

1a. Six pairs of gill slits 2
1b. Seven pairs of gill slits . . . . *Heptranchias perlo* p. 99
2a. Lower jaw with six rows of large, comblike teeth on each side; distance between end of dorsal fin base and origin of dorsal caudal fin lobe about equal to dorsal fin base length . . . . *Hexanchus griseus* p. 100
2b. Lower jaw with five rows of large, comblike teeth on each side; distance between end of dorsal fin base and origin of dorsal caudal fin lobe greater than dorsal fin base length . . . . *Hexanchus vitulus* p. 101

Heptranchias perlo (Bonnaterre 1788)
Sharpnose sevengill shark

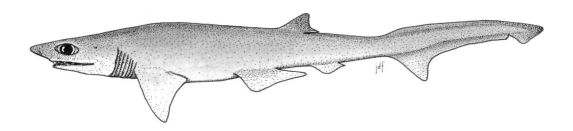

Heptranchias perlo is moderately slender, with a narrow, pointed head. It is distinguished from the other species of the family by the following combination of characters. Mouth is narrow and strongly arched. Upper jaw teeth are small and narrow, with a long cusp and often small mesial and lateral cusplets. Lower jaw teeth are comblike, with a few short, mesial cusplets, a high cusp, and seven or eight progressively smaller lateral cusplets. Eye is relatively large. Gill slits are large and number seven. Caudal peduncle is relatively long; distance from end of dorsal fin base to origin of dorsal caudal lobe is about twice length of dorsal fin base. Color is brownish gray dorsally and lighter ventrally. Body lacks spots, but dorsal and upper caudal lobe are black tipped (more evident in young than in older individuals).

This species probably occurs worldwide in tropical to temperate seas between 27 and 1,720 m. It occurs in the Gulf of Mexico and the Caribbean Sea in the western Atlantic. Food consists of squids and bony fishes. Litters range from 9 to 20 young. Maximum known size is 137 cm TL; males mature at about 85 cm TL, females mature at about 89 to 93 cm TL, and young are about 26 cm TL at birth.

REFERENCES: Bigelow and Schroeder 1948a; Applegate et al. 1979; Castro 1983; Boeseman 1984; Compagno 1984.

Hexanchus griseus (Bonnaterre 1788)
Sixgill shark

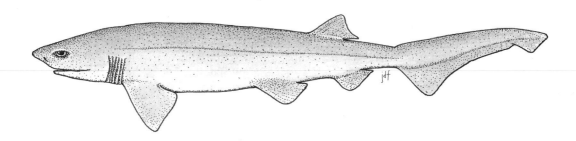

Hexanchus griseus is stout, with a relatively broad and blunt head. It is distinguished from the other species of the family by the following combination of characters. Mouth is narrow and strongly arched. Upper jaw teeth are relatively narrow, with a long pointed cusp and often series of progressively smaller lateral cusplets. Lower jaw has six large, comblike teeth on each side, with medial cusp only slightly higher than adjacent cusplet, and cusplets gradually decreasing in size laterally. Eye is relatively small. Gill slits are large and number six. Caudal peduncle is relatively short; distance between end of dorsal fin base and origin of dorsal caudal lobe is about equal to length of dorsal fin base. Color is dark gray to brown dorsally and lighter ventrally.

This species occurs worldwide in tropical to temperate seas. In the western Atlantic it occurs in the northern Gulf of Mexico and the Caribbean Sea. It has been captured from the surface to 1,875 m and is more common at shallow depths at higher latitudes. Food consists of pelagic and benthic organisms, such as squids, crustaceans, sharks, rays, chimaeras, bony fishes, and seals. Litters range from 22 to 108. Maximum known size is about 482 cm TL; males mature at about 325 cm TL, females mature at about 450 to 482 cm TL, and young are about 65 to 70 cm TL at birth.

REFERENCES: Bigelow and Schroeder 1948a; Castro 1983; Boeseman 1984; Compagno 1984; Branstetter and McEachran 1986a; C. R. Robins et al. 1986.

Hexanchus vitulus Springer and Waller 1969
Bigeye sixgill shark

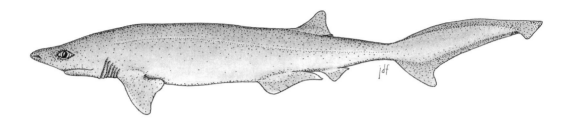

Hexanchus vitulus is relatively slender bodied, with a narrow and pointed head. It is distinguished from the other species of the family by the following combination of characters. Mouth is large and strongly arched. Upper jaw has relatively narrow teeth with a long pointed cusp and often series of poorly defined lateral cusplets. Lower jaw has five large, comblike teeth on each side, with cusp relatively larger than adjacent cusplet, and cusplets gradually decreasing in size laterally. Eye is relatively large. Gill slits are large and number six. Caudal peduncle is relatively long; distance between end of dorsal fin base and origin of dorsal caudal fin lobe is much longer than dorsal fin base length. Color is gray dorsally and lighter ventrally.

This species occurs worldwide in tropical seas between 90 and 600 m. In the western Atlantic it occurs from the Bahamas, the Greater Antilles, southern Florida, the Gulf of Mexico, Nicaragua, and Costa Rica. Food consists of small- to medium-sized fishes and probably benthic invertebrates. Litters number about 13. Maximum known size is 180 cm TL; males mature at 123 to 157 cm TL, females mature at 142 to 178 cm TL, and young are 43 cm TL at birth.

REFERENCES: Springer and Waller 1969; Applegate et al. 1979; Castro 1983; Compagno 1984; C. R. Robins et al. 1986; Bonfil et al. 1990.

SQUALIFORMES

Squaliformes are considered to be the sister group of Squatiniformes, Pristiophoriformes, Torpediniformes, Pristiformes, Rajiformes, and Myliobatiformes. Generally this order is divided into
three families (Compagno 1984). Recently, however, Shirai (1992)
split one of the three families (Squalidae) into six families. Nelson
(1994) accepted the sequencing of Shirai but reduced the six families to three. Compagno's classification is utilized herein because
Shirai's classification has not been tested and because some of his
families are nearly as morphologically variable as the entire order.
Thus it is difficult either to construct a key for or to morphologically define his families. Two of the three families occur in the
Gulf of Mexico.

Key to the Families of the Gulf of Mexico
(Adapted from Compagno 1984)

1a.   First dorsal fin originates posterior to pelvic fin origin
. . . . Echinorhinidae p. 102
1b.   First dorsal fin originates anterior to pelvic fin origin
. . . . Squalidae p. 104

ECHINORHINIDAE   Bramble sharks

Bramble sharks are rather stout and cylindrical in cross section,
with a moderately depressed head, two spineless dorsal fins, and
no anal fin. They are distinguished from the other families of the
order by the following combination of characters. Nostrils are
well separated from each other and from mouth. Anterior nasal
flap is short. Mouth is broadly arched, with short labial folds.
Teeth are similar in both jaws, are compressed, bladelike, and have
a single cusp and up to three cusplets. Spiracle is small and is located far posterior to eye. Dorsal fins are smaller than pelvic fin.
First dorsal fin originates slightly posterior to origin of pelvic fin.
Second dorsal fin is about equal in size to first dorsal fin. Pectoral
fin has angular rear tip. Caudal fin is moderately low and long
and lacks subterminal notch. Body is covered with relatively close-
set denticles or with scalloped bucklerlike denticles.

Bramble sharks occur worldwide in tropical to warm temperate seas between 11 and 900 m on or near the bottom. Food consists of crabs, octopods, squids, and a large variety of benthic
fishes. They are ovoviviparous. There are two species in a single
genus, and one species occurs in the Gulf of Mexico.

Echinorhinus brucus   (Bonnaterre 1788)
Bramble shark

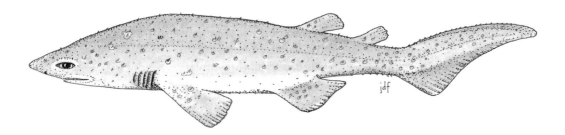

Echinorhinus brucus is stout and cylindrical, with a moderately blunt and depressed snout and posteriorly located dorsal fins. It is distinguished from the other species of the family by the following combination of characters. Snout is relatively short, less than mouth width. Anterior nasal flap is short. Mouth is broadly arched, with short labial folds. Teeth are compressed and bladelike in both jaws, with a single cusp and up to three cusplets. Upper jaw has 20 to 26 tooth rows, and lower jaw has 22 to 26. Dorsal fins are relatively small and are not preceded by spine. Origin of first dorsal fin is posterior to pelvic fin base. Posterior corner of pectoral fin is not expanded into narrow, acute lobe. Body and fins are sparsely covered with thornlike denticles that range from small to bucklerlike in size. Base of denticles has radiating ridges but is not stellate, and occasionally several are fused together to form plates with multiple cusps. Underside of snout of adults is covered with long denticles. Color is dark gray or brown to black dorsally and light or whitish ventrally.

This species occurs worldwide in tropical to warm temperate seas except for the eastern Pacific. In the western Atlantic it occurs off Virginia, in the northeastern Gulf of Mexico, and off Argentina. It has been captured from 18 to 900 m but is most abundant from 366 to 900 m. Food consists of crabs, small sharks, and bony fishes. Litters range from 15 to 24 young. Maximum known size is 310 cm TL; males mature at 150 cm TL, females mature at 213 to 230 cm TL, and young are born at 29 to 90 cm TL.

REFERENCES: Musick and McEachran 1969; Castro 1983; Compagno 1984; C. R. Robins et al. 1986.

SQUALIDAE   Dogfish sharks

The dogfish sharks are slender to rather stout, with a conical to moderately depressed head and a low to moderately high hetero-cercal caudal fin. They are distinguished from the other families of the order by the following combination of characters. Nostril is well separated from mouth, and anterior flap is short. Mouth is arched to transverse, with short to very long labial furrow. Teeth consist of a single cusp and often cusplets, and vary from non-bladelike in both jaws, to bladelike in both jaws, to bladelike in lower jaw and needlelike in upper jaw. Spiracle is small to very large and is often above level of eye. First dorsal fin originates anterior to pelvic fin origin. Anal fin is absent. Caudal fin has moderate to long dorsal lobe and long to no ventral lobe.

Dogfish sharks occur worldwide from tropical to polar seas, although they are absent from shallow tropical seas. In polar seas they occur from shallow waters to 6,000 m. Many are benthic, while others are epipelagic, mesopelagic, and possibly bathypelagic. They feed on cephalopods, crustaceans, sharks, bony fishes, and marine mammals. Development is ovoviviparous. There are 72 recognized species in 22 genera, and 20 species in 9 genera occur in the Gulf of Mexico.

Key to the Species of the Gulf of Mexico
(Adapted from Castro 1983; Compagno 1984; Springer and Burgess 1985)

1a. Both dorsal fins preceded by a spine 2
1b. Second dorsal fin and generally first dorsal fin not preceded by a spine 17
2a. Teeth similarly shaped in both jaws 3
2b. Teeth in lower jaw much broader and differently shaped than those of upper jaw 5
3a. Second dorsal fin as large or nearly as large as first dorsal fin; anterior nasal flap with a distinct secondary lobe (Fig. 25) . . . . *Squalus asper* p. 124
3b. Second dorsal fin considerably smaller than first dorsal fin; anterior nasal flap with a small or no secondary lobe 4
4a. Distance between tip of snout and inner edge of nostril equal to or less than distance between nostril and upper labial furrow; pectoral fin with deeply concave rear margin and acutely pointed posterior free tip (Fig. 26) . . . . *Squalus cubensis* p. 125
4b. Distance between tip of snout and inner edge of nostril greater than distance between nostril and upper labial furrow; pectoral fin with slightly to moderately concave rear margin and rounded posterior free tip (Fig. 27) . . . . *Squalus mitsukurii* p. 126

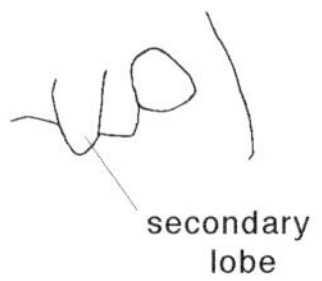

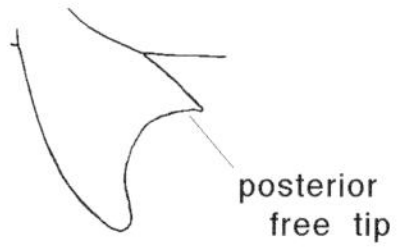

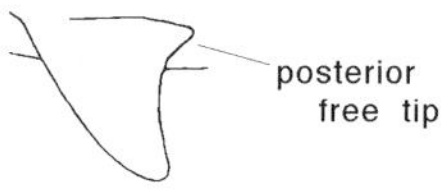

secondary lobe

FIG 25

posterior free tip

FIG 26

posterior free tip

FIG 27

5a. Teeth of upper jaw with large cusp and several smaller cusplets (Fig. 28) 6

5b. Teeth of upper jaw with single bladelike cusp and no cusplets (Fig. 29) 11

6a. Dermal denticles craterlike, low without median spine (Fig. 30) . . . . *Etmopterus bigelowi* p. 114

6b. Dermal denticles with central stout to slender spine (Fig. 31) 7

7a. Dermal denticles on dorsal and lateral parts of body arranged in longitudinal or nearly longitudinal rows . . . . *Etmopterus bullisi* p. 115

7b. Dermal denticles on dorsal and lateral parts of body randomly arranged 8

8a. Ventral side of snout nearly free of dermal denticles . . . . *Etmopterus virens* p. 119

8b. Ventral side of snout fully scaled 9

9a. Body black or gray dorsally and ventrally, without prominent markings (pelvic markings may or may not be evident); tip of appressed pectoral fin not extending to level of spine of first dorsal fin 10

9b. Prominent black markings present on lighter background; tip of appressed pectoral fin reaching level of spine of first dorsal fin. . . . . *Etmopterus hillianus* p. 117

10a. Pectoral fin notably short and broad, its distal margin fringed with horny rays (ceratotrichia) normally about one-sixth to one-half as long as fin length, most ceratotrichia free of connecting membranes; color in life black, with markings very obscure or absent; markings may be evident after storage in preservatives. . . *Etmopterus schultzi* p. 118

10b. Pectoral fin not notably short and broad, its distal margin occasionally fringed, but some to most ceratotrichia connected by membranes; color grayish, with pelvic and caudal markings visible but not prominent . . . . *Etmopterus gracilispinis* p. 116

11a. Preoral snout length greater than distance between mouth and pectoral fin origin; dermal denticles on upper sides with slender pedicels and pitchfork-shaped crowns . . . . *Deania profundorum* p. 113

11b. Preoral snout length less than distance between mouth and pectoral fin origin; dermal denticles on upper sides without pitchfork-shaped crowns 12

12a. Teeth of upper jaw relatively broad and bladelike (Fig. 32); teeth of lower jaw low and wide; rear tip of pectoral fin short and angular to elongated and acutely pointed 13

12b. Teeth of upper jaw narrow, not bladelike (Fig. 33); teeth of lower jaw high and wide; rear tip of pectoral fin short and broadly rounded. 16

13a. Lateral trunk denticles overlapping, with flat, leaflike crowns on elevated pedicels extending above denticle

FIG 28

FIG 29

FIG 30

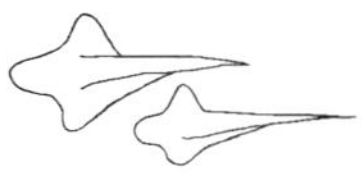

FIG 31

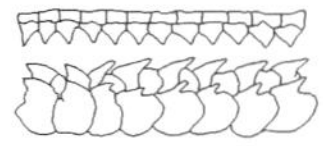

FIG 32

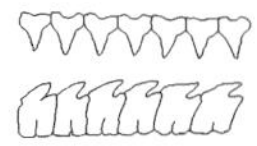

FIG 33

bases, and with medial and lateral cusps on posterior ends
. . . . *Centrophorus* c.f. *ascus* p. 107

13b. Lateral trunk denticles nonoverlapping, with flat crowns
on bases without pedicels, and with or without posterior
medial cusps. 14

14a. Dermal denticles of adult specimens without cusps; crowns
broadly rounded posteriorly. 15

14b. Dermal denticles of adult specimens with medial cusps;
crowns angular, with posterior thornlike extension
. . . . *Centrophorus uyato* p. 110

15a. Distance between dorsal fins about equal to distance from
tip of snout to axil of pectoral fin
. . . . *Centrophorus granulosus* p. 108

15b. Distance between dorsal fins distinctly shorter than distance from tip of snout to axil of pectoral fin
. . . . *Centrophorus* c.f. *tessellatus* p. 109

16a. Lower teeth with relatively low, approximately oblique
cusps (Fig. 33) . . . . . *Centroscymnus cryptacanthus* p. 111

16b. Lower teeth with relatively high, approximately erect cusps
(Fig. 34). . . . . *Scymnodon squamulosus* p. 122

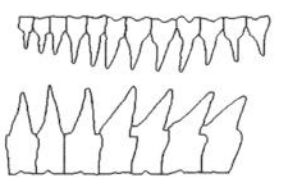

17a. End of first dorsal fin base distinctly anterior to origin of
pelvic fin. 18

17b. End of first dorsal fin base close to rear tip of pelvic fin
. . . . 19

18a. Second dorsal fin base twice as long or longer than length
of first dorsal fin base; upper caudal fin lobe short, caudal
fin paddlelike . . . . *Squaliolus laticaudus* p. 123

18b. Second dorsal fin base about as long as first dorsal fin base;
upper caudal fin lobe relatively long, caudal fin not paddlelike. . . . . *Dalatias licha* p. 112

19a. Lower jaw with 25 to 31 rows of teeth; height of dorsal
fins less than height of dorsal lobe of caudal fin; dark ring
around branchial region (gill region)
. . . . *Isistius brasiliensis* p. 120

19b. Lower jaw with about 19 rows of teeth; height of dorsal
fins about equal to height of dorsal lobe of caudal fin; no
dark ring around branchial region (gill area)
. . . . *Isistius plutodus* p. 121

FIG 34

Centrophorus c.f. *ascus*   Garman 1906

This undescribed species is moderately elongate, with a depressed and moderately long snout, pectoral fins with narrowly expanded rear lobes, and a moderately short, high caudal fin. It is distinguished from the other species of the family by the following combination of characters. Snout is slightly longer than mouth width and shorter than distance from mouth to origin of pectoral fin. Anterior nasal flap is short. Teeth are bladelike, without cusplets, and form interlocked cutting edges. Those of upper jaw are moderately broad, with erect to slightly oblique and acute cusps. Teeth of lower jaw are broader than those of upper jaw and have oblique, asymmetrical cusps. Gill slits are moderately broad and all are about same size. Both dorsal fins are preceded by relatively large grooved spine. Origin of first dorsal fin is over inner margin of pectoral fin. Second dorsal fin is about as high as first dorsal fin, and its base is three-fourths that of first. Distance between dorsal fins is about equal to distance from tip of snout to midbase of pectoral fin. Posterior corner of pectoral fin is expanded into narrow acute lobe that extends to level of first dorsal fin spine. Length of inner margin of pectoral fin is shorter than distance from second dorsal fin spine to origin of upper caudal fin lobe. Upper caudal fin lobe is relatively long, ventral lobe is moderately developed, and subterminal notch is distinct. Dermal denticles on sides of body are partially overlapping and have low, thick pedicles and leaflike crowns bearing one central and two lateral cusps. Color is light gray to grayish brown.

Centrophorus ascus occurs in the western Pacific at depths greater than 200 m. The species resembling *C. ascus* in the northern Gulf of Mexico is thought to be a distinct, undescribed species (George Burgess, pers. com., March 1994). Maximum known size is 81 cm TL.

REFERENCES: Bigelow and Schroeder 1957; Compagno 1984.

Centrophorus granulosus (Bloch and Schneider 1801)
Gulper shark

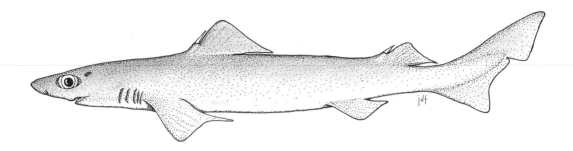

Centrophorus granulosus is rather slender, with a moderately long, broad snout; pectoral fins with narrowly expanded rear lobes; and a moderately long, high caudal fin. It is distinguished from the other species of the family by the following combination of characters. Snout is moderately long, about equal to mouth width but shorter than distance from mouth to origin of pectoral fin. Anterior nasal flap is short. Teeth are bladelike and form interlocked cutting edge in both jaws. Those of upper jaw are moderately broad, with erect to slightly oblique cusps. Teeth of lower jaw are broader than those of upper jaw, and have oblique, asymmetrical cusps. Upper jaw has 33 to 40 tooth rows, and lower jaw has 30. Both dorsal fins are preceded by a long, grooved spine. Origin of first dorsal fin is above axil of pectoral fin. Second dorsal fin is nearly as high as first dorsal fin, and its base is about three-fourths that of first dorsal fin. Distance between dorsal fins is about equal to distance from tip of snout to axil of pectoral fin. Posterior corner of pectoral fin is expanded into narrow acute lobe that extends posterior to origin of first dorsal fin. Length of inner margin of pectoral fin is greater that distance from second dorsal spine to origin of upper caudal fin lobe. Upper lobe of caudal fin is relatively long, ventral lobe is moderately developed, and subterminal notch is distinct. Posterior margins of fins are not fringed. Dermal denticles on sides of body are nonoverlapping, low, and blocklike, with broad, transversely rhomboidal crowns on bases without pedicels. Color is light brown dorsally and lighter ventrally.

This species occurs worldwide in tropical to temperate seas between 100 and 1,200 m but is apparently rare outside the Atlantic. In the western Atlantic it occurs from North Carolina to the northern Gulf of Mexico. Maximum known size is about 150 cm TL; young are born at about 30 to 42 cm TL.

REFERENCES: Bigelow et al. 1955; Bigelow and Schroeder 1957; Applegate et al. 1979; Castro 1983; Compagno 1984; McEachran and Branstetter 1984.

Centrophorus c.f. *tessellatus*   Garman 1906

This undescribed species is rather slender, with a moderately long, broad snout; pectoral fins with narrowly expanded rear corners; and a moderately long and high caudal fin. It is distinguished from the other species of the family by the following combination of characters. Snout is slightly longer than mouth width but shorter than distance from mouth to origin of pectoral fin. Anterior nasal flap is short. Teeth are bladelike, lack cusplets, and form interlocking cutting edge in both jaws. Teeth of upper jaw are moderately broad, with erect to slightly oblique cusps. Those of lower jaw are broader than those of upper jaw and have oblique, asymmetrical cusps. Both dorsal fins are preceded by a long, grooved spine. Origin of first dorsal fin is above axil of pectoral fin. Second dorsal fin is nearly as high as first dorsal fin, and its base is about three-fourths that of first. Distance between dorsal fins is slightly less than distance from tip of snout to pectoral fin origin. Posterior corner of pectoral fin is expanded into narrow acute lobe that extends beyond first dorsal spine. Length of inner margin is shorter than distance from second dorsal spine to origin of upper caudal fin lobe. Upper caudal lobe is moderately long, ventral lobe is moderately developed, and subterminal notch is distinct. Dermal denticles on sides of body are nonoverlapping and blocklike, with broad, rhomboidal crowns on bases without pedicels. Color is light gray to brownish gray.

Centrophorus tessellatus occurs in the western and central Pacific between 260 and 728 m. The species resembling *C. tessellatus* in the Gulf of Mexico is thought to represent a distinct, undescribed species (George Burgess, pers. com., March 1994). Maximum known size is 89 cm TL.

REFERENCES: Bigelow and Schroeder 1957; Compagno 1984.

Centrophorus uyato (Rafinesque 1810)
Little gulper shark

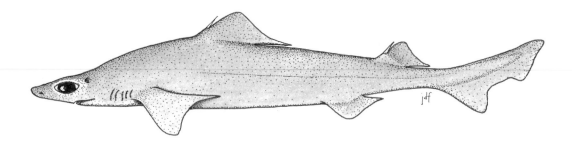

Centrophorus uyato is slender, with a rather long, moderately slender snout; pectoral fins with narrowly expanded rear corners; and a moderately long and high caudal fin. It is distinguished from the other species of the family by the following combination of characters. Snout is relatively long, longer than mouth width and about equal to distance from mouth to pectoral fin origin. Anterior nasal flap is short. Teeth are bladelike, lack cusplets, and form interlocking cutting edge in both jaws. Those of upper jaw are moderately broad and have slightly oblique to oblique cusps. Teeth of lower jaw are broader than those of upper jaw and have asymmetrical oblique cusps. Upper jaw has 36 to 39 tooth rows, and lower jaw has 32 to 33. Both dorsal fins are preceded by a long, grooved spine. Origin of first dorsal fin is posterior to axil of pectoral fin. Second dorsal fin is nearly as high as first dorsal fin, and its base is about three-fourths that of first dorsal fin. Distance between dorsal fins is about equal to distance from tip of snout to axil of pectoral fin. Posterior corner of pectoral fin is expanded into narrow acute lobe that extends distally to origin of first dorsal fin. Length of inner margin is about equal to distance from second dorsal spine to origin of dorsal caudal fin lobe. Upper caudal fin lobe is moderately long, ventral lobe is moderately developed, and subterminal notch is distinct. Dermal denticles on sides of body are nonoverlapping and blocklike, with rhomboidal-shaped crowns without pedicels. Color is uniform grayish brown.

This species occurs nearly worldwide in tropical to warm temperate seas between 50 and 1,400 m, but it appears to be most abundant in the Atlantic. In the western Atlantic it occurs in the Gulf of Mexico. Food consists of squids and bony fishes. Litters are thought to be limited to one young. Maximum size is about 100 cm TL; males mature at about 81 to 94 cm TL, females mature at about 75 to 89 cm TL, and young are about 40 to 50 cm TL at birth.

REFERENCES: Bigelow and Schroeder 1957; Applegate et al. 1979; Castro 1983; Compagno 1984; McEachran and Branstetter 1984.

Centroscymnus cryptacanthus   Regan 1906

Centroscymnus cryptacanthus is moderately stout bodied, with a moderately long and depressed head, small dorsal fin spines, and a caudal fin with a distinct subterminal notch. It is distinguished from the other species of the family by the following combination of characters. Snout is about equal to mouth width and to distance from mouth to first gill slit. Anterior nasal flap is short. Teeth in upper jaw are very slender, have acute cusps but no cusplets, and are not bladelike. Teeth of lower jaw are compressed and bladelike, have oblique cusps and no cusplets, and form interlocked cutting edge. Upper labial furrows are shorter than distance between them. Both dorsal fins are preceded by a small, grooved spine that is often buried in fins. First dorsal fin is distinctly smaller than second and extends forward as prominent ridge. Second dorsal fin is longer than distance from end of its base to origin of dorsocaudal fin lobe. Pectoral fin is short, with broadly rounded free corner and inner margin.

Anal fin is larger than, and originates anterior to, second dorsal fin. Caudal lobe has relatively long dorsal lobe and short ventral lobe. Dermal denticles on sides of body are large, with smooth, oval, partially ridged, cuspidate crowns. Color is black to dark brown.

This species occurs in the Atlantic and western Pacific Oceans near the bottom between 400 and 1,164 m. In the western North Atlantic it occurs in the northern Gulf of Mexico. This species was previously split into two species, *C. cryptacanthus* from the Atlantic Ocean and *C. owstoni* from the western Pacific and the Gulf of Mexico; however, recent opinion suggests that they are synonymous (George Burgess, pers. com., March 1994). Maximum known size is 104 cm TL; males mature at 72 to 84 cm, and females mature at 102 to 104 cm TL.

REFERENCES: Bigelow and Schroeder 1957; Compagno 1984.

Dalatias licha   (Bonnaterre 1788)
Kitefin shark

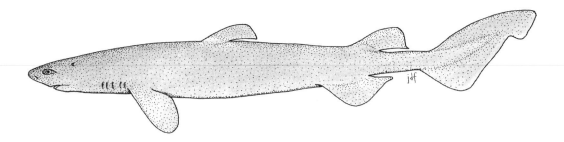

Dalatias licha is moderately slender, with a short, blunt snout and a relatively high caudal fin. It is distinguished from the other species of the family by the following combination of characters. Snout is relatively short, about equal to mouth width, and is considerably shorter than distance from mouth to pectoral fin origin. Anterior nasal flap is short. Teeth of upper jaw are narrow, with hooked cusps. Teeth of lower jaw are bladelike, with broad, triangular, serrated cusps, and form interlocked cutting edge. Upper jaw has 16 to 21 tooth rows, and lower jaw has 17 to 20. Dorsal fins are not preceded by a spine. Origin of first dorsal fin is posterior to free tip of pectoral fin. Second dorsal fin is higher than first dorsal fin, and its base is longer than that of first dorsal fin. Distance between dorsal fins is slightly greater than distance from tip of snout to axil of pectoral fin. Pectoral fin has broadly rounded rear corner. Dorsal lobe of caudal fin is well developed. Posterior margins of fins are not fringed. Dermal denticles on sides of body are low and flat with a single cusp. Color is uniform dark gray.

This species occurs worldwide in tropical to temperate seas, except that it is apparently absent from the eastern Pacific. It has been captured from 37 to 1,000 m but is most common below 200 m. In the western Atlantic it has been reported from Georges Bank and the northern Gulf of Mexico. Food consists of siphonophores, polychaetes, crustaceans, squids, octopods, sharks, skates, and bony fishes. Litters range from 10 to 16 young. Maximum size is about 159 to 182 cm TL; males mature at about 77 to 121 cm TL, females mature at about 117 to 159 cm TL, and young are about 30 cm TL at birth.

REFERENCES: Bigelow and Schroeder 1948a, 1957; Castro 1983; Compagno 1984; McEachran and Branstetter 1984; C. R. Robins et al. 1986.

Deania profundorum   (Smith and Radcliffe 1912)

Deania profundorum is moderately slender, with a greatly elongated, flattened snout and a subcaudal keel on ventral surface of caudal peduncle. It is distinguished from the other species of the family by the following combination of characters. Snout is over one-half head length and longer than distance from mouth to pectoral fin origin. Anterior nasal flap is short. Teeth are moderately broad to broad and lack cusplets. Those of upper jaw are moderately broad, with erect, acute cusps, and form noninterlocked cutting edge. Teeth of lower jaw are broader than those of upper jaw, have oblique asymmetrical cusps, and form interlocked cutting edge. Upper jaw has 26 to 31 tooth rows, and lower jaw has 26 to 30. Both dorsal fins are preceded by a grooved spine; first spine is short, and second is long and curved. First dorsal fin is short and high and originates over inner margin of pectoral fin. Second dorsal fin is slightly larger than first dorsal fin and originates over midbase of pelvic fin. Pectoral fin has narrowly rounded rear corner. Caudal fin has moderately long dorsal lobe, poorly developed ventral lobe, and well-defined subterminal notch. Dermal denticles on sides of body have stellate bases, high pedicels, and tricuspidate and triridged erect crowns. Color is gray to brown.

This species occurs in the western Pacific, western Indian and Atlantic Oceans on or near the bottom from 275 to 1,785 m. Food consists of squids, crustaceans, and bony fishes. It is ovoviviparous, and litter size ranges from five to seven young. Maximum known size is 76 cm TL.

REFERENCES: Bigelow and Schroeder 1957; Springer 1959; Castro 1983; Compagno 1984.

Etmopterus bigelowi Shirai and Tachikawa 1993
Smooth lanternshark

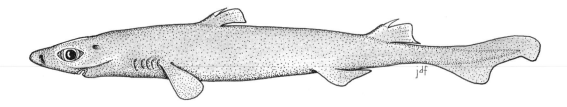

Etmopterus bigelowi is relatively slender, with a moderately long snout and a moderately short, low caudal fin. It is distinguished from the other species of the family by the following combination of characters. Snout is moderately long, greater than mouth width but slightly shorter than distance from mouth to origin of pectoral fin. Anterior nasal flap is short. Teeth of upper jaw are narrow, with relatively broad, erect median cusps and two to four pairs of lateral cusplets. Teeth of lower jaw are broad, with narrow, obliquely directed cusps, and form interlocked cutting edge. Upper jaw has 19 to 24 tooth rows, and lower jaw has 25 to 39. Dorsal fins are preceded by a spine. Origin of first dorsal fin is above to slightly posterior to rear tip of pectoral fin. Second dorsal fin is higher and broader based than first dorsal fin. Distance between dorsal fins is greater than distance from tip of snout to first gill slit. Pectoral fin has broadly rounded rear corner. Dorsal lobe of caudal fin is shorter than distance from tip of snout to distal margin of pectoral fin. Posterior margins of fins are not broadly fringed. Dermal denticles on sides of body have low, flat crowns and four-pointed bases. Color is uniform grayish to dusky brown except for pale yellow spot on head over pineal eye and inconspicuous black markings on lateral side of head, on lower surface of pectoral fin, above pelvic fin, and at origin of lower caudal lobe.

This species occurs in the Atlantic, Indian, and western Pacific Oceans. In the western Atlantic it occurs in the northern Gulf of Mexico and the Caribbean Sea, and off Suriname, Brazil, Uruguay, and Argentina. It has been captured on or near the bottom from 163 to 1,000 m, and in open water from 110 to 700 m. Food consists of squids, small squalid sharks, bony fish eggs, and lanternfishes. Maximum known size is about 47 cm TL; males mature at about 31 to 39 cm TL, and females mature at about 38 to 47 cm TL.

REFERENCES: Bigelow et al. 1955; Bigelow and Schroeder 1957; Krefft 1968; Castro 1983; Compagno 1984; McEachran and Branstetter 1984 (all above as *E. pusillus*); Shirai and Tachikawa 1993.

Etmopterus bullisi Bigelow and Schroeder 1957
Lined lanternshark

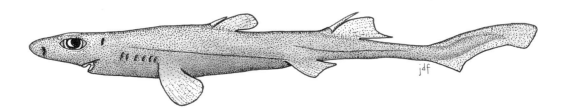

Etmopterus bullisi is slender, with a rather acute snout and a long tail. It is distinguished from the other species of the family by the following combination of characters. Snout is relatively long, greater than mouth width and nearly as long as distance from mouth to origin of pectoral fin. Anterior nasal flap is short. Teeth of upper jaw are narrow, with median cusps and two pairs of lateral cusplets. Teeth of lower jaw are broad, bladelike, with narrow oblique cusps and lateral blade, and form interlocked cutting edge. Upper jaw has 18 to 20 tooth rows, and lower jaw has 27 to 31. Dorsal fins are preceded by spine. Origin of first dorsal fin is above free tip of pectoral fin. Second dorsal fin is higher and longer based than first dorsal fin. Distance between dorsal fins is less than distance from tip of snout to first gill slit. Pectoral fin has broadly rounded rear corner. Dorsal lobe of caudal fin is well developed but shorter than distance from tip of snout to tip of pectoral fin. Posterior margins of fins are not fringed. Dermal denticles along sides of body have slender hooked crowns and are arranged in regular longitudinal rows. Color is dark gray dorsally and abruptly black ventrally, with narrow, elongate, black area above and behind pelvic fin base, and pale yellow spot on head over pineal eye.

This species occurs in the western North Atlantic from North Carolina to the Straits of Florida and off Honduras between 200 and 350 m. According to George Burgess (pers. com., March 1994), it also occurs in the Gulf of Mexico. Food consists of small crustaceans and squids. Maximum known size is 23 to 24 cm TL, although mature specimens have not been reported.

REFERENCES: Bigelow and Schroeder 1957; Castro 1983; Compagno 1984.

Etmopterus gracilispinis Krefft 1968
Broadband dogfish shark

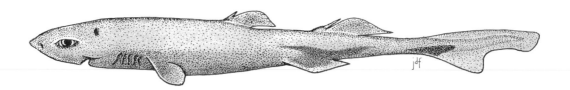

Etmopterus gracilispinis is relatively stout, with a moderately long, rounded snout and a short, low tail. It is distinguished from the other species of the family by the following combination of characters. Snout is moderately long, greater than mouth width but slightly shorter than distance from mouth to origin of pectoral fin. Anterior nasal flap is short. Teeth of upper jaw are narrow, with median cusps and two lateral pairs of cusplets. Teeth of lower jaw are broad and bandlike, with narrow oblique cusps and lateral blades, and form interlocked cutting edge. Upper jaw has about 27 tooth rows, and lower jaw has about 28. Dorsal fins are preceded by spine. Origin of first dorsal fin is posterior to free tip of pectoral fin. Second dorsal fin is higher and longer based than first dorsal fin. Distance between dorsal fins is less than distance from tip of snout to first gill slit. Pectoral fin has broadly rounded rear corner. Dorsal lobe of caudal fin is relatively short, about equal to head length. Posterior margins of fins are not broadly fringed. Dermal denticles along sides of body have very slender, hooked crowns and are widely and randomly spaced. Color is blackish brown dorsally, grading to black ventrally, with indistinct broad, elongate black area above and behind pelvic fin base, elongate black marks on caudal fin base, and pale yellow spot on head.

This species occurs in the Atlantic Ocean. In the western Atlantic it occurs from Virginia, Florida, Uruguay, and Argentina. According to George Burgess (pers. com., March 1994), it also occurs in the Gulf of Mexico. It has been captured near the bottom from 100 to 1,000 m, but it is thought to ascend in the water column during the night to depths of 70 to 490 m. Maximum known size is 33 cm TL; males mature at about 26 cm TL, females mature at about 33 cm TL, and young are born at about 13 cm TL.

REFERENCES: Krefft 1968, 1980; Schwartz and Burgess 1975; Castro 1983; Compagno 1984.

Etmopterus hillianus (Poey 1861)
Blackbelly dogfish shark

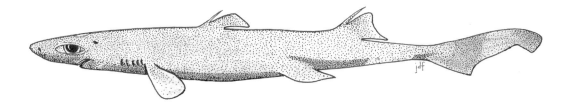

Etmopterus hillianus is moderately stout, with a relatively long, rounded snout and a relatively long, low caudal fin. It is distinguished from the other species of the family by the following combination of characters. Snout is moderately long, greater than mouth width but slightly shorter than distance from mouth to origin of pectoral fin. Anterior nasal flap is short. Teeth of upper jaw are narrow, with median cusps and generally fewer than three pairs of lateral cusplets. Teeth of lower jaw are broad and bandlike, with narrow horizontally directed cusps, and form interlocked cutting edge. Upper jaw has 24 tooth rows, and lower jaw has 36. Dorsal fins are preceded by spine. Origin of first dorsal fin is posterior to rear tip of pectoral fin. Second dorsal fin is higher and broader based than first dorsal fin. Distance between dorsal fins is greater than distance from tip of snout to first gill slit. Pectoral fin has broadly rounded rear corner. Dorsal lobe of caudal fin is about equal to head length. Pos-terior margins of fins are not broadly fringed. Dermal denticles on sides of body have slender, hooked crowns and are widely and randomly spaced. Color is gray to dark brown dorsally and black ventrally, with broad, elongate, black area above and behind pelvic fin base, black band on caudal fin base and on caudal fin tip, and pale yellow spot on head over pineal eye.

This species occurs in the western North Atlantic from Virginia to southern Florida, and from Bermuda, Cuba, the northern Gulf of Mexico, and St. Kitts. It has been captured from 380 to 717 m. Litters range from four to five young. Maximum known size is about 50 cm TL; males mature at about 25 to 27 cm TL, females mature at about 30 cm TL, and young are about 9 cm TL at birth.

REFERENCES: Bigelow and Schroeder 1948a, 1957; Schwartz and Burgess 1975; Castro 1983; Compagno 1984; C. R. Robins et al. 1986.

Etmopterus schultzi Bigelow, Schroeder, and Springer 1953
Fringefin lanternshark

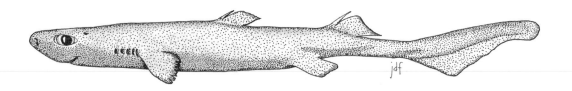

Etmopterus schultzi is relatively slender, with a moderately short snout; short, broad pectoral fins; and a moderately short tail. It is distinguished from the other species of the family by the following combination of characters. Snout length is less than mouth width and shorter than distance from mouth to origin of pectoral fin. Anterior nasal flap is short. Teeth of upper jaw are narrow, with median cusps and two to three pairs of cusplets. Teeth of lower jaw are broad, with horizontally directed cusps, and form interlocked cutting edge. Upper jaw has 32 to 38 tooth rows, and lower jaw has 32. Both dorsal fins are preceded by spine. Origin of first dorsal fin is posterior to rear tip of pectoral fin. Second dorsal fin is higher and broader based than first dorsal fin. Distance between dorsal fins is about equal to distance from tip of snout to first gill slit. Pectoral fin has broadly rounded rear corner. Dorsal lobe of caudal fin is relatively long, about equal to head length. Posterior margins of fins are broadly fringed with naked ceratotrichia. Fringes on pectoral fin represent one-sixth to one-half fin length. Dermal denticles on sides of body have very slender, hooked crowns and are widely and randomly spaced. Color is black to light brown dorsally and dusky gray ventrally, with elongate dusky markings above and behind pelvic fin base, elongate black markings on caudal fin base, and pale yellow spot on head over pineal eye.

This species occurs in the western North Atlantic in the northern Gulf of Mexico from Florida to Texas, where it is very abundant. It has been captured on or near the bottom from 384 to 732 m. Food consists of squids. Maximum known size is about 30 cm TL; males mature at about 27 cm TL, and females mature at about 28 to 30 cm TL.

REFERENCES: Bigelow et al. 1953; Bigelow and Schroeder 1957; Castro 1982; Compagno 1984; Springer and Burgess 1985.

Etmopterus virens Bigelow, Schroeder, and Springer 1953
Green lanternshark

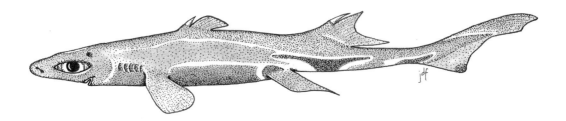

Etmopterus virens is moderately slender, with a moderately short, rounded snout and a relatively long tail. It is distinguished from the other species of the family by the following combination of characters. Snout length is about equal to mouth width and about equal to distance from mouth to origin of pectoral fin. Anterior nasal flap is short. Teeth of upper jaw are narrow and have median cusps and two pairs of cusplets. Teeth of lower jaw have narrow horizontally directed cusps and form interlocked cutting edge. Upper jaw has 29 to 34 tooth rows, and lower jaw has 24 to 32. Both dorsal fins are preceded by spine. Origin of first dorsal fin is above inner margin of pectoral fin. Second dorsal fin is higher and broader based than first dorsal fin. Distance between dorsal fins is about equal to distance from tip of snout to first gill slit. Pectoral fin has broadly rounded rear corner. Dorsal lobe of caudal fin is about equal to head length. Posterior margins of fins are not broadly fringed.

Dermal denticles on sides of body have short, stout, conical, hooked crowns and are widely and randomly spaced. Color is dark brown or grayish black dorsally and black ventrally, with pale yellow spot on head over pineal eye. Body is marked with elongate, broad black band posterior to pelvic fin and elongate black markings on caudal fin.

This species occurs in the western North Atlantic in the northern Gulf of Mexico from Florida to Texas, and in the Caribbean Sea off Nicaragua. It has been captured on or near the bottom from 348 to 465 m. Food consists of squids and octopods. Litters consist of one to three young. Maximum known size is about 23 cm TL; males mature at about 20 to 23 cm TL, females mature at about 23 cm TL, and young are about 9 cm TL at birth.

REFERENCES: Bigelow et al. 1953; Bigelow and Schroeder 1957; Springer 1967; Castro 1983; Compagno 1984.

Isistius brasiliensis (Quoy and Gaimard 1824)
Cookie-cutter shark

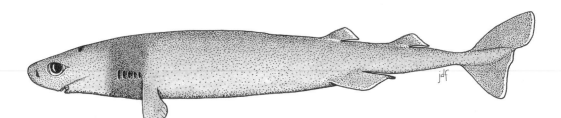

Isistius brasiliensis is moderately slender, with a moderately short snout and a short, broad caudal fin. It is distinguished from the other species of the family by the following combination of characters. Snout length is shorter than mouth width and shorter than distance from mouth to origin of pectoral fin. Anterior nasal flap is short. Teeth of upper jaw are narrow, have acute, erect cusps, and lack cusplets. Teeth of lower jaw are bladelike, with high, broad, erect cusps, and form interlocked cutting edge. Upper jaw has 31 to 37 tooth rows, and lower jaw has 25 to 31. Neither dorsal fin is preceded by spine. Origin of first dorsal fin is slightly anterior to origin of pelvic fin. Second dorsal fin is slightly higher than first dorsal fin, but bases are about equal. Distance between dorsal fins is less than distance between tip of snout and first gill slit but greater than twice base of first dorsal fin. Pectoral fin has abruptly rounded rear tip. Upper lobe of caudal fin is shorter than head length. Posterior margins of fins are not broadly fringed. Dermal denticles are flat and blocklike. Color is grayish brown, with fins light edged and dark ring around the gill slits.

This species occurs circumtropically. In the western Atlantic it has been reported from the Bahamas, the northern Gulf of Mexico, and southern Brazil between 85 and 3,500 m. It apparently moves toward the surface during the night. Food consists of tissue from large squids, fishes (including tunas, wahoos, dolphins, marlins, and swordfishes), and porpoises and whales. A combination of bandlike teeth and the ability to produce bioluminescence apparently enables this shark to excise plugs of tissue from large predators. Maximum known size is about 50 cm TL; males mature at about 31 to 37 cm TL, and females mature at about 38 to 44 cm TL.

REFERENCES: Bigelow and Schroeder 1948a, 1957; Strasburg 1963; Garrick and Springer 1964; Jones 1971; Castro 1983; Compagno 1984; Castro-Aguirre and García-Domínguez 1985; C. R. Robins et al. 1986; Retzer 1990.

Isistius plutodus Garrick and Springer 1964
Largetooth cookie-cutter shark

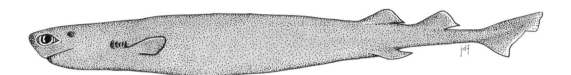

Isistius plutodus is moderately slender, with a short snout and a short, low tail. It is distinguished from the other species of the family by the following combination of characters. Snout length is shorter than mouth width and about equal to eye length. Anterior nasal flap is short. Teeth of upper jaw are narrow, with acute, erect cusps, and lack cusplets. Teeth of lower jaw are bladelike, with high, broad, erect cusps, and form interlocked cutting edge. Upper jaw has 29 tooth rows, and lower jaw has 19. Neither dorsal fin is preceded by spine. Origin of first dorsal fin is slightly anterior to origin of pelvic fin. Second dorsal fin is slightly higher and slightly broader based than first dorsal fin. Distance between dorsal fins is less than distance from tip of snout to first gill slit and about equal to length of base of first dorsal fin. Pectoral fin has broadly rounded rear tip. Dorsal lobe of caudal fin is shorter than head length. Posterior margins of fins are not broadly fringed. Dermal denticles are flat and blocklike. Color is uniform dark brown except for pale brown band on ventral side of head from mouth to gill slits.

This species occurs in the western North Atlantic from the northern Gulf of Mexico off Alabama, and in the western North Pacific off Okinawa, Japan. It has been captured in midwater. The holotype has a large plug of bony fish flesh in its stomach, thus it probably feeds like *I. brasiliensis*. Maximum known size is about 42 cm TL.

REFERENCES: Garrick and Springer 1964; Castro 1983; Compagno 1984.

Scymnodon squamulosus (Günther 1877)

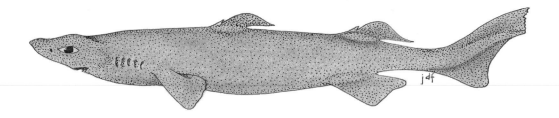

Scymnodon squamulosus is moderately slender and oval in cross section, with a moderately long snout and a small, grooved spine preceding each dorsal fin. It is distinguished from the other species of the family by the following combination of characters. Snout is depressed, pointed, and shorter than distance between mouth and pectoral fin origin. Anterior nasal flap is short. Mouth is small and nearly straight. Teeth in upper jaw are small, with very narrow, erect cusps, and without cusplets. Teeth in lower jaw are large and bladelike, with broad, erect to slightly oblique cusps and small cusplet on each side of cusp, and form interlocked cutting edge. Upper jaw has 57 to 59 tooth rows, and lower jaw has 31 to 33. Dorsal fins are small. First dorsal fin originates posterior to inner margin of pectoral fin. Second dorsal fin is slightly larger than first, and base of second dorsal fin is about 1.5 times as long as that of first. Pectoral fin has short, broadly rounded rear corner. Caudal fin is asymmetrical, with long upper lobe, well-developed subterminal notch, and short, poorly developed lower lobe.

Dermal denticles on sides of body have five to seven transverse ridges. Color is uniform brown.

This species occurs in the tropical to temperate Atlantic Ocean and possibly the Indian Ocean near the bottom between 550 and 1,450 m. It has occasionally been captured in oceanic waters between the surface and 550 m. In the western Atlantic it occurs in the northern Gulf of Mexico, off Suriname, and off southern Brazil. This species was formerly divided into two species, *S. squamulosus* from the western Pacific and *S. obscurus* from the Atlantic and western Indian Oceans; however, recent opinion suggests that they are synonymous (George Burgess, pers. com., March 1994). Food consists of benthic invertebrates and fishes. Development is ovoviviparous. Maximum known size of males is 51 cm TL and of females is 59 cm TL.

REFERENCES: Bigelow and Schroeder 1957; Compagno 1984; McEachran and Branstetter 1984 (all above as *S. obscurus*).

Squaliolus laticaudus Smith and Radcliffe 1912

Squaliolus laticaudus is slender and spindle shaped, with a long, conical snout; a slender caudal peduncle; and a high, almost symmetrical caudal fin. It is distinguished from the other species of the family by the following combination of characters. Snout is about one-half head length and about equal to distance from mouth to origin of pectoral fin. Anterior nasal flap is short. Teeth in upper jaw are narrow, with erect, acute cusps and without cusplets. Teeth of lower jaw are broad and bladelike, with high, moderately broad, asymmetrical but nearly erect cusps that form interlocked cutting edge. Upper jaw has 22 to 31 tooth rows, and lower jaw has 16 to 21. First dorsal fin is very short, originates near posterior margin of pectoral fin, and is preceded by small embedded or partially exposed spine. Second dorsal fin is low but is about twice as long as first dorsal fin, originates over pelvic fin base, and lacks spine. Pectoral fin is short, with slightly convex posterior margin. Caudal fin has short and similarly shaped dorsal and ventral lobes and well-developed subterminal notch. Dermal denticles on sides of body are flat and blocklike, with bases lacking pedicels and crowns lacking posterior cusps. Photophores are distributed over body but are most dense on ventral side. Color is black to blackish brown, and fins have light margins.

This species occurs in the western Pacific, western Indian, and Atlantic Oceans in the water column between 200 and 500 m. In the western Atlantic it occurs from Bermuda, the Gulf of Mexico, and Brazil. It makes diel vertical migrations, swimming up to about 200 m during the night and retreating to the lower part of its range during the day. Food consists of squids and midwater fishes such as gonostomatids, idiacanthids, and myctophids. Maximum known size is 25 cm TL; males mature at 15 cm TL and reach 22 cm TL, and females mature at 17 to 20 cm TL.

REFERENCES: Bigelow and Schroeder 1957; Seigel et al. 1977; Seigel 1978; Castro 1983; Compagno 1984.

Squalus asper   Merrett 1973
Roughskin dogfish

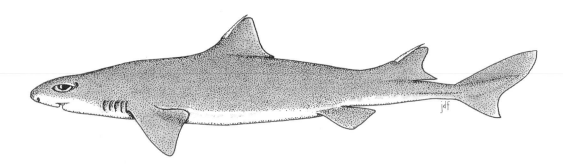

Squalus asper is stout, with a moderately long, broad snout and a short tail. It is distinguished from the other species of the family by the following combination of characters. Snout length is slightly less than to about equal to mouth length, and shorter than distance from mouth to origin of pectoral fin. Anterior nasal flap has broad, posteriorly directed secondary lobe. Teeth are similarly shaped in both jaws. Teeth are bladelike, with oblique cusps and no cusplets. Upper jaw has 24 to 28 tooth rows, and lower jaw has 22 to 24. Both dorsal fins are preceded by spine. Origin of first dorsal fin is above to posterior to rear tip of pectoral fin. Second dorsal fin is about equal in size to first dorsal fin. Distance between dorsal fins is greater than distance from tip of snout to origin of pectoral fin. Pectoral fin is broad and triangular, with broadly rounded rear tip. Dorsal lobe of caudal fin is shorter than head length.

Posterior margins of fins are not broadly fringed. Dermal denticles on sides of body are relatively large and tricuspidate, with scalloped posterior margins. Color is gray to brown dorsally and lighter ventrally.

This species occurs in the tropical western Atlantic, western Indian, and central Pacific Oceans on or near the bottom from 214 to 600 m. In the western Atlantic it occurs off South Carolina and in the northern Gulf of Mexico. Food consists of squids and small bony fishes. Litters range from 21 to 22 young. Maximum known size is about 118 cm TL; males mature at about 85 to 90 cm TL, females mature at about 89 to 118 cm TL, and young range from 25 to 28 cm TL at birth.

REFERENCES: Merrett 1973; Castro 1983; Compagno 1984.

Squalus cubensis Howell Rivero 1936
Cuban dogfish

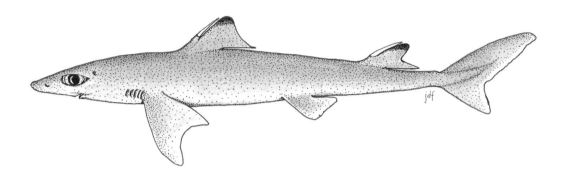

Squalus cubensis is relatively slender, with a moderately long, broad snout and a moderately long caudal fin. It is distinguished from the other species of the family by the following combination of characters. Snout length is greater than mouth width but shorter than distance from mouth to origin of pectoral fin. Anterior nasal flap has narrow, posteriorly directed secondary lobe. Teeth are bladelike, with oblique cusps and no cusplets, and are similarly shaped in both jaws. Upper and lower jaws have 26 tooth rows. Both dorsal fins are preceded by spine. Origin of first dorsal fin is anterior to rear corner of pectoral fin. Second dorsal fin is shorter and has narrower base than first dorsal fin. Distance between dorsal fins is greater than distance from tip of snout to first gill slit. Pectoral fin has acutely angled rear corner. Dorsal lobe of caudal fin is shorter than head length. Posterior margins of fins are not broadly fringed. Dermal denticles on sides of body are small, low, and unicuspidate. Color is dark gray dorsally and light gray ventrally. Dorsal fins are black tipped, and other fins are white edged.

This species occurs in the western Atlantic from North Carolina to Florida, Cuba, and Hispaniola; in the northern Gulf of Mexico from Florida to Mexico; and off southern Brazil and Argentina. It has been captured on or near the bottom from 60 to 380 m. Litters consist of 10 young. Maximum known size is about 110 cm TL; males and females mature at about 50 to 75 cm TL.

REFERENCES: Bigelow and Schroeder 1948a, 1957; Hoese and Moore 1977; Applegate et al. 1979; Sadowsky and Soares Moreira 1981; Castro 1983; Compagno 1984; C. R. Robins et al. 1986; Bonfil et al. 1990.

Squalus mitsukurii Jordan and Snyder 1903
Shortspine dogfish

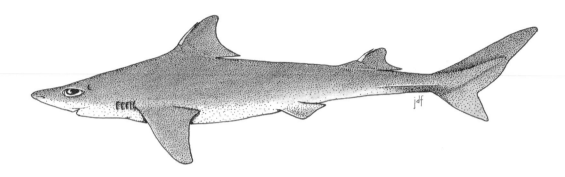

Squalus mitsukurii is fairly stout, with a moderately long, broad, rounded snout and a long caudal fin. It is distinguished from the other species of the family by the following combination of characters. Snout length is slightly greater than mouth width. Anterior nasal flap has small, narrow, posteriorly directed secondary lobe. Teeth are similarly shaped in both jaws, bladelike, with oblique cusps and no cusplets. Upper jaw has 17 tooth rows, and lower jaw has 23. Both dorsal fins are preceded by spine. Origin of first dorsal fin is above axil of pectoral fin. Second dorsal fin is shorter and narrower based than first dorsal fin. Distance between dorsal fins is greater than head length. Pectoral fin is broad and triangular, with acutely angled rear corner. Dorsal lobe of caudal fin is about equal to head length. Posterior margins of fins are not broadly fringed. Dermal denticles on sides of body are relatively small, low, and tricuspidate. Color is grayish brown dorsally and white ventrally.

This species occurs in the tropical to temperate Atlantic, western Indian, and Pacific Oceans on or near the bottom from 330 to 394 m. In the western Atlantic it occurs from North Carolina to the northern Gulf of Mexico and off Argentina. Specimens from the Gulf of Mexico and several other areas may represent an undescribed species. This species was previously misidentified as *Squalus blainvillei*. Food consists of crustaceans, squids, and small bony fishes. Litters consist of four to nine young. Maximum known size is about 110 cm TL; males mature at about 65 to 89 cm TL, females mature at about 72 cm TL, and young are about 22 to 26 cm TL at birth.

REFERENCES: Bigelow and Schroeder 1957; Applegate et al. 1979; Castro 1983 (all above as *S. blainvillei*); Compagno 1984; Bonfil et al. 1990 (as *S. blainvillei*).

SQUATINIFORMES

Squatiniformes are the sister group of Pristiophoriformes, Torpediniformes, Pristiformes, Rajiformes, and Myliobatiformes. The single family within the order occurs in the Gulf of Mexico.

SQUATINIDAE   Angelsharks

Angelsharks are dorsoventrally flattened (depressed), with greatly expanded pectoral fins and pelvic fins. They are distinguished from all other families of neoselachians by the following combination of characters. Mouth is terminal. Teeth are similarly shaped in both jaws. Eye and spiracle are located on top of head. Gill slits are laterally located. Pectoral fin is free from head, and anterior margin of pectoral fin is adjacent to gill slits. Anal fin is lacking, and two small dorsal fins are located on stout tail. Pelvic fin is laterally expanded and originates slightly behind axil of pectoral fin. Caudal fin is well developed and slightly hypocercal.

Angelsharks occur worldwide in tropical to temperate seas either on or near the bottom from the shore zone to 1,300 m. They are associated with continents but are absent from much of the Indian Ocean and from the Red Sea. Food consists of bivalves, gastropods, cephalopods, crustaceans, and small bony fishes. Embryonic development is ovoviviparous. There are 12 species recognized, and 1 of these occurs in the Gulf of Mexico.

Squatina dumeril Lesueur 1818
Atlantic angelshark

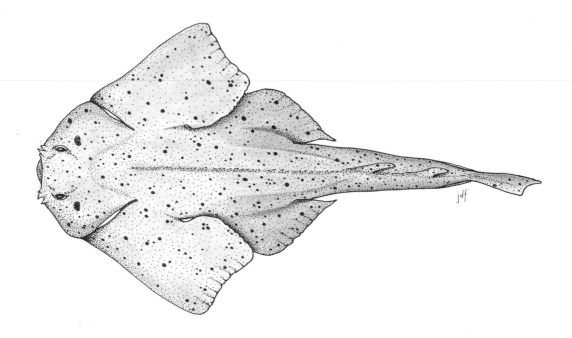

Squatina dumeril is greatly depressed, with a flat, blunt snout and a moderately developed tail that has well-developed dorsal and ventral lobes. It is distinguished from the other species of the family by the following combination of characters. Anterior nasal barbel is simple, with narrow, tapering tip. Teeth are conical, with broad bases and smooth crowns. Upper jaw has 20 tooth rows, and lower jaw has 18. Dermal folds on sides of head are simple, without angular lobes. Distance between eye and spiracle is about one and one-half times eye diameter. Free tip of pectoral fin is acutely angled. Moderate-sized thorns occur along midline of back and tail to origin of first dorsal fin, and between dorsal fins. Denticles on sides of body have hooked, three-ridged crowns. Color is light gray to reddish brown dorsally, often with dark blotches, and white ventrally.

This species occurs in the western North Atlantic from southern New England to Florida, the northern Gulf of Mexico from Florida to Mexico, and off Jamaica, Nicaragua, and Venezuela. It has been captured from near shore to 1,290 m. Food consists of mollusks, crustaceans, skates, and bony fishes. Litters consist of up to 16 young. The young are born in the summer over shallow depths (18 to 26 m). Maximum known size is about 152 cm TL; males and females mature at about 92 to 107 cm TL, and young range from 28 to 30 cm TL at birth.

REFERENCES: Bigelow and Schroeder 1948a; Hoese 1962; Hoese and Moore 1977; Applegate et al. 1979; Castro 1983; Compagno 1984; C. R. Robins et al. 1986.

TORPEDINIFORMES

This order and the Pristiformes, Rajiformes, and Myliobatiformes compose the Batoidea (rays). Torpediniformes are considered to be the sister group to the other taxa of Batoidea. The order contains four families, and two of these occur in the Gulf of Mexico.

Key to the Families of the Gulf of Mexico

1a. Mouth wide and little protrusible; upper and lower jaws not bound together by labial cartilages
. . . . Torpedinidae p. 133
1b. Mouth narrow and greatly protrusible to form a short tube; upper and lower jaws bound together by labial cartilages . . . . Narcinidae p. 129

NARCINIDAE

Narcinids are anteriorly flattened and posteriorly stout bodied, with a rounded snout and a stout tail with a well-developed caudal fin. They are distinguished from the other families of the order by the following combination of characters. Snout is moderately long, broad, and evenly convex to obtusely rounded. Pectoral fin is moderately laterally expanded, is attached to side of head, and extends to level of nostril to form disc. Disc is longer than it is broad and is relatively thick at margin. Anterior margin of nostril is extended to form broad curtain in front of mouth. Mouth is narrow, transverse, and protrusible into short tube. Mouth is surrounded by deep groove. Teeth are small, consist of single cusp, and are in quincunx arrangement. Spiracle is well developed, and posterior margin is smooth, corrugated, or has papillae. Pectoral fin radials extend anteriorly to anterior margin of nasal capsules. Electric organ is kidney shaped and is located posterolateral to eye. Pelvic fin is laterally expanded, with broadly rounded to acutely angled lateral corner and straight to slightly convex or concave posterolateral margin. Dorsal fins are large and similarly shaped. Caudal fin is well developed and consists of dorsal and ventral lobes confluent around tip of vertebral column. Body and fins are naked.

Narcinids occur nearly worldwide in tropical to temperate seas. They have not been reported from the eastern Atlantic. Food consists of benthic invertebrates and small bony fishes. Embryonic development is ovoviviparous. There are about 15 species in 4 genera, and 2 species in separate genera occur in the Gulf of Mexico.

Key to the Species of the Gulf of Mexico

1a. Eye minute, often covered with skin; entire inner margin of pelvic fin connected to side of tail
.... *Benthobatis marcida* p. 131
1b. Eye normally developed; distal section of inner margin of pelvic fin free of side of tail .... *Narcine brasiliensis* p. 132

Benthobatis marcida Bean and Weed 1909
Deep-sea electric ray

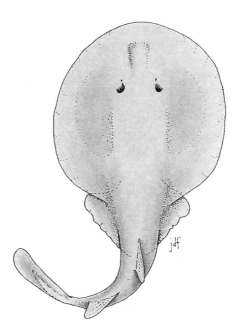

Benthobatis marcida has an oval-shaped disc, a relatively long snout, and a relatively long tail. It is distinguished from the other species of the family by the following combination of characters. Snout is relatively long, preorbital length is 14% of TL. Mouth is transverse, and width is slightly less than preoral length. Upper jaw has 12 to 20 tooth rows. Teeth have subquadrangular bases and short acute cusps. Eye is minute and entirely covered with skin. Spiracle is transverse to slightly oblique, is located posterior to eye by distance equal to length of spiracle, and has smooth margin. Gill slits are small; first four are equal to or less than one-half mouth width. Pelvic fin originates slightly anterior to axil of pectoral fin and is slightly overlapped by posterior margin of pectoral fin. Anterior margin of pelvic fin is nearly straight and equal to about one-third distance from origin of fin to posterior tip. Inner margin of pelvic fin is connected to side of tail over entire length. Dorsal fins are of similar size and shape. First dorsal fin originates anterior to posterior tip of pelvic fin. Interspace between dorsal fins is 80% of base length of first dorsal fin. Interspace between second dorsal fin and dorsal caudal fin lobe is from two-thirds to one base length of second dorsal fin. Caudal fin is oval shaped. Color is light tan, occasionally with darker or lighter spots dorsally, and white, yellowish white, or brownish white ventrally.

This species occurs in the western North Atlantic from South Carolina, Florida, Cuba, and the northern Gulf of Mexico. It has been captured from 274 to 920 m. Two specimens from Cuba had crustacean remains in their stomachs. Maximum known size is 490 mm TL; young are less than 81 to 87 mm TL at birth.

REFERENCE: Bigelow and Schroeder 1953a.

Narcine brasiliensis   (Olfers 1831)
Lesser electric ray

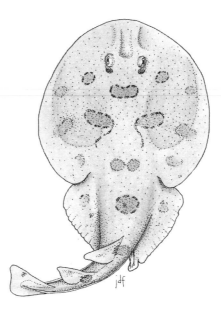

Narcine brasiliensis has a nearly uniformly convex disc, a moderately long snout, and a stout tail. It is distinguished from the other species of the family by the following combination of characters. Snout is moderately long, preorbital length is 11% to 13% of TL. Nostril is nearly transverse and largely covered by nasal curtain. Nasal curtain is rectangular with rounded corners. Mouth is transverse and about one-half of preoral length. Tooth rows in upper and lower jaws vary from 17 to 33 or 34 in juveniles and adults respectively. Eye is developed and is about two-thirds diameter of spiracle. Spiracle is immediately posterior to eye, is transverse to slightly oblique, and has 12 to 20 rounded papillae. Gill slits are small; first four are about one-fourth mouth length. Pelvic fin originates at axil of pectoral fin and is slightly overlapped by posterior section of pectoral fin. Anterior margin of pelvic fin is about 50% to 58% of distance from origin to posterior margin of fin. First dorsal fin originates posterior to insertion of pelvic fin by distance equal to one-half base of first dorsal fin. Interspace between dorsal fins is 36% to 74% of first dorsal fin base. Interspace between second dorsal fin and dorsal caudal fin lobe is 43% to 65% of second dorsal fin base. Caudal fin resembles equilateral triangle, posterior margin is nearly vertical, and ventral corners are abruptly rounded. Color is dark brown, grayish brown, or reddish orange dorsally. Ventral surface is white to yellowish or greenish, with posterior margins of disc and pelvic fins dusky. Dorsal surface varies from plain colored to irregularly patterned with vague dark blotches or bars. Bars frequently occur across head anterior to eyes, posterior section of head, and posterior part of disc and tail. Juveniles usually have numerous dark rings, oval loops, or dark blotches with lighter centers.

This species occurs in the western Atlantic from Cape Lookout, North Carolina (rare); northern Florida; throughout the Gulf of Mexico to southern Brazil; and rarely off northern Argentina. It has been captured from the shoreline to 37 m. Food consists of polychaetes. Litters range from 4 to 15 young. Maximum known size is 450 mm TL; males mature at 225 to 250 mm TL, females mature at 271 to 320 mm TL, and young are 110 to 120 mm TL at birth.

REFERENCES: Gunter 1945; Bigelow and Schroeder 1953a; Hoese and Moore 1977; C. R. Robins et al. 1986.

TORPEDINIDAE

Torpedinid electric rays are anteriorly flattened and posteriorly stout bodied, with a relatively blunt snout and a well-developed caudal fin. They are distinguished from the other families of the order by the following combination of characters. Snout is short and slightly convex to slightly concave. Pectoral fin is laterally expanded, is attached to side of head, and extends to level of nostril to form disc. Disc is broader than it is long and relatively thick at margin. Anterior margin of nostril is greatly expanded to form broad curtain in front of mouth. Mouth is broad, transverse, and only slightly protractile. Mouth is not surrounded by groove. Teeth are small, consist of single cusp, and are in quincunx arrangement. Spiracle is well developed, transverse, and its posterior margin is smooth or possesses papillae or knobs. Pectoral radials extend anteriorly to level of anterior margin of nasal capsules. Electric organ is kidney shaped and is located posterolateral to eye. Pelvic fin is laterally expanded, with broadly rounded lateral corner and straight to moderately convex posterolateral margin. First dorsal fin is considerably larger than second dorsal fin and originates anterior to origin of pelvic fin. Caudal fin is well developed, is subtriangular shaped, and consists of equal-sized dorsal and ventral lobes that are confluent around tip of vertebral column. Body and fins are naked in all but one species.

Torpedinids occur worldwide in tropical to temperate seas. Food consists largely of fishes. Embryonic development is ovoviviparous. There are about 13 species in a single genus, and 1 species occurs in the Gulf of Mexico.

Torpedo nobiliana Bonaparte 1835
Atlantic torpedo

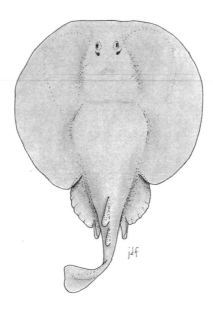

Torpedo nobiliana has a subcircular disc, a short snout, and a stout tail. It is distinguished from the other species of the family by the following combination of characters. Snout is short and truncate, and preorbital length is 7% to 8% of TL. Anterior margin is broad and varies from slightly convex to slightly concave. Nostril is moderately oblique, close to but separate from mouth, and largely covered by nasal curtain. Nasal curtain is subrectangular, is about 3 times as broad as it is long, and has irregular posterior margin. Eye is developed and about one-third as long as spiracle. Spiracle has smooth margin. Mouth is broad, moderately arched, and slightly less than preoral length. Number of tooth rows in upper and lower jaws varies from 38 to 66 in juveniles and adults respectively. Gill slits are small; second through fourth are equal to one-third mouth length. Pelvic fin originates near axil of pectoral fin and is slightly overlapped by distal part of pectoral fin. Anterior and posterior margins of pelvic fin are broadly convex. First dorsal fin is triangular, with rounded corners and nearly straight distal margin. End of first dorsal fin base is posterior to axil of pelvic fin.

Interspace between dorsal fins is about 75% of first dorsal fin base. Second dorsal fin is about one-half to two-thirds size of first dorsal fin. Interspace between second dorsal fin and dorsal caudal fin lobe is equal to or greater than twice second dorsal fin base. Caudal fin resembles equilateral triangle, posterior margin is nearly vertical, and dorsal and ventral corners are broadly rounded. Body and fins are naked. Color is dark brown to purplish brown with or without obscure dark spots dorsally and white with a dark margin ventrally.

This species occurs in the North Atlantic from tropical to temperate latitudes. In the western Atlantic it occurs from southern Nova Scotia to North Carolina, and rarely from the Florida Keys, the northern Gulf of Mexico, Cuba, Trinidad, Panama, and Venezuela. It has been captured from the shoreline to 530 m. Food consists of bony fishes. Litter size is unknown. Maximum known size is 180 cm TL; and young are 20 to 25 cm TL at birth.

REFERENCES: Bigelow and Schroeder 1953a, 1962, 1965; Hoese and Moore 1977; Stehmann and Bürkel 1984a.

PRISTIFORMES

Pristiformes are considered to be the sister group of Rajiformes and Myliobatiformes. The single family in the order occurs in the Gulf of Mexico.

PRISTIDAE Sawfishes

Sawfishes are elongate and moderately depressed anteriorly, with a snout prolonged into a long, narrow, flattened blade bearing a series of teeth, and a stout tail bearing two dorsal fins and a caudal fin. They are distinguished from the other families of elasmobranchs by the following combination of characters. Rostral teeth are embedded in sockets in rostrum. Teeth have triangular, flattened, and smooth-edged crowns. Nostril and anterior nasal flap are widely separated from each other and from mouth. Nostril is not connected to mouth by nasoral groove. Jaw teeth are small, with short, pointed cusps, and are in quincunx arrangement. Spiracle is located posterior to eye and is obliquely directed. Gill slits are on ventral surface. Pectoral fin is relatively small and connected to side of head anterior to first gill slit but is posterior to mouth. Posterior tip of pectoral fin is anterior to axil of pelvic fin. Origin of first dorsal fin varies from distinctly anterior to origin of pelvic fin to posterior to axil of pelvic fin. Dorsal fin bases are well separated. Body of adults is covered with small dermal denticles.

Sawfishes occur worldwide in tropical and warm temperate seas, although they are absent around the oceanic islands of the western Pacific. They are also found in tropical freshwater with oceanic connections. There are six recognized species in two genera, and two species in a single genus occur in the Gulf of Mexico.

Key to the Species of the Gulf of Mexico

1a. Caudal fin with a distinct ventral lobe; rostrum with 20 or fewer pairs of teeth . . . . *Pristis pristis* p. 137
1b. Caudal fin without a distinct ventral lobe; rostrum with more than 23 pairs of teeth. . . . . . . *Pristis pectinata* p. 136

Pristis pectinata   Latham 1794
Smalltooth sawfish

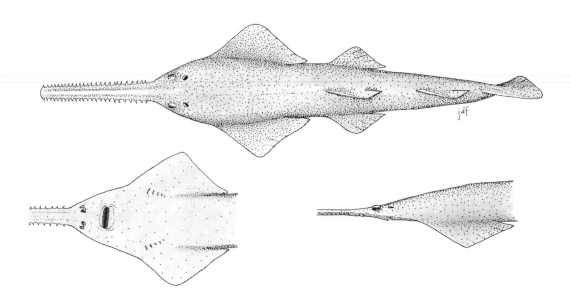

Pristis pectinata is moderately depressed anteriorly, with relatively large dorsal fins and a moderately developed caudal fin. It is distinguished from the other species of the family by the following combination of characters. Rostrum has 24 to 32 pairs of teeth and is about 25% of TL. Rostral teeth are narrow, triangular, and have groove running along posterior margin. Upper jaw has about 88 to 128 tooth rows. Jaw teeth are dome shaped, with obtuse, transverse cutting edge. Dorsal fins are of similar shape and size. First dorsal fin originates above origin of pelvic fin. Distance between dorsal fin bases is about 1.5 times base of first dorsal fin. Distance between second dorsal fin and origin of caudal fin is slightly less than base of second dorsal fin. Length of dorsal caudal lobe is about 15% of TL. Ventral lobe of caudal fin is poorly developed. Body is uniformly and densely covered with dermal denticles. Color is dark brownish gray to blackish dorsally and white to grayish white to pale yellow ventrally.

This species occurs in the tropical to warm temperate western Atlantic from New York (rare), New Jersey (rare), northern Florida, the Gulf of Mexico, the Caribbean, and Bermuda to central Brazil. It is found near shore, including bays, estuaries, and freshwater habitats with saltwater connections. This species has been captured in the lower Mississippi River; the St. Johns River of Florida; the Esequito, Atrato, and San Juan Rivers of Colombia; and in the Amazon River. Food consists of benthic invertebrates and bony fishes. The saw is apparently used to dislodge benthic invertebrates and to disable fishes. Embryonic development is ovoviviparous. Litters range from 15 to 20 young. Maximum known size is 550 cm TL; females are mature at 460 cm TL, and young are 60 cm TL at birth.

REFERENCES: Baughman 1943a; Bigelow and Schroeder 1953a; Hoese and Moore 1977; C. R. Robins et al. 1986.

Pristis pristis (Linnaeus 1758)
Largetooth sawfish

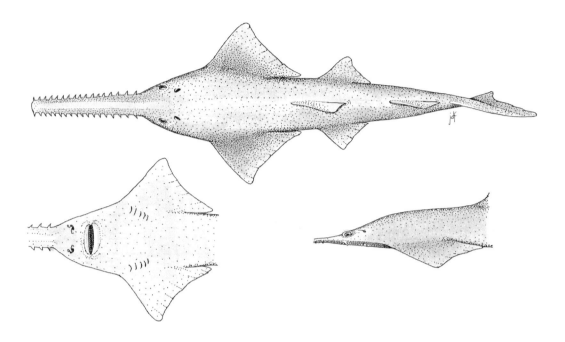

Pristis pristis is moderately depressed anteriorly, with relatively large dorsal fins and a moderately developed caudal fin. It is distinguished from the other species of the family by the following combination of characters. Rostrum has 16 to 20 pairs of teeth and is about 20% of TL. Rostral teeth are narrow, triangular, and have groove running along the posterior margin. Upper jaw has about 80 to 90 tooth rows. Teeth are dome shaped, with obtuse, transverse cutting edge. Dorsal fins are of similar shape and size and have strongly concave posterior margins. First dorsal fin originates above rear corner of pectoral fin. Distance between dorsal fins is about equal to 1.6 times base of first dorsal fin. Distance between second dorsal fin and origin of caudal fin is about equal to base of second dorsal fin. Length of dorsal caudal lobe is about 16% to 18% of TL. Ventral lobe of caudal fin is well developed. Body is sparsely covered with dermal denticles. Color is dark gray to golden brown dorsally and grayish white ventrally.

This species occurs worldwide in tropical to warm temperate seas. In the western Atlantic it occurs from southern Florida, the Gulf of Mexico, the Caribbean, and to central Brazil. It was formerly called *P. perotteti*. This species is limited to inshore habitats, including bays, estuaries, and freshwater with connections to the sea. It has been captured in the Río Colorado in Costa Rica; in Lake Nicaragua and Río San Juan in Nicaragua; and in the Amazon River of Brazil. Food consists of benthic invertebrates and bony fishes. The saw is apparently used to dislodge benthic invertebrates and to disable fishes. Embryonic development is ovoviviparous. Maximum known size is 610 cm TL, and young are 60 cm TL at birth.

REFERENCES: Baughman 1943a, b; Bigelow and Schroeder 1953a; Thorson 1976; Hoese and Moore 1977 (all above as *P. perotteti*); C. R. Robins et al. 1986.

RAJIFORMES

Rajiformes are considered to be the sister group of the Myliobatiformes. The order contains two families, and both occur in the Gulf of Mexico.

Key to the Families of the Gulf of Mexico

1a. Tail stout to moderately stout and confluent with trunk; two relatively large dorsal fins; first dorsal fin originates at about midlength of tail . . . . Rhinobatidae p. 138
1b. Tail moderately slender to very slender, and distinct from trunk; two, one, or no dorsal fins; when present, dorsal fins are relatively small; first dorsal fin originates posterior to midlength of tail . . . . Rajidae p. 141

RHINOBATIDAE   Guitarfishes

Guitarfishes are anteriorly flattened but posteriorly relatively stout bodied, with a wedge-shaped snout and a moderately developed caudal fin without a well-developed ventral lobe. They are distinguished from the other families of the order by the following combination of characters. Snout is moderately to greatly prolonged. Pectoral fin is moderately laterally expanded and attached to head from nostril to about one-half length of snout. Expansion of anterior margin of nostril extends from just posterior to nostril to just anterior to mouth. When anterior expansion extends posteriorly to near mouth, right and left expansions are united to form broad nasal curtain in front of mouth. Mouth is short and nearly straight to slightly arched. Teeth are small, molariform, and in quincunx arrangement. Spiracle is well developed and generally possesses tufts of gill filaments along anterior margin and one to several folds along posterior margin. Pectoral fin extends posteriorly to or slightly posterior to origin of pelvic fin. Pelvic fin is only moderately expanded laterally. Dorsal fins and caudal fin are well developed. First dorsal fin originates from posterior to rear tip of pelvic fin to near midlength of tail. Second dorsal fin originates along posterior one-half of tail. Body and fins are covered with minute dermal denticles. Area over tip of snout, along inner margin of orbits, over shoulder girdle, and along dorsal midline to first dorsal fin often have series of thorns or thornlets.

Guitarfishes occur worldwide in tropical to warm temperate seas except for the oceanic islands of the western Pacific. They are limited to coastal waters and are occasionally found in freshwaters with access to the sea. Food consists of benthic invertebrates and small bony fishes. Embryonic development is ovoviviparous. There are about 37 to 39 recognized species in 4 genera, and 1 species occurs in the Gulf of Mexico.

Rhinobatos lentiginosus (Garman 1880)
Atlantic guitarfish

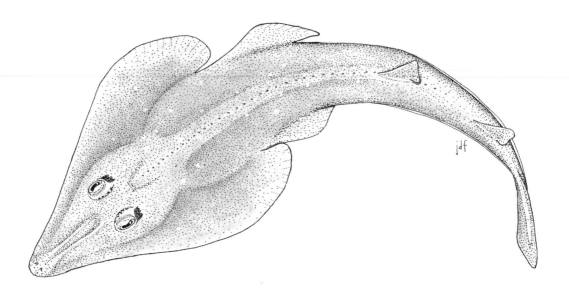

Rhinobatos lentiginosus is anteriorly flattened and posteriorly stout bodied, with a long, triangular-shaped snout and a moderately developed, slightly upturned caudal fin. It is distinguished from the other species of the family by the following combination of characters. Rostral ridges are narrowly separated and converge slightly toward rostral tip. Rostral cartilage is expanded distally, and tip of rostrum is spatulate. Lobelike expansion of anterior margin of nostril is poorly developed; it extends only about one-half length of inner one-half of nostril. Length of nostril is equal to or slightly greater than distance between nostrils and slightly greater than one-half of mouth width. Preorbital length is 4 to 5 times interorbital distance. Preoral length is 2.7 to 3 times mouth width. Posterior margin of spiracle possesses two well-developed folds or ridges. First dorsal fin originates posterior to pelvic fin tip by a distance equal to length of base of first dorsal fin. Distance between dorsal fins is about equal to twice length of first dorsal fin base. Teeth in jaws are small, with rectangular to pentagonal

bases and rounded cusps, and are in quincunx arrangement. Upper jaw has 56 to 80 tooth rows. Body is covered with small, close-set dermal denticles. Tip of snout, orbital rim, midline from nuchal region to origin of first dorsal fin, and scapular region possess blunt thorns. Thorns are lacking on rostral ridges. Color is gray to olive brown or chocolate brown dorsally and pale yellow to white ventrally. Generally, dorsal surface is freckled with many small white spots. However, specimens from the Gulf of Mexico often lack, or are sparsely covered with, white spots.

This species occurs in the western North Atlantic from Cape Lookout, North Carolina, to Florida and throughout the Gulf of Mexico to Yucatán, Mexico. It is an inshore species found from the shoreline to about 18 m. Maximum known size is 76 cm TL; males mature at 48 to 51 cm TL.

REFERENCES: Bigelow and Schroeder 1953a; Hoese and Moore 1977; C. R. Robins et al. 1986.

RAJIDAE Skates

Skates are extremely flattened and laterally expanded, with a moderately acute to very obtuse snout and a moderately slender to very slender tail with a poorly developed caudal fin. They are distinguished from the other families of the order by the following combination of characters. Snout is little to strongly prolonged. Pectoral fin is extremely laterally expanded and attached to side of head from about midlength of snout to near tip of snout. Anterior margin of nostril is greatly expanded to form nasal curtain that is continuous in front of mouth and covers medial section of nostril. Posterolateral margin of nasal curtain is often fringed. Mouth is moderately broad and ranges from nearly transverse to strongly arched. Teeth are small, numerous, and generally in quincunx arrangement; they are arranged in rows in mature males. Spiracle is located just posterior to eye. Anterior margin of spiracle bears tufts of gill filaments. Pectoral fin extends posterior to origin of pelvic fin. Pelvic fin is slightly to moderately laterally expanded and usually divided into anterior and posterior lobes united by posterior concave margin. Tail is distinctly narrower than disc and generally tapers posteriorly. Two dorsal fins are generally present, but occasionally there is one or no dorsal fin. Dorsal fins are small, similar in size and shape, and located near tip of tail. Body and tail range from densely covered with dermal denticles to naked. Thorns often occur on snout, head, along midline of disc and tail, and over scapular region. Mature males, in addition, possess clawlike thorns (alar thorns) on outer corners of disc.

Skates occur worldwide from tropical to polar seas, although they are unknown from the oceanic western Pacific. At temperate latitudes they occur from the shoreline to 2,000 m, but at tropical and polar latitudes they range from the outer half of the continental shelf to 3,000 m. They have not been reported from low-salinity waters. Food consists of a wide variety of benthic invertebrates and fishes. Embryonic development is oviparous. Eggs are encapsulated in horny egg capsules soon after fertilization and are shed to the bottom, where they remain until hatching several months to nearly one year later. There are about 229 species in about 17 genera, and 22 to 24 species in 6 or 7 genera occur in the Gulf of Mexico.

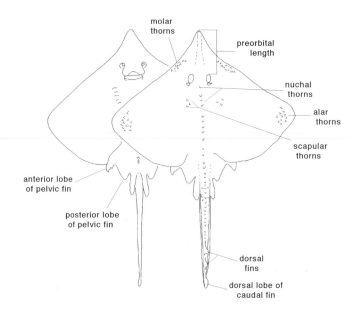

Key to the Species of the Gulf of Mexico

1a. Pelvic fin consisting of single laterally directed lobe; posterior margin of pelvic fin transverse
.... *Pseudoraja fischeri* p. 164

1b. Pelvic fin usually consisting of anterior and posterior lobes; posterior margin of pelvic fin diagonal and weakly to strongly concave............................... 2

2a. Anterior and posterior lobes of pelvic fin separate, anterior lobe fingerlike (Fig. 35) 3

2b. Anterior and posterior lobes of pelvic fin continuous, connected by series of radials and fin membrane (Fig. 36) ... 6

3a. Preorbital length greater than 15% of TL; dorsal fins lacking.. 4

3b. Preorbital length usually less than 15% of TL; two dorsal fins present.................................... 5

4a. Distal section of snout laterally expanded into leaflike structure............. *Anacanthobatis folirostris* p. 146

4b. Distal section of snout evenly attenuating to filament and not laterally expanded
.... *Anacanthobatis longirostris* p. 147

5a. Nuchal region of dorsal disc without thorn(s); ventral side of tail of specimens greater than 250 mm TL smooth, without dermal denticles .... *Cruriraja poeyi* p. 150

5b. Nuchal region of dorsal disc with one or more thorns; ventral side of tail of specimens greater than 250 mm TL covered with dermal denticles........ *Cruriraja rugosa* p. 151

6a. Anterior margin of snout very obtuse; anterolateral margin of ventral side of disc with band of clawlike denticles.... 7

6b. Anterior margin of snout acute to moderately obtuse; anterolateral margin of ventral side of disc without band of clawlike denticles 8

7a. Lateral aspects of disc with narrow spatulate-like lobe projecting from margin of disc; anterolateral margin of disc convex; dorsal surface of disc gray with blackish blotches . . . . *Dactylobatus armatus* p. 152

7b. Lateral aspects of disc without narrow spatulate-like lobe; anterolateral margin of disc concave; dorsal surface of disc tan, generally with several pairs of prominent white markings outlined with dark pigment . . . . *Dactylobatus clarki* p. 153

8a. Tip of snout flexible; rostral cartilage distally very slender; anterior pectoral rays extending nearly to tip of snout . . . 9

8b. Tip of snout firm; rostral cartilage moderately stout to stout; anterior pectoral rays distinctly separated from tip of snout 13

9a. Anterior lobe of pelvic fin 65% to 80% of posterior lobe of pelvic fin; tail width at base slightly greater than orbit diameter 10

9b. Anterior lobe of pelvic fin 80% to 100% of posterior lobe of pelvic fin; tail width at base less than orbit diameter 11

10a. Ventral surface sooty gray to black over central part of disc or over entire disc except for pale areas around mouth, gill slits, and cloaca; several rows of thorns from level of maximum disc width to axil of pelvic fin . . . . *Breviraja spinosa* p. 149

10b. Ventral surface light tan to yellowish white over central part of disc; at most, single row of thorns from level of maximum disc width to axil of pelvic fin . . . . *Breviraja colesi* p. 148

11a. Distinct interspace between second dorsal fin and dorsal lobe of caudal fin; dorsal surface of disc uniformly colored . . . . *Fenestraja ishiyamai* p. 159

11b. Second dorsal fin and dorsal lobe of caudal fin confluent; dorsal surface of disc generally spotted, blotched, or mottled. 12

12a. Dorsal fins and dorsal surface of tail with dark crossbars; snout relatively obtuse, maximum angle in front of spiracle 130° to 135°; thorns on dorsal surface of tail relatively small and arranged in single row . . . . *Fenestraja plutonia* p. 160

12b. Dorsal fins and dorsal surface of tail plain colored; snout angular, maximum angle in front of spiracle 100° to 110°; thorns on dorsal surface of tail relatively large and arranged in three rows . . . . *Fenestraja sinusmexicanus* p. 161

13a. Snout moderately elongated to strongly elongated, anterolateral margin of disc concave (line connecting tip of snout
to anterior aspect of lateral corner of disc does not inter-
sect disc; Fig. 37); ampullar pores on ventral surface of disc
generally darkly pigmented. 14

13b. Snout generally not elongated, anterolateral margin of disc
straight to slightly convex (line connecting tip of snout to
anterior aspect of lateral corner of disc intersects disc;
Fig. 38); ampullar pores on ventral surface of disc not
darkly pigmented 18

14a. Midbelt of disc without thorns. 15

14b. Midbelt of disc with at least single nuchal thorn 17

15a. Tail with three rows of thorns 16

15b. Tail with one row of thorns. . . . . . *Dipturus teevani* p. 158

16a. Midline of tail with 31 to 48 thorns; thorns on tail with
compressed hook-shaped crowns; distance between dorsal
fins shorter than base of first dorsal fin; only one thorn
between dorsal fins. . . . . *Dipturus oregoni* p. 157

16b. Midline of tail with 13 to 26 thorns; thorns on tail without
compressed and hook-shaped crowns; distance between
dorsal fins about equal to length of first dorsal fin base;
three to six thorns between dorsal fins
. . . . *Dipturus olseni* p. 156

17a. Midbelt of disc with continuous row of thorns extending
from nuchal region to tail. . . . . . . *Dipturus garricki* p. 155

17b. Nuchal thorn only thorn along midbelt of disc
. . . . *Dipturus bullisi* p. 154

18a. Dorsal surface of disc with various color patterns (ocelli,
spots, bars, rosettes); ventral surface of disc light colored
. . . . 19

18b. Dorsal surface of disc plain colored; ventral surface of disc
as dark or darker than dorsal side 23

19a. Dorsal surface of disc with ocellus near base of each pecto-
ral fin. 20

19b. Dorsal surface of disc without ocellus near base of each
pectoral fin. 21

20a. Lateral margin of snout distinctly concave; preorbital snout
length about 5 times length of eye; no thorns over scapular
region of disc . . . . *Raja texana* p. 168

20b. Lateral margin of snout only slightly concave; preorbital
snout length about 3 times length of eye; one or more
thorns over scapular region of disc. . . . *Raja ackleyi* p. 165

21a. Dorsal surface of disc with many irregular dark spots and
transverse, oblique narrow bars; several thorns on scapular
and nuchal region of disc, but thorns never forming a triangular patch. . . . . *Raja eglanteria* p. 166

21b. Dorsal surface of disc peppered with small dark and light

FIG 37

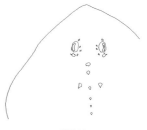

FIG 38

spots or with spots concentrated into dark rosettes; thorns
on scapular and nuchal region of disc forming triangular
patch 22

22a. Dorsal surface with dark and pale spots; specimens mature
between 350 and 418 mm TL
. . . . *Leucoraja lentiginosa* p. 163

22b. Dorsal surface with diffuse to concentrated rosette pattern
of dark spots; specimens mature between 248 and 335 mm
TL . . . . *Leucoraja garmani* p. 162

23a. Preorbital snout length about 10% of TL; snout obtuse
and bluntly rounded. . . . . *Rajella fuliginea* p. 169

23b. Preorbital snout length about 15% of TL; snout acutely
angled. . . . . *Rajella purpuriventralis* p. 170

Anacanthobatis folirostris   (Bigelow and Schroeder 1951)

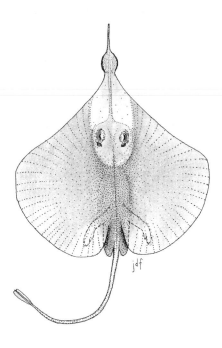

Anacanthobatis folirostris has a heart-shaped disc, a greatly elongated snout bearing a leaf-shaped lateral expansion, and a very slender tail that lacks dorsal fins. It is distinguished from the other species of the family by the following combination of characters. Snout is greatly elongated; preorbital length is about 21% to 22% of TL. Snout is abruptly expanded at about distal one-third of length, margin of expansion is strongly convex, and distal extreme of snout is filamentous. Mouth is slightly arched. Upper jaw has 22 to 26 tooth rows. Pectoral radials extend to about mid-length of snout. Anterior lobe of pelvic fin is limblike and externally separated from posterior lobe. Posterior lobe of pelvic fin is laterally connected to medial margin of pectoral fin.

Tail is about 50% to 52% of TL and lacks lateral folds. Caudal fin has relatively well-developed dorsal and ventral lobes, which are separated distally by tip of vertebral column. Body is completely devoid of dermal denticles and thorns. Color is ash gray dorsally and pale gray ventrally.

This species occurs in the western North Atlantic from the northern Gulf of Mexico. It has been captured from 300 to 512 m. Maximum known size is 576 mm TL for males and 620 mm TL for females.

REFERENCES: Bigelow and Schroeder 1951a, 1953a, 1965, 1968b (all as *Spingeria folirostris*); Hulley 1973.

Anacanthobatis longirostris   Bigelow and Schroeder 1962

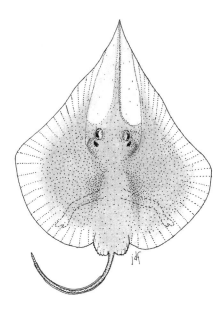

Anacanthobatis longirostris has a heart-shaped disc, a greatly elongated snout, and a very slender tail. It is distinguished from the other species of the family by the following combination of characters. Snout is greatly elongated; preorbital length is about 24% to 30% of TL. Snout tapers to fine filament. Mouth is moderately arched. Upper jaw has 28 tooth rows. Pectoral radials extend to about distal one-fifth of snout. Anterior lobe of pelvic fin is limblike and externally separated from posterior lobe. Lateral margin of posterior lobe of pelvic fin is partially joined to medial margin of pectoral fin. Tail is about 42% of TL and possesses lateral folds that extend to near tip of tail. Cau-

dal fin has relatively well-developed dorsal and ventral lobes, which are separated distally by tip of vertebral column. Body is completely devoid of dermal denticles and thorns. Color is purplish dorsally and light gray ventrally except for tip of snout, which is black.

This species occurs in the western North Atlantic from the northern Gulf of Mexico, the Bahamas, and the Greater and Lesser Antilles. It has been captured from 520 to 1,052 m. Maximum known size is 745 mm TL.

REFERENCES: Bigelow and Schroeder 1962, 1965, 1968b; Hulley 1973.

Breviraja colesi   Bigelow and Schroeder 1948

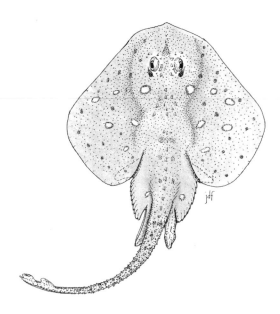

Breviraja colesi has a heart-shaped disc, with a relatively short, obtuse snout and a moderately slender tail with two dorsal fins and a poorly developed caudal fin. It is distinguished from the other species of the family by the following combination of characters. Snout is relatively short (preorbital length is about 8% to 10% of TL) and obtuse (maximum snout angle is 135°). Pectoral radials extend nearly to tip of snout. Oronasal pit is located anterior to mouth and dorsal to nasal curtain. Mouth is moderately arched on either side of symphysis. Upper jaw has 42 to 50 tooth rows. Anterior pelvic lobe is connected to posterior pelvic lobe by fin membrane and is about two-thirds length of posterior lobe. Lateral margin of pelvic fin is deeply incised. Tail is about 60% of TL and has lateral folds extending from axil of pelvic fin tip near tip. Caudal fin is poorly developed and consists of short dorsal lobe. Dorsal surface of disc and tail is nearly uniformly covered with small dermal denticles. Small thorns occur on rostral ridge, along orbital rim, in triangular patch over nuchal and scapular region, in single row along midline of disc, and in three to five irregular rows along midbelt of tail to origin of first dorsal fin. Ventral surface is naked. Color is pale brown dorsally, with scattered spots and blotches of dark brown and more or less symmetrically arranged pale, eye-sized spots surrounded by dark brown pigment, and yellowish to whitish ventrally. Tail is same color as disc but dorsally has numerous brown markings and crossbars.

This species occurs in the western North Atlantic from the east coast of Florida, Cuba, and the Bahamas. One specimen housed at the National Museum of Natural History, Smithsonian Institution (USNM), is listed from the southern Gulf of Mexico, but this locality may be in error. This species has been captured from 220 to 415 m. Maximum known size is 400 mm TL, and males mature at 320 mm TL.

REFERENCES: Bigelow and Schroeder 1948b, 1953a, 1962; McEachran and Compagno 1982; McEachran and Matheson 1985.

Breviraja spinosa Bigelow and Schroeder 1950

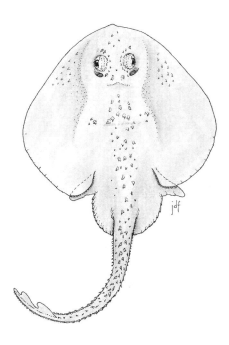

Breviraja spinosa has a heart-shaped disc, with a relatively short, obtuse snout and a moderately slender tail with two dorsal fins and a poorly developed caudal fin. It is distinguished from the other species of the family by the following combination of characters. Snout is relatively short (preorbital length is about 6% to 9% of TL) and obtuse (maximum snout angle is about 139° to 145°). Pectoral radials extend to near tip of snout. Mouth is moderately arched on either side of symphysis. Upper jaw has 40 to 44 tooth rows. Oronasal pit is located anterior to mouth and dorsal to nasal curtain. Anterior pelvic lobe is connected to posterior lobe by fin membrane and is about two-thirds length of posterior lobe. Lateral margin of pelvic fin is deeply incised. Tail is 58% to 60% of TL and has lateral folds extending along posterior one-third of length. Dorsal fins are of similar shape and size and are confluent at bases. Caudal fin is poorly developed and consists of dorsal lobe. Dorsal surface of disc and tail is nearly uniformly covered with dermal denticles except for naked areas over body cavity and on posterior margins of disc and pelvic fin. Moderate-sized thorns occur on orbital rim, in triangular patch over nuchal and scapular region, and in three rows along midbelt of disc and tail anterior to origin of first dorsal fin. Ventral surface is naked. Color is tan without markings dorsally and yellowish white ventrally except for sooty-gray blotches on central part of disc.

This species occurs in the western North Atlantic from North Carolina to the Florida Keys. One specimen housed at the National Museum of Natural History, Smithsonian Institution (USNM), is listed from the northern Gulf of Mexico, but this record may be in error. This species has been captured from 366 to 671 m. Maximum known size is 330 mm TL, and males mature at 330 mm TL.

REFERENCES: Bigelow and Schroeder 1950, 1953a, 1962; McEachran and Compagno 1982; McEachran and Matheson 1985.

Cruriraja poeyi   Bigelow and Schroeder 1948

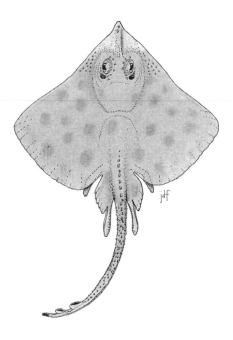

Cruriraja poeyi has a diamond-shaped disc, with a moderately long, acute snout and a slender tail with two dorsal fins and a moderately well-developed caudal fin. It is distinguished from the other species of the family by the following combination of characters. Snout is moderately long (preorbital length is about 11% to 12% of TL) and acute (maximum snout angle is about 85° to 100°). Pectoral fin radials extend to about midlength of tip of snout. Mouth is almost transverse to slightly arched on either side of symphysis. Upper jaw has 46 to 50 tooth rows. Oronasal pit is absent. Anterior lobe of pelvic fin is limblike, externally separated from posterior lobe, and about as long as posterior lobe. Lateral margin of posterior lobe of pelvic fin is free of posterior medial margin of pectoral fin. Tail is about 57% to 58% of TL and has lateral folds extending from near base to near tip of tail. Dorsal fins are of similar size and shape and are separated by interspace equal to one-half first dorsal fin base. Caudal fin consists of dorsal lobe about as long as second dorsal fin base. Dorsal surface of disc and tail are devoid of dermal denticles except along anterior margin and along midbelt of disc from scapular region to base of tail. Moderate-sized thorns occur near tip of rostrum, along orbital rim, and along midline from midlength of disc to origin of first dorsal fin. Midrow thorns on tail are flanked by one or two irregular rows of thorns. Two or three thorns occur between dorsal fins. Color is pale brown dorsally, usually with dark brown round spots about one-half diameter of orbit, and dark brown ventrally. Anterior margins of dorsal fins and tip of caudal fin are black.

This species occurs in the western North Atlantic from Cuba, the Bahamas, southern Florida, and the Florida Keys. It has been captured from 366 to 870 m. Maximum known size is 343 mm TL.

REFERENCES: Bigelow and Schroeder 1948b, 1953a, 1962, 1965.

Cruriraja rugosa Bigelow and Schroeder 1958

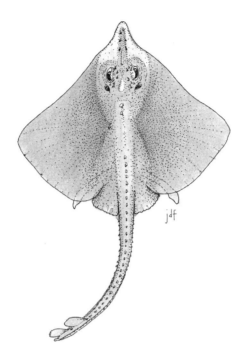

Cruriraja rugosa has a diamond-shaped disc, with a moderately long, acute snout and a slender tail. It is distinguished from the other species of the family by the following combination of characters. Snout is moderately long (preorbital length is about 12% of TL) and moderately acute (greatest snout angle is about 87°). Pectoral fin radials extend to about one-third length of snout. Mouth is almost transverse to slightly arched on each side of symphysis. Upper jaw has 43 tooth rows. Oronasal pit is absent. Anterior lobe of pelvic fin is limblike, externally separated from posterior lobe, and slightly longer than posterior lobe. Lateral margin of posterior lobe of pelvic fin is free of posterior medial margin of pectoral fin. Tail is about 60% of TL and has lateral folds extending from about midlength of tail to near tip of tail. Dorsal fins are of similar size and shape and are separated by interspace equal to about one-fourth first dorsal fin base length. Caudal fin consists of poorly developed dorsal lobe. Dorsal surface of disc and tail is nearly uniformly covered with dermal denticles. Moderate-sized thorns occur along rostrum, over orbital rim, over nuchal region, and from posterior third of disc to origin of first dorsal fin. One thorn is located between dorsal fins. Color is brownish dorsally, without spots or other markings, and pale brownish to bluish ventrally.

This species occurs in the western North Atlantic from the Gulf of Mexico to Venezuela, and off Haiti and Grenada. It has been captured from 366 to 915 m. Maximum known size is 485 mm TL.

REFERENCES: Bigelow and Schroeder 1958, 1962, 1965, 1968b.

Dactylobatus armatus   Bean and Weed 1909

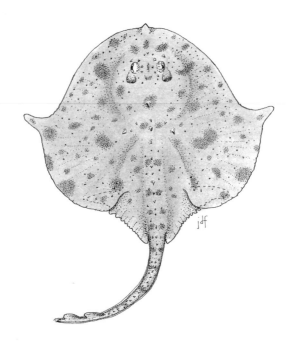

Dactylobatus armatus has a nearly circular disc with a spatulate-shaped lobe projecting from each lateral margin; a moderately short, very obtuse snout; and a moderately slender tail with two dorsal fins and a poorly developed caudal fin. It is distinguished from the other species of the family by the following combination of characters. Snout is moderately short (preorbital length is about 11% to 12% of TL) and very obtuse (maximum snout angle is about 140°). Pectoral radials extend to level of tip of snout but are separated from tip by hyaline-like interspace. Mouth is slightly arched on either side of symphysis. Upper jaw has 54 to 66 tooth rows. Oronasal pit is absent. Anterior lobe of pelvic fin is connected to posterior lobe by fin membrane and is nearly as long as posterior lobe. Lateral margin of pelvic fin is evenly concave. Tail length is about 52% of TL and has lateral folds extending from posterior tip of pelvic fin to near tip of tail. Dorsal fins are of similar shape and size and are confluent at bases. Caudal fin consists of poorly devel-oped dorsal lobe. Dorsal surface of disc and tail is sparsely covered with dermal denticles. Moderate-sized thorns occur on orbital rim, over nuchal and scapular region, and along midbelt of disc and tail to origin of first dorsal fin. Midbelt has regular medial row and one irregular lateral row of thorns. Ventral surface is naked except for irregular double row of hooked denticles running along anterior margin of disc from either side of snout to spatulate-shaped lobes. Color is brownish gray with various-sized blackish spots and blotches dorsally and yellowish white ventrally.

This species occurs in the western North Atlantic from South Carolina to southern Florida, the Gulf of Mexico, and off Nicaragua, Colombia, and Venezuela. It has been captured from 338 to 685 m. Maximum known size is 316 mm TL.

REFERENCES: Bigelow and Schroeder 1953a, 1968a.

Dactylobatus clarki   (Bigelow and Schroeder 1958)

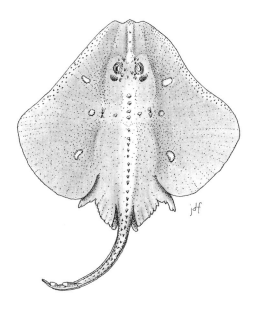

Dactylobatus clarki has a heart-shaped disc, with a long, very obtuse snout and a moderately slender tail with two dorsal fins and a moderately developed caudal fin. It is distinguished from the other species of the family by the following combination of characters. Snout is long (preorbital length is about 14% of TL) and very obtuse (maximum snout angle is about 134°). Pectoral radials extend to level of tip of snout but are separated from rostrum by a distinct hyaline-like interspace. Mouth is slightly arched on either side of symphysis. Upper jaw has 60 to 63 tooth rows. Oronasal pit is absent. Anterior lobe of pelvic fin is connected to posterior lobe by fin membrane and is about two-thirds length of posterior lobe. Lateral margin of pelvic fin is weakly incised. Tail is about 47% of TL and has lateral folds extending over entire length. Dorsal fins are of similar size and shape and are separated by interspace equal to one-third first dorsal fin base. Caudal fin is moderately developed and consists solely of long, low dorsal lobe. Dorsal surface of disc and tail is sparsely covered with small dermal denticles. Band of thornlets extends along anterior margin from tip of snout to near outer corner of disc. Moderate-sized thorns occur on rostrum, on orbital rim, over nuchal and scapular region, and along midline from scapular region to origin of first dorsal fin. Tail has lateral row of thorns on each side of midrow thorns. Ventral surface is naked except for band of hooked denticles extending from tip of snout to outer corner of disc. Color is pale brown with dark markings dorsally and white ventrally, with irregular grayish band along posterior margin of disc and posterior margin of pelvic fin. Dorsal surface also generally has several symmetrically arranged and irregularly shaped white markings outlined with dark margin.

This species occurs in the western North Atlantic from the east coast of Florida, the Gulf of Mexico, and off Nicaragua, Panama, Colombia, Venezuela, Suriname, and French Guiana. It has been captured from 366 to 915 m. Maximum known size is 747 mm TL.

REFERENCES: Bigelow and Schroeder 1958, 1962, 1965, 1968a (all as *Raja clarki*).

Dipturus bullisi   (Bigelow and Schroeder 1962)

Dipturus bullisi has a lozenge-shaped disc, with a long, acute snout and a moderately wide tail with two dorsal fins and a moderately developed caudal fin. It is distinguished from the other species of the family by the following combination of characters. Snout is long (preorbital length is 19% to 20% of TL) and slightly acute (maximum snout angle is 85° to 92°). Pectoral radials extend to about two-fifths of snout length. Mouth is moderately arched on each side of symphysis. Upper jaw has 31 to 36 tooth rows. Oronasal pit is absent. Anterior lobe of pelvic fin is connected to posterior lobe by fin membrane and is about four-fifths length of posterior lobe. Lateral margin of pelvic fin is deeply incised. Tail is 46% to 50% of TL and has lateral folds extending over most of length of tail. Dorsal fins are of similar size and shape and are separated by interspace equal to one-half of first dorsal fin base. Caudal fin is moderately developed and consists of low dorsal lobe equal in length

to second dorsal fin base. Dorsal surface is devoid of dermal denticles. Thorns on disc are limited to two preorbital, one postorbital, and one nuchal. Tail has single row of 12 to 15 thorns extending from base to origin of first dorsal fin and one thorn between dorsal fins. Ventral surface is naked except for dermal denticles on snout and along anterior margin of disc. Color is uniform light brown dorsally and dark brown ventrally. Ampullar pores are dark pigmented on ventral surface of snout and just posterior to lower jaw.

This species occurs in the western Atlantic from the Dry Tortugas, Florida, and off Nicaragua, Colombia, Venezuela, Suriname, and French Guiana. It has been captured from 183 to 549 m. Maximum known size is 770 mm TL, and males are mature at 759 mm TL.

REFERENCES: Bigelow and Schroeder 1962, 1965, 1968b (all as *Raja bullisi*).

Dipturus garricki   (Bigelow and Schroeder 1958)

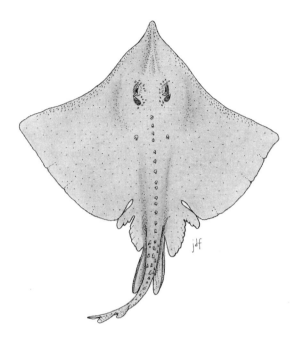

Dipturus garricki has a lozenge-shaped disc, with a long, acute snout and a moderately slender tail with two dorsal fins and a moderately developed caudal fin. It is distinguished from the other species of the family by the following combination of characters. Snout is long (preorbital length is 18% of TL) and acute (maximum snout angle is 74° to 78°). Pectoral radials extend to about midlength of snout. Mouth is moderately arched on each side of symphysis. Upper jaw has 35 tooth rows. Oronasal pit is absent. Anterior pelvic lobe is connected to posterior lobe by fin membrane and is 58% of length of posterior lobe. Lateral margin of pelvic fin is deeply incised. Tail is 45% of TL, is distinctly narrower at midlength than at base, and has lateral folds extending from tip of posterior pelvic lobe to near tip of tail. Dorsal fins are of similar size and shape and are separated by interspace equal to one-third of first dorsal fin base. Caudal fin is moderately developed and consists of long, low dorsal lobe. Dorsal surface is devoid of dermal denticles except for snout and anterior margin of disc. Small thorns occur on orbital rim and between spiracles. Several large thorns occur on nuchal region, one or two occur on scapular region, and row of large thorns extends along midline from nuchal region to origin of first dorsal fin. Midrow thorns on tail are flanked by two irregular rows of thorns, and two thorns are located between dorsal fins. Ventral surface is naked except for dermal denticles on snout and along anterior margin of disc. Color is brown dorsally and dusky bluish ventrally.

This species occurs in the western North Atlantic in the northern Gulf of Mexico and off Nicaragua. It has been captured from 275 to 476 m. Maximum known size is 1,065 mm TL.

REFERENCES: Bigelow and Schroeder 1958, 1965 (as *Raja garricki*).

Dipturus olseni   (Bigelow and Schroeder 1951)

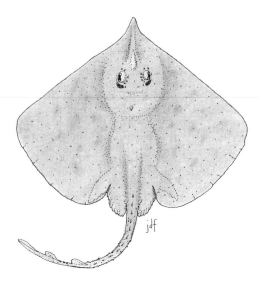

Dipturus olseni has a lozenge-shaped disc, with a moderately long, slightly acute snout and a moderately slender tail with two dorsal fins and a well-developed caudal fin. It is distinguished from the other species of the family by the following combination of characters. Snout is moderately long (preorbital length is 16% to 17% of TL) and slightly acute (maximum snout angle is 90°). Pectoral radials extend to midlength of snout. Mouth is moderately arched on either side of symphysis. Upper jaw has 34 to 41 tooth rows. Anterior pelvic lobe is connected to posterior lobe by fin membrane and is about equal in length to posterior lobe. Lateral margin of pelvic fin is deeply incised. Tail is 51% to 53% of TL, is distinctly narrower at midlength than at base, and has lateral folds extending nearly entire length of tail. Dorsal fins are of similar size and shape and are separated by interspace equal to first dorsal fin base. Caudal fin is well developed and consists of long, relatively high dorsal lobe and long, low ventral caudal lobe. Dorsal surface is devoid of dermal denticles. Small thorns occur on orbital rim and along midline of tail from axil of pectoral fin to origin of first dorsal fin. Midrow thorns on tail are flanked by two irregular rows of thorns, and three or more thorns occur between dorsal fins. Color is dark brown with small, vague dark spots dorsally and gray to black ventrally. Ampullar pores are light pigmented dorsally and dark pigmented ventrally.

This species occurs in the western North Atlantic from the northern Gulf of Mexico. It has been captured from 55 to 384 m. Maximum known size is 568 mm TL, and males mature at 511 mm TL.

REFERENCES: Bigelow and Schroeder 1951b, 1953a, 1962, 1968b; Hoese and Moore 1977; C. R. Robins et al. 1986 (all as *Raja olseni*).

Dipturus oregoni   (Bigelow and Schroeder 1958)

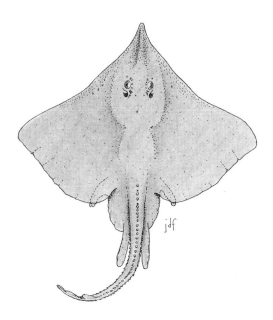

Dipturus oregoni has a lozenge-shaped disc, with a long, acute snout and a moderately slender tail with two dorsal fins and a moderately developed caudal fin. It is distinguished from the other species of the family by the following combination of characters. Snout is long (preorbital length is 17% to 18% of TL) and acute (maximum snout angle is 72°). Pectoral radials extend to about midlength of snout. Mouth is moderately arched on each side of symphysis. Upper jaw has 36 tooth rows. Oronasal pit is absent. Anterior lobe of pelvic fin is connected to posterior lobe by fin membrane and is 75% of length of posterior lobe. Lateral margin of pelvic fin is deeply incised. Tail is 50% of TL, is distinctly narrower at midlength than at base, and has lateral folds extending from tip of posterior lobe of pelvic fin to near tip of tail. Dorsal fins are of similar size and shape and are separated by interspace equal to 36% of first dorsal fin base length. Caudal fin is moderately developed and consists of long, low dorsal lobe. Dorsal surface is devoid of dermal denticles except on snout, on cranium, and along anterior margin. Small thorns occur on orbital rim and along anterior margin of disc. Tail has median row and two lateral rows of laterally flattened, hook-shaped thorns. Ventral surface is devoid of denticles except on snout and along anterior margin of disc. Color is brownish dorsally and bluish gray to pale brown ventrally. Ampullar pores on ventral surface anterior to abdomen are dark pigmented.

This species occurs in the western North Atlantic from the northern Gulf of Mexico. It has been captured from 475 to 1,079 m. Maximum known size is 1,440 mm TL.

REFERENCE: Bigelow and Schroeder 1958 (as *Raja oregoni*).

Dipturus teevani   (Bigelow and Schroeder 1951)

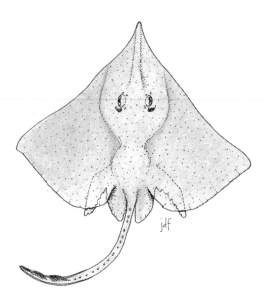

Dipturus teevani has a lozenge-shaped disc, with a long, acute snout and a moderately slender tail with two dorsal fins and a moderately developed caudal fin. It is distinguished from the other species of the family by the following combination of characters. Snout is long (preorbital length is 22% of TL) and acute (maximum snout angle is 70°). Pectoral fin radials extend anteriorly to two-fifths of snout length. Mouth is moderately arched on either side of symphysis. Upper jaw has 36 to 38 tooth rows. Oronasal pit is absent. Anterior pelvic lobe is connected to posterior lobe by fin membrane and is longer than posterior lobe. Lateral margin of pelvic fin is deeply incised. Tail is 48% to 53% of TL, is nearly as wide at midlength as at base, and has lateral folds extending from posterior tip of pelvic fin to near tip of tail. Dorsal fins are of similar size and shape and are confluent at bases. Caudal fin is moderately developed and consists of long dorsal lobe. Dorsal surface is devoid of dermal denticles except on snout. Dorsal surface is devoid of thorns except for one or two on anterior margin of orbit, one on posterior margin of orbit, and a row of thorns along midline of tail to origin of first dorsal fin. Ventral surface is naked except for dermal denticles on snout and along anterior margin of disc. Color is pale brown dorsally, with black dorsal and caudal fins, and cream to dusky ventrally. Ampullar pores are dark pigmented on ventral surface anterior to mouth.

This species occurs in the western North Atlantic from the northern Gulf of Mexico, the Bahamas, Honduras, Nicaragua, and Colombia. It has been captured from 320 to 732 m. Maximum known size is 840 mm TL, and males mature at 632 mm TL. *Raja floridana* is considered to be a synonym of this species (Jacob and McEachran 1994).

REFERENCES: Bigelow and Schroeder 1951b, 1953, 1965, 1968 (as *Raja floridana,* in part); Jacob and McEachran 1994 (all as *Raja teevani*).

Fenestraja ishiyamai   (Bigelow and Schroeder 1962)

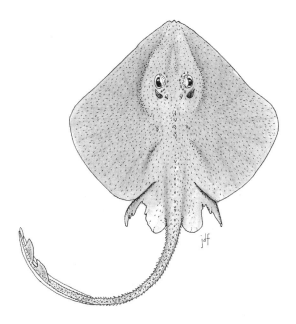

Fenestraja ishiyamai has a heart-shaped disc, with a moderately long, slightly obtuse snout and a slender tail with two dorsal fins and a poorly developed caudal fin. It is distinguished from the other species of the family by the following combination of characters. Snout is moderately long (preorbital length is 11% of TL) and slightly obtuse (maximum snout angle is about 115°). Pectoral fin radials extend to near tip of snout. Upper jaw has 34 tooth rows. Oronasal pit is absent. Anterior lobe of pelvic fin is connected to posterior lobe by fin membrane and is about equal in length to posterior lobe. Lateral margin of pelvic fin is deeply incised. Tail is about 62% of TL and has lateral folds extending from posterior tip of pelvic fin to near tip of tail. Dorsal fins are of similar size and shape and are confluent at bases. Caudal fin is poorly developed and consists of dorsal lobe. Dorsal surface of disc and tail is more or less uniformly covered with slender dermal denticles. Relatively small thorns occur on orbital rim, between spiracles, over nuchal and scapular region, and along midline from scapular region to origin of first dorsal fin. Midrow thorns on tail are flanked by two lateral rows of small thorns. Ventral surface is naked. Color is grayish brown dorsally and pinkish white ventrally.

This species occurs in the western North Atlantic from southeastern Florida to the Florida Keys (Dry Tortugas), off Cuba, the Bahamas, and Nicaragua. It has been captured from 503 to 950 m. Maximum known size is 362 mm TL.

REFERENCES: Bigelow and Schroeder 1962, 1965 (both as *Breviraja ishiyamai*); McEachran and Compagno 1982; McEachran 1984 (both as *Gurgesiella ishiyamai*).

Fenestraja plutonia (Garman 1881)

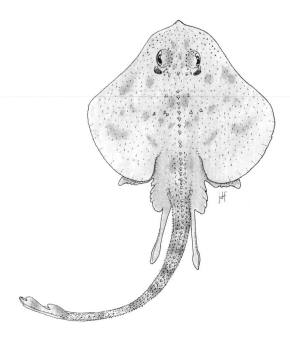

Fenestraja plutonia has a heart-shaped disc, with a short, obtuse snout and a moderately slender tail with two dorsal fins and a poorly developed caudal fin. It is distinguished from the other species of the family by the following combination of characters. Snout is short (pre-orbital length is 7% to 8% of TL) and obtuse (maximum snout angle is 130° to 135°). Pectoral fin radials extend nearly to tip of snout. Upper jaw has 32 to 34 tooth rows. Oronasal pit is absent. Anterior pelvic lobe is connected to posterior lobe by fin membrane and is of equal length or longer than posterior lobe. Lateral margin of pelvic fin is deeply incised. Tail is 64% to 67% of TL and has lateral folds extending along posterior one-half of tail. Dorsal fins are of similar size and shape and are confluent at bases. Caudal fin is poorly developed and consists of dorsal lobe. Dorsal surface of disc and tail is more or less uniformly covered with slender dermal denticles. Small- to moderate-sized thorns occur on orbital rim, between spiracles, over nuchal and scapular region, and along midline from scapular region to origin of first dorsal fin. Midrow thorns on tail are flanked by two lateral rows of small thorns. Thorns on posterior one-half of tail grade into denticles. Color is pale yellowish brown to grayish brown or purplish brown dorsally and yellowish white ventrally. Dorsal surface is marked with dark spots and blotches, and tail has several irregular bands.

This species occurs in the western North Atlantic from North Carolina to the Dry Tortugas in the Florida Keys, off Cuba, in the northern Gulf of Mexico, and off Venezuela and Guyana. It has been captured from 293 to 1,024 m. Maximum known size is 270 mm TL.

REFERENCES: Bigelow and Schroeder 1953a, 1962, 1968b (all as *Beviraja plutonia*); McEachran and Compagno 1982; McEachran 1984 (both as *Gurgesiella plutonia*).

Fenestraja sinusmexicanus   (Bigelow and Schroeder 1950)

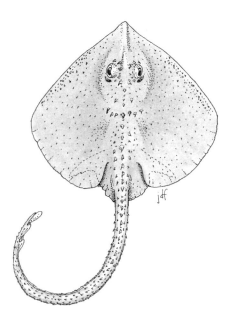

Fenestraja sinusmexicanus has a heart-shaped disc, with a moderately long, slightly obtuse snout and a slender tail with two dorsal fins and a poorly developed caudal fin. It is distinguished from the other species of the family by the following combination of characters. Snout is moderately long (preorbital length is 9% to 10% of TL) and obtuse (maximum snout angle is 100° to 110°). Pectoral fin radials extend nearly to tip of snout. Upper jaw has 40 to 46 tooth rows. Oronasal pit is absent. Anterior pelvic lobe is connected to posterior lobe by fin membrane and is equal to or longer than posterior lobe. Lateral margin of pelvic fin is deeply incised. Tail is 65% to 67% of TL and has lateral folds extending from posterior lobe of pelvic fin to near tip of tail. Dorsal fins are of similar size and shape and are confluent or separated by interspace equal to one-third first dorsal fin base. Caudal fin is poorly developed and consists of dorsal lobe. Dorsal surface is more or less uniformly covered with dermal denticles. Moderate-sized thorns occur on orbital rim, in triangular patch over scapular and nuchal region, and along midbelt from scapular region to origin of first dorsal fin. Midbelt of disc and tail has three rows of thorns. Ventral surface is naked. Color is brownish purple dorsally, with or without irregular dark blotches or spots, and yellowish white ventrally.

This species occurs in the western North Atlantic in the Gulf of Mexico, and off Cuba, Nicaragua, and Venezuela. It has been captured from 59 to 1,096 m. Maximum known size is 360 mm TL.

REFERENCES: Bigelow and Schroeder 1950, 1953a, 1962, 1965, 1968b (all as *Breviraja sinusmexicanus*); McEachran and Compagno 1982; McEachran 1984 (as *Gurgesiella sinusmexicanus*).

Leucoraja garmani   (Whitley 1939)
Rosette skate

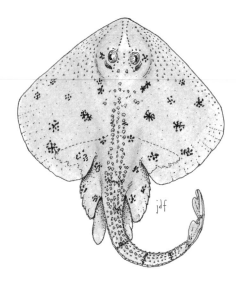

Leucoraja garmani has a heart-shaped disc, with a moderately short, obtuse snout and a moderately broad tail with two dorsal fins (type specimen has three dorsal fins) and a poorly developed caudal fin. It is distinguished from the other species of the family by the following combination of characters. Snout is moderately short (preorbital length is 9% to 10% of TL) and obtuse (maximum snout angle is 112° to 120°). Pectoral radials extend to about three-fourths snout length. Mouth is moderately to rather strongly arched. Upper jaw has 44 to 55 tooth rows. Oronasal pit is absent. Anterior pelvic lobe is connected to posterior lobe by fin membrane and is about 48% to 56% of posterior lobe. Lateral margin of pelvic fin is deeply incised. Tail length is 59% to 61% of TL and has lateral folds extending most of tail length. Dorsal fins are similar in size and shape and are separated by interspace equal to 10% to 38% of first dorsal fin base length. Caudal fin is poorly developed and consists of moderately long dorsal lobe and short ventral lobe. Dorsal surface is more or less uniformly covered with dermal denticles in juveniles but is largely devoid of denticles in adults. Small thorns occur on rostrum and orbital rim. Large thorns occur in triangular patch on nuchal and scapu-lar regions, and along midbelt in two to five rows from nuchal region to origin of first dorsal fin. Midrow thorns on medial section of tail are small or absent in adults. Ventral surface is naked except for dermal denticles on tip of snout of adults. Color is buff or brown dorsally, with small dark to black spots concentrated to form symmetrical rosette patterns, and white to pale yellow ventrally. Dark spots are concentrated to form bars on tail.

This species occurs in the western North Atlantic from Cape Hatteras to the Dry Tortugas between 66 and 366 m. Maximum known size is 335 mm TL. The species was formerly divided into four subspecies that occur (1) from Cape Cod to Cape Hatteras, (2) from Cape Hatteras to the Florida Keys, (3) in the Gulf of Mexico, and (4) from Yucatán to Nicaragua (McEachran 1977). These four subspecies are herein treated as distinct species.

REFERENCES: Bigelow and Schroeder 1951b, 1953a, 1954b, 1962, 1965, 1968b; McEachran 1970, 1977 (as *Raja lentiginosa* in part); McEachran and Musick 1975; McEachran and Compagno 1982; C. R. Robins et al. 1986 (all as *Raja garmani*).

Leucoraja lentiginosa   (Bigelow and Schroeder 1951)
Freckled skate

Leucoraja lentiginosa has a heart-shaped disc, with a moderately short, obtuse snout and a moderately broad tail with two dorsal fins and a poorly developed caudal fin. It is distinguished from the other species of the family by the following combination of characters. Snout is moderately short (preorbital length is 8.5% to 9.7% of TL) and obtuse. Pectoral radials extend to about three-fourths snout length. Mouth is moderately to rather strongly arched. Upper jaw has 44 to 51 tooth rows. Oronasal pit is absent. Anterior pelvic lobe is connected to posterior lobe by fin membrane and is distinctly shorter than posterior lobe. Lateral margin of pelvic fin is deeply incised. Tail length is 58.8% to 60.8% of TL and has lateral folds extending most of tail length. Dorsal fins are similar in size and shape and are separated by less than one-half length of first dorsal fin base length. Caudal fin is poorly developed and consists of moderately long dorsal lobe and short ventral lobe. Dorsal surface is more or less uniformly covered with denticles in juveniles but is largely devoid of denticles in adults. Small thorns occur on rostrum and orbital rim. Large thorns occur in triangular patch on nuchal and scapular regions and along midbelt in two to five rows from nuchal region to origin of first dorsal fin. Midrow thorns on medial section of tail are small or absent in adults. Ventral surface is naked except for denticles on tip of snout of adults. Color is buff to brown dorsally, freckled with small light and dark spots, and white to pale yellow ventrally.

This species occurs in the western North Atlantic in the Gulf of Mexico between 53 to 588 m. Maximum known size is 418 mm TL, and maturity is reached between 350 and 418 mm TL. It was formerly considered a subspecies of *Raja garmani* (McEachran 1977) but is herein considered a distinct species.

REFERENCES: Bigelow and Schroeder 1951b, 1953a, 1954b, 1962, 1965, 1968b; McEachran and Musick 1975; Hoese and Moore 1977; McEachran 1977 (as subspecies of *R. garmani*); McEachran and Compagno 1982; C. R. Robins et al. 1986 (all as *Raja lentiginosa*).

Pseudoraja fischeri   Bigelow and Schroeder 1954

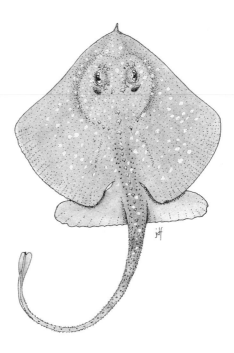

Pseudoraja fischeri has a heart-shaped disc, with a moderately short snout bearing a narrow conical process and a moderately slender tail with no dorsal fins and a well-developed caudal fin. It is distinguished from the other species of the family by the following combination of characters. Snout is moderately short (preorbital length is 8% to 9% of TL) and obtuse (maximum snout angle is 120°). Pectoral radials extend nearly to tip of snout. Upper jaw has 28 to 30 tooth rows. Oronasal pit is located anterior to upper jaw above nasal curtain. Pelvic fin is greatly laterally expanded and consists of single lateral lobe with transverse anterior and posterior margins. Tail is 61% to 62% of TL and has lateral folds extending along posterior one-third of length. Caudal fin is well developed, with more or less equally developed dorsal and ventral lobes distally separated by tip of vertebral column. Dorsal surface is more or less uniformly covered with dermal denticles. Moderate-sized thorns occur on orbital rim, over nuchal and scapular region, and along midline from nuchal region to origin of dorsal caudal lobe. Midrow thorns on tail are flanked by two rows of small thorns. Ventral surface is naked. Color is ashy gray to sooty gray scattered with pale spots dorsally and ash gray with irregular sooty areas over abdominal area ventrally. Ampullar pores on dorsal surface of disc are darkly pigmented.

This species occurs in the western North Atlantic from the Gulf of Mexico and the Lesser Antilles, and off Honduras and Panama. It has been captured from 412 to 576 m. Maximum known size is 576 mm TL.

REFERENCES: Bigelow and Schroeder 1954a, 1962, 1965; Hulley 1972; McEachran and Compagno 1979.

Raja ackleyi   Garman 1881

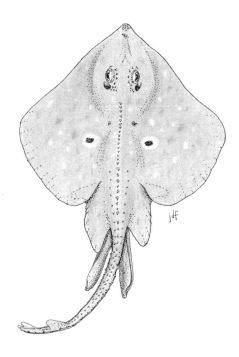

Raja ackleyi has a heart-shaped disc, with a moderately long, slightly obtuse snout and a moderately wide tail with two dorsal fins and a poorly developed caudal fin. It is distinguished from the other species of the family by the following combination of characters. Snout is moderately long (preorbital snout length is 12% to 15% of TL) and slightly obtuse (maximum snout angle is 97° to 112°). Pectoral radials extend to distal one-third of snout. Upper jaw has 42 to 48 tooth rows. Mouth is moderately arched on either side of symphysis. Oronasal pit is absent. Anterior pelvic lobe is connected to posterior lobe by fin membrane and is about one-half length of posterior lobe. Lateral margin of pelvic fin is moderately incised. Tail is 52% to 54% of TL and has lateral folds extending entire length. Dorsal fins are of similar size and shape and are separated by interspace equal to one-half of first dorsal fin base. Caudal fin is poorly developed and consists of

dorsal lobe. Dorsal surface is largely devoid of dermal denticles. Moderate-sized thorns occur on rostrum, on orbital rim, between spiracles, and along midline from nuchal region to origin of first dorsal fin. Each side of tail has additional irregular row of thorns. Ventral surface has dermal denticles on snout to level of mouth. Color is yellowish brown dorsally, scattered with small light and dark spots, and white ventrally. Dorsal surface also has oval dark spot surrounded by pale margin at base of each pectoral fin.

This species occurs in the western Atlantic from southern Florida, the Gulf of Mexico, and off Yucatán Bank, Mexico. It has been captured from 32 to 384 m. Maximum known size is 410 mm TL.

REFERENCES: Bigelow and Schroeder 1953a; C. R. Robins et al. 1986.

Raja eglanteria Bosc 1800
Clearnose skate

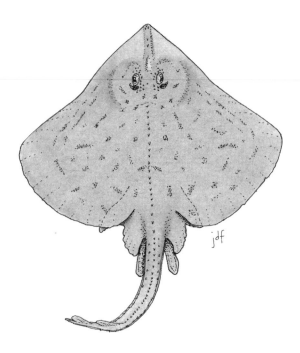

Raja eglanteria has a spade-shaped disc, with a moderately long, slightly obtuse snout and a moderately wide tail. It is distinguished from the other species of the family by the following combination of characters. Snout is moderately long (preorbital length is 14% to 15% of TL) and obtuse (maximum snout angle is 90° to 100°). Pectoral radials extend slightly anterior to midlength of snout. Mouth is slightly arched on either side of symphysis. Upper jaw has 46 to 54 tooth rows. Oronasal pit is absent. Anterior lobe of pelvic fin is connected to posterior lobe by fin membrane and is about 50% of length of posterior lobe. Lateral margin of disc is moderately incised. Tail is 49% to 52% of TL and has lateral folds extending nearly entire length of tail. Dorsal fins are of similar size and shape and are separated by interspace equal to one-third of first dorsal fin base length. Caudal fin is poorly developed and consists of moderately short and low dorsal lobe. Dorsal surface

is more or less uniformly but sparsely covered with dermal denticles, except mature males retain dermal denticles only along anterior section of disc. Medium-sized thorns occur on neurocranium anterior to orbits, on orbital rim, and between spiracles, and larger thorns occur on scapular region and along midline from nuchal region to origin of first dorsal fin. Tail has irregular row of thorns on each side, and several thorns occur between dorsal fins. Ventral surface is naked except for dermal denticles on snout and along anterior margin. Females also have patch of dermal denticles on axil of pectoral fin. Color is brown to gray dorsally, with darker brown spots, transverse and diagonal bars, and lighter spots, and whitish to yellowish ventrally.

This species occurs in the western North Atlantic from Massachusetts (occasionally as far north as the Gulf of Maine) to northern Florida and the northern Gulf of Mexico. In the Gulf of Mexico it is more common east than west of the Mississippi River. It has been captured from the shore zone (mostly in the northern part of its range) to 119 m. Food consists largely of polychaetes, amphipods, shrimps, crabs, and bony fishes. Maximum known size is 785 mm TL; males are mature at 535 to 770 mm TL, females are mature at 600 to 780 mm TL, and young are 125 to 144 mm TL at hatching.

REFERENCES: Bigelow and Schroeder 1953; Fitz and Daiber 1963; Robinson 1969; McEachran and Musick 1975; Hoese and Moore 1977; C. R. Robins et al. 1986.

Raja texana Chandler 1921
Roundel skate

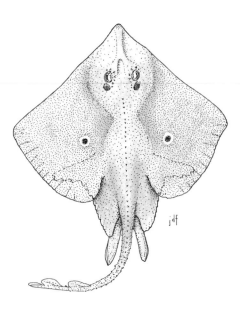

Raja texana has a lozenge-shaped disc; a moderately long, slightly obtuse snout; and a moderately slender tail with two dorsal fins and a moderately developed caudal fin. It is distinguished from the other species of the family by the following combination of characters. Snout is moderately long (preorbital length is 14% to 18% of TL) and slightly obtuse (maximum snout angle is 90° to 106°). Pectoral radials extend to midlength of snout. Mouth is moderately arched on either side of symphysis. Upper jaw has 44 to 48 tooth rows. Oronasal pit is absent. Anterior pelvic lobe is connected to posterior lobe by fin membrane and is 67% to 72% of length of posterior lobe. Lateral margin of pelvic lobe is moderately incised. Tail is 54% to 55% of TL and has lateral folds extending nearly entire length of tail. Dorsal fins are similar in size and shape and are separated by interspace of 30% to 100% of first dorsal fin length. Caudal fin is moderately developed and consists of long, moderately low dorsal lobe. Dorsal surface is devoid of dermal denticles except on tip of snout, rostrum, area between spiracles, and along midbelt of disc to origin of first dorsal fin in adult specimens. Moderate-sized thorns occur on orbital rim and along midline of disc from nuchal region to origin of first dorsal fin. Midrow thorns are flanked by one or two irregular rows of thorns. Ventral surface is naked except for dermal denticles on snout and along anterior margin of disc. Color is dark brown dorsally, with ocellus on medial part of each pectoral fin, and white to yellowish white ventrally. Ocelli have dark brown to black center and are bordered with light yellow ring. Young specimens often have indistinct light spots and blotches scattered over dorsal aspect of disc.

This species occurs in the western North Atlantic in the Gulf of Mexico, the Yucatán Bank, and off the southeastern coast of Florida. It has been captured from 15 to 110 m. Maximum known size is 537 mm TL, and males mature at 470 mm TL.

REFERENCES: Gunter 1945; Bigelow and Schroeder 1953a; Castro-Aguirre et al. 1970; Hoese and Moore 1977; C. R. Robins et al. 1986.

Rajella fuliginea   (Bigelow and Schroeder 1954)

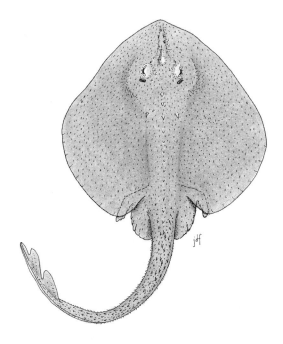

Rajella fuliginea has a heart-shaped disc, with a moderately short, obtuse snout and a moderately broad tail with two dorsal fins and a poorly developed caudal fin. It is distinguished from the other species of the family by the following combination of characters. Snout is moderately short (preorbital length is 10% of TL) and obtuse (maximum snout angle is 125° to 130°). Pectoral radials extend to three-fourths length of snout. Mouth is nearly transverse to moderately arched. Upper jaw has 40 to 45 tooth rows. Oronasal pit is absent. Anterior lobe of pelvic fin is connected to posterior lobe by fin membrane and is 90% of length of posterior lobe. Lateral margin of pelvic fin is deeply incised. Tail length is 56% to 65% of TL and has lateral folds extending along posterior one-third of tail. Dorsal fins are of similar size and shape and are confluent at bases. Caudal fin is poorly developed and consists of short and low dorsal caudal lobe. Dorsal sur-face is uniformly and densely covered with small dermal denticles. Moderate-sized thorns occur on orbital rim, in triangular patch on nuchal and scapular region, and along midline from nuchal region to first dorsal fin. Ventral surface is naked except for dermal denticles uniformly distributed on tail. Color is dark ashy gray to brownish gray dorsally and sooty gray ventrally.

This species occurs in the western North Atlantic from the northern Gulf of Mexico and off Colombia and Venezuela. It is very similar to *Raja bigelowi* Stehmann, and if the two species are judged to be synonymous, the range of *R. fuliginea* would extend to the temperate North Atlantic. *Raja fuliginea* has been captured from 731 to 1,280 m. Maximum known size is 445 mm TL.

REFERENCES: Bigelow and Schroeder 1954a, 1962, 1965 (as *Raja fuliginea*).

Rajella purpuriventralis   (Bigelow and Schroeder 1962)

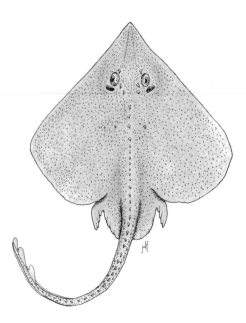

Rajella purpuriventralis has a spade-shaped disc, with a long, slightly acute snout and a moderately slender tail with a poorly developed caudal fin. It is distinguished from the other species of the family by the following combination of characters. Snout is long (preorbital length is 16% of TL) and slightly acute (maximum snout angle is 85° to 105°). Pectoral radials extend to about three-fourths snout length. Mouth is slightly arched on each side of symphysis. Upper jaw has 42 tooth rows. Oronasal pit is absent. Anterior pelvic lobe is connected to posterior lobe by fin membrane and is 80% of length of posterior lobe. Lateral margin of pelvic fin is deeply incised. Tail is 53% of TL and has lateral folds extending along posterior one-third of tail. Dorsal fins are of similar size and shape and are confluent at bases. Caudal fin is poorly developed and consists of small

dorsal lobe. Dorsal surface is uniformly covered with small dermal denticles. Thorns are limited to one stout preorbital, two postorbital, several scapular, and a row of thorns extending along midline from nuchal region to origin of first dorsal fin. Midrow thorns on tail are flanked by two irregular rows of thorns. Ventral surface is naked except for denticles along sides of medial part of tail and entire ventral surface of distal part of tail. Color is dark gray dorsally and blackish ventrally.

This species occurs in the western North Atlantic from the northern Gulf of Mexico, Panama, Suriname, and French Guiana. It has been captured from 732 to 2,010 m. Maximum known size is 510 mm TL.

REFERENCES: Bigelow and Schroeder 1962, 1965 (as *Raja purpuriventralis*).

MYLIOBATIFORMES

The order contains about eight or nine families, but the phylogenetic interrelationships of these families have not been clarified. Six families occur in the Gulf of Mexico, and of these, Dasyatidae and Urolophidae are primitive, with Dasyatidae sister to the more-derived Gymnuridae, Myliobatidae, Rhinopteridae, and Mobulidae. Gymnuridae is considered to be the sister group of the latter three families, and Myliobatidae may not be monophyletic without inclusion of Rhinopteridae and Mobulidae.

Key to the Families of the Gulf of Mexico

1a. Well-developed caudal fin present . . . . Urolophidae p. 183
1b. Caudal fin absent 2
2a. Head level with disc; without subrostral lobes or cephalic fins; eye and spiracle on top of head 3
2b. Head elevated above level of disc; with subrostral lobes or cephalic fins ventral to head; eye and spiracle on side of head 4
3a. Disc less than one and one-half times as broad as long; transverse curtain on roof of mouth with a fringed margin; floor of mouth with several fleshy papillae; tail longer than disc width; dorsal fin absent . . . . Dasyatidae p. 172
3b. Disc greater than one and one-half times as broad as long; transverse curtain on roof of mouth with a smooth margin; floor of mouth without fleshy papillae; tail shorter than disc width; dorsal fin present or absent
. . . . Gymnuridae p. 185
4a. Anterior subdivision of pectoral fin forming narrow finlike projection (cephalic fin) on each side of head
. . . . Mobulidae p. 193
4b. Anterior subdivision of pectoral fin forming either single fleshy lobe below front of head or forming a pair of fleshy lobes connected basally below head 5
5a. Single subrostral lobe located below front of head
. . . . Myliobatidae p. 188
5b. Pair of subrostral lobes located below front of head
. . . . Rhinopteridae p. 191

DASYATIDAE Stingrays

Stingrays are extremely flattened and laterally expanded, with a moderately long and acute to a short and obtuse snout and a very long, slender, whiplike tail. They are distinguished from the other families of the order by the following combination of characters. Snout is moderately long and acute to very short and obtuse. Pectoral fin is greatly laterally expanded and extends to tip of snout to form disc. Disc is broad, as long as it is broad to moderately broader than it is long, and relatively thin at margin. Anterior part of head is not elevated above disc. Anterior margin of nostril is greatly expanded to form curtain that is continuous across narrow isthmus in front of mouth and covers medial portion of nostrils. Posterior lateral margin of curtain is fringed. Mouth is straight to slightly arched. Floor of mouth has row of fleshy papillae. Teeth are numerous, with single conical cusps, and are in quincunx arrangement. Spiracle is located just posterior to eye on top of head. Posterior margin of spiracle lacks folds and ridges. Pectoral fin extends distinctly posterior to origin of pelvic fin and dorsally covers most of pelvic fin. Pelvic fin is laterally expanded and is not divided into anterior and posterior lobes. Tail is distinct from disc and is very slender, whiplike, and generally considerably longer than disc width. Most species bear one to several serrated spines on proximal section of tail, and many species have longitudinal folds on dorsal or ventral or both sides of tail. Body is generally naked or has small- to medium-sized thorns or large tubercles on dorsal surface of disc and tail.

Stingrays occur worldwide in tropical to temperate seas. They are most frequently captured close to shore but occasionally are found to 110 m. Most species occur in marine to brackish waters, but some species are restricted to freshwater. All but one or two species are benthic. Food consists of a wide variety of benthic invertebrates and bony fishes. Embryonic development is ovoviviparous. There are about 50 species in 7 genera, and 7 species in 3 genera occur in the Gulf of Mexico.

Key to the Species of the Gulf of Mexico
(Adapted in part from Bigelow and Schroeder 1953a)

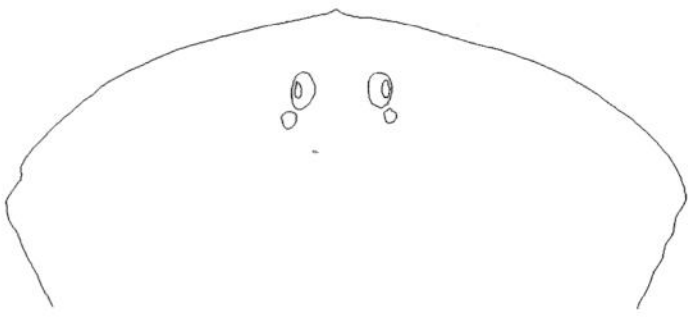

1a. Anterior margin of disc evenly convex to nearly straight
(Fig. 39) 2

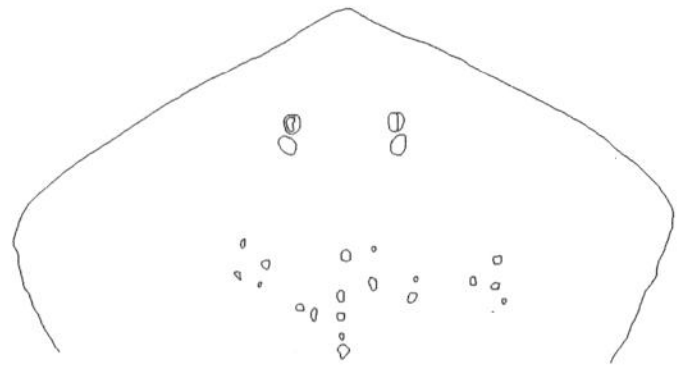

1b. Anterior margin of disc subangular, with tip of snout forming apex of angle (Fig. 40) 3

2a. Dorsal surface of disc uniformly covered with tubercles;
ventral surface of disc creamy white to yellowish, often
with variously colored blotches and dusky margin
. . . . *Himantura schmardae* p. 182

2b. Dorsal surface of disc mostly naked; ventral surface of disc
uniformly brown to black
. . . . *Pteroplatytrygon violacea* p. 181

3a. Outer corners of disc broadly and evenly rounded 4

3b. Outer corners of disc narrowly rounded to subangular
. . . . 5

4a. Preorbital length longer than distance between spiracles;
anterior margin of disc on either side of snout concave
. . . . *Dasyatis sabina* p. 177

4b. Preorbital length shorter than distance between spiracles;
anterior margin of disc on either side of snout straight to
weakly convex . . . . *Dasyatis say* p. 179

5a. Snout projecting beyond remainder of anterior margin of
disc; anterior margin of disc on either side of snout concave to level of spiracle. . . . . *Dasyatis guttata* p. 176

5b. Snout not projecting beyond remainder of anterior margin
of disc; anterior margin of disc on either side of snout
straight to slightly concave to level of spiracle 6

6a. Longitudinal fold along ventral side of tail about as wide
as height of tail (Fig. 41); dorsal side of tail with longitudinal ridge posterior to serrated spine; lateral sides of tail
lack conspicuous tubercles . . . . *Dasyatis americana* p. 174

6b. Longitudinal fold along ventral side of tail about one-half
as wide as height of tail (Fig. 42); dorsal side of tail without longitudinal ridge; lateral sides of tail have conspicuous
tubercles or thorns in large juveniles and adults
. . . . *Dasyatis centroura* p. 175

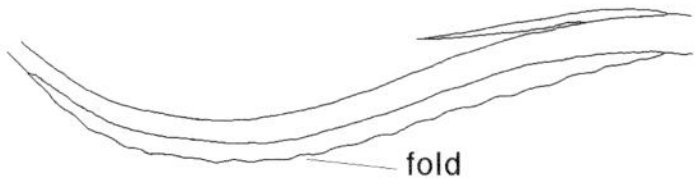

FIG 39

FIG 40

fold

FIG 41

fold

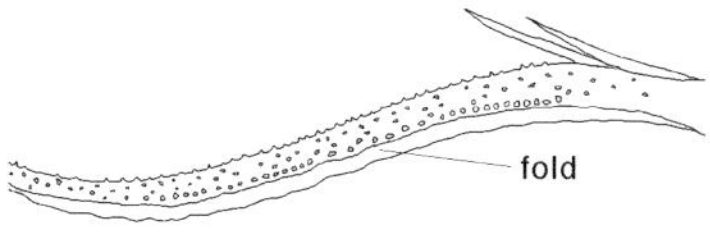

FIG 42

Dasyatis americana   Hildebrand and Schroeder 1928
Southern stingray

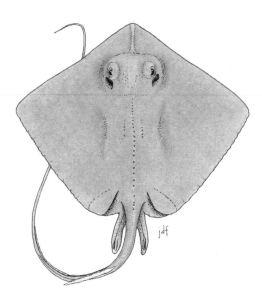

Dasyatis americana has a lozenge-shaped disc; a moderately long, angular snout; and a long, whiplike tail. It is distinguished from the other species of the family by the following combination of characters. Snout is moderately long (preorbital length is 17% to 18% of disc width [DW]) and obtuse (maximum snout angle is about 135°). Anterior margin of disc on either side of snout to level of eye is straight to slightly concave. Outer corners of disc are abruptly rounded to subangular. Mouth is slightly arched on either side of symphysis. Upper jaw is slightly projecting at symphysis, and lower jaw is slightly indented at symphysis. Floor of mouth has transverse row of three fleshy papillae. Additional slender papilla occasionally occurs lateral to fleshy papillae. Upper jaw has 39 to 56 tooth rows. Teeth of juveniles and females have tetragonal bases and flat to rounded cusps. Teeth of mature males have tetragonal bases and low, conical cusps. Anterior margin of pelvic fin is nearly straight in small specimens and slightly convex in larger specimens. Outer corner of pelvic fin is abruptly rounded, and posterior margin is evenly convex. One or more serrated spines are located on proximal section of tail. Tail bears fleshy dorsal keel distal to serrated spine. Ventral surface of tail bears broad tail fold, which is equal to tail height at level of serrated spine. Denticles occur between orbits and spiracles, on nuchal and scapular region, along midbelt of disc, and on dorsal and lateral aspects of tail. Dermal denticles may cover entire dorsal surface of disc in mature specimens. Tubercles occur along midline of disc and on scapular region, and are most numerous on mature species. Color is gray, dark brown, or olive green dorsally and white with gray to brown disc margin ventrally.

This species occurs in the western North Atlantic from New Jersey to Rio de Janeiro, Brazil, including the Gulf of Mexico, the Antilles, and the Bahamas. It is most frequently captured near shore but also is found in estuaries and rivers. Food consists of bivalves, gastropods, polychaetes, crustaceans, and bony fishes. Litters range from three to five young. Maximum known size is 150 cm DW; males mature at 51 cm DW, females mature at 75 to 80 cm DW, and young are 17 to 18 cm DW at birth.

REFERENCES: Hildebrand and Schroeder 1928; Bigelow and Schroeder 1953a; Cervigón 1966; Böhlke and Chaplin 1968; Brockmann 1975; Hoese and Moore 1977; Snelson and Williams 1981; C. R. Robins et al. 1986.

Dasyatis centroura (Mitchill 1815)
Roughtail stingray

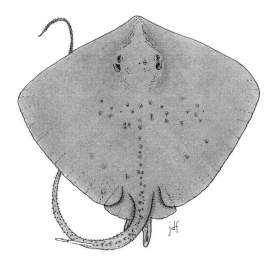

Dasyatis centroura has a lozenge-shaped disc; a moderately long, angular snout; and a long, slender, whiplike tail. It is distinguished from the other species of the family by the following combination of characters. Snout is moderately long (preorbital length is 16% to 17% of disc width [DW]) and obtuse (maximum snout angle is 130° to 140°). Anterior margin on either side of snout to level of eye is straight to slightly concave. Outer corners of disc are abruptly rounded to subangular. Mouth is moderately arched on either side of symphysis. Upper jaw is slightly projecting at symphysis, and lower jaw is slightly indented at symphysis. Floor of mouth has row of six fleshy papillae. Upper jaw has 51 tooth rows. Teeth of juveniles and females have tetragonal bases and flat to rounded cusps. Teeth of mature males have tetragonal bases and low, conical cusps. Anterior margin of pelvic fin is nearly straight to slightly convex. Outer corner of pelvic fin is abruptly rounded, and posterior margin is straight to evenly convex. One or more serrated spines are located on anterior part of tail. Tail lacks dorsal fleshy keel posterior to serrated spine. Ventral surface of tail bears relatively narrow fold that at level of serrated spine is about one-half tail height. Body of specimens less than 50 cm DW is naked. Specimens greater than 50 cm DW possess small patch of denticles on tip of snout, behind spiracles, on base of tail, and on posterior corner of disc, and have large tubercles or bucklers on midline and central part of disc and on dorsal and lateral sides of tail. Bucklers range in size up to diameter of eye. Color is dark brown to olive dorsally and white or whitish ventrally.

This species occurs in the tropical to warm temperate eastern Atlantic and warm temperate western Atlantic. In the western Atlantic it occurs from Georges Bank, off Massachusetts, to southern Florida, the northeastern Gulf of Mexico, the Bahamas, and off Uruguay. The eastern Atlantic population and the Uruguay population may represent distinct species. In the western North Atlantic it is most frequently captured near shore to 91 m, but the Bahaman specimen was taken at 274 m. Food consists of polychaetes, cephalopods, crustaceans, and bony fishes. Litters range from two to six young. Maximum known size is 210 cm DW; males mature at 130 to 150 cm DW, females mature at 140 to 160 cm DW, and young range from 34 to 37 cm DW at birth.

REFERENCES: Bigelow and Schroeder 1953a; Bullis and Struhsaker 1961; Struhsaker 1969; Hoese and Moore 1977; McEachran and Capapé 1984a; C. R. Robins et al. 1986.

Dasyatis guttata   (Bloch and Schneider 1801)

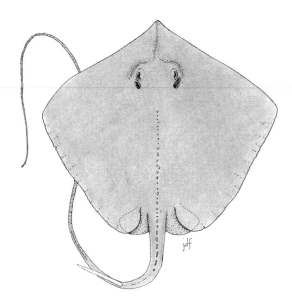

Dasyatis guttata has a lozenge-shaped disc; a relatively long, angular snout; and a long, slender, whiplike tail. It is distinguished from the other species of the family by the following combination of characters. Snout is relatively long (preorbital length is 23% to 26% of disc width [DW]) and moderately obtuse (maximum snout angle is 105° to 115°). Anterior margin of disc on either side of snout to level of eye is weakly concave. Outer corners of disc are abruptly rounded to subangular. Mouth is moderately arched on either side of symphysis. Upper jaw is slightly projecting at symphysis, and lower jaw is slightly indented at symphysis. Floor of mouth has transverse row of three stout papillae. Upper jaw has 34 to 46 tooth rows. Teeth of juveniles and females have tetragonal bases and flat to rounded cusps. Teeth of mature males are unknown. Anterior margin of pelvic fin is slightly convex. Outer corner of pelvic fin is abruptly rounded, and posterior margin is evenly convex. One or more serrated spines are located on anterior part of tail. Tail bears fleshy, dorsal ridge posterior to serrated spine. Lower surface of tail bears fold that at level of serrated spine is about two-thirds to four-fifths height of tail. Denticles occur on dorsal and lateral sides of tail posterior to serrated spine. Thorns or tubercles occur along midline from nuchal region to origin of serrated spine. Large specimens also possess heart-shaped tubercles along midbelt of disc from anterior margin of orbit to base of tail. Color is brown to olivaceous dorsally, with or without dark spots, and pale yellowish white ventrally. Ventral tail fold and dorsal keel are black.

This species occurs in the western Atlantic from the southern Gulf of Mexico, the Antilles, and from Panama to Santos, Brazil. It is probably an inshore species, but little is known of its habitat, feeding habits, or reproductive biology. Maximum known size is 180 to 200 cm DW.

REFERENCES: Bigelow and Schroeder 1953a; Cervigón 1966; Thorson 1983.

Dasyatis sabina (Lesueur 1824)
Atlantic stingray

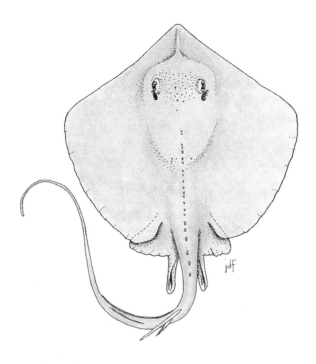

Dasyatis sabina has a spade-shaped disc; a relatively long snout; and a long, slender, whip-like tail. It is distinguished from the other species of the family by the following combination of characters. Snout is relatively long (preorbital length is 25% to 27% of disc width [DW]) and moderately obtuse (maximum snout angle is 107° to 122°). Anterior margin of disc on either side of snout to level of eye is concave. Outer corners of disc are broadly rounded, and posterior margin is moderately convex. Mouth is arched on either side of symphysis. Upper jaw is slightly projecting at symphysis, and lower jaw is slightly indented at symphysis. Floor of mouth has transverse row of three stout papillae. Upper jaw has 28 to 36 tooth rows. Teeth of juveniles and females have quadrangular bases and flat to slightly rounded cusps. Teeth of mature males have quadrangular bases and long, slender, conical cusps. Anterior margin of pelvic fin is more or less straight and about as long as distance from its origin to posterior margin. Outer corner of pelvic fin is abruptly rounded, and posterior margin is evenly convex. Tail bears low, dorsal, fleshy ridge posterior to serrated spine. Lower surface of tail bears fold that at level of serrated spine is about equal to tail height. Denticles occur on head between orbits and spiracles. Tubercles or thorns occur along dorsal midline from nuchal region to origin of serrated spine and on scapular region. Color is brown to yellowish brown dorsally, occasionally with dark stripe along midline, and whitish, occasionally with a darker margin, ventrally.

This species occurs in the western Atlantic from Chesapeake Bay to southern Florida and the Gulf of Mexico. It has been reported from Grenada, Suriname, and Brazil, but these records may refer to other species. This species occurs in freshwater in the Mississippi River, Lake Pontchartrain, and St. John's River, Florida. It is generally captured from the shoreline to 20 m. Food consists of polychaetes, crustaceans, and bony fishes. Litters range from one to three young. Maximum known size is 458 to 610 mm DW; females mature at 160 to 176 mm DW, and young are 100 mm DW at birth.

REFERENCES: Gunter 1945; Bigelow and Schroeder 1953a; Sage et al. 1972; Hoese and Moore 1977; Schwartz and Dahlberg 1978; Snelson and Williams 1981; Schmid et al. 1988.

Dasyatis say (Lesueur 1817)
Bluntnose stingray

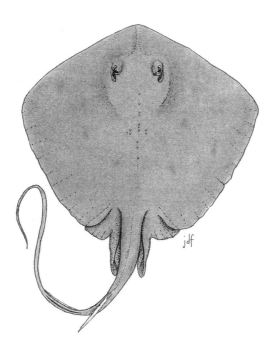

Dasyatis say has a lozenge-shaped disc; a moderately long snout; and a long, slender, whip-like tail. It is distinguished from the other species of the family by the following combination of characters. Snout is moderately long (preorbital length is 15% to 17% of disc width [DW]) and obtuse (maximum snout angle is 130°). Anterior margin on either side of snout to level of eye is straight to slightly convex. Outer corners of disc are rather broadly rounded. Mouth is moderately arched on either side of symphysis. Upper jaw is slightly projecting at symphysis, and lower jaw is slightly indented at symphysis. Floor of mouth has transverse row of three stout papillae flanked by single small papilla on each side. Upper jaw has 36 to 50 tooth rows. Teeth of juveniles and females have quadrangular bases and rounded cusps. Teeth of adult males have quadrangular bases and broad, triangular cusps. Anterior margin of pelvic fin is nearly straight and as long as distance from origin of fin to posterior margin.

Outer corner of pelvic fin is abruptly rounded, and posterior margin is nearly straight. Tail bears dorsal fold posterior to serrated spine. Ventral surface of tail bears fold that is slightly wider than the dorsal fold and tail height. Denticles occur along midbelt of disc and on dorsal and lateral aspects of tail in mature specimens. Relatively small thorns or tubercles occur along midline of disc from nuchal region to origin of serrated tail spine. Thorn number increases with growth. One or two thorns also occur on scapular region. Ventral surface is naked. Color is grayish brown, olivaceous brown, reddish brown, or dusky green dorsally. Occasionally dorsal surface is marked with bluish spots, is darker near lateral and posterior margins, or is narrowly edged with white. Ventral surface is white to whitish. Occasionally ventral surface is marked with dark blotches or has dark margin.

This species occurs in the western Atlantic from Massachusetts (rare), New Jersey (rare),

Virginia, and Chesapeake Bay to southern Brazil, and possibly Uruguay and northern Argentina. It occurs throughout the Antilles and northern Gulf of Mexico but is unrecorded from the coast of Mexico and coasts of Central America, Colombia, and Venezuela. This species is captured from the shoreline to 9 m and also occurs in estuaries. Food consists of polychaetes, bivalve and gastropod mollusks, and bony fishes. Litters range from two to four young. Maximum known size is 100 cm DW, and young are 15 to 16 cm DW at birth.

REFERENCES: Bigelow and Schroeder 1953a; Hoese and Moore 1977; Snelson and Williams 1981; C. R. Robins et al. 1986; Schmid et al. 1988; Snelson et al. 1988.

Pteroplatytrygon violacea   (Bonaparte 1832)
Pelagic stingray

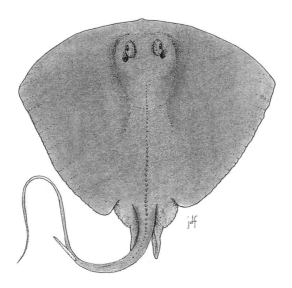

Pteroplatytrygon violacea has a broad, wedge-shaped disc; a moderately long, very obtuse snout; and a long, tapering tail. It is distinguished from the other species of the family by the following combination of characters. Snout is moderately long (preorbital length is 8% to 15% of disc width [DW]) and very obtuse (maximum snout angle is 158° to 169°). Anterior disc forms broad arch. Outer corners are abruptly rounded, and posterolateral margin is straight to slightly convex and slopes medially. Mouth is slightly arched. Upper jaw is very slightly projecting at symphysis, and lower jaw is very slightly indented at symphysis. Floor of mouth has transverse row of 10 to 12 fleshy papillae. Upper jaw has 28 to 34 tooth rows. Teeth of adults have quadrangular bases and low acute cusps. Anterior margin of pelvic fin is more or less straight and about 60% to 70% of distance from origin of fin to posterior margin. Outer corner of pelvic fin is broadly rounded. Tail is relatively thick at base but tapers greatly to origin of serrated spine. Tail lacks dorsal ridge or fold. Ventral tail fold is narrow and extends from origin to tip of serrated spine. Larger specimens are covered with denticles dorsally but are naked ventrally. Row of thorns extends from nuchal region to origin of serrated spine. Color is dark purple to dark green dorsally and slightly lighter grayish purple to greenish blue ventrally.

This species is probably circumtropical. In the western Atlantic it occurs from the Grand Banks and Flemish Cap to Cape Hatteras, North Carolina; the northern Gulf of Mexico off Texas; and off the Lesser Antilles. It is pelagic and is generally captured from the edge of the continental and insular shelves to oceanic waters. Food consists of squids, coelenterates, medusae, crustaceans, and bony fishes. Many of these prey are associated with pelagic Sargassum weed. Litters consist of 9 to 13 young. Maximum known size is 800 mm DW; males mature at 478 mm DW, and females mature at 400 to 500 mm DW. Size of young at birth is unknown.

REFERENCES: Bigelow and Schroeder 1962, 1965; Scott and Tibbo 1968; Wilson and Beckett 1970; Branstetter and McEachran 1983; McEachran and Capapé 1984a; C. R. Robins et al. 1986; Scott and Scott 1988 (all above as *Dasyatis violacea*).

Himantura schmardae   (Werner 1904)

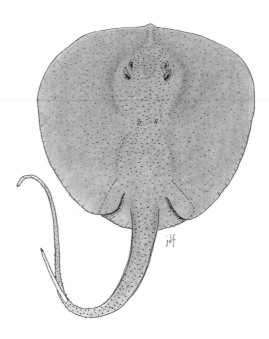

Himantura schmardae has an oval-shaped disc; a long, very obtuse snout; and a relatively short, moderately slender tail. It is distinguished from the other species of the family by the following combination of characters. Snout is relatively long (preorbital length is 19% to 20% of disc width [DW]) and obtuse (anterior margin is nearly straight). Anterior margin on either side of snout is broadly rounded. Mouth is moderately arched on either side of symphysis. Upper jaw is slightly projecting at symphysis, and lower jaw is slightly indented at symphysis. Floor of mouth has transverse row of five papillae. Upper jaw has 28 to 36 tooth rows. Teeth have oval to elliptical bases and flat or rounded cusps. Cusps have central, transverse depression, with scalloped margins. Anterior margin of pelvic fin is straight and slightly shorter than distance from origin of fin to posterior margin. Outer corner of pelvic fin is abruptly rounded, and posterior margin is evenly convex. Serrated tail spine is located on posterior one-half of tail. Tail lacks dorsal ridge but proximally has ventral ridge and ridge on each side. Small tubercles uniformly cover dorsal surface of disc and dorsal and lateral aspects of tail. Relatively large tubercles occur on scapular region. All tubercles are blunt and have four arborescent ridges radiating from apex of crown. Color is dark brown or grayish olive dorsally and yellowish to creamy white ventrally. Tail is sooty to blackish posteriorly.

This species occurs in the western Atlantic from the southern Gulf of Mexico, Cuba, Jamaica, Panama, Trinidad, and Suriname. It is most often captured in shallow water, but little is known of its habits. Maximum known size is 1.2 m DW.

REFERENCES: Bigelow and Schroeder 1953a; Cervigón 1966.

UROLOPHIDAE Round stingrays

The round rays are greatly flattened and laterally expanded, with a moderately short snout and a relatively stout, short tail. They are distinguished from the other families of the order by the following combination of characters. Snout is moderately short to short and obtuse. Pectoral fin is greatly expanded, is attached to side of head, and extends to tip of snout to form disc. Disc is from about as broad as it is long to about 1.3 times as broad as it is long, and relatively thin at margin. Head is not elevated from disc. Anterior margin of nostril is greatly expanded into curtain that is continuous across narrow isthmus anterior to mouth and covers medial part of nostrils. Posterolateral section of curtain is generally fringed. Mouth is slightly arched on either side of symphysis. Floor of mouth has transverse row of papillae. Teeth are small, numerous, and in quincunx arrangement. Spiracle is located just posterior to eye on top of head. Pectoral fin extends distally posterior to origin of pelvic fin. Pelvic fin is moderately laterally expanded and is not divided into anterior and posterior lobes. Tail is distinct from disc, moderately slender, and from slightly greater than, to slightly less than, disc length. One to several serrated spines occur on distal one-half of tail. One dorsal fin is present or absent. Small caudal fin is continuous or discontinuous around tip of vertebral column.

The round stingrays occur in the tropical to warm temperate seas of the western Atlantic, eastern Pacific, and Indo-West Pacific. Most species are limited to inshore waters. Little is known of their feeding habits or reproductive biology, although all species are probably ovoviviparous. There are about 35 species in 4 genera, and 1 species occurs in the Gulf of Mexico.

Urobatis jamaicensis   (Cuvier 1816)
Yellow stingray

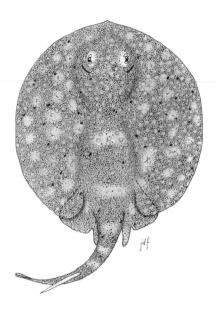

Urobatis jamaicensis has an oval-shaped disc; a moderately short snout; and a relatively short, broad tail. It is distinguished from the other species of the family by the following combination of characters. Snout is of moderate length (preorbital length is 11% to 12% of disc length) and obtuse (maximum snout angle is 140°). Anterior margin of disc is straight to slightly convex. Outer corners of disc are broadly rounded. Disc is 0.9 times as broad as it is long. Mouth is nearly straight. Floor of mouth has transverse row of three to five papillae. Upper jaw has 30 to 34 tooth rows. Teeth of juveniles and females have broad, oval bases and low, deeply furrowed cusps. Teeth of mature males have moderately broad bases and long, conical cusps. Anterior margin of pelvic fin is nearly straight and 60% to 65% of distance from origin of fin to posterior margin. Outer corner of pelvic fin is broadly rounded, and posterior margin is moderately convex. Tail is relatively short, 46% to 48% of TL. Tail lacks dorsal fin but has low keel on each side.

Body is naked except for small denticles along midbelt of disc and tail. Dorsal surface is patterned with fine reticulations of dark green to grayish brown on a lighter background, or pattern consists of small, pale whitish, yellowish, or golden spots on dark background. Ventral surface is yellowish, greenish, or brownish white and marked with small dots of dorsal coloration on tail and along margin of disc.

This species occurs in the western North Atlantic from Cape Lookout, North Carolina, to southern Florida, the Gulf of Mexico, the Bahamas, and the Antilles. It is generally captured near shore, including bays and estuaries. Food consists of crustaceans and probably other benthic organisms and bony fishes. Litters range from two to four young. Maximum known size is 70 cm TL.

REFERENCES: Bigelow and Schroeder 1953a; Böhlke and Chaplin 1968; Robinson 1969; Hoese and Moore 1977; C. R. Robins et al. 1986 (all above as *Urolophus jamaicensis*).

GYMNURIDAE Butterfly rays

Butterfly rays are greatly flattened and laterally expanded, with short, obtuse snouts and very slender, short tails. They are distinguished from the other families of the order by the following combination of characters. Snout is relatively short and obtuse. Pectoral fin is greatly expanded, is attached to side of head, and extends to tip of snout to form disc. Disc is more than 1.5 times as broad as it is long and is relatively thin at margin. Head is not elevated from disc. Anterior margin of nostril is greatly expanded to form curtain that is continuous across narrow isthmus anterior to mouth and covers medial part of nostrils. Posterolateral sections of curtain are finely fringed or smooth. Mouth is slightly arched on either side of symphysis. Floor of mouth lacks papillae. Teeth are numerous and are arranged in quincunx. Spiracle is located just posterior to eye on top of head. Inner posterior margin of spiracle either has or lacks tentacle-like lobe. Pectoral fin extends distinctly posterior to origin of pelvic fin. Pelvic fin is moderately laterally expanded and is not divided into anterior and posterior lobes. Tail is distinct from disc, very slender, and shorter than disc length. Tail either has or lacks one or more serrated spines and single dorsal fin.

Butterfly rays occur worldwide in tropical to temperate seas. They are generally captured in shallow coastal water, including estuaries. Food consists of bivalve mollusks, crustaceans, and bony fishes. Embryonic development is ovoviviparous. There are about 14 species in 2 genera, and 1 or 2 species in a single genus occur in the Gulf of Mexico.

Key to the Species of the Gulf of Mexico

1a. Tail with one or more serrated spines
. . . .*Gymnura altavela* p. 186
1b. Tail without serrated spines. . . . . *Gymnura micrura* p. 187

Gymnura altavela (Linnaeus 1758)
Spiny butterfly ray

Gymnura altavela has a very broad, lozenge-shaped disc; a short, blunt snout; and a very slender, short tail. It is distinguished from the other species of the family by the following combination of characters. Snout is short (preorbital length is 7% to 8% of disc width [DW]) and obtuse (maximum snout angle is 135°). Anterior margin of disc is slightly convex to level of eye and slightly concave from eye to level of spiracle. Outer corners of disc are abruptly rounded. Mouth is moderately arched laterally but straight medially. Upper jaw has 98 to 138 tooth rows. Teeth possess high, conical cusps. Inner posterior margin of spiracle has tentacle-like structure. Anterior margin of pelvic fin is more or less straight and slightly shorter than distance from origin of fin to posterior margin. Outer corner of pelvic fin is abruptly rounded, and posterior margin is convex. Tail length is about one-fourth disc width. Tail lacks dorsal fin, but has one or more serrated spines at base and dorsal and ventral ridge along entire length. Body of juveniles and subadults is naked. Adults have denticles on central part of disc. Color is dark brown dorsally, with small, darker spots or light spots and blotches, and white ventrally. Tail of small specimens is marked with pale crossbars.

This species occurs in tropical to temperate waters of the Atlantic. In the western Atlantic it occurs from southern Massachusetts to Rio de la Plata, Argentina, from the shoreline to 55 m. It has not been reported from the Gulf of Mexico but likely occurs there on rare occasions. Litters consist of four young. Maximum known size is 2,082 mm DW for specimens in the western Atlantic.

REFERENCES: Bigelow and Schroeder 1953a; Daiber and Booth 1960; McEachran and Capapé 1984b; C. R. Robins et al. 1986.

Gymnura micrura (Bloch and Schneider 1801)
Smooth butterfly ray

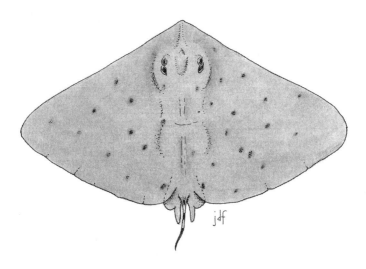

Gymnura micrura has a very broad, lozenge-shaped disc; a short, blunt snout; and a very slender, short tail. It is distinguished from the other species of the family by the following combination of characters. Snout is moderately short (preorbital length is 12% to 13% of disc width [DW]) and obtuse (maximum snout angle is 120° to 140°). Anterior margin of disc is weakly convex on either side of snout to level of eye and weakly concave from level of eye to level of spiracle. Outer corners of disc are narrowly rounded to subangular. Mouth is moderately arched laterally but straight medially. Upper jaw has 60 to 120 tooth rows. Number of tooth rows increases with growth. Teeth possess short, conical cusps. Anterior margin of pelvic fin is more or less straight and shorter than distance from origin of fin to posterior margin. Outer corner of pelvic fin is abruptly rounded, and posterior margin is more or less straight. Tail length is about one-fourth disc width. Tail lacks dorsal fin and serrated spines but has low dorsal and ventral ridges. Body is naked. Color is gray, brown, light green, or purple dorsally, in a dotted or vermicular pattern of alternating light and dark shades. Tail has three or four crossbars. Ventral surface is white with an outer grayish margin.

This species occurs in the tropical to warm temperate western Atlantic from southern New England (rare), Maryland, and Chesapeake Bay to Rio de Janeiro, Brazil, including the Gulf of Mexico. It is generally captured near shore, and occurs in estuaries but has not been reported from freshwater. Food consists of bivalve mollusks; crustaceans such as copepods, shrimps, and crabs; and bony fishes. Litter size is unknown. Maximum known size is 90 to 120 cm DW; males mature at 42 cm DW, females mature at 26 to 27 cm DW, and young are 16 to 22 cm DW at birth.

REFERENCES: Gunter 1945 (as *Pteroplatea micrura*); Bigelow and Schroeder 1953a; Daiber and Booth 1960; Cervigón 1966; Hoese and Moore 1977; Snelson and Williams 1981; C. R. Robins et al. 1986.

MYLIOBATIDAE Eagle rays

The eagle rays are extremely flattened and laterally expanded, with a very slender, long, whiplike tail. They are distinguished from the other families of the order by the following combination of characters. Pectoral fin is greatly expanded and attached to head to form disc. Head is elevated from disc. Anterior section of pectoral fin forms subrostral lobe anterior to head. Lobe is joined or narrowly separated from main portion of pectoral fin. Disc is much broader than it is long and is moderately thin at margin. Anterior margin of nostril is greatly expanded into curtain that is continuous across narrow isthmus in front of mouth and covers medial portion of nostrils. Posterolateral margin of curtain is fringed. Mouth is straight to slightly arched and has fringed curtain on roof. Floor of mouth has transverse row of papillae. Teeth are flattened and pavementlike, and occur in one to seven series. If there is more than one series, median series is largest. Spiracle is located posterior to eye on side of head. Posterior margin of spiracle lacks folds or ridges. Pectoral fin extends posterior to origin of pelvic fin and dorsally covers most of pelvic fin. Pelvic fin is slightly to moderately laterally expanded and is not divided into anterior and posterior lobes. Tail is distinct from disc, very slender, and considerably longer than disc width. Tail has small dorsal fin near its base and either has or lacks one or more serrated spines posterior to dorsal fin. Caudal fin and longitudinal folds are absent on tail.

Eagle rays occur worldwide in tropical to temperate seas, generally on continental and insular shelves. They also occur in bays and estuaries. Food consists of benthic mollusks and crustaceans. Embryonic development is ovoviviparous. There are about 24 species in 4 genera, and 2 species in separate genera occur in the Gulf of Mexico.

Key to the Species of the Gulf of Mexico

1a. Each jaw with single series of teeth
. . . . *Aetobatus narinari* p. 189
1b. Each jaw with more than 1, usually 7, series of teeth
. . . . *Myliobatis freminvillei* p. 190

Aetobatus narinari   (Euphrasen 1790)
Spotted eagle ray

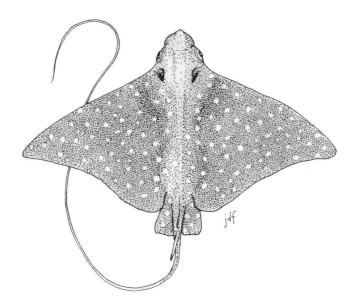

Aetobatus narinari has a broad, lozenge-shaped disc; an angular snout; and a very slender, long, whiplike tail. It is distinguished from the other species of the family by the following combination of characters. Snout is moderately short (preorbital length is 6% to 7% of disc width [DW]) and rounded. Rostral section of pectoral fin is separated from main section of fin. Disc is 2.1 times as broad as it is long. Anterior margins of disc, on either side of snout, are slightly convex, outer corners are abruptly rounded, and posterior margins are concave. Mouth is nearly straight. Nasal curtain is indented medially at isthmus. Floor of mouth has transverse row of six papillae. Teeth are in single series. Pelvic fin is relatively narrow and extends considerably posterior to posterior margin of pectoral fin. Dorsal fin is located over insertion of pelvic fin. Base of dorsal fin is about equal to one-half of distance between exposed nostrils. Body is naked. Dorsally color is olivaceous to dark brown, marked with small white, greenish, or yellow spots. Occasionally dorsal margin of disc is completely dark. Ventrally color is white, except for subrostral lobe and posterior margins of pelvic fins, which are dusky.

This species occurs worldwide in tropical to temperate seas. In the western Atlantic it occurs from North Carolina to southern Brazil, including the Gulf of Mexico, the Bahamas, the Antilles, and Bermuda. It is most frequently captured close to shore. Food consists of polychaetes, mollusks, crustaceans, and bony fishes. This ray is reported to be very destructive to clam and oyster beds. There are generally four young per litter. Maximum known size is 230 cm DW, and young range from 179 to 360 mm DW at birth.

REFERENCES: Bigelow and Schroeder 1953a; Cervigón 1966; Böhlke and Chaplin 1968; Hoese and Moore 1977; Snelson and Williams 1981; C. R. Robins et al. 1986.

Myliobatis freminvillei   Lesueur 1824
Bullnose ray

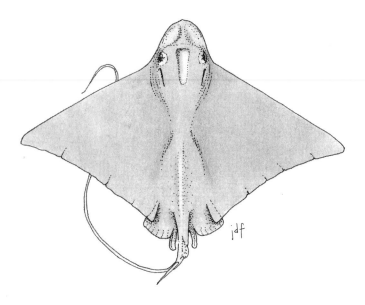

Myliobatis freminvillei has a lozenge-shaped disc; an angular snout; and a very slender, long, whiplike tail. It is distinguished from the other species of the family by the following combination of characters. Snout is moderately short (preorbital length is 7% to 10% of disc width [DW]). Rostral section of pectoral fin is narrowly connected to main section of fin at level of head. Disc is 1.6 to 1.8 times as broad as it is long. Anterior margins of disc, on either side of snout, are straight to slightly convex, outer corners are acutely angled, and posterior margins are concave. Mouth is nearly straight. Nasal curtain has straight, coarsely fringed posterior margin. Roof of mouth has transverse curtain with fringed margin. Floor of mouth has transverse row of five to six papillae. Teeth are in series of seven transverse hexagonal plates. Plates of median row are 2.5 times to 5 times as broad as they are long. Plates of juveniles are less broad than those of adults. Pelvic fin is relatively broad and extends moderately beyond posterior margin of pectoral fin. Dorsal fin originates at or slightly posterior to posterior margin of pelvic fin. Length of dorsal fin base is equal to distance between exposed nostrils. Body is naked in juveniles, but adults have oval-shaped tubercles along midline on scapular region. Mature males also have tubercle on margin of orbit. Color is gray to reddish brown or dusky brown dorsally and white to light gray or light brown ventrally. Teeth are green.

This species occurs in the western Atlantic from Cape Cod (rare) and New York to southern Brazil, including the Gulf of Mexico. It is most frequently encountered close to shore. Food consists of bivalve and gastropod mollusks and crustaceans. Litters generally consist of six young. Maximum known size is 860 mm DW; males mature at 600 to 700 mm DW, and young are 25 mm DW at birth.

REFERENCES: Bigelow and Schroeder 1953a; Cervigón 1966; C. R. Robins et al. 1986.

RHINOPTERIDAE   Cow-nosed rays

The cow-nosed rays are extremely flattened and laterally expanded, with a deeply incised snout and a very slender, long, whiplike tail. They are distinguished from the other families of the order by the following combination of characters. Pectoral fin is greatly expanded and attached to head to form disc. Disc is much broader than it is long. Anterior section of pectoral fin is greatly expanded laterally and extends, with interruption on sides of head, in front of head to form pair of subrostral lobes. Head is elevated from disc, and eye and spiracle are located on side of head. Anterior margin of nostril is greatly expanded into curtain that is continuous across narrow isthmus in front of mouth and covers medial section of nostrils. Nasal curtain is laterally expanded, posteriorly fringed, and not indented at isthmus. Mouth is straight, has transverse, finely fringed curtain on roof, and lacks transverse row of papillae on floor. Teeth are in six to eight series of flattened hexagonal plates. Median series of plates is largest. Posterior margin of spiracle lacks folds and ridges. Pectoral fin extends posteriorly distinctly beyond origin of pelvic fin and dorsally covers most of pelvic fin. Pelvic fin is slightly laterally expanded and is not divided into anterior and posterior lobes. Tail is considerably longer than disc width. Tail has small dorsal fin near base and one or more serrated spines posterior to dorsal fin. Tail lacks caudal fin and longitudinal folds.

Cow-nosed rays occur worldwide in tropical to warm temperate seas. They are most often captured on continental and insular shelves, but also occur in estuaries. Food consists of bivalve mollusks and crustaceans. Development is ovoviviparous. There are about five species in a single genus, and one species occurs in the Gulf of Mexico.

Rhinoptera bonasus (Mitchill 1815)
Cow-nosed ray

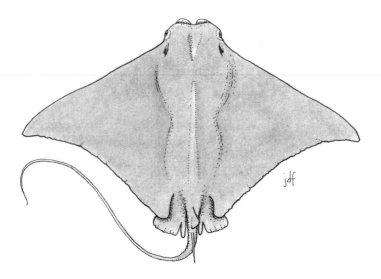

Rhinoptera bonasus has a lozenge-shaped disc; a bilobed snout (subrostral lobes); and a very slender, long, whiplike tail. It is distinguished from the other species of the family by the following combination of characters. Snout is bilobed and short (preorbital length is 2% of disc width [DW]). Disc is 1.7 times as broad as it is long. Anterior margins of disc, on either side of snout, are straight to weakly concave, outer corners are acutely angled, and posterior margins are concave. Teeth are normally in seven series of plates, but occasionally are in six or eight series. Plates of median series are twice as wide as those of adjacent series and 3 to 5 times as wide as those of outer series. Origin of dorsal fin is above axil of pelvic fin. Length of base of dorsal fin is about equal to distance between exposed nostrils. Body is naked. Color is brownish dorsally and white to yellowish white ventrally.

This species occurs in the western Atlantic from southern New England to southern Brazil, including the Gulf of Mexico and Cuba. It is most frequently encountered close to shore. Food consists of bivalve and gastropod mollusks, and crustaceans. Litters range from two to six young. Maximum known size is 91 cm DW; females mature at 78 cm DW, and young are 15 to 21 cm DW at birth.

REFERENCES: Bigelow and Schroeder 1953a; Hoese and Moore 1977; Snelson and Williams 1981; Smith and Merriner 1985, 1986, 1987; C. R. Robins et al. 1986; Schwartz 1990.

MOBULIDAE   Manta rays

Manta rays are greatly flattened and laterally expanded, with a broad head laterally connected to cephalic fins and a very slender, long, whiplike tail. They are distinguished from the other families of the order by the following combination of characters. Snout is very broad, straight to slightly convex, and very short. Head is slightly elevated but distinct from disc. Pectoral fin is greatly expanded and attached to head to form disc. Disc is much broader than it is long and relatively thin at margin. Anterior section of pectoral fin forms narrow, vertically oriented lobe (cephalic fin), is attached to side of head, and is separated from main section of pectoral fin. Anterior margin of nostril is greatly expanded into curtain that is continuous across broad isthmus in front of mouth and covers medial portion of nostrils. Mouth is moderately subterminal to terminal and broad to very broad. Roof of mouth has a transverse curtain, and roof and floor of mouth lack papillae. Teeth are present on either both jaws or on one jaw only. Spiracle is located posterior to eye on side of head, is smaller than eye, and is preceded by a groove. Gill slits are equal to one-third to one-half of mouth width. Inner sides of gill slits are covered by lamellae or gill plates attached to gill arches. Pectoral fin extends posteriorly to posterior margin of pelvic fin. Pelvic fin is slightly laterally expanded and is not divided into anterior and posterior lobes. Tail is distinct from body, very slender, and from moderately long to very long. Tail has small dorsal fin near base and either has or lacks one to several serrated spines posterior to dorsal fin. Caudal fin and longitudinal folds are absent from tail.

Manta rays occur worldwide in tropical to warm temperate seas. They are generally encountered near the surface over or near continental and insular shelves. Food consists of small planktonic and nektonic crustaceans and fishes, which are guided into the mouth by means of the cephalic fins as the ray moves through the water. In the mouth the organisms are strained from the water by means of lamellae or gill plates located on the medial sides of the gill slits. Development is ovoviviparous. There are about 13 species in 2 genera, and 3 species in 2 genera occur in the Gulf of Mexico.

Key to the Species of the Gulf of Mexico
(Adapted from Notabartolo-di-Sciara 1987a,b)

1a.   Mouth terminal; teeth on lower jaw only
. . . . *Manta birostris* p. 184
1b.   Mouth subterminal; teeth present on both jaws 2
2a.   Branchial filter plates fused . . . . *Mobula tarapacana* p. 196
2b.   Branchial filter plates separate
. . . . *Mobula hypostoma* p. 195

Manta birostris   (Walbaum 1792)
Atlantic manta

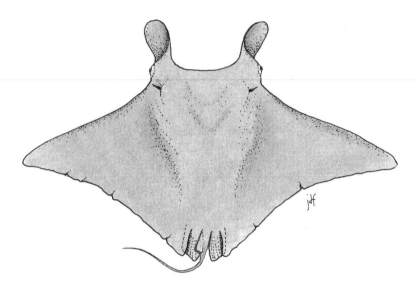

Manta birostris has a lozenge-shaped disc; a very broad head bordered by large cephalic fins; and a very slender, relatively short, whip-like tail. It is distinguished from the other species of the family by the following combination of characters. Head is relatively broad, and anterior margin of snout between cephalic fins is concave. Cephalic fins are about one-half as broad at base as they are long. Nasal curtain is rectangular, with rounded corners and a smooth posterior margin. Mouth is terminal, but lower jaw is somewhat projecting. Teeth are present only on lower jaw, and are in about 270 series in quincunx arrangement. Dorsal fin originates slightly anterior to axil of pectoral fin. Dorsal fin base is about one-third of mouth width. Serrated spines are either present or absent on tail. Body is covered with small denticles or tubercles. Color is reddish, olivaceous brown, or black dorsally and white ventrally. Dorsal surface is either plain colored or patterned with white spots, patches, or chevrons, and ventral surface varies from plain to blotched with gray.

This species occurs worldwide in tropical to warm temperate seas. The Atlantic manta generally is encountered near the surface over or near continental and insular shelves. In the western Atlantic it occurs from southern New England and Georges Bank (rare), and North Carolina to central Brazil, including the Gulf of Mexico, Bermuda, the Bahamas, and the Antilles. It is abundant over much of the year in the western Gulf around the Flower Gardens Reefs (Jeff Childs, pers. com., July 1996). Food consists of planktonic and nektonic crustaceans and fishes. Litter size is unknown. Maximum known size is 430 to 460 cm DW; young are 120 cm DW at birth.

REFERENCES: Bigelow and Schroeder 1953a; Cervigón 1966; Böhlke and Chaplin 1968; Hoese and Moore 1977; C. R. Robins et al. 1986; Notabartolo-di-Sciara and Hillyer 1989.

Mobula hypostoma (Bancroft 1831)
Devil ray

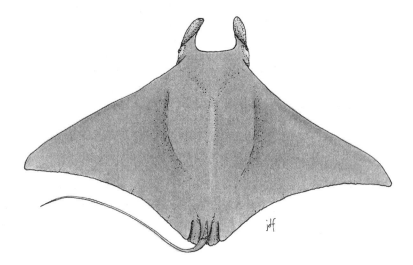

Mobula hypostoma has a lozenge-shaped disc; a relatively narrow head bordered by moderate-sized cephalic fins; and a very slender, relatively long, whiplike tail. It is distinguished from the other species of the family by the following combination of characters. Head is relatively narrow; anterior margin of snout, between cephalic fins, is slightly concave. Distance from tip of cephalic fin to spiracle is more than 13.4% of disc width (DW). Nasal curtain is rectangular, with corners forming right angles, and posterior margin is smooth. Mouth is subterminal and slightly arched. Teeth are present in both jaws but occupy less than 55% of upper jaw and less than 52% of lower jaw. Upper and lower jaws have 36 to 72 and 38 to 58 tooth rows respectively. Teeth of females and juveniles have oval, diamond-shaped, or rectangular-shaped bases and rounded cusps. Teeth of mature males have bases similar to those of females but have one to three long, pointed cusps. Branchial filter plates are not fused and have acorn-shaped terminal lobes, which are fused to distalmost lateral lobes. Lateral lobes of branchial filter plates are densely covered with denticles. Distance between first gill slits is about 14% of DW. Dorsal fin base is slightly less than one-half mouth width. Tail lacks serrated spines. Body is covered with denticles except for tail posterior to dorsal fin. Color is blackish brown dorsally and yellowish or grayish white ventrally.

This species occurs in the western Atlantic from Cape Lookout, North Carolina, to Mar del Plata, Argentina, including the Gulf of Mexico and the Antilles. It is generally encountered near the surface over continental and insular shelves. Food consists of small pelagic crustaceans and fishes. Little is known of its reproductive biology beyond an account of a pregnant female with a single embryo. Maximum known size is 120 cm DW; males mature at 114 cm DW, females mature at 111 cm DW, and young are 55 cm DW at birth.

REFERENCES: Bigelow and Schroeder 1953a; C. R. Robins et al. 1986; Notabartolo-di-Sciara 1987a,b; Notabartolo-di-Sciara and Hillyer 1989.

Mobula tarapacana   (Philippi 1893)

Mobula tarapacana has a lozenge-shaped disc; a narrow head bordered by moderate-sized cephalic fins; an elongated neck; and a moderately long, whiplike tail. It is distinguished from the other species of the family by the following combination of characters. Head is relatively narrow, and anterior margin of snout, between cephalic fins, is lunate. Distance from tip of cephalic fins to spiracle is 16% to 21.9% of disc width (DW). Nasal curtain is rectangular, with posterior margin slightly concave and partially overlapping upper tooth band. Mouth is subterminal and slightly arched. Teeth are present in both jaws and occupy 69% to 71% of jaw length. Upper and lower jaws have 94 to 135 and 107 to 153 tooth rows respectively. Teeth are large, with subhexagonal and pitted crowns, and buccal margin is comblike. Spiracle is located in elongated horizontal slit, above plane of pectoral fins. Branchial filter plates are fused together along their lateral edges, and terminal lobes have broadly rounded apical margins. Distance between first gill slits is 8.7% to 10.3% of DW, and distance between fifth gill slits is 3.8% to 4.7% of DW. Dorsal fin base origin is posterior to axil of pectoral fin, and length is slightly less than one-half mouth width. Tail lacks serrated spine. Body is densely covered with denticles. Dorsal surface is brown to olivaceous green, and ventral surface is white anteriorly and gray posteriorly with distinct line of demarcation.

This species occurs worldwide in tropical seas. In the western Atlantic it occurs in the southern Caribbean Sea and has recently been reported from the Flower Gardens Reefs in the western Gulf of Mexico (Jeff Childs, pers. com., July 1996). Food consists of copepods, hiperiid amphipods, brachiurans, euphausids, caridean shrimps, and fishes. Maximum known size is 305 cm DW.

References: Notabartolo-di-Sciara 1987a,b; Notabartolo-di-Sciara and Hillyer 1989.

ACIPENSERIFORMES

This order and the Polypteriformes constitute the only living representatives of the Chondrostei, the sister group of the remainder of the Actinopterygii (ray-finned fishes). The Acipenseriformes include two families, and one of these occurs in the Gulf of Mexico.

ACIPENSERIDAE   Sturgeons

Sturgeons are elongate, moderately slender, and robust, with a semiconical or depressed snout and a heterocercal caudal fin. They are distinguished from the other family of the order by the following combination of characters. Snout is moderately long to long. Mouth is inferior and preceded by four barbels in transverse series. Jaws are protrusible and lack teeth in adults. Spiracle is present or absent. Gill arches are covered by suboperculum; operculum is absent. First pectoral ray is ossified. Dorsal fin and anal fin are posterior to pelvic fin. Caudal fin has fleshy axis extending obliquely upward to near tip of fin. Dorsal lobe of caudal fin is longer than ventral lobe and tapers to acute tip. Ventral lobe of caudal fin has broadly rounded posterior margin. Body is covered with five rows of bony scutes. Dorsal margin of caudal fin has row of spinelike scales (fulcral scales).

Sturgeons are widespread in the Northern Hemisphere, with species either limited to freshwater or anadromous. Food consists mostly of benthic invertebrates, including polychaete and oligochaete worms, mollusks, insects, and crustaceans, but they occasionally eat fishes, birds, and newborn seals. Embryonic development is oviparous, and spawning takes place in freshwater or brackish water during the spring. Eggs are large, at least 2.5 mm in diameter, demersal, and adhesive. Fecundity varies with size and with species and may exceed seven million eggs in large specimens. There are 24 species in 4 genera, and 1 species occurs in the Gulf of Mexico.

Acipenser oxyrhynchus   Mitchill 1815
Atlantic sturgeon

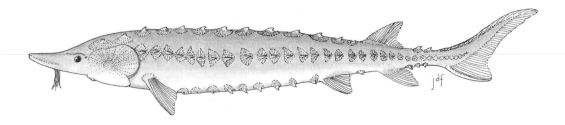

Acipenser oxyrhynchus is elongate, moderately slender, and robust, with a semiconical snout and a moderately elevated heterocercal caudal fin. It is distinguished from the other species of the family by the following combination of characters. Snout is slightly longer than one-half head length. Head length is 31% to 34% of FL (distance from tip of snout to posterior end of median fin rays). Four long, slender barbels are located at midlength of ventral snout in transverse series. Spiracle is present between eye and dorsal margin of suboperculum. Gill membranes are joined to isthmus. Gill rakers on first arch range from 18 to 20. Bony scutes are strongly developed; those of dorsal row are squarish, broader than long, and possess keel bearing two strong hooks. Skin between dorsal and lateral rows of scutes bears dermal ossifications. Preanal scutes are in double row. Color is bluish black dorsally, grading to whitish ventrally. Median part of scutes in dorsal row is white.

This species occurs in the western North Atlantic from Labrador to St. Johns River, Florida, and from the Suwannee River, Florida, to the Mississippi River in the Gulf of Mexico. It was recorded from Bermuda and from French Guiana over one hundred years ago. The Gulf of Mexico population is considered a separate subspecies (*A. oxyrhynchus desotoi*) and apparently spawns in the Mississippi River and other rivers flowing into the northeastern Gulf of Mexico. The Gulf subspecies is apparently limited to inshore waters of the northeastern Gulf of Mexico. The Atlantic subspecies feeds on benthic invertebrates, which it roots out of the bottom with its snout. Prey include polychaetes, chironomid larvae, isopods, amphipods, bivalve mollusks, shrimps, and small fishes. Fecundity ranges from 800,000 to 2,400,000 eggs. Maximum known size is 310 cm TL. Recorded lengths of the Gulf of Mexico subspecies range from 50 to 60 cm FL.

REFERENCES: Vladykov 1955; Vladykov and Greeley 1963; Huff 1975; Hoese and Moore 1977; Lee et al. 1980; Wooley 1985; Wooley and Crateau 1985; C. R. Robins et al. 1986; Bowen and Avise 1990; Boschung 1992.

SEMIONOTIFORMES

Semionotiformes are generally considered to be the sister group of the remainder of Neopterygii, although the evidence is somewhat equivocal. There is a single extant family, and it occurs in the Gulf of Mexico.

LEPISOSTEIDAE   Gars

Gars are elongate, moderately slender to slender, and robust, with an elongated, conical snout and an abbreviated heterocercal caudal fin. They are distinguished from the other families of fishes by the following combination of characters. Nasal openings and sac are located at end of snout. Both jaws bear small-, medium-, and large-sized teeth. Upper jaw has two rows of enlarged teeth, and lower jaw has single row. Outer margins of upper and lower jaws have row of needlelike teeth. Pectoral fin is located low on flank immediately posterior to opercular opening. Pelvic fin is located at about midlength of body. Single dorsal fin is located above anal fin just anterior to caudal peduncle. Fins lack spines, and rays of dorsal and anal fins are equal to number of supporting radials. Fleshy axis of caudal fin extends obliquely upward only slightly distal to base of tail. Dorsal margin of caudal fin is covered with fulcral scales. Body of adults is covered with rhombic ganoid scales. Scales are diagonally attached to one another by peg-and-socket articulations. Ganoin also covers dermal bones of head. Anus is bordered by three modified scales.

Gars are currently limited to North American waters, although fossil specimens are known from Europe, India, and Africa. They are considered freshwater fishes, but several species are occasionally caught in brackish or marine waters. Food consists mostly of fishes. Embryonic development is oviparous, and spawning takes place in freshwater. Eggs are negatively buoyant and adhesive and adhere to the bottom. Yolk sac larvae remain attached to the bottom by means of adhesive suckers attached to the tip of the lower jaw. There are seven species in two genera, and three species in the two genera occur in the Gulf of Mexico.

Key to the Species of the Gulf of Mexico
(Adapted from Suttkus 1963)

1a. Gill rakers large and laterally compressed; 59 to 66 gill rakers on first gill arch; palatines (bones immediately medial to upper jaw) of mature specimens with fanglike teeth. *Atractosteus spatula* p. 201

1b. Gill rakers small and pear shaped; 14 to 33 gill rakers on first gill arch; palatines of adult specimens without fanglike teeth. 2

2a. Snout length 79% to 83% of dorsal head length; outer tooth row of premaxilla with two or four teeth
. . . . *Lepisosteus osseus* p. 203

2b. Snout length less than 75% of dorsal head length; outer tooth row of premaxilla with one tooth
. . . . *Lepisosteus oculatus* p. 202

Atractosteus spatula (Lacepède 1803)
Alligator gar

Atractosteus spatula is moderately slender and robust, with a relatively short, broad snout and a relatively broad, fanlike caudal fin. It is distinguished from the other species of the family by the following combination of characters. Snout is 16% to 21% of SL (distance from tip of snout to last scale at dorsal base of tail). Snout width is 5% to 7% of SL. Large fanglike teeth are present on palatines (bones lining lateral aspect of roof of mouth). Gill rakers on first arch are relatively large and laterally compressed and range from 59 to 66. Interorbital distance is 7% to 9% of length. Lateral line scales range from 58 to 62, diagonal scale rows between insertion of pelvic fin and origin of dorsal fin number 34 to 38, and predorsal scales number 49 to 54. Color is olivaceous brown dorsally and whitish ventrally. Specimens 50 mm SL have light median dorsal stripe from tip of snout to origin of dorsal fin and from insertion of dorsal fin to base of caudal fin. Dorsal stripe is bordered on either side by broad dark brown stripe from posterior margin of eye to base of caudal fin. Specimens larger than 50 mm SL but less than 500 mm SL have numerous dark spots on sides of body.

This species occurs in the lower reaches of the Missouri, Ohio, and Mississippi Rivers; along the coast of the Gulf of Mexico from Veracruz to Choctawhatchee Bay, Florida; and from inland and coastal waters of Nicaragua and Costa Rica. Food consists of blue crabs, various fishes (including striped mullet), and water birds (including ducks and water turkey). Little is known about its reproductive biology, but in Louisiana it apparently spawns in the spring and summer. Maximum known size is over 300 cm SL.

REFERENCES: Gunter 1945; Suttkus 1963; Wiley 1976; Hoese and Moore 1977; Lee et al. 1980; Boschung 1992.

Lepisosteus oculatus (Winchell 1864)
Spotted gar

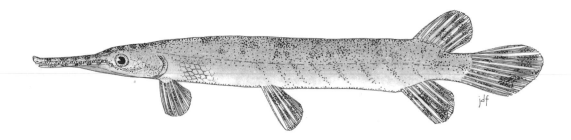

Lepisosteus oculatus is moderately slender and robust, with a moderately long, broad snout and a relatively broad, fan-shaped caudal fin. It is distinguished from the other species of the family by the following combination of characters. Snout is 16% to 23% of SL (distance from tip of snout to last scale at dorsal base of caudal fin). Snout width is 4% to 5% of SL. Large fanglike teeth are absent on palatines (bones lining lateral aspects of roof of mouth). Outer tooth row of premaxillary has single tooth. Gill rakers on first arch are relatively small and pear shaped and range from 15 to 24. Interorbital distance is 5% to 6% of length. Lateral line scales range from 53 to 59, diagonal scale rows between insertion of pelvic fin and origin of dorsal fin number 27 to 32, and predorsal scale rows number to 54. Color varies in intensity, generally is dark dorsally and light ventrally. Young have complete flank stripe running from lower jaw through eye to base of tail. Stripe joins with preopercular stripe on lower jaw.

Flank stripe is usually broken into series of blotches in adults. Head is pigmented with many large, dark blotches dorsally. Dark belly stripes run along each side to anal fin, where they join and run to base of caudal fin. Occasionally adults have uniformly dark bellies.

This species occurs in eastern North America from the Great Lakes southward in the Mississippi and other Gulf of Mexico drainages from western Florida (Choctawhatchee River) to central Texas (Copano Bay). It occurs in brackish waters of the Gulf of Mexico. Food consists of crustaceans (including blue crabs) and bony fishes. Little is known about its reproductive biology other than that it spawns in shallow water containing rooted aquatic vegetation. Maximum known size is 85 cm FL.

REFERENCES: Gunter 1945 (as *L. productus*); Suttkus 1963; Carlander 1969; Wiley 1976; Hoese and Moore 1977; Lee et al. 1980; Boschung 1992.

Lepisosteus osseus (Linnaeus 1758)
Longnose gar

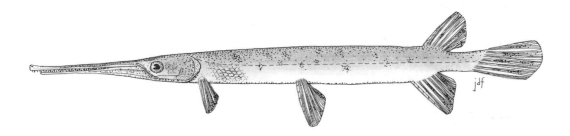

Lepisosteus osseus is slender and robust, with an extremely long and needlelike snout and a moderately broad, fan-shaped caudal fin. It is distinguished from the other species of the genus by the following combination of characters. Snout is 21% to 29% of SL (distance from tip of snout to last scale at dorsal base of caudal fin). Snout width is 3% to 4% of SL. Large fanglike teeth are absent on palatines (bones lining lateral aspects of roof of mouth). Outer tooth row of premaxillary has two to four teeth. Gill rakers on first arch are relatively small and pear shaped and range from 14 to 31. Interorbital distance is 4% to 5% of length and 11% to 13% of head length. Lateral line scales range from 57 to 63, diagonal scale rows from insertion of pelvic fin to origin of dorsal fin number 31 to 35, and predorsal scales number 47 to 55. Color varies with habitat but is generally olivaceous brown dorsally and whitish ventrally. Dark spots on body and fins are clearly defined on specimens from clear water but less defined on those from murky waters. Juveniles have mid-dorsal stripe, flank stripe from eye to base of caudal fin, and belly stripe. All stripes are dusky to dark brown. In adults dorsal stripe is missing, and flank stripes are missing or reduced to series of dark blotches.

This species occurs in North America along the eastern seaboard from Quebec to Florida, from the Great Lakes southward in the Mississippi River drainage, and in the Gulf of Mexico drainages to the northern Gulf coast from Texas to Florida. It is occasionally caught in marine coastal waters. Food consists of crustaceans (such as blue crabs) and bony fishes, including menhaden, anchovies, and sea catfishes. Spawning occurs during the late spring and summer in freshwater. Maximum known size is 150 cm TL.

REFERENCES: Suttkus 1963; Carlander 1969; Wiley 1976; Hoese and Moore 1977; Lee et al. 1980; Boschung 1992.

ELOPIFORMES

Elopiformes, Albuliformes, Notacanthiformes, Anguilliformes, and Saccopharyngiformes make up the Elopomorpha. Elopiformes are generalized and may be the sister group of the remainder of the Elopomorpha. The order includes two families, and both occur in the Gulf of Mexico.

Key to the Families of the Gulf of Mexico

1a. Body robust, slightly compressed; branchiostegal rays 27 to 35; dorsal fin rays 20 to 25; last dorsal fin ray not elongated . . . . Elopidae p. 204
1b. Body compressed; branchiostegal rays 23 to 27; dorsal fin rays 13 to 21; last dorsal fin ray elongated . . . . Megalopidae p. 206

ELOPIDAE Ladyfishes

Ladyfishes are elongate, slender, and robust, with a terminal mouth and a deeply forked caudal fin. They are distinguished from the other family of the order by the following combination of characters. Snout is moderately long. Head is moderately short and shallow. Mouth is slightly oblique and terminal. Both premaxilla and maxilla bear small teeth in upper jaw. Maxilla extends posterior to eye. Gular plate, located between limbs of lower jaw, is well developed. Eye is near dorsal profile of anterior one-half of head. Interorbital region is flat. Pectoral fin is located low on flank immediately posterior to opercular opening. Dorsal fin originates just posterior to midlength, is high anteriorly, and has strongly concave dorsal margin. Last ray of dorsal fin is not elongated. Pelvic fin originates ventral to, or slightly posterior to, origin of dorsal fin. Anal fin originates behind dorsal fin base and is similar in shape but smaller than dorsal fin. Caudal fin is high and deeply forked. Scales are small and form sheath on base of dorsal and anal fins. Lateral line is straight and extends onto base of caudal fin.

Ladyfishes occur worldwide in tropical to warm temperate seas. They are pelagic marine fishes but enter brackish waters. Food consists of crustaceans (such as shrimps) and bony fishes. Spawning occurs offshore and development is oviparous. Embryos develop into leptocephalous larvae, which are elongate, ribbon-like, transparent to slightly translucent, and have a long fin fold and a forked tail. There are six species in one genus, and one species occurs in the Gulf of Mexico.

Elops saurus Linnaeus 1766
Ladyfish

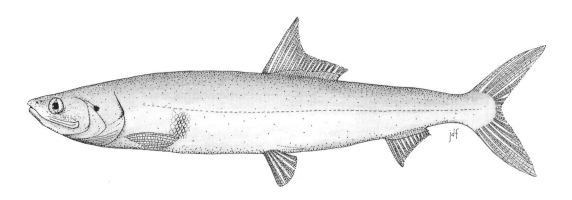

Elops saurus is elongate, slender, and robust, with a terminal mouth and a large, deeply forked caudal fin. It is distinguished from the other species of the family by the following combination of characters. Snout ranges from 6% to 7% of SL and is slightly longer than eye diameter. Branchiostegal rays vary from 26 to 32. Gill rakers are about two-thirds eye diameter and range from 6 to 8 and 10 to 15 on upper and lower limbs of first arch. Dorsal fin originates slightly posterior to origin of pelvic fin and has 21 to 25 rays. Anal fin originates about midway between origin of dorsal fin and origin of caudal fin and has 14 to 17 rays. Vertebrae range from 73 to 80, and lateral scale rows vary from 103 to 120. Axillary scales occur at base of pectoral and pelvic fins, and that at base of pectoral fin extends to about mid-length of fin. Color is silvery bluish to greenish dorsally and silvery laterally and ventrally. Dorsal and caudal fins are dusky, and pectoral, pelvic, and anal fins are pale.

This species occurs in the western North Atlantic from Cape Cod to Rio de Janeiro, Brazil, including Bermuda, the Gulf of Mexico, and the Antilles. It is common inshore and in bays, lagoons, and mangrove habitats. Food consists of crustaceans (including shrimps) and small bony fishes, including members of its own species and silversides. Spawning occurs offshore year-round. Leptocephalous larvae have a triangular snout and from 74 to 83 total myomeres, 66 to 77 preanal myomeres, and 59 to 66 predorsal myomeres between lengths of 14.3 to 38.3 mm SL. Larvae go through two phases of rapid growth separated by a stage of length decrease. Smallest known juvenile is 35 mm SL. Maximum known size is 91 cm TL.

REFERENCES: Gunter 1945; Whitehead 1962; Hildebrand 1963a; Eldred and Lyons 1966; Hoese and Moore 1977; Jones et al. 1978a; Lee et al. 1980; C. R. Robins et al. 1986; Boschung 1992.

MEGALOPIDAE Tarpons

Tarpons are elongate, moderately slender, and compressed, with a superior mouth and a deeply forked caudal fin. They are distinguished from the other family of the order by the following combination of characters. Snout is moderately long. Mouth is superior. Head is moderately short and deep. Both premaxilla and maxilla of upper jaw bear teeth. Maxilla extends posterior to eye. Gular plate, between arms of lower jaw, is well developed. Eye is near dorsal profile of anterior one-half of head. Gill membranes are free of isthmus. Pectoral fin is located low on flank immediately posterior to opercular opening. Pelvic fin originates anterior to or below dorsal fin origin. Dorsal fin originates just posterior to midlength, about midway between anterior margin of eye and base of caudal fin. Dorsal fin is high anteriorly, has strongly concave dorsal margin, and in specimens greater than 100 mm TL, last ray is elongated. Anal fin originates posterior to dorsal fin base, has strongly concave ventral margin, and in adults, last ray is elongated. Caudal fin is high and deeply forked. Scales are large, extend onto base of anal and caudal fins but not onto base of dorsal fin. Lateral line is decurved and has branched tubes.

Tarpons occur worldwide in tropical to warm temperate seas. They are coastal fishes that are also captured in brackish water and, occasionally, freshwater. Food consists of bony fishes. Spawning apparently takes place offshore. Development is oviparous, and embryos develop into leptocephalous larvae, which are elongate, ribbonlike, and transparent or slightly translucent, with a long fin fold and a forked tail. There are two species in a single genus, and one occurs in the Gulf of Mexico.

Megalops atlanticus Valenciennes 1847
Tarpon

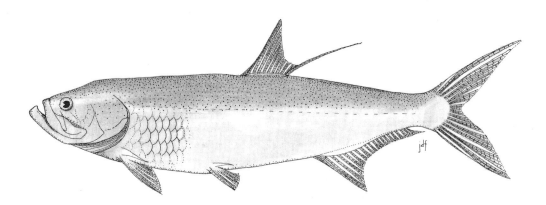

Megalops atlanticus is elongate, moderately slender, and compressed, with a superior mouth and a deeply forked caudal fin. It is distinguished from the other species of the family by the following combination of characters. Snout is 5% to 6% of SL and less than eye diameter in smaller specimens but greater than eye diameter in larger specimens. Branchiostegal rays number 23 to 27. Gill rakers are long and slender and range from 19 to 21 and 36 to 40 on the upper and lower limbs of first gill arch. Axil of pelvic fin is anterior to origin of dorsal fin. Dorsal fin originates about midway between anterior margin of eye and base of caudal fin and has 13 to 16 rays. Anal fin originates posterior to dorsal fin base and has 22 to 25 rays. Vertebrae range from 53 to 57, and lateral scale rows number 41 to 48. Single axillary scales occur at base of pectoral and pelvic fins; those at base of pectoral fin are about one-third length of fin. Color is silvery bluish or greenish dorsally and silvery laterally and ventrally.

This species occurs in the tropical to warm temperate waters of the Atlantic. In the western Atlantic it occurs from Nova Scotia to Brazil, including Bermuda, the Gulf of Mexico, the Bahamas, and the Antilles. It is an inshore marine species but also occurs in fresh and brackish waters. Young specimens are more common in fresh and brackish waters than are adults. Food of adults consists exclusively of fishes, such as anchovies, silversides, cutlassfishes, and mullets; while young feed on insects, copepods, ostracods, and shrimps, in addition to fishes. Spawning takes place offshore during the late spring and summer in the Gulf of Mexico. Leptocephalous larvae have a triangular snout and 54 to 57 total myomeres, 40 to 43 preanal myomeres, and 37 to 42 predorsal myomeres at 9.4 to 22 mm SL. Larvae have two periods of rapid length increase separated by a stage of length decrease. Smallest known juvenile is 25.2 mm SL. Maximum known size is about 240 cm TL.

REFERENCES: Gunter 1945; Wade 1962; Hildebrand 1963a; Hoese and Moore 1977; Jones et al. 1978a; Lee et al. 1980; C. R. Robins et al. 1986; Boschung 1992.

ALBULIFORMES

Albuliformes are thought to be the sister group of Notacanthiformes, and the two groups are sometimes placed in the same order. The single family of the order occurs in the Gulf of Mexico.

ALBULIDAE   Bonefishes

Bonefishes are elongate, slender, and slightly compressed, with a conical snout, an inferior mouth, and a deeply forked caudal fin. They are distinguished from the other families of ray-finned fishes by the following combination of characters. Snout is conical and projects anterior to inferior mouth. Mouth is small; maxilla does not extend to front of eye. Only premaxilla of upper jaw bears teeth. Head is moderately short and shallow. Gular plate, between arms of lower jaw, is very slender. Eye is near dorsal profile at about midlength of head. Gill membranes are free of isthmus. Pectoral fin is located low on flank immediately posterior to opercular opening. Origin of dorsal fin is about at midlength. Dorsal fin is high anteriorly and has concave dorsal margin. Pelvic fin originates posterior to origin of dorsal fin. Anal fin is small and originates posterior to dorsal fin base. Caudal fin is high and deeply forked. Scales are of moderate size. Lateral line is straight. Axillary scales occur at base of pectoral and pelvic fins.

Bonefishes occur worldwide in tropical to warm temperate seas. They are coastal fishes, and spawning takes place near shore. Development is oviparous, and embryos develop into leptocephalous larvae, which are elongate, ribbonlike, transparent to slightly translucent, and have a long fin fold and a forked caudal fin. There are six species in two genera, and one species occurs in the Gulf of Mexico.

Albula vulpes   (Linnaeus 1758)
Bonefish

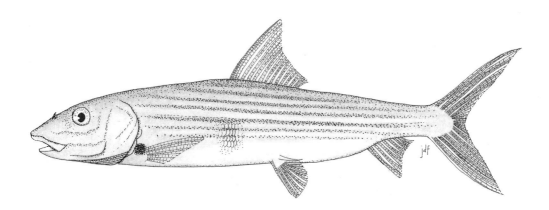

Albula vulpes is elongate, slender, and robust, with a conical snout, an inferior mouth, and a deeply forked caudal fin. It is distinguished from the other species of the family by the following combination of characters. Snout is 12% to 14% of SL and about 2 times eye diameter. Snout projects about one-third of its length beyond symphysis of upper jaw. Maxilla does not extend to eye. Branchiostegal rays number 13 or 14. Gill rakers are very short and stout, and range from 7 to 8 and 9 to 10 on upper and lower limbs of first gill arch. Dorsal fin has 17 or 18 rays, and last ray is not elongated. Anal fin has 8 or 9 rays. Vertebrae range from 72 to 74, and lateral scale rows number from 65 to 71. Axillary scales of pectoral fin are one-half length of fin. Color is silvery bluish or greenish dorsally and bright silvery laterally and ventrally. Tip of snout is blackish.

This species occurs worldwide in tropical to warm temperate seas. In the western Atlantic it occurs from New Brunswick in the Bay of Fundy to Rio de Janeiro, Brazil, including Bermuda, the Gulf of Mexico, the Bahamas, and the Antilles. This is an inshore species but is apparently not common in brackish or freshwater. Food consists of benthic invertebrates (such as polychaetes, bivalve mollusks, squids, shrimps, and crabs) and small fishes. Infaunal prey are obtained by grubbing in soft bottoms. Spawning apparently takes place offshore. Leptocephalous larvae have a small triangular snout and 65 to 73 total myomeres, 62 to 72 preanal myomeres, and 40 to 61 predorsal myomeres. Larvae go through two stages of rapid length increase separated by a stage of length decrease. Smallest known juvenile is 23 mm SL. Maximum known size of adults is 77 cm TL.

REFERENCES: Hildebrand 1963b; Eldred 1967; Richards 1969; Hoese and Moore 1977; C. R. Robins et al. 1986; Boschung 1992.

NOTACANTHIFORMES

The order includes three families, and two of these occur in the Gulf of Mexico.

Key to the Families of the Gulf of Mexico
(Adapted from McDowell 1973)

1a. Teeth on premaxilla and maxilla of upper jaw; sensory canals of head cavernous; dorsal fin rays articulated and dorsal fin relatively short, shorter than length of longest ray . . . . Halosauridae p. 210
1b. Teeth on premaxilla but not on maxilla of upper jaw; sensory canals of head small; dorsal fin rays unarticulated and dorsal fin relatively long . . . . Notacanthidae p. 216

HALOSAURIDAE   Halosaurids

Halosaurids are elongate, slender, and moderately robust, with a spatulate snout projecting beyond mouth and a long, tapering tail without a distinct caudal fin. They are distinguished from the other families of the order by the following combination of characters. Mouth is subterminal, and upper jaw is bordered by premaxilla and maxilla, both of which bear teeth. Maxilla bears posteriorly directed spine on posterior dorsal edge that projects outward and downward when mouth is opened. Sensory canals on head are cavernous. Gill membranes are separate. Branchiostegal membranes are separate and overlapping and are supported by 9 to 23 rays. Eye is degenerate and is covered with transparent window continuous with skin of head. Pectoral fin is high on flank. Pelvic fin is abdominal and is connected basally to other pelvic fin by membrane. Dorsal fin is short and is located anterior to anal fin. Anal fin is long, extending from just posterior to anus to tip of attenuated tail. Lateral line of body is enlarged and cavernous and runs close to ventral profile. Entire body is covered with scales, including bases of dorsal and anal fins. Scales are relatively large and regularly arranged.

Halosaurids are found worldwide in the deep sea, except they are absent in the Arctic and Antarctic Oceans. Although they are rarely captured, they are probably common along the lower slope to the abyss. Food consists of small anthozoans, sipunculids, polychaetes, gastropods, bivalves, squids, crustaceans, and echinoderms. Embryonic development is oviparous. Fertilized eggs develop into leptocephalous (transparent to translucent, ribbonlike) larvae. Larvae are poorly known; those that have been captured came from depths of about 1,100 m and are about 194 mm TL. There are 15 species in 3 genera, and 4 species in 2 genera occur in the Gulf of Mexico.

Key to the Species of the Gulf of Mexico
(Adapted from McDowell 1973; Sulak 1986d)

1a. Vertex of head with scales; one lateral line scale per body scale in longitudinal row 2

1b. Vertex of head without scales; one lateral line scale per every two or three body scales in longitudinal row 3

2a. Maxillary spine separated from blade of maxilla for less than one-half length of blade; lining of mouth pale except for black stripe along inner side of lower jaw, median black spot anterior to tongue, and roof of mouth black . . . . *Halosaurus ovenii* p. 215

2b. Maxillary spine separated from blade of maxilla by fissure greater than one-half length of blade; lining of mouth uniformly black . . . . *Halosaurus guentheri* p. 214

3a. Origin of dorsal fin over pelvic fin base; generally 12 dorsal fin rays, including short, spinelike first ray . . . . *Aldrovandia affinis* p. 212

3b. Origin of dorsal fin posterior to pelvic fin base; generally 11 dorsal fin rays, including short, spinelike first ray . . . . *Aldrovandia gracilis* p. 213

Aldrovandia affinis   (Günther 1877)

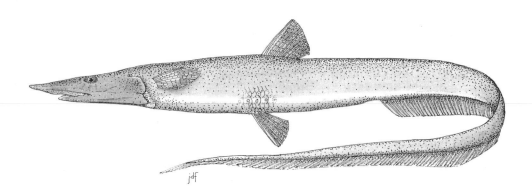

Aldrovandia affinis is elongate, slender, and moderately compressed, with a spatulate, projecting snout and a finely tapering tail. It is distinguished from the other species of the family by the following combination of characters. Preanal body depth is 10% to 12%, head length is 24% to 26%, snout length is 16% to 18%, and preoral snout length is 6% to 9% of gnathoproctal length (distance from tip of lower jaw to anus). Blade of maxilla is not ossified posterior to base of very small maxillary spine; base of spine is continuous with concave posterior margin of maxilla. Lower jaw length is less than distance from jaw articulation to posterior edge of preoperculum. Palatine tooth patches meet on midline. Branchiostegal rays number 10 or 11, and total gill rakers on first arch number 13 to 15. Pelvic fin base is only slightly anterior to dorsal fin origin. Dorsal fin has 11 to 13 rays, and first ray is reduced to short and unarticulated vestige. Modified lateral line scales (placques) are rectangular with rounded corners, and number 25 to 31 from gill cleft to anus. Body is covered with scales.

Head lacks scales except for lateral surface, excluding opercular bones. Color is light brown to nearly white, except for operculum, branchiostegal membranes, sides of body posterior to opercular opening, anal fin base, and midline of belly, which are dark brown to brownish lavender. Lateral line lacks pigment.

This species occurs nearly worldwide with exception of the polar and subpolar regions and the Mediterranean. In the western Atlantic it occurs from New England to the Gulf of Mexico and the Caribbean, and off the coast of South America (24°17′S to 40°48′30″W). Depths of capture range from 878 to 2,560 m. Food consists of polychaetes, bivalves, copepods, decapods, and detritus. Little is known about the reproductive biology other than that embryos develop into leptocephalous larvae. Maximum known size is 200 mm gnathoproctal length.

REFERENCES: Grey 1958; McDowell 1973; M. E. Anderson et al. 1985; Sulak 1986a,d.

Aldrovandia gracilis   Goode and Bean 1896

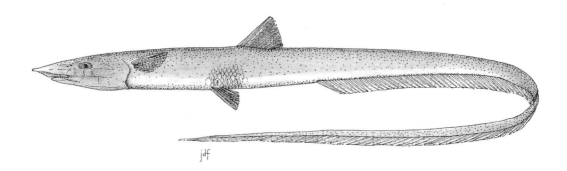

Aldrovandia gracilis is elongate, slender, and moderately compressed, with a spatulate, projecting snout and a finely tapering tail. It is distinguished from the other species of the family by the following combination of characters. Preanal body depth is 7% to 11%, head length is 25% to 32%, snout length is 15% to 20%, and preoral snout length is 5% to 7% of gnathoproctal length (distance from tip of lower jaw to anus). Blade of maxilla is not ossified posterior to base of very small maxillary spine; base of spine is continuous with concave posterior margin of maxilla. Lower jaw length is less than distance from jaw articulation to posterior edge of preoperculum. Palatine tooth patches do not meet on midline. Branchiostegal rays number 10 or 11, and total gill rakers on first arch number 14 to 16. Pelvic fin base is distinctly anterior to base of dorsal fin. Dorsal fin has 10 to 12 rays, and the first ray is short and unsegmented. Modified lateral line scales (placques) are in shape of vertical ovals and number 13 to 19 from gill cleft to anus. Placques are separated by one or two pairs of normal scale rows (one dorsal and one ventral to placque). Body is covered with scales. Head lacks scales except for lateral surface, excluding opercular bones. Color is grayish white to pale grayish tan except for snout, which is white; head, which is dark bluish; and sheath of lateral line, which is transparent.

This species occurs in the western North Atlantic from the Gulf of Mexico and the Caribbean Sea between 640 and 2,615 m. In the Gulf of Mexico it has not been reported west of Mobile, Alabama. Food consists of polychaetes, molluscan veligers, crustaceans, and detritus. Little is known about the reproductive biology of this species other than that embryos develop into leptocephalous larvae. Maximum known size is 210 mm gnathoproctal length.

REFERENCES: Grey 1958; McDowell 1973; M. E. Anderson et al. 1985.

Halosaurus guentheri   Goode and Bean 1896

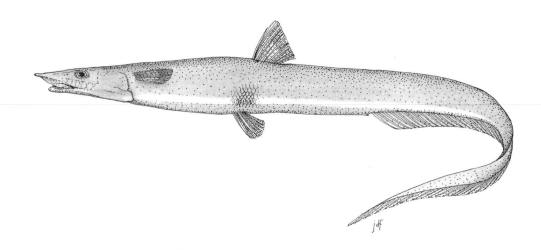

Halosaurus guentheri is elongate, slender, and cylindrical to slightly depressed, with a spatulate, projecting snout and a finely tapering tail. It is distinguished from the other species of the family by the following combination of characters. Preanal body depth is 8% to 12%, head length is 21% to 27%, snout length is 11% to 14%, and preoral snout length is 4% to 6% of gnathoproctal length (distance from tip of lower jaw to anus). Blade of maxilla is ossified posterior to base of large maxillary spine. Maxillary blade and maxillary spine are separated by fissure equal to two-thirds length of blade. Lower jaw is shorter than distance from jaw articulation to posterior edge of preoperculum. Palatine tooth patches meet at midline. Branchiostegal rays number 11 to 14, and total gill rakers on first arch number 11 to 13. Pelvic fin base is anterior to dorsal fin base and has one spine and 8 or 9 rays. Dorsal fin has 10 or 11 rays, and first 1 or 2 are unbranched. Modified lateral line scales (placques) are broader than they are long and number from 57 to 68 from gill cleft to anus. Placques are continuous and equal to number of body myomeres. Body is covered with scales. Top of head anterior to mid-distance between tip of lower jaw and sides of head and operculum are scaled. Color is grayish white with reticular pattern formed by dark spots on scale pockets. Dark spots are more intense dorsally than ventrally. Lateral line canals and mandibular and suborbital canals on head are unpigmented. Lining of mouth and branchial cavities are black.

This species occurs in the North Atlantic. In the western North Atlantic it occurs from New York (Hudson Canyon), the northern Gulf of Mexico, and the Caribbean Sea. It has been captured from 640 to 1,335 m. Food consists of polychaetes, gastropods, bivalves, echinoderms, and crustaceans. Maximum known size is 240 mm gnathoproctal length.

REFERENCE: McDowell 1973.

Halosaurus ovenii   Johnson 1864

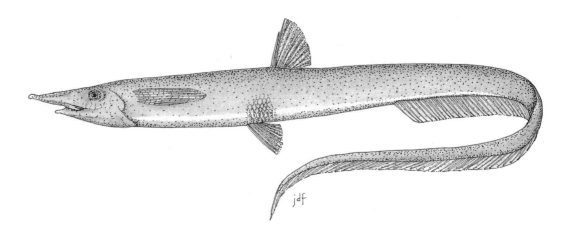

Halosaurus ovenii is elongate, slender, and moderately compressed, with a spatulate, projecting snout and a finely tapering tail. It is distinguished from the other species of the family by the following combination of characters. Preanal body depth is 7% to 13%, head length is 19% to 24%, snout length is 10% to 13%, and preoral snout length is 4% to 6% of gnathoproctal length (distance from tip of lower jaw to anus). Blade of maxilla is ossified posterior to base of large maxillary spine. Maxillary spine and maxillary blade are separated by fissure slightly less than one-half blade length. Lower jaw is shorter than distance from jaw articulation to posterior margin of preoperculum. Palatine tooth patches meet on midline. Branchiostegal rays number 14 to 16, and total gill rakers on first arch number 11 to 14. Pelvic fin base is anterior to dorsal fin base and has one spine and 8 or 9 rays. Dorsal fin has 9 or 10 rays, and first one or two are unbranched. Modified lateral line scales (placques) are slightly broader than they are long and number from 59 to 68 from gill cleft to anus. Placques are continuous and equal in number to body myomeres. Body is covered with scales. Top of head anterior to tip of lower jaw and sides of head and operculum are scaled. Color is pinkish tan, with sides of body and operculum silvery, and belly gray. Posterior one-half of each scale pocket is more pigmented than anterior one-half, forming subtle checkered pattern on back. Lateral line and sensory pores on head are pale. Lining of mouth is colorless except for roof and floor in front of tongue, which have black stripes. Lining of pharynx and branchial cavity are black.

This species occurs in the Atlantic Ocean between 400 and 1,700 m. In the western Atlantic it occurs from the Gulf of Mexico and the Caribbean Sea. Food consists of sipunculids, polychaetes, and crustaceans. Maximum known size is 450 to 500 mm TL, 180 mm gnathoproctal length.

REFERENCES: McDowell 1973; Sulak 1986a,d.

NOTACANTHIDAE   Notacanthid eels

Notacanthid eels are elongate, moderately deep bodied, and compressed, with a spatulate snout projecting beyond mouth and a long, tapering tail without a distinct caudal fin. They are distinguished from the other families of the order by the following combination of characters. Mouth is subterminal, and upper jaw is formed by premaxilla and maxilla, but maxilla contributes very little to margin of mouth and is toothless. Maxilla has single large, posteriorly directed spine on posterodorsal edge that projects outward and downward when mouth is opened. Sensory canals on head, except for rostral commissure, are of small diameter. Gill membranes are partially restricted. Branchiostegal membranes are fused anteriorly. Eye is degenerate and covered with transparent window continuous with skin of head. Pectoral fin has short, fleshy base and is high on flank. Pelvic fin is abdominal and is connected basally to other pelvic fin by membrane. Dorsal rays are separate and spinelike, except last one, which is divided into spinelike anterior, and raylike posterior, branch. Anal fin consists of anterior spinelike rays that are partially separated from each other, and posterior soft rays that are not branched and are broadly connected to each other. Lateral line of body consists of small pores. Entire body except for snout, lower branchiostegal membrane, and medial part of pectoral fin base is covered with scales. Scales are relatively small.

Notacanthid eels occur worldwide in the deep sea from 125 to 3,500 m just above the substrate. Food consists of bryozoans, hydrozoans, sea anemones, polychaetes, copepods, and amphipods. Embryonic development is oviparous. Fertilized eggs are thought to develop into leptocephalous larvae, but larvae are unknown. There are 10 species in 3 genera, and 2 species in separate genera occur in the Gulf of Mexico.

Key to the Species of the Gulf of Mexico
(Adapted from McDowell 1973; Sulak 1986c)

1a. Dorsal fin with 28 to 36 spines; mandibular, palatine, and premaxillary teeth clawlike
. . . . *Polyacanthonotus merretti* p. 218
1b. Dorsal fin with 6 to 15 spines; premaxillary teeth clawlike, mandibular and palatine teeth needlelike (slender, slightly compressed, and slightly curved)
. . . . *Notacanthus chemnitzii* p. 217

Notacanthus chemnitzii Bloch 1788
Snubnosed spiny eel

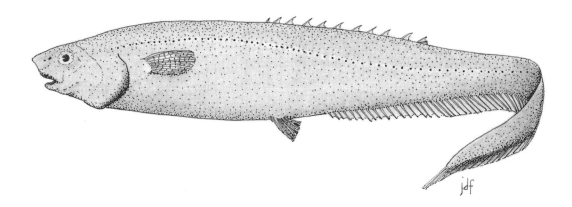

Notacanthus chemnitzii is elongate, moderately deep bodied, and compressed, with a spatulate snout projecting beyond mouth and a long, tapering tail without a distinct caudal fin. It is distinguished from the other species of the family by the following combination of characters. Preanal depth is 25% to 41%, head length is 25% to 35%, and snout length is 1% to 14% of gnathoproctal length (distance from tip of lower jaw to anus). Premaxillary teeth number 19 to 37 and are clawlike, compressed, with tip abruptly expanded, and broader than proximal shaft. Expanded tips of premaxillary teeth are in contact to form continuous cutting edge. Palatine and dentary teeth are needlelike and slightly compressed or curved, and are in two or more complete rows. Palatine tooth patches meet along midline. Posterior end of maxilla is bent ventrally at right angle to remainder of bone. Maxillary spine projects posteriorly from expanded bent part of bone. Branchiostegal rays number 7 to 9, and total gill rakers on first arch number 12 to 17. Pelvic fin base is ventral to first dorsal spine and has one fulcral spine and 9 or 10 rays. Two or 3 pelvic rays are modified into spines. Dorsal fin consists of 9 to 12 independent spines. Lateral line pores number 39 to 54 from gill cleft to level of anus. Color is pale tan or pale gray to dark brown, with lips, opercular margin, and more posterior part of anal fin nearly black.

This species possibly occurs worldwide, with exception of the tropics, between 128 to 1,001 m. In the western Atlantic it occurs from Labrador to the Gulf of Mexico. Food consists of sea anemones and actinarians. Maximum known size is 1,200 mm TL, 443 mm gnathoproctal length.

REFERENCES: McDowell 1973; Sulak 1986b,c.

Polyacanthonotus merretti   Sulak, Crabtree, and Hureau 1984

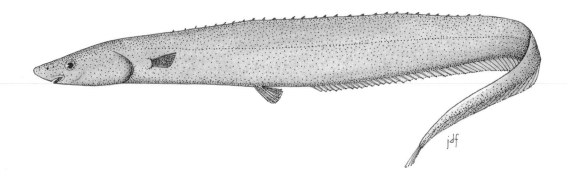

Polyacanthonotus merretti is elongate, moderately slender, and compressed, with a spatulate snout projecting beyond mouth and widely separated anterior and posterior nares. It is distinguished from the other species of the family by the following combination of characters. Posterior border of mouth extends to or beyond anterior margin of eye. Head length is 31% to 41%, predorsal length is 42% to 51%, and preanal length is 104% to 113% of gnathoproctal length (distance from tip of lower jaw to anus). Snout length is 28% to 37%, and eye diameter is 12% to 18% of head length. Internarial distance is 67% to 103% of eye diameter. Premaxillary, palatine, and dentine teeth are clawlike. Palatine tooth patches meet along midline. Maxillary spine projects posteriorly from slightly expanded bent part of maxillary. Branchiostegal rays number 7 or 8. Gill rakers on first arch number 4 or 5 on epibranch and 8 to 14 on lower limb. Pectoral fin is anterior to first dorsal spine and has 8 to 12 rays. Dorsal fin consists of 28 to 36 separate spines. Pelvic fins are nearly separated from each other and bases are posterior to first dorsal spine; each pelvic fin has one or two fulcral spines and 6 to 8 rays. Lateral line pores from gill cleft to anus number from 48 to 56. Total ver-tebrae number 224 to 245, vertebrae to dorsal fin origin number 11 to 16, vertebrae under dorsal fin base number 82 to 91, vertebrae to anal fin origin number 49 to 57, and vertebrae between pectoral fin insertion and dorsal fin origin number 1 to 7. Color is pale bluish gray except for margin of operculum, branchiostegal fold, and inside of mouth, which are black, and posterior section of anal fin, which is dark smoky gray. Mature males have slightly larger nares and eyes than females and immature males, and nares of mature males are dark pigmented but colorless in females and immature males.

This species occurs in the deep waters of the tropical and warm temperate Atlantic from 594 to 2,000 m. In the western Atlantic it occurs from New Jersey to the Guianas, including the Gulf of Mexico, the Bahamas, and the Caribbean Sea. Food consists of hydroids, coelenterates, polychaetes, amphipods, and mysids. Females mature between 84 and 119 mm gnathoproctal length and have between 1,932 and 5,709 eggs. Maximum known size is 119 mm gnathoproctal length or 300 mm TL.

REFERENCES: McDowell 1973 (as *P. africanus*); Sulak et al. 1984; Crabtree et al. 1985.

ANGUILLIFORMES

Interrelationships of the 15 families of the order are poorly known, but as a temporary measure, Robins (1989) recognized three suborders (Anguilloidei, Muraenoidei, and Congroidei). Anguilloidei comprise Anguillidae, Moringuidae, and Heterenchelyidae, and Muraenoidei comprise Myrocongridae, Chlopsidae, and Muraenidae. Both suborders share a primitive osteological character, but there is little evidence to unite them into a monophyletic group. Congroidei are in turn subdivided into three superfamilies, Synaphobranchoidea and Ophichthoidea, each with a single family, and Congroidea, with seven families. Colocongridae, Congridae, Derichthyidae, Muraenoscocidae, Nemichthyidae, Nettastomatidae, and Serrivomeridae are classified within Congroidea. Eleven of the 15 families occur in the Gulf of Mexico.

Key to the Families of the Gulf of Mexico

(Adapted from Robins 1989)

1a. Body very elongate and ribbonlike; anus at throat; jaws either very elongate and nonocclusible distally or very short and beaklike . . . . Nemichthyidae p. 285

1b. Body elongate but not ribbonlike; anus usually posterior to throat (under pectoral fin in some cosmopolitan synaphobranchid species); jaws very elongate to short—if long, occlusible distally 2

2a. Jaws very elongate and slender; maxillary with tiny granular or conical teeth 3

2b. Jaws not elongate and slender; teeth variably developed . . 4

3a. Jaws very slender and fragile; pectoral fin present . . . . Serrivomeridae p. 325

3b. Jaws slender but strong; pectoral fin generally absent—if present, upper jaw projects beyond lower jaw, and dorsal fin originates above opercular openings . . . . Nettastomatidae p. 314

4a. No caudal fin visible externally; dorsal and anal fins not confluent; posterior nostril at rim of mouth and covered by flap . . . . Ophichthidae (in part) p. 251

4b. Caudal fin visible; dorsal, caudal, and anal fins confluent; posterior nostril variously located 5

5a. Anterior branchiostegal rays greatly overlapping those of opposite side, not articulated basally to hyoid arch, branchial region often appearing enlarged or inflated; posterior nostril at rim of mouth in most species . . . . Ophichthidae (in part) p. 251

5b. Anterior branchiostegal rays not overlapping those of opposite side, all at least loosely articulated basally to hyoid arch; posterior nostril variously located 6

6a. Scales present over most of body 7
6b. Head and body naked 8
7a. Jaws equal or upper jaw protruding beyond lower; no
flange on upper lip; gill openings low on body, sometimes
united ventrally; body usually dark brown, with blackish
belly; peritoneum black
. . . . Synaphobranchidae (in part) p. 242
7b. Lower jaw protruding beyond upper; flange on upper lip;
gill openings lateral, extending to level of lower one-half of
pectoral fin; body variously colored, with belly usually pale
. . . . Anguillidae p. 220
8a. Eye generally small to minute, or if well developed, dorsal
and anal fins with high anterior lobe, margin falcate 9
8b. Eye normally developed; margin of dorsal and anal fins not
falcate 10
9a. Vomer and front part of dentary with large compound
teeth . . . . Synaphobranchidae (in part) p. 242
9b. No large compound teeth on vomer or dentary
. . . . Moringuidae p. 223
10a. Pectoral fin absent . . . . Muraenidae p. 228
10b. Pectoral fin present (except in *Heteroconger luteolus*). . . 11
11a. Lateral line incomplete, only one or two pores present in
branchial region. . . . . Chlopsidae p. 226
11b. Lateral line complete, with pores over most of body length
. . . . 12
12a. Body short and stout (depth between 10% and 25% of
TL); anus well behind midlength; most lateral line pores in
short tubes . . . . Colocongridae p. 283
12b. Body elongate (depth usually less than 10% of TL); anus
usually near or anterior to midpoint; lateral line pores not
tubular . . . . Congridae p. 291

ANGUILLIDAE   Freshwater eels

Freshwater eels are moderately elongate and broadly rounded in cross section, with anus slightly anterior to midlength and well-developed dorsal and anal fins confluent with caudal fin. They are distinguished from the other families of the order by the following combination of characters. Snout is moderately short and acute to rounded. Jaws are short, with lower jaw projecting beyond upper. Upper and lower lips have flanges. Jaw teeth are granular and in bands. Vomerine tooth patch is long. Anterior nostril is tubular and near tip of snout. Posterior nostril is round and anterior to midheight of eye. Eye is large. Gill openings are on sides of body and extend dorsally to midbase of pectoral fin. Pectoral fin is well developed and broadly rounded. Dorsal fin originates between gill openings and anus. Pelvic fin is absent. Lateral line is complete on head and trunk. Frontal commissures and adnasal pores are absent. Scales are small and embedded.

Freshwater eels occur in the tropical to temperate waters of the North Atlantic, Indian, and western Pacific Oceans. All species are catadromous and spend most of their lives in freshwater or along the coastline and estuaries. Upon reaching maturity, individuals leave these waters for the open oceans, where spawning takes place. Eggs and larvae (ribbonlike leptocephali) are pelagic in tropical waters for extended periods of time (up to two years in some cases). The leptocephali leave the oceanic currents, undergo metamorphosis, and take up residence in freshwater or inshore brackish to marine waters. Food consists of benthic invertebrates and fishes. The leptocephali are moderate to moderately small (maximum size about 80 mm SL), with body depth about one-fifth SL, gut simple, anus about three-quarters SL, kidney ending behind midpoint of gut, dorsal fin originating slightly before level of anus, and no melanophores on head or body. There are 15 species in one genus, and 1 species occurs in the Gulf of Mexico.

Anguilla rostrata   (Lesueur 1817)
American eel

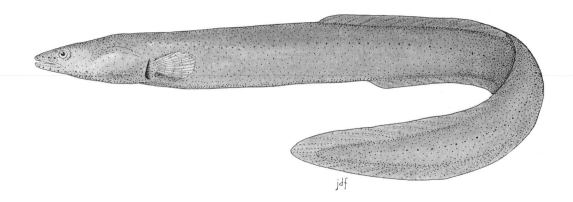

Anguilla rostrata is moderately elongate and broadly rounded in cross section, with large eyes and well-developed pectoral fins. It is distinguished from the other species of the family by the following combination of characters. Snout is 14% to 20%, eye is 9% to 23%, interorbital width is 13% to 21%, and mouth length is 19% to 27% of head length. Head length is 11% to 16%, predorsal length is 32% to 36%, distance between dorsal and anal fin origin is 6% to 12%, and preanal length is 39% to 47% of TL. Jaw teeth are small, granular, and in bands. Intermaxillary tooth patch is continuous with maxillary and vomerine teeth. Vomerine tooth patch is long. Branchiostegal rays number 9 to 13, pectoral fin rays number 14 to 20, and lateral line pores to anus number 31 to 33. Total vertebrae number 103 to 112, and precaudal vertebrae number 41 to 45. Infraorbital pores number four, with first on upper lip behind anterior nostril. Supraorbital pores number four, with first near edge of upper lip. Supratemporal pores are absent. Color is brownish to yellowish green in juveniles and gray to black dorsally and white ventrally in adults.

This species occurs in the western North At-lantic from Greenland to the West Indies, including Bermuda and the Gulf of Mexico. In the Gulf of Mexico it occurs along the northern and eastern coasts to at least Veracruz. This species remains in the larval (leptocephalous) stage for about one year. Metamorphosis into the transparent glass-eel stage occurs near the edge of the continental shelf and lasts until the individuals arrive at their freshwater or coastal habitat. The glass eels transform into elvers with adult coloration. The eels remain in fresh or brackish waters for a variable number of years, during which time they undergo most of their growth. At the end of the growth stage the eels stop feeding and start to mature. At this time they start their migration to the Sargasso Sea, where they spawn. The migration takes place at unknown depths. Maximum known size is 1,500 mm TL; males mature at about 300 to 350 mm TL, and females mature above 400 mm TL.

REFERENCES: Ege 1939; Hoese and Moore 1977; Tesch 1977; Lee et al. 1980; C. R. Robins et al. 1986; Smith 1989a,l; Boschung 1992.

MORINGUIDAE   Spaghetti eels

Spaghetti eels are moderately elongate and cylindrical, with anus near or slightly posterior to midlength, and low dorsal and anal fins confluent with caudal fin. They are distinguished from the other families of the order by the following combination of characters. Snout is conical. Jaws are of moderate length. Upper lip lacks flange, and lower lip has or lacks groove separating it from remainder of lower jaw. Anterior nostril has low tube or lacks tube, and posterior nostril is in front of eye. Eye is generally reduced. Jaw teeth are conical, small to moderately large, and in one or two series. Intermaxillary teeth are arranged in two rows or arches. Vomerine teeth are continuous with maxillary teeth. Gill openings are low on body and separated by isthmus. Pectoral fin is present but small. Dorsal fin originates at or behind midlength. Anal fin originates at or behind anus. Lateral line pores are present on lower jaw and along body to at least origin of anal fin. Pelvic fin and scales are absent.

Spaghetti eels occur worldwide in tropical seas except for the eastern Atlantic. All species burrow headfirst into the bottom. The leptocephali are small (maximum about 60 to 70 mm SL), with body one-quarter to one-third SL, gut moderately short and looped or arched just before anus, one or more expanded melanophores associated with loop or arch, and dorsal fin originating about at level of anus. There are seven species in two genera, and two species in separate genera occur in the Gulf of Mexico.

Key to the Species of the Gulf of Mexico
(Adapted from Smith 1989b)

1a.   Upper jaw extends beyond lower jaw; dorsal fin originates slightly anterior to anus; lateral line terminates near anus
. . . . *Neoconger mucronatus* p. 225
1b.   Lower jaw extends beyond upper jaw; dorsal fin originates posterior to anus; lateral line is complete
. . . . *Moringua edwardsi* p. 224

Moringua edwardsi (Jordan and Bollman 1889)
Spaghetti eel

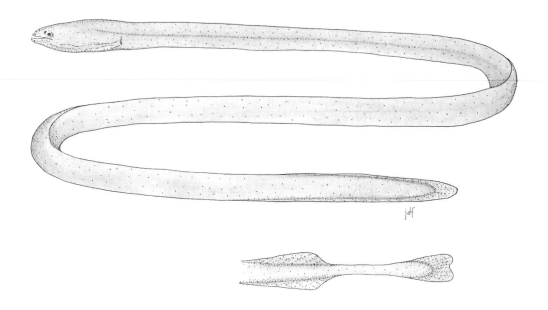

Moringua edwardsi is very elongate and cylindrical, except slightly compressed near tip of tail, with anus located posterior to midlength. It is distinguished from the other species of the family by the following combination of characters. Lower jaw extends beyond upper jaw. Snout is 13% to 16%, eye is 2% to 9%, and mouth length is 14% to 22% of head length. Head length is 7% to 12%, predorsal length is 74% to 78%, distance between anus and anal fin origin is 6% to 10%, and preanal length is 66% to 71% of TL. Jaw teeth are of moderate size, conical, and recurved at tips. Intermaxillary teeth are relatively large and arranged in semicircle of six teeth. Vomerine teeth are smaller than intermaxillary teeth and are arranged in single series. Branchiostegal rays number 11, and lateral line pores to anus number 68 to 75. Lateral line pores are absent on head. Total vertebrae number 109 to 123, predorsal vertebrae number 74 to 84, and preanal vertebrae number 74 to 84. Juveniles are wormlike, with reduced eye buried beneath skin. Mature males and females have large, fully functional eye, and dorsal and anal fins elevated anteriorly and posteriorly. Posterior elongation of fins results in truncated or emarginate tail. Eye and pectoral fin are larger in males than in females. Color in juveniles is uniform yellow to orange dorsally and yellowish white ventrally. Color in adults is dark gray to black dorsally and pale ventrally.

This species occurs in the tropical western Atlantic from Bermuda, the Bahamas, southern Florida to Venezuela, and Bahia, Brazil, including the Gulf of Mexico and the Caribbean Sea. It has been captured from the surface to 22 m and is common in clear water and sandy bottoms. This species is uncommon in the western Gulf of Mexico. Maximum known size is 512 mm TL; males mature at 114 to 149 mm TL, and females mature at 193 to 500 mm TL. Juveniles range from 110 to 150 mm TL (males) and from 200 to 500 mm TL (females). Juveniles are fossorial, and adults are free swimming.

REFERENCES: Böhlke and Chaplin 1968; C. R. Robins et al. 1986; Smith 1989b,i.

Neoconger mucronatus   Girard 1858
Ridged eel

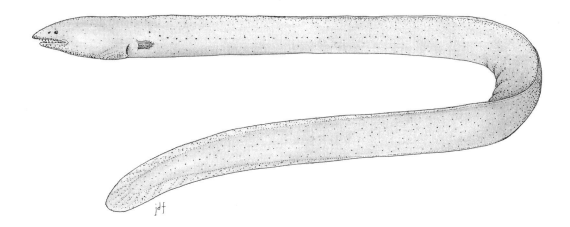

Neoconger mucronatus is moderately elongate and cylindrical, except tip of tail is slightly compressed, with anus near midlength. It is distinguished from the other species of the family by the following combination of characters. Upper jaw extends beyond lower jaw. Snout is 18% to 22%, eye is 3% to 8%, and mouth length is 26% to 35% of head length. Head length is 9% to 11%, predorsal length is 37% to 54%, and preanal length is 48% to 53% of TL. Jaw teeth are of moderate size, conical, recurved at tips, and in one or two series. Intermaxillary teeth are relatively large, in two irregular rows, and continuous with maxillary and vomerine teeth. Vomerine teeth are in single row and extend nearly to posterior end of maxillary teeth. Branchiostegal rays number 18, pectoral fin rays number 15 to 34, and lateral line pores to anus number 21 to 41. Lateral line pores are present on lower jaw and along body to anus. Total vertebrae number 96 to 107, predorsal vertebrae number 32 to 48, preanal vertebrae number 43 to 55, and precaudal vertebrae number 49 to 58. Male specimens have larger eyes, longer pectoral fins, and shorter predorsal and preanal lengths than females. Color is uniform gray to brown, with occasional dark reticulations.

This species occurs in the western Atlantic from the Gulf of Mexico, the Caribbean Sea, and the coast of northern Brazil. It has been captured from 3 to 183 m. Most captures have been on soft mud bottoms. Maximum known size is 302 mm TL.

REFERENCES: Smith and Castle 1972; Hoese and Moore 1977; C. R. Robins et al. 1986; Smith 1989b,i; Boschung 1992.

CHLOPSIDAE False moray eels

False moray eels are moderately elongate and compressed, with anus anterior to midbody, and dorsal, caudal, and anal fins well developed and confluent. They are distinguished from the other families of the order by the following combination of characters. Snout is moderate to short and projects slightly beyond lower jaw. Upper lip lacks upturned flange, and lower lip has or lacks downturned flange. Anterior nostril is tubular and near tip of snout. Posterior nostril opens on lower side of snout, on edge of upper lip, or inside of upper lip. Jaw teeth are small and conical to long and needlelike, and in two or more series. Intermaxillary teeth are in round patch or in several transverse rows. Vomerine teeth are in one or two series. Eye is large. Gill openings are reduced to small porelike openings. Pectoral fin is present or absent. Dorsal fin originates over to slightly behind gill openings. Pelvic fin is absent. Head pores are usually reduced on head to preoperculo-mandibular canal of five to seven pores, infraorbital canal of four pores, and supraorbital canal of three pores. Lateral line pores on trunk are obsolete except for few in branchial region. Scales are absent.

False moray eels occur worldwide in tropical to subtropical waters on continental shelves. Little is known of their biology because of their cryptic habitats. Leptocephali are small to moderate in size (maximum size less than 100 mm SL), with body about one-quarter to one-third as deep as it is long, dorsal fin originating at about anterior one-fifth of length, tail bluntly pointed, gut simple and terminating into anus slightly anterior to midlength, kidney terminating at or just before anus, and pigment consisting of small to moderately large melanophores on midline and often on sides of body. The family contains about 16 species in eight genera, and 1 species occurs in the Gulf of Mexico.

Kaupichthys nuchalis   Böhlke 1967
Collared eel

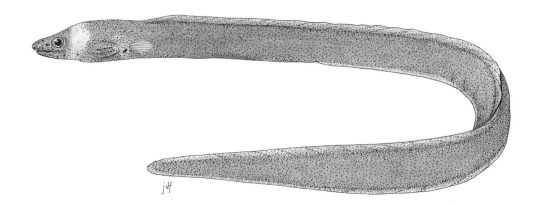

Kaupichthys nuchalis is moderately elongate, with reduced pectoral fins and dorsal fin originating behind gill openings. It is distinguished from the other species of the family by the following combination of characters. Snout is of moderate length and tapers anteriorly. Posterior nostril is above upper lip and is not covered with flap. Snout length is 20% to 24%, eye is 8% to 14%, mouth length is 33% to 40%, and pectoral fin length is 10% to 21% of head length. Head length is 10% to 12%, predorsal length is 11% to 14%, preanal length is 32% to 36%, and depth at anus is 3% to 5% of TL. Teeth in upper jaw are slender and in three or four rows anteriorly and in fewer rows posteriorly, with inner teeth larger than outer teeth. Teeth in lower jaw are slender and in three rows anteriorly and in two rows posteriorly, with inner teeth much larger than outer teeth. Intermaxillary teeth are in round patch. Vomerine teeth are continuous with intermax-illary teeth and in two rows. Lateral line pores are limited to two branchial pores. Branchiostegal rays number eight or nine. Total vertebrae number 119 to 125, predorsal vertebrae number 7 or 8, and preanal vertebrae number 33 to 37. Color is brown, with underside of head and throat pale, and pale area expanded dorsally in nuchal region to form band. Pores are surrounded by pale area.

This species occurs in the western North Atlantic from the northern Gulf of Mexico on the West Flower Gardens Reef off Texas, the Bahamas, and islands of the Caribbean Sea. It has been captured around coral reefs and is thought to live in sponges. It ranges from near shore to 77 m, and possibly from 604 to 732 m. Maximum known size is 163 mm TL.

REFERENCES: Böhlke 1967; Böhlke and Chaplin 1968; Böhlke and Smith 1968; Bright and Cashman 1974; Smith 1989c,o.

MURAENIDAE   Moray eels

Moray eels are moderately slender to relatively stout, with reduced gill openings and without pectoral fins. They are distinguished from the other families of the order by the following combination of characters. Snout is short to relatively long. Anterior
nostril is tubular, and posterior nostril is porelike and located near
upper margin of eye. Jaw teeth are variable, ranging from elongate fangs to molariform. Teeth also occur on ethmovomer (intermaxillary teeth) and upper and lower pharyngeal bones. Opercular bones are reduced. Eye is moderate to large. Gill openings are
located midlaterally. Dorsal, caudal, and anal fins are confluent.
Origin of dorsal fin is generally above or anterior to gill opening,
and origin of anal fin is just behind anus; but occasionally both
fins originate near tip of tail. Head pores are reduced.

Moray eels occur worldwide in tropical to subtropical, and occasionally warm temperate, seas. Most are marine and limited to
shallow-water reef habitats, but some occur in freshwater and
others occur in deep water. All species are benthic as adults. The
leptocephali are small to moderate sized (generally less than 100
mm SL), with body about one-seventh to one-sixth SL; posterior
nostril (when developed) located near upper margin of eye; pectoral fin reduced; caudal fin broadly rounded; gut simple; anus
located at one-half to three-quarters of SL; and pigment, when
present, located on gut, dorsal midline, head, base of fins, and
subcutaneously on underside of dorsal nerve cord. The family
contains about 200 species in more than 15 genera, and 12 species in 5 genera occur in the Gulf of Mexico.

Key to the Species of the Gulf of Mexico
(Adapted from E. Böhlke et al. 1989)

1a. Dorsal and anal fins restricted to tip of tail
. . . . *Anarchias similis* p. 230
1b. Dorsal and anal fins originate near or anterior to anus. . . 2
2a. Some teeth molariform, others conical, none caniniform
. . . . *Echidna catenata* p. 231
2b. No teeth molariform, at least some conical 3
3a. Jaws not curved and elongate, closing completely; inner
row of teeth, if present, not greatly enlarged. 5
3b. Jaws arched and elongate, meeting only at tips; inner row
of teeth elongate fangs 4
4a. Posterior nostril large and elongate (in adults), distinctly
anterior to eye; 2 to 5 inner teeth in lower jaw; color variably patterned or uniformly brown; jaw pores not outlined
with white spots . . . . *Enchelycore nigricans* p. 233

4b. Posterior nostril not elongated, near anterodorsal margin of eye; 6 to 14 inner teeth in lower jaw; color uniformly brown; jaw pores outlined with white spots . . . .*Enchelycore carychroa* p. 232

5a. Posterior nostril tubular, located on anterodorsal margin of eye; teeth in adults uniserial, slender, without serrations; gill openings within black spot . . . . *Muraena retifera* p. 241

5b. Posterior nostril flush or nearly flush with head profile; teeth uniserial or multiserial, with or without serrations; gill openings with body coloration 6

6a. Snout elongate and acute, tapering sharply from bulbous nape; jaws elongate; center of eye slightly anterior to midjaw length; teeth smooth; anterior teeth caniniform 7

6b. Snout short and blunt, not tapering sharply from nape; jaws short; center of eye above or behind midjaw length; teeth smooth or serrate, anterior teeth short and pointed or wedge shaped 10

7a. Color dark brown to black . . . .*Gymnothorax funebris* p. 234

7b. Color boldly patterned with reticulations, spots, or blotches 8

8a. Color pattern of large, spotted polygonal areas separated by dark reticulations . . . . *Gymnothorax polygonius* p. 238

8b. Color pattern of spots, mottling, or blotches 9

9a. Color pattern of dark overlapping spots on pale background; fin edges pale in small specimens and dark in large specimens . . . . *Gymnothorax moringa* p. 236

9b. Color pattern of diffuse dark spots and blotches; fin edges pale . . . . *Gymnothorax vicinus* p. 240

10a. Head and body spotted dorsally and ventrally; tail dark with three or four large white spots . . . .*Gymnothorax kolpos* p. 235

10b. Head and body spotted dorsally, pale ventrally; tail not noticeably dark 11

11a. Color pattern of upper body consists of small, more or less uniform-sized, well-separated pale spots on dark background . . . . *Gymnothorax nigromarginatus* p. 237

11b. Color pattern of upper body consists of pale polygonal spots of various sizes on dark background . . . .*Gymnothorax saxicola* p. 239

Anarchias similis (Lea 1913)
Pygmy eel

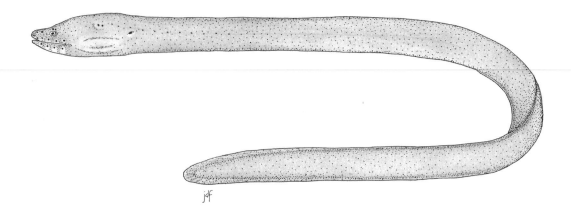

Anarchias similis is elongate and laterally compressed, with dorsal and anal fins restricted to tip of tail. It is distinguished from the other species of the family by the following combination of characters. Snout is short, subconical, and broad. Jaws close completely. Anterior nostril is tubular, and posterior nostril is rimmed, located above center of eye, and continuous with enlarged posteriormost supraorbital pore. Eye is moderate and centered slightly anterior to midpoint of upper jaw. Jaw teeth are numerous, conical, slender, and biserial anteriorly and uniserial posteriorly. Teeth along inner series of upper jaw number 2 to 5. Intermaxillary teeth are arranged in outer band of 7 to 10 small teeth and three inner rows of enlarged, depressible teeth. Vomerine teeth are separated from intermaxillary teeth and consist of single row of 3 to 11 small, sharp teeth. Gill openings are small, slitlike, and about at mid-depth of body. Head pores are developed and consist of four infraorbital, four supraorbital, six mandibular, and two branchial. Snout is 13% to 17%, eye is 7.3% to 10%, and upper jaw is 31% to 42% of head length. Head length is

11% to 13%, preanal length is 42% to 45%, depth at gill openings is 3.7% to 7.8%, and depth at anus is 2.7% to 5.2% of TL. Total vertebrae number 104 to 113, predorsal vertebrae number 94 to 104, and preanal vertebrae number 95 to 106. Lower jaw has pale marks, and head pores are in white spots. Body color is uniformly dark brown; dark with scattered pale spots; dark with small, distinct pale spots and diffuse, larger pale spots; or of bold overall pattern of irregular pale markings.

This species occurs in the tropical to warm temperate Atlantic between 27 and 97 m, and rarely as shallow as 5.5 m. In the western Atlantic it occurs from Georgia and Bermuda to southern Brazil, including the eastern Gulf of Mexico and the Lesser Antilles. It is often associated with boulders and eel grass. Maximum known size is 206 mm TL; males mature at 99 to 206 mm TL, and females mature at 76 to 136 mm TL.

REFERENCES: C. R. Robins et al. 1986 (as *A. yoshiae*); E. Böhlke et al. 1989; Smith 1989m.

Echidna catenata   (Bloch 1795)
Chain moray

Echidna catenata is moderately elongate and laterally compressed posteriorly, with a short, blunt snout and rather short jaws that close completely. It is distinguished from the other species of the family by the following combination of characters. Snout is subconical and broad. Jaws are subequal. Anterior nostril is tubular and near tip of snout. Posterior nostril is small and round, has raised crenate margin, and is open above anterior margin of eye. Eye is moderate in size and located at midpoint of upper jaw. Jaw teeth are molariform or conical and biserial to multiserial, with maxillary tooth rows shorter than lower jaw tooth rows. Upper jaw has 1 anterior median tooth, 6 to 11 teeth on each side, and one to three median rows of large teeth in intermaxillary series and two short rows of maxillary teeth. Lower jaw has two short rows of teeth, with those of outer row blunt and numbering 9 to 12 and those of inner row pointed and numbering 4 to 8. Vomerine teeth are conical to molariform and in two rows of 4 to 11 teeth anteriorly and a single row of 1 to 4 posteriorly. Lower jaw has two short rows of teeth, with outer row blunt and numbering 9 to 12 and inner row pointed and numbering 4 to 8. Gill openings are small, slitlike, and midlateral. Head pores are developed, small, and consist of three supraorbital, four infraorbital, six mandibular, and two branchial. Snout is 15% to 20%, eye is 7% to 10%, and upper jaw is 28% to 37% of head length. Head length is 12% to 14%, preanal length is 53% to 57%, depth at gill openings is 5.5% to 7.9%, and depth at anus is 5% to 7.3% of TL. Total vertebrae number 114 to 122, predorsal vertebrae number 5 to 7, and preanal vertebrae number 56 to 61. Color pattern is highly variable and consists of contrasting reticulations forming chainlike pattern. Ground color is brown to black, with pale yellow to white narrow chains. Pale chain pattern varies in relative width of chains.

This species occurs in the tropical to subtropical central and western Atlantic. In the western Atlantic it occurs from Bermuda and southern Florida to eastern Venezuela, including the Dry Tortugas, Florida, and the southwestern Gulf of Mexico. It is usually found in shallow water—less than 2 m—around reefs and rocky areas. The southwestern Gulf of Mexico record is from an unpublished manuscript by P. J. Cotter of Corpus Christi State University. Food consists of crustaceans (primarily small crabs) and small fishes. Maximum known size is 710 mm TL; males mature between 438 and 618 mm TL, and females mature between 475 and 680 mm TL.

REFERENCES: Randall 1968; C. R. Robins et al. 1986; Böhlke and Chaplin 1968; E. Böhlke et al. 1989.

Enchelycore carychroa   Böhlke and Böhlke 1976
Chestnut moray

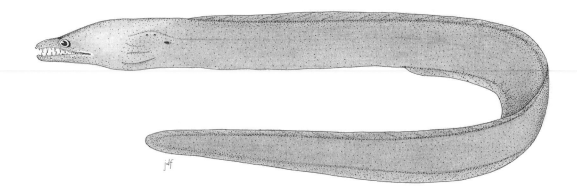

Enchelycore carychroa is relatively elongate, moderately stout, and compressed, with slender, elongate, arched jaws and anus slightly anterior to midlength. It is distinguished from the other species of the family by the following combination of characters. Snout is long and narrow. Jaws close only at tips. Anterior nostril is tubular, and posterior nostril is round or oval and located above anterior margin of eye, with slightly raised margin. Eye is large and centered at midpoint of jaws. Jaw teeth are conical, sharp, and prominent, with outer row of small, close-set teeth and inner row of large, depressible teeth. Intermaxillary teeth consist of outer ring of 11 to 17 small teeth and 3 to 5 inner, very long canines. Vomerine tooth patch is short and consists of small biserial teeth. Gill openings are small and slitlike and located at about midbody depth. Head pores are developed and consist of four infraorbital, three supraorbital, six mandibular, and two branchial. Snout is 16% to 21%, eye is 8.4% to 13%, and upper jaw is 37% to 50% of head length. Head length is 11% to 14%, predorsal length is 11% to 15%, preanal length is 38% to 44%, depth at gill opening is 4.4% to 6.5%, and depth at anus is 3.6% to 6.8% of TL. Total vertebrae number 128 to 140, predorsal vertebrae number 7 to 11, and preanal vertebrae number 45 to 51. Color is dark brown and gradually darker posteriorly. Corner of mouth, grooves in branchial region, margin of eye, and longitudinal lines on dorsal fin are blackish. Head pores are on white spots.

This species occurs in the tropical Atlantic Ocean between the shoreline and 54 m. In the western Atlantic it occurs from Bermuda, the Bahamas, the Florida Keys, and the northwestern Gulf of Mexico to Brazil. In the Gulf of Mexico it inhabits the Flower Gardens Reefs. Maximum known size is 335 mm TL; males mature between 195 and 325 mm TL, and females mature between 169 and 296 mm TL.

REFERENCES: Böhlke and Chaplin 1968 (as *Enchelycore* sp.); Böhlke and Böhlke 1976; C. R. Robins et al. 1986; E. Böhlke et al. 1989.

Enchelycore nigricans (Bonnaterre 1788)
Viper moray

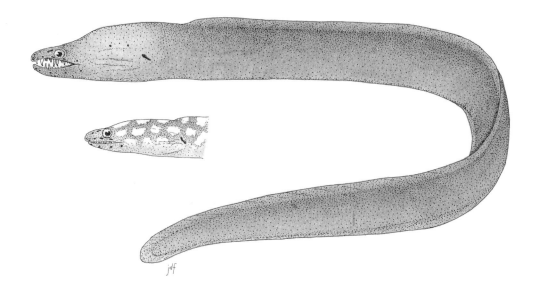

Enchelycore nigricans is relatively elongate, moderately stout, and compressed, with slender, elongate, arched jaws and anus slightly anterior to midlength. It is distinguished from the other species of the family by the following combination of characters. Snout is long and narrow. Jaws close only at tips. Anterior nostril is tubular. Posterior nostril is round or oval and located above eye in young and greatly elongate and located in front of eye in adults. Eye is large and centered at midpoint of jaws. Jaw teeth are conical and sharp, with those of outer row small and recurved and those of inner row long, slender, and depressible. Intermaxillary teeth consist of outer ring of 13 to 19 alternating large and small teeth; intermediate series of long, depressible canines; and inner series of 3 or 4 long, depressible fangs. Vomerine teeth are small and in single row. Gill openings are small and slitlike, and located at about midbody depth. Head pores are developed and consist of four infraorbital, three supraorbital, six mandibular, and two branchial, although numbers of pores increase with growth. Snout is 15% to 21%, eye is 7.7% to 12%, and upper jaw is 37% to 52% of head length. Head length is 11% to 14%, predorsal length is 10%

to 13%, preanal length is 45% to 50%, depth at gill openings is 3.8% to 6.3%, and depth at anus is 3.6% to 5.8% of TL. Total vertebrae number 141 to 148, predorsal vertebrae number 6 to 10, and preanal vertebrae number 58 to 63. Small specimens are pale, with brownish bands and streaks forming polygonal-shaped blocks, and dark areas between eyes and dark nuchal band. Large specimens are uniformly dark brown or dark with faint, darker marblings.

This species occurs in the tropical and subtropical Atlantic Ocean. In the western Atlantic it occurs from Bermuda, the Bahamas, the Florida Keys, on offshore reefs in the Gulf of Mexico, throughout the West Indies, and around offshore islands of Central and South America to central Brazil. It has been captured from near shore to 24 m. Maximum known size is 930 mm TL, and females mature between 548 and 707 mm TL.

REFERENCES: Böhlke and Chaplin 1968; Bright and Cashman 1974; Castro-Aguirre and Márquez-Espinoza 1981; E. Böhlke et al. 1989.

Gymnothorax funebris   Ranzani 1840
Green moray

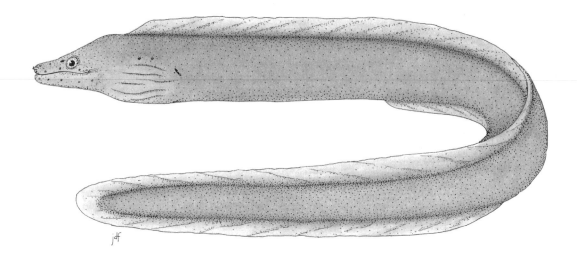

Gymnothorax funebris is moderately elongate, moderately stout, and laterally compressed posteriorly, with uniform coloration. It is distinguished from the other species of the family by the following combination of characters. Snout is elongate, acute, and narrows sharply from bulbous nape. Jaws are elongate. Anterior nostril is tubular, and posterior nostril is porelike, raised in adults and teardrop shaped in largest specimens. Eye is moderate in size and centered at midpoint of jaws. Teeth are smooth. Upper jaw has row of 10 to 18 triangular, posteriorly directed teeth and short anterior inner series of 1 to 3 long, slender teeth. Lower jaw has 1 to 4 long, slender teeth followed by series of 11 to 20 triangular, posteriorly directed teeth. Intermaxillary teeth consist of row of 5 or 6 large, stout teeth flanked by 0 to 6 small teeth continuous with upper jaw teeth. Vomerine teeth are separated from intermaxillary teeth and are small, conical, and biserial anteriorly and uniserial posteriorly. Gill openings are slitlike and are located at about mid-depth of body. Head pores are developed and number four infraorbital, three supraorbital, six mandibular, and two branchial.

Snout is 14% to 20%, eye is 6% to 11%, and upper jaw is 33% to 44% of head length. Head length is 13% to 16%, predorsal length is 10% to 12%, preanal length is 43% to 49%, depth at gill openings is 4.4% to 10%, and depth at anus is 4.5% to 8% of TL. Total vertebrae number 137 to 142, predorsal vertebrae number 4 to 7, and preanal vertebrae number 57 to 61. Color is uniform dark green to brown. Dorsal, anal, and caudal fins are dusky to pale. Head pores, gill openings, and anus may be darker than remainder of body.

This species occurs in the western Atlantic from Bermuda, the Bahamas, the Florida Keys, the western Gulf of Mexico, throughout the Caribbean Sea, and off South America to southern Brazil. It is common in rocky tide pools and in shallow coral reefs but occasionally is found in brackish water and mangrove areas. Maximum known size is 1,890 mm TL.

REFERENCES: Böhlke and Chaplin 1968; Castro-Aguirre and Márquez-Espinoza 1981; C. R. Robins et al. 1986; E. Böhlke et al. 1989.

Gymnothorax kolpos   Böhlke and Böhlke 1980
Blacktail moray

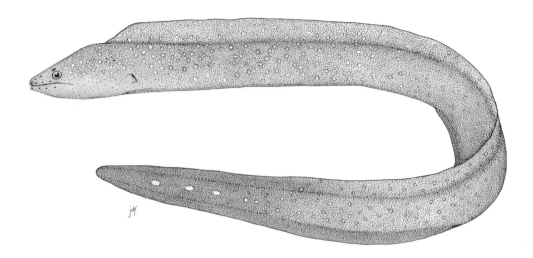

Gymnothorax kolpos is moderately elongate and laterally compressed posteriorly, with small ocellated white spots. It is distinguished from the other species of the family by the following combination of characters. Snout is short and blunt and does not narrow sharply from nape. Jaws are elongate. Anterior nostril is tubular, and posterior nostril is porelike. Eye is moderate in size and centered at midpoint of jaws. Upper jaw has 16 to 28 triangular, posteriorly directed teeth. Lower jaw has 26 to 38 slender teeth. Intermaxillary teeth consist of anterior median teeth and 4 large, compressed teeth on each side. Vomerine teeth number 0 to 7 and are separated from intermaxillary teeth. Gill openings are slitlike and are located just below mid-depth of body. Head pores number three (occasionally five) infraorbital, three supraorbital, six (occasionally five) mandibular, and two (occasionally one) branchial. Snout is 16% to 22%, eye is 6.4% to 9.7%, and upper jaw is 31% to 48% of head length. Head length is 11% to 13%, predorsal length is 7.2% to 11%, preanal length is 41% to 47%, depth at gill openings is 2.8% to 5.5%, and depth at anus is 4.1% to 7% of TL. Color is medium greenish brown, increasingly darker posteriorly, with posterior third of tail brownish black. Total vertebrae number 159 to 167, predorsal vertebrae number 5 to 7, and preanal vertebrae number 60 to 65. Head and body are covered with distinct, pale, ocellated spots that increase in size and become less numerous posteriorly.

This species occurs in the western North Atlantic Ocean from North Carolina and Georgia, in the eastern Gulf of Mexico from the Straits of Florida to Texas, and in Campeche Bay. It is captured from 48 to 230 m and most frequently between 75 and 100 m. Maximum known size is 925 mm TL.

REFERENCES: Böhlke and Böhlke 1980; C. R. Robins et al. 1986; E. Böhlke et al. 1989; Boschung 1992.

Gymnothorax moringa (Cuvier 1829)
Spotted moray

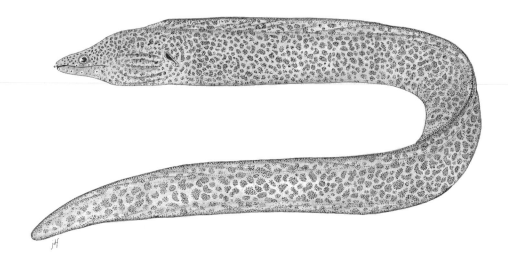

Gymnothorax moringa is moderately elongate and laterally compressed posteriorly, with a contrasting pattern of dark, overlapping spots on a pale background. It is distinguished from the other species of the family by the following combination of characters. Snout is elongate, acute, and narrows sharply from bulbous nape. Jaws are elongate. Anterior nostril is tubular, and posterior nostril is round to teardrop shaped and raised above and in front of eye. Eye is moderate in size and centered at midpoint of jaws. Teeth are smooth. Upper jaw has row of 14 to 18 triangular, posteriorly directed teeth and short anterior inner series of 1 or 2 slender teeth (missing in large specimens). Lower jaw has 15 to 24 triangular, posteriorly directed, uniserial teeth. Intermaxillary teeth consist of row of 5 or 6 large teeth flanked by 0 to 7 fanglike teeth and 3 long, slender fangs along midline. Vomerine teeth are separated from intermaxillary teeth, are uniserial, and number 5 to 11. Gill openings are slitlike and are located at about midbody depth. Head pores number four infraorbital, one supraorbital, six mandibular, and two branchial. Snout is 17% to 23%, eye is 8% to 12%, and upper jaw is 37% to 47% of head length. Head length is 13% to 15%, predorsal length is 11% to 13%, preanal length is 42% to 47%, depth at gill openings is 4.9% to 9.1%, and depth at anus is 4.9% to 8.8% of TL. Total vertebrae number 134 to 142, predorsal vertebrae number 4 to 7, and preanal vertebrae number 50 to 57. Color is highly variable, usually pale dark green with pattern of dark overlapping spots, occasionally predominately pale with dark markings reduced or predominately dark with light areas reduced. Often large specimens have row of round dark spots along body above midline. Margins of fins are pale in small and large pale specimens but dark in large dark specimens. Anterior nostril is pale, and head pores on lower jaw are set in white spots.

This species occurs in the western Atlantic Ocean off South Carolina and from Bermuda to Brazil, including the Gulf of Mexico and the Caribbean Sea. It has been captured from near shore to 90 m and occasionally at 200 m. Maximum known size is 2,000 to 3,000 mm TL; males mature between 575 and 940 mm TL, and females mature between 595 and 1,025 mm TL.

REFERENCES: Böhlke and Chaplin 1968; Hoese and Moore 1977; C. R. Robins et al. 1986; E. Böhlke et al. 1989; Smith 1989m; Boschung 1992.

Gymnothorax nigromarginatus (Girard 1858)
Blackedge moray

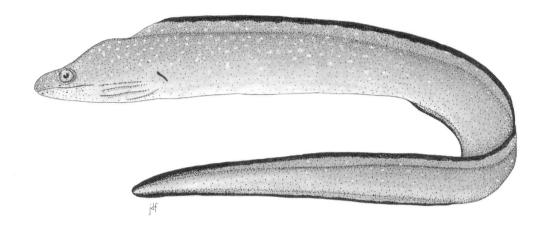

Gymnothorax nigromarginatus is moderately elongate and laterally compressed posteriorly, with small white spots on brown background and vertical fins with black margin. It is distinguished from the other species of the family by the following combination of characters. Snout is short and blunt and does not narrow sharply from nape. Jaws are short. Anterior nostril is tubular, and posterior nostril is rimmed pore. Eye is large and centered at midpoint of jaws. Teeth are serrate. Upper jaw has 8 to 12 teeth, and lower jaw has 9 to 16 teeth. Intermaxillary teeth consist of single tooth at tip of snout and 4 pairs of increasingly larger teeth, but median teeth are absent. Vomerine teeth are very small, conical, and uniserial. Gill openings are small, round to elliptical, and located slightly below mid-depth of body. Head pores number three infraorbital, one supraorbital, six mandibular, and two branchial. Snout is 14% to 22%, eye is 7.4% to 14%, and upper jaw is 34% to 54% of head length. Head length is

11% to 15%, predorsal length is 10% to 13%, preanal length is 39% to 45%, depth at gill openings is 5.4% to 7.3%, and depth at anus is 4% to 6.5% of TL. Total vertebrae number 137 to 147, predorsal vertebrae number 5 to 8, and preanal vertebrae number 45 to 52. Color is medium brown with uniform-sized, well-separated, small, white to yellow spots. Belly is pale. Eye is surrounded by dark ring; dorsal fin has dark margin, often slightly undulated; and anal fin has uniform dark edge.

This species occurs in the western North Atlantic from the northern Gulf of Mexico west of Mobile Bay, the west coast of Yucatán, and Honduras. It has been captured from 10 to 91 m. Maximum known size is 620 mm TL; males mature between 404 and 555 mm TL, and females mature between 328 and 620 mm TL.

REFERENCES: Ginsburg 1951; Hoese and Moore 1977; C. R. Robins et al. 1986; E. Böhlke et al. 1989; Boschung 1992.

Gymnothorax polygonius Poey 1875
Polygon moray

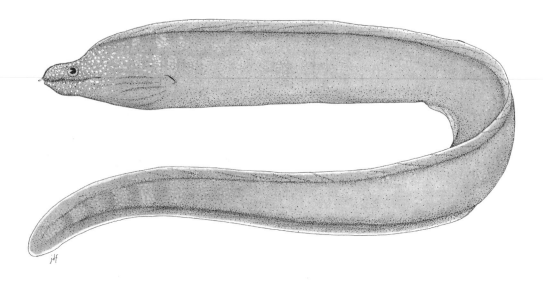

Gymnothorax polygonius is moderately elongate and laterally compressed posteriorly, with a color pattern of spotted polygons separated by dark reticulations. It is distinguished from the other species of the family by the following combination of characters. Snout is elongate, acute, and narrows sharply from bulbous nape. Jaws are elongate. Anterior nostril is tubular, and posterior nostril is round or teardrop shaped and located above anterior margin of eye. Eye is moderate in size and centered at midpoint of jaws. Teeth are smooth. Upper jaw has 8 to 12 teeth, and lower jaw has 16 to 25 teeth. Intermaxillary teeth consist of row of 5 or 6 teeth flanked by few tiny teeth and 0 to 3 fangs along midline. Vomerine teeth are uniserial, number 5 to 12, and are separated from intermaxillary teeth. Gill openings are slitlike and are located at about midbody depth. Head pores number four infraorbital, three supraorbital, six mandibular, and two branchial. Snout is 19% to 22%, eye is 7% to 11%, and upper jaw is 38% to 54% of head length. Head length is 13% to 16%, predorsal length is 10%

to 13%, preanal length is 44% to 49%, depth at gill openings is 5.8% to 8.9%, and depth at anus is 5% to 7% of TL. Total vertebrae number 135 to 142, predorsal vertebrae number 4 to 6, and preanal vertebrae number 51 to 55. Color is brown, with large, light polygonal, squarish, or intermediate patterns regularly arranged on body. Light-patterned areas are made of light spots separated by lilac brown coloration. Head coloration consists of pale spots separated by dark reticulations. Dorsal and anal fins have light margins.

This species occurs in the tropical to warm temperate Atlantic Ocean. In the western Atlantic it occurs from Bermuda, North Carolina, the Bahamas, Cuba, Puerto Rico, Campeche Bank in the Gulf of Mexico, and Brazil. Depths of capture range from about 10 to 256 m. Maximum known size is 835 mm TL; males mature at about 642 mm TL, and females mature between 575 and 722 mm TL.

REFERENCES: Böhlke and Chaplin 1968; E. Böhlke et al. 1989.

Gymnothorax saxicola   Jordan and Davis 1891
Honeycomb moray

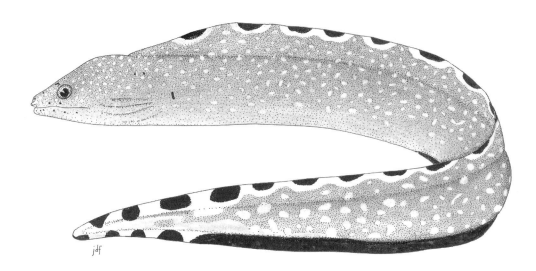

Gymnothorax saxicola is moderately elongate and laterally compressed posteriorly, with color pattern of polygonal spots enclosed by brown reticulations and dorsal fin patterned with bold undulating black-and-white margin. It is distinguished from the other species of the family by the following combination of characters. Snout is short, blunt, and does not narrow sharply from nape. Jaws are short. Anterior nostril is tubular, and posterior nostril is rimmed pore located above anterior one-half of eye. Eye is large and is located at midlength of jaws. Teeth are large, triangular, and serrate. Upper jaw has 8 to 12 teeth, and lower jaw has 9 to 16 teeth. Intermaxillary teeth consist of single tooth at tip of snout and four pairs of increasingly larger teeth. Vomerine teeth are very small, conical, and uniserial. Gill openings are small, rounded to elliptical, and located slightly below mid-depth of body. Head pores number three infraorbital, three supraorbital, six mandibular, and two branchial. Snout is 16% to 22%, eye is 7.1% to 15%, and upper jaw is 38% to 51% of head length. Head length is 13% to 16%, predorsal length is 10% to 16%, preanal length is 41% to 50%, depth at gill

openings is 4.6% to 9 %, and depth at anus is 4.1% to 7.2% of TL. Total vertebrae number 134 to 147, predorsal vertebrae number 4 to 7, and preanal vertebrae number 47 to 59. Color is brown to yellowish brown, with pale to yellowish irregular spots forming honeycomb pattern on back and sides. Large specimens occasionally have series of round spots along midbody depth. Margin of dorsal fin has pattern of saddle-shaped black areas outlined by undulating bright white stripe along middle and edge of fin. Anal fin is dark except for posterior end that is white with several saddle-shaped black areas.

This species occurs in the western North Atlantic from North Carolina to Florida and along the northeastern Gulf of Mexico to Mobile Bay. It has been captured from near shore to 86 m and occasionally from 128 to 213 m. Maximum known size is 620 mm TL; males mature between 406 and 555 mm TL, and females mature between 295 and 620 mm TL.

REFERENCES: Hoese and Moore 1977; C. R. Robins et al. 1986; E. Böhlke et al. 1989; Boschung 1992.

Gymnothorax vicinus   (Castelnau 1855)
Purplemouth moray

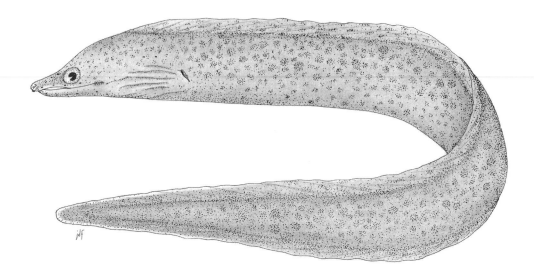

Gymnothorax vicinus is moderately elongate and laterally compressed posteriorly, with a mottled coloration, a pale edge along posterior section of medial fins, and a dark slash at angle of mouth. It is distinguished from the other species of the family by the following combination of characters. Snout is elongate, acute, and narrows sharply from bulbous nape. Jaws are elongate. Anterior nostril is tubular, and posterior nostril is slightly raised and located above and slightly behind anterior margin of eye. Eye is large and centered near midpoint of jaws. Teeth are smooth. Upper jaw has outer series of 15 to 21 teeth and inner series of 1 to 3 teeth. Lower jaw has 11 to 13 teeth, with anterior 4 enlarged and flanked by 2 to 8 tiny teeth. Intermaxillary teeth consist of lateral series of 5 or 6 teeth flanked by 3 to 9 tiny teeth and 3 median fangs. Vomerine teeth are uniserial, number 6 to 14, and are separated from intermaxillary teeth. Gill openings are slitlike and are located at about midbody depth. Head pores number four infraorbital, three supraorbital, six mandibular, and two branchial. Snout is 17% to 22%, eye is 8.1% to 12%, and upper jaw is 33% to 48% of head length.

Head length is 13% to 16%, predorsal length is 10% to 13%, preanal length is 41% to 47%, depth at gill openings is 4.6% to 8%, and depth at anus is 5.2% to 7.1% of TL. Total vertebrae number 128 to 140, predorsal vertebrae number 3 to 6, and preanal vertebrae number 48 to 53. Color ranges from mottled pattern of overlapping dark spots to almost uniform brown with faint freckles of darker colors. Posterior one-third of dorsal fin and entire anal fin have pale edges. Dark horizontal slash is located at inner corner of mouth, and interior of mouth is pigmented.

This species occurs in the tropical Atlantic Ocean between 9 and 73 m near reefs and rocky areas. In the western Atlantic it occurs off Bermuda, Florida, the northern Gulf of Mexico, throughout the Caribbean Sea, and off Central and northern South America. Maximum known size is 1,200 mm TL, and females mature between 380 and 785 mm TL.

REFERENCES: Hoese and Moore 1977; Castro-Aguirre and Márquez-Espinoza 1981; C. R. Robins et al. 1986; E. Böhlke et al. 1989; Smith 1989m; Boschung 1992.

Muraena retifera Goode and Bean 1882
Reticulate eel

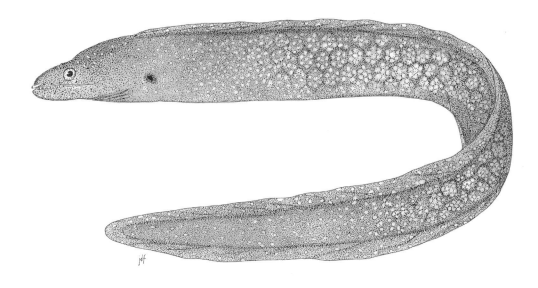

Muraena retifera is elongate and laterally compressed posteriorly, with a color pattern of large, closely set rosettes. It is distinguished from the other species of the family by the following combination of characters. Snout is of moderate length and subconical. Jaws are elongate. Anterior nostril is tubular, and posterior nostril is tubular and located above and anterior to anterior margin of eye. Eye is moderate in size and centered above midgape of jaws. Teeth are strong, pointed with smooth edges, and uniserial in adults. Upper jaw has 7 to 14 large, triangular teeth decreasing in size posteriorly. Lower jaw has 12 to 19 teeth decreasing in size posteriorly. Intermaxillary teeth consist of outer series of 5 or 6 stout teeth and median series of two or three depressible fangs. Vomerine teeth number 7 to 17 and are separated from intermaxillary teeth. Gill openings are small, slitlike, and located at about midbody depth. Head pores number four infraorbital, three supraorbital, six mandibular, and two branchial. Snout is 16% to 22%, eye is 7% to 12%, and upper jaw is 38% to 50% of head length. Head length is 12% to 16%, predorsal length is 7% to 13%, preanal length is 43% to 50%, depth at gill openings is 5.3% to 11%, and depth at anus is 5.2% to 10% of TL. Total vertebrae number 128 to 135, predorsal vertebrae number 4 to 6, and preanal vertebrae number 52 to 58. Color pattern consists of close-set rosettes of light brown blotches on medium brown to blackish background. Blotches are peppered with small white dots. Head is brown with white spots. Gill openings are surrounded by black blotch.

This species occurs in the western Atlantic from North Carolina to Florida, the eastern Gulf of Mexico off Florida and Yucatán, and Venezuela and southern Brazil. It has been captured from 21 to 91 m. Maximum known size is 895 mm TL, and females mature between 535 and 895 mm TL.

REFERENCES: Williams and Shipp 1980; C. R. Robins et al. 1986; E. Böhlke et al. 1989; Boschung 1992.

SYNAPHOBRANCHIDAE   Cutthroat eels

Cutthroat eels are relatively stout and moderately slender, with a large terminal mouth and well-developed pectoral fins. They are distinguished from the other families of the order by the following combination of characters. Snout is short and blunt to long and acute. Gape of mouth usually extends to level of posterior margin of eye. Anterior nostril is short simple tube located near fleshy tip of snout. Posterior nostril is located anterior to, at, or below mid-height of eye. Eye is moderately large to reduced. Gill openings are small to moderate in size, and ventrally located at or below level of insertion of pectoral fin. Dorsal, anal, and caudal fins are confluent. Caudal fin is small. Most species have embedded scales, usually elongate and arranged in basket-weave pattern. Swim bladder is present, but pyloric caecae are absent.

Cutthroat eels occur worldwide along continental shelves and slopes. The leptocephali are moderately small to large (from less than 100 to 200 mm SL), with telescopic eyes. The family contains about 24 species in eight genera, and 7 species in five genera occur in the Gulf of Mexico.

Key to the Species of the Gulf of Mexico

(Adapted from Robins and Robins 1989)

1a. Lower jaw longer than upper jaw, vomerine teeth weak
and in one or two rows 2

1b. Lower jaw shorter than upper jaw, vomerine teeth moderate to much enlarged 5

2a. Body covered with small scales; gill openings united ven-
trally 3

2b. Body naked; gill openings separate but low on body
. . . . *Haptenchelys texis* p. 246

3a. Scales elongate to oval (Fig. 43)
. . . . *Synaphobranchus affinis* p. 248

3b. Scales rounded 4

4a. Scales large, polygonal or rounded (Fig. 44); dorsal fin origin about one snout length anterior to midpoint of body;
vomerine teeth uniserial except for anterior patch of several
biserial teeth . . . . *Synaphobranchus oregoni* p. 250

4b. Scales small, rounded or oval, and irregularly arranged
(Fig. 45); dorsal fin origin near midpoint of body; vomerine
teeth irregularly biserial anteriorly
. . . . *Synaphobranchus brevidorsalis* p. 249

5a. Body with embedded scales arranged in basket-weave pattern . . . . *Ilyophis brunneus* p. 247

5b. Body without scales 6

6a. Anus anteriorly located, distance from gill slit to anus less
than head length . . . . *Dysomma anguillare* p. 244

6b. Anus moderately anteriorly located, distance from gill slit
to anus equal to head length or longer
. . . . *Dysommina rugosa* p. 245

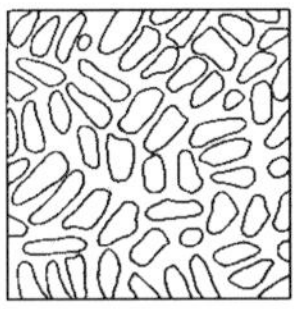

FIG 43

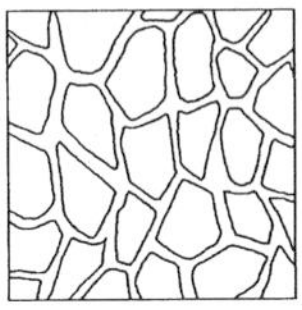

FIG 44

FIG 45

Dysomma anguillare Barnard 1923

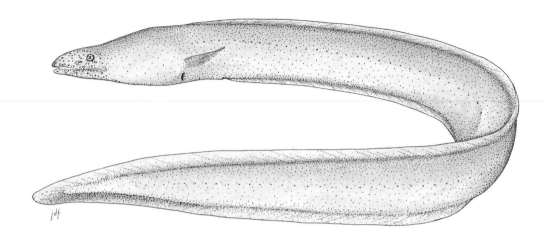

Dysomma anguillare is moderately stout, with a fleshy, plicate snout and an anteriorly located anus. It is distinguished from the other species of the family by a combination of the following characters. Snout is slightly tapered anteriorly and overhangs lower jaw. Eye is rather small. Teeth in upper jaw are small and multiserial. Teeth in lower jaw are large, widely spaced, in single series, and number about 10. Intermaxillary teeth number 2. Vomer has 4 compound teeth. Gill openings are small and extend to near insertion of pectoral fin. Dorsal fin originates above pectoral fin base. Anus is located behind tip of pectoral fin. Head pores number five infraorbital, three supraorbital, and six mandibular. Snout length is 21% to 28%, and jaw length is 36% to 44% of head length. Head length is 12% to 16%, predorsal length is 11% to 14%, and preanal length is 16% to 22% of TL. Total vertebrae number 119 to 130, precaudal vertebrae number 58 to 63, and caudal vertebrae number 59 to 66. Pectoral fins rays number 10 or 11. Color is pallid, tan dorsally and white ventrally. Ventral one-half of caudal fin is dark.

This species occurs in the western North Atlantic, western Pacific, and Indian Oceans generally at depths less than 100 m. In the western Atlantic it occurs from Florida, the Gulf of Mexico, and the Caribbean Sea. Maximum known size is 426 mm TL.

REFERENCES: Robins and Robins 1976, 1989; Castle 1986; Smith 1989h.

Dysommina rugosa   Ginsburg 1951

Dysommina rugosa is moderately stout, with a fleshy, papillose snout, relatively large circular eyes, and a posteriorly located anus. It is distinguished from the other species of the family by the following combination of characters. Snout is slightly tapered anteriorly and overhangs lower jaw. Eye is covered by skin. Teeth are lacking in premaxilla, and maxillary and dentary teeth are very small and arranged in many irregular rows. Vomer has four large compound teeth. Gill openings are crescentic and about equal to diameter of eye. Dorsal fin originates posterior to pectoral fin base. Anus is located less than 1.5 head lengths posterior to gill slits. Head pores number five infraorbital, three supraorbital, and six preoperculomandibular. Snout length is 31% to 39% and lower jaw length is 48% to 56% of head length. Head length is 12% to 15%, predorsal length is 17% to 20%, preanal length is 26% to 33%, and body depth is 4.8% to 8.6% of TL. Total vertebrae number 127 to 134. Color in preservative is brown, with head and dorsal aspect of body slightly lighter than remainder of body. Pectoral, dorsal, and anal fins are pale.

This species occurs in the western Atlantic, central Pacific, and southwestern Indian Oceans between 260 and 775 m. In the western Atlantic it occurs off the Carolinas to the Straits of Florida, the northern Gulf of Mexico, and the Caribbean Sea. Maximum known size is 352 mm TL.

REFERENCES: Ginsburg 1951; Robins and Robins 1989.

Haptenchelys texis   Robins and Martin 1976

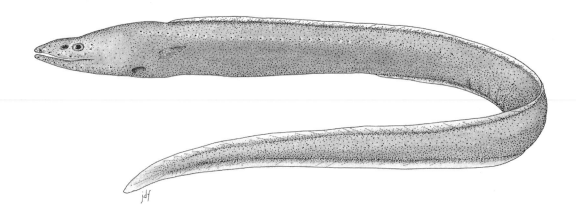

Haptenchelys texis is moderately slender, with separate gill openings and dorsal fin origin above pectoral fin base. It is distinguished from the other species of the family by the following combination of characters. Snout is fleshy and very slightly overhangs lower jaw. Eye is well developed. Gape of mouth extends to posterior margin of eye. Jaw teeth are small and in irregular series, with innermost series slightly enlarged. Intermaxillary tooth patch is more or less continuous with vomerine teeth. Vomerine teeth are small and in irregular row. Gill openings are separate, crescentic, and horizontally oriented on ventral surface of pharynx. Pectoral fin is small. Head pores number six to eight infraorbital, three supraorbital, and seven to nine preoperculo-mandibular. Snout length is 34% to 38% and jaw length is 73% to 84% of head length. Predorsal length is 14% to 17%, preanal length is 32% to 40%, and body depth is 4.1% to 5.5% of TL. Total vertebrae number 125 to 132. Pectoral fin rays number 15 to 17. Color is dark brown.

This species occurs in the North Atlantic Ocean. In the western Atlantic it occurs in the Gulf of Mexico, the Bahamas, and the Caribbean Sea. Depths of capture range from 2,160 to 4,086 m. Maximum known size is 511 mm TL.

REFERENCES: Robins and Martin 1976; Anderson et al. 1985; Robins and Robins 1989.

Ilyophis brunneus Gilbert 1891
Ooze eel

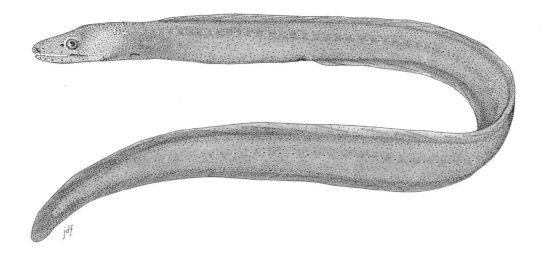

Ilyophis brunneus is moderately slender, with a moderately long abdomen and embedded scales. It is distinguished from the other species of the family by the following combination of characters. Snout is moderately long and slightly tapered. Eye is moderate sized. Gape of mouth extends about one eye diameter beyond posterior margin of eye. Jaw teeth are surrounded by papillae and are small, conical, and in bands, with inner row largest. Intermaxillary teeth are arranged in elongate patch. Vomerine teeth are in irregular biserial series. Gill openings are ventral, below pectoral fin base, and separate, with horizontal base. Pectoral fin is small but not attenuate. Dorsal fin origin is above tip of pectoral fin. Anus is located about two head lengths posterior to gill slits. Infraorbital pores number five, supraorbital pores number three, and preoperculo-mandibular pores number nine. Snout length is 31% to 37% and jaw length is 44% to 56% of head length. Head length is 8% to 11%, predorsal length is 11% to 12%, abdominal length (distance from posterior end of gill opening to fleshy protuberance around anus) is 16% to 20%, and body depth is 3% to 5% of TL. Total vertebrae number 145 to 151. Color is dark brown, with white lateral line pores. Peritoneum is black.

This species occurs in the Atlantic, Pacific, and southwestern Indian Oceans. In the western Atlantic it occurs from the Middle Atlantic Bight (39°04′N) to southern Brazil (31°35′S), including the Gulf of Mexico, where it is abundant in the northern and eastern sections. Depths of capture range from 700 to 1,100 m in the Gulf of Mexico and from 1,109 to 2,745 m in the Middle Atlantic Bight. Food consists of bivalve mollusks, brachyuran crabs, shrimps, and galatheids. Maximum known size is 1,360 mm TL, and females mature between 342 and 400 mm TL.

REFERENCES: Grey 1956; Castle 1964, 1986; Robins 1971; Robins and Robins 1976, 1989; Boschung 1992.

Synaphobranchus affinis Günther 1877

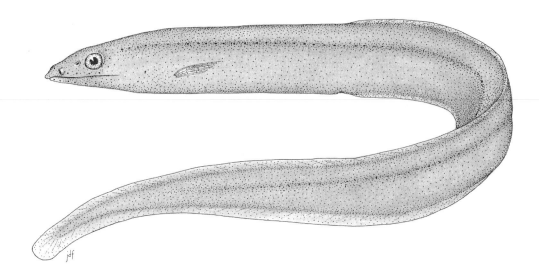

Synaphobranchus affinis is moderately slender and compressed, with lower jaw longer than upper jaw but with fleshy tip of snout overhanging tip of lower jaw. It is distinguished from the other species of the family by the following combination of characters. Snout has fleshy, acute, proboscis-like tip. Eye is large and oval shaped. Jaw teeth are small, pointed, and in bands, with innermost teeth longest. Intermaxillary teeth are larger than other teeth and are arranged in narrow patch. Vomerine teeth are minute and uniserial. Gape of mouth extends about eye diameter posterior to posterior margin of eye. Gill openings are midventral and open through common median slit. Pectoral fin tapers to point. Dorsal fin is above anus or slightly posterior. Infraorbital pores number 10, supraorbital pores number 5, and preoperculo-mandibular pores number 12. Snout length is 27% to 36%, eye is 9% to 17%, and length of lower jaw is 47% to 59% of head length. Predorsal length is 27% to 37%, preanal length is 27% to 31%, and body depth is 5% to 10% of TL. Total vertebrae number 125 to 140, precaudal vertebrae number 51, and caudal vertebrae number 66. Pectoral fin rays number 14 to 17. Scales are oval shaped, embedded, and arranged in basketweave pattern. Color is grayish to brownish, with pinkish dorsal surface.

This species occurs worldwide from tropical to temperate seas. In the western Atlantic it occurs from the Middle Atlantic Bight to the Straits of Florida, the northeastern Gulf of Mexico, the Bahamas, and the Caribbean Sea. Depths of capture range from 403 to 1,190 m. Food consists of crustaceans and small fishes. Maximum known size is 460 mm TL.

REFERENCES: Robins 1971; Robins and Robins 1976, 1989; Martin 1984; Castle 1986.

Synaphobranchus brevidorsalis Günther 1887

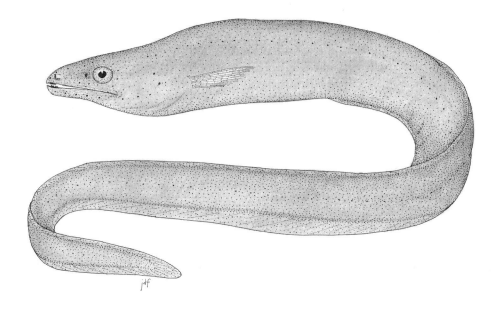

Synaphobranchus brevidorsalis is moderately slender and compressed, with lower jaw longer than upper jaw but with fleshy tip of snout overhanging tip of lower jaw. It is distinguished from the other species of the family by the following combination of characters. Snout has acute proboscis-like tip. Eye is large and oval shaped. Jaw teeth are small and pointed, with innermost teeth largest. Intermaxillary teeth are larger than other teeth and are arranged in narrow patch. Vomerine teeth are irregularly biserial anteriorly and uniserial posteriorly. Gape of mouth extends to slightly more than eye diameter beyond posterior margin of eye. Gill openings are midventral and open through common median slit. Pectoral fin tapers to point and is 1.5 to 2 times as long as snout length. Dorsal fin origin is posterior to level of anus at about midlength. Lower jaw length is 72% to 98% and eye length is 11% to 16% of head length. Head length is 10% to 14%, predorsal length is 45% to 52%, and body depth is 5.7% to 8% of TL. Total vertebrae number 130 to 140, precaudal vertebrae number 60 to 68, and caudal vertebrae number 64 to 78. Pectoral fin rays number 14 to 17. Scales are round to oval, embedded, and irregularly arranged. Color is brown, often lighter dorsally than ventrally.

This species occurs worldwide in tropical to warm temperate seas. In the western Atlantic it occurs from the Middle Atlantic Bight to southern Brazil but is rare in the Gulf of Mexico. Depths of capture range from 545 to 1,635 m. Maximum known size is 1,175 mm TL.

REFERENCES: Robins 1971; Martin 1984; Robins and Robins 1989.

Synaphobranchus oregoni Castle 1960

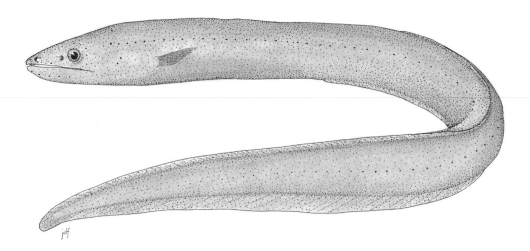

Synaphobranchus oregoni is moderately slender and compressed, with lower jaw longer than upper jaw but with fleshy tip of snout overhanging tip of lower jaw. It is distinguished from the other species of the family by the following combination of characters. Snout has acute proboscis-like tip. Eye is large and oval shaped. Jaw teeth are small and pointed, with innermost teeth largest. Intermaxillary teeth are enlarged, irregularly arranged, and biserial anteriorly. Gape of mouth extends to one eye diameter past posterior margin of eye or beyond. Gill openings are midventral and open through common median slit. Pectoral fin tapers to point. Dorsal fin origin is about one head length posterior to level of anus. Infraorbital pores number 10, supraorbital pores number 5, preoperculo-mandibular pores number 12, and supratemporal pores number 5. Snout length is 24% to 36%, eye is 12% to 19%, and lower jaw length is 49% to 67% of head length. Body depth is 5% to 12% of TL.

Total vertebrae number 140 to 150, precaudal vertebrae number 55 to 61, and caudal vertebrae number 82 to 87. Scales are large, polygonal or rounded, embedded, and in basket-weave pattern. Color is brown, often with reddish or orangish cast in large specimens. Abdomen, branchial region, bases of fins, and caudal fin are darker than remainder of body. Peritoneum is black.

This species occurs in the western North Atlantic from the Middle Atlantic Bight, the Straits of Florida, the Gulf of Mexico, and the Caribbean Sea. It is common in the Gulf of Mexico, especially on soft bottoms of the western Gulf, but rare over the remainder of its range. It has been captured from 545 to at least 1,200 m. Food consists of crustaceans, squids, and fishes. Maximum known size is 700 mm TL.

REFERENCES: Castle 1960; Robins 1971; Martin 1984; Robins and Robins 1989.

OPHICHTHIDAE Snake eels

Snake eels are moderately elongate and from oval anteriorly and compressed posteriorly to compressed throughout length. They are distinguished from the other families of the order by the following combination of characters. Snout is short to moderately elongate. Posterior nostril is usually within mouth or pierces upper lip. Teeth are variable and are present in jaws and ethmovomer. Tongue is adnate, not free. Jaws are not elongate and slender. Branchiostegal rays are numerous and broadly overlapping along ventral midline, are free of hyoid arch, and form basketlike structure. Caudal fin is generally absent, and tail terminates as a hardened tip. When caudal fin is present, it is confluent with dorsal and anal fins.

Snake eels occur worldwide in tropical to warm temperate seas. Leptocephali are moderately elongate (less than 150 mm SL), with variable number of gut loops or swellings, two or three liver lobes, gall bladder attached to last liver lobe, gut abruptly expanded between esophagus and intestine, kidney terminating 0 to 15 myomeres anterior to anus, and pigment on dorsal surface of gut. The family contains more than 250 species in 52 genera, and 28 species in 15 genera occur in the Gulf of Mexico.

Key to the Species of the Gulf of Mexico
(Adapted from McCosker et al. 1989)

1a. Tip of tail flexible, caudal fin rays visible, confluent with dorsal and anal fins; gill openings constricted and lateral 2

1b. Tip of tail hard or fleshy point; dorsal and anal fins not confluent; gill openings unconstricted and midlateral to ventral 4

2a. Posterior nostril before eye, above upper lip and not covered by flap; pectoral fin minute and flaplike . . . . *Pseudomyrophus nimius* p. 282

2b. Posterior nostril labial, within lip or opening into mouth or along lip and covered with flap; pectoral fin either present and well developed or absent 3

3a. Dorsal fin origin above or behind anus; maxillary stout and abutting pterygoid, not tapering posteriorly; vomerine teeth absent . . . . *Ahlia egmontis* p. 255

3b. Dorsal fin origin anterior to midtrunk region; maxillary thin and tapering posteriorly, not closely associated with pterygoid; vomerine teeth present (Fig. 46) . . . . *Myrophis punctatus* p. 272

4a. Dorsal fin present, origin on nape above supraoccipital; pectoral fin absent; gill openings inferior, parallel, or con-

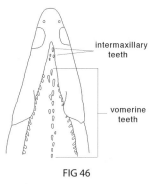

intermaxillary teeth

vomerine teeth

FIG 46

verging anteriorly; isthmus narrower than length of gill
openings. 5

4b. Dorsal fin present or absent—when present, origin behind
nape; pectoral fin present or absent; gill openings inferior
or lateral 7

5a. Anal fin absent . . . . *Letharchus velifer* p. 270

5b. Anal fin present 6

6a. Body depth 2.6% to 3.5% of TL; 7 to 11 maxillary teeth;
11 to 17 dentary teeth; head 7% to 8.8% of TL
. . . . *Callechelys muraena* p. 260

6b. Body depth 1.7% to 2.2% of TL; 4 or 5 maxillary teeth;
9 to 11 dentary teeth; head 5.6% to 7.1% of TL
. . . . *Callechelys guineensis* p. 261

7a. Pectoral fin present and as large or larger than eye; vertical
fins generally elevated; coloration variable 16

7b. Pectoral fin absent or vestigial; vertical fins reduced or
absent; coloration without large spots 8

8a. Gill openings entirely ventral; head pores developed; two
supratemporal pores and three preopercular pores (Fig. 47);
all fins absent 9

8b. Gill openings low but lateral; head pores reduced; three
supratemporal and two preopercular pores; at least dorsal
fin present 10

9a. Posterior nostril inside mouth, with irregular margin but
without flap; anterior nostril not tubular; eye minute
. . . . *Ichthyapus ophioneus* p. 268

9b. Posterior nostril outside of mouth and with flap; anterior
nostril tubular; eye moderately developed
. . . . *Apterichtus kendalli* p. 257

10a. Pectoral fin small, lappetlike, located on upper corner of
gill opening 11

10b. Pectoral fin absent 12

11a. Series of small pale spots above each lateral line pore along
body, tail, and branchial region (may be diffuse in large
specimens); pectoral fin base 13% to 32% of length of gill
openings . . . . *Bascanichthys scuticaris* p. 259

11b. No pale spots above lateral line pores; pectoral fin base
greater that 25% of length of gill openings
. . . . *Bascanichthys bascanium* p. 258

12a. Underside of snout not grooved; intermaxillary teeth
inconspicuous (Fig. 46) 13

12b. Underside of snout grooved; intermaxillary teeth conspicuous. 14

13a. Anterior nostril porelike, without raised rim
. . . . *Caralophia loxochila* p. 262

13b. Anterior nostril tubular, projecting beyond upper lip
. . . . *Ethadophis akkistikos* p. 265

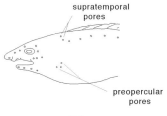

supratemporal
pores

preopercular
pores

FIG 47

14a. Anterior nostril within short tube, extending distinctly beyond underside of snout . . . *Gordiichthys ergodes* p. 266

14b. Anterior nostril not tubular, but partially set off by groove from underside of snout 15

15a. Body depth 1.1% to 1.3% of TL; preanal vertebrae 92 to 98 and total vertebrae 168 to 176; lateral line pores 161 to 166 . . . . *Gordiichthys leibyi* p. 268

15b. Body depth 0.8% to 1% of TL; preanal vertebrae 105 to 111 and total vertebrae 193 to 206; lateral line pores 186 to 189 . . . . *Gordiichthys irretitus* p. 267

16a. Anterior jaw teeth long and fanglike, extending outside of mouth when mouth closed; lower jaw extends beyond snout . . . . *Aplatophis chauliodus* p. 256

16b. Anterior jaw teeth not fanglike, not extending outside of mouth when mouth is closed; lower jaw does not extend beyond snout 17

17a. Teeth molariform or granular; pectoral fin with broad base, extending length of gill openings . . . . *Myrichthys breviceps* p. 271

17b. Teeth pointed; pectoral fin with narrow base, at level of upper one-half of gill openings 18

18a. Eye anterior to middle of upper jaw; some teeth long and fanglike 19

18b. Eye over middle of upper jaw; teeth not long and fanglike 20

19a. Color pattern consisting of large brown spots on pale background; two preopercular pores on light background (Fig. 48); dorsal fin origin posterior to pectoral fin tip by distance less than pectoral fin length . . . . *Echiophis intertinctus* p. 263

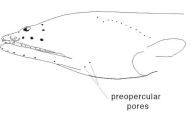

preopercular pores

FIG 48

19b. Color pattern consisting of small brown spots on tan background; three preopercular pores set in dark spots (Fig. 49); dorsal fin origin posterior to pectoral fin tip by distance greater than pectoral fin length . . . . *Echiophis punctifer* p. 264

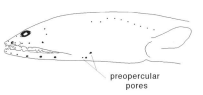

preopercular pores

FIG 49

20a. Teeth of upper jaw uniserial anteriorly (small juveniles) or throughout length (large juveniles and adults); body depth behind gill openings 1.5% to 1.8% of TL . . . .*Ophichthus melanoporus* p. 276

20b. Teeth of upper jaw biserial for most of length; body depth behind gill openings 2.3% to 7.7% of TL 21

21a. Dorsal fin origin distinctly posterior to tip of pectoral fin 22

21b. Dorsal fin origin above, slightly posterior to, or slightly anterior to tip of pectoral fin 24

22a. Body dark, lacking bands and spots . . . . *Ophichthus cruentifer* p. 273

Ahlia egmontis (Jordan 1884)
Key worm eel

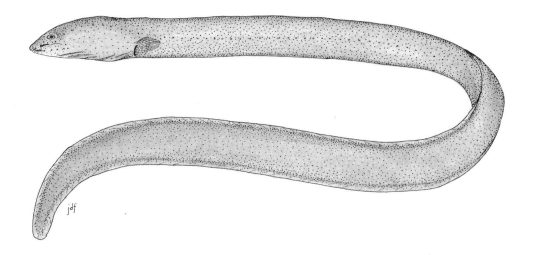

Ahlia egmontis is moderately elongate and laterally compressed, with well-developed pectoral fin and caudal fin, and dorsal fin originating above or behind anus. It is distinguished from the other species of the family by the following combination of characters. Snout is broad and subconical and overhangs lower jaw. Anterior nostril is tubular, with lateral interior projection. Posterior nostril is located along edge of lip, beneath flap, and opens into mouth. Jaw teeth are small, conical, and recurved, with 11 to 25 on upper jaw and 12 to 19 on lower jaw. Intermaxillary teeth consist of outer circle of 6 to 9 stout teeth and several smaller inner teeth. Vomerine teeth are absent. Gill openings are constricted, shorter than length of pectoral fin base, and crescent shaped. Infraorbital pores number six, supraorbital pores number five, and supratemporal pores number three. Snout is 17% to 21%, eye is 5.6% to 7.7%, and mouth length is 23% to 30% of head length. Head length is 7.9% to 10%, predorsal length is 44% to 49%, trunk length is 33% to 36%, and depth behind gill openings is 1.8% to 3.7% of TL. Total vertebrae number 155 to 167, predorsal vertebrae number 65 to 72, and preanal vertebrae number 60 to 66. Color is pale to tan, with scattered melanophores dorsally. Mature males are darker, especially on tail, fins, and branchial area, with reddish brown nuchal band.

This species occurs in the western Atlantic from North Carolina to the Guianas, including Bermuda, the eastern Gulf of Mexico, and the West Indies. It has been captured from near shore to 37 m, and is common in eel-grass beds and on sandy bottoms around coral reefs. Maximum known size is 433 mm TL; males mature between 142 and 343 mm TL, and females mature between 276 and 387 mm TL.

REFERENCES: Hoese and Moore 1977; C. R. Robins et al. 1986; McCosker et al. 1989; Leiby 1989.

Aplatophis chauliodus   Böhlke 1956
Tusky eel

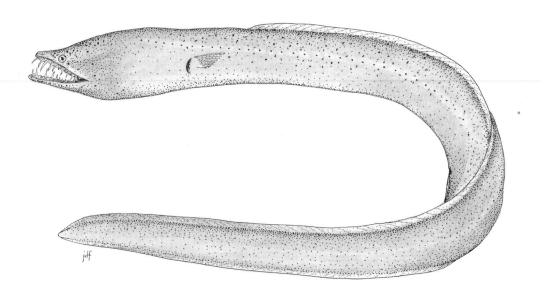

Aplatophis chauliodus is relatively stout, and cylindrical anteriorly and compressed posteriorly, with anus slightly posterior to midlength and tail ending as a hard, finless blunt tip. It is distinguished from the other species of the family by the following combination of characters. Snout is short. Jaws are elongate, with lower jaw projecting beyond upper jaw. Anterior nostril is tubular. Posterior nostril is short broad tube opening ventrally behind anterior nostril. Eye is small. Anterior teeth are fanglike and project outside closed mouth. Jaw teeth are variable; upper jaw has outer row of 17 to 20 short, conical teeth and inner row of 11 to 13 long, depressible teeth. Lower jaw has 3 or 4 long fangs anteriorly, outer row of 19 to 38 posteriorly, and inner row of 9 to 20 depressible teeth. Intermaxillary teeth consist of outer ring of large, fanglike teeth and 2 median teeth. Vomerine teeth are small, conical, and uniserial; are continuous with intermaxillary teeth; and number 2 to 7. Tongue is enlarged as fleshy lure. Dorsal fin originates posterior to pectoral fin. Head pores are minute, with six infraorbital and three supraorbital. Snout is 13% to 17%, eye is 4% to 6.3%, mouth length is 32% to 40%, and pectoral fin length is 13% to 17% of head length. Head length is 14% to 16%, trunk length is 34% to 37%, predorsal length is 25% to 28%, and depth behind gill openings is 3.6% to 6.4% of TL. Total vertebrae number 110 to 115, predorsal vertebrae number 20 to 26, and preanal vertebrae number 53 to 56. Color is tan with brown speckling, fine spots on head, larger freckles on body, and pale belly.

This species occurs in the western North Atlantic from the northern Gulf of Mexico west of Mobile Bay, Puerto Rico, and Panama to the Guianas. It has been captured from near shore to 91 m. Maximum known size is 815 mm TL; males mature at 334 mm TL, and females mature at 439 mm TL.

REFERENCES: Böhlke 1956; McCosker et al. 1989; Leiby 1989; Boschung 1992.

Apterichtus kendalli   (Gilbert 1891)
Finless eel

Apterichtus kendalli is elongate and cylindrical, with a pointed snout and tail ending as a hard, finless sharp point, and without dorsal and anal fins. It is distinguished from the other species of the family by the following combination of characters. Snout is subconical, overhangs lower jaw, and is flattened and grooved ventrally. Lips lack barbels. Anterior nostril is tubular, and posterior nostril is slitlike and located along edge of lip. Eye is moderately developed. Teeth are pointed and uniserial in jaws and vomer. Intermaxillary teeth are large and separated from vomer teeth by gap. Gill openings are ventral and converge anteriorly. Isthmus is narrow. Head pores are well developed, with seven infraorbital, five supraorbital, and three supratemporal. Snout is 19% to 21%, eye is 5.7% to 9.4%, and mouth length is 38% to 40% of head length. Head length is 5.3% to 7.1%, trunk length is 38% to 43%, and depth behind gill openings is 1.5% to 1.9% of TL. Total vertebrae number 137 to 145, and preanal vertebrae number 61 to 63. Color is pale yellow to tan in preservative. Fresh specimens have fine melanophores on dorsal surface and two patches behind eyes surrounded by pale patch.

This species occurs in the tropical waters of the central and western Atlantic. In the western Atlantic it occurs from the east coast of Florida to Venezuela, including the Bahamas and the northeastern Gulf of Mexico. Depths of capture range from 6 to 401 m, but it is most frequently captured between 30 and 80 m in sandy bottoms. Maximum known size is 542 mm TL; females mature between 225 and 246 mm TL.

REFERENCES: Williams and Shipp 1980; C. R. Robins et al. 1986; McCosker et al. 1989; Leiby 1989; Boschung 1992.

Bascanichthys bascanium (Jordan 1884)
Sooty eel

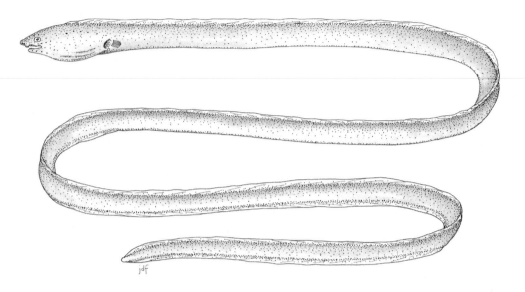

Bascanichthys bascanium is elongate, cylindrical anteriorly and compressed posteriorly, with anus posterior to midlength and tail ending as a hard, finless point. It is distinguished from the other species of the family by the following combination of characters. Snout is short and blunt, overhangs lower jaw, and is grooved on underside. Lips lack barbels. Anterior nostril is tubular. Posterior nostril opens into mouth. Eye is small. Jaw teeth are conical, recurved, and uniserial, with 15 or 16 in upper jaw and 15 to 18 in lower jaw. Intermaxillary teeth number 3 and form inverted V. Vomerine teeth are separate from intermaxillary teeth, number 21, and are in two irregular rows. Gill openings are low on sides, crescentic, and about as long as isthmus. Pectoral fin is flaplike, and pectoral fin base is 44% to 77% of length of gill opening. Infraorbital pores number six, supraorbital pores number four, and supratemporal pores number three. Snout is 13% to 15%, eye is 4% to 5.2%, and mouth length is 22% to 27% of head length. Head length is 4.6% to 6.3%, trunk is 50% to 52%, predorsal length is 2% to 22.8%, and depth behind gill openings is 1.2% to 1.8% of TL. Total vertebrae number 182 to 189, predorsal vertebrae number 1 or 2, and preanal vertebrae number 95 to 102. Color is dark dorsally and pale ventrally, with head and fins paler than body.

This species occurs in the western North Atlantic from North Carolina to Florida and in the eastern Gulf of Mexico to Texas and the Bay of Campeche along shallow sandy beaches to 24 m. It is not abundant east of Mobile Bay in the Gulf of Mexico. Maximum known size is 786 mm TL.

REFERENCES: Leiby and Yerger 1980; C. R. Robins et al. 1986; McCosker et al. 1989; Leiby 1989; Boschung 1992.

Bascanichthys scuticaris (Goode and Bean 1880)
Whip eel

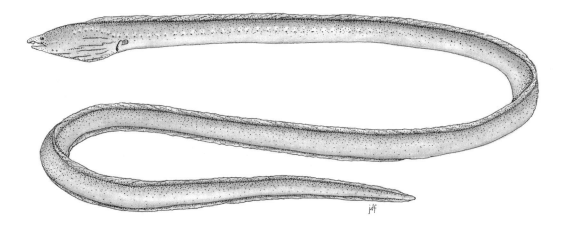

Bascanichthys scuticaris is elongate, cylindrical anteriorly and compressed posteriorly, with anus posterior to midlength and tail ending as a hard, finless point. It is distinguished from the other species of the family by the following combination of characters. Snout is short and blunt, overhangs lower jaw, and is grooved on underside. Lips lack barbels. Anterior nostril is tubular. Posterior nostril opens into mouth. Eye is small. Jaw teeth are conical, recurved, small, and mostly uniserial, with 16 to 23 in outer row and 6 to 12 in inner row of upper jaw and 16 to 19 in lower jaw. Intermaxillary teeth number 3 to 5 and form inverted V. Vomerine teeth are separated from intermaxillary teeth, number 11 to 18, and are in two irregular rows. Gill openings are low on sides, crescentic, and about as long as isthmus. Pectoral fin is minute, and base length is 13% to 32% of gill opening length. Infraorbital pores number six, supraorbital pores number four, and supratemporal pores number three. Snout is 14% to 15%, eye is 3.3% to 6.6%, and mouth length is 23% to 28% of head length. Head length is 5.4% to 6.5%, trunk length is 47% to 50%, predorsal length is 2.6% to 3.4%, and depth behind gill openings is 1.6% to 2.4% of TL. Total vertebrae number 159 to 167, predorsal vertebrae number 1 or 2, and preanal vertebrae number 83 to 89. Color is brown dorsally, with overlapping dots, and pale ventrally. Lateral line pores of branchial region and body are marked with white spots.

This species occurs in the western North Atlantic from North Carolina to the Gulf of Mexico along exposed sandy beaches to 46 m. It is most common from Cape San Blas, Florida, to the Florida Keys in the Gulf of Mexico. Maximum known size is 756 mm TL; males mature at 534 mm TL.

REFERENCES: Hoese and Moore 1977; Leiby and Yerger 1980; C. R. Robins et al. 1986; McCosker et al. 1989; Leiby 1989; Boschung 1992.

Callechelys muraena   Jordan and Evermann 1887
Blotched snake eel

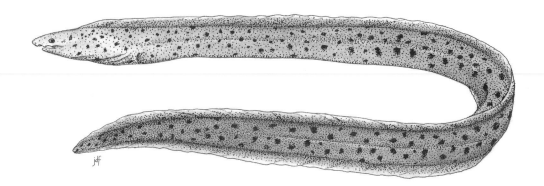

Callechelys muraena is moderately elongate and laterally compressed, with anus posterior to midlength and tail ending as a hard, finless point. It is distinguished from the other species of the family by the following combination of characters. Snout is acute and rounded, overhangs lower jaw, and is deeply grooved on underside. Lips lack barbels. Anterior nostril is tubular. Posterior nostril opens on underside of snout. Eye is moderately developed. Jaw teeth are moderately slender, conical, and uniserial, with 7 to 11 teeth on upper jaw and 11 to 17 teeth on lower jaw. Intermaxillary teeth consist of two pairs located in groove on underside of snout. Vomerine teeth number 8 to 12 and are separated from intermaxillary teeth. Gill openings are ventrolateral to ventral, converge anteriorly, and are longer than isthmus. Pectoral fin is absent. Infraorbital pores number six, supraorbital pores number four, and supratemporal pores number three. Snout is 13% to 17%, eye is 5.8% to 9.7%, and mouth length is 24% to 32% of head length. Head length is 7% to 8.8%, trunk length is 48% to 55%, predorsal length is 2.9% to 3.5%, and depth behind gill openings is 2.6% to 3.7% of TL. Total vertebrae number 139 to 144, and preanal vertebrae number 80 to 85. Color is pale tan on head and anterior trunk, grading to darker brown posteriorly, with numerous brown eye-sized spots and mottling on body. Head is pale yellowish without spots or mottling.

This species occurs in the western North Atlantic from North Carolina to Florida and the Gulf of Mexico, off Florida and the Yucatán Peninsula. It has been captured from 27 to 115 m. Maximum known size is 590 mm TL; males mature at about 379 mm TL, and females mature at about 317 mm TL.

REFERENCES: McCosker et al. 1989; Leiby 1989; Boschung 1992.

Callechelys guineensis (Osorio 1893)
Shorttail snake eel

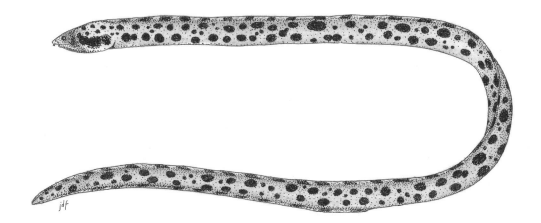

Callechelys guineensis is moderately elongate and laterally compressed, with anus posterior to midlength and tail ending as a hard, finless point. It is distinguished from the other species of the family by the following combination of characters. Snout is acute and rounded, overhangs lower jaw, and is deeply grooved on underside. Lips lack barbels. Anterior nostril is tubular. Posterior nostril opens on underside of snout. Eye is moderately developed. Jaw teeth are moderate in size, slender, conical, and uniserial, with 4 or 5 in upper jaw and 9 to 11 in lower jaw. Single pair of intermaxillary teeth occur in groove on underside of snout. Vomerine teeth number 6 to 9, are in two widely separated rows, and are separated from intermaxillary teeth. Gill openings are ventrolateral to ventral, converge anteriorly, and are longer than isthmus. Pectoral fin is absent. Infraorbital pores number six, supraorbital pores number four, and supratemporal pores number three. Snout is 11% to 17%, eye is 3.9% to 7.7%, and mouth length is 23% to 33% of head length. Head length is 5.6% to 6.7%, trunk length is 59% to 62%, predorsal length is 2% to 2.8%, and depth behind gill openings is 1.7% to 2.2% of TL. Total vertebrae number 172 to 182, and preanal vertebrae number 111 to 118. Color is cream to tan, with numerous brown to black spots. Spots on anterior head are equal to eye and those on rest of body are larger but variable in size. Belly is pale.

This species occurs in the tropical to warm temperate Atlantic Ocean from near shore to 36 m. In the western Atlantic it occurs from the eastern coast of Florida, the western coast of Florida in the Gulf of Mexico, the West Indies, and the Bahamas. Maximum known size is 1,080 mm TL; males mature at 722 mm TL.

REFERENCES: Böhlke and Chaplin 1968 (as *Callechelys perryae*); C. R. Robins et al. 1986 (as *C. perryae*); McCosker et al. 1989; Leiby 1989.

Caralophia loxochila Böhlke 1955
Slantlip eel

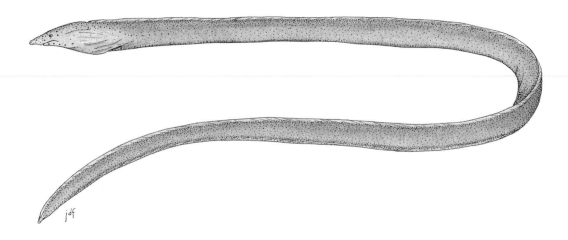

Caralophia loxochila is elongate and cylindrical throughout length, with anus posterior to midlength and tail ending as a hard, finless blunt point. It is distinguished from the other species of the family by the following combination of characters. Snout is subconical and blunt, overhangs lower jaw, and lacks groove on underside. Lips lack barbels. Anterior nostril is porelike with ventrolateral projection and is not tubular. Posterior nostril opens into mouth. Eye is small. Jaw teeth are bluntly conical, moderate in size, and uniserial, with 8 to 12 in upper jaw and 8 to 11 in lower jaw. Intermaxillary teeth number 4, are stout, and are arranged in arc. Vomerine teeth number 5 to 8, are in single row, and are separated from intermaxillary teeth. Gill openings are ventral, converge anteriorly, and are longer than isthmus. Pectoral fin is absent. Infraorbital pores number six, supraorbital pores number four, and supratemporal pores number three. Snout is 15% to 18%, eye is 3.2% to 4.4%, and mouth length is 23% to 30% of head length. Head length is 6.5% to 8.7%, trunk length is 43% to 47%, predorsal length is 4.3% to 5.2%, and depth behind gill openings is 12.6% to 2.3% of TL. Total vertebrae number 138 to 155, predorsal vertebrae number 2 or 3, and preanal vertebrae number 68 to 79. Color is brown, darker dorsally than ventrally, with pale fins.

This species occurs in the western Atlantic from the Gulf of Mexico off Florida, the Bahamas, and the Caribbean Sea to Brazil. It has been captured in coves and bays with ichthyocides over turtle-grass beds and sand from near shore to 3 m. Maximum known size is 456 mm TL; males mature between 350 and 456 mm TL.

REFERENCES: Böhlke 1955; Böhlke and Chaplin 1968; C. R. Robins et al. 1986; McCosker et al. 1989; Leiby 1989.

Echiophis intertinctus (Richardson 1848)
Spotted spoon-nose eel

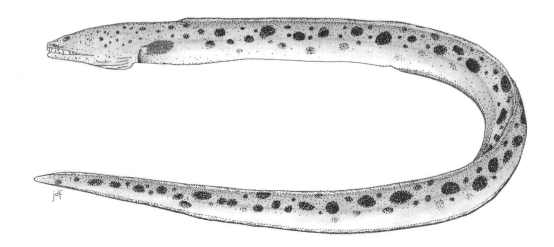

Echiophis intertinctus is relatively stout and cylindrical, with anus slightly posterior to mid-length and tail ending as a hard, finless blunt tip. It is distinguished from the other species of the family by the following combination of characters. Snout is short and subconical. Jaws are elongate and subequal. Lips lack barbels. Anterior nostril is tubular. Posterior nostril is in short tube. Eye is moderate sized. Jaw teeth are stout, conical, and biserial. Upper jaw has single row of 4 or 5 large to fanglike teeth anteriorly and biserial row posteriorly, with outer row of 14 to 26 large stout teeth generally interspersed with smaller teeth, and inner row of 8 to 14 small uniform teeth. Intermaxillary teeth consist of outer circle of 5 teeth and 2 stout median teeth. Vomerine teeth number 20 to 43 small teeth separated from intermaxillary teeth and are arranged in two converging rows. Dorsal fin originates behind pectoral fin tip. Snout is 11% to 14%, eye is 5.2% to 9.2%, mouth length is 40% to 48%, and pectoral fin length is 20% to 28% of head length. Head length is 11% to 12%, trunk length is 32% to 37%, predorsal length is 13% to 17%, and depth behind gill openings is 2.9% to 4.4% of

TL. Infraorbital pores number six, supraorbital pores number four, preopercular pores number two, and supratemporal pores number three. Total vertebrae number 125 to 128, predorsal vertebrae number 14 to 18, and preanal vertebrae number 53 to 58. Color is cream, slightly darker dorsally than ventrally, with faint tan to yellow stripe at base of median fins and two to three irregular rows of large brown spots above lateral line. Spots are larger than eye to larger than pectoral fin. Median fins are pale basally and spotted to striped marginally.

This species occurs in the western Atlantic from North Carolina to southern Florida, the Gulf of Mexico, and the Caribbean Sea to southern Brazil from near shore to 64 m. It occurs from the west coast of Florida to just west of Mobile Bay and off Yucatán in the Gulf of Mexico. Maximum known size is 1,030 mm TL; males mature between 478 and 863 mm TL, and females mature between 420 and 855 mm TL.

REFERENCES: Hoese and Moore 1976; C. R. Robins et al. 1986; McCosker et al. 1989; Leiby 1989; Boschung 1992.

Echiophis punctifer (Kaup 1860)
Stippled spoon-nose eel

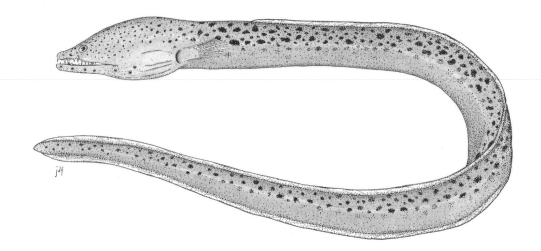

Echiophis punctifer is relatively stout and cylindrical, with anus slightly posterior to midlength and tail ending as a hard, finless blunt tip. It is distinguished from the other species of the family by the following combination of characters. Snout is short and subconical. Jaws are elongate and subequal. Lips lack barbels. Anterior nostril is tubular. Posterior nostril is in short tube. Eye is moderate sized. Jaw teeth are stout, conical, and biserial. Upper jaw teeth are uniserial anteriorly and biserial posteriorly, with 14 to 26 stout teeth in outer row and 8 to 14 small teeth in inner row. Lower jaw has 4 to 6 large teeth anteriorly and biserial row posteriorly, with 14 to 22 teeth in outer row and 14 to 26 small teeth in inner row. Intermaxillary teeth consist of outer circle of 5 teeth and 2 stout median teeth. Vomerine teeth are separated from intermaxillary teeth and are arranged in two rows. Head pores are small, with six infraorbital, four supraorbital, three preopercular, and three supratemporal. Snout is 11% to 14%, eye is 4.8% to 7.9%, mouth length is 42% to 52%, and pectoral fin length is 25% to 32% of head length. Head length is 11% to 13%, trunk length is 32% to 35%, predorsal length is 16% to 19%, and depth be-

hind gill openings is 3.2% to 5% of TL. Total vertebrae number 130 to 143, predorsal vertebrae number 16 to 19, and preanal vertebrae number 54 to 61. Color is tan, with brown stripe on each side of dorsal fin, faint brown to yellow stripe along lateral line, and reddish brown ventral stripe along base of anal fin. Numerous small brown spots, about equal to eye, form six to eight indistinct rows on body. Vertical fins are pale basally and spotted or striped marginally.

This species occurs in the tropical to warm temperate waters of the Atlantic Ocean from near shore to 100 m. In the western Atlantic it occurs in the western Gulf of Mexico, from Mobile Bay to Texas, and off Yucatán, and from the Caribbean Sea to southern Brazil. Maximum known size is 1,191 mm TL; males mature between 590 and 868 mm TL, and females mature between 620 and 1,191 mm TL. McCosker et al. (1989) synonymized *Echiophis mordax* with this species.

REFERENCES: Ginsburg 1951; Hoese and Moore 1976; C. R. Robins et al. 1986; McCosker et al. 1989; Leiby 1989; Boschung 1992.

Ethadophis akkistikos　McCosker and Böhlke 1984
Indifferent eel

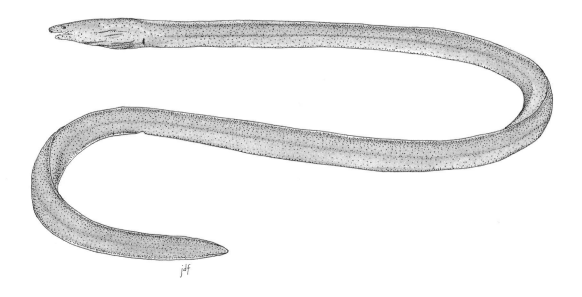

jdf

Ethadophis akkistikos is elongate, cylindrical anteriorly and compressed posteriorly, with anus posterior to midlength and tail ending as a hard, finless blunt point. It is distinguished from the other species of the family by the following combination of characters. Snout is short and rounded, overhangs lower jaw, and is not grooved on underside. Lips lack barbels. Anterior nostril is tubular. Posterior nostril opens into mouth. Eye is moderate in size. Jaw teeth are conical, small, and uniserial, with 11 to 16 in upper jaw and 12 to 16 in lower jaw. Four intermaxillary teeth are arranged in semicircle. Vomerine teeth number 8 to 14, are separated from intermaxillary teeth, and are in single row. Gill openings are low on body, crescentic, and shorter than isthmus. Pectoral fin is absent. Infraorbital pores number six, supraorbital pores number four, and supratemporal pores number three. Snout is 16% to 18%, eye is 3.4% to 4%, and mouth length is 26% to 29% of head length. Head length is 5.8% to 6.6%, trunk length is 52% to 55%, predorsal length is 4.4%, and depth posterior to gill openings is 1.5% to 2% of TL. Total vertebrae number 161 to 173, predorsal vertebrae number 3 or 4, and preanal vertebrae number 92 to 98. Color is pale yellow to tan, with few dark spots dorsally.

This species occurs in the western North Atlantic from the northern Gulf of Mexico and off Suriname at 30 to 60 m. Maximum known size is 316 mm TL, and females mature at 242 mm TL.

REFERENCES: McCosker and Böhlke 1984; McCosker et al. 1989; Leiby 1989; Boschung 1992.

Gordiichthys ergodes McCosker, Böhlke and Böhlke 1989
Irksome eel

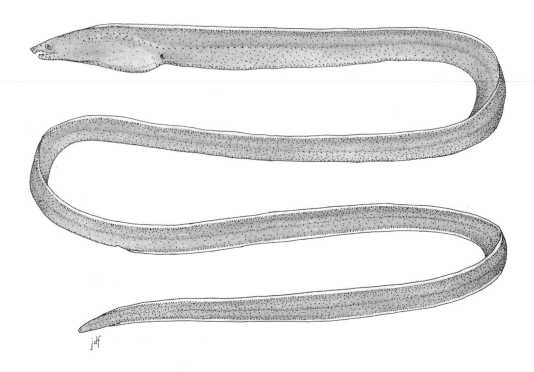

Gordiichthys ergodes is elongate and cylindrical, except compressed far posteriorly, with anus about at midlength and tail ending as a hard, finless blunt tip. It is distinguished from the other species of the family by the following combination of characters. Snout is short and blunt, overhangs lower jaw, and is grooved on underside. Lips lack barbels. Anterior nostril is tubular. Posterior nostril opens into mouth. Eye is small. Jaw teeth are conical, small, and uniserial, with 9 to 11 in upper jaw and 9 in lower jaw. Four intermaxillary teeth are arranged in chevron. Vomerine teeth number 11, are separated from intermaxillary teeth, and are in single row. Gill openings are low on body, crescentic, and shorter than isthmus. Pectoral fin is absent. Infraorbital pores number six, supraorbital pores number four, and supratemporal pores number three. Snout is 18%, eye is 4.6%, and mouth length is 30% of head length. Head length is 5.8%, trunk length is 50%, predorsal length is 3%, and depth posterior to gill openings is 1.7% of TL. Total vertebrae number 186, predorsal vertebrae number 1, and preanal vertebrae number 98. Color is reddish brown, and median fins are colorless.

This species occurs in the western North Atlantic. It is known from a single specimen from the northern Gulf of Mexico between Naples, Florida, and Biloxi, Mississippi. Maximum known size is 339 mm TL.

REFERENCE: McCosker et al. 1989.

Gordiichthys irretitus   Jordan and Davis 1891
Horsehair eel

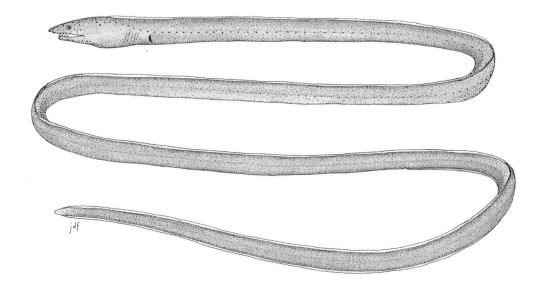

Gordiichthys irretitus is extremely elongate and cylindrical, except compressed far posteriorly, with anus posterior to midlength and tail ending as a hard, finless blunt tip. It is distinguished from the other species of the family by the following combination of characters. Snout is short and blunt, overhangs lower jaw, and is grooved on underside. Lips lack barbels. Anterior nostril is set in groove. Posterior nostril opens into mouth. Eye is small. Jaw teeth are conical, small, and uniserial, with 9 or 10 in upper jaw and 11 in lower jaw. Three intermaxillary teeth are arranged in triangle. Vomerine teeth number 7, are separated from intermaxillary teeth, and are in single row. Pectoral fin is absent. Infraorbital pores number six, supraorbital pores number four, and supratemporal pores number three. Snout is 19% to 21%, eye is 4% to 6%, and mouth length is 30% to 35% of head length. Head length is 4.5% to 5.4%, trunk length is 50% to 53%, and depth behind gill openings is 0.8% to 1% of TL. Total vertebrae number 193 to 206, predorsal vertebrae number 2, and preanal vertebrae number 105 to 111. Color is yellow to tan, with minute brown spots above midline, and median fins are colorless.

This species occurs in the western North Atlantic from the northeastern Gulf of Mexico off the west coast of Florida and Puerto Rico. It has been captured between 90 and 200 m. Maximum known size is 790 mm TL, and females mature at 730 mm TL.

REFERENCES: McCosker and Böhlke 1984; C. R. Robins et al. 1986; McCosker et al. 1989; Leiby 1989; Boschung 1992.

Gordiichthys leibyi   McCosker and Böhlke 1984
String eel

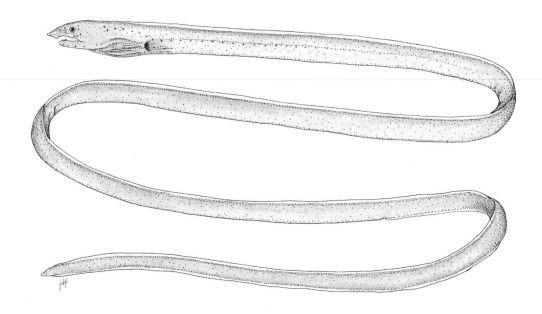

Gordiichthys leibyi is very elongate and cylindrical, except compressed far posteriorly, with anus posterior to midlength and tail ending as a hard, finless blunt tip. It is distinguished from the other species of the family by the following combination of characters. Snout is short and blunt, overhangs lower jaw, and is grooved on underside. Lips lack barbels. Anterior nostril is set in groove. Posterior nostril opens into mouth. Eye is small. Jaw teeth are conical, small, and uniserial, with 8 to 10 in upper jaw and 10 to 12 in lower jaw. Four intermaxillary teeth are arranged in triangle. Vomerine teeth number 6 to 8, are separated from intermaxillary teeth, and are in single row. Infraorbital pores number six, supraorbital pores number four, and supratemporal pores number three. Pectoral fin is absent. Snout is 18%

to 21%, eye is 4% to 5.3%, and mouth length is 28% to 32% of head length. Head length is 5% to 5.9%, trunk length is 51% to 53%, and depth behind gill openings is 1% to 1.2% of TL. Total vertebrae number 168 to 176, predorsal vertebrae number 2, and preanal vertebrae number 92 to 98. Color is yellow to tan, with minute spots above midline.

This species occurs in the western North Atlantic from the east coast of Florida to the northeastern Gulf of Mexico. It has been captured from 37 to 72 m. Maximum known size is 424 mm TL, and females mature at 274 mm TL.

REFERENCES: McCosker and Böhlke 1984; McCosker et al. 1989; Leiby 1989.

Ichthyapus ophioneus (Evermann and Marsh 1902)
Surf eel

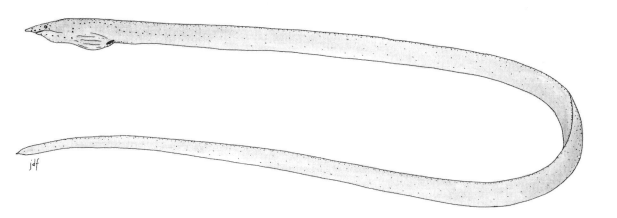

Ichthyapus ophioneus is elongate and cylindrical, with a pointed snout and tail ending as a hard, finless sharp point, and without dorsal and anal fins. It is distinguished from the other species of the family by the following combination of characters. Snout is relatively long and depressed and overhangs lower jaw. Lips lack barbels. Anterior nostril is convoluted, nontubular, and opens on underside of snout. Posterior nostril opens into mouth. Eye is small. Jaw teeth are pointed and uniserial, with about 24 to 30 in each jaw. Intermaxillary teeth consist of 5 to 7 teeth arranged in inverted V. Vomerine teeth are separated from intermaxillary teeth, and are biserial anteriorly and uniserial posteriorly. Gill openings are ventral. Pectoral fin is absent. Head pores are well developed, with seven infraorbital, five supraorbital, and five supratemporal. Snout is 13% to 19%, eye is 3.2% to 8.4%, and mouth

length is 25% to 30% of head length. Head length is 8% to 9.5%, trunk length is 27% to 30%, and depth behind gill opening is 1.4% to 2.8% of TL. Total vertebrae number 125 to 139, and preanal vertebrae number 43 to 51. Color is pale.

This species occurs in the western Atlantic from Bermuda, the Bahamas, southeastern Florida, the western Gulf of Mexico, and the Greater Antilles to central Brazil. The sole record from the Gulf of Mexico consists of two specimens captured at Alacran Reef, 22°30′N, 89°50′W at about 10 m. This species has generally been captured with ichthyocides in less than 15 m over sand. Maximum known size is 479 mm TL.

REFERENCES: Böhlke and Chaplin 1968; McCosker et al. 1989; Leiby 1989.

Letharchus velifer Goode and Bean 1882
Sailfin eel

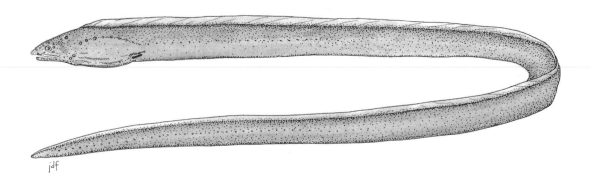

Letharchus velifer is moderately elongate and laterally compressed, with anus posterior to midlength and tail ending as a hard, finless point. It is distinguished from the other species of the family by the following combination of characters. Snout is acute and rounded, overhangs lower jaw, and lacks groove on underside. Lips lack barbels. Anterior nostril is pitlike, without raised rim. Posterior nostril opens into mouth. Eye is small. Jaw teeth are slender, pointed, and mostly uniserial, with 8 to 13 in outer row and 2 to 8 in inner row of upper jaw and 17 to 23 in lower jaw. Intermaxillary teeth are in short biserial patch. Vomerine teeth number 0 to 6 and are in single row. Gill openings are ventral, converge anteriorly, and are longer than isthmus. Pectoral and anal fins are absent. Infraorbital pores number six, supraorbital pores number five, and supratemporal pores number three. Snout is 8.9% to 13%, eye is 2.5% to 6.2%, and

mouth length is 18% to 27% of head length. Head length is 7.4% to 8.4%, trunk length is 50% to 56%, and depth behind gill openings is 1.9% to 2.9% of TL. Total vertebrae number 136 to 144, predorsal vertebrae number 1 or 2, and trunk vertebrae number 80 to 87. Color is dark brown, with darker mottling, except dorsal fin is white or pale in small specimens and has dark margin in large specimens. Head pores are pale on dark background.

This species occurs in the western North Atlantic from North Carolina to the northeastern Gulf of Mexico off northern Florida. It has been captured from 5 to 90 m. Maximum known size is 578 mm TL; males mature at 477 mm TL, and females mature between 192 and 492 mm TL.

REFERENCES: C. R. Robins et al. 1986; McCosker et al. 1989; Leiby 1989; Boschung 1992.

Myrichthys breviceps (Richardson 1848)
Sharptail eel

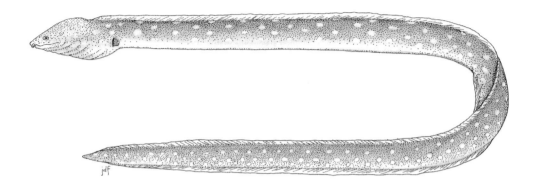

Myrichthys breviceps is elongate, cylindrical anteriorly and compressed posteriorly, with dorsal fin originating on head, pectoral fin broad based, and tail ending as a hard, finless point. It is distinguished from the other species of the family by the following combination of characters. Snout is short, acute, depressed, and has groove ventrally. Upper jaw overhangs lower jaw. Lips lack barbels, anterior nostril is tubular, and posterior nostril opens into mouth. Eye is of moderate size and above middle of upper jaw. Gill openings are vertical and semicircular. Jaw teeth are molariform, biserial in juvenile specimens and multiserial in adults. Vomerine teeth number 29 to 42 and are biserial anteriorly and multiserial posteriorly. Pectoral fin is short. Head pores are well developed, with six infraorbital, four supraorbital, five mandibular, two preopercular, and three supratemporal. Snout is 16% to 22%, eye is 6.4% to 8.4%, mouth length is 27% to 33%, and pectoral fin length is 5% to 7.9% of head length. Head length is 7.5% to 8.6%, predorsal length is 4.8% to 6.3%, trunk length is 30% to 34%, and depth behind gill openings is 2.5% to 3% of TL. Total vertebrae number 165 to 175, predorsal vertebrae number 2 or 3,

and preanal vertebrae number 61 to 65. Color is brown dorsally, including entire tail, and pale ventrally, with 30 to 35 pale spots on each side of dorsal fin more or less arranged in pairs, and one to three rows of pale spots in alternating rows on sides. Snout, cheeks, and nape have small spots, and dorsal fin has dark margin and is variously spotted. Small individuals, less than 80 mm TL, are not spotted. In life this species is green to brownish green, with pale spots with yellowish to yellow centers.

This species occurs in the western Atlantic from Bermuda, the Bahamas, the Florida Keys, the northern Gulf of Mexico, the Greater and Lesser Antilles, and islands off southern Brazil. It has been captured twice in the Gulf of Mexico—off Mobile Bay, Alabama, and the Dry Tortugas, Florida—and photographed from a submersible at the East Flower Gardens Reef in the northern Gulf of Mexico. Most specimens have been captured over sand and turtle grass at 3 to 9 m. Maximum known size is 783 mm TL.

REFERENCES: Böhlke and Chaplin 1968; Dennis and Bright 1988 (as *M. acuminatus*); McCosker et al. 1989.

Myrophis punctatus   Lütken 1852
Speckled worm eel

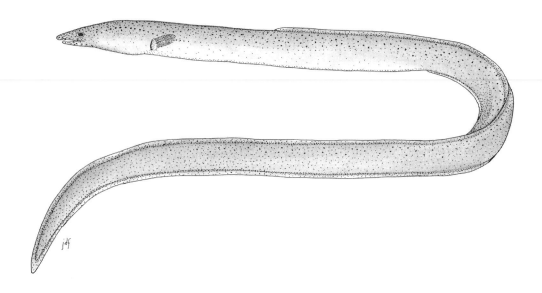

Myrophis punctatus is moderately elongate and laterally compressed, with well-developed pectoral fins and caudal fin. It is distinguished from the other species of the family by the following combination of characters. Snout is conical, overhangs snout, and lacks groove on underside. Lips lack barbels. Anterior nostril is tubular. Posterior nostril is located along edge to lip, beneath flap, and opens into mouth. Eye is well developed. Jaw teeth are small, conical, and at least partially biserial, with 23 to 25 close-set teeth in outer row and 6 to 12 longer teeth in inner row of upper jaw, and 26 to 28 small teeth in outer row and 6 or 7 teeth in inner row of lower jaw. Intermaxillary teeth consist of outer circle of 9 or 10 teeth and several inner teeth. Vomerine teeth are continuous with intermaxillary teeth and consist of 24 to 29 bi- or uniserial teeth. Gill openings are constricted and located anterior to base of pectoral fin. Head pores number six infraorbital, five supraorbital, one postorbital, and three supratemporal. Snout is 11% to 16%, eye is 5.9%

to 9.2%, and mouth length is 22% to 32% of head length. Head length is 9% to 12%, predorsal length is 23% to 28%, trunk length is 27% to 31%, and depth behind gill openings is 2.4% to 3.5% of TL. Total vertebrae number 141 to 154, predorsal vertebrae number 29 to 34, and preanal vertebrae number 51 to 55. Color is pale tan to dark brown, with numerous squarish brown freckles on dorsal and lateral aspects of head, chin, and body. Large specimens are darker than small specimens.

This species occurs in the western Atlantic Ocean from North Carolina to Brazil, including the Gulf of Mexico and the West Indies. It is most frequently captured inshore in protected areas to 7 m, including brackish waters, and has been captured at the surface at night. Maximum known size is 353 mm TL.

REFERENCES: Hoese and Moore 1977; C. R. Robins et al. 1986; McCosker et al. 1989; Leiby 1989; Boschung 1992.

Ophichthus cruentifer (Goode and Bean 1896)
Margined snake eel

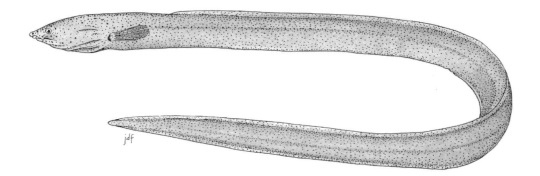

Ophichthus cruentifer is elongate, cylindrical anteriorly and laterally compressed posteriorly, with dorsal fin originating posterior to tip of pectoral fins and tail ending as a hard, finless point. It is distinguished from the other species of the family by the following combination of characters. Snout is subconical and overhangs lower jaw. Lips lack barbels. Anterior nostril is tubular and has dorsal groove. Posterior nostril opens outside of mouth and is covered with flap projecting below lip line. Eye is of moderate size. Jaw teeth are small, conical, and usually biserial, with 15 to 20 in outer row and 10 to 18 in inner row of upper jaw, and 17 to 25 in outer row and 3 to 13 in inner row of lower jaw. Large specimens have 2 to 5 additional teeth anteriorly in upper jaw. Intermaxillary teeth number about 5. Vomerine teeth are in three to seven pairs. Pectoral fin is well developed. Head pores are developed, with six infraorbital, five supraorbital, five or six mandibular, three preopercular, and three supra-temporal. Snout is 20% to 23%, eye is 5.6% to 9.2%, mouth length is 29% to 37%, and pectoral fin length is 20% to 30% of head length. Head length is 6.9% to 8.7%, predorsal length is 9.5% to 10%, trunk length is 31% to 34%, and depth behind gill openings is 2.3% to 3% of TL. Total vertebrae number 144 to 155, predorsal vertebrae number 14 to 19, and preanal vertebrae number 56 to 61. Color is grayish brown.

This species occurs in the western North Atlantic from Georges Bank and the Gulf of Maine to Florida, the Gulf of Mexico, and the Guianas. It has been captured from 36 to 1,350 m. Maximum known size is 467 mm TL; males mature at about 300 mm TL, and females mature between 200 and 467 mm TL.

REFERENCES: C. R. Robins et al. 1986; McCosker et al. 1989; Leiby 1989; Boschung 1992.

Ophichthus gomesii (Castelnau 1855)
Shrimp eel

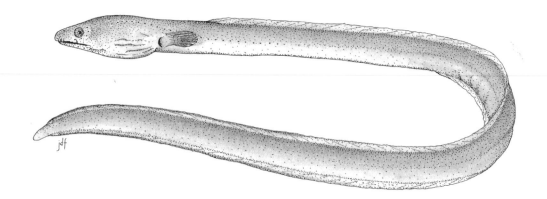

Ophichthus gomesii is moderately elongate, cylindrical anteriorly and laterally compressed posteriorly, with dorsal fin originating posterior to tip of pectoral fins and tail ending as a hard, finless point. It is distinguished from the other species of the family by the following combination of characters. Snout overhangs lower jaw. Lips lack barbels. Anterior nostril is tubular and has dorsal groove. Posterior nostril opens outside of mouth and is covered by flap projecting below lip line. Eye is moderate in size. Jaw teeth are small, conical, and biserial in young and triserial or quadriserial in adults. Intermaxillary teeth number 5 or 7 and are arranged in ring or inverted V. Vomerine teeth are slightly separated from intermaxillary teeth and are arranged in two or three rows extending as far as upper jaw teeth. Head pores are well developed, with six infraorbital, four supraorbital, six mandibular, two preopercular, and three supratemporal. Snout is 15% to 20%, eye is 8.6% to 12%, mouth is 35% to 53%, and pectoral fin length is 37% to 45% of head length. Head length is 9.6% to 14%, trunk length is 23% to 28%, predorsal length is 13% to 17%, and depth behind gill openings is 2.7% to 3.7% of TL. Total vertebrae number 138 to 153, predorsal vertebrae number 12 to 18, and preanal vertebrae number 44 to 52. Color is grayish brown to slate gray dorsally and pale ventrally, with head pores pale, inconspicuous, or outlined with dark spots. Vertical fins have dark margins posteriorly.

This species occurs in the western Atlantic from South Carolina to southern Brazil, including the northern Gulf of Mexico and the West Indies. It has been captured from near shore to 90 m and rarely from 421 to 457 m. Maximum known size is 665 mm TL; males mature between 330 and 570 mm TL, and females mature between 335 and 577 mm TL.

REFERENCES: Ginsburg 1951; Hoese and Moore 1977; Castro-Aguirre and Márquez-Espinoza 1981; C. R. Robins et al. 1986; McCosker et al. 1989; Leiby 1989; Boschung 1992.

Ophichthus hyposagmatus   McCosker and Böhlke 1984
Faint-saddled snake eel

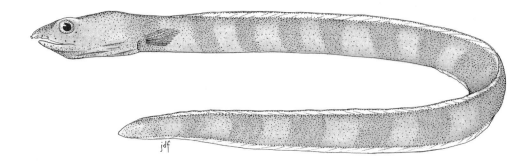

Ophichthus hyposagmatus is moderately elongate, relatively stout, cylindrical anteriorly and compressed posteriorly, with dorsal fin originating above tips of pectoral fins and tail ending as a hard, finless point. It is distinguished from the other species of the family by the following combination of characters. Snout overhangs lower jaw. Lips lack barbels. Anterior nostril is narrowly tubular, and posterior nostril opens outside of mouth and is covered anteriorly by small flap. Eye is large and bulbous. Jaw teeth are small, conical, and at least partially biserial, with 24 to 36 in outer row and 18 to 26 in inner row of upper jaw, and 25 to 32 in outer row and 4 anteriorly and 4 to 10 far posteriorly in inner row of lower jaw. Intermaxillary teeth number 4 and are arranged in inverted V. Vomerine teeth are slightly separated from intermaxillary teeth and consist of single pair followed by row of 12 to 18 teeth. Head pores are minute, with six infraorbital, four supraorbital, six or seven mandibular, three preopercular, and three supratemporal. Snout is 20% to 33%, eye is 12% to 14%,

mouth length is 35% to 42%, and pectoral fin length is 25% to 31%. Head length is 11% to 12%, trunk length is 31% to 35%, predorsal length is 14% to 16%, and depth behind gill openings is 2.9% to 4.5% of TL. Total vertebrae number 134 to 139, predorsal vertebrae number 12 or 13, and preanal vertebrae number 52 to 55. Color is yellow to pale tan and slightly darker dorsally than ventrally, with tan triangle between eyes and 15 to 16 faint tan saddles along body. Dorsal fin is dark edged.

This species occurs in the western North Atlantic from the northeastern Gulf of Mexico and the Caribbean Sea. It has not been captured west of Florida in the Gulf of Mexico. Only six specimens have been captured, and depths of capture range from 88 to 293 m. Maximum known size is 385 mm TL; males mature at about 357 mm TL, and females mature at about 385 mm TL.

REFERENCES: McCosker and Böhlke 1984; McCosker et al. 1989; Boschung 1992.

Ophichthus melanoporus Kanazawa 1963
Blackpored eel

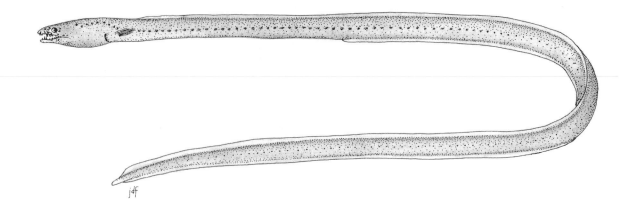

Ophichthus melanoporus is very elongate, cylindrical anteriorly and compressed posteriorly, with dorsal fin originating above tips of pectoral fins and tail ending as a hard, finless point. It is distinguished from the other species of the family by the following combination of characters. Snout barely overhangs lower jaw. Lips lack barbels. Anterior nostril is narrowly tubular, and posterior nostril opens outside of mouth and is covered by flap. Eye is moderate in size. Jaw teeth are needlelike and uniserial, with 12 to 17 in upper jaw and 20 to 26 in lower jaw. Intermaxillary teeth number 4 and are exposed when mouth is closed. Vomerine teeth are close to and stouter than intermaxillary teeth, number 8 to 11, and are in single row. Head pores are developed, with six infraorbital, five supraorbital, six mandibular, three preopercular, and three supratemporal. Snout is 14% to 18%, eye is 8.4% to 11%, mouth length is 36% to 44%, and pectoral fin length is 20% to 25% of head length. Head length is 6.3% to 7%, trunk is 22% to 24%, predorsal length is 8.2% to 9.4%, and depth behind gill opening is 1.5% to 1.8% of TL. Total vertebrae number 177 to 186, predorsal vertebrae number 11 to 14, and preanal vertebrae number 50 to 54. Color is yellow to tan, with small brown spots on dorsal surface. Most of head pores and lateral line pores are darkly pigmented. Fins are colorless.

This species occurs in the western North Atlantic from North Carolina to the Straits of Florida and in the northern Gulf of Mexico to Corpus Christi, Texas. It has been captured from 51 to 460 m. Maximum known size is 693 mm TL.

REFERENCES: Kanazawa 1963; C. R. Robins et al. 1986; McCosker et al. 1989; Leiby 1989.

Ophichthus menezesi   McCosker and Böhlke 1984
Blotchside snake eel

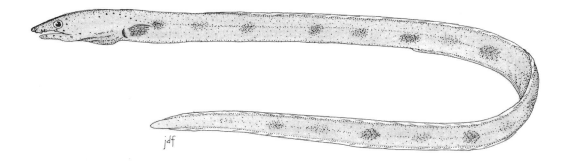

Ophichthus menezesi is moderately elongate, relatively stout bodied, cylindrical anteriorly and compressed posteriorly, with dorsal fin originating posterior to tips of pectoral fins and tail ending as a hard, finless point. It is distinguished from the other species of the family by the following combination of characters. Snout overhangs lower jaw. Lips lack barbels. Anterior nostril is tubular, and posterior nostril opens outside of mouth and is covered by small flap anteriorly. Eye is of moderate size. Jaw teeth are small, conical, and biserial in part, with 11 to 23 in outer row and 3 to 14 in inner row of upper jaw, and 19 to 25 in lower jaw. Intermaxillary teeth number 5 to 7 and form inverted chevron. Vomerine teeth are separated from intermaxillary teeth and are biserial anteriorly and uniserial posteriorly. Head pores are minute, with six infraorbital, five supraorbital, five mandibular, two preopercular, and three supratemporal. Snout is 23% to 26%, eye is 10% to 13%, mouth length is 34% to 38%, and pectoral fin length is 14% to 22% of head length. Head length is 7.5% to 8.9%, trunk length is 30% to 32%, predorsal length is 14% to 18%, and depth behind gill openings is 2.4% to 3% of TL. Total vertebrae number 150 to 156, predorsal vertebrae number 16 to 23, and preanal vertebrae number 55 to 58. Color is pale yellowish, with 16 to 25 round dark blotches on side. Fins are colorless.

This species occurs in the western Atlantic from the Gulf of Mexico to southern Brazil between 169 and 1,400 m. Only one specimen, from the west coast of Florida, has been reported from the Gulf of Mexico. Maximum known size is 281 mm TL.

REFERENCES: McCosker and Böhlke 1984; McCosker et al. 1989; Leiby 1989.

Ophichthus omorgmus McCosker and Böhlke 1984
Dotted-line snake eel

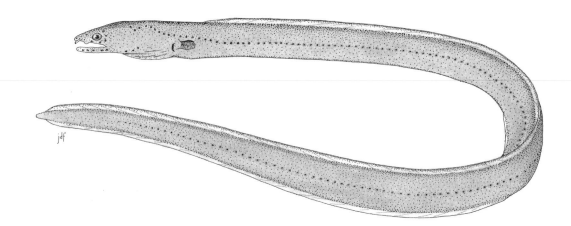

Ophichthus omorgmus is moderately elongate, relatively stout, cylindrical anteriorly and compressed posteriorly, with dorsal fin originating slightly behind tips of pectoral fins and tail ending as a hard, finless point. It is distinguished from the other species of the family by the following combination of characters. Snout overhangs lower jaw. Lips lack barbels. Anterior nostril is tubular, and posterior nostril opens outside of mouth and is covered by small flap anteriorly. Eye is large. Jaw teeth are small, conical, and biserial, with 21 in each row of upper jaw and about 20 in each row of lower jaw. Intermaxillary teeth number 4 and form chevron. Vomerine teeth are close to intermaxillary teeth and consist of single pair followed by 14 in single row. Head pores are developed, with six infraorbital, four supraorbital, six mandibular, three premaxillary, and three supratemporal. Snout is 19%, eye is

15%, mouth length is 36%, and pectoral fin length is 30% of head length. Head length is 9.7%, trunk length is 35%, predorsal length is 14%, and depth behind gill openings is 3.1% of TL. Total vertebrae number 141, predorsal vertebrae number 14, and preanal vertebrae number 56 or 57. Color is pale but slightly darker dorsally than ventrally, with head pores and lateral line pores dark pigmented. Dorsal and anal fins are pale, and dorsal fin has dark margin.

This species occurs in the western North Atlantic from the northeastern Gulf of Mexico off Florida and the Florida Keys. It has been captured from 183 to 271 m. Maximum known size is 453 mm TL; males mature at about 411 mm TL.

REFERENCES: McCosker and Böhlke 1984; McCosker et al. 1989.

Ophichthus ophis (Linnaeus 1758)
Spotted snake eel

Ophichthus ophis is moderately elongate and relatively robust, with dorsal fin originating above middle of tips of pectoral fins and tail ending as a hard, finless point. It is distinguished from the other species of the family by the following combination of characters. Snout slightly overhangs lower jaw. Lips lack barbels. Anterior nostril is tubular, with barbel on mesial rim. Posterior nostril is large, opens outside mouth, and is bordered by irregular, flangelike lip. Eye is large and elliptical. Jaw teeth are stout, conical, and biserial in jaws. Six outer intermaxillary teeth are slightly separated from anterior pair and posterior series of 12 to 17 vomerine teeth. Maxillary teeth number 8 to 15 in outer row and 10 to 19 in inner row. Lower jaw teeth number 14 to 23 in outer row and 14 to 19 in inner row. Head pores are small, with six infraorbital, five supraorbital, six mandibular, three preopercular, and three supratemporal. Snout is 16% to 20%, eye is 7.9% to 11%, mouth length is 33% to 42%, and pectoral fin length is 23% to 27% of head length. Head length is 9.9% to 12%, trunk length is 28% to 32%, predorsal length is 11% to 14%, and depth behind gill openings is 2.9% to 3.9% of TL. Total vertebrae number 161 to 167, predorsal vertebrae number 13 to 17, and preanal vertebrae number 57 to 64. Color is pale, with about 20 large, dark spots along midline; 25 to 35 small spots meeting dorsal fin base; and nape, snout, chin, and pectoral fin freckled with small, dark spots.

This species occurs in the tropical Atlantic Ocean. In the western Atlantic it occurs from southern Florida to Brazil, including the northern Gulf of Mexico, Bermuda, the Bahamas, and the Caribbean Sea, between the shoreline and 10 m. Maximum known size is about 2,000 mm TL; females mature between 977 and 1,241 mm TL.

REFERENCES: Cervigón 1966; Böhlke and Chaplin 1968; C. R. Robins et al. 1986; McCosker et al. 1989; Leiby 1989.

Ophichthus puncticeps (Kaup 1860)
Pale-spotted eel

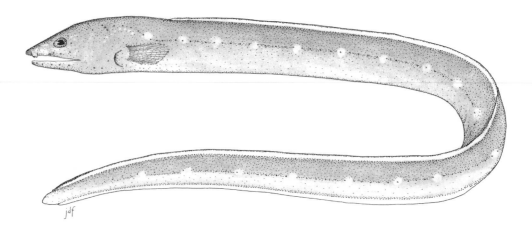

Ophichthus puncticeps is moderately elongate and relatively stout bodied, with dorsal fin originating anterior to or over tips of pectoral fins and tail ending as a hard, finless point. It is distinguished from the other species of the family by the following combination of characters. Snout slightly overhangs lower jaw. Lips lack barbels. Anterior nostril is tubular, and posterior nostril opens outside of mouth and is covered by short flap. Eye is moderate in size. Jaw teeth are of moderate size, conical, and biserial, with 17 to 25 in outer row and 13 to 24 in inner row of upper jaw, and 17 to 29 in outer and inner rows of lower jaw. Intermaxillary teeth are in three pairs. Vomerine teeth are slightly separated from intermaxillary teeth and are biserial anteriorly and uniserial posteriorly. Head pores are small, with six infraorbital, four supraorbital, six mandibular, three preopercular, and three supratemporal. Snout is 17% to 21%, eye is 9.4% to 12%, mouth length is 35% to 48%, and pectoral fin length is 30% to 45% of head length. Head length is 11% to 14%, trunk length is 30% to 35%, predorsal length is 15% to 18%, and depth behind gill openings is 3.7% to 5.9% of TL. Total vertebrae number 127 to 141, predorsal vertebrae number 12 to 17, and preanal vertebrae number 50 to 58. Color of large specimens is dark gray to brown, with dark brown stripe along lateral line punctuated by pale spots. Color of small specimens is gray dorsally fading to white ventrally, with series of 18 to 22 evenly spaced white or pale spots along side.

This species occurs in the western Atlantic from North Carolina to Suriname, including the northern Gulf of Mexico from Florida to Texas, and the West Indies. It has been captured from near shore to 219 m. Maximum known size is 927 mm TL; males mature between 387 and 498 mm TL, and females mature between 383 and 927 mm TL.

REFERENCES: C. R. Robins et al. 1986 (as *O. ocellatus*); McCosker et al. 1989; Leiby 1989; Boschung 1992.

Ophichthus rex   Böhlke and Caruso 1980
Giant snake eel

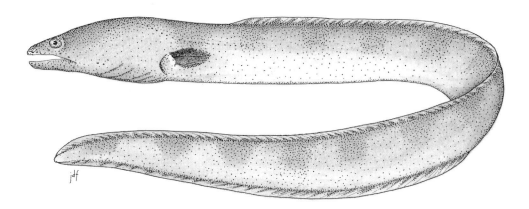

Ophichthus rex is moderately elongate and relatively stout, with dorsal fin originating behind tips of pectoral fins and tail ending as a hard, finless point. It is distinguished from the other species of the family by the following combination of characters. Snout is short and does not overhang lower jaw. Lips lack barbels. Anterior nostril is tubular, with notch in dorsal margin and ridge inside ventral margin. Posterior nostril opens outside of mouth and is covered by posteroventrally directed flap. Eye is of moderate size. Jaw teeth are stout, conical, and uniserial to multiserial, with number and rows increasing with growth. Intermaxillary teeth are arranged in semicircle, with number of teeth increasing with growth. Vomerine teeth are continuous with intermaxillary teeth, and number and series of teeth increase with growth. Head pores are small, with six infraorbital, five supraorbital, seven mandibular, three preopercular, and three supratemporal. Snout length is 17% to 21%, eye is 6% to

10%, mouth length is 35% to 44%, and pectoral fin length is 26% to 34% of head length. Head length is 11% to 13%, trunk length is 35% to 37%, predorsal length is 17% to 19%, and depth behind gill openings is 4.5% to 7.7% of TL. Total vertebrae number 115 to 121, predorsal vertebrae number 15 to 18, and preanal vertebrae number 45 to 47. Color is brown to slate gray, with 14 or 15 faint to dark saddles along body. Vertical fins are striped at base.

This species occurs in the western North Atlantic from the Gulf of Mexico. It has been captured from 22 to 366 m, where it occupies burrows on mud bottoms. Maximum known size is 2,100 mm TL; males mature between 722 and 896 mm TL, and females mature at about 1,687 mm TL.

REFERENCES: Hoese and Moore 1977 (as *Ophichthus* sp.); Böhlke and Caruso 1980; C. R. Robins et al. 1986; McCosker et al. 1989; Leiby 1989; Boschung 1992.

Pseudomyrophis nimius   Böhlke 1960
Elongate worm eel

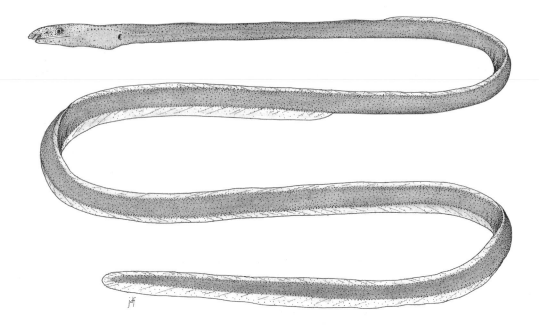

Pseudomyrophis nimius is extremely elongate and laterally compressed, with minute pectoral fins and a well-developed caudal fin. It is distinguished from the other species of the family by the following combination of characters. Snout is broad, overhangs lower jaw, and lacks groove on underside. Lips lack barbels. Anterior nostril is tubular. Posterior nostril is elongated slit located anterior to lower margin of orbit. Eye is of moderate size. Jaw teeth are small, conical, and mostly uniserial, with 17 to 20 in upper jaw, and 24 to 27 in outer row and 2 to 4 in inner row of lower jaw. Intermaxillary teeth consist of ring or patch of 7 or 8 teeth. Vomerine teeth are continuous with intermaxillary teeth and are triserial anteriorly and uniserial posteriorly. Gill openings are round, constricted, and located laterally. Infraorbital pores number six, supraorbital pores number five, and supratemporal pores number three. Visible lateral line pores number 143 to 160.

Snout is 20% to 25%, eye is 5.8% to 7.2%, and mouth length is 29% to 33% of head length. Head length is 5.2% to 6.1%, predorsal length is 24% to 28%, trunk length is 29% to 33%, and depth behind gill openings is 1% to 1.5% of TL. Total vertebrae number 211 to 217, predorsal vertebrae number 47 to 53, and preanal vertebrae number 71 to 75. Color is uniform brown to reddish brown with silvery-bluish cast and slightly darker along each side of lateral line.

This species occurs in the western North Atlantic in the northern Gulf of Mexico from Florida to Texas. It has been captured from 320 to 755 m. Maximum known size is 369 mm TL; males mature between 248 and 303 mm TL, and females mature between 297 and 348 mm TL.

REFERENCES: Böhlke 1960; McCosker et al. 1989; Leiby 1989.

COLOCONGRIDAE

Colocongrids are relatively short and strongly compressed, with well-developed dorsal and anal fins confluent with caudal fin. They are distinguished from the other families of the order by the following combination of characters. Snout is short, bluntly rounded, and projects slightly beyond lower jaw. Jaws are of moderate length, extending to posterior margin of eye. Upper and lower lips lack flanges. Anterior nostril has short tube and is located near tip of snout. Posterior nostril is large and round, with low, raised rim, and is located midway between tip of snout and eye at midheight of eye. Eye is large. Jaw teeth are small and conical. Maxillary teeth are in one or two series, with outer series larger and forming cutting edge, and teeth of inner series smaller and concealed by flesh. Mandibular teeth are in two or three series. Intermaxillary teeth are in two transverse series, with posterior series continuous with maxillary teeth. Vomerine teeth are lacking. Gill openings are vertical slits extending from middle to upper end of pectoral fin base. Pectoral fin is well developed. Dorsal fin originates slightly posterior to pectoral fin base. Lateral line pores are complete, and most open through low tubes. Pelvic fin and scales are absent.

Colocongrids occur in the tropical Atlantic and Indo-Pacific Oceans. They are benthic species but are not known to burrow. There are five species in a single genus, and one species occurs in the Gulf of Mexico.

Coloconger meadi Kanazawa 1957

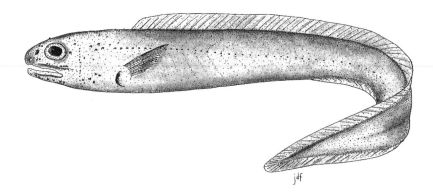

Coloconger meadi is relatively short and strongly compressed, with well-developed pectoral, dorsal, and anal fins. It is distinguished from the other species of the family by the following combination of characters. Snout is 19% to 27%, eye is 24% to 30%, and mouth length is 38% to 47% of head length. Head length is 17% to 21%, predorsal fin length is 20% to 23%, and preanal fin length is 58% to 65% of TL. Lateral line pores on head are numerous; anteriormost pores are normal, others open through fleshy tubes. Branchiostegal rays number 11 to 13, pectoral fin rays number 19 to 12, dorsal fin rays number 209 to 232, and lateral line pores to anus number 64 to 74.

Head pores number 12 to 23 infraorbital, 6 to 8 supraorbital, and 1 supratemporal. Total vertebrae number 152 to 157, predorsal vertebrae number 13 to 17, and preanal vertebrae number 80 to 84 for Gulf of Mexico specimens. Color is gray to brown, with sensory pores and papillae blackish.

This species occurs in the western Atlantic from the Gulf of Mexico, the Caribbean Sea, and off northern South America to the Guianas. It has been captured from 366 to 915 m. Maximum known size is 505 mm TL.

REFERENCES: Kanazawa 1957; Smith 1989d.

NEMICHTHYIDAE   Snipe eels

Snipe eels are elongate to very elongate and moderately to strongly compressed, with anus near pectoral fins and tail moderately attenuate to filiform. They are distinguished from the other families of the order by the following combination of characters. Upper and lower jaws of females and immature males are produced into nonocclusible, slender beaks. Jaws of mature males are short and beaklike. Anterior and posterior nostrils are close together in front of eye. Anterior nostril of females and immature males has low tube or no tube. Anterior nostril of mature male has long tube. Teeth are small, have recurved tips, and occur in jaws and along roof of mouth. Eye is large. Dorsal and anal fins are long and confluent with caudal fin. Pectoral fin is well developed. Lateral line pores are well developed on head and body. Pelvic fin and scales are absent.

Snipe eels occur worldwide in tropical to subtropical seas. All species are pelagic. Leptocephali are large (300 to 400 mm SL) and slender, with short dorsal fin, series of small melanophores along top of dorsal nerve cord, and small melanophores on top of intestine. The family contains nine species in three genera, and four species in three genera occur in the Gulf of Mexico.

Key to the Species of the Gulf of Mexico
(Adapted from Smith and Nielsen 1989)

1a. Anus distinctly posterior to pectoral fin base
. . . . *Avocettina infans* p. 287
1b. Anus below pectoral fin base 2
2a. Caudal region not filamentous; one row of lateral line pores; head with dermal ridges
. . . . *Labichthys carinatus* p. 288
2b. Caudal region filamentous; three rows of lateral line pores; head without dermal ridges 3
3a. Jaws produced into long, nonocclusible beak bearing teeth (females and immature males) 4
3b. Jaws short and toothless (mature males). 5
4a. Body dark or countershaded; no dark, subcutaneous vertical bars; postorbital pores 6 to 17 and arranged in staggered row (Fig. 50); preopercular pores 6 to 13 (usually more than 10) . . . . *Nemichthys scolopaceus* p. 290
4b. Body pale with cluster of black spots below stomach; dark, subcutaneous vertical bars between vertebrae; postorbital pores 5 to 14 (usually fewer than 10) and arranged in even row; preopercular pores 2 to 6
. . . . *Nemichthys curvirostris* p. 289

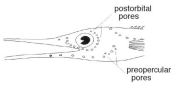

postorbital
pores

preopercular
pores

FIG 50

5a. Body dark brown; head rounded in profile, not sharply set
off from body; postorbital pores 11 to 19, arranged in
staggered row; preopercular pores 6 to 13
. . . . *Nemichthys scolopaceus* p. 290

5b. Body light brown; head angular in profile, set off from
body; postorbital pores 5 to 8, arranged in even row; preopercular pores 2 or 3 . . . . *Nemichthys curvirostris* p. 289

Avocettina infans   (Günther 1878)

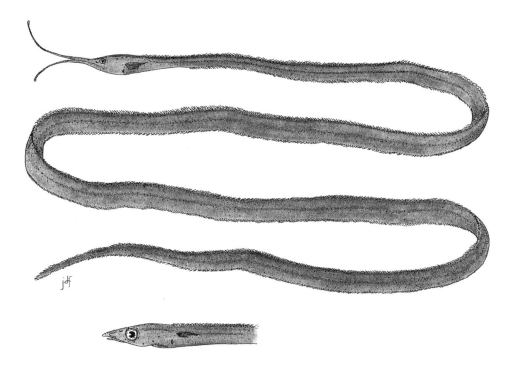

Avocettina infans is elongate and strongly compressed, with anus distinctly behind pectoral fins and tail not terminating as a long, slender filament. It is distinguished from the other species of the family by the following combination of characters. Upper jaw is longer than lower jaw, and tips of jaws are slightly expanded to form small spatulate knobs. Eye length is 24% to 47% of distance from postorbital margin to upper end of pectoral fin base. Predorsal length, measured from postorbital margin, is 21% to 39% of distance from posterior margin to anal fin origin. Dermal ridges are located behind eyes on occiput, behind anterior nostril, on snout, and on nape anterior to dorsal fin. Head pores number 8 to 14 infraorbital, 5 to 8 supraorbital, and 1 supratemporal. Pectoral fin rays number 14 to 18, dorsal fin rays number 279 to 432, and anal fin rays number 240 to 372. Anterior dorsal fin rays 9 to 15 are close-set, remainder are normally spaced. Lateral line pores number 181 to 201, preanal lateral line pores number 16 to 26, predorsal lateral line pores number 5 to 8, and prepectoral lateral line pores number 3 to 8. Total vertebrae number 187 to 202, predorsal vertebrae number 5 to 9, preanal vertebrae number 17 to 22, and precaudal vertebrae number 62 to 70. Color is brown and slightly darker brown along lateral line. Mature males have short jaws and dorsal fin originating slightly anterior to pectoral fin base.

This species occurs in the Atlantic and Pacific Oceans. In the western Atlantic it occurs from southern New England to northern Brazil, including the Gulf of Mexico and the Caribbean Sea. It has been captured in midwater nets generally between 1,200 and 2,000 m, and rarely at 170 m. Maximum known size is 800 mm TL.

REFERENCES: Nielsen and Smith 1978; Smith and Nielsen 1989; Smith 1989n.

Labichthys carinatus   Gill and Ryder 1883

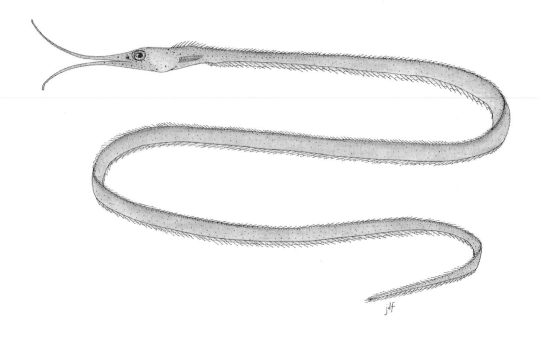

Labichthys carinatus is elongate and strongly compressed, with anus under pectoral fin base and an unfilamentous caudal region. It is distinguished from the other species of the family by the following combination of characters. Upper jaw is longer than lower jaw, and tips of jaws are expanded to form small spatulate knobs. Eye length is 33% to 44% of distance from postorbital margin to upper end of pectoral fin base. Dermal ridges are located behind eyes on occiput, medial to nostrils, behind anterior nostril, on snout, and on nape anterior to dorsal fin. Head pores are small, with 10 to 13 infraorbital and 5 or 6 supraorbital. Pectoral fin rays number 12 to 14. Anteriormost dorsal fin rays are closer together than remainder of rays. Lateral line pores are in single row and number 170 to 191, preanal lateral line pores number 8 to 13, and predorsal lateral line pores number 4 to 6. Total vertebrae number 172 to 181, predorsal vertebrae number 5 or 6, and preanal vertebrae number 9 to 11. Color is light brown, with anterior nostril tube dark. Mature males have short jaws and dorsal fin originating anterior to pectoral fin base.

This species occurs in the Atlantic, central Pacific, and western Indian Oceans. In the western Atlantic it occurs from Georges Bank and from Bermuda to southern Brazil, including the eastern Gulf of Mexico, the Caribbean Sea, and the Bahamas. It has generally been captured below 1,200 m. Maximum known size is 800 mm TL.

REFERENCES: Nielsen and Smith 1978; Smith and Nielsen 1989; Smith 1989n.

Nemichthys curvirostris (Strömman 1896)

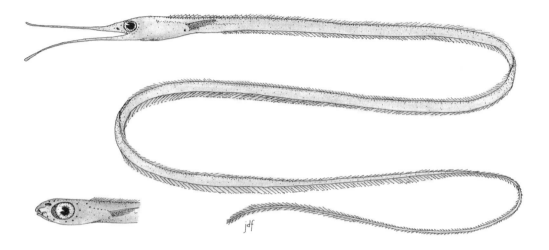

Nemichthys curvirostris is very elongate and slightly compressed, with anus under pectoral fin base and tail extended as a filament. It is distinguished from the other species of the family by the following combination of characters. Upper and lower jaws are about equal in length, and tips of jaws are not expanded into spatulate knobs. Eye length is 33% to 75% of distance from postorbital margin to upper end of pectoral fin base. Dermal ridges are lacking on head. Head pores are small, with 13 to 29 infraorbital, 5 to 14 supraorbital, 1 to 4 supratemporal, 5 to 14 postorbital, and 2 to 6 preopercular. Branchiostegal rays number 7 to 12, and pectoral fin rays number 8 to 12. Dorsal fin originates anterior to pectoral fin base. Lateral line pores are in three rows, with dorsal and ventral rows twice as numerous as median row. Predorsal vertebrae number 3 to 5, preanal vertebrae number 10 to 14, and precaudal vertebrae number 84 to 101. Color is pale yellow to white, with cluster of large black spots on abdomen in juveniles. Mature females are grayish, and mature males are light brown. Mature males have short, occlusible jaws.

This species occurs in the Atlantic, Pacific, and eastern Indian Oceans. In the western Atlantic it occurs from the east coast of the United States to the Antilles and the northern Gulf of Mexico. It has been captured from 100 to 2,000 m in open midwater nets. Maximum known size is 1,430 mm TL.

REFERENCES: Nielsen and Smith 1978; Smith and Nielsen 1989; Smith 1989n.

Nemichthys scolopaceus   Richardson 1848

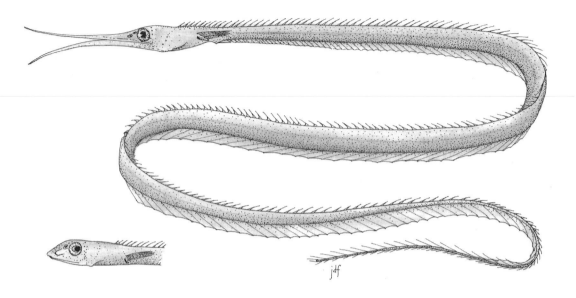

Nemichthys scolopaceus is very elongate and slightly compressed, with anus under pectoral fin base and tail extended as a filament. It is distinguished from the other species of the family by the following combination of characters. Upper jaw is only slightly longer than lower jaw, and tips of jaws are not expanded into spatulate knobs. Eye length is 18% to 51% of distance from postorbital margin to upper end of pectoral fin base. Dermal ridges are lacking on head. Head pores are small, with 13 to 43 infraorbital, 7 to 22 supraorbital, 2 to 8 supratemporal, 6 to 17 postorbital, and 6 to 13 preopercular. Branchiostegal rays number 7 to 15, and pectoral fin rays number 10 to 14. Dorsal fin originates anterior to pectoral fin base. Lateral line pores are in three rows, with dorsal and ventral rows twice as numerous as median row. Predorsal vertebrae number 2 to 5, preanal vertebrae number 9 to 15, and precaudal vertebrae number 77 to 105. Color is light dorsally and dark ventrally, with dark pigment on ventral midline below stomach in juveniles and uniformly dark brown to black in mature specimens. Mature males have short, occlusible jaws.

This species occurs worldwide in tropical to temperate seas. In the western Atlantic it occurs from southern New England to the mouth of the Amazon River, including the northern Gulf of Mexico, the Caribbean Sea, and the Bahamas. It has been captured above and below 1,000 m in open pelagic nets. Maximum known size is 1,000 mm TL.

REFERENCES: Nielsen and Smith 1978; Smith and Nielsen 1989; Smith 1989n.

CONGRIDAE   Conger eels

Conger eels are moderately stout to elongate, with dorsal and anal fins confluent with caudal fin, and pectoral fins usually present. They are distinguished from the other families of the order by the following combination of characters. Snout is short and blunt to long and slender. Most species have lips that conceal jaw teeth. Upper lip is usually separated by groove into inner and outer sections. Anterior nostril is tubular and near tip of snout. Posterior nostril is round to oval. Teeth are of variable shape and size and are located in jaws and ethmo-vomer. Eye is large. Gill slits are on sides of head and reach pectoral fin base, when fin is present. Dorsal fin originates near level of gill openings. Lateral line pores are present on head and are complete on body to tail. Pelvic fin and scales are absent.

Conger eels occur worldwide in tropical to temperate seas. The leptocephali are moderate to large (90 to 300 mm SL), with body moderately elongate, gut usually simple, preanal length about three-quarters SL or more, ventral pigment variable but always present, and lateral pigment variable to absent. The family contains about 150 species in 32 genera, and 20 species in 12 genera occur in the Gulf of Mexico.

Key to the Species of the Gulf of Mexico
(Adapted from Smith 1989f)

1a. Body very long and slender; pectoral and caudal fins reduced or absent; mouth short and oblique; lower jaw projecting beyond upper jaw
. . . . *Heteroconger luteolus* p. 304
1b. Body moderately stout to moderately slender; pectoral and caudal fins present and not reduced; mouth horizontal; jaws equal or upper jaw projecting beyond lower. 2
2a. Preanal length greater than 40% of TL; posterior nostril below midheight of eye; dorsal and anal fin rays unsegmented 3
2b. Preanal length usually less than 40% of TL; posterior nostril at or above midheight of eye; dorsal and anal fin rays segmented 6
3a. Posterior nostril covered by flap
. . . . *Parabathymyrus oregoni* p. 305
3b. Posterior nostril without flap 4
4a. Gill openings extend to midlength of pectoral fin base; jaw teeth in bands. 5
4b. Gill openings extend to or above upper end of pectoral fin base; jaw teeth in one or two series, forming cutting edge
. . . . *Paraconger caudilimbatus* p. 306

5a. Three supratemporal pores; two interorbital pores; three postorbital pores (Fig. 51) . . . *Ariosoma balearicum* p. 294

5b. Zero supratemporal and interorbital pores; zero to two postorbital pores (Fig. 52) . . . . . *Ariosoma selenops* p. 295

6a. Inner and outer rows of jaw teeth separated by groove; jaw teeth exposed when mouth closed 7

6b. Inner and outer rows of teeth not separated by groove; jaw teeth concealed when mouth closed 8

7a. Intermaxillary tooth patch longer than it is broad (Fig. 53); dorsal fin originates over or slightly behind pectoral fin base; stomach and intestine pale
. . . . *Xenomystax bidentatus* p. 312

7b. Intermaxillary tooth patch as broad as it is long; dorsal fin originates anterior to pectoral fin base; stomach and intestine black . . . . *Xenomystax congroides* p. 313

8a. Jaw teeth in one or two rows, outer row forming cutting edge; upper labial flange well developed 9

8b. Jaw teeth in bands or in two rows, not forming cutting edge; upper labial flange reduced or absent 10

9a. Three supratemporal pores; one or two postorbital pores
. . . . *Conger triporiceps* p. 301

9b. One supratemporal pore; zero postorbital pores
. . . . *Conger oceanicus* p. 300

10a. Tip of tail slightly stiffened; upper labial flange narrow but present (Fig. 54) 11

10b. Tip of tail soft and flexible; upper labial flange poorly developed or absent 12

11a. Second and seventh through thirteenth lateral line pores elevated above other pores; stomach black (Fig. 55)
. . . . *Gnathophis bathytopos* p. 302

11b. Only second lateral line pore elevated above other pores; stomach pale . . . . *Gnathophis bracheatopos* p. 303

12a. Vomerine teeth in single row, extending to posterior end of maxillary tooth patch . . . . . . *Uroconger syringinus* p. 311

12b. Vomerine teeth in more than two rows, at least anteriorly, and failing to reach posterior end of maxillary tooth patch
. . . . 13

13a. Vomerine tooth patch with few enlarged teeth or with granular teeth; if granular, patch extends less than one-half length of maxillary patch 14

13b. Vomerine tooth patch with small, conical teeth, extending at least two-thirds length of maxillary tooth patch
. . . . *Pseudophichthys splendens* p. 307

14a. Vomerine tooth patch round to slightly elongate, with small teeth; upper labial flange rudimentary; upper jaw pores small 15

14b. Vomerine tooth patch occasionally extending posteriorly as

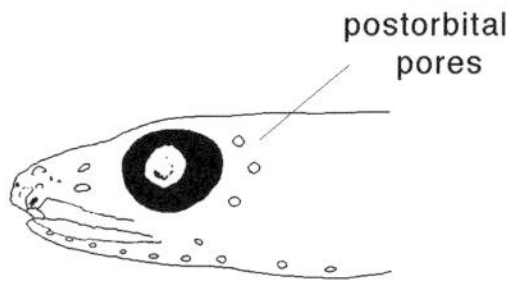

postorbital
pores

FIG 51

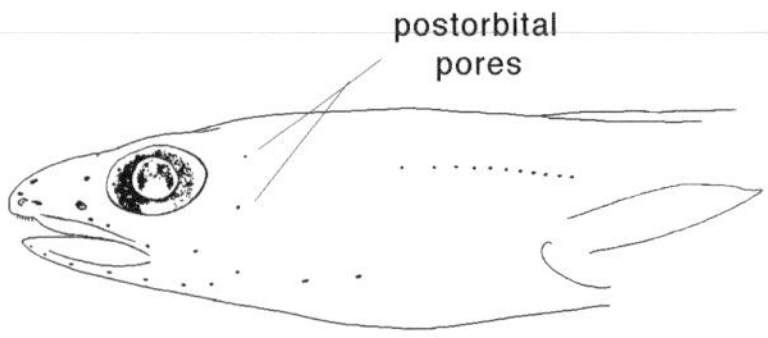

postorbital
pores

FIG 52

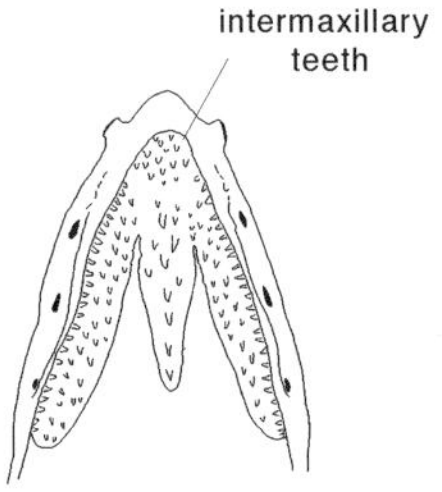

intermaxillary
teeth

FIG 53

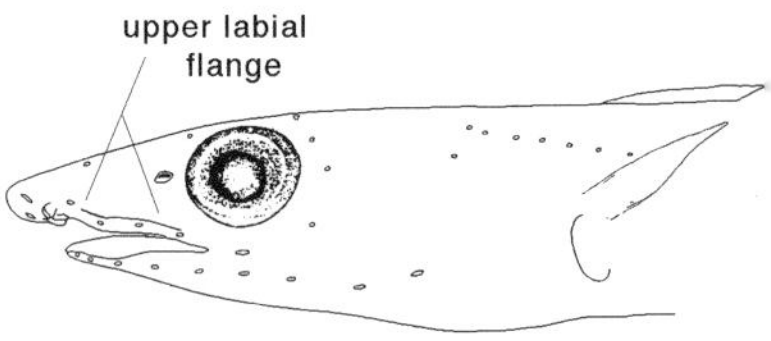

upper labial
flange

FIG 54

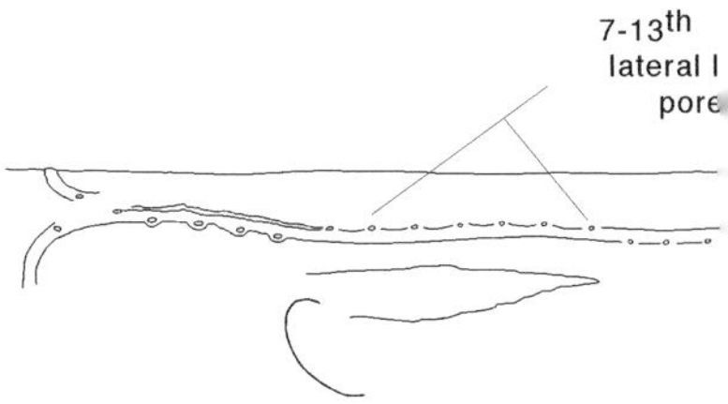

7-13th
lateral l
pore

FIG 55

row of teeth, with some enlarged teeth; upper labial flange absent; upper jaw pores enlarged 17

15a. Fourth supraorbital pore, between anterior and posterior nostrils, present (Fig. 56)
. . . . *Rhynchoconger gracilior* p. 309

15b. Fourth supraorbital pore, between anterior and posterior nostrils, absent (Fig. 57) 16

16a. Vomerine tooth patch equally as broad as it is long; stomach pale . . . . *Rhynchoconger flavus* p. 308

16b. Vomerine tooth patch slightly longer than it is broad; stomach black . . . . *Rhynchoconger guppyi* p. 310

17a. Upper jaw projecting beyond lower jaw; teeth moderately large 18

17b. Jaws nearly equal in length; anterior teeth fanglike
. . . . *Bathyuroconger vicinus* p. 299

18a. Posterior nostril at midheight of eye
. . . . *Bathycongrus dubius* p. 297

18b. Posterior nostril at dorsal margin of eye 19

19a. Preanal lateral line pores fewer than 39
. . . . *Bathycongrus vicinalis* p. 298

19b. Preanal lateral line pores 39 or more
. . . . *Bathycongrus bullisi* p. 296

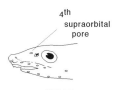

4th
supraorbital
pore

FIG 56

FIG 57

Ariosoma balearicum (Delaroche 1809)

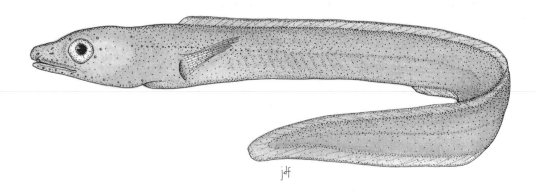

Ariosoma balearicum is moderately elongate, with a reduced, blunt, stiff tail. It is distinguished from the other species of the family by the following combination of characters. Snout is rounded and projects slightly beyond lower jaw. Upper and lower lips have well-developed flanges. Anterior nostril is tubular and near tip of snout, and posterior nostril is small and slightly below midheight of eye. Jaw teeth are small and in bands. Intermaxillary tooth patch is not separated from maxillary teeth and is about as broad as it is long. Vomerine tooth patch is elongate, extending to about midlength of maxillary tooth band, and is slightly separated from intermaxillary tooth patch. Infraorbital pores number eight, supraorbital pores number five or six, and supratemporal pores number three. Snout is 19% to 25%, eye is 16% to 24%, and mouth length is 26% to 32% of head length. Head length is 15% to 19%, predorsal length is 15% to 19%, and preanal length is 45% to 49% of TL. Gill openings are shorter than interbranchial space. Anus is slightly anterior to midlength. Branchiostegal rays number 7 to 10, pectoral fin rays number 10, and lateral line pores to anus number 46 to 52. Total vertebrae number 120 to 136, predorsal vertebrae number 7 to 10, preanal vertebrae number 49 to 54, and precaudal vertebrae number 62 to 66. Color is brown with dark-edged vertical fins. In life, lower flank is light brown with silvery or golden reflections. Stomach and intestines are pale.

This conger eel occurs in the western Atlantic from North Carolina to northern Brazil, including the Gulf of Mexico, the Caribbean Sea, and Bermuda. It has been captured from the surface to 732 m and is most common on the continental shelf on sandy bottoms. Maximum known size is 336 mm TL.

REFERENCES: C. R. Robins et al. 1986; Smith 1989f,k; Boschung 1992.

Ariosoma selenops   Reid 1934

Ariosoma selenops is moderately elongate, with relatively wide gill openings and a reduced, blunt, stiff tail. It is distinguished from the other species of the family by the following combination of characters. Snout is rounded and projects slightly beyond lower jaw. Upper and lower lips have well-developed flanges. Anterior nostril is tubular and near tip of snout, and posterior nostril is small and located below midheight of eye. Jaw teeth are small and in bands. Intermaxillary tooth patch is not separated from maxillary teeth and is broader than it is long. Vomerine tooth patch is elongate, extending to about midlength of maxillary tooth band, and is slightly separated from intermaxillary tooth patch. Infraorbital pores number seven, supraorbital pores number four, and supratemporal and interorbital pores are absent. Snout is 18% to 24%, eye is 18% to 22%, and mouth length is 27% to 32% of head length. Head length is 17% to 19%, predorsal length is 16% to 19%, and preanal length is 41% to 47% of TL. Gill openings are longer than interbranchial space. Anus is distinctly anterior to midlength. Branchiostegal rays number 10, pectoral fin rays number 13 to 16, and lateral line pores to anus number 51 to 59. Total vertebrae number 158 to 174, predorsal vertebrae number 7 to 12, preanal vertebrae number 57 to 62, and precaudal vertebrae number 94. Color is brown to yellowish brown, with median fins darker at margins. Stomach and intestines are pale.

This species occurs in the western Atlantic from the Bahamas to the mouth of the Amazon, including the northeastern Gulf of Mexico and the Caribbean Sea, between 220 and 549 m. In the Gulf of Mexico it has been captured twice off Alabama.

REFERENCES: Smith 1989f,k; Boschung 1992.

Bathycongrus bullisi   (Smith and Kanazawa 1977)

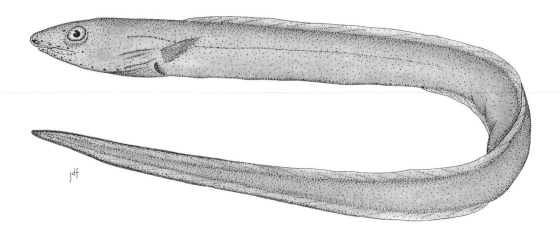

Bathycongrus bullisi is moderately elongate, with anus anterior to midlength and with a slender and attenuated tail. It is distinguished from the other species of the family by the following combination of characters. Snout projects beyond lower jaw. Lower lip has flange, and upper lip has rudimentary or no flange. Anterior nostril is tubular and near tip of snout. Posterior nostril is elliptical and located in front of upper margin of eye. Snout is 26% to 30%, eye is 15% to 19%, and mouth is 36% to 42% of head length. Head length is 35% to 40%, predorsal length is 39% to 49%, and preanal length is 37% to 41% of TL. Jaw teeth are moderately large and in narrow band tapering posteriorly, with outer teeth larger than inner teeth. Intermaxillary teeth are in three transverse rows and are separate from maxillary and vomerine teeth. Vomerine tooth patch is round, with one or two medial teeth enlarged.

Head pores along upper jaw, second and third supraorbital pores, and third preopercular-mandibular pores are enlarged. Pores on head number five infraorbital, three supraorbital, and one supratemporal. Pectoral fin rays number 12 to 15, and lateral line pores to anus number 39 to 45. Total vertebrae number 179 to 186, predorsal vertebrae number 10 to 13, and preanal vertebrae number 45 to 49. Color is brown to grayish brown, with vertical fins edged in black posteriorly. Stomach and intestine are black.

This species occurs in the western North Atlantic from the northern Gulf of Mexico to the mouth of the Amazon River. It has been captured from 55 to 549 m. Maximum known size is 606 mm TL.

REFERENCES: Smith and Kanazawa 1977; Smith 1989f (both as *Rhechias bullisi*).

Bathycongrus dubius   (Breder 1927)

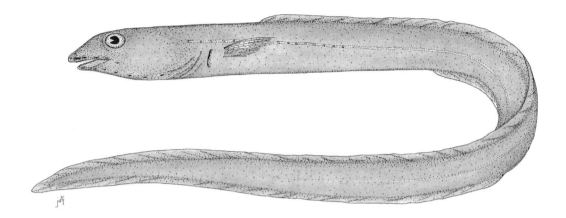

Bathycongrus dubius is moderately elongate, with anus anterior to midlength and with a slender, attenuated tail. It is distinguished from the other species of the family by the following combination of characters. Snout projects beyond lower jaw. Lower lip has flange, and upper lip has rudimentary or no flange. Anterior nostril is tubular and near tip of snout. Posterior nostril is elliptical and located in front of midheight of eye. Snout is 21% to 27%, eye is 14% to 20%, and mouth length is 29% to 36% of head length. Head length is 37% to 49%, predorsal length is 43% to 65%, and preanal length is 34% to 40% of TL. Jaw teeth are moderately small and in narrow bands, narrowing posteriorly, with outer teeth slightly larger than inner teeth. Intermaxillary teeth are in three or four series forming triangular patch. Vomerine tooth patch is round, with slightly larger median series. Head pores along upper jaw, second and third supraorbital pores, and third preopercular-mandibular pores are enlarged. Pores on head number five infraorbital, three supraorbital, and one supratemporal. Branchiostegal rays number 10 or 11, pectoral fin rays number 11 to 14, and lateral line pores to anus number 25 to 36. Total vertebrae number 120 to 145, predorsal vertebrae number 9 to 13, preanal vertebrae number 29 to 36, and precaudal vertebrae number 37 to 40. Color is brown or yellowish brown to gray.

This species occurs in the western North Atlantic from Georgia to the Guianas, including the Gulf of Mexico and the Caribbean Sea. It has been captured from 128 to 886 m. Maximum known size is 443 mm TL.

REFERENCES: Breder 1927; Smith 1989f,k (as *Rhechias dubia*).

Bathycongrus vicinalis   (Garman 1899)

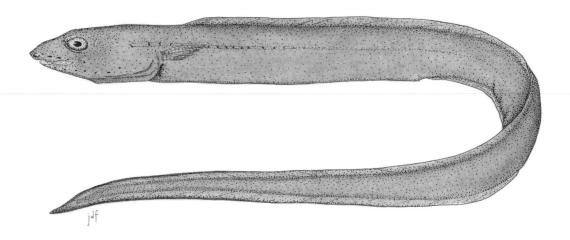

Bathycongrus vicinalis is moderately elongate, with anus at about anterior one-third of length and with a slender, attenuated tail. It is distinguished from the other species of the family by the following combination of characters. Snout projects beyond lower jaw. Lower lip has flange, and upper lip has rudimentary or no flange. Anterior nostril is tubular and near tip of snout. Posterior nostril is elliptical and located in front of upper margin of eye. Snout is 23% to 30%, eye is 14% to 20%, and mouth length is 33% to 43% of head length. Head length is 38% to 46%, predorsal length is 42% to 48%, and preanal length is 32% to 38% of TL. Jaw teeth are moderately large and in narrow bands, tapering posteriorly, with outer teeth larger than inner teeth. Intermaxillary teeth are in three transverse rows and are separated from maxillary and vomerine teeth. Vomerine tooth patch is round, with one or two median teeth enlarged. Head pores along upper jaw, second and third supraorbital pores, and third preopercular-mandibular pores are enlarged. Pores on head number five to eight infraorbital, three to six supraorbital, and one to three supratemporal. Branchiostegal rays number 9, pectoral fin rays number 15 to 18, and lateral line pores to anus number 33 to 38. Total vertebrae number 168 to 176, predorsal vertebrae number 10 to 12, preanal vertebrae number 40 to 47, and precaudal vertebrae number 47 to 51. Color is brown to grayish brown, with vertical fins edged in black posteriorly and stomach and intestine black.

This species occurs in the western North Atlantic from the eastern Gulf of Mexico to the mouth of the Amazon River, including the Bahamas and the West Indies. In the Gulf of Mexico it occurs off the east coast of Mexico and the west coast of Yucatán. It has been captured from 101 to 503 m. Maximum known size is 462 mm TL.

REFERENCES: Smith and Kanazawa 1977; Smith 1989f (both as *Rhechias vicinalis*).

Bathyuroconger vicinus (Vaillant 1888)

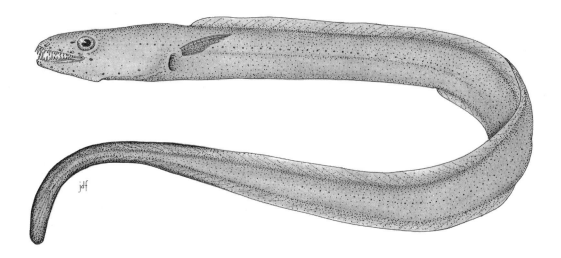

Bathyuroconger vicinus is moderately elongate, with an attenuate tail and delicate, rather transparent and loosely attached skin. It is distinguished from the other species of the family by the following combination of characters. Jaws are equal; fleshy part of snout does not project beyond lower jaw. Upper and lower lips lack flanges. Anterior nostril is tubular and near tip of snout. Posterior nostril is small and in front of midheight of eye. Snout is 24% to 31%, eye is 10% to 17%, and mouth length is 36% to 45% of head length. Head length is 23% to 38%, predorsal length is 34% to 41%, and preanal length is 36% of TL. Jaw teeth are strong, fanglike, and in narrow bands, with outer teeth longest. Intermaxillary teeth are enlarged, in two transverse rows, and separated from maxillary and vomerine teeth. Vomerine teeth consist of greatly enlarged central tooth,

flanked and followed by three smaller teeth. Head pores are enlarged, with five infraorbital, three supraorbital, and one supratemporal. Branchiostegal rays number 7 or 8, pectoral fin rays number 13 to 16, and lateral line pores to anus number 40 to 47. Total vertebrae number 179 to 206, predorsal vertebrae number 10 to 14, preanal vertebrae number 47 to 55, and precaudal vertebrae number 58 to 60. Color is brown to gray, with branchial chamber black and vertical fins edged in black posteriorly.

This species occurs in the Atlantic, Indian, and western Pacific Oceans. It occurs in the Gulf of Mexico and along the coasts of Central and South America to the Guianas in the western Atlantic. It has been captured from 229 to 1,318 m. Maximum known size is 880 mm TL.

REFERENCES: Smith 1989f,k.

Conger oceanicus (Mitchill 1818)
Conger eel

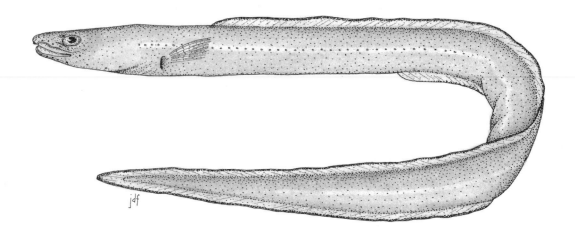

Conger oceanicus is moderately elongate, with dorsal fin originating posterior to pectoral fin base, anus anterior to midlength, and tail moderately slender and flexible. It is distinguished from the other species of the family by the following combination of characters. Fleshy part of snout projects slightly beyond lower jaw. Upper and lower lips have flanges, with upper one wide. Anterior nostril is tubular and near tip of snout. Posterior nostril is located near upper margin of orbit. Snout is 21% to 28%, eye is 12% to 19%, and mouth length is 34% to 40% of head length. Head length is 14% to 17%, predorsal length is 19% to 24%, and preanal length is 38% to 43% of TL. Jaw teeth are small, acute, and arranged in one or two rows, with outer row forming cutting edge. Intermaxillary tooth patch is rounded and not distinctly separated from maxillary and vomerine teeth. Vomerine tooth patch is short and triangular. Head pores are small, with five to eight infraorbital, three to four supraorbital, zero postorbital, and one supratemporal. Branchiostegal rays number 9, pectoral fin rays number 16 to 18, and lateral line pores to anus number 37 to 42. Total vertebrae number 143 to 147, predorsal vertebrae number 14 to 19, preanal vertebrae number 41 to 46, and precaudal vertebrae number 50. Color is brown to gray and slightly lighter ventrally, with vertical fins dark edged.

This species occurs in the western North Atlantic from Massachusetts to the eastern Gulf of Mexico. It has been captured from near shore to 577 m. The deepest captures are from the Gulf of Mexico. Spawning takes place in the southwestern Sargasso Sea south of the subtropical convergence zone, and may also occur close to the Bahamas and the Antilles. Maximum known size is 2,000 mm TL.

REFERENCES: Bigelow and Schroeder 1953b; Kanazawa 1958; C. R. Robins et al. 1986; Smith 1989f,k; Boschung 1992; McCleave and Miller 1994.

Conger triporiceps Kanazawa 1958

Conger triporiceps is moderately elongate, with dorsal fin originating posterior to pectoral fin base, anus anterior to midlength, and tail slender and flexible. It is distinguished from the other species of the family by the following combination of characters. Fleshy part of snout projects slightly beyond lower jaw. Upper and lower lips have flanges, with upper one wide. Anterior nostril is tubular and near tip of snout. Posterior nostril is located near upper margin of orbit. Jaw teeth are small, acute, and arranged in one or two rows, with outer forming cutting edge. Intermaxillary tooth patch is rounded and not distinctly separated from maxillary and vomerine teeth. Vomerine tooth patch is short and triangular. Snout is 24% to 29%, eye is 13% to 18%, and mouth length is 36% to 41% of head length. Head length is 12% to 15%, predorsal length is 15% to 19%, and preanal length is 32% to 34% of TL. Head pores are small, with five infraorbital, five supraorbital, one or two postorbital, and three supratemporal pores. Branchiostegal rays number 8, pectoral fin rays number 14 to 17, and lateral line pores to anus number 35 to 39. Total vertebrae number 156 to 160, predorsal vertebrae number 12 to 14, and preanal vertebrae number 38 to 40. Color is brown, with lower part of head and belly pale, lateral line pores pale, and median fins black edged.

This species occurs in the western Atlantic from Bermuda and south Florida to Brazil, including the northeastern Gulf of Mexico and the Caribbean Sea, in shallow water around coral reefs. In the Gulf of Mexico it has been captured off Pensacola, Florida, and Alabama. Spawning occurs in the southwestern Sargasso Sea south of the subtropical convergence zone, and possibly near the Bahamas, the Antilles, and in the Caribbean Sea.

REFERENCES: Kanazawa 1958; Böhlke and Chaplin 1968; C. R. Robins et al. 1986; Smith 1989f,k; Boschung 1992; McCleave and Miller 1994.

Gnathophis bathytopos   Smith and Kanazawa 1977
Blackgut conger

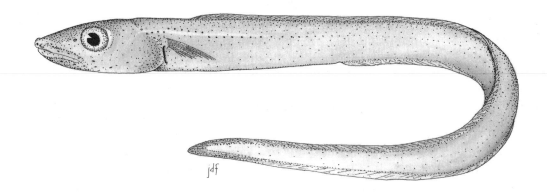

Gnathophis bathytopos is moderately elongate, with anus anterior to midlength and tail moderately blunt and slightly stiffened at tip. It is distinguished from the other species of the family by the following combination of characters. Snout projects beyond lower jaw and bears fleshy keel on underside of tip. Anterior nostril is tubular and located on underside near tip of snout. Posterior nostril is elliptical and located anterior to midheight of eye. Snout is 27% to 32%, eye is 18% to 22%, and mouth length is 36% to 37% of head length. Head length is 15% to 18%, predorsal length is 18% to 20%, and preanal length is 38% to 40% of TL. Jaw teeth are moderately small, conical, and in narrow bands. Intermaxillary tooth patch is longer than it is broad, visible when mouth is closed, and not separated from maxillary and vomerine teeth. Vomerine tooth patch is elongate, about one-third length of maxillary tooth band. Head pores are small, with eight infraorbital, six supraorbital, and three supratemporal. Branchiostegal rays number 8, pectoral fin rays number 10 to 13, and lateral line pores to anus number 27 to 37. Second and about seventh through thirteenth lateral line pores are elevated above remainder. Total vertebrae number 128 to 133, predorsal vertebrae number 9 or 10, preanal vertebrae number 34 to 36, and precaudal vertebrae number 40 to 43. Color is brownish, stomach is black, and intestine is pale.

This species occurs in the western Atlantic from Chesapeake Bay to Florida, the eastern Gulf of Mexico, and the Yucatán Channel. It has been captured from 90 to 366 m. Maximum known size is 351 mm TL.

REFERENCES: Smith and Kanazawa 1977; C. R. Robins et al. 1986; Smith 1989f; Boschung 1992.

Gnathophis bracheatopos Smith and Kanazawa 1977
Longeye conger

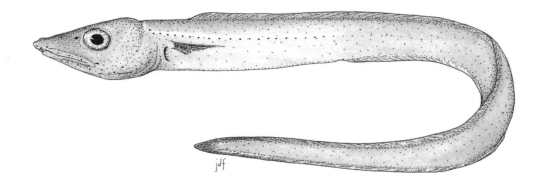

Gnathophis bracheatopos is moderately elongate, with anus anterior to midlength and tail moderately blunt and slightly stiffened at tip. It is distinguished from the other species of the family by the following combination of characters. Snout projects beyond lower jaw and bears fleshy keel on underside of tip. Upper lip has narrow flange. Anterior nostril is tubular and located on underside near tip of snout. Posterior nostril is elliptical and located anterior to midheight of eye. Snout is 31% to 35%, eye is 19% to 21%, and mouth length is 39% to 42% of head length. Head length is 16% to 18%, predorsal length is 17% to 19%, and preanal length is 36% to 40% of TL. Jaw teeth are moderately small, conical, and in narrow bands. Intermaxillary tooth patch is longer than it is broad, visible when mouth is closed, and not separated from maxillary and vomerine teeth. Vomerine tooth patch is elongate, about one-third length of maxillary tooth band. Head pores are small, with eight infraorbital, five or six supraorbital, and one to four supratemporal. Branchiostegal rays number 8, pectoral fin rays number 10 to 14, and lateral line pores to anus number 26 to 31. Second lateral line pore is elevated. Total vertebrae number 125 to 130, predorsal vertebrae number 7 to 9, preanal vertebrae number 30 to 34, and precaudal vertebrae number 40. Color is brown and slightly paler ventrally.

This species occurs in the western North Atlantic from North Carolina to the northeastern Gulf of Mexico off northwestern Florida. It has been captured from 55 to 110 m. Maximum known size is 352 mm TL.

REFERENCES: Smith and Kanazawa 1977; C. R. Robins et al. 1986; Smith 1989f; Boschung 1992.

Heteroconger luteolus   Smith 1989

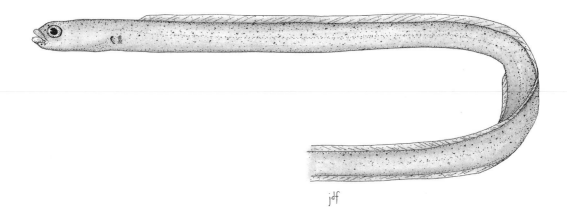

Heteroconger luteolus is very elongate and slightly compressed, with pectoral fins reduced. It is distinguished from the other species of the family by the following combination of characters. Snout is short, with lower jaw projecting beyond upper jaw. Mouth is oblique. Upper and lower labial flanges are well developed and continuous around snout and lower jaw. Anterior nostril and ethmoid pore are enclosed in upper flange. Posterior nostril is located anterior to midheight of eye. Snout is 12%, eye is 17% to 18%, and mouth length is 16% of head length. Head length is 18% and predorsal length is 23% of preanal length. Jaw teeth are in bands, and are small anteriorly but relatively large and directed forward posteriorly. Single, large, forwardly directed tooth occurs anterior to intermaxillary teeth. Intermaxillary tooth patch is broad anteriorly and continuous with vomerine teeth. Vomerine tooth patch is long. Head pores are reduced and number two infraorbital and three supraorbital. Lateral line pores to anus number 46. Predorsal vertebrae number 8 or 9, and preanal vertebrae number 52. Color is pale yellow, with tiny dark spots.

This species occurs in the western North Atlantic from the northeastern Gulf of Mexico (adults) and from the northwestern Gulf of Mexico and Campeche Bank (leptocephali). It has been captured from 33 to 37 m. Total length is unknown.

REFERENCES: Smith 1989f,k.

Parabathymyrus oregoni   Smith and Kanazawa 1977

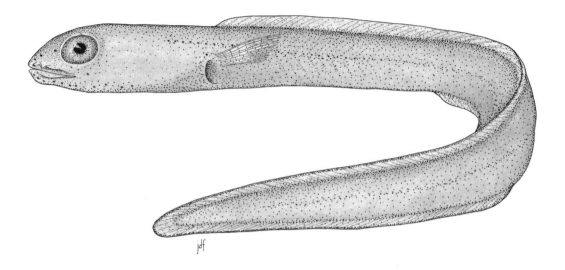

Parabathymyrus oregoni is moderately elongate, with a reduced, blunt, stiff tail. It is distinguished from the other species of the family by the following combination of characters. Snout is short, rounded, and projects slightly beyond lower jaw. Upper and lower lips have flanges, and upper flange is well developed. Anterior nostril is tubular and located near tip of snout. Posterior nostril is near lip, close to anterior nostril, and covered by flap. Snout is 17% to 19%, eye is 15% to 20%, and mouth length is 29% to 34% of head length. Head length is 17% to 19%, predorsal length is 17% to 21%, and preanal length is 41% to 45% of TL. Jaw teeth are small and in two or more series anteriorly and in single series posteriorly. Intermaxillary tooth patch is slightly longer than it is broad and is separated from maxillary and vomerine teeth. Vomerine teeth are in short row. Head pores are small, with four infraorbital and four supraorbital. Branchiostegal rays number 10, pectoral fin rays number 13 to 16, and trunk lateral line pores to anus number 45 to 48. Total vertebrae number 149 to 155, predorsal vertebrae number 10 to 12, preanal vertebrae number 50 to 54, and precaudal vertebrae number 67 to 70. Color is brown, with dark-edged vertical fins.

This species occurs in the western North Atlantic from the southern Gulf of Mexico, the Caribbean Sea, and off the coast of northern South America to French Guiana. It has been captured along the outer continental shelf. Holotype was captured at 210 m. Maximum known size is 330 mm TL.

REFERENCES: Smith and Kanazawa 1977; Smith 1989f,k.

Paraconger caudilimbatus   (Poey 1867)
Margintail conger

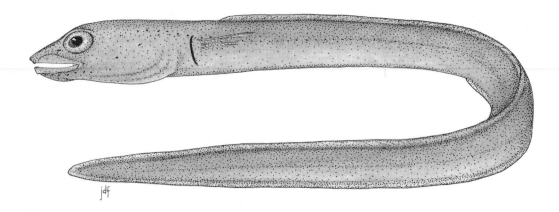

Paraconger caudilimbatus is moderately elongate, with a reduced, blunt, stiff tail. It is distinguished from the other species of the family by the following combination of characters. Snout is moderately tapered and projects slightly beyond lower jaw. Upper and lower lips have flanges, and upper flange is wide. Anterior nostril is tubular and located near tip of snout. Posterior nostril is anterior to midheight of eye. Snout is 10% to 22%, eye is 18% to 22%, and mouth length is 30% to 38% of head length. Head length is 16% to 18%, predorsal length is 18% to 22%, and preanal length is 39% to 46% of TL. Jaw teeth are small, acute, and in two to several rows, with outer row forming cutting edge. Intermaxillary tooth patch is square and separated from maxillary and vomerine teeth. Vomerine teeth are in short patch, about equally as broad as it is long.

Head pores are very small, with three infraorbital, five supraorbital, and three supratemporal. Branchiostegal rays number 9 or 10, pectoral fin rays number 12, and lateral line pores to anus number 40 to 43. Total vertebrae number 121 to 127, predorsal vertebrae number 11 to 13, and preanal vertebrae number 44 to 45. Color is brown to gray and slightly lighter ventrally, with vertical fins dark edged. Stomach and intestine are pale.

This species occurs in the western North Atlantic from Bermuda, southeastern Florida, the Bahamas, the Gulf of Mexico, and the Caribbean Sea. It has been captured from the surface to 70 m. Maximum known size is 461 mm TL.

REFERENCES: Kanazawa 1961; Hoese and Moore 1977; C. R. Robins et al. 1986; Smith 1989f; Boschung 1992.

Pseudophichthys splendens   (Lea 1913)

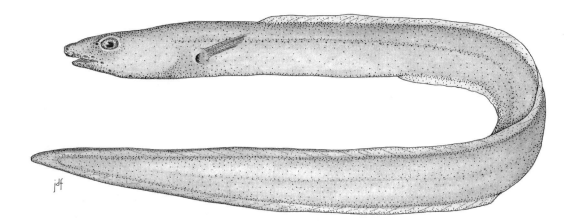

Pseudophichthys splendens is moderately elongate, with a swollen snout, an anus located at about two-fifths of length, and a rounded tail. It is distinguished from the other species of the family by the following combination of characters. Snout projects beyond lower jaw. Upper lip lacks labial flange. Anterior nostril is tubular and located near tip of snout. Posterior nostril is elliptical and located anterior to midheight of eye. Snout is 25% to 33%, eye is 13% to 19%, and mouth length is 24% to 33% of head length. Head length is 13% to 15%, predorsal length is 17% to 22%, and preanal length is 35% to 40% of TL. Jaw teeth are moderately small, conical, and in moderately broad to broad bands. Intermaxillary teeth are in several rows and are not separated from maxillary teeth. Vomerine teeth are in broad, elongate patch, nearly cover roof of mouth, and extend to almost end of maxillary tooth band.

Head pores are slightly enlarged and number five infraorbital and three supraorbital. Supratemporal pores are absent. Branchiostegal rays number 9, pectoral fin rays number 10 to 13, and lateral line pores to anus number 33 to 39. Total vertebrae number 130 to 136, predorsal vertebrae number 13 to 17, preanal vertebrae number 38 to 41, and precaudal vertebrae number 52. Color is gray to brown, with abdomen and inside of mouth black, and vertical fins dark edged posteriorly.

This species occurs in the tropical waters of the Atlantic Ocean. In the western Atlantic it occurs from the east coast of Florida to Central America, including the Gulf of Mexico and the West Indies. It has been captured from 37 to 1,647 m. Maximum known size is 387 mm TL.

REFERENCES: Smith 1989f,k; Boschung 1992.

Rhynchoconger flavus   (Goode and Bean 1896)
Yellow conger

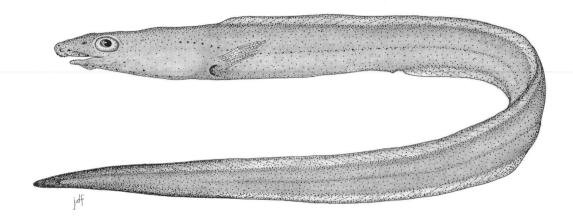

Rhynchoconger flavus is moderately elongate, with anus located at one-quarter to one-third of length and with an acutely pointed tail. It is distinguished from the other species of the family by the following combination of characters. Snout projects beyond lower jaw, and longitudinal fleshy keel occurs on underside of tip of snout. Upper lip has broad flange, and lower lip has narrow flange. Anterior nostril is tubular and located near anteroventral corner of snout. Posterior nostril is elliptical and located anterior to midheight of eye. Snout is 25% to 29%, eye is 19% to 21%, and mouth length is 34% to 40% of head length. Head length is 42% to 54% and predorsal length is 44% to 56% of preanal length. Jaw teeth are small, conical, and in narrow bands. Intermaxillary tooth patch is round, as long as or slightly longer than it is broad, exposed when mouth is closed, and slightly separated from maxillary and vomerine teeth. Vomerine tooth patch is short. Head pores are small, with those on up-per jaw located on flange, and number five infraorbital, three supraorbital, and one supratemporal. Branchiostegal rays number 8 or 9, pectoral fin rays number 12, and lateral line pores to anus number 26 to 34. Total vertebrae number 159 to 172, predorsal vertebrae number 6 to 9, preanal vertebrae number 31 to 37, and precaudal vertebrae number 43. Color is brown to yellowish brown, with vertical fins black edged posteriorly and stomach and intestine pale.

This species occurs in the western North Atlantic from the Gulf of Mexico to the mouth of the Amazon River at 26 to 183 m. It is rare east of Mobile Bay in the Gulf of Mexico, where it is generally limited to muddy inshore waters. Maximum known size is 1,500 mm TL.

REFERENCES: Hoese and Moore 1977 (as *Hildebrandia flava*); C. R. Robins et al. 1986 (as *H. flava*); Smith 1989f,k; Boschung 1992.

Rhynchoconger gracilior (Ginsburg 1951)
Whiptail conger

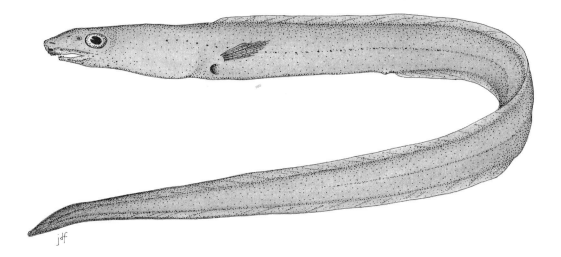

Rhynchoconger gracilior is moderately elongate, with anus located at one-quarter to one-third of length and with an acutely pointed tail. It is distinguished from the other species of the family by the following combination of characters. Snout projects beyond lower jaw, and longitudinal fleshy keel occurs under tip of snout. Upper lip has broad flange, and lower lip has narrow flange. Anterior nostril is tubular and is located near anteroventral corner of snout. Posterior nostril is elliptical and located anterior to midheight of eye. Snout is 23% to 28%, eye is 17% to 20%, and mouth length is 34% to 40% of head length. Head length is 44% to 54% and predorsal length is 45% to 53% of preanal length. Jaw teeth are small, conical, and in narrow bands. Intermaxillary tooth patch is broader than it is long, exposed when mouth is closed, and slightly separated from maxillary and vomerine teeth. Vomerine tooth patch is longer than it is broad. Head pores are small, with those of upper jaw located on flange, and number five infraorbital, four supraorbital, and one supratemporal. Branchiostegal rays number 8 to 10, pectoral fin rays number 9 to 13, and lateral line pores to anus number 23 to 27. Total vertebrae number 175 to 182, predorsal vertebrae number 6 or 7, preanal vertebrae number 29, and precaudal vertebrae number 41 to 42. Color is brown to yellowish, with vertical fins edged in black posteriorly, stomach black, and intestine pale.

This species occurs in the western North Atlantic from Georgia, the east coast of Florida, and the eastern Gulf of Mexico to Suriname, including the West Indies, at 82 to 458 m. It is most abundant in clear offshore waters and is rare west of Mobile Bay in the Gulf of Mexico. Maximum known size is 434 mm TL.

REFERENCES: Ginsburg 1951 (as *Congrina gracilior*); Hoese and Moore 1977 (as *Hildebrandia gracilior*); C. R. Robins et al. 1986 (as *H. gracilior*); Smith 1989f,k; Boschung 1992.

Rhynchoconger guppyi (Norman 1925)

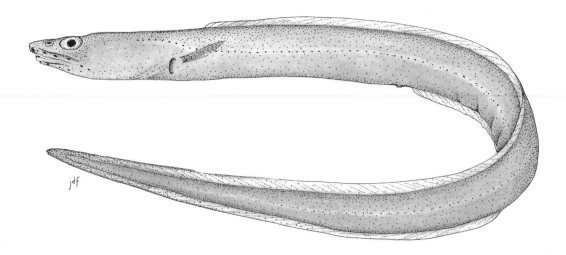

Rhynchoconger guppyi is moderately elongate, with anus located at one-quarter to one-third of length and with an acutely pointed tail. It is distinguished from the other species of the family by the following combination of characters. Snout projects beyond lower jaw and has longitudinal fleshy keel under tip of snout. Upper lip has broad flange, and lower lip has narrow flange. Anterior nostril is tubular and is located near anteroventral corner of snout. Posterior nostril is elliptical and is located anterior to midheight of eye. Snout is 20% to 27%, eye is 11% to 18%, and mouth length is 33% to 38% of head length. Head length is 40% to 48%, predorsal length is 38% to 49%, and preanal length is 25% to 32% of preanal length. Jaw teeth are small, conical, and in narrow band. Intermaxillary tooth patch is broader than it is long, exposed when mouth is closed, and slightly separated from maxillary and vomer- ine teeth. Vomerine tooth patch is longer than it is broad. Head pores are small, with those of upper jaw located on flange, and number five infrarorbital, three supraorbital, and one supratemporal. Branchiostegal rays number 7 or 8, pectoral fin rays number 11 to 13, and lateral line pores to anus number 24 to 33. Total vertebrae number 171 to 178, predorsal vertebrae number 6 to 8, and preanal vertebrae number 30 to 37. Color is brown to grayish brown, with vertical fins black edged posteriorly, stomach black, and intestine pale.

This species occurs in the western North Atlantic in the northern Gulf of Mexico and in the Caribbean Sea from Honduras to Tobago and throughout the Antilles between 137 and 458 m. Maximum known size is 945 mm TL.

REFERENCES: Smith and Kanazawa 1977; Smith 1989f,k.

Uroconger syringinus   Ginsburg 1954

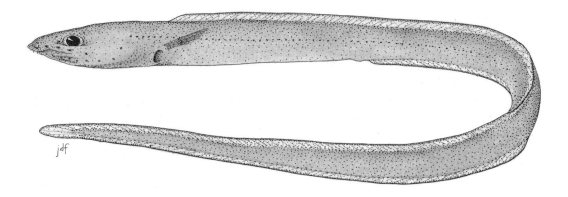

Uroconger syringinus is moderately elongated, with anus located at about one-third of length and with a greatly attenuated tail. It is distinguished from the other species of the family by the following combination of characters. Snout projects slightly beyond lower jaw. Flange is present on lower lip. Anterior nostril is tubular and located near tip of snout. Posterior nostril is elliptical and located anterior to midheight of eye. Snout is 25% to 30%, eye is 12% to 16%, and mouth length is 36% to 42% of head length. Head length is 36% to 42% and predorsal length is 39% to 43% of preanal length. Jaw teeth are moderately large, acute, and in two rows anteriorly but converging to single row posteriorly. Lower jaw has additional short, inner, rudimentary row. Intermaxillary tooth patch is relatively large, consists of two transverse rows, and is separated from maxillary and vomerine teeth. Vomerine teeth are in single row extending posterior to maxillary teeth. Three posteriormost head pores along upper jaw are enlarged and slitlike. Head pores number five to seven interorbital, three to five supraorbital, and one to three supratemporal. Branchiostegal rays number 9, pectoral fin rays number 11 or 12, and lateral line pores to anus number 40 to 46. Total vertebrae number 220 to 225, predorsal vertebrae number 11, preanal vertebrae number 46 to 49, and precaudal vertebrae number 86. Color is brown to grayish brown, with vertical fins black edged and stomach and intestine pale.

This species occurs in the tropical to warm temperate waters of the Atlantic Ocean. It occurs from the east coast of Florida to Suriname, including the Gulf of Mexico, the Bahamas, and rarely in the West Indies. It has been captured from 44 to 384 m. Maximum known size is 380 mm TL.

REFERENCES: Ginsburg 1954; Hoese and Moore 1977; Smith 1989f,k; Boschung 1992.

Xenomystax bidentatus   (Reid 1940)

Xenomystax bidentatus is moderately elongate, with a relatively acute snout and head, anus located at 30% to 40% of length, and a greatly attenuated caudal fin. It is distinguished from the other species of the family by the following combination of characters. Snout projects beyond lower jaw. Lips are reduced, teeth are exposed when mouth is closed, and labial flanges are absent. Anterior nostril is tubular and located behind intermaxillary tooth patch. Posterior nostril is elliptical and located less than its diameter in front of midheight of eye. Snout is 33% to 40%, eye is 10% to 16%, and mouth length is 53% to 58% of head length. Head length is 41% to 44% and predorsal length is 41% to 45% of preanal length. Jaw teeth are slender, conical, recurved, and in bands. Inner row of jaw teeth is separated from three to five irregular outer rows by groove. Intermaxillary tooth patch is triangular, slightly longer than it is broad, and separated from maxillary and vomerine teeth by broad, transverse groove. Vomer has median row of 10 to 14 enlarged teeth flanked by smaller teeth. Head pores are numerous, with eight infraorbital, six supraorbital, and three supratemporal. Branchiostegal rays number 7 or 8, pectoral fin rays number 9 to 11, and lateral line pores to anus number 31 to 34. Dorsal fin originates over or slightly posterior to pectoral fin base. Total vertebrae number 174 to 180, predorsal vertebrae number 6 or 7, preanal vertebrae number 32 to 35, and precaudal vertebrae number 46. Color is brown and slightly darker dorsally than ventrally. Medial fins are black posteriorly, and stomach, intestine, and swim bladder are pale.

This species occurs in the western Atlantic in the Caribbean Sea, the Straits of Florida, and the northeastern Gulf of Mexico between 384 and 860 m. It has been captured only once in the Gulf of Mexico off the coast of Alabama. Maximum known size is 525 mm TL.

REFERENCES: Smith 1989f,k; Boschung 1992.

Xenomystax congroides Smith and Kanazawa 1989

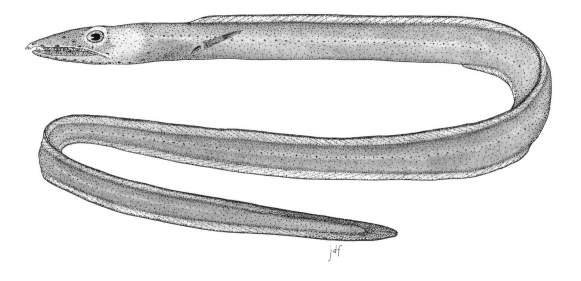

Xenomystax congroides is moderately elongate, with anus located at about 30% to 40% of length and with a greatly attenuated caudal fin. It is distinguished from the other species of the family by the following combination of characters. Snout projects beyond lower jaw. Lips are reduced, teeth are exposed when mouth is closed, and labial flanges are absent. Anterior nostril is tubular and located behind intermaxillary tooth patch. Posterior nostril is elliptical and located less than its diameter in front of midheight of eye. Snout is 30% to 37%, eye is 10% to 14%, and mouth length is 47% to 62% of head length. Head length is 36% to 40% and predorsal length is 30% to 38% of preanal length. Jaw teeth are slender, conical, recurved, and in bands. Inner row of jaw teeth is separated from outer two or three rows by groove. Intermaxillary tooth patch is short and rounded, as broad as it is long, and separated from maxillary and vomerine teeth by broad transverse groove. Vomer has several large, median teeth flanked by smaller teeth.

Head pores are numerous, with eight infraorbital, six supraorbital, and three supratemporal. Branchiostegal rays number 7 to 10, pectoral fin rays number 10 to 15, and lateral line pores to anus number 28 to 40. Dorsal fin originates anterior to pectoral fin base. Total vertebrae number 189 to 219, predorsal vertebrae number 4 to 6, preanal vertebrae number 32 to 40, and precaudal vertebrae number 50 to 60. Color is brown to yellowish brown, with vertical fins black edged posteriorly, mouth and branchial membrane dark, and stomach and intestine black.

This species occurs in the tropical to warm temperate waters of the Atlantic Ocean. In the western Atlantic it occurs from northeastern Florida to the mouth of the Amazon River, including the Gulf of Mexico, the Bahamas, and the West Indies. It has been captured from 140 to 825 m. Maximum known size is 876 mm TL.

REFERENCES: Smith 1989k; Smith and Kanazawa 1989; Boschung 1992.

NETTASTOMATIDAE   Duckbill eels

Duckbill eels are elongate, with a long, narrow snout and a slender tail. They are distinguished from the other families of the order by the following combination of characters. Jaws are acute, and upper jaw projects beyond lower jaw. Upper and lower lips lack flanges. Anterior nostril is tubular and located near tip of snout. Jaw teeth are variable in size and exposed when mouth is closed. Eye is well developed. Gill openings are lateral. Dorsal and anal fins are confluent with caudal fin. Dorsal fin originates near gill openings. Pectoral fin is present or absent. Anus is located anterior to midlength. Lateral line pores are complete on head and body. Pelvic fin and scales are absent.

Duckbill eels occur worldwide in tropical to warm temperate seas. The leptocephali are moderate to large (85 to 200 mm SL), with short gut possessing two distinct swellings or irregular undulations, long dorsal fin, and pigment on head, gut, and lateral midline. The family contains about 25 to 38 species in six genera, and 9 species in six genera occur in the Gulf of Mexico.

Key to the Species of the Gulf of Mexico
(Adapted from Smith 1989g)

1a. Pectoral fin present. 2
1b. Pectoral fin absent 4
2a. Pterygoid teeth present (except in very small specimens) (Fig. 58); lateral vomerine teeth close-set and numerous . . . . *Hoplunnis tenuis* p. 319
2b. Pterygoid teeth absent; lateral vomerine teeth widely spaced or absent. 3
3a. Lateral vomerine teeth present only in very small specimens; stomach pale. . . . . *Hoplunnis macrura* p. 318
3b. Lateral vomerine teeth absent; stomach black . . . .*Hoplunnis diomedianus* p. 317
4a. Posterior nostril at midheight of eye; pterygoid teeth present . . . . *Saurenchelys cognita* p. 323
4b. Posterior nostril above or below midheight of eye; pterygoid teeth absent 5
5a. Posterior nostril consists of slit on upper lip . . . . *Facciolella* sp. p. 316
5b. Posterior nostril above midheight of eye and located from in front of anterior margin of eye to behind occiput on dorsal surface of body 6
6a. Infraorbital pores number 11 to 13, with 8 to 10 along upper jaw; snout 32% to 37% of head length (Fig. 59); posterior nostril behind posterior margin of eye . . . . *Nettenchelys pygmaea* p. 322

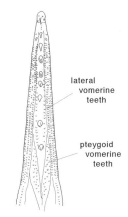

lateral
vomerine
teeth

pteygoid
vomerine
teeth

FIG 58

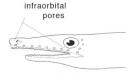

infraorbital
pores

FIG 59

6b. Infraorbital pores number 14 to 19, with 11 to 16 along
      upper jaw; snout 35% to 55% of head length; posterior
      nostril over or anterior to posterior margin of eye 7

7a. Supraorbital pores number 4 to 7; tip of snout without
      fleshy proboscis 8

7b. Supraorbital pores number 8 to 13; tip of snout with fleshy
      proboscis . . . . *Venefica procera* p. 324

8a. Two supraorbital pores between anterior naris and eye; lat-
      eral line pores 44 to 49 . . . . . *Nettastoma melanura* p. 320

8b. Three supraorbital pores between anterior naris and eye;
      lateral line pores 38 to 41 . . . . *Nettastoma syntresis* p. 321

Facciolella sp.

This unnamed *Facciolella* species is elongate, round in cross section anteriorly and compressed posteriorly, with upper jaw distinctly projecting beyond lower jaw and without pectoral fins. It is distinguished from the other species of the family by the following combination of characters. Snout is elongate. Posterior nostril is slitlike and located on upper lip in front of eye. Jaw teeth are small, conical, and in bands, with inner teeth slightly larger than outer teeth. Intermaxillary teeth are slightly larger than and continuous with maxillary teeth, and form spadelike patch. Vomerine teeth are separated from intermaxillary teeth and are in elongate band, with median teeth slightly larger than others. Pterygoid teeth are absent. Snout is 33% to 39%, eye is 7% to 9%, and upper jaw is 48% to 54% of head length. Head length is 11%, predorsal length is 11% to 13%, and preanal length is 30% to 33% of TL. Branchiostegal rays number 6 to 8, and lateral line pores to anus number 51 to 55. Infraorbital pores number nine, supraorbital pores number five, and supratemporal pores number zero to three. Total vertebrae number 243 to 256, predorsal vertebrae number 10 to 13, and preanal vertebrae number 53 to 57. Color is tan to dark brown or gray.

This species occurs in the western North Atlantic from Bermuda, the east coast of Florida, the northeastern Gulf of Mexico, Hispaniola, the Caribbean coast of Nicaragua to Venezuela, and southern Brazil. It has been captured from 75 to 3,109 m. Maximum known size is 627 mm TL.

REFERENCE: Smith 1989g.

Hoplunnis diomedianus   Goode and Bean 1896

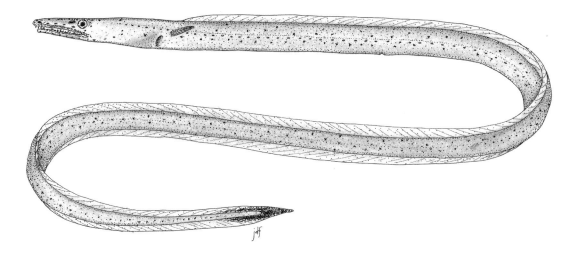

Hoplunnis diomedianus is elongate, round in cross section anteriorly and compressed posteriorly, with pectoral fins present and upper jaw projecting beyond lower jaw. It is distinguished from the other species of the family by the following combination of characters. Snout is moderately elongate and conical. Posterior nostril is slitlike and located near midheight of eye. Jaw teeth are in three rows, with those of inner row relatively large and those of outer row relatively small. Intermaxillary teeth are arranged in semicircle and number 6 or 7. Vomer has single row of large teeth and few or no lateral teeth. Pterygoid teeth are absent. Snout is 35% to 38%, eye is 8% to 12%, and upper jaw length is 52% to 56% of head length. Head length is 9% to 10%, predorsal length is 8% to 9%, and preanal length is 23% to 25% of TL. Branchiostegal rays number 5 to 7, pectoral fin rays number 9 or 10, and lateral line pores to anus number 33 to 38. Infraorbital pores number eight, supraorbital pores number five, and supratemporal pores number three. Total vertebrae number 221 to 234, predorsal vertebrae number 3 to 5, and preanal vertebrae number 35 to 41. Color is light yellow-brown, with sparse scattering of small dark spots above and below lateral line and densely concentrated spots on dorsal aspect of head. Vertical fins are edged in black posteriorly. Inner surfaces of branchial membrane and stomach are black, intestine is pale, and swim bladder is silvery.

This species occurs in the western Atlantic from North Carolina to southern Florida and in the northeastern and southern Gulf of Mexico between 33 and 203 m. It has only once been captured west of the Mississippi River in the Gulf of Mexico. Maximum known size is 543 mm TL.

REFERENCES: Lane and Stewart 1968; Hoese and Moore 1977; Smith and Castle 1982; Uyeno et al. 1983; Smith 1989g,j; Boschung 1992.

Hoplunnis macrura Ginsburg 1951

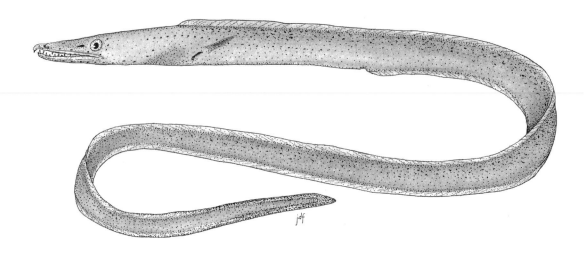

Hoplunnis macrura is elongate, round in cross section anteriorly and compressed posteriorly, with pectoral fins present and upper jaw projecting beyond lower jaw. It is distinguished from the other species of the family by the following combination of characters. Snout is moderately elongate and conical. Posterior nostril is slitlike and located near midlength of eye. Jaw teeth are in two rows, with those of inner row slightly larger than those of outer row. Intermaxillary teeth consist of one enlarged tooth flanked by one or two smaller teeth. Vomer has single row of greatly enlarged teeth; small lateral teeth occur only in small juveniles. Pterygoid teeth are absent. Snout is 32% to 40%, eye is 9% to 11%, and upper jaw is 50% to 57% of head length. Head length is 11% to 12%, predorsal length is 9% to 10%, and preanal length is 22% to 23% of TL. Branchiostegal rays number 7 or 8, pectoral fin rays number 10 or 11, and lateral line pores to anus number 32 to 37. Infraorbital pores number eight, supraorbital pores number five, and supratemporal pores number three. Total vertebrae number 227 to 245, predorsal vertebrae number 4 or 5, and preanal vertebrae number 34 to 38. Color is light yellowish brown, with small brown spots dorsally. Inner surface of branchial membrane is black. Vertical fins are edged in black posteriorly. Stomach and intestine are light.

This species occurs in the western North Atlantic from the western and southern Gulf of Mexico and from Colombia to the mouth of the Amazon River between 20 and 220 m. It has not been captured east of Pensacola, Florida, in the northern Gulf of Mexico. Maximum known size is 542 mm TL.

REFERENCES: Ginsburg 1951; Lane and Stewart 1968; Hoese and Moore 1977; Smith and Castle 1982; C. R. Robins et al. 1986; Smith 1989g,j; Boschung 1992.

Hoplunnis tenuis   Ginsburg 1951

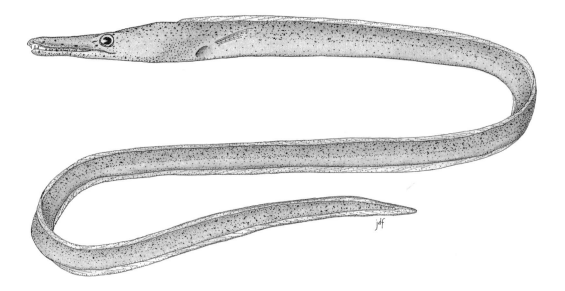

Hoplunnis tenuis is elongate, round in cross section anteriorly and compressed posteriorly, with pectoral fins present and upper jaw projecting slightly beyond lower jaw. It is distinguished from the other species of the family by the following combination of characters. Snout is moderately elongate and conical. Posterior nostril is slitlike and located near midheight of eye. Jaw teeth are in two rows anteriorly and three rows posteriorly, with those of inner row larger than those of outer row. Intermaxillary teeth consist of three irregular transverse rows. Vomer has single series of teeth; first several are small and remainder are fanglike. Band of small teeth flanks series of large teeth on vomer. Pterygoid has series of small teeth. Snout is 35% to 41%, eye is 8% to 11%, and upper jaw is 51% to 59% of head length. Head length is 10% to 11%, predorsal length is 8% to 10%, and preanal length is 25% to 26% of TL. Branchiostegal rays number 7 or 8, pectoral fin rays number 9 or 10, and lateral line pores to anus number 35 to 38. Infraorbital pores number eight, supraorbital pores number five, and supratemporal pores number three. Total vertebrae number 232 to 244, predorsal vertebrae number 3 to 6, and preanal vertebrae number 36 to 38. Color is light brown to tan, with small brown spots dorsally. Inner surface of branchial membrane is black. Vertical fins are edged in black posteriorly. Stomach and intestine are black.

This species occurs in the western North Atlantic from New Jersey to the Guianas and southern Brazil, including the Gulf of Mexico, the Bahamas, and the Caribbean Sea. It has been captured from 110 to 468 m. Maximum known size is 576 mm TL.

REFERENCES: Lane and Stewart 1968; Hoese and Moore 1977; Smith and Castle 1982; C. R. Robins et al. 1986; Smith 1989g,j; Boschung 1992.

Nettastoma melanura   Rafinesque 1810

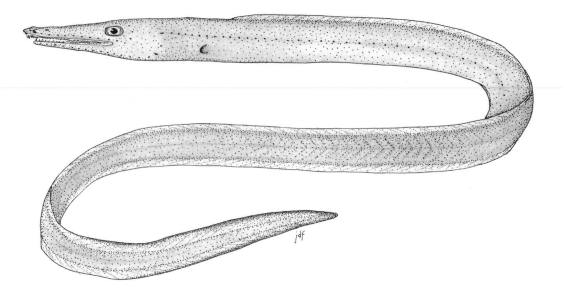

Nettastoma melanura is elongate, round in cross section and compressed posteriorly, with upper jaw projecting beyond lower jaw and pectoral fins lacking. It is distinguished from the other species of the family by the following combination of characters. Snout is slender, elongate, and slightly depressed. Posterior nostril is slitlike or crescent shaped and located above anterior margin of eye. Jaw teeth are conical, small, and in narrow bands, with inner teeth larger than outer teeth. Intermaxillary tooth patch is short and continuous with maxillary teeth. Vomerine tooth patch is elongate, with median teeth larger than lateral teeth and slightly separated from intermaxillary teeth. Pterygoid teeth are absent. Snout is 35% to 44%, eye is 8% to 11%, and upper jaw is 51% to 62% of head length. Head length is 35% to 42% and predorsal length is 33% to 40% of preanal length. Branchiostegal rays number 9, and lateral line pores to anus number 43 to 49. Infraorbital pores number 15 to 17, supraorbital pores number 5 or 6, and supratemporal pores number 3. Total vertebrae number 195 to 207, predorsal vertebrae number 4 to 8, and preanal vertebrae number 44 to 50. Color is brown to gray, with vertical fins edged in black.

This species occurs in the tropical to warm temperate waters of the Atlantic Ocean. In the western Atlantic it occurs from the east coast of Florida and the northern Gulf of Mexico to the Guianas. It has been captured from 329 to 860 m and rarely from 37 m and 1,647 m. Maximum known size is 773 mm TL.

REFERENCES: Böhlke and Smith 1968; Smith et al. 1981; Uyeno et al. 1983; Smith 1989g,j; Boschung 1992.

Nettastoma syntresis Smith and Böhlke 1981

Nettastoma syntresis is elongate, round in cross section and compressed posteriorly, with upper jaw projecting beyond lower jaw and pectoral fins absent. It is distinguished from the other species of the family by the following combination of characters. Snout is slender, elongate, and slightly depressed. Posterior nostril is slit-like or crescent shaped and located near anterodorsal margin of eye. Jaw teeth are conical, small, and in narrow bands, with inner teeth larger than outer teeth. Intermaxillary tooth patch is short and continuous with maxillary teeth. Vomerine tooth patch is elongate, with median teeth equal in size to outer teeth and slightly separated from intermaxillary teeth. Pterygoid teeth are absent. Snout is 41% to 44%, eye is 8% to 11%, and upper jaw is 57% to 63% of head length. Head length is 39% to 43% and predorsal length is 37% to 41% of preanal length. Branchiostegal rays number 7 or 8, and lateral line pores to anus number 38 to 41. Infraorbital pores number 15 or 16, supraorbital pores number 5 to 7, and supratemporal pores number 3. Total vertebrae number 201, predorsal vertebrae number 5 or 6, and preanal vertebrae number 40 or 41. Color is brown to gray, with vertical fins edged in black.

This species occurs in the tropical waters of the western North Atlantic off the Bahamas and Cuba and in the northeastern Gulf of Mexico. It has been captured once in the Gulf of Mexico at 620 m. Maximum known size is 550 mm SL.

REFERENCES: Smith et al. 1981; Smith 1989g.

Nettenchelys pygmaea   Smith and Böhlke 1981

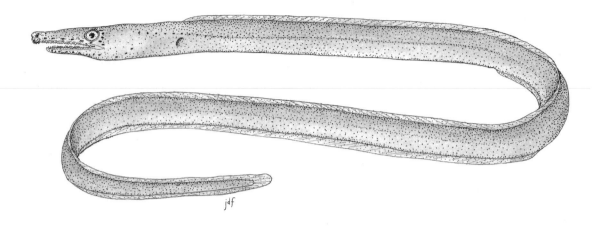

Nettenchelys pygmaea is elongate, round in cross section and compressed posteriorly, with upper jaw projecting beyond lower jaw and pectoral fins lacking. It is distinguished from the other species of the family by the following combination of characters. Snout is slender, elongate, and slightly depressed. Posterior nostril is located on top of head just behind posterior margin of eye. Jaw teeth are small, conical, and in bands, with those of innermost series larger than remainder. Intermaxillary tooth patch is short and continuous with maxillary teeth. Vomerine tooth patch is long, with anteriormost teeth enlarged and forming median row. Remaining vomerine teeth are separated from those of anterior row and from elliptical patch. Pterygoid teeth are absent. Snout is 34% to 37%, eye is 8% to 10%, and upper jaw length is 53% of head length. Head length is 30% to 33% and predorsal length is 33% to 35% of preanal length. Lateral line pores to anus number 40 to 42. Infraorbital pores number 11, supraorbital pores number 5, and supratemporal pores number 3. Total vertebrae number about 220 to 250, predorsal vertebrae number 7 or 8, and preanal vertebrae number 40 to 43. Color is brown, slightly darker dorsally than ventrally.

This species occurs in the western North Atlantic in the northern Gulf of Mexico and off Venezuela. Only four specimens have been captured, and these came from 128 to 280 m. Maximum known size is 201 mm TL.

REFERENCES: Smith et al. 1981; Smith 1989g,j: Boschung 1992.

Saurenchelys cognita Smith 1989

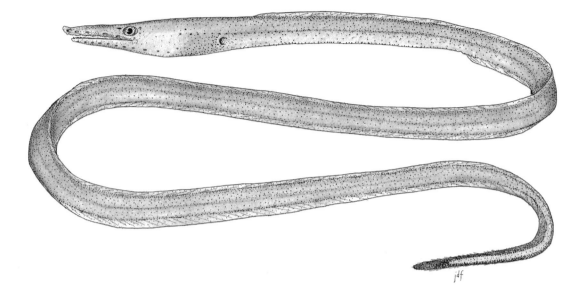

Saurenchelys cognita is elongate, round in cross section anteriorly and compressed posteriorly, with upper jaw projecting beyond lower jaw and pectoral fins lacking. It is distinguished from the other species of the family by the following combination of characters. Snout is slender, elongate, and slightly depressed. Posterior nostril is a longitudinal slit located anterior to midheight of eye. Jaw teeth are small, conical, and in narrow bands, with those of inner series larger than other teeth. Intermaxillary tooth patch is spade shaped, consists of about six transverse rows, and is continuous with maxillary teeth but separated from vomerine teeth. Vomerine tooth patch is long and consists of median row of enlarged teeth and two or three lateral rows of small teeth. Pterygoid teeth consist of long band of small teeth originating posterior to vomerine tooth patch and extending to end of maxillary tooth patch. Snout is 35% to 43%, eye is 8% to 11%, and

upper jaw is 49% to 51% of head length. Head length is 37% to 42%, predorsal length is 11%, and preanal length is 23% of TL. Branchiostegal rays number 7, and lateral line pores to anus number 31 or 32. Infraorbital pores number eight, supraorbital pores number three to six, and supratemporal pores number three. Total vertebrae number 199 to 209, predorsal vertebrae number 8 to 10, preanal vertebrae number 32 to 36, and precaudal vertebrae number 55. Color is light tan to gray, with vertical fins edged in black posteriorly.

This species occurs in the western North Atlantic from North Carolina to the east coast of Florida and the northwestern Gulf of Mexico west of Mobile Bay. It has been captured from 59 to 158 m.

REFERENCES: Smith and Castle 1982; Smith 1989g,j; Boschung 1992.

Venefica procera   (Goode and Bean 1883)

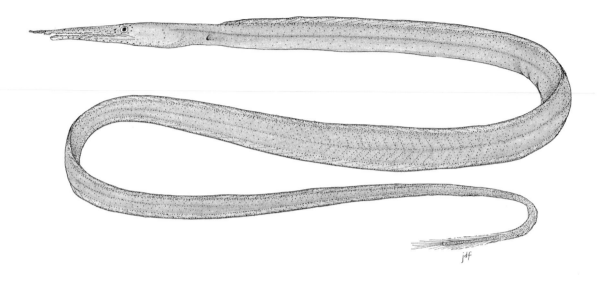

Venefica procera is elongate, round in cross section anteriorly and compressed posteriorly, with upper jaw projecting well beyond lower jaw and pectoral fins lacking. It is distinguished from the other species of the family by the following combination of characters. Tip of snout extends as slender proboscis, skin of proboscis is pitted, and pits are separated by dermal ridges. Snout is long, slender, and slightly depressed. Anterior nostril is located at base of proboscis. Posterior nostril is large, oblique, and located anterior to dorsal margin of eye. Jaw teeth are small, conical, and in narrow bands. Mandibular tooth patches meet at tip of snout, where they are expanded slightly to fit into gap between vomerine and intermaxillary teeth. Intermaxillary tooth patch is spade shaped and separated from vomerine teeth by crescent-shaped gap. Vomerine tooth patch is long. Pterygoid teeth are absent. Snout is 42%

to 55%, eye is 4% to 7%, and upper jaw is 53% to 67% of head length. Head length is 24% to 36%, predorsal length is 11%, and preanal length is 38% of TL. Branchiostegal rays number 5, and lateral line pores to anus number 60 to 64. Infraorbital pores number 16 to 19, supraorbital pores number 9 to 13, and supratemporal pores number 3 or 4. Total vertebrae number 200 to 205, predorsal vertebrae number 6 to 8, and preanal vertebrae number 57 to 62. Color is brown to gray, with vertical fins edged in black and stomach and intestine black.

This species occurs in the western North Atlantic from North Carolina to Suriname, including the Gulf of Mexico and the Caribbean Sea. It has been captured from 832 to 2,304 m. Maximum known size is 1,088 mm TL.

REFERENCE: Smith 1989g.

SERRIVOMERIDAE Sawtooth eels

Sawtooth eels are very slender, with moderately attenuate jaws and anus located anterior to midlength. They are distinguished from the other families of the order by the following combination of characters. Vomer projects beyond articulation with maxilla. Jaws are slender, but snout is less than one-half head length. Anterior nostril is tubular or nontubular, and anterior and posterior nostrils are close-set in front of eye. Jaw teeth are small, erect, and set in two or more rows. Vomerine teeth are compressed to conical and arranged in two rows. Eye is well developed. Dorsal and anal fins are confluent with caudal fin. Dorsal fin originates near anal fin origin, and anal fin originates just behind anus. Pectoral fin is small. Lateral line system is reduced; on head it consists of three small pores between nostrils and several series of infraorbital and supraorbital sensory papillae, and on body it consists of single series of sensory papillae. Pelvic fin and scales are absent.

Sawtooth eels occur worldwide in pelagic tropical to temperate seas. The leptocephali are small to moderate in size (generally less than 60 mm SL), with gut narrow; simple, short dorsal fin; and series of small melanophores on base of caudal fin, lateral caudal surface, and dorsal surface of eye. Depths of capture range from 500 to 1,000 m. The family contains nine species in two genera, and two species in the same genus occur in the Gulf of Mexico.

Key to the Species of the Gulf of Mexico
(Adapted from Tighe 1989a)

1a. Anterior tips of first four or five branchiostegal rays extending beyond their articulation with hyoid arch; dorsal fin rays 136 to 175; anal fin rays 119 to 156
. . . . *Serrivomer beanii* p. 326

1b. Anterior tips of first five branchiostegal rays not extending beyond their articulation with hyoid arch; dorsal fin rays 175 to 198; anal fin rays 165 to 192
. . . . *Serrivomer lanceolatoides* p. 327

Serrivomer beanii   Gill and Ryder 1883

Serrivomer beanii is very slender, subcylindrical to slightly compressed and tapering gradually to tail, with dorsal fin originating posterior to anus. It is distinguished from the other species of the family by the following combination of characters. Lower jaw extends slightly beyond upper jaw. Maxillary teeth are in two to four rows, with inner teeth largest. Mandibular teeth are in three to five rows, with inner row consisting of small teeth isolated from remainder, next row consisting of largest teeth, and outer row possessing small irregular teeth. Vomerine teeth are in two alternating rows of enlarged, erect, and laterally compressed teeth, and each tooth is 3 to 4 times as long as it is wide. Anterior tips of first four or five branchiostegal rays extend beyond their articulation with hyoid arch. Snout length is 36% to 40%, eye is 4% to 7%, and mouth length is 37% to 50% of head length. Head length is 11% to 17%, predorsal length is 27% to 34%, preanal length is 22% to 28%, and depth at anal fin origin is 0.9% to 2.5% of TL. Dorsal fin rays number 136 to 175, and anal fin rays number 119 to 156. Total vertebrae number 154 to 162, predorsal vertebrae number 27 to 31, preanal vertebrae number 20 to 22, and precaudal vertebrae number 77 to 103. Adults undergo metamorphosis in dentition, orbit diameter, and jaw structure. Vomerine teeth become arranged in groups of four to six teeth of descending length, orbit increases in size, maxillary teeth are reduced to single row of enlarged teeth, and premaxilla of males regresses in length. Color is brown to black, with iridescent silvery surface.

This species occurs in the Atlantic Ocean. In the western Atlantic it occurs from New England to Suriname, including the Gulf of Mexico and the Caribbean Sea, at mesopelagic depths. Captures of this species in the Gulf of Mexico and the Caribbean Sea are predominately juveniles. Juveniles are located between 550 and 1,000 m, and subadults and adults occur in the lower section of the mesopelagic realm. Food consists of euphausiids, shrimps, other crustaceans, and small fishes. Maximum known size is 745 mm TL; males mature between 510 and 640 mm TL, and females mature between 620 and 745 mm TL.

REFERENCES: Uyeno et al. 1983; Tighe 1989a,b.

Serrivomer lanceolatoides   (Schmidt 1916)

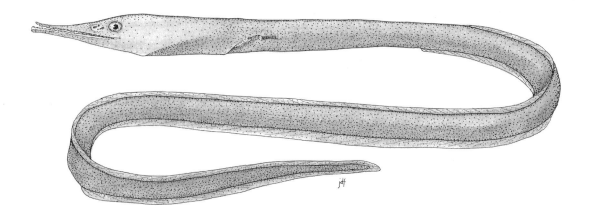

Serrivomer lanceolatoides is very slender, sub-cylindrical to slightly compressed and tapering gradually to tail, with dorsal fin originating posterior to anus. It is distinguished from the other species of the family by the following combination of characters. Lower jaw extends slightly beyond upper jaw. Maxillary teeth are in three or four rows, with inner teeth largest. Mandibular teeth are in four to six rows, with inner row consisting of small teeth slightly isolated from remainder, next row consisting of largest teeth, and outer row possessing small, irregular teeth. Vomerine teeth are in two alternating rows of enlarged, erect, and laterally compressed teeth, with each tooth about 2 times as long as it is wide. Anterior tips of first five branchiostegal rays do not extend beyond articulation with hyoid arch. Snout length is 30% to 40%, eye is 5% to 10%, and mouth length is 36% to 43% of head length. Head length is 15% to 18%, predorsal length is 30% to 41%, preanal length is 25% to 30%, and depth at anal fin origin is 1.4% to 3% of TL. Dorsal fin rays number 175 to 198, and anal fin

rays number 165 to 192. Total vertebrae number 154 to 163, predorsal vertebrae number 29 to 35, preanal vertebrae number 22 to 26, and precaudal vertebrae number 89 to 95. Color is dark brown to black. Adult males have few isolated vomerine teeth, single row of maxillary teeth, single row of recurved mandibular teeth, tubular anterior nostril, and posterior dorsal and anal fin rays prolonged and stiffened to form pseudocaudal fin.

This species occurs in the tropical and subtropical Atlantic Ocean. In the western Atlantic it occurs from southern New England to northern Brazil, including the Gulf of Mexico and the Caribbean Sea. Newly metamorphosed specimens have been captured between 500 and 900 m, juveniles between 650 and 850 m, and subadults and adults between 800 and 1,000 m. Maximum known size is 633 mm TL; males mature between 471 and 488 mm TL, and females mature between 500 and 633 mm TL.

REFERENCES: Tighe 1989a,b.

CLUPEIFORMES

Clupeiformes are thought to be the sister group of the euteleosteans based on the structure of the lower jaw. The order contains five families, and two of these occur in the Gulf of Mexico.

Key to the Families of the Gulf of Mexico

1a. Lower jaw extending, at most, to posterior margin of eye; snout not overhanging mouth . . . . Clupeidae p. 328
1b. Lower jaw extending distinctly posterior to eye; snout overhanging mouth. . . . . Engraulidae p. 347

CLUPEIDAE   Herrings and sardines

Herrings and sardines are fusiform to moderately deep bodied and slightly to strongly compressed, with a terminal mouth and a deeply forked caudal fin. They are distinguished from the other families of the order by the following combination of characters. Snout is moderately short to moderately long, generally equal to 1 or 2 times orbital width. Mouth is generally terminal but is slightly subterminal in some taxa. Jaw teeth are small to absent. Both premaxilla and maxilla contribute to upper margin of mouth. One or two supramaxillae are attached to posterodorsal aspect of maxilla. Eye is large, is located on anterior one-half of head, and often is partially covered by adipose eyelid. Pectoral fin is low on flank, immediately posterior to opercular flap. Dorsal fin is rather short and near midlength. Pelvic fin is slightly anterior to, beneath, or slightly posterior to base of dorsal fin. Anal fin is small and posterior to base of dorsal fin. Body, excluding head, is covered with moderate to small (rarely) scales. Most species have complete series of scutes along belly. Occasionally scutes are absent except for one at base of pelvic fin. Lateral line pores are absent.

Herrings and sardines occur worldwide from tropical to polar latitudes. They are generally present in coastal marine waters, but a number are anadromous and some live exclusively in freshwater. Most are schooling fishes that feed on plankton; however, a few are solitary and feed on fishes. Embryonic development is oviparous. Fertilized eggs are pelagic or demersal, and larvae are generally pelagic. There are about 181 species in 56 genera, and 16 species in 8 genera occur in the Gulf of Mexico.

Key to the Species of the Gulf of Mexico
(Adapted from Whitehead 1985)

1a. Belly free of scutes along midline except for W-shaped scute preceding pelvic fin 2

1b. Belly with scutes along midline before and behind pelvic scute that has ascending arms. 5

2a. Branchiostegal rays range from 11 to 18; pelvic fin posterior to dorsal fin base . . . . *Etrumeus teres* p. 338

2b. Branchiostegal rays range from 6 to 7; pelvic fin under dorsal fin base 3

3a. Premaxilla with teeth; gill rakers 20 to 26 (usually 22 to 24) on lower limb of first arch 4

3b. Premaxilla without teeth; gill rakers 24 to 28 on lower limb of first arch . . . . *Jenkinsia majua* p. 343

4a. Isthmus slender but with slight shoulder on each side anteriorly; pectoral fin rays 12 to 15 (Fig. 60)
. . . . *Jenkinsia lamprotaenia* p. 342

4b. Isthmus broadly triangular; pectoral fin rays 11 to 12 (Fig. 61). . . . . *Jenkinsia stolifera* p. 344

5a. Symphysis of upper jaw concave and rounded (Fig. 62) 6

5b. Symphysis of upper jaw concave and rounded but with distinct cleft (Fig. 63) 10

6a. Small bone bearing teeth (hypomaxilla) between premaxilla and toothed portion of maxilla (Fig. 64) 7

6b. No toothed bone (hypomaxilla) between premaxilla and tooth portion of maxilla. 9

7a. Black pigment at tip of dorsal fin; tooth plate on tongue (basihyal tooth plate) and tooth plate posterior to it (basibranchial tooth plate) narrow, width 10% of their combined length . . . . *Harengula humeralis* p. 340

7b. No black pigment at tip of dorsal fin; tooth plate on tongue (basihyal tooth plate) and tooth plate posterior to it (basibranchial tooth plate) broad, width 20% to 33% of their combined length. 8

8a. Gill rakers 28 to 34 (usually 30 to 32) on lower limb of first arch . . . . *Harengula clupeola* p. 339

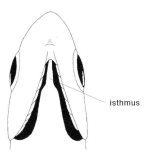

FIG 60

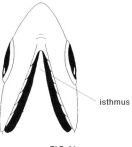

FIG 61

FIG 62

FIG 63

FIG 64

8b. Gill rakers 30 to 40 (usually 32 to 39) on lower limb of
first arch . . . . *Harengula jaguana* p. 341
9a. Last dorsal fin ray prolonged as filament
. . . . *Opisthonema oglinum* p. 345
9b. Last dorsal fin ray not prolonged as filament
. . . .*Sardinella aurita* p. 346
10a. Lower jaw flared outward (Fig. 65); mouth subterminal or
terminal; last dorsal fin ray filamentous 11
10b. Lower jaw not flared outward (Fig. 66); mouth terminal;
last dorsal fin ray not filamentous 12
11a. Mouth subterminal; more than 50 transverse scale rows on
body . . . . *Dorosoma cepedianum* p. 336
11b. Mouth terminal; fewer than 50 transverse scale rows on
body . . . . *Dorosoma petenense* p. 337
12a. Pelvic fin rays nine; paired scales along dorsal midline anterior to dorsal fin not enlarged or fringed; scales along
remainder of body not deeply overlapping 13
12b. Pelvic fin rays seven; paired scales along dorsal midline
anterior to dorsal fin enlarged and fringed; scales along
remainder of body deeply overlapping 14
13a. No teeth present in front of jaws; gill rakers 41 to 48 on
lower limb of first arch . . . . *Alosa alabamae* p. 331
13b. Teeth prominent at front of lower jaw; gill rakers 20 to 24
on lower limb of first arch. . . . . *Alosa chrysochloris* p. 332
14a. Scales 54 to 80 in lateral series; pelvic fin with oblique,
more or less straight posterior margin (inner rays distinctly
shorter than outer rays when fin is laid back); black spot
posterior to opercular flap but none along flank. 15
14b. Scales 42 to 48 in lateral series; pelvic fin with rounded
posterior margin (inner rays equal to or nearly equal to
outer rays when fin is laid back); black spot posterior to
opercular flap followed by series of spots along flank
. . . .*Brevoortia patronus* p. 334
15a. Scales 60 to 77 in lateral series; scutes 27 to 30 along belly;
tip of pectoral fin extends to within one or two scales of
pelvic fin base . . . . *Brevoortia gunteri* p. 333
15b. Scales 54 to 80 (usually 60 to 70) in lateral series; scutes
30 to 32 along belly; tip of pectoral fin extends to within
three to five scales of pelvic fin base
. . . . *Brevoortia smithi* p. 335

FIG 65

FIG 66

Alosa alabamae   Jordan and Evermann 1896
Alabama shad

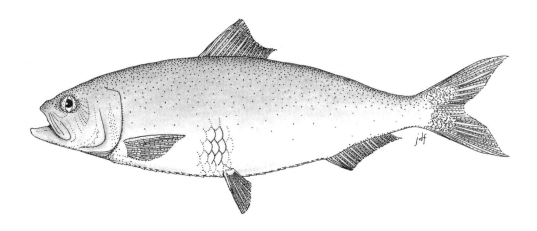

Alosa alabamae is compressed and rather deep bodied, with a large terminal mouth and a deeply forked caudal fin. It is distinguished from the other species of the family by the following combination of characters. Body depth is 26% to 36% and head length is 24% to 27% of SL. Symphysis of upper jaw is distinctly notched. Lower jaw is included in upper jaw when mouth is closed. Upper margin (within mouth) of lower jaw is oblique and not strongly arched. Snout is about equal to eye diameter. Suborbital bone (below eye) is deeper than it is long. Maxilla extends to midlength of eye. Vomer and tongue lack teeth. Teeth also lacking in jaws of adults. Lower limb of first gill arch has 41 to 48 gill rakers in adults. Dorsal fin has 16 to 20 rays, and last fin ray is not prolonged. Pelvic fin has 9 rays. Anal fin has 19 to 22 rays. Scales are deciduous and number 55 to 60 in transverse series. Paired scales along midline of back anterior to dorsal fin are not enlarged or fringed. Belly has 35 to 38 scutes with ascending arms. Axillary scale of pelvic fin is about 75% of pelvic fin length. Vertebrae number 55. Color is metallic greenish to bluish dorsally, grading to bright silvery laterally and ventrally.

This species occurs in the western North Atlantic in the eastern Gulf of Mexico, from Grand Isle, Louisiana, to Choctawhatchee River, Florida. It ascends the rivers in this area to spawn and has been captured from Hot Springs, Arkansas, to Freeport, Iowa, and Montgomery, Virginia. Because this species does not eat during its spawning run, nothing is known of its feeding habits. Maximum known size is 510 mm TL.

REFERENCES: Hildebrand 1963d; Hoese and Moore 1977; Lee et al. 1980; Whitehead 1985; C. R. Robins et al. 1986; Boschung 1992.

Alosa chrysochloris   (Rafinesque 1820)
Skipjack shad

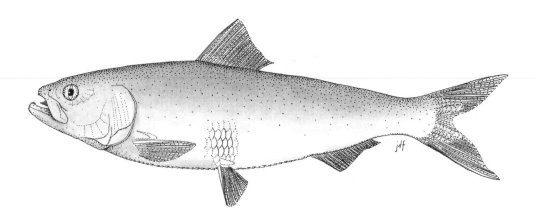

Alosa chrysochloris is compressed and moderately deep bodied, with a large terminal mouth and a deeply forked caudal fin. It is distinguished from the other species of the family by the following combination of characters. Body depth is 24% to 28% and head length is 25% to 28% of SL. Symphysis of upper jaw is distinctly notched. Lower jaw projects beyond upper jaw when mouth is closed. Upper margin (within mouth) of lower jaw is strongly arched. Maxilla extends to middle of eye. Suborbital bone (below eye) is longer than it is deep. Teeth are present in front of jaws in adults. Vomer lacks teeth, but tongue has teeth. Lower limb of first gill arch has 20 to 24 gill rakers. Dorsal fin originates closer to tip of snout than to base of caudal fin and has slightly concave dorsal margin and 16 to 21 rays, the last of which is not produced. Pelvic fin is under dorsal fin base and has 9 rays. Anal fin is posterior to dorsal fin base and has 18 to 21 rays. Scales are deciduous and in 51 to 60 transverse series. Paired scales along dorsal midline anterior to dorsal fin are of normal shape. Belly has 33 to 37 scutes with ascending arms along midline. Vertebrae number 53 to 55. Color is bluish green dorsally and silver laterally and ventrally.

This species occurs in the western North Atlantic in the northern Gulf of Mexico, from Corpus Christi, Texas, to Pensacola, Florida. It ascends rivers in this area to spawn and has been captured from Minnesota to Pittsburgh, Pennsylvania. Food consists of insects (for young) and fishes (for adults). Maximum known size is 450 mm TL.

REFERENCES: Gunter 1945 (as *Pomolobus chrysochloris*); Hildebrand 1963d; Hoese and Moore 1977; Lee et al. 1980; Whitehead 1985; C. R. Robins et al. 1986; Boschung 1992.

Brevoortia gunteri Hildebrand 1948
Finescale menhaden

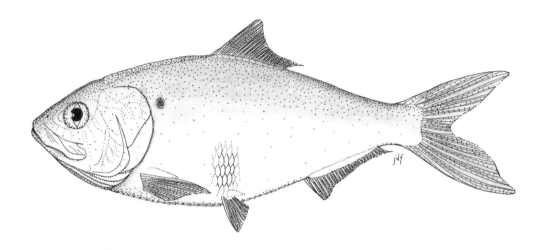

Brevoortia gunteri is compressed and deep bodied, with a large terminal mouth and a deeply forked caudal fin. It is distinguished from the other species of the family by the following combination of characters. Body depth is 37% to 45% and head length is 31% to 36% of SL. Symphysis of upper jaw is notched. Lower jaw is included in upper jaw when mouth is closed. Upper margin of lower jaw (within mouth) is nearly straight. Maxilla extends nearly to posterior margin of eye. Suborbital bone (below eye) is deeper than it is long. Jaws lack teeth in adults. Gill rakers are long, increase in number with growth, and those of upper limb overlap those of lower limb of first arch. Specimens 97 mm TL have about 97 gill rakers on lower limb, and specimens from 200 to 300 mm TL have 135 to 150 gill rakers on lower limb of first arch. Pectoral fin extends to within one to two vertical scale rows of pelvic fin base. Dorsal fin originates at about mid-distance between tip of snout and base of caudal fin, has concave dorsal margin, and has 17 to 20 rays, the last of which is slightly produced. Pelvic fin has straight posterior margin, inserts under base of dorsal fin, and has 7 rays. Anal fin is located posterior to dorsal fin base and has 20 to 25 rays. Scales are adherent and in 60 to 77 transverse rows. Scales along dorsal midline in front of dorsal fin are enlarged and fringed. Belly has 27 to 31 scutes with ascending arms. Vertebrae number 42 to 44. Color is dark gray dorsally through horizontal line extending from dorsal margin of eye to middle of caudal fin base. Side and belly are silvery. Adults have large, black shoulder spot that is not followed by additional spots. Dorsal and caudal fins are dusky, and margin of caudal fin is pale. Other fins are translucent.

This species occurs in the western North Atlantic in the northern and western Gulf of Mexico, from Chandeleur Bay, Louisiana, to Campeche Bay west of Punto Morros. This is an inshore species that also occurs in brackish water. Food consists of plankton obtained by filtering water through the fine sieve formed by the gill rakers. Spawning takes place in winter and early spring near shore and in bays. Maximum known size is 315 mm TL.

REFERENCES: Gunter 1945 (as *Brevoortia* sp.); Christmas and Gunter 1960; Hildebrand 1963d; Dahlberg 1970; Hoese and Moore 1977; Whitehead 1985; C. R. Robins et al. 1986; Boschung 1992.

Brevoortia patronus Goode 1878
Gulf menhaden

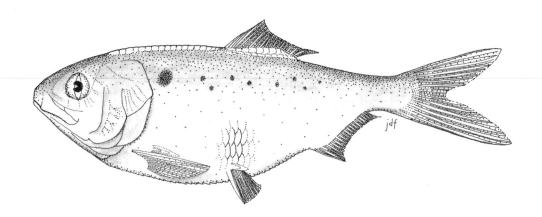

Brevoortia patronus is compressed and deep bodied, with a large terminal mouth and a deeply forked tail. It is distinguished from the other species of the family by the following combination of characters. Body depth is 33% to 45% and head length is 31% to 38% of SL. Symphysis of upper jaw is notched. Lower jaw is included in upper jaw when mouth is closed. Upper margin of lower jaw (within mouth) is nearly straight. Maxilla extends to posterior margin of pupil. Jaws lack teeth in adults. Suborbital bone (below eye) is deeper than it is long. Gill rakers are long, increase with size, and those of upper limb overlap those of lower limb on first arch. Gill rakers on lower limb of first gill arch increase from 40 to 50 in specimens ranging from 25 to 40 mm TL, from 135 to 150 in specimens above 200 mm TL. Pectoral fin extends to within one or two vertical scale rows of pelvic fin base. Dorsal fin originates about midway between tip of snout and base of caudal fin, has concave dorsal margin, and has 17 to 20 rays, the last 2 of which are produced. Pelvic fin has convex posterior margin, inserts under dorsal fin base, and has 7 rays. Anal fin is posterior to dorsal fin base and

has 20 to 23 rays. Scales are adherent and are in 42 to 48 transverse rows. Paired scales along dorsal midline anterior to dorsal fin are enlarged and fringed and number 24 to 33. Belly has 28 to 32 scutes with ascending arms. Vertebrae number 45 to 47. Color is bluish gray dorsally and silvery laterally and ventrally. Large dark spot, generally followed by series of smaller spots, is located posterior to upper margin of operculum. Fins are yellowish green.

This species occurs in the western North Atlantic in the Gulf of Mexico, from Caloosahatchee River, Florida, to Brazos Santiago, Texas, in inshore waters. It is rare east of Pensacola, Florida. Food consists of plankton obtained by filtering water through the fine sieve formed by the gill rakers. Spawning takes place in late autumn and early winter. Maximum known size is 300 mm TL.

REFERENCES: Gunter 1945 (as *Brevoortia tyrannus*); Christmas and Gunter 1960; Hildebrand 1963d; Dahlberg 1970; Hoese and Moore 1977; Whitehead 1985; C. R. Robins et al. 1986; Boschung 1992.

Brevoortia smithi   Hildebrand 1941
Yellowfin menhaden

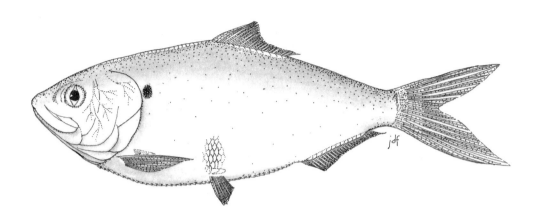

Brevoortia smithi is compressed and deep bodied, with a large terminal mouth and a deeply forked tail. It is distinguished from the other species of the family by the following combination of characters. Body depth is 36% to 43% and head length is 29% to 33% of SL. Symphysis of upper jaw is notched. Lower jaw is included in upper jaw when mouth is closed. Upper margin of lower jaw (within mouth) is nearly straight. Maxilla extends from below middle of eye to posterior margin of pupil. Suborbital bone (below eye) is deeper than it is long. Jaws of adults lack teeth. Gill rakers are long, increase in number with age, and those of upper limb overlap those of lower limb on first arch. Gill rakers range from 121 to 149 in adults. Pectoral fin usually extends to within three to five vertical scale rows of pelvic fin base. Dorsal fin originates about equidistant between tip of snout and base of caudal fin, has concave dorsal margin, and has 18 to 20 rays, the last of which is slightly produced. Pelvic fin has straight posterior margin, inserts slightly anterior to origin of dorsal fin, and has 7 rays. Anal fin is located posterior to dorsal fin base and has 22 to 23 rays. Scales are adherent, of

irregular size, and in 54 to 80 transverse rows. Paired scales along dorsal midline anterior to dorsal fin are enlarged and fringed and number 39 to 45. Belly has 30 to 32 scutes with ascending arms. Color is bluish gray dorsally and silvery laterally and ventrally. Single large dark spot occurs posterior to upper margin of operculum. Fins are golden.

This species occurs in the western North Atlantic from Beaufort, North Carolina, to the St. Lucie Estuary, Florida, and from Placida, Florida, to Chandeleur Sound, Louisiana, in the Gulf of Mexico. However, it is rare east of the Florida Panhandle. This species is found in coastal waters, including brackish bays and estuaries. Food consists of plankton obtained by filtering water through the fine sieve formed by the gill rakers. Spawning takes place from November through February or March along the east coast of the United States. Maximum known size is 330 mm TL.

REFERENCES: Christmas and Gunter 1960; Hildebrand 1963d; Dahlberg 1970; Hoese and Moore 1977; Whitehead 1985; C. R. Robins et al. 1986; Boschung 1992.

Dorosoma cepedianum (Lesueur 1818)
Gizzard shad

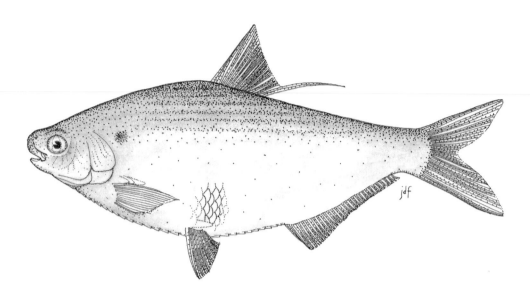

Dorosoma cepedianum is compressed and deep bodied, with a subterminal mouth and a deeply forked caudal fin. It is distinguished from the other species of the family by the following combination of characters. Body depth is 32% to 43% and head length is 26% to 33% of SL. Symphysis of upper jaw is notched. Maxilla extends nearly to anterior margin of eye. Suborbital bone (below eye) is longer than it is deep. Gill rakers are very long and fine, and increase in number with growth. Gill rakers on first arch number over 300 in specimens 65 mm TL, and number 412 in specimens 157 mm TL. Dorsal fin has nearly straight dorsal margin and 10 to 13 rays, the last of which is produced into filament. Pelvic fin inserts anterior to base of dorsal fin and has 7 to 8 rays. Anal fin has 25 to 36 rays. Scales are deciduous and in 52 to 70 transverse series. Midline from head to origin of dorsal fin is free of scales. Belly has 27 to 32 scutes with ascending arms. Vertebrae range from 48 to 51. Color is bluish dorsally and milky white with brassy overtones later-ally and ventrally. Large dark spot is located posterior to operculum, and six to eight horizontal dark stripes occur on upper side behind spot. Dorsal fin is uniformly dusky.

This species occurs in the Atlantic and Mississippi drainages of North America from the St. Lawrence River and South Dakota to the Río Panuco, Mexico. It inhabits quiet, open waters with connections to the sea. The youngest specimens are found in freshwater, and adults are found in fresh to salt water. Food consists of phytoplankton for juveniles and phytoplankton and zooplankton for adults. The gizzard shad spawns in quiet freshwater from late winter to summer. The eggs are demersal and adhesive. Maximum known size is 520 mm TL.

REFERENCES: Gunter 1945; Miller 1963; Nelson and Rothman 1973; Hoese and Moore 1977; Lee et al. 1980; Whitehead 1985; C. R. Robins et al. 1986; Boschung 1992.

Dorosoma petenense (Günther 1867)
Threadfin shad

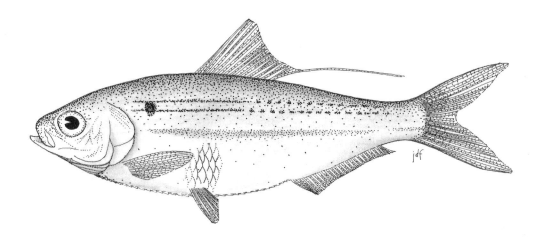

Dorosoma petenense is compressed and moderately deep bodied, with a small terminal mouth and a deeply forked caudal fin. It is distinguished from the other species of the family by the following combination of characters. Body depth is 33% to 42% and head length is 27% to 34% of SL. Symphysis of upper jaw is notched. Maxilla extends to anterior margin of orbit. Suborbital bone (below eye) is longer than it is deep. Gill rakers are very long and fine, and increase with growth, from about 300 at 66 mm TL to 440 at 80 mm TL. Dorsal fin has a concave dorsal margin and 11 to 14 rays, the last of which is produced into filament. Pelvic fin inserts anterior to dorsal fin base and has 7 or 8 rays. Anal fin has 17 to 27 rays. Scales are deciduous and in 41 to 48 transverse rows. Midline from head to origin of dorsal fin lacks scales. Belly has 23 to 29 scutes with ascending arms. Vertebrae range from 40 to 45. Color is bluish black to dark olivaceous with a golden hue dorsally and bright silvery laterally and ventrally. Large dark spot is located posterior to upper margin of operculum. Dorsal fin is dusky olive.

This species occurs in the western Atlantic and freshwater of eastern North America. It occurs from North Carolina to the east coast of Florida, in the Gulf of Mexico from Florida to the Rio Grande, and along the coast of Belize and Guatemala. It inhabits quiet, open waters with connections to the sea. The youngest specimens are found in fresh to brackish water, and adults are found from freshwater to full sea water. Food consists of phytoplankton and zooplankton. Spawning occurs in freshwater during the spring and summer. Maximum known size is 220 mm TL.

REFERENCES: Gunter 1945 (as *Signalosa mexicana*); Miller 1963; Nelson and Rothman 1973; Hoese and Moore 1977; Lee et al. 1980; Whitehead 1985; C. R. Robins et al. 1986; Boschung 1992.

Etrumeus teres   (DeKay 1842)
Round herring

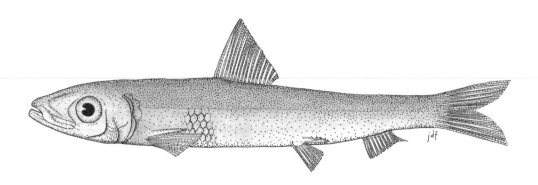

Etrumeus teres is elongate and robust, with a terminal mouth and a deeply forked caudal fin. It is distinguished from the other species of the family by the following combination of characters. Body depth is 16% to 19% and head length is 24% to 29% of SL. Symphysis of upper jaw is not notched. Maxilla extends to margin of eye. Jaws have minute teeth. Suborbital bone (below eye) is longer than it is deep. Gill rakers are moderately slender and number 14 on upper limb and 32 to 38 on lower limb of first arch. Dorsal fin originates closer to tip of snout than to base of caudal fin and has 16 to 20 rays, the last of which is not produced. Pelvic fin is located posterior to dorsal fin base and has 8 rays. Anal fin has 10 to 12 rays. Scales are highly deciduous and in 48 to 55 transverse rows. Scales along dorsal midline anterior to dorsal fin are normal. Belly lacks scutes except for W-shaped pelvic scute.

Vertebrae range from 48 to 56. Color is olive green dorsally and silver laterally and ventrally.

This species occurs in the western Atlantic, western Indian, western Pacific, and eastern Pacific Oceans. In the western Atlantic it occurs from the Bay of Fundy to south Florida and the Gulf of Mexico, and from Venezuela and the Guianas. This species is most common over shallow waters of the continental shelf but is uncommon in low-salinity waters. Food consists of zooplankton. Spawning takes place along the inner continental shelf during the winter in the warmer parts of its range. Maximum known size is 250 mm TL.

REFERENCES: Hildebrand 1963d; Hoese and Moore 1977; Jones et al. 1978b; Whitehead 1985; C. R. Robins et al. 1986; Boschung 1992.

Harengula clupeola   (Cuvier 1829)
False pilchard

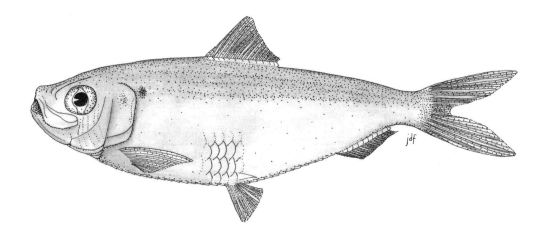

Harengula clupeola is compressed and moderately deep bodied, with a moderate-sized terminal mouth and a deeply forked caudal fin. It is distinguished from the other species of the family by the following combination of characters. Body depth is 26% to 31% and head length is 27% to 33% of SL. Symphysis of upper jaw is not notched. Maxilla extends slightly posterior to anterior margin of eye. Pointed teeth are absent on palatine. Small bone (hypomaxilla) bearing teeth is present in upper jaw between premaxilla and maxilla. Suborbital bone (below eye) is longer than it is deep. Gill rakers on upper limb do not overlap those of lower limb of first arch. Gill rakers number 28 to 35 on lower limb of first arch. Vertical anterior edge of shoulder girdle has bilobed dermal fold. Dorsal fin originates nearer to tip of snout than to base of caudal fin, has slightly concave dorsal margin, and has 17 to 20 rays, the last of which is not produced. Pelvic fin inserts nearer to insertion of pectoral fin than to origin of anal fin, and has 7 to 9 rays. Anal fin has 17 to 19 rays. Scales are adherent and in 40 to 43 transverse rows. Scales along dorsal margin anterior to dorsal fin are normal and number 11 to 14. Belly has 29 to 32 scutes with ascending arms. Color is dark brownish or greenish gray with silver overtones dorsally and silver laterally and ventrally. Faint yellow to orange spot occurs posterior to upper opercular margin, and distinct dark spot occurs in shoulder region behind opercular spot.

This species occurs in the western Atlantic from the Florida Keys, the Bahamas, and the Antilles to northern Brazil, including the Gulf of Mexico. It is usually found along the coast and in shallow bays and is rare or absent in the northern Gulf of Mexico. Food consists of zooplankton. Maximum known size is 172 mm TL.

REFERENCES: Gunter 1945; Rivas 1963; Böhlke and Chaplin 1968; Castro-Aguirre and Márquez-Espinoza 1981; Whitehead 1985; C. R. Robins et al. 1986; Boschung 1992.

Harengula humeralis (Cuvier 1829)
Redear sardine

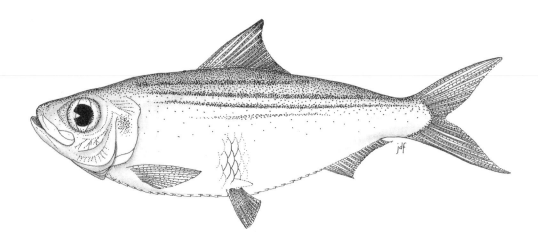

Harengula humeralis is compressed and moderately deep bodied, with a moderate-sized terminal mouth and a deeply forked caudal fin. It is distinguished from the other species of the family by the following combination of characters. Body depth is 26% to 31% and head length is 21% to 33% of SL. Symphysis of upper jaw is not notched. Maxilla extends to anterior margin of pupil. Pointed teeth are present on inner edge of palatine. Small bone (hypomaxilla) bearing teeth is present in upper jaw between premaxilla and maxilla. Suborbital bone (below eye) is longer than it is deep. Gill rakers on upper limb do not overlap those of lower limb of first arch. Gill rakers of lower limb of first arch number 26 to 32. Vertical anterior edge of shoulder girdle has bilobed dermal fold. Dorsal fin originates nearer to tip of snout than to base of caudal fin, has distinctly concave dorsal margin, and has 17 to 20 rays, the last of which is not produced. Pelvic fin inserts nearer to insertion of pectoral fin than to origin of anal fin, and has 7 to 9 rays.

Scales are deciduous and in 25 to 29 transverse rows. Scales along midline anterior to dorsal fin are normal and number 9 to 11. Belly has 25 to 29 scutes with ascending arms. Vertebrae number 40 to 44. Color is brownish gray with silvery overtones dorsally and silvery laterally and ventrally. Scales on side have longitudinal broken streaks, and reddish orange spot is present posterior to operculum. Tips of anterior dorsal fin rays are darkly pigmented.

This species occurs in the western North Atlantic from Bermuda, both coasts of Florida, the Bahamas, the Caribbean, and the Guianas. It has been reported only once from the western Gulf of Mexico off Isla Lobos between Tampico and Tuxpan, Mexico. It is limited to coastal waters. Maximum known size is 200 mm TL.

REFERENCES: Rivas 1963; Böhlke and Chaplin 1968; Castro-Aguirre and Márquez-Espinoza 1981; Whitehead 1985; C. R. Robins et al. 1986.

Harengula jaguana Poey 1865
Scaled sardine

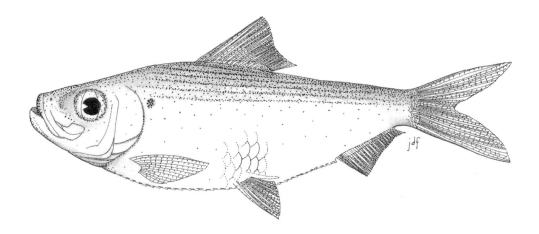

Harengula jaguana is compressed and moderately deep bodied, with a moderate-sized terminal mouth and a deeply forked caudal fin. It is distinguished from the other species of the family by the following combination of characters. Body depth is 30% to 35% and head length is 28% to 32% of SL. Symphysis of upper jaw is not notched. Maxilla extends slightly past anterior margin of pupil. Pointed teeth are absent on inner margin of palatine. Small bone (hypomaxilla) bearing teeth is present in upper jaw between premaxilla and maxilla. Suborbital bone (below eye) is deeper than it is long. Gill rakers on upper limb do not overlap those of lower limb of first arch. Gill rakers of lower limb of first arch number 30 to 40. Vertical anterior edge of shoulder girdle has bilobed dermal fold. Dorsal fin originates nearer to tip of snout than to base of caudal fin, has slightly concave dorsal margin, and has 17 to 20 rays, the last of which is not produced. Pelvic fin inserts about midway between insertion of pectoral fin and origin of anal fin, and has 7 to 9 rays. Anal fin has 17 to 19 rays. Scales on body are adherent and in 39 to 43 transverse rows. Scales along dorsal midline anterior to dorsal fin are normal and number 11 to 14. Belly has 30 to 32 scutes with ascending arms. Vertebrae number 40 to 44. Color is dark brownish or bluish gray with metallic reflections dorsally and silvery laterally and ventrally. Side of body has solid dark streaks. Spot behind operculum is faint to conspicuous.

This species occurs in the western Atlantic from New Jersey to southern Brazil, including Bermuda, the entire Gulf of Mexico, the Bahamas, and the Antilles. It is a coastal species but is also found in bays and estuaries. Maximum known size is 180 mm TL.

REFERENCES: Rivas 1963; Böhlke and Chaplin 1968 (as *H. pensacolae*); Hoese and Moore 1977 (as *H. pensacolae*); Lee et al. 1980; Castro-Aguirre and Márquez-Espinoza 1981; Whitehead 1985; C. R. Robins et al. 1986; Boschung 1992.

Jenkinsia lamprotaenia (Gosse 1851)
Dwarf herring

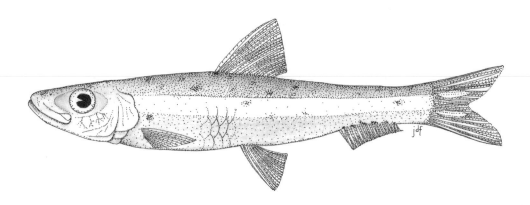

Jenkinsia lamprotaenia is slender and compressed, with a relatively small terminal mouth and a deeply forked caudal fin. It is distinguished from the other species of the family by the following combination of characters. Body depth is 15% to 18% and head length is 25% to 27% of SL. Symphysis of upper jaw is not notched. Maxilla extends to anterior margin of eye. Teeth are present in single series in premaxilla and maxilla. No teeth are present in lower jaw and few if any are present in roof of mouth. Only one supramaxilla is present on upper posterior margin of maxilla. Suborbital bone (below eye) is longer than it is deep. Gill rakers on upper limb do not overlap those of lower limb of first arch. Gill rakers on lower limb of first arch number 20 to 26. Isthmus, uniting lower aspect of shoulder girdle with lower part of gill arches, has blunt shoulders. Vertical anterior edge of shoulder girdle lacks bilobed dermal fold. Pectoral fin has 12 to 15 rays. Dorsal fin originates nearer to tip of snout than to base of caudal fin, has slightly convex dorsal margin, and has 9 to 13 rays, the last of which is not produced. Pelvic fin inserts slightly

closer to caudal fin base than to tip of snout, and has 8 rays. Anal fin has 13 to 16 rays. Scales are deciduous and in 33 to 37 transverse series. Scales along dorsal midline anterior to dorsal fin are normal. Belly lacks scutes except for W-shaped pelvic scute. Vertebrae number 40 to 43. Color is greenish dorsally, with distinct silvery band laterally, and white ventrally. Silver band is equal in width to eye diameter. Dark spots are present on and above silvery band, on back, on snout, and along base of anal fin.

This species occurs in the western North Atlantic off Bermuda and from south Florida to Venezuela, including the Gulf of Mexico, the Bahamas, and the Antilles. It is an inshore species but is also common in bays and estuaries. Food consists of zooplankton. Maximum known size is 75 mm TL.

REFERENCES: Hildebrand 1963d; Böhlke and Chaplin 1968; Hoese and Moore 1977; Whitehead 1985; C. R. Robins et al. 1986; Boschung 1992.

Jenkinsia majua   Whitehead 1963
Littleye herring

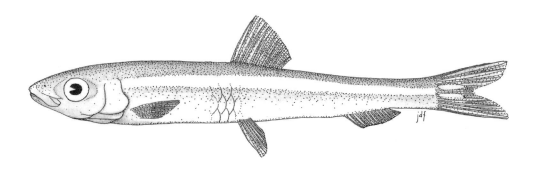

Jenkinsia majua is slender and compressed, with a relatively small terminal mouth and a deeply forked caudal fin. It is distinguished from the other species of the family by the following combination of characters. Body depth is 11% to 15% and head length is 21% to 24% of SL. Symphysis of upper jaw is not notched. Maxilla extends to anterior margin of eye. Teeth are absent on premaxilla but present on maxilla. No teeth are present in lower jaw and few if any are present in roof of mouth. Only one supramaxilla is present on upper posterior margin of maxilla. Suborbital bone (below eye) is longer than it is deep. Gill rakers on upper limb do not overlap those of lower limb of first arch. Gill rakers on lower limb of first arch number 24 to 28. Isthmus, uniting lower aspect of shoulder girdle with lower part of gill arches, has blunt shoulders. Vertical anterior edge of shoulder girdle lacks bilobed dermal fold. Pectoral fin has 12 to 14 rays. Dorsal fin originates closer to tip of snout than to caudal fin base, has slightly convex dorsal margin,

and has 9 to 11 rays, the last of which is not produced. Pelvic fin inserts closer to caudal fin base than to tip of snout, and has 8 rays. Anal fin has 11 to 13 rays. Scales are deciduous and in 35 to 40 transverse rows. Scales along dorsal midline anterior to dorsal fin are normal. Belly lacks scutes except for W-shaped pelvic scute. Vertebrae number 38. Color is greenish dorsally, with distinct silver band laterally, and white ventrally. Silvery band is distinct anteriorly and is narrower than eye.

This species occurs in the western North Atlantic from the Bahamas, the Antilles, the Florida Keys, and the Bay of Campeche in the Gulf of Mexico. It is a coastal marine species that schools and feeds on zooplankton. Maximum known size is 65 TL.

REFERENCES: Hildebrand 1963d; Böhlke and Chaplin 1968; Castro-Aguirre and Márquez-Espinoza 1981; Whitehead 1985; C. R. Robins et al. 1986.

Jenkinsia stolifera (Jordan and Gilbert 1884)
Shortband herring

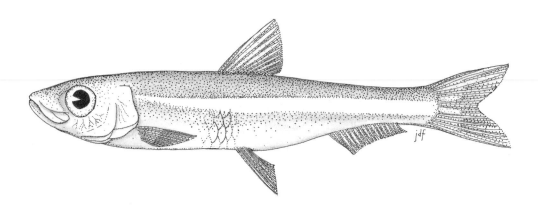

Jenkinsia stolifera is slender and compressed, with a relatively small mouth and a deeply forked caudal fin. It is distinguished from the other species of the family by the following combination of characters. Body depth is 14% to 19% and head length is 24% to 29% of SL. Symphysis of upper jaw is not notched. Maxilla extends to anterior margin of eye. Teeth are present in premaxilla and maxilla. Only one supramaxilla is attached to upper posterior margin of maxilla. No teeth are present in lower jaw and few if any are present in roof of mouth. Isthmus, uniting lower aspect of shoulder girdle with lower part of gill arches, is triangular and lacks shoulders. Suborbital bone (below eye) is longer than it is deep. Gill rakers on upper limb do not overlap those of lower limb of first gill arch. Gill rakers on lower limb of first arch number 20 to 24. Vertical anterior edge of shoulder girdle lacks bilobed dermal fold. Pectoral fin has 11 to 12 rays. Dorsal fin originates closer to tip of snout than to base of caudal fin, has slightly convex dorsal margin,

and has 9 to 13 rays, the last of which is not produced. Pelvic fin inserts slightly closer to caudal fin base than to tip of snout. Anal fin has 12 to 15 rays. Scales are deciduous and in 33 to 37 transverse rows. Scales along dorsal midline anterior to dorsal fin are normal. Belly lacks scutes except for W-shaped pelvic scute. Color is greenish dorsally, with distinct silvery band laterally, and silvery white ventrally. Silvery band is about one-half width of eye diameter and is absent or greatly reduced anteriorly.

This species occurs in the western North Atlantic from Florida, the Florida Keys, southwestern Florida in the Gulf of Mexico, the Bahamas, and Honduras to Venezuela. It is a coastal marine species that schools and feeds on zooplankton. Maximum known size is 75 mm TL.

REFERENCES: Böhlke and Chaplin 1968 (as *J. lamprotaenia*, in part); Whitehead 1985; C. R. Robins et al. 1986.

Opisthonema oglinum (Lesueur 1818)
Atlantic thread herring

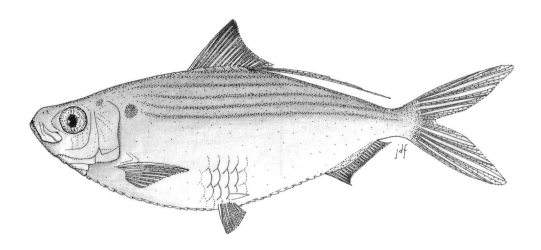

Opisthonema oglinum is compressed and moderately deep bodied, with a relatively small terminal mouth and a deeply forked caudal fin. It is distinguished from the other species of the family by the following combination of characters. Body depth is 30% to 40% and head length is 22% to 28% of SL. Symphysis of upper jaw is not notched. Maxilla extends to anterior margin of pupil. Teeth are lacking in jaws. Two supramaxillae are attached to dorsoposterior margin of maxilla. Isthmus, uniting lower aspect of shoulder girdle with lower part of gill arches, is triangular and lacks shoulders. Suborbital bone (below eye) is longer than it is deep. Gill rakers on upper limb do not overlap those of lower limb of first arch. Gill rakers of first arch number 28 to 46. Vertical anterior edge of shoulder girdle has bilobed dermal fold. Pectoral fin has 15 to 17 rays. Dorsal fin originates closer to tip of snout than to base of caudal fin, has slightly concave dorsal margin, and has 17 to 21 rays, the last of which is greatly produced into a filament. Pelvic fin inserts under base of dorsal fin, slightly closer to tip of snout than to base of caudal fin, and has 8 rays. Anal fin has 20 to 25 rays. Scales are deciduous and in 43 to 50 transverse rows. Scales along dorsal midline anterior to dorsal fin are normal. Belly has 32 to 36 scutes with ascending arms. Vertebrae number 45 to 48. Color is bluish to greenish with silvery overtones dorsally and silvery laterally and ventrally. Single black spot above operculum and another posterior to operculum followed by number of smaller spots are usually present. Six or seven dark stripes are present on side. Tips of dorsal and caudal fins are dark.

This species occurs in the western Atlantic from the Gulf of Maine to southern Brazil, including Bermuda, the entire Gulf of Mexico, the Bahamas, and the Antilles. It is a coastal, schooling, pelagic fish that feeds on zooplankton and nekton. Prey include copepods, small shrimps, crabs, and fishes. Spawning takes place from late winter to late summer in coastal waters. Maximum known size is 300 mm TL.

REFERENCES: Gunter 1945; Hildebrand 1963d; Böhlke and Chaplin 1968; Hoese and Moore 1977; Jones et al. 1978b; Lee et al. 1980; Whitehead 1985; C. R. Robins et al. 1986; Boschung 1992.

Sardinella aurita Valenciennes 1847
Spanish sardine

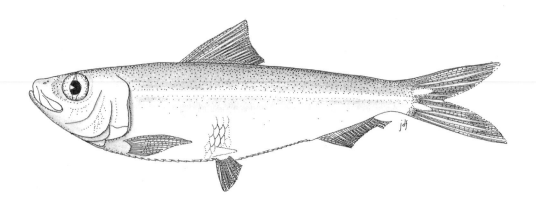

Sardinella aurita is compressed and relatively slender, with a moderately large terminal mouth and a deeply forked caudal fin. It is distinguished from the other species of the family by the following combination of characters. Body depth is 21% to 27% and head length is 22% to 27% of SL. Symphysis of upper jaw is not notched. Maxilla extends to about anterior margin of pupil. Teeth are absent in upper jaw, but several are present in lower jaw. Gill rakers of upper limb do not overlap those of lower limb of first arch. Gill rakers of lower limb of first arch increase with growth and number between 70 and 145 in adults. Gill rakers on lower limb of second and third arches are more or less flat. Vertical anterior edge of shoulder girdle possesses bilobed dermal fold. Pectoral fin has 15 to 16 rays. Dorsal fin originates closer to tip of snout than to base of caudal fin, has slightly concave dorsal margin, and has 17 to 19 rays, the last of which is not produced. Pelvic fin inserts under base of dorsal fin, closer to tip of snout than to base of caudal fin, and has 9 rays. Anal fin has 16 to 20 rays, and last two are distinctly produced. Scales are deciduous and in 41 to 46 transverse rows. Scales along dorsal midline anterior to dorsal fin are normal. Belly has 32 to 34 scutes with ascending arms. Vertebrae number 45 to 47. Color is bluish gray to greenish dorsally and bright silver to brassy laterally and ventrally. Spots and streaks on side are absent.

This species occurs in the tropical and warm temperate Atlantic Ocean. In the western Atlantic it occurs from Cape Cod to Argentina, including Bermuda, the entire Gulf of Mexico, the Bahamas, and the Antilles. It is a coastal pelagic species but ranges over the entire continental shelf. Food consists of zooplankton, especially copepods, and to some extent phytoplankton. Spawning occurs throughout the year in the Gulf of Mexico. Earlier studies suggested that two species occur in the Gulf of Mexico, *S. brasiliensis* and *S. aurita*. However, recent electrophoretic studies (Wilson and Alberdi 1991; Tringali and Wilson 1993) found only the latter species in the Gulf. Maximum known size is 380 mm TL.

REFERENCES: Hildebrand 1963d; Böhlke and Chaplin 1968; Hoese and Moore 1977 (as *Sardinella anchovia*); Jones et al. 1978b; Castro-Aguirre and Márquez-Espinoza 1981; Whitehead 1985; C. R. Robins et al. 1986; Wilson and Alberdi 1991; Tringali and Wilson 1993; Ditty et al. 1994.

ENGRAULIDAE   Anchovies

Anchovies are fusiform, slightly to strongly compressed, with a large subterminal mouth and a deeply forked caudal fin. They are distinguished from the other families of the order by the following combination of characters. Snout is generally short and blunt, and projects moderately to strongly beyond tip of jaws. Subterminal mouth is bordered by premaxilla and maxilla. Small teeth are generally present in jaws and in roof of mouth. Eye is large and is placed in anterior part of head. Two supramaxillae are generally attached to posterodorsal margin of maxilla. Pectoral fin is located low on flank, immediately posterior to gill openings. Dorsal fin is short and usually originates near midlength of body. Pelvic fin is located slightly beneath or slightly posterior to dorsal fin base and generally has seven rays. Body, with exception of head, is covered with deciduous scales. Lateral line is absent.

Anchovies occur worldwide from the tropics to temperate latitudes. They are generally caught in coastal marine waters, but some enter brackish water or freshwater, and some live permanently in freshwater. Most are schooling fishes that feed on zooplankton. Embryonic development is oviparous. Fertilized eggs and larvae are pelagic.

There are 139 species in 16 genera, and 8 to 10 species in 4 genera occur in the Gulf of Mexico.

Key to the Species of the Gulf of Mexico
(Adapted from Whitehead et al. 1988)

1a. Maxilla with blunt tip and posteriorly not extending to preoperculum (Fig. 67). 2
1b. Maxilla with pointed tip and posteriorly extending to preoperculum (Fig. 68) 4

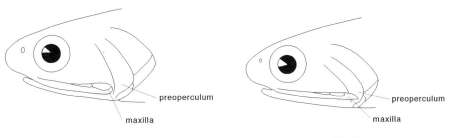

FIG 67   FIG 68

2a. Branchiostegal membrane broadly joined across isthmus and covering it (Fig. 69) . . . . *Cetengraulis edentulus* p. 357

2b. Branchiostegal membrane narrowly joined across isthmus and not covering it (Fig. 70) 3

3a. Pseudobranch, located on inner side of gill cover, shorter than eye length and not extending to inner surface of operculum . . . . *Anchoviella perfasciata* p. 356

3b. Pseudobranch, located on inner side of gill cover, longer than eye length and extending to inner surface of operculum . . . . *Engraulis eurystole* p. 358

4a. Pseudobranch, located on inner side of gill cover, longer than eye length and extending to inner surface of operculum; anal fin origin below or posterior to last dorsal fin ray base . . . . *Anchoa lyolepis* p. 353

4b. Pseudobranch, located on inner side of gill cover, shorter than eye length; anal fin origin below midlength of dorsal fin base or below origin of dorsal fin 5

5a. Anus located closer to tip of pelvic fin than to origin of anal fin 6

5b. Anus located closer to origin of anal fin than to tip of pelvic fin 8

6a. Gill rakers 23 to 30 on lower limb of first arch; anal fin with 16 to 22 rays 7

6b. Gill rakers 17 to 22 on lower limb of first arch; anal fin with 18 to 24 rays . . . . *Anchoa lamprotaenia* p. 352

7a. Maxillary tip very acute, extending posterior to suboperculum and projecting one-half eye diameter beyond second supramaxilla . . . . *Anchoa cubana* p. 350

7b. Maxillary tip acute, extending to or slightly beyond posterior margin of preoperculum and projecting less than one-half eye diameter beyond second supramaxilla . . . . *Anchoa parva* p. 355

8a. Gill rakers 16 to 19 on lower limb of first arch . . . . *Anchoa cayorum* p. 349

8b. Gill rakers 19 to 25 on lower limb of first arch. 9

9a. Anal fin with 20 to 24 rays; origin of anal fin below midlength of dorsal fin base . . . . *Anchoa hepsetus* p. 351

9b. Anal fin with 20 to 27 rays; origin of anal fin below origin of dorsal fin base . . . . *Anchoa mitchilli* p. 354

branchiostegal
membrane

FIG 69

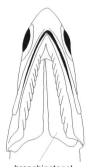

branchiostegal
membrane

FIG 70

Anchoa cayorum (Fowler 1906)
Key anchovy

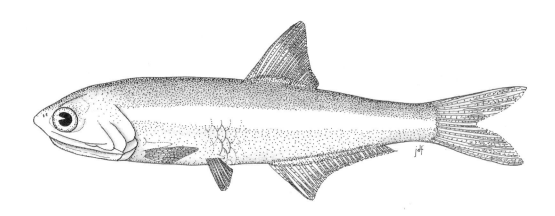

Anchoa cayorum is slender and moderately compressed, with a moderately short, pointed snout and a deeply forked caudal fin. It is distinguished from the other species of the family by the following combination of characters. Body depth is 19% to 23% and head length is 24% to 26% of SL. Snout length is slightly less than eye diameter. Maxilla has pointed tip and is long, extending posterior to supramaxilla and nearly reaching gill opening. Jaw teeth are small. Suborbital bone (below eye) is as long as or slightly longer than eye diameter. Pseudobranch (on inner surface of gill cover) is shorter than eye diameter and does not extend posteriorly onto operculum. Gill rakers on lower limb of first arch are slender and number 16 to 19. Upper lobe of third gill arch has gill rakers. Pectoral fin is falcate and nearly reaches base of pelvic fin. Dorsal fin originates posterior to midpoint between tip of snout and caudal fin base, and has 13 to 15 rays. Pelvic fin is slightly closer to base of pectoral fin than to origin of anal fin. Anal fin originates below midlength of dorsal fin base and has 26 to 28 rays. Anus is closer to anal fin origin than to tip of pelvic fin. Scales are deciduous and in 39 to 42 transverse rows. Vertebrae number 43. Color is translucent with silvery stripe along flank. Stripe is slightly narrower than eye diameter.

This species occurs in the western North Atlantic from the Florida Keys, the Bahamas, the Antilles, the east coast of Yucatán, Belize, and possibly Venezuela. It has not been reported from the Gulf of Mexico but probably penetrates into the Gulf by means of the Loop Current. It is an inshore schooling species that is apparently limited to clear water. Maximum known size is 85 mm TL.

REFERENCES: Hildebrand 1963c; Böhlke and Chaplin 1968; C. R. Robins et al. 1986; Whitehead et al. 1988.

Anchoa cubana (Poey 1868)
Cuban anchovy

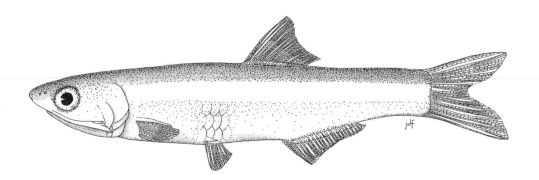

Anchoa cubana is very slender and moderately compressed, with a short, moderately pointed snout and a deeply forked caudal fin. It is distinguished from the other species of the family by the following combination of characters. Body depth is 15% to 18% and head length is 23% to 28% of SL. Snout length is about three-fourths eye length. Maxilla has pointed tip and is long, extending posterior to supramaxilla and reaching posterior margin of preoperculum. Jaw teeth are small. Suborbital bone (below eye) is slightly longer than eye diameter. Pseudobranch (on inner surface of gill cover) is shorter than eye diameter and does not extend onto operculum. Gill rakers on lower limb of first arch are slender and number 24 to 30. Upper lobe of third gill arch has gill rakers. Pectoral fin falls short of pelvic fin base by distance equal to eye diameter. Dorsal fin originates posterior to mid-distance between tip of snout and base of caudal fin, and has 14 to 16 rays. Pelvic fin is slightly closer to origin of anal fin than to pectoral fin base. Anal fin originates below midlength of dorsal fin base and has 19 to 24 rays. Anus is closer to pelvic fin tip than to anal fin origin. Scales are deciduous and in 42 to 45 transverse rows. Vertebrae number 44 to 45. Color is translucent with silvery stripe along flank. Stripe is about as broad as pupil diameter.

This species occurs in the western Atlantic from North Carolina to southern Florida, the northeastern Gulf of Mexico, the Antilles, and the east coast of Yucatán to southern Brazil. It is an inshore schooling species, occurring from the shoreline to 60 m. Maximum known size is 75 mm TL.

REFERENCES: Hildebrand 1963c; Hoese and Moore 1977; C. R. Robins et al. 1986; Whitehead et al. 1988; Boschung 1992.

Anchoa hepsetus (Linnaeus 1758)
Striped anchovy

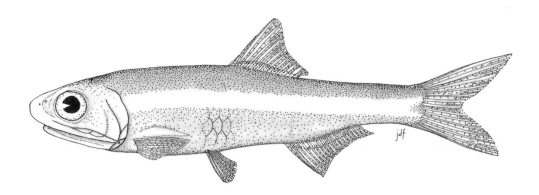

Anchoa hepsetus is slender and moderately compressed, with a short, pointed snout and a deeply forked caudal fin. It is distinguished from the other species of the family by the following combination of characters. Body depth is 19% to 22% and head length is 25% to 30% of SL. Snout length is about three-fourths eye length. Maxilla has pointed tip and is long, extending posterior to supramaxilla and reaching posterior margin of preoperculum. Jaw teeth are small. Suborbital bone (below eye) is slightly longer than eye diameter. Pseudobranch (on inner surface of gill cover) is shorter than eye diameter and does not extend posteriorly onto operculum. Gill rakers on lower limb of first arch are slender and number 19 to 25. Upper limb of third gill arch has gill rakers. Pectoral fin fails to reach pelvic fin base. Dorsal fin originates posterior to midpoint between tip of snout and base of caudal fin, and has 13 to 16 rays. Pelvic fin is nearly equidistant between origin of anal fin and pectoral fin base. Anal fin originates below midlength of dorsal fin base and has 20 to 24 rays. Anus is nearer to anal fin origin than to pelvic fin tip. Scales are deciduous and in 37 to 43 transverse rows. Color is translucent with silvery stripe along flank. Stripe width is about three-fourths of eye diameter.

This species occurs in the western Atlantic from Nova Scotia to southern Florida and the northern Gulf of Mexico, and off Venezuela to southern Brazil. It is a coastal schooling species, ranging from the shoreline to 70 m. It has a wide salinity tolerance and is frequently found in brackish-water bays and estuaries. Food consists of copepods, ostracods, and occasionally annelids. Spawning takes place in spring and summer on the inner continental shelf and occasionally in bays. Maximum known size is 150 mm TL.

REFERENCES: Gunter 1945; Hildebrand 1963c; Hoese and Moore 1977; Jones et al. 1978b; C. R. Robins et al. 1986; Whitehead et al. 1988; Boschung 1992.

Anchoa lamprotaenia   Hildebrand 1943
Bigeye anchovy

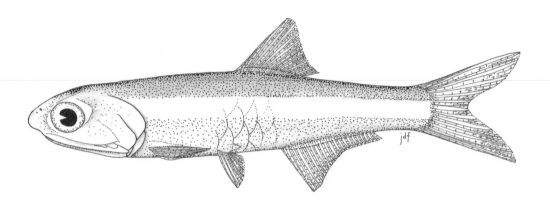

Anchoa lamprotaenia is slender and moderately compressed, with a short, pointed snout and a deeply forked caudal fin. It is distinguished from the other species of the family by the following combination of characters. Body depth is 19% to 23% and head length is 25% to 30% of SL. Snout length is about three-fourths eye length. Maxilla has pointed tip and is long, extending posterior to supramaxilla and reaching posterior margin of preoperculum. Jaw teeth are small. Suborbital bone (below eye) is longer than eye diameter. Pseudobranch (on inner surface of gill cover) is shorter than eye diameter and does not extend posteriorly onto operculum. Gill rakers on lower limb of first arch are slender and number 17 to 22. Upper limb of third gill arch has gill rakers. Pectoral fin is falcate and nearly reaches to pelvic fin base. Dorsal fin originates slightly posterior to mid-distance between tip of snout and base of caudal fin, and has 13 to 16 rays. Pelvic fin is slightly nearer to origin of anal fin than to base of pectoral fin. Anal fin originates below midlength of dorsal fin base and has 18 to 24 rays. Anus is nearer pelvic fin tip than to origin of anal fin. Scales are deciduous and in 38 to 41 transverse rows. Vertebrae number 39 to 42. Color is translucent with silvery stripe along flank. Stripe width is about three-fourths of eye diameter.

This species occurs in the western North Atlantic from southern Florida and the Florida Keys, the Bahamas, and the Antilles, and from the eastern coast of Yucatán to Venezuela or possibly Brazil. It has not thus far been captured in the Gulf of Mexico but probably penetrates into the Gulf by means of the Loop Current. It is a coastal schooling species apparently limited to high salinities. Food consists of zooplankton. Spawning occurs in June and July. Maximum known size is 92 mm TL.

REFERENCES: Hildebrand 1963c; Böhlke and Chaplin 1968; C. R. Robins et al. 1986; Whitehead et al. 1988.

Anchoa lyolepis (Evermann and Marsh 1900)
Dusky anchovy

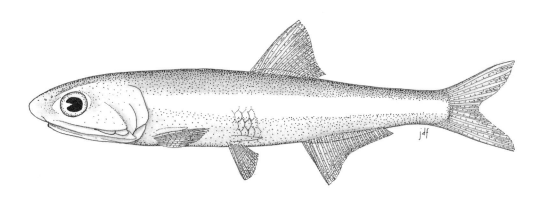

Anchoa lyolepis is slender and moderately compressed, with a pointed, relatively long snout and a deeply forked caudal fin. It is distinguished from the other species of the family by the following combination of characters. Body depth is 17% to 20% and head length is 27% to 32% of SL. Snout length is nearly as long as eye. Maxilla is long, extending posterior to supramaxilla to near opercular opening, and has pointed tip. Jaw teeth are small. Suborbital bone (below eye) is as long as distance from tip of snout to posterior margin of eye. Pseudobranch (on inner margin of gill cover) is longer than eye, extending posteriorly onto operculum. Gill rakers on lower limb of first arch are slender and number 19 to 27. Upper lobe of third gill arch has gill rakers. Pectoral fin is moderately falcate and does not reach base of pelvic fin. Dorsal fin originates slightly nearer to caudal fin base than to tip of snout, and has 12 to 15 rays. Pelvic fin inserts about equidistant between origin of anal fin and pectoral fin base. Anal fin originates below base of last dorsal fin ray and has 21 to 24 rays. Anus is nearer to origin of anal fin than to tip of pelvic fin. Scales are deciduous and in 40 to 44 transverse rows. Vertebrae number 41 to 43. Color is translucent with silvery stripe on flank. Stripe depth is about equal to eye diameter.

This species occurs in the western Atlantic from Cape Hatteras to southern Brazil, including the Gulf of Mexico and possibly Bermuda and the Antilles. It is a coastal schooling species captured from the shoreline to 23 m but is absent in low-salinity bays and estuaries. Maximum known size is 90 mm TL.

REFERENCES: Gunter 1945; Hildebrand 1963c; Castro-Aguirre and Márquez-Espinoza 1981; C. R. Robins et al. 1986; Whitehead et al. 1988; Boschung 1992.

Anchoa mitchilli   (Valenciennes 1848)
Bay anchovy

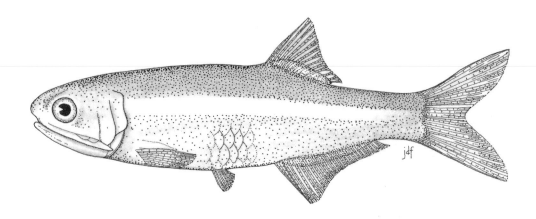

Anchoa mitchilli is moderately slender and moderately compressed, with a fairly blunt, short snout and a deeply forked caudal fin. It is distinguished from the other species of the family by the following combination of characters. Body depth is 16% to 27% and head length is 22% to 27% of SL. Snout length is about one-half head length. Maxilla is long, extending posterior to supramaxilla to posterior margin of preoperculum, and has pointed tip. Jaw teeth are small. Suborbital bone (below eye) is about as long as eye diameter. Pseudo-branch (on inner surface of gill cover) is shorter than eye diameter and does not extend posteriorly onto operculum. Gill rakers on lower limb of first arch are slender and number 21 to 25. Upper lobe of third gill arch has gill rakers. Pectoral fin is variable in length, either falling short of or reaching pelvic fin base. Dorsal fin originates distinctly nearer to caudal fin base than to tip of snout, and has 13 to 17 rays. Pelvic fin inserts nearer to anal fin origin than to pectoral fin base. Anal fin originates slightly posterior to origin of dorsal fin and has 20 to 27 rays. Anus is nearer to pelvic fin tip than to anal fin origin. Scales are deciduous and in 38 to 44 transverse rows. Vertebrae number 38 to 44. Color is translucent with silvery stripe on flank. Stripe is variable, may be absent anteriorly, is narrower than eye in southern populations, and as wide as eye in northern populations.

This species occurs in the western North Atlantic from the Gulf of Maine to Yucatán, including the entire Gulf of Mexico. It is an inshore schooling species that also occurs in brackish-water bays and estuaries. Food consists of gastropods, copepods, isopods, mysid shrimps, and small fishes. Spawning takes place in water less than 20 m deep from May to November or February off Texas and possibly year-round off Biscane Bay, Florida. Maximum known size is 100 mm TL.

REFERENCES: Gunter 1945; Hildebrand 1963c; Hoese and Moore 1977; Jones et al. 1978b; C. R. Robins et al. 1986; Whitehead et al. 1988; Boschung 1992.

Anchoa parva   (Meek and Hildebrand 1923)

Anchoa parva is moderately slender and compressed, with a moderately short, pointed snout and a moderately long, pointed maxilla. It is distinguished from the other species of the family by the following combination of characters. Body depth is 20% to 22.2% of SL. Snout length is slightly greater than one-half eye diameter. Maxilla has pointed tip and extends slightly beyond posterior margin of preoperculum. Jaw teeth are small. Suborbital bone (below eye) is slightly longer than eye diameter. Pseudobranch (on inner surface of gill cover) is shorter than eye diameter and does not extend onto operculum. Gill rakers on lower limb of first arch are slender and number 23 to 30. Upper lobe of third gill arch has gill rakers. Pectoral fin falls short of pelvic fin base by distance less than eye diameter. Dorsal fin originates posterior to mid-distance between tip of snout and base of caudal fin. Pelvic fin is about mid-distance between pectoral fin base and anal fin origin. Anal fin originates anterior to midbase of dorsal fin base and has 17 to 22 rays. Anus is closer to pelvic fin tip than to anal fin origin. Scales are deciduous. Color is translucent with silvery stripe along flank. Stripe is about as broad as pupil of eye but is little evident in preserved specimens.

This species occurs in the western Atlantic from the Caribbean Sea and the southern Gulf of Mexico. It is a coastal species that also occurs in brackish water and freshwater with connections to the sea. Maximum known size is 60 mm SL.

REFERENCES: Hildebrand 1963c; Castro-Aguirre 1978; Whitehead et al. 1988.

Anchoviella perfasciata   (Poey 1860)
Flat anchovy

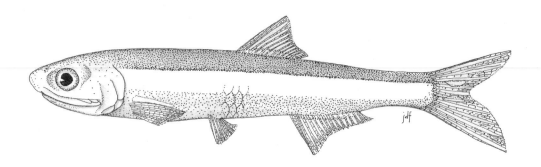

Anchoviella perfasciata is slender and strongly compressed, with a pointed, moderately short snout and a deeply forked caudal fin. It is distinguished from the other species of the family by the following combination of characters. Body depth is 15% to 18% and head length is 23% to 26% of SL. Snout length is about three-fourths eye diameter. Maxilla is short, extending slightly beyond supramaxilla and falling short of preoperculum by distance equal to one-half pupil diameter, and is bluntly tipped. Jaw teeth are small. Suborbital bone (below eye) is slightly longer than eye diameter. Pseudobranch (on inner surface of gill cover) is shorter than eye diameter and does not extend posteriorly onto operculum. Gill rakers on lower limb of first gill arch are slender and number 24 to 30. Upper limb of third gill arch has gill rakers. Pectoral fin falls short of pelvic fin base by distance equal to eye diameter. Dorsal fin has 12 to 15 rays, and though its origin varies, it generally originates midway between caudal fin base and tip of snout. Pelvic fin in-

serts about equidistant between origin of anal fin and pectoral fin base. Anal fin originates under or slightly posterior to base of last dorsal fin ray and has 13 to 18 rays. Scales are deciduous and in 40 to 44 transverse rows. Vertebrae number 42 to 44. Color is translucent with silver stripe on flank. Stripe width is about three-fourths eye diameter and has dark dorsal margin.

This species occurs in the western North Atlantic from Beaufort, North Carolina, to southern Florida, the northern Gulf of Mexico, the Antilles, and off Panama. It is rare to absent west of Louisiana in the Gulf of Mexico. This is a coastal schooling species limited to full-salinity waters. Maximum known size is 100 mm TL.

REFERENCES: Longley and Hildebrand 1941; Hildebrand 1963c; Hoese and Moore 1977; C. R. Robins et al. 1986; Whitehead et al. 1988.

Cetengraulis edentulus   (Cuvier 1829)

Cetengraulis edentulus is moderately deep bodied and compressed, with branchiostegal membrane expanded posteriorly to cover isthmus. It is distinguished from the other species of the family by the following combination of characters. Snout is rather pointed. Body depth is 25% to 34.4%, head length is 30% to 34.5%, snout length is 3.8% to 4.8%, and eye diameter is 6.5 to 8% of SL. Maxilla has blunt tip and is short, generally not extending beyond anterior margin of preoperculum. Upper jaw teeth are very small, and lower jaw lacks teeth. Suborbital bone (under eye) is as long as snout and eye and has acute posterior angle. Branchiostegal rays number 8. Gill rakers are long and slender; they number 30 to 36 on lower limb of first arch in specimens about 65 mm SL, and number 45 to 55 in specimens between 100 and 130 mm SL but can number up to 105 in specimens 130 mm SL. No gill rakers occur on posterior face of epibranch of third arch.

Pectoral fin is bluntly rounded and has 14 or 15 rays. Dorsal fin is near midpoint of body and has 14 to 16 rays. Pelvic fin inserts slightly closer to anal fin origin than to pectoral fin base. Anal fin originates under last one-third of dorsal fin base and has 18 to 24 rays. Scales are deciduous and in 40 to 43 transverse rows. Vertebrae number 42. Color in preservative is bluish gray dorsally and silvery ventrally and on side. Specimens up to 100 mm SL have silver stripe on flank.

This species occurs in the western Atlantic Ocean from the southern Gulf of Mexico, the Antilles, and along the coast of Costa Rica to southern Brazil in brackish waters. It frequently forms large schools. Maximum known size is about 130 mm SL.

REFERENCES: Hildebrand 1963b; Castro-Aguirre 1978; Whitehead et al. 1988.

Engraulis eurystole (Swain and Meek 1885)
Silver anchovy

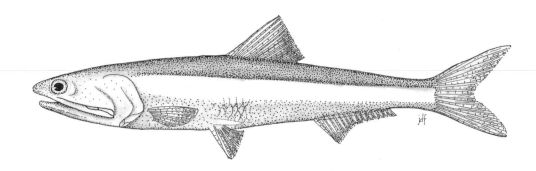

Engraulis eurystole is slender and moderately compressed, with a pointed, moderately short snout and a deeply forked caudal fin. It is distinguished from the other species of the family by the following combination of characters. Body depth is 15% to 19% and head length is 25% to 29% of SL. Snout length is slightly shorter than eye diameter. Maxilla is short, not extending beyond supramaxilla and only reaching anterior margin of preoperculum, and is bluntly tipped. Jaw teeth are small. Suborbital bone (below eye) is as long as distance from tip of snout to posterior margin of eye. Pseudobranch (on inner surface of gill cover) is longer than eye, extending posteriorly onto operculum. Gill rakers on lower limb of first gill arch are slender and number 27 to 43. Upper limb of third gill arch has gill rakers. Pectoral fin falls short of pelvic fin base by distance greater than eye diameter. Dorsal fin originates nearer to tip of snout than to base of caudal fin, and has 13 to 16 rays. Pelvic fin inserts nearer to pectoral fin base than to anal fin origin. Anal fin originates posterior to dorsal fin base and has 15 to 19 rays. Scales are deciduous and in 40 to 45 transverse rows. Vertebrae number 43 to 45. Color is translucent with silvery stripe on flank. Stripe is as wide as eye diameter and has dark dorsal margin.

This species occurs in the western North Atlantic from Massachusetts to Florida, the northeastern Gulf of Mexico to Mississippi Sound, and from Venezuela to northern Brazil. It is a coastal schooling species found from the shoreline to 65 m. Spawning occurs during the summer. Maximum known size is 150 mm TL.

REFERENCES: Hildebrand 1963c; Jones et al. 1978b; C. R. Robins et al. 1986; Whitehead et al. 1988.

SILURIFORMES

Siluriformes, Gonorhynchiformes, Cypriniformes, Characiformes, and Gymnotiformes make up the ostariophysians, one of the two basal groups of euteleosteans. The order contains about 31 families, and 1 of these occurs in the Gulf of Mexico.

ARIIDAE   Sea catfishes

Sea catfishes are relatively elongate, robust, depressed anteriorly, and compressed posteriorly, with barbels on head and a forked tail. They are distinguished from the other families of the order by the following combination of characters. Snout and head are rounded and conical to depressed. Mouth is terminal to slightly inferior. Upper jaw has one pair and lower jaw has two pairs of barbels, although one or more pairs are occasionally absent. Teeth in jaws and palatines are villiform, conical, granular, or molar-like, and arranged in bands. Teeth are present or absent in palatine. Nostrils are close-set, separated by only a narrow bridge of tissue, and posterior nostril is covered by flap of skin but lacks barbel. Head is covered with granular bony shield, with posterior extension reaching predorsal plate at base of dorsal fin. Gill membranes are united and attached to isthmus. Gill rakers are present on lateral aspect of all arches and on medial aspect of first and second arches. Branchiostegal rays number 5 to 9. Dorsal fin is short based and has very short spine followed by long, more or less serrated, pungent spine and 7 rays. Pectoral fin originates near ventral profile and has more or less serrated, pungent spine followed by 8 to 13 rays. Pelvic fin has 6 rays and is modified in mature females. Anal fin is short to moderate in length and has 16 to 22 rays. Adipose fin is shorter than dorsal fin, located above anal fin, and lacks rays. Lateral line is complete and posteriorly it branches onto dorsal and ventral lobes of caudal fin. Scales are absent. Physostomous swim bladder is enclosed in bone.

Sea catfishes occur worldwide in tropical to subtropical seas and occasionally penetrate into temperate seas in the summer. They are generally limited to coastal and estuarine waters over muddy to sandy bottoms, although some species enter freshwater and others are restricted to freshwater. There are about 139 to

145 species in about 20 genera, and at least 3 species in separate genera occur in the Gulf of Mexico. Some species form schools, and all of the marine and some of the freshwater species are mouth-brooders. Eggs are large, few in number, and generally brooded by males in the buccal cavity.

Key to the Species of the Gulf of Mexico

(Adapted from Taylor 1978)

1a. Two pairs of barbels, one on lower jaw and other on maxilla; maxillary barbels and filaments of dorsal and pectoral fins long, flattened, and ribbonlike
.... *Bagre marinus* p. 362

1b. Three pairs of barbels, two on lower jaw and other on maxilla; all barbels and filaments round in cross section and are not ribbonlike 2

2a. Teeth on palatines small, villiform, arranged in two patches on each side; gill rakers on inner surface of first two arches very small, number three to five, and occur on epibranch
.... *Arius felis* p. 361

2b. Teeth on palatines molariform and arranged in single patch on each side; gill rakers on inner surface of first two arches well developed and located on both epibranch and lower limb........................ *Cathorops* sp. p. 363

Arius felis (Linnaeus 1766)
Hardhead catfish

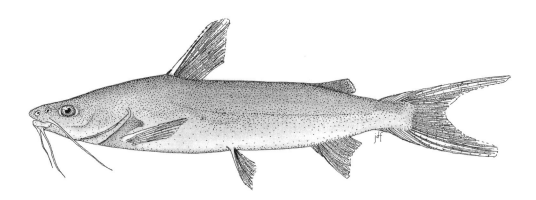

Arius felis is moderately slender, with a rounded head, an inferior mouth, and three pairs of barbels. It is distinguished from the other species of the family by the following combination of characters. Snout is moderately long and transversely rounded. Maxillary barbels extend to origin of pectoral fin and are round in cross section. Bony head shield is very rugose and extends anteriorly to level of eye. Supraoccipital process of head shield is broad at base, tapers rearward, is truncated posteriorly, and has slight medial keel. Long, narrow fleshy groove is present along midline of head and extends anteriorly to level of eye. Predorsal plate is crescent shaped. Teeth in jaws and palatines are villiform or granular. Teeth of palatine are in small anteromedial patch and in large posterolateral patch. Gill rakers on first arch number 13 to 16. Few tiny gill rakers occur on rear surface of first and second gill arches, mostly on upper limb. Dorsal and pectoral fins have strong, serrated erectile spine that lacks long terminal filaments. Pectoral fin rays range from 6 to 10 but usually number 10. Anal fin rays number 18 to 20, and posterior margin of anal fin is not deeply indented. Color is brown to dark brown or dark blue dorsally and whitish ventrally.

This species occurs in the western North Atlantic from North Carolina to Florida and throughout the Gulf of Mexico and off northern Yucatán. It is limited to turbid coastal waters over muddy to sandy bottoms, generally in brackish to marine waters, but it occasionally occurs in freshwater. Food consists mostly of benthic crustaceans. Spawning takes place from May through the first week of August in the northern Gulf of Mexico. Maximum known size is 610 mm TL.

REFERENCES: Gunter 1945 (as *Galeichthys felis*); Hoese and Moore 1977; Jones et al. 1978a; Taylor 1978 (as *Ariopsis felis*); Platania and Ross 1980; C. R. Robins et al. 1986; Boschung 1992.

Bagre marinus (Mitchill 1815)
Gafftopsail

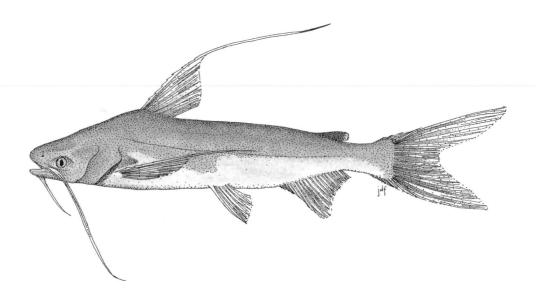

Bagre marinus is moderately slender, with an arched head, slightly inferior mouth, and two pairs of barbels. It is distinguished from the other species of the family by the following combination of characters. Snout is of moderate length and transversely rounded. Maxillary barbels extend about to pelvic fin base, and are flattened and ribbonlike. Bony head shield is obscure, and fleshy groove along midline of head is lacking. Supraoccipital process of head shield is relatively narrow and tapers slightly rearward toward contact with crescent-shaped predorsal plate. Teeth in jaws and palatines are villiform and in bands. Palatine teeth are in two patches on each side forming transverse arc, and each patch is wider than it is long. Dorsal and pectoral fins have strong, serrated erectile spines terminating as flattened, ribbonlike filament. Pectoral fin rays number 11 to 14, and anal fin rays number 22 to 28. Posterior margin of anal fin has V-shaped indentation. Color is bluish gray to dark brown dorsally and lighter ventrally.

This species occurs in the western Atlantic from Cape Cod to Brazil, including the Gulf of Mexico and the continental coast of the Caribbean Sea. It is generally found in brackish to marine coastal waters but occasionally occurs in freshwater in the tropics. Food consists of invertebrates and small fishes. Spawning occurs from May through August in the northern Gulf of Mexico. Fertilized eggs are brooded by the males. Maximum known size is 1,000 mm TL.

REFERENCES: Gunter 1945; Hoese and Moore 1977; Jones et al. 1978a; Taylor 1978; C. R. Robins et al. 1986; Boschung 1992.

Cathorops sp.

This ariid catfish is moderately slender, with a moderately flattened head, inferior mouth, and three pairs of barbels. It is distinguished from the other species of the family by the following combination of characters. Snout is moderately long and transversely rounded. Single pair of maxillary barbels are round in cross section and extend to pectoral fin base. Single pair of mental barbels occur on each side of mouth. Bony head shield is rugose and extends forward only to posterior margin of eye. Supraoccipital process of head is broad at base, narrow and truncated posteriorly, and has slight median keel. Predorsal plate, preceding base of dorsal fin spine, is small and crescent shaped. Long, rather broad, fleshy groove extends from anterior margin of head shield to snout. Teeth in jaws are villiform, and teeth in palatines are mostly molariform and in single oblique patch on each side of midline. Gill rakers are numerous and well developed on both lateral and medial surfaces of first two gill arches. Dorsal and pectoral fins are preceded by stout, serrated erectile spine that lacks terminal filament. Pectoral rays number 10. Posterior margin of anal fin is not deeply indented. Color is dark brown to bluish black dorsally and pale to whitish ventrally.

Three species of *Cathorops* occur in the tropical seas of the western Atlantic, and at least one of these occurs in the coastal and brackish waters of the southern Gulf of Mexico. Two additional species are limited to freshwater of Mexico and Central America. All of these species are poorly known, thus it is not possible to name the species that has been recorded from the southern Gulf of Mexico.

REFERENCES: Castro-Aguirre 1978; Taylor 1978.

OSMERIFORMES

Osmeriformes, Salmoniformes, and Esociformes make up the protacanthopterygians, the second of the basal groups of euteleosteans. This order is subdivided into two suborders, Argentinoidei and Osmeroidei. Six of the argentinoid families but none of the osmeroid families occur in the Gulf of Mexico. Argentinoids, in turn, are subdivided into two superfamilies: Argentinoidea, with families Argentinidae, Bathylagidae, Microstomatidae, and Opisthoproctidae; and Alepocephaloidea, with families Alepocephalidae, Leptochilichthyidae, and Platytroctidae.

Key to the Families of the Gulf of Mexico
(Adapted from Smith and Heemstra 1986)

1a. Eye tubular and directed anteriorly or dorsally; interorbital width less than one-half caudal peduncle depth; premaxilla reduced or absent; scalelike maxilla easily damaged or lost . . . . Opisthoproctidae p. 377

1b. Eye normal and directed laterally, or rarely, tubular and directed anteriorly; interorbital width equal to or greater than one-half caudal peduncle depth; premaxilla and maxilla normally developed 2

2a. Teeth absent in upper jaw; anal fin origin below last dorsal fin ray or posterior to dorsal fin base 3

2b. Teeth present in upper jaw; anal fin origin below or anterior to dorsal fin base 5

3a. Anal fin with 7 to 15 rays; swim bladder and postcleithra present 4

3b. Anal fin with 17 to 25 rays; swim bladder and postcleithra absent . . . . Bathylagidae p. 369

4a. Pectoral fin on ventrolateral aspect of body; lateral line not extending onto caudal fin . . . . Argentinidae p. 365

4b. Pectoral fin on lateral aspect of body; lateral line extending onto caudal fin . . . . Microstomatidae p. 373

5a. Large sac extending forward under shoulder girdle, containing luminous fluid and opening posteriorly through small tube between lateral line and pectoral fin base . . . . Platytroctidae p. 403

5b. No sac under shoulder girdle . . . . . Alepocephalidae p. 381

ARGENTINIDAE   Argentines

Argentines are elongate and polygonal in cross section, with a small terminal mouth and a deeply forked caudal fin. They are distinguished from the other families of the order by the following combination of characters. Snout length is moderately short to short, ranging from longer than eye to slightly less than eye diameter. Teeth are present on vomer, palatine, and tongue. Nostril is closer to eye than to tip of snout. Eye is large, located on side of head, and is tubular or nontubular. Branchiostegal rays number four to six. Pectoral fin is located on ventrolateral aspect of body posterior to gill slits. Dorsal fin originates closer to origin of pelvic fin than to origin of pectoral fin. Pelvic fin is located on abdomen. Adipose fin is present and is located dorsal to anal fin. Body is covered with deciduous scales that either have or lack spines on their posterior surface. Lateral line originates slightly below angle of operculum or near dorsal edge of operculum, and runs straight to base of caudal fin.

Argentines occur worldwide in tropical to temperate seas. They are generally captured on or over the outer continental shelf or slope. Most species are pelagic but closely associated with the bottom (benthopelagic). Food consists largely of crustaceans. Embryonic development is oviparous. Fertilized eggs and larvae are pelagic. There are about 19 species in two genera, and 3 species in two genera occur in the Gulf of Mexico.

Key to the Species of the Gulf of Mexico
(Adapted from Cohen 1964a, 1986a)

1a. Vomerine and palatine teeth in continuous band; teeth on anterior and lateral aspects of tongue; maxillae do not meet anteriorly 2

1b. Vomerine and palatine teeth not in continuous band, separated by distinct distance; teeth only on anterior aspect of tongue; maxillae meet or are in close proximity anteriorly . . . . *Glossanodon pygmaeus* p. 368

2a. Swim bladder generally with distinct silvery pigment visible through thin belly musculature; pectoral fin rays 18 to 21 (usually 19); body depth 9.7% to 15.7% ($\bar{x}$ = 12.2%) of SL; caudal peduncle depth 16.7% to 22.7% ($\bar{x}$ = 19.2%) of head length . . . . *Argentina striata* p. 367

2b. Swim bladder lacks silvery pigment; pectoral fin rays 16 to 19 (usually 17); body depth 8.3% to 13.4% ($\bar{x}$ = 10.5%) of SL; caudal peduncle depth 13.7% to 17.9% ($\bar{x}$ = 15.6%) of head length . . . . *Argentina georgei* p. 366

Argentina georgei   Cohen and Atsaides 1969

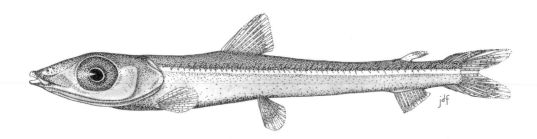

Argentina georgei is elongate and polygonal in cross section, with a moderately short snout and a deeply forked caudal fin. It is distinguished from the other species of the family by the following combination of characters. Body depth at dorsal fin origin is 8.3% to 13.4%, body depth at caudal peduncle is 4.3% to 5.6%, head length is 28.5% to 32.4%, snout length is 8.7% to 11.2%, and maxillary length is 5.2% to 6.6% of SL. Maxillae do not meet anteriorly. Palatine and head of vomer bear small, closely spaced, needlelike teeth in continuous band on anterior roof of mouth. No teeth occur in premaxilla, maxilla, or dentaries. Lower limb of first gill arch has six or seven gill rakers. Branchiostegal rays number 5. Tongue has eight large, recurved teeth along anterior and lateral margins. Pectoral fin is on ventrolateral aspect of trunk and possesses 17 to 18 rays. Dorsal fin originates anterior to pelvic fin and has 11 rays. Pelvic fin has 13 to 14 rays.

Anal fin is located below adipose fin and has 10 to 11 rays. Scales are deciduous and lack spines. Lateral line scales do not extend onto caudal fin. Swim bladder lacks external silvery pigment. Upper quarter of body is dark brown with black mid-dorsal stripe. Ventral aspect of body is light with large, dark chromatophores forming band midventrally from isthmus to vent. Some specimens lack ventral pigment and dark color shows through ventral musculature.

This species occurs in the western North Atlantic from the east coast of Florida to the Dry Tortugas, Bahamas Bank, and off the northern coast of Cuba, the Antilles, and Central America. Depth of capture ranges from 220 to 457 m. It is associated with mud and mud-shell bottoms at temperatures of 8.9°C to 16.7°C. Maximum known size is 146 mm SL.

REFERENCE: Cohen and Atsaides 1969.

Argentina striata   Goode and Bean 1896
Striated argentine

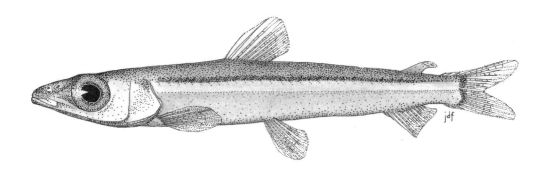

Argentina striata is elongate and polygonal in cross section, with a moderately short snout and a deeply forked caudal fin. It is distinguished from the other species of the family by the following combination of characters. Body depth at dorsal fin origin is 9.7% to 15.7%, body depth at caudal peduncle is 5.2% to 6.5%, head length is 26.1% to 32%, snout length is 8.5% to 10.6%, and maxillary length is 4.2% to 6.1% of SL. Maxillae do not meet anteriorly. Palatine and head of vomer bear small, closely spaced, needlelike teeth in continuous band. No teeth occur on premaxilla, maxilla, or dentaries. Lower limb of first gill arch has six or seven gill rakers. Branchiostegal rays number 5. Tongue has five to nine stout, recurved teeth on anterior and lateral margins. Pectoral fin is on ventrolateral aspect of body and possesses 18 to 21 rays. Dorsal fin originates anterior to pelvic fin and has 11 to 12 rays. Pelvic fin has 12 to 15 rays. Anal fin is located below adipose fin and has 11 to 15 rays. Scales are deciduous and lack spines. Lateral line scales do not extend onto caudal fin. Swim bladder is covered externally with silvery pigment. Vertebrae number from 47 to 51. Color is translucent to silvery with ventral two-thirds of body light brown. Brown band often runs above lateral line, and brown chromatophores often occur on throat. Peritoneum is black. Young specimens have a row of eight to nine dark blotches along upper one-third of body.

This species occurs in the western North Atlantic from Nova Scotia to Venezuela (to mouth of Orinoco River), including the entire Gulf of Mexico, and off Cuba and Brazil. Depth of capture ranges from 95 to 365 m. It is usually associated with mud bottoms at temperatures from 8.9°C to 15°C. Maximum known size is 200 mm SL.

REFERENCES: Cohen 1958a, 1964a; Cohen and Atsaides 1969; Rass 1971; C. R. Robins et al. 1986; Scott and Scott 1988; Boschung 1992.

Glossanodon pygmaeus   Cohen 1958

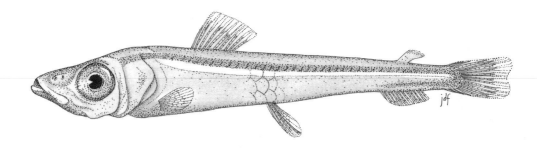

Glossanodon pygmaeus is elongate and polygonal in cross section, with a moderately short snout and a deeply forked caudal fin. It is distinguished from the other species of the family by the following combination of characters. Body depth at dorsal fin origin is 10.1% to 14%, body depth at caudal peduncle is 5.3% to 6.8%, head length is 27.2% to 30%, snout length is 8% to 10.2%, and maxillary length is 6.7% to 8.9% of SL. Maxillae meet or are separated by narrow space anteriorly. Palatine and head of vomer bear small, conical teeth. Teeth on vomer are set posteriorly relative to those of palatine and do form continuous band. No teeth occur on maxilla or dentaries. Tongue has two to six teeth along anterior margin. Lower limb of first gill arch has 21 to 23 gill rakers. Branchiostegal rays number 5. Anus is located anterior to origin of anal fin by distance of depth of caudal peduncle or more. Pectoral fin is on ventrolateral aspect of body and possesses 12 to 14 rays. Dorsal fin originates anterior to pelvic fin and has 10 to 12 rays. Pelvic fin has 10 to 12 rays. Anal fin is located below adipose fin and has 11 to 13 rays. Scales are deciduous and lack spines. Lateral line scales do not extend onto caudal fin. Vertebrae number 43. Color is uniform light tan, often with dark stripe on dorsolateral margin of body. Stripe may be reduced to lightly pigmented band. Poorly defined lateral and ventrolateral bands are formed by large brown chromatophores. Bands meet at caudal fin base, coloring caudal peduncle brown.

This species occurs in the western North Atlantic from South Carolina to southern Florida, in the northern Gulf of Mexico, and off Cuba, Nicaragua, Venezuela, and northern Brazil. It is most often captured over mud bottoms between 183 and 366 m; the known depth range is from 91 to 457 m. Maximum known size is 113 mm SL, and maturity occurs at about 77 mm SL.

REFERENCES: Cohen 1958a, 1964a; Rass 1971; Bekker et al. 1975; Boschung 1992.

BATHYLAGIDAE   Deep-sea smelts

Deepsea smelts are variable in body shape but are generally compressed and range from slender to robust with a narrow caudal peduncle to rather deep bodied with a deep caudal peduncle. They are distinguished from the other families of the order by the following combination of characters. Snout is short to very short, slightly less than eye diameter to less than one-half eye diameter. Teeth are present on head of vomer and lower jaw, and are present or absent on palatine. Eye is large, directed laterally or anterolaterally, and is not tubular. Branchiostegal rays number two. Interorbital width is more than one-half caudal peduncle depth. Parietal bones, forming posterior cranial roof, do not meet on midline. Pectoral fin is located on ventrolateral aspect of body posterior to gill slits. Postcleithrum is lacking from pectoral girdle. Dorsal fin base is anterior to pelvic fin and closer to origin of pelvic fin than to origin of pectoral fin. Pelvic fin is located on abdomen. Adipose fin is present or absent. Anal fin originates on posterior one-third of body and has relatively long base. Body is covered with deciduous scales.

Deep-sea smelts occur worldwide, with the possible exception of the South Pacific. They are apparently mesopelagic and bathypelagic, but little is known of their depth distribution. Larvae of some species have stalked eyes. There are about 15 species in a single genus, and 3 of these occur in the Gulf of Mexico.

Key to the Species of the Gulf of Mexico
(Adapted from Cohen 1984b)

1a. Gill openings large, extending to about midflank 2
1b. Gill openings reduced, not extending to midflank
. . . .*Bathylagus bericoides* p. 370
2a. Anal fin base equal to or less than caudal peduncle length; anal rays number 13 . . . . *Bathylagus greyae* p. 371
2b. Anal fin base longer than caudal peduncle length; anal fin rays number 19 to 21 . . . . . *Bathylagus longirostris* p. 372

Bathylagus bericoides   (Borodin 1929)

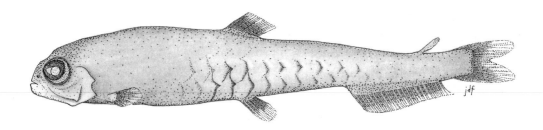

Bathylagus bericoides is slender and compressed, with a very short snout and a moderately forked tail. It is distinguished from the other species of the family by the following combination of characters. Body depth at dorsal fin origin is 14.8% to 16.6%, body depth at caudal peduncle is 5.9% to 7.1%, head length is 17% to 18.1%, and snout length is 2.8% to 3.5% of SL. Maxillae do not meet anteriorly. Head of vomer and palatine bear small, pointed teeth in single row, and dentary has minute, compressed teeth. Tongue lacks teeth. Gill slits do not extend dorsally to mid-body depth. Pectoral fin is on ventrolateral aspect of trunk and has 10 to 12 rays. Dorsal fin originates anterior to pelvic fin base and has 10 to 11 rays. Pelvic fin has 9 to 10 rays. Anal fin base is more than twice dorsal fin base length, is longer than caudal peduncle, and has 18 to 22 rays. Adipose fin is located dorsal to posterior one-half of anal fin base. Scales are decid-uous. Scale rows along side number about 50. Color is dusky, with margins of scale pockets pigmented with very dark, purplish, faintly iridescent pigment. Pigment is more pronounced ventrally. Head and fins are dusky.

This species has a very disjunct range. In the western North Atlantic it has been reported from Bermuda, the Bahamas, and the Gulf of Mexico. Specimens, thought to be the same species, have been reported from the mid–northern Pacific. It is apparently bathypelagic at depths below 1,000 m. Most specimens were captured between 1,200 and 1,700 m, although one was captured between the surface and 100 m at night in the Pacific, suggesting that it is a vertical migrator. Maximum known size is 183 mm SL.

REFERENCES: Cohen 1958a, 1964a, 1984b; Rass 1971.

Bathylagus greyae   Cohen 1958

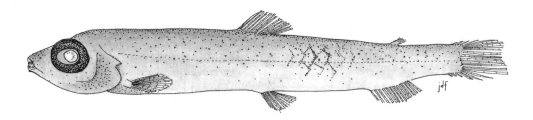

Bathylagus greyae is slender and compressed, with a short snout and a forked tail. It is distinguished from the other species of the family by the following combination of characters. Body depth at dorsal fin origin is 13.4% to 16.9%, body depth at caudal peduncle is 8.4%, head length is 25.3% to 29.6%, and snout length is 5.9% to 7% of SL. Maxillae do not meet anteriorly. Head of vomer bears small, conical teeth, and dentaries have small, compressed teeth and one spikelike tooth on either side of symphysis. Gill openings extend dorsally to midflank. Pectoral fin is located on ventrolateral aspect of body and has 12 to 13 rays. Dorsal fin originates anterior to pelvic fin and has 13 rays. Pelvic fin has 10 to 11 rays.

Anal fin base is slightly shorter than dorsal fin base, is shorter than caudal peduncle length, and has 13 rays. Adipose fin is located dorsal to midlength of anal fin base. Scales are deciduous, and there are about 45 to 50 lateral line scales. Color is brown dorsally and pale yellow ventrally. Operculum and snout are dusky. Margins of scale pockets are darkly pigmented.

This species occurs in the western North Atlantic off Bermuda and in the northern Gulf of Mexico. It has been captured from 500 to 550 m and between 1,646 m and the surface. Maximum known size is 160 mm SL.

REFERENCES: Cohen 1958a, 1964a, 1984b.

Bathylagus longirostris   Maul 1948

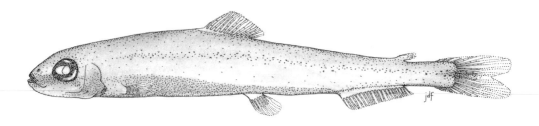

Bathylagus longirostris is slender and compressed, with a moderately short snout and a forked caudal fin. It is distinguished from the other species of the family by the following combination of characters. Body depth at dorsal fin origin is 14.1% to 16.9%, body depth at caudal peduncle is 5.2% to 6.6%, head length is 18.3% to 26.3%, and snout length is 4.1% to 5.6% of SL. Snout length is equal to or greater than one-half eye length. Maxillae do not meet anteriorly, and posteriorly they extend to level of anterior margin of orbit. Head of vomer and palatine bear about 35 conical teeth, and dentary bears numerous compressed teeth. Gill openings extend dorsally to mid-flank. Pectoral fin is located on ventrolateral aspect of body and has 9 to 12 rays. Dorsal fin originates anterior to pelvic fin and has 10 to 12 rays. Pelvic fin has 9 to 10 rays. Anal fin base is slightly less than twice dorsal fin base length and has 19 to 21 rays. Adipose fin is lo-cated dorsal to insertion of anal fin. Scales are deciduous, and there are about 40 to 50 lateral line scales. Color is light tan with large brown chromatophores forming an irregular band along midline of body. Snout is dusky, operculum is metallic blue-black, and fins are clear. Scale pockets are not pigmented. Peritoneum is dark and shows through belly.

This species has a very disjunct distribution. It has been recorded from the central North Pacific off Hawaii, the Indian Ocean, and from the western North Atlantic from New Jersey, Bermuda, the Bahamas, and in the northeastern Gulf of Mexico off Pensacola, Florida. It is a pelagic species most frequently captured between 914 and 1,829 m but has been captured at 70 m from the surface. Maximum known size is 175 mm SL.

REFERENCES: Cohen 1958a, 1964a, 1984b; Rass 1971; Bekker et al. 1975.

MICROSTOMATIDAE

Microstomatids are elongate, slender, and subcylindrical in cross section, with a blunt to acute snout and a forked caudal fin. They are distinguished from the other families of the order by the following combination of characters. Snout length is less than eye length to less than one-half eye length. Teeth are present on vomer, palatine, and dentaries and are lacking on premaxilla, maxilla, and tongue. Nostril is on upper corner of snout. Eye is large, located on side of head, and is generally not tubular. Branchiostegal rays number two to four. Pectoral fin is located on lateral aspects of body posterior to gill slits. Dorsal fin originates closer to origin of pelvic fin than to origin of pectoral fin. Pelvic fin is located on abdomen. Adipose fin is present or absent. Body is covered with deciduous scales. Lateral line originates near dorsal edge of operculum and runs straight onto caudal fin. Lateral line scales are larger and less easily dislodged than scales of remainder of body.

Microstomatids occur worldwide in tropical to temperate seas. They are mesopelagic. Food consists of zooplankton. Embryonic development is oviparous, and eggs and larvae are pelagic. There are 15 to 17 species in three genera, and 3 species in separate genera occur in the Gulf of Mexico.

Key to the Species of the Gulf of Mexico
(Adapted from Cohen 1964a, 1984a)

1a. Eye of adults tubular. . . *Xenophthalmichthys danae* p. 376
1b. Eye of adults not tubular 2
2a. Adipose fin present; predorsal length is less than 60% of SL; pelvic fin insertion posterior to origin of dorsal fin
. . . . *Nansenia groenlandica* p. 375
2b. Adipose fin absent; predorsal length greater than 60% of SL; pelvic fin insertion anterior to origin of dorsal fin
. . . . *Microstoma microstoma* p. 374

Microstoma microstoma   (Risso 1810)

Microstoma microstoma is very elongate and subcylindrical in cross section, with a short snout and a deeply forked caudal fin. It is distinguished from the other species of the family by the following combination of characters. Body depth at dorsal fin origin is 7.3% to 7.7%, body depth at caudal peduncle is 4.3% to 5%, head length is 18.9% to 20.2%, and snout length is 3.3% to 4.7% of SL. Head of vomer and possibly palatine possess delicate, needlelike teeth. Maxilla is largely concealed by orbital bones and lacks teeth. Dentaries have compressed, close-set teeth. Tongue lacks teeth. Lower limb of first gill arch has 14 gill rakers. Branchiostegal rays number 2. Pectoral fin is on lateral aspect of body and has 7 to 8 rays. Dorsal fin originates posterior to pelvic fin and has 9 to 11 rays. Pelvic fin has 10 to 11 rays. Anal fin originates posterior to dorsal fin insertion.

Adipose fin is absent. Scales are deciduous. Lateral line scales are wider and more adherent than body scales and extend onto caudal fin. Color is silvery, with operculum, caudal peduncle, and ventral midline of body anterior to pelvic fin dark.

This species occurs in the North Atlantic and eastern Pacific. In the western Atlantic it has been captured only once in the western Gulf of Mexico off Tampico, Mexico. It is apparently a pelagic species most frequently captured in surface waters over depths greater than 1,000 m. The specimen from the Gulf of Mexico was captured at the surface with a dip net over a depth of 2,195 m. Maximum known size is 197 mm SL.

REFERENCES: Grey 1956; Cohen 1958a, 1964a; Rass 1971.

Nansenia groenlandica (Reinhardt 1839)

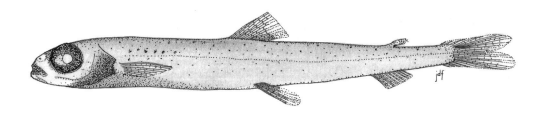

Nansenia groenlandica is elongate, slender, and subcylindrical in cross section, with a short, blunt snout and a forked caudal fin. It is distinguished from the other species of the family by the following combination of characters. Body depth at dorsal fin origin is 10% to 13%, prepectoral length is 18% to 22%, and head length is about 18% of TL. Snout length is less than one-half eye length. Maxilla is scalelike, mostly covered by preorbital bones, and extends to near anterior margin of eye. Palatine, vomer, and dentaries bear short, conical teeth in single row. Teeth are lacking on premaxilla, maxilla, and tongue. First gill arch has 35 to 45 gill rakers. Branchiostegal rays number 3. Pectoral fin is located on lower one-third of body and has 11 to 13 rays. Dorsal fin originates anterior to insertion of pelvic fin and has 9 to 10 rays. Pelvic fin has 10 to 12 rays. Anal fin originates anterior to adipose fin and has 8 to 10 rays. Vertebrae number 42 to 45. Color is brown, with vertical bars on caudal fin of juveniles.

This species occurs in the North Atlantic and eastern Pacific. In the western North Atlantic it occurs from the west coast of Greenland, on Flemish Cap off Newfoundland, on Browns Bank off Nova Scotia, and in the Gulf of Mexico. It is mesopelagic and most frequently captured between 300 and 1,000 m. In the eastern Atlantic it spawns in the spring and summer. The smallest larvae were captured in water ranging from 8 to 10 m. Maximum known size is 245 mm TL.

REFERENCES: Cohen 1958b, 1964a, 1984a; Ahlstrom et al. 1984; Scott and Scott 1988.

Xenophthalmichthys danae   Regan 1925

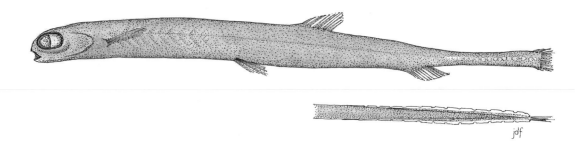

Xenophthalmichthys danae is elongate, sub-cylindrical anteriorly, and moderately compressed posteriorly, with a small mouth and anteriorly directed tubular eyes. It is distinguished from the other species of the family by the following combination of characters. Body depth between head and pelvic fin is 6% to 11.5%, body depth of caudal peduncle is 2.7% to 4.5%, head length is 14.6% to 17.5%, and snout length is 1.2% to 2.3% of SL. Eye is large and projects over margin of head. Small teeth occur in dentaries, vomer, and palatine. Gill membranes are united and free from isthmus. Pectoral fin base is on upper flank, and rays number 7 and are relatively long. Pelvic fin is abdominal, slightly anterior to midlength, and fin rays number 7. Dorsal fin originates posterior to midlength and has 10 or 11 rays. Anal fin originates about one head length posterior to dorsal fin insertion and has 9 or 10 rays. Lateral line scales are large and archlike, forming cylinder over lateral line organs. Color is dark brownish and brassy ventrally and on side. Gill covers are silvery.

This species occurs in the tropical Atlantic Ocean between 500 and 1,000 m. It occurs in the Gulf of Mexico and the Caribbean Sea in the western Atlantic. Maximum known size is 88 mm SL.

REFERENCES: Bertelsen 1958; Cohen 1964a; Rass 1971; Bekker et al. 1975.

OPISTHOPROCTIDAE Spookfishes

Spookfishes are slender and subcylindrical or short and laterally compressed, with a small terminal mouth and a forked caudal fin. They are distinguished from the other families of the order by the following combination of characters. Snout is acute and moderately long to long. Premaxilla is reduced or absent. Maxilla is scalelike and easily damaged or lost. Eye is large, tubular (except in one genus), and anteriorly or dorsally directed. Teeth are lacking on premaxilla and maxilla in all species and are lacking on dentaries in most species. Gill membranes are broadly united and free of isthmus. Pectoral fin is on lower side of body. Dorsal fin origin is anterior to anal fin origin. Pelvic fin is abdominal in position and occasionally located on side of body. Adipose fin is present or absent. Body is covered with large, deciduous scales. Lateral line runs straight to base of caudal fin. Photophores and other luminous tissue, often associated with eyes, are present in some species. Swim bladder is present or absent.

The spookfishes occur worldwide in tropical to temperate seas. All species are thought to be mesopelagic or bathypelagic. There are about 10 species in six genera, and 3 species in two genera occur in the Gulf of Mexico.

Key to the Species of the Gulf of Mexico
(Adapted from Cohen 1964a)

1a. Body short and laterally compressed
. . . . *Opisthoproctus grimaldii* p. 380
1b. Body elongate and subcylindrical 2
2a. Pectoral fin extending more than one-half distance from pectoral fin base to origin of anal fin
. . . . *Dolichopteryx binocularis* p. 378
2b. Pectoral fin extending less than one-half distance from pectoral fin base to origin of anal fin
. . . . *Dolichopteryx longipes* p. 379

Dolichopteryx binocularis   Beebe 1932

Dolichopteryx binocularis is slender, subcylindrical anteriorly, and slightly compressed posteriorly, with eyes directed dorsally and relatively elongated pectoral fins. It is distinguished from the other species of the family by the following combination of characters. Body depth behind head is 5.9%, head length is 20%, snout length is 12%, and pectoral fin length is 64.7% of SL. Snout is relatively long and acute. Nostril is closer to eye than to tip of snout. Premaxilla is absent, and maxilla is scalelike and lacks teeth. Lower jaw has small teeth in single series. Vomerine teeth are slightly larger than those of lower jaw and are posteriorly directed. Eye is tubular and slightly oblique to perpendicular axis, and has small accessory eye on tube. Gill membranes are broadly united and are separated from isthmus. Branchiostegal rays number 2. Pectoral fin rays number 14, with upper 5 or 6 rays elongated, filamentous, and extending to midlength. Dorsal, pelvic, and anal fins are posteriorly located, with 15, 9, and 11 rays respectively. Adipose fin is lacking. Scales are thin and number 58 along lateral line. Ventral surface of body is covered with tubercles. Color is transparent white, with darker snout, five large ventral blotches, and midline of dark chromatophores.

This species occurs in the tropical Atlantic Ocean. In the western Atlantic it occurs off Bermuda, and in the Caribbean Sea and the Gulf of Mexico.

REFERENCE: Cohen 1964a.

Dolichopteryx longipes (Vaillant 1888)

Dolichopteryx longipes is slender, subcylindrical anteriorly, and slightly compressed posteriorly, with eyes directed dorsally and pelvic fins elongated. It is distinguished from the other species of the family by the following combination of characters. Body depth behind head is 12.6% to 14.3%, head length is 29% to 32.4%, snout length is 13.9% to 15%, and pectoral fin length is about 14% to 15% of SL. Snout is relatively long and acute. Nostril is closer to tip of snout than to eye. Premaxilla is absent, and maxilla is scalelike and lacks teeth. Lower jaw has small teeth in single series. Vomerine teeth are small, needlelike, and in band about six or seven teeth wide. Eye is tubular and slightly oblique to perpendicular axis, and small accessory eye occurs on tube. Gill membranes are broadly united and are separate from isthmus. Branchiostegal rays number 2. Pectoral fin rays number 13. Dorsal, pelvic, and anal fins are posteriorly located, with 10 or 11, 8 or 9, and 8 or 9 rays respectively. Adipose fin is present or absent. Scales are thin. Color is transparent, with series of four pairs of blotches in lining of ventral part of peritoneal cavity on either side of gut, line of chromatophores along body below lateral line to about level of dorsal fin, two dark blotches at base of caudal fin, and snout dusky. Gut is unpigmented.

This species occurs in the tropical Atlantic and eastern Pacific. In the western Atlantic it occurs from Bermuda, the Bahamas, the Greater Antilles, and in the Gulf of Mexico. It is a deep-sea pelagic species most frequently captured below 1,000 m, but the Gulf of Mexico specimens have been captured between 310 and 460 m. Maximum known size is 95 mm SL.

REFERENCES: Cohen 1964a; Cohen 1984c.

Opisthoproctus grimaldii   Zugmayer 1911

Opisthoproctus grimaldii is short and laterally compressed, with eyes directed dorsally and anal fin distinct from caudal fin. It is distinguished from the other species of the family by the following combination of characters. Body depth behind head is 43.2% to 45.4%, head length is 43% to 44.3%, snout length is 17.2% to 18.6%, pectoral fin length is 19.5% to 21.8%, and sole length is 73% to 77.9% of SL. Snout is long and beaklike. Nostrils are paired and located at end of papillae supported by nasal bones. Premaxilla is absent, and maxilla is scalelike and lacks teeth. Teeth are lacking in lower jaw. Vomer has six or seven teeth. Eyes are tubular, directed dorsally, and are less in diameter and in height than snout length. First gill arch has 20 small, widely spaced gill rakers. Branchiostegal rays number 2. Ventral side of body is flattened and keel-like, and forms sole reflecting organ that extends anteriorly along ventral midline behind anterior margin of orbit. Pectoral fin is located on pedicel on side of body and has 11 rays. Dorsal and pelvic fins are posteriorly located and have 14 and 10 rays respectively. Anal fin is distinct, clearly separated from caudal fin, and has 8 rays. Adipose fin is present. Caudal fin is broad based and deeply forked. Scales are large, deciduous, cycloid, and cover sole in addition to body. Diverticulum of rectum contains luminescent bacteria, and light from bacteria is spread along sole reflecting organ on ventral edge of belly. Head is transparent dorsally and peppered with large melanophores ventrally. Similar melanophores occur on body and fins with exception of adipose fin. Sole generally has four dusky blotches.

This species occurs in the Atlantic and western Pacific Oceans between 200 and 600 m. In the western Atlantic it occurs off the Bahamas and in the northern Gulf of Mexico. Food consists of siphonophores. Eggs and larvae are pelagic. Maximum known size is 60 mm SL.

REFERENCES: Cohen 1964a, 1984c; Heemstra 1986a.

ALEPOCEPHALIDAE Smoothheads

Smoothheads are elongate, slightly slender to eel-like, and slightly to moderately compressed, with a terminal mouth and a moderately to deeply forked caudal fin. They are distinguished from the other families of the order by the following combination of characters. Snout is moderately short to long, less than twice mouth length in all but four species. Mouth ranges from small and tube-like to fairly large and greater than one-half of head length. Eye is large and located on side of head. Teeth are small and feeble, and are present in premaxilla and dentaries of most genera and in maxilla and palatine of many genera. Tongue lacks teeth. Gill membranes are free of isthmus and overlap on midline. Gill rakers are numerous and moderately long to long. Branchiostegal rays number 5 to 8. Shoulder sac apparatus and papilla are lacking. Pectoral fin is located below midflank, is small to rudimentary, and has 4 to 18 rays. Pelvic fin is located on abdomen when present. Dorsal fin is located posterior to midlength of body and posterior to insertion of pelvic fin. Anal fin generally originates near origin of dorsal fin. Adipose fin is absent. Scales are present or absent but are almost always lacking on head. When present, scales are cycloid, thin, and deciduous. Luminous organs are usually absent, but when present, they are located on nodules or on raised skin. Swim bladder is absent. Pyloric caecae range from 2 to 21.

Smoothheads occur worldwide from the tropics to high latitudes at great depths. Most species appear to be bathypelagic, but some appear to be benthopelagic (located slightly above the bottom) or benthic. They are most common below 1,000 m and have been reported to depths of 5,490 m. There are about 60 species in 22 genera, and 19 species in 13 genera occur in the Gulf of Mexico.

Key to the Species of the Gulf of Mexico
(Adapted from Markle and Quéro 1984)

1a. Body completely scaleless (except for occasional presence of lateral line scales). 2
1b. Body completely (with exception of head) or partially scaled. 7
2a. Lateral line located in tube supported by ringlike scales; anal fin with 18 to 22 rays 3
2b. Lateral line, if present, without ringlike scales; anal fin usually with fewer or more than 18 to 22 rays. 4
3a. Photophores absent; lateral line with 43 to 48 modified ringlike scales (on specimens greater than 154 mm SL); body with papillae near lateral line, along bases of vertical fins, and along all fin rays . . . . *Rouleina attrita* p. 398

15a. Lower jaw with distinct conical knob at tip, directed ventrally . . . . *Bajacalifornia megalops* p. 387

15b. Lower jaw without distinct conical knob at tip 16

16a. Anal fin rays 13 to 17; more than 29 gill rakers on first
arch 18

16b. Anal fin rays 9 to 13; fewer than 31 gill rakers on first gill
arch 17

17a. Pectoral fin rays 11 or 12; total gill rakers on first arch 20
to 23. . . . . *Bellocia koefoedi* p. 390

17b. Pectoral fin rays 15 to 17; total gill rakers on first arch 27
to 31. . . . . *Bellocia michaelsarsi* p. 381

18a. Scales present on cheek and operculum; scales above lateral line about same size as those of lateral line; 48 to 61
transverse scale rows above lateral line; orbit diameter 1.6
to 1.9 times greater than snout length
. . . .*Bathytroctes squamosus* p. 389

18b. Scales absent on cheek and operculum; scales above lateral
line smaller than those of lateral line; 59 to 77 transverse
scale rows above lateral line; orbit diameter 1.2 to 1.6
times greater than snout length
. . . . *Bathytroctes microlepis* p. 388

Alepocephalus agassizii   Goode and Bean 1883

Alepocephalus agassizii is moderately elongate, moderately slender, and compressed, with an acute snout, relatively large eyes, and scales on body. It is distinguished from the other species of the family by the following combination of characters. Snout is shorter than eye, and posterior margin of eye is anterior to midpoint of head. Head length is much greater than body depth. Maxilla extends to near posterior margin of pupil. Two supramaxillae are present on dorsal margin of maxilla. Teeth are present in premaxilla, lower jaw, and palatine, and are absent in maxilla and vomer. First gill arch has 7 to 10 gill rakers on epibranch, 1 in corner, and 14 to 20 on lower limb. Pectoral fin is not fanlike, upper rays are longer than lower rays, and rays number from 10 to 12. Origin of dorsal fin is about over origin of anal fin. Dorsal fin rays number 15 to 18, and anal fin rays number 16 to 18. Pelvic fin has single splint bone and 6 to 8 rays. Body is covered with small scales. Lateral line scales number 80 to 90. Area between gill slits and pectoral fin base is scaled. Pyloric caecae number 15 to 23. Color is generally purplish brown but is black when scales and skin are intact.

This species occurs in the temperate to subtropical North Atlantic. In the western Atlantic it occurs from Davis Strait to about 15°N, including the northern Gulf of Mexico between 600 and 2,400 m. Food consists of ctenophores, and to a lesser extent, crustaceans, echinoderms, and polychaetes. Fecundity ranges up to 9,150 eggs. Maximum known size is 79 mm SL.

REFERENCE: Markle and Quéro 1984.

Alepocephalus productus   Gill 1883

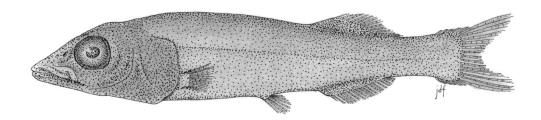

Alepocephalus productus is moderately elongate, moderately slender, and compressed, with a relatively long, acute snout, relatively small eyes, and scales on body. It is distinguished from the other species of the family by the following combination of characters. Snout is longer than eye length, and posterior margin of eye is slightly closer to edge of operculum than to snout. Head length is much greater than body depth. Maxilla extends to about anterior margin of pupil. Two supramaxillae are present on dorsal margin of maxilla. Teeth are present in premaxilla, dentaries, and palatine, and are absent in maxilla and vomer. First gill arch has 7 gill rakers on epibranch, 1 in corner, and 16 on lower limb. Pectoral fin is not fanlike, upper rays are longer than lower rays, and rays number 10. Origin of dorsal fin is slightly anterior to origin of anal fin, and base length of

dorsal fin is greater than that of anal fin. Dorsal and anal fins have 17 rays. Pelvic fin has splint bone and 7 rays. Body is covered with small scales. Lateral line scales number 58. Transverse scale rows from first lateral scale to origin of dorsal fin number fewer than 40 and more than 30. Area between gill slits and pectoral fin base is scaled. Trunk vertebrae number 24, and caudal vertebrae number 26 to 28. Pyloric caecae number 14 to 15. Color is brown.

This species occurs in the North Atlantic. In the western North Atlantic it occurs in the Caribbean Sea and the northeastern Gulf of Mexico. It is benthopelagic at 2,000 to 2,500 m. Maximum known size is 430 mm SL.

REFERENCES: Grey 1956, 1958; Rass 1971; Markle and Quéro 1984.

Asquamiceps caeruleus   Markle 1980

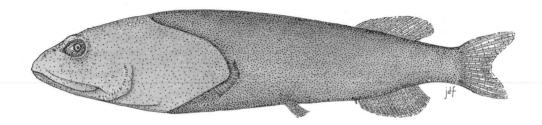

Asquamiceps caeruleus is moderately elongate, moderately slender, and compressed, with a relatively long, acute snout and a moderately forked caudal fin. It is distinguished from the other species of the family by the following combination of characters. Snout length is longer than eye length and is 7% to 10% of SL. Head length is 37% to 45% of SL. Maxilla extends to posterior margin of orbit. One supramaxilla is present on dorsal margin of maxilla. Dentary has minute uniserial teeth to level of posterior margin of orbit. Teeth are lacking in maxilla, palatine, and vomer. First gill arch has 7 to 9 gill rakers on epibranch, 1 in corner, and 14 to 17 on lower limb. Branchiostegal rays number 5 to 7. Opercular flap extends to base of pectoral fin. Posterior edge of flap consists of bands of muscle and connective tissue. Pectoral fin is fanlike and has 14 to 16 rays. Origin of dorsal fin is over origin of anal fin, and base length is slightly greater than that of anal fin. Dorsal fin has 16 to 18 rays, and anal fin has 15 to 17 rays. Pelvic fin has 5 rays. Body, exclusive of head, is covered with irregularly arranged scales. Mid-dorsal and midventral scales are smaller than those along side, are crowded, and form ridge for short distance anterior to dorsal fin and pelvic fin respectively. Raised pores occur on preoperculum, dentaries, between and over orbits, and on posterior part of head. Lateral line is lacking. Trunk vertebrae number 21 to 22, and caudal vertebrae number 20 to 22. Pyloric caecae number 9 to 11. Color is black on body and cobalt blue on head, except skin on unscaled bases of pectoral, pelvic, dorsal, anal, and caudal fins is light blue.

This species occurs in the tropical to temperate waters of the Atlantic and Indian Oceans. In the western Atlantic it occurs in the western Gulf of Mexico. All known specimens were caught in nonclosing nets between 1,900 m and the surface and between 2,740 m and the surface. Maximum known size is 337 mm SL.

REFERENCE: Markle 1980.

Bajacalifornia megalops (Lütken 1898)

Bajacalifornia megalops is moderately elongate, moderately slender, and compressed, with large eyes and a ventrally directed conical knob at tip of snout. It is distinguished from the other species of the family by the following combination of characters. Snout length ranges from 90% to 130% of orbit diameter, greater than eye diameter in smaller specimens and slightly less than eye diameter in larger specimens. Head length is of moderate size and is greater than body depth. Orbit diameter is 7.2% to 10.8% of SL. Maxilla has teeth along ventral margin and extends to posterior margin of pupil. Teeth are in single row in upper and lower jaws. Gill rakers on first arch number 5 to 7 on epibranch, 1 in corner, and 17 to 21 on lower limb. Pectoral fin is small and has 12 to 17 rays. Dorsal fin originates distinctly anterior to anal fin origin and has 14 to 19 rays. Pelvic fin inserts posterior to midlength and has 7 to 9 rays. Anal fin has 13 to 16 rays. Pyloric caecae number 11 to 26, trunk vertebrae number 31 to 32, and tail vertebrae number 19 to 20. Body, exclusive of head, is covered with moderate-sized scales. Color is brownish.

This species occurs in the Atlantic, Indian, and eastern Pacific Oceans in tropical to temperate seas. In the western Atlantic it occurs along the eastern seaboard of the United States from about 40°N to the Gulf of Mexico and the Caribbean Sea. Larvae and juveniles are mesopelagic and bathypelagic between 250 and 3,182 m, and adults are benthopelagic from 820 to 1,425 m. Maximum known size is 28 cm SL.

REFERENCES: Parr 1952b (as *B. drakei*); Markle and Quéro 1984; Markle 1986.

Bathytroctes microlepis Günther 1878

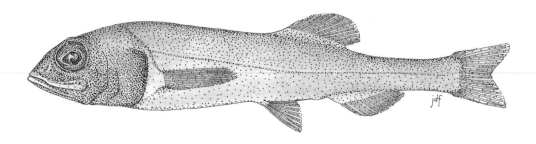

Bathytroctes microlepis is moderately elongate, moderately slender, and compressed, with a short, blunt snout and a moderately forked caudal fin. It is distinguished from the other species of the family by the following combination of characters. Orbit length is 1.2 to 1.6 times snout length. Head length is 26% to 28% of SL and is slightly greater than body depth. Head profile is arched over eyes. Maxilla extends to about posterior margin of pupil. Two supramaxillae are present on dorsal margin of maxilla. Teeth are small, conical, and uniserial, and are found in palatine, vomer, and both jaws. First gill arch has 8 to 12 gill rakers on epibranch and 21 to 24 on lower limb. Branchiostegal rays number 7 or 8. Pectoral fin is not fanlike and has 10 to 14 rays. Origin of dorsal fin is distinctly anterior to origin of anal fin. Dorsal fin has 15 to 17 rays, and anal fin has 15 to 16 rays. Pelvic fin has 8 rays. Body, exclusive of head, is covered with scales, and those above lateral line are smaller than lateral line scales. Scales are absent on cheek and operculum. Lateral line scales number 47 to 49. Transverse scale rows above lateral line number 59 to 77. Pectoral fin is surrounded by normal scales; there is no naked area between gill slit and base of pectoral fin. Pyloric caecae number 13. Color is brownish.

This species occurs in the North Atlantic, the South China Sea, and the eastern South Pacific. In the western North Atlantic it occurs in the eastern Gulf of Mexico. It is benthopelagic, has been caught between 1,100 and 3,984 m, and is most common below 1,900 m. Nothing is known of its reproductive biology other than that ova reach 3.5 mm in diameter. Maximum known size is 300 mm SL.

REFERENCES: Grey 1958; Markle and Quéro 1984; Anderson et al. 1985.

Bathytroctes squamosus   Alcock 1890

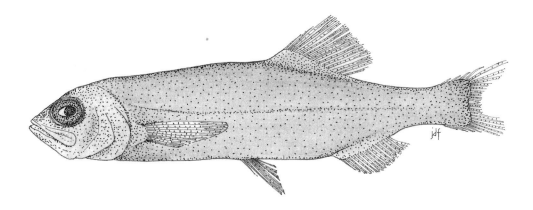

Bathytroctes squamosus is moderately elongate, moderately slender, and compressed, with a short, blunt snout and a moderately forked caudal fin. It is distinguished from the other species of the family by the following combination of characters. Snout length is shorter than eye length. Head length is about 27% of SL. Head profile is arched over eye. Maxilla extends to about posterior margin of pupil. Two supramaxillae occur on dorsal margin of maxilla. Teeth are arranged in single series in upper and lower jaws. First gill arch has 8 to 10 gill rakers on epibranch and 21 to 24 on lower limb. Branchiostegal rays number 7 or 8. Pectoral fin is not fanlike and possesses 11 to 13 rays. Origin of dorsal fin is distinctly anterior to origin of anal fin. Dorsal fin has 17 rays, and anal fin has 14 rays. Pelvic fin has 8 rays. Body, exclusive of head, is covered with scales. Lateral line scales number 48 to 51. Transverse scale rows above lateral line number 48 to 61. Color is dark brown.

This species occurs in the western North Atlantic and the tropical Indian Ocean. In the western North Atlantic it occurs in the eastern Gulf of Mexico, where it has been captured at 2,104 to 2,194 m. Maximum known size is 235 mm SL.

REFERENCES: Grey 1958 (as *Grimatroctes bullisi,* in part); Markle 1986.

Bellocia koefoedi   (Koefoed 1927)

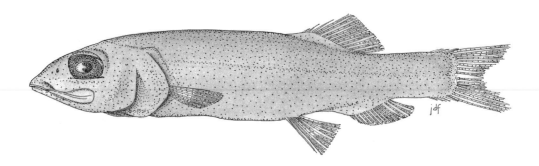

Bellocia koefoedi is moderately elongate, moderately slender, and compressed, with a moderately long, acute snout and a moderately forked caudal fin. It is distinguished from the other species of the family by the following combination of characters. Snout length is greater than eye length and is about 12.4% of SL. Head length is about 40% of SL. Head profile is slightly curved over eye. Maxilla extends to posterior margin of orbit. Two supramaxillae occur on dorsal margin of maxilla. Teeth are arranged in single series in upper and lower jaws. First gill arch has 5 or 6 gill rakers on epibranch, 1 in corner, and 14 to 17 on lower limb. Branchiostegal rays number 8. Pectoral fin is not fanlike—upper rays are longer than lower rays—and has 11 or 12 rays. Origin of dorsal fin is distinctly anterior to origin of anal fin. Dorsal fin has 12 to 16 rays, and anal fin has 9 to 13 rays. Pelvic fin has 7 to 9 rays. Body, exclusive of head, is covered with scales. Transverse scale rows number about 40 to 43. Color is brownish.

This species occurs in the North Atlantic. In the western North Atlantic it occurs in the Gulf of Mexico. It has been captured from 2,500 to 5,850 m and is most frequently taken between 2,800 and 3,300 m. Maximum known size is 400 mm SL.

REFERENCES: Markle and Quéro 1984; Anderson et al. 1985 (as *Nomoctes koefoedi*).

Bellocia michaelsarsi   (Parr 1951)

Bellocia michaelsarsi is moderately elongate, moderately slender, and compressed, with a moderately long, acute snout and a moderately forked caudal fin. It is distinguished from the other species of the family by the following combination of characters. Snout length is about equal to eye diameter. Head profile is straight over eye. Maxilla extends to about posterior margin of eye. Two supramaxillae occur on dorsal margin of maxilla. Teeth are arranged in single row in upper and lower jaws. Gill rakers on first gill arch number 7 to 9 on epibranch, 1 in corner, and 19 to 25 on lower limb. Branchiostegal rays number 7 or 8. Pectoral fin is not fanlike—upper rays are longer than lower fin rays—and possesses 15 to 17 rays. Dorsal fin originates distinctly anterior to anal fin origin and has 12 to 16 rays, and anal fin has 9 to 13 rays. Pelvic fin inserts slightly anterior to dorsal fin origin and has 7 to 9 rays. Body, exclusive of head, is covered with scales. Pyloric caecae number 7 to 15. Color is brownish.

This species occurs in the Atlantic Ocean from tropical to temperate seas between 2,600 and 4,000 m. It is thought to be bathypelagic or benthopelagic. In the western Atlantic it occurs along the eastern seaboard of the United States and in the Gulf of Mexico. There is only a single record from the Gulf of Mexico.

REFERENCES: Markle and Quéro 1984; Anderson et al. 1985 (as *Nomoctes michaelsarsi*).

Conocara macroptera   (Vaillant 1888)

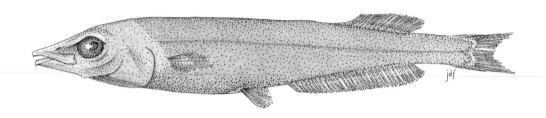

Conocara macroptera is elongate, slender, and posteriorly compressed, with a moderately long, acute snout, a fleshy fold along back and above and below caudal peduncle, and a body covered with scales. It is distinguished from the other species of the family by the following combination of characters. Snout length is longer than eye length and is about 9% or 10% of SL. Head length is 30% to 33% of SL. Premaxilla does not form visorlike plate. Maxilla extends to or just distal to anterior margin of eye. One supramaxilla is located on dorsal margin of maxilla. Teeth occur in premaxilla, palatine, and dentary but not in maxilla or vomer. Epibranch of first gill arch has one gill raker. Pectoral fin is not fanlike—upper rays are longer than lower rays—and rays number 8 to 10. Origin of dorsal fin is posterior to origin of anal fin, and dorsal fin base is shorter than anal fin base. Dorsal fin has 18 to 21 rays, and anal fin has 37 to 39 rays. Pelvic fin has 6 or 7 rays. Body, with exception of head, is covered with small and barely imbricated scales. Color is pale brown to black.

This species occurs in the Atlantic. In the western Atlantic it is known from the Bahamas, the eastern Gulf of Mexico, and Brazil. It is benthopelagic between 800 and 2,200 m, and most common between 1,200 and 1,800 m. Maximum known size is 340 mm SL. *Conocara macdonaldi* Goode and Bean is a junior synonym of this species.

REFERENCE: Markle and Quéro 1984.

Conocara murrayi   (Koefoed 1927)

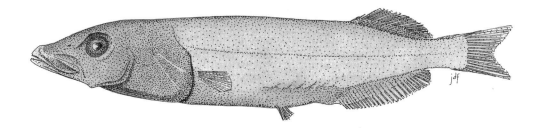

Conocara murrayi is moderately elongate, deep bodied, and posteriorly compressed, with a relatively long, acute snout, a fleshy fold on back and above and below caudal peduncle, and a body covered with scales. It is distinguished from the other species of the family by the following combination of characters. Snout length is greater than eye length and is 13% to 15% of SL. Head length is 37% to 41% of SL. Head profile is straight over eye. Premaxilla does not form visorlike plate. Maxilla extends to anterior margin of eye. One supramaxilla is located on dorsal margin of maxilla. Teeth are of moderate size, curved inward, and uniserial in dentaries, premaxilla, and palatine. Teeth are absent in maxilla and vomer. Epibranch of first gill arch has three to five gill rakers. Pectoral fin is not fanlike and has 8 or 9 rays. Origin of dorsal fin is posterior to origin of anal fin, and dorsal fin base is shorter than anal fin base. Dorsal fin has 19 to 22 rays, and anal fin has 21 to 28 rays. Pelvic fin has 5 or 6 rays. Body is covered with small and barely imbricated scales. Color is brownish.

This species occurs in the North Atlantic, Indian, and western South Pacific Oceans. It is benthopelagic at depths of 1,200 to 2,600 m, and is most common below 2,000 m. In the western North Atlantic it occurs in the eastern Gulf of Mexico, although this record is based on a single juvenile specimen and thus is questionable. Nothing is known of its reproductive biology other than that ova reach 3.9 mm in diameter. Maximum known size is about 340 mm SL.

REFERENCES: Grey 1958; Rass 1971; Markle and Quéro 1984.

Leptoderma macrops Vaillant 1886

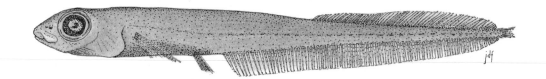

Leptoderma macrops is very elongate, slender, and slightly compressed, with a short, blunt snout and a very small caudal fin. It is distinguished from the other species of the family by the following combination of characters. Snout projects anterior to mouth, is less than eye diameter, and is about 3.8% to 5.3% of SL. Head length is about 17% to 21% of SL. Maxilla extends to anterior margin of eye. One supramaxilla occurs on dorsal margin of maxilla. Small, conical teeth occur in premaxilla, anterior section of maxilla, and dentaries. Teeth are lacking in vomer and palatine. First gill arch has 0 to 1 gill raker on epibranch and 11 to 14 on lower limb. Branchiostegal rays number 4 to 6. Pectoral fin is not fanlike—upper rays are longer than lower rays—and has 7 to 9 rays. Origin of dorsal fin is posterior to origin of anal fin, dorsal fin base is shorter than anal fin base, and both bases are continu-ous with small caudal fin. Dorsal fin has 57 to 67 rays, and anal fin has 78 to 85 rays. Pelvic fin has 5 or 6 rays. Head, body, and fins are covered with loose skin that is free of scales. Skin is covered with numerous papillae that are regularly arranged along lateral line, anal fin and dorsal fin bases, and along midline of back and on head. Trunk vertebrae number 17 to 19, and caudal vertebrae number 62 to 65. Pyloric caecae number two. Color is dark filmy to semiglossy black.

This species occurs in the Atlantic. In the western Atlantic it occurs from the eastern Gulf of Mexico, the Caribbean Sea, and off Brazil. It is benthopelagic at depths between 500 and 2,000 m. Maximum known size is 240 mm SL.

REFERENCES: Mead and Böhlke 1953 (as *Leptoderma springeri*); Grey 1956; Rass 1971; Markle and Quéro 1984; Markle 1986.

Narcetes stomias (Gilbert 1890)

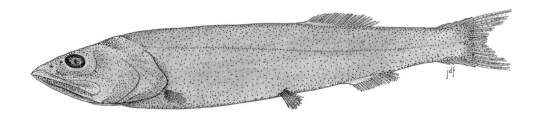

Narcetes stomias is moderately elongate, moderately slender, and compressed, with a moderately short, pointed snout and dorsal fin in advance of anal fin. It is distinguished from the other species of the family by the following combination of characters. Snout length is about equal to eye length. Maxilla extends considerably posterior to orbit. Two supramaxillae are located on dorsal margin of maxilla. Dentaries and premaxilla have several series of teeth, vomer has one to five pairs of teeth, and maxilla and palatine have one to several series of teeth. Teeth are lacking on either side of symphysis of lower jaw. First gill arch has 3 to 5 gill rakers on epibranch, 1 in corner, and 10 to 14 on lower limb. Branchiostegal rays number 8 or 9. Pectoral fin is small, is not fanlike, and has 9 to 11 rays. Dorsal fin base is longer than anal fin base. Dorsal fin has 18 to 20 rays, and anal fin has 14 to 17 rays. Pelvic fin has bony splint and 8 to 9 rays. Body is covered with deciduous scales that are seldom present on specimens. Lateral line scales number 53 to 73, and transverse scale rows anterior to dorsal fin origin number 30 to 47. Trunk vertebrae number 25 to 28, and caudal vertebrae number 21 to 23. Pyloric caecae range from 8 to 11. Color is blackish.

This species occurs in the North Atlantic. In the western North Atlantic it occurs from New England to the eastern Gulf of Mexico and the Caribbean Sea. It has been captured from 1,500 to 2,300 m and is most abundant between 1,800 and 2,100 m. Maximum known size is 530 mm SL.

REFERENCES: Grey 1956, 1958; Rass 1971; Markle and Quéro 1984; Markle 1986.

Photostylus pycnopterus   Beebe 1933

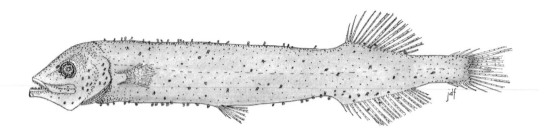

Photostylus pycnopterus is elongate, slender, and compressed, with a moderately short, pointed snout and light organs on raised stalks. It is distinguished from the other species of the family by the following combination of characters. Snout length is slightly longer than eye length. Head length is about 17% of SL. Maxilla extends near to posterior margin of eye. One supramaxilla is present on dorsal margin of maxilla. Premaxilla, maxilla, and dentaries have single series of small teeth. Palatine has two small teeth, and vomer lacks teeth. Branchiostegal rays number 6. Pectoral fin is not fanlike and has 17 to 20 rays. Origin of dorsal fin is over origin of anal fin, and dorsal fin has shorter base than anal fin. Dorsal fin has 12 to 15 rays, and anal fin has 16 to 19 rays. Pelvic fin has 6 or 7 rays. Body is naked. Small light organs are scattered over head and body. Pyloric caecae number three. Color is brownish.

This species occurs worldwide between 40°N and 35°S at depths of 1,000 to 2,000 m. In the western Atlantic it occurs in the Gulf of Mexico. Nothing is known of its reproductive biology other than that ova reach 1.8 mm in diameter. Maximum known size is 110 mm SL.

REFERENCES: Bekker et al. 1975; Markle and Quéro 1984.

Rinoctes nasutus   (Koefoed 1927)

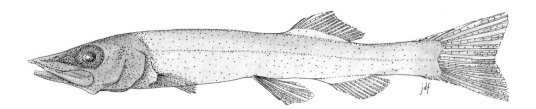

Rinoctes nasutus is elongate, slender, and posteriorly compressed, with a long, acute snout and dorsal fin anterior to anal fin. It is distinguished from the other species of the family by the following combination of characters. Snout length is 9.1% to 12.4% of SL and greater than orbit length. Head length is 28.4% to 33.6% of SL. Premaxilla is produced into beak projecting anterior to tip of lower jaw. Maxilla extends to anterior margin of eye. Two supramaxillae are present on dorsal margin of maxilla. Premaxilla, maxilla, dentaries, palatine, and vomer bear teeth. Premaxillary teeth are in two rows, and those of outer row are larger than those of inner row. First gill arch has 4 gill rakers on epibranch, 1 in corner, and 15 to 17 on lower limb. Branchiostegal rays number 6 or 7.

Pectoral fin is not fanlike and has 8 rays. Bases of dorsal and anal fins are about equal length. Dorsal fin has 11 to 15 rays, and anal fin has 10 to 13 rays. Pelvic fin has 7 rays. Body is naked. Color is blackish on head and pale yellowish on body.

This species occurs in the North Atlantic. In the western North Atlantic it occurs in the Gulf of Mexico. It is benthopelagic at depths of 2,000 to 4,156 m and is most abundant below 3,650 m. Food consists of crustaceans, worms, and sponges. Ova range up to 4.5 mm in diameter. Maximum known size is 217 mm SL.

REFERENCES: Markle and Merrett 1980; Markle 1984.

Rouleina attrita (Vaillant 1888)

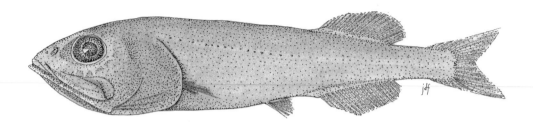

Rouleina attrita is moderately elongate, moderately slender, and posteriorly compressed, with a moderately long, blunt snout and large eyes located on anterior part of head. It is distinguished from the other species of the family by the following combination of characters. Snout length is about equal to eye length. Head length is about 33% of SL. Maxilla extends beyond posterior margin of eye. Two supramaxillae are present on dorsal margin of maxilla. Premaxilla, maxilla, and dentaries bear row of small teeth. Teeth are absent in palatine and vomer. First gill arch has 7 or 8 gill rakers on epibranch, 1 in corner, and 16 to 20 on lower limb. Branchiostegal rays number 5 or 6. Pectoral fin is small, not fanlike, and has 6 or 7 rays. Origin of dorsal fin is over origin of anal fin, and bases of fins are about equal. Dorsal and anal fins have 18 to 21 rays. Pelvic fin has 6 or 7 rays. Trunk vertebrae number 19 to 22, and caudal vertebrae number 22 to 26. Pyloric caecae number 7 to 11. Body is naked except for lateral line scales that are ringlike. Lateral line scales number 43 to 48. Skin contains small fluid-filled compartments. Color is black.

This species occurs in the Atlantic, eastern Pacific, and western South Indian Oceans. In the western North Atlantic it occurs from Newfoundland and the eastern United States to Panama and Venezuela, including the Gulf of Mexico and the Lesser Antilles. It is benthopelagic and is generally captured between 1,400 and 2,100 m. Maximum known size is 380 mm SL.

REFERENCES: Rass 1971; Markle 1978 (as *Rouleina mollis*), 1986; Markle and Quéro 1984.

Rouleina maderensis   Maul 1948

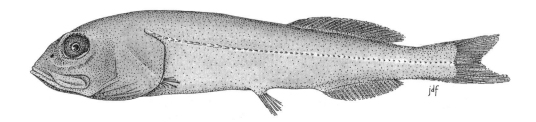

Rouleina maderensis is moderately elongate, moderately slender, and posteriorly compressed, with a moderately long, blunt snout, large eyes located on anterior part of head, and light organs on body. It is distinguished from the other species of the family by the following combination of characters. Snout length is about equal to eye length. Head length is about 33% of SL. Maxilla extends posterior to eye. Two supramaxillae are present on dorsal margin of maxilla. Premaxilla, maxilla, and dentaries bear row of small teeth. No teeth are present in palatine or vomer. First gill arch has 6 or 7 gill rakers on epibranch, 1 in corner, and 17 on lower limb. Branchiostegal rays number 6. Pectoral fin is small and has 5 to 7 rays. Origin of dorsal fin is over origin of anal fin, and fin bases are about of equal length. Dorsal and anal fins have 20 to 22 rays. Pelvic fin has 5 or 6 rays. Trunk vertebrae number 20 to 22, and caudal vertebrae number 26 to 28. Body is naked except for lateral line scales that are ringlike. Lateral line scales number 50 to 56. Skin contains small fluid-filled compartments and is covered with numerous light organs located mostly below lateral line. Color is black.

This species occurs in the North Atlantic and eastern South Pacific Oceans. In the western North Atlantic it occurs off the northeastern United States, in the Straits of Florida, the Gulf of Mexico, the Lesser Antilles, and off Costa Rica and Panama. It is benthopelagic at depths of 600 to 1,200 m. Nothing is known of its reproductive biology other than that ova reach 3.7 mm in diameter. Maximum known size is 320 mm SL.

REFERENCES: Markle 1978, 1986; Markle and Quéro 1984.

Talismania antillarum   (Goode and Bean 1896)

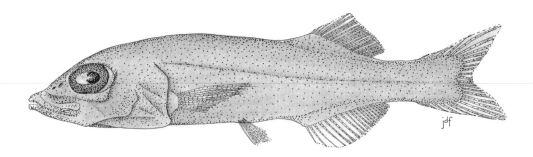

Talismania antillarum is moderately elongate, moderately slender, and posteriorly compressed, with a moderately long, acute snout, large eyes, and body covered with scales. It is distinguished from the other species of the family by the following combination of characters. Snout length is slightly shorter than eye length and is 7% to 10% of SL. Head length is 29% to 34% of SL. Maxilla extends slightly beyond anterior margin of eye. Two supramaxillae are present on dorsal margin of maxilla. Premaxilla, maxilla, dentaries, and palatine bear single row of teeth. Teeth are present or absent in vomer. First gill arch has 8 gill rakers on epibranch, 1 in corner, and 21 on lower limb. Branchiostegal rays number 7. Pectoral fin is of moderate size, is not filamentous, and has 15 to 16 rays. Origin of dorsal fin is above origin of anal fin, and fin bases are about equal length. Dorsal fin has 19 to 22 rays, and anal fin has 20 to 22 rays. Pelvic fin has 7 to 9 rays. Trunk vertebrae number 16 to 17, and caudal vertebrae number 28 to 31. Lateral line scales number 45. Color is brownish.

This species occurs in the western North Atlantic, eastern Atlantic, eastern South Pacific, and Indian Oceans. In the western North Atlantic it occurs in the Gulf of Mexico off the Mississippi Delta, and off the Bahamas, Nicaragua, Colombia, and the Antilles. It is benthopelagic at depths of 455 to 1,460 m. Maximum known size is 150 mm SL.

REFERENCE: Markle and Quéro 1984.

Talismania homoptera   (Vaillant 1888)

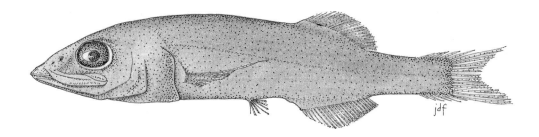

Talismania homoptera is moderately elongate, moderately slender, and posteriorly compressed, with a moderately long, acute snout, upper pectoral fin rays filamentous, and body covered with scales. It is distinguished from the other species of the family by the following combination of characters. Snout length is slightly longer than eye and is 10% to 12% of SL. Head length is 32% to 37% of SL. Maxilla extends to posterior margin of eye. Two supramaxillae are present on dorsal margin of maxilla. Premaxilla, maxilla, dentaries, and palatine bear single row of teeth. Vomer has well-developed teeth. First gill arch has 8 gill rakers on epibranch, 1 in corner, and 17 on lower limb. Branchiostegal rays number 7 or 8. Pectoral fin has 11 to 13 rays, with upper rays filamentous and thickened. Origin of dorsal fin is over origin of anal fin, and fin bases are about equal length. Dorsal fin has 21 to 24 rays, and anal fin has 20 to 24 rays. Pelvic fin has 7 rays. Body, excluding head, is covered with scales. Lateral line scales number 52 to 55. Trunk vertebrae number 17 to 19, and caudal vertebrae number 29 to 32. Pyloric caecae number 10 or 11. Color is blackish with black wartlike spot on base of sixth dorsal fin ray.

This species occurs in the North Atlantic and tropical eastern Atlantic. In the western North Atlantic it occurs in the northern Gulf of Mexico, the Caribbean, and off Suriname. It is benthopelagic at depths of 560 to 1,690 m. Maximum known size is 290 mm SL.

REFERENCES: Parr 1952a (as *Talismania oregoni*); Markle and Quéro 1984.

Xenodermichthys copei (Gill 1884)

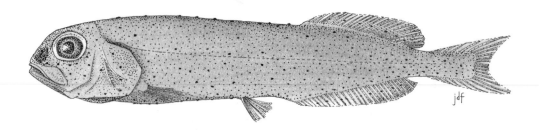

Xenodermichthys copei is moderately elongate, relatively deep bodied, and compressed, with a short, blunt snout and nodular light organs on head and body. It is distinguished from the other species of the family by the following combination of characters. Snout length is less than eye length. Head length is 20% to 25% of SL. Maxilla extends to about center of eye. One supramaxilla is present on dorsal margin of maxilla. Premaxilla and dentaries have minute teeth. First gill arch has 6 to 8 gill rakers on epibranch, 1 in corner, and 16 to 18 on lower limb. Pectoral fin is not fanlike and has 7 or 8 rays. Origin of dorsal fin is over origin of anal fin, and fin bases are about equal length. Dorsal fin has 27 to 31 rays, and anal fin has 26 to 30 rays. Pelvic fin has 6 rays. Body is naked. Trunk vertebrae number 16 to 19, and caudal vertebrae number 30 to 32. Pyloric caecae number four to seven. Color is black.

This species occurs in the Atlantic, eastern Pacific, and Indian Oceans. In the western North Atlantic it occurs off Virginia and Bermuda and in the Gulf of Mexico, off the Dry Tortugas and Pensacola, Florida. It is mesopelagic and has been captured between 100 and 1,000 m, generally near continental or insular slopes. Food consists of copepods, amphipods, euphausiids, decapod zoea, ostracods, and small cephalopods. Spawning occurs from September to November either near or on the bottom. Ova range up to 2.7 mm in diameter, and fecundity is low; a single 15.6-cm female had 151 ova. Maximum known length is 170 mm SL.

REFERENCES: Rass 1971; Markle and Quéro 1984; Markle 1986.

PLATYTROCTIDAE   Tubeshoulders

Tubeshoulders are slightly slender to slender, and moderately compressed to compressed, with a terminal mouth and a forked caudal fin. They are distinguished from the other families of the order by the following combination of characters. Snout is moderately long to short and acute. Mouth is moderate to large, and greater than one-half head length in some species. Teeth are rudimentary to small and are present in premaxilla and maxilla, usually in dentaries, and are present or absent in palatine and vomer. Forwardly directed tusks on premaxilla occur in some species. Eye is large and located on side of head. Gill membranes are free of isthmus and overlap along midline. Gill rakers are generally numerous. Large, round black sac is present under upper aspect of shoulder girdle. Sac opens to exterior by means of tube or papilla above pectoral fin base. Tube is usually supported by modified scales. Sac contains luminous fluid. Pectoral fin originates below midflank and is small or rudimentary. Dorsal fin is located posterior to midlength and posterior to insertion of pelvic fin. Pelvic fin is usually present, and when present, is small and located on belly. Anal fin originates near or posterior to origin of dorsal fin. Adipose fin is absent. Scales are generally present on body and rarely on dorsal part of head. Luminescent organs (photophores) are generally present. Swim bladder is absent.

Tubeshoulders occur worldwide from the tropics to high latitudes at great depths. Most species are mesopelagic or bathypelagic, but some are benthopelagic. There are about 31 species in 12 genera, and 4 species in separate genera occur in the Gulf of Mexico.

Key to the Species of the Gulf of Mexico
(Adapted from Parr 1960; Quéro et al. 1984)

1a. Body deep and strongly compressed; upper and lower body margins formed into keels, lower keel deeper than caudal peduncle . . . . *Platytroctes apus* p. 407
1b. Body relatively elongate and moderately compressed; upper and lower body margins not formed into keels 2
2a. Photophores present on body; lateral line very distinct, with greatly enlarged scales . . . . . *Holtbyrnia innesi* p. 405
2b. Photophores absent on body; lateral line indistinct, without enlarged scales 3
3a. Symphysis of lower jaw with pair of horizontal, divergent spines; premaxilla without forward-directed tusk . . . . *Barbantus curvifrons* p. 404
3b. Symphysis of lower jaw without pair of horizontal, divergent spines; premaxilla with strong, forward-directed tusk . . . . *Mentodus facilis* p. 406

Barbantus curvifrons   (Roule and Angel 1931)

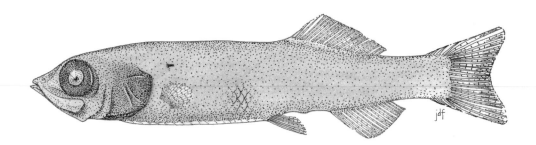

Barbantus curvifrons is moderately elongate, slender, and compressed, with an acute snout and a forked tail. It is distinguished from the other species of the family by the following combination of characters. Snout length is less than eye length and is 5.3% to 6.9% of SL. Head length is 27% to 29% of SL. Upper jaw extends to posterior margin of pupil. Symphysis of lower jaw has horizontal spine projecting laterally on each side. Premaxilla, maxilla, and dentaries have single series of minute teeth. Palatine and vomer have one or two tiny fangs. Forwardly directed teeth (tusks) are absent on premaxilla, and lateral, horizontally directed teeth are lacking in lower jaw. Gill rakers on first arch number from 17 to 20. Branchiostegal rays number 7 or 8. Pectoral fin is low on flank, short, and has 20 or 21 rays. Dorsal fin originates posterior to pelvic fin origin and has 15 to 21 rays. Pelvic fin is inserted on belly at about midlength and has 7 or 8 rays. Anal fin originates below midlength of dorsal fin base and has 14 to 17 rays. Body is covered with moderate-sized scales, with about 45 to 55 in lateral series, 7 to 10 from dorsal fin base to lateral line, and 7 to 10 from lateral line to anal fin base. Lateral line scales are similar to other scales. Photophores are absent. Color is uniform dark except scales along belly are opalescent.

This species occurs in the tropical western Pacific, the Gulf of California, the eastern Atlantic, and the Gulf of Mexico. It has been captured from 800 to deeper than 1,000 m in open water. Maximum known size is 130 mm SL.

REFERENCES: Parr 1960; Quéro et al. 1984.

Holtbyrnia innesi   (Fowler 1934)

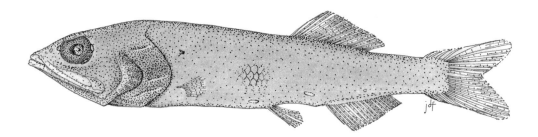

Holtbyrnia innesi is moderately elongate, slender, and compressed, with an acute snout and a forked caudal fin. It is distinguished from the other species of the family by the following combination of characters. Snout length is slightly less than eye length and is 7.7% of SL. Head length is 35% of SL. Upper jaw extends considerably posterior to orbit. Small teeth occur in premaxilla, maxilla, and dentaries. Premaxilla also has prominent, forwardly directed tooth (tusk). Symphysis of lower jaw lacks horizontal spine, but anterior part of lower jaw has series of forwardly directed teeth. First gill arch has 15 or 16 gill rakers on lower limb and 6 or 7 on epibranch. Branchiostegal rays number 8. Pectoral fin is low on flank, short, and has 16 to 20 rays. Dorsal fin originates posterior to pelvic fin insertion and has 18 to 20 rays. Pelvic fin is inserted on belly posterior to midlength and has 9 rays. Anal fin originates at about midlength of dorsal fin base and has 15 to 17 rays. Body is covered with small scales, with 94 to 104 in lateral series. Lateral line scales are similar to other scales. Photophores are present on body. Two whitish bodies occur on posterior rim of orbit separated by distance equal to diameter of lower body. Color is dark except for light color of photophores.

This species occurs in the Pacific and western North Atlantic Oceans. In the western North Atlantic it occurs off the eastern United States and in the southern Gulf of Mexico, at about 1,000 m. Maximum known size is 210 mm SL.

REFERENCES: Parr 1960; Matsui and Rosenblatt 1986.

Mentodus facilis   (Parr 1951)

Mentodus facilis is moderately elongate and slender, with an acute snout and a heart-shaped head in cross section. It is distinguished from the other species of the family by the following combination of characters. Snout length is less than eye length and is 6.5% to 8.4% of SL. Head length is 32.2% to 34.9%, orbit diameter is 13.3% to 14%, upper jaw length is 15.1% to 16.8%, and predorsal length is 65.3% to 65.5% of SL. Premaxilla has single tusk and seven vertical teeth. Upper jaw extends to posterior margin of pupil. Two supramaxillae occur along dorsal margin of maxilla. Maxilla and lower jaw have single row of small, widely spaced teeth. Vomer has pair of teeth, and palatine lacks teeth. Dorsal margin of gill opening is at same height as tube of shoulder organ. Gill rakers on first arch number 20 or 21. Branchiostegal rays number 7.

Pectoral fin is low on flank, is fanlike, and has 18 to 20 rays. Dorsal fin originates posterior to pelvic fin base and has 18 rays. Pelvic fin is inserted on belly at about midlength and has 6 or 7 rays. Anal fin originates below fifth or sixth dorsal fin ray and has 15 to 17 rays. Body is covered with moderate-sized scales, with about 40 to 57 in lateral series and 6 or 7 from dorsal fin base to lateral line. Lateral line scales are not tubular. Photophores are absent. Color is dark and is darkest over anterior half of body.

This species occurs worldwide in tropical and subtropical seas at mesopelagic depths. In the western Atlantic it occurs in the Gulf of Mexico and the Caribbean Sea. Maximum known size is about 98 mm SL.

REFERENCES: Parr 1960; Matsui and Rosenblatt 1987; Sazonov and Miya 1996.

Platytroctes apus   Günther 1878

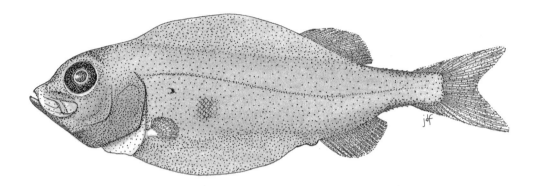

Platytroctes apus is relatively deep bodied and very compressed, with an acute snout and a deeply forked caudal fin. It is distinguished from the other species of the family by the following combination of characters. Snout length is slightly less than eye length and is about 7% of SL. Head length is about 30% of SL. Upper jaw extends to about anterior margin of pupil. Premaxilla lacks prominent anteriorly directed tooth (tusk). Symphysis of lower jaw lacks horizontal spine, and anterior part of lower jaw lacks series of forwardly directed teeth. Gill rakers on first gill arch number 29 to 40, including 8 to 11 on epibranch. Branchiostegal rays number 5 or 6. Upper and lower profiles of body are formed by fleshy keels, and keel along belly is as deep as caudal peduncle. Pec-toral fin is low on flank, short, and has 19 to 25 rays. Dorsal fin is posteriorly located and has 17 to 21 rays. Pelvic fin is absent. Anal fin is below dorsal fin and has 15 to 19 rays. Body is covered with mostly keeled scales, which number 85 to 107 in lateral series. Photophores are absent. Color is uniform dark with black band on upper and lower edges of caudal peduncle.

This species occurs worldwide in tropical to temperate seas from 385 m to deeper than 1,000 m. In the western North Atlantic it occurs in the mid-Atlantic and in the southern Gulf of Mexico. Maximum known size is 180 mm SL.

REFERENCES: Parr 1960; Quéro et al. 1984.

STOMIIFORMES

Stomiiformes and the Ateleopodiformes make up the Stenopterygii, the basal taxon of the neoteleosteans. The order is subdivided into two suborders, Gonostomatoidei and Phosichthyoidei. Gonostomatoids consist of two families, Gonostomatidae and Sternoptychidae, and both occur in the Gulf of Mexico. Phosichthyoids consist of two superfamilies, Phosichthyoidea, with one family (Phosichthyidae), and Stomioidea, with six families (Astronesthidae, Chauliodontidae, Idiacanthidae, Malacosteidae, Melanostomiidae, and Stomiidae), and all families occur in the Gulf of Mexico. Fink (1985) proposed lumping the six families of stomioids into a single family (Stomiidae) based on the shared possession of derived characters. However, herein the six are treated separately because they have long been recognized and because Fink's classification has not been corroborated or widely used.

Key to the Families of the Gulf of Mexico
(Adapted from Morrow 1964a; Weitzman 1986)

1a. True gill rakers present throughout development; jaw teeth small and about same size; no postorbital photophore or light organ; serial photophores with lumen and duct 2

1b. True gill rakers present only in larvae (replaced by spinelike teeth or totally absent in juveniles and adults); jaw teeth moderate to large (except small in few species of Astronesthidae), generally with one to several fangs in each jaw; postorbital photophore or light organ present (at least in males); serial photophores without lumen and duct 4

2a. Branchiostegal rays 10 to 16; photophores on branchiostegal membrane (BR) 7 to 16; photophores in ventral series posterior to anal fin origin (AC) never clumped into compound light organs 3

2b. Branchiostegal rays 6 to 10; photophores on branchiostegal membrane (BR) 6 or, rarely, 7; 2 or more photophores in ventral series posterior to anal fin origin (AC) clumped into compound light organ and surrounded with silvery pigment . . . . Sternoptychidae p. 426

3a. Photophores present on isthmus; total number of photophores in ventral series less than 65 . . . . Phosichthyidae p. 440

3b. Photophores generally absent on isthmus, but if present, total number of photophores greater than 65 (photophores absent in one species of *Cyclothone*) . . . . Gonostomatidae p. 409

GONOSTOMATIDAE Bristlemouths

Bristlemouths are moderately elongate to elongate, and moderately slender to very slender, with a large to very large horizontal mouth and generally two rows of photophores. They are distinguished from the other families of the order by the following combination of characters. Upper jaw extends posterior to eye and possesses fine teeth. Teeth in premaxilla are uniserial, and those of lower jaw are biserial. Chin barbel is absent. Two supramaxillae are present on dorsal margin of maxilla. Vomer and palatine generally bear teeth. Branchiostegal rays number 12 to 17, with 4 to 6 on epihyal. Gill rakers are well developed. Pectoral fin is located below midflank. Dorsal fin origin is generally located at or posterior to midlength of body. Pelvic fin is located on abdomen. Anal fin is located below or anterior to dorsal fin and generally is longer than dorsal fin. Dorsal adipose fin is present or absent. Photophores are usually present on isthmus, on branchiostegal membrane, near orbit, and in ventral and lateral rows on body. Ventral row consists of prepectoral series (IP), prepelvic series (PV), and postpelvic series (VAV). Lateral row (OA) consists of prepelvic series (OV) and postpelvic series (VAL).

Bristlemouths occur worldwide at mesopelagic and bathypelagic depths. Many species are diel vertical migrators and ascend to the epipelagic zone at night. Premetamorphic larvae are generally found near the surface. Postmetamorphic larvae sink as they develop. Food consists of crustaceans and small fishes. There are about 26 species in six genera, and 13 species in six genera occur in the Gulf of Mexico.

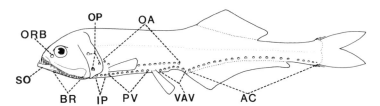

Generalized Gonostomatidae for Photophore ID (See p. 1073)

Key to the Species of the Gulf of Mexico
(Adapted from Badcock 1984a)

1a. Photophores on isthmus between elements of lower jaw; OA extend posteriorly over origin of anal fin; more than 27 AC. 2

1b. Photophores absent on isthmus; OA terminate at or near anal fin origin; fewer than 25 AC. 3

2a. Anal fin rays exceed 54; more than 38 AC; dorsal fin origin nearer to tip of snout than to caudal fin base
. . . . *Diplophos taenia* p. 421

2b. Anal fin rays 36 to 41; AC 28 to 30; dorsal fin origin nearer to caudal fin base than to tip of snout
. . . . *Manducus maderensis* p. 424

3a. Body with single row of conspicuous photophores; branchiostegal rays 15 to 17 4

3b. Body with two rows of conspicuous photophores or no conspicuous rows of photophores; fewer than 15 branchiostegal rays 5

4a. Origin of dorsal fin slightly posterior to origin of anal fin; pair of SO at symphysis of lower jaw; more than 27 anal fin rays . . . . *Bonapartia pedaliota* p. 413

4b. Origin of dorsal fin slightly anterior to anal fin origin; no SO at symphysis of lower jaw; fewer than 26 anal fin rays
. . . . *Margrethia obtusirostra* p. 425

5a. Anus closer to anal fin origin than to pelvic fin insertion; 3 or more VAV anterior to anus; pair of SO present at symphysis of lower jaw, often associated with white glandular patch 6

5b. Anus closer to pelvic fin base than to anal fin origin, or midway between; only 1 or 2 VAV anterior to anus or body photophores absent; no SO present at symphysis of lower jaw 7

6a. White glandular patch just posterior to SO, and associated with suborbital organ (ORB) and OA; gill rakers on first arch number 18 to 21 . . . . . *Gonostoma elongatum* p. 423

6b. No white glandular patch just posterior to SO, or associated with suborbital organ (ORB) or OA; fewer than 19 gill rakers on first arch . . . . *Gonostoma atlanticum* p. 422

7a. One gill raker in corner between epibranch and lower limb of first arch; total of 14 gill rakers on first arch; 8 or 9 BR; 1 VAV anterior to anus; no teeth on vomer . . . .*Cyclothone alba* p. 415

7b. No gill raker in corner between epibranch and lower limb of first arch; more than 14 gill rakers on first arch; 9 to 11 BR; 2 VAV anterior to anus; teeth present on vomer. 8

8a. Gill filaments fused basally into broad crescent-shaped band along hypobranch and lower limb of first arch (Fig. 71); generally 1 AC between last anal fin ray and first procurrent caudal fin ray 9

8b. Gill filaments free or basally fused in straight, narrow band along hypobranch and lower limb of first arch (Fig. 72); more than 1 AC between last anal fin ray and first procurrent caudal fin ray 11

9a. VAV evenly spaced, first 2 not closer together than remainder of series; branchiostegal membrane uniform dark with pigment evenly distributed over membrane (Fig. 73) . . . .*Cyclothone microdon* p. 417

9b. First 2 VAV closer together than remainder of series; pigment on branchiostegal membrane concentrated basal to photophores, along medial free edge of membrane, and over branchiostegal rays. 10

10a. Three or rarely four gill rakers on hypobranch of first arch; OA 7; membrane between posteriormost branchiostegal rays transparent or with single stellate melanophore between each ray (Fig. 74); three pyloric caecae . . . .*Cyclothone braueri* p. 416

10b. Four gill rakers on hypobranch of first arch; OA 8; membrane between posteriormost branchiostegal rays with scattering of punctate melanophores (Fig. 75); four pyloric caecae . . . . *Cyclothone pseudopallida* p. 420

11a. Photophores present on head and trunk; opercular and precaudal glands present 12

11b. Photophores absent on head and trunk; opercular and precaudal glands absent . . . . *Cyclothone obscura* p. 418

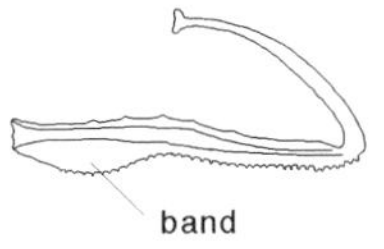

band

FIG 71

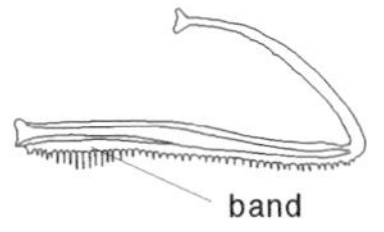

band

FIG 72

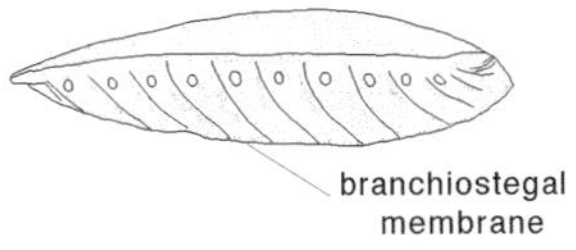

branchiostegal membrane

FIG 73

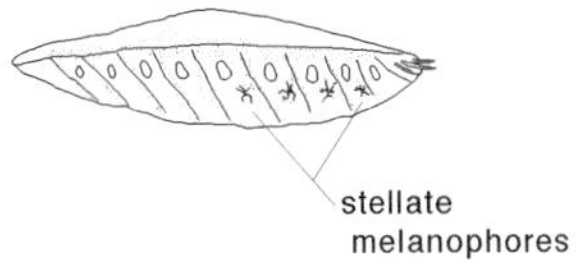

stellate melanophores

FIG 74

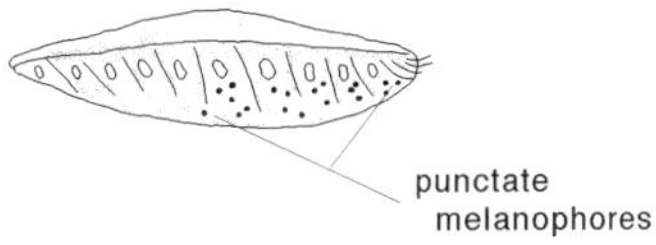

punctate melanophores

FIG 75

12a. Premaxillary teeth of uneven length, one or more (usually fourth) greatly enlarged; precaudal glands weakly developed; area between anus and anal fin origin transparent to slightly pigmented . . . . *Cyclothone pallida* p. 419

12b. Premaxillary teeth of even length, not greatly enlarged; precaudal glands well developed; area between anus and anal fin origin lightly to darkly pigmented
. . . .*Cyclothone acclinidens* p. 414

Bonapartia pedaliota   Goode and Bean 1896

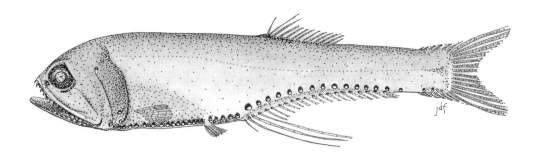

Bonapartia pedaliota is moderately elongate and moderately slender, with a large mouth and a single row of photophores. It is distinguished from the other species of the family by the following combination of characters. Premaxilla has two to four relatively long teeth and two or three small teeth between larger ones. Lower jaw has three to nine relatively long teeth and two to four relatively small teeth between them. Pseudobranch is poorly developed. Gill filaments are free and stouter than first few gill rakers on first arch. Gill rakers on first arch number 16 to 18, with 3 on hypobranch. Branchiostegal rays number 15 to 17, with 5 on epihyal. Dorsal fin origin is posterior to anal fin origin. Anterior rays of both dorsal and especially anal fins are elongated. Dorsal fin rays number 16 to 20, and anal fin rays number 28 to 31, and last ray of each fin is not split to base. Dorsal adipose fin is absent. Anus is closer to anal fin origin than to pelvic fin origin. Scales are deciduous. Symphysis of lower jaw has pair of SO; orbital photophore (ORB) is on anterior margin of orbit. Isthmus lacks photophores. BR number 11 to 13 and OP number 3. IV number 14 or 15, and VAV number 5. AC number 16 to 18, with 2 located posterior to anal fin. Color is dark dorsally and silvery on operculum and peritoneum.

This species occurs in the tropical to subtropical North Atlantic from the surface to 700 m. In the western Atlantic it occurs from south of Newfoundland, off Bermuda, South Carolina, Florida, the Bahamas, the Virgin Islands, and the Gulf of Mexico. Little is known of its reproductive biology other than that larvae sink as they develop, and photophores develop over a size range of 9 to 35 mm SL. Food consists of euphausiids. Maximum known size is 83 mm SL.

REFERENCES: Grey 1964; Rass 1971; Bekker et al. 1975; Murdy et al. 1983; Badcock 1984a; Schaefer et al. 1986b.

Cyclothone acclinidens   Garman 1899

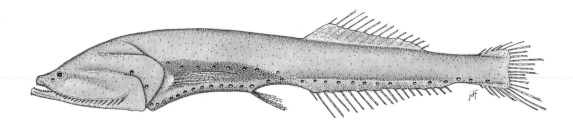

Cyclothone acclinidens is elongate and slender, with a very large mouth and a double row of photophores. It is distinguished from the other species of the family by the following combination of characters. Premaxillary teeth are uniserial and of moderate and about equal size. Teeth on posterior section of maxilla are curved anteriorly. Vomer has teeth. Pseudobranch is absent. Gill filaments are short and are not fused at base. Gill rakers of first arch number 23 to 25, with 5 on hypobranch and none at corner of lower limb and epibranch. Branchiostegal rays number 13 or 14, with 5 or 6 on epihyal. Dorsal fin is opposite anal fin. Anterior rays of dorsal and anal fins are moderately elongated. Dorsal fin has 13 or 14 rays, and anal fin has 18 to 20 rays. Last dorsal and anal fin rays are not split to base. Dorsal adipose fin is absent. Anus is about midway between pelvic fin base and anal fin origin. Photophores are lacking from symphysis of lower jaw and from isthmus. One orbital photophore (ORB) is located on anterior margin of orbit. OP num-
ber 2, and BR number 9 or 10. IP number 3, PV number 10 or 11, and VAV number 4 or 5, with 2 or 3 of these anterior to urogenital openings. OA number 9, and AC number 14 to 16, with 2 located between last anal fin ray and first procurrent caudal ray. Opercular gland is poorly developed, and supracaudal gland is much larger than infracaudal gland. Color is uniform brown.

This species occurs in tropical waters worldwide. In the western Atlantic it occurs from New Jersey to the equator, including the Gulf of Mexico and the Caribbean Sea. Juveniles and adults are generally captured between 300 and 1,200 m, while larvae are generally captured from the surface to 70 m. Food consists of copepods. Maximum known size is 36 mm SL for males and 60 mm SL for females.

REFERENCES: Mukhacheva 1964, 1980a; Bekker et al. 1975; Badcock 1984a; Schaefer et al. 1986b.

Cyclothone alba   Brauer 1906

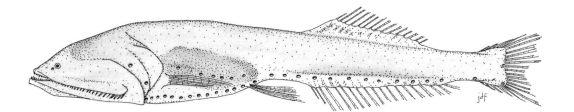

Cyclothone alba is elongate and slender, with a very large mouth and a double row of photophores. It is distinguished from the other species of the family by the following combination of characters. Premaxillary teeth are uniserial and of moderate and about equal size. Teeth on posterior section of maxilla are slanted anteriorly and are slightly irregular in size. Vomer lacks teeth. Pseudobranch is absent. Gill filaments are short and fused basally into broad, crescent-shaped band along hypobranch. Gill rakers of first arch number 14, with 1 in corner between lower limb and epibranch. Branchiostegal rays number 12, including 5 on epihyal. Dorsal fin is opposite anal fin. Anterior rays of dorsal and anal fin are moderately elongate. Dorsal fin has 12 to 14 rays, and anal fin has 17 to 20 rays. Last dorsal and anal fin rays are not split to base. Dorsal adipose fin is absent. Anus is closer to pelvic fin base than to anal fin origin. Photophores are lacking from symphysis of lower jaw and from isthmus. One orbital photophore (ORB) is located on anterior margin of orbit. OP number 2, and BR number 8 or 9. IP number 3, PV number 10, and VAV number 3 or 4, and are evenly spaced with 1 preceding urogenital openings. OA number 6, and AC number 12, with last located between last anal ray and first procurrent caudal ray. Opercular and precaudal glands are inconspicuous. Color is white, with few melanophores. Branchiostegal membrane between last several rays is transparent or has single stellate melanophore between each ray.

This species occurs worldwide in tropical seas. It has been captured from the northern Sargasso Sea to the Gulf of Mexico and the Caribbean Sea in the western Atlantic. Juvenile and adult specimens are generally captured between 300 and 600 m. Larvae are usually taken between 25 and 150 m. Maximum known size is 29 mm SL for males and 34 mm SL for females.

REFERENCES: Grey 1964; Mukhacheva 1964; Bond and Tighe 1974; Bekker et al. 1975; Badcock 1984a; Schaefer et al. 1986b.

Cyclothone braueri Jespersen and Tåning 1926

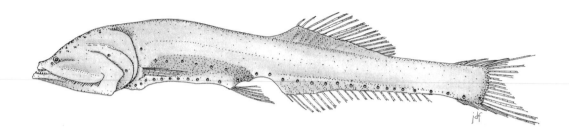

Cyclothone braueri is elongate and slender, with a very enlarged mouth and a double row of photophores. It is distinguished from the other species of the family by the following combination of characters. Premaxillary teeth are uniserial and of moderate and equal size. Teeth on posterior section of maxilla are slanted anteriorly and of rather unequal length. Pseudobranch is absent. Gill filaments are short and fused basally into broad, crescent-shaped band along hypobranch. Gill rakers of first arch number 15 to 18, with 3 or, rarely, 4 on hypobranch and none in corner between lower limb and epibranch. Branchiostegal rays number 13 or 14, with 5 or 6 on epihyal. Dorsal fin is opposite anal fin. Anterior rays of dorsal and anal fins are moderately elongate. Last dorsal and anal fin rays are not split at base. Dorsal adipose fin is absent. Anus is closer to pelvic fin base than to anal fin origin. Dorsal fin has 13 or 14 rays, and anal fin has 18 to 20 rays. Photophores are lacking from symphysis of lower jaw and from isthmus. Orbital photophore (ORB) is located on anterior margin of orbit. OP number 2, and BR number 8 to 10.

IP number 3, PV number 10, and VAV number 4, with first 2 more closely spaced than remainder. OA number 7, and AC number 13 or 14, with last one located between last anal ray and first procurrent caudal fin ray. Opercular and precaudal glands are inconspicuous. Color is white, with stellate melanophores located on dorsal one-half of body. Branchiostegal membrane between last several rays is transparent or has single stellate melanophore between each pair of rays.

This species occurs worldwide in tropical to temperate seas. In the western Atlantic it occurs in the Gulf of Mexico. Juveniles and adults are most common between 250 and 900 m. Larvae are most common at 10 to 50 m. Food consists of copepods. Spawning takes place from April to October. Ripe eggs are 0.5 mm in diameter, and fecundity ranges from 100 to 900 eggs.

REFERENCES: Mukhacheva 1964; Rass 1971; Bond and Tighe 1974; Bekker et al. 1975; Badcock 1984a; Schaefer et al. 1986b.

Cyclothone microdon   (Günther 1878)

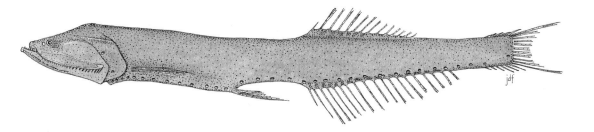

Cyclothone microdon is elongate and slender, with a very large mouth and a double row of photophores. It is distinguished from the other species of the family by the following combination of characters. Premaxillary teeth are uniserial and of moderate and equal size. Teeth in posterior section of maxilla are slanted anteriorly and are rather unequal in length. Pseudobranch is absent. Gill filaments are short and are fused basally into broad, crescent-shaped band along hypobranch. Gill rakers of first arch number 19 to 22, with 4 or 5 on hypobranch and none in corner between lower limb and epibranch. Branchiostegal rays number 12 to 14, with 5 or 6 on epihyal. Dorsal fin is opposite anal fin. Anterior rays of dorsal and anal fins are moderately elongated. Last dorsal and anal fin rays are not split to base. Dorsal adipose fin is absent. Anus is closer to pelvic fin base than to anal fin origin. Dorsal fin has 13 or 14 rays, and anal fin has 17 to 20 rays. Photophores are lacking on symphysis of lower jaw and from isthmus. One orbital photophore (ORB) is on anterior margin of orbit. OP number 2, and BR number 9 or 10. IP number 2 or 3, PV number 10, and VAV number 5, with 3 or 4 anterior to genital pore. OA number 8 or 9, and AC number 14 or 15, with last located between last anal ray and first procurrent caudal fin ray. Glandular tissue between opercular photophores is poorly developed, and supracaudal gland is small but distinct. Color is dark brown.

This species occurs worldwide in tropical to temperate seas. In the western Atlantic it occurs from 60°N to the Caribbean Sea, including the Gulf of Mexico. Juveniles and adults are generally caught from 500 to 2,700 m. Larvae occur from the surface to 50 m. Food consists mainly of copepods. Individuals are protandric hermaphrodites; all individuals are functional males, then switch to functional females at 22 to 42 mm SL. Spawning occurs during the summer and fall. Ripe eggs are about 0.5 mm in diameter, and fecundity ranges from 2,000 to 10,000 eggs. Maximum known size is 49 mm SL for males and 66 SL mm for females.

REFERENCES: Mukhacheva 1964; Rass 1971; Bekker et al. 1975; Badcock 1984a; Schaefer et al. 1986b.

Cyclothone obscura   Brauer 1902

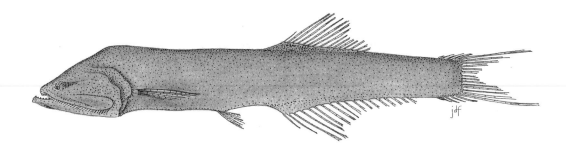

Cyclothone obscura is elongate and slender, with a very large mouth and without photophores. It is distinguished from the other species of the family by the following combination of characters. Premaxillary teeth are uniserial and of even length. Teeth in posterior section of maxilla are slanted anteriorly and are of irregular length. Vomer has teeth. Pseudobranch is absent. Gill filaments are short and are not fused basally. Gill rakers on first arch number 23 to 29, with 5 or 6 on hypobranch and none in corner between lower limb and epibranch. Branchiostegal rays number 13 or 14, with 5 on epihyal. Anterior rays of dorsal and anal fins are elongate. Dorsal adipose fin is absent.

Anus is midway between pelvic fin base and origin of anal fin. Dorsal fin has 13 to 15 rays, and anal fin has 17 to 19 rays. Last rays of dorsal and anal fins are not split to base. Photophores are lacking on head and body. Opercular and precaudal glands are lacking. Color is uniform dark brown.

This species occurs worldwide in tropical to subtropical seas between 900 and 3,000 m, and apparently is not a vertical migrator. In the western Atlantic it occurs in the Gulf of Mexico.

REFERENCES: Mukhacheva 1964; Bekker et al. 1975; Badcock 1984a.

Cyclothone pallida Brauer 1902

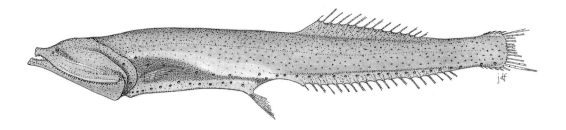

Cyclothone pallida is elongate and slender, with a very large mouth and a double row of photophores. It is distinguished from the other species of the family by the following combination of characters. Premaxillary teeth are uniserial, with at least one (usually fourth) greatly enlarged. Teeth on posterior section of maxilla are slanted anteriorly and are rather unequal in length. Pseudobranch is absent. Gill filaments are moderately short and are not fused basally. Gill rakers of first arch number 22 to 25, with 4 or 5 on hypobranch and none in corner between lower limb and epibranch. Branchiostegal rays number 14 or 15, with 5 or 6 on epihyal. Dorsal fin is opposite anal fin. Anterior rays of dorsal and anal fins are slightly elongate. Last dorsal and anal fin rays are not split to base. Dorsal adipose fin is absent. Anus is closer to pelvic fin base than to anal fin origin. Dorsal fin has 12 to 14 rays, and anal fin has 17 or 18 rays. Photophores are lacking on symphysis of lower jaw and from isthmus. One orbital photophore (ORB) is located on anterior margin of orbit. OP number 2, and BR number 10 or 11. IP number 3, PV number 10, and VAV number 5, with 2 or 3 posterior ones anterior to genital pore. OA number 8, and AC number 14 or 15, with last 2 or 3 located between last anal fin ray and first procurrent caudal fin ray. Supracaudal and infracaudal glands are weak but distinctly developed. Color is light to dark brown, with dorsal and anal rays pigmented. Meningeal pigment over brain extends anteriorly to level of posterior margin of eye or to pineal body.

This species occurs worldwide in tropical to subtropical seas. In the western Atlantic it occurs from about 40°N to the Gulf of Mexico and the Caribbean Sea. Juveniles and adults are most frequently captured between 400 and 1,000 m. Maximum known size is 48 mm SL for males and 70 mm SL for females.

REFERENCES: Mukhacheva 1964; Bekker et al. 1975; Badcock 1984a; Schaefer et al. 1986b.

Cyclothone pseudopallida Mukhacheva 1964

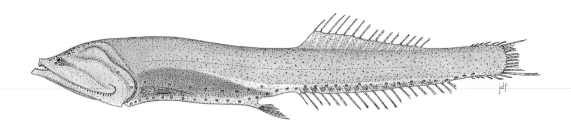

Cyclothone pseudopallida is elongate and slender, with a very large mouth and two rows of photophores. It is distinguished from the other species of the family by the following combination of characters. Premaxillary teeth are uniserial and of moderate and equal size. Teeth on posterior section of maxilla are slanted anteriorly and are rather unequal in length. Pseudobranch is absent. Vomer has teeth. Gill filaments are moderately short and are fused basally in narrow band along hypobranch and lower limb. Gill rakers of first arch number 18 to 20, with 4 on hypobranch and none in corner between lower limb and epibranch. Branchiostegal rays number 13 or 14, with 6 on epihyal. Dorsal fin is opposite anal fin. Anterior rays of dorsal and anal fins are slightly elongate. Last rays of dorsal and anal fins are not split to base. Dorsal adipose fin is absent. Anus is closer to pelvic fin base than to anal fin origin. Dorsal fin has 13 or 14 rays, and anal fin has 19 to 20 rays. Photophores are lacking on symphysis of lower jaw and from isthmus. One orbital photophore (ORB) is on anterior margin of orbit. OP number 2, and BR number 10. IP number 3, PV number 10, and VAV number 5, with 2 anterior to anus. OA number 8, and AC number 14, with last 1 or 2 between last anal fin ray and first procurrent caudal fin ray. Opercular gland is inconspicuous and supracaudal gland is confined to procurrent rays. Color is whitish, with dorsal one-half of body slightly brownish. Branchiostegal membrane between last several rays is transparent, with scattering of punctate melanophores. Meningeal pigment over brain consists of many punctate melanophores.

This species occurs worldwide in tropical seas. In the western Atlantic it occurs from about 60°N to equatorial waters, including the Gulf of Mexico and the Caribbean Sea. Juveniles and adults are most frequently captured from 300 to 900 m. Maximum known size is 43 mm SL for males and 58 mm SL for females.

REFERENCES: Mukhacheva 1964; Bond and Tighe 1974; Bekker et al. 1975; Badcock 1984a; Schaefer et al. 1986b.

Diplophos taenia   Günther 1873

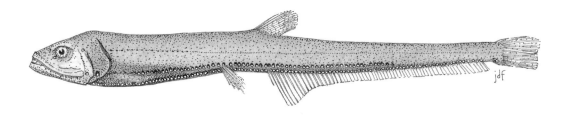

Diplophos taenia is very elongate and slender, with a large mouth and two rows of photophores. It is distinguished from the other species of the family by the following combination of characters. Premaxillary teeth are uniserial, straight, and of moderate and equal size. Teeth on posterior section of maxilla are straight and alternate between long and short. Pseudobranch is present. Vomer has few teeth. Palatine has row of small teeth. Gill filaments are long and free at base. Gill rakers of first arch number 11 or 12. Branchiostegal rays number 14 or 15, with 4 on epihyal. Dorsal adipose fin is absent. Anus is closer to anal fin origin than to pelvic fin insertion. Dorsal fin has 9 to 11 rays, and anal fin has 57 to 68 rays. Last dorsal and anal fin rays are split to base. Photophores are present on symphysis of lower jaw and isthmus. One orbital photophore (ORP) is near anterior margin of orbit. OP number 3, and BR number 10 to 13. IV number 44 to 51, with last on pelvic fin base, and VAV number 14 to 16. OA number 66 to 71, with last extending over anal fin. AC number 45 to 51, with last 2 close together and separated by distinct space from others of series. Accessory photophores occur on head, anterior and posterior to symphyseal photophore, between posteriormost branchiostegal rays, anterior to pectoral fin, and along side of body. Color is black on dorsal surface and silvery on flank.

This species occurs worldwide in tropical seas. In the western Atlantic it occurs along the eastern seaboard of the United States to Florida, from Bermuda, the Bahamas, the Gulf of Mexico, and the Caribbean Sea. Juveniles and adults are generally caught between 300 and 800 m during the day and much closer to the surface during the night. Postlarvae occur near the surface. Food consists of euphausiids and copepods. Maximum known size is 276 mm SL.

REFERENCES: Grey 1964; Johnson 1970; Murdy et al. 1983; Badcock 1984a; Schaefer et al. 1986b.

Gonostoma atlanticum Norman 1930

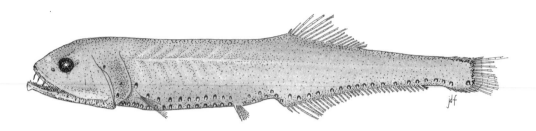

Gonostoma atlanticum is moderately elongate and moderately slender, with a large mouth and two rows of photophores. It is distinguished from the other species of the family by the following combination of characters. Premaxillary teeth are uniserial and consist of large, fanglike teeth separated by small teeth. Teeth in maxilla are similar to those in premaxilla. Vomer has one or two small teeth on each side, and palatine has single row of teeth. Pseudobranch is poorly developed. Gill filaments are long and free at base. Gill rakers on first arch number 17 or 18, with 6 or 7 on epibranch, 7 on lower limb, and 4 on hypobranch. Branchiostegal rays number 14. Dorsal adipose fin is absent. Anus is closer to anal fin origin than to pelvic fin insertion. Dorsal fin has 16 to 18 rays, and anal fin has 27 to 31 rays. Last dorsal and anal fin rays are split to base. Photophores are absent on isthmus but are present on symphysis of lower jaw. One or-

bital photophore (ORB) is near anterior margin of orbit. OP number 3, and BR number 9. IV number 16, and VAV number 4 or 5. OA number 13 or 14, and AC number 18 to 20, with 2 between last anal fin ray and first procurrent caudal fin ray. Two supracaudal and one infracaudal gland are present. Color is dark dorsally and silvery on flank.

This species occurs worldwide in tropical seas. In the western Atlantic it occurs from southern Florida and the Gulf of Mexico to the equator. Juveniles and adults are mainly caught between 300 and 500 m during the day and between 50 and 200 m during the night. Postlarvae are found at shallow depths. Food consists of copepods and euphausiids. Maximum known size is 68 mm SL.

REFERENCES: Grey 1964; Rass 1971; Bekker et al. 1975; Murdy et al. 1983; Badcock 1984a; Schaefer et al. 1986b.

Gonostoma elongatum   Günther 1878

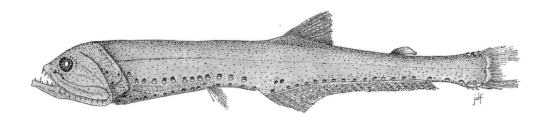

Gonostoma elongatum is elongate and slender, with a large mouth and two rows of photophores. It is distinguished from the other species of the family by the following combination of characters. Premaxillary teeth are uniserial and consist of large, fanglike teeth separated by small teeth. Teeth in posterior section of maxilla are similar to those of premaxilla, except fanglike teeth are larger than those of premaxilla. Vomer has 1 or 2 teeth on each side, and palatine has row of 12 to 15 small teeth. Pseudobranch is poorly developed. Gill filaments are long and free at base. Gill rakers on first arch number 18 to 21, with 4 on hypobranch. Branchiostegal rays number 13 or 14. Dorsal adipose fin is present. Anus is closer to anal fin origin than to pelvic fin insertion. Dorsal fin has 12 to 15 rays, and anal fin has 29 to 32 rays. Last dorsal and anal fin rays are split to base. Photophores are absent on isthmus but are present at symphysis of lower jaw. One orbital photophore (ORB) is located near anterior margin of orbit. OP number 3, and BR number 8 or 9. IV number 15, and VAV number 4 to 6. OA number 13 or 14, with first 2 elevated above others. AC number 21 to 23, with second and third elevated above others. One or two supracaudal and two infracaudal glands are present. White glandular masses are associated with symphyseal photophore, ORB, and OA. Color is dark with flank slightly silvery.

This species occurs worldwide in tropical to subtropical seas. In the western Atlantic it occurs from south of Newfoundland and off Bermuda to the northeastern coast of South America, including the entire Gulf of Mexico and the Caribbean Sea. Juveniles and adults are generally caught between 500 and 1,200 m or deeper during the day and between 50 and 400 m during the night. Food consists of crustaceans and small fishes. All individuals develop into functional males and later become functional females (protandric hermaphroditism). Spawning takes place mainly in spring and summer. Maximum known size is 178 mm SL for males and 275 mm SL for females, and males mature at 110 mm SL and females mature at 200 mm SL.

REFERENCES: Grey 1964; Rass 1971; Bekker et al. 1975; Murdy et al. 1983; Badcock 1984a; Schaefer et al. 1986b.

Manducus maderensis (Johnson 1890)

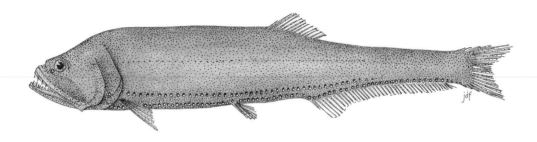

Manducus maderensis is elongate and moderately slender, with a large mouth and two rows of photophores. It is distinguished from the other species of the family by the following combination of characters. Premaxillary teeth are uniserial, with 3 to 7 enlarged teeth separated by small teeth. Premaxilla is equal in length to maxilla. Teeth on posterior section of maxilla are straight, close-set, and shorter than enlarged premaxillary teeth. Pseudobranch is present. Vomer has 1 to 6 small teeth on each side, and palatine has row of 9 to 15 small teeth. Gill filaments are long and free at base. Gill rakers on first arch number 12 to 14. Branchiostegal rays number 13, with 4 on epihyal. Dorsal adipose fin is absent. Anus is closer to anal fin origin than to pelvic fin insertion. Dorsal fin has 12 or 13 rays, and anal fin has 36 to 41 rays. Last dorsal and anal fin rays are split to base. Photophores are present on symphysis of lower jaw and on isthmus. One orbital photophore (ORB) is near anterior margin of orbit.

OP number 3, and BR number 8 to 9. IV number 30 to 33, with last on pelvic fin base, and VAV number 12 to 14. OA number 45 to 48 and extend over anal fin. AC number 28 to 30 and are evenly spaced. Accessory photophores occur above toothed section of maxillary, posterior to symphyseal photophore, and along lateral line anterior to pectoral fin. Color is dark on dorsal aspect and silvery on flank.

This species occurs in the tropical Atlantic. In the western Atlantic it occurs from the eastern seaboard of the United States, the Bahamas, the Straits of Florida, the Gulf of Mexico, Suriname, and Brazil. It has been reported only once from the Gulf of Mexico. Juveniles and adults most frequently are captured between 400 and 800 m during the day and up to the surface at night. Postlarvae are found near the surface. Maximum known size is 279 mm SL.

REFERENCES: Grey 1964; Badcock 1984a; Schaefer et al. 1986b; Smith et al. 1991.

Margrethia obtusirostra   Jespersen and Tåning 1919

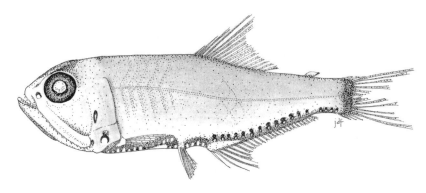

Margrethia obtusirostra is relatively short and moderately deep bodied, with large eyes and a single row of photophores. It is distinguished from the other species of the family by the following combination of characters. Premaxillary teeth are uniserial and consist of small to very small teeth slanted anteriorly, with small teeth separated by smaller teeth. Teeth in posterior section of maxilla are slightly larger than those of premaxilla but are similarly shaped and oriented. Vomer has small teeth, and palatine has long row of small teeth. Pseudobranch consists of 8 to 10 filaments. Gill filaments are relatively long and are not fused at base. Gill rakers on first arch number 14 to 16, with 3 on hypobranch. Branchiostegal rays number 16, with 5 on epihyal. Dorsal adipose fin is present. Anus is closer to anal fin origin than to pelvic fin insertion. Dorsal fin has 15 or 16 rays, and anal fin has 23 to 25 rays. Anterior rays of both fins are elongate, and last ray of each is split to base. Photophores are absent on symphysis of lower jaw and on isthmus. One orbital photophore (ORB) is located near anterior margin of orbit. OP number 3, and BR number 11 or 12. IV number 14 to 15, with last 2 located ventral to others, and VAV number 4. AC number 16 to 18, with anterior 12 or 13 located over anal fin base. Color is dark dorsally, operculum is silvery, and flank is lighter.

This species occurs in the tropical to subtropical Atlantic Ocean between 100 and 600 m, and apparently does not make diel migrations. In the western Atlantic it occurs from southeastern Florida and Bermuda to Venezuela, including the Gulf of Mexico and the Caribbean Sea. Food consists of crustaceans and small fishes. Spawning takes place in summer and fall. Maximum known size is 83 mm SL.

REFERENCES: Grey 1964; Rass 1971; Bekker et al. 1975; Murdy et al. 1983; Badcock 1984a; Schaefer et al. 1986b.

STERNOPTYCHIDAE   Hatchetfishes

Hatchetfishes are moderately elongate to short, and slightly deep bodied to very deep bodied, with a moderate-sized oblique mouth to a relatively large, almost vertical mouth and two or more rows of photophores. They are distinguished from the other families of the order by the following combination of characters. Upper jaw extends from anterior to posterior margin of orbit and bears small to fine teeth. Teeth on upper jaw and lower jaw are in one to three rows. Teeth are present or absent on vomer and palatine. Two supramaxillae are located on dorsal margin of maxilla. Branchiostegal rays number 6 to 10, with 3 on epihyal. Gill rakers are well developed in adults. Pseudobranch is present. Pectoral fin is located below midflank and has four radials. Pelvic fin is located on abdomen. Dorsal fin origin is anterior to, at, or posterior to midlength, and either is preceded by or precedes pelvic fin insertion. Anal fin origin precedes or is preceded by dorsal fin origin and is generally considerably longer than dorsal fin base. Dorsal adipose fin is usually present, and when present, usually has long base. Photophores are both discrete (do not share same photogenic masses) and compound (share photogenic masses). Photophores are present at symphysis of lower jaw, near orbit, on operculum, on branchiostegal membrane, and on lower and midflank. One photophore is located near orbit, and three to six are on branchiostegal membrane.

Hatchetfishes occur worldwide in mesopelagic and bathypelagic depths, but some are apparently benthopelagic. Some species are vertical migrators, while others are nonmigrators. Younger individuals are generally found in shallower water than larger individuals. Food consists of zooplankton. All species are dioecious. There are about 49 species in 10 genera, and 11 species in 6 genera occur in the Gulf of Mexico.

Key to the Species of the Gulf of Mexico
(Adapted from Badcock 1984b)

1a. Body compressed and deep, depth from 50% to 125% of SL; dorsal blade moderately to well developed; abdominal keel well developed; postabdominal spines posterior to abdominal keel well developed. 2
1b. Body moderately elongate and slightly deep bodied, depth from 13% to 27% of SL; dorsal blade, abdominal keel, and postabdominal spines absent or inconspicuous 9
2a. Dorsal blade consists of several spines; eye tubular and directed dorsally; PV 12. 3
2b. Dorsal blade consists of one or two spines; eye not tubular and directed laterally; PV 10 7

Generalized Sternoptychidae for Photophore ID (See p. 1073)

3a. VAV, AC_1, and AC_2 series distinctly separated, with photophores of each series sharing common photogenic mass, all three series elevated with respect to posterior 6 OA; anal fin rays divided into anterior and posterior groups by central AC_1 4

3b. VAV, AC_1, and AC_2 series not distinctly separated, photophores of each series not sharing common photogenic mass, and all three series on about same level as posterior 6 OA; anal fin rays not separated into anterior and posterior groups by central AC_1 6

4a. Single posteriorly directed postabdominal spine with serrated edges and small posterodorsal spine; posterior two fused spines of dorsal blade bear barbs; dorsal fin rays 8; anal fin with 6 rays in anterior and 5 rays in posterior group .... *Argyropelecus hemigymnus* p. 432

4b. Two separate postabdominal spines, one directed posteroventrally and other directed anteroventrally; posterior fused spines of dorsal blade without barbs; dorsal fin rays 9 or 10; anal fin with 7 rays in anterior and 5 rays in posterior group 5

5a. Upper preopercular spine extends beyond posterior margin of preoperculum; anteroventrally directed postabdominal spine blunt; no enlarged teeth in lower jaw; median superficial caudal chromatophore dorsal to AC_2 .... *Argyropelecus sladeni* p. 433

5b. Upper preopercular spine extends little if any beyond posterior margin of preoperculum; anteroventrally directed postabdominal spine pointed; enlarged teeth in lower jaw; no median superficial caudal chromatophore dorsal to AC_2 .... *Argyropelecus aculeatus* p. 429

6a. Body profile with fleshy elevations between third and fourth fused spines of dorsal blade and posterior to dorsal blade; adults with distinct postorbital spine; snout with angular profile . . . . *Argyropelecus gigas* p. 431

6b. Body profile without elevation between third and fourth fused spines of dorsal blade and posterior to dorsal blade; adults without postorbital spine; snout with evenly convex profile . . . . *Argyropelecus affinis* p. 430

7a. Dorsal blade consists of single spine with serrated anterior margin; 3 BR; 5 IP; ORB ventral to eye, externally indistinct and directed into mouth 8

7b. Dorsal blade small and consists of two spines and lacks serrated margin; 6 BR; 6 IP; ORB anterior to eye, externally distinct and directed into eye . . . . *Polyipnus clarus* p. 435

8a. First AC_1 slightly elevated and nearer to anteroventral margin of remainder of series than to trunk midline . . . . *Sternoptyx diaphana* p. 437

8b. First AC_1 distinctly elevated and midway between anteroventral margin of remainder of series and trunk midline or higher . . . . *Sternoptyx pseudobscura* p. 438

9a. AC_1 divided into three to six groups, each with 2 to 4 photophores; IP divided into two groups, of 3 and 4 photophores; gill rakers on first arch with 2 to 4 and 12 or 13 on epibranch and lower limb respectively . . . . *Valenciennellus tripunctulatus* p. 439

9b. AC_1 divided into two or three groups, each with 5 or more photophores; IP in single group of 6 photophores; gill rakers on first arch with 3 to 7 and 15 to 24 on epibranch and lower limb respectively 10

10a. Dorsal fin origin posterior to midlength of body; anal fin rays not subdivided by AC photophores into separate ray groups . . . . *Maurolicus weitzmani* p. 434

10b. Dorsal fin origin slightly anterior to midlength of body; anal fin rays subdivided by AC photophores into two separate ray groups . . . . *Sonoda megalophthalma* p. 436

Argyropelecus aculeatus Valenciennes 1850

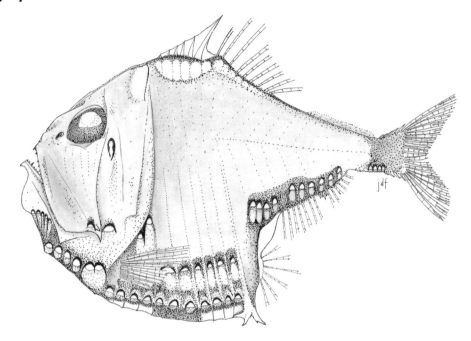

Argyropelecus aculeatus is short and very deep bodied, with a moderate-sized, vertical mouth and dorsally directed eyes. It is distinguished from the other species of the family by the following combination of characters. Jaws have relatively large, recurved teeth, and lower jaw has two enlarged canine teeth. Gill rakers on first arch number 15 to 17. Branchiostegal rays number 10, with 3 on epihyal. Upper preopercular spine is short, extending slightly beyond posterior edge of preoperculum. Lower preopercular spine is short and curves ventrolaterally. Post-temporal spine is small. Dorsal blade is long and is derived from seven dorsal fin radials, with exposed parts of posterior two radials fused. Abdominal keel is well developed. Postabdominal spines are well developed. Posteroventrally directed postabdominal spine is larger than anteroventral spine. Mid-anterior projection of anteroventral postabdominal spine extends to or near to anterior margin of posterior ventral keel scale. Spinelets are present along anterior five dorsal blade spines, dorsal rim of dorsal blade, and along ventral keel. Pectoral fin has 9 or 10, dorsal fin has 9, pelvic fin has 6, and anal fin has 7 anterior and 5 posterior fin rays. Dorsal adipose fin is present and has long base. ORB is pigmented and directed toward eye lens. BR number 6, and OP number 3. IP number 6, PV number 12, and VAV number 4. OA are in two groups of 2 and 6. AC are in two groups of 6 and 4. VAV, AC_1, and AC_2 photophores are compound (share common photogenic mass). Vertebrae number 35 or 36. Color is dark on dorsal surface and silvery on flank.

This species occurs in subtropical waters worldwide. In the western Atlantic it occurs along the eastern seaboard of the United States to southern Florida, in the Gulf of Mexico and the Caribbean Sea, and off southern Brazil to Uruguay. It is caught in mesopelagic waters between 100 and 600 m and is most abundant between 300 and 600 m during the day and between 100 and 300 m during the night. Food consists of ostracods, copepods, decapod larvae, and fish larvae, and feeding takes place at dusk. Life span appears to be two years. Maximum known size is 83 mm SL.

REFERENCES: Schultz 1964; Bright and Pequegnat 1969; Baird 1971, 1986; Rass 1971; Murdy et al. 1983; Badcock 1984b; Howell and Krueger 1987.

Argyropelecus affinis   Garman 1899

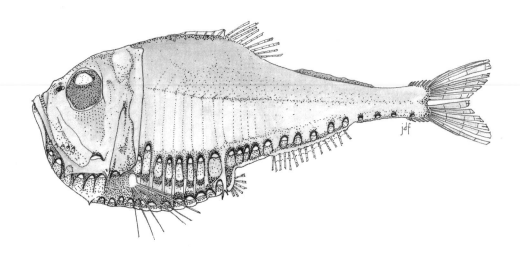

Argyropelecus affinis is short and moderately deep bodied, with a moderate-sized, vertical mouth and dorsally directed, tubular eyes. It is distinguished from the other species of the family by the following combination of characters. Jaws have relatively short, recurved teeth, with those of lower jaw slightly longer than those of upper jaw. Gill rakers on first arch number 18 to 20. Branchiostegal rays number 10, with 3 on epihyal. Upper preopercular spine is short, extending slightly beyond edge of preoperculum. Lower preopercular spine is long and curves anteriorly in adults. Dorsal blade is low (height is less than one-third length), is derived from seven dorsal fin radials, and exposed parts of posterior two radials are fused. Abdominal keel is shallow. Postabdominal spines are short and of equal length. Spinelets are absent along anterior margin of dorsal blade and on ventral keel. Pectoral fin has 10 to 12, dorsal fin has 9, pelvic fin has 6, and anal fin has 13 rays. Dorsal adipose fin is long based. ORB

is pigmented and directed toward eye lens. BR number 6, and OP number 3. IP number 6, PV number 12, and VAV number 4. OA are in two groups of 2 and 6 photophores. AC are in two loose aggregations of 6 and 4 photophores. VAV and AC photophores are discrete (do not share common photogenic mass). Vertebrae number 38 to 40. Color is dark on dorsal surface and silver on flank.

This species occurs worldwide in tropical to subtropical seas between 300 and 600 m and apparently is not a vertical migrator. In the western Atlantic it occurs off the southeastern United States, in the northern Gulf of Mexico, and off Venezuela. Food consists of copepods, ostracods, euphausiids, salps, and chaetognaths. Maximum known size is 72 mm SL.

REFERENCES: Schultz 1964; Bright and Pequegnat 1969; Baird 1971; Rass 1971; Murdy et al. 1983; Badcock 1984b.

Argyropelecus gigas   Norman 1930

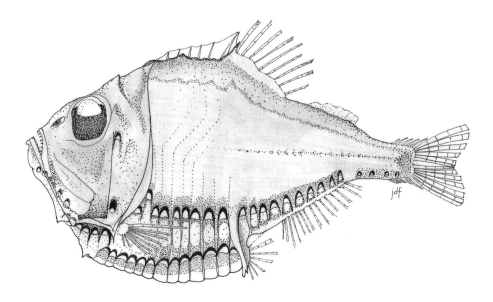

Argyropelecus gigas is short and deep bodied, with a moderately large, vertical mouth and dorsally directed, tubular eyes. It is distinguished from the other species of the family by the following combination of characters. Jaws have small, recurved teeth, with a pair of canines in premaxillae. Gill rakers of first arch are well developed and number 18 to 22. Branchiostegal rays number 10, with 3 on epihyal. Upper preopercular spine is short, extending posteriorly to operculum. Lower preopercular spine is long and curves anteriorly in adults. Dorsal blade is high (its height is greater than one-third its length), is derived from seven dorsal fin radials, and exposed parts of posterior two radials are fused. Abdominal keel is deep. Postabdominal spines are short and of equal length. Spinelets are absent on anterior margin of dorsal blade and on ventral keel. Pectoral fin has 10 or 11, dorsal fin has 9, pelvic fin has 6, and anal fin has 13 rays. Dorsal adipose fin is long based. ORB is pigmented. BR number 6, and OP number 3. IP number 6, PV number 12, and VAV number 4. OA are in two groups of 2 and 6 photophores. AC are in two loose aggregations of 6 and 4 photophores. VAV and AC photophores are discrete (do not share common photogenic mass). Vertebrae number 36 to 39. Color is dark dorsally and silvery on flank.

This species occurs worldwide in tropical to subtropical seas between 300 and 650 m and is not a vertical migrator. In the western Atlantic it occurs off the eastern seaboard of the United States, south of about 40°N, and in the Gulf of Mexico. Maximum known size is 120 mm SL.

REFERENCES: Schultz 1964; Bright and Pequegnat 1969; Baird 1971, 1986; Rass 1971; Murdy 1983; Badcock 1984b.

Argyropelecus hemigymnus   Cocco 1829

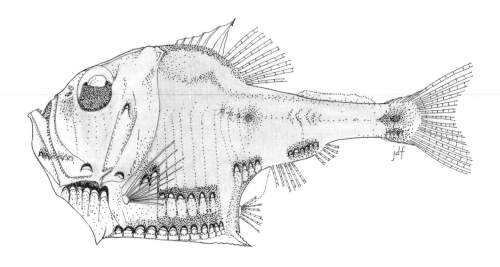

Argyropelecus hemigymnus is short and deep bodied, with a moderately large, vertical mouth and dorsally directed, tubular eyes. It is distinguished from the other species of the family by the following combination of characters. Jaws have small to minute teeth. Gill rakers of first arch are long and number 19 to 23. Branchiostegal rays number 10, with 3 on epihyal. Upper preopercular spine is long, extending beyond posterior margin of preoperculum. Lower preopercular spine is long and vertically directed. Dorsal blade is long, is derived from seven dorsal fin radials, and exposed parts of posterior two radials are fused and bear barbs. Abdominal keel is well developed. Single postabdominal spine has serrated edges and small posterodorsal spine. Spinelets are absent on anterior margin of dorsal blade and ventral keel. Pectoral fin has 10 or 11, dorsal fin has 8, pelvic fin has 6, and anal fin has 6 anterior and 5 posterior rays. Dorsal adipose fin has long base. ORB is pigmented and directed toward eye lens. BR number 6, and OP number 3. IP number 6, PV number 12, and VAV number 4. OA are in two groups of 2 and 6 photophores. AC are in two distinct groups of 6 and 4 photophores. VAV and AC_1 and AC_2 photophores are compound (share common photogenic mass). Vertebrae number 36 to 39. Color is dark dorsally and silvery on flank.

This species occurs worldwide in tropical to warm temperate seas between 50 and 800 m. In the western Atlantic it occurs off the eastern seaboard of the United States south of 40°N to the Gulf of Mexico and the Caribbean Sea, and off southern Brazil. Subadults and adults are captured between 200 and 800 m during the day and from 100 to 600 m during the night. Premetamorphic postlarvae occur from 50 to 300 m, and postmetamorphic postlarvae occur from 300 to 600 m. Food consists of calanoid copepods, ostracods, and small fishes. Life span appears to be slightly over one year. Spawning occurs throughout the year with peaks in early to midsummer throughout its range. Ripe eggs are 0.92 to 188 mm in diameter, and fecundity ranges from 50 to 500 eggs. Maximum known size is 28 mm SL for males and 39 mm SL for females.

REFERENCES: Schultz 1964; Bright and Pequegnat 1969; Baird 1971, 1986; Rass 1971; Murdy et al. 1983; Badcock 1984b; Howell and Krueger 1987.

Argyropelecus sladeni   Regan 1908

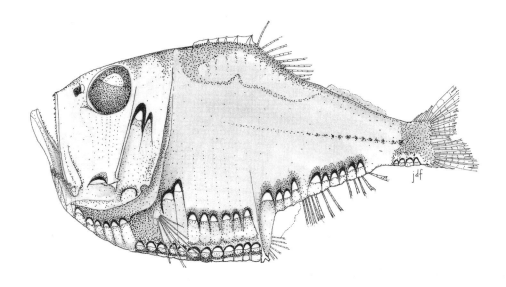

Argyropelecus sladeni is short and deep bodied, with a moderately large, vertical mouth and dorsally directed, tubular eyes. It is distinguished from the other species of the family by the following combination of characters. Jaws have small, recurved teeth. Gill rakers are of medium to long length and number 17 to 21. Branchiostegal rays number 10, with 3 on epihyal. Upper preopercular spine is long and usually directed posterodorsally. Lower preopercular spine is directed ventrally, or often ventroposteriorly. Dorsal blade is low (height is about 3 times length), is derived from seven dorsal fin radials, and exposed parts of posterior two radials are fused. Abdominal keel is well developed. Postabdominal spines are of equal size, one is directed anteroventrally and is blunt, and other is directed posteroventrally. Spinelets are absent on anterior margin of dorsal blade and on ventral keel. Pectoral fin has 10 or 11, dorsal fin has 9, pelvic fin has 6, and anal fin has 7 anterior and 5 posterior rays.

Dorsal adipose fin has long base. ORB is pigmented. BR number 6, and OP number 3. IP number 6, PV number 12, and VAV number 4. OA are in two groups of 2 and 6 photophores. AC are in two distinct groups of 6 and 4 photophores. VAV, AC_1, and AC_2 photophores are compound (share common photogenic masses). Vertebrae number 35 to 37. Color is dark dorsally and silvery on flank.

This species occurs worldwide in tropical to subtropical seas. In the western Atlantic it occurs off the eastern seaboard of the United States south of 45°N to 40°N, in the Straits of Florida, the northern and western Gulf of Mexico, the Caribbean Sea, and off the northern coast of South America to southern Brazil. It is mesopelagic from depths of 350 to 600 m during the day and 100 to 375 m during the night. Maximum known size is 60 mm SL.

REFERENCES: Schultz 1964; Baird 1971, 1986.

Maurolicus weitzmani   Parin and Kobyliansky 1993

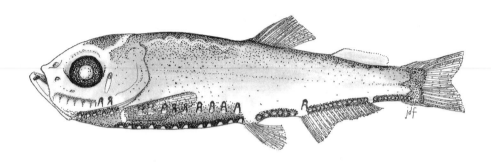

Maurolicus weitzmani is moderately elongated and moderately deep bodied, with a large head and laterally directed nontubular eyes. It is distinguished from the other species of the family by the following combination of characters. Teeth in upper jaw are minute and uniserial, and teeth in lower jaw are minute and biserial anteriorly and uniserial posteriorly. Gill rakers on first arch number 21 to 26. Branchiostegal rays number 10, with 3 on epihyal. Preoperculum lacks spines. Head length is 29.5% to 33%, eye diameter is 9.5% to 11.5%, upper jaw is 17% to 19%, and body depth is 22.5% to 25.5% of SL. Dorsal blade, abdominal keel, and postabdominal spines are absent. Dorsal fin origin is posterior to midlength. Pectoral fin has 17 or 18, dorsal fin has 9 to 12, pelvic fin has 7, and anal fin has 22 to 28 rays. Dorsal adipose fin is broad based. ORB is in front of eye. BR number 6, and OP number 3. IP number 6, PV number 12 or 13, and VAV number 6.

OA are in two groups of 2 and 7 photophores. AC number 22 to 26 (usually 23 or 24), and first photophore is elevated. Vertebrae number 32 or 33. Color is silvery with dorsal surface dark and with undulating dorsolateral light brown strip. Stomach and posterior aspect of intestine are not pigmented.

This species occurs in the tropical to warm temperate Atlantic Ocean. In the western Atlantic it occurs from the Bay of Fundy to the Gulf of Mexico. It is mesopelagic at 200 to 400 m during the day and in the upper 100 m during the night. Food consists of copepods and euphausiids. Maximum known size is 52 mm SL.

REFERENCES: Grey 1964; Rass 1971; Murdy et al. 1983; Badcock 1984b; Weitzman 1986b; Howell and Krueger 1987; Boschung 1992 (all above as *M. muelleri*); Parin and Kobyliansky 1996.

Polyipnus clarus   Harold 1994

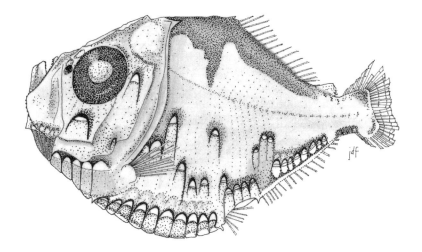

Polyipnus clarus is short and deep bodied, with a moderate-sized, vertical mouth and laterally directed, nontubular eyes. It is distinguished from the other species of the family by the following combination of characters. Jaws have minute teeth. Gill rakers are medium sized to large and number 19 to 21. Branchiostegal rays number 10. Preopercular spine is very short and triangulate. Dorsal blade is small and results from fusion between first dorsal radial and seventh supraneural. Abdominal keel is well defined. Postabdominal spines are distinct and directed posteroventrally. Spinelets are absent on anterior dorsal blade and on ventral keel. Pectoral fin has 13 to 15, dorsal fin has 15 or 16, pelvic fin has 7, and anal fin has 16 or 17 rays. Dorsal adipose fin has short base. ORB is pigmented and directed into eye. BR number 6, and OP number 3. IP number 6, PV number 10, and VAV number 5, with first elevated above others. OA are isolated or grouped at different levels: first two are located above pectoral fin base; third is dorsal to these; fourth, fifth, and sixth are located on lower abdomen; seventh is dorsal to fourth, fifth, and sixth; and last three are above anal fin. AC are in two distinct groups of 9 and 4 photophores. Vertebrae number 32 or 33. Color is dark dorsally and silvery on flank, with short, dark, triangular-shaped pigment bar extending from dorsum to one-half distance to midline, and dark pigment spots on lateral midline.

This species occurs in the western Atlantic from the Gulf of Maine, the Straits of Florida, the Gulf of Mexico, and the Caribbean Sea. It is mesopelagic between 39 and 833 m and most common between 300 and 400 m. Maximum known size is 56 mm SL.

REFERENCES: Schultz 1964; Bright and Pequegnat 1969; Baird 1971, 1986; Rass 1971; Murdy et al. 1983; Badcock 1984b (in part); Boschung 1992 (all as *P. asteroides*); Harold 1994.

Sonoda megalophthalma Grey 1959

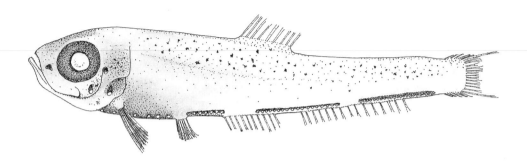

Sonoda megalophthalma is moderately elongate and moderately slender, with a moderately large mouth and laterally directed, nontubular eyes. It is distinguished from the other species of the family by the following combination of characters. Teeth are minute and uniserial in upper jaw, and bi- or triserial in anterior part of lower jaw. Gill rakers on first arch number 18 to 21, with 3 on epibranch. Preoperculum lacks spines. Dorsal blade, abdominal keel, and postabdominal spines are absent. Pectoral fin has 13 to 15, dorsal fin has 8 or 9, and anal fin has 8 or 9 anterior and 14 to 16 posterior rays. Dorsal adipose fin is absent. ORB is anteroventral to eye. BR number 6 or 7, and OP number 3. IP number 6, PV number 10, and VAV number 7 or 8. OV number 2, and VA number 4 or 5. AC are in two groups of 16 to 21 and 19 to 24 photophores. Vertebrae number 40. Color is light with scattering of black melanophores, except lower part of head, operculum, and abdomen are dark.

This species occurs in the western North Atlantic from the Gulf of Mexico and the Caribbean Sea off Nicaragua. It has been captured at depths of 503 and 548 m. Maximum known size is 60 mm SL.

REFERENCES: Grey 1964; Rass 1971; Weitzman 1986b.

Sternoptyx diaphana Hermann 1781

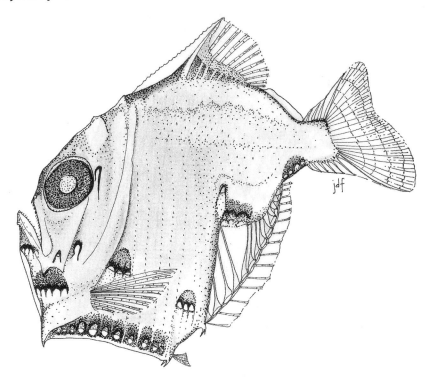

Sternoptyx diaphana is short and deep bodied, with a small, vertical mouth and laterally directed, nontubular eyes. It is distinguished from the other species of the family by the following combination of characters. Jaws have short teeth. Gill rakers on first arch number six to eight. Branchiostegal rays number 6, with 3 on epihyal. Preoperculum has single ventrally directed spine. Dorsal blade is derived from one supraneural and has serrated anterior projection. Abdominal keel is well defined. Postabdominal spines are well developed. Pectoral fin rays number 10 or 11. Dorsal fin is shorter than dorsal blade and has 9 to 11 rays. Dorsal adipose fin has long base. Anal fin rays number 13 to 15. Anterior anal radial is elongate and bears external spine. ORB is unpigmented and ventral to eye. BR number 3, and OP number 3. IP number 5, PV number 10, and VAV number 3. OA are in two groups of 1 and 3 photophores. VAV and AC are distinctly separated. First AC photophore is nearer to remainder of group than to midline of body. Vertebrae number 29 or 30. Color is dark dorsally and silvery on flank.

This species occurs worldwide in tropical to temperate seas between 300 and 1,100 m and apparently is not a vertical migrator. It is most abundant between 700 and 1,000 m, with smaller specimens located shallower than larger specimens. In the western Atlantic it occurs off the eastern seaboard of North America from south of 45°N to the Straits of Florida, the Gulf of Mexico, the Caribbean Sea, and off Brazil. Food consists of copepods, ostracods, euphausiids, amphipods, and fishes. Life span appears to be slightly over one year. Maximum known size is 46 mm SL in the Gulf of Mexico.

REFERENCES: Schultz 1964; Bright and Pequegnat 1969; Baird 1971, 1986; Rass 1971; Badcock and Baird 1980; Murdy et al. 1983; Badcock 1984b; Howell and Krueger 1987.

Sternoptyx pseudobscura Baird 1971

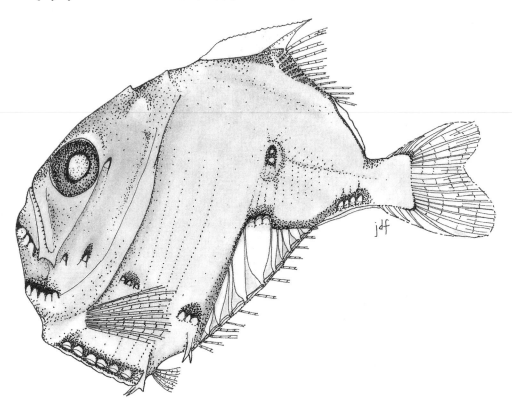

Sternoptyx pseudobscura is short and deep bodied, with a small, almost vertical mouth and laterally directed, nontubular eyes. It is distinguished from the other species of the family by the following combination of characters. Jaws have moderate-sized, recurved teeth. Gill rakers on first arch number seven to nine. Branchiostegal rays number 6, with 3 on epihyal. Preoperculum has single, ventrally directed spine. Dorsal blade is long, is about same length as dorsal fin, has serrated dorsal margin, and is derived from one supraneural. Abdominal keel is well developed. Postabdominal spines are well developed. Pectoral fin has 9 to 11, dorsal fin has 9 to 12, and anal fin has 13 to 15 rays. Anterior anal radial is long and bears external spine. Dorsal adipose fin has long base. ORB is unpigmented and ventral to eye. BR and OP each number 3. IP number 5, PV number 10, and VAV number 3. OA are in two groups of 1 and 3 photophores. AC are in two distinct groups of 3 and 4 photophores. First AC is located near trunk midline. Vertebrae number 28 to 31. Color is dark dorsally and silvery on flank.

This species occurs worldwide in tropical to subtropical seas between 800 and 1,500 m and apparently is not a vertical migrator. In the western Atlantic it occurs in the Straits of Florida, the northern Gulf of Mexico, the Caribbean Sea, and off Brazil. Food consists of copepods, ostracods, euphausiids, amphipods, and decapod crustaceans. Maximum known size is 55 mm SL.

REFERENCES: Schultz 1964; Baird 1971, 1986; Badcock and Baird 1980; Murdy et al. 1983; Badcock 1984b; Howell and Krueger 1987.

Valenciennellus tripunctulatus (Esmark 1871)

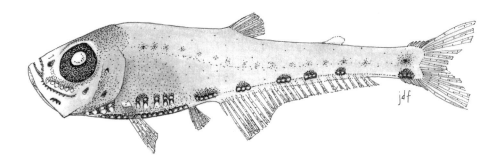

Valenciennellus tripunctulatus is moderately elongated and moderately slender, with a moderate-sized, nearly vertical mouth and dorsally directed, moderately tubular eyes. It is distinguished from the other species of the family by the following combination of characters. Teeth in premaxilla and lower jaw are minute and uniserial, and those in maxilla are larger and of unequal size. Gill rakers on first arch number 14 to 16. Branchiostegal rays number 10, with 3 on epihyal. Preoperculum lacks spines. Dorsal blade, abdominal keel, and post-abdominal spines are absent. Pectoral fin has 16 or 17, dorsal fin has 7 or 8, pelvic fin has 6 or 7, and anal fin has 24 or 25 rays. Dorsal adipose fin has relatively short base. ORB is anterior to eye. BR number 6, and OP number 3. IP are subdivided into two groups of 3 and 4 photophores, VP number 15 to 18, and VAV number 5. OA number 5, and AC are in three to six groups of generally 2 to 4 photophores, with posterior group comprised of 4 photophores. Vertebrae number 32 or 33. Head and abdomen are blackish brown, and back and tail are translucent. Series of distinct melanophores runs along dorsolateral aspect of flank.

This species occurs worldwide in tropical to temperate seas between 100 and 700 m and apparently is not a vertical migrator. It is most common between 351 and 550 m. In the western Atlantic it occurs from Bermuda and the eastern coast of Florida to the Gulf of Mexico and the Virgin Islands. Food consists of copepods and ostracods. Spawning may take place year-round. Fecundity ranges from 100 to 360 eggs. Life span appears to be about one year. Maximum known size is 35 mm SL in the Gulf of Mexico.

REFERENCES: Grey 1964; Rass 1971; Murdy et al. 1983; Badcock 1984b; Weitzman 1986b; Howell and Krueger 1987.

PHOSICHTHYIDAE Lightfishes

Lightfishes are moderately elongate to elongate, and moderately deep bodied to very slender, with a small to very large mouth and two rows of photophores. They are distinguished from the other families of the order by the following combination of characters. Upper jaw extends to midlength of eye or posterior to eye and bears fine teeth. Teeth in premaxilla are uniserial or biserial, and those of lower jaw are biserial anteriorly and uniserial posteriorly. Teeth are present or absent in vomer and palatine. Two supramaxillae are present on dorsal margin of maxilla. Chin barbel is absent. Branchiostegal rays number 10 to 21, with 4 to 7 on epihyal. Gill rakers are well developed in adults. Pectoral fin is located below midflank. Pelvic fin is located on abdomen. Dorsal fin origin is located near midlength and generally is anterior to pelvic fin insertion. Anal fin is located over posterior section of or behind dorsal fin base and ranges from equal in length to longer than dorsal fin base. Photophores are discrete (do not share photogenic masses) and are present on isthmus, near eye, on branchiostegal membrane, and in two rows on side of body.

Lightfishes occur worldwide, generally in mesopelagic or bathypelagic waters, although some are benthopelagic. Some species are diel vertical migrators, while others apparently do not migrate. Premetamorphic and metamorphic larvae are located near the surface. Food consists of zooplankton. All species are dioecious. There are about 18 species in seven genera, and 7 species in five genera occur in the Gulf of Mexico.

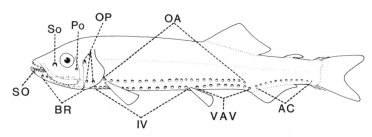

Generalized Phosichthyidae for Photophore ID (See p. 1073)

Key to the Species of the Gulf of Mexico
(Adapted from Badcock 1984c)

1a. Two orbital photophores, 1 So, 1 Po; teeth in premaxilla uniserial 2
1b. One So, no Po; teeth in premaxilla biserial. 6
2a. Anal fin origin over or slightly posterior to last dorsal fin ray; 8 or 9 BR 3
2b. Anal fin origin distinctly posterior to dorsal fin base; 11 to 18 BR . . . . *Ichthyococcus ovatus* p. 442

3a. Anal and dorsal fin bases about equal length; anal rays number 12 to 16; AC number 12 to 16, with 6 or 7 of these over anal fin base; IV level 4

3b. Anal fin base about twice length of dorsal fin base; anal fin rays number 22 to 30; AC number 19 to 21, with 13 to 15 of these over anal fin base; eighth and/or ninth IV elevated above others of series . . . . *Pollichthys mauli* p. 443

4a. Anus under seventh to ninth VAV; streak of black pigment at lower jaw symphysis; eyes laterally oriented and not tubular; interorbital width at least 13% of head length; head length equal to or greater than length of AC row; OA number 22 to 24. 5

4b. Anus under sixth or seventh VAV; no pigment at lower jaw symphysis; eye slightly tubular and directed dorsolaterally; interorbital width less than 11% of head length; head length less than length of AC row; OA number 21 to 23 . . . . *Vinciguerria attenuata* p. 445

5a. Pair of photophores at symphysis of lower jaw (in specimens greater than 20 mm); 21 to 23 gill rakers on first arch. . . . . *Vinciguerria nimbaria* p. 446

5b. No photophores at symphysis of lower jaw; 14 to 16 gill rakers on first arch . . . . *Vinciguerria poweriae* p. 447

6a. Body with two photophore rows; dorsal adipose fin present; 7 or 8 VAV; ninth or tenth IV elevated above others of series; 1 or 2 AC elevated; OA not extending to anal fin base; 12 to 14 dorsal fin rays . . . . *Polymetme corythaeola* p. 444

6b. Body with more than two photophore rows; dorsal adipose fin absent; 9 to 12 VAV; IV and AC level; OA extending to caudal fin base; 14 to 16 dorsal fin rays . . . . *Yarrella blackfordi* p. 448

Ichthyococcus ovatus   (Cocco 1838)

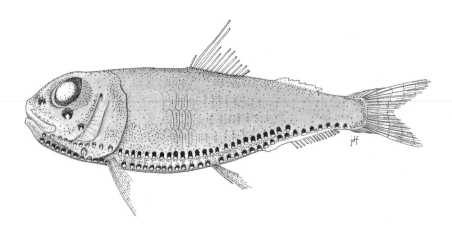

Ichthyococcus ovatus is relatively short and moderately deep bodied, with a relatively small mouth, large eyes, and two rows of photophores. It is distinguished from the other species of the family by the following combination of characters. Premaxillary teeth are uniserial, of uniform size, and small. Teeth in posterior section of maxilla are small, close together, and slanted posteriorly. Vomer has few minute teeth, and palatine lacks teeth. Pseudobranch is absent. Gill filaments are long and are not fused at base. Gill rakers on first arch number 20 to 25 and are of moderate length. Branchiostegal rays number 10, with 4 on epihyal. Dorsal adipose fin base is about equal to anal fin base. Very small ventral adipose fin precedes anal fin. Anus is closer to origin of anal fin than to pelvic fin insertion. Dorsal fin and anal fin bases are about equal in length. Dorsal fin has 11 or 12 rays, and anal fin has 15 to 17 rays. Last dorsal and anal fin rays are split to base. Photophores are absent from symphysis of lower jaw. So is located anterior to eye, and Po is located midventral to eye. OP number 3, and BR number 11 or 12. IV number 24 to 26, and VAV plus AC number 21 to 24. OA number 23 to 26. Vertebrae number 40 to 42. Color is dark on dorsal surface, scale pockets are edged with dark pigment, and peritoneum is silvery.

This species occurs in the subtropical Atlantic Ocean and the Mediterranean Sea. In the western Atlantic it occurs along the eastern seaboard of the United States from 40°N to Florida, off Bermuda, and in the Gulf of Mexico and the Caribbean Sea. Juveniles and adults are mainly captured between 200 and 500 m and apparently do not make diel migrations. Premetamorphic larvae are caught between the surface and 150 m, and postmetamorphic larvae are caught between 400 and 750 m. Spawning may take place year-round, with a peak in late spring to early summer. Maximum known size is 50 mm SL.

REFERENCES: Grey 1964; Rass 1971; Bekker et al. 1975; Mukhacheva 1980b; Murdy et al. 1983; Badcock 1984c; Schaefer et al. 1986a.

Pollichthys mauli (Poll 1953)

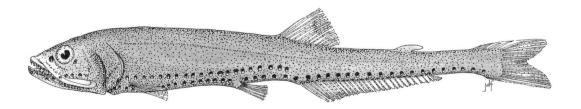

Pollichthys mauli is long and very slender, with a large mouth, small eyes, and two rows of photophores. It is distinguished from the other species of the family by the following combination of characters. Premaxillary teeth are uniserial, and consist of evenly spaced, moderately large teeth separated by one or two smaller teeth. Teeth on posterior section of maxilla are similar to those on premaxilla except that smaller teeth are relatively larger than those of premaxilla. Vomer has few or no teeth, and palatine has short row of small teeth. Gill filaments are moderately long and are not fused at base. Gill rakers on first arch number 4 to 6 on epibranch and 11 to 13 on lower limb. Branchiostegal rays number 12, with 4 on epihyal. Dorsal adipose fin base is rather long. Anus is closer to anal fin origin than to pelvic fin insertion. Dorsal fin is anterior to anal fin, and dorsal fin base is considerably shorter than anal fin base. Dorsal fin rays number 10 to 12, and anal fin rays number 24 to 26. Last dorsal and anal fin rays are usually split to base. Photophores are present at symphysis of lower jaw. So is located anterior to eye, and Po is located posterolateral to eye. OP number 3, and BR number 8. IV number 21 or 22, and VAV number 7 to 9. OA number 19 to 21, and AC number 18 to 21.

This species occurs worldwide in tropical to subtropical seas. In the western Atlantic it occurs from the eastern seaboard of the United States from about 40°N to the Bahamas, southern Florida, the Gulf of Mexico, and the Caribbean Sea. Juveniles and adults are generally caught between 300 and 600 m during the day and from the surface to 200 m at night. Premetamorphic postlarvae are generally caught near the surface. Food consists of euphausiids. Spawning takes place during the summer. Maximum known size is 60 mm SL.

REFERENCES: Grey 1959, 1964; Rass 1971; Bekker et al. 1975; Murdy et al. 1983; Badcock 1984c; Schaefer et al. 1986a; Boschung 1992.

Polymetme corythaeola   (Alcock 1898)

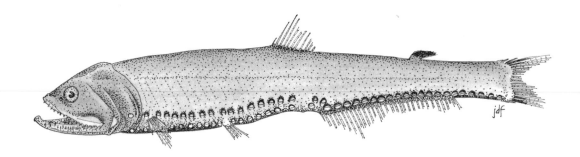

Polymetme corythaeola is long and slender, with a large mouth, moderate-sized eyes, and two rows of photophores. It is distinguished from the other species of the family by the following combination of characters. Premaxillary teeth are biserial, with teeth of outer row straight and of unequal length, and those of inner row curved inwardly. Teeth in posterior section of maxilla are widely spaced, erect, and increasingly larger posteriorly. Vomer has one to three teeth on each side, and palatine has row of three to six teeth. Gill filaments are of moderate length and are not fused at base. Gill rakers on first arch number 16 or 17. Branchiostegal rays number 13, with 4 on epihyal. Dorsal adipose fin is short based. Anus is closer to anal fin origin than to pelvic fin insertion. Dorsal fin origin is anterior to anal fin origin, and dorsal fin base is less than one-half anal fin base. Dorsal fin rays number 12 to 14, and anal fin rays number 30 to 33. Last dorsal and anal fin rays are split to base. Photophores are present at symphysis of lower jaw. So is located an-teroventral to eye. OP number 3, and BR number 9 or 10. IV number 21, with tenth elevated above others, and VAV number 8. OA number 17, and AC number 24 or 25, with 17 or 18 over anal fin base. Glandular tissue is present on iris of eye. Vertebrae number 43 to 45. Color is dark dorsally and silvery on flank.

This species occurs worldwide in tropical to subtropical seas. In the western Atlantic it occurs off the eastern seaboard of the United States from about 40°N to southern Florida, the Gulf of Mexico, the Caribbean Sea, and southward to the equatorial coast of South America. Juveniles and adults are found from 165 to 760 m but are generally caught from 300 to 500 m. This species probably does not make diel vertical migrations. Maximum known size is 216 mm SL.

REFERENCES: Grey 1964; Rass 1971; Murdy et al. 1983; Badcock 1984c; Schaefer et al. 1986a; Boschung 1992.

Vinciguerria attenuata   (Cocco 1838)

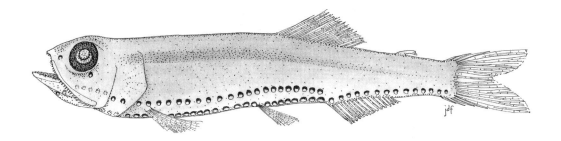

Vinciguerria attenuata is moderately elongate and moderately slender, with a large mouth, slightly tubular eyes, and two rows of photophores. It is distinguished from the other species of the family by the following combination of characters. Premaxillary teeth are uniserial, with several moderately long teeth separated by short teeth. Teeth on posterior section of maxilla are evenly spaced and moderately long, and they slightly increase in size posteriorly. Vomer has one small tooth on each side, and palatine has three or four teeth. Gill filaments are relatively long and are not fused at base. Gill rakers on first arch number 5 on epibranch and 14 or 15 on lower limb. Branchiostegal rays number 12, with 4 on epihyal. Dorsal adipose fin has short base. Anus is closer to anal fin origin than to pelvic fin insertion. Dorsal fin origin is anterior to anal fin origin, and dorsal fin base is about equal to anal fin base. Dorsal fin rays number 13 to 15, and anal fin rays number 13 to 16. Photophores are absent on symphysis of lower jaw. So is located anterior to eye, and Po is located posteroventral to eye. OP number 3, and BR number 8. IV number 22 to 24, and VAV number 7 to 10. OA number 21 to 23, and AC number 12 to 14. Color is dark dorsally and silvery on flank. Lower jaw symphysis, premaxilla, and fin rays lack pigment streaks.

This species occurs worldwide in tropical to warm temperate seas. In the western Atlantic it occurs from the eastern seaboard of the United States from about 40°N to the equator, including the Gulf of Mexico and the Caribbean Sea. Juveniles and adults are most commonly captured between 250 and 300 m. Premetamorphic postlarvae are most frequently captured from 250 to 300 m. Metamorphic postlarvae are generally taken between 300 and 700 m. Food consists of copepods. Peak spawning occurs in early spring to summer. Maximum known size is 46 mm SL.

REFERENCES: Grey 1964; Bekker et al. 1975; Badcock 1984c; Schaefer et al. 1986a.

Vinciguerria nimbaria (Jordan and Williams 1895)

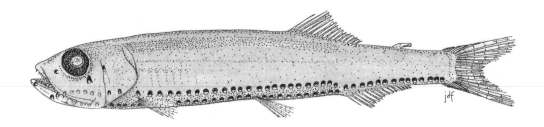

Vinciguerria nimbaria is moderately elongate and moderately slender, with a large mouth, moderate-sized nontubular eyes, and two rows of photophores. It is distinguished from the other species of the family by the following combination of characters. Premaxillary teeth are uniserial, widely spaced, and of unequal length. Teeth in posterior section of maxilla are slightly larger than premaxillary teeth and are of unequal size. Vomer has one or two minute teeth on each side, and palatine has short row of minute teeth. Gill filaments are relatively long and are not fused at base. Gill rakers on first arch number 6 or 7 on epibranch and 15 to 17 on lower limb. Branchiostegal rays number 11. Dorsal adipose fin has short base. Anus is closer to anal fin origin than to pelvic fin insertion. Dorsal fin origin is anterior to anal fin origin, and dorsal fin base is about equal to anal fin base. Dorsal fin rays number 13 to 15, and anal fin rays number 13 to 16. Photophores are absent on symphysis of lower jaw. So is located anterior to eye, and Po is located ventral to eye.

OP number 3, and BR number 8. IV number 22 or 23, and VAV number 9 to 11. OA number 23 or 24, and AC number 13 or 14. Color of dorsal surface is dark, and flank is silvery. Symphysis of lower jaw is streaked with dark pigment, and premaxilla is pigmented.

This species occurs worldwide in tropical to warm temperate seas. In the western Atlantic it occurs along the eastern seaboard of the United States from about 42°N to the Gulf of Mexico and the Caribbean Sea. Juveniles and adults are generally captured between 200 and 400 m during the day and in the upper 100 m at night. Premetamorphic postlarvae occur in the upper 50 m, and postmetamorphic postlarvae are most frequent between 300 and 400 m. Food consists of copepods. Maximum known size is 48 mm SL.

REFERENCES: Grey 1964; Rass 1971; Murdy et al. 1983; Badcock 1984c; Schaefer et al. 1986a.

Vinciguerria poweriae (Cocco 1838)

Vinciguerria poweriae is moderately elongate and moderately slender, with a large mouth, large nontubular eyes, and two rows of photophores. It is distinguished from the other species of the family by the following combination of characters. Premaxillary teeth are uniserial, widely spaced, and of unequal length. Teeth in posterior section of maxilla are slightly larger than those of premaxilla and of unequal size. Vomer has very small teeth on each side, and palatine has four small teeth. Gill filaments are relatively long and are not fused at base. Gill rakers on first arch number 3 or 4 on epibranch and 11 to 14 on lower limb. Branchiostegal rays number 11. Dorsal adipose fin has short base. Anus is closer to anal fin base than to pelvic fin insertion. Dorsal fin is slightly anterior to anal fin, and dorsal fin base is slightly longer than anal fin base. Dorsal fin rays number 13 to 15, and anal fin rays number 12 to 14. Photophores are absent at symphysis of lower jaw. So is located anterior to eye, and Po is located posteroventral to eye. OP number 3, and BR number 8. IV number 22 to 24, and VAV number 8 to 10. OA number 22 to 24, and AC number 12 to 14. Color is dark dorsally and silvery on flank, with pigment streak above premaxilla and, in specimens 20 mm SL and larger, with one at lower jaw symphysis.

This species occurs worldwide in tropical to warm temperate seas. In the western Atlantic it occurs off the eastern seaboard of the United States from about 43°N to the Gulf of Mexico and the Caribbean Sea. Juveniles and adults occur between 300 and 600 m by day and from 50 to 350 m at night. Premetamorphic larvae occur in the upper 100 m, and postmetamorphic larvae are found between 350 and 600 m. Food consists of copepods. Spawning mainly takes place in spring and summer. Maximum known size is 43 mm SL.

REFERENCES: Grey 1964; Rass 1971; Bekker et al. 1975; Murdy et al. 1983; Badcock 1984c; Schaefer et al. 1986a, Boschung 1992.

Yarrella blackfordi   Goode and Bean 1896

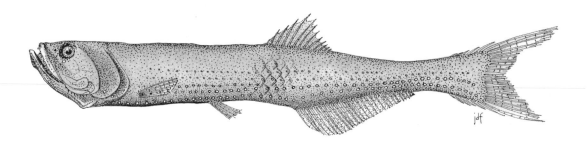

Yarrella blackfordi is elongate and slender, with a large mouth, moderate-sized nontubular eyes, and five rows of photophores. It is distinguished from the other species of the family by the following combination of characters. Premaxillary teeth are biserial; outer row consists of widely spaced, moderately large teeth separated by several very small teeth, and inner row consists of evenly sized and spaced teeth curved inwardly. Teeth on posterior section of maxilla are moderate sized, evenly spaced, inwardly curved, and separated by small teeth. Vomer has one to three small teeth on each side, and palatine has row of three to five teeth. Gill filaments are of moderate length and are not fused at base. Gill rakers on first arch number 6 or 7 on epibranch and 12 to 14 on lower limb. Branchiostegal rays number 14 to 16. Dorsal adipose fin is absent. Anus is closer to anal fin origin than to pelvic fin insertion. Dorsal fin is anterior to anal fin, and dorsal fin base is shorter than anal fin base. Dorsal fin rays number 14 to 17, and anal fin rays number 28 to 31. Photophores are lacking from symphysis. So is located anterior to eye. OP number 3, and BR number 12 to 13. IV number 12 or 13, and VAV number 12. OA extend to base of caudal fin and number 52 or 53. AC number 25 to 27. Three rows of small photophores are located dorsal to lateral row of photophores. Dorsalmost row of photophores extends to pelvic fin insertion; second and third rows extend to caudal fin base. Color is uniform blackish, including lining of mouth and gill covers, and branchiostegal membranes.

This species occurs in the tropical and subtropical Atlantic. In the western Atlantic it occurs from the Straits of Florida, the Gulf of Mexico, and the Caribbean Sea off Cuba and Colombia. It is frequently captured from 380 to 732 m at or near the bottom. All specimens have been captured in bottom trawls. Based on a single individual, this species feeds on crustaceans. Maximum known size is 322 mm SL.

REFERENCES: Grey 1964; Rass 1971; Schaefer et al. 1986a.

ASTRONESTHIDAE Snaggletooths

Snaggletooths are elongate, moderately slender to slender, and compressed, with a terminal, horizontal mouth and a chin barbel. They are distinguished from the other families of the order by the following combination of characters. Snout is short, and mouth is very large and generally with stout, fanglike teeth. Premaxilla is in contact with maxilla. Narrow supramaxilla is located on posterodorsal margin of maxilla. Vomer and palatine bear teeth. Pectoral fin is located below midflank. Dorsal fin origin is posterior to pelvic fin insertion but distinctly anterior to anal fin origin. Pelvic fin is located on abdomen or on flank above abdomen. Dorsal adipose fin is present. Scales and hexagonal markings on body, possibly representing scale pockets, are absent. Two rows of prominent photophores are present on body. AC runs from over anal fin base to caudal fin base. PV series and VAV series are not continuous. Numerous small photophores are located over head and body, and luminescent tissue is located on head and body of some species. Postorbital light organ (Po) consists of single or double photophores and is located posterior to eye.

Snaggletooths occur worldwide in mesopelagic waters. They are most common below 500 m, but some apparently migrate near or to the surface at night. Some may be benthopelagic as adults. Food consists of crustaceans and fishes. There are about 35 species in five genera, and 11 of these in three genera occur in the Gulf of Mexico.

Key to the Species of the Gulf of Mexico
(Adapted from Gibbs 1964a; Goodyear and Gibbs 1970; Gibbs 1984a)

1a. Ventral series of photophores arranged in regular continuous row; PV fewer than 27; OV fewer than 25 2
1b. Ventral series of photophores arranged in one to five irregular groups; PV more than 32; OV more than 33
. . . . *Heterophotus ophistoma* p. 461
2a. Teeth on maxilla slender, distinctly separate, and not slanting posteriorly 3
2b. Teeth on maxilla comblike, closely spaced, and slanting posteriorly 4
3a. AC curved dorsally posterior to anal fin base; VAL fewer than 18 . . . . *Borostomias elucens* p. 459
3b. AC straight, not curved dorsally posterior to anal fin base; VAL usually 19 or more. . . *Borostomias mononema* p. 460
4a. Serial photophores few and relatively widely spaced; 5 or 6 OV and 7 or 8 VAL; 5 IP, 6 PV, and 7 or 8 VAV; 7 AC
. . . . *Astronesthes indicus* p. 453

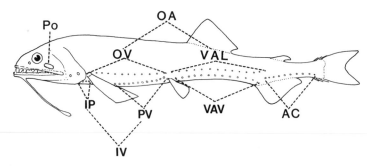

Generalized Astronesthidae for Photophore ID (See p. 1073)

4b. Serial photophores numerous and closely spaced, at least 11 OV and 17 VAL; 8 IP, 10 PV, and 13 VAV; 9 AC. 5
5a. IP forming U-shaped curve near pectoral fin base. 6
5b. IP forming straight line or slightly curved over pectoral fin base 7
6a. Dorsal fin with 18 or more rays; tip of chin barbel without swelling (Fig. 76); operculum of large specimens covered with patch of white luminous tissue . . . . *Astronesthes macropogon* p. 454
6b. Dorsal fin with 17 or fewer rays; tip of chin barbel with elongate swelling (Fig. 77); operculum of large specimens covered by little or no white luminous tissue . . . . *Astronesthes niger* p. 456
7a. Chin barbel very small (Fig. 78); body silvery colored . . . .*Astronesthes micropogon* p. 455
7b. Chin barbel well developed; body colored black. 8
8a. Chin barbel without terminal bulb or swelling (Fig. 79); dorsal fin origin distinctly posterior to pelvic fin insertion . . . . *Astronesthes richardsoni* p. 457
8b. Chin barbel with terminal bulb or flattened tip; dorsal fin origin over or slightly posterior to pelvic fin insertion . . . 9
9a. Chin barbel with flattened, leaflike tip (Fig. 80) . . . .*Astronesthes cyclophotus* p. 451
9b. Chin barbel with terminal bulb 10
10a. Bulb of chin barbel uniformly colored and with two filaments arising from sides (Fig. 81); 23 to 25 VAL; 21 to 24 VAV; 11 to 14 dorsal fin rays . . . .*Astronesthes similus* p. 458
10b. Bulb of chin barbel darkly pigmented on ventral half and lightly pigmented on dorsal half, and without filaments on sides (Fig. 82); 25 to 29 VAL; 26 to 28 VAV; 15 to 17 dorsal fin rays . . . . *Astronesthes gemmifer* p. 452

FIG 76

FIG 77

FIG 78

FIG 79

FIG 80

FIG 81

FIG 82

Astronesthes cyclophotus   Regan and Trewavas 1929

Astronesthes cyclophotus is moderately elongate and moderately slender, with enlarged, fanglike teeth in the jaws and a chin barbel possessing a terminal leaflike structure. It is distinguished from the other species of the family by the following combination of characters. Snout is not upturned at tip. Chin barbel is flattened distally into narrow fragile structure that tapers to acute point. Maxillary teeth are comblike and number about 20. Gill rakers are replaced by groups of short teeth. Vomer has one tooth on each side, and palatine has four to six teeth. Dorsal fin origin is slightly posterior to pelvic fin insertion, and anal fin origin is under insertion of dorsal fin base. Dorsal fin has 15 or 16, anal fin has 12 to 15, pectoral fin has 8 or 9, and pelvic fin has 7 rays. Serial photophores are in unbroken, more or less straight line. IP number 9 or 10, PV number 17 to 19, and VAV number 17 or 18. OV number 15 to 18, and VAL number 18 to 20. AC number 11 or 12. Po organ is very small and located near edge of fleshy orbit. Luminous patches occur on head. Color is black except for barbel that is pale and has few melanophores.

This species occurs in the North Atlantic Ocean in subtropical to temperate seas and has been captured between the surface and 140 m at night. Food consists of copepods, euphausiids, and ostracods. In the western Atlantic it occurs in the northeastern Gulf of Mexico. Maximum known size is 61 mm SL.

REFERENCES: Morrow and Gibbs 1964; Sutton and Hopkins 1996, in press.

Astronesthes gemmifer   Goode and Bean 1896

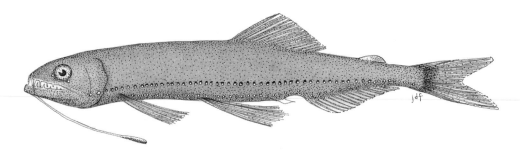

Astronesthes gemmifer is moderately elongate and moderately slender, with enlarged, fang-like teeth in the jaws and a long, slender chin barbel. It is distinguished from the other species of the family by the following combination of characters. Snout is not upturned at tip. Chin barbel is long and slender and slightly to considerably longer than head. Tip of barbel is expanded to form spoon-shaped bulb that is darkly pigmented ventrally and pale dorsally. Maxillary teeth are comblike, closely spaced, slanted posteriorly, and number 36 to 45. Gill rakers are replaced by groups of short teeth. Vomer has one tooth on each side, and palatine has 9 to 12 teeth. Dorsal fin origin is slightly posterior to insertion of pelvic fin, and distance from dorsal fin origin to caudal fin base is 50% to 55% of SL. Dorsal fin has 15 to 17 rays, and anal fin has 16 to 19 rays. Serial photophores are not broken into small groups, and those of ventral row curve only slightly on base of pectoral fin. IP number 10 to 12, PV number 15 to 18, and VAV number 26 to 28. OV number 17 to 19, and VAL number 25 to 29. AC number 9 to 11. Po organ is much smaller than eye and is located near edge of fleshy orbit. Luminous patches are lacking from top of head and from body. Color is black.

This species occurs worldwide in tropical to temperate seas from the surface to 2,400 m. In the western Atlantic it occurs along the Atlantic seaboard of North America from 44°25′N southward to Bermuda, the Gulf of Mexico, and the Caribbean Sea. Young specimens are generally captured near the surface. Maximum known size is 170 mm SL.

REFERENCES: Gibbs 1964a, 1984a; Rass 1971.

Astronesthes indicus Brauer 1902

Astronesthes indicus is moderately elongate and moderately slender, with enlarged, fanglike teeth in jaws and a long, slender chin barbel. It is distinguished from the other species of the family by the following combination of characters. Snout is not upturned at tip. Chin barbel is long and slender, from slightly shorter than to about one and one-half times head length. Tip of barbel is expanded in form of thin flaps or moderately swollen bulb, bearing either longitudinal crease or thin lateral flaps. Maxillary teeth are comblike, closely spaced, slanted posteriorly, and number 16 to 24. Gill rakers are replaced with groups of small teeth. Vomer has one tooth on each side, and palatine has 8 to 12 teeth. Dorsal fin origin is distinctly posterior to pelvic fin insertion, and distance from dorsal fin origin to caudal fin base is 40% to 45% of SL. Dorsal fin has 14 to 17 rays, and anal fin has 13 to 16 rays. Ventral adipose fin is located anterior to anus. Serial photophores are not broken into small groups but are few in number, and those of ventral row are curved only slightly over base of pectoral fin. IP number 5, PV number 5, and VAV number 7 to 9. OV number 5 or 6, and VAL number 6 to 8. AC number 7 to 9. Po organ is minute. Large specimens possess luminous patches on dorsal and ventral aspects of operculum and over pelvic fin. Color is black.

This species occurs in tropical and subtropical seas worldwide, generally between the surface and 100 m, but it has been captured to 2,000 m. Most specimens are captured at night from the surface to 100 m. In the western Atlantic it occurs in the Gulf of Mexico and the Caribbean Sea. Food consists of euphausiids and copepods. Maximum known size is 100 mm SL.

REFERENCES: Gibbs 1964a, 1984a, 1986b; Rass 1971; Sutton and Hopkins in press.

Astronesthes macropogon Goodyear and Gibbs 1970

Astronesthes macropogon is moderately elongate and moderately slender, with enlarged, fanglike teeth in the jaws and a moderately long, slender chin barbel. It is distinguished from the other species of the family by the following combination of characters. Snout is not upturned at tip. Chin barbel is about one-half head length. Tip of barbel is slightly swollen in large specimens but lacks swelling in small specimens. Maxillary teeth are comblike, closely spaced, and slanted posteriorly. Gill rakers are replaced by 15 to 19 groups of teeth. Vomer teeth are weakly developed or absent, and palatine teeth number two to seven. Dorsal fin origin is distinctly posterior to insertion of pelvic fin, and distance from dorsal fin origin to caudal fin base is 39% to 51% of SL. Dorsal fin has 18 to 21 rays, and anal fin has 13 to 15 rays. Ventral adipose fin is located anterior to anus. Photophores are small and not broken into small groups, and those of ventral row form a U-shaped curve near base of pectoral fin. IP number 8 to 10, PV number 12 to 15, and VAV number 17 to 20. OV number 12 to 15, and VAL number 19 to 22. AC number 9 to 11. Po organ is small and located near orbital margin. Luminous patches are developed on operculum and nostrils, and occasionally on dorsum between head and dorsal fin. Color is dark.

This species occurs in the Atlantic Ocean between 30°N and 30°S, including the Gulf of Mexico, and is generally associated with land masses. It has been captured from the surface to 2,000 m but is most frequently captured between the surface and 500 m. Food consists of euphausiids and fishes. Maximum known size is 139 mm SL.

REFERENCES: Goodyear and Gibbs 1970; Bekker et al. 1975; Gibbs 1984a; Sutton and Hopkins in press.

Astronesthes micropogon Goodyear and Gibbs 1970

Astronesthes micropogon is moderately elongate and moderately slender, with enlarged, fanglike teeth in the jaws and a minute chin barbel. It is distinguished from the other species of the family by the following combination of characters. Snout is not upturned at tip. Chin barbel is less than 1 mm long and tapers to a point. Maxillary teeth are comblike, closely spaced, and slanted posteriorly. Gill rakers are replaced by 13 to 18 groups of small teeth. Teeth on vomer are well developed, and palatine teeth number two to seven. Dorsal fin origin is over pelvic fin insertion, and distance from dorsal fin origin to caudal peduncle is 40.5% to 50.4% of SL. Dorsal fin has 17 to 20 rays, and anal fin has 14 to 16 rays. Ventral adipose fin is located anterior to anus. Serial photophores are not broken into small groups and are relatively large; those of ventral row are curved very slightly near base of pectoral fin. IP number 8 to 10, PV number 13 to 15, and VAV number 17 to 21. OV number 13 to 15, and VAL number 18 to 21. AC number 10 to 12. Color is silvery.

This species occurs in the Atlantic Ocean between 30°N and 10°S, including the Gulf of Mexico and the Caribbean Sea, and is associated with oceanic rather than continental waters. In the Gulf of Mexico it is known from 25°02′N to 29°06′N and 79°48′W to 88°18′W. It has been captured from the surface to 700 m. Food consists of euphausiids and myctophids. Maximum known size is 79 mm SL.

REFERENCES: Goodyear and Gibbs 1970; Gibbs 1984a; Sutton and Hopkins in press.

Astronesthes niger   Richardson 1845

Astronesthes niger is moderately elongate and moderately slender, with enlarged, fanglike teeth in the jaws and a long, slender chin barbel. It is distinguished from the other species of the genus by the following combination of characters. Snout is not upturned at tip. Chin barbel is slightly less than, to 1.7 times, head length. Distal one-third to one-half of barbel is swollen. Maxillary teeth are comblike, closely spaced, slanted posteriorly, and number 11 to 17. Gill rakers are replaced with groups of small teeth. Vomer has single tooth on each side, and palatine usually has 4 or 5 prominent teeth and 6 to 10 small teeth. Dorsal fin origin is slightly to moderately posterior to pelvic fin insertion, and distance from dorsal fin origin to caudal fin base is 46% to 57% of SL. Dorsal fin has 15 to 17 rays, and anal fin has 12 to 15 rays. Ventral adipose fin is located anterior to anus. Serial photophores are not broken into small groups, and those of ventral row form U-shaped pattern near base of pectoral fin. IP number 8 or 9, PV number 12 to 15, and VAV number 18 to 21. OV number 13 to 15, and VAL number 19 to 22. AC number 10 to 12. Po organ is smaller than eye and located near rim of fleshy orbit. Luminescent patches occur on head anterior to eye, on upper jaw above nares, above eye, on body above pectoral fin, and above lateral photophore row. Color is black.

This species occurs worldwide in tropical to subtropical seas between the surface and 1,000 m, but is most commonly captured between the surface and 100 m at night. In the western Atlantic it occurs along the eastern seaboard of North America from about 40°N to the equator, including the Gulf of Mexico and the Caribbean Sea. Food consists of euphausiids, amphipods, and myctophids. Maximum known size is 160 mm SL.

REFERENCES: Gibbs 1964a, 1984a, 1986b; Rass 1971; Sutton and Hopkins in press.

Astronesthes richardsoni   (Poey 1852)

Astronesthes richardsoni is moderately elongate and moderately slender, with enlarged, fanglike teeth in the jaws and a moderately long chin barbel. It is distinguished from the other species of the family by the following combination of characters. Snout is not upturned at tip. Chin barbel is one-half to slightly greater than one-half head length. Tip of barbel is not expanded. Maxillary teeth are closely spaced, slanted posteriorly, and number 11 to 18. Gill rakers are replaced by groups of small teeth. Vomer has 1 small tooth on each side, and palatine has up to 4 small teeth anteriorly. Dorsal fin is distinctly posterior to pelvic fin insertion, and distance from dorsal fin origin to caudal fin base is 43% to 46% of SL. Dorsal fin has 12 to 14 rays, and anal fin has 13 to 18 rays. Ventral adipose fin is located anterior to anus. Serial photophores are not broken into small groups, and those of ventral row are straight.

IP number 10 or 11, PV number 15 to 27, and VAV number 19 to 22. OV number 14 or 15, and VAL number 19 to 22. AC number 11 or 12. Po organ is considerably smaller than eye and is located on margin of fleshy orbit. Luminous patches are present on margin of preoperculum. Color is black.

This species occurs in the tropical Atlantic Ocean between the surface and 1,000 m, and is most abundant between the surface and 300 m. In the western Atlantic it has been captured in the western Gulf of Mexico (20°48′N, 95°48′W) and the Caribbean Sea. Food consists of euphausiids and fishes. Maximum known size is 145 mm SL.

REFERENCES: Gibbs 1964a; Bekker et al. 1975; Murdy et al. 1983; Sutton and Hopkins in press.

Astronesthes similus   Parr 1927

Astronesthes similus is moderately elongate and moderately slender, with enlarged, fanglike teeth in the jaws and a relatively long, slender chin barbel. It is distinguished from the other species of the family by the following combination of characters. Snout is not upturned at tip. Chin barbel is about equal to one and one-fourth times head length. Tip of barbel is expanded into bulb, is longer than it is wide, and bears two filaments originating at about one-half bulb length. Maxillary teeth are comblike, closely spaced, slanted posteriorly, and number 15 to 22. Gill rakers are replaced by groups of small teeth. Vomer has 1 or 2 small teeth on each side, and palatine has 4 or 5 small teeth anteriorly. Dorsal fin origin is moderately posterior to insertion of pelvic fin, and distance from dorsal fin origin to caudal fin base is 49% to 52% of SL. Dorsal fin has 11 to 14 rays, and anal fin has 18 to 21 rays. Ventral adipose fin is located anterior to anus. Serial photophores are not broken into small groups, and those of ventral row are straight. IP number 10 or 11, PV number 15 to 17, and VAV number 21 to 24. OV number 15 to 17, and VAL number 23 to 25. AC number 10 to 12. Po organ is much smaller than eye and located near margin of fleshy orbit. Luminous patches are absent on head and body. Color is black.

This species occurs in the western Atlantic Ocean in the eastern Gulf of Mexico and the Caribbean Sea. It has been captured from the surface to 850 m but is most frequently encountered between the surface and 200 m. Food consists of myctophids. Maximum known size is 150 mm SL.

REFERENCES: Parr 1927b; Regan and Trewavas 1929; Gibbs 1964a; Rass 1971; Murdy et al. 1983.

Borostomias elucens (Brauer 1906)

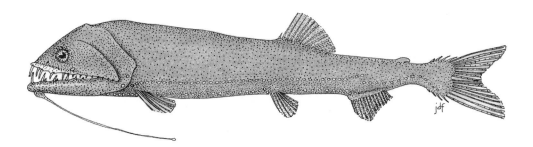

Borostomias elucens is moderately elongate and moderately slender, with enlarged, fang-like teeth in the jaws and a long, slender chin barbel. It is distinguished from the other species of the family by the following combination of characters. Chin barbel is about one and one-half times head length. Tip of barbel is expanded into an elongate bulb that is spherical to twice as long as it is wide, and rarely has one or two filaments. Fanglike jaw teeth are straight and relatively larger than other jaw teeth. Maxillary teeth are widely spaced and erect, with first only slightly smaller than last premaxillary tooth, and number 8 to 10. Gill rakers are replaced by one to several groups of small teeth. Vomer has small tooth on each side, and palatine has 9 teeth. Dorsal fin origin is over or slightly posterior to pelvic fin insertion, and distance from dorsal fin origin to cau-dal fin base is 45% to 48% of SL. Dorsal fin has 13 or 14 rays, and anal fin has 13 to 16 rays. Ventral adipose fin is absent. Serial photophores are not broken up into small groups, and those of ventral row are straight. IP number 10 to 12, PV number 22 or 23, and VAV number 14 or 15. OV number 21 to 27, and VAL number 15 or 16. AC number 12 to 14. Po organ is single, equal to or slightly shorter than eye, and sometimes obscured by black pigment. Color is black except bulb of chin barbel is white.

This species occurs worldwide in tropical seas between 250 and 1,650 m. In the western Atlantic it occurs in the Gulf of Mexico and the Caribbean Sea. Maximum known size is 350 mm SL.

REFERENCES: Gibbs 1964a, 1984a; Rass 1971.

Borostomias mononema   (Regan and Trewavas 1929)

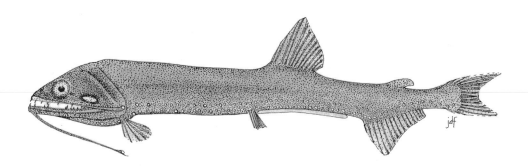

Borostomias mononema is moderately elongate and moderately slender, with enlarged, fanglike teeth in the jaws and a moderately long chin barbel. It is distinguished from the other species by the following combination of characters. Chin barbel is slightly less than head length. Tip of barbel consists of bulbous black proximal part and narrow pale distal part, usually with one or more filaments. Bulb is less than twice as long as it is wide. Fanglike teeth of jaws are slightly larger than other jaw teeth and are curved. Maxillary teeth are widely spaced, slightly curved anteriorly, and number 10 to 12. Gill rakers are replaced by several groups of small teeth. Dorsal fin is slightly posterior to insertion of pelvic fin, and distance from dorsal fin origin to caudal fin base is 45% of SL. Dorsal fin has 13 rays, and anal fin has 18 rays. Ventral adipose fin is absent. Serial photophores are not broken into small groups, and those of ventral row are straight. IP number 10 or 11, PV number 25 or 26, and VAV number 22 to 25. OV number 20 to 25, and VAL number 21 to 25. AC number 12 and are curved dorsally posterior to anal fin base. Po organ is double, with small anterior and large posterior parts. Color is black.

This species occurs worldwide in tropical seas. In the western Atlantic it occurs in the Gulf of Mexico (26°36′N, 90°41′W) and the Caribbean Sea. It has been captured from the surface to 670 m in the Gulf of Mexico. Food consists of fishes. Maximum known size is 300 mm SL.

REFERENCES: Regan and Trewavas 1929; Gibbs 1964a, 1984a, 1986b; Rass 1971 (as *Diplolychnus mononema*); Sutton and Hopkins in press.

Heterophotus ophistoma Regan and Trewavas 1929

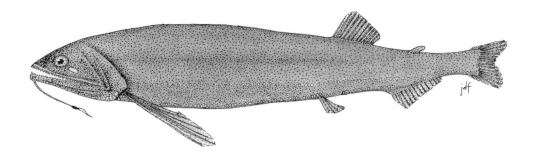

Heterophotus ophistoma is moderately elongate and relatively slender, with short, slender teeth in the jaws and a moderately long chin barbel. It is distinguished from the other species of the family by the following combination of characters. Chin barbel is slightly longer than one-half head length. Tip of barbel consists of swollen dark bulb with single photophore on each side, and terminal white swelling equal in length to black bulb and bearing single filament. Jaw teeth are small, erect, and not fang- or comblike. Maxillary teeth number 31 to 36. Gill rakers are replaced by several groups of short teeth. Vomer has 1 tooth on each side, and palatine has 14 to 20 teeth. Dorsal fin origin is posterior to pelvic fin insertion, and distance from dorsal fin origin to caudal fin base is 32% to 33% of SL. Dorsal fin has 11 to 13 rays, and anal fin has 12 to 17 rays. Ventral adipose fin is absent. Serial photophores are arranged into discontinuous small groups, and those of ventral row are straight. IP number 10 or 11, PV number 32 to 35, and VAV number 13 or 14. OV number 33 to 36, and VAL number 16 to 20. AC number 13 to 15. Po organ is about as long as eye and is single. Color is black.

This species occurs in the tropical and subtropical western and central Atlantic between the surface and 850 m. In the western Atlantic it occurs in the Gulf of Mexico and the Caribbean Sea. Food consists of cephalopods. Maximum known size is 300 mm SL.

REFERENCES: Regan and Trewavas 1929; Gibbs 1964a, 1986b; Rass 1971.

CHAULIODONTIDAE   Viperfishes

Viperfishes are very elongate and slender, with very large jaws bearing fanglike teeth and a short-based, anteriorly located dorsal fin. They are distinguished from the other families of the order by the following combination of characters. Upper jaw extends to near anterior margin of preoperculum. Premaxilla is not protractile. Maxilla has fine teeth in posterior one-half of length. Vomer lacks teeth, and palatine has few minute teeth. Chin barbel is tiny in young specimens and absent in adult specimens. Gill rakers are replaced by teeth in adult specimens. Floor of mouth is present, membrane connects halves of lower jaw to isthmus. Pectoral fin is located immediately posterior to opercular flap below midflank. Dorsal fin origin is anterior to pelvic fin insertion, and first ray is greatly elongated. Pelvic fin is located anterior to midlength on abdomen. Ventral adipose fin is located anterior to anal fin. Anal fin is located below dorsal adipose fin. Photophores are present anterior and posterior to eye, on branchiostegal membrane, in ventral row from isthmus to caudal fin, and above ventral row from opercular flap to near anal fin origin. Small luminous organs occur in wavy row between ventral and lateral rows and on each body scale. Body is covered with hexagonal pigmented areas representing scale pockets. In life, body is covered with gelatinous membrane.

Viperfishes occur worldwide from tropical to temperate seas between 20 and 2,800 m. Species are mesopelagic or bathypelagic, and all are asynchronous vertical migrators. Food consists of fishes and, to a lesser extent, crustaceans. There are eight species in a single genus, and two species occur in the Gulf of Mexico.

Key to the Species of the Gulf of Mexico
(Adapted from Morrow 1964a)

1a. Distance from snout tip to origin of dorsal fin is 17% to 28% of SL; dorsal fin origin over fourth to eighth OV
. . . .*Chauliodus sloani* p. 464
1b. Distance from snout tip to origin of dorsal fin is 24% to 33% of SL; dorsal fin origin over ninth to eleventh OV
. . . .*Chauliodus danae* p. 463

Chauliodus danae Regan and Trewavas 1929

Chauliodus danae is very elongate and slender, with a relatively posteriorly positioned dorsal fin. It is distinguished from the other species of the family by the following combination of characters. Body depth is 4.7% to 9% and head length is 11.9% to 14.3% of SL. Premaxilla has 4 fanglike teeth; second is longest, fourth is larger than third, and second and often third and fourth are barbed. Lower jaw has 5 to 10 teeth; first is largest, second is small, third is larger than second, and remainder are progressively smaller posteriorly. Branchiostegal rays number 12 to 16. Pectoral fin has 12 to 14 rays. Dorsal fin originates between 24% and 33% of SL, over ninth to eleventh photophore of lateral series, and has 5 or 6 rays, with first considerably longer than remainder. Anal fin has 10 to 12 rays. IP number 9 or 10, PV number 17 to 21, and VAV number 22 to 27. OV number 17 to 20, and VAL number 22 to 26. AC number 8 to 12. Preorbital and postorbital photophores and 12 minute suborbital photophores are present. Small photophores also occur on branchiostegal membrane and operculum, at bases of pectoral, pelvic, and anal fins, and beneath scales. Color is dark, occasionally paler ventrally, and body has five rows of hexagonal pigmented areas marking scale pockets.

This species occurs in the subtropical to temperate North Atlantic Ocean. In the western Atlantic it occurs from about 48°N to the Gulf of Mexico and the Caribbean Sea. During the day it ranges from 500 to 3,500 m, and during the night part of the population ranges from near the surface to 500 m. Spawning takes place year-round but is most common in the spring. Food consists of midwater fishes. Maximum known size is 160 mm SL.

REFERENCES: Morrow 1961, 1964a; Rass 1971; Parin and Novikova 1974; Gibbs 1984b; Sutton and Hopkins in press.

Chauliodus sloani   Bloch and Schneider 1801

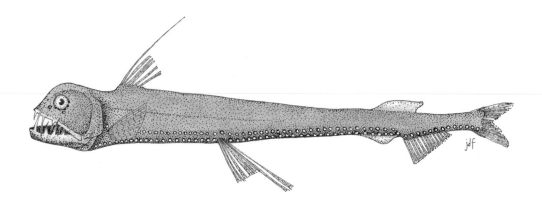

Chauliodus sloani is very elongate and slender, with a relatively anteriorly positioned dorsal fin. It is distinguished from the other species of the family by the following combination of characters. Body depth is 5.8% to 10.5% and head length is 10.5% to 16.3% of SL. Premaxilla has four fanglike teeth; second is longest, fourth is longer than third, and second and often third and fourth are barbed. Lower jaw has five to nine teeth; first is longest, second is small, third is larger than second, and remainder are progressively smaller posteriorly. Branchiostegal rays number 14 to 17. Pectoral fin has 11 to 14 rays. Dorsal fin originates between 17% and 28% of SL, over fourth to eighth photophore of lateral series, and has 5 to 7 rays, with first considerably longer than remainder. Anal fin has 10 to 13 rays. IP number 8 to 11, PV number 17 to 23, and VAV number 23 to 30. OV number 17 to 22, and VAL number 23 and 29. AC number 9 to 13. Preorbital and postorbital photophores and minute suborbital photophores are present. Small photophores also occur on branchios-tegal membrane; operculum; pectoral, pelvic, and anal fin bases; and beneath scales. Color is black to brown or dusky green to silvery. Body is marked with five rows of hexagonal pigmented areas outlining scale pockets.

This species occurs worldwide from tropical to temperate seas. In the western Atlantic it occurs from Browns Bank, 43°N, to Florida, the Gulf of Mexico, the Bahamas, and the Caribbean Sea. During the day it ranges from 1,000 to 1,800 m, and during the night the majority of the population ranges from near the surface to 800 m. In the eastern Gulf of Mexico it ranges between 450 and 700 m during the daytime. Food consists mostly of myctophid fishes. Spawning takes place year-round with a peak in late winter to early spring. Maximum known size is over 300 mm SL.

REFERENCES: Morrow 1961, 1964a; Rass 1971; Parin and Novikova 1974; Bekker et al. 1975; Murdy et al. 1983; Gibbs 1984b, 1986a; Boschung 1992; Sutton and Hopkins 1996, in press.

IDIACANTHIDAE Black dragonfishes

Black dragonfishes are very elongate and very slender, with very long jaws bearing fanglike teeth and very long-based, posteriorly located dorsal and anal fins. They are distinguished from the other families of the order by the following combination of characters. Upper jaw extends to near anterior margin of preoperculum. Premaxilla is not protractile. Teeth in premaxilla and lower jaw of females are depressible and fanglike. Males lack teeth. Vomer has single tooth, and palatine has two or three teeth. Chin barbel is present in females but absent in males. Gill arches lack gill rakers and teeth. Floor of mouth is present, membrane connects halves of lower jaw to isthmus. Pectoral fin is absent in juveniles and adults. Dorsal fin is very long, originates at midlength, and extends to near caudal peduncle. Pelvic fin is located on abdomen at about midlength in females but is absent in males. Anal fin is very long, about one-half as long as dorsal fin, and extends to near caudal peduncle. Adipose fins are absent. Photophores are present posterior to eye, on branchiostegal membrane, in ventral row from isthmus to caudal fin base, and in lateral row from opercular flap to anal fin origin. Small luminous organs are scattered over head and body. Body lacks scales and hexagonal pigmented rows (scale pockets).

Black dragonfishes occur worldwide from tropical to temperate seas between 250 and 2,000 m. Larvae inhabit subsurface waters and descend to greater depths after metamorphosis. Females are located between 500 and 2,000 m during the day and in the upper 250 m during the night. Males appear to remain between 1,000 and 2,000 m day and night. Food consists of midwater fishes. There are four species in a single genus, and one species occurs in the Gulf of Mexico.

Idiacanthus fasciola Peters 1877

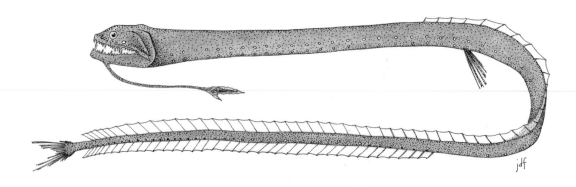

Idiacanthus fasciola is very elongate and very slender, with a very long-based dorsal fin. It is distinguished from the other species of the family by the following combination of characters. Body depth is 2.9% to 4.7% and head length is 5.8% to 8.35% of SL. Females have 8 to 11 fanglike premaxillary teeth, 4 to 6 fanglike and 4 smaller maxillary teeth, and about 16 fanglike mandibular teeth. Chin barbel of females is 2 times head length, with distal end expanded to form narrow leaflike appendage with small flap and filament at base. Dorsal fin originates at about 31% to 34.3% of SL and has 54 to 74 rays. Pelvic fin base is anterior to midlength, and fin has 6 rays. Anal fin is about one-half length of dorsal fin and has 39 to 49 rays. Dorsal and anal fin rays have lateral spinelike projections. IV number 31 to 36, and VAV number 15 to 18. OV number 21 to 25, and VAL number 30 to 36. AC number 13 to 18. Postorbital luminous organ is smaller than eye in females but is equal to or larger than eye in males. White luminous tissue is present in three longitudinal rows on each side. Fin rays are lined with luminous tissue. Color is black to dark brownish black.

This species occurs worldwide in subtropical to temperate seas. In the western Atlantic it occurs along the eastern seaboard of the United States from about 40°N to the Straits of Florida, the Gulf of Mexico, and the Caribbean Sea. Females are captured from 500 to 2,000 m during the day and from near the surface to 250 m during the night. Males apparently inhabit the water column between 1,000 and 2,000 m night and day. Larvae are found in subsurface waters until they undergo metamorphosis and seek greater depths. Spawning takes place at great depths. Fecundity is about 14,000 eggs. Larvae have their eyes at the end of long, slender stalks and have pectoral fins. Food consists of myctophids and other midwater fishes. Males resemble postlarval females except that their digestive tract is degenerate. Apparently males do not feed. Maximum known size of males is 32 to 44 mm SL and of females is 290 mm SL.

REFERENCES: Gibbs 1964b, 1984f; Rass 1971; Murdy et al. 1983; Hulley 1986a; Sutton and Hopkins in press.

MALACOSTEIDAE   Loosejaws

The loosejaws are moderately elongate and moderately slender, with very large jaws bearing fanglike teeth and moderately long-based, posteriorly located dorsal and anal fins. They are distinguished from the other families of the order by the following combination of characters. Jaws extend almost to end of head. Teeth in premaxilla are small to medium sized and needlelike. Teeth in lower jaw are long and fanglike. Maxilla has minute denticle-like teeth. Vomer lacks teeth, and palatine either has or lacks small teeth. Floor of mouth is absent, there is no membrane connecting halves of lower jaw to isthmus. Chin barbel is present or absent. Pectoral fin is located below midflank or is absent. Dorsal and anal fins are located just anterior to caudal peduncle and have about equal base lengths. Pelvic fin insertion is abdominal at about mid-length. Adipose fins are absent. Photophores are present anterior to and below eye, in ventral row from isthmus to caudal fin base, and in lateral row from opercular flap to anal fin origin. Luminous organ is located posterior to eye. Minute photophores are scattered over head and body. Body lacks scales and hexagonal pigment areas representing scale pockets. Body is usually black.

Loosejaws occur worldwide from tropical to temperate seas at depths from near the surface to 4,000 m. They are usually found below 500 m during the day and at shallower depths during the night. Food consists of midwater crustaceans and fishes. There are 15 species in three genera, and 7 species in three genera occur in the Gulf of Mexico.

Key to the Species of the Gulf of Mexico
(Adapted from Gibbs 1984e)

1a. Pectoral fin present; suborbital and postorbital luminous organs present; two rows of photophores on each side of isthmus. 2
1b. Pectoral fin absent; preorbital and postorbital luminous organs present; one row of photophores on each side of isthmus . . . . *Photostomias guernei* p. 475
2a. Chin barbel present; snout longer than eye diameter; two pairs of nares on each side of snout 3
2b. Chin barbel absent; snout shorter than eye diameter; single nostril on each side of snout . . . . *Malacosteus niger* p. 474
3a. PV photophores loosely grouped into two assemblages . . . . *Aristostomias lunifer* p. 470
3b. PV photophores in close-set groups or nonlinear clusters . 4
4a. Pectoral fin rays 14 to 17 . . . . *Aristostomias polydactylus* p. 471

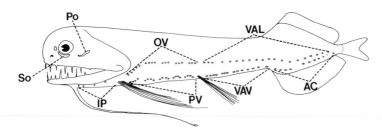

Generalized Malacosteidae for Photophore ID (See p. 1073)

Aristostomias grimaldii Zugmayer 1913

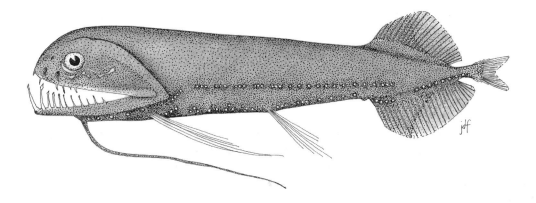

Aristostomias grimaldii is moderately elongate and moderately slender, with pectoral fins and a slender chin barbel bearing a poorly defined bulb. It is distinguished from the other species of the family by the following combination of characters. Body depth is 16% to 21% and head length is 25% to 30% of SL. Snout length is 22% to 30% and eye diameter is 16% to 20% of head length. Two nares are present on each side of snout. Premaxilla has about six rather small teeth, maxilla lacks teeth, and lower jaw has two fangs anteriorly fitting into grooves in upper jaw, followed by progressively smaller teeth. Palatine has small, depressible teeth. Chin barbel is 30% to 60% of SL and has slight swelling at tip. Pectoral fin has 7 to 10, dorsal fin has 21 to 26, pelvic fin has 6, and anal fin has 26 to 32 rays. IP number 8, PV number 14 to 16, and VAV number 15 to 17.

OV number 16, VAL number 15 or 16, and AC number 10 or 11. Three pairs of photophores are located between last two pairs of IP. So is crescent shaped, and Po is slightly elongate. Row of small luminous spots and patches extends from eye to postorbital organ. Head and body are covered with numerous minute light organs. Color is black.

This species occurs worldwide in tropical to subtropical seas. In the western Atlantic it occurs from the eastern seaboard of the United States to Florida, the Gulf of Mexico, and the Caribbean Sea at depths from 25 to 800 m. Food consists of midwater fishes. Maximum known size is 150 mm SL.

REFERENCES: Morrow 1964c; Gibbs 1984e; Sutton and Hopkins in press.

Aristostomias lunifer Regan and Trewavas 1930

Aristostomias lunifer is moderately elongate and moderately slender, with pectoral fins and a long, slender chin barbel possessing an elongate, slender, tapering bulb. It is distinguished from the other species of the family by the following combination of characters. Body depth is 14% to 16% and head length is 22% to 23% of SL. Snout length is 21% to 23% and eye diameter is 18% to 19% of head length. Two nares occur on each side of snout. Premaxilla has about 7 rather long, fixed teeth; maxilla has about 24 minute, oblique denticles; and lower jaw has one fang, fitting into groove in upper jaw, followed by 16 or 17 relatively small teeth. Palatine has row of about 8 small teeth. Chin barbel extends past pelvic fin base, with bulb nearly spherical in young, and slender, elongated, and tapering to acute tip in adults, with maximum width just slightly broader than stem. Pectoral fin has 7 or 8, dorsal fin has 20 to 24, pelvic fin has 6, and anal fin has 26 to 29 rays. PV photophores are divided into loose groupings. IP number 8, PV number 17, and VAV number 14 or 15. OV number 18 or 19, VAL number 16 to 18, and AC number 10 to 12. So is crescent shaped and slightly longer than one-half eye diameter. Po is below and behind eye. Head and body are scattered with small light organs. Color is black.

This species occurs worldwide in tropical waters. In the western Atlantic it occurs from Cape Hatteras and Bermuda to the eastern Caribbean Sea, the Bahamas, and the northeastern Gulf of Mexico. Food consists of midwater fishes. Maximum known size is 170 mm SL.

REFERENCES: Morrow 1964; Gibbs 1984; Goodyear and Gibbs 1986; Sutton and Hopkins in press.

Aristostomias polydactylus   Regan and Trewavas 1930

Aristostomias polydactylus is moderately elongate and moderately slender, with pectoral fins and a moderately long, slender barbel bearing a cylindrical bulb. It is distinguished from the other species of the family by the following combination of characters. Body depth is about 14% to 20% and head length is 25.6% to 33.3% of SL. Snout length is 25% to 33% and eye diameter is 14% to 20% of head length. Two nares are present on each side of snout. Premaxilla has 8 teeth, and maxilla has minute denticles on posterior one-half of ventral margin. Lower jaw has 16 barbed teeth, and first 2 are much larger than remainder and fit into grooves in upper jaw. Chin barbel is slender, about 40% to 75% of SL, and terminates as elongated, cylindrical bulb. Pectoral fin has 14 to 17, dorsal fin has 21 to 26, pelvic fin has 6, and anal fin has 26 to 29 rays. IP number 8, PV number 15 to 17, and VAV number 15 to 18. OV number 15 to 17, VAL number 17 or 18, and AC number 10. Three pairs of photophores are located between last two pairs of IP. So is crescent shaped and about 50% to 65% of eye diameter in length. Po is oval and about equal to eye diameter in length. Small luminescent spots are present anterior to and below eye, dense streak of luminous tissue is located between suborbital and postorbital luminous organs, and luminous spots occur posterior to opercular flap. Color is black.

This species occurs in the western North Atlantic from the Gulf of Mexico and the Caribbean Sea between 25 and 1,000 m. Food consists of myctophids. Maximum known size is 60 mm SL.

REFERENCES: Morrow 1964c; Rass 1971; Goodyear and Gibbs 1986; Sutton and Hopkins in press.

Aristostomias tittmanni   Welsh 1923

Aristostomias tittmanni is moderately elongate and moderately slender, with pectoral fins and a slender chin barbel bearing a club-shaped bulb. It is distinguished from the other species of the family by the following combination of characters. Body depth is 14.7% to 15.9% and head length is 27.9% to 29.5% of SL. Snout length is 29.1% to 29.3% and eye diameter is 15% to 20% of head length. Two nares are present on each side of snout. Premaxilla has 6 small to moderate-sized, fanglike teeth, and maxilla has 12 small, oblique denticles. Palatine has row of 4 small teeth. Lower jaw has 7 to 11 barbed fangs, with first 2 larger than remainder and fitting into grooves in upper jaw. Chin barbel is 60% to 75% of SL and terminates as a club-shaped bulb. Pectoral fin has 6 or 7, dorsal fin has 20 to 23, pelvic fin has 6, and anal fin has 24 to 29 rays. IP number 8, PV number 17 to 19, and VAV number 15 or 16. OV number 18 to 20, VAL number 14 to 16, and AC number 9 to 11. Three pairs of photophores are located between last two pairs of IP photophores. So is crescent shaped and 40% to 80% of eye diameter in length, and Po is oval shaped and 50% to 60% of eye diameter in length. Series of luminous spots are located between eye and postorbital organ, and in front of and below eye. Small light organs are scattered over head and body. Color is dark brown to black.

This species occurs in the North Atlantic and southwestern Pacific from near the surface to 2,000 m. In the western Atlantic it occurs from the eastern seaboard of the United States to the Gulf of Mexico and the Caribbean Sea. Food consists of myctophids and possibly other midwater fishes. Maximum known size is 215 mm SL.

REFERENCES: Morrow 1964c; Rass 1971; Gibbs 1984e; Sutton and Hopkins in press.

Aristostomias xenostoma   Regan and Trewavas 1930

Aristostomias xenostoma is moderately elongate and moderately slender, with pectoral fins and a slender barbel bearing a well-defined bulb. It is distinguished from the other species of the family by the following combination of characters. Body depth is 15.3% to 21% and head length is 25% to 30% of SL. Snout length is 22.8% and eye diameter is 29.6% of head length. Two nares are present on each side of snout. Premaxilla has 8 or 9 teeth, and maxilla has minute denticles along posterior one-half of ventral margin. Palatine has about 6 very small teeth. Lower jaw has 16 to 18 barbed teeth, with first 2 larger and fitting into grooves in upper jaw. Chin barbel is about 75% of SL and has terminal bulb with swollen base in adults. Barbel is about 20% of SL and bulb is swollen at tip in juvenile specimens. Pectoral fin has 6 to 9, dorsal fin has 21 to 23, pelvic fin has 6, and anal fin has 26 to 29 rays. IP number 8, PV number 14 to 17, and VAV number 15 to 18. OV number 14 to 18, VAL number 14 to 16, and AC number 9 to 11. Three pairs of photophores are located between last two pairs of IP. So is crescent shaped and 70% to 100% of eye diameter in length, and Po is oval and much smaller than suborbital organ. Few luminous spots often are located posterior to So or between it and Po, but luminous streak extending posterior to eye is absent. Small light organ occurs near posterior end of lower jaw. Head and body are scattered with small light organs. Vertebrae number 50. Color is brown to black.

This species occurs in the tropical Atlantic. In the western Atlantic it occurs in the eastern Gulf of Mexico and the Caribbean Sea from 50 to 2,000 m. Food consists of myctophids and possibly other midwater fishes. Maximum known size is 150 mm SL.

REFERENCES: Morrow 1964c; Rass 1971; Sutton and Hopkins in press.

Malacosteus niger Ayres 1848

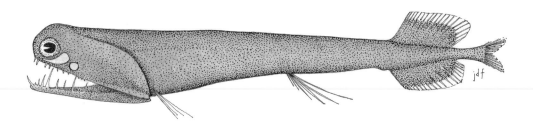

Malacosteus niger is moderately elongate and moderately slender, and has pectoral fins but lacks a chin barbel. It is distinguished from the other species of the family by the following combination of characters. Body depth is 10.4% to 17.4% and head length is 26% to 29.3% of SL. Snout length is 7.1% and eye diameter is 14.5% to 23.8% of head length. One nostril is present on each side of snout. Premaxilla has 21 to 28 small teeth, and maxilla has minute, oblique denticles on posterior one-half of ventral margin. Palatine lacks teeth. Lower jaw has 27 to 38 teeth arranged in five groups of one large tooth followed by about 4 smaller teeth. Pectoral fin has 3 to 5, dorsal fin has 14 to 20, pelvic fin has 6, and anal fin has 17 to 23 rays. Serial photophores are inconspicuous, IC number 12 to 27, and OA number 7 to 15. Two rows of photophores are found on each side of isthmus. So is crescent shaped and nearly as long as eye diameter, and Po is spherical, small, and located distinctly posterior to eye. Head and body are scattered with numerous small light organs. Vertebrae number 49. Color is black.

This species occurs worldwide in tropical to temperate seas. In the western Atlantic it occurs from the eastern seaboard of North America to Florida, the Gulf of Mexico, the Caribbean Sea, and southward to 20°S. Eyes of this species are sensitive to red light rays. Food consists of copepods, euphausiids, penaeidean crustaceans, and midwater fishes. Maximum known size is 240 mm SL.

REFERENCES: Morrow 1964c; Rass 1971; Murdy et al. 1983; Gibbs 1984e; Goodyear and Gibbs 1986; Sutton and Hopkins in press.

Photostomias guernei Collett 1889

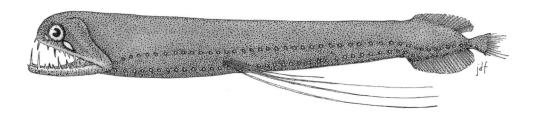

Photostomias guernei is elongate and slender, and lacks pectoral fins and a chin barbel. It is distinguished from the other species of the family by the following combination of characters. Body depth is 7.7% to 13.9% and head length is 16% to 22.1% of SL. Snout length is 12.4% and eye diameter is 13.8% to 25.2% of head length. Two nares are present on each side of snout. Premaxilla has 6 to 10 small- to moderate-sized teeth, and maxilla has up to about 30 small denticles on posterior one-half of ventral margin. Palatine has single row of 2 to 7 teeth. Lower jaw has 2 large anterior teeth and up to 38 posterior teeth about same size as those of premaxilla. Dorsal fin has 22 to 29, pelvic fin has 6, and anal fin has 25 to 33 rays.

IP number 7, PV number 13 to 16, and VAV number 21 to 25. OV number 12 to 17, VAL number 20 to 23, and AC number 12 to 15. Preorbital luminous organ is present, So is absent, and Po is triangular shaped and longer than it is wide. Vertebrae number 52 to 58. Color is black.

This species occurs in the tropical to temperate North Atlantic. It occurs in the Gulf of Mexico in the western Atlantic. Food consists strictly of penaeidean shrimp (*Sergestes*). Maximum known size is 135 mm SL.

REFERENCES: Morrow 1964c; Rass 1971; Bekker et al. 1975; Murdy et al. 1983; Gibbs 1984e; Sutton and Hopkins in press.

MELANOSTOMIIDAE   Scaleless dragonfishes

Scaleless dragonfishes are moderately to very elongate and moderately to very slender, with a large horizontal mouth and a moderately long to very long chin barbel. They are distinguished from the other families of the order by the following combination of characters. Upper jaw extends considerably posterior to eye. Jaw teeth are small, and sharp to fanglike. Chin barbel varies from less than length of head to considerably longer than body and varies from simple to very complex, with filaments and bulbs of various shapes and sizes. Vomer either lacks or has teeth, and palatine usually has teeth. Gill rakers are absent in adults. Floor of mouth is present, membrane connects sides of lower jaw. Pectoral fin is located below midflank or, occasionally, is absent. Pelvic fin is abdominal or located near midline of flank. Dorsal and anal fins are located near base of tail. Dorsal adipose fin is absent in one genus. Two rows of photophores are present along ventrolateral sides of body. Other light organs are variously located on head and are scattered over body. Scales and hexagonal markings are absent on body. Color is black or occasionally iridescent blue, green, or bronze.

Scaleless dragonfishes occur worldwide in mesopelagic to bathypelagic depths. They usually are located below 500 m during the day, but some migrate to near the surface during the night. Food consists of relatively large midwater crustaceans and fishes. There are about 160 species in 16 genera, and 58 species in 9 genera occur in the Gulf of Mexico.

Key to the Species of the Gulf of Mexico
(Adapted from Morrow and Gibbs 1964; Gibbs et al. 1983; Gomon and Gibbs 1985; Gibbs 1986d)

1a. Anal fin base considerably longer than dorsal fin base; anal fin origin anterior to dorsal fin origin 32
1b. Anal fin base about equal to dorsal fin base; anal fin origin opposite dorsal fin origin 2
2a. Pelvic fin insertion near midflank 3
2b. Pelvic fin insertion near ventral midline 9
3a. Pectoral fin rays 13 or fewer. 4
3b. Pectoral fin rays 16 or more 7
4a. Pectoral fin rays 2 . . . . *Bathophilus pawneei* p. 487
4b. Pectoral fin rays 5 or more 5
5a. Pectoral fin rays 6 to 9; pelvic fin rays 8 to 13
. . . . *Bathophilus longipinnis* p. 485
5b. Pectoral fin rays 7 or 8 or more; pelvic fin rays 9 or 10, or 16 to 20 6

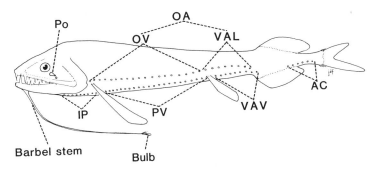

Generalized Melanostomiidae for Photophore ID (See p. 1073)

6a. Pectoral fin rays 7 or 8; pelvic fin rays 16 to 20
. . . . *Bathophilus schizochirus* p. 489
6b. Pectoral fin rays 11 to 13; pelvic fin rays 9 or 10
. . . . *Bathophilus digitatus* p. 484
7a. Pectoral fin rays 16 to 19 . . . *Bathophilus proximus* p. 488
7b. Pectoral fin rays more than 23 8
8a. Pectoral fin rays 24 or 25; pelvic fin rays 15
. . . . *Bathophilus altipinnis* p. 483
8b. Pectoral fin rays 31 to 57; pelvic fin rays 16 to 24
. . . . *Bathophilus nigerrimus* p. 486
9a. Preorbital, suborbital, and postorbital luminous organs
present; suborbital organ crescent shaped
. . . . *Pachystomias microdon* p. 532
9b. Preorbital and suborbital luminous organs absent, or preorbital luminous organ absent and suborbital luminous
organ minute; postorbital luminous organ present, or present in males and absent in females 10
10a. Loop or narrow line of luminous tissue on each side of
body . . . . *Grammatostomias circularis* p. 518
10b. Loop or narrow line of luminous tissue on side of body
absent. 11
11a. Lower jaw long, projecting beyond snout and strongly
curved upward; pectoral fin rays 0 to 3 12
11b. Lower jaw about equal to upper jaw, not projecting
beyond snout and not strongly curved upward; pectoral fin
rays 4 to 12 19
12a. Dorsal and anal fin rays covered with thick black skin, with
only tips of rays visible in adults; IV number 42 to 48. . . 13
12b. Dorsal and anal fin rays not covered with black skin, rays
clearly visible; IV number 30 to 37. 14
13a. Two short pectoral fin rays; distal appendage of chin barbel
without pigment (Fig. 83)
. . . . *Photonectes parvimanus* p. 539
13b. Single long pectoral fin ray; distal appendages of chin barbel pigmented (Fig. 84). . . . . *Photonectes margarita* p. 537

distal appendage

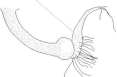

FIG 83

distal appendage

FIG 84

14a. Pectoral fin with two or three rays 15
14b. Pectoral fin absent 17
15a. Tip of snout with luminous spot. 16
15b. Tip of snout without luminous spot
. . . . *Photonectes braueri* p. 534
16a. Chin barbel with slightly swollen bulb bearing long translucent appendage that ends in second bulb with two short terminal filaments (Fig. 85) . . . . . . *Photonectes dinema* p. 535

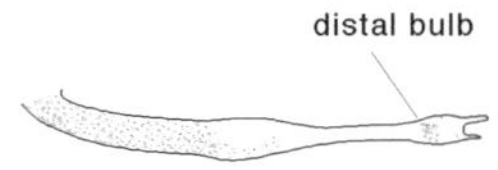

distal bulb

FIG 85

16b. Chin barbel with large white bulb bearing long translucent
appendage that ends in very small white bulb lacking
filaments (Fig. 86) . . . . *Photonectes leucospilus* p. 536

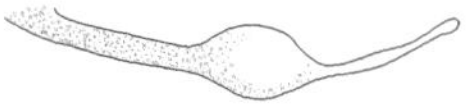

FIG 86

17a. Lateral or midventral band of bluish luminous tissue absent;
no superficial luminous tissue under lower jaw; no light
organs inside lower jaw. . . *Photonectes phyllopogon* p. 540
17b. Lateral or midventral band of bluish luminous tissue present; superficial luminous tissue on underside of lower jaw
present or absent; three pairs of light organs inside lower
jaw present or absent 18
18a. Three pairs of light organs inside lower jaw; luminous tissue on underside of lower jaw absent; blue band present on
side . . . . *Photonectes mirabilis* p. 538
18b. Light organs inside lower jaw absent; superficial luminous
tissue present on underside of lower jaw; midventral blue
band present. . . . . *Photonectes achirus* p. 533
19a. Pectoral fin with 1 long ray separated from 3 to 5 shorter
rays. . . . . *Echiostoma barbatum* p. 490
19b. Pectoral fin with 3 to 12 rays of about equal length, and
none separated from remainder 20
20a. Body depth 10% of SL or less; PV number 39 or more;
chin barbel increasing in length with growth, from one-
half SL to greater than SL; pectoral fin rays 10 to 12 . . . 21
20b. Body depth greater than 10% of SL; PV number 30 or
fewer; chin barbel about equal to head length; pectoral fin
rays 3 to 7 26
21a. Stem of chin barbel without basal filaments 22
21b. Stem of chin with basal filaments 23
22a. PV number 41; chin barbel with median series of minute
filaments on distal part of stem and proximal part of bulb;
bulb with pairs of minute filaments on distal part (Fig. 87)
. . . . *Leptostomias haplocaulus* p. 523

FIG 87

22b. PV number 45 to 48; chin barbel without median series of
filaments; bulb without distal filaments (Fig. 88)
. . . . *Leptostomias bermudensis* p. 520

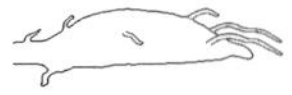

FIG 88

23a. Bulb without basal filaments 24
23b. Bulb with basal filaments 25
24a. Stem of chin barbel with two basal filaments; bulb without
filaments (Fig. 89) . . . . *Leptostomias leptobolus* p. 524

FIG 89

24b. Stem of chin barbel with one basal filament; bulb with one minute, nearly terminal tubercle (Fig. 90) . . . . *Leptostomias analis* p. 519

FIG 90

25a. Distal part of bulb longitudinally divided into two parts (Fig. 91) . . . . *Leptostomias bilobatus* p. 521

25b. Bulb not longitudinally divided (Fig. 92) . . . . *Leptostomias gladiator* p. 522

FIG 91

26a. Chin barbel ending in one or two bulbous swellings without expanded and flattened process (Fig. 93) . . . . *Melanostomias tentaculatus* p. 530

26b. Chin barbel ending in expanded and flattened process through which axis of stem is visible and is associated with luminous bodies or accumulations of luminous material on one or both sides of axis. 27

FIG 92

27a. Length of expanded part of barbel tip about twice width, free end occasionally pointed but never attenuated into filament 28

27b. Length of expanded part of barbel 5 or more times width, free end often attenuated into filament 29

FIG 93

28a. Single ovoid luminous body beside axis in expanded part of barbel (Fig. 94) . . . . *Melanostomias margaritifer* p. 527

28b. Two or more luminous bodies beside axis in expanded part of barbel (Fig. 95) . . . . *Melanostomias valdiviae* p. 531

FIG 94

29a. Axis of expanded part of barbel wide proximally and tapering almost to point distally (Fig. 96) . . . . *Melanostomias melanops* p. 529

29b. Axis of expanded part of barbel about same width over length or expanded and then narrowed distally 30

FIG 95

30a. Axis of expanded part of barbel lined on each side with row of small and discrete or fused luminous bodies (Fig. 97) . . . . *Melanostomias biseriatus* p. 525

30b. Axis of expanded part of barbel not lined on each side with luminous bodies. 31

FIG 96

31a. Terminal barbel filament present (Fig. 98) . . . . *Melanostomias melanopogon* p. 528

31b. Terminal barbel filament absent (Fig. 99) . . . . *Melanostomias macrophotus* p. 526

FIG 97

32a. First pectoral fin ray separated from and longer than other rays; snout blunt and not protrusible . . . . *Flagellostomias boureei* p. 517

32b. First pectoral fin ray, when present, not separated from and usually no longer than remainder of rays; snout tapering and protrusible. 33

FIG 98

33a. Pectoral fin absent . . . . *Eustomias lipochirus* p. 505

33b. Pectoral fin present. 34

34a. Pectoral fin with 9 to 16 rays 35

34b. Pectoral fin with 1 to 7 rays 36

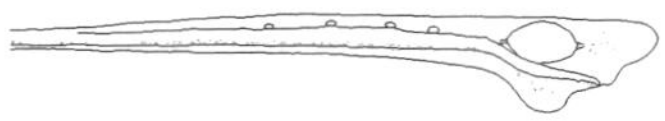

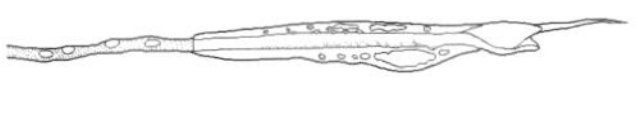

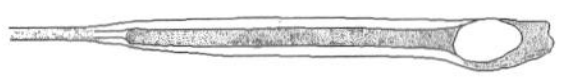

FIG 99

35a. Chin barbel with two minute to long filaments proximal to single terminal bulb and without yellowish spots on stem (Fig. 100) . . . . *Eustomias braueri* p. 496

FIG 100

35b. Chin barbel without filaments proximal to bulb and with light yellowish spots on stem (Fig. 101) . . . . *Eustomias macrurus* p. 508

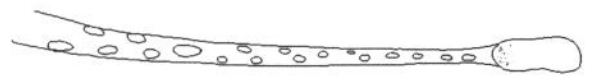

FIG 101

36a. Stem of chin barbel with one to three simple or dendritic branches or filaments proximal to terminal bulb(s) 37

36b. Stem of chin barbel without branches or filaments proximal to first terminal bulb 45

37a. Chin barbel with single, thin, tapering filament just before first terminal bulb. 38

37b. Chin barbel usually with two or three branches, either well before bulb or just after it, occasionally with single branch with filaments or branches 39

38a. Bulb of chin barbel with distal appendage resembling bunch of grapes (Fig. 102); other distal appendages either simple or dendritic . . . . *Eustomias acinosus* p. 491

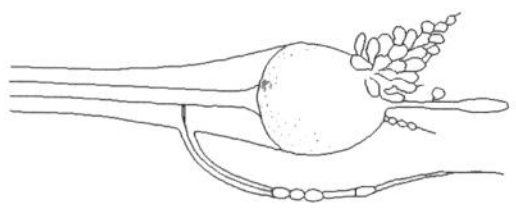

FIG 102

38b. Bulb of chin barbel with simple and dendritic distal appendages but without distal appendage resembling bunch of grapes (Fig. 103). . . . . *Eustomias enbarbatus* p. 499

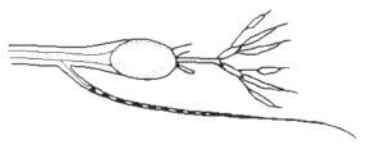

FIG 103

39a. Chin barbel with single branch on stem anterior to terminal bulbs (arising from single stem) 40

39b. Chin barbel with two or more branches on stem anterior to terminal bulbs (often arising close together). 41

FIG 104

40a. Terminal bulb of chin barbel abruptly enlarged to about 3 times diameter of stem directly preceding it and constricted before distal end; branch from stem simple, ending in bulblet or with many side branches (Fig. 104) . . . .*Eustomias dentriticus* p. 498

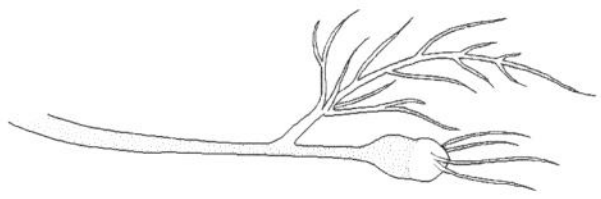

40b. Terminal bulb of chin barbel gradually enlarged and usually less than 3 times diameter of stem directly preceding it and slightly tapering distally; branch from stem with two side branches and ending in prominent bulb (Fig. 105) . . . . *Eustomias fissibarbis* p. 501

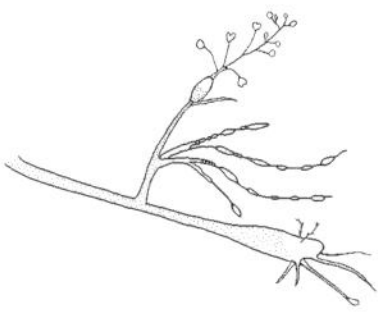

FIG 105

41a. Main stem of chin barbel distal to branches with one or more small proximal swellings and long unswollen section ending in smaller swelling; stem distal to branches, preceding terminal swelling, at least 10 times longer than terminal swelling (Fig. 106) . . . . *Eustomias filifer* p. 500

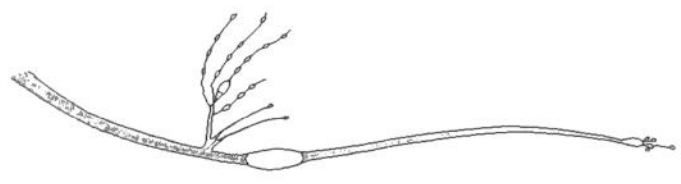

FIG 106

41b. Main stem of chin barbel distal to branches with single distal bulbous swelling at tip (constricted at tip in *E. schmidti*) or without swelling; stem beyond branches preceding bulb not more than 2 times length of bulb 42

42a. Terminal bulb of main stem of chin barbel distinctly constricted at tip; middle branch of stem short and bulbous (Fig. 107) . . . . *Eustomias schmidti* p. 514

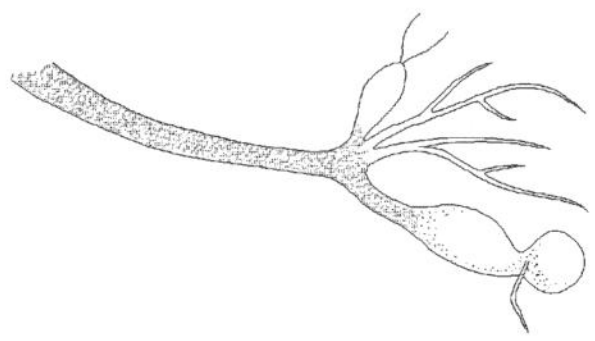

FIG 107

42b. Terminal bulb of main stem of chin barbel not constricted at tip; middle branch of stem variable, either absent, small, and filamentous or long and dendritic 43

43a. Terminal bulb of chin barbel very small, hardly distinct from main stem (Fig. 108)
. . . . *Eustomias parvibulbus* p. 512

FIG 108

43b. Terminal barbel of chin barbel well developed 44

44a. Terminal barbel of chin barbel swollen and globular (Fig. 109) . . . . *Eustomias bigelowi* p. 494

44b. Terminal barbel of chin barbel swollen and elongated, about twice as long as it is wide (Fig. 110)
. . . . *Eustomias binghami* p. 495

FIG 109

45a. Photophores of OV and VAL series partly in pairs
. . . . *Eustomias obscurus* p. 511

45b. Photophores of OV and VAL series more or less evenly spaced 46

46a. Chin barbel with two or more prominent distal swellings
. . . . 47

FIG 110

46b. Chin barbel with one distal swelling and often bearing elaborate appendages 55

47a. Chin barbel with long distal extension beyond distal bulb, at least 5 times length of terminal bulb and often bearing lateral filaments, or much branched at tip 48

47b. Chin barbel without terminal filaments arising from distal bulb (minute lateral filamentous projection often present) or with one or more short filaments arising from terminal bulb (all usually less than 3 times terminal bulb length)
. . . . 52

48a. Two pectoral fin rays . . . . *Eustomias polyaster* p. 513

48b. Three pectoral fin rays 49

FIG 111

49a. Terminal bulb of chin barbel with three or more terminal filaments (sometimes arising from very short stem) (Fig. 111) . . . . *Eustomias kreffti* p. 503

49b. Terminal bulb of chin barbel with single terminal filament and with or without branches 50

50a. Terminal bulb of chin barbel bearing one or more branches on terminal filament that are relatively long compared to length of main filament (Fig. 112)
. . . . *Eustomias arborifer* p. 492

FIG 112

50b. Terminal bulb of chin barbel either lacking branches on terminal filament or bearing relatively short filaments compared to main filament 51

51a. Terminal bulb of chin barbel with four or more short branches near base of terminal filament, each branch with internal bulblets, and usually swollen tip (Fig. 113)
. . . . *Eustomias micraster* p. 510

FIG 113

51b. Terminal bulb of chin barbel with no, or at most, one simple branch near base of terminal filament (Fig. 114)
. . . . *Eustomias bibulbosus* p. 493

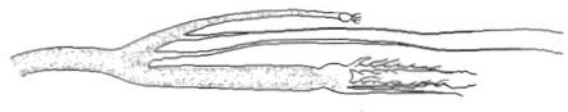

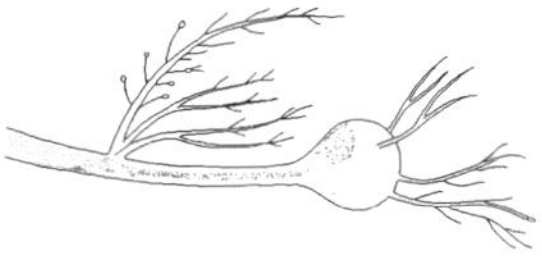

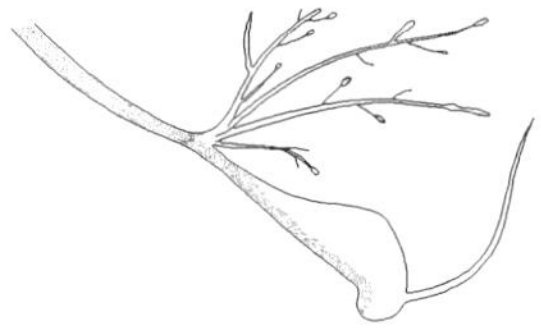

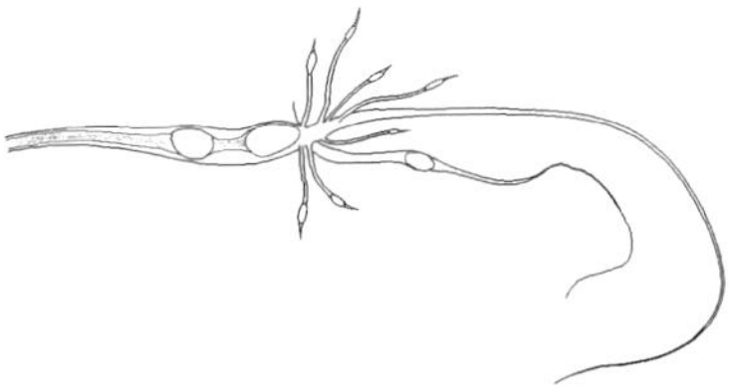

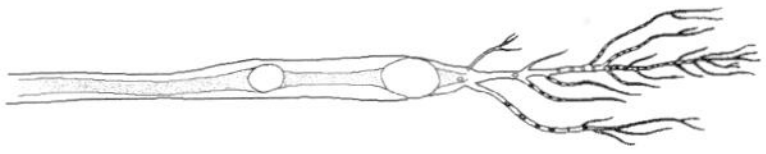

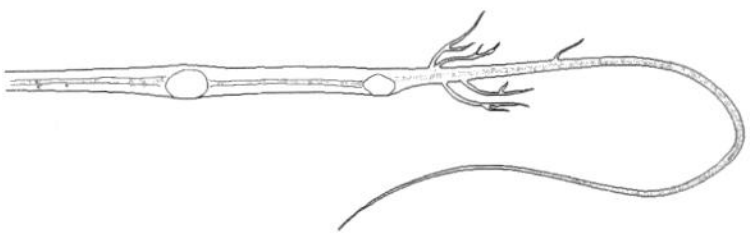

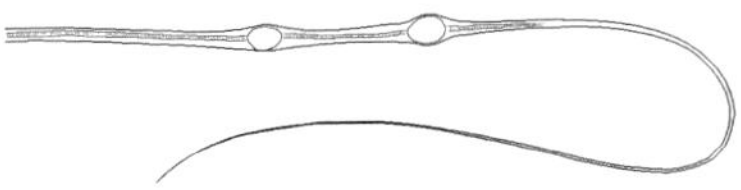

FIG 114

52a. No filament arising from terminal bulb of chin barbel
(but minute lateral filamentous projection often present)
(Fig. 115)............... *Eustomias hypopsilus* p. 502

52b. One or more short filaments arising from terminal bulb (all
usually less than 3 times terminal bulb length 53

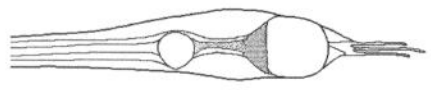

53a. Two pectoral fin rays 54

53b. Three pectoral fin rays ... *Eustomias melanostigma* p. 509

54a. Proximal end of terminal bulb of chin barbel covered with
prominent black cap (Fig. 116)
.... *Eustomias brevibarbatus* p. 497

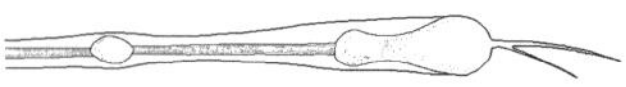

54b. Proximal end of terminal bulb of chin without black cap
(Fig. 117)................. *Eustomias variabilis* p. 515

55a. Length of terminal bulb of chin barbel more than 3 times
width 56

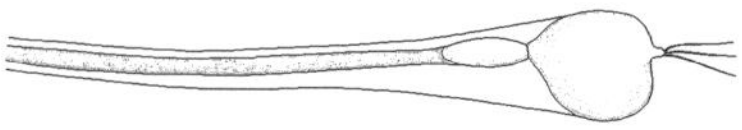

55b. Length of terminal bulb of chin barbel seldom greater than
2 times width (Fig. 118)..... *Eustomias xenobolus* p. 516

56a. Three pectoral fin rays; terminal bulb of chin barbel 3 to 4
times longer than it is wide (Fig. 119)
.... *Eustomias longibarba* p. 506

56b. Two pectoral fin rays; terminal bulb of chin barbel about 6
times longer than it is wide..................... 57

57a. Terminal bulb of chin barbel constricted along length; terminal bulb bearing small distal filament (Fig. 120)
.... *Eustomias leptobolus* p. 504

57b. Terminal bulb of chin barbel not constricted along length;
terminal bulb bearing distal papilla (Fig. 121)
.... *Eustomias macrophthalmus* p. 507

FIG 115

FIG 116

FIG 117

FIG 118

FIG 119

FIG 120

FIG 121

Bathophilus altipinnis   Beebe 1933

Bathophilus altipinnis is elongate and moderately slender, with a moderately long snout, a relatively short chin barbel, and pelvic fins located near midflank. It is distinguished from the other species of the family by the following combination of characters. Body depth is 15.3% to 17% and head length is 20% to 21.5% of SL. Snout length is 26.5% of head length. Lower jaw is about equal to upper jaw and is not curved upward at tip. Upper jaw has one large and one small tooth followed by one flexible fang and seven moderate to small teeth. Lower jaw has moderate-sized, fixed tooth and one large depressible tooth followed by eight small to minute teeth. Vomer lacks teeth, and palatine has two teeth on each side. Chin barbel is filamentous, about twice as long as head, and terminates as two minute filaments. Pectoral fin inserts low on body and has 24 or 25 rays. Dorsal fin and anal fins both have 15 rays. Pelvic fin consists of 15 rays. Rays of both pectoral and pelvic fins are filamentous and are not connected by membranes. IP number 5, PV number 13, and VAV number 11. OV number 13, VAL number 11, and AC number 10. Preorbital and suborbital luminous organs are absent. Po is located behind and below eye and is nearly as long as eye. Body is covered with small light organs. Color is black with silvery green sheen.

This scaleless dragonfish occurs in the western Atlantic off Bermuda and in the northeastern Gulf of Mexico at 1,463 m. Maximum known size is 58.6 mm SL.

REFERENCES: Morrow and Gibbs 1964; Sutton and Hopkins 1996.

Bathophilus digitatus (Welsh 1923)

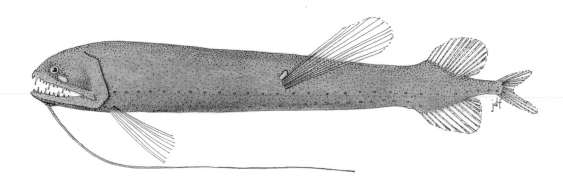

Bathophilus digitatus is elongate and slender, with a moderately long, blunt snout; a long and slender chin barbel; and pelvic fins located near midline of flank. It is distinguished from the other species of the family by the following combination of characters. Body depth is about 10% and head length is 21.8% of SL. Lower jaw is about equal to upper jaw and is not turned up at tip. Premaxilla has 4 stout, fixed teeth, and first protrudes through skin of snout. Lower jaw has 10 teeth, second of which is largest. Chin barbel is about 50% of SL or longer, when complete. Barbel lacks bulb and filaments. Pectoral fin consists of 11 to 13 free rays. Dorsal fin has 14 rays, and anal fin has 15 rays. Pelvic fin consists of 9 or 10 free filamentous rays. IP number 10 or 11, PV number 15 or 16, and VAV number 12 or 13. OV number 14 to 16, and VAL number 10 to 12. Preorbital and suborbital luminous organs are absent. Po is about twice diameter of eye. Entire body is covered with small photophores. Color is blackish with an iridescent blue, green, or bronze cast. Barbel lacks pigment.

This species occurs worldwide in tropical to subtropical seas between the surface and 500 m. In the western Atlantic it occurs off Bermuda, Cuba, the Bahamas to the Lesser Antilles, and in the Gulf of Mexico. Food consists of myctophids. Maximum known size is 170 mm SL.

REFERENCES: Morrow and Gibbs 1964; Barnett and Gibbs 1968; Gibbs 1984d, 1986d; Sutton and Hopkins 1996, in press.

Bathophilus longipinnis (Pappenheim 1914)

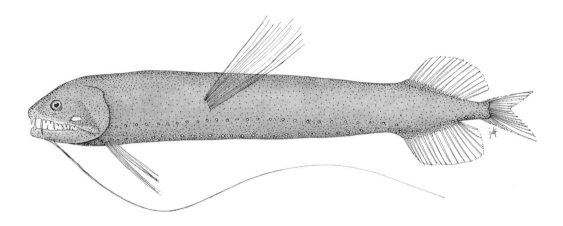

Bathophilus longipinnis is elongate and slender, with a moderately long, blunt snout; a long chin barbel; and pelvic fins located near midline of flank. It is distinguished from the other species of the family by the following combination of characters. Body depth is 9% to 15% and head length is 18% to 25% of SL. Lower jaw is about equal in length to upper jaw and is not upturned at tip. Premaxilla has seven or eight teeth, with second and fifth longest. Lower jaw has seven to nine teeth, with first longest. Chin barbel is slender and nearly as long as body. Barbel has number of distal swellings but lacks bulbs and filaments. Pectoral fin consists of 6 to 9 free rays. Dorsal fin has 14 to 16 rays, and anal fin has 12 to 16 rays. Pelvic fin consists of 8 to 13 free filamentous rays. IP number 6, PV number 14 or 15, and VAV number 11 to 13. OV number 13 to 16, VAL number 10 to 12, and AC number 5. Preorbital and suborbital luminous organs are absent. Po is about equal to eye diameter. Entire body is covered with small photophores. Color is black. Barbel is yellowish white.

This species occurs worldwide in tropical to subtropical seas from near the surface to 1,000 m. In the western Atlantic it occurs along the eastern seaboard of the United States to the Straits of Florida, Bermuda, the Gulf of Mexico, and the Caribbean Sea. Food consists of midwater fishes. Maximum known size is 110 mm SL.

REFERENCES: Morrow and Gibbs 1964; Barnett and Gibbs 1968; Gibbs 1986d; Sutton and Hopkins 1996, in press.

Bathophilus nigerrimus Giglioli 1882

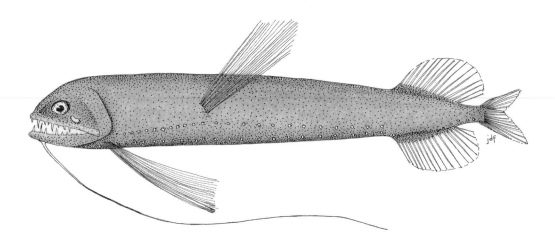

Bathophilus nigerrimus is elongate and moderately slender, with a moderately long, blunt snout; a long chin barbel; and pelvic fins located near midline of flank. It is distinguished from the other species of the family by the following combination of characters. Body depth is 16% to 20% and head length is 21.5% to 25% of SL. Lower jaw is about equal to upper jaw and is not turned up at tip. Premaxilla has 8 to 9 teeth, and first, second, and fifth are moderately long to long. Lower jaw has 9 or 10 teeth of variable length. Chin barbel is very long and lacks bulbs and filaments. Pectoral fin consists of 31 to 57 free rays. Dorsal and anal fins have 13 to 15 rays. Pelvic fin has 16 to 24 free rays. IP number 4, PV number 12 or 13, and VAV number 11 or 12. OV number 13, VAL number 9 to 12, and AC number 5. Pre-orbital and suborbital luminous organs are absent. Po is kidney shaped and about equal to eye diameter. Entire body is covered with small photophores. Color is black with iridescent blue, green, or bronze cast.

This species occurs worldwide in tropical to subtropical seas between the surface and 500 m. In the western Atlantic it occurs along the eastern seaboard of the United States from 40°N to the Straits of Florida, the Gulf of Mexico, and the Caribbean Sea. Food consists of myctophids. Maximum known size is 120 mm SL.

REFERENCES: Morrow and Gibbs 1964; Barnett and Gibbs 1968; Rass 1971; Gibbs 1984d, 1986d; Sutton and Hopkins 1996, in press.

Bathophilus pawneei   Parr 1927

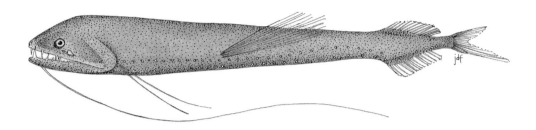

Bathophilus pawneei is elongate and moderately slender, with a moderately long snout, a long chin barbel, and pelvic fins located near midline. It is distinguished from the other species of the family by the following combination of characters. Body depth is 10% to 18% and head length is 15.1% to 18.4% of SL. Lower jaw is about as long as upper jaw and is not curved upward at tip. Premaxilla has 8 to 13 teeth; first 2 are large, and remainder are small. Lower jaw has 2 large anterior teeth and 10 to 13 small teeth. Chin barbel is as long as body or longer and lacks bulbs and filaments. Pectoral fin consists of 2 filamentous rays. Dorsal fin has 14 to 17 rays, and anal fin has 15 to 18 rays. Pelvic fin has 12 to 15 free rays. IP number 5, PV number 12 to 15, and VAV number 13 to 15. OV number 11 to 14, VAL number 13 to 15, and AC number 6 or 7. Preorbital and suborbital luminous organs are absent. Po is slightly shorter than eye diameter and is preceded by small roundish organ. Entire body is covered with small photophores. Vertebrae number 45. Color is black with iridescent blue, green, or bronze cast.

This species occurs worldwide in tropical seas. In the western Atlantic it occurs off the east coast of Florida, the Bahamas, the Gulf of Mexico, and the Caribbean Sea. It has been caught from near the surface to 1,500 m but is most abundant between 100 and 500 m at night. Food consists of midwater fishes. Maximum known size is 124 mm SL.

REFERENCES: Morrow and Gibbs 1964; Barnett and Gibbs 1968; Rass 1971; Sutton and Hopkins 1996, in press.

Bathophilus proximus   Regan and Trewavas 1930

Bathophilus proximus is elongate and moderately slender, with a moderately long snout, a moderately long to long chin barbel, and pelvic fins that are located near midflank. It is distinguished from the other species of the family by the following combination of characters. Body depth is 16.6% to 17.1% and head length is 20% to 21.1% of SL. Snout length is 27.9% of head length. Lower jaw is about as long as upper jaw and is not turned upward at tip. Chin barbel is simple and extends beyond pelvic fin base. Pectoral fin inserts near ventral midline and has 16 to 19 rays. Dorsal fin and anal fin each have 16 rays. Pelvic fin has 16 rays. Pectoral and pelvic rays are filamentous and are not connected by membranes. IP number is unknown, PV number 13, and VAV number 13. OV number 10, VAL number 10, and AC number 5. Preorbital and suborbital luminous organs are absent. Po is higher than it is long and about equal to eye diameter in height. Color is black.

This species occurs in the western Atlantic off Bermuda and in the northeastern Gulf of Mexico. Food consists of myctophids. Maximum known size is 55 mm SL.

REFERENCES: Regan and Trewavas 1930; Morrow and Gibbs 1964; Sutton and Hopkins 1996, in press.

Bathophilus schizochirus   Regan and Trewavas 1930

Bathophilus schizochirus is elongate and moderately slender, with a moderately long snout, a very long and simple chin barbel, and pelvic fin bases near midflank. It is distinguished from the other species of the family by the following combination of characters. Body depth is 13.3% and head length is 18.9% to 20% of SL. Lower jaw is about as long as upper jaw and is not curved upward. Premaxilla has series of long, slender, fixed teeth followed by series of depressible teeth, with first, second, and fifth longer than remainder. Maxilla has series of small, oblique denticles. Lower jaw has one fixed tooth followed by depressible fang and one small fixed tooth and series of depressible teeth of variable lengths. Chin barbel is longer than body and lacks bulb or filaments. Pectoral fin rays are divided into two groups of 3 and 4 or 5 long, free rays. Dorsal fin has 14 or 15 and anal fin has 15 or 16 rays. Pelvic fin has 16 to 20 long, free rays. IP number 5, PV number about 14, and VAV number 11. OV number 13 or 14, VAL number 8 or 9, and AC number 5. Po is bean shaped and about as long as eye. Color is black.

This species occurs in the North Atlantic. In the western Atlantic it occurs in the Caribbean Sea and in the northeastern Gulf of Mexico. Maximum known size is 72 mm SL.

REFERENCES: Morrow and Gibbs 1964; Sutton and Hopkins 1996.

Echiostoma barbatum   Lowe 1843

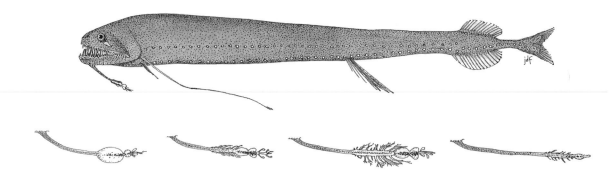

Echiostoma barbatum is elongate and very slender, with a short, blunt, rounded snout; a relatively short chin barbel; and abdominal pelvic fins. It is distinguished from the other species of the family by the following combination of characters. Body depth is 10% to 17% and head length is 14% to 17.1% of SL. Lower jaw is about equal in length to upper jaw and is not upturned at tip. Premaxilla has 9 to 11 curved, barbed fangs. Lower jaw has 15 to 35 fanglike, barbed teeth. Chin barbel is usually shorter than head length. Barbel has slender axis and two terminal bulbs in young specimens. Bulbs are largely replaced by series of terminal filaments in adults. Pectoral fin consists of 1 long ray distally separated from 3 short rays. Dorsal fin has 11 to 14 rays, and anal fin has 13 to 18 rays. Pelvic fin has 8 rays. IP number 10, PV number 25 to 28, and VAV number 14 to 18.

OV number 24 to 27, VAL number 13 to 18, and AC number 11 to 13. Preorbital and suborbital luminous organs are absent. Po is one-half length or longer than eye diameter. Color is black.

This species occurs worldwide in tropical to subtropical seas. In the western Atlantic it occurs along the eastern seaboard of the United States from about 36°N to Argentina, about 40°S, including the Gulf of Mexico and the Caribbean Sea. It has been captured between 200 and 1,900 m. Food consists of midwater fishes and shrimps. Maximum known size is 370 mm SL.

REFERENCES: Morrow and Gibbs 1964; Krueger and Gibbs 1966; Rass 1971; Gibbs 1984d, 1986d; Boschung 1992; Sutton and Hopkins 1996, in press.

Eustomias acinosus   Regan and Trewavas 1930

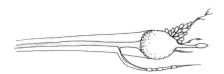

Eustomias acinosus is elongate and slender, with a long, tapering, protrusible snout; a relatively long chin barbel bearing several simple to complex appendages; and abdominal pelvic fins. It is distinguished from the other species of the family by the following combination of characters. Body depth is 9% to 11% and head length is 13% to 14.2% of SL. Lower jaw is about as long as upper jaw and is not upturned at tip. Premaxilla has six fanglike teeth. Lower jaw has seven fanglike teeth. Chin barbel is 25% to 50% of SL. Barbel has slender axis, and terminal bulb is preceded by a long, simple filament and followed by an appendage resembling a bunch of grapes and other appendages that are either simple or dendritic. Pectoral fin consists of 3 or 4 rays. Dorsal fin has 21 to 23 rays, and anal fin has 35 to 37 rays. Pelvic fin has 7 rays. IP number 7, PV number 26 or 27, and VAV number 11 or 12. OV number 26 or 27, VAL number 11 to 13, and AC number 19 to 23. Preorbital and suborbital luminous organs are absent. Po is present. Color is black. Barbel stem has little or no pigment.

This species occurs in the tropical Atlantic Ocean. In the western Atlantic it occurs east of Bermuda and in the Gulf of Mexico. Food consists of midwater fishes. Maximum known size is 185 mm SL.

REFERENCES: Morrow and Gibbs 1964; Sutton and Hopkins 1996, in press.

Eustomias arborifer Parr 1927

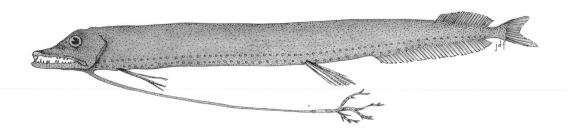

Eustomias arborifer is elongate and slender, with a long, tapering, protrusible snout; a relatively long chin barbel bearing two terminal bulbs separated by a short interspace; and abdominal pelvic fins. It is distinguished from the other species of the family by the following combination of characters. Body depth is 5% to 8% of SL. Lower jaw is slightly longer than upper jaw but not distinctly upturned at tip. Premaxilla has 12 or 13 teeth. Lower jaw has 14 to 21 fanglike teeth. Chin barbel is 70% to 90% of SL in males and 46% to 51% of SL in females. Barbel has slender stem and two terminal bulbs separated by interspace equal to one-half to one and one-half distal bulb lengths, with short to long terminal filament and two to several well-developed side branches arising close to distal end of bulb. All terminal branches possess internal bulblets that are as wide as or wider than terminal branches. Deep ventral groove on belly is absent. Pectoral fin consists of 3 free rays. Dorsal fin has 21 to 25 rays, and anal fin has 35 to 42 fin rays. Pelvic fin rays number 7. IP number 7, PV number 31 to 34, and VAV number 16 to 19. OV number 30 to 34, VAL number 17 to 19, and AC number 17 to 21. Preorbital and suborbital luminous organs are absent. Po is about one-third of orbit diameter. Color is black. Barbel stem has little or no external pigment.

This species occurs in the tropical to subtropical Atlantic Ocean. In the western Atlantic it occurs in the northern Gulf of Mexico, the Caribbean Sea, and off the coast of Brazil. Food consists of midwater fishes. Maximum known size is 150 mm SL for males and 179 mm SL for females.

REFERENCES: Morrow and Gibbs 1964 (as *E. bibulbosus*); Gibbs et al. 1983; Sutton and Hopkins 1996, in press.

Eustomias bibulbosus Parr 1927

Eustomias bibulbosus is elongate and slender, with a long, tapering, protrusible snout; a long chin barbel bearing two terminal bulbs and a single terminal filament; and abdominal pelvic fins. It is distinguished from the other species of the family by the following combination of characters. Lower jaw is about as long as upper jaw and is not upturned at tip. Chin barbel is 60% to 85% of SL. Barbel has slender stem, two widely separated terminal bulbs, and a single, long filament (22% to 33% of SL) with no, or rarely one or 2, short branches. Distal bulb is usually 1 to 1.5 times length of proximal bulb, and bulbs are separated by distance equal to 2.2% to 4.2% of SL. Deep groove on belly is absent. Pectoral fin consists of 3 free rays. Dorsal fin has 22 to 25 rays, and anal fin has 35 to 42 rays. Pelvic fin has 7 rays. IP number 7, PV number 31 to 35, and VAV number 16 to 19. OV number 30 to 35, VAL number 17 to 20, and AC number 18 to 20. Preorbital and suborbital luminous organs are absent. Color is black. Barbel has no external pigment, but axis of stem is black and external chevron-shaped or roundish striated areas are pigmented in specimens larger than 80 mm SL.

This species occurs in the western Atlantic between 25°N and 40°N, including the eastern Gulf of Mexico, between 100 and 2,134 m. Maximum known size is 149 mm SL.

REFERENCES: Morrow and Gibbs 1964 (in part); Gibbs et al. 1983.

Eustomias bigelowi Welsh 1923

Eustomias bigelowi is elongate and slender, with a long, tapering, protrusible snout; a moderately short chin barbel bearing a single terminal bulb; and abdominal pelvic fins. It is distinguished from the other species of the family by the following combination of characters. Body depth is 6.7% to 9.1% and head length is 11.4% to 14.4% of SL. Lower jaw is about as long as upper jaw. Chin barbel is 11.2% to 12.9% of SL. Barbel has slender stem, three branches, and globular terminal bulb. Branches are located medial to bulb and are slightly shorter to slightly longer than distance from base of branches to tip of barbel, and bear several side branches. Terminal bulb bears several branched filaments near tip. Deep groove is located on belly between PV 3 and PV 13. Pectoral fin consists of 2 tightly bound rays. Dorsal fin has 22 to 26 rays, and anal fin has 37 to 42 rays. Pelvic fin has 7 rays. IP number 7, PV number 27 to 30, and VAV number 14 or 16. OV number 26 to 29, VAL number 14 to 17, and AC number 20 to 22. Color is black. Barbel stem is pigmented to origin of branches or to near distal bulb.

This species occurs in the western Atlantic from Bermuda, the Straits of Florida, the Bahamas, Puerto Rico, and the northeastern Gulf of Mexico. Maximum known size is 134 mm SL.

REFERENCES: Morrow and Gibbs 1964; Gibbs et al. 1983; Sutton and Hopkins 1996.

Eustomias binghami   Parr 1927

Eustomias binghami is elongate and slender, with a long, tapering, protrusible snout; a moderately short chin barbel bearing a single terminal bulb; and abdominal pelvic fins. It is distinguished from the other species of the family by the following combination of characters. Body depth is 7.4% to 12.4% and head length is 10.5% to 15.8% of SL. Lower jaw is about as long as upper jaw. Chin barbel is 18.3% of SL. Barbel has two or three branches arising from stem and a single terminal bulb. Branches bear several to many filaments, and filaments often end in bulblets. Terminal bulb is twice as long as it is wide and has one prominent filament and several minor filaments. Deep groove extends along belly from PV 3 to PV 13. Pectoral fin has 2 tightly bound rays. Dorsal fin has 23 to 25 rays, and anal fin has 39 to 46 rays. Pelvic fin has 7 rays. IP number 7, PV number 24 or 25, and VAV number 14 or 15. OV number 24 to 26, VAL number 13 to 16, and AC number 20 to 22. Color is black. Barbel stem, branches, and one side of bulb are pigmented.

This species occurs in the tropical to subtropical North Atlantic Ocean between 75 and 1,700 m. In the western Atlantic it occurs off Bermuda and in the northeastern Gulf of Mexico. Maximum known size is 144 mm SL.

REFERENCES: Morrow and Gibbs 1964; Gibbs et al. 1983; Sutton and Hopkins 1996.

Eustomias braueri   Zugmayer 1911

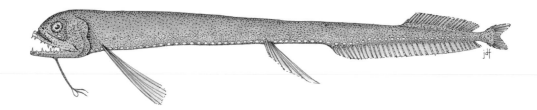

Eustomias braueri is elongate and slender, with a long, tapering, protrusible snout; a moderately short chin barbel bearing an ovoid, white terminal bulb; and abdominal pelvic fins. It is distinguished from the other species of the family by the following combination of characters. Body depth is 7.7% to 11% and head length 12.5% to 16.6% of SL. Lower jaw is about equal to length of upper jaw and is not upturned at tip. Premaxilla has 8 teeth. Lower jaw has 13 teeth. Chin barbel is 12% to 17% of SL. Barbel has slender stem and one ovoid terminal bulb, with two filaments varying in length from very short to 3 times length of bulb. Deep ventral groove extends from isthmus to behind pectoral fin base. Pectoral fin consists of 11 to 16 rays. Dorsal fin has 22 to 30 rays, and anal fin has 36 to 41 rays. Pelvic fin rays number 8. IP number 7, PV number 25 to 28, and VAV number 16. OV number 25 to 29, VAL number 15 to 18, and AC number 20 to 22. Preorbital and suborbital luminous glands are absent. Po is present. Color is black, with irregular, roundish white spots on lower side of body in large specimens. Barbel stem is darkly pigmented.

This species occurs in the tropical to warm temperate Atlantic. In the western Atlantic it occurs in the Gulf of Mexico, the Caribbean Sea, and off the northern coast of South America between 8°S and 11°S. There is only one record of this species from the Gulf of Mexico. Maximum known size is 135 mm SL.

REFERENCES: Morrow and Gibbs 1964; Gibbs 1984d.

Eustomias brevibarbatus   Parr 1927

Eustomias brevibarbatus is elongate and slender, with a long, tapering, protrusible snout; a moderately long chin barbel bearing two or three terminal bulbs; and abdominal pelvic fins. It is distinguished from the other species of the family by the following combination of characters. Body depth is 7.5% to 10% and head length is 10.3% to 14.4% of SL. Lower jaw is about equal in length to upper jaw and is not upturned at tip. Premaxilla has 10 to 12 teeth. Lower jaw has 10 to 15 teeth. Chin barbel is 13% to 40% of SL. Barbel has slender stem and two or three terminal bulbs. Distal bulb is largest and bears two or more short, terminal filaments that are variously branched or unbranched. Deep ventral groove on belly is lacking. Pectoral fin consists of 2 long, free rays. Dorsal fin has 20 to 26 rays, and anal fin has 33 to 38 rays. Pelvic fins rays number 7. IP number 7 or 8, PV number 32 to 34, and VAV number 14 to 17. OV number 31 to 35, VAL number 14 to 18, and AC number 15 to 18. Preorbital and suborbital luminous organs are absent. Po is present. Vertebrae number 63 to 66. Color is black. Barbel stem is lightly to moderately pigmented, and distal bulb is often lightly pigmented along base and side.

This species occurs in the western Atlantic from the Gulf of Mexico and the Caribbean Sea. It has been captured between 20 and 2,000 m and is most frequently taken above 200 m at night. Food consists of midwater fishes. Maximum known size is 149 mm SL.

REFERENCES: Morrow and Gibbs 1964; Rass 1971; Murdy et al. 1983; Gomon and Gibbs 1985; Sutton and Hopkins 1996, in press.

Eustomias dentriticus   Regan and Trewavas 1930

Eustomias dentriticus is elongate and slender, with a long, tapering, protrusible snout; a moderately short chin barbel bearing a single terminal barbel; and abdominal pelvic fins. It is distinguished from the other species of the family by the following combination of characters. Body depth is 8.5% to 9.1% and head length is 11.8% to 12.5% of SL. Lower jaw is about as long as upper jaw. Chin barbel is 11% to 12% SL. Barbel has slender stem, single branch arising from stem, and distal bulb constricted near its distal end and bearing two to four simple or branched filaments at tip. Branch is as long as distance from its base to tip of bulb or twice as long, and bears small distal bulb and several short branches or bears numerous branches over length. Deep groove extends along belly from PV 3 to PV 13. Pectoral fin consists of 2 tightly bound rays. Dorsal fin has 23 rays, pelvic fin has 7 rays, and anal fin has 38 to 40 rays. IP number 7, PV number 28 to 30, and VAV number 13 to 15. OV number 29 or 30, VAL number 13 to 16, and AC number 19 to 22. Color is black. Barbel stem and proximal section of barbel are pigmented.

This species occurs in the North Atlantic in tropical to subtropical waters. In the western Atlantic it occurs in the Caribbean Sea off St. Croix and in the northeastern Gulf of Mexico. Food consists of midwater fishes. Maximum known size is 89 mm TL.

REFERENCES: Morrow and Gibbs 1964; Gibbs et al. 1983; Sutton and Hopkins 1996, in press.

Eustomias enbarbatus Welsh 1923

Eustomias enbarbatus is elongate and slender, with a long, tapering, protrusible snout; a moderately long chin barbel bearing a single terminal bulb; and abdominal pelvic fins. It is distinguished from the other species of the family by the following combination of characters. Body depth is 7.1% to 7.4% and head length is 12.1% to 13.1% of SL. Premaxilla has 6 to 8 teeth, with second fanglike. Lower jaw has 9 to 11 teeth on each side. Chin barbel is 27.5% to 34.9% of SL. Barbel has slender stem, single filament, and terminal bulb bearing several short filaments or single stem of variable length with side branches. Deep groove on belly is absent. Pectoral fin consists of 3 free rays. Dorsal fin has 21 to 23 rays, and anal fin has 34 to 36 rays. Pelvic fin has 7 rays. IP number 7, PV number 26 or 27, and VAV number 11 to 13. OV number 25 to 28, VAL number 12 or 13, and AC number 18 to 20. Color is black. Barbel is unpigmented.

This species occurs in the tropical Atlantic Ocean. In the western Atlantic it occurs off Bermuda and in the northeastern Gulf of Mexico. Maximum known size is 122.5 mm SL.

REFERENCES: Morrow and Gibbs 1964; Gibbs et al. 1983; Sutton and Hopkins 1996.

Eustomias filifer   (Gilchrist 1906)

Eustomias filifer is elongate and slender, with a long, tapering, protrusible snout; a moderate-length chin barbel bearing several branches; and abdominal pelvic fins. It is distinguished from the other species of the family by the following combination of characters. Body depth is 9% to 10% and head length is 11.1% to 14.3% of SL. Lower jaw is about as long as upper jaw and is not curved upward at tip. Premaxilla has 9 teeth. Lower jaw has 10 teeth. Chin barbel is 20% to 43% of SL. Barbel has slender stem, three branches arising from proximal part of stem, and large distal bulb. Bulb has long, narrow stem bearing small bulb. Deep ventral groove extends from isthmus to pectoral fin base. Pectoral fin consists of 1 long and 1 short rudimentary ray bound together in black membrane. Dorsal fin has 20 to 25 rays, and anal fin has 40 to 45 rays. Pelvic fin has 7 rays. IP number 7 or 8, PV number 27 or 28, and VAV number 14 or 15. OV number 27 to 29, VAL number 13 to 15, and AC number 21 to 23. Preorbital and suborbital luminous organs are absent. Po is present. Color is black. Axis of barbel is black, and external tissue has row of black dots and strips of colorless reflecting material.

This species occurs in the Atlantic Ocean. In the western Atlantic it occurs from about 40°N to 28°N, including the northern Gulf of Mexico and the Caribbean Sea, and from 12°S to 35°S, off South America. Food consists of midwater fishes. Maximum known size is 230 mm SL.

REFERENCES: Morrow and Gibbs 1964; Gibbs 1984d, 1986d; Sutton and Hopkins 1996.

Eustomias fissibarbis (Pappenheim 1914)

Eustomias fissibarbis is elongate and very slender, with a long, tapering snout; a relatively short chin barbel bearing a single branch; and abdominal pelvic fins. It is distinguished from the other species of the family by the following combination of characters. Body depth is 5.5% to 8.3% and head length is 12.8% to 13.2% of SL. Lower jaw is about as long as upper jaw and is not upturned at tip. Premaxilla has 9 to 10 teeth. Lower jaw has 10 to 11 teeth. Chin barbel is 12% to 16% of SL. Barbel has slender stem, subterminal branch that gives rise to three ornate secondary branches, and terminal bulb bearing filaments. Two lateral secondary branches of subterminal branch are bifurcated, and medial branch bears apical bulb and dendritic appendage. Pectoral fin consists of 2 closely bound rays. Dorsal fin has 22 to 26 rays, and anal fin has 36 to 41 rays. Pelvic fin has 7 rays. IP number 7, PV number 27 to 29, and VAV number 13 to 15. OV number 26 to 29, VAL number 14 to 16, and AC number 19 to 21. Preorbital and suborbital luminous organs are absent. Po is present. Color is black. Stem of barbel is lightly to darkly pigmented, and terminal bulb is lightly to darkly pigmented along proximal one-half of length.

This species occurs in the North Atlantic. In the western Atlantic it occurs from Bermuda, the Bahamas, the Gulf of Mexico, and the Caribbean Sea. Food consists of myctophids. Maximum known size is 130 mm SL.

REFERENCES: Morrow and Gibbs 1964; Rass 1971; Sutton and Hopkins 1996, in press.

Eustomias hypopsilus   Gomon and Gibbs 1985

Eustomias hypopsilus is elongate and very slender, with a long, tapering, protrusible snout; a moderately long chin barbel bearing two terminal bulbs separated by short interspace; and abdominal pelvic fins. It is distinguished from the other species of the family by the following combination of characters. Body depth is 8.8% and head length is 13.5% of SL. Lower jaw is about as long as upper jaw and is not upturned at tip. Premaxilla has 9 to 11 teeth. Lower jaw has 10 teeth. Chin barbel is 11% to 47% of SL. Barbel has slender stem and two terminal bulbs separated by distance 1.2% to 3.7% of SL. Distal bulb is 0.5% to 1.5% of SL (about same size as proximal bulb), is ovoid but not bilobate, and lacks terminal filament. Deep ventral groove on belly is absent. Pectoral fin consists of 2 free rays. Dorsal fin has 21 to 26 rays, and anal fin has 33 to 40 rays. Pelvic fin has 7 rays. IP number 7, PV number 32 to 36, and VAV number 15 to 19. OV number 31 to 36, VAL number 13 to 18, and AC number 33 to 40. Preorbital and suborbital luminous organs are absent. Po in males is 1.6% to 1.9% of SL. Vertebrae number 64 to 66. Color is black. Axis of barbel stem is lightly to darkly pigmented, and external chevron-shaped or round striated areas on stem are unpigmented.

This species occurs in the western North Atlantic in the northern Gulf of Mexico, the Straits of Florida, and off the Guianas. Maximum known size is 164 mm SL.

REFERENCES: Gomon and Gibbs 1985; Boschung 1992; Sutton and Hopkins 1996.

Eustomias kreffti   Gibbs, Clarke, and Gomon 1983

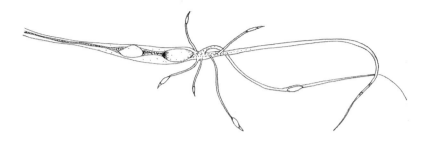

Eustomias kreffti is elongate and slender, with a long, tapering, protrusible snout; a long chin barbel bearing two terminal bulbs and many terminal filaments; and abdominal pelvic fins. It is distinguished from the other species of the family by the following combination of characters. Body depth is 7.6% and head length is 12.2% of SL. Lower jaw is about as long as upper jaw and is not upturned at tip. Premaxilla has 12 or 13 teeth, with second fanglike. Lower jaw has about 30 short, slanting teeth. Chin barbel is 37% to 44% of SL. Barbel has slender stem, two terminal bulbs separated by short distance, three to nine short bulblet-tipped filaments, and two long filaments arising near tip of bulb or from short stem. Bulbs are separated by distance equal to 0.4 to 1.6 times length of distal bulb, and distal bulb is slightly larger than proximal bulb. Deep groove on belly is absent. Pectoral fin consists of 3 free rays. Dorsal fin has 23 to 26 rays, and anal fin has 33 to 39 rays. Pelvic fin has 7 rays. IP number 7, PV number 30 to 34, and VAV number 16 to 20. OV number 30 to 34, VAL number 18 or 19, and AC number 17 to 20. Preorbital and suborbital luminous organs are absent. Po is 26% to 43% of orbit diameter. Color is black. Barbel has no external color, but stem is pigmented.

This species occurs in the tropical Atlantic Ocean. In the western Atlantic it occurs in the northeastern Gulf of Mexico and off northeastern Brazil. Maximum known size is 125.2 mm SL.

REFERENCES: Gibbs et al. 1983; Sutton and Hopkins 1996.

Eustomias leptobolus   Regan and Trewavas 1930

Eustomias leptobolus is elongate and very slender, with a long, tapering, protrusible snout; a moderately long chin barbel bearing a long and slender terminal bulb; and abdominal pelvic fins. It is distinguished from the other species of the family by the following combination of characters. Body depth is 8.3% and head length is 11.6% of SL. Premaxilla has 7 to 15 teeth. Lower jaw has 9 or 10 teeth. Chin barbel is 46% to 49% of SL. Barbel has slender stem and single, large, elongate terminal barbel with constriction before tip. Bulb is 33% to 35% of SL and bears simple, minute terminal filament. Deep ventral groove on belly is absent. Pectoral fin consists of 2 free rays. Dorsal fin has 23 or 24 rays, and anal fin has 36 or 37 rays. Pelvic fin has 7 rays. IP number 7, PV number 33 or 34, and VAV number 15 or 16. OV number 33, VAL number 16 or 17, and AC number 17 or 18. Preorbital and suborbital luminous organs are absent. Po is present. Vertebrae number 65 to 67. Color is black. Barbel stem is darkly pigmented, but external chevron-shaped or roundish striated areas on stem are not pigmented.

This species occurs in the western Atlantic from the Straits of Florida and the northern Gulf of Mexico. It has been caught between the surface and 400 m in nonclosing nets. Maximum known size is 95 mm SL.

REFERENCES: Morrow and Gibbs 1964; Rass 1971; Gomon and Gibbs 1985.

Eustomias lipochirus Regan and Trewavas 1930

Eustomias lipochirus is elongate and slender, with a long, tapering, protrusible snout and a relatively short chin barbel bearing an asymmetrical projection, and without pectoral fins. It is distinguished from the other species of the family by the following combination of characters. Body depth is 7.8% to 8.5% and head length is 12.5% to 14.7% of SL. Lower jaw is about equal to upper jaw in length and is not upturned at tip. Premaxilla and lower jaw have few, mostly depressible teeth. Chin barbel is 8% to 15% of SL. Barbel has slender stem, generally two very small branches, and single terminal bulb with lump or digitiform protuberance on one side of terminal end. Deep ventral groove extends along belly. Dorsal fin has 23 or 24 rays, and anal fin has 38 to 40 rays. Pelvic fin is abdominal and has 7 rays. IP number 7, PV number 28 or 29, and VAV number 12 or 13. OV number 28 or 29, VAL number 13 or 14, and AC number 19 or 20. Preorbital and suborbital luminous organs are absent. Po is present. Color is black. Barbel stem and bulb are unpigmented, or stem is pigmented proximally to origin of branches.

This species occurs in the tropical Atlantic. In the western Atlantic it occurs off Bermuda and in the Gulf of Mexico and the Caribbean Sea. Maximum known size is 88 mm SL.

REFERENCES: Morrow and Gibbs 1964; Gibbs 1986d; Sutton and Hopkins 1996.

Eustomias longibarba Parr 1927

Eustomias longibarba is elongate and very slender, with a long, tapering, protrusible snout; a long chin barbel bearing a slender terminal bulb; and abdominal pelvic fins. It is distinguished from the other species of the family by the following combination of characters. Body depth is 6.4% to 8.2% and head length is 12.2% to 13.6% of SL. Lower jaw is about as long as upper jaw and is not upturned at tip. Premaxilla has 10 to 13 teeth. Lower jaw has 12 to 15 teeth. Chin barbel is 40% to 78% of SL. Barbel has slender stem and single, elongate terminal bulb 1.1% to 2.3% of SL bearing simple, digitate terminal projection. Deep ventral groove on belly is absent. Pectoral fin consists of 3 rays. Dorsal fin has 23 to 26 rays, and anal fin has 35 to 39 rays. Pelvic fin has 7 rays. IP number 7, PV number 32 to 35, and VAV number 16 to 20. OV number 32 to 35, VAL number 17 to 19, and AC number 16 to 20. Preorbital and suborbital luminous organs are absent. Po is about 1% of SL. Vertebrae number 66 to 68. Color is black. Barbel stem has little external pigment.

This species occurs in the North Atlantic. In the western Atlantic it occurs off Bermuda, in the Straits of Florida, the northern Gulf of Mexico, and the Caribbean Sea, and off Brazil. Maximum known size is 129 mm SL.

REFERENCES: Morrow and Gibbs 1964; Gibbs et al. 1983; Gibbs 1984d.

Eustomias macrophthalmus   Parr 1927

Eustomias macrophthalmus is elongate and slender, with a long, tapering, protrusible snout; a very long chin barbel bearing a very long terminal bulb; and abdominal pelvic fins. It is distinguished from the other species of the family by the following combination of characters. Body depth is 6.3% to 8.7% and head length is 13.3% of SL. Lower jaw is about equal to length of upper jaw and is not upturned at tip. Premaxilla has 7 to 15 teeth, and lower jaw has 9 to 18 teeth. Chin barbel is 7.6% to 9.3% of SL. Barbel has slender stem and single, elongate terminal bulb with minute terminal filament. Bulb is 4.3% to 7% of SL and 6 times longer than it is wide. Ventral groove on belly is absent. Pectoral fin consists of 2 free rays. Dorsal fin has 20 to 25 rays, and anal fin has 35 to 37 rays. Pelvic fin rays number 7. IP number 7, PV number 31 to 34, and VAV number 17. OV number 32 to 34, VAL number 17, and AC number 17 or 18. Preorbital and suborbital luminous organs are absent. Po is 34% to 67% of eye diameter. Color is black. Barbel stem is lightly pigmented, and bulb is unpigmented.

This species occurs in the western Atlantic off the Bahamas and in the Gulf of Mexico and the Caribbean Sea. It has been captured from near the surface to 1,800 m. Maximum known size is 111 mm SL.

REFERENCES: Morrow and Gibbs 1964; Gomon and Gibbs 1985.

Eustomias macrurus   Regan and Trewavas 1930

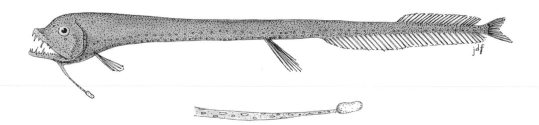

Eustomias macrurus is elongate and slender, with a long, tapering, protrusible snout; a moderately short chin barbel bearing a terminal bulb; and abdominal pelvic fins. It is distinguished from the other species of the family by the following combination of characters. Body depth is 4.9% and head length is 13.3% of SL. Premaxilla has six teeth, with second fanglike. Lower jaw has eight teeth on each side. Chin barbel is 13.3% of SL. Barbel has slender stem and single terminal bulb but lacks branches and filaments. Ventral groove on belly extends from PV 5 to PV 8. Pectoral fin consists of 9 rays. Dorsal fin has 25 to 29 rays, and anal fin has 45 rays. Pelvic fin has 7 rays. IP number 7, PV number 28 or 29, and VAV number 16 or 17. OV number 28 or 29, VAL number 16 to 18, and AC number 24 or 25. Color is black. Barbel lacks external pigment.

This species occurs in the western and central Atlantic Ocean in tropical areas. In the western Atlantic it occurs off Bermuda and Puerto Rico and in the northeastern Gulf of Mexico. Maximum known size is 112.5 mm SL.

REFERENCES: Morrow and Gibbs 1964; Gibbs et al. 1983; Sutton and Hopkins 1996.

Eustomias melanostigma   Regan and Trewavas 1930

Eustomias melanostigma is elongate and slender, with a long, tapering, protrusible snout; a moderately long chin barbel bearing two terminal bulbs and several terminal filaments; and abdominal pelvic fins. It is distinguished from the other species of the family by the following combination of characters. Body depth is 7.7% to 9.6% and head length is 12.1% to 12.5% of SL. Lower jaw is about as long as upper jaw and is not upturned at tip. Premaxilla has 13 teeth, and lower jaw has 16 teeth on each side. Chin barbel is 31% to 82% of SL. Barbel has slender stem, two terminal bulbs, and three to seven terminal filaments arising together on distal bulb or arising on short stem on distal bulb. Terminal bulbs are separated by a distance equal to 1.7 to 3.8 times length of distal bulb, terminal filaments lack bulblets, and one is thicker and longer than remainder. Ventral groove on belly is absent. Pectoral fin consists of 3 free rays. Dorsal fin has 23 to 26 rays, and anal fin has 36 to 40 rays. Pelvic fin has 7 rays. IP number 7, PV number 31 to 34, and VAV number 17 to 20. OV number 31 to 35, VAL number 18 to 21, and AC number 17 to 20. Preorbital and suborbital luminous organs are absent. Vertebrae number 67 to 69. Color is black. Barbel has no external color, but axis of stem and filaments is pigmented.

This species occurs in the Atlantic, Indian, and western Pacific Oceans. In the western Atlantic it occurs in the Caribbean Sea, the Straits of Florida, and the northeastern Gulf of Mexico. Food consists of myctophids. Maximum known size is 135.8 mm SL.

REFERENCES: Morrow and Gibbs 1964; Gibbs et al. 1983; Sutton and Hopkins 1996, in press.

Eustomias micraster   Parr 1927

Eustomias micraster is elongate and slender, with a long, tapering, protrusible snout; a long chin barbel bearing two terminal bulbs and a single terminal filament; and abdominal pelvic fins. It is distinguished from the other species of the family by the following combination of characters. Lower jaw is about as long as upper jaw and is not upturned at tip. Chin barbel is less than 60% of SL. Barbel has slender stem, two widely separated terminal bulbs, and a single, long filament with four or more short bulblet-bearing branches near terminal bulb. Distal bulb is shorter than proximal bulb in large specimens but longer than proximal bulb in small specimens. Deep groove on belly is absent. Pectoral fin consists of 3 free rays. Dorsal fin has 22 to 25 rays, and anal fin has 32 to 40 rays. Pelvic fin has 7 rays. IP number 7, PV number 29 to 32, and VAV number 17 or 18. OV number 29 to 32, VAL number 17 to 20, and AC 18 or 19. Preorbital and suborbital luminous organs are absent. Color is black. Barbel has no external color, but axis of stem is pigmented.

This species occurs in the western Atlantic Ocean from the Bahamas to the Lesser Antilles and the northeastern Gulf of Mexico. Food consists of midwater fishes. Maximum known size is 223.5 mm SL.

REFERENCES: Morrow and Gibbs 1964 (as *E. bibulbosus*, in part); Gibbs et al. 1983; Sutton and Hopkins 1996, in press.

Eustomias obscurus   Vaillant 1888

Eustomias obscurus is elongate and very slender, with a long, tapering, protrusible snout; a relatively long chin barbel bearing a single or double terminal bulbs; and abdominal pelvic fins. It is distinguished from the other species of the family by the following combination of characters. Body depth is 5.2% to 8.2% and head length is 11.2% to 12.3% of SL. Premaxilla has 12 to 14 teeth, first of which is fanglike. Lower jaw has 11 to 20 teeth on each side. Chin barbel is 23.5% to 49% of SL. Barbel has slender stem without branches or filaments and single or double terminal bulbs. Apex of single bulb or terminal bulb bears three to eight filaments that arise separately or have common stem. Deep groove on belly is lacking. Pectoral fin consists of 3 free rays. Dorsal fin has 23 to 30 rays, and anal fin has 34 to 46 rays. Pelvic fin has 7 rays. Photophores of OV and VAL series are partially grouped into pairs. IP number 7 to 9, PV number 33 to 35, and VAV number 14 to 18. OV number 30 to 37, VAL number 14 to 19, and AC number 19 to 23. Color is black. Barbel has little pigment.

This species occurs in the Atlantic Ocean. In the western Atlantic it occurs in the northeastern Gulf of Mexico. Maximum known size is 205.9 mm SL.

REFERENCES: Morrow and Gibbs 1964 (as *E. chabanaudi*, in part); Gibbs et al. 1983; Gibbs 1984d; Sutton and Hopkins 1996 (consider *E. chabanaudi* to be distinct from *E. obscurus*).

Eustomias parvibulbus Parr 1927

Eustomias parvibulbus is elongate and slender, with a long, tapering, protrusible snout; a short chin barbel bearing a terminal bulb; and abdominal pelvic fins. It is distinguished from the other species of the family by the following combination of characters. Body depth is 10.2% and head length is 15% of SL. Lower jaw is about as long as upper jaw and is not upturned at tip. Premaxilla has 10 teeth, with second fanglike. Lower jaw has 12 teeth. Chin barbel is 15.7% of SL. Barbel has slender stem, three branches arising near middle of stem, and terminal bulb bearing three hairy filaments. Two lateral branches are slender and relatively long, and middle branch is relatively thick and has distal bulblet. Ventral groove on belly extends from PV 3 to PV 13. Pectoral fin consists of 2 closely bound rays. Dorsal fin has 23 rays, and anal fin has 40 rays. Pelvic fin has 7 rays. IP number 7, PV number 28, and VAV number 18. OV number 28, VAL number 16, and AC number 21. Preorbital and suborbital luminous organs are absent. Color is black. Barbel is externally colored.

This species occurs in the northwestern Atlantic off the Bahamas and in the northeastern Gulf of Mexico at about 1,700 m. Food consists of myctophids. Maximum known size is 198 mm SL.

REFERENCES: Morrow and Gibbs 1964; Gibbs et al. 1983 (as *E. bigelowi*); Sutton and Hopkins 1996, in press.

Eustomias polyaster   Parr 1927

Eustomias polyaster is elongate and very slender, with a long, tapering, protrusible snout; a moderately long chin barbel bearing several terminal bulbs and a terminal appendage; and abdominal pelvic fins. It is distinguished from the other species of the family by the following combination of characters. Body depth is 6.2% to 9.1% and head length is 11.5% to 14.3% of SL. Premaxilla has 11 to 15 teeth. Lower jaw has 14 to 18 teeth. Chin barbel is 37% to 52% of SL. Barbel has slender shaft and two or more terminal bulbs separated by a distance of 0.8% to 2.6% of SL. Distal bulb is 1.3 to 3 times longer than proximal bulb and is bilobate or notched distally. Terminal filament is 8% to 19% of SL, originates from longer lobe of distal bulb, and has numerous bulblets and side branches. In large specimens, some bulblets in terminal filament exceed size of proximal bulb. Ventral groove on belly is absent. Pectoral fin consists of 2 free rays. Dorsal fin has 23 to 26 rays, and anal fin has 33 to 38 rays. Pelvic fin has 7 rays. IP number 7, PV number 32 to 35, and VAV number 15 to 17. OV number 32 to 35, VAL number 16 to 18, and AC number 17 or 18. Preorbital and suborbital luminous organs are absent. Po is 1.6% to 2% of SL. Vertebrae number 65 to 67. Color is black. Barbel stem is light to darkly pigmented, and external chevron-shaped or roundish striated areas on stem are unpigmented.

This species occurs in the North Atlantic. In the western Atlantic it occurs from the northern and southern Sargasso Sea, the Bahamas to the northern Gulf of Mexico off the Mississippi Delta, and the Caribbean Sea. Maximum known size is 142 mm SL.

REFERENCES: Morrow and Gibbs 1964; Gomon and Gibbs 1985.

Eustomias schmidti   Regan and Trewavas 1930

Eustomias schmidti is elongate and slender, with a long, tapering, protrusible snout; a moderately short chin barbel bearing three branches; and abdominal pelvic fins. It is distinguished from the other species of the family by the following combination of characters. Body depth is 8.5% to 10% and head length is 11.6% to 14.2% of SL. Lower jaw is about as long as upper jaw. Chin barbel is 5% to 17% of SL. Barbel has slender stem and three branches of variable complexity medial to terminal bulb. Lateral branches are secondarily branched, and medial branch is swollen, slightly shorter than lateral branches, and has one or two terminal filaments. Terminal bulb is constricted to produce distal knob, and one or more filaments arise from constriction. Deep ventral groove on belly is relatively short. Pectoral fin consists of 2 rays enclosed in black membrane. Dorsal fin has 22 to 26 rays, and anal fin has 36 to 44 rays. Pelvic fin has 7 rays. IP number 7 or 8, PV number 27 or 28, and VAV number 14 or 15. OV number 27 to 29, VAL number 14 to 16, and AC number 20 to 23. Preorbital and suborbital luminous organs are absent. Po is present. Color is black. Barbel stem is pigmented.

This species occurs in the North Atlantic. In the western Atlantic it occurs from about 40°N to 35°S, including Bermuda, the Gulf of Mexico, and the Caribbean Sea. Food consists of midwater fishes. Maximum known size is 210 mm SL.

REFERENCES: Morrow and Gibbs 1964; Gibbs 1984d; Sutton and Hopkins 1996, in press.

Eustomias variabilis Regan and Trewavas 1930

Eustomias variabilis is elongate and slender, with a long, tapering, protrusible snout; a moderately short chin barbel bearing two or three terminal bulbs; and abdominal pelvic fins. It is distinguished from the other species of the family by the following combination of characters. Body depth is 8% to 10% of SL. Premaxilla has 10 to 12 teeth. Lower jaw has 10 to 15 teeth. Chin barbel is 18% to 41% of SL. Barbel has slender stem and two to four terminal bulbs, with proximal and distal bulbs separated by a distance of 4% to 6.2% of SL. Proximal bulb is 0.3% to 1.3% of SL, and distal bulb is 0.6% to 2.1% of SL. Distal bulb bears terminal filaments 0.3% to 4.9% of SL that either possess or lack swollen bulblets. Deep ventral groove on belly is absent. Pectoral fin consists of 2 free rays. Dorsal fin has 22 to 24 rays, and anal fin has 33 to 37 rays. Pelvic fin has 7 rays. IP number 7 or 8, PV number 31 to 34, and VAV number 14 to 17. OV number 31 to 34, VAL number 16 to 18, and AC number 16 to 18. Preorbital and suborbital luminous organs are absent. Po is present. Vertebrae number 63 to 66. Color is black. Barbel stem is well pigmented and external chevron-shaped or roundish striated areas on stem are unpigmented.

This species occurs in the western North Atlantic from the Straits of Florida, the northern Gulf of Mexico, the Bahamas, the Caribbean Sea, and off the northern coast of South America. Maximum known size is 145 mm SL.

REFERENCES: Morrow and Gibbs 1964 (as *Eustomias brevibarbatus,* in part); Gomon and Gibbs 1985; Sutton and Hopkins 1996.

Eustomias xenobolus   Regan and Trewavas 1930

Eustomias xenobolus is elongate and very slender, with a long, tapering, protrusible snout; a moderately short chin barbel bearing a single terminal bulb with three short filaments; and abdominal pelvic fins. It is distinguished from the other species of the family by the following combination of characters. Body depth is 7.1% to 9.1% and head length is 12.5% of SL. Chin barbel is 22% to 57% of SL. Barbel has slender stem and single terminal bulb ranging from 0.5% to 1.4% of SL. Bulb consists of slender proximal part about width of stem and globular distal part much wider than proximal part. Distal part of bulb has one to three terminal filaments 0.4 to 2.1 times bulb length and with or without side branches. Deep groove on belly is absent. Pectoral fin consists of 2 free rays.

Dorsal fin has 22 to 25 rays, and anal fin has 36 to 37 rays. Pelvic fin has 7 rays. IP number 7, PV number 34, and VAV number 14 to 16. OV number 33 or 34, VAL number 16 or 17, and AC number 17 or 18. Preorbital and suborbital luminous organs are absent. Po is present. Vertebrae number 65. Color is black. Barbel stem has little or no pigment, but axis of stem is darkly pigmented.

This species occurs in the western Atlantic from the Gulf of Mexico and the Caribbean Sea. Maximum known size is 170 mm SL.

REFERENCES: Morrow and Gibbs 1964; Gomon and Gibbs 1985; Sutton and Hopkins 1996.

Flagellostomias boureei   (Zugmayer 1913)

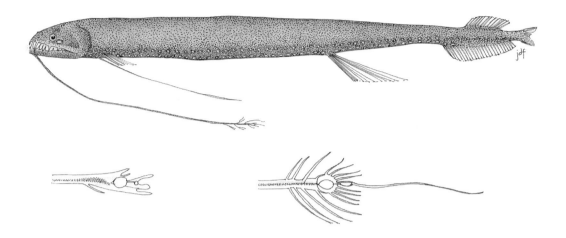

Flagellostomias boureei is elongate and very slender, with a blunt, nonprotrusible snout; a long chin barbel bearing a swollen bulb and filaments; and abdominal pelvic fins. It is distinguished from the other species of the family by the following combination of characters. Body depth is 6.2% to 11.1% and head length is 11.4% to 15.4% of SL. Lower jaw is neither longer than upper jaw nor upturned at tip. Premaxilla has six fanglike teeth. Lower jaws have one large, fanglike tooth and four smaller teeth. Chin barbel is 50% to 75% of SL. Barbel has slender stem, preterminal filaments, and swollen bulb bearing variable number of filaments. Pectoral fin consists of 1 long, free ray and 8 to 11 short, joined rays. Long pectoral ray has bulb and filament at tip. Dorsal fin has 14 to 17 rays, and anal fin has 21 to 26 rays. Pelvic fin has 7 rays. IP number 8 to 10, PV number 31 to 34, and VAV number 14 to 16. OV number 30 to 32, VAL number 12 to 17, and AC number 15 to 18. Preorbital and suborbital luminous organs are absent. Po is present in males and is about twice as long as it is wide. Vertebrae number about 65. Color is black.

This species occurs worldwide in subtropical to warm temperate seas. In the western Atlantic it occurs in subtropical and warm temperate waters north of 15°N and south of 28°S, including the Gulf of Mexico and the Caribbean Sea. Maximum known size is 320 mm SL.

REFERENCES: Morrow and Gibbs 1964; Murdy et al. 1983; Gibbs 1984d, 1986d; Sutton and Hopkins 1996.

Grammatostomias circularis Morrow 1959

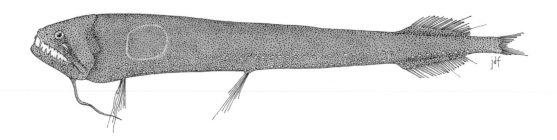

Grammatostomias circularis is elongate and slender, with a tapering, nonprotrusible snout; a moderately long and simple chin barbel; and abdominal pelvic fins. It is distinguished from the other species of the family by the following combination of characters. Body depth is 10.5% and head length is 15.6% of SL. Lower jaw is about as long as upper jaw and is not upturned at tip. Premaxilla has 11 teeth, and lower jaw has 18 teeth, with anterior teeth largest in both jaws. Chin barbel is up to 7 times SL when complete. End of barbel is thought to be unmodified. Pectoral fin has 9 rays. Dorsal fin has 21 rays, and anal fin has 23 rays. Pelvic fin has 8 rays. IP number 7, PV number 18, and VAV number 21, with last one above anal fin base. OV number 18, VAL number 19 or 20, and AC number 13. Pre-orbital luminous organ is absent. Suborbital organ and Po are present, and Po is about 5 times longer than it is wide. Side of body has circular line of luminous tissue behind pectoral fin insertion. Head and body are scattered with numerous small, luminous organs. Luminous tissue also occurs on anterior pectoral rays. Vertebrae number 56. Color is black.

This species occurs in the tropical to subtropical Atlantic Ocean. In the western Atlantic it occurs along the eastern seaboard of the United States from 32°N to 19°N, in the Gulf of Mexico and the Caribbean Sea, and off northern South America from 19°S to 32°S. Maximum known size is 136 mm SL.

REFERENCES: Morrow and Gibbs 1964; Gibbs 1984d; Sutton and Hopkins 1996.

Leptostomias analis   Regan and Trewavas 1930

Leptostomias analis is elongate and very slender, with a short, blunt, nonprotrusible snout; a long chin barbel bearing a single filament on the stem and on the bulb; and abdominal pelvic fins. It is distinguished from the other species of the family by the following combination of characters. Body depth is 7.1% and head length is 11.1% of SL. Premaxilla has one or two moderate-sized teeth followed by a fang-like tooth and several outer fixed and inner depressible teeth. Lower jaw has single series of teeth, with first four erect and remainder oblique. Chin barbel is nearly as long as body. Barbel has slender stem; single small filament at base of stem; and elongate, slender bulb bearing single swollen filament near tip. Belly lacks groove. Pectoral fin is small and consists of 10 unbranched rays. Dorsal fin has 21 rays, and anal fin has 28 rays. Pelvic fin has 8 rays. IP number 10, PV number 40, and VAV number 22. OV number 40, VAL number 22, and AC number 14. Preorbital and suborbital luminous organs are absent. Po is present in males. Color is black, and barbel has black stem.

This species occurs in the western North Atlantic in the Caribbean Sea off St. Croix and in the northeastern Gulf of Mexico. Maximum known size is 168 mm SL.

REFERENCES: Morrow and Gibbs 1964; Sutton and Hopkins 1996.

Leptostomias bermudensis Beebe 1932

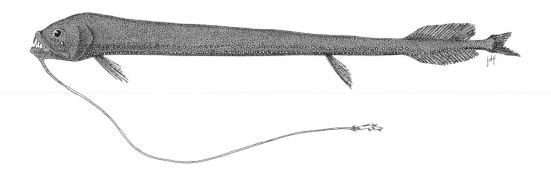

Leptostomias bermudensis is elongate and very slender, with a short, blunt, nonprotrusible snout; a long chin barbel bearing an elongated, asymmetrical bulb; and abdominal pelvic fins. It is distinguished from the other species of the family by the following combination of characters. Body depth is 6.3% to 7.1% and head length is 8.3% to 9.1% of SL. Lower jaw is neither longer than upper jaw nor upturned at tip. Premaxilla has six teeth. Lower jaw has minute, depressible teeth anteriorly, followed by one large fang, moderate-sized depressible teeth, and three small teeth posteriorly. Chin barbel is 59% to 72% of SL. Barbel consists of slender stem, three small filaments widely spaced on distal one-fourth of stem, and banana-shaped bulb with small filaments. Pectoral fin consists of 9 to 11 unbranched rays of equal length. Dorsal fin has 20 rays, and anal fin has 24 or 25 rays. Pelvic fin has 7 rays. IP number 10, PV number 45 to 48, and VAV number 21. OV number 46 to 48, VAL number 22, and AC number 12. Preorbital and suborbital luminous organs are absent. Po is small and roundish. Color is black.

This species occurs in the western North Atlantic off Bermuda and in the Gulf of Mexico and the Caribbean Sea. Food consists of myctophids. Maximum known size is 267 mm SL.

REFERENCES: Morrow and Gibbs 1964; Sutton and Hopkins 1996, in press.

Leptostomias bilobatus   (Koefoed 1956)

Leptostomias bilobatus is elongate and very slender, with a short, blunt, nonprotrusible snout; a long chin barbel bearing two long filaments on stem and two short filaments on bulb; and abdominal pelvic fins. It is distinguished from the other species of the family by the following combination of characters. Body depth is 6% to 9% and head length is 10.9% to 12.3% of SL. Lower jaw is neither longer than upper jaw nor upturned at tip. Premaxilla has 7 teeth. Lower jaw has 10 teeth. Chin barbel is 65% to 75% of SL. Barbel consists of slender stem, two long, slender filaments arising near base of stem, and one terminal bulb. Bulb is split distally into two segments and has pair of filaments arising near base and two pairs of short filaments arising near base of each distal portion of bulb. Pectoral fin consists of 9 un-branched rays of equal length. Dorsal and anal fin bases are about equal length. Dorsal fin has 20 or 21 rays, and anal fin has 25 or 26 rays. Pelvic fin has 7 rays. IP number 11, PV number 42 to 45, and VAV number 21 to 23, with last 4 or 5 located over anal fin base. OV number 42, VAL number 23 or 24, and AC number 11 or 12. Preorbital and suborbital luminous organs are absent. Po is small and roundish. Color is black.

This species occurs in the North Atlantic. It occurs in the Gulf of Mexico in the western Atlantic. Food consists of myctophids. Maximum known size is 110 mm SL.

REFERENCES: Morrow and Gibbs 1964; Rass 1971; Sutton and Hopkins 1996, in press.

Leptostomias gladiator   (Zugmayer 1911)

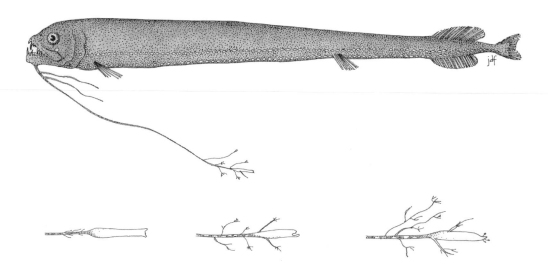

Leptostomias gladiator is elongate and very slender, with a short blunt, nonprotrusible snout; a long chin barbel bearing one or two filaments on stem and one to several filaments on bulb; and abdominal pelvic fins. It is distinguished from the other species of the family by the following combination of characters. Body depth is 5.5% to 10.1% and head length is 10% to 13.4% of SL. Lower jaw is neither longer than upper jaw nor upturned at snout. Premaxilla has seven or eight teeth. Lower jaw has five to eight teeth. Chin barbel is 33% to 75% of SL. Barbel consists of slender stem, one or two filaments at base of stem and other filaments along stem and base of bulb, and one long slender bulb with short tubercles or bulbed filaments. Pectoral fin consists of 11 unbranched rays of equal length. Dorsal fin has 19 to 22 rays, and anal fin has 23 to 29 rays.

Pelvic fin has 7 rays. IP number 10, PV number 39 to 44, and VAV number 20 to 22, with last 4 located over anal fin base. OV number 39 to 42, VAL number 20 to 22, and AC number 13. Preorbital and suborbital luminous organs are absent. Po is small and roundish. Vertebrae number 77. Color is black.

This species occurs worldwide in subtropical to warm temperate seas. In the western Atlantic it occurs from the eastern seaboard of the United States between 40°N and 25°N, in the Gulf of Mexico and the Caribbean Sea, and off the east coast of South America from 10°S to 40°S. Food consists of myctophids. Maximum known size 370 mm SL.

REFERENCES: Morrow and Gibbs 1964; Rass 1971; Gibbs 1984d, 1986d; Sutton and Hopkins 1996, in press.

Leptostomias haplocaulus   Regan and Trewavas 1930

Leptostomias haplocaulus is very elongate and slender, with a short, blunt, nonprotrusible snout; a long chin barbel bearing series of filaments on stem; and abdominal pelvic fins. It is distinguished from the other species of the family by the following combination of characters. Body depth is 7.4% and head length is 10.5% of SL. Premaxilla has one or two moderate-sized teeth followed by a fanglike tooth and several erect outer and several depressible inner teeth. Chin barbel lacks filaments on base of stem but possesses filaments at base of elongate bulb and along surface of bulb. Groove on belly is absent. Pectoral fin is small and consists of 10 rays. Dorsal fin has 19 rays, and anal fin has 23 rays. Pelvic fin has 7 rays. IP number 10, PV number 41, and VAV number 21. OV number 4, VAL number 20, and AC number 11. Preorbital and suborbital luminous organs are absent. Po is present in males. Color is black, and belly has black stem.

This species occurs in the northwestern Atlantic off Bermuda and in the northeastern Gulf of Mexico. Maximum known size is 100 mm SL.

REFERENCES: Morrow and Gibbs 1964; Sutton and Hopkins 1996.

Leptostomias leptobolus   Regan and Trewavas 1930

Leptostomias leptobolus is very elongate and slender, with a short, blunt, nonprotrusible snout; a very long chin barbel bearing filaments on base of stem; and abdominal pelvic fins. It is distinguished from the other species of the family by the following combination of characters. Body depth is 7.7% and head length is 11.1% to 11.8% of SL. Premaxilla has one or two moderate-sized teeth followed by a fanglike tooth and several fixed outer and depressible inner teeth. Lower jaw has small tooth followed by a fanglike tooth and several small, fixed outer and depressible inner teeth. Chin barbel is about 75% of SL. Barbel has slender stem bearing two filaments near base and elongate bulb lacking filaments. Belly lacks groove. Pectoral fin is small and has 10 unbranched rays. Dorsal fin has 20 rays, and anal fin has 25 rays. Pelvic fin has 7 rays. IP number 10, PV number 43, and VAV number 20. OP number 42 or 43, VAL number 20, and AC number 12 or 13. Preorbital and suborbital luminous organs are absent. Po is present in males. Color is black.

This species occurs in the western North Atlantic off Bermuda, in the Caribbean Sea off Dominica, and in the northeastern Gulf of Mexico. Food consists of myctophids and other midwater fishes. Maximum known size is 115 mm SL.

REFERENCES: Morrow and Gibbs 1964; Sutton and Hopkins 1996, in press.

Melanostomias biseriatus   Regan and Trewavas 1930

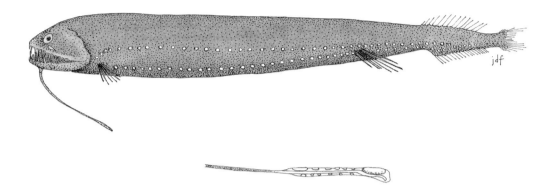

Melanostomias biseriatus is elongate and moderately slender, with a short, blunt, nonprotrusible snout; a moderately long chin barbel bearing long slender expanded section; and abdominal pelvic fins. It is distinguished from the other species of the family by the following combination of characters. Body depth is 10.6% to 15% and head length is 13.1% to 14.9% of SL. Lower jaw is about equal in length to upper jaw and is not upturned at tip. Premaxilla has eight long, barbed teeth. Lower jaw has eight or nine long, barbed teeth. Chin barbel is 20% to 40% of SL. Barbel has slender stem and narrow, flattened distal tip terminating as prominent ovoid bulb. Distal tip bears two narrow flattened wings, each with row of discrete opaque bodies. Pectoral fin consists of 5 rays and is poorly developed. Dorsal fin has 13 to 15 rays, and anal fin has 17 to 19 rays. Pelvic fin has 7 rays. IP number 10, PV number 27 to 29, and VAV number 12 to 14. OV number 26 to 28, VAL number 12 or 13, and AC number 9 to 11. Preorbital and suborbital luminous organs are absent. Po is about equal to eye diameter and is triangular shaped. Color is black. Barbel stem is black, and tip of barbel is unpigmented.

This species occurs in the tropical to subtropical Atlantic between 40 and 1,800 m. In the western Atlantic it occurs in the Bahamas, the Gulf of Mexico, and the Caribbean Sea. Food consists of midwater fishes. Maximum known size is 250 mm SL.

REFERENCES: Morrow and Gibbs 1964; Gibbs 1984d; Sutton and Hopkins 1996, in press.

Melanostomias macrophotus   Regan and Trewavas 1930

Melanostomias macrophotus is elongate and moderately slender, with a short, blunt, non-protrusible snout; a moderately short chin barbel bearing an expanded and pigmented distal section; and abdominal pelvic fins. It is distinguished from the other species of the family by the following combination of characters. Body depth is 10% to 11% of SL. Lower jaw is about as long as upper jaw and is not upturned at tip. Premaxilla has eight long, barbed teeth. Lower jaw has eight or nine long, barbed teeth. Chin barbel is about 23% to 33% of SL. Barbel has slender stem and flattened, moderately narrow distal tip with narrow lateral wings and oval-shaped distal bulb. Pectoral fin is poorly developed and consists of 6 rays. Dorsal fin has 13 to 16 rays. Pelvic fin has 7 rays. IP number 10, PV number 26 to 29, and VAV number 15. OV number 26, VAL number 13, and AC number 9. Preorbital and suborbital luminous organs are absent. Po is about equal to eye diameter and is triangular shaped. Color is black. Barbel is black except that narrow proximal band, outer edges of flattened wings, and distal bulb are unpigmented.

This species occurs in the tropical to subtropical Atlantic and Pacific Oceans. In the western Atlantic it occurs in the Gulf of Mexico and the Caribbean Sea, and along the coast of South America to 28°S. Maximum known size is 230 mm SL.

REFERENCES: Morrow and Gibbs 1964 (as *Melanostomias melanopogon*); Gibbs 1984d.

Melanostomias margaritifer   Regan and Trewavas 1930

Melanostomias margaritifer is elongate and moderately slender, with a short, blunt, non-protrusible snout; abdominal pelvic fins; and a moderately long chin barbel bearing a flattened terminal section with a luminous body. It is distinguished from the other species of the family by the following combination of characters. Body depth is about 10% and head length is 13.8% of SL. Lower jaw is about equal to upper jaw in length and is not upturned at tip. Premaxilla has about eight, maxilla has four or five, and lower jaw has eight or nine long, depressible, barbed teeth. Chin barbel is 2 to 2.5 times head length. Barbel has slender stem and relatively slender distally expanded section bearing single ovoid luminous body. Length of expanded section of barbel is less than 2 times width. Pectoral fin is short and consists of 5 rays. Dorsal fin has 15 or 16 rays, and anal fin has 18 rays. Pelvic fin has 7 rays. IP number 10, PV number 27 or 28, and VAV number 13 or 14. OV number 27, VAL number 13, and AC number 10. Preorbital and suborbital luminous organs are absent. Po is triangular shaped and about as long as eye diameter. Color is black.

This species occurs in the Caribbean Sea off Jamaica and Puerto Rico, and in the northeastern Gulf of Mexico. Maximum known size is 80 mm SL.

REFERENCES: Morrow and Gibbs 1964; Sutton and Hopkins 1996.

Melanostomias melanopogon   Regan and Trewavas 1930

Melanostomias melanopogon is elongate and moderately slender, with a short, blunt, non-protrusible snout; a moderately short chin barbel bearing a long, slender distal section that lacks luminous material; and abdominal pelvic fins. It is distinguished from the other species of the family by the following combination of characters. Body depth is 10% to 11.1% and head length is 13.3% to 15% of SL. Premaxilla has about eight, maxilla has four or five, and lower jaw has eight or nine mostly long, depressible, barbed teeth. Chin barbel is 25.9% of SL. Barbel has slender stem and long, slender distal expanded section that broadens to near tip and bears single ovoid bulb. Pectoral fin is small and consists of 5 rays. Dorsal fin has 13 rays, and anal fin has 17 rays. Pelvic fin has 7 rays. IP number 10, PV number 28, and VAV number 15. OV number 26, VAL number 13, and AC number 9. Preorbital and suborbital luminous organs are absent. Po luminous organ is triangular and about as long as eye diameter. Color is black, and barbel is lightly to darkly pigmented.

This species occurs in the northwestern Atlantic off the Bahamas, the Lesser Antilles, Jamaica, St. Croix, and in the northeastern Gulf of Mexico. Maximum known size is 82 mm SL.

REFERENCES: Morrow and Gibbs 1964; Sutton and Hopkins 1996.

Melanostomias melanops   Brauer 1902

Melanostomias melanops is elongate and moderately slender, with a short, blunt, nonprotrusible snout; a long chin barbel that distally tapers to a filament; and abdominal pelvic fins. It is distinguished from the other species of the family by the following combination of characters. Body depth is 11.8% to 14.2% and head length is 14.1% to 14.5% of SL. Lower jaw is about equal to upper jaw in length and is not upturned at tip. Premaxilla has eight long, barbed teeth. Lower jaw has eight or nine long, barbed teeth. Chin barbel is 25% to 45% of SL. Barbel has slender stem and flattened, narrow distal tip bearing terminal filamentous extension. Distal tip bears flattened wings, each with small spherical or elongate opaque bodies. Pectoral fin is poorly developed and consists of 5 rays. Dorsal fin has 11 to 16 rays, and anal fin has 17 or 18 rays. Pelvic fin has 7 or 8 rays. IP number 11, PV number 26 to 29, and VAV number 13 or 14. OV number 27 or 28, VAL number 11 or 12, and AC number 9 or 10. Preorbital and suborbital luminous organs are absent. Po is about equal to eye diameter and is triangular shaped. Color is black. Stem of barbel is unpigmented except for base, and tip of barbel is unpigmented or has irregular dark patches.

This species occurs worldwide in tropical to subtropical seas. In the western Atlantic it occurs along the eastern seaboard of the United States from about 40°N to 28°N, in the Gulf of Mexico and the Caribbean Sea, and along the east coast of South America from 10°S to 30°S. Food consists of myctophids. Maximum known size is 260 mm SL.

REFERENCES: Morrow and Gibbs 1964; Gibbs 1984d; Sutton and Hopkins 1996, in press.

Melanostomias tentaculatus (Regan and Trewavas 1930)

Melanostomias tentaculatus is elongate and moderately slender, with a short, blunt, nonprotrusible snout; a long chin barbel bearing a nonterminal bulb; and abdominal pelvic fins. It is distinguished from the other species of the family by the following combination of characters. Body depth is 11.6% to 14.3% and head length is 12.5% to 16.7% of SL. Lower jaw is about as long as upper jaw and is not upturned at tip. Premaxilla has eight long, barbed teeth. Lower jaw has eight or nine long, barbed teeth. Chin barbel is 25% to 50% of SL. Barbel has slender stem and elongate bulb beside distal aspect of stem. Stem extends distal to bulb to form distal tentacle. Bulb is occasionally preceded by small bulb. Pectoral fin consists of 5 rays and is poorly developed. Dorsal fin has 16 or 17 rays, and anal fin has 19 or 20 rays. Pelvic fin has 7 rays. IP number 10, PV number 25 to 27, and VAV number 14 or 15. OV number 24 or 25, VAL number 14, and AC number 9 or 10. Preorbital and suborbital luminous organs are absent. Po is about equal to eye diameter and is triangular shaped. Color is black. Barbel stem is black, and bulb and tentacle are unpigmented.

This species occurs worldwide in the tropical to subtropical seas. In the western Atlantic it occurs from the eastern seaboard of the United States from about 35°N to the east coast of Brazil to about 8°S, including the Gulf of Mexico and the Caribbean Sea. Food consists of myctophids. Maximum known size is nearly 240 mm SL.

REFERENCES: Morrow and Gibbs 1964; Gibbs 1984d; Sutton and Hopkins 1996, in press.

Melanostomias valdiviae Brauer 1902

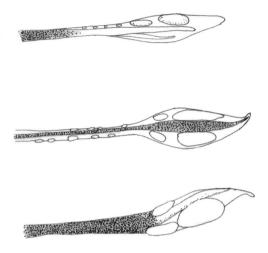

Melanostomias valdiviae is elongate and moderately slender, with a short, blunt, nonprotrusible snout; a moderately short chin barbel bearing a relatively short terminal expanded section; and abdominal pelvic fins. It is distinguished from the other species of the family by the following combination of characters. Body depth is 9.6% to 12.7% and head length is 11.7% to 15.3% of SL. Lower jaw is about as long as upper jaw and is not upturned at tip. Premaxilla has eight long, barbed teeth. Lower jaw has eight or nine long, barbed teeth. Chin barbel is 8.9% to 23.2% of SL. Barbel has slender stem and short, broad tip. Tip has wing on either side of axis, and each wing contains one or two spherical to long, opaque bodies, with one side of distal end of tip tapering to form short pointed filament. Pectoral fin is poorly developed and consists of 4 or 5 rays. Dorsal fin has 12 to 16 rays, and anal fin has 16 to 19 rays. Pelvic fin has 7 rays. IP number 10 or 11, PV number 27, and VAV number 12 to 15. OV number 23 to 26, VAL number 11 to 15, and AC number 9 or 10. Preorbital and suborbital luminous organs are absent. Po is about equal to eye diameter and is triangular shaped. Color is black. Barbel is black, and tip of barbel is unpigmented.

This species occurs worldwide in tropical to warm temperate seas. In the western Atlantic it occurs from about 40°N to about 8°N, including the Gulf of Mexico and the Caribbean Sea, and off eastern South America from 10°S to 40°S. Food consists of myctophids. Maximum known size is 230 mm SL.

REFERENCES: Morrow and Gibbs 1964; Gibbs 1984d, 1986d; Sutton and Hopkins 1996.

Pachystomias microdon   (Günther 1878)

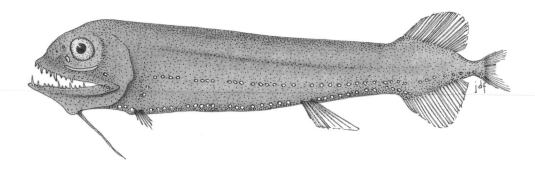

Pachystomias microdon is moderately elongate and relatively deep bodied, with large eyes; a relatively short, simple chin barbel; and abdominal pelvic fins. It is distinguished from the other species of the family by the following combination of characters. Body depth is 13.8% to 20% and head length is 21.4% to 32% of SL. Jaws are slender and slightly curved upward. Premaxilla has 11 to 14 slender, uniserial teeth. Maxilla has small, oblique teeth, and lower jaw has single series of slender teeth of variable length. Chin barbel is shorter than head length in adults but about equal to one-half body length in juveniles. Barbel tapers to filament and lacks bulb or filaments. Pectoral fin is small and has 5 or 6 rays. Dorsal fin has 21 to 24 rays, and anal fin has 25 to 29 rays. Pelvic fin has 7 to 9 rays. Serial photophores are broken into loose groupings. IP number 8 or 9, PV number 14 to 17, and VAV number 12 to 14. OV number 17 or 18, VAL number 14 or 15, and AC number 8 or 9. Suborbital luminous organ is subdivided into short anterior part and long, slender posterior part. Po is very small and located below and behind eye. Color is black.

This species occurs in the Atlantic and southwestern Pacific Oceans. In the western Atlantic it occurs off Nova Scotia and from Bermuda to St. Lucia in the Caribbean Sea and in the northeastern Gulf of Mexico. Eyes of this species are sensitive to red light rays. Food consists of myctophid fishes. Maximum known size is 215 mm SL.

REFERENCES: Morrow and Gibbs 1964; Gibbs 1984d, 1986d; Sutton and Hopkins 1996, in press.

Photonectes achirus   Regan and Trewavas 1930

Photonectes achirus is elongate and slender, with a short, blunt, nonprotrusible snout and a short chin barbel bearing a small bulb and a slender unpigmented appendage, but without pectoral fins. It is distinguished from the other species of the family by the following combination of characters. Body depth is 11.8% to 16.7% and head length is 15.4% to 16.7% of SL. Lower jaw is longer than upper jaw and is curved upward at tip. Premaxilla has five or six erect teeth and seven or eight oblique teeth. Chin barbel is 50% to 67% of head length. Barbel has slender stem, small bulb, and slender, unpigmented terminal appendage. Dorsal fin has 15 to 17 rays, and anal fin has 18 or 19 rays. Pelvic fin has 7 rays. IV number 31 to 34, and VAV number 12 or 13. OV number 19 to 21, VAL number 11 or 12, and AC number 9 to 11. Po is as long as eye diameter. Color is black, with bluish midventral luminous stripe extending to pelvic fin base.

This species occurs in the northwestern Atlantic in the Caribbean Sea and the northeastern Gulf of Mexico between 75 and 500 m. Maximum known size is 62 mm SL.

REFERENCES: Morrow and Gibbs 1964; Sutton and Hopkins 1996.

Photonectes braueri   (Zugmayer 1913)

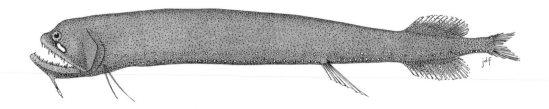

Photonectes braueri is elongate and slender, with a short, blunt, nonprotrusible snout; a short chin barbel bearing a terminal bulb with a minute terminal appendage; and abdominal pelvic fins. It is distinguished from the other species of the family by the following combination of characters. Body depth is 10.8% to 12.5% and head length is 11.9% to 15.4% of SL. Lower jaw is longer than upper jaw and is curved upward at tip. Premaxilla has 10 long teeth. Lower jaw has 34 or 35 teeth arranged in series of 4 that increase in size posteriorly. Chin barbel is about one-half head length in small specimens and about 20% of head length in large specimens. Barbel has short stem and relatively large, pear-shaped bulb bearing small ovoid terminal appendage. Pectoral fin has 2 rays. Dorsal and anal fin bases are about equal in length, and fin rays are not covered with thick skin. Dorsal fin has 15 to 18 rays, and anal fin has 17 to 21 rays. Pelvic fin has 7 rays.

IP number 10 or 11, PV number 21 to 23, and VAV number 14 or 15. OV number 20 to 23, VAL number 12 to 14, and AC number 10 to 12. Preorbital and suborbital luminous organs are absent. Po is longer than eye diameter. Head and body are covered with small light organs. Color is black. Barbel stem is black, and bulb is unpigmented.

This species occurs in subtropical to warm temperate waters of the Atlantic and Indian Oceans. In the western Atlantic it occurs between 23°N and 32°N, in the Gulf of Mexico and waters off Bermuda, and between 8°S and 40°S off South America. There is only a single confirmed record of this species from the Gulf of Mexico. Maximum known size is 280 mm SL.

REFERENCES: Morrow and Gibbs 1964; Murdy et al. 1983 (as *P.* c.f. *braueri*); Gibbs 1984d, 1986d.

Photonectes dinema   Regan and Trewavas 1930

Photonectes dinema is elongate and moderately slender, with a short, blunt, nonprotrusible snout; a short chin barbel bearing a terminal bulb and long appendage; and abdominal pelvic fins. It is distinguished from the other species of the family by the following combination of characters. Body depth is 10.5% to 15.4% and head length is 14.3% to 21.5% of SL. Lower jaw is longer than upper jaw and is upturned at tip. Premaxilla has 8 or 9 long teeth. Lower jaw has 22 to 28 small irregular teeth. Chin barbel is 25% to 66% of head length. Barbel has short stem and small terminal bulb bearing terminal appendage about as long as bulb, and is bifurcated distally. Pectoral fin consists of 2 or 3 short rays. Dorsal and anal fin bases are about equal in length, and fin rays are not covered with thick skin. Dorsal fin has 15 to 18 rays, and anal fin has 18 to 21 rays. Pelvic fin has 6 or 7 rays. IP number 9 to 11, PV number 19 or 20, and VAV number 14 to 18. OV number 17 to 20, VAL number 14 to 17, and AC number 11 or 12. Preorbital and suborbital luminous organs are absent. Po is about as long as eye diameter. Tip of snout has luminous spot, and small light organs are scattered over head and body. Vertebrae number 50. Color is black. Barbel stem is black, and bulb and terminal appendage are unpigmented.

This species occurs in subtropical to warm temperate waters of the North Atlantic. In the western Atlantic it occurs between 36°N and 23°N, including the Gulf of Mexico. Maximum known size is 250 mm SL.

REFERENCES: Morrow and Gibbs 1964; Gibbs 1984d.

Photonectes leucospilus   Regan and Trewavas 1930

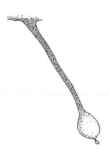

Photonectes leucospilus is elongate and moderately slender, with a short, blunt, nonprotrusible snout; a short chin barbel bearing a large terminal bulb and a long terminal appendage; and abdominal pelvic fins. It is distinguished from the other species of the family by the following combination of characters. Body depth is 11.1% to 12.5% and head length is 14.3% of SL. Lower jaw is longer than upper jaw and is upturned at tip. Premaxilla has 8 long teeth. Lower jaw has about 20 teeth. Chin barbel is 50% to 66% of head length. Barbel has short, thick stem and large bulb with single terminal appendage ending in small swelling. Pectoral fin has 2 or 3 rays. Dorsal and anal fin bases are about equal in length, and fin rays are not covered with thick skin. Dorsal fin has 16 rays, and anal fin has 18 to 20 rays. Pelvic fin has 7 rays. IP number 10, PV number 23 or 24, and VAV number 14 or 15. OV number 21 to 23, VAL number 12 to 14, and AC number 10 to 12. Preorbital and suborbital luminous organs are absent. Po is about one-half eye diameter. Tip of snout has luminous spot. Color is black. Barbel stem is black, and bulb and terminal appendage are unpigmented.

This species occurs in the western North Atlantic off Bermuda and in the Gulf of Mexico. It has been captured to 1,000 m. Food consists of midwater fishes. Maximum known size is 50 mm SL.

REFERENCES: Morrow and Gibbs 1964; Sutton and Hopkins 1996, in press.

Photonectes margarita   (Goode and Bean 1896)

Photonectes margarita is elongate and moderately slender, with a short, blunt, nonprotrusible snout; a short chin barbel bearing a terminal bulb with filaments; and abdominal pelvic fins. It is distinguished from the other species of the family by the following combination of characters. Body depth is 6.9% to 15% and head length is 12.6% to 15.3% of SL. Lower jaw is longer than upper jaw and is upturned at tip. Premaxilla has 5 to 8 long teeth. Lower jaw has 20 to 25 teeth in groups of 3 to 6 and size of teeth increases posteriorly. Chin barbel is shorter than, to slightly longer than, head length. Barbel has thick stem and terminal bulb. In small specimens bulb is large and bears about six short filaments, and in large specimens bulb is very small and bears various short minor filaments and single long major filament bearing secondary filaments. Pectoral fin consists of 1 long ray, or is absent. Dorsal fin has 15 to 18 rays, anal fin has 19 to 24 rays, and all fin rays are covered with thick skin. Pelvic fin has 7 rays. IP number 8 to 11, PV number 30 to 35, and VAV number 11 to 13. OV number 28 to 34, VAL number 11 to 14, and AC number 11 or 12. Preorbital and suborbital luminous organs are absent. Po is small (young) to equal to eye diameter (adults). Body is covered with vertical rows of small photophores. Vertebrae number 62 or 63. Color is black. Barbel stem is pigmented, and bulb is unpigmented.

This species occurs in the western North Atlantic from 47°40′N to the Gulf of Mexico and the Caribbean Sea. It has been captured from near the surface to 2,000 m. Food consists of midwater fishes and shrimps. Maximum known size is 320 mm SL.

REFERENCES: Morrow and Gibbs 1964; Rass 1971; Murdy et al. 1983; Sutton and Hopkins 1996, in press.

Photonectes mirabilis Parr 1927

Photonectes mirabilis is elongate and slender, with a short, blunt, nonprotrusible snout and a moderately short chin barbel bearing an elongated bulb, but without pectoral fins. It is distinguished from the other species of the family by the following combination of characters. Body depth is 12.9% to 15% and head length is 13.3% to 14.4% of SL. Lower jaw is longer than upper jaw and is curved upward at tip. Premaxilla has 7 teeth, with second and fifth longest. Maxilla has 4 teeth and 15 oblique denticles. Lower jaw has 25 small teeth. Chin barbel is about as long as head. Barbel has slender stem, moderately elongated bulb, and terminal appendage longer than remainder of barbel. Appendage has two white spots proximally, followed by short branch terminating as white bulb. Dorsal fin has 16 or 17 rays, and anal fin has 19 or 20 rays. Pelvic fin is abdominal, has 7 rays, and is located closer to caudal fin base than to posterior margin of opercular margin. IP number 9 or 10, PV number 24, and VAV number 11. OV number 21 to 24, VAL number 10, and AC number 11. Preorbital and suborbital luminous organs are absent. Po is located below and behind eye and is longer than eye diameter. Color is black.

This species occurs in the northwestern Atlantic Ocean from Cape Hatteras and Bermuda to the Bahamas and the northeastern Gulf of Mexico between 150 and 1,200 m. Maximum known size is 60 mm SL.

REFERENCES: Morrow and Gibbs 1964; Sutton and Hopkins 1996.

Photonectes parvimanus   Regan and Trewavas 1930

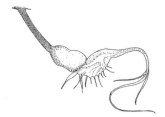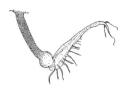

Photonectes parvimanus is elongate and slender, with a short, blunt, nonprotrusible snout; a short chin barbel bearing a comblike terminal appendage; and abdominal pelvic fins. It is distinguished from the other species of the family by the following combination of characters. Body depth is 8.3% to 12.5% and head length is 12.5% to 15.2% of SL. Lower jaw is longer than upper jaw and is upturned at tip. Premaxilla has 9 long teeth. Lower jaw has 26 small teeth in groups of 3 to 5. Chin barbel is about one-half head length. Barbel has short, moderately stout stem and swollen, ovoid bulb with complex terminal appendage. Terminal appendage is generally longer than bulb, broad basally, tapering to slender filament distally, and with fringing near bulb. Pectoral fin consists of 2 minute rays. Dorsal and anal fin bases are about equal in length, and fin rays are covered with thick skin. Dorsal fin has 17 to 19 rays, and anal fin has 22 to 24 rays. Pelvic fin has 7 rays. IP number 10 or 11, PV number 34 to 38, and VAV number 12 to 14. OV number 34 to 36, VAL number 12 to 14, and AC number 10 to 13. Preorbital and suborbital luminous organs are absent. Po is about equal to eye diameter. Vertebrae number 63. Color is black. Barbel stem is pigmented, and bulb and appendage are unpigmented.

This species occurs in the tropical to warm temperate Atlantic and Pacific Oceans. In the western Atlantic it occurs from 33°N to 23°N, including the Gulf of Mexico. It has been captured from the surface to 800 m. Maximum known size is 250 mm SL.

REFERENCES: Morrow and Gibbs 1964; Gibbs 1984d, 1986d; Sutton and Hopkins 1996.

Photonectes phyllopogon   Regan and Trewavas 1930

Photonectes phyllopogon is elongate and slender, with a short, blunt, nonprotrusible snout and a moderately short chin barbel bearing a large, round bulb and a leaflike terminal appendage, but without pectoral fins. It is distinguished from the other species of the family by the following combination of characters. Body depth is 11.8% and head length is 16.7% of SL. Lower jaw is longer than upper jaw and is curved upward at tip. Premaxilla has single row of curved teeth. Lower jaw has two or three oblique teeth on each side. Chin barbel is 66% of head length. Barbel has slender stem, large rounded white bulb, and terminal appendage consisting of cylindrical stalk and distal leaflike translucent expansion with serrated edges and bearing four terminal filaments. Dorsal fin has 20 rays, and anal fin has 22 rays. Pelvic fin is abdominal, is located closer to caudal fin base than to posterior margin of operculum, and has 7 rays. IV number 30, and VAV number 11. OV number 19, VAL number 12, and AC number 12. Color is black, and dorsal and anal fins are not covered with thick black skin.

This species occurs in the northwestern Atlantic in the Caribbean Sea and the northeastern Gulf of Mexico at 150 m or deeper. Maximum known size is 45 mm SL.

REFERENCES: Morrow and Gibbs 1964; Sutton and Hopkins 1996.

STOMIIDAE   Scaly dragonfishes

Scaly dragonfishes are very elongate and very slender, with very large jaws bearing fanglike teeth and a moderately long-based, posteriorly placed dorsal fin. They are distinguished from the other families of the order by the following combination of characters. Upper jaw extends to near anterior margin of preoperculum. Premaxilla is protractile. Chin barbel is long and slender, with terminal bulb and filaments at tip. Maxilla has numerous small teeth on posterior one-half of ventral margin. Vomer has pair of teeth, and palatine has one to three teeth. Gill rakers are replaced by teeth. Floor of mouth is present, membrane connects halves of lower jaw to isthmus. Pectoral fin is located below midflank. Pelvic fin is inserted closer to caudal fin base than to snout. Dorsal fin has short to moderate length base and is located just anterior to caudal peduncle. Anal fin base is about equal to or slightly longer than dorsal fin base and is located below dorsal fin. Adipose fin is absent. Photophores are present below eye, on branchiostegal membrane, in ventral row from isthmus to caudal fin base, and in lateral row from opercular flap to anal fin origin. Small luminous organs are scattered over head and body. Body is covered with five or six rows of hexagonal pigmented areas representing scale pockets. In life, body is covered with gelatinous membrane.

Scaly dragonfishes occur worldwide from tropical to temperate seas at depths near the surface to 2,000 m. Food consists of midwater fishes and, to a lesser extent, crustaceans. There are 11 species in two genera, and 3 species in two genera occur in the Gulf of Mexico.

Key to the Species of the Gulf of Mexico
(Adapted from Morrow 1964a)

1a. Chin barbel equal to head length or shorter; pelvic fin rays five, connected by membranes; large photophores of ventral row 100 or fewer 2

1b. Chin barbel 6 to 11 times head length; pelvic fin rays four or five, free of membranes; large photophores of ventral row 170 or more . . . . *Stomias longibarbatus* p. 544

2a. Chin barbel shorter than 50% of head length; five rows of hexagonal pigment patterns above lateral row of large photophores . . . . *Stomias brevibarbatus* p. 543

2b. Chin barbel longer than 50% of head length; six rows of hexagonal pigment patterns above lateral row of large photophores . . . . *Stomias affinis* p. 542

Stomias affinis   Günther 1887

Stomias affinis is very elongate and very slender, with a moderately short barbel and six rows of hexagonal pigmented areas. It is distinguished from the other species of the family by the following combination of characters. Body depth is 5.7% to 9.5% and head length is 9.9% to 11.2% of SL. Premaxilla has one small tooth, followed by one long fang and three or four small teeth. Maxilla has many minute oblique teeth on posterior one-half of ventral margin. Lower jaw has three or four small teeth near symphysis, followed by one large tooth and four or five progressively smaller teeth. Longest mandibular tooth is shorter than longest premaxillary tooth. Vomer has one tooth on each side, and palatine has two teeth. Chin barbel is slender, about as long as head length, and has terminal luminous bulb with three slender filaments. Pectoral fin has 6 or 7, dorsal fin has 16 to 21, pelvic fin has 4 or 5, and anal fin has 18 to 25 rays. IP number 9 to 12, PV number 41 to 46, and VAV number 5 to 9. OV number 40 to 46, VAL number 4 to 9, and AC number 14 to 18. Postorbital luminous organ is small and round. Small photophore is located on each branchiostegal ray, and small photophores are associated with each of six longitudinal rows of hexagonal pigmented areas. Three dorsalmost rows have 1 photophore per hexagon; fourth row has 2 or 3 photophores per hexagon, horizontally arranged; fifth row has 2 photophores per hexagon, vertically arranged; and sixth row has 3 photophores per hexagon, vertically arranged. Vertebrae number 66 to 72. Color is black to dark brown.

This species occurs worldwide in tropical to warm temperate seas. In the western Atlantic it occurs from Hudson Canyon, 39°N, to northern South America, including the Gulf of Mexico and the Caribbean Sea. Food consists of myctophids and, to a lesser extent, other midwater fishes and shrimps (*Sergestes*). Maximum known size is 204 mm SL.

REFERENCES: Morrow 1964b; Rass 1971; Gibbs 1969, 1984c; Sutton and Hopkins in press.

Stomias brevibarbatus Ege 1918

Stomias brevibarbatus is very elongate and very slender, with a short barbel and five rows of hexagonal pigment patterns above lateral row of large photophores. It is distinguished from the other species of the family by the following combination of characters. Snout is short, and lower jaw projects slightly beyond upper jaw. Body depth is 5% to 10.9% and head length is 10% to 13.9% of SL. Premaxilla has 1 small tooth, followed by relatively large tooth and 9 to 11 small teeth. Maxilla has minute, posteriorly directed teeth. Lower jaw has toothless space on either side of symphysis, followed by 14 to 20 small teeth. Vomer has 1 tooth on each side, and palatine has 2 teeth. Chin barbel is about 30% of head length and possesses spherical bulb, about one-third barbel length, with two pairs of short, simple filaments. Pectoral fin has 7 to 9, dorsal fin has 16 to 20, pelvic fin has 5, and anal fin has 19 to 22 rays.

IP number 9 to 12, PV number 32 to 35, and VAV number 12 to 16. OV number 32 to 35, VAL number 13 to 17, and AC number 14 or 15. Po organ is elongate and located slightly behind eye. Small photophore is located on each branchiostegal ray, and small photophores are associated with each of five longitudinal rows of hexagonal areas. Upper two rows have 1 small photophore per haxagon; third row has 7 to 10 photophores per hexagon; fourth row has 17 or 18 photophores per hexagon; and fifth row has 14 to 20 small photophores per hexagon. Vertebrae number 64 to 68. Color is black to dark brown.

This species occurs in the Atlantic Ocean in tropical to warm temperate seas at mesopelagic depths. Maximum known size is 200 mm SL.

REFERENCES: Morrow 1964a; Gibbs 1969, 1984c.

Stomias longibarbatus   (Brauer 1902)

Stomias longibarbatus is very elongate and very slender, with a very long barbel and six rows of hexagonal pigment areas above large lateral photophores. It is distinguished from the other species of the family by the following combination of characters. Snout is short, and lower jaw extends slightly beyond upper jaw. Body depth is 3% to 5% and head length is 5.3% to 7% of SL. Premaxilla has one small tooth, followed by one large fang and four small teeth. Maxilla has many small teeth. Lower jaw has small tooth near symphysis, followed by two progressively larger teeth and two or three small teeth. Vomer has one tooth on each side, and palatine has two teeth. Chin barbel is 6 to 11 times longer than head and terminates as spindle-shaped bulb bearing many complex filaments. Bulb and filaments appear to be luminous. Pectoral fin has 6 or 7 rays, dorsal fin has 13 or 14 rays, pelvic fin has 4 or 5 rays, and anal fin has 15 to 18 rays. IP number 11 or 12, PV number 80 to 86, and VAV number 58 to 67. OV number 79 to 85, VAL number 56 to 68, and AC number 19 to 22. Po organ is ovoid and surrounded by bluish rim. Single small photophore is associated with each branchiostegal ray, and small photophores are associated with six horizontal rows of hexagonal pigment areas. Uppermost row has single photophore per hexagon; second has 1 or 2 photophores per hexagon; and third, fourth, fifth, and sixth each have single photophore per hexagon. Color is bluish black with metallic sheen in life, and black dorsally, light silvery laterally, and black on belly in preservative.

This species occurs worldwide in tropical to warm temperate seas in the lower mesopelagic and upper bathypelagic zones. In the western Atlantic it occurs off Bermuda and in the Gulf of Mexico. Maximum known size is 400 mm SL.

REFERENCES: Morrow 1964a; Gibbs 1969, 1984c.

ATELEOPODIFORMES

Ateleopodiformes and Stomiiformes constitute the Stenopterygii, the basal group of the neoteleosteans. The single family of this order occurs in the Gulf of Mexico.

ATELEOPODIDAE

Ateleopodids are elongate and tapering, with a relatively large, broad head; reduced pelvic fins; and a long anal fin that is continuous with reduced caudal fin. They are distinguished from the other families of the order by the following combination of characters. Snout is moderately long, overhangs mouth, and has convex dorsal profile. Mouth is inferior, large, and horizontal to slightly oblique. Premaxilla is protractile. Small villiform teeth are present or absent in premaxilla. Maxilla, vomer, and palatine lack teeth. Eye is moderate to small in size. Four gill arches are present; slit is located behind fourth gill arch. Gill arches on first arch are short, bear small teeth, and number 7 to 10. Branchiostegal rays number 7 to 9. Pectoral fin is moderate to large and is located at midflank or slightly below midflank. Dorsal fin is short based and originates over or behind pectoral fin base. Pelvic fin is located below or slightly anterior to pectoral fin base and consists of 1 free ray, followed by 6 or 7 rays (in young of some species) or by 3 rudimentary rays. Anal fin originates anterior to or slightly posterior to midlength and consists of more than 50 rays. Caudal fin is reduced. Scales are either present or absent on body. Lateral line is indistinct, consisting of mucous canals in shallow depressions. Swim bladder is absent.

Ateleopodids occur in the Atlantic, Indian, and western Pacific Oceans in tropical to warm temperate seas near or on the bottom. There are about 12 species in two or three genera, and 2 species in the same genus occur in the Gulf of Mexico.

Key to the Species in the Gulf of Mexico
(Adapted from Howell Rivero 1935)

1a. Caudal fin rays 14; eye diameter 9.4% to 12.1% of head length; body depth 14.1% to 15% of TL
. . . . *Ijimaia loppei* p. 547

1b. Caudal fin rays 5; eye diameter about 6.9% of head length, body depth about 11.6% of TL
. . . . *Ijimaia antillarum* p. 546

Ijimaia antillarum   Howell Rivero 1936

Ijimaia antillarum is elongate, tapering, and posteriorly compressed, with a large, robust head; relatively small eyes; a short trunk; and a long tail. It is distinguished from the other species of the family by the following combination of characters. Head surface is rugose, and snout has convex dorsal profile and overhangs mouth. Mouth is horizontal. Angle of lower jaw has spiny protuberance on outer surface. Gill rakers on first arch number 10. Branchiostegal rays number 7. Head length is about 15% and body depth is about 11.6% of TL. Snout length is about 36.4%, eye length is about 6.9%, and mouth is about 25% of head length. Pectoral fin has 14 rays. Dorsal fin originates behind axil of pectoral fin and has 9 rays. Pelvic fin is slightly longer than snout length and has 1 visible ray and 2 additional undeveloped rays buried in integument. Anal fin has 75 rays. Caudal fin is about one-half head length and has 5 rays. Lateral line consists of separate pores and runs length of body. Vertebrae number 126. Color is light brown and mottled with dark brown over most of body. Pelvic fin is white, and the other fins are brown. Mouth and opercular cavities are white.

This species occurs in the western Atlantic off the coast of Cuba and in the Gulf of Mexico between 439 and 549 m. Maximum known size is 1,636 mm TL.

REFERENCE: Howell Rivero 1935.

Ijimaia loppei   Roule 1922

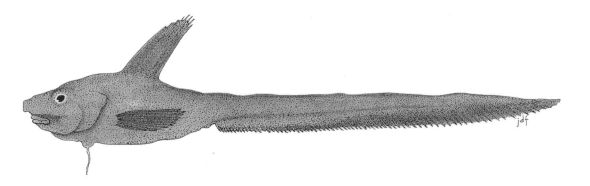

Ijimaia loppei is elongate, tapering, and posteriorly compressed, with a large, robust head; a short trunk; and an elongate tail. It is distinguished from the other species of the family by the following combination of characters. Head surface is covered with gelatinous tissue and is rugose. Snout has convex dorsal profile, and mouth is large, subterminal, and horizontal to slightly oblique. Eye is of moderate size. Gill rakers on first arch number 8 to 10. Branchiostegal rays number 7. Head is 15.8% to 16.1% and body depth is 14.1% to 15% of TL. Eye length is 9.4% to 12.1% of head length. Pectoral fin has 13 or 14 rays. Dorsal fin originates over pectoral fin base and has 9 to 10 rays. Pelvic fin is thoracic and consists of 1 partially split ray. Continuous anal-caudal fin has 80 to 87 rays. Body lacks scales except for lateral line scales. Lateral line is poorly developed and runs along midflank. Color is black, with white pelvic fins.

This species occurs in the Atlantic Ocean at tropical to subtropical latitudes on the bottom between 30 and 692 m. In the western Atlantic it occurs from the Gulf of Mexico and in the Caribbean Sea off Suriname. Food consists of ophiuroids and fishes. Maximum known size is 2,000 mm SL.

REFERENCES: Roule 1922; Howell Rivero 1935; Paxton 1986; Smith 1986 (in part as *Ateleopus barnardi*).

AULOPIFORMES

Aulopiformes are the sister group of the remainder of the neoteleosteans. The order is subdivided into four suborders: Giganturoidei with a single family (Giganturidae), Aulopoidei with a single family (Aulopodidae), Chlorophthalmoidei with four families (Chlorophthalmidae, Ipnopidae, Notosudidae, and Scopelarchidae), and Alepisauroidei with seven families (Synodontidae, Pseudotrichonotidae, Paralepididae, Anotopteridae, Evermannellidae, Omosudidae, and Alepisauridae). Eleven of these families occur in the Gulf of Mexico.

Key to the Families of the Gulf of Mexico
(Adapted from Smith and Heemstra 1986)

1a. Pelvic fin thoracic . . . . Aulopodidae p. 553
1b. Pelvic fin subthoracic, abdominal, or absent. 2
2a. Origin of soft-rayed dorsal fin at or behind midlength . . . 3
2b. Origin of soft-rayed dorsal fin in front of midlength. 6
3a. Eye tubular, directed anteriorly; pectoral fin above gill openings and with 30 to 34 rays . . . . . Giganturidae p. 549
3b. Eye not tubular, directed laterally; pectoral fin behind gill openings and with 10 to 17 rays 4
4a. Anal fin rays 14 to 16; lateral line absent in specimens larger than 4 to 5 cm . . . . Omosudidae p. 588
4b. Anal fin rays 16 to 50; lateral line present 5
5a. Anal fin rays 16 to 21; dorsal fin origin at about midlength . . . . Notosudidae p. 568
5b. Anal fin rays 20 to 50; dorsal fin origin distinctly behind midlength . . . . Paralepididae p. 590
6a. Deciduous scales present on body; teeth in upper jaw at least partially biserial to multiserial 7
6b. Scales lacking except for lateral line scales; teeth in upper jaw in single row 10
7a. Eye tubular, directed dorsally or anterodorsally; upper jaw teeth partially biserial; tongue with single row of large fixed teeth . . . . Scopelarchidae p. 575
7b. Eye not tubular; upper jaw teeth biserial or multiserial; tongue with or without teeth 8
8a. Jaw teeth needlelike or lanceolate; tongue with numerous long curved teeth; gill rakers rudimentary or minute and spinelike. . . . . Synodontidae p. 604
8b. Jaw teeth absent or small; tongue without teeth; gill rakers lathlike (except in *Bathytyphlops*) 9
9a. Maxilla extending beyond middle of eye . . . . Ipnopidae p. 558

9b. Maxilla not extending beyond middle of eye
. . . . Chlorophthalmidae p. 555
10a. Dorsal fin base more than one-half of body length and
with more than 30 rays . . . . Alepisauridae p. 582
10b. Dorsal fin base less than one-half of body length and with
10 to 13 rays . . . . Evermannellidae p. 584

GIGANTURIDAE Giganturids

Giganturids are moderately elongate to very slender and moderately to strongly compressed, with horizontal tubular eyes, a pouchlike stomach, and a deeply forked and extended caudal fin bearing a greatly elongated ventral lobe. They are distinguished from the other families of the order by the following combination of characters. Snout is short to very short and convex to truncated. Olfactory organs consist of single papilla emerging from deep groove in front of eyes. Mouth extends to below middle of pectoral fin base. Maxilla is toothless and excluded from gape of mouth by premaxilla. Supramaxillae are absent. Jaw teeth are moderate to long, sharply recurved, depressible, and arranged in two or three rows. Tubular eye is directed forward. Branchiostegal rays are absent in adults. Gill rakers are absent. Pectoral fin base is broad, horizontal, and high on body above gill opening. Dorsal fin origin is posterior to midlength. Pelvic fin and girdle are lacking in adults. Anal fin originates below posterior section of dorsal fin base or posterior to dorsal fin base. Dorsal adipose fin is absent in juveniles and adults but is present in larvae. Caudal fin is deeply forked, and middle rays of lower lobe are greatly elongated. All fin rays are unsegmented, but some are branched. Body lacks scales and luminous organs. Swim bladder is absent.

Larvae are short, deep bodied, globose, and translucent but colorless. Head is massive, with steep forehead and pointed snout. Body is deepest at center of operculum and tapers toward caudal peduncle. Teeth are in two rows, with those in outer row relatively short and broad based and those of inner row consisting of prominent canines. Eye is small and round. Branchiostegal rays are well developed and number 10. Gill membranes are continuous ventrally and are free of isthmus.

Giganturids occur worldwide in tropical seas. They are mesopelagic or bathypelagic. Food consists of midwater fishes. Black lining of esophagus and stomach may serve to prevent the escape of luminescence from luminescent prey. There are two species in a single genus, and both occur in the Gulf of Mexico.

Key to the Species of the Gulf of Mexico

(Adapted from Johnson 1986b; Johnson and Bertelsen 1991)

1a. Juveniles and adults 2

1b. Larvae 3

2a. Pectoral fin rays 30 to 33; anal fin rays 8 to 10; caudal peduncle depth greater than 8% of SL
. . . . *Gigantura chuni* p. 551

2b. Pectoral fin rays 36 to 42; anal fin rays 11 to 14; caudal peduncle depth less than 4% of SL
. . . . *Gigantura indica* p. 552

3a. Least depth of caudal peduncle 12% to 16% of SL; anal fin rays (specimens less than or equal to 4.5 mm) 8 to 10
. . . . *Gigantura chuni* p. 551

3b. Least depth of caudal peduncle 7.5% to 11.5% of SL; anal fin rays (specimens less than or equal to 4.5 mm) 11 to 14
. . . . *Gigantura indica* p. 552

Gigantura chuni   Brauer 1901

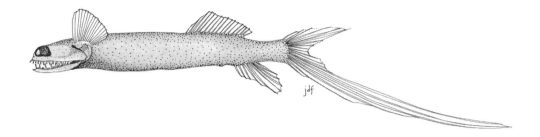

Gigantura chuni is moderately elongate, relatively deep bodied, and compressed, with a very short snout and a relatively deep caudal peduncle. It is distinguished from the other species of the family by the following combination of characters. Body depth increases with growth; depth at dorsal fin origin ranges from 8.9% to 20%, at anal fin origin ranges from 7.2% to 14%, and at caudal peduncle ranges from 8.1% to 11% of SL. Head length is 20% to 30%, snout length is 2.5% to 5.4%, diameter of eye is 5.5% to 8.5%, and length of upper jaw is 15% to 33% of SL. Gills are located above angle of jaws. Upper jaw has about 14 enlarged, recurved, depressible canine teeth and smaller teeth of irregular size lateral to larger teeth. Lower jaw has series of 12 enlarged, recurved, depressible canine teeth and smaller teeth of irregular size lateral to larger teeth. Pectoral fin has 30 to 33 rays. Dorsal fin has 16 to 19 rays and originates anterior to posterior one-third of body. Anal fin has 8 to 10 rays and originates beneath posterior one-fourth of dorsal fin base. Caudal peduncle is oval in cross section. Color is black to grayish brown in preservative, and iridescent silvery in life.

This species occurs in tropical seas of the Atlantic, Indian, and western and central Pacific Oceans. In the western Atlantic it occurs along the southeastern coast of the United States and in the Gulf of Mexico and the Caribbean Sea. It is thought to be mesopelagic and has been captured in open midwater nets between the surface and 1,830 m. Food consists of mesopelagic fishes, such as *Cyclothone*, *Gonostoma*, and *Chauliodus*. It is a synchronous hermaphrodite. Transformation between larval and juvenile stages takes place between 28 and 37 mm SL. Maximum known length is 177 mm SL.

REFERENCES: Walthers 1961, 1964 (as *G. vorax*); Rass 1971 (as *G. vorax*); Johnson 1986b; Johnson and Bertelsen 1991.

Gigantura indica   Brauer 1901

Gigantura indica is very slender and slightly compressed, with a very short snout and a relatively slender caudal peduncle. It is distinguished from the other species of the family by the following combination of characters. Body depth does not obviously increase with increase in growth; depth at dorsal fin origin ranges from 4.6% to 9.9%, at anal fin origin ranges from 4.2% to 7.4%, and at caudal peduncle ranges from 2% to 3.6% of SL. Length of head is 12% to 19%, snout length is 1.5% to 3.5%, eye diameter is 3.2% to 5.8%, and upper jaw length is 7.9% to 15% of SL. Gills extend onto throat region. Premaxilla and lower jaw have enlarged, recurved, depressible canine teeth and smaller teeth of irregular size lateral to larger teeth. Pectoral fin has 36 to 42 rays. Dorsal fin has 16 to 19 rays and originates just posterior to midlength of body. Anal fin has 11 to 14 rays and originates posterior to dorsal fin base. Caudal peduncle is about of equal depth and width. Color is black to grayish brown in preservative, and iridescent silvery in life.

This species occurs worldwide in tropical and subtropical seas. In the western Atlantic it occurs along the southeastern United States and in the Gulf of Mexico and the Caribbean Sea at mesopelagic depths. Transformation between larval and juvenile stages takes place between 25 and 55 mm SL. Maximum known size is 232 mm SL.

REFERENCES: Walthers 1964 (as *Bathyleptus indicus*); Johnson 1986b (as *Rosaura indica*); Johnson and Bertelsen 1991.

AULOPODIDAE Flagfins

Flagfins are moderately elongate, moderately slender, and slightly compressed anteriorly, with a large mouth and a high dorsal fin originating on first one-third of body. They are distinguished from the other families of the order by the following combination of characters. Snout is shorter than to slightly longer than orbit diameter. Upper jaw is bordered by premaxilla. Jaws, vomer, palatine, and tongue have recurved needlelike teeth. Two well-developed supramaxillae are present on maxilla. Gill rakers are lath shaped. Eye is large, nontubular, and laterally directed. Pectoral fin is inserted just below midflank. Pelvic fin is thoracic. Dorsal fin originates over or slightly posterior to pelvic fin insertion. Anal fin originates on posterior one-half of body. Dorsal adipose fin is present and has short base. Caudal fin is deeply forked. Scales occur on cheeks, gill covers, body, and base of caudal fin.

Flagfins occur in tropical to warm temperate seas worldwide, except for the eastern Pacific Ocean. They are benthic on continental shelves and slopes. Food consists of fishes. Individuals are dioecious, and eggs and larvae are pelagic. There are nine species in two genera, and one species occurs in the Gulf of Mexico.

Aulopus nanae Mead 1958

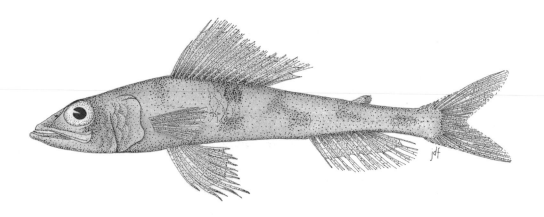

Aulopus nanae is moderately elongate and moderately slender, with a relatively short dorsal fin and a relatively long anal fin. It is distinguished from the other species of the family by the following combination of characters. Snout is relatively long and depressed. Body depth is 16.6%, head length is 30%, snout length is 8.3%, and eye diameter is 6.9% of SL. Teeth in jaws are in broad bands, with those on inner row longer than others. First gill arch has 3 gill rakers on epibranch, 1 in corner, and 10 on lower limb. Pectoral fin rays number 12 or 13. Dorsal fin has 15 fin rays, and base is shorter than distance from insertion of dorsal fin to origin of dorsal adipose fin. Anal fin has 12 fin rays, and last 2 rays are longer than depth of body at origin of anal fin. Predorsal scales number 12, and lateral line scales number 48. Vertebrae number 47. Head is purple, and body is yellowish with purple blotches. Pectoral and anal fins are colorless, pelvic fin is reddish, anterior dorsal fin rays are black, and rest of rays are dusky. In life, scales of body are opalescent and iridescent with transverse bands, and belly is silvery.

This species occurs in the western Atlantic from the eastern Gulf of Mexico and the Caribbean Sea. It has been captured off Tortugas, Florida, and off northwestern Cuba to 183 m. Maximum known size is 223 mm SL.

REFERENCES: Mead 1958, 1966a.

CHLOROPHTHALMIDAE   Greeneyes

Greeneyes are moderately slender, nearly oval in cross section anteriorly, and compressed posteriorly, with a moderately large mouth and subthoracic pelvic fins. They are distinguished from the other families of the order by the following combination of characters. Snout is moderately long, broad, and depressed. Mouth is terminal and nonprotrusible. Teeth occur in jaws, vomer, and palatine, and are small to minute, conical, slightly recurved, and mostly repressible. Upper jaw is bordered by premaxilla. Maxilla is vertically expanded and free distally. One supramaxilla is located on dorsal margin of maxilla. Lower jaw terminates as bony knob at symphysis. Eye is large, nontubular, and laterally directed, with keyhole-shaped pupil and lensless aphaktic space. Interorbital space is narrow to moderately narrow and flat or slightly concave. Gill membranes are joined across isthmus by broad fold. Gill rakers are lath shaped. Branchiostegal rays number eight. Pectoral fin inserts below midflank. Dorsal fin originates on anterior one-half of body. Dorsal adipose fin is well developed and located above anal fin base. Pelvic fin is subthoracic. Caudal fin is forked, with upper and lower lobes of equal length. Scales are cycloid and deciduous and cover body, cheeks, head, and base of caudal fin. Lateral line is complete and terminates at base of middle caudal ray.

Greeneyes occur worldwide in tropical to temperate seas and are closely associated with bottom between 50 and 1,000 m. All species are monoecious. Larvae are epipelagic or mesopelagic. Food consists of polychaetes, crustaceans, squids, and fishes, although feeding habits are unknown for most species.

There are 20 species in two genera, and 2 species in separate genera occur in the Gulf of Mexico.

Key to the Species of the Gulf of Mexico
(Adapted from Mead 1966e)

1a. Horizontal diameter of eye equal to or greater than snout length; anus close to bases of inner pelvic fin rays; vomerine teeth small . . . . *Chlorophthalmus agassizi* p. 556

1b. Horizontal diameter of eye equal to or less than snout length; anus distinctly posterior to bases of inner pelvic fin rays; vomer with two fanglike teeth
. . . . *Parasudis truculenta* p. 557

Chlorophthalmus agassizi   Bonaparte 1840
Shortnose greeneye

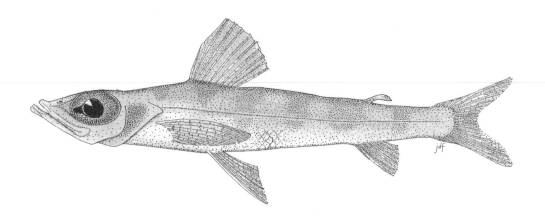

Chlorophthalmus agassizi is moderately elongate and moderately slender, with a relatively short mouth and large eyes. It is distinguished from the other species of the family by the following combination of characters. Body depth is 12.6% to 18.8%, head length is 27% to 33.5%, and snout length is 8.4% to 10% of SL. Teeth in jaws are small and arranged in bands. Similar teeth occur in vomer and palatine. Eye is directed dorsolaterally and has keyhole-shaped pupil. Gill rakers number 19 to 22 on lower limb of first arch. Pectoral fin is of moderate length and has 15 to 17 rays. Dorsal fin originates just posterior to pelvic fin insertion and has 10 or 11 rays. Pelvic fin is subthoracic in location and has 8 or 9 rays. Anal fin is located beneath dorsal adipose fin and has 7 to 9 rays. Caudal fin is forked, and upper and lower lobes are of about equal length. Scales are present on cheeks, operculum, body, and base of caudal fin. Lateral line scales number 50 to 55. Vertebrae number 47. Color is light brown to yellow, with dark blotches on side of trunk and black mid-dorsal stripe. Eye is greenish.

This species occurs in tropical to warm temperate waters of the Atlantic Ocean. In the western Atlantic it occurs from Cape Cod to Suriname, including the Gulf of Mexico and the Caribbean Sea. It has been captured on mud and clay bottoms from 50 to 1,000 m. Young specimens have been captured near the surface. Maximum known size is 200 mm SL.

REFERENCES: Mead 1966e; Sulak 1984c; C. R. Robins et al. 1986; Boschung 1992.

Parasudis truculenta (Goode and Bean 1896)
Longnose greeneye

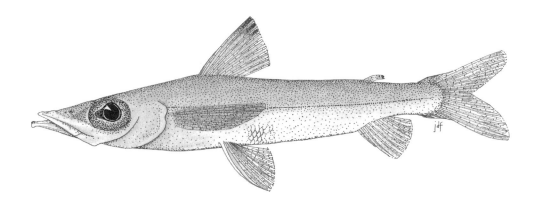

Parasudis truculenta is moderately elongate and moderately slender, with large eyes and a relatively small mouth. It is distinguished from the other species of the family by the following combination of characters. Body depth is 14.9% to 18.4%, head length is 31.6% to 33.9%, and snout length is 12.5% to 13.6% of SL. Teeth in jaw are small and arranged in rows anteriorly. Vomer has conical and fang-like teeth, and palatine has patch of recurved teeth. Eye is directed dorsolaterally. Gill rakers are lathlike, and number 1 on epibranch and 11 to 13 on lower limb of first arch. Pectoral fin is of moderate length and has 15 or 16 rays. Dorsal fin originates anterior to pelvic fin base and has 10 rays. Pelvic fin is subthoracic and has 9 rays. Anal fin is located beneath dorsal adipose fin and has 9 rays. Caudal fin is forked, and upper and lower lobes are of about equal length. Scales are present on cheeks, gill covers, body, and base of caudal fin. Scales in longitudinal series number 78 to 85. Vertebrae number 38. Color is light brown, with edge of each scale outlined by black line in skin below. Tip of dorsal fin is black.

This species occurs in the tropical to warm temperate waters of the Atlantic Ocean. In the western Atlantic it occurs from Nantucket, Massachusetts, to the northern coast of Brazil north of the Amazon, including the Gulf of Mexico and the Caribbean Sea. It is considered to be benthic and has been captured from 183 to 479 m. Food consists of squids and midwater fishes. Maximum known size is 225 mm SL.

REFERENCES: Mead 1966e; Uyeno et al. 1983; C. R. Robins et al. 1986; Boschung 1992.

IPNOPIDAE

Ipnopids are moderately slender to slender, nearly oval in cross section anteriorly, and compressed in cross section posteriorly, with a large mouth, subthoracic pelvic fins, and often very elongated fin rays. They are distinguished from the other families of the order by the following combination of characters. Snout is depressed and flattened dorsally. Mouth is terminal, occasionally curved upward at tip, and nonprotrusible. Teeth occur in jaws and usually in vomer and palatine, and are minute, needlelike, and mostly depressible. Maxilla is vertically expanded and free distally. One supramaxilla is located on dorsal margin of maxilla. Lower jaw terminates as bony knob at symphysis. Eye is minute, laterally directed, and horizontally elliptical; or broad, flat, dorsally directed, and lensless; or minute, vestigial, and covered with skin and scales. Interorbital space is broad and slightly concave. Gill rakers are lathlike or knoblike. Branchiostegal rays number 8 to 17. Pectoral fin is either undivided and high on flank or on midflank and divided into two parts, with or without prolonged rays. Dorsal fin origin is on anterior one-half of body. Dorsal adipose fin is located behind anal fin base or is absent. Pelvic fin is subthoracic, with anterior rays occasionally fused and prolonged. Caudal fin is forked, with upper and lower lobes of about equal length or with lower lobe much longer. Scales are cycloid, with smooth or occasionally pectinate margin, and deciduous and cover body, cheeks, base of caudal fin, and occasionally sides of head. Lateral line is complete and terminates at base of caudal fin.

Ipnopids occur worldwide in tropical to temperate seas on the bottom between 476 and 6,000 m. All species are monoecious. Larvae are epipelagic or mesopelagic. Food consists of crustaceans, squids, and fishes, although the feeding habits are unknown for most species. There are 29 species in six genera, and 8 species in three genera occur in the Gulf of Mexico.

Key to the Species of the Gulf of Mexico
(Adapted from Mead 1966e)

1a. Caudal fin and paired fins with elongated and specialized rays 2

1b. Caudal fin and paired fins without elongated and specialized rays except caudal fin elongated in *Ipnops murrayi* 6

2a. Pectoral fin not superficially divided into parts and without greatly elongated rays, none extend beyond anal fin rays; anterior pelvic fin rays and lower caudal fin rays exceed SL; no dorsal adipose fin . . . . *Bathypterois grallator* p. 561

2b. Pectoral fin superficially divided into two parts and with uppermost pectoral fin rays extending beyond anal fin rays; anterior pelvic fin rays and lower caudal fin rays less than SL; dorsal adipose fin usually present 3

3a. Body with three dark bands; area under dorsal fin white; caudal fin dark; all rays of upper part of pectoral fin well developed; lower part of pectoral fin with fewer than six rays . . . . *Bathypterois viridensis* p. 564

3b. Body uniform black or white with two dark spots on caudal fin base; lower rays of upper part of pectoral fin poorly developed; lower part of pectoral fin with more than six rays 4

4a. Scales posterior to base of lower part of pectoral fin with toothlike projections; lowermost ray of lower part of pectoral fin elongated and distinctly thicker than next fin ray . . . . *Bathypterois quadrifilis* p. 563

4b. Scales posterior to base of lower part of pectoral fin without toothlike projections; lowermost ray of lower part of pectoral fin not more elongated or thicker than next ray 5

5a. Ventral procurrent rays of caudal fin separated from first principal ray and forming subcaudal notch . . . . *Bathypterois phenax* p. 562

5b. Ventral procurrent rays of caudal fin not separated from first principal ray and not forming subcaudal notch . . . . *Bathypterois bigelowi* p. 560

6a. Top of head covered with thin flattened membrane bone covering degenerate eyes . . . . *Ipnops murrayi* p. 567

6b. Top of head covered with scales; eyes minute, laterally directed, and located above upper jaw 7

7a. Dorsal fin rays 12 or 13; anal fin rays 12 to 14; pectoral fin rays 12 to 15; lateral line scales 64 to 66 . . . . *Bathytyphlops marionae* p. 565

7b. Dorsal fin rays 11 to 13; anal fin rays 14 to 17; pectoral fin rays 12 to 14; lateral line scales 67 to 70 . . . . *Bathytyphlops sewelli* p. 566

Bathypterois bigelowi Mead 1958

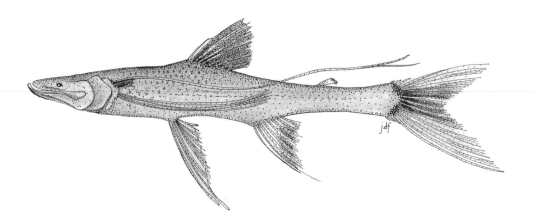

Bathypterois bigelowi is moderately elongate and moderately slender, with upper pectoral rays thickened and elongated and separated from lower rays, and interior pelvic rays and lower caudal fin rays greatly elongated. It is distinguished from the other species of the family by the following combination of characters. Body depth is 12.9% to 15.8%, head length is 20% to 24.1%, and snout length is 7.6% to 8.6% of SL. Teeth in jaws are minute and in bands. Few small teeth occur on vomer and palatine. Tongue lacks teeth. Eye is minute and laterally directed. Branchiostegal rays number 10 to 12. First gill arch has 10 to 12 gill rakers on epibranch and 22 to 28 on lower limb. Pectoral fin consists of 2 rudimentary upper rays; 2 thickened, stiffened, and greatly produced rays that are united over most of length; 3 well-developed but short rays joined by black membrane; 2 or 3 rudimentary rays; and 8 to 10 moderately long lower rays. Dorsal fin originates over or posterior to insertion of pelvic fin and has 11 to 13 rays. Pelvic fin has 8 rays, with 2 first rays produced and thickened at tip. Anal fin originates posterior to last dorsal fin ray and has 8 to 10 rays. Dorsal adipose fin is well developed. Lower 2 principal caudal fin rays are simple and elongated. Ventral procurrent caudal fin rays are not separated from first principal ray and do not form subcaudal notch. Scales are present on body, except for gular fold, and number 48 to 55 in lateral line. Vertebrae number 49 to 52. Color is white, with two dark spots at base of caudal fin, and occasionally irregularly mottled with pale red-violet, yellow, or blue. Each scale pocket has one or more dark pigment specks forming triangular or diamond-shaped pigment areas on dorsal one-half of body. Large spot is present at base of each lobe of caudal fin.

This species occurs in the western Atlantic along the east coast of Florida and the Straits of Florida, and in the Gulf of Mexico and the Caribbean Sea. It has been captured from 377 to 986 m where bottom temperatures range from 4.2°C to 11.1°C. Maximum known size is 130 mm SL.

REFERENCES: Mead 1959, 1966c; Sulak 1977.

Bathypterois grallator   (Goode and Bean 1886)
Tripodfish

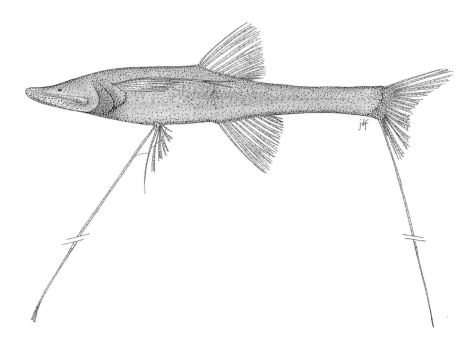

Bathypterois grallator is moderately elongate and moderately slender, with upper pectoral fin rays slender, slightly elongated, and superficially connected to lower rays, and interior pelvic rays and lower caudal fin rays greatly elongated. It is distinguished from the other species of the family by the following combination of characters. Body depth is 12.9% to 15.6%, head length is 26.1% to 28.7%, and snout length is 7.9% to 8.6% of SL. Teeth in jaws are recurved, barbed at tips, and arranged in a broad band, with those of premaxilla larger than those of lower jaw. Teeth also occur in vomer. Eye is minute and laterally directed. Branchiostegal rays number 10 or 11. Gill rakers on first arch number 8 or 9 on epibranch, 1 in corner, and 19 to 23 on lower limb. Pectoral fin consists of 2 rudimentary upper rays, 7 to 10 moderately long but gradually shorter rays, and 1 or 2 rudimentary lower rays. Dorsal fin has 12 or 13 rays and originates posterior to pelvic fin insertion and just anterior to anal fin origin. Pelvic fin has 8 rays, with first one greatly produced. Anal fin has 12 or 13 rays.

Dorsal adipose fin is absent. Caudal fin has lower principal ray greatly elongated, but ventral procurrent rays are not modified into separate subcaudal notch. Scales are present on body, including gular fold, and lateral line scales number 52 to 54. Vertebrae number 53 or 54. Color is black, with scale pockets and lateral line pores outlined in white.

This species occurs in the tropical to warm temperate Atlantic, Indian, and western and central Pacific Oceans. In the western Atlantic it occurs along the eastern seaboard of the United States from about 40°N to the Gulf of Mexico and the Caribbean Sea. It has been captured from 878 to 3,980 m. Adults are benthic, as presumably are juveniles, although one transforming postlarva was captured at 3,000 m in 4,407 m of water. Food consists of copepods and other small crustaceans. Maximum known size is 300 mm SL or longer.

REFERENCES: Mead 1966c; Sulak 1977, 1984c; Anderson et al. 1985; Crabtree et al. 1991.

Bathypterois phenax Parr 1928
Blackfin spiderfish

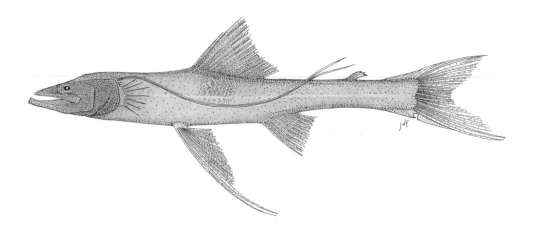

Bathypterois phenax is moderately elongate and moderately slender, with upper pectoral fin rays thickened, greatly elongated, and superficially separated from lower rays, and interior pelvic fin rays and lower caudal fin rays elongated. It is distinguished from the other species of the family by the following combination of characters. Body depth is 11.7% to 15.1%, head length is 23% to 24.1%, and snout length is 7.4% to 8.3% of SL. Teeth in jaws are small, conical, and arranged in bands. Teeth also occur in palatine and occasionally in vomer. Eye is minute and directed laterally. First gill arch has 10 to 12 gill rakers on epibranch, 1 in corner, and 27 or 28 on lower limb. Branchiostegal rays number 12 or 13. Pectoral fin consists of 2 rudimentary upper rays; 2 thickened, stiffened, and greatly produced rays that are united for most of length; 1 short ray; 3 rudimentary rays; and 7 to 9 long lower rays. Dorsal fin originates behind pelvic fin insertion and has

14 or 15 rays. Pelvic fin has 9 rays, with first 2 stiffened and elongated. Anal fin has 9 rays. Dorsal adipose fin is present. Caudal fin has lower ray or rays elongated. Last ventral procurrent caudal ray is separated from first principal ray by notch and is curved upward to form subcaudal notch. Scales are present on body, except for gular fold. Lateral line scales number 55 to 60. Vertebrae number 53 or 54. Color is black, with scale pockets and lateral line pores outlined in white.

This species occurs in the tropical to warm temperate Atlantic. In the western Atlantic it occurs off the east coast of the United States from about 39°N to the Gulf of Mexico and the Caribbean Sea. It has been captured from 827 to 2,651 m. Maximum known size is 180 mm SL.

REFERENCES: Mead 1966c; Sulak 1977, 1986e.

Bathypterois quadrifilis   Günther 1878

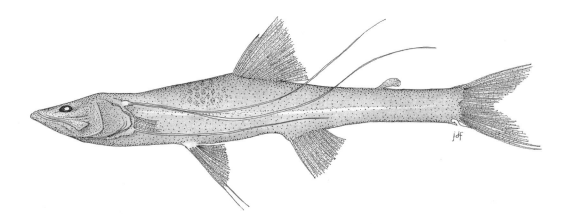

Bathypterois quadrifilis is moderately elongate and moderately slender, with upper pectoral rays thickened, greatly elongated, and superficially separated from lower rays, and interior pelvic fin rays and lower caudal fin rays moderately elongated. It is distinguished from the other species of the family by the following combination of characters. Body depth is 13.2% to 15.6%, head length is 19.7% to 21.4%, and snout length is 6.2% to 7.1% of SL. Teeth in jaws are small, conical, and arranged in bands. Teeth also occur in palatine and occasionally in vomer. Eye is minute and directed laterally. Branchiostegal rays number 11 or 12. Gill rakers on first arch number 11 or 12 on epibranch, 1 in corner, and 28 to 30 on lower limb. Pectoral fin consists of 2 rudimentary upper rays; 2 thickened, stiffened, and greatly produced rays that are united for about one-half of length; 1 short ray; 2 or 3 rudimentary rays; and 7 to 9 produced lower rays. Dorsal fin originates posterior to axil of pelvic fin and has 12 to 15 rays. Pelvic fin has 9 rays, with first 2 rays stiffened and elongated. Anal fin has 8 or 9 rays. Dorsal adipose fin is present. Caudal fin has lowermost rays elongated. Last procurrent ray is separated from first lower principal ray by notch, and procurrent ray is bent upward to form hook. Scales are present on body, except for gular fold, and those behind pectoral fin base have toothlike projections. Lateral line scales number 57 to 63. Vertebrae number 54 to 59. Color is black, with scale pockets and lateral line pores outlined in white.

This species occurs in the tropical to warm temperate Atlantic Ocean. In the western Atlantic it occurs from North Carolina to Recife, Brazil, including the Gulf of Mexico and the Caribbean Sea. It has been captured from 462 to 1,408 m at temperatures of 4.3°C to 7.8°C. Maximum known length is 180 mm SL.

REFERENCES: Mead 1966c; Sulak 1977; Uyeno et al. 1983.

Bathypterois viridensis   (Roule 1916)

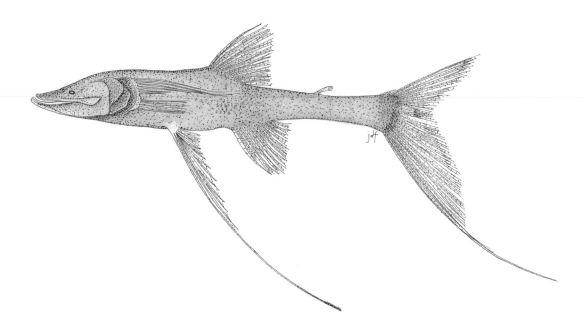

Bathypterois viridensis is moderately elongate and moderately slender, with upper pectoral fin rays slender, elongated, and superficially separated from lower rays, and interior pelvic fin rays and lower caudal fin rays greatly elongated. It is distinguished from the other species of the family by the following combination of characters. Body depth is 12.8% to 17.3%, head length is 24.7% to 29.1%, and snout length is 8.1% to 9.8% of SL. Teeth in jaws are recurved, barbed at tips, and arranged in a broad band. Teeth also occur on vomer, palatine, and tongue. Eye is minute and laterally directed. Branchiostegal rays number 12 or 13. Gill rakers on first arch number 11 on epibranch, 1 in corner, and 27 or 28 on lower limb. Pectoral fin has 2 rudimentary upper rays, 7 elongate rays, 1 rudimentary ray, and 5 or 6 elongated lower rays. Dorsal fin originates over or slightly posterior to base of inner pelvic fin rays and has 12 or 13 rays. Pelvic fin has 8 rays, with first one greatly produced and

thickened. Anal fin has 10 to 12 rays. Dorsal adipose fin is present. Caudal fin has lower 2 principal rays greatly elongated, with tips usually thickened. Last ventral procurrent ray is not modified into subcaudal notch and hook. Scales are present on body, including gular fold. Lateral line scales number 51 to 56. Vertebrae number 50 to 52. Color is white with three dark bands, with body below dorsal fin white and caudal fin dark.

This species occurs in the tropical to warm temperate Atlantic. In the western Atlantic it occurs from the eastern seaboard of the United States from about 44°N to northern Brazil, 4°N, including the Gulf of Mexico and the Caribbean Sea. It has been captured from 476 to 1,477 m at temperatures of 5.6°C to 11.1°C. Maximum known size is 222 mm SL.

REFERENCES: Mead 1966c; Sulak 1977; Uyeno et al. 1983.

Bathytyphlops marionae   Mead 1958

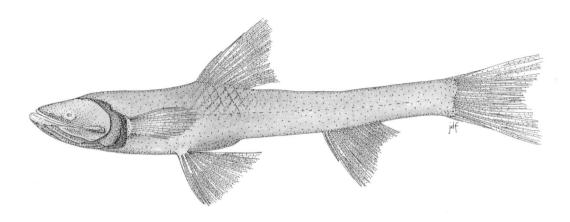

Bathytyphlops marionae is moderately elongate and moderately slender, with small eyes covered with skin, and pectoral and caudal fins lacking greatly elongated rays. It is distinguished from the other species of the family by the following combination of characters. Body depth is 11.4% to 16%, head length is 22.4% to 23.1%, snout length is 6.6% to 7.5%, and anal fin base is 12.1% to 14.4% of SL. Teeth in jaws consist of denticles, except symphyses of both jaws lack teeth. Vomer and palatine have patches of similar teeth. Eye is broad, flat, dorsally directed, vestigial, and covered with skin. Branchiostegal rays number 15 to 17. Gill rakers on first arch consist of 6 platelike basal ossifications on epibranch, 1 stout gill raker in corner, and 12 to 14 platelike basal ossifications on lower limb. Pectoral fin is of moderate length and has 12 or 13 rays. Dorsal fin originates posterior to insertion of pelvic fin and has 12 or 13 rays. Pelvic fin is subthoracic and consists of 8 rays. Anal fin originates posterior to insertion of dorsal fin and has 12 to 14 rays. Dorsal adipose fin is absent. Caudal fin is forked, and upper and lower lobes are of equal length. Scales are present on body; cheeks, sides, and top of head; and base of caudal fin. Lateral line scales number 64 or 65. Vertebrae number 63 or 64. Color is pale with dark edges around scale pockets, and head is dark.

This species occurs in the tropical Atlantic, western Indian, and Pacific Oceans. In the western Atlantic it occurs in the Gulf of Mexico and the Caribbean Sea. It is benthic and has been captured from 850 to 2,650 m. Food consists of benthic mysid shrimps and copepods. Larvae occur at the surface at night. Maximum known size is 280 mm SL.

REFERENCES: Mead 1966c; Nielsen 1966; Berry and Robins 1967 (as *Macristiella perlucens*); Sulak 1974, 1986e; Merrett 1980; Shcherbachev 1980; Uyeno et al. 1983.

Bathytyphlops sewelli   (Norman 1939)

Bathytyphlops sewelli is moderately elongate and moderately slender, with small eyes covered with skin, and pectoral and caudal fins lacking greatly elongated rays. It is distinguished from the other species of the family by the following combination of characters. Body depth is 11.6% to 13.2%, head length is 21.5% to 22.8%, snout length is 6.7% to 7.5%, and anal fin base is 16.1% to 18.1% of SL. Jaws have denticle-like teeth on either side of symphysis. Vomer and palatine have patches of denticle-like teeth. Eye is broad, flat, dorsally directed, covered with skin, and becomes less conspicuous with age. Branchiostegal rays number 14 to 16. Gill rakers on first arch are clublike ossifications and number 6 or 7 on epibranch, 1 in corner, and 11 to 13 on lower limb. Gill raker in corner is longer and stouter than other gill rakers. Dorsal fin originates posterior to insertion of pelvic fin and has 11 to 13 rays. Pectoral fin has 12 to 14 rays. Pelvic fin is subthoracic and consists of 8 rays. Anal fin originates posterior to insertion of dorsal fin and has 14 to 17 rays. Dorsal adipose fin is absent. Caudal fin is forked, and upper and lower lobes are of equal length. Scales are present on body, cheeks and top of head, and base of caudal fin. Lateral line scales number 65 to 70. Vertebrae number 65 to 70. Color is pale, with dark edges around scales pockets and dark head.

This species occurs in the tropical and temperate Atlantic and Indian Oceans close to the bottom between 2,980 and 4,186 m. In the western Atlantic it occurs in the southern Caribbean Sea off Colombia and in the eastern Gulf of Mexico between 3,459 and 4,186 m. Food consists of mysids and decapod crustaceans. Maximum known size is 300 mm SL.

REFERENCES: Nielsen 1966; Sulak 1974; Merrett 1980; Shcherbachev 1980; Anderson et al. 1985.

Ipnops murrayi Günther 1878

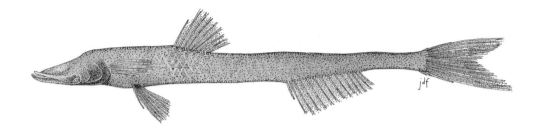

Ipnops murrayi is elongate and slender, with a depressed and spatulate snout and eyes represented by dorsally directed placques. It is distinguished from the other species of the family by the following combination of characters. Body depth is 8.9% and head length is 20% of SL. Jaw teeth are villiform and arranged in bands. Vomer and palatine have small to minute teeth. Eye is represented by light-sensitive tissue lying under membranous bones; lens is lacking and retinal rods are small. Branchiostegal rays number 10 or 11. Gill rakers are lath-like, and first arch has 3 on epibranch, 1 in corner, and 17 on lower limb. Pectoral fin is of moderate size and has 13 rays. Dorsal fin has 9 rays. Pelvic fin is subthoracic and has 8 rays. Anal fin originates posterior to dorsal fin and has 14 rays. Dorsal adipose fin is absent. Caudal fin is forked, with ventral lobe longer than dorsal lobe. Scales are present on cheeks, sides of head, body, and base of caudal fin but not on membrane bones over eyes. Lateral line scales number 53. Vertebrae number 55 to 61. Color is black, with margins of each scale pocket colorless, and head, branchiostegal membrane, and pharyngeal and abdominal lining black. Color fades to dark brown in preservative.

This species occurs in the tropical to warm temperate Atlantic. In the western Atlantic it occurs in the Gulf of Mexico and off Bequia Island, Brazil. It has been captured on the bottom from 1,463 to 3,518 m. Maximum known size is 152 mm SL.

REFERENCES: Grey 1958; Mead 1966d; Nielsen 1966; Anderson et al. 1985.

NOTOSUDIDAE

Notosudids are elongate, slender, and slightly compressed, with dorsal fin located near midlength of body and dorsal and anal fins of about equal length. They are distinguished from the other families of the order by the following combination of characters. Snout is acutely pointed, spatulate, and moderately long to long. Head length is moderately long to short. Premaxilla excludes maxilla from gape of mouth. Teeth in premaxilla are small and uniserial in young, in narrow band in adults. Teeth in lower jow are arranged in two distinct bands, with teeth of inner band larger than those of outer band. Vomer and palatine teeth are small and are arranged in two or three patches. Eye is large, nontubular, and laterally directed. Gill rakers are long and lathlike. Pectoral fin is small to large and is located on or above midflank. Dorsal fin is short and originates near midlength of body. Pelvic fin originates slightly anterior to or below dorsal fin base. Anal fin is short and located on last quarter of body. Dorsal adipose fin is located above anal fin. Caudal fin is forked and has 19 principal rays. Lateral line is well developed. Body and head, including cheeks, is covered with cycloid scales. Light organs are absent.

Notosudids occur worldwide in tropical to temperate seas from the epipelagic to the upper bathypelagic realm. Some species occur near the bottom on continental and insular slopes. Adults are active swimmers and feed on zooplankton. All species are thought to be hermaphroditic. The family contains 19 species in three genera, and 5 species in two genera occur in the Gulf of Mexico.

Key to the Species of the Gulf of Mexico
(Adapted from Bertelsen, Krefft, and Marshall 1976)

1a. Pelvic fin inserts below or immediately in front of dorsal fin origin; posterior infraorbital bones forming simple half tubes, without posterior expansions; skeleton weakly ossified; abdominal body wall thin and transparent; vertebrae 47 to 50 . . . . *Ahliesaurus berryi* p. 570

1b. Pelvic fin inserts distinctly anterior to dorsal fin origin; posterior infraorbital bones with lobed posterior expansions; skeleton moderately ossified; abdominal body wall relatively thick and opaque. 2

2a. Gill rakers on first arch 19 to 22 3

2b. Gill rakers on first arch 15 to 18 4

3a. Gill rakers on first arch 20 or 22; pectoral fin rays 12 or 13; pyloric caecae 12 or 13
. . . . *Scopelosaurus mauli* p. 573

3b. Gill rakers on first arch 19 or 20; pectoral fin rays 14 to 22;
     pyloric caecae 18 to 30. . . . . . *Scopelosaurus lepidis* p. 572
4a. Gill rakers on first arch 15 to 18; pyloric caecae 12 to 16;
     vertebrae 53 to 56 . . . . *Scopelosaurus smithii* p. 574
4b. Gill rakers on first arch 15 to 18; pyloric caecae 20 to 32;
     vertebrae 54 to 57 . . . . *Scopelosaurus argenteus* p. 571

Ahliesaurus berryi Bertelsen, Krefft, and Marshall 1976

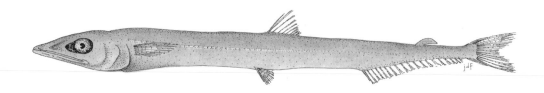

Ahliesaurus berryi is very elongate, slender, and oval in cross section anteriorly and slightly compressed posteriorly, with a spatulate snout and a relatively small head. It is distinguished from the other species of the family by the following combination of characters. Body depth is 5.3% to 8.6%, snout length is 6.1% to 7.9%, maxillary length is 11.4% to 14.5%, and head length is 19% to 23.1% of SL. Maxilla extends beyond posterior margin of orbit. Jaw teeth are small, in single band in premaxilla and in double band in lower jaw. Vomer and palatine have minute, pointed teeth. Gill rakers are long and lathlike, with 1 on epibranch, 1 in corner, and 13 on lower limb. Posterior circumorbital bones are shaped as simple half tubes. Pectoral fin is very short and has 10 or 11 rays. Dorsal fin originates over midlength and has 10 or 11 rays. Pelvic fin inserts below or immediately in front of dorsal fin origin and has 9 rays. Anal fin originates along last quarter of length and has 19 to 21 rays. Dorsal adipose fin is located above anal fin base. Caudal fin is forked. Scales are large and deciduous. Lateral line scales number 46, vertebrae number 47 to 50, and pyloric caecae number 8 to 11. Color in preservative is olive brown, with scale pockets blackish and two ventral black bands formed by peritoneum. Opercular bones and interior of mouth are black.

This species occurs in the tropical to warm temperate Atlantic and in the southern warm temperate regions of the Pacific and Indian Oceans at deep mesopelagic and bathypelagic depths. Larvae and newly metamorphosed juveniles are epipelagic. Food consists of zooplankton such as copepods. Mature adults lose their teeth and gill rakers prior to spawning. Maximum known size is 280 mm SL.

REFERENCES: Bertelsen et al. 1976; Krefft 1984; Krefft 1986.

Scopelosaurus argenteus (Maul 1954)

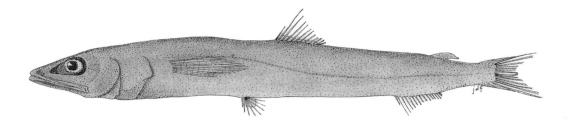

Scopelosaurus argenteus is elongate, slender, and slightly compressed posteriorly, with posterior infraorbital bones forming both a prominent anterior crest bordering eyes and a posterior, expanded, lobed lamella. It is distinguished from the other species of the family by the following combination of characters. Body depth is 8.3% to 11.9%, snout length is 7.1% to 8.1%, upper jaw length is 12.5% to 15.9%, head length is 25.7% to 28.8%, and pectoral fin length is 9.3% to 18.6% of SL. Jaw teeth are small, in single band in premaxilla, and in double band in lower jaw. Vomer and palatine have patches of small teeth. Gill rakers number 1 on epibranch, 1 in corner, and 13 to 16 on lower limb. Pectoral fin inserts above midline and has 12 to 14 rays. Dorsal fin originates at about midlength and has 12 or 13 rays. Pelvic fin inserts distinctly anterior to dorsal fin origin and has 9 rays. Anal fin has 17 or 18 rays.

Dorsal adipose fin is located above end of anal fin base. Caudal fin is forked. Scales are cycloid and deciduous. Lateral line scales number 57 or 58, vertebrae number 54 to 57, and pyloric caecae number 20 to 32. Color is light but is not silvery despite name.

This species occurs in the tropical to warm temperate Atlantic Ocean at mesopelagic depths both in the water column and near the bottom. Small larvae, identified as this species, have been captured in the eastern Gulf of Mexico off Florida. However, small larvae of this species cannot be distinguished from those of *S. lepidus*. Larvae are epipelagic between 50 and 100 m. Food consists of zooplankton. Maximum known size is 215 mm SL.

REFERENCES: Bertelsen et al. 1976; Krefft 1984.

Scopelosaurus lepidus   (Krefft and Maul 1955)

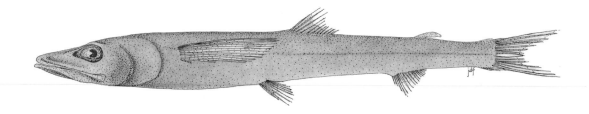

Scopelosaurus lepidus is elongate, slender, and slightly compressed posteriorly, with posterior infraorbital bones forming both a prominent anterior crest bordering eyes and a posterior, expanded, lobed lamella. It is distinguished from the other species of the family by the following combination of characters. Body depth is 7.2% to 13.3%, snout length is 6.7% to 10%, upper jaw is 12.7% to 16.2%, head length is 24.5% to 27.7%, and pectoral fin length is 18.6% to 30.6% of SL. Jaw teeth are small, in single band in premaxilla and in double band in lower jaw. Vomer and palatine have patches of small teeth. Gill rakers are long and lathlike and number 1 on epibranch, 1 in corner, and 17 or 18 on lower limb. Pectoral fin inserts above midline and has 13 to 15 rays. Dorsal fin originates at midlength and has 10 to 12 rays. Pelvic fin inserts distinctly anterior to dorsal fin origin and has 9 rays. Anal fin has 17 to 19 rays. Dorsal adipose fin is located above end of anal fin base. Caudal fin is forked.

Scales are cycloid and deciduous. Lateral line scales number 60 to 64, vertebrae number 58 to 61, and pyloric caecae number 18 to 30. Color is jet black; pectoral fin has large black patch basally and large whitish band distally. Specimens often lose scales and pigmented skin in capture and appear light in color.

This species occurs throughout the Atlantic Ocean but is most common in the eastern Atlantic at mesopelagic depths both in the water column and near the bottom. It has not been reported from the Gulf of Mexico, but larvae resembling both this species and *S. argenteus* were captured off Florida. Larvae of these two species cannot be distinguished. Larvae occur between 70 and 200 m. Food consists of copepods for small specimens, and euphausiids, hyperiids, and mesopelagic fishes for large specimens. Maximum known size is 365 mm SL.

REFERENCES: Bertelsen et al. 1976; Krefft 1984.

Scopelosaurus mauli Bertelsen, Krefft, and Marshall 1976

Scopelosaurus mauli is elongate, slender, and slightly compressed posteriorly, with posterior infraorbital bones forming both a prominent anterior crest bordering eyes and a posterior, expanded, lobed lamella. It is distinguished from the other species of the family by the following combination of characters. Body depth is 6.4% to 8.8%, snout length is 7.3% to 8.2%, upper jaw length is 13.3% to 14.3%, head length is 27.1% to 29%, and pectoral fin length is 16.2% to 25.1% of SL. Jaw teeth are small, in single band in premaxilla, and in double band in lower jaw. Vomer and palatine have patches of small teeth. Gill rakers are long and lathlike and number 1 on epibranch, 1 in corner, and 18 to 20 on lower limb. Pectoral fin inserts above mid-depth and has 12 or 13 rays. Dorsal fin originates at about midlength and has 10 or 11 rays. Pelvic fin inserts distinctly anterior to dorsal fin base and has 9 rays, and anal fin has 17 to 20 rays. Dorsal adipose fin is located above posterior section of anal fin base. Caudal fin is forked. Scales are cycloid and deciduous. Vertebrae number 55 to 57, and pyloric caecae number 12 or 13. Color in preservative is brown, with scale pockets dark distally and opercular bones black.

This species occurs in tropical and subtropical seas in the western Atlantic, western Pacific, and western Indian Oceans at mesopelagic depths. In the western Atlantic it occurs from about 40°N to the southern Caribbean Sea, including the eastern Gulf of Mexico. Both adults and larvae have been captured in the Gulf of Mexico. Maximum known size is 99.5 mm SL.

REFERENCES: Bertelsen et al. 1976; Belianina 1981.

Scopelosaurus smithii Bean 1925

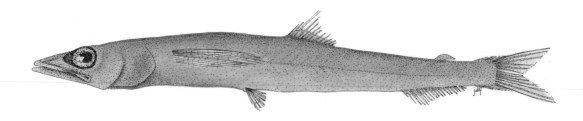

Scopelosaurus smithii is elongate, slender, and slightly compressed posteriorly, with posterior infraorbital bones forming both a prominent anterior crest bordering eyes and a posterior, expanded, lobed lamella. It is distinguished from the other species of the family by the following combination of characters. Body depth is 7.9% to 9.9%, head length is 25.5% to 28.9%, snout length is 6.6% to 9%, upper jaw length is 12.1% to 15.2%, pectoral fin length is 18.6%, and caudal peduncle depth is 5.1% of SL. Jaw teeth are small, in single band in premaxilla, and in double band in lower jaw. Vomer and palatine have patches of small teeth. Gill rakers number 1 on epibranch, 1 in corner, and 12 to 16 on lower limb. Pectoral fin inserts above midline of body and has 11 to 14 rays. Dorsal fin originates at about midlength and has 10 to 12 rays. Pelvic fin inserts anterior to dorsal fin base and has 9 rays. Anal fin has 17 to 19 rays. Dorsal adipose fin is located above end of anal fin base. Caudal fin is forked. Lateral line scales number 54 to 57, vertebrae number 53 to 56, and pyloric caecae number 12 to 16. Color is bright silver with bluish iridescence.

This species occurs worldwide in tropical seas, including the eastern Gulf of Mexico. Adults occur near the bottom between 200 and 600 m, and young occur in epipelagic and mesopelagic realms between 50 and 200 m. Maximum known size is 222 mm SL.

REFERENCES: Marshall 1966; Uyeno et al. 1983; Krefft 1984, 1986.

SCOPELARCHIDAE Pearleye fishes

Pearleyes are moderately elongate, moderately slender, and moderately compressed, with lanceolate teeth in lower jaw, hooked teeth on tongue, and tubular eyes. They are distinguished from the other families of the order by the following combination of characters. Snout is moderately long to moderately short, and acute to moderately blunt. Mouth is terminal, upper jaw extends past middle of eye, and lower jaw is arched anteriorly. Upper jaw is bordered by premaxilla that has small uniserial teeth. Lower jaw has two series of teeth, with inner row large and often barbed. Teeth are present on vomer, palatine, and tongue. Supramaxillae are present on dorsal margin of maxillary. Eye is directed dorsally or occasionally anterodorsally. Gill rakers consist of bony plates bearing short spines termed "gill teeth." Pectoral fin inserts on lower flank. Dorsal fin originates at about mid-distance between gill opening and anal fin origin. Pelvic fin is abdominal. Anal fin base is longer than dorsal fin base. Dorsal adipose fin is well developed. Caudal fin is forked. Body and posterior part of head are covered with cycloid scales. Lateral line scales are large and consist of bony plates pierced by a moderate to large pore and a bony covering (tympanum) over posterior part of bony plate that partially covers pore. Luminous tissue is present in some species. Swim bladder is absent.

Pearleyes occur in tropical seas worldwide. They are mesopelagic and bathypelagic between 500 and 1,000 m. Food consists of midwater fishes. All species are thought to be synchronous hermaphrodites. There are 17 species in four genera, and 5 species in three genera occur in the Gulf of Mexico.

Key to the Species of the Gulf of Mexico
(Adapted from Johnson 1974a,b)

1a. Adults: Distinct stripes extending forward from caudal peduncle both above and below lateral line; pectoral fin longer than pelvic fin; pectoral fin rays 18 to 22; no concentration of pigment on upper lobe of caudal fin. Larvae 20 mm SL or longer: Accessory pigment spots or areas absent; origin of pectoral fin buds midlateral at or below level of intestine 2

1b. Adults: No distinct stripes extending forward from caudal peduncle above and below lateral line; pectoral fin equal to or shorter than pelvic fin; pectoral fin rays 20 to 25; upper lobe of caudal fin with distinct concentration of pigment. Larvae 20 mm SL or longer: Accessory pigment spots or areas present; origin of pectoral fin buds midlateral in abdomen body wall, above level of intestine 4

2a. Pigment lacking on pectoral fin; anal fin rays generally more than 25. . . . . *Scopelarchus guentheri* p. 580

2b. Pigment present on pectoral fin; anal fin rays generally fewer than 25. 3

3a. Anal fin rays 21 or more; lateral line scales 45 or more (specimens 40 mm or longer)
. . . . *Scopelarchus analis* p. 579

3b. Anal fin rays 22 or fewer; lateral line scales 44 or fewer (specimens 40 mm or longer)
. . . . *Scopelarchus michaelsarsi* p. 581

4a. Adults: Pelvic fin insertion behind origin of dorsal fin. Larvae 20 mm SL or longer: Mid-dorsal and midventral accessory pigment spots and areas distinctly posterior to end of adipose and anal fin bases
. . . . *Scopelarchoides danae* p. 578

4b. Adults: Pelvic fin insertion anterior to origin of dorsal fin. Larvae 20 mm SL or longer: Mid-dorsal and midventral accessory pigment spots and areas distinctly anterior to end of adipose and anal fin bases
. . . . *Rosenblattichthys hubbsi* p. 577

Rosenblattichthys hubbsi Johnson 1974

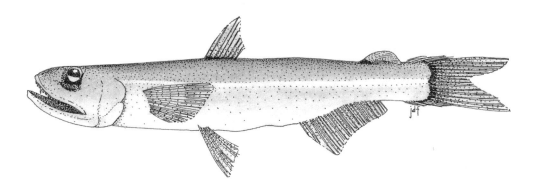

Rosenblattichthys hubbsi is relatively short, deep, and robust, with pelvic fins about equal in length to pectoral fins and inserting slightly anterior to dorsal fin origin. It is distinguished from the other species of the family by the following combination of characters. Snout is longer than orbit diameter. Body depth is 17% and head length is 22.7% of SL. Premaxilla has 52 teeth, and lower jaw has 40 teeth in lateral row and 4 in medial row. Palatine has single irregular series of teeth, and tongue has 9 teeth. Pectoral fin inserts below midflank and has 21 rays. Dorsal fin originates just behind pelvic fin insertion and has 8 rays. Anal fin rays number 24. Lateral line scales number 53, and vertebrae number 49. Body is uniformly pigmented with small, scattered melanophores and lacks stripes or other pigment patterns. Fin rays are covered with scattered melanophores.

This species occurs in the western Atlantic from the Gulf of Mexico, the Caribbean Sea, and the coast of northern Brazil between 124 and 627 m. Maximum known size is 144.5 mm SL.

REFERENCES: Johnson 1974a,b, 1984a, 1986a; Belianina 1981.

Scopelarchoides danae Johnson 1974

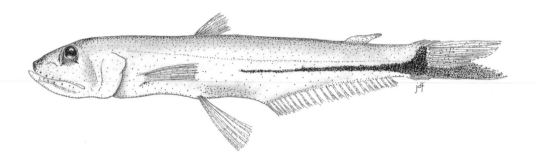

Scopelarchoides danae is moderately elongate and moderately slender, with pelvic fins longer than pectoral fins and a stripe below the lateral line. It is distinguished from the other species of the family by the following combination of characters. Snout is slightly longer than eye diameter. Body depth is 10.9% to 16.2%, head length is 18.9% to 21.8%, and snout length is 7.8% to 9.3% of SL. Premaxilla has 30 to 69 teeth. Lower jaw has 17 to 39 teeth in lateral row and 6 to 8 larger teeth in medial row. Palatine has 8 to 13 teeth, and tongue has 8 to 16 teeth. Pectoral fin inserts just below midflank and has 20 to 22 rays. Dorsal fin originates over pelvic fin insertion and has 7 or 8 rays. Anal fin rays number 24 to 27. Lateral line scales number 50 to 52. Vertebrae number 48 to 50. Color consists of dermal pigment forming stripe below lateral line from pelvic fin to caudal peduncle. Stripe increases in width posteriorly. Bases of anterior dorsal fin rays are weakly pigmented, and lower lobe of caudal fin is strongly pigmented. Peritoneum is black.

Larvae less than 16 mm SL have single peritoneal section of pigment located in anterior region of abdominal cavity, dorsomedial to gut. Larvae longer than 16 mm SL have two paired peritoneal pigment sections in addition to single section. Peritoneal sections fuse in larvae 45 mm SL and longer. Larvae also have midventral spot behind last anal ray, mid-dorsal spot behind adipose fin, slashlike bar at fork of caudal fin, and intestinal spot midventrally behind anus.

This species occurs worldwide in tropical seas. It occurs in the Gulf of Mexico and the Caribbean Sea in the western Atlantic. Adults are most numerous between 300 and 500 m at night and below 500 m during the day. Adolescents are most abundant between 100 and 200 m, and larvae are generally captured in less than 100 m. Maximum known size is 122 mm SL.

REFERENCES: Johnson 1974a, 1982, 1986a; Belianina 1981; Uyeno et al. 1983.

Scopelarchus analis (Brauer 1902)

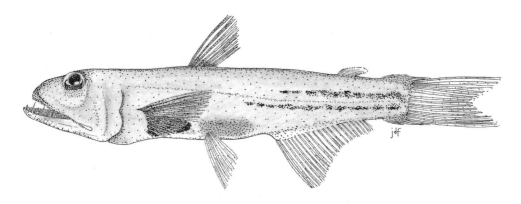

Scopelarchus analis is moderately elongate and moderately slender, with pectoral fins longer than pelvic fins and a stripe above and below lateral line. It is distinguished from the other species of the family by the following combination of characters. Snout is slightly less than to slightly longer than eye diameter. Body depth is 14.2% to 22.8% and head length is 20.4% to 26.2% of SL. Premaxilla has 23 to 133 teeth. Lower jaw has 15 to 33 teeth in lateral row and 6 to 13 larger teeth in medial row. Palatine has 10 to 17 teeth, and tongue has 9 to 15 teeth. Pectoral fin inserts below midflank and has 18 to 22 rays. Dorsal fin originates anterior to pelvic fin and has 7 to 9 rays. Anal fin rays number 21 to 26. Lateral line scales number 45 to 50. Vertebrae number 44 to 49. Color consists of dermal pigment forming stripes above and below lateral line. Dorsal fin is pigmented at base and along anterior fin rays, and pectoral fin is pigmented on base and often on rays and membrane. Peritoneum is black. Larvae have single anterior peritoneal section, two posterior paired sections, and two dermal pigment stripes above and below lateral line.

This species occurs worldwide in tropical to warm temperate seas. In the western Atlantic it occurs off the southeastern United States, the Bahamas, the Gulf of Mexico, and the Caribbean Sea. It has been captured from near the surface to 800 m. Adults are generally taken below 300 m. Larvae are most abundant in the upper 100 m. Maximum known size is 126 mm SL.

REFERENCES: Johnson 1974a, 1982, 1984a, 1986a.

Scopelarchus guentheri Alcock 1896

Scopelarchus guentheri is moderately elongate and moderately slender, with pectoral fins longer than pelvic fins and a stripe above and below lateral line. It is distinguished from the other species of the family by the following combination of characters. Snout is slightly less than to slightly longer than eye diameter. Body depth is 10.8% to 17.4% and head length is 28.3% to 23.3% of SL. Premaxilla has 28 to 81 teeth, with number of teeth increasing with size. Lower jaw has 14 to 25 teeth in lateral row and 7 to 18 teeth in medial row. Palatine has 9 to 14 teeth, and tongue has 8 to 13 teeth. Pectoral fin inserts below midflank and has 18 to 21 rays. Dorsal fin originates anterior to pelvic fin and has 7 or 8 rays. Anal fin has 24 to 29 rays. Lateral line scales number 47 to 52, and vertebrae number 47 to 51. Color consists of dermal pigment forming stripes above and below lateral line. Dorsal fin is pigmented at base and along anterior fin rays. Peritoneum is black. Larvae have single unpaired anterior peritoneal section, two posterior paired sections, and two dermal pigment stripes above and below lateral line.

This species occurs worldwide in tropical to warm temperate seas. In the western Atlantic it occurs off southern Florida, in the Gulf of Mexico, and in the Caribbean Sea. It has been captured between the surface and 300 m. Larvae are most abundant between the surface and 150 m. Maximum known size is 49.5 mm SL.

REFERENCES: Johnson 1974b, 1986a.

Scopelarchus michaelsarsi Koefoed 1955

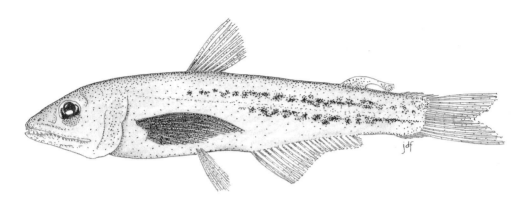

Scopelarchus michaelsarsi is moderately elongate and relatively deep bodied, with pectoral fins longer than pelvic fins and a stripe above and below lateral line. It is distinguished from the other species of the family by the following combination of characters. Snout length is less than eye diameter. Body depth is 19% to 24.1% and head length is 23.2% to 27.3% of SL. Premaxilla has 38 to 75 teeth. Lower jaw has 17 or 22 teeth in lateral row and 8 or 9 larger teeth in medial row. Palatine has 12 to 16 teeth, and tongue has 7 to 12 teeth. Pectoral fin inserts below midflank and has 18 to 21 rays. Dorsal fin originates slightly anterior to pelvic fin insertion and has 7 to 9 rays. Anal fin rays number 18 to 21. Lateral line scales number 40 to 44. Vertebrae number 40 to 44. Dermal pigment is limited to one stripe above and one below lateral line extending from level of pelvic fin base to caudal peduncle. Scale pockets are edged with pigment above lateral line. Dorsal fin is pigmented at base and over anterior fin rays. Pectoral fin is densely pigmented. Larval pigment is located in single anterior peritoneal segment, two posterior paired peritoneal segments, and in two dermal pigment stripes above and below lateral line.

This species occurs worldwide in tropical to warm temperate waters, with exception of the eastern North Atlantic. It has been captured from less than 200 m to 500 m. Adults have never been captured at depths less than 256 m at night, and most have been taken below 500 m. Larvae have been captured in less than 200 m at night. Maximum known size is 101.5 mm SL.

REFERENCES: Johnson 1974a, 1982, 1986a.

ALEPISAURIDAE Lancetfishes

Lancetfishes are very elongate, very slender, and subcylindrical in cross section, with a long terminal mouth and a very long sail-like dorsal fin. They are distinguished from the other families of the order by the following combination of characters. Snout is long, about twice orbit diameter. Upper jaw is bordered by premaxilla that has single series of small teeth. Lower jaw has single row of variable-sized canine teeth. Palatine has one or two erect, long, daggerlike teeth anteriorly and one or two daggerlike teeth and five to nine triangular teeth posteriorly. Supramaxillae are absent. Eye is nontubular and laterally directed. Gill rakers consist of tufts of small filaments. Pectoral fin originates low on flank. Dorsal fin originates over middle or over posterior margin of gill cover. Pelvic fin is abdominal. Dorsal adipose fin is short based. Caudal fin is deeply forked. Body lacks scales.

Lancetfishes occur worldwide in tropical to temperate seas. They are pelagic from near the surface to greater than 1,000 m. Food consists of squids, copepods, crustaceans, tunicates, and fishes. There are two species in a single genus, and one species occurs in the Gulf of Mexico.

Alepisaurus ferox Lowe 1833
Longnose lancetfish

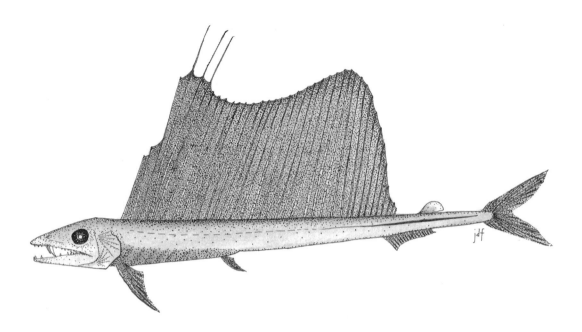

Alepisaurus ferox is very elongate and very slender, with a long snout and a dorsal fin that is high anteriorly and has several free rays. It is distinguished from the other species of the family by the following combination of characters. Body depth is 8% to 12.5% and head length is 16% to 23% of SL. Snout length is 33% to 50% and eye diameter is 17% to 20% of head length. Dorsal fin originates over posterior margin of operculum, has emarginate profile, and possesses several elongated anterior fin rays. Dorsal fin has 36 to 45, pectoral fin has 12 to 15, pelvic fin has 8 to 10, and anal fin has 14 to 18 fin rays.

This species occurs in the tropical to warm temperate waters of the Atlantic and Pacific Oceans. In the western Atlantic it occurs from the Gulf of Maine to the Gulf of Mexico and the Caribbean Sea. It has been captured from near the surface to below 1,000 m. Food consists of cephalopods, crustaceans, tunicates, and fishes. Maximum known size is about 200 cm SL.

REFERENCES: Gibbs and Wilimowsky 1966; Rass 1971; Post 1984a; Heemstra and Smith 1986.

EVERMANNELLIDAE Sabertooth fishes

Sabertooth fishes are moderately elongate, moderately slender, and moderately compressed, with a saberlike tooth in each palatine and abdominal pelvic fins. They are distinguished from the other families of the order by the following combination of characters. Snout is short and blunt. Upper jaw is indented at symphysis and is bordered by premaxilla that bears small uniserial teeth. Lower jaw has barbed, biserial or unbarbed, uniserial teeth. Vomer has two small teeth, and palatine has single series of teeth decreasing in size posteriorly; anteriormost tooth is enormous. Single supramaxilla is present on dorsal margin of maxilla. Eye is small and nontubular, to large and subtubular, to tubular. Gill rakers consist of bony plates bearing teeth. Pectoral fin inserts just above ventral contour of body. Dorsal fin originates anterior to midlength of body, over or anterior to base of pelvic fin. Anal fin base is longer than dorsal fin base, and origin is posterior to midlength of body. Dorsal adipose fin is well developed. Caudal fin is deeply forked. Body and head lack scales. Luminous tissue is present in some species.

Sabertooth fishes occur in tropical to warm temperate seas worldwide. They are mesopelagic in the upper 1,000 m. Food consists of squids and fishes. All species are thought to be synchronous hermaphrodites. There are seven species in three genera, and three species in separate genera occur in the Gulf of Mexico.

Key to the Species of the Gulf of Mexico
(Adapted from Johnson 1982)

1a. Eye nontubular and directed laterally; aperture diameter in adipose eyelid less than eye lens diameter
. . . . *Odontostomops normalops* p. 582

1b. Eye semitubular to tubular and directed dorsolaterally or dorsally; aperture diameter in adipose eyelid greater than eye lens diameter 2

2a. Eye semitubular and directed dorsolaterally; aperture diameter of adipose eyelid slightly greater than eye lens diameter; jaw teeth nonbarbed; anteriormost palatine saberlike fang is 7.1% to 10% of SL
. . . . *Coccorella atlantica* p. 585

2b. Eye tubular and directed dorsally; aperture diameter of adipose eyelid considerably greater than eye lens diameter; some jaw teeth barbed; anteriormost palatine saberlike fang is 4.6% to 7.3% of SL . . . . *Evermannella indica* p. 586

Coccorella atlantica (Parr 1928)

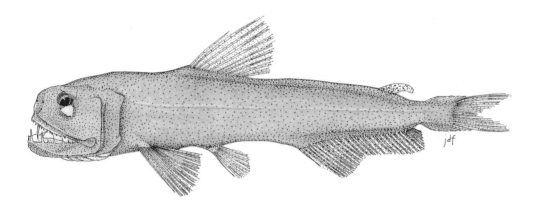

Coccorella atlantica is moderately elongate and moderately slender, with semitubular eyes and a very long, saberlike tooth in each palatine. It is distinguished from the other species of the family by the following combination of characters. Snout is high, angular, and vertical anteriorly. Body depth at anal fin origin is 14.4% to 21%, head length is 19.6% to 24.3%, and interorbital width is 3.2% to 4.7% of SL. Teeth in jaws and palatine are not barbed. Anteriormost palatine tooth is 7.1% to 10% of SL. Teeth in lower jaw are uniserial. Eye is directed dorsolaterally, and horizontal eye diameter is about equal to interorbital width. Aperture diameter of adipose eyelid is slightly greater than eye lens diameter. Pectoral fin rays number 11 to 13. Dorsal fin originates anterior to pelvic fin base and has 10 to 13 rays. Anal fin originates posterior to dorsal fin base and has 26 to 30 rays. Frontal canal commissure has six pores. Vertebrae number 48 to 50. Luminous tissue is associated with ventral wall of pyloric caecae and intestine. Color is dark brown on head, body, and fins, with brassy green iridescent layers along flank, between eyes, and on cheeks. White glistening spot is located on side of eye.

This species occurs worldwide in subtropical to warm temperate seas. In the western Atlantic it occurs off the east coast of the United States, the Bahamas, the Gulf of Mexico, the Caribbean Sea, and off the coast of South America. Adults are generally captured below 500 m, but juveniles and adults are taken between 100 and 400 m. Larvae are found between 50 and 125 m. Food consists of squids and fishes. Maximum known size is 185 mm SL.

REFERENCES: Rofen 1966c; Johnson 1982, 1984b, 1986c.

Evermannella indica   Brauer 1906

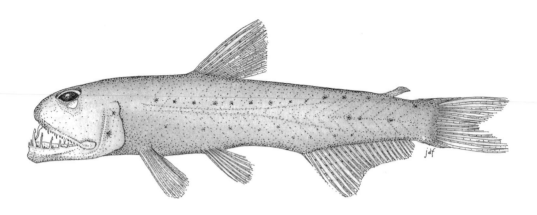

Evermannella indica is moderately elongate and moderately slender, with tubular eyes and a moderately long, saberlike tooth in each palatine. It is distinguished from the other species of the family by the following combination of characters. Snout is low and rounded. Body at anal fin origin is 13.6% to 17.3%, head length is 21.6% to 26.5%, and interorbital width is 0.8% to 2% of SL. Some teeth in jaws and palatine are barbed. Anteriormost palatine tooth is 4.6% to 7.3% of SL. Teeth in lower jaw are biserial. Eye is directed dorsally. Horizontal eye diameter is considerably greater than interorbital width. Aperture diameter of adipose eyelid is considerably greater than eye lens diameter. Frontal canal commissure has six pores. Pectoral fin rays number 11 or 12. Dorsal fin originates anterior to pelvic fin base and has 27 to 29 rays. Anal fin originates posterior to dorsal fin base and has 27 to 29 rays. Vertebrae number 49 or 50. Color is light brown, with numerous melanophores scattered over head and body and with brassy iridescent coloration overlying dermal pigmentation on cheek and flank. White glistening spot is located on side of eye.

This species occurs in tropical to subtropical seas worldwide. In the western Atlantic it occurs off Bermuda, the southeast coast of the United States, the Gulf of Mexico, the Bahamas, the Caribbean Sea, and off the northern coast of South America. Adults are generally captured below 400 m, mostly between 500 and 800 m, but occasionally in the upper 200 m. Larvae and small juveniles are most frequently taken in the upper 50 to 100 m. Food consists of midwater fishes. Maximum known size is 127 mm SL.

REFERENCES: Rofen 1966c; Johnson 1982, 1984b, 1986c; Murdy et al. 1983.

Odontostomops normalops   (Parr 1928)

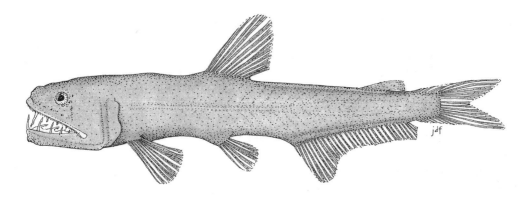

Odontostomops normalops is moderately elongate and moderately slender, with non-tubular eyes and a moderately long, saberlike tooth in each palatine. It is distinguished from the other species of the family by the following combination of characters. Snout is relatively high and truncate. Body depth at anal fin origin is 13.5% to 17%, head length is 19.7% to 24.7%, and interorbital width is 3.6% to 5.2% of SL. Some lower jaw and palatine teeth are barbed. Anteriormost palatine tooth is 5.3% to 6.9% of SL. Lower jaw teeth are biserial. Eye is directed laterally. Horizontal diameter of eye is considerably greater than interorbital width. Aperture diameter of adipose eyelid is considerably less than eye lens diameter. Frontal canal commissure has six pores. Pectoral fin rays number 11 to 13. Dorsal fin originates anterior to pelvic fin base and has 11 to 13 rays. Anal fin originates posterior to dorsal fin base and has 30 to 35 rays. Vertebrae number 48 to 52. Color is dark brown, with brassy iridescent coloration overlying head and flank. No white glistening spot is found on side of eye.

This species occurs worldwide in tropical to subtropical seas. In the western Atlantic it occurs off the east coast of the United States, from the Gulf of Mexico, the Bahamas, the Caribbean Sea, and off the northeast coast of South America. Most adults are captured below 400 m, but they are often encountered between 100 and 400 m. Larvae and small juveniles are frequently captured in the upper 50 to 100 m. Food consists of midwater fishes. Maximum known size is 123 mm SL.

REFERENCES: Rofen 1966c; Belianina 1981; Johnson 1982, 1984b, 1986c.

OMOSUDIDAE Omosudids

Omosudids are moderately elongate, moderately slender, and compressed, with a large head and a massive lower jaw. They are distinguished from the other families of the order by the following combination of characters. Snout is moderately long, slightly convex, and acute. Lower jaw is terminal and truncated. Premaxilla and maxilla are fused, with maxilla excluded from gape. One supramaxilla is present on dorsal margin of maxilla. Teeth occur on premaxilla, dentaries, and palatine. Eye is large and nontubular. Gill membranes are free of isthmus. Gill rakers consist of short spines termed "gill teeth." Pectoral fin is low on flank, and pelvic fin is abdominal. Dorsal fin is relatively small and originates slightly posterior to midlength of body, slightly anterior to pelvic fin insertion. Anal fin is relatively small and originates posterior to anal fin base. Dorsal adipose fin is located above anal fin base. Adults possess longitudinal dermal keel midlaterally below adipose fin. Caudal fin is deeply forked, and upper and lower lobes are about equal in length. Body lacks scales and luminous organs. Lateral line is apparently vestigial in adults. Swim bladder is absent.

Omosudids occur worldwide in tropical seas. They are meso- to bathypelagic in open waters. Food consists of squids and pelagic fishes. Individuals are dioecious. Family is monotypic, containing a single species, which occurs in the Gulf of Mexico.

Omosudis lowei Günther 1887

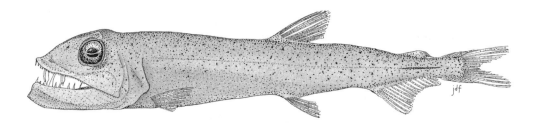

Omosudis lowei is moderately elongate, moderately slender, and compressed, with a large head and a massive lower jaw. It is distinguished by the following combination of characters. Body depth is 16.6% to 25.9%, head length is 27.3% to 32.5%, and snout length is 9.9% to 11.6% of SL. Premaxilla has single row of 30 to 80 minute retrorse teeth, with number increasing with growth. Lower jaw has single row of 10 to 17 prominent, fixed, canine teeth, with fifth tooth enormous and lanceolate. Palatine has single row of 1 to 4 upright fixed teeth; anterior 2 are largest. Branchiostegal rays number 7. Pectoral fin has 12 or 13 rays, dorsal fin has 9 to 11 rays, pelvic fin has 8 rays, and anal fin has 13 or 14 rays. Vertebrae number 39 to 41. Color is light iridescent, with brown dorsal band and scattering of melanophores. Peritoneum is silvery.

This species occurs worldwide in tropical to warm temperate seas. In the western Atlantic it occurs off the east coast of the United States from about 36°N, and from Bermuda to southern Florida, the Bahamas, the Gulf of Mexico, and the Caribbean Sea. Adults are most frequently captured between 700 and 1,800 m. Postlarvae are captured at depths above 1,000 m at night and below about 1,000 m during the day. Food consists of squids, hatchetfishes (*Sternoptyx*), and lanternfishes (myctophids). Maximum known size is 200 to 250 mm SL.

REFERENCES: Rofen 1966b; Rass 1971; Post 1984b; Maul 1986d.

PARALEPIDIDAE   Barracudinas

Barracudinas are elongate, slender, and subcylindrical to laterally compressed, with a pointed snout and a short dorsal fin located posterior to midlength. They are distinguished from the other families of the order by the following combination of characters. Snout is acutely pointed and long to very long. Mouth is terminal, but lower jaw projects as fleshy process. Premaxilla and maxilla are joined by connective tissue, and premaxilla excludes maxilla from gape of mouth. One small supramaxilla is present on dorsal margin of maxilla. Teeth occur in premaxilla, mandible, palatine, and occasionally on vomer. Teeth in jaws and palatine are uniserial or biserial. Eye is large, nontubular, and laterally directed. Gill rakers consist of long filaments or small fixed spines called "gill teeth." Pectoral fin inserts on flank and generally lacks prolonged rays. Pelvic fin is abdominal and inserts near dorsal fin origin. Dorsal fin originates at about midlength of body and is short based. Anal fin originates posterior to dorsal fin insertion and is long based. Dorsal adipose fin is present, and ventral adipose fin is often present. Caudal fin is deeply forked, and upper and lower lobes are about equal length. Body either has or lacks scales and luminous organs. Lateral line scales are covered with ossified plates (tympana). Swim bladder is absent.

Barracudinas occur worldwide from tropical to polar seas but are most abundant in the tropics. They are mesopelagic as adults but are epipelagic as young. Adults are rapid swimmers, and some species have been observed to swim vertically at high speeds through mesopelagic realm. Food consists of fishes and other pelagic organisms. Some species are synchronous hermaphrodites. The family contains about 56 species in 12 genera, and 12 species in 7 genera occur in the Gulf of Mexico.

Key to the Species of the Gulf of Mexico
(Adapted from Rofen 1966a)

1a. Pectoral fin longer than anal fin base; large teeth in lower jaw fixed, with serrated edges. 2
1b. Pectoral fin shorter than anal fin base; large teeth in lower jaw fixed or depressible, with smooth edges. 3
2a. Lateral line scalelike sections with four to seven pores above and below (Fig. 122); vertebrae 59 or 60 and prehaemal vertebrae 33 . . . . *Sudis hyalina* p. 601
2b. Lateral line scalelike sections with three pores above and below; vertebrae 53 or 54 and prehaemal vertebrae 28 to 30 . . . . *Sudis atrox* p. 600
3a. Body and much of head covered with deciduous scales; teeth of lower jaw minute or absent in adults
. . . . *Paralepis atlantica* p. 596

FIG 122

3b. Body and head naked except for lateral line scales; teeth of lower jaw well developed 4

4a. Anterior lateral line scales elongate, longer than they are high; distance between dorsal and caudal fin origins about 33% of SL 5

4b. Anterior lateral line scales about equal in height and length; distance between dorsal and caudal fin origins greater than 33% of SL 7

5a. Pelvic fin about equidistant between tip of pectoral fin and dorsal fin insertion; dorsal fin origin near midlength (body length equals tip of operculum to base of caudal fin) . . . . *Stemonosudis bullisi* p. 592

5b. Pelvic fin closer to dorsal fin insertion than to tip of pectoral fin; dorsal fin origin distinctly posterior to midlength (body length equals tip of operculum to base of caudal fin) 6

6a. Anal fin rays 36 to 38 . . . . . . *Stemonosudis gracilis* p. 598

6b. Anal fin rays 41 to 47. . . . *Stemonosudis intermedia* p. 599

7a. Pelvic fin extending to anal fin origin; dorsum with one to four bold black saddles 8

7b. Pelvic fin not extending to anal fin origin; dorsum posterior to dorsal fin plain colored, without black saddles. 9

8a. Pectoral fin rays 11; anal fin rays 28; dorsum with four saddle markings . . . . *Uncisudis quadrimaculata* p. 603

8b. Pectoral fin rays 12 or 13; anal fin rays 30 or 31; dorsum with one saddle marking . . . . *Uncisudis advena* p. 602

9a. Anal fin rays 41 to 45; prominent black spot immediately anterior to eye; dorsal fin origin about equidistant between pelvic fin insertion and anal fin origin . . . . *Lestrolepis intermedia* p. 595

9b. Anal fin rays 26 to 32; no prominent black spot anterior to eye; dorsal fin origin closer to pelvic fin insertion than to anal fin origin. 10

10a. Pelvic fin near or ventral to base of dorsal fin, horizontal distance between origin of dorsal fin and origin of pelvic fin less than eye diameter . . . . *Lestidium atlanticum* p. 594

10b. Pelvic fin distinctly anterior to base of dorsal fin, horizontal distance between origin of dorsal fin and origin of pelvic fin usually greater than eye diameter. 11

11a. Anus about on vertical with origin of dorsal fin; fewer than 10 expanded pigment cells across mid-dorsal color band . . . .*Lestidiops jayakari* p. 593

11b. Anus distinctly anterior to origin of dorsal fin; more than 20 small pigment cells across mid-dorsal color band . . . . *Lestidiops affinis* p. 592

Lestidiops affinis (Ege 1930)

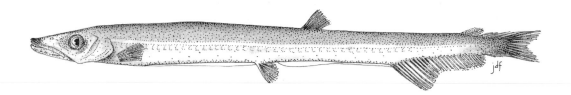

Lestidiops affinis is elongate, slender, and moderately compressed, with lower jaw curved upward and dorsal fin distinctly posterior to pelvic fin insertion. It is distinguished from the other species of the family by the following combination of characters. Body depth is 6.1% to 7.9%, head length is 16.7% to 18.1%, and snout length is 7.1% to 7.6% of SL. Premaxilla has 2 to 4 depressible canine teeth anteriorly and 12 to 26 small, fixed uniserial teeth posteriorly. Lower jaw has 7 or 8 moderate-sized canine teeth, each accompanied by one small, fixed canine tooth. Vomer lacks teeth. Anteriorly palatine has 2 to 14 large, depressible canine teeth, each accompanied by 1 short, fixed tooth, and posteriorly palatine has 2 to 7 short, fixed uniserial teeth. Gill membranes are joined near anterior margin of eye and are free of isthmus. Pectoral fin inserts on lower flank and has 10 to 12 rays. Dorsal fin originates posterior to anus and has 8 to 10 rays. Pelvic fin is anterior to midlength and has 9 rays. Anal fin has 27 to 29 rays. Scales are lacking except for embedded lateral line scales. Lateral line sections are diamond shaped, with anterior ends somewhat prolonged (1.75 times longer than they are high), and number 58 to 61. Tympana (osseous scale plates on lateral line scales) are Y-shaped, narrow posteriorly and forked anteriorly. Luminous organ is absent. Vertebrae number 75 to 83. Body is unpigmented except for dense, narrow, dorsal band of melanophores; dark brassy pigment covering snout, head, and upper side of caudal peduncle; and midventral line of 8 to 14 stellate chromatophores.

This species occurs in the tropical to warm temperate Atlantic. In the western Atlantic it occurs from New Jersey, about 40°N, to northern Brazil, about 10°S, including the eastern Gulf of Mexico, the Bahamas, and the Caribbean Sea. It is most common in the Sargasso Sea. It has been captured from the surface to 2,000 m. Adults and adolescents occur from 200 to 2,000 m. Postlarvae are found from the surface to 200 m. Food consists of planktonic crustaceans. Maximum known size is 103 mm SL.

REFERENCES: Rofen 1966a; Rass 1971; Murdy et al. 1983; Post 1984c.

Lestidiops jayakari (Boulenger 1889)

Lestidiops jayakari is elongate, slender, and moderately compressed, with lower jaw curved upward and dorsal fin distinctly posterior to pelvic fin insertion. It is distinguished from the other species of the family by the following combination of characters. Body depth is 6.7% to 9.1%, head length is 22%, and snout length is 7.6% to 10.2% of SL. Premaxilla has 3 or 4 depressible canine teeth anteriorly, followed by 55 small, fixed canine teeth posteriorly. Lower jaw has 7 or 8 moderately large, depressible canine teeth, each accompanied by one short, fixed canine tooth. Vomer lacks teeth. Anteriorly palatine has 3 or 4 large, depressible, hooked canine teeth, each accompanied by 1 short fixed tooth. Gill membranes are joined near anterior margin of eye and are free of isthmus. Pectoral fin inserts on lower flank and has 11 or 12 rays. Dorsal fin originates above anus and has 10 rays. Pelvic fin is posterior to midlength and has 9 rays. Anal fin has 28 to 30 rays. Scales are lacking except for embedded lateral line scales. Lateral line scale sections are diamond shaped, about 1.75 times longer than they are high, and number 56 to 76. Tympana (osseous scale plates) are Y-shaped, narrow posteriorly and forked anteriorly. Luminous organs are absent. Vertebrae number 78 to 82. Body is light colored with dark dorsal band formed by many irregular bands of small pigment cells.

This species occurs worldwide in tropical to warm temperate seas except for the eastern Pacific. In the western Atlantic it occurs off the eastern United States from about 36°N to 27°N, and from the northern Gulf of Mexico and the Caribbean Sea. Adults and adolescents have been captured from 200 to 2,000 m, and postlarvae and juveniles have been captured from the surface to about 200 m. No adults have been reported from the western Atlantic. Maximum known size is 187 mm SL.

REFERENCES: Rofen 1966a; Rass 1971; Post 1984c, 1986a.

Lestidium atlanticum Borodin 1928

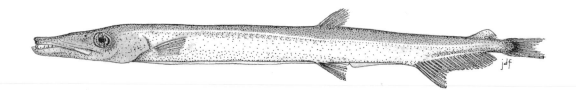

Lestidium atlanticum is elongate, slender, and compressed, with lower jaw curved upward and dorsal fin closer to pelvic fin than to anus. It is distinguished from the other species of the family by the following combination of characters. Body depth is 8%, head length is 22.4% to 22.9%, and snout length is 10.1% to 12.4% of SL. Premaxillary teeth consist of 2 or 3 depressible canines and 27 to 78 small uniserial teeth. Lower jaw has 7 or 8 widely spaced canines, each followed by 1 short fixed canine. Vomer lacks teeth. Anteriorly palatine has 3 large depressible teeth, each accompanied by 1 short fixed tooth, and posteriorly palatine has single row of 6 to 14 short fixed teeth. Gill membranes are joined in front of eyes and are free of isthmus. Pectoral fin inserts slightly below midbody depth and has 12 rays. Dorsal fin originates just anterior to pelvic fin insertion and has 9 or 10 rays. Pelvic fin inserts below first dorsal fin ray and has 9 rays. Anal fin has 29 or 30 rays. Scales are lacking except for embedded lateral scales. Lateral line scale sections are diamond shaped, about 1.5 times longer than they are high, and number 120. Vertebrae number 80 to 83. Body is unpigmented except for light brown band along dorsal surface, light pigment on side of caudal peduncle, and line of melanophores along upper and lower border of lateral line sections. Luminous organ is present in midventral musculature that extends from head to pelvic fin insertion.

This species is circumtropical with exception of the eastern Pacific. In the western Atlantic it occurs from the southeastern United States, from about 35°N, to Brazil, about 20°S, including the eastern Gulf of Mexico, the Bahamas, and the Caribbean Sea. It has been captured from the surface to the bathypelagic zone. Postlarvae have been captured from the surface to 1,200 m. Smallest postlarvae occur at the shallowest depths. Maximum known size is 196 mm SL.

REFERENCES: Rofen 1966a; Rass 1971; Murdy et al. 1983; Uyeno et al. 1983; Post 1986a.

Lestrolepis intermedia   (Poey 1868)

Lestrolepis intermedia is elongate, slender, and moderately compressed, with lower jaw curved upward and dorsal fin closer to origin of anal fin than to pelvic fin insertion. It is distinguished from the other species of the family by the following combination of characters. Body depth is 5.7% to 6.8%, head length is 19.4% to 20.3%, and snout length is 10.4% to 11% of SL. Premaxilla has 3 depressible canine teeth anteriorly and 55 to 96 small, fixed uniserial teeth posteriorly. Lower jaw has 6 to 9 moderate-sized canine teeth, each accompanied by one short, fixed canine tooth. Vomer lacks teeth. Anteriorly palatine has 4 to 8 large depressible teeth, each accompanied by one short fixed tooth. Gill membranes are joined anterior to posterior tip of upper jaw and are free of isthmus. Pectoral fin inserts on lower flank and has 11 rays. Dorsal fin originates posterior to anus and has 9 rays. Pelvic fin inserts at about midlength. Anal fin has 41 or 42 rays. One pair of luminous ducts extend on either side of ventral midline from gill covers to base of pelvic fin. Scales are lacking except for embedded lateral line scales. Lateral line scale sections are diamond shaped, about 1.75 times longer than they are high, and number 69 to 77. Tympana (osseous scale plates) are Y-shaped, narrow posteriorly and forked anteriorly. Vertebrae number 91 to 93. Body is colorless except for mid-dorsal band of stellate chromatophores, two ventral black streaks between pectoral fin and pelvic fin, and prominent black spot anterior to eye.

This species occurs worldwide in tropical to warm temperate seas, except it is absent in the eastern Pacific. In the western Atlantic it occurs from the southeastern United States, from about 35°N, to French Guiana, about 5°N, including the northern and eastern Gulf of Mexico, the Bahamas, and the Caribbean Sea. It has been captured from the surface to about 200 m. Food consists of bathypelagic fishes. Maximum known size is 148 mm SL.

REFERENCES: Rofen 1966a; Rass 1971; Uyeno et al. 1983; Post 1986a; Boschung 1992.

Paralepis atlantica Krøyer 1868

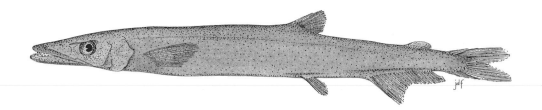

Paralepis atlantica is moderately elongate, moderately slender, and moderately compressed, with lower jaw curved upward and dorsal fin slightly anterior to pelvic fin insertion. It is distinguished from the other species of the family by the following combination of characters. Body depth is 11.9% to 18.6%, head length is 21.8% to 31%, and snout length is 10.3% to 15.6% of SL. Premaxilla has 0 to 5 minute depressible canine teeth anteriorly and 0 to 60 tiny fixed teeth posteriorly. Lower jaw has 1 to 9 tiny, fixed, uniserial canine teeth in smaller adults, but larger adults lack lower jaw teeth. Vomer either lacks or has single median depressible canine tooth. Anteriorly palatine has total of 1 to 6 short, slender fixed and depressible teeth, and posteriorly palatine has total of 8 to 20 short fixed and depressible canine teeth in one or two rows. First gill arch has 7 to 10 "gill teeth" on epibranch, 16 to 19 on lower limb, and 9 to 12 on hypobranch. Gill membranes are joined at about midsnout length and are free of isthmus. Pectoral fin inserts on lower one-third of flank and has 15 to 17 rays. Dorsal fin originates anterior to anus and has 9 to 11 rays. Pelvic fin inserts posterior to midlength of body and has 9 rays. Anal fin has 20 to 22 rays. Luminous organs are absent.

Scales are present on head anterior to midsnout length, on body, and on bases of fins. Lateral line sections are covered with four to six horizontal rows of body scales, and body scales are not pierced by pores of lateral line. Lateral line segments are longer than they are wide and number 55 to 62. Skin and deciduous scales are silvery. Vertebrae, for North Atlantic specimens, number 63 to 66. Color beneath scales is reddish brown or bluish brown. Gill membranes are dark brown to black, and peritoneum is black.

This species occurs in all oceans from the tropics to the Arctic and Antarctic. In the western Atlantic it occurs off the eastern United States, from about 38°N, to the Gulf of Mexico, Bermuda, and the Caribbean Sea. It has been captured from 66 to 2,166 m in the Atlantic Ocean. Small postlarvae are most common between 100 and 200 m, and large postlarvae are most common between 700 and 1,700 m. Food consists of euphausiid shrimps and pelagic fishes. Maximum known size is 560 mm SL.

REFERENCES: Rofen 1966a; Rass 1971; Murdy et al. 1983 (as *P. c.f. atlantica*); Uyeno et al. 1983; Post 1984a.

Stemonosudis bullisi   Rofen 1963

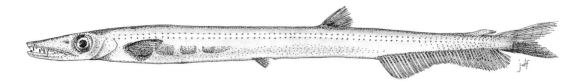

Stemonosudis bullisi is elongate, slender, and moderately compressed, with lower jaw slightly upturned and dorsal fin origin closer to origin of anal fin than to pelvic fin insertion. It is distinguished from the other species of the family by the following combination of characters. Body depth is 7.3%, head length is 18.3%, and snout length is 10.2% of SL. Premaxilla has 2 depressible canine teeth anteriorly and 14 fixed uniserial teeth posteriorly. Lower jaw has 8 large depressible canine teeth, each accompanied by one short fixed canine. Vomer lacks teeth. Anteriorly palatine has 3 depressible canine teeth, each accompanied by 1 short fixed tooth, and posteriorly palatine has single row of fine, short fixed teeth. First gill arch has 1 "gill tooth" in corner, 11 on lower limb, and 5 on hypobranch. Gill membranes are joined near end of upper jaw and are free of isthmus. Pectoral fin inserts near midflank and has 11 rays. Dorsal fin is located posterior to anus and has 9 rays. Pelvic fin inserts anterior to mid-length of body and has 9 rays. Anal fin has 41 rays. Luminous organs are absent. Scales are absent except for embedded lateral line scales. Lateral line scale sections are elliptical shaped, at least twice as long as they are high, and number 68 to 72. Tympana (osseous scale plates) are Y-shaped, convex, and relatively broad posteriorly and slightly concave anteriorly. Vertebrae number 84. Body is lightly pigmented, with narrow mid-dorsal band from occiput to procurrent caudal rays, light dusky pigmentation on lower regions of flank, and dense pigmentation on head at occiput and anterior one-half of snout.

This species occurs in the western North Atlantic from the northeastern Gulf of Mexico between 814 and 997 m. Maximum known size is 61.7 mm SL, but specimen was immature.

REFERENCES: Rofen 1963, 1966a; Rass 1971.

Stemonosudis gracilis   (Ege 1933)

Stemonosudis gracilis is very elongate, slender, and moderately compressed, with lower jaw slightly upturned and dorsal fin origin about mid-distance between pelvic fin insertion and anal fin origin. It is distinguished from the other species of the family by the following combination of characters. Body depth is 4.1%, head length is 16.8% to 17.2%, and snout length is 9.3% to 9.4% of SL. Premaxilla has 3 or 4 depressible canine teeth anteriorly and 20 or 21 fixed teeth posteriorly. Lower jaw has 10 or 11 fixed teeth in outer row and 11 to 17 depressible teeth in inner row. Vomer lacks teeth. Anteriorly palatine has 3 fixed teeth, each accompanied by 1 longer depressible canine tooth, and posteriorly palatine has closely spaced, short, fixed canine teeth. "Gill teeth" are not developed. Gill membranes are joined anterior to eye and are free of isthmus. Pectoral fin inserts on lower one-half of flank and has 11 or 12 rays. Dorsal fin originates posterior to mid-length and posterior to anus and has 10 rays. Pelvic fin inserts posterior to midlength of body and has 9 rays. Anal fin has 36 or 37 rays. Luminous organs are absent. Scales are absent on body, and embedded lateral line scales are not developed on specimens (postlarvae and juveniles) available for study. Vertebrae number 98 to 107. Body is lightly pigmented, with 4 or 5 saddlelike patches on back, 4 or 5 ventral patches between dorsal fin and caudal fin, and 14 or 15 peritoneal spots.

This species occurs worldwide in tropical to subtropical seas except for the eastern Pacific. In the western Atlantic it occurs in the Gulf of Mexico and the Caribbean Sea, between 25°N and 5°N. It has been captured from near the surface to 1,300 m. Maximum known size is 96 mm SL for a juvenile specimen.

REFERENCES: Rofen 1966a; Rass 1971 (both as *Stemonosudis gracile*); Post 1986a.

Stemonosudis intermedia (Ege 1933)

Stemonosudis intermedia is very elongate, slender, and moderately compressed, with lower jaw straight and dorsal fin closer to pelvic fin insertion than to anal fin origin. It is distinguished from the other species of the family by the following combination of characters. Body depth is 2.3% to 4.9%, head length is 13% to 16.5%, and snout length is 7.6% to 9.4% of SL. Premaxilla has 3 or 4 depressible canine teeth anteriorly and 16 to 28 fixed teeth posteriorly. Lower jaw has 9 fixed canine teeth in outer series and 9 depressible teeth in inner series. Vomer lacks teeth. Anteriorly palatine has 3 or 4 depressible canine teeth, each accompanied by 1 shorter fixed tooth, and posteriorly 4 to 6 fixed uniserial canine teeth. First gill arch has 2 or 3 "gill teeth" on epibranch, 1 in corner, 18 to 23 on lower limb, and 3 or 4 on hypobranch. Pectoral fin inserts on lower one-third of flank and has 11 or 12 rays. Dorsal fin originates posterior to midlength and has 10 rays. Pelvic fin inserts posterior to midlength and has 8 or 9 rays. Luminous organs are absent. Scales are absent except for embedded lateral line scales. Lateral line scale sections are elliptical shaped, at least twice as long as they are high, and number 86 to 92. Tympana (osseous scale plates) are Y-shaped, convex posteriorly, and relatively broad and slightly concave anteriorly. Vertebrae number 111 to 114. Body is lightly pigmented, with series of alternating dorsal and ventral spots, mid-dorsal band from head to caudal fin, and spots on midventral region. Larvae and juveniles have 16 to 18 peritoneal spots.

This species occurs in the western Atlantic off the eastern United States, from about 40°N, to the Gulf of Mexico and the Caribbean Sea. It has been captured from near the surface to 800 m. Young appear to be most abundant in the upper 100 m. Food consists of midwater fishes, e.g., *Lestidiops* sp. Maximum known size is 138 mm SL for an adolescent specimen; adults are not known.

REFERENCES: Rofen 1966a; Rass 1971.

Sudis atrox   Rofen 1963

Sudis atrox is elongate and moderately compressed, with lower jaw distinctly upturned, a large compressed head, and relatively long pectoral fins. It is distinguished from the other species of the family by the following combination of characters. Premaxillary teeth are minute and fixed, number 23, and have serrated edges in adults. Lower jaw has 2 retrorse teeth; outer row of 3 or 4 long, antrorse, compressed, fixed canine teeth; and inner row of depressible teeth. Vomer lacks teeth, and palatine has 4 short curved teeth anteriorly and 1 fixed retrorse canine tooth posteriorly. Gill rakers on first arch consist of bony plate bearing small teeth. Pectoral fin inserts just below midflank, extends to pelvic fin, and has 14 rays. Dorsal fin originates slightly posterior to pelvic fin insertion and has 11 rays. Pelvic fin has 9 rays, and anal fin has 21 rays. Scales are lacking except for two series on preoperculum and embedded lateral line scales. Lateral line scalelike sections are diamond shaped with rounded corners. Each scale section has three pores above and below. Tympana (osseous scale plates) are broad, with irregular upper and lower edges and indented anterior edges. Vertebrae number 53 or 54. Body is light colored, with top of head and snout brownish black. Anteriorly trunk is covered with evenly spaced small black spots above lateral line, and posteriorly spots extend below lateral line. Lateral line sections have two or three expanded melanophores along upper margin. Pectoral fin is mottled with black pigment anteriorly and along upper edge. Caudal fin has black vertical line at base. Peritoneum is black. Pectoral fin is relatively short in early postlarvae but extends to pelvic fin insertion in specimens between 16 and 20 mm SL. Postlarvae have six peritoneal pigment sections and uniform coloration on dorsal surface.

This species occurs in the eastern Pacific and western Atlantic Oceans. In the western Atlantic it occurs off the east coast of North America, from 37°40′N, to southern Brazil, 23°08′S, including the Gulf of Mexico and the Caribbean Sea. Specimens have been captured between 30 and 2,250 m in nonopening and nonclosing midwater trawls. All specimens captured in the western Atlantic have been postlarvae, less than 50 mm SL. Maximum known size is 75 mm SL.

REFERENCES: Rofen 1963a; Shores 1969; Rass 1971.

Sudis hyalina Rafinesque 1810

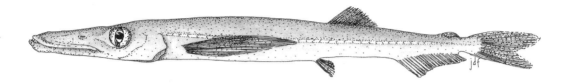

Sudis hyalina is elongate and moderately compressed, with lower jaw upturned, a large compressed head, and relatively long pectoral fins. It is distinguished from the other species of the family by the following combination of characters. Body depth is 10.2% to 11.1%, head length is 28% to 31.1%, and snout length is 16.2% to 18.6% of SL. Premaxilla is minute and has serrated edges in adults. Lower jaw has two rows of teeth; outer row consists of 2 very small antrorse canine teeth, followed by 5 to 8 large, fixed, compressed, triangular canine teeth, and inner row consists of large depressible teeth. All large mandibular teeth have serrated edges in adults. Vomer lacks teeth, and palatine possesses large, fixed conical tooth followed by 2 or 3 large, depressible canine teeth and 0 to 14 very small, fixed retrorse teeth in single row. "Gill teeth" number 8 to 11 on epibranch, 1 in corner, 24 or 25 on lower limb, and 9 to 23 on hypobranch. Pectoral fin inserts just below midflank, is equal in length to snout length, and has 14 or 15 rays. Dorsal fin originates slightly posterior to pelvic fin insertion and has 13 rays. Pelvic fin has 9 rays, and anal fin has 21 to 23 rays. Scales are lacking except for two series on preoperculum and embedded lateral line scales. Lateral line scale sections are diamond shaped with rounded corners and number 51 to 77. Each scale section has four to seven pores above and below. Tympana (osseous scale plates) are broad, with irregular upper and lower edges and indented anterior edges. Vertebrae number 59 or 60. Body is unpigmented except for light pigment band on dorsal surface and fine pigment on caudal peduncle. Head has light pigmentation on snout, along lower jaw, and on dorsal surface. Peritoneum is black. Pectoral fin extends to or beyond pelvic fin insertion in postlarvae and juveniles. Peritoneal pigment sections number seven or eight, and dorsal trunk pigmentation is concentrated into nine blotches in postlarvae.

This species occurs in the Atlantic Ocean. In the western Atlantic it occurs from 41°40′N to 32°56′S, including the Gulf of Mexico and the Caribbean Sea. It has been taken at depths of 35 to 217 m with nonopening and nonclosing nets. All specimens collected in the western Atlantic have been postlarvae, less than 50 mm SL. Maximum known size is about 400 mm SL.

REFERENCES: Rofen 1966a; Shores 1969; Murdy et al. 1983; Post 1984c.

Uncisudis advena (Rofen 1963)

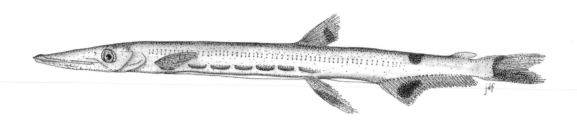

Uncisudis advena is elongate, slender, and moderately compressed, with lower jaw slightly curved upward and dorsal fin origin slightly anterior to pelvic fin insertion. It is distinguished from the other species of the family by the following combination of characters. Body depth is 6% to 7.3%, head length is 23.3% to 25.6%, and snout length is 13.2% to 14.7% of SL. Premaxilla has 3 depressible canine teeth anteriorly and 14 to 20 fixed uniserial teeth posteriorly. Lower jaw has 6 or 7 moderate-sized depressible canine teeth, each accompanied by 1 short fixed tooth. Vomer lacks teeth. Anteriorly palatine has 2 to 4 large depressible canine teeth, each accompanied by 1 short fixed canine tooth, and posteriorly palatine has 2 to 4 fixed uniserial teeth. First gill arch has 1 or 2 "gill teeth" on epibranch, 1 in corner, and 16 to 22 on lower limb. Gill membranes are joined at end of upper jaw and are free of isthmus. Pectoral fin inserts on lower one-third of flank and has 12 or 13 rays. Dorsal fin originates anterior to anus and has 10 rays. Pelvic fin inserts posterior to midlength of body and has 9 rays. Anal fin has 30 or 31 rays. Luminous organs are absent. Scales are absent except for embedded lateral line scales. Lateral line scale sections are diamond shaped, about 1.5 times longer than they are high, and number 57 to 60. Tympana (osseous scale plates) are Y-shaped, narrow posteriorly and forked anteriorly. Vertebrae number 75 to 78. Body is sparsely pigmented except for solid black saddle on dorsum anterior to adipose fin, middorsal band from occiput to black saddle, melanophores of lateral line, and seven peritoneal pigment sections.

This species occurs in the western North Atlantic from the eastern Gulf of Mexico and off the east coast of Florida. It has been caught between 813 and 997 m. Maximum known size is 62 mm SL, but specimen was immature.

REFERENCES: Rofen 1963, 1966a; Rass 1971 (all above as *Pontosudis advena*); Post 1969.

Uncisudis quadrimaculata   (Post 1969)

Uncisudis quadrimaculata is elongate, slender, and moderately compressed, with lower jaw slightly curved upward and dorsal fin origin slightly posterior to pelvic fin origin. It is distinguished from the other species of the family by the following combination of characters. Body depth is 6.6% to 6.8%, head length is 24% to 24.5%, and snout length is 13.4% to 13.6% of SL. Premaxilla has 4 unequal-sized depressible canine teeth anteriorly and small recurved teeth in single row posteriorly. Lower jaw has 6 moderate-sized depressible canine teeth, each with 1 short fixed tooth. Vomer lacks teeth. Gill membranes are joined at end of upper jaw and are free of isthmus. First gill arch has 4 "gill teeth" on epibranch, 1 in corner, and 16 to 19 on lower limb. Pectoral fin inserts on lower one-third of flank and has 11 rays. Dorsal fin has 10 rays. Pelvic fin inserts posterior to midlength of body and has 9 rays. Anal fin has 28 rays. Luminous organs are absent. Scales are absent except for embedded lateral line scales. Lateral line scale sections are diamond shaped, about 1.5 times longer than they are high, and number 60 to 62. Tympana (osseous scale plates) are Y-shaped, narrow posteriorly and forked anteriorly. Vertebrae number 75 or 76. Body is sparsely covered except for four saddles on dorsal surface and melanophores of lateral line.

This species occurs in the western Atlantic in the Gulf of Mexico and off the coast of northern South America. It has been caught between 500 and 520 m. Maximum known size is 77 mm SL.

REFERENCE: Post 1969.

SYNODONTIDAE   Lizardfishes

Lizardfishes are moderately elongate, moderately slender to slender, and cylindrical to slightly compressed, with a large oblique mouth and pelvic fins anterior to dorsal fin origin. They are distinguished from the other families of the order by the following combination of characters. Snout is short to moderately long. Premaxilla forms upper margin of mouth. Maxilla is rudimentary or absent, and supramaxillae are absent. Teeth are of moderate size, usually carniform and depressible, and occur in premaxilla, lower jaw, vomer (when present), palatine, and tongue. Eye is of moderate size, directed laterally, and nontubular. Gill rakers consist of bony plates and small spines ("gill teeth"). Gill membranes unite anterior to corner of mouth and are free of isthmus. Pectoral fin is inserted at about midflank. Dorsal fin originates over or posterior to pelvic fin insertion. Pelvic fin is generally subthoracic. Anal fin originates posterior to dorsal fin base. Dorsal adipose fin is usually present. Caudal fin is emarginate to deeply forked. Scales are cycloid and cover body, cheeks, and gill covers. Bases of pectoral, dorsal, pelvic, and caudal fins are enlarged and modified. Lateral line is nearly straight and terminates at bases of middle rays of caudal fin. Larvae and postlarvae have patches of dark pigment, or peritoneal sections, resulting from midventral and paired lateral windows in skin revealing black-pigmented peritoneum.

Lizardfishes are demersal with exception of two genera and occur worldwide in tropical to temperate seas. Most species occur on continental shelves, but some species are found from the lower continental slope, rise, and abyss to depths of 1,000 to 4,800 m. Larvae are generally epipelagic. Most species are dioecious, but some are hermaphroditic. There are about 55 species in five genera, and 9 species in four genera occur in the Gulf of Mexico.

Key to the Species of the Gulf of Mexico
(Adapted from Anderson et al. 1966)

1a.   Scales of lateral line enlarged . . . *Bathysaurus mollis* p. 606
1b.   Scales of lateral line not enlarged 2
2a.   Pelvic fin rays 8; inner rays of pelvic fin longer than outer rays; palatine with single series of teeth 3
2b.   Pelvic fin rays 9; inner rays of pelvic fin about equal to outer rays; palatine with two series of teeth 4
3a.   Anal fin origin about mid-distance between insertion of pectoral fin and caudal fin base; anal fin origin closer to pelvic fin insertion than to caudal fin base; anal fin base more than 23% of SL . . . . *Trachinocephalus myops* p. 614
3b.   Anal fin origin nearer to caudal fin base than to pectoral

fin insertion; anal fin origin closer to caudal fin base than
to pelvic fin insertion; anal fin base less than 18% of SL
. . . . 6

4a.   Lower jaw shorter than upper jaw, not visible dorsally
      when mouth is closed . . . . *Saurida normani* p. 609
4b.   Lower jaw longer than upper jaw, distinctly visible dorsally
      when mouth is closed. 5
5a.   Scales in lateral line 40 to 50 . . . *Saurida brasiliensis* p. 607
5b.   Scales in lateral line 51 to 60 . . . . *Saurida caribbaea* p. 608
6a.   Scales in lateral line 43 to 53 7
6b.   Scales in lateral line 54 to 65 8
7a.   Anterior rays of dorsal fin extending to but not beyond
      posterior rays when fin is depressed; lower jaw rounded
      anteriorly, without fleshy knob; shoulder girdle with black
      patch under operculum . . . . . . *Synodus intermedius* p. 611
7b.   Anterior rays of dorsal fin extending beyond posterior rays
      when fin is depressed; lower jaw with fleshy knob at tip;
      shoulder girdle without black patch under operculum
      . . . . *Synodus poeyi* p. 612
8a.   Anal fin rays 11 to 13 (rarely 10 to 14); anal fin base 82.5%
      to 125% of dorsal fin base length; tip of pectoral fin not
      extending beyond pelvic fin base; predorsal scales 20 to 30
      . . . . *Synodus foetens* p. 610
8b.   Anal fin rays 8 to 10 (rarely 11); anal fin base 53% to 68%
      of dorsal fin base length; tip of pectoral fin extending
      beyond pelvic fin base; predorsal scales 15 to 18
      . . . . *Synodus synodus* p. 613

Bathysaurus mollis   Günther 1878

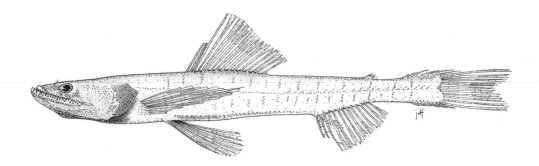

Bathysaurus mollis is moderately elongate, moderately slender, slightly depressed anteriorly, and compressed posteriorly, with a relatively long dorsal fin and a large horizontal mouth. It is distinguished from the other species of the family by the following combination of characters. Snout is long, depressed, and rounded in cross section. Body depth is 8.5% to 10.8%, head length is 22.3% to 23.9%, and snout length is 5.8% to 6.2% of SL. Lower jaw extends beyond upper jaw. Teeth in jaws are conical, recurved, and mostly depressible and are arranged in broad bands. Area at symphysis of lower jaw lacks teeth. Teeth also occur in vomer, palatine, tongue, and branchial arches. Branchiostegal rays number 8. Pectoral fin has 16 or 17 rays, and central rays are elongate. Dorsal fin originates anterior to midlength and posterior to pelvic fin insertion and has 15 to 17 rays. Anal fin has shorter base than dorsal

fin and has 11 to 13 rays. Dorsal adipose fin is present. Cycloid scales are present on cheeks, gill covers, body, and base of caudal fin. Lateral line scales are somewhat enlarged, and no axillary scales occur at bases of paired fins. Vertebrae number 50 to 52. Color is generally white, with peritoneum, branchial and buccal regions dark, but very large specimens are dark. Small specimens have faint vertical bars, and these sometimes persist in adults.

This species occurs worldwide in tropical to temperate seas from 50°N to 20°S between 1,554 and 4,700 m, except possibly the tropical eastern Pacific. It occurs in the Gulf of Mexico and the Caribbean Sea in the western Atlantic. Maximum known size is 400 to 650 mm SL.

REFERENCES: Mead 1966b; Sulak 1977, 1986e; Anderson et al. 1985.

Saurida brasiliensis Norman 1935
Largescale lizardfish

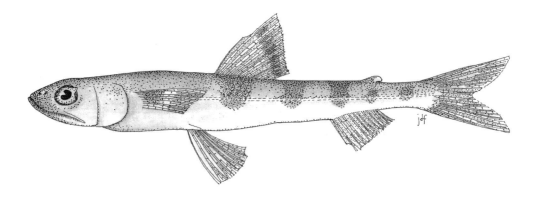

Saurida brasiliensis is moderately elongate, moderately slender, and almost cylindrical, with a relatively short dorsal fin and a large oblique mouth. It is distinguished from the other species of the family by the following combination of characters. Snout is blunt, narrow, and about equal to eye diameter. Body depth is 9.2% to 15.2%, head length is 22.4% to 26.5%, and snout length is 4.4% to 6.3% of SL. Lower jaw extends beyond upper jaw. Teeth are arranged in bands in upper and lower jaws, with inner teeth largest. Bands of similar teeth occur on tongue and branchial arches, and in two bands in palatine. Branchiostegal rays number 13 to 16. Pectoral fin has 11 to 13 rays, and when depressed, tip of fin extends to or beyond pelvic fin base. Dorsal fin has 9 to 12 rays, and when depressed, tips of anterior rays extend beyond tips of all succeeding rays. Pelvic fin has 9 rays, and median rays are usually longer than outer rays. Anal fin has 10 to 13 rays, and base is shorter than dorsal fin base. Dorsal adipose fin is present. Scales are present on cheeks, gill cover, body, and base of caudal fin. Lateral line scales are not enlarged and number 43 to 47. Enlarged axillary scales occur at base of pectoral and pelvic fins. Vertebrae number 44. Color is brownish on dorsal parts of head and trunk to lateral line. Three faint brown saddles occur at origin of dorsal fin, posterior end of dorsal fin base, and anterior to adipose fin. About six faint brown blotches are present on lateral line. Lower parts of head and body are light. Dorsal fin has dark submarginal stripe. Juveniles have 10 large black spots on lower side and an elongate black blotch on lower edge of operculum.

This species occurs in the tropical and warm temperate waters of the western North Atlantic and possibly from the tropical waters of the eastern Atlantic. In the western Atlantic it occurs from the coast of North Carolina to the Florida Keys, throughout the Gulf of Mexico and the western Caribbean to southern Brazil. It has been captured on the bottom from 18 to 410 m but is most abundant in less than 183 m. Size at maturity is 80 mm SL, and maximum known size is 115 mm SL.

REFERENCES: Longley and Hildebrand 1941; Anderson et al. 1966; Hoese and Moore 1977; Castro-Aguirre and Márquez-Espinoza 1981; C. R. Robins et al. 1986; Boschung 1992.

Saurida caribbaea   Breder 1927
Smallscale lizardfish

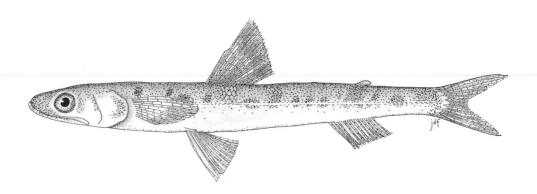

Saurida caribbaea is moderately elongate, moderately slender, and almost cylindrical, with a relatively short dorsal fin and a large oblique mouth. It is distinguished from the other species of the family by the following combination of characters. Snout is blunt, narrow, and about equal to eye diameter. Body depth is 9.3% to 13.2%, head length is 23% to 24.6%, and snout length is 4.8% to 7.3% of SL. Lower jaw extends beyond upper jaw. Teeth are arranged in bands in upper and lower jaws, with inner teeth longest. Similar teeth occur on tongue and branchial arches, and in two bands in palatine. Branchiostegal rays number 13 to 16. Pectoral fin has 12 or 13 rays, and when depressed, tip of fin extends to or beyond pelvic fin base. Dorsal fin has 10 to 12 rays, and when depressed, tips of anterior rays extend beyond all succeeding rays. Pelvic fin has 9 rays, and median rays are longer than outer rays. Anal fin has 11 or 12 rays, and base is usually shorter than dorsal fin base. Dorsal adipose fin is present. Scales cover cheeks, gill covers, body, and base of caudal fin. Lateral line scales number 51 to 60 and are not enlarged. Enlarged axillary scales occur at bases of pectoral and pelvic fins. Color is light brownish on dorsal parts of head and trunk to lateral line. Dark blotches, but not saddlelike markings, are present on back, and irregular brown spots occur above and on lateral line. Ventral parts of head and trunk are yellowish white. Dorsal fin is dusky with dark stripe distally.

The species occurs in the western Atlantic off northeastern Florida and from the Gulf of Mexico to the Guianas, the Bahamas, and Cuba between 4 and 460 m. In the Gulf of Mexico it is most common east of the Mississippi River and in the eastern section of Campeche Bay. Maximum known size is 130 mm SL.

REFERENCES: Anderson et al. 1966; Hoese and Moore 1977; Uyeno et al. 1983; C. R. Robins et al. 1986; Boschung 1992.

Saurida normani   Longley 1935
Shortjaw lizardfish

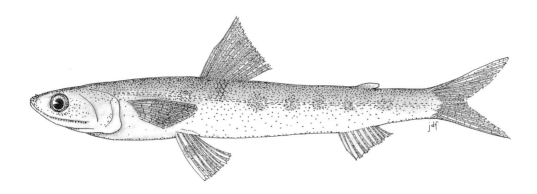

Saurida normani is moderately elongate, moderately slender, and almost cylindrical, with a relatively short dorsal fin and a large oblique mouth. It is distinguished from the other species of the family by the following combination of characters. Snout is blunt, narrow, and slightly shorter than eye diameter. Body depth is 11.7% to 15.1%, head length is 22.7% to 26.7%, and snout length is 4.2% to 5.7% of SL. Upper jaw extends beyond lower jaw. Teeth are arranged in bands in upper and lower jaws, with inner teeth longest. Similar teeth occur on tongue and branchial arches, and in two bands in palatine. Branchiostegal rays number 13 to 16. Pectoral fin has 13 or 14 rays, and when depressed, tip of fin extends to or beyond pelvic fin base. Dorsal fin has 10 to 12 rays, and when depressed, tips of anterior rays extend beyond all succeeding rays. Pelvic fin has 9 rays, and medial rays are longer than outer rays. Anal fin has 9 to 11 rays, and base is shorter than dorsal fin base. Dorsal adipose fin is present. Scales cover cheeks, gill cover, body, and base of caudal fin. Lateral line scales number 51 to 56 and are not enlarged. Enlarged axillary scales occur on bases of pectoral and pelvic fins. Vertebrae number 49. Color is grayish on dorsal parts of head and trunk to lateral line. Five or six dark blotches occur along lateral line. Belly is silvery. Dorsal and caudal fins are dusky, and anterior edge of pelvic fin has dark blotch.

This species occurs in the western North Atlantic from North Carolina to the Florida Keys and in the eastern Gulf of Mexico, the western Caribbean to the Guianas, the Bahamas, and off Cuba. It has been captured on the bottom from 40 to 550 m. Maximum known size is 450 mm SL.

REFERENCES: Longley and Hildebrand 1941; Anderson et al. 1966; Böhlke and Chaplin 1968; Castro-Aguirre and Márquez-Espinoza 1981; C. R. Robins et al. 1986; Boschung 1992.

Synodus foetens (Linnaeus 1766)
Inshore lizardfish

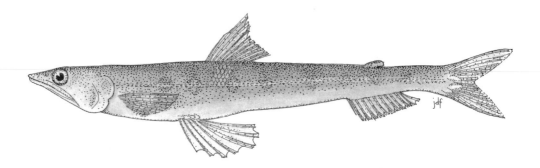

Synodus foetens is moderately elongate, moderately slender, and cylindrical, with a short dorsal fin and a large oblique mouth. It is distinguished from the other species of the family by the following combination of characters. Snout is conical and slightly longer than eye diameter. Body depth is 9.8% to 14.4%, head length is 20.6% to 26.3%, and snout length is 4.4% to 8% of SL. Upper jaw extends beyond lower jaw. Lower jaw has a fleshy tip. Teeth in jaws are compressed, pointed, and in narrow band, with inner teeth largest and depressible. Palatine has single row of teeth. Tongue has depressible teeth. Branchiostegal rays number 12 to 18. Pectoral fin has 12 to 15 rays, and when depressed, tips of rays usually fail to reach pelvic fin insertion. Dorsal fin has 10 to 13 rays, and when depressed, tips of anterior rays extend beyond some or all of succeeding rays. Pelvic fin has 8 rays, and medial rays are longest. Anal fin has 10 to 14 rays, and base is usually longer than dorsal fin base. Dorsal adipose fin is present. Scales occur on cheeks, gill covers, body, and base of caudal fin. Lateral line scales number 56 to 65 and are not enlarged but are keeled on caudal peduncle. Enlarged axillary

scales are present at bases of pectoral and pelvic fins. Color is grayish on head and upper trunk, with about eight faint diamond-shaped blotches on side of some specimens. Belly is white. Larvae and postlarvae have 6 large, evenly spaced peritoneal sections along side of belly anterior to anal fin and about 13 small spots along anal fin base.

This species occurs in the western Atlantic from the coast of Massachusetts to the Florida Keys and from Bermuda, the Gulf of Mexico, the Caribbean Sea, and the West Indies to the mouth of the Amazon River. It has been captured on the bottom from near shore to 183 m and is most common in shallow water. It also occurs along beaches and in lagoons and estuaries. Young are most abundant in inshore areas. Food consists of a wide variety of fishes. Maximum known size is 405 mm SL.

REFERENCES: Longley and Hildebrand 1941; Gunter 1945; Anderson et al. 1966; Böhlke and Chaplin 1968; Hoese and Moore 1977; Castro-Aguirre and Márquez-Espinoza 1981; Uyeno et al. 1983; C. R. Robins et al. 1986; Boschung 1992.

Synodus intermedius (Spix and Agassiz 1829)
Sand diver

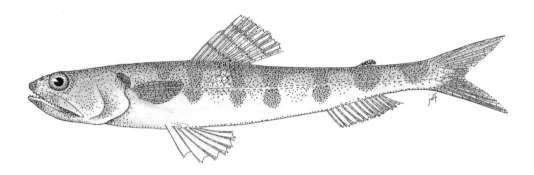

Synodus intermedius is moderately elongate, moderately slender, and cylindrical, with a relatively short dorsal fin and a large oblique mouth. It is distinguished from the other species of the family by the following combination of characters. Snout is conical and about as long as eye diameter. Body depth is 10.2% to 16.2%, head length is 23.4% to 29.6%, and snout length is 3.1% to 7.9% of SL. Upper jaw extends beyond lower jaw. Lower jaw has round tip. Teeth in jaws are compressed, pointed, and in narrow band, with inner teeth largest and depressible. Palatine has single band of teeth. Tongue has depressible teeth. Branchiostegal rays number 12 to 18. Pectoral fin has 11 to 13 rays, and when depressed, tips of rays extend beyond origin of pelvic fin. Dorsal fin has 11 to 13 rays, and when depressed, tips of anterior rays extend to but not beyond tips of succeeding rays. Pelvic fin has 8 rays, and medial rays are longest. Anal fin has 10 to 13 rays, and base is shorter than or equal to dorsal fin base. Dorsal adipose fin is present. Lateral line scales number 45 to 52 and are not enlarged but are keeled on caudal peduncle.

Enlarged axillary scales occur at bases of pectoral and pelvic fins. Color is brownish gray on head and upper trunk, with about eight bands extending below lateral line. Small patches of pigment occur between bands. Belly is light. Black oval spot is located on shoulder girdle, partially below upper margin of operculum. Young specimens are more intensely colored.

This species occurs in the western Atlantic from North Carolina to the Florida Keys, the Gulf of Mexico, Bermuda, the Bahamas, the West Indies, and the Caribbean Sea to the Guianas. In the Gulf of Mexico it is more abundant east of Mobile Bay and in the eastern section of Campeche Bay. It has been captured from the shoreline to 320 m but is most common between 36 and 108 m. Food consists of shrimps and fishes. Maximum known size is 450 mm SL.

REFERENCES: Longley and Hildebrand 1941; Anderson et al. 1966; Böhlke and Chaplin 1968; Hoese and Moore 1977; Uyeno et al. 1983; C. R. Robins et al. 1986.

Synodus poeyi Jordan 1887
Offshore lizardfish

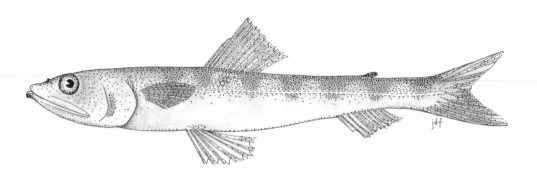

Synodus poeyi is moderately elongate, moderately slender, and cylindrical, with a relatively short dorsal fin and a large oblique mouth. It is distinguished from the other species of the family by the following combination of characters. Snout is conical and shorter than eye diameter. Body depth is 8.8% to 18.5%, head length is 22.1% to 28.3%, and snout length is 2.6% to 6.5% of SL. Lower jaw extends beyond upper jaw and has fleshy knob. Teeth in jaws are compressed, pointed, and in narrow band, with inner teeth largest and depressible. Palatine has single row of teeth. Tongue has depressible teeth. Branchiostegal rays number 12 to 18. Pectoral fin has 10 to 12 rays, and when depressed, tips of rays extend beyond origin of pelvic fin. Dorsal fin has 10 to 12 rays, and when depressed, tips of anterior rays extend to or beyond tips of some of succeeding rays. Pelvic fin has 8 rays, and medial rays are longest. Anal fin has 9 to 12 rays, and base is shorter than dorsal fin base. Dorsal adipose fin is present. Lateral line scales number 43 to 48 and are not enlarged but are keeled on caudal peduncle. Enlarged axillary scales occur on bases of pectoral and pelvic fins. Color is grayish brown on head and trunk above lateral line, with about eight obscure darker blotches on side along lateral line. Belly and lower side of trunk are white. Blotches are more distinct in young specimens.

This species occurs in the western Atlantic from North Carolina to the Florida Keys, the Gulf of Mexico, the West Indies, and the Caribbean Sea to the Guianas. It has been captured on the bottom from 27 to 320 m but is most common in less than 180 m. Maximum known size is 200 mm SL.

REFERENCES: Longley and Hildebrand 1941; Anderson et al. 1966; Hoese and Moore 1977; C. R. Robins et al. 1986; Boschung 1992.

Synodus synodus (Linnaeus 1758)
Red lizardfish

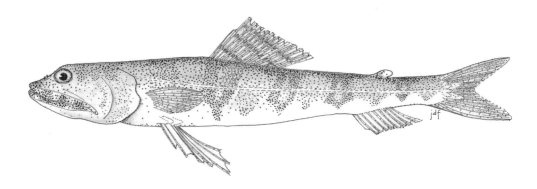

Synodus synodus is moderately elongate, moderately slender, and cylindrical, with a moderately long dorsal fin and a large oblique mouth. It is distinguished from the other species of the family by the following combination of characters. Snout is conical and longer than eye diameter. Body depth is 11.6% to 16.1%, head length is 27.2% to 30.6%, and snout length is 5.5% to 7.9% of SL. Upper jaw extends beyond lower jaw, and lower jaw has fleshy tip. Teeth in jaw are compressed, pointed, and in narrow band, with inner teeth largest and depressible. Palatine has single row of teeth. Tongue has depressible teeth. Branchiostegal rays number 12 to 18. Pectoral fin has 11 or 12 rays, and when depressed, tips of rays extend beyond pelvic fin base. Dorsal fin has 12 to 14 rays, and when depressed, tips of anterior rays do not extend to or beyond tips of any succeeding rays. Pelvic fin has 8 rays, and medial rays are longest. Anal fin has 8 to 10 rays, and base is shorter than dorsal fin base. Dorsal adipose fin is present. Lateral line scales number 54 to 59 and are not enlarged but are keeled on caudal peduncle. Enlarged axillary scales occur on bases of pectoral and pelvic fins. Color is light gray on head and trunk above lateral line, with small dark spot near tip of snout, blotches on sides of jaws, dark patch on shoulder girdle, and broad brown saddles at origin of dorsal fin, posterior to dorsal fin, anterior to adipose fin, and between adipose fin and caudal fin. Less distinct bands are found between saddles, and broad band is located at nape. Belly and lower side are white. Postlarvae have 12 or 13 pairs of small peritoneal sections.

This species occurs in the tropical to warm temperate waters of the Atlantic. In the western Atlantic it occurs in the Gulf of Mexico, predominantly along the west coast of Florida and in eastern Campeche Bay, and off the Bahamas and the West Indies to Uruguay. It has been captured on the bottom from near shore to 90 m and is frequently associated with rocky and reef areas in shallow water. Maximum known size is 300 mm SL in the Gulf of Mexico.

REFERENCES: Longley and Hildebrand 1941; Anderson et al. 1966; Böhlke and Chaplin 1968; C. R. Robins et al. 1986; Sulak 1986e; Boschung 1992.

Trachinocephalus myops (Forster 1801)
Snakefish

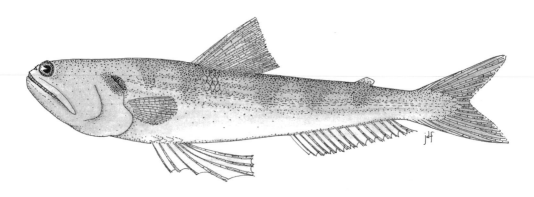

Trachinocephalus myops is moderately elongate, moderately slender, and slightly compressed, with a long anal fin and a large, strongly oblique mouth. It is distinguished from the other species of the family by the following combination of characters. Snout is blunt and very short, considerably shorter than eye diameter. Body depth is 15.5% to 21.5%, head length is 25.2% to 28.6%, and snout length is 2.2% to 3.1% of SL. Lower jaw extends beyond upper jaw and has round tip. Teeth in jaws are large, compressed, pointed, and in narrow row, with inner ones largest and depressible. Palatine has single band of teeth. Tongue has large depressible teeth. Branchiostegal rays number 14. Pectoral fin has 11 to 13 rays, and when depressed, tips of rays extend beyond pelvic fin origin. Dorsal fin has 11 to 13 rays, and when depressed, tips of anterior rays extend to tips of some of succeeding rays. Pelvic fin has 8 rays, and medial rays are much longer than outer rays. Anal fin has 14 to 16 rays, and base is considerably longer than dorsal fin base. Dorsal adipose fin is present. Lateral line scales number 53 to 59 and are not enlarged. Enlarged axillary scales occur on bases of pectoral and pelvic fins. Color is mottled grayish brown on head and upper trunk to below lateral line, with about five indistinct broad saddles of dark brown on body midway between head and dorsal fin origin, at dorsal fin origin, posterior to dorsal fin base, midway between dorsal fin base and adipose fin, and below adipose fin. Operculum has black spot at upper corner. Belly is pale yellowish white.

This species occurs worldwide in tropical waters. In the western Atlantic it occurs from Massachusetts to the Florida Keys, Bermuda, the northern Gulf of Mexico, and the Bahamas and West Indies to Brazil. It has been captured from near shore to 388 m but is most common between 36 and 91 m and is common on reefs. Maximum known size is 300 mm SL.

REFERENCES: Longley and Hildebrand 1941; Anderson et al. 1966; Böhlke and Chaplin 1968; Hoese and Moore 1977; Uyeno et al. 1983; C. R. Robins et al. 1986; Boschung 1992.

MYCTOPHIFORMES

Myctophiformes are the sister group of the Acanthomorpha (Lampridiformes, Polymixiiformes, Paracanthopterygii, and Acanthopterygii). The order includes two families, and both occur in the Gulf of Mexico.

Key to the Families of the Gulf of Mexico

1a. Photophores small, buttonlike, circular in shape, covered by modified scale; luminescent tissue patches, scales, or glands often present at or along bases of fins (one species without photophores). . . . . Myctophidae p. 615

1b. Photophores large, oval in shape, covered by unmodified scale; no other luminescent tissue, scales, or glands (one species without photophores) . . . . . . Neoscopelidae p. 677

MYCTOPHIDAE   Lanternfishes

Lanternfishes are typically small (less than 300 mm SL), slender to deep bodied, and compressed, with large heads and eyes. They are distinguished from the other family of the order by the following combination of characters. Snout is short and acute to blunt. Mouth is subterminal to terminal and large to very large, with premaxilla excluding maxilla from upper jaw. Jaws have bands of closely set teeth, with inner teeth largest. Palatine has narrow band of teeth, vomer generally has patch of minute teeth on each side, and pharyngobranchs bear enlarged teeth. Small supramaxilla is located on dorsal margin of maxilla. Eye is generally laterally directed but occasionally dorsolaterally directed. Gill rakers are lathlike or absent (*Centrobranchus*). Pectoral fin is on lower one-half of flank. Dorsal fin originates anterior to midlength. Pelvic fin is abdominal and has six to eight rays. Anal fin originates from midway to just posterior to dorsal fin base and has moderately long to long base. Dorsal adipose fin is present. Caudal fin is forked. First dorsal, first anal, upper pectoral, and outermost pelvic fin rays are preceded by rudimentary spine. Body is covered with cycloid, or occasionally ctenoid, scales. Round or kidney-shaped photophores are present on head and trunk of all but one species. Luminous organs occur on head and/or caudal peduncle. Luminous tissue patches, scales, or glands often occur at bases of fins. Swim bladder is generally present but may be regressed in adults or may become filled with oil or fatty tissue.

Lanternfishes occur worldwide from the equator to the Arctic and Antarctic in mesopelagic to bathypelagic depths. Many mesopelagic species migrate to the upper 100 m or to the surface at night, although vertical migration may be limited to certain life stages. Food consists of copepods, amphipods, ostracods, euphausiids, chaetognaths, and fish eggs and larvae. There are about 235 species in 32 genera, and 53 species in 17 genera occur in the Gulf of Mexico.

Key to the Species of the Gulf of Mexico

(Adapted from Nafpaktitis et al. 1977; Hulley 1984b)

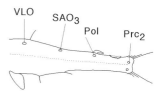

FIG 123

1a. VLO, SAO_3, and Pol close to dorsal margin of body (Fig. 123); 2 Prc; Prc_2 above lateral line
. . . . *Notolychnus valdiviae* p. 670

1b. No photophores near dorsal margin of body; two or more Prc; Prc_2 below lateral line 2

2a. PLO slightly above (less than its diameter above) level of upper end of pectoral fin base 3

2b. PLO more than its diameter above level of upper end of pectoral fin base 4

3a. Gill rakers essentially absent (represented by spiny keels)
. . . . *Centrobranchus nigroocellatus* p. 627

3b. Gill rakers lathlike . . . . *Gonichthys cocco* p. 648

FIG 124

4a. PVO_2 on level or below level of upper end of pectoral fin base (Fig. 124) 6

4b. PVO_2 above level of upper end of pectoral fin base (Fig. 125) 5

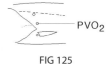

FIG 125

5a. Gill rakers on first arch 13 to 15
. . . . *Notoscopelus caudispinosus* p. 671

5b. Gill rakers on first arch 19 to 23
. . . . *Notoscopelus resplendens* p. 672

6a. Two Prc 7

6b. More than two Prc 19

7a. PVO photophores horizontal, PVO_1 not more than its diameter ventral to level of PVO_2; VO_2 elevated 8

7b. PVO photophores diagonal, PVO_1 more than its diameter below PVO_2; VO level 9

8a. Prc_2 much higher than Prc_1, located its diameter or less below lateral line; jaw teeth small and simple
. . . . *Benthosema suborbitale* p. 624

8b. Prc_2 horizontal to or slightly higher than Prc_1, located twice its diameter or more below lateral line; premaxillary teeth flattened and lanceolate, outer teeth of lower jaw close-set and flattened . . . . *Diogenichthys atlanticus* p. 647

9a. Two Pol 10

9b. One Pol 14

10a. Last AOa, Pol_1, and Pol_2 in straight line or nearly so, line

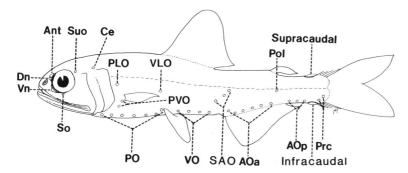

Generalized Myctophidae for Photophore ID (See p. 1073)

through anterior margin of last AOa and Pol_2 in contact with Pol_1 11

10b. Last AOa, Pol_1, and Pol_2 not in straight line, line through anterior margin of last AOa and Pol_2 passes behind Pol_1 12

11a. Prc_2 low, distance between Prc_1 and Prc_2 equal to or less than distance between Prc_2 and lateral line; distance between posterior end of dorsal fin base and Prc_2 less than distance between tip of snout and base of pelvic fin .... *Hygophum benoiti* p. 649

11b. Prc_2 high, distance between Prc_1 and Prc_2 much greater than distance between Prc_2 and lateral line; distance between posterior end of dorsal fin base and Prc_2 greater than distance between tip of snout and base of pelvic fin .... *Hygophum reinhardtii* p. 652

12a. VLO in contact with or less than its diameter below lateral line; SAO_1 anterior to or directly above VO_2 .... *Hygophum hygomii* p. 650

12b. VLO midway between base of pelvic fin and lateral line, or higher; SAO_1 behind VO_2 13

13a. SAO_1 anterior to vertical line through VO_3; VO_4, SAO_2, and SAO_3 in straight line; pectoral fin, when depressed, extending beyond AOa_1; gill rakers 19 to 21; supracaudal luminous gland consisting of five to seven scalelike structures .... *Hygophum macrochir* p. 651

13b. SAO_1 behind or directly above VO_3; VO_4, SAO_2, and SAO_3 not in straight line, VO_4 anterior to line through SAO_2 and SAO_3; pectoral fin, when depressed, not extending to AOa_1; gill rakers 16 to 18; supracaudal luminous gland without distinct scalelike structures .... *Hygophum taaningi* p. 653

14a. SAO strongly angular; SAO_1 anterior to or directly above VO_3 .... *Symbolophorus rufinus* p. 673

14b. SAO form straight line or slightly curved line; SAO_1 behind VO_3 15

15a. Gill rakers 14 to 16; SAO form slightly curved line
.... *Myctophum asperum* p. 666

15b. Gill rakers 18 or more; SAO form straight or nearly
straight line 16

16a. Gill rakers 18 to 22; AO 12 to 15; pectoral fin rays 13 or
14.. 17

16b. Gill rakers 22 to 25; AO 9 to 12; pectoral fin rays 16 to 18
.... 18

17a. Posterodorsal margin of operculum sharply angled in late
juveniles and adults; scales cycloid
.... *Myctophum nitidulum* p. 667

17b. Posterodorsal margin of operculum evenly rounded in all
postmetamorphic stages; scales ctenoid
.... *Myctophum affine* p. 665

18a. Body deep; head nearly as deep as it is long; upper part of
posterior opercular margin smooth; scales ctenoid
.... *Myctophum selenops* p. 669

18b. Body slender; head distinctly longer than it is deep; upper
part of posterior opercular margin serrate; scales cycloid
.... *Myctophum obtusirostre* p. 668

19a. First PO and two PVO in straight, ascending line; first
three VO in straight, ascending line; males with supracaudal and females with infracaudal or caudal luminous
glands absent; four Prc......................... 20

19b. First PO and two PVO not in straight, ascending line; first
three VO not in straight, ascending line; both sexes with
supracaudal and infracaudal luminous glands; three or
four Prc 38

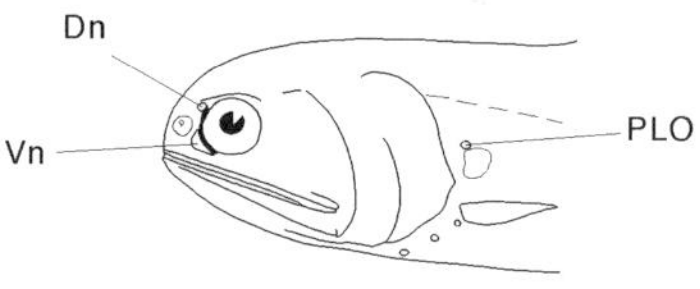

20a. Dn and Vn present; caudal luminous glands absent; usually
luminous scale at PLO (Fig. 126) 21

20b. Only Dn present; males with supracaudal and females with
infracaudal luminous glands; no luminous scale at PLO
.... *Lobianchia gemellarii* p. 664

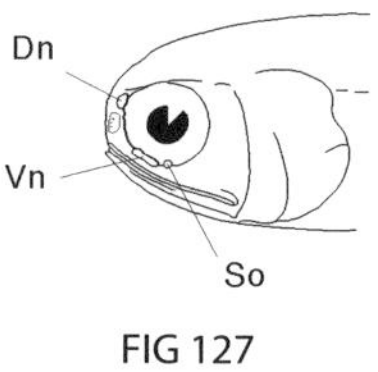

21a. So on ventral margin of orbit, separate from Vn, or connected to it by strand of dark tissue (Fig. 127); inner series
of teeth in posterior section of premaxilla with broad bases
and strongly recurved cusps (Fig. 128); vomer with few or
no teeth 22

21b. So absent; inner series of teeth in posterior section of premaxilla of various sizes, sometimes distinctly recurved;
vomer with small round to oval patch of teeth on each side
.... 25

22a. So behind vertical through posterior margin of pupil; Vn
longer than horizontal diameter of pupil (Fig. 129); no
luminous scale at PLO.... *Diaphus brachycephalus* p. 651

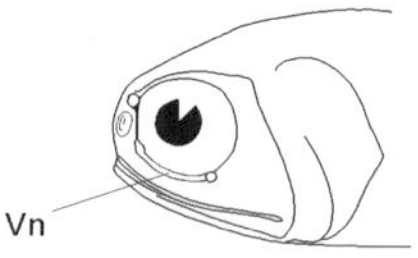

22b. So anterior to vertical through posterior margin of pupil;
Vn elongate but shorter than horizontal diameter of pupil,
or small and round; luminous scale at PLO present 23

23a. Five or more (usually six) AOp and AOp continuous or

FIG 126

FIG 127

FIG 128

FIG 129

nearly continuous with Prc, distance between Prc_1 and Prc_3 greater than between last AOp and Prc_1 (Fig. 130); gill rakers 20 to 22. . . . . *Diaphus subtilis* p. 644

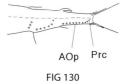

FIG 130

23b. Five or less (usually four) AOp and AOp not continuous with Prc, distance between Prc_1 and Prc_3 equal to or less than distance between last AOp and Prc_1. 24

24a. Five to seven (usually six) AOa; AOa_1 elevated, its ventral margin above level of dorsal margin of next two of series; SAO forming straight to slightly curved line (Fig. 131); large luminous scale at PLO; gill rakers 22 to 25
. . . . *Diaphus rafinesquii* p. 642

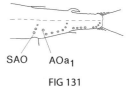

FIG 131

24b. Five or rarely six AOa; AOa_1 in straight line with next two of series, or slightly raised and forming gentle curve with next two photophores; SAO forming distinctly angular line; small luminous scale at PLO; gill rakers 15 to 18
. . . . *Diaphus mollis* p. 639

25a. Dn small, thin, poorly developed, shallowly embedded, and directed laterally; Vn small, completely separated from Dn, located on ventral orbital margin or on anteroventral aspect of orbit and connected to Dn by narrow streak of luminous tissue between eye and nasal apparatus. 26

25b. Dn well developed, in deep recess above nasal apparatus, and directed forward; Vn restricted to anteroventral aspect of orbit, or extending along anterior margin of orbit and often reaching Dn. 28

26a. Vn small, round to oval, one-half size of body photophore, separated from Dn, located on ventral orbital margin, near vertical through anterior margin of pupil; PLO anterior to vertical through upper end of pectoral fin base and 1 or 2 times its diameter below lateral line (Fig. 132); SAO form angle; AOa_1 not elevated. . . . . . . *Diaphus dumerilii* p. 632

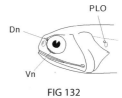

FIG 132

26b. Vn at anteroventral aspect of orbit, larger than Dn and connected to it by thin streak of luminous tissue; PLO behind vertical through upper end of pectoral fin base; SAO form slight angle or straight line; AOa_1 elevated above AOa_2 and AOa_3. 27

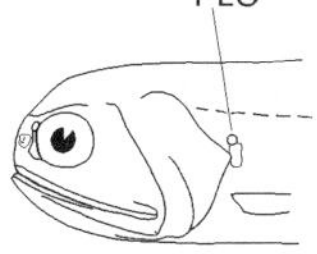

27a. PLO closer to lateral line than to pectoral fin base (Fig. 133); VLO midway between lateral line and pelvic fin base; SAO_3 and Pol in contact with lateral line; AOp_1 entirely posterior to anal fin base; gill rakers 20 to 23
. . . . *Diaphus garmani* p. 635

FIG 133

27b. PLO closer to pectoral fin base than to lateral line (Fig. 134); VLO closer to lateral line than to pelvic fin base; SAO_3 and Pol 1 to 1.5 times their diameter below lateral line; AOp_1 directly over pelvic fin base; gill rakers 13 or 14 . . . . *Diaphus problematicus* p. 641

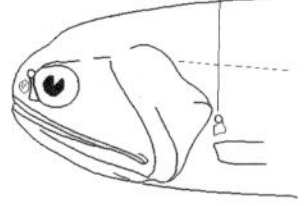

FIG 134

28a. Dn smaller than nasal rosette; Vn extending dorsally to or beyond level of Dn or restricted to below nostril but connected to Dn by strand of dark tissue. 29

28b. Dn equal in size or larger than nasal rosette; Vn extending along front of eye and meeting Dn 34

29a. Vn extending dorsally between eye and nasal rosette and reaching Dn 30

29b. Vn not extending dorsally beyond lower margin of nasal rosette 31

30a. Vn not extending along ventral orbital margin, its posterior end, at most, reaching vertical through anterior margin of pupil; elongate luminous organ along dorsal margin of orbit absent; anterior end of supraorbital frontal ridge produced into forward-directed spine; PLO closer to pectoral fin base than to lateral line (Fig. 135); SAO_3 and Pol in contact with lateral line
. . . . *Diaphus splendidus* p. 643

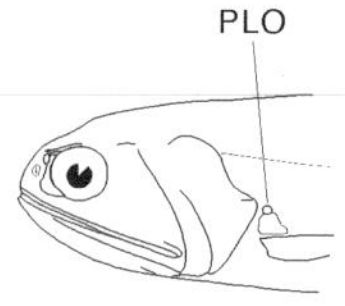

PLO

FIG 135

30b. Vn extending along ventral orbital margin, its posterior end extending to or behind vertical through center of lens; luminous organ extending along entire or nearly entire dorsal orbital margin; anterior end of supraorbital frontal ridge not produced into spine; PLO midway between pectoral fin base and lateral line or closer to lateral line (Fig. 136); SAO_3 and Pol not in contact with lateral line
. . . . *Diaphus adenomus* p. 629

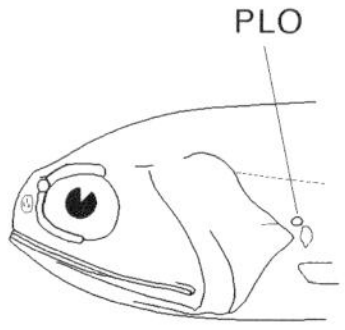

PLO

FIG 136

31a. SAO_1 above level of VO_5; upper jaw extending less than diameter of eye behind posterior margin of orbit; pelvic fin extending to origin of anal fin 32

31b. SAO_1 on same level as VO_5; upper jaw extending more than diameter of eye behind posterior margin of orbit; pelvic fin extending beyond origin of anal fin 33

VLO

FIG 137

32a. Body photophores of moderate size, those of AOp series separated by distance greater than one-half diameter of a photophore; VLO midway between lateral line and pelvic fin base or closer to lateral line (Fig. 137); gill rakers 20 to 22. . . . . *Diaphus taaningi* p. 645

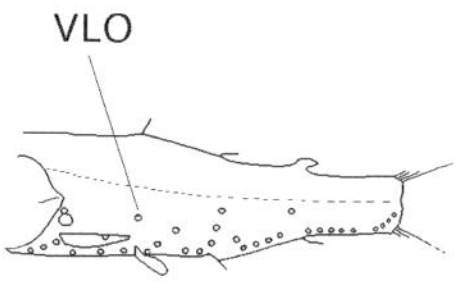

32b. Body photophores large, those of AOp series separated by distance equal to or less than one-half diameter of a photophore; VLO closer to pelvic fin base than to lateral line (Fig. 138); gill rakers 18. . . . . *Diaphus bertelseni* p. 630

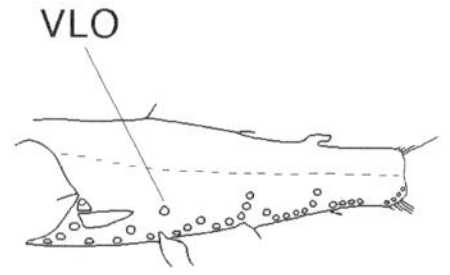

VLO

FIG 138

33a. Vn extending along most of ventral border of eye; dorsal margin of Vn with budlike projections (Fig. 139); dorsal and anal fin bases overlapping . . . *Diaphus luetkeni* p. 637

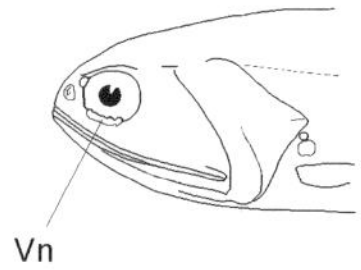

33b. Vn roundish or oval, located on ventral orbital margin, near center of pupil (Fig. 140); dorsal and anal fin bases not overlapping . . . . *Diaphus termophilus* p. 646

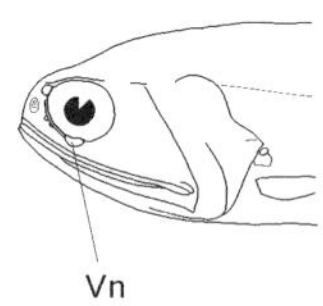

Vn

FIG 139

34a. Ant present. 35

34b. Ant absent . . . . *Diaphus lucidus* p. 636

35a. Vn not reaching vertical through anterior margin of pupil; head longer than it is deep; body photophores of normal size. 36

Vn

FIG 140

35b. Vn extending beyond vertical through center of pupil
(Fig. 141); head nearly as deep as it is long; body photophores of small size. . . . . . *Diaphus metopoclampus* p. 638

36a. Dn extending little if any above level of dorsal eye margin;
PLO midway between lateral line and pectoral fin base or
higher; SAO_3 and Pol less than their diameter below lateral
line. 37

36b. Dn extending distinctly higher than dorsal eye margin; PLO
closer to pectoral fin base than to lateral line (Fig. 142);
SAO_3 and Pol 1.5 to 3 times their diameter below lateral
line . . . . *Diaphus effulgens* p. 633

37a. Vn not extending behind nasal rosette (Fig. 143); diameter
of eye less than 10% of SL; inner series of teeth of lower
jaw larger than other teeth; gill rakers 17 or 18
. . . . *Diaphus fragilis* p. 634

37b. Vn extending behind nasal rosette to medial ethmoid crest
(Fig. 144); diameter of eye more than 10% of SL; inner
series of teeth of lower jaw not larger than other teeth; gill
rakers 26 to 29 . . . . *Diaphus perspicillatus* p. 640

38a. Caudal luminous glands large, undivided, and bordered by
black pigment (Fig. 145); three Prc or none 39

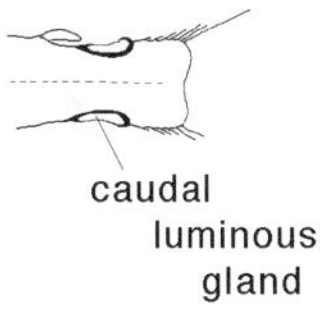

38b. Caudal luminous glands consisting of overlapping scalelike
structures, not bordered by black pigment (Fig. 146); three
or four Prc 43

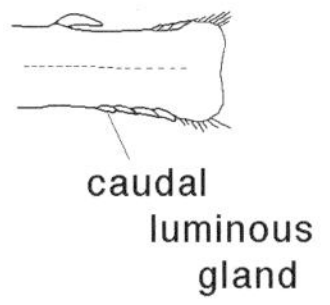

39a. Dorsal fin origin directly over or anterior to pelvic fin base
. . . . 40

39b. Dorsal fin origin behind pelvic fin base. 41

40a. PO_4 highly elevated, almost directly above PO_3; total gill
rakers on first arch 13 to 15, usually 14
. . . . *Lampadena luminosa* p. 655

40b. PO_{1-5} all low, more or less in straight line; total gill rakers
on first arch 16 to 18, usually 17
. . . . *Lampadena anomala* p. 654

41a. Primary photophores absent
. . . . *Taaningichthys paurolychnus* p. 676

41b. Primary photophores present 42

42a. VO 3 to 5; AO 2 to 5; Pol behind adipose fin base; distance
between Prc_1 and Prc_2 equal to or less than diameter of
photophores . . . . *Taaningichthys bathyphilus* p. 674

42b. VO 8 to 10; AO 9 to 13; Pol under or anterior to adipose
fin base; distance between Prc_1 and Prc_2 greater than diameter of photophores . . . . . . *Taaningichthys minimus* p. 675

43a. PO_4 not elevated; luminous scalelike structures midventrally between pelvic fin bases or between pelvic fin bases
and anus; 4 Prc . . . . *Ceratoscopelus warmingii* p. 628

43b. PO_4 elevated; no luminous scalelike structure midventrally
between pelvic fin bases or between pelvic fin bases and
anus; 3 or 4 Prc 44

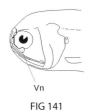

Vn

FIG 141

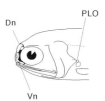

Dn   PLO

Vn

FIG 142

Vn

FIG 143

Vn

FIG 144

caudal
luminous
gland

FIG 145

caudal
luminous
gland

FIG 146

44a. Four VO; SAO forming distinct angle; line through SAO_1 and SAO_2 not intersecting photophores of VO series; no luminous tissue other than photophores and caudal glands at bases of fins; 4 Prc; SAO_3, Pol_2, and PLO in contact with or below lateral line 45

44b. Five VO; SAO forming slight angle; line through SAO_1 and SAO_2 intersecting photophores of VO series; patches of luminous tissue at bases of fins; 3 or 4 Prc; SAO_3, Pol_2, and, often, PLO slightly above lateral line 50

45a. Pectoral fin not extending beyond pelvic fin base; VLO in contact with or less than twice its diameter below lateral line 46

45b. Pectoral fin extending beyond pelvic fin base; VLO more than 3 times its diameter below lateral line (except *Lampanyctus alatus*, which has long pectoral fins and VLO in contact with lateral line). 48

46a. Prc continuous with AOp; AO 9 to 12; lateral line organs 33; pectoral fin rays 11 or 12
. . . . *Lampanyctus cuprarius* p. 658

46b. Prc usually separate from AOp; AO 12 to 16; lateral line organs 35 to 38; pectoral fin rays 14 47

47a. SAO_1 behind VO_3; lateral line organs 37 or 38; dorsal fin rays 16 to 18; anal fin origin anterior to vertical through middle of dorsal fin base . . . . *Lampanyctus lineatus* p. 659

47b. SAO_1 in front of VO_3; lateral line organs 35 or 36; dorsal fin rays 13 to 15; anal fin origin behind vertical through middle of dorsal fin base . . . . *Lampanyctus ater* p. 657

48a. One cheek photophore; luminous tissue at base of adipose fin . . . . *Lampanyctus alatus* p. 656

48b. No cheek photophore; no luminous tissue at base of adipose fin. 49

49a. SAO_1 behind VO_3; Prc separated from AOp; Prc_2, Prc_3, and Prc_4 in straight line . . . . . *Lampanyctus nobilis* p. 660

49b. SAO_1 in front of or over VO_3; Prc continuous with AOp; Prc_2, Prc_3, and Prc_4 not in straight line
. . . .*Lampanyctus tenuiformis* p. 661

50a. Four Prc; no crescent of whitish tissue on posterior half of iris; jaws extending 1 or more times diameter of eye beyond posterior margin of orbit 51

50b. Three Prc; crescent of whitish tissue on posterior half of iris; jaws extending one-half diameter of eye or less beyond posterior margin of orbit 52

51a. No luminous tissue under pectoral fin base and at pelvic fin base; gill rakers 14 or 15
. . . .*Lepidophanes guentheri* p. 663

51b. Luminous tissue under pectoral fin base and at pelvic fin base; gill rakers 12 . . . . *Lepidophanes gaussi* p. 662

52a. VLO more than twice its diameter below lateral line; VO_2 below line connecting PO_4 and SAO_1; patches of luminous tissue along base of anal fin
. . . . *Bolinichthys supralateralis* p. 626

52b. VLO in contact with or less than its diameter below lateral line; VO_2 at or slightly above line connecting PO_4 and SAO_1; patches of luminous tissue on top of head, above and below pectoral fin base, at pelvic fin base, and along dorsal and anal fin bases
. . . . *Bolinichthys photothorax* p. 625

Benthosema suborbitale   (Gilbert 1913)

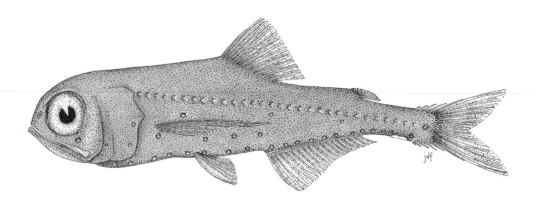

Benthosema suborbitale is short, compressed, and somewhat deep bodied, with a moderate-sized mouth and an anal fin base longer than dorsal fin base. It is distinguished from the other species of the family by the following combination of characters. Snout is slightly blunt. Jaws extend less than one-half eye diameter beyond posterior margin of orbit, and maxilla is expanded posteriorly. Head is 33% and eye is 12% of SL. Posterior margin of operculum tapers to obtuse angle above pectoral fin base. Gill rakers number 13 to 15. Dorsal fin originates posterior to pelvic fin base and has 11 to 14 rays. Pectoral fin extends to first or second AOa and has 12 to 14 rays. Anal fin originates under posterior one-half of dorsal fin base and has 16 or 17 rays. Dn and Vn are poorly developed. Two PVO are nearly horizontal, with PVO_1 over PO_3. PLO is above upper end of pectoral fin base. Five PO are present. VLO is anterior to pelvic fin base and closer to lateral line than to pelvic fin base. Four VO are present, with VO_2 highly elevated over VO_1. SAO form angle, with SAO_1 above or slightly behind VO_3, and SAO_3 over AOa_1 and very close to lateral line. Single Pol is near lateral line. AOa number 6, and AOp number 4 to 6, with first over anal fin base. Two Prc are present, and Prc_2 is in contact with lateral line.

Supracaudal luminous gland is present in males and infracaudal luminous gland is present in females.

This species occurs in tropical to subtropical waters worldwide. In the western North Atlantic it occurs from Cape Cod to northern Brazil, including the Gulf of Mexico and the Caribbean Sea. It is very abundant in the Gulf of Mexico. Daytime depths range from 375 to 750 m, and nighttime depths range from 10 to 100 m, occasionally to 250 m, with a portion of the population, mainly juveniles, remaining at daytime depths. Maximum known size is 39 mm SL, and maturity is reached at about 24 to 26 mm SL. Life span is approximately 10 months, with an average larval period of 40 days. Maturity in females is reached in about 4 months at a size of 23 mm SL. Fecundity ranges from 150 to 300 eggs and increases with body size. Spawning is repetitive, with interspawn periods of 14 days for the youngest females and 1.5 days for the largest females. Spawning generally occurs after midnight between 25 and 50 m.

REFERENCES: Nafpaktitis et al. 1977; Hulley 1984b, 1986b; Gartner et al. 1987; Gartner 1991, 1993.

Bolinichthys photothorax   (Parr 1928)

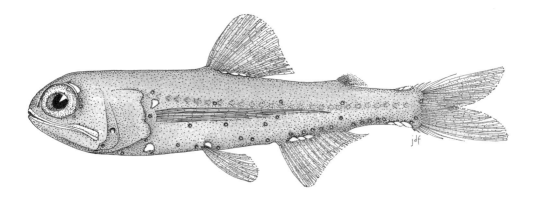

Bolinichthys photothorax is moderately slender and compressed, with a moderate-sized mouth and an anal fin base slightly longer than dorsal fin base. It is distinguished from the other species of the family by the following combination of characters. Snout is slightly blunt. Jaws extend about one-half eye diameter beyond posterior margin of orbit, and maxilla is slightly expanded posteriorly. Head is 31.3% to 33.3% and upper jaw is 19.2% to 20.8% of SL. Posterodorsal opercular margin is concave, and posterior margin is pointed or serrated. Gill rakers number 19 to 23. Dorsal fin originates over pelvic fin base and has 12 to 14 rays. Pectoral fin extends to last AOa and has 12 to 14 rays. Anal fin originates posterior to dorsal fin base and has 13 to 15 rays. Vn is poorly developed. PVO_2 is over and slightly posterior to PVO_1 and anterior to midbase of pectoral fin. PLO is immediately above or below lateral line. Five PO are present, with PO_3 and PO_4 elevated. VLO is in contact with or within its diameter below lateral line. Five VO are present, with VO_2 elevated and VO_3, VO_4, and VO_5 in straight descending line. SAO form slightly curved line to moderate angle, with SAO_1 over or slightly anterior to VO_5, and SAO_3 over anal fin base and above lateral line. Pol_1 is close to AOa series, and Pol_2 is above lateral line. AOa number five to seven, with first one somewhat depressed, and AOp number three to six and are located posterior to anal fin base. Three Prc are present, with first two located near ventral contour and third above level of lateral line. Supracaudal and infracaudal luminous glands are present on both sexes and consist of two or three and two to four scalelike structures respectively. Top of head has four pairs of patches of luminous tissue, and other patches occur above pectoral fin base, above PVO_1, above pelvic fin base, and along anal and dorsal fin bases. Crescent-shaped whitish tissue occurs on posterior half of iris.

This species occurs in the tropical to subtropical waters of the Atlantic and western Indian Oceans. In the western Atlantic it occurs from Cape Cod to southern Brazil, including the Gulf of Mexico and the Caribbean Sea. It is abundant in the Gulf of Mexico. Daytime depths range from 425 to 750 m, and nighttime depths range from 40 to 500 m. Maximum known size is 65 mm SL, and maturity is reached at about 56 to 60 mm SL.

REFERENCES: Nafpaktitis et al. 1977; Hulley 1986b; Gartner et al. 1987.

Bolinichthys supralateralis (Parr 1928)

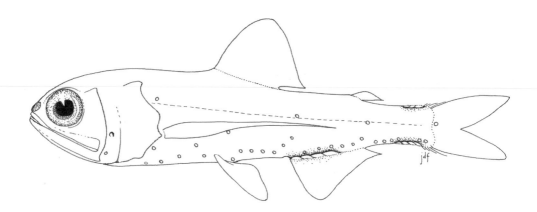

Bolinichthys supralateralis is moderately slender and compressed, with a moderate-sized mouth, and dorsal and anal fin bases of approximately equal length. It is distinguished from the other species of the family by the following combination of characters. Snout is slightly blunt. Jaws extend about one-half eye diameter beyond posterior margin of orbit, and maxilla is expanded posteriorly. Head is 33.3% to 35.7% and upper jaw is 21.3% to 23.4% of SL. Posterodorsal opercular margin is concave, and posterior margin is pointed or serrated. Gill rakers number 19 or 20. Dorsal fin originates over or slightly anterior to pelvic fin base and has 13 to 15 rays. Pectoral fin extends to last AOa and has 13 or 14 rays. Anal fin originates posterior to dorsal fin base and has 13 to 15 rays. Vn is poorly developed and located on anterior aspect of orbit. PVO_2 is above and slightly posterior to PVO_1. PLO is in contact with or above lateral line. Five PO are present, with PO_3 and PO_4 elevated. VLO is closer to lateral line than to pelvic fin base. Five VO are present, with VO_2 slightly elevated and VO_3, VO_4, and VO_5 in straight line. SAO form very slight angle, with SAO_1 above and slightly behind VO_5, and SAO_3 over anal fin base and above lateral line. AOa number four to six,

with first depressed, and AOp number three to five and are behind anal fin base. Three Prc are present, with first two near ventral contour and third above level of lateral line. Supracaudal and infracaudal glands occur in both sexes and consist of two or three and three to six scalelike structures respectively. Luminous patches occur on base of anal fin. Crescent-shaped whitish tissue is located on posterior half of iris.

This species occurs in the tropical to warm temperate Atlantic, western Pacific, and western Indian Oceans. In the western Atlantic it occurs from Cape Cod to northern Argentina, including the Gulf of Mexico and the Caribbean Sea. It is less common in the Gulf of Mexico than *B. photothorax*. Daytime depths range from 250 to 750 m, and nighttime depths range from 40 to 650 m for smaller specimens and from 500 to 750 m for larger specimens, which are taken at the greatest depths during the night and may not migrate. Maximum known size is 110 mm SL, and maturity is reached at about 90 mm SL.

REFERENCES: Nafpaktitis et al. 1977; Uyeno et al. 1983; Hulley 1984b, 1986b; Gartner et al. 1987.

Centrobranchus nigroocellatus (Günther 1873)

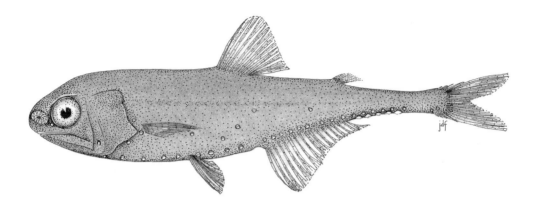

Centrobranchus nigroocellatus is elongate and slender, with a subterminal, moderate-sized mouth, an anal fin base longer than dorsal fin base, and a slender caudal peduncle. It is distinguished from the other species of the family by the following combination of characters. Snout is pointed. Jaws extend less than one-half diameter of eye beyond posterior margin of orbit, and maxilla is not expanded posteriorly. Posterior margin of operculum tapers to acute angle at PVO_2. Gill rakers are absent. Dorsal fin originates posterior to pelvic fin base and has 10 or 11 rays. Pectoral fin extends to VLO and has 13 to 15 rays. Anal fin originates under posterior end of dorsal fin base and has 16 to 19 rays. Dn and Vn are present on anterodorsal and anteroventral margins of orbit. PVO_2, PVO_1, and PO_2 are in straight or nearly straight line. PLO is near upper end of pectoral fin base. Five PO are present. VLO is about midway to slightly higher than midway between lateral line and pelvic fin base. Four VO are present. SAO form nearly straight line, with SAO_1 anterior to or over VO_3, and SAO_3 anterior to or over anal fin origin and below lateral line. Pol is below lateral line and over last AOa. AOa number 4 to 6 and are level, and AOp number 8 to 11, with first 3 or 4 over anal fin base. Two Prc are present, and Prc_2 is its diameter behind Prc_1. Males have supracaudal gland consisting of four to seven overlapping scalelike structures, and females have infracaudal gland consisting of three to six nonoverlapping oval patches.

This species occurs in the tropical to subtropical waters of the Atlantic, southern Pacific, and western Indian Oceans. In the western Atlantic it occurs from Cape Cod to southern Brazil, including the Gulf of Mexico and the Caribbean Sea. Daytime depths range from 375 to 800 m, and nighttime depths are mainly at and near the surface but can extend to 150 m. Maximum known size is 50 mm SL, and maturity is reached at about 34 mm SL.

REFERENCES: Nafpaktitis et al. 1977; Hulley 1986b; Gartner et al. 1987.

Ceratoscopelus warmingii (Lütken 1892)

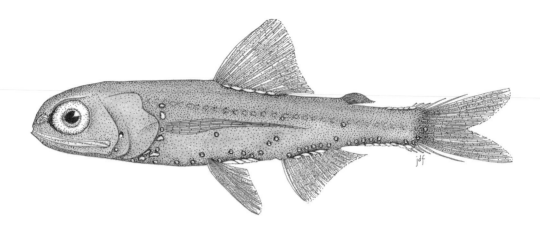

Ceratoscopelus warmingii is moderately slender and compressed, with a moderately large mouth, and dorsal and anal fin bases of about equal length. It is distinguished from the other species of the family by the following combination of characters. Snout is slightly blunt. Jaws extend about one-half eye diameter beyond posterior margin of orbit, and maxilla is slightly expanded posteriorly. Posterodorsal margin of operculum is concave, and posterior margin is convex. Gill rakers number 13 to 15. Dorsal fin originates over pelvic fin base and has 13 to 15 rays. Pectoral fin extends to AOa_2 or AOa_3 and has 13 to 15 rays. Anal fin originates on or slightly anterior to end of dorsal fin base and has 13 to 15 rays. Vn is located between nasal rosette and anterior margin of orbit. PVO_2 is above and slightly posterior to PVO_1. PLO is in contact with or just below lateral line. Five PO are present, with PO_5 displaced dorsolaterally. VLO is about midway between lateral line and pelvic fin base. Five VO are present, with VO_2, VO_3, and VO_5 elevated above others. SAO form nearly straight line, with SAO_1 above and slightly behind VO_5, and SAO_3 over or slightly anterior to anal fin origin and in contact with lateral line. AOa number five to seven, with AOa_1 depressed, and AOp number four to six and are behind anal fin base. Pol photophores are in nearly straight line with last AOa. Four Prc are present, with first three in curved line and close together, and with Prc_4 at level of lateral line. Supracaudal and infracaudal organs are present and consist of two to four scalelike structures and five to seven scalelike structures respectively. Numerous luminous scalelike structures and patches of luminous tissue are found on body, including series of scalelike structures from between pelvic fin bases to anus.

This species occurs in the tropical to subtropical waters of the Atlantic, western Indian, and western Pacific Oceans. In the western Atlantic it occurs from Cape Cod to northern Argentina, including the Gulf of Mexico and the Caribbean Sea. It is abundant in the Gulf of Mexico. Daytime depths range from 425 to 1,100 m, and nighttime depths mainly range from near the surface to 200 m, with a deep group comprised mostly of juveniles remaining at daytime depths. Maximum known size is 55 mm SL for males and 70 mm SL for females. Life span is approximately one year. Females mature in six months at about 55 mm SL. Fecundity ranges from 3,300 to 13,000 eggs and increases with body size. Spawning occurs about every seven days for about three months.

REFERENCES: Nafpaktitis et al. 1977; Uyeno et al. 1983; Hulley 1984b, 1986b; Gartner et al. 1987; Gartner 1993.

Diaphus adenomus Gilbert 1905

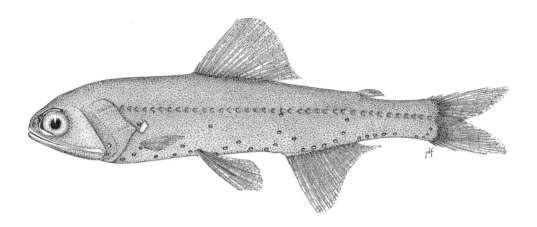

Diaphus adenomus is moderately slender and compressed, with a large mouth, and dorsal and anal fin bases of about equal length. It is distinguished from the other species of the family by the following combination of characters. Snout is blunt. Jaws extend about diameter of eye beyond posterior margin of orbit, and maxilla is not expanded posteriorly. Head is 28.5% to 33.5% of SL. Posterior margin of operculum tapers to acute angle above PLO. Gill rakers number 17. Dorsal fin originates over pelvic fin base and has 14 or 15 rays. Pectoral fin extends to or slightly beyond PO_4 and has 11 or 12 rays. Anal fin originates behind dorsal fin base and has 15 or 16 rays. Dn is small and shallow, and Vn extends along ventral and anterior border of orbit to Dn. Another luminous organ extends along dorsal margin of orbit to Dn, and it and Vn are outlined in black pigment and extend posteriorly to posterior margin of pupil. PVO_1, PVO_2, and PO_1 are in nearly straight line, and PVO_2 is anterior to midbase of pectoral fin. PLO is midway between lateral line and pectoral fin base. Five PO are present, and PO_4 is elevated.

VLO is midway between lateral line and pelvic fin base, or closer to lateral line. Five VO are present, with VO_1, VO_2, and VO_3 progressively elevated. SAO form straight line or nearly straight line, with SAO_1 above and behind VO_5, and SAO_3 anterior to anal fin base and within its diameter below lateral line. Pol is within its diameter below lateral line. AOa number six or seven, with AOa_1 elevated, and AOp number four to six, with AOp_1 over or behind anal fin base. Four more or less evenly spaced Prc form gentle curve, with Prc_4 below lateral line. Luminous scale is present at PLO.

This species occurs in the tropical waters of the Atlantic and Pacific Oceans. It occurs in the Gulf of Mexico, the Bahamas, and the Caribbean Sea in the western Atlantic. In the Gulf of Mexico this species was captured off the Mississippi River. Daytime depths range from 500 to 600 m, and nighttime depths are at 180 m. Most captures are near the bottom.

REFERENCES: Nafpaktitis 1974; Nafpaktitis et al. 1977; Hulley 1984b.

Diaphus bertelseni Nafpaktitis 1966

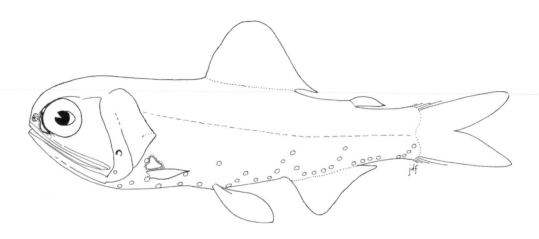

Diaphus bertelseni is moderately slender and compressed, with a moderately large mouth, and dorsal and anal fin bases about equal in length. It is distinguished from the other species of the family by the following combination of characters. Snout is blunt. Jaws extend 0.6 to 0.9 times eye diameter beyond posterior margin of orbit. Head length is 33% to 35% and upper jaw length is 23.1% to 24.5% of SL. Maxilla is not expanded posteriorly. Posterior margin of operculum tapers to angle above PLO. Gill rakers number 18. Dorsal fin originates slightly anterior to pelvic fin base and has 14 or 15 rays. Pectoral fin extends past PO_4 and has 11 rays. Anal fin originates behind base of dorsal fin and has 15 rays. Dn is round, directed forward, and is one-third to one-half size of nasal rosette. Vn is elongate, located between nasal rosette and anteroventral border of orbit, and reaches at most to anterior margin of pupil. PVO_1, PVO_2, and PO_1 are in straight line. PLO is closer to base of pectoral fin than to lateral line. Five PO are present, with PO_4 elevated. VLO is closer to base of pelvic fin than to lateral line. Five VO are present, with

VO_1, VO_2, and VO_3 progressively elevated. SAO form straight to nearly straight line, with SAO_1 posterior to VO_5, and SAO_3 over origin of anal fin and 3 to 3.5 times its diameter below lateral line. Pol is 2 or more times its diameter below lateral line. AOa number six, with first and last elevated. AOp number four, with first over or behind anal fin base. Four Prc form ascending arc, with Prc_4 2.5 to 3 times its diameter below lateral line. Large luminous scale is located at PLO.

This species occurs in the tropical to subtropical waters of the Atlantic and Pacific Oceans. In the western Atlantic it occurs from New York to southern Brazil, including the Gulf of Mexico and the Caribbean Sea. It is rare in the Gulf of Mexico. Daytime depths range from 200 to 300 m, and nighttime depths range from 60 to 175 m. Maximum known size is 80 mm SL.

REFERENCES: Nafpaktitis 1966, 1968; Nafpaktitis et al. 1977; Hulley 1984b, 1986b; Gartner et al. 1987.

Diaphus brachycephalus Tåning 1928

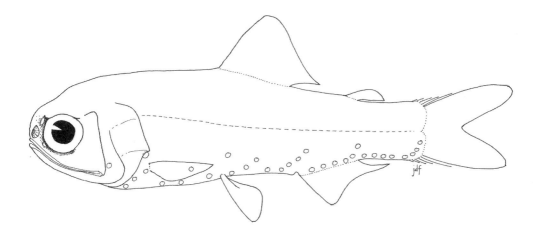

Diaphus brachycephalus is moderately deep bodied and compressed, with a moderately large mouth, and dorsal and anal fin bases of about equal length. It is distinguished from the other species of the family by the following combination of characters. Snout is blunt. Jaws extend 0.3 to 0.4 times eye diameter beyond posterior margin of orbit, and maxilla is not expanded posteriorly. Head length is 34% to 38% of SL. Operculum is angular posteriorly and rounded posterodorsally. Gill rakers number 18 to 21. Dorsal fin originates over pelvic fin base and has 12 or 13 rays. Pectoral fin extends to or slightly beyond PO_5 and has 10 to 12 rays. Anal fin originates behind dorsal fin base and has 13 or 14 rays. Dn is small, round, and directed forward. Vn is about 1.5 times diameter of pupil and extends along anteroventral and ventral margin of eye. So is small, round, immediately posterior to Vn, and below posterior margin of pupil. PVO_1, PVO_2, and PO_1 are in straight line. PLO is closer to pectoral fin base than to lateral line. Five PO are present, with PO_4 elevated. VLO is closer to pelvic fin base than to lateral line. Five VO

are present, with VO_1, VO_2, and VO_3 progressively elevated. SAO form straight to nearly straight line, with SAO_1 slightly behind VO_5, and SAO_3 over anal fin base and 3 times its diameter below lateral line. Pol is about 2 times its diameter below lateral line. AOa number four to six, with AOa_1 often slightly raised and AOa_5 raised. AOp number three to five and are located behind anal fin base. Four Prc form ascending arc, with Prc_4 2 to 3 times its diameter below lateral line.

This species occurs in the tropical to subtropical waters of the Atlantic and eastern Indian Oceans. In the western Atlantic it occurs from Cape Cod to southern Brazil, including the Gulf of Mexico and the Caribbean Sea. It is uncommon in the Gulf of Mexico. Daytime depths range from 175 to 550 m, and nighttime depths range from the surface to 300 m. Maximum known size is 60 mm SL, and maturity is reached at about 30 mm SL.

REFERENCES: Nafpaktitis 1968; Nafpaktitis et al. 1977; Hulley 1984b, 1986b; Gartner et al. 1987.

Diaphus dumerilii   (Bleeker 1856)

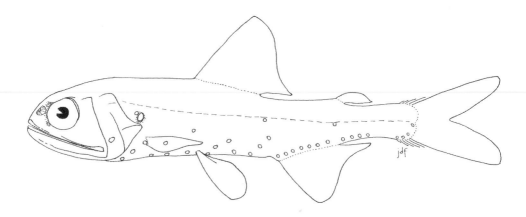

Diaphus dumerilii is moderately slender and compressed, with a large mouth, and dorsal and anal fin bases of about equal length. It is distinguished from the other species of the family by the following combination of characters. Snout is blunt. Jaws extend 0.7 to 1.0 times eye diameter beyond posterior margin of orbit, and maxilla is not expanded posteriorly. Head is 30% to 33.5% of SL. Posterior margin of operculum tapers to acute angle. Gill rakers number 19 to 27. Dorsal fin originates over pelvic fin base and has 14 or 15 rays. Pectoral fin extends to base of pelvic fin and has 11 or 12 rays. Anal fin originates posterior to dorsal fin base and has 14 or 15 rays. Dn is irregularly shaped and is laterally directed. Vn is small, round to oval, one-half size of body photophore, and located below anterior margin of pupil. PVO_1, PVO_2, and PO_1 are in straight line. PLO is 1 to 2 times its diameter below lateral line. Five PO are present, with PO_4 elevated. VLO is midway between pelvic fin base and lateral line. Five VO are present, with VO_1, VO_2, and VO_3 progressively elevated. SAO form obtuse angle, with SAO_1 behind VO_5, and SAO_3 over and slightly anterior to SAO_2

and in contact with lateral line. Pol is in contact with lateral line. AOa number six to eight, with last often slightly elevated. AOp number four to seven, with first occasionally over anal fin base. Four Prc form gentle curve, with Prc_4 about 2 times its diameter below lateral line. Luminous scale is present at PLO.

This species occurs in the tropical waters of the Atlantic and western Pacific Oceans. In the western Atlantic it occurs from Cape Cod to northern Argentina, including the Gulf of Mexico and the Caribbean Sea. It is very abundant in the Gulf of Mexico. Daytime depths range from 225 to 750 m, and nighttime depths range from the surface to 155 m. Maximum known size is 86 mm SL, and maturity is reached at about 52 mm SL, during the second year of life. Life span is about two years. First year is spent in the mesopelagic realm, and second year is spent near the bottom.

REFERENCES: Nafpaktitis 1968; Nafpaktitis et al. 1977; Uyeno et al. 1983; Hulley 1984b, 1986b; Gartner et al. 1987; Gartner 1991, 1993; Boschung 1992.

Diaphus effulgens   (Goode and Bean 1896)

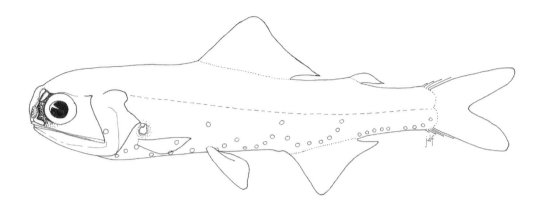

Diaphus effulgens is moderately slender and compressed, with a moderately large mouth, and dorsal and anal fin bases of equal length. It is distinguished from the other species of the family by the following combination of characters. Snout is blunt. Jaws extend 0.5 to 0.7 times diameter of eye beyond posterior orbital margin, and maxilla is not expanded posteriorly. Head is 28.5% to 33% of SL. Operculum tapers to acute point at PLO. Gill rakers number 19 to 22. Dorsal fin originates slightly in advance of pelvic fin base and has 15 or 16 rays. Pectoral fin does not extend to pelvic fin base and has 11 or 12 rays. Anal fin originates at or slightly behind end of dorsal fin base and has 14 or 15 rays. Dn is larger than nasal rosette, is directed forward, and extends above dorsal margin of orbit. Vn is very large, is in contact with Dn, and extends along anteroventral margin of orbit to anterior margin of pupil. Ant is located above Dn and is triangular shaped. PVO_1, PVO_2, and PO_1 are in straight line, with PVO_2 just anterior to lower end of pectoral fin base. PLO is nearer to base of pectoral fin than to lateral line. Five PO are present, and PO_4 is elevated. VLO photophore is midway between lateral line and pelvic fin base or slightly lower.

Five VO are present, with VO_1, VO_2, and VO_3 progressively elevated. SAO form straight line, with SAO_1 behind VO_5, and SAO_3 above anal fin origin and 1.5 to 2 times its diameter below lateral line. Pol is 1.5 to 2 times its diameter below lateral line. AOa number five to seven, with AOa_1 elevated above and in front of AOa_2, and last AO elevated. AOp number five or six, with first AOp behind anal fin base. Four Prc form gentle curve, with Prc_4 about 2 to 3 times its diameter below lateral line. Luminous scale is present at PLO.

This species occurs in the Atlantic, central South Pacific, and Indian Oceans. In the western Atlantic it occurs from southern New England to the Caribbean Sea, including the eastern Gulf of Mexico off the Florida Escarpment. It is not common in the Gulf of Mexico. Daytime depths range from 300 to 850 m, and nighttime depths range from 90 to 330 m; however, large specimens may remain at daytime depths during the night. Maximum known size is 150 mm SL.

REFERENCES: Nafpaktitis 1968; Nafpaktitis et al. 1977; Hulley 1986b; Gartner et al. 1987.

Diaphus fragilis Tåning 1928

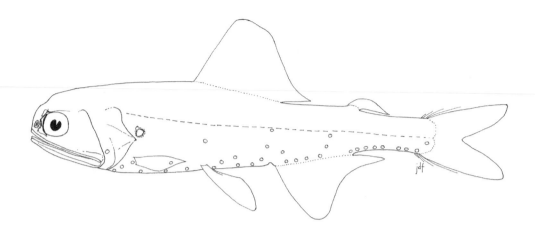

Diaphus fragilis is moderately slender and compressed, with a large mouth, and dorsal and anal fin bases about equal in length. It is distinguished from the other species of the family by the following combination of characters. Snout is blunt. Jaws extend 0.7 to 1.0 times diameter of eye beyond posterior orbit margin, and maxilla is not expanded posteriorly. Head is 28% to 32.5% of SL. Operculum tapers to acute angle below PLO. Gill rakers number 17 to 19. Dorsal fin originates slightly in advance of pelvic fin base and has 17 to 19 rays. Pectoral fin does not extend to pelvic fin base and has 11 to 13 rays. Anal fin originates slightly anterior to end of dorsal fin base and has 17 to 18 rays. Dn is equal in size to nasal rosette and is directed forward. Vn is continuous with Dn along anterior and anteroventral aspect of orbit and extends to near anterior margin of pupil. Ant is located above Dn. PVO_1, PVO_2, and PO_1 are in straight line, with PVO_2 anterior to lower end of pectoral fin base. PLO is closer to lateral line than to pectoral fin base. Five PO are present, and PO_4 is elevated. VLO is midway between lateral line and pelvic fin base or slightly higher. Five VO are present, with VO_1, VO_2, and VO_3 progressively elevated.

SAO form straight line, with SAO_1 above VO_5, and SAO_3 over or slightly anterior to anal fin base and less than its diameter below lateral line. Pol is less than its diameter below lateral line. AOa number six or seven, with AOa_1 elevated above and slightly in front of AO_2, and last AO elevated. AOp number four to six, with first AOp over or just behind anal fin base. Four Prc form gentle arc, with Prc_4 about 2 times its diameter below lateral line. Luminous scale is located at PLO.

This species occurs in the tropical waters of the Atlantic, western and central Pacific, and Indian Oceans. In the western Atlantic it occurs from New Jersey to central Brazil, including the Gulf of Mexico and the Caribbean Sea. It is abundant in the Caribbean but is uncommon in the Gulf of Mexico. Daytime depths range from 350 to 750 m, and nighttime depths range from 40 to 200 m. Maximum known size is 90 mm SL, and maturity is reached by about 65 to 70 mm SL.

REFERENCES: Nafpaktitis 1968; Nafpaktitis et al. 1977; Uyeno et al. 1983; Hulley 1986b; Gartner et al. 1987.

Diaphus garmani Gilbert 1906

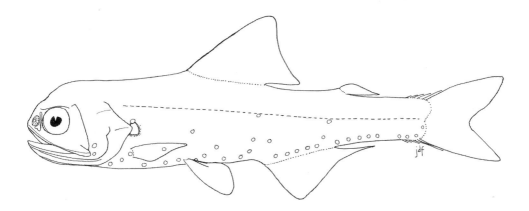

Diaphus garmani is moderately slender and compressed, with a large mouth and an anal fin base slightly longer than dorsal fin base. It is distinguished from the other species of the family by the following combination of characters. Snout is blunt. Jaws extend about one eye diameter beyond posterior orbit margin, and maxilla is not expanded posteriorly. Head is 27.5% to 30.5% of SL. Operculum tapers to acute angle just below PLO. Gill rakers number 20 to 23. Dorsal fin originates over pelvic fin base and has 14 to 16 rays. Pectoral fin extends to pelvic fin base and has 11 or 12 rays. Anal fin originates posterior to dorsal fin base and has 15 to 17 rays. Dn is small, is located dorsolateral to nasal rosette, is directed antero-laterally, and extends ventrally to meet attenuated section of Vn. Vn is smaller than or equal in size to Dn (males) or larger than Dn (females) and fails to reach anterior margin of pupil. PVO_1, PVO_2, and PO_1 are in straight line. PLO is closer to lateral line than to pectoral fin base. Five PO are present, and PO_4 is elevated. VLO is midway between lateral line and pelvic fin base. Five VO are present, with VO_1, VO_2, and VO_3 progressively elevated. SAO form straight or nearly straight line, with SAO_1 posterior to VO_5, and SAO_3 over or slightly behind anal fin origin and in contact with lateral line. Pol is in contact with lateral line. AOa number six to eight, with first and last elevated. AOp number four to seven and are behind anal fin base. Four Prc form arc, with Prc_4 about 1.5 times its diameter below lateral line. Large luminous scale is located at PLO.

This species occurs in the tropical waters of the Atlantic, western Pacific, and western Indian Oceans. In the western Atlantic it occurs from North Carolina to northern Brazil, including the Gulf of Mexico and the Caribbean Sea. It is not abundant in the Gulf of Mexico. Daytime depths range from 325 to 750 m, and nighttime depths range from 15 to 150 m. Maximum known size is 60 mm SL, and maturity is reached at about 40 mm SL.

REFERENCES: Nafpaktitis 1968; Nafpaktitis et al. 1977; Uyeno et al. 1983; Hulley 1986b; Gartner et al. 1987.

Diaphus lucidus (Goode and Bean 1896)

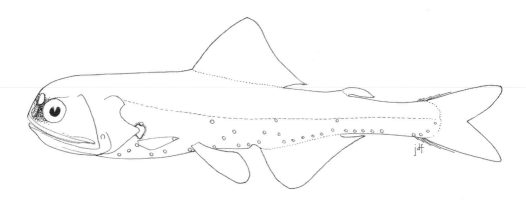

Diaphus lucidus is moderately slender and compressed, with a large mouth, and dorsal and anal fin bases about equal in length. It is distinguished from the other species of the family by the following combination of characters. Snout is blunt. Jaws extend 0.9 to 1.2 times eye diameter beyond posterior margin of orbit, and maxilla is not expanded posteriorly. Head is 27.5% to 30.5% of SL. Posterior margin of operculum tapers to acute angle just below PLO. Gill rakers number 16 to 19. Dorsal fin originates over or slightly anterior to pelvic fin base and has 17 rays. Pectoral fin extends beyond PO_4 and has 11 or 12 rays. Anal fin originates anterior to end of dorsal fin base and has 17 or 18 rays. Dn is rounded, about one-half diameter of eye, and directed forward. Vn extends along anterior and anteroventral border of orbit, and dorsally is in contact with Dn. PVO_1, PVO_2, and PO_1 are in straight line. PLO is midway between lateral line and pectoral fin base. Five PO are present, and PO_4 is elevated. VLO is closer to lateral line than to pelvic fin base. Five VO are present, with VO_1, VO_2, and VO_3 progressively elevated. SAO form straight line, with SAO_1 posterior to VO_5, and SAO_3 above or posterior to anal fin origin and within its diameter of lateral line. Pol is within its diameter of lateral line. AOa number seven or eight, and first and last are elevated. AOp number four to six, and first is over but usually behind anal fin base. Four Prc form arc, with Prc_4 1.5 to 3 times its diameter below lateral line. Large luminous scale is located at PLO.

This species occurs in the tropical waters of the Atlantic, southwestern Pacific, and Indian Oceans. In the western Atlantic it occurs from New Jersey to northern Brazil, including the Gulf of Mexico and the Caribbean Sea. It is abundant in the Gulf of Mexico. Daytime depths range from 425 to 750 m, and nighttime depths range from 40 to 550 m. Maximum known size is 115 mm SL, and maturity is reached at about 90 to 100 mm SL.

REFERENCES: Nafpaktitis 1968; Nafpaktitis et al. 1977; Hulley 1984b, 1986b; Gartner et al. 1987.

Diaphus luetkeni (Brauer 1904)

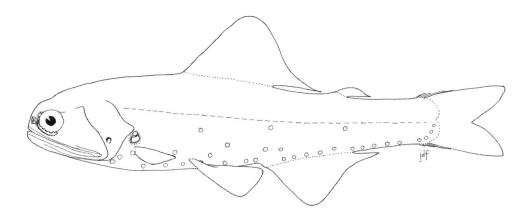

Diaphus luetkeni is moderately slender and compressed, with a very large mouth and a dorsal fin base that is slightly longer than anal fin base. It is distinguished from the other species of the family by the following combination of characters. Snout is blunt. Jaws extend about 1.2 to 1.5 times eye diameter beyond posterior orbital margin, and maxilla is not expanded posteriorly. Head is 31.5% to 34% of SL. Posterior opercular margin tapers to acute angle just above PLO. Gill rakers number 20 to 23. Dorsal fin originates over or slightly posterior to pelvic fin base and has 15 to 17 rays. Pectoral fin reaches slightly beyond PO_4 and has 11 rays. Anal fin originates anterior to end of dorsal fin base and has 14 to 16 rays. Dn is oblong, about one-third size of nasal rosette, directed forward, and located dorsal to nasal rosette. Vn extends along ventral margin of orbit and bears three to five projections along its dorsal border. PVO_1, PVO_2, and PO_1 are in straight line. PLO is closer to pectoral fin base than to lateral line. Five PO are present, and PO_4 is elevated. VLO is slightly closer to lateral line than to pelvic fin base. Five VO are present, with VO_1, VO_2, and VO_3 progressively elevated. SAO form straight to nearly straight line, with SAO_1 posterior to and on same level as VO_5, and SAO_3 over or slightly anterior to anal fin base and about its diameter below lateral line. Pol is about its diameter below lateral line. AOa number five to seven, with first and last elevated. AOp number four to six, with AOp_1 usually over anal fin base. Four Prc form gentle curve, with Prc_4 1.5 times its diameter below lateral line. Small luminous scale is located at PLO.

This species occurs in the tropical waters of the Atlantic, western Pacific, and Indian Oceans. In the western Atlantic it occurs from Massachusetts to northern Brazil, including the Gulf of Mexico and the Caribbean Sea. It is abundant in the Gulf of Mexico. Daytime depths range from 375 to 750 m, and nighttime depths range from 40 to 325 m. Maximum known size is 60 mm SL, and maturity is reached at about 42 to 45 mm SL.

REFERENCES: Nafpaktitis 1968; Nafpaktitis et al. 1977; Hulley 1986b; Gartner et al. 1987.

Diaphus metopoclampus   (Cocco 1829)

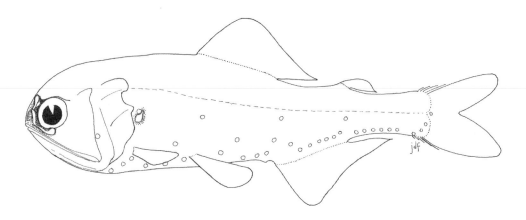

Diaphus metopoclampus is relatively deep bodied and compressed, with a moderately large mouth, and dorsal and anal fin bases about equal in length. It is distinguished from the other species of the family by the following combination of characters. Snout is very blunt. Jaws extend 0.6 to 0.9 times eye diameter beyond posterior margin of orbit, and maxilla is not posteriorly expanded. Head is 27% to 33% of SL. Operculum is truncated posteriorly. Gill rakers number 22 to 26. Dorsal fin originates over pelvic fin base and has 15 or 16 rays. Pectoral fin extends past PO_4 and has 10 or 11 rays. Anal fin originates anterior to or at end of dorsal fin base and has 14 to 16 rays. Dn is large, extends along dorsal margin of orbit, and is directed anteriorly. Vn is large and extends along anterior and much of ventral orbital margin, with posterior end slightly expanded. Ant is triangular and in contact with Dn. PVO_1, PVO_2, and PO_1 are in straight line. PLO is closer to lateral line than to pectoral fin base. Five PO are present, and PO_4 is elevated. VLO is closer to lateral line than to pelvic fin base. Five VO are present, with VO_1, VO_2, and VO_3 progressively elevated. SAO form straight line, with SAO_1 posterior to VO_5, and SAO_3 above or behind anal fin origin and less than its diameter below lateral line. Pol is less than to equal to its diameter below lateral line. AOa number five to seven, and first and last are elevated. AOp number five to seven, with first behind, but occasionally over, anal fin base. Four Prc form straight to nearly straight line, with Prc_4 within its diameter below lateral line.

This species occurs in the tropical to subtropical waters of the Atlantic, western Pacific, and southwestern Indian Oceans. In the western Atlantic it occurs from the northeastern United States to southeastern Florida, in the southwestern Gulf of Mexico, and from southern Brazil, Uruguay, and northern Argentina. It is not abundant in the Gulf of Mexico. Daytime depths range from 375 to 850 m, and nighttime depths range from 90 to 850 m. Maximum known size is 75 mm SL, and maturity is reached at 55 to 60 mm SL.

REFERENCES: Nafpaktitis 1968; Nafpaktitis et al. 1977; Hulley 1984b; 1986b.

Diaphus mollis Tåning 1928

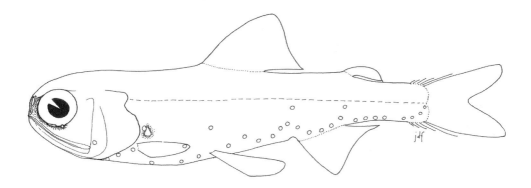

Diaphus mollis is moderately slender and compressed, with a moderate-sized mouth, and dorsal and anal fin bases of about equal length. It is distinguished from the other species of the family by the following combination of characters. Snout is blunt. Jaws extend 0.3 to 0.5 times eye diameter beyond posterior margin of orbit, and maxilla is not posteriorly expanded. Head is 29.5% to 33% of SL. Operculum is truncated posteriorly. Gill rakers number 15 to 18. Dorsal fin originates over pelvic fin base and has 13 rays. Pectoral fin extends to PO_4 and has 10 or 11 rays. Anal fin originates posterior to dorsal fin base and has 12 or 13 rays. Dn is round, smaller than nasal rosette, and directed forward. Vn is large (males) to moderate (females) in size and is located on ventral margin of eye. So is small, round, and located anterior to posterior margin of pupil. PVO_1, PVO_2, and PO_1 are in straight line. PLO is closer to pectoral fin base than to lateral line. Five PO are present, and PO_4 is elevated. VLO is midway between lateral line and pelvic fin base or lower. Five VO are present, with VO_1, VO_2, and VO_3 progressively elevated. SAO form obtuse angle, with SAO_1 above and behind VO_5, and SAO_3 slightly anterior to origin of anal fin and 1 to 1.5 times its diameter below lateral line. Pol is about its diameter below lateral line. AOa number four to six, with first and last elevated. AOp number three to five and are behind anal fin base. Four Prc form ascending arc, and Prc_4 is 2 times its diameter below lateral line. Small luminous organ is located at PLO.

This species occurs in the tropical to subtropical waters of the Atlantic, southwestern Pacific, and western Indian Oceans. In the western Atlantic it occurs from Cape Cod to northern Argentina, including the Gulf of Mexico and the Caribbean Sea. Daytime depths range from 300 to 800 m, and nighttime depths range from 33 to 350 m. Maximum known size is 60 m SL, and sexual maturity is attained at about 30 mm SL.

REFERENCES: Nafpaktitis 1968; Nafpaktitis et al. 1977; Hulley 1984b, 1986b; Gartner et al. 1987.

Diaphus perspicillatus (Ogilby 1898)

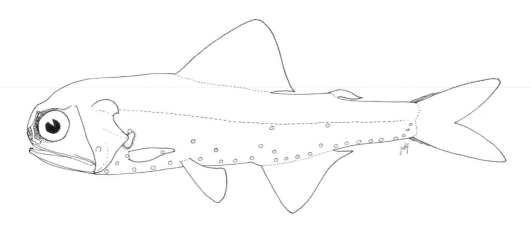

Diaphus perspicillatus is moderately slender and compressed, with a moderately large mouth and a dorsal fin base slightly longer than anal fin base. It is distinguished from the other species of the family by the following combination of characters. Snout is blunt. Jaws extend 0.6 to 0.8 times diameter of eye beyond posterior orbital margin, and maxilla is not expanded posteriorly. Head is 31% to 35% of SL. Posterior margin of operculum tapers to acute angle near PLO. Gill rakers number 26 to 29. Dorsal fin originates anterior to pelvic fin base and has 15 to 17 rays. Pectoral fin extends almost to pelvic fin base and has 11 or 12 rays. Anal fin originates behind dorsal fin base and has 14 or 15 rays. Dn is large, triangular, and directed anteriorly. Vn is large and extends from Dn to anteroventral margin of orbit. PVO_1, PVO_2, and PO_1 are in straight line. PLO is midway between lateral line and pectoral fin base. Five PO are present, and PO_4 is elevated. VLO is closer to pelvic fin base than to lateral line. Five VO are present, with VO_1, VO_2, and VO_3 progressively elevated. SAO form straight to nearly straight line, with SAO_1 behind and slightly above VO_5, and SAO_3 above or slightly anterior to anal fin origin and in contact with lateral line. Pol is in contact with lateral line. AOa number five to seven, with first and last elevated. AOp number four to six, and first is elevated and generally behind, but occasionally over, anal fin base. Four Prc form slight arc, with Prc_4 1.5 to 2.5 times its diameter below lateral line. Luminous scale is located at PLO.

This species occurs in the tropical waters of the Atlantic, western Pacific, and western Indian Oceans. In the western Atlantic it occurs from Cape Cod to southern Brazil, including the Gulf of Mexico and the Caribbean Sea. It is not abundant in the Gulf of Mexico. Daytime depths range from 375 to 750 m, and nighttime depths range from the surface to 125 m. Maximum known size is 70 mm SL, and maturity is reached at about 50 to 58 mm SL.

REFERENCES: Nafpaktitis 1968; Nafpaktitis et al. 1977; Hulley 1986b; Gartner et al. 1987.

Diaphus problematicus   Parr 1928

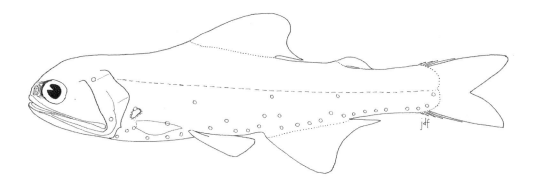

Diaphus problematicus is moderately slender and compressed, with a very large mouth, and dorsal and anal fin bases of about equal length. It is distinguished from the other species of the family by the following combination of characters. Snout is moderately blunt. Jaws extend 1.2 to 1.5 times diameter of eye beyond posterior margin of orbit, and maxilla is not expanded posteriorly. Head is 26.5% to 30.5% of SL. Posterior margin of operculum tapers to acute angle slightly above PLO. Gill rakers number 13 or 14. Dorsal fin originates slightly anterior to pelvic fin base and has 16 or 17 rays. Pectoral fin fails to reach pelvic fin base and has 11 or 12 rays. Anal fin originates under posterior section of dorsal fin base and has 16 to 18 rays. Dn is small and heart shaped. Vn is triangular, located on anteroventral aspect of orbit, and connected to Dn by thin streak of luminous tissue. Small luminous organ is located dorsal and medial to Dn. PVO_1, PVO_2, and PO_2 are in straight line. PLO is closer to base of pectoral fin than to lateral line. Five PO are present, and PO_4 is elevated. VLO is closer to lateral line than to pelvic fin base.

Five VO are present, with VO_1, VO_2, and VO_3 progressively elevated. SAO form straight to nearly straight line, with SAO_1 posterior to VO_5, and SAO_3 over origin of anal fin base and 1 to 1.5 times its diameter below lateral line. Pol is 1 to 1.5 times its diameter below lateral line. AOa number six or seven, and first and last are elevated. AOp number four to six, and first is over anal fin base. Four Prc form arc, and Prc_4 is 1 to 1.5 times its diameter below lateral line. Luminous scale is located at PLO.

This species occurs in the tropical waters of the Atlantic, western Pacific, and eastern Indian Oceans. In the western Atlantic it occurs from New Jersey to central Brazil, including the Gulf of Mexico and the Caribbean Sea. It is abundant in the southern Gulf of Mexico. Daytime depths range from 375 to 750 m, and nighttime depths range from 40 to 225 m. Maximum known size is 90 mm SL, and maturity is reached at about 68 to 74 mm SL.

REFERENCES: Nafpaktitis 1968; Nafpaktitis et al. 1977; Uyeno et al. 1983; Hulley 1986b; Gartner et al. 1987.

Diaphus rafinesquii (Cocco 1838)

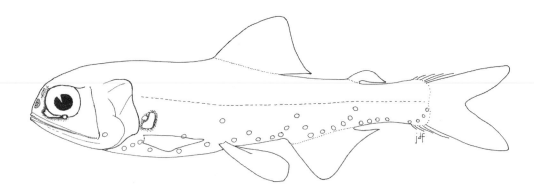

Diaphus rafinesquii is moderately slender and compressed, with a moderately large mouth, and dorsal and anal fin bases of about equal length. It is distinguished from the other species of the family by the following combination of characters. Snout is blunt. Jaws extend 0.5 to 0.6 times eye diameter beyond posterior orbital margin, and maxilla is not expanded posteriorly. Head is 30.5% to 32.5% of SL. Operculum is truncated posteriorly. Gill rakers number 22 to 24. Dorsal fin originates over pelvic fin base and has 13 or 14 rays. Pectoral fin extends to PO_5 and has 10 or 11 rays. Anal fin originates posterior to dorsal fin base and has 13 to 15 rays. Dn is rounded and directed anteriorly. Vn is elongated, extends along ventral border of eye from anterior margin of orbit to middle of lens, and is wider anteriorly than posteriorly. So is round and surrounded by black pigment. PVO_1, PVO_2, and PO_1 are in straight line. PLO is closer to pectoral fin base than to lateral line. Five PO are present, and PO_4 is elevated. VLO is midway between lateral line and pelvic fin base. Five VO are pres-ent, with VO_1, VO_2, and VO_3 progressively elevated. SAO form straight to nearly straight line, with SAO_1 above and slightly behind VO_5, and SAO_3 over anal fin base and 1 to 1.5 times its diameter below lateral line. Pol is about its diameter below lateral line. AOa number five to seven, and first and last two are elevated. AOp number three to five and are behind anal fin base. Four Prc form ascending arc, with Prc_4 2 or 3 times its diameter below lateral line. Large luminous scale is located at PLO.

This species occurs in the subtropical to temperate waters of the North Atlantic. It occurs from Nova Scotia to Florida and the Gulf of Mexico in the western Atlantic. Daytime depths range from 400 to 750 m, and nighttime depths range from 40 to 200 m for smaller specimens, and from 300 to 600 m for larger specimens. Large specimens apparently do not migrate. Maximum known size is 90 mm SL, and maturity is reached at about 65 mm SL.

REFERENCES: Nafpaktitis 1968; Nafpaktitis et al. 1977; Hulley 1984b; Gartner et al. 1987.

Diaphus splendidus   (Brauer 1904)

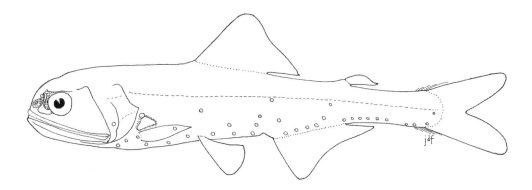

Diaphus splendidus is moderately slender and compressed, with a very large mouth and an anal fin base slightly longer than dorsal fin base. It is distinguished from the other species of the family by the following combination of characters. Snout is moderately blunt. Jaws extend 1.2 to 1.5 times eye diameter beyond posterior orbital margin, and maxilla is not posteriorly expanded. Head is 28% to 31% of SL. Posterior opercular margin tapers to angle near PLO. Gill rakers number 17 to 20. Dorsal fin originates over or slightly anterior to pelvic fin base and has 14 or 15 rays. Pectoral fin extends nearly to pelvic fin base and has 11 or 12 rays. Anal fin originates over or slightly posterior to dorsal fin base and has 15 to 17 rays. Dn is round and directed anteriorly. Vn is triangular and extends from Dn to below anterior margin of orbit. Small luminous organ is located ventromedial to Dn. PVO_1, PVO_2, and PO_1 are in straight line. PLO is closer to base of pectoral fin than to lateral line. Five PO are present, and PO_4 is elevated. VLO is closer to lateral line than to pelvic fin base. Five VO are present, and VO_1, VO_2, and VO_3 are progressively elevated. SAO form slight angle, with SAO_2 slightly behind SAO_1, SAO_1 slightly posterior to VO_5, and SAO_3 over anal fin origin and in contact with lateral line. Pol is in contact with lateral line. AOa number six or seven, with first and last elevated. AOp number five to seven, with first over anal fin base. Four Prc form arc, with Prc_4 0.5 to 1 times its diameter below lateral line. Large luminous scale is located at PLO.

This species occurs in the tropical to subtropical waters of the Atlantic, western Pacific, and Indian Oceans. In the western Atlantic it occurs from New York to southern Brazil, including the Gulf of Mexico and the Caribbean Sea. Daytime depths range from 500 to 650 m, and nighttime depths range from 50 to 250 m. Maximum known size is 90 mm SL, and maturity is reached at about 50 to 55 mm SL.

REFERENCES: Nafpaktitis 1968; Nafpaktitis et al. 1977; Hulley 1986b; Gartner et al. 1987.

Diaphus subtilis   Nafpaktitis 1968

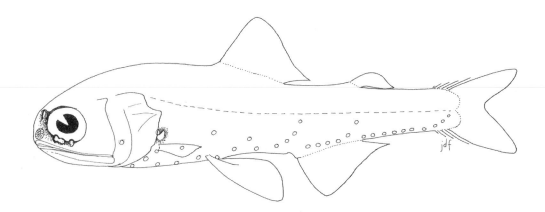

Diaphus subtilis is moderately slender and compressed, with a moderately large mouth, and dorsal and anal fin bases of about equal length. It is distinguished from the other species of the family by the following combination of characters. Snout is very blunt. Jaws extend 0.3 to 0.5 times eye diameter beyond posterior margin of orbit, and maxilla is not expanded posteriorly. Head is 31.5% to 34% of SL. Operculum is truncated posteriorly. Gill rakers number 20 to 23. Dorsal fin originates over or slightly posterior to pelvic fin base and has 12 or 13 rays. Pectoral fin extends to PO_5 and has 10 to 12 rays. Anal fin originates posterior to dorsal fin base and has 13 rays. Dn is round and is directed anteriorly. Vn is elongated and located along ventral margin of orbit. So is small and located posterior to Vn. PVO_1, PVO_2, and PO_1 are in straight line. PLO is closer to pectoral fin base than to lateral line. Five PO are present, and PO_4 is elevated. VLO is midway between lateral line and pelvic fin base. Five VO are present, with VO_1, VO_2, and VO_3 pro-gressively elevated. SAO form straight to nearly straight line, with SAO_1 posterior to VO_5, and SAO_3 over or slightly posterior to anal fin origin and 1 to 1.5 times its diameter below lateral line. Pol is about its diameter below lateral line. AOa number five or six, with first and last little if any elevated. AOp number five to seven, with first behind anal fin base. Four Prc form slightly curved line, with Prc_4 its diameter below lateral line. Small luminous scale is located at PLO.

This species occurs in the tropical to subtropical waters of the Atlantic Ocean. In the western Atlantic it occurs from New Jersey to the Guianas, including the Gulf of Mexico and the Caribbean Sea. Daytime depths range from 375 to 750 m, and nighttime depths range from 40 to 550 m. Maximum known size is 85 mm SL, and maturity is reached at about 70 mm SL.

REFERENCES: Nafpaktitis 1968; Nafpaktitis et al. 1977; Hulley 1984b, 1986b; Gartner et al. 1987.

Diaphus taaningi   Norman 1930

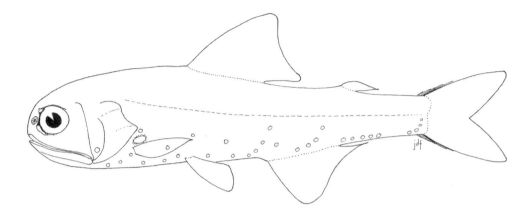

Diaphus taaningi is moderately slender and compressed, with a moderately large mouth, and dorsal and anal fin bases of about equal length. It is distinguished from the other species of the family by the following combination of characters. Snout is blunt. Jaws extend 0.5 to 0.6 times eye diameter beyond posterior orbital margin, and maxilla is not expanded posteriorly. Head is 28.5% to 30.5% of SL. Posterior opercular margin tapers to acute angle slightly above PLO. Gill rakers number 19 to 23. Dorsal fin originates over or slightly posterior to pelvic fin base and has 14 rays. Pectoral fin extends to base of pelvic fin and has 11 rays. Anal fin originates posterior to dorsal fin base and has 14 or 15 rays. Dn is small, round, and directed forward. Vn is elongate and extends from behind nasal rosette to anterior margin of pupil. PVO_1, PVO_2, and PO_1 are in straight line. PLO is closer to pectoral fin base than to lateral line. Five PO are present, and PO_4 is elevated. VLO is midway between lateral line and pelvic fin base. Five VO are present and VO_1,

VO_2, and VO_3 are progressively elevated. SAO usually form straight line, with SAO_1 posterior to VO_5, and SAO_3 over anal fin base and 1.5 to 2 times its diameter below lateral line. Pol is 1.5 to 2 times its diameter below lateral line. AOa number five or six, with first and last elevated. AOp number four to six, with first occasionally over but usually posterior to anal fin base. Four Prc form slight curve, with Prc_4 about 3 times its diameter below lateral line. Roundish luminous scale is located at PLO.

This species occurs in the tropical and subtropical waters of the Atlantic Ocean. In the western Atlantic it occurs from Cape Cod to Venezuela, including the Gulf of Mexico and the Caribbean Sea. Daytime depths range from 325 to 475 m, and nighttime depths range from 40 to 250 m. Maximum known size is 50 mm SL, and maturity is reached at about 40 mm SL.

REFERENCES: Nafpaktitis 1968; Nafpaktitis et al. 1977; Uyeno et al. 1983; Hulley 1986b; Gartner et al. 1987; Boschung 1992.

Diaphus termophilus Tåning 1928

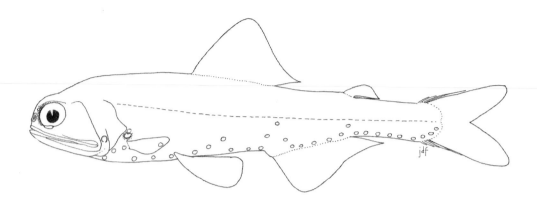

Diaphus termophilus is moderately slender and compressed, with a large mouth and an anal fin base slightly longer than dorsal fin base. It is distinguished from the other species of the family by the following combination of characters. Snout is moderately blunt. Jaws extend 1.1 to 1.2 times eye diameter beyond posterior orbital margin, and maxilla is not expanded posteriorly. Head is 32% to 34% of SL. Posterior opercular margin tapers to angle slightly above PLO. Gill rakers number 23 to 26. Dorsal fin originates slightly posterior to pelvic fin base and has 13 or 14 rays. Pectoral fin extends nearly to pelvic fin base and has 11 or 12 rays. Anal fin originates slightly posterior to dorsal fin base and has 15 rays. Dn is small, oblong, and directed anteriorly. Vn is large, elliptical, on ventral margin of orbit, and connected by strand of dark tissue to Dn. PVO_1, PVO_2, and PO_1 are in straight line, with PVO_2 anterior to pectoral fin base. PLO is closer to pectoral fin base than to lateral line. Five PO are present, with PO_4 elevated. VLO is midway between lateral line and pelvic fin base. Five VO are pres-

ent, with VO_1, VO_2, and VO_3 progressively elevated. SAO form straight to nearly straight line, with SAO_1 behind and about on same level as VO_5, and SAO_3 over anal fin base and 2 to 2.5 times its diameter below lateral line. Pol is about 1.5 times its diameter below lateral line. AOa number five or six, and first and last are elevated. AOp number four or five and are posterior to anal fin base. Four Prc form arc, with Prc_4 2 times its diameter below lateral line. Small luminous scale is located at PLO.

This species occurs in the tropical waters of the Atlantic and western Pacific Oceans. In the western Atlantic it occurs from southeastern Florida to Venezuela, including the Gulf of Mexico and the Caribbean Sea. Daytime depths range from 325 to 850 m, and nighttime depths range from 40 to 225 m. Maximum known size is 80 mm SL, and maturity is reached at about 63 mm SL.

REFERENCES: Nafpaktitis 1968; Nafpaktitis et al. 1977; Hulley 1984b; Gartner et al. 1987.

Diogenichthys atlanticus   (Tåning 1928)

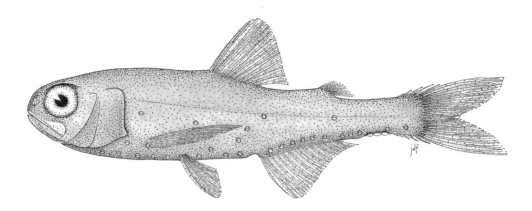

Diogenichthys atlanticus is moderately slender and compressed, with a relatively short mouth and an anal fin base longer than dorsal fin base. It is distinguished from the other species of the family by the following combination of characters. Snout is moderately blunt. Jaws extend to about posterior margin of orbit, and maxilla is expanded posteriorly. Head length is 32% to 35% of SL. Posterior margin of operculum is convex dorsally and straight to slightly concave ventrally. Gill rakers number 12 to 14. Dorsal fin originates posterior to pelvic fin base and has 11 or 12 rays. Pectoral fin extends to about SAO_2 and has 12 or 13 rays. Anal fin originates posterior to dorsal fin base and has 15 or 16 rays. Dn is present. PVO_1 and PVO_2 are horizontal to nearly horizontal. PLO is about midway between lateral line and pectoral fin base or higher. Five PO are present and on same level. VLO is midway between lateral line and pelvic fin base. Four VO are present, with VO_3 in line with SAO_1 and SAO_2. SAO_3 is behind line connecting VO_3, SAO_1, and SAO_2 and in contact with lateral line. Pol is in contact with lateral line. AOa number five to seven, and AOp number two to four, with first occasionally over anal fin base. Two Prc are present, with Prc_2 slightly higher than Prc_1 and separated from Prc_1 by distance equal to distance between last AOp and Prc_1. Males have large supracaudal luminous gland, and females have small infracaudal luminous gland.

This species occurs in the tropical to subtropical waters of the Atlantic, Pacific, and western Indian Oceans. In the western Atlantic it occurs from Cape Cod to northern Brazil, Uruguay, and northern Argentina, including the Gulf of Mexico and the Caribbean Sea. It is abundant in the Gulf of Mexico. Daytime depths range from 450 to 1,250 m, and nighttime depths range from 18 to 1,050 m. Larvae and small juveniles do not migrate. Maximum known size is 29 mm SL, and size at maturity is about 20 mm SL.

REFERENCES: Nafpaktitis et al. 1977; Hulley 1984b, 1986b; Gartner et al. 1987; Boschung 1992.

Gonichthys cocco (Cocco 1829)

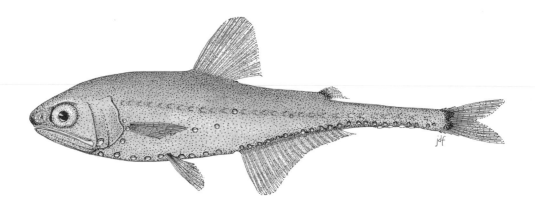

Gonichthys cocco is relatively slender and compressed, with a moderately large, subterminal mouth and an anal fin base much longer than dorsal fin base. It is distinguished from the other species of the family by the following combination of characters. Snout is projecting and acute. Jaws extend about 0.5 to 0.6 times eye diameter beyond posterior margin of orbit, and maxilla is not expanded posteriorly. Posterior opercular margin tapers to blunt angle below PLO. Gill rakers number 9 to 11. Dorsal fin originates posterior to pelvic fin base and has 11 or 12 rays. Pectoral fin extends beyond pelvic fin base and has 13 to 15 rays. Anal fin originates near end of dorsal fin base and has 20 to 23 rays. Dn and Vn are present on anterodorsal and anteroventral orbital margin respectively. PVO_1, PVO_2, and PO_2 are in straight line. PLO is at upper end of pectoral fin base. Five PO are present. VLO is closer to pelvic fin base than to lateral line. Four VO are present. SAO form obtuse angle, with SAO_1 approximately over VO_2, and SAO_3 over or slightly anterior to anal fin base and about its diameter below lateral line. Pol is about its diameter below lateral line. AOa number 4 to 8, and AOp number 10 to 14, with 5 to 7 over anal fin base. Two Prc are almost continuous with AOp. Males have series of six or seven rounded luminous organs outlined in black forming supracaudal gland, and females have four to six separate oval patches forming infracaudal gland.

This species occurs in the tropical to subtropical waters of the Atlantic. In the western Atlantic it occurs from Cape Cod to southern Brazil, including the Gulf of Mexico. It is abundant in the Gulf of Mexico. Daytime depths range from 425 to 1,000 m, and nighttime depths range from the surface to 200 m for larger specimens and from 750 to 900 m for smaller specimens. Most of the deepest captures are juveniles that apparently do not migrate. Maximum known size is 60 mm SL, and maturity is reached at about 38 mm SL.

REFERENCES: Nafpaktitis et al. 1977; Hulley 1984b, 1986b; Gartner et al. 1987.

Hygophum benoiti (Cocco 1838)

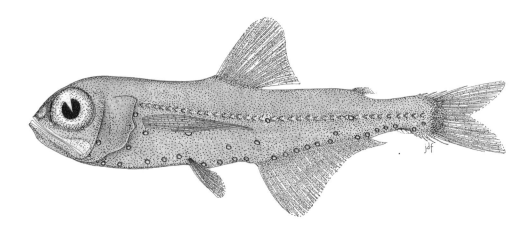

Hygophum benoiti is relatively slender and compressed, with a relatively small mouth and an anal fin base distinctly longer than dorsal fin base. It is distinguished from the other species of the family by the following combination of characters. Snout is acute. Jaws extend slightly past posterior orbital margin, and maxilla is broadly expanded posteriorly. Operculum has angular posterior margin. Gill rakers number 18 to 20. Dorsal fin originates posterior to pelvic fin base and has 12 to 14 rays. Pectoral fin extends to near anal fin base and has 13 to 15 rays. Anal fin originates under posterior end of dorsal fin base and has 19 to 21 rays. Dn, Vn, and Suo are present, and Vn is larger than Dn. PVO_1, PVO_2, and PO_1 are in line. PLO is about equidistant between lateral line and pectoral fin base. Five PO are present. VLO is midway between lateral line and pelvic fin base. Four VO are present. SAO form obtuse angle, with SAO_1 anterior to VO_3, SAO_2 and SAO_3 in line with VO_4, and SAO_3 in contact with lateral line. Two Pol are in line with last AOa, and Pol_2 is in contact with lateral line. AOa number five to seven, and AOp number five to seven, with two or three over anal fin base. Two Prc are separate from AOp and well below lateral line. Males have a single undivided supracaudal luminous gland outlined with black tissue. Females have an infracaudal luminous gland that may be subdivided into three or four components, and occasionally have a poorly developed supracaudal gland.

This species occurs in the subtropical to temperate waters of the Atlantic Ocean. In the western Atlantic it occurs from Cape Cod to southern Florida, and in the northern Gulf of Mexico. It is common in the Gulf of Mexico. Daytime depths range from 250 to 1,050 m, and nighttime depths range from the surface to 1,000 m. Maximum known size is 55 mm SL, and maturity is reached at about 40 mm SL.

REFERENCES: Nafpaktitis et al. 1977; Hulley 1984b; Gartner et al. 1987.

Hygophum hygomii (Lütken 1892)

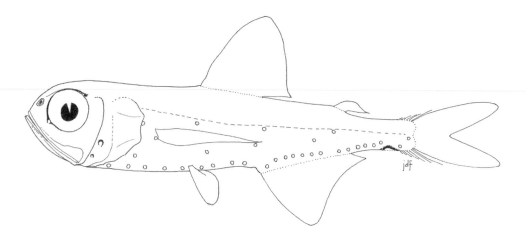

Hygophum hygomii is moderately slender and compressed, with a relatively short mouth and an anal fin base distinctly longer than dorsal fin base. It is distinguished from the other species of the family by the following combination of characters. Snout is moderately blunt. Jaws extend to posterior margin of orbit, and maxilla is broadly expanded posteriorly. Operculum is truncated posteriorly. Gill rakers number 19 to 21. Dorsal fin originates over pelvic fin base and has 13 to 15 rays. Pectoral fin extends to AOa_1 and has 15 or 16 rays. Anal fin originates under posterior end of dorsal fin and has 20 to 22 rays. Dn, Vn, and Suo are present. PVO_1, PVO_2, and PO_1 are in straight line. PLO is closer to upper end of pectoral fin base than to lateral line. Five PO are present. VLO is within its diameter below lateral line. Four VO are present. SAO form obtuse angle, with SAO_1 anterior to VO_2, and SAO_3 posterior to anal fin origin and in contact with lateral line.

Pol_1 is anterior to last AOa, and Pol_2 is in contact with lateral line. AOa number six to eight, and AOp number five to seven, with two over anal fin base. Two Prc are separated from AOp series, and Prc_2 is about one-half its diameter below lateral line. Males have single, small, heart-shaped supracaudal luminous gland, and females have one or two small lanceolate infracaudal patches.

This species occurs in subtropical to temperate waters worldwide. In the western Atlantic it occurs from Cape Cod to eastern Florida and Cuba, in the northern Gulf of Mexico, and from southern Brazil to northern Argentina. Daytime depths range from 400 to 850 m, and nighttime depths range from the surface to 1,050 m. Maximum known size is 68 mm SL for immature specimens.

REFERENCES: Nafpaktitis et al. 1977; Hulley 1984b, 1986b; Gartner et al. 1987.

Hygophum macrochir (Günther 1864)

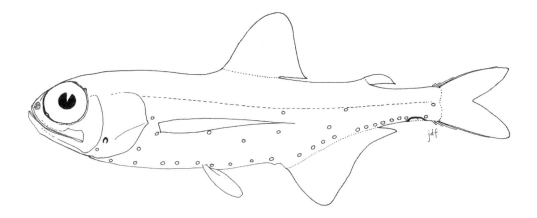

Hygophum macrochir is moderately slender and compressed, with a relatively small mouth and an anal fin base distinctly longer than dorsal fin base. It is distinguished from the other species of the family by the following combination of characters. Snout is moderately blunt. Jaws extend slightly beyond posterior orbital margin, and maxilla is broadly expanded posteriorly. Posterior margin of operculum is broadly convex, with blunt angular protrusion below PLO photophore. Gill rakers number 19 to 21. Dorsal fin originates slightly behind pelvic fin base and has 12 to 14 rays. Pectoral fin extends posterior to SAO_2 and has 13 to 15 rays. Anal fin originates near end of dorsal fin base and has 18 to 20 rays. Dn, Vn, and Suo are present. PVO_1, PVO_2, and PO_1 are in straight line. PLO is closer to upper end of pectoral fin base than to lateral line. Five PO are present. VLO is midway between lateral line and pelvic fin base. Four VO are present. SAO form obtuse angle, with SAO_1 anterior to VO_3, and SAO_3 directly over or posterior to anal fin origin and in contact with lateral line. Pol_1 is anterior to last AOa, and Pol_2 is in contact with lateral line. AOa number four to six, and AOp number five to seven, with two to four over anal fin base. Two Prc are separated from AOp series, and Prc_2 is in contact with lateral line. Males have supracaudal luminous gland consisting of five to seven scalelike structures, and females have infracaudal luminous gland consisting of one to three patches of luminous tissue.

This species occurs in the tropical waters of the Atlantic Ocean. In the western Atlantic it occurs from southeastern Florida and the Gulf of Mexico to northern Argentina. It is rare in the Gulf of Mexico. Daytime depths range from 275 to 750 m, and nighttime depths range from the surface to 125 m. Maximum known size is 60 mm SL, and maturity is reached at about 45 to 55 mm SL.

REFERENCES: Nafpaktitis et al. 1977; Gartner et al. 1987.

Hygophum reinhardtii (Lütken 1892)

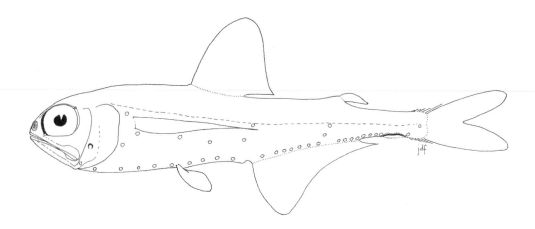

Hygophum reinhardtii is moderately slender and compressed, with a relatively small mouth and an anal fin base distinctly longer than dorsal fin base. It is distinguished from the other species of the family by the following combination of characters. Snout is slightly blunt. Jaws extend slightly beyond posterior margin of orbit, and maxilla is broadly expanded posteriorly. Operculum has evenly convex posterior margin. Gill rakers number 17 to 20. Dorsal fin originates slightly posterior to pelvic fin base and has 13 or 14 rays. Pectoral fin extends to about first AOa and has 13 to 15 rays. Anal fin originates at posterior end of dorsal fin base and has 22 to 24 rays. Dn, Vn, and Suo are present. PVO_1, PVO_2, and PO_1 are in straight line. PLO is usually slightly closer to upper end of pectoral fin base than to lateral line. Five PO are present. VLO is midway between lateral line and pelvic fin base. Four VO are present. SAO form obtuse angle, with SAO_1 behind VO_2, and SAO_3 slightly posterior to anal fin origin and in contact with lateral line.

Pol_1 is posterior to last AOa, and Pol_2 is in contact with lateral line. AOa number six to eight, and AOp number six to nine, with three or four over anal fin base. Two Prc are separate from AOp series, and Prc_2 is immediately below lateral line. Males have supracaudal luminous organ consisting of four to six scalelike structures, and females have infracaudal luminous organ consisting of three or four oval patches.

This species occurs in the subtropical waters of the Atlantic and Pacific Oceans. In the western Atlantic it occurs from New York to Venezuela, including the Gulf of Mexico and the Caribbean Sea, and from central Brazil to Uruguay. Daytime depths range from 475 to 1,100 m, and nighttime depths range from the surface to 250 m. Maximum known size is 46 mm SL, and maturity is reached at about 40 to 45 mm SL.

REFERENCES: Nafpaktitis et al. 1977; Hulley 1984b, 1986b; Gartner et al. 1987.

Hygophum taaningi Bekker 1965

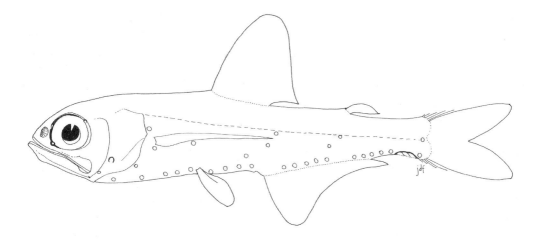

Hygophum taaningi is moderately slender and compressed, with a relatively small mouth and an anal fin base distinctly longer than dorsal fin base. It is distinguished from the other species of the family by the following combination of characters. Snout is slightly acute. Jaws extend slightly beyond posterior margin of orbit, and maxilla is broadly expanded posteriorly. Posterodorsal margin of operculum is angular. Gill rakers number 16 to 18. Dorsal fin originates over or slightly posterior to pelvic fin base and has 13 or 14 rays. Pectoral fin extends to about SAO_2 and has 13 or 14 rays. Anal fin originates slightly anterior to end of dorsal fin base and has 19 or 20 rays. Dn, Vn, and Suo are present. PVO_1, PVO_2, and PO_1 are in straight line. PLO is midway between lateral line and pectoral fin base. Five PO are present. VLO is slightly closer to lateral line than to pelvic fin base. Four VO are present. SAO form slight obtuse angle, with SAO_1 posterior to or over VO_3, and SAO_3 posterior to anal fin origin and in contact with lateral line. Pol_1 is slightly ante-

rior to last AOa, and Pol_2 is in contact with lateral line. AOa number four to six, and AOp number four to six, with two or three over anal fin base. Two Prc are separate from AOp series, and Prc_2 is in contact with lateral line. Males have long supracaudal luminous gland, and females have infracaudal luminous gland consisting of two or three small, elongate patches.

This species occurs in the subtropical waters of the Atlantic Ocean. In the western Atlantic it occurs from New York to Venezuela, including the northern Gulf of Mexico and the Caribbean Sea. Daytime depths range from 475 to 1,000 m, and nighttime depths range from near the surface to 250 m, and between 650 and 1,250 m. All of those captured from 650 to 1,250 m during the night have been juveniles. Maximum known size is 50 mm SL, and maturity is reached at about 40 mm SL.

REFERENCES: Nafpaktitis et al. 1977; Hulley 1984b; Gartner et al. 1987.

Lampadena anomala   Parr 1928

Lampadena anomala is relatively slender and compressed, with a large mouth, dorsal and anal fin bases of about equal length, and body photophores poorly developed. It is distinguished from the other species of the family by the following combination of characters. Snout is moderately blunt. Jaws extend about eye diameter beyond posterior margin of orbit, and maxilla is not expanded posteriorly. Posterior margin of operculum tapers to acute angle above PLO. Gill rakers number 16 to 18. Dorsal fin originates slightly in advance of pelvic fin base and has 14 to 16 rays. Pectoral fin extends to VO_2 or VO_3 and has 16 to 18 rays. Anal fin originates posterior to dorsal fin base and has 13 or 14 rays. Vn is small. PVO_1 is on or slightly behind vertical through center of PVO_2. PLO is 2 to 3 times its diameter below lateral line. Five PO are present, with none highly elevated. VLO is closer to lateral line than to pelvic fin base. VO number 3. SAO form slight angle, with SAO_1 posterior to last VO and about mid-distant between this photophore and SAO_2. SAO_3 is above origin of anal fin and about twice its diameter below lateral line. Pol is twice its diameter below lateral line. AOa number three or four, and AOp number two and are behind anal fin base. Prc_1 and Prc_2 are separated from AOp series and are separated from each other by photophore diameter. Supracaudal and infracaudal luminous glands are large, bordered with black pigment, and present in both sexes.

This species occurs in the tropical to subtropical Atlantic, western Indian, and central Pacific Oceans. In the western Atlantic it occurs from 32°N to 39°S, including the eastern Gulf of Mexico, the Caribbean Sea, and Bermuda between 450 and 2,000 m. Maximum known size is 150 mm SL.

REFERENCES: Nafpaktitis and Paxton 1968; Nafpaktitis et al. 1977; Hulley 1986b.

Lampadena luminosa   (Garman 1899)

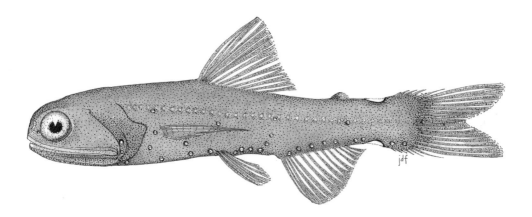

Lampadena luminosa is relatively slender and compressed, with a large mouth, and dorsal and anal fin bases of equal length. It is distinguished from the other species of the family by the following combination of characters. Snout is moderately blunt. Jaws extend about eye diameter beyond posterior margin of orbit, and maxilla is not expanded posteriorly. Posterior margin of operculum tapers to acute angle above PLO. Gill rakers number 13 to 15. Dorsal fin originates slightly in advance of pelvic fin base and has 14 or 15 rays. Pectoral fin extends to VO_2 or VO_3 and has 15 to 17 rays. Anal fin originates posterior to dorsal fin base and has 13 to 15 rays. Vn is small. PVO_1 is slightly anterior to PVO_2. PLO is closer to lateral line than to pectoral fin base. Five PO are present, with PO_4 highly elevated and above PO_3. VLO is closer to lateral line than to pelvic fin base. VO number four or five. SAO form slight angle, with SAO_1 posterior to last VO and about mid-distant between this photophore and SAO_2. SAO_3 is anterior to anal fin base and within its diameter below lateral line. Pol is within its diameter below lateral line. AOa number five to seven, and AOp number two and are behind anal fin base. Three Prc are separated from AOp series, and Prc_3 is at level of lateral line. Supracaudal and infracaudal luminous glands are large, bordered with black pigment, and present in both sexes.

This species occurs in tropical to subtropical waters worldwide. In the western Atlantic it occurs from Cape Cod to Uruguay, including the Gulf of Mexico and the Caribbean Sea. Daytime depths range from 425 to 850 m, and nighttime depths range from 40 to 225 m. Maximum known size is 180 mm SL, and maturity is reached at about 150 mm SL.

REFERENCES: Nafpaktitis and Paxton 1968; Nafpaktitis et al. 1977; Uyeno et al. 1983; Hulley 1986b; Gartner et al. 1987.

Lampanyctus alatus Goode and Bean 1896

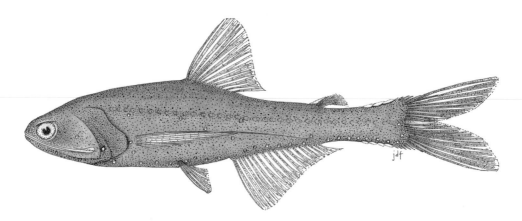

Lampanyctus alatus is relatively slender and compressed, with a large mouth and an anal fin base slightly longer than dorsal fin base. It is distinguished from the other species of the family by the following combination of characters. Snout is acute. Jaws extend more than eye diameter beyond posterior margin of orbit, and maxilla is slightly expanded posteriorly. Posterior margin of operculum is concave dorsally and convex with serrations ventrally. Gill rakers number 13 to 15. Dorsal fin originates posterior to pelvic fin base and has 11 to 13 rays. Pectoral fin extends nearly to end of anal fin base and has 11 to 13 rays. Anal fin originates at about end of dorsal fin base and has 16 to 18 rays. Vn is small. One photophore is present on cheek. PVO_2 is above and anterior to POV_1. PLO is 0.5 to 1.5 times its diameter below lateral line. Five PO are present, with PO_4 elevated to level of PVO_2. VLO is about its diameter below lateral line. Four VO are present, with VO_2 slightly elevated. SAO form obtuse angle, with SAO_1 slightly anterior to or over VO_3 and higher than SAO_2. SAO_3 is behind anal fin origin and immediately below lateral line. Two Pol are in straight line with last AOa, and Pol_2 is less than its diameter below lateral line. AOa number five to seven, and AOp number six to eight and are behind anal fin base

and continuous with four Prc. Prc_4 is anterior to Prc_3 and in contact with lateral line. Supracaudal and infracaudal luminous glands consist of two to four and four or five luminous scalelike structures respectively, and are present in both sexes. Luminous gland at base of adipose fin is better developed in males than in females. Secondary photophores are present at anterior margin of orbit.

This species occurs in the tropical to warm temperate waters of the Atlantic, western Pacific, and Indian Oceans. In the western Atlantic it occurs from Cape Cod to northern Brazil, including the Gulf of Mexico and the Caribbean Sea. It is very abundant in the Gulf of Mexico. Daytime depths range from 275 to 1,000 m, and nighttime depths range from 40 to 300 m. Maximum known size is 60 mm SL, and sexual maturity is reached at about 36 mm SL for females. Fecundity ranges from 400 to 900 eggs and increases with body size. The smallest mature females spawn about every four days, and the largest spawn every other day. Spawning takes place at night between 25 and 50 m.

REFERENCES: Nafpaktitis et al. 1977; Hulley 1984b, 1986b; Gartner et al. 1987; Gartner 1991, 1993.

Lampanyctus ater   Tåning 1928

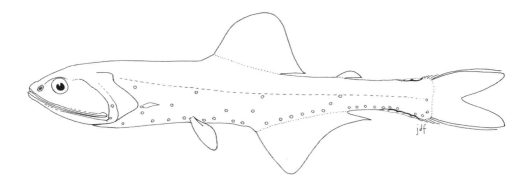

Lampanyctus ater is relatively slender and compressed, with a large mouth and an anal fin base slightly longer than dorsal fin base. It is distinguished from the other species of the family by the following combination of characters. Snout is acute. Jaws extend more than eye diameter beyond posterior orbital margin, and maxilla is slightly expanded posteriorly. Posterior margin of operculum forms acute angle. Gill rakers number 10 to 12. Dorsal fin originates posterior to pelvic fin base and has 13 to 15 rays. Pectoral fin is very short, extending just past PO_2. Anal fin originates under posterior one-half of dorsal fin base and has 18 or 19 rays. Vn is small. PVO_2 is above and from slightly in front to slightly behind PVO_1. PLO is 1.5 to 2 times its diameter below lateral line. Five PO are present, with PO_4 elevated and over or slightly behind PO_3. VLO is about its diameter below lateral line. Four VO are present. SAO form obtuse angle, with SAO_1 in front of VO_3 and level with SAO_2. SAO_3 is over or slightly posterior to anal fin origin and in contact with lateral line. Two Pol are in straight line with last AOa, and Pol_2 is in contact with lateral line. AOa number six to eight, and AOp number six to eight and first is behind or over anal fin base. Four Prc are separated from AOp series, with first three forming arc, and fourth over Prc_3 at level of lateral line. Supracaudal and infracaudal luminous glands are present in both sexes, and infracaudal gland consists of five to seven poorly defined scalelike structures.

This species occurs in the subtropical waters of the Atlantic, western Pacific, and Indian Oceans. In the western Atlantic it occurs from New York to northeastern Florida and the Gulf of Mexico, and from southern Brazil to northern Argentina. Daytime depths range from 550 to 1,550 m, and nighttime depths range from 51 to 250 m and from 801 to 850 m. Maximum known size is 129 mm SL, and maturity is reached at about 90 mm SL.

REFERENCES: Nafpaktitis et al. 1977; Hulley 1984b, 1986b; Gartner et al. 1987.

Lampanyctus cuprarius   Tåning 1928

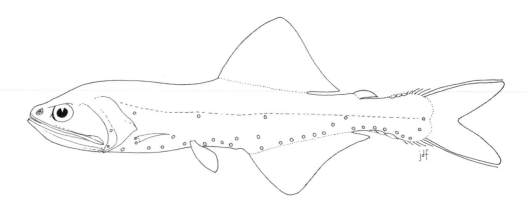

Lampanyctus cuprarius is moderately slender and compressed, with a large mouth and an anal fin base slightly longer than dorsal fin base. It is distinguished from the other species of the family by the following combination of characters. Snout is moderately acute. Jaws extend more than eye diameter beyond posterior margin of orbit, and maxilla is slightly expanded posteriorly. Posterior margin of operculum forms acute angle slightly above pectoral fin base. Gill rakers number 11 or 12. Dorsal fin originates posterior to pelvic fin base and has 16 to 18 rays. Pectoral fin is very short, extends just past PO_3, and has 11 or 12 rays. Anal fin originates under anterior one-half of dorsal fin base and has 17 to 19 rays. Vn is small. PVO_2 is above and either slightly anterior or slightly posterior to PVO_1. PLO is 0.5 to 1.5 times its diameter below lateral line. Five PO are present, with PO_4 elevated and behind PO_3. VLO is immediately below lateral line. Four VO are present and form arch. SAO form obtuse angle, with SAO_1 behind VO_3 and lower than SAO_2, and SAO_3 over or slightly behind AOa and in contact with lateral line. Two Pol are in straight line with last AOa, and Pol_2 is in contact with lateral line. AOa number five to seven, with AOa_1 distinctly separated from AOa_2. AOp number four to six, with first usually over anal fin base. Four Prc are continuous with AOp series, with first three forming arc, and last on level with lateral line. Supracaudal and infracaudal luminous glands are found in both sexes and consist of two or three and three or four poorly defined scalelike structures respectively. Minute secondary photophores are present on caudal fin rays and on posterior margins of enlarged lateral line scales.

This species occurs in the subtropical waters of the Atlantic Ocean. In the western Atlantic it occurs from Cape Cod to Venezuela, including the Gulf of Mexico and the Caribbean Sea, and from central to southern Brazil. Daytime depths range from 600 to 1,200 m, and nighttime depths range from 40 to 1,000 m. Food consists of amphipods, calanoid copepods, ostracods, and euphausiids. Maximum known size is 110 mm SL, and maturity is reached at about 70 to 75 mm SL.

REFERENCES: Nafpaktitis et al. 1977; Hulley 1984b.

Lampanyctus lineatus Tåning 1928

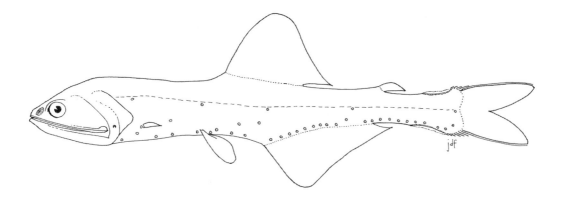

Lampanyctus lineatus is slender and compressed, with a very large mouth and an anal fin base slightly longer than dorsal fin base. It is distinguished from the other species of the family by the following combination of characters. Snout is acute. Jaws extend more than twice eye diameter beyond posterior margin of orbit, and maxilla is abruptly expanded posteriorly. Posterior margin of operculum tapers to acute angle slightly above pectoral fin base. Gill rakers number 17 to 19. Dorsal fin originates posterior to pelvic fin base and has 16 to 18 rays. Pectoral fin is small, extends just past PO_3, and has 12 to 14 rays. Anal fin originates under anterior one-half of dorsal fin base and has 19 to 22 rays. Vn is small. PVO_2 is above and behind PVO_1. PLO is about its diameter below lateral line. Five PO are present, with PO_4 elevated and over or slightly behind PO_3. VLO is its diameter below lateral line. Four VO are present. SAO form obtuse angle, with SAO_1 behind VO_3 and lower than SAO_2, and SAO_3 over first AOa and in contact with lateral line. Two Pol are nearly in line with last AOa, and Pol_2 is in contact with lateral line. AOa number seven or eight, with first often separated from second. AOp number six to eight, with first often over anal fin base. Four Prc are distinct from AOp series, with first three forming arc, and last at level of lateral line. Supracaudal and infracaudal luminous glands are found in both sexes and consist of three or four and four to six luminous scalelike structures respectively.

This species occurs in the subtropical waters of the Atlantic, western Pacific, and western Indian Oceans. In the western Atlantic it occurs from Cape Cod to Venezuela, including the Gulf of Mexico and the Caribbean Sea. Daytime depths range from 650 to 1,150 m, and nighttime depths range from 60 to 350 m for smaller specimens and from 900 to 1,000 m for larger specimens. Maximum known size is 235 mm SL, and maturity is reached at about 152 mm SL.

REFERENCES: Nafpaktitis et al. 1977; Hulley 1984b, 1986b; Gartner et al. 1987.

Lampanyctus nobilis Tåning 1928

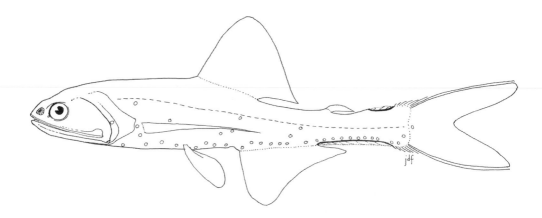

Lampanyctus nobilis is slender and compressed, with a very large mouth, and dorsal and anal fin bases of about equal length. It is distinguished from the other species of the family by the following combination of characters. Snout is acute. Jaws extend about twice eye diameter beyond posterior orbital margin, and maxilla is slightly expanded posteriorly. Posterior margin of operculum tapers to acute angle above PLO. Gill rakers number 13 to 15. Dorsal fin originates posterior to pelvic fin base and has 14 to 16 rays. Pectoral fin extends to third or fourth AOa and has 13 to 15 rays. Anal fin originates under posterior one-third of dorsal fin base and has 18 or 19 rays. Vn is small. PVO_2 is above and in front of PVO_1. Five PO are present, with PO_4 slightly elevated and behind PO_3. VLO is closer to lateral line than to pelvic fin base. Four VO are present. SAO form slight angle, with SAO_1 behind VO_3 and below SAO_2, and SAO_3 over or slightly anterior to anal fin origin and at level of lateral line. Two Pol are in straight line, with last AOa and Pol_2 in contact with lateral line. AOa number 5 to 8, and AOp number 8 to 10, with first and occasionally second over anal fin base. Four Prc are separate from AOp series; Prc_2, Prc_3, and Prc_4 are in straight line; and Prc_4 is on level with lateral line. Supracaudal and infracaudal luminous glands are present in both sexes and consist of 3 or 4 and 8 to 10 scalelike structures respectively.

This species occurs in tropical waters worldwide. In the western Atlantic it occurs from New York to central Brazil, including the Gulf of Mexico and the Caribbean Sea. Daytime depths range from 475 to 750 m, and nighttime depths range from 40 to 325 m. Maximum known size is 113 mm SL, and maturity is reached at about 82 to 84 mm SL.

REFERENCES: Nafpaktitis et al. 1977; Uyeno et al. 1983; Hulley 1986b; Gartner et al. 1987.

Lampanyctus tenuiformis   Brauer 1906

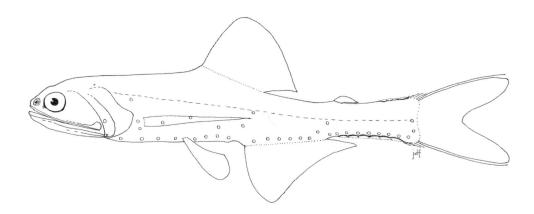

Lampanyctus tenuiformis is moderately slender and compressed, with a very large mouth and an anal fin base longer than dorsal fin base. It is distinguished from the other species of the family by the following combination of characters. Snout is acute. Jaws extend slightly less than twice eye diameter beyond posterior margin of orbit, and maxilla is slightly expanded posteriorly. Posterior margin of operculum is concave dorsally and convex ventrally. Gill rakers number 14. Dorsal fin originates posterior to pelvic fin base and has 13 or 14 rays. Pectoral fin extends to origin of anal fin and has 13 rays. Anal fin originates under posterior one-third of dorsal fin base and has 17 or 18 rays. Vn is small. PVO_2 is above and anterior to PVO_1. PLO is 1.5 to 2.5 times its diameter below lateral line. Five PO are present, with PO_4 highly elevated and behind PO_3. VLO is closer to lateral line than to pelvic fin base. Four VO are present. SAO form obtuse angle, with SAO_1 over or slightly anterior to VO_3, and SAO_3 over or anterior to anal fin origin and in contact with lateral line. Two Pol are nearly in straight line with last AOa, and Pol_2 is within its diameter of lateral line. AOa number six or seven, and AOp number six or seven, with first behind, but occasionally over, anal fin base. Four Prc are continuous with AOp series, with first three forming arc, and last on level with lateral line. Supracaudal and infracaudal luminous glands are present in both sexes and consist of two or three and seven to nine scalelike structures respectively.

This species occurs in tropical waters worldwide. In the western Atlantic it occurs from the Gulf of Mexico and the Caribbean Sea to northern Brazil. Daytime depths range from 300 to 750 m, and nighttime depths range from 40 to 325 m. Maximum known size is 122 mm SL.

REFERENCES: Nafpaktitis et al. 1977; Hulley 1986b; Gartner et al. 1987.

Lepidophanes gaussi   (Brauer 1906)

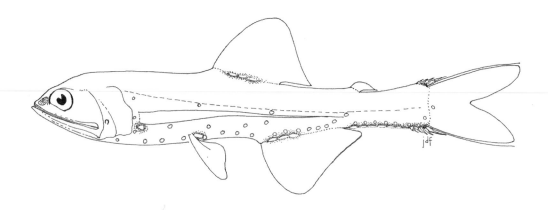

Lepidophanes gaussi is moderately slender and compressed, with a large mouth, and dorsal and anal fin bases of about equal length. It is distinguished from the other species of the family by the following combination of characters. Snout is acute. Jaws extend about 1.5 times eye diameter beyond posterior orbital margin, and maxilla is slightly expanded posteriorly. Posterior margin of operculum is concave posterodorsally and convex posteriorly. Gill rakers number 12. Dorsal fin originates posterior to pelvic fin base and has 13 or 14 rays. Pectoral fin extends to about end of anal fin base and has 12 or 13 rays. Anal fin originates anterior to end of dorsal fin base and has 13 to 15 rays. Vn is small. PVO_2 is above or slightly anterior to PVO_1. PLO is slightly anterior to PVO and is its diameter or less below lateral line. Five PO are present, with PO_4 elevated and behind PO_3. VLO is posterior to pelvic fin base and in contact with lateral line. Five VO are present, with VO_2 elevated. SAO form obtuse angle, with SAO_1 over VO_4–VO_5 interspace, and SAO_3 behind SAO_2 and in contact with lateral line. Two Pol are in straight line with last AOa,

and Pol_2 is in contact with lateral line. AOa number five or six, and AOp number five or six and all are behind anal fin base. Four Prc are separated from AOp series, with first three forming arc, and last on level with lateral line. Luminous tissue is present at bases of pectoral, pelvic, dorsal, and anal fins, one or two roundish photophores are located in front of dorsal procurrent caudal rays, and series of poorly developed patches of luminous tissue occur on ventral aspect of caudal peduncle.

This species occurs in the subtropical waters of the Atlantic Ocean. In the western Atlantic it occurs from Cape Cod to the northern Caribbean Sea, including the northern Gulf of Mexico, and from central Brazil to Uruguay. It is extremely rare in the Gulf of Mexico. Daytime depths range from 425 to 1,100 m, and nighttime depths range from the surface to 800 m. Maximum known size is 50 mm SL, and size at maturity is about 35 mm SL.

REFERENCES: Nafpaktitis et al. 1977; Hulley 1984b.

Lepidophanes guentheri   (Goode and Bean 1896)

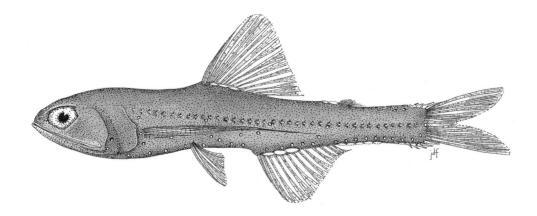

Lepidophanes guentheri is moderately slender and compressed, with a large mouth, and dorsal and anal fin bases of about equal length. It is distinguished from the other species of the family by the following combination of characters. Snout is acute. Jaws extend about eye diameter beyond posterior orbital margin, and maxilla is slightly expanded posteriorly. Margin of operculum is concave posterodorsally and rounded posteriorly. Gill rakers number 14 or 15. Dorsal fin originates posterior to pelvic fin base and has 13 to 15 rays. Pectoral fin extends to near end of anal fin base and has 12 or 13 rays. Anal fin originates anterior to end of dorsal fin base and has 14 or 15 rays. Vn is small. PVO_2 is above and slightly anterior to PVO_1. PLO is in straight line with PVO_1 and PVO_2, and is its diameter or less below lateral line. Five PO are present, with PO_4 elevated and behind PO_3. VLO is behind pelvic fin base and in contact with lateral line. Five VO are present, with VO_2 elevated. SAO form obtuse angle, with SAO_1 over VO_4–VO_5 interspace, and SAO_3 behind SAO_2 and in contact with lateral line. Two Pol are in straight line with last AOa. AOa number five or six, with first separated from second. AOp number five or six and all are behind anal fin base. Four Prc

are occasionally continuous with AOp series, with first three forming arc, and last on level with lateral line. One to three pairs of roundish photophore-like structures occur in front of dorsal procurrent caudal rays, five to seven scalelike luminous structures occur infracaudally, and luminous patches occur at bases of dorsal and anal fins.

This species occurs in the tropical waters of the Atlantic Ocean. In the western Atlantic it occurs from Cape Cod to northern Argentina, including the Gulf of Mexico. It is one of the most abundant myctophids in the Gulf of Mexico. Daytime depths range from 425 to 950 m, and nighttime depths range from 40 to 175 m. Maximum known size is 78 mm SL, and maturity is reached at about 43 mm SL in females. Maturity is reached at about 4 months, and life span is about 14 months. Fecundity ranges from 650 to 2,300 eggs and increases with body size. Spawning frequency ranges from every 10 days for the smallest mature females to every 4 days for the largest females, and occurs at night between 25 and 75 m.

REFERENCES: Nafpaktitis et al. 1977; Hulley 1984b, 1986b; Gartner et al. 1987; Gartner 1991, 1993.

Lobianchia gemellarii   (Cocco 1838)

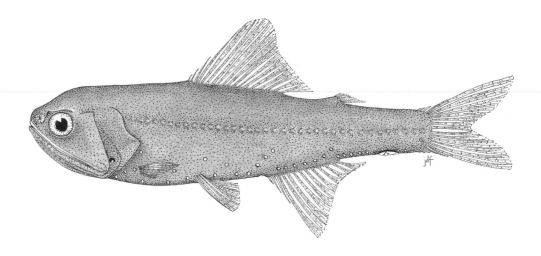

Lobianchia gemellarii is moderately slender and compressed, with a very large mouth and a dorsal fin base slightly longer than anal fin base. It is distinguished from the other species of the family by the following combination of characters. Snout is blunt. Jaws extend 1.3 to 1.5 times eye diameter beyond posterior orbital margin, and maxilla is slightly expanded posteriorly. Posterior margin of operculum tapers to acute angle above PLO. Gill rakers number 15 to 21. Dorsal fin originates slightly anterior to pelvic fin base and has 17 or 18 rays. Pectoral fin extends to PO_4 and has 11 or 12 rays. Anal fin originates slightly anterior to end of dorsal fin base and has 13 to 15 rays. Dn is small and inconspicuous. PVO_1 and PVO_2 are in straight line with PO_1. PLO is slightly closer to pectoral fin base than to lateral line. Five PO are present, with PO_4 elevated and behind PO_3. VLO is closer to pelvic fin base than to lateral line. Five VO are present, with VO_1, VO_2, and VO_3 progressively elevated. SAO form straight line with last VO, and SAO_3 is slightly closer to lateral line than to anal fin base. Single Pol is anterior to end of anal fin base, continuous with last AOa, and midway between lateral line and anal fin base. AOa number five or six, with last one or two elevated. AOp number six, with first usually behind anal fin base. Four Prc are evenly spaced and well below lateral line. Males have supracaudal luminous gland consisting of six scalelike structures flanked by five pairs of triangular luminous structures. Females have infracaudal luminous glands consisting of two heart-shaped structures flanked by two pairs of triangular luminous structures.

This species occurs in the tropical to subtropical waters of the Atlantic, Pacific, and western Indian Oceans. In the western Atlantic it occurs from Cape Cod to Uruguay, including the Gulf of Mexico and the Caribbean Sea. It is abundant in the Gulf of Mexico. Daytime depths range from 300 to 800 m, and nighttime depths range from 25 to 300 m. Maximum known size is 60 mm SL, and maturity is reached at about 40 to 45 mm SL.

REFERENCES: Nafpaktitis et al. 1977; Hulley 1984b, 1986b; Gartner et al. 1987.

Myctophum affine (Lütken 1892)

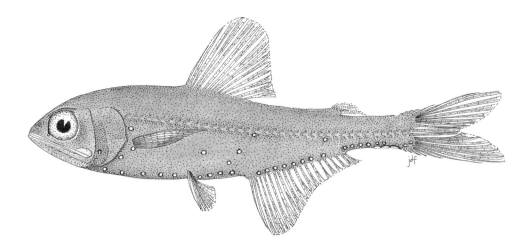

Myctophum affine is moderately slender and compressed, with a moderately large mouth and an anal fin base longer than dorsal fin base. It is distinguished from the other species of the family by the following combination of characters. Snout is blunt. Jaws extend slightly beyond posterior margin of orbit, and maxilla is moderately expanded posteriorly. Posterior margin of operculum is obtusely angled, and posterodorsal margin is convex. Gill rakers number 18 to 22. Dorsal fin originates over pelvic fin base and has 12 or 13 rays. Pectoral fin extends to VO_2 and has 13 or 14 rays. Anal fin originates below or slightly behind end of dorsal fin base and has 18 to 20 rays. Dn and Vn are small. PVO_1, PVO_2, and PO_1 form straight line. PLO is midway between lateral line and pectoral fin base. Five PO are present. VLO is midway between lateral line and pelvic fin base. Four VO are present. SAO form straight line with VO_3, and SAO_3 is about 0.5 times its diameter below lateral line. Single Pol is about 0.5 times its diameter below lateral line. AOa number seven to nine, and AOp number four to six, with first usually over anal fin base. Two Prc are separate from AOp series, with Prc_2 slightly higher than Prc_1. Males have supracaudal luminous gland consisting of seven or eight overlapping scale-like structures, and females have infracaudal luminous structure consisting of three or four oval to lanceolate patches.

This species occurs in the tropical waters of the Atlantic Ocean. It occurs from Cape Cod to the Caribbean Sea and the Gulf of Mexico in the western Atlantic, and it is common in the Gulf of Mexico. Daytime depths range from 300 to 650 m, and nighttime depths range from the surface to 275 m. Maximum known size is about 79 mm SL, and maturity is reached at about 46 to 58 mm SL. Fecundity ranges from 550 to 3,000 eggs and increases with body size.

REFERENCES: Nafpaktitis et al. 1977; Gartner et al. 1987; Gartner 1993.

Myctophum asperum   Richardson 1845

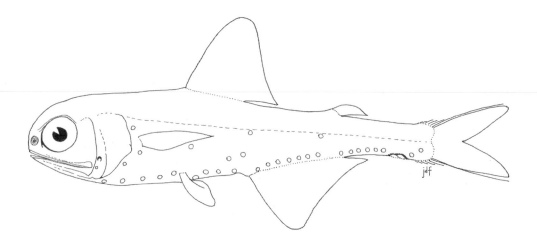

Myctophum asperum is moderately slender and compressed, with a moderately large mouth and an anal fin base longer than dorsal fin base. It is distinguished from the other species of the family by the following combination of characters. Snout is blunt. Jaws extend slightly beyond posterior orbital margin, and maxilla is slightly expanded posteriorly. Posterior margin of operculum is obtusely angled. Gill rakers number 14 to 16. Dorsal fin originates over pelvic fin base and has 12 to 14 rays. Pectoral fin extends to VO_3 and has 14 or 15 rays. Anal fin originates posterior to dorsal fin base and has 17 or 18 rays. Dn and Vn are small. PVO_1, PVO_2, and PO_1 are in straight line. PLO is midway between lateral line and pectoral fin base. Five PO are present. VLO is midway between lateral line and pelvic fin base. Four VO are present. SAO form obtuse angle, with SAO_1 anterior to VO_4, and SAO_3 slightly anterior to anal fin origin and immediately below lateral line. Single Pol is immediately below lateral line. AOa number six to eight, with first usually slightly depressed. AOp number five to seven, with first usually over anal fin base. Two Prc are separated from AOp series, with Prc_2 1.5 to 2 times its diameter above Prc_1. Males have supracaudal luminous gland consisting of five or six overlapping scalelike structures, and females have infracaudal luminous gland consisting of one to three heart-shaped patches.

This species occurs in tropical waters worldwide. In the western Atlantic it occurs from Cape Cod to northern Brazil, including the Gulf of Mexico and the Caribbean Sea. Daytime depths range from 425 to 750 m, and nighttime depths are at or near the surface. Maximum known size is 85 mm SL, and size at maturity is about 70 to 77 mm SL.

REFERENCES: Nafpaktitis et al. 1977; Hulley 1986b; Gartner et al. 1987.

Myctophum nitidulum Garman 1899

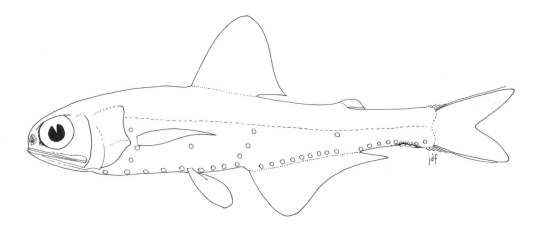

Myctophum nitidulum is moderately slender and compressed, with a moderately large mouth and an anal fin base longer than dorsal fin base. It is distinguished from the other species of the family by the following combination of characters. Snout is blunt. Jaws extend slightly beyond posterior orbital margin, and maxilla is slightly expanded posteriorly. Posterior margin of operculum forms obtuse angle, and posterodorsal margin is sharply angular. Gill rakers number 18 to 22. Dorsal fin originates over pelvic fin base and has 13 or 14 rays. Pectoral fin extends to VO_2 and has 13 or 14 rays. Anal fin originates over or slightly anterior to end of dorsal fin base and has 19 or 20 rays. Dn and Vn are small. PVO_1, PVO_2, and PO_1 are in straight line. PLO is closer to upper end of pectoral fin base than to lateral line. Five PO are present. VLO is midway between lateral line and pelvic fin base. Four VO are present. SAO form straight line, with SAO_1 over or slightly posterior to VO_4, and SAO_3 over or slightly posterior to anal fin origin and about 0.5 times its diameter below lateral line.

Single Pol is located about 0.5 times its diameter below lateral line. AOa number 8 to 10, and AOp number 4 to 6, with first usually over anal fin base. Two Prc are separate from AOp series, with Prc_2 slightly above Prc_1. Males have supracaudal luminous gland consisting of six or seven overlapping scalelike structures, and females have infracaudal luminous gland consisting of three to five oval-shaped patches.

This species occurs in tropical to subtropical waters worldwide. In the western Atlantic it occurs from Cape Cod to northern Argentina, including the Gulf of Mexico and the Caribbean Sea. Daytime depths range from 475 to 850 m, and nighttime depths range from the surface to 200 m for larger specimens and from 400 to 950 m for smaller specimens. All captures at night are juveniles. Maximum known size is 99 mm SL, and maturity is reached at about 55 mm SL.

REFERENCES: Nafpaktitis et al. 1977; Uyeno et al. 1983; Hulley 1984b, 1986b; Gartner et al. 1987.

Myctophum obtusirostre Tåning 1928

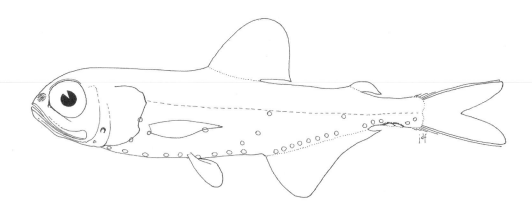

Myctophum obtusirostre is moderately slender and compressed, with a moderately large mouth and an anal fin base much longer than dorsal fin base. It is distinguished from the other species of the family by the following combination of characters. Snout is moderately obtuse. Jaws extend to just below to slightly beyond posterior margin of orbit, and maxilla is moderately expanded posteriorly. Posterior opercular margin forms obtuse, blunt angle, and posterodorsal margin is truncate and serrated. Gill rakers number 22 to 25. Dorsal fin originates over pelvic fin base and has 12 or 13 rays. Pectoral fin extends about to VO_3 and has 16 to 18 rays. Anal fin originates under or slightly posterior to end of dorsal fin base and has 17 to 19 rays. Dn and Vn are small. PVO_1, PVO_2, and PO_1 are in straight line. PLO is closer to upper end of pectoral fin base than to lateral line. Five PO are present. VLO is midway between lateral line and pelvic fin base. Four VO are present. SAO form obtuse angle, with SAO_1 slightly anterior to VO_4, and SAO_3 over or slightly posterior to anal fin origin and immediately below lateral line. Single Pol is immediately below lateral line. AOa number six to eight, with first often depressed. AOp number three to five, with first over anal fin base. Two Prc are separated from AOp series, with Prc_2 its diameter above and behind Prc_1. Males have supracaudal luminous gland consisting of three or four large, and series of small overlapping, scalelike structures, and females have infracaudal luminous gland consisting of two or three lanceolate patches.

This species occurs in the tropical waters of the Atlantic, western and central Pacific, and Indian Oceans. In the western Atlantic it occurs off New York and New Jersey, in the Gulf of Mexico and the Caribbean Sea, and off the northern and central coasts of South America. Daytime depths range from 325 to 750 m, and nighttime depths range from the surface to 125 m. Maximum known size is 90 mm SL, and size at maturity is about 75 mm SL.

REFERENCES: Nafpaktitis et al. 1977; Uyeno et al. 1983; Hulley 1986b; Gartner et al. 1987.

Myctophum selenops Tåning 1928

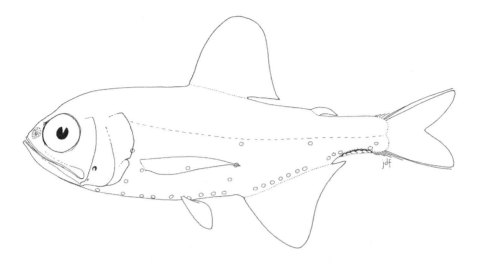

Myctophum selenops is moderately deep bodied and compressed, with a moderately large mouth and an anal fin base much longer than dorsal fin base. It is distinguished from the other species of the family by the following combination of characters. Snout is moderately blunt. Jaws extend slightly beyond posterior orbital margin, and maxilla is moderately expanded posteriorly. Posterior and posterodorsal margins of operculum are convex. Gill rakers number 22 to 24. Dorsal fin originates about over pelvic fin base and has 12 to 14 rays. Pectoral fin extends to near anal fin origin and has 16 to 18 rays. Anal fin originates under end of dorsal fin base and has 17 or 18 rays. Dn and Vn are small. PVO_1, PVO_2, and PO_1 are in straight line. PLO is closer to upper end of pectoral fin base than to lateral line. Five PO are present. VLO is closer to pelvic fin base than to lateral line. Five VO are present. SAO are nearly in straight line, with SAO_1 posterior to VO_4, and SAO_3 over anal fin origin and about 0.5 times its diameter below lateral line. Single Pol is about its diameter below lateral line. AOa number six or seven and are close together. AOp number three or four, and first is usually over anal fin base. Two Prc are widely separated from AOp series, with Prc_2 above and less than its diameter from Prc_1. Males and females have supracaudal luminous gland consisting of five or six overlapping scalelike structures in males and four similar but smaller structures in females.

This species occurs in the tropical to subtropical waters of the Atlantic, western and central Pacific, and Indian Oceans. In the western Atlantic it occurs from Cape Cod to northern Brazil, including the Gulf of Mexico and the Caribbean Sea, and from Uruguay to northern Argentina. It is rare in the Gulf of Mexico. Daytime depths range from 225 to 450 m, and nighttime depths range from 40 to 225 m. Juveniles occupy the lower depths during the night. Maximum known size is 72 mm SL, and size at maturity is about 50 mm SL.

REFERENCES: Nafpaktitis et al. 1977; Hulley 1984b, 1986b; Gartner et al. 1987.

Notolychnus valdiviae   (Brauer 1904)

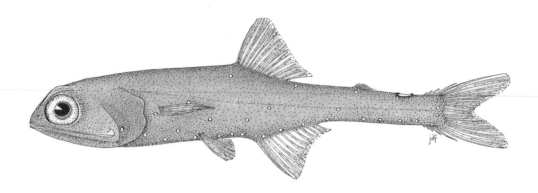

Notolychnus valdiviae is relatively slender and compressed, with a large mouth, and dorsal and anal fin bases of about equal length. It is distinguished from the other species of the family by the following combination of characters. Snout is acute. Jaws extend slightly less than eye diameter beyond posterior margin of orbit, and maxilla is abruptly expanded posteriorly. Posterior margin of operculum is rounded. Gill rakers number 10 or 11. Dorsal fin originates posterior to pelvic fin base and has 10 to 12 rays. Pectoral fin extends to VO_2 and has 12 or 13 rays. Anal fin originates about under midbase of dorsal fin and has 12 to 14 rays. Dn is small. PVO_2 is above and behind PVO_1. PLO is in contact with, or within its diameter below, horizontal septum. Five PO are present, with PO_3 and PO_4 elevated, and PO_4 nearly in contact with lateral line. VLO is about 2 times its diameter below dorsal fin origin. Four VO are present, with VO_1 elevated and over or slightly anterior to VO_2. SAO form slight angle, with SAO_1 usually slightly posterior to VO_4, and SAO_3 near end of dorsal fin base. Pol_1 is just below horizontal septum, and Pol_2 is 1 to 2 times its diameter below adipose fin base. AOa number four, with last behind anal fin base. AOp number three or four and are widely spaced. Two Prc are present, with second above first and above horizontal septum. Both sexes have undivided supracaudal luminous gland, but it is larger in males.

This species occurs in tropical to subtropical waters worldwide. In the western Atlantic it occurs from Cape Cod to northern Argentina, including the Gulf of Mexico and the Caribbean Sea. It is one of the most abundant myctophids in the Gulf of Mexico. Daytime depths range from 375 to 850 m, and nighttime depths range from 25 to 800 m. Juveniles are migratory, and adults are migratory, partially migratory, or nonmigratory. Food consists largely of copepods, ostracods, and euphausiids. Maximum known size is 25 mm SL, and maturity is reached at about 18 mm SL for females. Sexual maturity is reached at about four months, and life span is about six months (J. V. Gartner, Jr., pers. com., June 19, 1995). Fecundity ranges from 60 to 100 eggs and increases with body size. Spawning frequency is every three days for the smallest females and every one and one-half days for the largest females, and takes place around midnight between 50 and 75 m.

REFERENCES: Nafpaktitis et al. 1977; Hulley 1984b, 1986b; Gartner et al. 1987, 1989; Gartner 1993.

Notoscopelus caudispinosus (Johnson 1863)

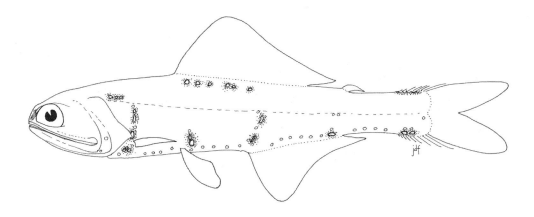

Notoscopelus caudispinosus is relatively slender and compressed, with a large mouth and a dorsal fin base much longer than anal fin base. It is distinguished from the other species of the family by the following combination of characters. Snout is moderately blunt. Jaws extend more than eye diameter beyond posterior orbital margin, and maxilla is slightly expanded posteriorly. Posterior margin of operculum tapers to acute angle slightly above pectoral fin base. Gill rakers number 14 or 15. Dorsal fin originates slightly anterior to pelvic fin base and has 25 to 27 rays. Pectoral fin is very small, extends to pelvic fin base, and has 11 to 13 rays. Anal fin originates posterior to midbase of dorsal fin and has 20 or 21 rays. Dn consists of small dorsal component and large ventral component extending along anterodorsal orbital margin. Vn is small. PVO_2 is above PVO_1 and pectoral fin base. PLO is immediately below lateral line. Five PO are present, with PO_2, PO_3, and PO_4 separated from PO_1 and PO_5, and PO_5 is elevated. VLO is midway between lateral line and pelvic fin base or closer to lateral line. Five VO are present, with VO_5 slightly elevated. SAO form slight angle, with SAO_1 posterior to VO_5, and SAO_3 about over SAO_2 and in contact with lateral line. Pol number one to three. AOa number six to eight, with first depressed and last elevated. AOp number three to five and all are behind anal fin base. Three Prc are present, with Prc_1 and Prc_2 close together and just above ventral contour, and Prc_3 within 1 to 1.5 times its diameter below lateral line. Males have supracaudal luminous gland consisting of six to eight scalelike segments.

This species occurs in the tropical to subtropical waters of the Atlantic, central Pacific, and Indian Oceans. In the western Atlantic it occurs from Cape Cod to southern Brazil, including the Gulf of Mexico and the Caribbean Sea. Daytime depths range from 600 to 1,150 m, and nighttime depths range from the surface to 175 m. Maximum known size is 140 mm SL.

REFERENCES: Nafpaktitis et al. 1977; Hulley 1984b, 1986b; Gartner et al. 1987.

Notoscopelus resplendens (Richardson 1845)

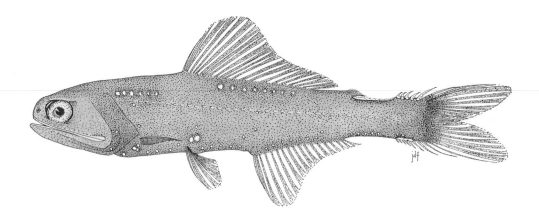

Notoscopelus resplendens is relatively slender and compressed, with a large mouth and a dorsal fin base much longer than anal fin base. It is distinguished from the other species of the family by the following combination of characters. Snout is moderately blunt. Jaws extend more than eye diameter beyond posterior margin of orbit, and maxilla is slightly expanded posteriorly. Posterior margin of operculum tapers to acute angle above pectoral fin base. Gill rakers number 19 to 23. Dorsal fin originates slightly anterior to pelvic fin base and has 21 to 23 rays. Pectoral fin reaches pelvic fin base and has 12 or 13 rays. Anal fin originates slightly posterior to dorsal fin base and has 18 to 20 rays. Dn consists of small dorsal section and large ventral section. Vn is small. PVO_2 is above PVO_1 and pectoral fin base. PLO is 1 to 2 times its diameter below lateral line. Five PO are present, with PO_2, PO_3, and PO_4 separated from PO_1 and PO_5, and PO_5 is elevated. VLO is midway between lateral line and pelvic fin base or higher. Five VO are present, with VO_5 often elevated. SAO form slight angle, with SAO_1 over or slightly behind VO_5, and SAO_3 above SAO_2 and in contact with lateral line. Pol number two or three and are located close together just below lateral line. AOa number seven to nine and form wavy line. AOp number four to seven and all are behind anal fin base. Three Prc are present, with Prc_1 and Prc_2 close together and just above ventral contour, and Prc_3 1.5 to 2 times its diameter below level of lateral line. Males have supracaudal luminous gland consisting of eight or nine scale-like segments.

This species occurs in the tropical to subtropical waters of the Atlantic, western Pacific, and western Indian Oceans. In the western Atlantic it occurs from Cape Cod to Argentina, including the Gulf of Mexico and the Caribbean Sea. It is abundant in the Gulf of Mexico. Daytime depths range from 325 to 2,000 m, and nighttime depths range from the surface to 800 m. Maximum known size is 95 mm SL, and size at maturity is about 66 mm SL.

REFERENCES: Nafpaktitis et al. 1977; Hulley 1984b, 1986b; Gartner et al. 1987.

Symbolophorus rufinus   (Tåning 1928)

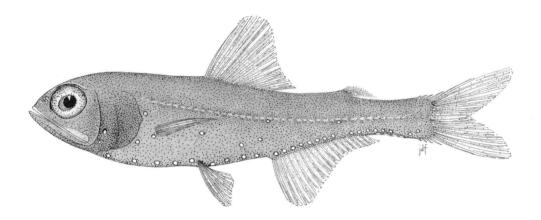

Symbolophorus rufinus is moderately slender and compressed, with a relatively small mouth and an anal fin base much longer than dorsal fin base. It is distinguished from the other species of the family by the following combination of characters. Snout is moderately blunt. Jaws extend just behind posterior margin of orbit, and maxilla is moderately expanded posteriorly. Posterior margin of operculum is rounded except for obtuse angle below PLO. Gill rakers number 20 to 22. Dorsal fin originates over pelvic fin base and has 14 to 15 rays. Pectoral fin extends past VO_2 and has 14 to 16 rays. Anal fin originates near end of dorsal fin base and has 20 or 21 rays. Dn is small and often poorly defined, and Vn is small but clearly defined. PVO_1 is above PO_2, and PVO_2 precedes PO_3. PLO is midway between lateral line and pectoral fin base. Five PO are present, with PO_5 slightly elevated. VLO is midway between lateral line and pelvic fin base. Four VO are present. SAO form obtuse angle, with SAO_1 slightly anterior to VO_3, and SAO_3 over ori-gin of anal fin and immediately below lateral line. Pol is immediately below lateral line. AOa number seven to nine, and AOp number five or six, with one or two over anal fin base. Prc_2 is slightly above Prc_1. Males have supracaudal luminous gland consisting of five or six semi-circular patches, and females have infracaudal luminous gland consisting of three or four nonoverlapping oval-shaped patches.

This species occurs in the tropical to sub-tropical waters of the Atlantic and western Indian Oceans. In the western Atlantic it occurs from the southwestern United States to southern Brazil, including the Gulf of Mexico and the Caribbean Sea. It is rare in the Gulf of Mexico. Daytime depths range from 425 to 850 m, and nighttime depths range from the surface to 200 m. Maximum known size is 87 mm SL, and maturity is reached at about 70 to 75 mm SL.

REFERENCES: Nafpaktitis et al. 1977; Gartner et al. 1987.

Taaningichthys bathyphilus (Tåning 1928)

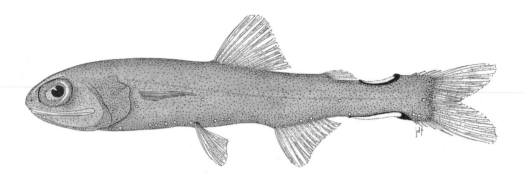

Taaningichthys bathyphilus is slender and compressed, with a relatively small mouth, and dorsal and anal fin bases of about equal length. It is distinguished from the other species of the family by the following combination of characters. Snout is moderately blunt. Jaws extend moderately beyond posterior margin of orbit, and maxilla is slightly expanded posteriorly. Posterior margin of operculum is convex. Gill rakers number 9 to 14. Dorsal fin originates posterior to pelvic fin base and has 11 to 14 rays. Pectoral fin extends to pelvic fin base and has 12 to 14 rays. Anal fin originates posterior to dorsal fin base and has 12 to 14 rays. Vn is small and poorly defined. PVO_2 is above and slightly anterior to PVO_1. PLO is usually closer to horizontal septum than to pectoral fin base. PO number five to seven and are unevenly spaced. VLO is closer to horizontal septum than to pelvic fin base. VO range from three to 5. Single SAO is behind last VO at about its diameter below horizontal septum. Single Pol is located just below horizontal septum. AOa number one to four, and AOp number one or two. Three Prc are present, with Prc_1 and Prc_2 close together near ventral contour, and Prc_3 at level of horizontal septum. Males and females possess large undivided supracaudal and infracaudal luminous glands. Posterior part of iris of eye is covered with crescent of whitish tissue.

This species occurs in tropical waters worldwide. In the western Atlantic it occurs from the southeastern United States, the Gulf of Mexico, and the Caribbean Sea. Daytime depths range from 800 to 1,550 m, and nighttime depths range from 800 to 1,000 m. It is considered a bathypelagic species that does not undergo vertical migrations. Maximum known size is 80 mm SL, and size at maturity is about 57 to 61 mm SL.

REFERENCES: Nafpaktitis et al. 1977; Hulley 1984b, 1986b; Gartner et al. 1987.

Taaningichthys minimus   (Tåning 1928)

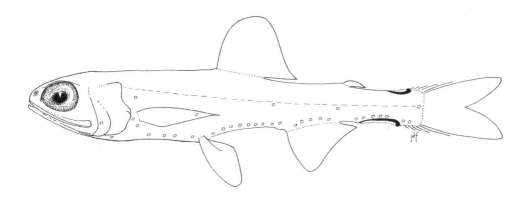

Taaningichthys minimus is slender and compressed, with a relatively small mouth, and dorsal and anal fins of about equal length. It is distinguished from the other species of the family by the following combination of characters. Snout is moderately blunt. Jaws extend moderately beyond posterior orbital margin, and maxilla is slightly expanded posteriorly. Posterior margin of operculum tapers to blunt point. Gill rakers number 15 to 18. Dorsal fin originates posterior to pelvic fin base and has 11 to 13 rays. Pectoral fin extends beyond pelvic fin base and has 15 to 17 rays. Anal fin originates posterior to dorsal fin base and has 11 to 14 rays. Vn is small and poorly defined. PVO_2 is above and slightly anterior to PVO_1. PLO is midway between horizontal septum and pectoral fin base. PO number five to seven and are unevenly spaced. VLO is closer to horizontal septum than to pelvic fin base. VO range from 8 to 10 and form wavy line. Single SAO is over or anterior to last VO and is 1.5 times its diameter below horizontal septum. Single Pol is located about 1.5 times its diameter below horizontal septum. AOa number five to seven, and AOp number four to six. Three Prc are present, with Prc_1 and Prc_2 close together and near ventral contour, and Prc_3 at level of horizontal septum. Males and females possess large undivided supracaudal and infracaudal luminous glands. Posterior part of iris of eye is covered with crescent of whitish tissue.

This species occurs in the subtropical waters of the Atlantic, eastern Pacific, and Indian Oceans. In the western Atlantic it occurs from New York to Venezuela, including the Gulf of Mexico and the Caribbean Sea. However, it is uncommon in the Gulf of Mexico. Daytime depths range from 600 to 800 m, and nighttime depths range from 51 to 500 m. Maximum known size is 65 mm SL, and maturity is reached at about 40 mm SL.

REFERENCES: Nafpaktitis et al. 1977; Hulley 1984b, 1986b; Gartner et al. 1987.

Taaningichthys paurolychnus Davy 1972

Taaningichthys paurolychnus is slender and compressed, with a relatively small mouth, and dorsal and anal fins of about the same length. It is distinguished from the other species of the family by the following combination of characters. Snout is moderately blunt. Jaws extend moderately beyond posterior orbital margin, and maxilla is slightly expanded posteriorly. Posterior margin of operculum tapers to blunt point. Gill rakers number 12 to 16. Dorsal fin originates posterior to pelvic fin base and has 11 to 13 rays. Pectoral fin extends beyond pelvic fin base and has 13 to 15 rays. Anal fin originates posterior to dorsal fin base and has 11 to 14 rays. Primary photophores are absent. Small secondary photophores are present on head and between rays of caudal fin. Caudal luminous glands are present, with supracaudal gland ranging from one-third to one-half of infracaudal gland, and infracaudal gland extending length of caudal peduncle. Posterior part of iris of eye is covered with crescent of whitish tissue.

This species occurs worldwide in tropical to subtropical seas at bathypelagic depths. In the western Atlantic it occurs in the Sargasso Sea and the eastern Gulf of Mexico off the Florida Escarpment. It is rarely captured, possibly because of its great depth range. Maximum known size is 95 mm SL, and maturity occurs at 65 mm ST.

REFERENCES: Nafpaktitis et al. 1977; Gartner et al. 1987.

NEOSCOPELIDAE

Neoscopelids are slightly elongate, moderately slender, and compressed, with moderate-sized heads and small to large eyes. They are distinguished from the other family of the order by the following combination of characters. Snout is short and acute. Mouth is terminal and large, with premaxilla excluding greatly expanded maxilla from upper jaw. Jaws have bands of villiform teeth. Palatine, vomer, and basibranchs have bands of villiform teeth. Single long, slender supramaxilla is located along dorsal margin of maxilla. Eye is laterally directed. Gill rakers are well developed and lathlike. Pectoral fin inserts on lower one-half of flank. Dorsal fin originates anterior to midlength, about over pelvic fin base. Pelvic fin originates posterior to pectoral fin base. Anal fin originates well posterior to dorsal fin base and has moderately short base. Dorsal adipose fin is present. Caudal fin is forked. First dorsal, first anal, uppermost pectoral, and outermost pelvic rays are preceded by rudimentary spine in some but not all species. Body is covered with cycloid or, occasionally, ctenoid scales. Lateral line organs are weakly developed. Luminous organs and photophores are present or absent. Swim bladder is generally present.

Neoscopelids occur worldwide in tropical to subtropical seas. Some species are mesopelagic, while others are benthopelagic. There are six species in three genera, and two species in a single genus occur in the Gulf of Mexico.

Key to the Species of the Gulf of Mexico
(Adapted from Nafpaktitis 1977)

1a. Upper series of photophores behind pectoral fin base (LO) number 20 to 22 and extend to end of anal fin base; gill rakers on first arch number 14 or 15
. . . . *Neoscopelus microchir* p. 679

1b. Upper series of photophores behind pectoral fin base (LO) number 12 to 14 and do not reach anal fin origin; gill rakers on first arch number 10 or 11
. . . . *Neoscopelus macrolepidotus* p. 678

Neoscopelus macrolepidotus   Johnson 1863

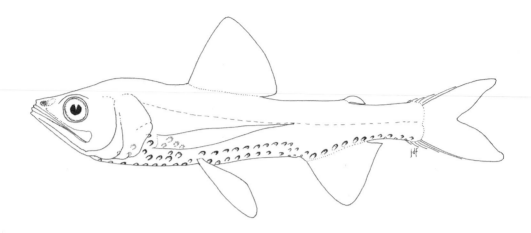

Neoscopelus macrolepidotus is rather fusiform and compressed, with a conical head and large eyes. It is distinguished from the other species of the family by the following combination of characters. Dorsal profile of head is straight to slightly concave. Mouth is oblique. Upper jaw extends to posterior margin of orbit. Lower jaw projects slightly beyond upper jaw. Upper and lower jaws have inner series of enlarged, conical, and depressible teeth and outer band of close-set, villiform teeth. Vomer, palatine, and ectopterygoids have bands of small teeth. Eye is 20% to 22% of head length. Gill rakers on first arch number two on epibranch, one in corner, and seven or eight on lower limb. Those on lower limb are dentigerous plates. Dorsal fin originates slightly anterior to pelvic fin base and has 12 or 13 rays. Pectoral fin extends to near anal fin origin and has 18 or 19 rays. Anal fin has 11 to 13 rays, and base length is equal to or shorter than dorsal fin base. Adipose fin base is over or slightly behind middle of anal fin base. Photophores are arranged in midventral series and in several bilateral series on trunk, and in single series along periphery of tongue. Those in lateral row behind pectoral fin base (LO) extend almost to anal fin origin and number 12 to 14. Large cycloid scales cover body. Swim bladder is present. Vertebrae number 30 or 31. Color is light brown, with operculum, back, and ventral photophore regions dark brown, or head and ventral half of body silvery iridescent. Color in life is dark red, with silvery white belly.

This species occurs in the tropical to subtropical waters of the Atlantic, western Indian, and western Pacific Oceans. In the western Atlantic it occurs in the Straits of Florida and the northern Gulf of Mexico, and off Nicaragua and Suriname. It has been captured from 300 to 800 m near the bottom. Maximum known size is 250 mm SL, and size at maturity is about 150 mm SL.

REFERENCES: Nafpaktitis 1977; Uyeno et al. 1983; Hulley 1984a, 1986c; Burgess and Branstetter 1985.

Neoscopelus microchir Matsubara 1943

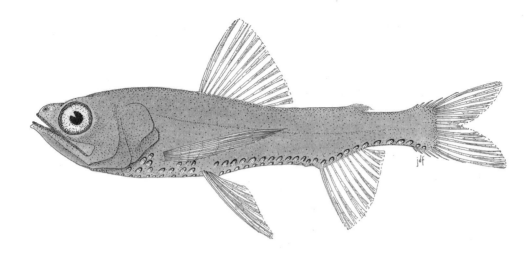

Neoscopelus microchir is rather fusiform and compressed, with a conical head and large eyes. It is distinguished from the other species of the family by the following combination of characters. Dorsal profile of head is straight. Mouth is oblique. Upper jaw extends to slightly behind posterior margin of orbit. Lower jaw projects slightly beyond upper jaw. Upper and lower jaws have inner series of enlarged, conical, and depressible teeth, and outer band of close-set, villiform teeth. Vomer, palatine, and ectopterygoids have bands of small teeth. Eye is 23% to 25% of head length. Gill rakers on first arch number 3 on epibranch, 1 in corner, and 10 or 11 on lower limb. Those on lower limb are dentigerous plates. Dorsal fin originates over, to slightly anterior to, pelvic fin base and has 12 or 13 rays. Pectoral fin extends to near anus and has 16 or 17 rays. Anal fin has 10 to 12 rays, and base is shorter than dorsal fin base. Adipose fin base is over posterior one-half of anal fin base. Photophores are arranged in midventral series and in several bilateral series on trunk, and in single series along periphery of tongue. Those of lateral series posterior to pectoral fin base (LO) extend to end of anal fin base and number 20 to 22. Large cycloid scales cover body. Swim bladder is present. Vertebrae number 30 or 31. Color is light brown, with operculum, back, and ventral photophore regions dark brown, or head and ventral half of body silvery iridescent. Color in life is dark red, with belly silvery white.

This species occurs in the tropical to subtropical waters of the Atlantic, Indian, and western Pacific Oceans. In the western Atlantic it occurs in the Straits of Florida and the northern Gulf of Mexico, and off Jamaica and Honduras. It has been captured from 250 to 700 m near the bottom. Maximum known size is 305 mm SL, and size at maturity is about 120 mm SL.

REFERENCES: Nafpaktitis 1977; Hulley 1984a, 1986c; Burgess and Branstetter 1985.

LAMPRIDIFORMES

Lampridiformes are thought to be the sister group to the remainder of the Acanthomorpha (Polymyxiformes, Paracanthopterygii, and Acanthopterygii). The composition of the order has changed slightly and may change in the future with further study. The order contains 7 families, and 5 of these occur in the Gulf of Mexico.

Key to the Families of the Gulf of Mexico
(Adapted from Heemstra 1986)

1a. Body oval shaped; all fins well developed; caudal fin forked
. . . . .Lamprididae p. 681

1b. Body elongate; pelvic, anal, and caudal fins present or absent. 2

2a. Eye tubular, directed forward or upward; mouth greatly protrusible; lower jaw length equal to head length
. . . . Stylephoridae p. 687

2b. Eye not tubular, directed laterally; mouth more or less protrusible; lower jaw shorter than head length. 3

3a. Anus near caudal fin; maxilla width less than one-half eye diameter; upper jaw slightly protrusible
. . . . .Lophotidae p. 683

3b. Anus near middle of body; maxilla width greater than one-half eye diameter; upper jaw very protrusible. 4

4a. Body greatly elongated, depth 1.7% to 6.7% of SL; dorsal fin with about 400 rays, rays without minute spines or prickles along lateral edges . . . . Regalecidae p. 685

4b. Body moderately elongate, depth 10% to 25% of SL; dorsal fin with 150 to 200 rays, rays with minute spines or prickles along lateral edges . . . . Trachipteridae p. 689

LAMPRIDIDAE   Opahs

The opahs are compressed and deep bodied, with long dorsal and anal fins and protrusible jaws. They are distinguished from the other families of the order by the following combination of characters. Dorsal profile of head is convex, and snout is of moderate length. Mouth is terminal, relatively small, and strongly oblique. Eye is laterally located and is of moderate size. Jaws have minute teeth in juveniles but lack teeth in adults. Gill rakers are well developed. Branchiostegal rays number six. Pectoral fin is long and rather falcate and inserts horizontally above midflank. Dorsal fin lacks spines and consists of high, recurved anterior lobe and short posterior section. Pelvic fin inserts slightly behind pectoral fin base and is long and falcate. Anal fin is similar in length to dorsal fin but lacks recurved anterior lobe. Caudal peduncle is slender and of moderate length. Caudal fin is well developed and deeply forked. Scales are cycloid, minute, and deciduous. Lateral line is well developed and strongly arched over pectoral fin base. Swim bladder is well developed and anteriorly bifurcate.

Opahs occur worldwide in tropical to temperate oceanic seas at lower epipelagic depths. They feed on squids and fishes. Swimming is accomplished by flapping of the pectoral fins. There are two species in a single genus, and one species occurs in the Gulf of Mexico.

Lampris guttatus   (Brünnich 1788)
Opah

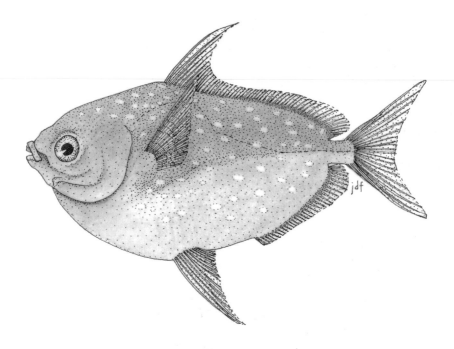

Lampris guttatus is compressed and deep bodied, with protrusible jaws and long dorsal and anal fins. It is distinguished from the other species of the family by a combination of the following characters. Body depth of specimens greater than 50 cm SL is 58% to 68% of SL. Gill rakers on first arch number 2 on epibranch and 14 on lower limb. Pectoral fin has 22 to 25, dorsal fin has 49 to 58, pelvic fin has 13 to 17, and anal fin has 38 to 41 rays. Pelvic fin inserts posterior to pectoral fin origin. Color is purple to pink, with opaque whitish spots over body. Fins and anterior part of snout are red. Small juveniles lack spots.

This species occurs worldwide in tropical to temperate oceanic waters at epipelagic to mesopelagic depths. It has been captured to depths of 400 m. In the western Atlantic it occurs from the Grand Banks to the West Indies, including the Gulf of Mexico. Food consists of squids and fishes, including some benthic species. Maximum known size is 180 cm SL and 100 kg.

REFERENCES: Palmer and Oelschlager 1976; Rosenblatt and Johnson 1976; Heemstra 1986a; Palmer 1986a; C. R. Robins et al. 1986; Boschung 1992.

LOPHOTIDAE Crestfishes

The crestfishes are very elongate, compressed, and ribbonlike, with slightly protrusible jaws, tapering trunk and tail, and rudimentary or no pelvic fins. They are distinguished from the other families of the order by the following combination of characters. Head has elevated occipital crest. Mouth is small and terminal, and jaw teeth are conical and in one to three irregular rows. Small patch of teeth occurs in vomer. Pectoral fin is small and has horizontal base on lower flank. Dorsal fin originates on occipital crest of head anterior to level of mouth and extends to near caudal fin. Anteriormost dorsal fin rays are elongate and filamentous. Pelvic fin is very small and inserts laterally below or slightly posterior to pectoral fin base or is absent. Anal fin is short and is located near caudal fin. Caudal fin is short and pointed. Skin is covered with small, thin, deciduous scales. Lateral line is covered with smooth plates. Swim bladder is present, and ink sac located posterior to swim bladder empties into cloaca.

Crestfishes occur worldwide in tropical to warm temperate seas at mesopelagic depths. There are between two and six species in two genera, and one species occurs in the Gulf of Mexico.

Lophotus lacepede Bosc 1817
Crestfish

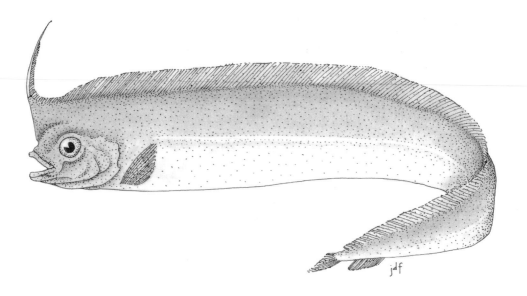

Lophotus lacepede is very elongate, compressed, and ribbonlike, with the head produced dorsally and anterior dorsal fin rays moderately elongated. It is distinguished from the other species of the family by the following combination of characters. Anterior profile of head is vertical or inclined slightly forward. Single nostril is present on each side of front of snout. Jaw teeth are arranged in three irregular rows in both jaws. Gill rakers on first arch number three or four on epibranch and seven to nine on lower limb. Pectoral fin has 14 to 17 rays. Dorsal fin originates above mouth and has 220 to 263 rays, with first ray elongated and swollen. Pelvic fin is minute, located on side of body behind pectoral fin base, and consists of 5 or 6 rays. Anal fin has 12 to 20 rays. Scales are very thin, oblong, and cycloid. Vertebrae number 124 to 153. Color is silvery, occasionally with silvery spots. Fins are red to pinkish.

This species occurs worldwide in tropical to warm temperate seas at mesopelagic depths. In the western Atlantic it occurs from Florida to Brazil, including the eastern Gulf of Mexico off Florida. Food consists of squids and fishes, such as engraulids. Maximum known size is 189 cm SL.

REFERENCES: Goin and Erdman 1951; Heemstra 1986b; Palmer 1986d; C. R. Robins et al. 1986.

REGALECIDAE Oarfishes

Oarfishes are very elongate and compressed, with a very protrusible upper jaw, a very long dorsal fin, and a caudal fin that is reduced or absent. They are distinguished from the other families of the order by the following combination of characters. Snout is short to moderately long, and concave to convex in dorsal profile. Mouth is small and strongly oblique. Eye is small to moderate in size and is located laterally. Gill rakers on first arch are numerous. Pectoral fin has vertical base on lower or midflank and is poorly developed. Dorsal fin originates either anterior to or slightly posterior to center of eye and extends to near base of tail. First few dorsal rays are elongated and leaf shaped. Pelvic fin has one to five rays. Anal fin is absent. Scales are absent. Lateral line runs along lower flank and consists of tube. Swim bladder is absent.

Oarfishes occur worldwide in tropical to temperate oceanic waters at epipelagic or mesopelagic depths. There are two species in separate genera, and one species occurs in the Gulf of Mexico.

Regalecus glesne   Ascanius 1772
Oarfish

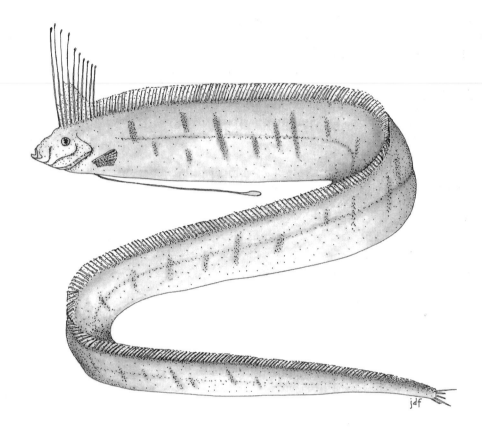

Regalecus glesne is very elongate and compressed, with very protrusible jaws, a very long dorsal fin, and a reduced or rudimentary caudal fin. It is distinguished from the other species of the family by the following combination of characters. Head is short, and dorsal profile anterior to dorsal fin is strongly concave. Single nostril is located on each side of snout just in front of maxillary symphysis. Mouth is toothless or has small teeth at front of lower jaw. Gill rakers on first arch number 7 on epibranch and 36 on lower limb. Pectoral fin is short and has horizontal base and 14 rays. Dorsal fin originates anterior to center of eye and has 10 to 12 elongated rays with fleshy membrane at tips, and 400 succeeding shorter rays. Pelvic fin in adults consists of single elongate ray fringed with paddlelike membrane at tip of fin. Caudal fin of juveniles has 4 free rays, and caudal fin of adults is rudimentary. Color is silvery with oblique dusky bars, head is bluish, and fins are deep red.

This species occurs worldwide in tropical to warm temperate seas at lower epipelagic and mesopelagic depths. In the western Atlantic it occurs from Bermuda to Florida and the Gulf of Mexico. It swims vertically with head up by undulatory movements of the body. Food consists of squids, euphausid crustaceans, and fishes. Maximum known size is about 8 m SL, but there are unconfirmed reports of specimens over twice this length.

REFERENCES: Trunov 1982; Heemstra 1986c; Palmer 1986b; C. R. Robins et al. 1986.

STYLEPHORIDAE

The stylephorids are elongate, moderately to extremely compressed, and ribbonlike, with tubular eyes, highly protrusible jaws, and a very long dorsal fin. They are distinguished from the other species of the family by the following combination of characters. Snout is of moderate length, with a concave dorsal profile. Mouth is small, with lower jaw extending beyond upper jaw. Premaxilla lacks teeth, but maxilla has partially biserial row of teeth. Gill rakers are short and spikelike. Operculum is small and thin. Preoperculum has oblique ridge terminating in posteriorly directed vertical spine. Pectoral fin has horizontal base and is located on flank. Dorsal fin originates at nape and extends to near caudal fin base, with first two rays longer than remainder of rays. Pelvic fin inserts below pectoral fin base and consists of a single ray. Anal fin is short and originates just anterior to midlength. Caudal fin is divided into upper and lower portions, with upper lobe consisting of five to seven rays directed obliquely upward and lower portion consisting of two very long and stout rays. Scales are lacking. Lateral line is a simple segmented tube arching downward from base of pectoral fin and running ventrally along body and onto caudal fin between the elongated lower rays. Stomach is divided into two chambers.

Stylephorids occur worldwide at mesopelagic or bathypelagic depths. They are inactive swimmers that generally hover vertically in the water column with head up. Food consists of copepods obtained by pipettelike feeding. They are capable of very rapid protrusion and inflation of mouth cavity. The family consists of a single species, and it occurs in the Gulf of Mexico.

Stylephorus chordatus Shaw 1791
Tube-eye

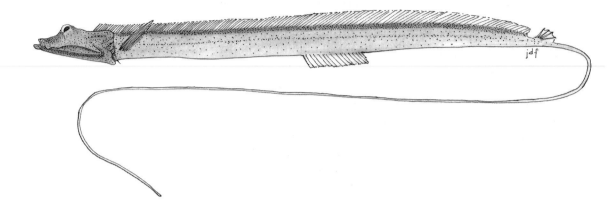

Stylephorus chordatus is elongate, moderately to extremely compressed, and ribbonlike, with a highly protrusible mouth, tubular eyes, and an elongate dorsal fin. It is distinguished by the following combination of characters. Gill rakers number seven to nine. Pectoral fin has 10 or 11, dorsal fin has 110 to 124, pelvic fin has 1, and anal fin has 14 to 17 ray(s). Vertebrae number 50 to 53. Color is silvery, with head dark violet and eyes silvery.

This species occurs worldwide in tropical to subtropical seas at mesopelagic to bathypelagic depths. In the western Atlantic it occurs from southern Florida to the Lesser Antilles, including the Gulf of Mexico. Specimens occasionally wash ashore along the south Florida coast. It swims in a vertical position with head upward and may make vertical migrations. The elongate caudal filament may function as a sea anchor to increase stability. Food consists of copepods. Maximum known size is 280 mm SL.

REFERENCES: Hulley 1986; Johnson and Berman 1986; C. R. Robins et al. 1986.

TRACHIPTERIDAE   Ribbonfishes

Ribbonfishes are elongate and ribbonlike, with a very protractile upper jaw, a relatively deep head, and a tapering trunk. They are distinguished from the other families of the order by the following combination of characters. Head is short and has paper-thin bones. Snout slopes strongly to mouth. Mouth is small, almost vertical, and subterminal. Jaws, vomer, and usually palatine have few pointed teeth. Pectoral fin inserts horizontally and is short in adults but elongate in juveniles. Dorsal fin originates above or slightly posterior to eye and extends to near caudal fin base. Pelvic fin inserts on ventral midline below pectoral fin base and consists of three to nine rays. Anal fin is absent. Caudal fin is either horizontal or in two lobes, with upper one pointing obliquely upward and lower one rudimentary. All elongated fin rays are reduced with growth. Skin is covered with bony tubercles pierced with numerous pores in adults. Juveniles are either naked or covered with deciduous cycloid scales. Lateral line consists of bony plates, each of which is armed with a single spine, and runs diagonally downward to caudal fin base or extends onto lower caudal fin lobe. Swim bladder is rudimentary or absent.

Ribbonfishes occur worldwide in tropical to temperate oceanic waters at mesopelagic depths. They probably assume a vertical posture by means of undulatory action of dorsal fin. Food consists of squids and fishes. There are about eight species in three genera, and two species in separate genera occur in the Gulf of Mexico.

Key to the Species of the Gulf of Mexico
(Adapted from Heemstra and Kannemeyer 1986; Palmer 1986c)

1a. Lateral line runs along ventral edge of tail and consists of row of elongate, bony plates; ventral margin of body scalloped in specimens less than 80 cm SL, more or less straight in larger specimens; body depth 34.5% to 66.7% of distance from snout to anus; young stages with bulbous flaps on dorsal and anal fins; lower caudal fin lobe not reduced to stump in adults. . . . . *Zu cristatus* p. 691
1b. Lateral line runs above ventral edge of tail and consists of row of bony tubercles; ventral margin of body straight; body depth 24.4% to 27% of distance from snout to anus; young stages without bulbous flaps on dorsal and pelvic fins; lower caudal fin lobe reduced to stump in adults
. . . . *Trachipterus arcticus* p. 690

Trachipterus arcticus (Brünnich 1771)
Deal fish

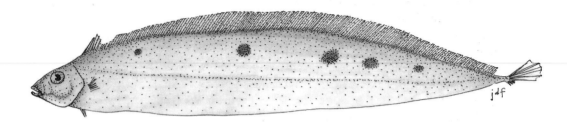

Trachipterus arcticus is elongate and oval shaped, with ventral margin of body straight and greatest depth of body at one-quarter to one-third of length. It is distinguished from the other species of the family by the following combination of characters. Head is short, and dorsal profile is convex. Palatine bones lack teeth. Pectoral fin has 9 to 11 rays. Dorsal fin consists of 5 or 6 elongate rays followed by 144 to 184 shorter rays. Pelvic fin has 5 or 6 rays in young but may be absent in adults. Caudal fin is fan shaped and has 8 rays in upper lobe and 5 or 6 rays in short lower lobe. Lateral line runs above ventral margin of tail.

Color is silvery, with one to five dark spots along body. Dorsal fin is red. Spots are absent on large specimens.

This species occurs in the North Atlantic in warm temperate seas at mesopelagic depths. In the western Atlantic it occurs from New York to south Florida and in the Gulf of Mexico. Food consists of squids and small fishes. Maximum known size is 2.5 m SL, but specimens are rare longer than 1 m SL. The western Atlantic population may represent a new species.

REFERENCES: Palmer 1961, 1986c; C. R. Robins et al. 1986; Boschung 1992.

Zu cristatus (Bonelli 1819)
Scalloped ribbonfish

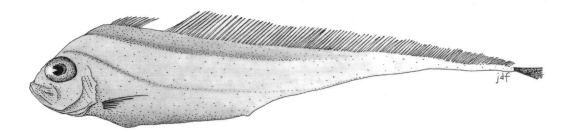

Zu cristatus is elongate, moderately compressed, and tapering, with a scalloped ventral margin in juvenile specimens. It is distinguished from the other species of the family by the following combination of characters. Dorsal profile anterior to dorsal fin is straight to slightly convex. Upper jaw has 12 to 18 canine teeth, and lower jaw has 8 to 16. Vomer has 4 teeth, and palatine has 1 to 3 teeth. Eye diameter is 13% to 16% of distance between snout and anus. Body depth in adults is 20% to 26% of SL. Body in prejuveniles is abruptly constricted behind anus. Pectoral fin has 10 to 12 rays. Dorsal fin originates over posterior margin of orbit and consists of 5 or 6 elongate rays followed by 125 to 145 shorter rays. Pelvic fin has 5 to 7 rays that are long in juveniles but rudimentary in adults. Caudal fin consists of upper lobe of 8 to 12 rays and lower lobe of 1 to 5 rays. Lateral line runs along ventral margin of tail, and lateral line scales along tail are spiny and resemble bucklers. Vertebrae number 63 to 69. Adults are silvery gray and slightly paler ventrally, with scarlet dorsal fin and reddish black caudal fin. Juveniles have greatly elongated anterior dorsal fin rays, pelvic fin rays, and lowermost caudal fin ray. They are silvery, with about six wavy, dark vertical bars on upper part of body, four bars on lower part of body, and six complete bars on tail; caudal fin is largely black.

The scalloped ribbonfish occurs in the tropical to warm temperate Atlantic and Indo-West Pacific Oceans at epipelagic and mesopelagic depths. In the western Atlantic it occurs from Bermuda and south Florida to Cuba and the northern Gulf of Mexico. Food consists of squids and small fishes. Maximum known size is 1 m SL.

REFERENCES: Fitch 1964; Uyeno et al. 1983; Heemstra and Kannemeyer 1986, 1986; C. R. Robins et al. 1986; Boschung 1992.

POLYMIXIIFORMES

Polymixiiformes are the sister group of the Paracanthopterygii and Acanthopterygii. The order includes one family that is present in the Gulf of Mexico.

POLYMIXIIDAE   Beardfishes

The beardfishes are moderately deep bodied and moderately compressed, with large eyes and two chin barbels on the posterior section of the lower jaw. Snout is blunt and projects beyond lower jaw. Maxilla extends beyond posterior margin of orbit and is very broad posteriorly. Mouth is large and horizontal. Jaws have close-set, villiform teeth. Palatine, vomer, tongue, and endopterygoids have short teeth. Two supramaxillae are located on dorsal margin of maxilla. Branchiostegal rays number 7, with 3 modified and curving around base of barbels. Gill rakers are located on epibranch and lower limb of first arch. Pectoral fin inserts on lower one-half of flank. Dorsal fin is long and elevated anteriorly but is low posteriorly, and has four to six spines and 26 to 38 rays. Pelvic fin inserts slightly anterior to dorsal fin origin, is subthoracic (not connected with pectoral girdle), and consists of 1 spinelike ray and 7 rays. Anal fin is of moderate length, is elevated anteriorly, and has four short spines and 13 to 17 rays. Caudal fin is deeply forked and has 16 branched rays, and spines on dorsal and ventral bases. Head and body are covered with ctenoid scales. Swim bladder is present and is physoclistous.

Beardfishes occur worldwide in warm seas on continental shelves and slopes from depths of 80 to 770 m. There are about five species in a single genus, and two species occur in the Gulf of Mexico.

Key to the Species of the Gulf of Mexico
(Adapted from Woods and Sonoda 1973)

1a. Segmented dorsal fin rays 27 to 30; gill rakers on first arch 16 to 22, with 9 to 13 on lower limb
. . . . *Polymixia lowei* p. 693

1b. Segmented dorsal fin rays 34 to 37; gill rakers on first arch 10 to 13, with 7 to 9 on lower limb
. . . . *Polymixia nobilis* p. 694

Polymixia lowei Günther 1859
Beardfish

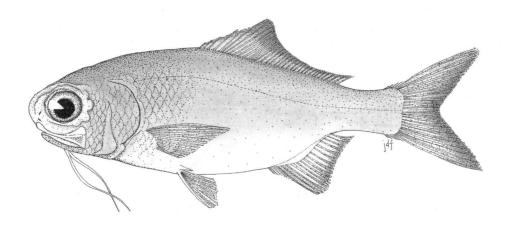

Polymixia lowei is of moderate depth and is moderately compressed, with a tapering caudal peduncle and a relatively short dorsal fin. It is distinguished from the other species of the family by the following combination of characters. Adipose snout is rounded and extends beyond premaxilla. Lower jaw is short and fits inside upper jaw. Head is 32% to 38%, snout length is 5.4% to 7.2%, eye is 10.5% to 13%, chin barbel is 22.5% to 30.6%, and body depth is 36% of SL. Preoperculum extends obliquely posteroventrally, with upper portions membranous and lower portions and angles weakly serrated. Posterior margin of operculum is rounded and with small, triangular, membranous spines. Gill rakers are slender, short, and number 6 to 8 on epibranch, 1 in corner, and 9 to 12 on lower limb. Dorsal fin has five slender spines and 27 to 30 rays. Pectoral fin has 1 spinelike ray and 14 rays. Pelvic fin has 1 spinelike ray and 6 rays. Anal fin has four slender spines and 14 to 16 rays. Lateral line scales number 33 to 35. Vertebrae number 29 or 30. Color is bluish gray, with snout light grayish, barbels white basally, breast and belly white, and dorsal and caudal fins black tipped.

This species occurs in the western Atlantic from New Jersey to French Guiana, including the northern Gulf of Mexico and the Caribbean Sea. Food consists of crustaceans and fishes. Maximum known size is 198 mm SL.

REFERENCES: Woods and Sonoda 1973; Uyeno et al. 1983; C. R. Robins et al. 1986; Boschung 1992.

Polymixia nobilis Lowe 1838
Stout breadfish

Polymixia nobilis is of moderate depth and is moderately compressed, with a thick, slightly tapering caudal peduncle and a relatively long dorsal fin. It is distinguished from the other species of the family by the following combination of characters. Adipose snout is rounded. Lower jaw is short and fits inside upper jaw. Head is 34% to 36.7%, snout is 6.7% to 8.6%, eye is 9.9% to 13.3%, chin barbel is 23% to 33%, and body depth is 36% to 40% of SL. Preoperculum extends obliquely posteroventrally, with angles serrated. Posterior margin of operculum is rounded. Gill rakers are slender, short, and number three on epibranch, one in corner, and six to nine on lower limb of first arch. Dorsal fin has four or five slender spines and 34 to 37 rays. Pectoral fin has 1 spinous ray and 14 to 15 rays. Pelvic fin has 1 spinous ray and 6 rays. Anal fin has three or four spines and 15 or 16 rays. Lateral line scales number 34 to 37. Vertebrae number 29. Color is dark brownish gray, with operculum dark and dorsal, anal, and caudal rays dusky. Tips of anterior dorsal fin rays and tips of caudal fin rays are dark to black.

This species occurs in the tropical Atlantic Ocean. In the western Atlantic it occurs in the Gulf of Mexico and the Caribbean Sea at 100 to 770 m. Maximum known size is 350 mm SL.

REFERENCES: Woods and Sonoda 1973; Heemstra 1986g; Hureau 1986.

OPHIDIIFORMES

Ophidiiformes, Percopsiformes, Gadiformes, Batrachoidiformes, and Lophiiformes make up the Paracanthopterygii that, in turn, are the sister group of the Acanthopterygii. The percopsiforms are freshwater fishes that do not occur in the Gulf of Mexico. The ophidiiforms are considered the sister group of the remaining paracanthopterygians, but the interrelationships within the order remain poorly known and it may not be monophyletic. It comprises the Ophidioidei and Bythitoidei. The ophidioids consist of the Carapidae and Ophidiidae, both of which occur in the Gulf. The bythitoids consist of three families, and two of these, Bythitidae and Aphyonidae, occur in the Gulf. The bythitoids may be more closely related to the gadiforms, batrachoidiforms, and lophiiforms than to the ophidioids, but herein they are treated as ophidiiforms, pending additional research.

Key to the Families of the Gulf of Mexico
(Adapted from Cohen and Nielsen 1978)

1a. Anterior nostril widely separated from upper lip in most (Fig. 147); median basibranchial tooth plates present or absent; pelvic fin, when present, at level of preoperculum or anterior to preoperculum; males without intromittent organ 2

1b. Anterior nostril slightly separated from upper lip in most (Fig. 148); median basibranchial tooth plate absent; pelvic fin, when present, at level of preoperculum; males with intromittent organ 3

2a. Supramaxilla absent; anal fin rays longer than corresponding dorsal fin rays . . . . Carapidae p. 696

2b. Supramaxilla present; anal fin rays equal to or shorter than corresponding dorsal fin rays . . . . Ophidiidae p. 700

3a. Scales generally present; swim bladder present; precaudal vertebrae 9 to 22 . . . . Bythitidae p. 742

3b. Scales absent; swim bladder absent; precaudal vertebrae 26 to 48 . . . . Aphyonidae p. 738

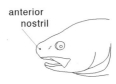

anterior nostril

FIG 147

anterior nostril

FIG 148

CARAPIDAE Pearlfishes

Pearlfishes are slender and distinctly tapering posteriorly, with anal fin rays distinctly longer than corresponding dorsal fin rays, and anus anteriorly located. They are distinguished from the other families of the order by the following combination of characters. Snout is acute to slightly blunt and equal to or slightly overhanging lower jaw. Mouth is large and from nearly horizontal to distinctly oblique. Anterior nostril is widely separated from upper lip. Chin barbel is absent. Teeth range from small and villiform to fanglike and occur in jaws, vomer, and palatine. Opercular spine is present. Fin spines are absent. Pectoral fin ranges from rather large to absent and, when present, is located at or below mid-flank. Dorsal fin originates from above pectoral fin base to posterior to appressed pectoral fin and ranges from longer than anal fin to shorter than anal fin. Pelvic fin is generally absent, but when present, consists of two filamentous rays. Scales are absent. Swim bladder is present.

Carapids occur worldwide in tropical to temperate seas from near shore to 1,600 m. Species are benthic and either free living or inquilines within shallow-water invertebrate hosts such as bivalves, holothurians, and asteroids. All species have a unique larval form, "vexillifer," that is pelagic and has a highly modified first dorsal fin ray or vexillum. Vexillum is extremely elongate and often is ornamented with fleshy protuberances and pigment. The vexillum is also motile, well vascularized and innervated by cranial nerves, and is lost at metamorphosis. Development is oviparous. There are 31 species in seven genera, and 3 species in separate genera occur in the Gulf of Mexico.

Key to the Species of the Gulf of Mexico
(Adapted from Markle and Olney 1990)

1a. Dorsal fin origin anterior to anal fin origin; pectoral fin rays 24 or 25 . . . . *Snyderidia canina* p. 699

1b. Dorsal fin origin posterior to anal fin origin; pectoral fin rays 17 to 20 2

2a. Upper and lower jaws with one to several large symphyseal fangs; cardiform teeth absent . . . *Echiodon dawsoni* p. 698

2b. Upper and lower jaws without enlarged symphyseal fangs; cardiform teeth present . . . . . *Carapus bermudensis* p. 697

Carapus bermudensis (Jones 1874)
Pearlfish

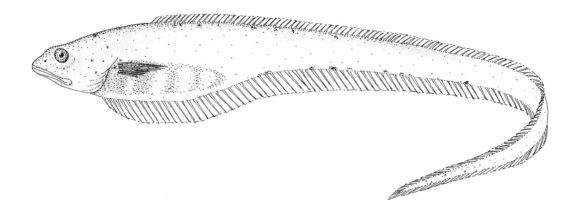

Carapus bermudensis is elongate and uniformly tapering posteriorly, with a very short trunk and anus located under throat. It is distinguished from the other species of the family by the following combination of characters. Snout is moderately acute and slightly overhangs lower jaw. Eye is of moderate size. Premaxillary teeth are small, conical, and in several series, with innermost along anterior one-third of length slightly enlarged and slightly recurved, and outermost cardiform. Innermost teeth of lower jaw are short, blunt, and in several rows, and outermost are enlarged and conical. Vomer has median row of five to nine large teeth flanked by row of short, blunt teeth. Palatine teeth are short, blunt, and progressively smaller from front to back. Maxilla is free and movable. Pectoral fin is slender and has 17 to 20 rays. Dorsal fin originates over 17th to 25th anal ray. Pelvic fin is absent. Precaudal vertebrae number 17 or 18. Dorsal fin rays to 31st vertebra number 36 to 45, and anal fin rays to 31st vertebra number 53 to 62. Color in life is translucent with silvery bands along flank, with vertebral column pigmented and silvery patch on cheek. Color in preservative is tan, with stellate melanophores on cheek, at pectoral fin base, and along side and tail. Large melanophores form saddlelike patterns dorsally from nape to tip of tail.

This species occurs in the western Atlantic from the Carolinas and Bermuda to central Brazil, including the Gulf of Mexico and the Caribbean Sea. It generally occurs on or near shallow grass beds to 34 m, and it occupies the body cavity of sea cucumbers during the day and forages during the night. However, dark-pigmented specimens of this species occur between 48 and 235 m, where they are associated with deep-water sea cucumbers. Vexillifer larvae are very elongate and have vexillum well separated from first normal dorsal fin ray, and ring of stellate melanophores anterodorsal to nasal rosette. Maximum known size is 197 mm SL and 26.1 mm head length.

REFERENCES: Smith and Tyler 1969; Dawson 1971b; Haburay et al. 1974; Hoese and Moore 1977; Trott 1981; C. R. Robins et al. 1986; Markle and Olney 1990; Boschung 1992; Tyler et al. 1992.

Echiodon dawsoni   Williams and Shipp 1982
Chain pearlfish

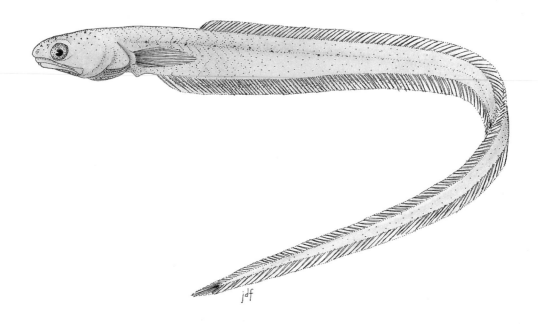

Echiodon dawsoni is elongate and moderately tapering posteriorly, with a very short trunk, symphyseal fangs in jaws, and anus located under throat. It is distinguished from the other species of the family by the following combination of characters. Snout is moderately acute and slightly overhangs lower jaw. Eye is of moderate to large size. Upper and lower jaws have one or two large, curved fangs on either side of symphysis and several series of small, conical teeth posterior to fangs; fangs and smaller teeth are separated by toothless space (diastema). Vomer has patch of small, conical teeth. Palatine teeth are small, conical, and in several series. Maxilla is movable. Pectoral fin is moderately slender and has 17 to 20 rays. Dorsal fin originates over 11th or 12th anal fin ray. Pelvic fin is absent. Precaudal vertebrae number 21 to 25. Dorsal fin rays number 28 to 35 to 31st vertebra, and anal fin rays number 39 to 43 to 31st vertebra. Color in preservative is cream to tan, with large stellate melanophores over brain, ventral margin of eye, snout, lower jaw, and vertebral column.

This species occurs in the western Atlantic from Cape Cod and Bermuda to southern Brazil, including the Gulf of Mexico and the Caribbean Sea between 76 and 173 m. It is thought to be free living and not an inquiline. Vexillifer larvae are very elongate and have vexillum adjacent to first normal dorsal fin ray, short gut that does not trail from body, head length less than 10% of body length, short anal fin radials that are not visible through body, and vexillum lacking wavy ventral contour.

REFERENCES: Olney and Markle 1979; Williams and Shipp 1982; Markle and Olney 1990; Boschung 1992.

Snyderidia canina   Gilbert 1905

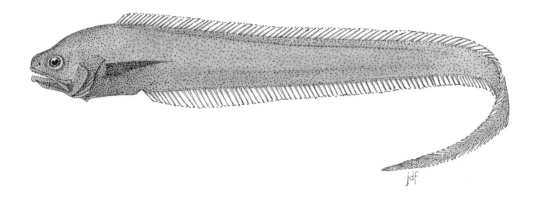

Snyderidia canina is moderately elongate and tapering posteriorly from origin of dorsal fin, with dorsal fin origin anterior to anal fin origin. It is distinguished from the other species of the family by the following combination of characters. Snout is moderately acute, and lower jaw projects beyond upper jaw. Eye is of moderate size. Premaxilla has large, fanglike teeth anteriorly and three or four rows of short, sharply pointed, depressible teeth posteriorly. Lower jaw has one or two large canine teeth anteriorly and short, stout teeth that increase in size posteriorly. Vomer has one large canine tooth and cluster of short, strong teeth. Palatine has single row of teeth. Maxilla is movable and lacks sheath posteriorly. Gill rakers on first arch number 3 on inner row and 12 rudimentary rakers on outer row. Pectoral fin is long and pointed and has 24 or 25 rays. Dorsal fin originates at about one-fourth of length of appressed pectoral fin. Pelvic fin is absent. Anus is located at about one-half length of appressed pectoral fin. Precaudal vertebrae number 15. Lateral line is absent on body. Color is brownish, with numerous rows of small black spots. Peritoneum and lining of mouth and gill cavities are black.

This species occurs in tropical to warm temperate seas worldwide at 260 to 909 m, except for the eastern Pacific. In the western Atlantic it occurs in the Gulf of Mexico and the Caribbean Sea. It has not been found in sea cucumbers, but large sea cucumbers were collected in a trawl with the specimens of this species. The specimens may have left their hosts in the trawl (C. R. Robins, pers. com., July 1995). Maximum known size is 351 mm TL and 48 mm head length, but the caudal part of the body is missing in many specimens.

REFERENCES: Robins and Nielsen 1970 (as *Snyderidia bothrops*); Olney and Markle 1979; Uyeno et al. 1983; Williams 1983; Markle and Olney 1990.

OPHIDIIDAE   Cusk-eels

Cusk-eels are relatively robust to moderately slender, and compressed and tapering posteriorly, with dorsal fin rays as long as or longer than anal fin rays, and scales present on body. They are distinguished from the other families of the order by the following combination of characters. Snout is acute to moderately blunt and is equal to or slightly overhangs lower jaw. Mouth is large and horizontal or oblique, with upper jaw extending to or beyond posterior margin of eye. Supramaxilla is present on posterodorsal margin of maxilla. Chin barbel is present or absent. Teeth are granular or variously enlarged and occur in jaws, vomer, and palatine. Opercular spine is present or absent. Fin spines are absent. Pectoral fin varies from small to extremely large and is located at or below midflank. Dorsal fin origin ranges from above pectoral fin base to above appressed pectoral fin tip. Pelvic fin, when present, consists of one or two filamentous rays. Anal fin originates immediately behind anus and urogenital openings. Scales are cycloid or are nonimbricate prickles. Swim bladder is present.

Cusk-eels occur worldwide in tropical to temperate seas. Species are benthic or benthopelagic from the shoreline to 8,000 m. Development is oviparous, and larvae lack vexillum. There are about 209 species in 46 genera, and 35 species in 19 genera occur in the Gulf of Mexico.

Key to the Species of the Gulf of Mexico
(Adapted in part from Cohen and Nielsen 1978; C. R. Robins et al. 1986)

1a. Barbels on snout and chin . . . . *Brotula barbata* p. 711
1b. Barbels absent on snout and chin 2
2a. Scales on body small, nonimbricate (nonoverlapping)
    prickles . . . . *Brotulotaenia brevicauda* p. 712
2b. Scales on body cycloid 3
3a. Pelvic fin consists of two rays located beneath eye 4
3b. Pelvic fin consists of one or two rays located below pre-
    operculum, or is absent 17
4a. Operculum with strong spine, extending far beyond rear
    margin of head 16
4b. Operculum with or without strong spine, but if present,
    not projecting far beyond rear margin of head 5
5a. Body scales in regular rows and rounded 6
5b. Body scales set at oblique angles to each other and elongate
    or elliptical 10
6a. Body without color pattern except for dark edge on dorsal
    fin, and occasionally, on anal fin
    . . . . *Lepophidium brevibarbe* p. 716

29b. Head relatively slender; dorsal profile of head straight; preopercular spines well developed
. . . . *Monomitopus magnus* p. 723

30a. Eye diameter less than snout length 31

30b. Eye diameter equal to or greater than snout length 32

31a. Snout distinctly inflated; maxilla sheathed; developed gill rakers 12 or more . . . . . *Barathrodemus manatinus* p. 706

31b. Snout not inflated; maxilla not sheathed; developed gill rakers 7 . . . . *Bassogigas gillii* p. 707

32a. Preoperculum with one spine at angle 33

32b. Preoperculum with two spines at angle. 34

33a. Body and fins lack pigment patterns, ocelli and stripes absent. . . . . *Neobythites unicolor* p. 727

33b. Body and fins with pigment patterns, body and dorsal fin with series of blotches . . . . *Neobythites gilli* p. 725

34a. Upper part of body marbled with brownish pigment; dorsal fin with black band . . . . *Neobythites marginatus* p. 726

34b. Upper part of body with two indistinct dark bands; dorsal fin without black band . . . . . *Neobythites elongatus* p. 724

Acanthonus armatus   Günther 1878

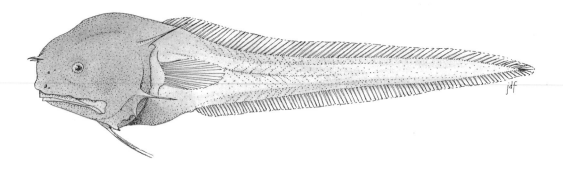

Acanthonus armatus is big headed, tapers posteriorly from posterior part of head, and has a bifid spine on snout and prominent preopercular and opercular spines. It is distinguished from the other species of the family by the following combination of characters. Snout is strongly rounded and overhangs mouth. Mouth is large, nearly horizontal, and extends considerably beyond eye. Eye is small. Small, conical, slightly recurved teeth occur in jaws, vomer, and palatine. Single basibranchial tooth plate is present. Gill rakers on first arch number 4 or 5 on epibranch and 16 to 22 on lower limb. Branchiostegal rays number 8 or 9. Head length is 24% to 30%, snout length is 9.1% to 10%, eye length is 2.1% to 2.6%, predorsal length is 25.5% to 32.5%, and preanal length is 29% to 37.5% of SL. Pectoral fin is of moderate size and has 16 to 19 rays. Dorsal fin originates above pectoral fin base and has 100 to 108 rays. Pelvic fins are located close together below or slightly posterior to orbits, and each consists of 2 filamentous rays. Anal fin has 93 to 99 rays, and caudal fin has 8 rays. Body and head are covered with small scales. Trunk vertebrae number 9 or 10, and caudal vertebrae number 51 to 55. Color is black to dark brown on ventral side of head, operculum, and peritoneum. Branchial cavity and remainder of head are black, and tail is yellowish.

This species occurs worldwide in tropical seas from 1,957 to 4,417 m. In the western Atlantic it occurs in the Gulf of Mexico and the Bahamas. Food consists of polychaetes, crustaceans, and fishes. Maximum known size is 335 mm SL.

REFERENCES: Grey 1956; Nielsen 1965; Anderson et al. 1985.

Barathrites sp.

Barathrites sp. is moderately elongate, with a rather small head, a long abdomen, and an attenuated caudal fin. It is distinguished from the other species of the family by the following combination of characters. Snout is blunt and overhangs lower jaw. Mouth is large and nearly horizontal. Jaws have narrow bands of very small, conical teeth. Vomer has diamond-shaped patch of very small conical teeth, and palatine has three or four rows of very small conical teeth. Single small basibranchial tooth patch is present. Gill rakers on first arch number five to seven, and rudiments number six. Branchiostegal rays number 7. Head length is 15.6% to 16.4%, predorsal length is 19.7% to 25.4%, preanal length is 42.8% to 43.2%, and body depth at anus is 15% to 15.8% of SL. Snout length is 27.7% to 28.7% and eye diameter is 16.7% to 17.2% of head length. Opercular spine is short, conical, and pointed. Pectoral fin is large and has 25 or 26 rays. Dorsal fin originates just posterior to pectoral fin base and has 113 or 114 rays. Pelvic fin is located under preoperculum and consists of 2 filamentous rays. Anal fin has 86 rays. Caudal fin extends beyond dorsal and anal fin contours and has 8 rays. Body and anterior one-half of dorsal and anal fin membranes are covered with scales. Precaudal vertebrae number 18. Body color is pale.

This species is represented by two specimens, one 127 mm SL and the other 148 mm SL, from the northeastern Gulf of Mexico, TCWC 6332.01 and TCWC 6335.05. The specimens are distinct from the two recognized species of *Barathrites* in several characters and may represent a new species or a variant of either of the nominal species. They were captured at 28°51′N, 87°36′W at 2,070 m.

REFERENCES: Nybelin 1957; Nielsen 1986b.

Barathrodemus manatinus   Goode and Bean 1883

Barathrodemus manatinus is moderately elongate and compressed, with an inflated snout, a short abdomen, and an attenuated tail. It is distinguished from the other species of the family by the following combination of characters. Snout is blunt and greatly overhangs lower jaw. Mouth is large and nearly horizontal. Maxilla extends far beyond posterior margin of orbit and is sheathed. Teeth in jaws are very small, pointed, and in narrow bands. Teeth in vomer and palatine are larger than jaw teeth and are conical. Vomerine teeth are arranged in triangular patch, and palatine teeth are in broad bands. Median basibranchial teeth are located in two patches. Gill rakers on first gill arch number 5 on epibranch, 1 in corner, and 13 on lower limb. Branchiostegal rays number 8. Head length is 19.6% to 20.4%, predorsal length is 20.2% to 21.3%, preanal length is 35.8% to 38.4%, and body depth is 12% to 13.5% of SL. Snout length is 4.5% to 6.9% and eye diameter is 7.7% to 9% of head length. Opercular spine is short, straight, conical, and sharply pointed. Pectoral fin extends to near anus and has 18 to 20 rays. Dorsal fin originates above pectoral fin base and has about 106 rays. Pelvic fin inserts under preoperculum and consists of 2 filamentous rays. Anal fin has about 86 rays. Dorsal and anal fins are about as high as one-half body depth and extend to near caudal fin base. Caudal fin has 9 rays. Body is covered with small scales. Color is pale brown in preservative.

This species occurs in the western Atlantic from about 37°N to the northern Gulf of Mexico and the Caribbean Sea between 1,183 and 2,250 m. Maximum known size is about 170 mm SL.

REFERENCES: Goode and Bean 1896; Cohen and Nielsen 1978.

Bassogigas gillii   Goode and Bean 1896

Bassogigas gillii is moderately elongate and tapering posteriorly, with a moderate-sized head and a long snout. It is distinguished from the other species of the family by the following combination of characters. Snout is acute and does not overhang lower jaw. Mouth is large and slightly oblique. Maxilla is posterodorsally sheathed. Teeth are granular, close-set, and occur in jaws and vomer in inverted-V-shaped patch. Gill rakers on first arch number seven to nine. Two median basibranchial tooth patches are present. Opercular spine is stout. Basibranchial rays number 8. Pectoral fin is moderate in size but less than one-half head length and has 27 to 31 rays. Dorsal fin originates posterior to pectoral fin base and has 106 rays. Pelvic fins are located close together under preopercula, and each consists of 2 filamentous rays. Anal fin has 84 rays. Lateral line is distinct. Trunk vertebrae number 15 or 16. Color is grayish brown, with fins slightly darker.

This species occurs in the tropical waters of the Atlantic Ocean at 2,022 m. In the western Atlantic it has been captured off Delaware and in the Gulf of Mexico off Louisiana and Alabama. Maximum known size is 850 mm TL.

REFERENCES: Grey 1956; Cohen and Nielsen 1978; Nielsen and Cohen 1986.

Bassozetus compressus Günther 1878

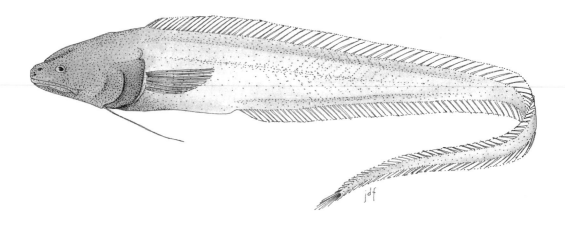

Bassozetus compressus is relatively slender and tapering posteriorly, with a terminal mouth, a slightly depressed snout, a moderately arched head, and a compressed body. It is distinguished from the other species of the family by the following combination of characters. Snout is blunt and somewhat inflated. Mouth is large, slightly oblique, with maxilla extending posterior to eye. Eye is very small, about one-half snout length. Jaws, vomer, and palatine have band of villiform teeth, with vomerine band V-shaped. First gill arch has 15 developed gill rakers on lower limb. Single median basibranchial tooth plate is present. Pectoral fin is short and has about 23 rays. Dorsal fin originates above gill opening and has 138 rays. Pelvic fin is located beneath preoperculum and consists of single ray that extends to pectoral fin base. Anal fin has about 92 rays. Head and body are covered with relatively large scales, with about 16 in oblique series from anal fin origin to dorsal fin. Lateral line is indistinct. Color is blackish, with head, peritoneum, and fins black.

This species occurs in the western Atlantic and western Pacific between 1,911 and 4,592 m. In the western Atlantic it occurs in the Gulf of Mexico. This species may be a composite of two or three species (Jørgen G. Nielsen, pers. com., October 23, 1996).

REFERENCES: Günther 1878 (as *Bathynectes compressus*); Goode and Bean 1896.

Bassozetus robustus   Smith and Radcliffe 1913

Bassozetus robustus is moderately robust anteriorly and tapering posteriorly, with a terminal mouth, a strongly arched head, and a compressed body. It is distinguished from the other species of the family by the following combination of characters. Snout is blunt and somewhat inflated. Mouth is large and slightly oblique, with maxilla extending well posterior to eye. Eye is small, less than one-half snout length. Jaws, vomer, and palatine have broad bands of villiform teeth, with vomerine band V-shaped. First gill arch has 12 to 14 developed gill rakers on lower limb. Opercular spine is weak, broad, and covered with integument. Free edge of preoperculum and vertical edge of operculum are crenate. Single median basibranchial tooth plate is present. Snout length is about 26%, eye diameter is about 10%, and upper jaw is about 54% of head length. Pectoral fin is relatively short and has 25 rays. Dorsal fin originates anterior to pectoral fin base and has 120 rays. Pelvic fin is located beneath preoperculum and consists of single ray that extends to anus. Anal fin has about 102 rays, and caudal fin has 9 rays. Head and body are covered with small, deciduous scales, with about 32 in oblique series from anal fin origin to dorsal fin. Lateral line is indistinct. Color in alcohol is brownish yellow on upper part of body and dusky on lower part of body and lips, with operculum and branchiostegal rays black.

This species occurs in the western Pacific and western Atlantic Oceans. In the western Atlantic it occurs in the Gulf of Mexico above 2,000 m. Maximum known size is about 360 mm TL.

REFERENCES: Smith and Radcliffe 1913; Grey 1956, 1958 (as *B. normalis*); Jørgen G. Nielsen, pers. comm., October 23, 1996.

Bathyonus pectoralis   Goode and Bean 1885

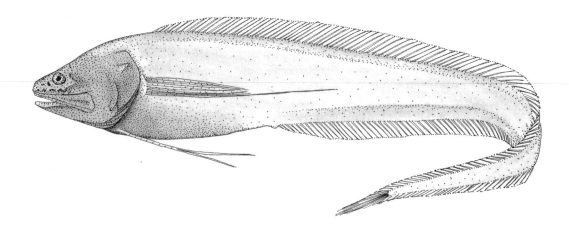

Bathyonus pectoralis is relatively slender and tapering posteriorly, with a moderate-sized head and a broad, flat, sharply pointed opercular spine. It is distinguished from the other species of the family by the following combination of characters. Snout is blunt and does not overhang lower jaw. Mouth is large, nearly horizontal, and extends well beyond eye. Villiform teeth occur in jaws, vomer, and palatine. Eye is small. Branchiostegal rays number 8. First gill arch has 5 gill rakers, including 4 rudiments, on epibranch and 18 gill rakers on lower limb. Head is 17.5% to 18.6%, snout length is 4.5% to 5%, eye diameter is 2% to 2.2%, predorsal length is 22.1% to 22.3%, preanal length is 40.4% to 42%, body depth is 12.8% to 13.1%, and pelvic fin is 10.3% to 15% of SL. Pectoral fin has 17 rays, with lower rays free of membranes and elongated, and next to lowermost ray extends considerably posterior to vent. Dorsal fin originates above pectoral fin base and has about 93 rays. Pelvic fin is under preoperculum and consists of 2 filamentous rays. Anal fin has 73 rays, and caudal fin has 6 rays. Color is pale, with head, opercular region, and peritoneum dark.

This species occurs in the western Atlantic from the Gulf of Mexico and the Caribbean Sea at 604 to 2,615 m. Maximum known size is 215 mm TL.

REFERENCES: Goode and Bean 1896; Grey 1958.

Brotula barbata (Bloch and Schneider 1801)
Bearded brotula

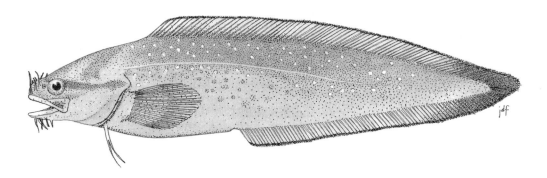

Brotula barbata is rather stout bodied and tapering posteriorly, with three barbels on each side of snout and lower jaw. It is distinguished from the other species of the family by the following combination of characters. Snout is acute and equal to lower jaw. Mouth is moderate in size and nearly horizontal. Small, blunt teeth occur in jaws, vomer, and palatine. Basibranchial tooth patch is absent. First gill arch has three rudimentary gill rakers on epibranch and five rudiments and three gill rakers on lower limb. Opercular spine is present. Branchiostegal rays number 8. Head length is 22.2% to 24.4%, snout length is 4.1% to 5.7%, interorbital length is 3.3% to 4.2%, predorsal length is 23.9% to 27.1%, preanal length is 45.9% to 53%, and body depth is 16.3% to 20% of SL. Pectoral fin is broad based and has 25 or 26 rays. Dorsal fin originates posterior to pectoral fin base and has 112 to 117 rays. Pelvic fin is located beneath preoperculum and consists of 2 filamentous rays. Anal fin has 86 to 94 rays, and caudal fin has 9 to 11 rays. Body is covered with small scales. Color is reddish to olive brown, with occasional spots or freckles. Young are covered with dark spots and stripes on cheeks, but these are lost with growth.

This species occurs in the western Atlantic from Bermuda and Florida to northern South America, including the entire Gulf of Mexico and the Caribbean Sea, from near shore to the upper slope. Maximum known size is 600 mm TL.

REFERENCES: Longley and Hildebrand 1941; Hubbs 1944; Hoese and Moore 1977; Castro-Aguirre and Márquez-Espinoza 1981; Uyeno et al. 1983; C. R. Robins et al. 1986; Boschung 1992.

Brotulotaenia brevicauda Cohen 1974

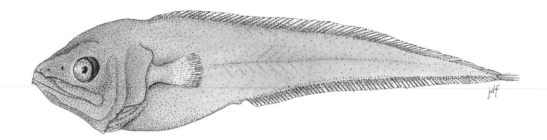

Brotulotaenia brevicauda is elongate, compressed, and tapering posteriorly behind head, with small pectoral fins and no pelvic fins. It is distinguished from the other species of the family by the following combination of characters. Snout is moderately blunt and relatively long. Mouth is large and moderately oblique. Teeth occur in jaws, vomer, and palatine. First gill arch has four gill rakers and 10 to 12 tubercles. Opercular spine is absent. Branchiostegal rays number 7. Basibranchial tooth patch is absent. Head length is 24.2% to 31.3%, snout length is 7% to 9.7%, eye diameter is 3.2% to 6.9%, predorsal length is 20.9% to 26.3%, preanal length is 43.5% to 50.3%, and body depth at vent is 11.6% to 18.1% of SL. Pectoral fin is small and has 21 to 24 rays. Dorsal fin originates anterior to pectoral fin base and has 79 to 84 rays. Anal fin has 58 to 64 rays, and caudal fin has 9 rays. Body and head are covered with minute, adherent, nonimbricate, prickly scales. Lateral line is well developed on head. Trunk vertebrae number 13, and total vertebrae number 63 to 66. Color is dark brown to black, with belly purple. Small specimens have five to seven pairs of dusky blotches along dorsal and anal fin bases.

This species occurs in the tropical to temperate Atlantic. In the western Atlantic it occurs off Bermuda, in the western Gulf of Mexico, and in the Caribbean Sea between the surface and 2,650 m. It is thought to be mesopelagic or bathypelagic. Maximum known size is 300 mm SL.

REFERENCES: Cohen 1974; Nielsen 1986b.

Dicrolene intronigra   Goode and Bean 1883

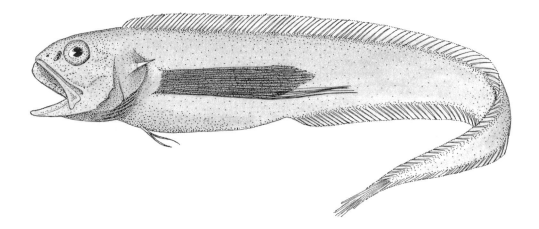

Dicrolene intronigra is moderately slender, moderately compressed, and tapering posteriorly, with a strong, slightly curved opercular spine and three spines on preoperculum. It is distinguished from the other species of the family by the following combination of characters. Snout is rather blunt and slightly overhangs lower jaw. Head has strong supraorbital spine directed posterodorsally. Mouth is nearly horizontal and large; upper jaw extends beyond eye. Eye is just slightly smaller than snout length. Teeth are villiform and occur in jaws, vomer, and palatine. Gill rakers on first gill arch number 4 plus 3 or 4 rudiments on epibranch, and 11 plus 4 or 5 rudiments on lower limb. Branchiostegal rays number 8. Head is 16.4% to 18.4%, snout length is 4.1% to 4.9%, eye diameter is 2.5% to 3%, predorsal length is 20.9% to 21.5%, preanal length is 36.8% to 41.6%, body depth is 13.5% to 14.8%, and outer and inner pelvic fins are 6.5% to 9% and 4.3% to 6.4% respectively of SL. Pectoral fin is long, has 26 rays, and lowermost 6 or 9 rays are free of membranes and elongated. Dorsal fin has about 100 rays. Pelvic fins are located close together under preopercula, and each consists of 2 filamentous rays. Anal fin has 85 rays, and caudal fin has 6 or 7 rays. Body is covered with small deciduous scales, and scales also occur on posterior section of maxilla. Lateral line is close to dorsal fin base and is obsolete on posterior one-third of body. Lateral scale rows number 110 to 120. Color is brownish.

This species occurs in the Atlantic Ocean between 200 and 1,495 m. In the western Atlantic it occurs off the southeastern United States, in the Gulf of Mexico, and in the Caribbean Sea. Maximum known size is about 300 mm TL.

REFERENCES: Goode and Bean 1896; Uyeno et al. 1983; Nielsen and Cohen 1986.

Dicrolene kanazawai   Grey 1958

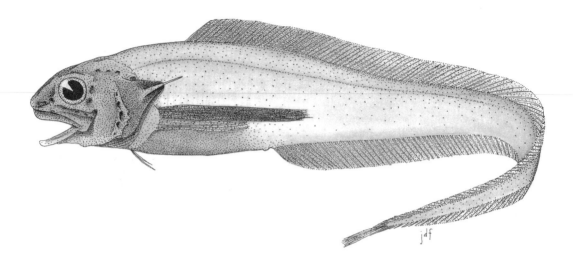

Dicrolene kanazawai is relatively slender, moderately compressed, and tapering posteriorly, with a stout and slightly curved opercular spine. It is distinguished from the other species of the family by the following combination of characters. Snout is moderately blunt, slightly swollen, and slightly overhangs lower jaw. Mouth is moderately long and almost horizontal. Eye is large. Villiform teeth occur in jaws, vomer, and palatine. First gill arch has 5 rudiments on epibranch and 11 gill rakers plus 6 rudiments on lower limb. Preoperculum has four small spines along posterior margin. Opercular spine extends considerably beyond opercular membrane. Head length 18.9% to 20.9%, snout length is 4.9% to 5.9%, predorsal length is 22.2% to 24.8%, preanal length is 35% to 38.8%, body depth is 13% to 16.9%, and pelvic fin length is about 7.2% of SL. Pectoral fin is large and consists of 23 to 26 attached upper rays and 5 to 8 free lower rays. Dorsal fin originates posterior to pectoral fin base and has 105 to 108 rays. Pelvic fin is located under preoperculum and consists of 2 filamentous rays. Anal fin has 82 to 89 rays, and caudal fin has 6 or 7 rays. Body and head are covered with small scales. Color is brown, with faint reddish tinge dorsally, and head and belly are black. Pectoral fin is largely black, and other fins are gray.

This species occurs in the western Atlantic from the Gulf of Mexico and the Caribbean Sea between 2,070 and 2,367 m. Maximum known size is 254 mm SL.

REFERENCE: Grey 1958; Anderson et al. 1985.

Lamprogrammus niger   Alcock 1891

Lamprogrammus niger is relatively deep bodied and compressed, with a large, cavernous, poorly ossified head; two weak, flat opercular spines; and enlarged lateral line scales covering vertically oriented, spindle-shaped neuromasts. It is distinguished from the other species of the family by the following combination of characters. Snout is blunt, short, and does not overhang lower jaw. Mouth is large, moderately oblique, and extends well beyond eye. Villiform, slightly recurved teeth are arranged in bands in jaws, vomer, and palatine. Median basibranchial tooth plate is absent. Eye is rather moderate in size. Branchiostegal rays number 8. Preoperculum has deep notches on posterior margin but lacks flexible spines. First gill arch has 3 or 4 short gill rakers on epibranch and 13 or 14 mostly long and slender gill rakers on lower limb. Head is 17.3% to 20.9%, snout length is 4.9% to 5.9%, eye diameter is 1.8% to 2.3%, predorsal length is 19.5% to 21.6, preanal length is 35.6% to 37.9%, and body depth is 16.1% to 18.4% of SL. Pectoral fin fails to reach vent and has 16 to 19 rays. Dorsal fin originates above pectoral fin base and has 105 to 115 rays. Pelvic fin is lacking in adults and is represented by rudimentary stub in juveniles. Anal fin has 84 to 91 rays, and caudal fin has 8 rays. Body is covered with relatively large, deciduous cycloid scales. Lateral lines scales are covered by small scales. Trunk vertebrae number 12 to 14. Color is blackish brown.

This species is probably circumtropical between 800 and 2,615 m. In the western Atlantic it occurs in the Gulf of Mexico and the Caribbean Sea from 604 to 2,615 m. Maximum known size is 550 mm TL.

REFERENCES: Goode and Bean 1896; Cohen and Nielsen 1978; Uyeno et al. 1983; Nielsen and Cohen 1986.

Lepophidium brevibarbe (Cuvier 1829)
Blackedge cusk-eel

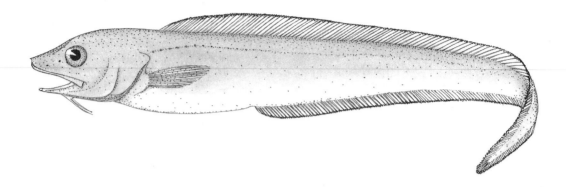

Lepophidium brevibarbe is relatively slender, compressed posteriorly, and tapering to a pointed caudal fin, with a well-developed, forwardly directed spine on snout and filamentous pelvic fins located beneath eyes. It is distinguished from the other species of the family by the following combination of characters. Snout is moderately blunt and slightly overhangs jaws. Mouth is slightly oblique and large; upper jaw extends to near posterior margin of eye. Eye is large. Villiform teeth occur in jaws, vomer, and palatine, with those in outer row of jaws somewhat enlarged. Medial basibranchial tooth plate is absent. First gill arch has four gill rakers on epibranch and seven on lower limb. Operculum has strong spine at dorsoposterior margin hidden by integument. Branchiostegal rays number 7. Head is 19.5% to 20.4%, snout length is 4.3% to 4.9%, eye diameter is 3.6% to 3.7%, predorsal length is 23.6% to 25.3%, preanal length is 36.7% to 46.6%, body depth is 14% to 14.1%, and outer and inner pelvic fin rays are 8% and 4.9% respectively of SL. Pectoral fin is of moderate size. Dorsal fin orig-inates over pectoral fin base and has 126 to 131 rays. Pelvic fin consists of 2 filamentous rays. Anal fin has 103 to 110 rays, and caudal fin has 9 rays. Body and head are covered with small, slightly imbricate scales arranged in regular rows. Vertebrae usually number 71 or 72 and comprise 15 trunk, and 56 or 57 caudal, vertebrae. Color is tan to sooty brown dorsally and white ventrally, with dorsal fin and occasionally anal fin dark edged.

This species occurs in the western Atlantic from southeastern Florida and the Gulf of Mexico to Brazil at 6 to 90 m. It is absent in the Bahamas and is rare in the Antilles. Spawning occurs during two peaks, summer and fall, and individuals live about two years in the northwestern Gulf of Mexico. Maximum known size is 260 mm TL.

REFERENCES: Nichols and Breder 1922; Robins 1959; Hoese and Moore 1977; Uyeno et al. 1983; C. R. Robins et al. 1986; Retzer 1991; Boschung 1992.

Lepophidium jeannae   Fowler 1941
Mottled cusk-eel

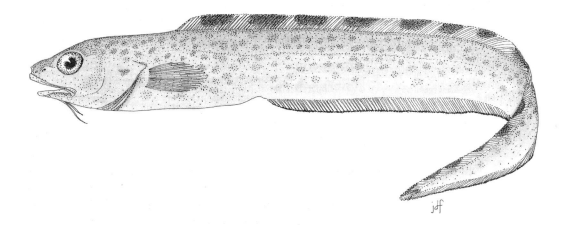

Lepophidium jeannae is relatively slender, posteriorly compressed, and tapering to a pointed caudal fin, with a well-developed, forwardly directed spine on the snout and numerous small, dusky spots on dorsal part of body. It is distinguished from the other species of the family by the following combination of characters. Snout is moderately blunt and extends slightly beyond upper jaw. Mouth is slightly oblique and large; upper jaw extends to near posterior margin of eye. Eye is large. Villiform teeth occur in jaws, vomer, and palatine. Medial basibranchial tooth plate is absent. First gill arch has two rudiments on epibranch and four gill rakers plus two or three rudiments on lower limb. Operculum has strong spine at dorsoposterior margin hidden by integument. Branchiostegal rays number 7. Head is 21%, snout length is 5%, orbit length is 5%, predorsal length is 21% to 23%, preanal length is 36% to 39%, body depth at anal fin origin is 10%, and outer and inner pelvic rays are 8% to 11% and 6% to 8% respectively of SL. Pectoral fin is of moderate size and has 20 or 21 rays. Dorsal fin has 135 to 139 rays. Pelvic fin consists of 2 filamentous rays of unequal length located under eye. Anal fin has 112 to 116 rays, and caudal fin has 9 rays. Body and head are covered with small, slightly imbricate scales arranged in regular rows. Pyloric caecae number 3, and trunk and caudal vertebrae number 14 or 15 and 59 or 60 respectively. Color is pale, with numerous irregular dusky spots scattered on upper two-thirds of body. Most spots are smaller than pupil of eye. Dorsal fin margin alternates dark and pale, with dark blotches extending to near fin base. Anal fin is dusky with black border. Caudal fin is dark along outer rays and pale along middle rays.

This species occurs in the western Atlantic from North Carolina to southern Florida and the Gulf of Mexico at 18 to 90 m. It is rare to 280 m. Maximum known size is 300 mm TL.

REFERENCES: Robins 1959, 1960; Hoese and Moore 1977; C. R. Robins et al. 1986; Retzer 1991; Boschung 1992.

Lepophidium pheromystax   Robins 1960

Lepophidium pheromystax is relatively slender, posteriorly compressed, and tapering to a pointed caudal fin, with a well-developed, forwardly directed spine on the snout and filamentous pelvic fins located beneath eyes. It is distinguished from the other species of the family by the following combination of characters. Snout is moderately blunt and extends slightly beyond upper jaw. Mouth is slightly oblique and large; upper jaw extends to near posterior margin of eye. Eye is large. Villiform teeth occur in jaws, vomer, and palatine. Jaw teeth of outer row are largest, and vomerine and palatine teeth are short and blunt. Medial basibranchial tooth patch is absent. First gill arch has four rudiments on epibranch and four gill rakers and two or three rudiments on lower limb. Operculum has strong flattened spine at dorsoposterior margin hidden by integument. Branchiostegal rays number 7. Head is 19% to 22%, snout length is 4% to 5%, orbit diameter is 6% to 7%, predorsal length is 20% to 23%, preanal length is 35% to 40%, body depth at dorsal fin origin is 11% to 14%, and outer and inner pelvic fin rays are 6% to 10% and 5% to 8% respectively of SL. Pectoral fin is of moderate size and has 20 to 22 rays. Dorsal fin originates above pectoral fin base and has 125 to 132 rays. Pelvic fin consists of 2 filamentous rays. Anal fin has 104 to 110 rays, and caudal fin has 9 rays. Body and head, to level of anterior interorbital region, are covered with slightly imbricate scales arranged in regular rows. Pyloric caecae number one to four, and trunk and caudal vertebrae number 14 or 15 and 54 to 57 respectively. Color is yellowish brown, slightly darker dorsally than ventrally, with numerous spots, up to size of eye, arranged in two rows. Upper row consists of about 15 spots that extend vertically from dorsal fin base to pale lateral line. Lower row is located on flank below lateral line. Small spots occur between large spots. Dorsal fin has series of U-shaped black spots. Anal fin is dusky with black border.

This species occurs in the western Atlantic from Campeche Bay in the southern Gulf of Mexico, and from northern South America between 4°02′N, 50°20′W and 7°55′N, 57°25′W at 46 to 92 m. Food consists of small crustaceans and occasionally small benthic fishes. Maximum known size is 218 mm TL.

REFERENCES: Robins 1960; Uyeno et al. 1983.

Lepophidium profundorum   (Gill 1863)
Fawn cusk-eel

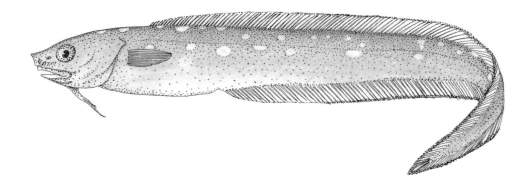

Lepophidium profundorum is relatively slender, posteriorly compressed, and tapering to a pointed caudal fin, with a well-developed, forwardly directed spine on snout and a row of white spots on dorsal half of body. It is distinguished from the other species of the family by the following combination of characters. Snout is moderately blunt and extends slightly anterior to jaws. Mouth is slightly oblique and large; upper jaw extends to near posterior margin of eye. Eye is large. Villiform teeth occur in jaws, vomer, and palatine. First gill arch has two gill rakers on epibranch and five to seven on lower limb. Operculum has strong spine at dorsoposterior margin hidden by integument. Branchiostegal rays number 7. Head is 17%, predorsal length is 21% to 22%, preanal length is 34%, and body depth at anal fin origin is 10% of SL. Snout length is 22% to 23%, orbit diameter is 27%, outer pelvic fin ray is 4.9% to 5.4%, and inner pelvic fin ray is 3.3% to 3.7% of head length. Pectoral fin is of moderate size and has 22 or 23 rays. Dorsal fin originates above pectoral fin origin and has 134 to 136 rays. Anal fin has 114 or 115 rays, and caudal fin has 9 rays. Body is covered with small, slightly imbricate scales arranged in regular rows. Pyloric caecae number three, and trunk and caudal vertebrae number 16 or 17 and 58 respectively. Color is brownish yellow, with row of numerous, subcircular white spots about size of pupil on dorsal one-half of body.

This species occurs in the western Atlantic from Georges Bank to northern South America and in the eastern and southern Gulf of Mexico at 55 to 365 m. Maximum known size is 230 mm TL. *Lepophidium cervinum* is a junior synonym.

REFERENCES: Hildebrand and Schroeder 1928; Bigelow and Schroeder 1953b (both as *L. cervinum*); Castro-Aguirre and Márquez-Espinoza 1981; Uyeno et al. 1983; Robins 1986; C. R. Robins et al. 1986; Boschung 1992.

Lepophidium staurophor   Robins 1958
Barred cusk-eel

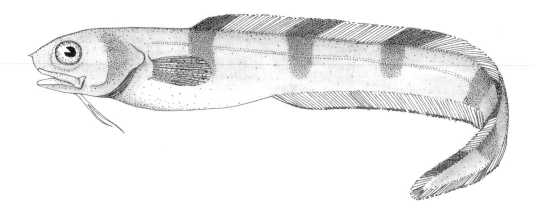

Lepophidium staurophor is relatively slender, posteriorly compressed, and tapering to a pointed caudal fin, with a well-developed, forwardly directed spine on snout and prominent black bands on dorsal part of body. It is distinguished from the other species of the family by the following combination of characters. Snout is moderately blunt and extends slightly anterior to jaws. Mouth is slightly oblique and large; upper jaw extends to near posterior margin of eye. Eye is large. Villiform teeth occur in jaws, vomer, and palatine. Vomerine tooth patch is inverted-V-shaped. Jaw teeth of outer row are slightly enlarged. First gill arch has 4 gill rakers on epibranch and 8 to 11 on lower limb. Operculum has strong spine at dorsoposterior margin hidden by integument. Branchiostegal rays number 7. Head is 17% to 22%, snout length is 19% to 21%, eye diameter is 11% to 13%, predorsal length is 22% to 24%, preanal length is 36% to 40%, depth of body at anal fin origin is 9% to 10%, and outer pelvic rays are 22% to 23% of SL. Pectoral fin is of moderate size and has 22 or 23 rays. Dorsal fin originates over midlength of pectoral fin and has 140 to 147 rays. Pelvic fin is located under eye and consists of 2 filamentous rays of unequal length. Anal fin has 122 to 127 rays, and caudal fin has 9 rays. Body and head are covered with small, slightly imbricate scales arranged in regular rows. Pyloric caecae number three. Color is tan to slightly reddish, with four or five prominent black bands on dorsal part of body. First band passes through anterior 3 to 7 dorsal fin rays; second band is located above anal fin origin; third band, and occasionally first and second, extend onto ventral one-half of body; and fourth band usually encircles body. Dorsal fin has five or six black blotches.

This species occurs in the western Atlantic from the eastern Gulf of Mexico and the western Caribbean Sea between 100 and 420 m. Maximum known size is 260 mm TL.

REFERENCES: Robins 1959; C. R. Robins et al. 1986.

Luciobrotula corethromycter   Cohen 1964

Luciobrotula corethromycter is moderately slender and tapering posteriorly, with a depressed snout bearing fleshy flaps and ridges at tip and a relatively large head. It is distinguished from the other species of the family by the following combination of characters. Tip of snout has fleshy mound of tissue bearing series of broad, fleshy flaps that are covered with single broad, fleshy lappet on each side. Mouth is large and extends about one eye diameter beyond eye. Anterior naris is tubular and located near tip of snout, and posterior naris is large, circular, and located at about midlength of snout. Eye is small, and iris is much smaller than lens. Small, granular teeth occur in broad bands in jaws, vomer, and palatine. There are one large unpaired and four paired branchial tooth patches. First gill arch has one gill raker in corner, two gill rakers on lower limb, and granular tooth patches. Posterior margin of preoperculum is free and lacks spines. Opercular spine is broad, bluntly tipped, and buried in flesh. Branchiostegal rays number 8. Head length is 22.2% to 25%, snout length is 5.6% to 6.7%, orbit length is 2.2% to 2.7%, predorsal length is 30.7% to 33.1%, preanal length is 50.8% to 57%, and depth is 13.8% to 16.9% of SL. Pectoral fin is relatively short, broad, and paddlelike and has 27 or 28 rays. Dorsal fin originates over posterior one-third to one-half of pectoral fin and has 92 to 103 rays. Pelvic fins originate close together and posterior to tip of symphysis of cleithra, slightly anterior to pectoral fin base. Anal fin has 70 to 77 rays. Caudal fin is distinctly narrower at base than confluent dorsal and anal rays and has 10 to 12 rays. Head (except for snout), body, and bases of pectoral, dorsal, and anal fins are covered with small cycloid scales. Scales on fin bases are smaller than other scales. Lateral line tube is incomplete and runs from upper edge of opercular opening dorsal to midline to about level of vent. Vertebrae number 53 to 56. Color is brown, with belly and fins (except for pelvic fins) darker brown.

This species occurs in the western Atlantic from the Gulf of Mexico and the Caribbean Sea between 549 and 914 m. In the Gulf of Mexico it has been captured off the Mississippi River, west of the Florida Keys, and off Campeche. Food consists of caridean shrimp. Maximum known size is 534 mm SL.

REFERENCES: Cohen 1964b, 1974; Cohen and Nielsen 1978; Uyeno et al. 1983.

Monomitopus agassizii   (Goode and Bean 1896)

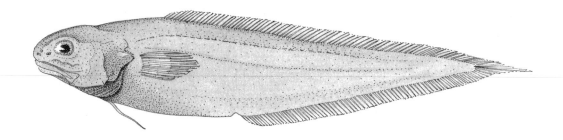

Monomitopus agassizii is moderately slender and tapering posteriorly, with a relatively deep head, two or three weak spines on lower angle of preoperculum, and a strong opercular spine. It is distinguished from the other species of the family by the following combination of characters. Snout is moderately acute and extends beyond jaws. Mouth is slightly oblique and large; upper jaw extends posterior to margin of orbit. Eye is large. Villiform teeth occur in jaws, vomer, and palatine. Vomer tooth patch is inverted-V-shaped, with slightly enlarged apex. Single median basibranchial tooth plate is present. First gill arch has 28 to 33 gill rakers. Branchiostegal rays number 8 or 9. Head is 20.8% to 23.2%, snout length is 4.7% to 6.1%, eye diameter is 4.5% to 6%, predorsal length is 22.6% to 24.9%, preanal length is 38.9% to 43.7%, and body depth is 16.3% to 19.2% of SL. Pectoral fin is of moderate size and has 30 to 35 rays. Dorsal fin originates above pectoral fin and has 100 to 106 rays. Pelvic fin is located under preoperculum and consists of a single filamentous ray. Anal fin has 83 to 89 rays, and caudal fin has 8 rays. Head and body are covered with deciduous scales. Lateral line is indistinct on trunk. Pyloric caecae number seven, and trunk vertebrae number 12 to 14. Color is pale.

This species occurs in the western Atlantic from the Gulf of Mexico and the Caribbean Sea between 48 and 1,125 m. Maximum known size is 193 mm TL.

REFERENCES: Goode and Bean 1896; Uyeno et al. 1983.

Monomitopus magnus   Carter and Cohen 1985

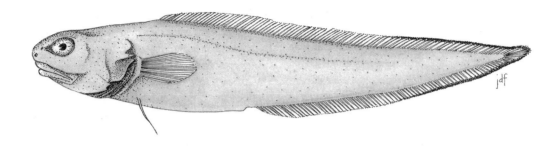

Monomitopus magnus is moderately slender and tapering posteriorly, with a relatively slender head, two spines on lower angle of preoperculum, and a strong, bifurcated opercular spine. It is distinguished from the other species of the family by the following combination of characters. Snout is moderately acute and extends beyond jaws. Mouth is slightly inferior, slightly oblique, and large; upper jaw extends beyond posterior margin of orbit. Eye is large. Villiform teeth occur in jaws, vomer, and palatine. Vomer tooth patch is inverted-V-shaped, with enlarged and rounded apex. Palatine tooth patch is elongated, rounded anteriorly, and tapering posteriorly. First gill arch has 4 rudiments on epibranch and 10 or 11 gill rakers plus 4 rudiments on lower limb. Branchiostegal rays number 8. Head is 23% to 24%, snout length is 5.3% to 6%, eye diameter is 4.7% to 5%, predorsal length is 25% to 28%, preanal length is 40% to 47%, body depth at vent is 16% to 19%, and pelvic fin ray is 7%

to 10% of SL. Pectoral fin is moderately small and has 27 to 31 rays. Dorsal fin has 104 to 108 rays. Pelvic fin is under preoperculum and consists of single filamentous ray. Anal fin has 85 to 92 rays, and caudal fin has 8 rays. Body and head are covered with small deciduous scales. Lateral line is distinct, with 56 to 59 scales on trunk. Pyloric caecae number nine. Trunk vertebrae number 15, and caudal vertebrae number 46 to 49. Color is brown, with opercular flap dark, mouth cavity dark brown, and dorsal and anal fins with dark posterior margins.

This species occurs in the western Atlantic off the east coast of Florida, off northern Cuba, and in the eastern Gulf of Mexico off the Florida Keys between 731 and 930 m. Food consists of euphausiid shrimps, gammaridian amphipods, and fishes, including midwater myctophids. Maximum known size is 535 mm SL.

REFERENCE: Carter and Cohen 1985.

Neobythites elongatus   Nielsen and Retzer 1994

Neobythites elongatus is elongate, compressed, and tapering posteriorly, with a long, flat spine on posterodorsal section of operculum and two small spines at lower angle of preoperculum. It is distinguished from the other species of the family by the following combination of characters. Snout is blunt, less than eye diameter, and slightly overhangs jaws. Mouth is slightly oblique and large, and upper jaw extends well beyond posterior margin of orbit. Eye is moderately large. Granular teeth occur in jaws, vomer, and palatine. Vomerine tooth patch is inverted-V-shaped. First gill arch has 2 short and 3 or 4 long gill rakers on epibranch, 0 or 1 long gill raker in corner, and 0 to 6 short and 9 to 11 long gill rakers on lower limb. Head length is 21.5% to 23%, eye diameter is 4.7% to 5.7%, predorsal length is 20.5% to 26%, preanal length is 37% to 41%, pelvic fin length is 12% to 14%, and body depth is 14% to 16% of SL. Pectoral fin is relatively small and has 23 to 25 rays. Dorsal fin originates posterior to pectoral fin base and has 101 to 104 rays. Pelvic fin is located beneath preoperculum and consists of 2 filamentous rays that extend two-thirds of distance from insertion to anal fin origin. Anal fin has 86 to 90 rays. Head and body are covered with small deciduous scales. Lateral line is distinct. Color is brownish, with upper surface marbled and slightly darker than lower surface. Ocelli and stripes are lacking.

This species occurs in the western Atlantic in the Gulf of Mexico and the Caribbean Sea between 229 and 549 m. Maximum known size is 135 mm SL.

REFERENCE: Nielsen and Retzer 1994.

Neobythites gilli   Goode and Bean 1885

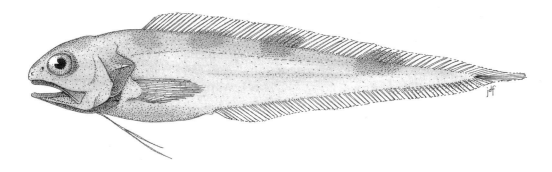

Neobythites gilli is relatively elongate, compressed, and tapering posteriorly, with a long, flat spine on operculum and a small hidden spine at lower angle of preoperculum. It is distinguished from the other species of the family by the following combination of characters. Snout is rounded and blunt and slightly overhangs jaws. Mouth is slightly oblique, terminal, and large; upper jaw extends beyond posterior margin of orbit. Eye is of moderate size. Villiform teeth occur in jaws, vomer, and palatine. Vomerine tooth patch is inverted-V-shaped. First gill arch has 11 gill rakers and 3 rudiments on lower limb. Branchiostegal rays number 8. Head is 19.1% to 21.9%, snout length is 4.8% to 5.4%, eye diameter is 4% to 4.5%, predorsal length is 24.5% to 25.2%, preanal length is 40.1% to 41.7%, body depth is 19.2% to 19.5%, and pelvic fin length is 16.9% to 19.8% of SL. Pectoral fin is of moderate size. Dorsal fin originates slightly posterior to pectoral fin base. Pelvic fins are located close together under preopercula, and each consists of 2 filamentous rays. Head and body are covered with small deciduous scales. Scale rows between dorsal fin base and lateral line number seven. Color is light yellow, slightly darker dorsally than ventrally, and with series of irregular brown blotches above lateral line and two large dark blotches extending from dorsum to dorsal fin. First dorsal fin blotch is posterior to level of anus, and second is at midlength of tail.

This species occurs in the western Atlantic from Cape Hatteras to Brazil, including the Gulf of Mexico, between 97 and 640 m. However, two additional and very similar species occur in the Caribbean Sea and may be confused with this species (Jorgen Nielsen, pers. com., May 1991). Maximum known size is 150 mm TL.

REFERENCES: Goode and Bean 1896; Hoese and Moore 1977; Uyeno et al. 1983; Boschung 1992.

Neobythites marginatus   Goode and Bean 1886

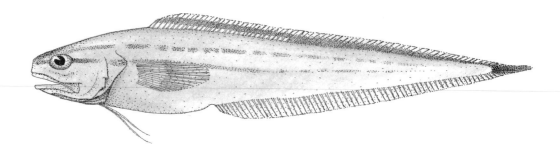

Neobythites marginatus is elongate, compressed, and tapering posteriorly, with a long, flat spine on posterodorsal section of operculum and two small spines at lower angle of preoperculum. It is distinguished from the other species of the family by the following combination of characters. Snout is blunt and slightly overhangs jaws. Mouth is slightly oblique and large; upper jaw extends beyond posterior margin of orbit. Eye is moderately small. Villiform teeth occur in jaws, vomer, and palatine. Vomerine tooth patch is inverted-V-shaped. First gill arch has about seven gill rakers and three rudiments on lower limb. Pectoral fin is of moderate size. Dorsal fin originates posterior to pectoral fin base. Pelvic fin is located beneath preoperculum and consists of 2 filamentous rays. Head and body are covered with small deciduous scales, with about 123 vertical scale rows and 7 between dorsal fin base and lateral line. Color is light yellowish brown, with two indistinct narrow bands of dark brown from snout to anterior two-thirds of tail.

This species occurs in the western Atlantic in the Gulf of Mexico and the Caribbean Sea between 329 and 549 m.

REFERENCE: Goode and Bean 1896.

Neobythites unicolor Nielsen and Retzer 1994

Neobythites unicolor is elongate, compressed, and tapering posteriorly, with a long, flat spine on posterodorsal section of operculum and one small spine at lower angle of preoperculum. It is distinguished from the other species of the family by the following combination of characters. Snout is blunt, about equal to eye diameter, and slightly overhangs jaws. Mouth is slightly oblique and large, upper jaw extends well beyond posterior margin of orbit. Eye is moderately large. Granular teeth occur in jaws, vomer, and palatine. Vomerine tooth patch is inverted-V-shaped. First gill arch has three short and three long gill rakers on epibranch, one long gill raker in corner, and six short and eight or nine long gill rakers on lower limb. Head length is 21.5% to 24%, eye diameter is 4.6% to 5.5%, predorsal length is 24% to 27.5%, preanal length is 35% to 42.5%, pelvic fin length is 17% to 22%, and body depth is 16.5% to 18% of SL. Pectoral fin is of moderate size and has 27 or 28 rays. Dorsal fin originates posterior to pectoral fin base and has 97 to 101 rays. Pelvic fins are located beneath preoperculum and consist of 2 filamentous rays that extend nearly to anus. Anal fin has 82 to 86 rays. Head and body are covered with small deciduous scales. Lateral line is indistinct. Color is yellowish, with minute black spots on lower part of head and body, and on posterior section of dorsal, anal, and caudal fins. Ocelli and stripes are lacking.

This species occurs in the western Atlantic in the Gulf of Mexico and the Caribbean Sea between 240 and 348 m. Maximum known size is 104 mm SL.

REFERENCE: Nielsen and Retzer 1994.

Ophidion beani Jordan and Gilbert 1883
Longnose cusk-eel

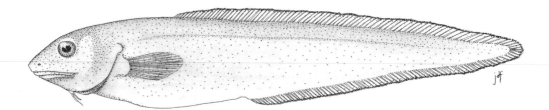

Ophidion beani is moderately long and slender, with head profile rounded, pelvic fins under eyes, and body plain colored except for dark margin on dorsal fin. It is distinguished from the other species of the family by the following combination of characters. Snout is moderately blunt, slightly overhangs jaws, and has small, blunt, and anteriorly directed spine. Mouth is terminal, almost horizontal, and moderately large, with upper jaw extending to near posterior margin of orbit. Eye is large. Villiform teeth occur in jaws, vomer, and palatine. Outer teeth of jaws are slightly larger than inner teeth. Vomerine tooth patch is triangular shaped, with apex slightly swollen, and vomerine and palatine teeth are broad, blunt, and short. First gill arch has two or three rudiments on epibranch and five or six gill rakers on lower limb. Operculum has strong spine at dorsoposterior margin hidden by integument. Head is 18.6%, snout length is 5.4%, eye diameter is 3.1%, predorsal length is 28.1%, pre-anal length is 37.8%, body depth at dorsal fin origin is 15.5%, and outer and inner pelvic fin rays are 7.6% and 3.6% respectively of SL. Pectoral fin is moderately small and rounded. Dorsal fin originates posterior to appressed pectoral fin and has 115 to 125 rays. Pelvic fin consists of 2 flattened rays. Anal fin has 96 to 100 rays, and caudal fin has 9 rays. Body is covered with elongate scales set at oblique angles, and head lacks scales. Trunk vertebrae number 16, and caudal vertebrae number 50 or 51. Color is brown, with black margin on dorsal fin and occasionally on anal fin.

This species occurs in the western Atlantic from South Carolina to the northeastern Gulf of Mexico and along the Atlantic coast of Mexico between 16 and 75 m. Maximum known size is 250 mm TL.

REFERENCES: C. R. Robins et al. 1986; Boschung 1992.

Ophidion grayi (Fowler 1948)
Blotched cusk-eel

Ophidion grayi is moderately long and slender, with head profile rounded, pelvic fins located under eyes, and body marked with dark spots and blotches. It is distinguished from the other species of the family by the following combination of characters. Snout is moderately blunt, slightly overhangs jaws, and has small, blunt, anteriorly directed spine. Mouth is terminal, nearly horizontal, and moderately large; upper jaw extends nearly to posterior margin of eye. Eye is large. Villiform teeth occur in jaws, vomer, and palatine. Outer jaw teeth are slightly larger than inner teeth. Vomerine tooth patch is triangular, and vomerine and palatine teeth are broad, blunt, and short. First gill arch has two rudiments on epibranch and four gill rakers on lower limb. Operculum has strong spine on dorsoposterior margin hidden by integument. Head is 18.7% to 19.8%, snout length is 5.1% to 5.7%, eye diameter is 3.5% to 3.7%, predorsal length is 26.8% to 27.7%, preanal length is 43.8% to 45%, body depth at dorsal fin origin is 16.1% 17.2%, and outer and inner pelvic fin rays are 10.6% to 12.3% and 5.8% to 6.9% respectively of SL. Pectoral fin is of moderate size and rounded. Dorsal fin originates anterior to appressed pectoral fin and has 133 to 144 rays. Pelvic fin consists of 2 flattened rays. Anal fin has 98 to 105 rays, and caudal fin has 9 rays. Body is covered with elongate scales set at oblique angles, and head is naked. Trunk vertebrae number 16, and caudal vertebrae number 48 or 49. Color is light tan, with dark brown spots and blotches arranged in two irregular horizontal rows. Upper row extends vertically from dorsal midline to lateral line, and lower row extends from lateral line to just below midflank. Some of upper row spots and blotches are coalesced into horizontal blotches. Top of head and dorsal fin have scattered small dark brown spots. Margin of dorsal fin is blotched or bordered with black pigment. Anal fin is clear with black margin.

This species occurs in the western Atlantic from South Carolina to the Gulf of Mexico between 10 and 60 m. It is more common in the northeastern than in the northwestern Gulf of Mexico. Spawning takes place during the winter in the northern Gulf of Mexico. Maximum known size is 300 mm TL.

REFERENCES: Robins 1957; Hoese and Moore 1977; C. R. Robins et al. 1986; Retzer 1991; Boschung 1992.

Ophidion holbrooki (Putnam 1874)
Bank cusk-eel

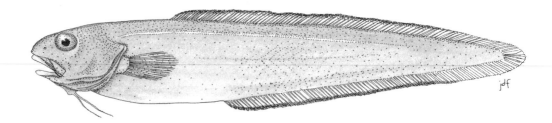

Ophidion holbrooki is moderately long and slender, with head profile nearly straight, pelvic fins located under eye, and body plain colored except for black margin on dorsal fin. It is distinguished from the other species of the family by the following combination of characters. Snout is moderately blunt; slightly overhangs jaws; and has small, blunt, anteriorly directed spine. Mouth is subterminal, nearly horizontal, and moderately large; upper jaw extends nearly to posterior margin of eye. Eye is large. Villiform teeth occur in jaws, vomer, and palatine. Outer jaw teeth are slightly larger than inner teeth. Vomerine tooth patch is triangular shaped, with apex slightly swollen. Teeth in vomer and palatine are relatively broad, blunt, and short. First gill arch has two rudiments on epibranch and four gill rakers on lower limb. Operculum has flat spine at dorsoposterior margin hidden by integument. Head is 17.4% to 18.4%, snout length is 3.8% to 4.7%, eye diameter is 3.4% to 3.9%, predorsal length is 26.8% to 27.4%, preanal length is 37.2% to 37.4%, body depth at dorsal fin origin is 14.5% to 15.6%, and outer and inner pelvic fin rays are 12.3% to 13.4% and 7.9% to 9.2% respectively of SL. Pectoral fin is moderately small and rounded. Dorsal fin originates slightly anterior to tip of appressed pectoral fin and has 120 to 136 rays. Pelvic fin consists of 2 slightly flattened rays. Anal fin has 98 to 111 rays, and caudal fin has 9 fin rays. Body is covered with elongate scales set at oblique angles. Color is brown, with dorsal fin and occasionally anal fin black edged. Trunk vertebrae number 16, and caudal vertebrae number 50 or 51.

This species occurs in the western Atlantic from North Carolina to southern Brazil, including the Gulf of Mexico, between the shoreline and 75 m. It is common in the northeastern, but uncommon in the northwestern, Gulf of Mexico. Maximum known size is 300 mm TL.

REFERENCES: Nichols and Breder 1922; Hoese and Moore 1977; C. R. Robins et al. 1986; Boschung 1992.

Ophidion marginatum   DeKay 1842
Striped cusk-eel

Ophidion marginatum is moderately long and slender, with head profile straight anterior to postorbital region, pelvic fins located under eyes, and body marked with two or three complete horizontal stripes. It is distinguished from the other species of the family by the following combination of characters. Snout is moderately acute and slightly overhangs jaws. Mouth is nearly horizontal and large; upper jaw extends near to posterior margin of eye. Eye is large. Villiform teeth occur in jaws, vomer, and palatine. Vomer tooth patch is triangular, with apex slightly swollen. First gill arch has four or five gill rakers on lower limb. Operculum has strong spine at dorsoposterior margin hidden by integument. Head is 16.3% to 16.8% and body depth is 12.2% to 13.6% of SL. Snout length is 24.7% to 28.6% and eye diameter is 30.3% to 32.8% of head length. Pectoral fin is moderately large, broadly rounded, and has 21 rays. Dorsal fin originates over or slightly behind midlength of appressed pectoral fin and has 147 to 158 rays. Pelvic fin consists of 2 moderately flattened rays. Anal fin has 118 to 124 rays, and caudal fin has 9 rays. Body is covered with elongate scales set at oblique angles, and head is naked. Trunk vertebrae number 15, and caudal vertebrae number 53 or 54. Color is grayish green dorsally, golden on side, and white on belly, with two or three complete dark stripes along side. Side of head is punctuated with brown spots, lateral line is outlined by dark band, and dorsal fin is pale green with black margin. Anal fin has black margin. Males have prominent crest on nape.

This species occurs in the western North Atlantic from New York to northern Florida and from the west coast of Florida and the coast of Alabama in the Gulf of Mexico. Maximum known size is 230 mm SL.

REFERENCES: Hildebrand and Schroeder 1928; Fritzsche 1978; C. R. Robins et al. 1986; Boschung 1992.

Ophidion welshi (Nichols and Breder 1922)
Crested cusk-eel

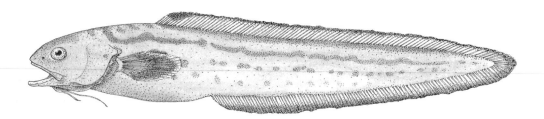

Ophidion welshi is moderately long and slender, with head profile straight anterior to postorbital region, pelvic fins located under eyes, and body marked with three complete to nearly complete horizontal stripes. It is distinguished from the other species of the family by the following combination of characters. Snout is moderately acute and slightly overhangs jaws. Mouth is nearly terminal, horizontal, and moderately large; upper jaw extends to near posterior margin of eye. Eye is large. Villiform teeth occur in jaws, vomer, and palatine. Vomerine tooth patch is triangular, with apex slightly swollen. First gill arch has two rudiments on epibranch and four gill rakers on lower limb. Operculum has strong spine at dorsoposterior margin hidden by integument. Head is 17.4% to 17.7%, snout length is 4.2% to 4.3%, eye diameter is 3% to 3.2%, predorsal length is 27.1% to 27.8%, preanal length is 35.4% to 41.3%, body depth at dorsal fin origin is 13.4% to 15.3%, and outer and inner pelvic fin rays are 12.1% to 12.6% and 5.8% to 6.3% respectively of SL. Pectoral fin is moderate in size and rounded. Dorsal fin originates above midlength of appressed pectoral fin and has 138 to 146 rays. Pelvic fin consists of 2 moderately flattened rays. Anal fin has 114 to 121 rays, and caudal fin has 9 rays. Body is covered with elongate scales set at oblique angles to each other, and head is naked. Trunk vertebrae number 16, and caudal vertebrae number 50 or 51. Color is pale tan, with three horizontal rows of brownish gray spots along dorsal one-half of body. Uppermost row is generally fused into stripe on either side of dorsal fin. Middle row is partially to completely fused into stripe and is located on or below lateral line. Dorsal fin has long black blotch anteriorly near fin origin and black margin posterior to blotch. Anal fin has black margin. Males have prominent crest on nape.

This species occurs in the western Atlantic from Georgia to south Florida and throughout the Gulf of Mexico between seashore and 55 m. In the northwestern Gulf of Mexico spawning takes place in the fall, and life span is about two years. Males at maturity develop prominent crest at nape. Maximum known size is 284 mm TL.

REFERENCES: Courtenay 1971; Hoese and Moore 1977; C. R. Robins et al. 1986; Retzer 1991; Boschung 1992.

Otophidium omostigmum (Jordan and Gilbert 1882)
Polka-dot cusk-eel

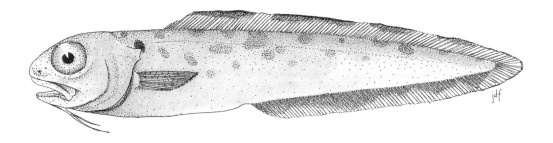

Otophidium omostigmum is moderately slender and relatively short, with a moderately convex head profile and a dark shoulder spot preceding brown spots and blotches on upper flank. It is distinguished from the other species of the family by the following combination of characters. Snout is moderately blunt, slightly overhangs jaws, and has short, sharp spine directed anterodorsally at about 45°. Mouth is slightly horizontal, subterminal, and moderately large; upper jaw extends nearly to posterior margin of eye. Eye is very large. Villiform teeth occur in jaws, vomer, and palatine. Outer jaw teeth are slightly larger than inner teeth. Vomerine tooth patch is inverted-V-shaped, and vomerine and palatine teeth are moderately broad, blunt, and short. First gill arch has two or three rudiments on epibranch and four short gill rakers on lower limb. Operculum has strong spine at dorsoposterior margin hidden by integument. Head is 21.2% to 24.4%, snout length is 5.4% to 6.4%, eye diameter is 5.6% to 6.6%, predorsal length is 26.1% to 28.5%, preanal length is 43.3% to 45.5%, body depth at dorsal fin origin is 16.8% to 17.2%, and outer and inner pelvic fins rays are 8.7% to 10.9% and 6.2% to 7.7% respectively of SL. Pectoral fin is moderately small, bluntly pointed, and has 16 to 18 rays. Dorsal fin originates above midlength of appressed pectoral fin and has 102 to 105 rays. Pelvic fin consists of 2 moderately flattened rays. Anal fin has 82 to 85 rays, and caudal fin has 9 rays. Body is covered with oblong scales set at oblique angles, and head is naked. Precaudal vertebrae number 14, and caudal vertebrae number 43 to 45. Color is tan, with pupil-sized black shoulder spot, and two series of black-brown blotches on upper one-half of body. Upper rows of spots and blotches meet along dorsal midline to form saddlelike marks. Lower row of spots and blotches is on or below lateral line. Dorsal fin has several black blotches, and anal fin is black along base.

This species occurs in the western Atlantic from North Carolina to southern Florida, along the northern Gulf of Mexico, and in the Lesser Antilles between 10 and 50 m. It is uncommon in the northwestern Gulf of Mexico. Maximum known size is 105 mm TL.

REFERENCES: Robins 1957; C. R. Robins et al. 1986; Boschung 1992.

Penopus macdonaldi   Goode and Bean 1896

Penopus macdonaldi is slender and tapering posteriorly to an acutely tipped caudal fin, with a long, acute snout; small eyes; and a strong, curved opercular spine. It is distinguished from the other species of the family by the following combination of characters. Snout is depressed and distinctly projects beyond jaws. Mouth is nearly horizontal, inferior, and large; upper jaw extends well beyond eye. Villiform teeth occur in jaws, vomer, and palatine. Eye is minute. First gill arch has three or four rudiments on epibranch, two gill rakers in corner, and six to eight gill rakers on lower limb. Branchiostegal rays number eight. Preoperculum has four or five small, weak spines at lower angle. Operculum has long, slender, sharply curved spine and two or three small, flattened spines on lower angle. Head is 20.7% to 22.4%, snout length is 7.9%, eye length is 1.4%, predorsal length is 26.1%, preanal length is 39.8% to 43%, depth is 9.4%, and length of pelvic fin is 7.2% of SL. Pectoral fin is narrow based and has 18 rays. Dorsal fin originates posterior to pectoral fin base. Pelvic fin is located under preoperculum and consists of 2 filamentous rays. Caudal fin has 8 rays. Body is covered with small, subrectangular, cycloid scales. Head is naked except for scales on cheeks. Lateral line is indistinct but consists of three rows anterior to anal fin. Trunk vertebrae number 18 or 19. Color is pale yellowish, with abdomen and head (except snout) black, pectoral fins dusky, and other fins colorless.

This species occurs in the tropical Atlantic Ocean to about 3,536 m. In the western Atlantic it occurs in the northeastern Gulf of Mexico between 2,104 and 2,194 m. Maximum known size is 113 mm TL.

REFERENCES: Grey 1956, 1958; Carter and Sulak 1984; Anderson et al. 1985.

Porogadus catena   (Goode and Bean 1885)

Porogadus catena is relatively slender, elongate, compressed, and tapering to a pointed caudal fin, with a large head, enlarged head pores, small spines on preoperculum, and a large spine on dorsoposterior margin of operculum. It is distinguished from the other species of the family by the following combination of characters. Snout is acute and compressed. Mouth is slightly subterminal, slightly oblique, and large; upper jaw extends beyond posterior margin of orbit. Eye is large. Narrow band of villiform teeth occurs in jaws, vomer, and palatine. First gill arch has 3 rudiments on epibranch, 1 gill raker in corner, and 15 gill rakers on lower limb. Preoperculum has four spines on posterior margin. Opercular spine is weak and flattened. Head length is 46.2% to 51.4%, head depth is 27.5% to 34.7%, snout length is 12.5% to 16.9%, orbit length is 6.8% to 12%,

predorsal length is 42.5% to 56.8%, and body depth is 19.2% to 26.6% of gnathoproctal length. Pectoral fin is narrow based and has 15 to 17 rays. Dorsal fin originates over pectoral fin base. Pelvic fin is located below preoperculum and consists of 2 filamentous rays. Body and head are covered with small, subrectangular, cycloid scales. Lateral line consists of three rows of pores. Color is blackish brown, with head and abdomen darker and fins colorless.

This species occurs worldwide in tropical seas between 1,500 and 3,500 m. In the western Atlantic it occurs in the Gulf of Mexico at 2,683 m.

REFERENCES: Goode and Bean 1896; Grey 1956 (as *P subarmatus*); Carter and Sulak 1984; Anderson et al. 1985.

Porogadus miles   Goode and Bean 1885

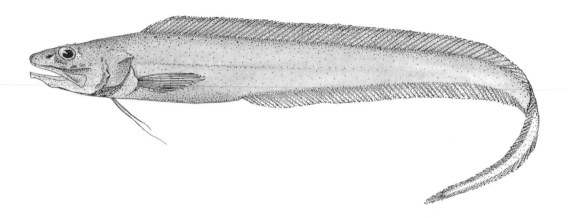

Porogadus miles is relatively slender, elongate, compressed, and tapering to a pointed caudal fin, with a relatively large head, large mucous cavities beneath orbital region and on posterior margin of preoperculum, and a lateral line consisting of three rows of circular pores. It is distinguished from the other species of the family by the following combination of characters. Snout is acute, depressed, and slightly overhangs jaws. Mouth is slightly subterminal, nearly horizontal, and large; upper jaw extends posterior to orbit. Eye is large. Villiform teeth occur in jaws, vomer, and palatine. Vomerine tooth patch is inverted-V-shaped. Basibranchial tooth patch is single. First gill arch has 3 rudiments on epibranch, 1 gill raker in corner, and 14 long gill rakers on lower limb. Preoperculum has four or five well-developed spines along posterior margin. Opercular spine is well developed and flattened. Head length is 47.9% to 56.7%, head depth is 24.5% to 30.9%, snout length is 13.9% to 18%, predorsal length is 55% to 64%, preanal length is 88.7%, and body depth is 25.1% to 30.9% of gnathoproctal length. Pectoral fin is narrow based and has 14 to 16 rays. Dorsal fin originates above pectoral fin base and has about 170 rays. Pelvic fin is located below preoperculum and consists of 2 filamentous rays. Anal fin has about 135 rays, and caudal fin has 6 rays. Body is covered with very small, subrectangular, cycloid scales. Color is brown, with belly and head darker, pectoral and dorsal fins dark brown, and other fins gray.

This species occurs worldwide in tropical to temperate seas between about 1,200 and 5,054 m. In the western Atlantic it occurs off the east coast of the United States at 38°N, 73°W and in the Gulf of Mexico between 2,104 and 2,194 m. Maximum known size is 291 mm TL.

REFERENCES: Goode and Bean 1896; Grey 1956, 1958; Nielsen and Cohen 1986; Carter and Sulak 1984; Anderson et al. 1985.

Xyelacyba myersi   Cohen 1961

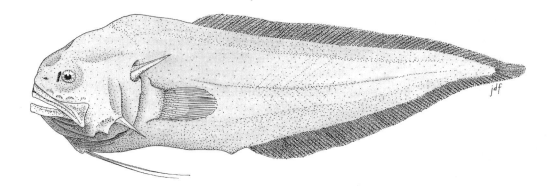

Xyelacyba myersi is relatively deep bodied, short, and compressed, with stout preopercular and opercular spines, and pelvic fins located below eyes. It is distinguished from the other species of the family by the following combination of characters. Snout is blunt and rounded. Mouth is terminal, oblique, and large; upper jaw extends beyond posterior margin of orbit. Eye is small. Villiform teeth occur in jaws, vomer, and palatine. Jaws have edentulous space at symphysis. Head of vomer has three rows of teeth, and lateral extensions of vomer and palatine have single row of teeth. Three basibranchial tooth patches are present. First gill arch has 4 or 5 rudiments on epibranch, 1 gill raker in corner, and 15 to 17 gill rakers plus 4 rudiments on lower limb. Preoperculum has three spines, with dorsalmost spine largest. Operculum has large, posterodorsally directed spine at upper angle. Head length is 21.9% to 22.4%, snout length is 6.2% to 6.3%, eye diameter is 2.8% to 3.8%, preanal length is 31.9% to 44.8%, body depth is 26.3% to 29.1%, and pelvic fin length is 17.5% to 24.8% of SL. Pectoral fin is broad based and has 19 rays. Dorsal fin originates above pectoral fin base and has 87 rays. Pelvic fin consists of 2 filamentous rays. Anal fin has 71 rays, and caudal fin has 9 rays. Body and head are covered with deciduous scales. Lateral line is indistinct posterior to vent. Vertebrae number 49. Scale pockets are dark brown, unpaired fins and belly are very dark, ventral surface of head is dark brown, and remainder of head is white.

This species occurs in the Atlantic and Pacific Oceans. In the western Atlantic it occurs in the northeastern Gulf of Mexico and the Bahamas between 1,555 and 2,012 m. Maximum known size is 464 mm SL.

REFERENCE: Cohen 1961.

APHYONIDAE

Aphyonids are moderately slender to slender, taper posteriorly, and have a large head, poorly developed eyes, and confluent dorsal, caudal, and anal fins. They are distinguished from the other families of the order by the following combination of characters. Snout is rather blunt. Mouth is moderate to large, and terminal to slightly superior or slightly inferior. Anterior nostril is immediately above upper lip or widely separated from upper lip. Chin barbel is absent. Teeth range from small to fanglike but are generally small and occur in jaws and on vomer, and are present or absent in palatine. Opercular spines are weak to absent. Fins lack spines. Pectoral fin is broad based and located on lower midbody. Dorsal fin originates anterior to posterior one-half of body but is always longer based than anal fin. Pelvic fin, when present, is located under preoperculum or further posteriorly and consists of one ray. Caudal fin is bluntly to acutely pointed. Scales are absent, and body is enveloped in thick gelatinous envelope, visible only in freshly caught specimens. Lateral line canals occur on head and body. Swim bladder is absent. Abdominal vertebrae range from 26 to 48.

Aphyonids occur worldwide in tropical to temperate seas, generally between 700 and 5,600 m. Species are either bathypelagic or benthic. Fecundity ranges from 20 to 70 eggs in pelagic species and from 1,000 to 1,500 eggs in benthic species. Development is viviparous, and newborn larvae are apparently well developed and occur at same depths as adults. There are 21 species in six genera, and 3 species in separate genera occur in the Gulf of Mexico.

Key to the Species of the Gulf of Mexico
(Adapted from Cohen and Nielsen 1978)

1a. Palatine teeth present; long gill rakers on first arch 24 to 33; caudal fin rays 9 or 10 . . . . *Barathronus bicolor* p. 740

1b. Palatine teeth absent; long gill rakers on first arch 0 to 14; caudal fin rays 6 to 8 2

2a. Long gill rakers on first arch
. . . . *Aphyonus gelatinosus* p. 739

2b. No long gill rakers on first arch
. . . . *Sciadonus pedicellaris* p. 741

Aphyonus gelatinosus   Günther 1878

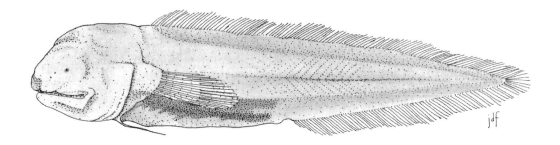

Aphyonus gelatinosus is moderately slender and compressed posteriorly, with a swollen head, a horizontal mouth, and a bifurcated opercular spine. It is distinguished from the other species of the family by the following combination of characters. Snout is swollen and projects slightly beyond lower jaw. Anterior and posterior nostrils are midway between upper jaw and eye. Eye is very small and is located beneath skin. Premaxilla has about five relatively large teeth medially and five small teeth laterally. Lower jaw has band of conical teeth. Vomer has anterior row of six to eight small teeth and posterior row of six to eight large teeth. First gill arch has 3 or 4 long, and 9 or 10 short, gill rakers. Head is 25%, snout is 8.4% to 8.7%, predorsal length is 28% to 30%, and preanal length is 52% to 56% of SL. Pectoral fin has 17 or 18 rays, dorsal fin has 106 to 116 rays, anal fin has 65 to 68 rays, and caudal fin has 7 or 8 rays. Lateral line papillae occur on lower jaw and along midline of body. Vertebrae number 84 and comprise 31 to 33 trunk, and 51 to 53 tail, vertebrae. Mature males have copulatory apparatus consisting of long penis and clasper, located medially below penis. Color is light yellow in preservative, with peritoneum dark brown.

This species occurs in the western Atlantic and southwestern Pacific Oceans and is benthic between 914 and 2,560 m. In the western Atlantic it occurs in the Gulf of Mexico. Fecundity is about 800 eggs. Maximum known size is 132 mm SL.

REFERENCES: Grey 1956; Nielsen 1969, 1986c,d.

Barathronus bicolor   Goode and Bean 1886

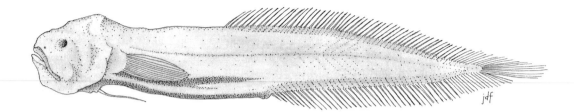

Barathronus bicolor is slender and compressed, with a large head and a very oblique mouth. It is distinguished from the other species of the family by the following combination of characters. Snout is blunt and does not project beyond lower jaw. Anterior and posterior nostrils are about midway between upper lip and eye. Eye is small and located below skin. Small, knoblike teeth occur in premaxilla. Lower jaw has small, knoblike teeth closely placed along anterior third of length, and large, fanglike teeth in single row along posterior section. Vomer has two or three lateral rows of small, blunt teeth between two large, fanglike teeth. First gill arch has 28 to 33 gill rakers. Pectoral fin rays number 22 to 25, dorsal fin rays number 65 to 78, anal fin rays number 52 to 59, and caudal fin rays number 9 or 10. Lateral line papillae occur on head and along midline of body. Vertebrae number 70 to 75 and comprise 31 to 35 trunk, and 38 to 41 tail, vertebrae. Mature males have copulatory apparatus consisting of very long penis; clasper is absent. Females possess small claspers behind and on either side of genital openings. Body is colorless, except peritoneum is very dark.

This species occurs in the western Atlantic in the Gulf of Mexico and the Caribbean Sea and is benthic between 366 and 1,406 m. Fecundity is about 600 eggs, and spawning apparently takes place year-round. Maximum known size is 140 mm SL; males mature at about 85 mm SL, and females mature at about 90 mm SL.

REFERENCES: Grey 1959; Nielsen 1969, 1986d; Uyeno et al. 1983.

Sciadonus pedicellaris   Garman 1899

Sciadonus pedicellaris is long, slender, and compressed posteriorly, with an almost horizontal mouth, very small eyes, and small pelvic fins. It is distinguished from the other species of the family by the following combination of characters. Head is about twice as wide as body. Lower jaw projects beyond upper jaw. Anterior nostril is tubular and near upper lip. Posterior nostril is porelike and midway between anterior nostril and eye. Indistinct eyes are located beneath skin. Fine teeth occur in upper and lower jaws and in vomer. Teeth are lacking from symphyses of upper and lower jaw. Palatine lacks teeth. First gill arch has 14 small dentigerous gill rakers, 3 on hypobranch and 11 on lower limb; long gill rakers are lacking. Branchiostegal rays number 9 or 10. Head is 15.5%, upper jaw length is 8.8% to 9%, lower jaw length is 11%, predorsal length is 28.5% to 30.5%, and preanal length is 68% to 70% of SL. Pectoral fin is located on elongated pedicel and has 12 to 14 rays. Dorsal fin has about 90 to 93 rays, and anal fin has 46 rays. Pelvic fin is thoracic and consists of 1 ray. Lateral line papillae are limited to snout and lower jaw. Trunk vertebrae number 43 or 44, and caudal vertebrae number 38 or 39. Color is reddish brown in preservative.

This species occurs in the North Atlantic and tropical eastern Pacific Oceans from 1,847 to 4,600 m. In the western North Atlantic it occurs in the northern Gulf of Mexico. Maximum known size is 102 mm SL.

REFERENCES: Nielsen 1969; Cohen and Nielsen 1978.

BYTHITIDAE

Bythitids are moderately elongate, taper posteriorly, and have small cycloid scales, and dorsal and anal fins either confluent or free of caudal fin. They are distinguished from the other species of the family by the following combination of characters. Snout is moderately blunt to blunt and equal to or slightly overhanging lower jaw. Anterior nostril is immediately above upper lip in most. Chin barbel is absent. Teeth are present in jaws and vomer, and are present or absent in palatine. First gill arch has six or fewer gill rakers. Fins lack spines. Pectoral fin is broad based with short peduncle or narrow based with long peduncle, and is located on midbody or lower one-half of flank. Dorsal fin originates from near nape to above anus but is always longer based than anal fin. Pelvic fins, when present, are located close together below preopercula, and each consists of one filamentous ray or two fleshy rays. Anal fin originates immediately behind anus. Scales are generally present on head and body. Abdominal vertebrae range from 9 to 22.

Bythitids occur worldwide in tropical to temperate seas. Most species are benthic from near shore to the abyss, but a few species are bathypelagic or found in freshwater caves. All species have internal fertilization and viviparous development. Larval stages are pelagic. There are 90 species in 31 genera, and 6 species in 5 genera occur in the Gulf of Mexico.

Key to the Species of the Gulf of Mexico
(Adapted from Cohen and Nielsen 1978)

1a. Caudal fin free of dorsal and anal fins 2
1b. Caudal fin continuous with dorsal and anal fins 3
2a. Branchiostegal rays eight; body scales barely imbricate; scales absent on head . . . . *Gunterichthys longipenis* p. 745
2b. Branchiostegal rays seven; body scales imbricate; scales present on head. . . . . *Ogilbia cayorum* p. 746
3a. Scales absent on head. 4
3b. Scales present on head . . . . *Cataetyx laticeps* p. 743
4a. Body completely scaled
. . . . *Diplacanthopoma brachysoma* p. 744
4b. Body naked or incompletely scaled. 5
5a. Scales absent on body
. . . . *Saccogaster rhamphidognatha* p. 747
5b. Scales present on body . . . . *Saccogaster staigeri* p. 748

Cataetyx laticeps   Koefoed 1927

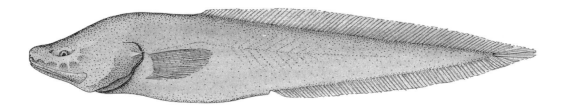

Cataetyx laticeps is relatively slender, tapers posteriorly, and has a blunt knob buried in skin behind posterior nostril and a strong opercular spine. It is distinguished from the other species of the family by the following combination of characters. Snout is strongly depressed and projects slightly beyond lower jaw. Eye is small and directed dorsolaterally. Teeth occur in jaws, vomer, and palatine. Vomerine tooth patch is triangular. First gill arch has three gill rakers. Branchiostegal rays number 8. Head is 25%, snout length is 5.4%, eye diameter is 2%, predorsal length is 35.1%, preanal length is 56.3%, body depth is 13.5%, and length of pelvic fins is 7.5% of SL. Pectoral fin is broad based and has short peduncle and 22 to 29 rays. Dorsal fin originates posterior to pectoral fin base and has 91 to 107 rays. Pelvic fin consists of 1 filamentous ray. Anal fin has 74 to 87 rays, and caudal fin has 8 to 11 rays. Head and body are scaled. Vertebrae number 60 or 61. Color is dark brown.

This species occurs in the Atlantic Ocean between 1,050 and 2,830 m. In the western Atlantic it occurs in the Gulf of Mexico. Maximum known size is 650 mm TL.

REFERENCES: Koefoed 1927; Cohen and Nielsen 1978; Nielsen 1986a; Cohen 1986e.

Diplacanthopoma brachysoma   Günther 1887

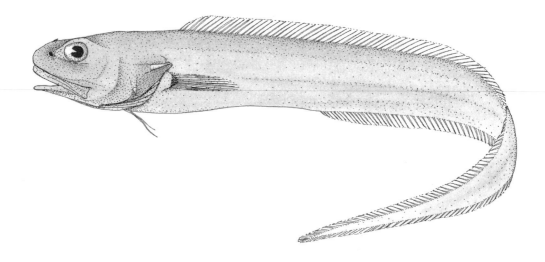

Diplacanthopoma brachysoma is elongate, compressed, and tapering posteriorly, with head naked and body completely scaled. It is distinguished from the other species of the family by the following combination of characters. Snout is moderately blunt and slightly overhangs jaws. Mouth is slightly oblique and large; upper jaw extends beyond posterior margin of orbit. Eye is large. Villiform teeth occur in jaws, vomer, and palatine. Vomerine tooth patch is inverted-V-shaped. First gill arch has one gill raker and four rudiments on epibranch and three gill rakers and eight or nine rudiments on lower limb. Operculum has single horizontal spine extending to near tip of opercular flap, and single, short, vertical spine directed ventrally. Head is 20.7% to 23.7%, snout length is 4.1% to 4.7%, eye diameter is 3.4% to 4.5%, predorsal length is 27.7% to 29.1%, preanal length is 46.9% to 52.2%, body depth is 12% to 16.2%, and pelvic fin is 7.4% to 11.4% of SL. Pectoral fin is narrow based and of moderate size. Dorsal fin originates above pectoral fin base. Pelvic fins are located together under preopercula, and each consists of two filamentous rays. Dorsal, caudal, and anal fins are confluent. Scales on body are small and deciduous. Lateral line is indistinct. Color is light brown dorsally and pale ventrally.

This species occurs in the western Atlantic in the Gulf of Mexico and off the coast of Brazil at 439 to 752 m. Maximum known size is about 220 mm SL.

REFERENCE: Goode and Bean 1896.

Gunterichthys longipenis Dawson 1966
Gold brotula

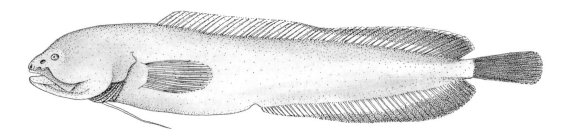

Gunterichthys longipenis is moderately elongate, compressed, and tapering slightly posteriorly, with a scaleless head and dorsal and anal fins separated from caudal fin. It is distinguished from the other species of the family by the following combination of characters. Snout is blunt and narrowly rounded. Anterior nostril is tubelike and located near upper lip. Pronounced fold overhangs thin, skirtlike lower lip. Eye is small but distinct, and covered with skin. Jaws have bands of villiform teeth, with those of inner row near symphysis of upper jaw enlarged, and those of inner row of lower jaw enlarged and depressible. Vomer has inverted-V-shaped patch of 11 pointed, depressible teeth, and palatine has two longitudinal series of small, conical teeth. Gill rakers on first arch number 14 to 22. Branchiostegal rays number 8. Head is 25% to 29%, predorsal length is 34% to 38%, preanal length is 54% to 57%, and body depth at anal fin origin is 16% to 18% of SL. Snout is 19% to 20% and eye diameter is 5% to 6% of head length. Pectoral fin is broad based with short peduncle, and has 18 to 22 rays. Dorsal fin originates slightly posterior to pectoral fin base and has 64 to 68 rays.

Pelvic fin consists of single filamentous ray. Anal fin has 45 to 50 rays, and caudal fin has convex posterior margin and 13 or 14 rays. Lateral line is inconspicuous. Scales are lacking on head and present on body but are scarcely overlapping. Vertebrae number 39 to 43. Mature males have copulatory organs consisting of long, pointed, distally hardened intromittent organ and pair of broad, hardened claspers. Color in life is pale gold, with distal part of body translucent, dorsal fin anteriorly freckled and posteriorly dark brown with pale margin, and anal fin dark posteriorly. Color in alcohol is pale beige, with dorsal and anal fins colorless or pale gray and pectoral and pelvic fins beige.

This species occurs in the western Atlantic from the northern Gulf of Mexico from the Florida Keys to Texas. It burrows into the soft mud bottoms of lagoons and estuaries. Maximum known size is 75 mm TL.

REFERENCES: Dawson 1966, 1971a; Moore 1975; Hoese and Moore 1977; C. R. Robins et al. 1986; Tolley and Peebles 1987; Boschung 1992.

Ogilbia cayorum   Evermann and Kendall 1898
Key brotula

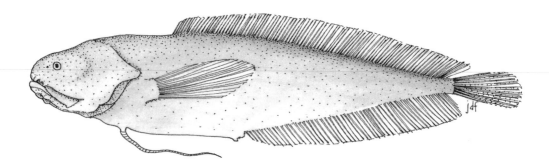

Ogilbia cayorum is moderately elongate, compressed, and moderately tapering posteriorly, with distal section of maxilla expanded vertically, head partially scaled, and dorsal and anal fins separated from caudal fin. It is distinguished from the other species of the family by the following combination of characters. Snout is slightly blunt and convex. Anterior nostril is close to upper lip. Maxilla is expanded vertically near posterior margin. Jaw, vomerine, and palatine teeth are villiform and arranged in bands. Eye is small. Gill membranes are free of isthmus. Operculum has single sharp spine. Branchiostegal rays number seven. Gill rakers on first arch number 12 to 18. Dorsal fin rays number 58 to 73, anal fin rays number 49 to 55, and lateral scale rows number 87 to 90. Pelvic fin is thoracic in position and consists of two filamentous rays. Vertebrae number 38 to 44.

Intromittent organs of males have two sets of pseudoclaspers, with larger one compressed and ear shaped.

This species occurs in the western Atlantic around tropical coral reefs, including the eastern Gulf of Mexico. Maximum known size is about 70 mm SL. The genus *Ogilbia* contains an unknown number of species that differ in details of dermal ridges and papillae on head, and in color. Several of these undescribed species may occur in the Gulf of Mexico. All species are secretive, occur on coral reefs, have internal fertilization, and are viviparous.

REFERENCES: Cervigón 1966; Böhlke and Chaplin 1968; Suarez 1975; Ogren and Brusher 1977; Cohen and Nielsen 1978; C. R. Robins et al. 1986; Boschung 1992.

Saccogaster rhamphidognatha   Cohen 1987

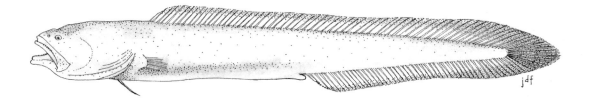

Saccogaster rhamphidognatha is relatively elongate and compressed, with an antrorse, hooklike projection at the posteroventral angle of the maxilla, and without scales. It is distinguished from the other species of the family by the following combination of characters. Snout is moderately blunt and slightly overhangs lower jaw. Anterior nostril is small pore directly above upper lip, and posterior nostril is equal in size to clear window over eye. Premaxilla has outer band of granular teeth and inner band of enlarged, needlelike teeth. Lower jaw has narrow outer row of small, slightly compressed teeth and inner row of slightly compressed teeth. Vomer has inverted-U-shaped band of small pointed teeth continuous with teeth on palatine. Head length is 21%, predorsal length is 24%, preanal length is 55%, and body depth at vent is 10% of SL. Snout length is 27% and eye diameter is 7.1% of head length. Pectoral fin is narrow based and has short peduncle and 12 rays. Dorsal fin originates over pectoral fin base and has 77 rays. Pelvic fin consists of single ray. Anal fin originates on posterior one-half of body and has 49 rays. Caudal fin has 12 rays. Lateral line is obsolete on body, and on head consists of one supraorbital pore, two infraorbital pores, and two mandibular pores. Males have copulatory organ consisting of prominent penis protruding distally from elongated protuberance. Vertebrae number 58 and comprise 20 trunk, and 38 tail, vertebrae. Color is pale, with vertical fins brownish distally.

This species occurs in the western Atlantic in the northern Gulf of Mexico off the Mississippi Delta at 210 m. It is known from a single specimen of 59.7 mm SL.

REFERENCE: Cohen 1987.

Saccogaster staigeri   Cohen and Nielsen 1972

Saccogaster staigeri is moderately elongate and compressed, with scales on sides of body. It is distinguished from the other species of the family by the following combination of characters. Snout is moderately blunt and slightly overlaps lower jaw. Anterior nostril is a small pore directly above upper lip. Eye is small. Premaxilla has about 20 needlelike teeth medially and a narrow band of granular teeth laterally. Lower jaw has outer series of small teeth in narrow band and inner row of pointed teeth. Vomer has about 10 needlelike teeth, and palatine has 8 to 10 sharp-pointed teeth in single row. Head is 27%, predorsal length is 30% to 31%, pre-anal length is 60% to 61%, and body depth at vent is 11% to 16% of SL. Snout length is 24% and eye diameter is 8% to 10.2% of head length. Pectoral fin is narrow based and has short peduncle and 18 rays. Dorsal fin has 87 or 88 rays. Pelvic fin consists of single filament. Anal fin has 54 or 55 rays. Lateral line is indistinct. Vertebrae number 51 to 53. Mature males have copulatory organ consisting of long penis protruding from elongated protuberance. Color is pale.

This species occurs in the western Atlantic Ocean from the Gulf of Mexico and off the east coast of Florida between 201 and 347 m. Only two specimens have been captured. Maximum known size is 91 mm SL.

REFERENCE: Cohen and Nielsen 1972.

GADIFORMES

Gadiformes are thought to be a monophyletic group that is the sister group of the Batrachoidiformes and Lophiiformes, but despite considerable research, there is little agreement as to the number of families or the composition of the families of the order. Cohen (1984) recognized 10 families, Markle (1989) recognized 13 families, and Nelson (1994) recognized 12 families, and the composition and sequencing of the families among these studies vary to some degree. Because of the disagreement, herein the classification of Nelson (1994) is accepted. Seven of the 12 families of Nelson occur in the Gulf of Mexico.

Key to the Families of the Gulf of Mexico
(Adapted from Cohen et al. 1990)

1a. Anterior dorsal fin consisting of more than one ray and originating on posterior margin of head or behind head; lateral line usually on midflank. 2

1b. Anterior dorsal fin consisting of single ray originating on top of head and widely separated from remaining dorsal fin(s); lateral line near dorsal midline
. . . . Bregmacerotidae p. 750

2a. Top of head with pair of more or less well-developed anteroposteriorly converging bony ridges. 3

2b. Top of head without pair of anteroposteriorly converging bony ridges. 4

3a. Anus and urogenital openings close together; luminescent organ absent . . . . Merlucciidae p. 799

3b. Anus and urogenital openings widely separated; luminescent organ present . . . . Steindachneriidae p. 801

4a. Tail fin absent or (rarely) microsopic
. . . . Macrouridae p. 761

4b. Tail fin present 5

5a. Caudal peduncle very slender, with numerous procurrent caudal rays extending nearly to posterior dorsal and anal fin rays . . . . Melanonidae p. 797

5b. Caudal peduncle very slender to rather broad, without numerous procurrent caudal rays extending nearly to posterior dorsal and anal fin rays. 6

6a. Vomer with few or no teeth; caudal peduncle very slender; swim bladder with anterior projections attached to rear of cranium . . . . Moridae p. 803

6b. Vomer with teeth; caudal peduncle moderately slender to broad; swim bladder without anterior projections or, if projection present, not connected to cranium
. . . . Phycidae p. 755

BREGMACEROTIDAE Codlets

The codlets are moderately elongate and compressed, with the first dorsal fin consisting of a single ray on top of the head, and jugular pelvic fins having several elongated rays. They are distinguished from the other families of the order by the following combination of characters. Snout is moderately short and blunt. Mouth is terminal and extends posterior to anterior margin of orbit. Teeth are minute, are arranged in one or two series in jaws, and also occur in vomer. Chin barbel is absent. Eye is of moderate size, and upper portion is covered with transparent membrane. Dorsal side of head lacks V-shaped ridge. Gill rakers are present. Gill membranes extend to level of pectoral fin base, are narrowly united below throat, and are free of isthmus. Branchiostegal rays number seven. Pectoral fin is located at midflank or above midflank, and is rather small but broadly based. First dorsal fin consists of one long ray that fits into groove when depressed and is widely separated from second dorsal fin. Second dorsal fin is long based and notched over middle third of length. Pelvic fin is located under head and consists of five to seven rays, with outer two or three thickened and elongated to at least anal fin origin. Anal fin is located below second dorsal fin and resembles it in shape. Anal and second dorsal fins are separated by short distance from caudal fin. Caudal fin is bilobed. Scales are cycloid, thin, and deciduous. Lateral line is tubular and runs along dorsal margin of body. Swim bladder is physoclistous, lacks anterior projections, and is not joined to the cranium.

Codlets occur worldwide in tropical and subtropical seas. All species are epipelagic or mesopelagic to 2,000 m. Some species occur in coastal waters and estuaries. There are about 16 species in a single genus, and 4 species occur in the Gulf of Mexico.

Key to the Species of the Gulf of Mexico

1a. Second dorsal fin rays greater than 46; anal fin rays greater than 48; body heavily pigmented (brown) 2
1b. Second dorsal fin rays fewer than 49; anal fin rays fewer than 50; body transparent to sparsely pigmented 3
2a. Second dorsal fin rays greater than 56; anal fin rays greater than 57 . . . . *Bregmaceros mcclellandii* p. 754
2b. Second dorsal fin rays 47 to 56; anal fin rays 49 to 58 . . . . *Bregmaceros atlanticus* p. 751
3a. Second dorsal fin rays 40 to 44; anal fin rays 41 to 46 . . . . *Bregmaceros houdei* p. 753
3b. Second dorsal fin rays 45 to 48; anal fin rays 45 to 49 . . . . *Bregmaceros cantori* p. 752

Bregmaceros atlanticus   Goode and Bean 1886

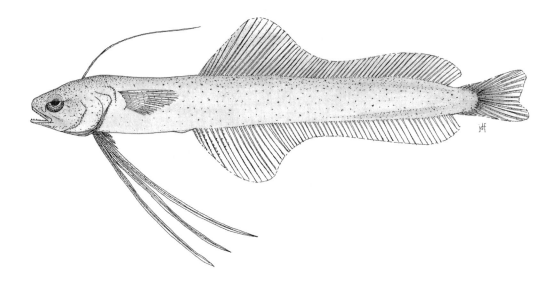

Bregmaceros atlanticus is moderately elongate and compressed posteriorly, with relatively long and symmetrical second dorsal and anal fins. It is distinguished from the other species of the family by the following combination of characters. Snout is moderately blunt. Jaws are slightly oblique, terminal, and extend beyond anterior margin of orbit. Teeth are minute and occur in jaws and vomer. Head length is 14.9% to 17.5%, predorsal length is 33.7% to 40%, preanal length is 34.5% to 38.5%, and body depth is 10.9% to 14.3% of SL. Eye diameter is 1 to 1.3 times snout length and 0.9 to 1.2 times interorbital distance. Head length is 3.9 to 5 times interorbital distance. Second dorsal fin has 47 to 56 rays (49 to 53 in cleared and stained specimens). Anal fin has 49 to 58 rays (54 to 57 in cleared and stained specimens). Caudal fin is emarginate. Myomeres number 50 to 55, and vertebrae number 53 to 55. Color is brown, and fins usually have chromatophores but occasionally are colorless.

This species occurs in tropical to warm temperate waters of the Atlantic and western Indian Oceans between 50 and 2,000 m. In the western Atlantic it occurs from New Jersey to the Guianas, including the Gulf of Mexico and the Caribbean Sea. Maximum known size is 67 mm TL.

REFERENCES: D'Ancona and Cavinato 1965; Belianina 1980; Houde 1984; Milliken and Houde 1984; Saksena and Richards 1986; Smith 1986a; Boschung 1992.

Bregmaceros cantori Milliken and Houde 1984

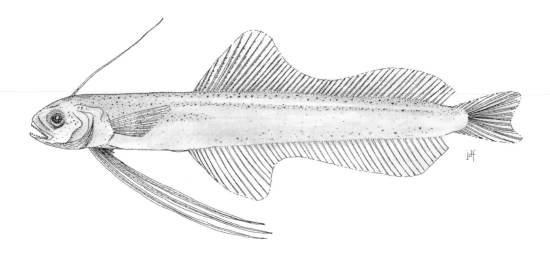

Bregmaceros cantori is moderately elongate and compressed posteriorly, with relatively short and symmetrical second dorsal and anal fins. It is distinguished from the other species of the family by the following combination of characters. Snout is moderately blunt. Jaws are slightly oblique, terminal, and extend beyond anterior margin of pupil. Teeth are minute and occur in jaws and vomer. Head length is 15.6% to 19.6%, predorsal length is 37% to 43.5%, preanal length is 35.7% to 41.7%, and body depth is 13.9% to 18.2% of SL. Eye diameter is 1 to 1.24 times snout length and 1.2 to 2.1 times interorbital width. Head length is 4 to 6.7 times interorbital width. Second dorsal fin has 45 to 48 rays, and anal fin has 45 to 49 rays. Myomeres and vertebrae number 45 to 48. Color is nearly transparent in fresh specimens and white to yellowish in preserved specimens, with line of brown pigment extending from posterodorsal margin of operculum to base of caudal fin dorsal to midline. Scattered brown chromatophores occur on base and fin rays of posterior one-third of second dorsal fin. Second line of melanophores extends from base of second dorsal fin onto head and forms figure-eight pattern on head. Smallest larvae are lightly pigmented, with melanophore at angle of jaw and melanophores on ventral surface of visceral mass. Larger larvae (5 to 10 mm SL) lose melanophores on visceral mass but have large melanophore over forebrain.

This species occurs in the western and possibly the eastern Atlantic. In the western Atlantic it occurs from the Carolinas to the Straits of Florida, in the Gulf of Mexico and the Caribbean Sea, and off the coast of Brazil. Adults are known from the Cariaco Trench off Venezuela and in the Gulf of Mexico off the Mississippi River and in Campeche Bay. Maximum known size is 57.1 mm SL.

REFERENCES: Houde 1984; Milliken and Houde 1984; Saksena and Richards 1986.

Bregmaceros houdei   Saksena and Richards 1986

Bregmaceros houdei is moderately elongate and compressed posteriorly, with relatively short and symmetrical second dorsal and anal fins. It is distinguished from the other species of the family by the following combination of characters. Snout is moderately acute. Jaws are slightly oblique, terminal, and extend beyond anterior margin of pupil. Teeth are minute and occur in jaws and vomer. Head length is 21.3% to 25.5%, predorsal length is 25.6% to 45.2%, and body depth is 13% to 16% of SL. Eye diameter is 0.7 to 0.9 times snout length and 0.9 to 1.3 times interorbital width. Head length is 3.5 to 5.3 times interorbital width. Second dorsal fin has 40 to 44 rays (45 to 48 in cleared and stained specimens). Anal fin has 41 to 46 rays (46 to 50 in cleared and stained specimens). Caudal fin has convex posterior margin and 31 to 33 rays. Myomeres number 44 to 47, and vertebrae number 47 to 50. Color is limited to dark melanophores located on anterior half of body. Smallest larvae (1.7 to 3.5 mm SL) have large, stellate chromatophores at angle of jaw, scattered over hindbrain, and at base of first dorsal fin ray. Larger larvae (5 to 10 mm SL) have additional chromatophores on midbrain, hindbrain, and on ventral surface of anterior half of visceral mass. Juvenile specimens have chromatophores scattered over anterior third of body.

This species occurs in the western Atlantic in the eastern Gulf of Mexico and the Caribbean Sea west of the Lesser Antilles, generally at less than 50 m. Maximum known size is 16.4 mm SL for a juvenile specimen. This species may be paedomorphic.

REFERENCES: Houde 1984; Saksena and Richards 1986.

Bregmaceros mcclellandii   Thompson 1840

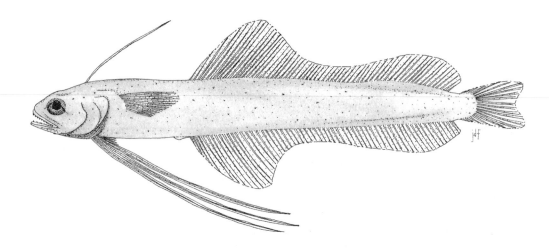

Bregmaceros mcclellandii is moderately slender and compressed posteriorly, with relatively long and symmetrical second dorsal and anal fins. It is distinguished from the other species of the family by the following combination of characters. Snout is moderately blunt. Jaws are slightly oblique, terminal, and extend beyond anterior margin of pupil. Teeth are minute and occur in jaws and vomer. Head length is 14.5% to 16.4%, predorsal length is 35.7% to 41.7%, preanal length is 33.3% to 35.7%, and body depth is 11.9% to 16.4% of SL. Eye diameter is 0.7 to 1 times snout length and 0.5 to 0.9 times interorbital length. Head length is 2.4 to 4.8 times interorbital width. Second dorsal fin has 57 to 65 rays, and anal fin has 58 to 69 rays. Caudal fin is emarginate. Myomeres number 52 to 59, and vertebrae number 58. Color is brown, slightly darker dorsally than ventrally. Fins are pigmented except for anal fin.

This species occurs worldwide in tropical to warm temperate seas, except it is absent in the eastern Pacific. In the western Atlantic it occurs from Cape Cod to northern Brazil, including the Gulf of Mexico and the Caribbean Sea. It has been captured from near the surface to 500 m. Maximum known size is 96 mm TL.

REFERENCES: D'Ancona and Cavinato 1965; Belianina 1980; Milliken and Houde 1984; Saksena and Richards 1986.

PHYCIDAE

Phycids are moderately slender to moderately fusiform, with two dorsal fins, one anal fin, and a caudal fin separated from last dorsal and anal fins. They are distinguished from the other families of the order by the following combination of characters. Snout is short to moderately long and depressed. Mouth is large, horizontal to moderately oblique, and slightly subterminal. Chin barbel is usually present, and several paired and single barbels are often present on snout. Eye is large to rather small. Teeth are generally in villiform bands on jaws, vomer, and palatine. Fins lack spines. Pectoral fin has moderately narrow to rather broad base and is inserted high on flank. First dorsal fin originates at rear of or behind head and is either short and triangular or consists of single ray followed by number of fleshy filaments. Second dorsal fin is shorter and longer based than first dorsal fin. Pelvic fins are widely separated and located anterior to pectoral fin base. Anal fin is long and not indented. Caudal peduncle is moderately deep. Scales are small and cycloid. Lateral line is generally complete but occasionally interrupted and extends to base of tail. Physoclistous swim bladder is present and either lacks or has anterior projections that are free of rear of cranium.

Phycids occur in the Atlantic, western Pacific, and western Indian Oceans. All species are benthic. Food consists of a wide range of invertebrates and fishes. There are 27 species in five genera, and 5 species in two genera occur in the Gulf of Mexico.

Key to the Species of the Gulf of Mexico
(Adapted from Cohen et al. 1990)

1a. First dorsal fin ray followed by row of small, fleshy filaments; three barbels on snout
. . . . *Enchelyopus cimbrius* p. 756
1b. First dorsal fin ray followed by remaining fin rays of first dorsal fin; no barbels on snout 2
2a. Scale rows between dorsal fin base and lateral line 18 to 21
. . . .*Urophycis earllii* p. 753
2b. Scales rows between dorsal fin base and lateral line fewer than 13. 3
3a. Upper limb of first gill arch (epibranch) with two gill rakers
. . . . *Urophycis floridanus* p. 759
3b. Upper limb of first gill arch (epibranch) with three gill rakers. 4
4a. Head with series of dark spots; first dorsal fin with dark blotch and white margin. . . . . *Urophycis regia* p. 760
4b. Head without series of dark spots; first dorsal fin without dark blotch or white margin . . . . *Urophycis cirrata* p. 757

Enchelyopus cimbrius   (Linnaeus 1776)
Rockling

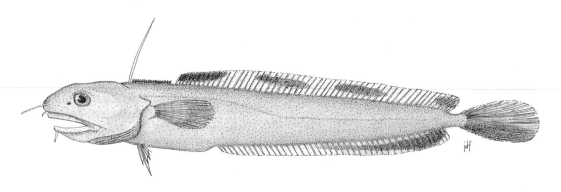

Enchelyopus cimbrius is moderately slender and slightly tapering posteriorly, with three barbels on snout and the first dorsal fin ray followed by a row of small, fleshy filaments. It is distinguished from the other species of the family by the following combination of characters. Snout is moderately blunt. Jaws are inferior and horizontal. Head is about 16% to 17%, predorsal length is 14% to 15%, and pelvic fin is 7% to 9% of TL. Snout length is 24% to 27%, upper jaw is 44% to 48%, lower jaw is 49% to 56%, and eye is 22% to 24% of head length. Gill rakers number 9 or 10. Pectoral fin has rounded margin and 15 or 16 rays. First dorsal fin ray is located above upper section of gill slit, is about as long as head, and is followed by 50 fleshy filaments. Second dorsal fin originates over midlength of pectoral fin and has 45 to 53 equal-length rays. Pelvic fin is located anterior to pectoral fin base and has 5 rays. Anal fin has 37 to 41 rays. Caudal fin has oval margin. Lateral line is interrupted along entire length. Scales are small. Vertebrae number 54. Color is dark olive to dusky brown dorsally and white ventrally, with small brown spots. First dorsal fin ray is blackish, and second dorsal fin has elongate dark blotches.

The species occurs in the North Atlantic, and in the western Atlantic it occurs from southwestern Greenland and Newfoundland south to northern Florida and the northern Gulf of Mexico. It is found from near shore to 650 m and is demersal. There is one record in the Gulf of Mexico at 1,325 m, but this depth is questionable. Adults are sedentary bottom dwellers. Food consists of shrimps, isopods, and other small crustaceans, and to a lesser extent, small fishes. Sexual maturity is reached by age three at 250 mm TL. Fecundity ranges from 5,000 to 45,000 eggs. Maximum known size is 410 mm TL, and maximum known age is nine years.

REFERENCES: Bigelow and Schroeder 1953b; Svetovidov 1962; Cohen and Russo 1979; Cohen et al. 1990.

Urophycis cirrata   (Goode and Bean 1896)
Gulf hake

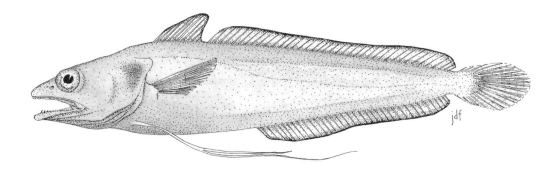

Urophycis cirrata is moderately slender and moderately fusiform, with a short, triangular first dorsal fin, a long second dorsal fin, and long pelvic rays. It is distinguished from the other species of the family by the following combination of characters. Snout is slightly blunt and projects slightly beyond jaws. Jaws are subterminal, slightly oblique, and extend beyond posterior margin of orbit. Head is 21% to 23%, predorsal length is 23% to 25%, and pelvic fin is 36% to 46% of TL. Snout length is 24% to 25%, upper jaw is 51% to 52%, lower jaw is 45% to 46%, eye length is 19%, and caudal peduncle depth is 14.7% to 16% of head length. Gill rakers number three (rarely two) on upper limb of first arch. Pectoral fin is bluntly pointed and fails to reach anus. First dorsal fin originates over pectoral fin base and has 10 rays. Second dorsal fin originates immediately behind first dorsal fin and has 66 rays. Pelvic fin has 2 long rays that extend posterior to origin of anal fin. Anal fin has 57 rays. Second dorsal fin and anal fin are narrowly separated from caudal fin. Caudal fin has convex posterior margin. Lateral line is continuous. Scales number 93 from opercular flap to caudal fin base and 6 to 9 from dorsal fin base to lateral line. Color is pale brown, with diffuse dusky blotch on operculum, dark-edged dorsal and anal fins, and without dark spots on head.

This species occurs in the western North Atlantic from the Gulf of Mexico and off the Caribbean coast of South America to the mouth of the Orinoco River and perhaps southward to Rio de Janeiro, Brazil, between 27 and 684 m (most common between 360 and 470 m). It is generally associated with mud bottoms. Maximum known size is 570 mm TL.

REFERENCES: Svetovidov 1962; Hoese and Moore 1977; C. R. Robins et al. 1986; Cohen et al. 1990; Boschung 1992.

Urophycis earllii   (Bean 1880)
Carolina hake

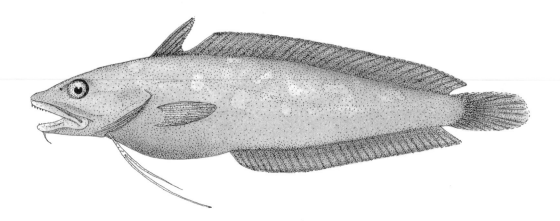

Urophycis earllii is moderately fusiform, with a short, triangular first dorsal fin, a long second dorsal fin, and a moderately long chin barbel. It is distinguished from the other species of the family by the following combination of characters. Snout is slightly blunt and projects slightly beyond jaws. Jaws are subterminal, slightly oblique, and extend beyond posterior margin of orbit. Head is 22%, predorsal length is 26%, and pelvic fin is 30% of TL. Snout length is 24%, upper jaw is 48%, lower jaw is 45%, eye length is 18%, and caudal peduncle depth is 20% of head length. Gill rakers number two on epibranch. Pectoral fin is bluntly pointed, fails to reach anus, and has 15 rays. First dorsal fin originates over pectoral fin base and has 10 rays. Second dorsal fin originates immediately behind first dorsal fin base and has 60 to 63 rays. Pelvic fin has 2 rays that fall just short of anus. Anal fin has 50 to 56 rays. Second dorsal fin and anal fin are narrowly separated from caudal fin. Caudal fin has convex posterior margin. Lateral line is continuous. Scales number 153 to 175 from opercular flap to caudal fin base and 18 to 21 from dorsal fin base to lateral line. Color is generally dark, with side mottled.

This species occurs in the western North Atlantic from Cape Hatteras, North Carolina, to northeastern Florida and the northeastern Gulf of Mexico off Alabama from near shore to about 81 m. It is generally associated with hard bottoms. Maximum known size is 450 mm TL.

REFERENCES: Hildebrand and Cable 1938; Svetovidov 1962; Cohen et al. 1990; Boschung 1992.

Urophycis floridanus (Bean and Dresel 1884)
Southern hake

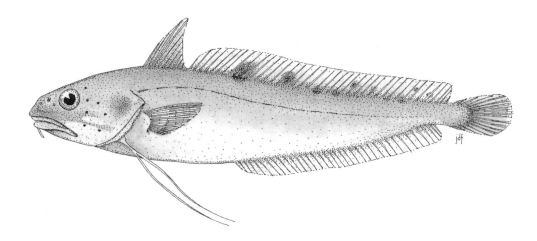

Urophycis floridanus is moderately fusiform, with a short, triangular first dorsal fin, a long second dorsal fin, and a short chin barbel. It is distinguished from the other species of the family by the following combination of characters. Snout is moderately blunt and projects slightly beyond jaws. Jaws are subterminal, slightly oblique, and extend beyond posterior margin of orbit. Head is 22%, predorsal length is 23% to 24%, and pelvic fin is 24% to 30% of TL. Snout length is 25% to 26%, upper jaw is 48% to 49%, lower jaw is 52%, eye length is 20% to 23%, and caudal peduncle depth is 15.8% to 17.7% of head length. Gill rakers number two on epibranch. Pectoral fin is pointed and fails to reach anus. First dorsal fin originates over pectoral fin base and has 12 or 13 rays. Second dorsal fin originates immediately behind first dorsal fin and has 59 rays. Pelvic fin has 2 long rays that extend to anus. Anal fin has 49 to 52 rays. Second dorsal fin and anal fin are narrowly separated from caudal fin. Caudal fin has convex posterior margin. Lateral line is continuous. Scales number 110 to 120 from opercular flap to caudal fin base and 9 to 12 from dorsal fin base to lateral line. Vertebrae number 50. Color is brown to bluish dorsally and silvery ventrally; lateral line is dark with row of pale spots. Series of dark spots occur on head, dusky blotch is located on operculum, and first dorsal fin is partially black.

This species occurs in the western North Atlantic from Beaufort, North Carolina, to the northern Gulf of Mexico westward to northern Mexico on the continental shelf to 400 m. It is most common at less than 300 m. Food consists of polychaetes, crustaceans, and fishes. Maximum known size is 350 mm TL.

REFERENCES: Hildebrand and Cable 1938; Svetovidov 1962; Hoese and Moore 1977; C. R. Robins et al. 1986; Cohen et al. 1990; Boschung 1992.

Urophycis regia (Walbaum 1792)
Spotted hake

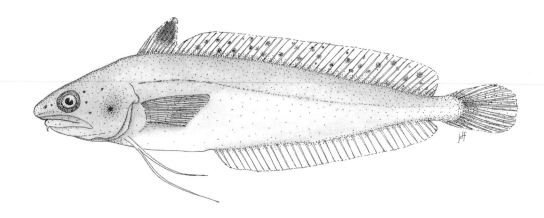

Urophycis regia is moderately slender and moderately fusiform. It is distinguished from the other species of the family by the following combination of characters. Snout is moderately blunt and projects slightly beyond jaws. Jaws are subterminal, slightly oblique, and extend beyond posterior margin of orbit. Head is 21%, predorsal length is 23%, and pelvic fin is 23% of TL. Snout length is 25%, upper jaw is 49%, lower jaw is 55%, and eye length is 24% of head length. Gill rakers number 14 or 15, with 3 (rarely 2) on epibranch. Pectoral fin is bluntly pointed, fails to reach anus, and has 16 rays. First dorsal fin originates over pectoral fin base and has 8 or 9 rays. Second dorsal fin originates immediately behind first dorsal fin base and has 46 to 51 rays. Pelvic fin has 2 rays that extend to origin of anal fin. Anal fin has 43 to 49 rays. Second dorsal fin and anal fin are narrowly separated from caudal fin. Caudal fin has slightly convex posterior margin. Lateral line is continuous. Scales number 85 to 97 from opercular flap to base of caudal fin and 9 to 12 from dorsal fin base to lateral line. Vertebrae number 46. Color is brown, darker dorsally than ventrally, with pores on head dark, first dorsal fin black with white margin, lateral line darker than body, and operculum with blotch.

This species occurs in the western North Atlantic from southern New England to the northeastern Gulf of Mexico from near shore to 420 m. It is most common between 110 and 185 m, and juveniles undergo part of their development in estuaries. Food consists of crustaceans, squids, and fishes. Maximum known size is 410 mm TL.

REFERENCES: Hildebrand and Schroeder 1928; Hildebrand and Cable 1938; Bigelow and Schroeder 1953b; Svetovidov 1962; Hoese and Moore 1977; C. R. Robins et al. 1986; Cohen et al. 1990; Boschung 1992.

MACROURIDAE Grenadiers

Grenadiers are elongate, with a compact head and trunk; a long, tapering, compressed tail; and long, continuous dorsal and anal fins. They are distinguished from the other families of the order by the following combination of characters. Snout is bluntly rounded to sharply pointed. Mouth is large and terminal to small and subterminal. Jaws are usually protrusible. Chin barbel is usually present. Eye is moderate to large (small in *Squalogadus*). Teeth range from enlarged canines to villiform bands, and occur in premaxilla and lower jaw. Gill rakers are short and tuberculate to long and slender. Branchiostegal rays number 6 or 7 (rarely 8). Pectoral fin has narrow base and is inserted high on flank. Two dorsal fins are usually present. First dorsal fin is high, generally with first 2 rays spinous. Second dorsal fin is very long, with 80 or more rays. Pelvic fin is narrow based and thoracic or jugular in position, with 5 to 17 rays. Anal fin is very long, with 80 or more rays, and meets dorsal fin at tip of tail. Scales are cycloid, but exposed portion often has sharp spinules. Physoclistous swim bladder is usually present. Lateral line usually extends to tip of tail.

Grenadiers occur worldwide from tropical to polar latitudes. Most species are benthopelagic between 100 and 4,000 m. A few are bathypelagic. Food consists of a wide range of pelagic and benthic invertebrates and fishes. Eggs are spawned near the bottom and presumably float upward and develop near the seasonal thermocline. There are four subfamilies and three of these—Bathygadinae (with two genera, *Bathygadus* and *Gadomus,* both in the Gulf), Macrouroidinae (two genera and *Squalogadus* in the Gulf), and Macrourinae (remainder of the genera in the Gulf)—occur in the Gulf of Mexico. The family comprises about 300 species in 30 to 38 genera, and 29 species in 12 genera occur in the Gulf of Mexico.

Key to the Species of the Gulf of Mexico
(Adapted in part from Marshall and Iwamoto 1973; Cohen et al. 1990)

1a.   Single dorsal fin, with anterior section not elevated; pelvic fin small and with 5 rays
. . . . *Squalogadus modificatus* p. 772

1b.   Two dorsal fins, first elevated; pelvic fin with 6 to 17 rays
. . . . 2

2a.   Second dorsal fin originating close to first dorsal fin and better developed than anal fin; outer gill rakers on first arch slender and lathlike; outer gill slit not restricted by integument connecting first gill arch to operculum. 3

2b. Second dorsal fin distinctly separated from first dorsal fin and less developed than anal fin; outer gill rakers on first arch generally tuberculate; outer gill slit restricted by integument connecting first gill arch to operculum 8

3a. Chin barbel less than one-third of orbit diameter or absent; teeth in jaws small but not shagreenlike 4

3b. Chin barbel usually greater than one-half of orbit diameter; teeth in jaws small to minute, often shagreenlike 6

4a. Pelvic fin rays 9 or 10; orbit diameter 17.3% to 21.2% of head length. . . . . *Bathygadus favosus* p. 766

4b. Pelvic fin rays 7 or 8; orbit diameter 24.7% to 34.4% of head length. 5

5a. Outer gill filaments on first gill arch darkly pigmented; chin barbel absent; interorbital width 24.7% to 33.9% of head length . . . . *Bathygadus melanobranchus* p. 768

5b. Outer gill filaments on first gill arch unpigmented; small chin barbel usually present; interorbital width 19.7% to 25% of head length. . . . . *Bathygadus macrops* p. 767

6a. Outer 2 rays of pelvic fin elongated; pectoral fin rays 22 to 27 . . . . *Gadomus arcuatus* p. 769

6b. Outer ray of pelvic fin elongated; pectoral fin rays 14 to 20 7

7a. Gill rakers on lower limb of first arch 27 to 31; pectoral fin rays 14 to 16; interorbital width 21% to 25% of head length. *Gadomus longifilis* p. 771

7b. Gill rakers on lower limb of first arch 20 or 21; pectoral fin rays 18 to 20; interorbital width 15% to 17% of head length . . . . *Gadomus dispar* p. 770

8a. Branchiostegal rays 6 9

8b. Branchiostegal rays 7 or 8 16

9a. Gill rakers absent on lateral side of first gill arch 10

9b. Gill rakers present on lateral side of first gill arch. 12

10a. Scales on trunk and tail with spinules on section forming toothed keel; abdomen fully scaled . . . . *Caelorinchus occa* p. 775

10b. Scales on trunk and tail without median keel; abdomen with scaleless black area on midventral line 11

11a. Terminal scute of snout lanceolate, projecting distally beyond lateral scutes (Fig. 149); naked area on abdomen more or less diamond shaped, width at least 40% of length . . . . *Caelorinchus caribbaeus* p. 774

11b. Terminal scute of snout relatively short, projecting slightly beyond lateral scutes (Fig. 150); naked area on abdomen oval or lanceolate, width 30% of length or less . . . . *Caelorinchus caelorhincus* p. 773

12a. Pelvic fin rays 12 to 14; inner gill rakers of first arch 15 or 16 . . . . *Coryphaenoides mediterraneus* p. 778

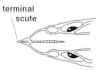

terminal scute

FIG 149

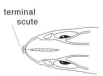

terminal scute

FIG 150

12b. Pelvic fin rays 8 to 12; inner gill rakers of first arch 9 to 16
. . . . 13

13a. Interorbital width less than 20% of head length; chin barbel thick, fleshy, and conical
. . . . *Coryphaenoides zaniophorus* p. 781

13b. Interorbital width greater than 20% of head length; chin
barbel slender. 14

14a. Pelvic fin rays 8 . . . . *Coryphaenoides alateralis* p. 777

14b. Pelvic fin rays 9 to 12. 15

15a. Snout to origin of second dorsal fin 180% to 205% of head
length; chin barbel 6% to 9% of head length; interorbital
width 23% to 25% of head length; orbit black rimmed
. . . . *Coryphaenoides mexicanus* p. 779

15b. Snout to origin of second dorsal fin 153% to 160% of
head length; chin barbel 10% to 23% of head length;
interorbital width 26% to 30% of head length; orbit without black rim. . . . . *Coryphaenoides rudis* p. 780

16a. Striae (alternating black and silvery lines) on gular membrane, sides of isthmus, over shoulder girdle, and in triangular patch above pelvic fin; integument of head membranes transparent 17

16b. No striae (alternating black and silvery lines) on gular
membrane, sides of isthmus, over shoulder girdle, or above
pelvic fin; integument of head membranes thick and translucent or opaque 19

17a. Orbit 20% to 25% of head length
. . . . *Hymenocephalus aterrimus* p. 782

17b. Orbit 28% to 40% of head length 18

18a. Chin barbel minute or absent
. . . . *Hymenocephalus billsamorum* p. 783

18b. Chin barbel small but distinctly developed, more than 7%
of head length. . . . . *Hymenocephalus italicus* p. 784

19a. Anus and urogenital openings surrounded by narrow to
broad margin of naked skin (periproct), and periproct
closer to anal fin origin than to pelvic fin; no black-
pigmented fossa (accessory structure for light organ)
anterior to anus 20

19b. Anus and urogenital openings surrounded by narrow to
broad margin of naked skin (periproct), and periproct distinctly separated from anal fin origin, usually closer to
pelvic fin than to anal fin; small- to medium-sized, black-
pigmented fossa (accessory structure for light organ) often
anterior to anus 22

20a. Spinous ray of first dorsal fin smooth; pelvic fin origin
below first dorsal fin base and posterior to pectoral fin
origin . . . . *Trachonurus sulcatus* p. 795

20b. Spinous ray of first dorsal fin weakly to strongly serrated; pelvic fin origin below or anterior to pectoral fin origin 21

21a. Head swollen by expansive lateral line canals; head almost entirely scaled, without broad naked areas; series of enlarged scales along second dorsal fin . . . . *Cetonurus globiceps* p. 776

21b. Head not swollen by expansive lateral line canals; head mostly scaled, but underside of snout partially naked; no enlarged scales along second dorsal fin . . . . *Sphagemacrurus grenadae* p. 794

22a. First dorsal fin spine smooth 23

22b. First dorsal fin spine weakly to strongly serrated 24

23a. Upper jaw less than 35% of head length; barbel very small; no separate naked fossa anterior to periproct . . . . *Kumba* sp. p. 785

23b. Upper jaw more than 40% of head length; barbel moderate to large; naked fossa anterior to periproct . . . . *Malacocephalus laevis* p. 787

24a. Lower jaw teeth large, widely spaced, and in single row . . . . *Malacocephalus occidentalis* p. 788

24b. Lower jaw teeth small to moderate in size, closely spaced, and in one or more rows 25

25a. Snout and suborbital region completely and uniformly covered with small, finely spinulated scales; tip of snout without tuberculate scale; upper jaw length greater than one-third of head length 26

25b. Snout and suborbital region with naked areas, especially ventrally, often extending onto ventral suborbital region, mandible, and lower margin of preoperculum; tip of snout often with tuberculate scale; upper jaw usually less than one-third of head length (except *Nezumia atlantica*) . . . 27

26a. Premaxillary teeth in narrow band extending posteriorly beyond maxillary process; mandibular teeth in one to three irregular series; snout with blackish tip, or entire leading edge blackish; inner gill rakers on first arch 13 to 20; upper jaw 35% to 53% of head length; pores of cephalic lateral line small and inconspicuous . . . . *Ventrifossa macropogon* p. 796

26b. Premaxillary teeth in narrow band that fails to reach posterior margin of maxillary process; mandibular teeth in narrow to broad band; snout tip and leading edge not darkly pigmented; inner gill rakers on first arch 8 to 10; upper jaw 33% to 41% of head length; pores of cephalic lateral line system conspicuous or inconspicuous . . . . *Kuronezumia bubonis* p. 786

27a. Pelvic fin rays 6 or 7. . . . . *Nezumia suilla* p. 793

27b. Pelvic fin rays 8 or more. 28

28a. Pelvic fin rays 13 or more. . . *Nezumia longebarbata* p. 792
28b. Pelvic fin rays 8 to 10 29
29a. Snout blunt, protruding slightly beyond mouth; suborbital region flat, almost vertical; chin barbel more than 20% of head length, or two-thirds orbital diameter (Fig. 151) . . . . *Nezumia atlantica* p. 790

chin
barbel

FIG 151

29b. Snout acutely pointed, protruding distinctly beyond mouth; suborbital region angular in cross section; chin barbel less than 21% of head length, or less than two-thirds orbital diameter 30
30a. First dorsal fin with distinct blackish tip; chin barbel 9% to 17% of head length . . . . *Nezumia aequalis* p. 789
30b. First dorsal fin uniformly dark or dusky; chin barbel 3% to 8% of head length . . . . *Nezumia cyrano* p. 791

Bathygadus favosus   Goode and Bean 1886

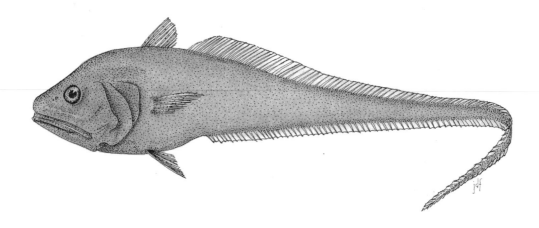

Bathygadus favosus is elongate and attenuated, with a large, terminal mouth; relatively small eyes; and closely spaced dorsal fins. It is distinguished from the other species of the family by the following combination of characters. Snout is blunt and concave anterior to eye. Jaws extend distinctly beyond posterior margin of orbit, and premaxilla has short, ascending process and is only slightly protrusible. Head is cavernous and 15% to 20% of TL. Snout length is 28% to 33%, orbit is 17% to 21%, premaxilla is 51% to 55%, and body depth at dorsal fin origin is 73% to 95% of head length. Chin barbel is absent. Jaw teeth are small, recurved, and depressible, and are in relatively broad band in premaxilla and relatively narrow band in lower jaw. First gill slit is unrestricted. Gill rakers are lathlike and number 4 to 6 on epibranch and 19 to 22 on lower limb of first arch. Pectoral fin is relatively short and has 15 to 17 rays. First dorsal fin has 9 to 11 rays, first of which is splintlike and second, slender and spinous. Second dorsal fin originates very close to insertion of first dorsal fin and has longer rays than anal fin. Pelvic fin has 9 or 10 relatively short rays. Scales lack spinules. Abdominal area lacks naked area and light organ. Swim bladder has two retia mirabilia and lacks drumming muscles. Color is dark on head and brown on trunk and tail, with lining of body, gill, and buccal cavities black.

This species occurs in the subtropical to tropical Atlantic Ocean. In the western Atlantic it occurs in the Straits of Florida, the Gulf of Mexico, and the Caribbean Sea at 770 to 2,745 m, but is most common from 770 to 1,700 m. Maximum known size is 465 mm TL.

REFERENCES: Grey 1956; Marshall 1973; Geistdoerfer 1986; Iwamoto 1986; Cohen et al. 1990.

Bathygadus macrops   Goode and Bean 1885

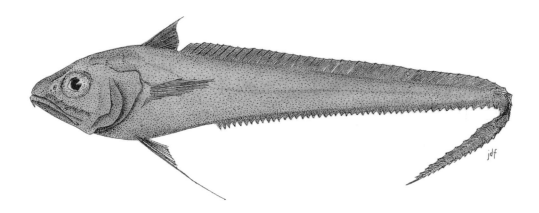

Bathygadus macrops is elongate and attenuated, with a large, terminal mouth; relatively large eyes; and closely spaced dorsal fins. It is distinguished from the other species of the family by the following combination of characters. Snout is slightly acute and straight to slightly concave anterior to eye. Jaws do not reach posterior margin of orbit, and premaxilla has short ascending process and is only slightly protrusible. Head is firm, not cavernous, and 15% to 20% of TL. Snout length is 23% to 27%, orbit is 27% to 34%, length of premaxilla is 54% to 56%, chin barbel is 0% to 8.6%, and depth of body at origin of first dorsal fin is 70% to 81% of head length. Jaw teeth are small, recurved, and depressible, and are in relatively broad bands in both jaws. First gill slit is unrestricted. Gill rakers are lathlike and number 6 or 7 on epibranch and 19 to 21 on lower limb of first arch. Pectoral fin is of moderate length and has 17 to 20 rays. First dorsal fin has 10 to 13 rays, first of which is splintlike and second, slender and spinous. Second dorsal fin originates very close to insertion of first dorsal fin and has longer rays than anal fin. Pelvic fin has 8 rays, with first ray slightly elongated. Scales lack spinules. Abdominal area lacks naked area and light organ. Swim bladder has two retia mirabilia but lacks drumming muscles. Color is light yellow to pale brown, with fins, branchiostegal membranes, gular membranes, buccal cavity, gill cavity, and body cavity dark. Outer gill filaments are unpigmented.

This species occurs in the tropical Atlantic Ocean. In the western Atlantic it occurs in the Gulf of Mexico and the Caribbean Sea at 347 to 777 m. Maximum known size is about 500 mm TL.

REFERENCES: Iwamoto 1970; Marshall 1973; Cohen et al. 1990; Boschung 1992.

Bathygadus melanobranchus Vaillant 1888

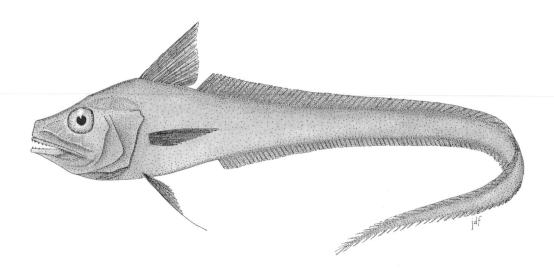

Bathygadus melanobranchus is elongate and attenuated, with a large, terminal mouth; relatively large eyes; and closely spaced dorsal fins. It is distinguished from the other species of the family by the following combination of characters. Snout is slightly acute to slightly blunt and straight anterior to eye. Jaws do not reach posterior margin of orbit, and premaxilla has short ascending process and is only slightly protrusible. Head is firm, not cavernous, and 15% to 20% of TL. Snout length is 25% to 29%, orbit is 25% to 30%, premaxilla length is 46% to 57%, and depth of body at dorsal fin origin is 72% to 80% of head length. Chin barbel is absent. Jaw teeth are small, recurved, and depressible, and in wide band in premaxilla and narrow band in dentaries. First gill slit is unrestricted. Gill rakers are lathlike and number 6 or 7 on epibranch and 21 to 24 on lower limb of first arch. Pectoral fin is of moderate length and has 16 to 20 rays. First dorsal fin has 11 to 13 rays, first of which is splintlike and second, smooth and spinous. Second dorsal fin origi-

nates very close to insertion of first dorsal fin and has longer rays than anal fin. Pelvic fin has 8 rays, with first ray slightly elongated. Scales lack spinules. Abdominal area lacks naked area and light organ. Swim bladder has two retia mirabilia and lacks drumming muscles. Color is rather pale to darkish, with fins gray to black, and linings of mouth, gills, and abdomen black. Gill filaments have dark median stripe.

This species occurs in the subtropical to tropical Atlantic. In the western Atlantic it occurs in the Gulf of Mexico, the Caribbean Sea, and off Suriname at 450 to 2,560 m but generally from 700 to 1,400 m. Food consists of pelagic copepods, mysid shrimps, and chaetognaths. Maximum known size is about 400 mm TL.

REFERENCES: Parr 1946a; Grey 1956; Iwamoto 1970, 1986; Marshall 1973; Uyeno et al. 1983; Geistdoerfer 1986; Cohen et al. 1990; Boschung 1992.

Gadomus arcuatus (Goode and Bean 1886)
Doublethread grenadier

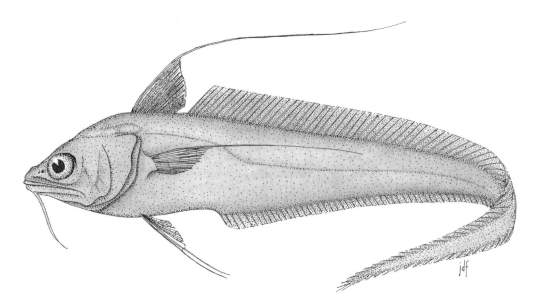

Gadomus arcuatus is elongate and attenuated, with a large, terminal mouth; a long chin barbel; and long leading rays of the dorsal, pectoral, and pelvic fins. It is distinguished from the other species of the family by the following combination of characters. Snout is moderately acute and slightly concave anterior to eye. Jaws reach almost to posterior margin of orbit, and premaxilla has short ascending process and is only slightly protrusible. Head is firm, not cavernous, and about 20% of TL. Snout length is 28% to 30%, orbit is 18% to 27%, premaxilla length is 52% to 57%, chin barbel is 66% to 87%, and body depth at dorsal fin origin is 80% to 91% of head length. Jaw teeth are very small and in wide bands in premaxilla and in narrow bands in dentaries. First gill slit is unrestricted. Gill rakers are lathlike and number 4 to 6 on epibranch and 18 to 21 on lower limb of first arch. Pectoral fin has 22 to 27 rays and is of moderate length, except second ray

is greatly elongated. First dorsal fin has 10 to 13 rays, first of which is splintlike and second, smooth, spinous, and greatly elongated. Second dorsal fin originates very close to insertion of first dorsal fin and has longer rays than anal fin. Pelvic fin has 8 rays, with first 2 rays greatly elongated. Scales lack spinules and cover head except for gular and branchiostegal membranes. Abdominal area lacks naked area and light organ anterior to anus. Swim bladder has four retia mirabilia and lacks drumming muscles. Color is brownish, with membranes of fins, mouth, and gill chambers blackish.

This species occurs in the tropical North Atlantic. In the western Atlantic it occurs in the Gulf of Mexico, the Caribbean Sea, and off the northeastern coast of South America at 610 to 1,370 m. Maximum known size is 580 mm TL.

REFERENCES: Marshall 1973; Uyeno et al. 1983; Geistdoerfer 1986; Cohen et al. 1990.

Gadomus dispar   (Vaillant 1888)

Gadomus dispar is elongate and attenuated, with a large, terminal mouth; a long chin barbel; and long leading rays of the dorsal, pectoral, and pelvic fins. It is distinguished from the other species of the family by the following combination of characters. Snout is moderately acute and nearly straight to slightly concave. Jaws reach nearly to posterior margin of eye, and premaxilla has short ascending process and is only slightly protrusible. Head is firm, not cavernous, and 15% to 20% of TL. Snout is 22.6% to 27.3%, orbit is 26.8% to 31.6%, premaxilla length is 51.6% to 56.3%, barbel length is 83.9% to 103.2%, and body depth at origin of dorsal fin is 67.7% to 85.3% of head length. Jaw teeth are very small and in broad band in premaxilla and in narrow band in lower jaw. First gill slit is unrestricted. Gill rakers are lathlike and number 4 or 5 on epibranch and 20 or 21 on lower limb of first arch. Pectoral fin has 19 or 20 rays and is moderately long. First dorsal fin has 12 or 13 rays, first of which is splintlike and second, spinous and slightly longer than remainder. Second dorsal fin is very close to insertion of first dorsal fin and has longer rays than anal fin. Pelvic fin has 8 rays, with first ray elongated. Scales lack spinules and cover head except for gular and branchiostegal membranes. Abdominal area lacks naked area and light organ. Swim bladder has four retia mirabilia and lacks drumming muscles. Color is dusky brown. Membranes of mouth and gill cavities are dark except for light-colored areas on branchiostegal membranes.

This species occurs in the tropical and subtropical Atlantic Ocean. In the western Atlantic it occurs in the Caribbean Sea and the eastern Gulf of Mexico between 548 and 640 m. There is only one record of this species from the Gulf of Mexico. Maximum known size is 272 mm TL.

REFERENCES: Marshall 1973; Cohen et al. 1990.

Gadomus longifilis (Goode and Bean 1885)

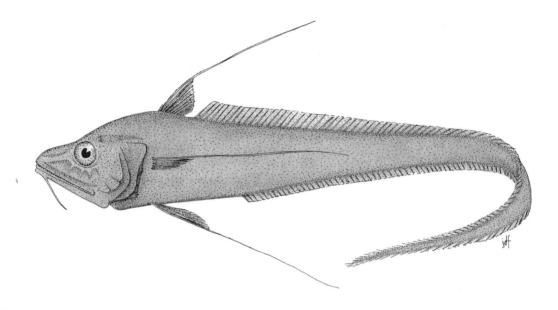

Gadomus longifilis is elongate and attenuated, with a large, terminal mouth; a long chin barbel; and long leading rays of the dorsal, pectoral, and pelvic fins. It is distinguished from the other species of the family by the following combination of characters. Snout is moderately acute and straight to slightly concave. Jaws reach almost to posterior margin of orbit, and premaxilla has short ascending process and is only slightly protrusible. Head is firm, not cavernous, and about 15% of TL. Snout length is 26% to 29%, orbit is 23% to 28%, premaxilla length is 53% to 60%, chin barbel is 32% to 40%, and body depth at first dorsal fin origin is 66% to 77% of head length. Jaw teeth are very small and in bands in both jaws. First gill slit is unrestricted. Gill rakers are lathlike and number 6 to 8 on epibranch and 27 to 29 on lower limb. Pectoral fin has 14 to 16 rays and is relatively short, except second ray is greatly elongated. First dorsal fin has 9 to 11 rays, first of which is splintlike and second, slender, spinous, and greatly elongated. Second dorsal fin is very close to insertion of first dorsal fin and has longer rays than anal fin. Pelvic fin has 8 rays, with first ray greatly elongated. Scales lack spinules and cover head except for gular and branchiostegal membranes. Abdominal area lacks naked area and light organ anterior to anus. Swim bladder has four retia mirabilia and lacks drumming muscles. Color is brownish, with membranes of mouth and gill chambers brown to black. Gill lamellae have dark median stripe.

This species occurs in the subtropical to tropical Atlantic. In the western Atlantic it occurs off the east coast of Florida, the Straits of Florida, the Gulf of Mexico, and the Caribbean Sea at 630 to 2,168 m. Maximum known size is 300 mm TL.

REFERENCES: Grey 1956; Marshall 1973; Uyeno et al. 1983; Geistdoerfer 1986.

Squalogadus modificatus   Gilbert and Hubbs 1916

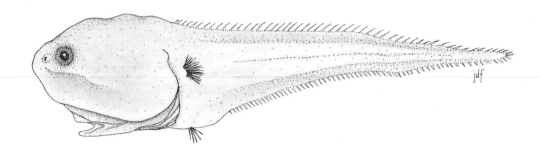

Squalogadus modificatus is moderately elongate and attenuated, with a large, round head; a subterminal mouth; and a low single dorsal fin. It is distinguished from the other species of the family by the following combination of characters. Snout is broadly rounded. Jaws are moderately large; premaxilla is small and very protrusible. Head is swollen due to expansion of lateral line system and is 25% to 30% of TL. Snout length is 28% to 32%, orbit is 9% to 12%, premaxilla length is 23% to 27%, and depth of body at dorsal fin insertion is about 60% of head length. Chin barbel is absent. Jaw teeth are minute, pointed, and in relatively broad band in premaxilla and in narrow band in lower jaw. First gill slit is unrestricted. Gill rakers are styliform and number 7 or 8 on epibranch and 19 to 22 on lower limb of first arch. Branchiostegal rays number 7. Pectoral fin is short and has 23 to 26 rays. Dorsal fin originates on nape and has rays about equal in length to those of anal fin. Anal fin originates immediately behind anus. Pelvic fin is small and has 5 rays. Scales are small, have one or several upright spinules, and cover head except for parts of gular and branchiostegal membranes. Abdominal area lacks naked area and light organ. Swim bladder has three retia mirabilia, but these are regressed in adults. Color is dark brown, with gular and branchiostegal membranes and buccal and gill cavities black.

This species occurs in the tropical Atlantic and western Pacific Oceans and is either benthopelagic or bathypelagic. In the western Atlantic it occurs in the Gulf of Mexico. Maximum known size is 350 mm TL.

REFERENCES: Grey 1956; Marshall 1973.

Caelorinchus caelorhincus (Risso 1810)
Saddled grenadier

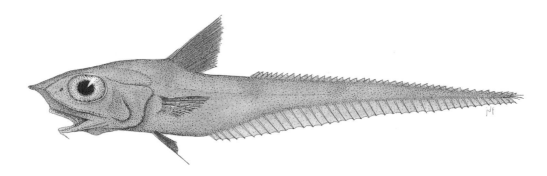

Caelorinchus caelorhincus is elongate and attenuated, with a triangular snout, stout suborbital ridges on scales, and an oval or lanceolate naked area on abdomen. It is distinguished from the other species of the family by the following combination of characters. Snout bears terminal scute that is wider than it is long. Jaws are subterminal, and premaxilla has long ascending process and is very protrusible. Snout length is 32% to 40%, orbit is 31% to 37%, premaxilla length is 24% to 32%, chin barbel is 5% to 10%, and body depth at first dorsal fin origin is 50% to 73% of head length. Teeth are small and in broad bands in both jaws. First gill slit is greatly restricted. Gill rakers are absent on outer side of first arch and number 7 to 12 on inner side of first arch. Branchiostegal rays number 6. Pectoral fin is of moderate length and has 17 to 20 rays. First dorsal fin has 10 or 11 rays, first of which is splintlike and second, smooth and spinous. Second dorsal fin is distinctly separated from first and has shorter rays than anal fin. Pelvic fin has 7 rays, with first ray slightly elongated. Abdomen has large oval or lanceolate naked area extending slightly anterior to pelvic fin base. Width of naked area is at most 30% of its length. Anus and urogenital openings are surrounded by narrow naked black area (periproct) and are located just anterior to anal fin origin. Scales are covered with small, moderately fine, moderately reclining spinules. Head is mostly scaled except for median naked strip under snout. Color is pale grayish to dusky, sometimes with three dark saddle marks equally spaced on dorsum.

This species occurs in the warm temperate to tropical Atlantic Ocean. In the western Atlantic it occurs from Nova Scotia to Suriname, including the Gulf of Mexico, at 90 to 850 m but usually from 200 to 500 m. Food consists of polychaetes, gastropods, cephalopods, copepods, amphipods, isopods, cumaceans, and fishes.

REFERENCES: Marshall and Iwamoto 1973; Uyeno et al. 1983; Geistdoerfer 1986; Cohen et al. 1990; Boschung 1992.

Caelorinchus caribbaeus (Goode and Bean 1885)
Blackfin grenadier

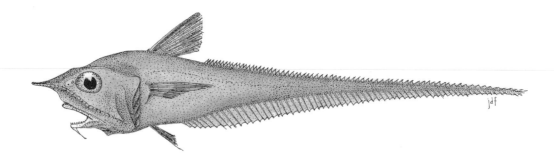

Caelorinchus caribbaeus is elongate and attenuated, with a triangular snout, stout suborbital ridges on enlarged scales, and a diamond-shaped naked area on the abdomen. It is distinguished from the other species of the family by the following combination of characters. Snout bears terminal lanceolate scute projecting beyond lateral scutes. Jaws are subterminal, and premaxilla has long ascending process and is very protrusible. Snout length is 37% to 55%, orbit is 30% to 34%, premaxilla length is 26% to 30%, chin barbel is 8% to 11%, and body depth at first dorsal fin origin is 51% to 66% of head length. Teeth are small and in wide bands in both jaws. First gill slit is greatly restricted. Gill rakers are absent on outer side of first arch and number 9 to 11 on inner side of first arch. Branchiostegal rays number 6. Pectoral fin is moderate in length and has 17 to 20 rays. First dorsal fin has 11 or 13 rays, first of which is splintlike and second, smooth and spinous. Second dorsal fin is distinctly separated from first and has shorter rays than anal fin. Pelvic fin has 7 rays. Abdominal area has broad, diamond-shaped, black naked area associated with light organ, extending slightly anterior to pelvic fin base. Width of naked area is 40% of its length. Anus and urogenital openings are surrounded by narrow naked black area (periproct) and are located just anterior to anal fin origin. Scales have fine, conical spinules, except those on posterior and ventral sections of trunk and tail have broader spinules. Scales are narrow along median nasal ridge and are absent or sparse in broad band on either side of leading edge of snout. Underside of head is mostly scaled except for median naked strip under snout. Color is dusky, with silvery tinge on abdomen and operculum. Mouth lining is white.

This species occurs in the subtropical and tropical western Atlantic, including the Gulf of Mexico, at 200 to 700 m but usually from 300 to 400 m. It is absent from the Straits of Florida. Maximum known size is 300 mm TL.

REFERENCES: Marshall and Iwamoto 1973; Uyeno et al. 1983; Cohen et al. 1990.

Caelorinchus occa   (Goode and Bean 1885)

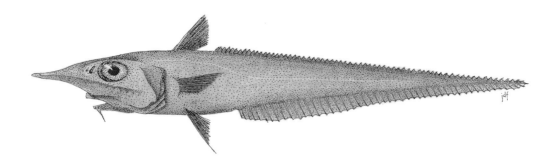

Caelorinchus occa is elongate and attenuated, with a very long triangular snout, stout suborbital ridges, and abdomen without a naked area. It is distinguished from the other species of the family by the following combination of characters. Snout bears elongate, pointed scute that lacks lateral protuberances. Jaws are subterminal, and premaxilla has long ascending process and is very protrusible. Snout length is 44% to 47%, orbit is 23% to 27%, premaxilla length is 21% to 26%, chin barbel is 5% to 9%, and body depth at first dorsal fin origin is 36% to 54% of head length. Jaw teeth are small and in broad bands in both jaws. First gill slit is greatly restricted. Gill rakers are absent on outer side of first arch and number seven to nine on inner side of first arch. Branchiostegal rays number 6. Pectoral fin is relatively short and has 17 to 20 rays. First dorsal fin has 9 to 11 rays, first of which is splintlike and second, smooth and spinous. Second dorsal fin is distinctly separated from first and has shorter rays than anal fin. Pelvic fin has 7 rays, with first ray slightly elongated. Abdomen lacks naked area anterior to anus. Anus and urogenital openings are surrounded by narrow naked black area and are located just anterior to anal fin origin. Scales have prominent median keel consisting of several closely appressed, stout, sharp spinules and one to three divergent keel-like lateral rows of spinules. Head is scaled except for areas below suborbital ridges, which are naked. Color is dusky to brownish, with abdomen darker, mouth and gill cavities blackish, and first dorsal fin dusky.

This species occurs in the tropical Atlantic. In the western Atlantic it occurs off Bermuda, the Gulf of Mexico, the southern Caribbean Sea, and Suriname at 600 to 1,000 m. Maximum known size is over 500 mm TL.

REFERENCES: Parr 1946a; Marshall and Iwamoto 1973; Uyeno et al. 1983; Cohen et al. 1990; Boschung 1992.

Cetonurus globiceps (Vaillant 1888)

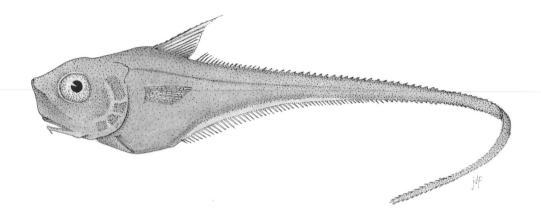

Cetonurus globiceps is elongate and attenuated, with a large, inflated head; a relatively small mouth; and a short trunk. It is distinguished from the other species of the family by the following combination of characters. Snout is broad and blunt. Jaws are subterminal and fail to reach posterior margin of orbits. Head is about 20% of TL. Snout length is 33% to 41%, orbit is 26% to 31%, premaxilla length is 25% to 31%, chin barbel is 2% to 6%, and body depth at first dorsal fin origin is 71% to 89% of head length. Jaws have band of small, pointed teeth. First gill slit is greatly restricted. Gill rakers are tuberculate and number 11 to 14 on first arch. Pectoral fin is of moderate length and has 16 to 19 rays. First dorsal fin has 9 to 12 rays, first of which is splintlike and second, serrated and spinous. Second dorsal fin is distinctly separated from first and has shorter rays than anal fin. Pelvic fin has 8 to 10 rays. Abdomen lacks naked area and light organ ante-rior to anus. Anus and urogenital openings are surrounded by broad, naked black area (periproct) and are located just anterior to anal fin origin. Scales are small and have slender spinules, except that those on either side of second dorsal fin are large and densely covered with spinules. Color is brown to dark brown, with gular and branchiostegal membranes darker, and mouth, gill, and abdominal cavities black.

This species occurs in the warm temperate to tropical Atlantic, Indian, and western Pacific Oceans. In the western Atlantic it occurs in the Gulf of Mexico and the eastern Caribbean Sea at 1,097 to 1,828 m. Food consists of copepods and fishes. Maximum known size is 450 mm TL.

REFERENCES: Grey 1956; Iwamoto 1966; Marshall 1973; Sazonov and Shcherbachev 1985; Geistdoerfer 1986.

Coryphaenoides alateralis   Marshall and Iwamoto 1973

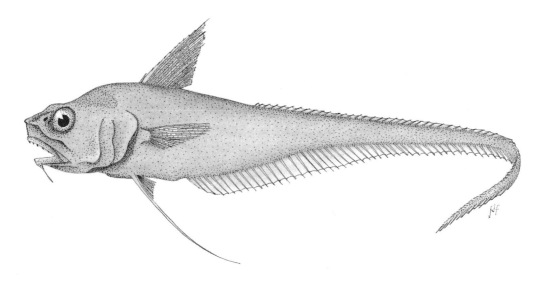

Coryphaenoides alateralis is elongate and attenuated, with a moderately blunt snout, depressed head over orbits, and a serrated second ray of the first dorsal fin. It is distinguished from the other species of the family by the following combination of characters. Snout is slightly acute and slightly convex anterior to orbits. Jaws are subterminal, long, and extend to posterior margin of orbits. Head length is 20% of TL. Snout length is 30%, orbit is 21%, premaxilla length is 42%, chin barbel is 23%, and body depth at first dorsal fin origin is 89% of head length. Premaxilla has outer series of widely spaced, enlarged teeth and inner band of small, conical teeth; lower jaw has moderately broad band of small teeth. First gill slit is greatly restricted. Gill rakers are tuberculate and number 10 on first arch. Branchiostegal rays number 6. Pectoral fin is of moderate length and has 21 to 23 rays. First dorsal fin has 13 rays, first of which is splintlike and second, serrated and spinous. Second dorsal fin is widely separated from first and has shorter rays than anal

fin. Pelvic fin has 8 rays, with first ray thickened and greatly elongated. Abdomen has no naked area or light organ anterior to anus. Anus and urogenital openings are surrounded by narrow naked black area (periproct) and are just anterior to anal fin origin. Scales are densely covered with relatively long, greatly reclined and slender spinules. Scales cover head except for branchiostegal and gular membranes, broad band along both sides of lower jaw, and narrow margin above upper lip. Color is brown, with ventral surface of head and posteriormost portion of tail lighter. Orbits have narrow black rim. First dorsal fin and mouth and gill cavities are black.

This species occurs in the western North Atlantic off the eastern coast of the United States, near Hudson Canyon, and in the eastern Gulf of Mexico between 1,035 and 1,116 m. Maximum known size is 265 mm TL.

REFERENCES: Marshall and Iwamoto 1973; Crabtree 1983; Cohen et al. 1990.

Coryphaenoides mediterraneus (Giglioli 1893)

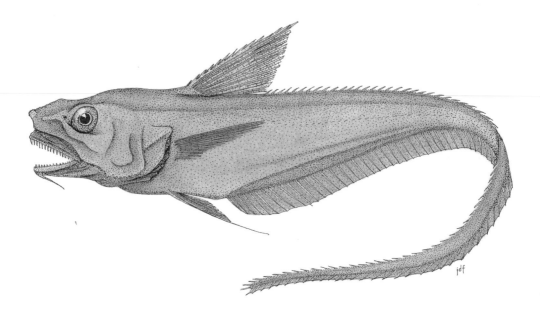

Coryphaenoides mediterraneus is elongate and attenuated, with a blunt snout armed with a transverse median ridge of weakly tuberculated scales, a subterminal mouth, and a serrated second ray of first dorsal fin. It is distinguished from the other species of the family by the following combination of characters. Snout is slightly acute and convex anterior to orbits. Jaws are subterminal, moderately long, and extend to posterior margin of orbits. Head is 15% to 17% of TL. Snout length is 25% to 29%, orbit is 17% to 23%, premaxilla length is 37% to 45%, chin barbel is 27% to 37%, and body depth at first dorsal fin origin is 70% to 96% of head length. Premaxilla has outer series of enlarged teeth and four or five inner rows of small teeth; lower jaw has single row of teeth. First gill slit is greatly restricted. Gill rakers are tuberculate and number 10 or 11 on first arch. Pectoral fin is moderately long and has 19 to 22 rays. First dorsal fin has 10 to 12 rays, first of which is splintlike and second, serrated and spinous. Second dorsal fin is distinctly separated from first and has shorter rays than anal fin. Pelvic fin has 12 to 14 rays, with first ray elongated. Abdomen has no naked area or light organ anterior to anus. Anus and urogenital openings are surrounded by narrow naked area (periproct) and are located just anterior to anal fin origin. Scales are covered with spinules forming parallel ridges on sides of body. Head and snout are covered with scales except for gular and branchiostegal membranes, underside of snout, and lunate areas on dorsal surface of snout. Swim bladder has six retia mirabilia and lacks drumming muscles. Color is brown to dark brown, with opercular region and branchiostegal and gular membranes blackish.

This species occurs in the warm temperate to tropical Atlantic. In the western Atlantic it occurs in the Gulf of Mexico at 1,200 to 2,300 m. Maximum known size is 730 mm TL.

REFERENCES: Grey 1956; Marshall and Iwamoto 1973 (as *Chalinura mediterranea*); Geistdoerfer 1986 (as *Chalinura mediterranea*); Cohen et al. 1990.

Coryphaenoides mexicanus (Parr 1946)

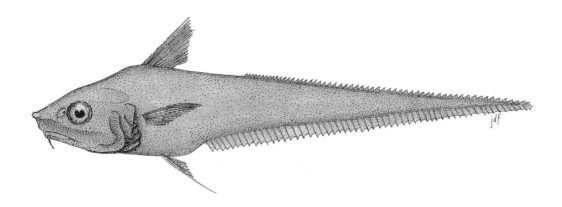

Coryphaenoides mexicanus is elongate and attenuated, with a broadly acute snout, a straight profile over orbits, and a serrated second ray of first dorsal fin. It is distinguished from the other species of the family by the following combination of characters. Snout is acute and slightly convex anterior to orbits. Jaws are subterminal, moderately long, and fail to reach posterior margin of orbits. Head length is about 20% of TL. Snout length is 30% to 34%, orbit is 26% to 29%, premaxilla length is 26% to 29%, chin barbel is 6% to 9%, and body depth at first dorsal fin origin is 75% to 83% of head length. Jaws have relatively broad band of small, pointed teeth, with outermost teeth in upper jaw somewhat enlarged. First gill slit is greatly restricted. Gill rakers are tuberculate and number nine on first arch. Branchiostegal rays number 6. Pectoral fin is of moderate length and has 19 to 21 rays. First dorsal fin has 11 to 13 rays, first of which is splintlike and second, serrated and spinous. Second dorsal fin is distinctly separated from first and has shorter rays than anal fin. Pelvic fin has 9 or 10 rays, with first ray elongated. Abdomen has no naked area or light organ anterior to anus. Anus and urogenital openings are surrounded by narrow naked black area (periproct) and are located just anterior to anal fin origin. Scales are covered with moderate number of strong, moderately broad spinules. Tip and angles of snout have round, scutelike scales, with radially arranged spinules. Head and snout are uniformly scaled except for branchiostegal and gular membranes. Color is brown, with darker brown around nostrils and orbits.

This species occurs in the western North Atlantic in the northern Gulf of Mexico at 730 to 1,600 m. Maximum known size is 400 mm TL.

REFERENCES: Parr 1946a; Marshall and Iwamoto 1973; Cohen et al. 1990.

Coryphaenoides rudis   Günther 1878

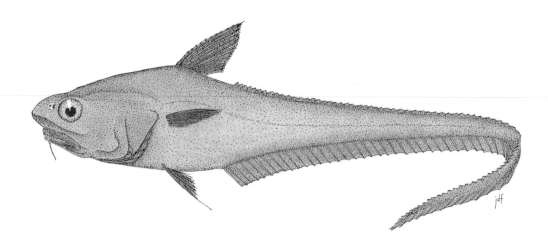

Coryphaenoides rudis is elongate and attenuated, with a blunt, slightly depressed head over the orbits and a serrated second ray of first dorsal fin. It is distinguished from the other species of the family by the following combination of characters. Snout is slightly acute in young but rounded in adults, and slightly convex anterior of orbits. Jaws are subterminal, moderately long, and extend to posterior margin of orbits. Head is about 20% of TL. Snout length is 23% to 29%, orbit is 16% to 26%, premaxilla length is 37% to 43%, chin barbel is 10% to 23%, and body depth at first dorsal fin origin is 80% to 100% of head length. Premaxilla has outer series of enlarged teeth and moderately broad inner band of small teeth. Dentaries have narrow band of small teeth. First gill slit is greatly restricted. Gill rakers are tuberculate and number 10 on first arch. Pectoral fin is of moderate length and has 19 to 20 rays. First dorsal fin has 12 or 13 rays, first of which is splintlike and second, serrated and spinous. Second dorsal fin is distinctly separated from first and has shorter rays than anal fin. Pelvic fin has 9 to 11 rays, with first ray elongated. Abdomen has no naked area or light organ anterior to anus. Anus and urogenital openings are surrounded by narrow black area (periproct) and are located just anterior to anal fin origin. Scales are densely covered with small spinules. Head and snout are entirely and evenly covered with scales. Color is brown to light brown, with tips of fins and branchiostegal rays dark brownish to black.

This species occurs in the tropical North Atlantic. In the western Atlantic it occurs in the Gulf of Mexico and the Caribbean Sea at 600 to 3,508 m. Food consists of squids. Maximum known size is 1,100 mm TL.

REFERENCES: Marshall and Iwamoto 1973; Anderson et al. 1985; Cohen et al. 1990 (all as *C. macrocephalus*); Sazonov and Iwamoto 1992; Shcherbachev and Iwamoto 1995.

Coryphaenoides zaniophorus (Vaillant 1888)

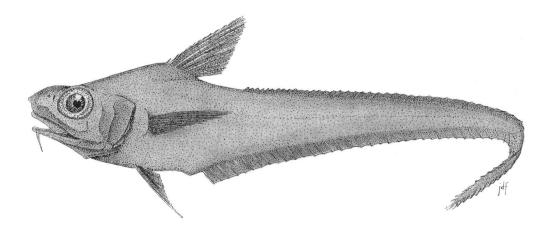

Coryphaenoides zaniophorus is elongate and attenuated, with a slightly acute snout, a concave profile over orbits, and a serrated second ray of first dorsal fin. It is distinguished from the other species of the family by the following combination of characters. Snout is short and moderately convex anterior to orbits. Jaws are subterminal, moderately small, and extend to anterior margin of orbits. Head is 15% to 20% of TL. Snout length is 28% to 31%, orbit is 29% to 33%, premaxilla length is 23% to 28%, chin barbel is 14% to 19%, and body depth at first dorsal fin origin is 91% to 102% of head length. Jaws have band of small, pointed teeth, with those in outer row of upper jaw enlarged. First gill slit is greatly restricted. Gill rakers are tuberculate and number 11 or 12 on first arch. Branchiostegal rays number 6. Pectoral fin is of moderate length and has 22 to 24 rays. First dorsal fin has 11 to 13 rays, first of which is splintlike and second, serrated and spinous. Second dorsal fin is distinctly separated from first and has shorter rays than anal fin. Pelvic fin has 9 or 12 rays, with first ray elongated. Abdomen has no naked area or light organ anterior to anus. Anus and urogenital openings are surrounded by narrow naked black area (periproct) and are located just anterior to anal fin origin. Scales are covered with numerous short, stout spinules in V-shaped rows. Scales cover head and snout. Tip of snout has stout terminal and lateral scutes. Color is medium to dark brown, with fins blackish.

This species occurs in the warm temperate to tropical Atlantic. In the western Atlantic it occurs along the east coast of the United States off Chesapeake Bay, and in the Gulf of Mexico and the Caribbean Sea, at 400 to 2,165 m. Food consists of polychaetes, copepods, gammarian amphipods, ostracods, isopods, mysids, and echinoderms. Maximum known size is at least 400 mm TL.

REFERENCES: Parr 1946a; Marshall and Iwamoto 1973 (as *Corypaenoides colon*); Merrett and Marshall 1981; Geistdoerfer 1986; Cohen et al. 1990.

Hymenocephalus aterrimus   Gilbert 1905

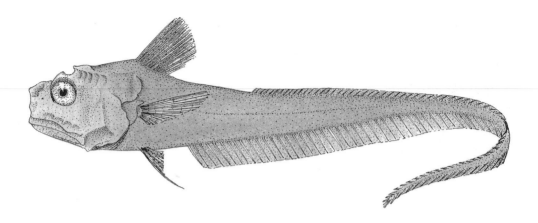

Hymenocephalus aterrimus is elongate and attenuated, with a large, cavernous head; a subterminal mouth; and deciduous scales. It is distinguished from the other species of the family by the following combination of characters. Snout is high, with thin, membranous, fragile median protuberance. Jaws are large and extend to posterior margin of orbits. Head is 20% to 25% of TL. Snout length is 30% to 35%, orbit is 20% to 25%, premaxilla length is 46% to 56%, and body depth at first dorsal fin origin is 70% to 80% of head length. Chin barbel is lacking. Jaws have small, depressible teeth in narrow bands. First gill slit is greatly restricted. Gill rakers are tuberculate and number 20 to 25 on first arch. Branchiostegal rays number 7. Pectoral fin is moderately long and has 14 to 17 rays. First dorsal fin has 10 to 13 rays, first of which is splintlike and second, smooth and spinous. Second dorsal fin is widely separated from first and has shorter rays than anal fin.

Pelvic fin has 13 or 14 rays, with first ray elongated. Abdomen has long, tubular light organ that consists of prepelvic and preanal lenslike windows connected by narrow naked black strip. Anus and urogenital pores are located just anterior to anal fin origin. Scales are large and thin, and lack spinules. Swim bladder has two retia mirabilia. Abdominal region and head are black, tail and upper part of trunk are blackish brown, and head membranes are transparent. Isthmus, shoulder girdle, and chest are patterned with striae consisting of fine, parallel black lines over silver ground color.

This species occurs in the tropical western Atlantic and off the Hawaiian Islands. In the western Atlantic it occurs in the Straits of Florida, the Gulf of Mexico, the Caribbean Sea, and off northern South America at 457 to 914 m. Maximum known size is 200 mm TL.

REFERENCE: Marshall and Iwamoto 1973.

Hymenocephalus billsamorum   Marshall and Iwamoto 1973

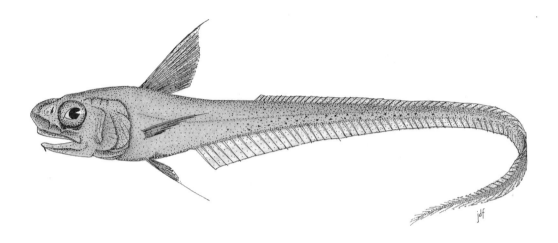

Hymenocephalus billsamorum is very elongate and attenuated, with a moderate-sized head, a subterminal mouth, and a very slender body. It is distinguished from the other species of the family by the following combination of characters. Snout is moderately blunt. Jaws are large and extend to posterior margin of orbits. Head is about 15% of TL. Snout length is 26% to 35%, orbit is 28% to 37%, premaxilla length is 51% to 59%, and body depth at first dorsal fin origin is 60% to 74% of head length. Chin barbel is rudimentary. Jaws have narrow band of small, pointed teeth. First gill slit is greatly restricted. Gill rakers are tuberculate and number 23 to 28 on first arch. Branchiostegal rays number 7. Pectoral fin is of moderate length and has 14 to 17 rays. First dorsal fin has 10 to 13 rays, first of which is splintlike and second, smooth and spinous. Second dorsal fin is distinctly separated from first and has shorter rays than anal fin. Pelvic fin has 12 to 14 rays, with first ray elongated. Abdomen has long tubular light organ consisting of prepelvic and preanal lenslike windows connected by narrow naked black strip. Anus and urogenital pores are just anterior to anal fin origin. Scales are large and deciduous. Swim bladder has two retia mirabilia. Head is brownish, with dark band behind leading edge of snout. Posterior parts of trunk and tail are dark with small, densely distributed melanophores dorsally, and light with large, sparsely distributed melanophores ventrally. Isthmus, shoulder girdle, and chest are patterned with striae, consisting of fine, parallel dark lines over silvery ground color.

This species occurs in the western Atlantic from the Straits of Florida, the Gulf of Mexico, the Caribbean Sea, and off Rio de Janeiro, Brazil, at 400 to 900 m. Maximum known size is 150 mm TL.

REFERENCE: Marshall and Iwamoto 1973.

Hymenocephalus italicus Giglioli 1884

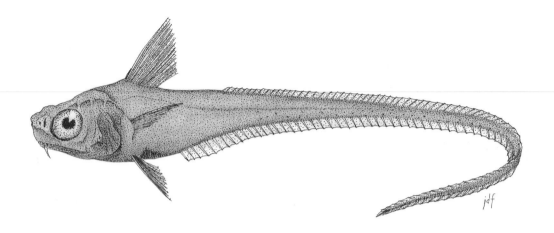

Hymenocephalus italicus is very elongate and attenuated, with a moderate-sized head, a subterminal mouth, and a very slender body. It is distinguished from the other species of the family by the following combination of characters. Snout is blunt. Jaws are large and extend to posterior margin of orbits. Head is 15% of TL. Snout is 23% to 29%, orbit is 32% to 38%, premaxilla length is 44% to 54%, chin barbel is 10% to 15%, and body depth at first dorsal fin origin is 61% to 80% of head length. Jaws have narrow band of small, blunt, depressible teeth. First gill slit is greatly restricted. Gill rakers are tuberculate and number 21 to 25. Branchiostegal rays number 7. Pectoral fin is of moderate length and has 13 to 16 rays. First dorsal fin has 11 to 14 rays, first of which is splintlike and second, smooth and spinous. Second dorsal fin is distinctly separated from first and has shorter rays than anal fin. Pelvic fin has 10 to 12 rays, with first ray elongated. Abdomen has long, tubular light organ consisting of prepelvic and preanal lenslike windows connected by narrow naked black strip. Anus and urogenital pores are located just anterior to anal fin origin. Scales are large, decid-

uous, and may have spinules. Swim bladder has two retia mirabilia. Jaws, gill covers, branchiostegal membranes, and nape are dark, with remainder of head light. Abdomen is dark, and posterior parts of trunk and tail are dark with small, densely distributed melanophores dorsally, and light with large, sparsely distributed melanophores ventrally. Isthmus, shoulder girdle, and chest are patterned with striae consisting of fine, parallel dark lines over silvery ground color.

This species occurs in the warm temperate to tropical Atlantic Ocean. In the western Atlantic it occurs in the Straits of Florida, the Gulf of Mexico, the Caribbean Sea, and off northern South America to northern Brazil at 100 to 800 m. Food consists of pelagic copepods, euphausiids, and gammarid amphipods, and to a lesser degree, shrimps, ostracods, cumaceans, and small fishes. Maximum known size is 200 mm TL.

REFERENCES: Marshall and Iwamoto 1973; Uyeno et al. 1983; Geistdoerfer 1986; Cohen et al. 1990.

Kumba sp.

This undescribed species is elongate and attenuated, with a large, firm head; a blunt snout; and a relatively short upper jaw. It is distinguished from the other species of the family by the following combination of characters. Head is not inflated. Snout is about equal to orbit diameter and lacks terminal or lateral scutes. Jaws are subterminal and extend to posterior margin of eye. Head is about 20% of TL. Snout length is 29.1%, orbit diameter is 30.3%, premaxilla length is 33.9%, barbel length is 8%, and body depth at first dorsal fin origin is 72% of head length. Teeth in jaws are villiform and arranged in four to six rows, with those in outer row of upper jaw relatively large. First gill slit is greatly restricted. Gill filaments are short. Gill rakers on first arch are tuberculate and number 11 on inner side of first arch. Branchiostegal rays number 7. First dorsal fin has 13 rays, first of which is splintlike and second, smooth. Second dorsal fin is distinctly separated from first and has shorter rays than anal fin. Pelvic fin has 8 rays. Abdomen has teardrop-shaped naked black area associated with light organ located anterior to anus. Anus and urogenital openings are surrounded by oval-shaped naked black area (periproct) and are located in middle one-third of space between anal and pelvic fin bases. Scales are covered with parallel series of spinules, with those on upper surface of suborbital region small, in several rows, and bearing small, erect spinules forming comblike rows. Scales are lacking on areas of snout and head, with naked area on upper part of snout extending to anterior margin of orbits. Color is probably dark.

This species occurs in the western North Atlantic from the western Gulf of Mexico. It is represented by a single specimen captured off Brownsville, Texas, at 1,280 m. Maximum known size is about 129 mm TL.

REFERENCE: Iwamoto and Sazonov 1994.

Kuronezumia bubonis (Iwamoto 1974)

Kuronezumia bubonis is elongate and attenuated, with a blunt snout, a moderate-sized subterminal mouth, and a light organ enlarged into a bulbous, scaly, wartlike structure anterior to anus. It is distinguished from the other species of the family by the following combination of characters. Snout is short and not produced. Upper jaw extends to about center of eye. Head is about 15% of TL. Snout is 26% to 32%, orbit is 23% to 31%, premaxilla length is 35% to 41%, chin barbel is 20% to 29%, and body depth is 88% to 109% of head length. Jaw teeth are villiform and arranged in broad bands. First gill slit is greatly restricted. Gill rakers are tuberculate and number 8 to 10 on inner side of first arch. Branchiostegal rays number 7. Pectoral fin rays number 23 to 26. First dorsal fin has 12 or 14 rays, first of which is splintlike and second, serrated. Second dorsal fin is distinctly separated from first and has shorter rays than anal fin. Pelvic fin has 11 to 13 rays. Abdomen has enlarged naked area associated with light organ located anterior to anus and between pelvic fin bases. Anus and urogenital openings are surrounded by oval-shaped naked black area (periproct). Small scales are covered with nearly erect, slender spinules. Snout is almost entirely covered with small scales. Scales on suborbital region are small, uniform, and do not form ridge. Pyloric caecae number 35 to 39. Abdominal vertebrae number 13. Color is brown to black, with ventral surfaces of head, gill covers, and abdomen black or brownish black.

This species occurs in the western Atlantic, central and western Pacific, and Indian Oceans at 585 to 1,300 m. In the western Atlantic it occurs in the Gulf of Mexico and the Caribbean Sea. Maximum known size is 730 mm TL.

REFERENCES: Iwamoto 1974; Uyeno et al. 1983; Cohen et al. 1990; Sazonov and Iwamoto 1992; Shcherbachev et al. 1992.

Malacocephalus laevis   (Lowe 1843)

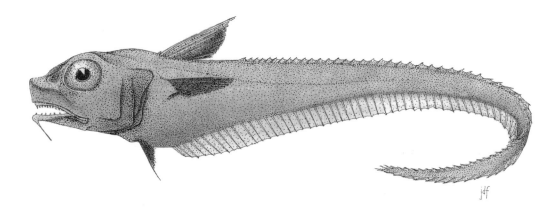

Malacocephalus laevis is elongate and attenuated, with a rounded snout, large jaws, and a laterally compressed head. It is distinguished from the other species of the family by the following combination of characters. Snout is relatively short and not produced. Jaws are subterminal and extend to near posterior margin of orbits. Head is 15% to 20% of TL. Snout length is 23% to 28%, orbit is 31% to 35%, premaxilla length is 46% to 50%, chin barbel is 22% to 27%, and body depth at first dorsal fin origin is 74% to 83% of head length. Upper jaw has two rows of teeth, with those of outer row enlarged and widely spaced. Lower jaw has one row of widely spaced canine teeth. First gill slit is greatly restricted. Gill rakers are tuberculate and number 11 to 13 on inner side of first arch. Branchiostegal rays number 7. Pectoral fin rays have 15 to 21 rays. First dorsal fin has 11 to 15 rays, first of which is splintlike and second, smooth and spinous. Second dorsal fin is distinctly separated from first and has shorter rays than anal fin. Pelvic fin has 8 to 10 rays. Abdomen has bean-shaped naked black area associated with light organ located between pelvic fin bases. Anus and urogenital openings are surrounded by oval-shaped naked black area (periproct) and are located closer to pelvic fin insertion than to anal fin origin. Scales are covered with nearly erect, slender spinules. Head is covered with scales except for gular membrane. Branchiostegal rays are covered with patches of scales. Swim bladder has two retia mirabilia. Color is grayish with silvery pigment over ventral part of body, with blackish gill covers, gular and branchiostegal membranes, and abdomen.

This species occurs in the warm temperate to tropical Atlantic and Indian Oceans, and possibly off Baja California in the eastern Pacific. In the western Atlantic it occurs in the Gulf of Mexico, the Caribbean Sea, and off the northern South American coast to northern Brazil at 200 to 1,000 m. Maximum known size is 520 mm TL.

REFERENCES: Marshall 1973; Geistdoerfer 1986; Iwamoto 1986; Cohen et al. 1990.

Malacocephalus occidentalis   Goode and Bean 1885

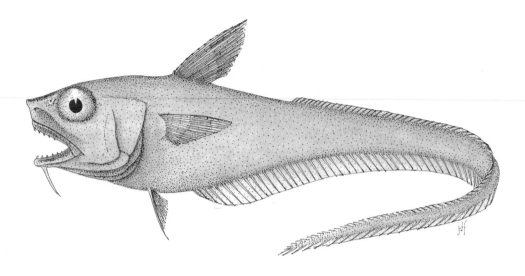

Malacocephalus occidentalis is elongate and attenuated, with a weakly pointed snout, large jaws, and a laterally compressed head. It is distinguished from the other species of the family by the following combination of characters. Snout is relatively short and slightly produced. Jaws are subterminal and extend to near posterior margin of orbits. Head is about 15% of TL. Snout length is 26% to 29%, orbit is 28% to 35%, premaxilla length is 31% to 41%, chin barbel is 31% to 44%, and body depth at first dorsal fin origin is 82% to 100% of head length. Upper jaw has broad band of teeth, with those of outer row enlarged and widely spaced. Lower jaw has one row of widely spaced teeth. First gill slit is greatly restricted. Gill rakers are tuberculate and number 11 to 13 on inner side of first arch. Branchiostegal rays number 7. Pectoral fin has 20 to 25 rays. First dorsal fin has 13 to 15 rays, first of which is splintlike and second, serrated and spinous. Second dorsal fin is distinctly separated from first and has shorter rays than anal fin. Pelvic fin has 7 or 8 rays. Abdomen has semicircular-shaped naked black area associated with light organ located anterior to pelvic fin base. Anus and urogenital openings are surrounded by oval-shaped naked black area and are located near insertion of pelvic fin. Scales are densely covered with small spinules. Head is covered with scales except for gular and part of branchiostegal membranes. Four lowermost branchiostegal rays are covered with scales. Swim bladder has two retia mirabilia. Color is brown dorsally and silvery ventrally.

This species occurs in the warm temperate to tropical Atlantic Ocean. In the western Atlantic it occurs from Cape Cod to Uruguay, including the Straits of Florida, the Gulf of Mexico, and the Caribbean Sea, at 200 to 600 m. Maximum known size is 450 mm TL.

REFERENCES: Parr 1946a; Marshall 1973; Uyeno et al. 1983; Cohen et al. 1990.

Nezumia aequalis   (Günther 1878)

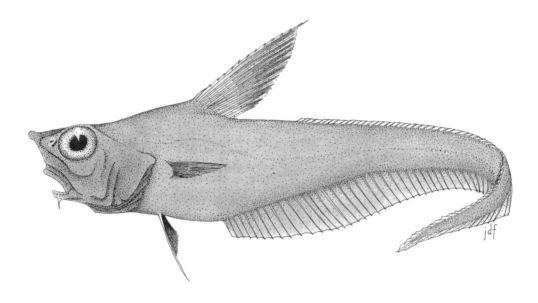

Nezumia aequalis is elongate and attenuated, with a pointed snout and a moderately deep body. It is distinguished from the other species of the family by the following combination of characters. Snout bears terminal scutelike scale. Jaws are moderately short, subterminal, and fail to extend to posterior margin of orbits. Head is 15% to 18% of TL. Snout length is 26% to 34%, orbit is 28% to 39%, premaxilla length is 28% to 36%, chin barbel is 10% to 17%, and body depth at first dorsal fin origin is 67% to 102% of head length. Jaws have broad band of small teeth. First gill slit is greatly restricted. Gill rakers are tuberculate and number 9 to 12 on first arch. Branchiostegal rays number 7. Pectoral fin has 15 to 23 rays. First dorsal fin has 11 to 15 rays, first of which is splintlike and second, serrated and spinous. Second dorsal fin is widely separated from first and has shorter rays than anal fin. Pelvic fin has 7 to 9 rays. Abdomen has small naked black area between pelvic fin bases associated with light organ. Anus and urogenital openings are surrounded by naked black area (periproct) and are located midway between pelvic fin base and anal fin origin. Scales are covered with broad, flat spinules. Head is covered with scales except for area along either side of ventral snout, and gular and branchiostegal membranes. Row of stout, scutelike scales extends from angle of snout to preoperculum, forming ridge. Swim bladder has two retia mirabilia. Color is bluish to violet, with distal part of first dorsal fin black, inner part of pelvic fin black, pectoral fin dusky, and anal fin dusky.

This species occurs in the temperate to tropical Atlantic Ocean. In the western Atlantic it occurs from the Davis Strait to northern Brazil, including the Gulf of Mexico and the Caribbean Sea, at 200 to 1,000 m. Food consists of polychaetes, mysids, and amphipods. Maximum known size is 300 mm TL.

REFERENCES: Parr 1946a; Marshall and Iwamoto 1973; Uyeno et al. 1983; Geistdoerfer 1986; Cohen et al. 1990.

Nezumia atlantica (Parr 1946)

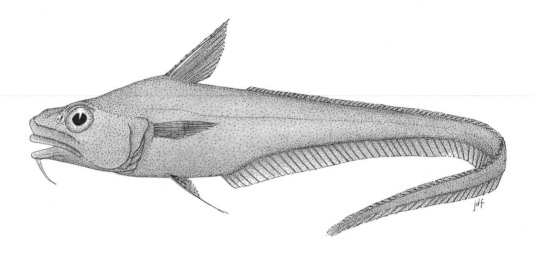

Nezumia atlantica is elongate and attenuated, with a relatively long snout and a relatively long upper jaw. It is distinguished from the other species of the family by the following combination of characters. Snout is blunt and slightly produced. Jaws are subterminal and fail to extend to posterior margin of orbits. Head is about 20% of TL. Snout length is 24% to 29%, orbit is 27% to 31%, premaxilla length is 36% to 44%, chin barbel is 20% to 29%, and body depth at first dorsal fin origin is 70% to 89% of head length. Jaws have three or four rows of conical teeth, with those in outer row of premaxilla enlarged. First gill slit is greatly restricted. Gill rakers are tuberculate and number 9 to 11. Branchiostegal rays number 7. Pectoral fin has 19 to 25 rays. First dorsal fin has 12 to 15 rays, first of which is splintlike and second, serrated and spinous. Second dorsal fin is distinctly separated from first and has shorter rays than anal fin. Pelvic fin has 9 or 10 rays. Abdomen has small, round naked black area between pelvic fin bases associated with light organ. Anus and urogenital openings are surrounded by naked black area (periproct) and are located between pelvic fin base and anal fin origin. Scales are covered with broad, flattened spinules. Head is covered with scales except for ventral snout, and gular and branchiostegal membranes. Swim bladder has two retia mirabilia. Color is brownish black.

This species occurs in the Gulf of Mexico, the Caribbean Sea, and along the northern coast of South America to Suriname at 366 to 1,097 m. Maximum known size is 450 mm TL.

REFERENCES: Parr 1946a; Marshall and Iwamoto 1973 (both as *Ventrifossa atlantica*); Uyeno et al. 1983; Cohen et al. 1990.

Nezumia cyrano   Marshall and Iwamoto 1973

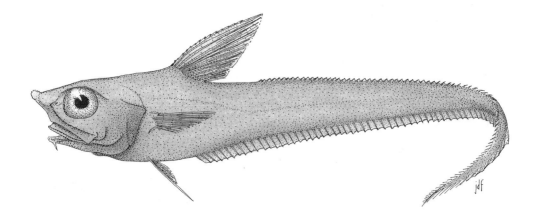

Nezumia cyrano is elongate and attenuated, with a relatively acute snout and a slender body. It is distinguished from the other species of the family by the following combination of characters. Snout is of moderate length and bears two large scutelike scales at tip. Jaws are subterminal, relatively short, and fail to reach posterior margin of orbits. Head length is 15% to 20% of TL. Snout length is 32% to 36%, orbit is 30% to 36%, premaxilla length is 20% to 21%, chin barbel is 3% to 8%, and body depth at first dorsal fin origin is 65% to 77% of head length. Jaws have wide band of small teeth, with those in outer row of premaxilla enlarged. First gill slit is greatly restricted. Gill rakers are tuberculate and number 6 to 10 on first arch. Branchiostegal rays number 7. Pectoral fin has 18 to 22 rays. First dorsal fin has 11 to 13 rays, first of which is splintlike and second, serrated and spinous. Second dorsal fin is distinctly separated from first and has shorter rays than anal fin. Pelvic fin has 8 to 10 rays. Abdomen has small, circular naked black area between pelvic fin bases associated with light organ. Anus and urogenital openings are surrounded by naked black area (periproct) and are located between pelvic fin base and anal fin origin. Scales are covered with broad, flattened spinules. Head is covered with scales except for median section of ventral snout, and gular and branchiostegal membranes. Row of stout, scutelike scales extends from angle of snout to preoperculum, forming ridge. Swim bladder has two retia mirabilia. Color is brownish violet, with snout pale and gill covers, gular and branchiostegal membranes, and abdomen blackish.

This species occurs in the western Atlantic in the Gulf of Mexico, the Caribbean Sea, and off the northern coast of South America to Suriname at 640 to 1,324 m. Maximum known size is 280 mm TL.

REFERENCES: Marshall and Iwamoto 1973; Uyeno et al. 1983; Boschung 1992.

Nezumia longebarbata (Roule and Angel 1933)

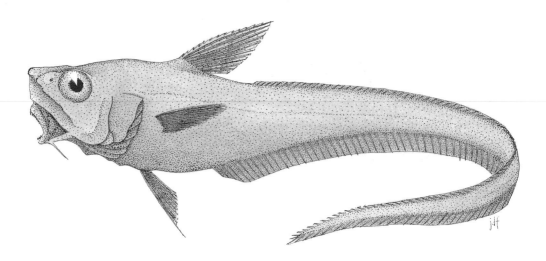

Nezumia longebarbata is elongate and attenuated, with a blunt snout and a deep head. It is distinguished from the other species of the family by the following combination of characters. Snout is relatively short and slightly produced. Jaws are subterminal, relatively short, and fail to reach posterior margin of orbits. Head length is 17% to 20% of TL. Snout length is 28% to 31%, orbit is 28% to 32%, premaxilla length is 26% to 33%, chin barbel is 17% to 25%, and body depth at first dorsal fin origin is 84% to 92% of head length. Jaws have broad band of small teeth, with those in outer row of premaxilla enlarged. First gill slit is greatly restricted. Gill rakers are tuberculate and number 9 or 10 on first arch. Branchiostegal rays number 7. Pectoral fin has 21 to 24 rays. First dorsal fin has 10 or 12 rays, first of which is splintlike and second, serrated and spinous. Second dorsal fin is widely separated from first and has shorter rays than anal fin. Pelvic fin has 13 rays. Abdomen has small naked black area between pelvic fin bases associated with light organ. Anus and urogenital openings are surrounded by naked black area (periproct) and are located between pelvic fin base and anal fin origin. Scales are densely covered with conical to lanceolate spinules arranged in rows. Head is covered with scales except for ventral side of snout. Snout has median and lateral scutelike scales. Row of stout, scutelike scales extends from angle of snout to preoperculum, forming ridge. Swim bladder has two retia mirabilia. Color is brown, with bluish tinge over abdomen and ventral region blackish.

This species occurs in the tropical to temperate Atlantic Ocean. In the western Atlantic it occurs off the eastern coast of the United States near Hudson Canyon and in the Gulf of Mexico between 1,463 and 1,960 m. Maximum known size is 71 mm TL, but no mature specimens are known.

REFERENCES: Marshall and Iwamoto 1973; Haedrich and Polloni 1974; Geistdoerfer 1986.

Nezumia suilla   Marshall and Iwamoto 1973

Nezumia suilla is elongate and attenuated, with an acute snout and a relatively slender body. It is distinguished from the other species of the family by the following combination of characters. Snout is of moderate length and slightly produced. Jaws are subterminal, relatively short, and fail to reach posterior margin of orbits. Head length is 15% to 20% of TL. Snout length is 28% to 32%, orbit is 29% to 34%, premaxilla length is 26% to 29%, chin barbel is 8% to 21%, and body depth at first dorsal fin origin is 73% to 81% of head length. Jaws have band of small teeth, with those in outer row of premaxilla enlarged. First gill slit is greatly restricted. Gill rakers are tuberculate and number 7 to 9 on first arch. Branchiostegal rays number 7. Pectoral fin has 19 to 22 rays. First dorsal fin has 11 to 13 rays, first of which is splintlike and second, serrated and spinous. Second dorsal fin is distinctly separated from first and has shorter rays than anal fin. Pelvic fin has 7 rays. Abdomen has small naked black area between pelvic fin bases associated with light organ. Anus and urogenital openings are surrounded by naked black area (periproct) and are located between pelvic fin base and anal fin origin. Scales are covered with moderately broad to broad spinules. Head is covered with scales except for ventral side of snout, and gular and branchiostegal membranes. Snout has median and lateral scutelike scales. Row of stout, scutelike scales extends from angle of snout to preoperculum, forming ridge. Swim bladder has two retia mirabilia. Color is brown, with ventral side of head and gill covers darker; abdomen bluish; and pelvic fin, periproct, and gular and branchiostegal membranes blackish.

This species occurs in the western Atlantic from the Gulf of Mexico, the Caribbean Sea, and off the northern coast of South America to Suriname at 900 to 1,500 m. Maximum known size is 350 mm TL.

REFERENCES: Marshall and Iwamoto 1973; Uyeno et al. 1983.

Sphagemacrurus grenadae   (Parr 1946)

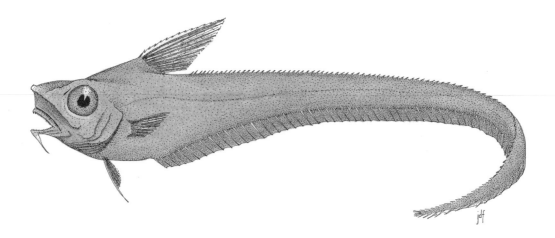

Sphagemacrurus grenadae is elongate and attenuated, with a short snout, a compressed body, and a short abdomen. It is distinguished from the other species of the family by the following combination of characters. Snout is blunt and slightly acute, with a strong, terminal, scutelike scale. Jaws are short, subterminal, and do not extend to posterior margin of orbits. Head is about 15% of TL. Snout length is 29% to 31%, orbit is 31% to 34%, premaxilla length is 29% to 32%, chin barbel is 19% to 26%, and body depth at first dorsal fin origin is 94% to 107% of head length. Jaws have band of small, pointed teeth. First gill slit is greatly restricted. Gill rakers are tuberculate and number 7 to 9 on first arch. Branchiostegal rays number 7. Pectoral fin has 18 to 22 rays. First dorsal fin has 12 or 13 rays, first of which is splintlike and second, strongly serrated and spinous. Second dorsal fin is distinctly separated from first and has shorter rays than anal fin. Pelvic fin has 11 rays, with first ray slightly elongated. Abdomen lacks naked area and light organ anterior to anus. Anus and urogenital openings are surrounded by broad naked black area (periproct) and are located well anterior to anal fin origin. Scales are densely covered with spinules arranged in parallel rows. Head is fully scaled except for ventral side of snout, and gular and branchiostegal membranes. Swim bladder has two retia mirabilia. Color is dark brown to black, with buccal cavity, gill cavities, and peritoneum black.

This species occurs in the western North Atlantic off the east coast of the United States in Hudson Canyon, in the Gulf of Mexico, and in the Caribbean Sea at 1,000 to 1,960 m. Maximum known size is 250 mm TL.

REFERENCES: Parr 1946a; Marshall 1973; Haedrich and Polloni 1974; Geistdoerfer 1986; Cohen et al. 1990.

Trachonurus sulcatus (Goode and Bean 1885)

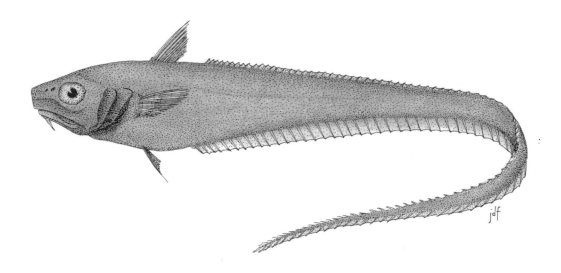

Trachonurus sulcatus is slender, elongate, and attenuated, with a relatively small head, short jaws, and a very long tail. It is distinguished from the other species of the family by the following combination of characters. Snout is rounded and relatively compressed. Jaws are short and extend to about anterior margin of orbits. Head is about 15% of TL. Snout length is 23% to 29%, orbit is 25% to 32%, premaxilla length is 28% to 36%, chin barbel is 9% to 19%, and body depth at first dorsal fin origin is 74% to 82% of head length. Jaws have narrow band of relatively small, pointed teeth. First gill slit is greatly restricted. Gill rakers are tuberculate and number 5 or 6 on first arch. Branchiostegal rays number 7. Pectoral fin is short and has 15 to 17 rays. First dorsal fin has 9 to 11 rays, first of which is splintlike and second, smooth and spinous. Second dorsal fin is widely separated from first and has shorter rays

than anal fin. Pelvic fin has 7 rays. Anus and urogenital openings are surrounded by broad naked black area (periproct) that extends anteriorly to insertion of pelvic fin. Scales have few upright spinules. Head and snout are fully scaled except for branchiostegal membranes and parts of gular membrane. Color is brown to black.

This species occurs in the warm temperate to tropical Atlantic Ocean. In the western Atlantic it occurs off the southeastern United States, the Gulf of Mexico, and the Caribbean Sea at 700 to 1,500 m. Maximum known size is 455 mm TL. Marshall (1973) considered this species to be synonymous with *Trachonurus villosus* (Günther).

REFERENCES: Parr 1946a; Marshall 1973; Geistdoerfer 1986 (as *T. villosus*); Cohen et al. 1990.

Ventrifossa macropogon   Marshall 1973

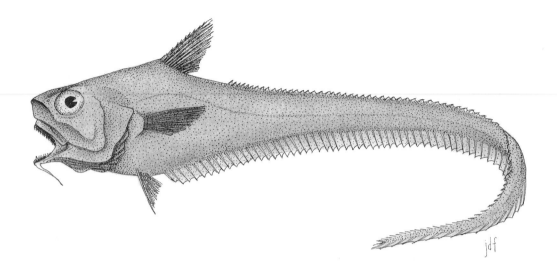

Ventrifossa macropogon is elongate and attenuated, with an acute snout, large jaws, and a relatively long chin barbel. It is distinguished from the other species of the family by the following combination of characters. Snout is relatively short and slightly produced. Jaws are subterminal and extend to near posterior margin of orbits. Head is 16% to 18% of TL. Snout length is 23% to 29%, orbit is 28% to 38%, premaxilla length is 40% to 48%, chin barbel is 38% to 43%, and body depth at first dorsal fin origin is 79% to 109% of head length. Upper jaw has broad band of teeth, with those of outer row enlarged and widely spaced. Lower jaw has two to four rows of teeth. First gill slit is greatly restricted. Gill rakers are tuberculate and number 8 to 12 on inner side of first arch. Branchiostegal rays number 7. Pectoral fin has 20 to 22 rays. First dorsal fin has 13 to 16 rays, first of which is splintlike and second, serrated and spinous. Second dorsal fin is distinctly separated from first and has shorter rays than anal fin. Pelvic fin has 9 or 10 rays. Abdomen has small, oval-shaped naked black area associated with light organ and located anterior to pelvic fin base. Anus and urogenital openings are surrounded by oval-shaped naked black area (periproct) and are located near pelvic fin insertion. Scales have slender, conical spinules. Head is covered with scales except for gular and branchiostegal membranes. Swim bladder has two retia mirabilia. Color is brown, with head dark brown, buccal membrane light, and first dorsal fin blackish.

This species occurs in the western Atlantic Ocean from the east coast of Florida to Suriname, including the northeastern Gulf of Mexico and the Caribbean Sea, at 439 to 1,000 m. Maximum known size is 450 mm TL.

REFERENCES: Marshall 1973; Cohen et al. 1990.

MELANONIDAE Pelagic cods

The pelagic cods are relatively slender and tapered posteriorly, with a single dorsal fin and numerous procurrent caudal rays on the caudal peduncle. They are distinguished from the other families of the order by the following combination of characters. Snout is blunt, and mouth extends to near posterior margin of orbits. Teeth are of moderate size and occur in narrow band in jaws, vomer, and palatine. Chin barbel is lacking. Eye is of moderate size. Dorsal side of head lacks V-shaped ridge. Pectoral fin is narrow based and located at midflank. Dorsal fin originates above pectoral fin base, and second ray is slightly elongated. Pelvic fin is thoracic, with base slightly anterior to pectoral fin base. Anal fin is long based and unnotched. Caudal fin is small and sharply rounded, with numerous procurrent rays extending anterior to near dorsal and anal fin insertion. Swim bladder is not connected to cranium.

Pelagic cods occur worldwide in tropical to warm temperate seas and in subantarctic seas, and are mesopelagic or bathypelagic. There are two species in a single genus, and one species occurs in the Gulf of Mexico.

Melanonus zugmayeri   Norman 1930

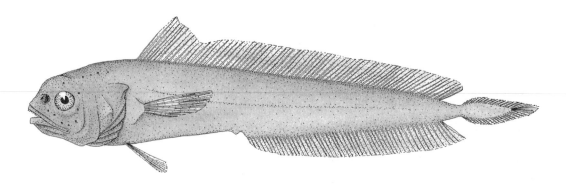

Melanonus zugmayeri is relatively slender and tapered posteriorly. It is distinguished from the other species of the family by the following combination of characters. Snout is blunt, and mouth is moderately oblique. Upper jaw extends to near posterior margin of orbits. Teeth are relatively stout, with pair in anterior section of upper jaw and anterior teeth in lower jaw enlarged. Vomer has two parallel rows of teeth, and palatine has a single row of teeth. Pectoral fin has 13 rays and is about 67% of head length. Head length is 25% and body depth is 19% to 21% of SL. Snout length is 29%, eye diameter is 20% to 21%, and interorbital width is 43% of head length. Dorsal fin has about 70 rays, pelvic fin has 7 rays, and anal fin has about 50 rays.

This species occurs worldwide in tropical to warm temperate seas. In the western Atlantic it occurs from the Carolinas to Venezuela, including the Gulf of Mexico and the Caribbean Sea. Maximum known size is about 150 mm TL.

REFERENCES: Uyeno et al. 1983; Howes 1991.

MERLUCCIIDAE

The merlucciids are moderately fusiform, with a large, terminal mouth, two dorsal fins, and a separate caudal fin. They are distinguished from the other families of the order by the following combination of characters. Head is one-third to one-fourth of body length. Snout is long and depressed, with lower jaw projecting slightly beyond upper jaw. Mouth extends to about middle of eyes. Teeth are long and pointed, occur in two rows in upper and lower jaws, and also occur in vomer. Chin barbel is absent. Eye is large. Dorsal side of head has low, V-shaped ridge converging posteriorly and extending from above eyes to rear of skull. Gill rakers are present. Branchiostegal rays number 7. Pectoral fin is high on flank and long. First dorsal fin is short, triangular shaped, and has spinous anterior rays. Second dorsal fin is long and partially divided by notch at midlength. Pelvic fin is located slightly anterior to pectoral fin base and has 7 rays. Caudal fin is truncate. Scales are small, thin, and cycloid. Lateral line is continuous.

Merlucciids occur in the northern and southern Atlantic, eastern Pacific, and western South Pacific Oceans. All species are benthic on continental shelves and upper slopes. Some species occur inshore and enter estuaries. Food consists mainly of crustaceans in young and fishes in larger individuals. There are 13 species in a single genus, and 1 species occurs in the Gulf of Mexico.

Merluccius albidus (Mitchill 1818)
Offshore hake

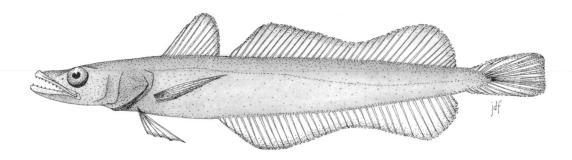

Merluccius albidus is slender and fusiform, with an acute, depressed snout; a large mouth; and a distinct caudal fin. It is distinguished from the other species of the family by the following combination of characters. Snout is relatively long and very slightly arched. Mouth is terminal, slightly oblique, and extends posterior to anterior margin of orbits. Teeth are large, sharp, and in two irregular rows in jaws, with outer teeth fixed and widely spaced and inner teeth larger, depressible, and moderately widely spaced. Gill openings extend above pectoral fin base. Gill rakers are short and thick, with blunt tips, and number 8 to 11 on first arch. Head length is 27% to 32% and maximum body depth is 17.5% to 20% of SL. Snout length is 31% to 37.2%, interorbital width is 20.8% to 26.5%, and eye diameter is 15.4% to 22.9% of head length. Pectoral fin is narrow based and pointed, extends to anus, and has 12 to 17 rays. First dorsal fin is short based and triangular shaped, and has one spine and 10 to 12 rays. Second dorsal fin originates immediately posterior to first, is notched at about mid-length, and has 35 to 39 rays. Anal fin is shaped similarly to second dorsal fin and has 35 to 41 rays. Caudal fin is emarginate, with upper and lower rays longer than middle rays. Caudal fin of juveniles is rounded, with middle rays longer than upper or lower rays. Anus and urogenital openings are located close together near anal fin origin. Scales are relatively large and number 104 to 119 along lateral line. Vertebrae number 51 to 55. Color is silvery white.

This species occurs in the western Atlantic from New England to northern Brazil, including the Gulf of Mexico and the Caribbean Sea, at 80 to 1,170 m. It is most common between 160 and 640 m. This species feeds off the bottom at night largely on fishes such as myctophids, clupeids, and engraulids, although it also eats crustaceans and squids. Juveniles feed mostly on shrimps. Spawning takes place from late spring to early fall. Fecundity ranges up to 340,000 eggs. Maximum known size is 400 mm TL for males and 700 mm TL for females.

REFERENCES: Ginsburg 1954; Karnella 1973; Rohr and Gutherz 1977; Vergara 1978; Inada 1981; Uyeno et al. 1983; Cohen et al. 1990; Boschung 1992.

STEINDACHNERIIDAE

This family is monotypic, and the single species occurs in the Gulf of Mexico.

Steindachneria argentea   Goode and Bean 1896
Luminous hake

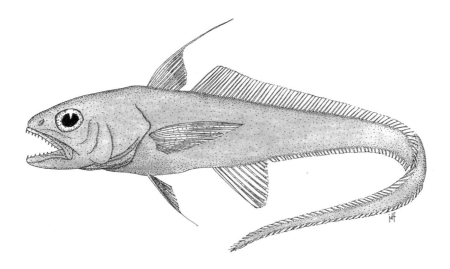

Steindachneria argentea is long and attenuated, with a blunt, compressed snout; a caudal fin continuous with dorsal and anal fins; and an abdominal light organ. It is distinguished from the other species of the family by the following combination of characters. Snout is relatively short and convex. Mouth is moderately oblique, with upper jaw extending beyond anterior margin of orbits. Jaw teeth are large, sharp, and in two irregular rows, with those in outer row enlarged and widely spaced and those in inner row small and narrowly spaced in upper jaw. Teeth in both rows are enlarged and widely spaced in lower jaw. Vomerine teeth are arranged in U-shaped row. Gill openings extend above pectoral fin base. Gill rakers are slender and number 5 on epibranch and 13 to 15 on lower limb. Head is 18.2% to 19.2% of TL. Snout length is 21.7% to 23.8%, eye diameter is 26.3% to 27.8%, and interorbital width is 22.2% to 25.2% of head length. Pectoral fin is narrow based and pointed and extends beyond anus. First dorsal fin is short based and has one spine elongated into a filiform ray and 7 to 9 rays. Second dorsal fin originates close to first dorsal fin base and has 123 or more rays that decrease in length posteriorly. Pelvic fin is located under pectoral fin and has 8 rays, with first ray elongated. Anal fin originates slightly posterior to second dorsal fin origin and has elevated anterior portion of 10 to 12 rays followed by lower portion with 109 to 111 rays. Caudal fin is very reduced. Scales are small and cycloid, with six rows between second dorsal fin base and lateral line. Color is silvery; dorsal surface has a slightly brownish tinge; and belly has a slightly purplish tinge. Inside of mouth is dark.

This species occurs in the western North Atlantic in the Gulf of Mexico and the Caribbean Sea along the outer continental shelf and slope to 500 m. It is usually found on soft bottoms. Maximum known size is 277 mm TL.

REFERENCES: Goode and Bean 1896; Hoese and Moore 1977; Uyeno et al. 1983; C. R. Robins et al. 1986; Cohen et al. 1990; Boschung 1992.

MORIDAE Moras

The moras are moderately fusiform and tapered posteriorly, with a large, terminal to subterminal mouth; two or three dorsal fins; and one or two anal fins. They are distinguished from the other families of the order by the following combination of characters. Snout is acute to moderately blunt. Mouth extends beyond anterior margin of orbits. Narrow band of teeth occurs in each jaw, but teeth are few or lacking on vomer. Chin barbel is present or absent. Eye is moderate to large in size. Dorsal side of head lacks V-shaped ridge. Gill rakers are present. Fins lack spines. Pectoral fin is just below to just above midflank and is moderately long. First dorsal fin is short based and originates above pectoral fin origin, or consists of single ray located above pectoral fin origin. Second dorsal fin is generally long based and narrowly separated from first dorsal fin, but is occasionally widely separated from first dorsal fin base. Pelvic fins are thoracic, with bases widely separated. Anal fin is long based, often notched at about midlength, and separated from caudal fin. Caudal fin is rounded, truncate, or emarginate. Scales are cycloid. Swim bladder is connected by two anterior projections to rear of cranium.

Moras occur worldwide on continental shelves to lower slopes, although some species enter estuaries. Species are benthopelagic or demersal to 2,500 m. There are about 100 species in about 18 genera, and 4 species in 3 genera occur in the Gulf of Mexico.

Key to the Species of the Gulf of Mexico
(Adapted from Cohen et al. 1990)

1a. Ventral light organ absent between anus and pelvic fin base
.... 2
1b. Ventral light organ present between anus and pelvic fin
base 3
2a. Gill rakers on lower limb of first arch 10 to 13
.... *Laemonema barbatulum* p. 805
2b. Gill rakers on lower limb of first arch more than 13
.... *Laemonema* sp. p. 806
3a. Chin barbel present .... *Physiculus fulvus* p. 807
3b. Chin barbel absent .... *Gadella imberbis* p. 804

Gadella imberbis (Vaillant 1888)

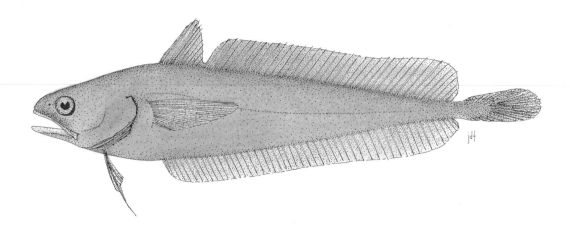

Gadella imberbis is moderately fusiform and tapered posteriorly, with two dorsal fins and an abdominal light organ, but without a chin barbel. It is distinguished from the other species of the family by a combination of the following characters. Snout is moderately blunt and rounded. Mouth is moderately oblique and extends to posterior margin of orbits. Teeth in jaws are large and irregular in size, and arranged in two or three rows in upper jaw and in one or two rows in lower jaw. Vomer lacks teeth. Gill rakers are short and spiny, and number 3 or 4 on epibranch and 4 to 10 on lower limb. Head length is 18% to 24%, predorsal length is 25% to 29.5%, preanal length is 27.4% to 31.4%, and body depth is 18.3% to 25% of SL. Snout length is 24.4% to 33%, upper jaw length is 46.9% to 58.2%, orbit diameter is 21% to 24.8%, and caudal peduncle depth is 12% to 15% of head length. Pectoral fin extends beyond anal fin origin and has 25 to 26 rays. First dorsal fin is short based and has 9 to 11 rays. Second dorsal fin originates immediately behind first and has 54 to 61 rays. Pelvic fins are widely separated and located anterior to pectoral fin base, with outer 2 rays filamentous and extending beyond anal fin origin. Anal fin is not notched and has 63 to 66 rays. Caudal fin is rounded. Scales are small and number 81 to 88 from opercular flap to caudal fin base, and 6 or 7 from second dorsal fin base to lateral line. Light organ is circular and closer to anus than to line connecting anterior rays of pelvic fins. Vertebrae number 49 to 51. Color is pale tan, with abdominal area bluish, and gular region and branchiostegal membrane dark brown.

This species occurs in the Atlantic, and in the western Atlantic it occurs in the Gulf of Mexico, the Caribbean Sea, and off the coast of Brazil at 200 to 800 m. Maximum known size is about 200 mm SL.

REFERENCES: Goode and Bean 1896; Uyeno et al. 1983; Paulin 1989; Boschung 1992 (as *Brosmiculus imberbis*).

Laemonema barbatulum   Goode and Bean 1883

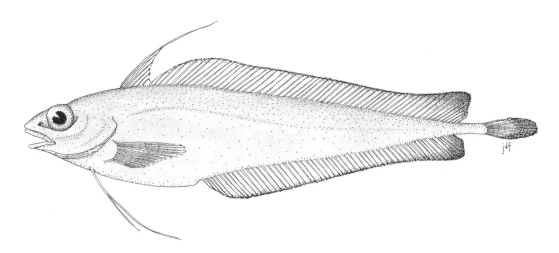

Laemonema barbatulum is moderately fusiform and tapered posteriorly, with two dorsal fins and a short chin barbel, but no abdominal light organ. It is distinguished from the other species of the family by the following combination of characters. Snout is moderately blunt and slightly convex. Mouth is terminal, but upper jaw slightly overhangs lower jaw. Chin barbel is shorter than eye diameter. Jaws extend to about midlength of orbits. Upper jaw has outer row of enlarged canine teeth and two or three inner rows of villiform teeth. Lower jaw has two rows of cardiform teeth, with those of outer row larger than those of inner row. Vomer has small oval patch of cardiform teeth. Operculum has single flat spine on upper posterior margin. Gill rakers are rather long and slender, and number 3 to 6 on epibranch and 10 to 13 on lower limb. Head length is 18.8% to 26.7%, snout length is 4.5% to 8.2%, lower jaw length is 7.7% to 12.7%, orbit diameter is 5.2% to 8.9%, predorsal length is 21.1% to 28.9%, preanal length is 35% to 56.5%, body depth is 13.8% to 38.1%, and caudal peduncle depth is 1.7% to 3.6% of SL. Pectoral fin has 19 to 23 rays. First dorsal fin is short and has 6 (rarely 7) rays, first of which is beneath skin and second is longest. Second dorsal fin originates immediately behind first, has 57 to 63 rays, and lacks notch. Pelvic fins are widely separated, originate anterior to pectoral fin base, and have 2 elongated rays that fail to reach anus and 2 or 3 short rays beneath skin. Anal fin lacks notch and has 54 to 63 rays. Caudal fin is slightly rounded. Lateral line scales number 128 to 140, and scales between second dorsal fin base and lateral line number 12 to 15. Vertebrae number 50 to 56, with 13 to 15 trunk, and 37 to 42 caudal, vertebrae. Color is pale tan, with dorsal and anal fins edged with black.

This species occurs in the western Atlantic from 40°17′N to 2°37′S, including the Gulf of Mexico, between 50 and 1,620 m. Maximum known size is 400 mm SL.

REFERENCES: Goode and Bean 1896; Springer and Bullis 1956; Bullis and Thompson 1965; Uyeno et al. 1983; Melendez and Markle 1997.

Laemonema sp.

Laemonema sp. is moderately fusiform and tapered posteriorly, with two dorsal fins and a short chin barbel, but no abdominal light organ. It is distinguished from the other species of the family by the following combination of characters. Snout is moderately blunt and slightly convex. Mouth is terminal, but upper jaw slightly overhangs lower jaw. Jaws extend to about midlength of orbit. Upper jaw has outer row of enlarged cardiform teeth and five or six inner rows of villiform teeth. Lower jaw has outer row of enlarged cardiform teeth and two or three rows of villiform teeth. Vomer has small oval patch of small teeth. Operculum has single, wide, flat spine on upper posterior margin. Gill rakers are rather long and slender, and number 7 to 9 on epibranch and 17 to 20 on lower limb. Head is 20% to 24%, orbit diameter is 6.4% to 8.3%, interorbital width is 3.4% to 4.7%, upper jaw length is 9.2% to 11.73%, predorsal length is 21.4% to 27.6%, preanal length is 37.8% to 45.7%, body depth is 14% to 20.6%, and caudal peduncle depth is 1.7% to 2.5% of SL. Pectoral fin is pointed, extends to anus, and has 19 to 22 rays. First dorsal fin is short and has 5 or 6 rays, first of which is beneath skin. Second dorsal fin originates immediately behind first, has 66 to 73 rays, and lacks notch. Pelvic fins are widely separated, originate anterior to pectoral fin base, have 2 rays, and extend to fourth or fifth anal rays. Anal fin has 65 to 71 rays. Caudal fin is slightly rounded. Scales are of moderate size and number 125 to 140 in lateral series. Vertebrae number 56 to 59, with 15 to 17 trunk, and 39 to 43 caudal, vertebrae. Color is light gray to pinkish white, with fins dusky brown to whitish pale tan. First dorsal fin has black tip.

This species occurs in the western Atlantic from Canada to southern Brazil, including the Gulf of Mexico and the coasts of French Guiana and Suriname, between 180 to 792 m. Maximum known size is about 262 mm SL.

REFERENCES: Goode and Bean 1896 (in part as *Laemonema barbatulum*); Melendez and Markle 1997.

Physiculus fulvus   Bean 1884
Metallic codling

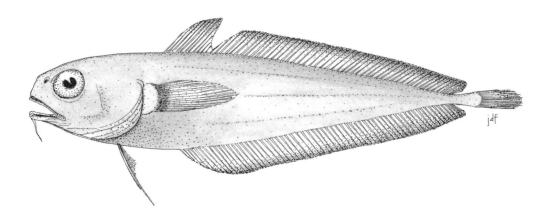

Physiculus fulvus is moderately elongate and slightly compressed, with a short chin barbel and two dorsal fins. It is distinguished from the other species of the family by the following combination of characters. Snout is obtusely rounded and does not project beyond mouth. Mouth is moderately oblique and terminal, with upper jaw extending beyond anterior margin of orbits. Teeth in jaws are in narrow bands, and outer teeth are slightly larger. Vomer lacks teeth. Gill rakers are moderately long and slender, and number 2 or 3 on epibranch and 8 to 11 on lower limb of first arch. Head is 25.3% to 28%, predorsal length is 27.9% to 29.6%, preanal length is 33.7% to 34.4%, and body depth is 20.1% to 20.7% of SL. Snout length is 27% to 30.7%, upper jaw length is 44.5% to 60%, and caudal peduncle depth is 9.1% to 10.1% of head length. Pectoral fin has 21 to 26 rays. First dorsal fin is short based and has 9 to 12 rays. Second dorsal fin originates immediately behind first and has 57 to 61 rays. Pelvic fin is slightly anterior to pectoral fin base, and outer 2 rays are filamentous and extend beyond anal fin origin. Anal fin is not indented and has 59 to 68 rays. Caudal fin is rounded. Scales are small and number 70 to 84 along lateral line and 6 or 7 between dorsal fin base and lateral line. Light organ is moderately large and located midway between line connecting anterior pelvic fin rays and anus. Vertebrae number 47 to 50. Color is pinkish tan, with abdominal region bluish, silvery tinge extending from abdomen to sides of body and head, and lips and gular region dark brown.

This species occurs in the western Atlantic from Cape Cod to North Carolina, in the northeastern Gulf of Mexico, the Caribbean Sea, and off Suriname to northern Brazil at 200 to 475 m. Maximum known size is 133 mm SL.

REFERENCES: Goode and Bean 1896; Uyeno et al. 1983; Paulin 1989; Boschung 1992.

BATRACHOIDIFORMES

Batrachoidiformes are the sister group of Lophiiformes. The order contains one family, and it occurs in the Gulf of Mexico.

BATRACHOIDIDAE Toadfishes

The toadfishes are depressed anteriorly and compressed posteriorly, with a large head and mouth. They are distinguished from the other families by the following combination of characters. Snout is short. Mouth is terminal and is bordered by both premaxilla and maxilla. Mouth and head are occasionally covered with fleshy tentacles, barbels, fleshy tabs, or cirri. Jaws, vomer, and palatine have bands of sharp to blunt, moderately sized teeth, and occasionally canine teeth in anterior section of jaws. Eye is of moderate size and is located on upper side of head. Gill filaments are present on three gill arches. Operculum has three to five strong spines, usually hidden in skin, and occasionally most prominent opercular spine is hollow and has poison gland at base. Subopercular spine is present or absent. Opercular opening is somewhat restricted, extending from above pectoral fin base to above pelvic fin base. Branchiostegal rays number six. Pectoral fin is broad based and fan shaped. Upper pectoral fin rays have glands in some species. Axillary pore or foramen occurs behind pectoral fin base in some species. First dorsal fin is located above pectoral fin base and has two to four short, stout spines. Dorsal fin spines are occasionally hollow and associated with poison glands. Second dorsal fin is slightly longer than anal fin base. Pelvic fin is jugular, located anterior to pectoral fin base, and consists of one spine and two or three soft rays. Anal fin has long base and lacks spines. Caudal fin is convex. Skin is covered with small, embedded, cycloid scales; is partially covered with scales; or is naked. One to four lateral line canals occur on body, with pores usually surrounded by low bifid tentacle. Photophores are associated with lateral line canals in some species. Swim bladder is present.

Toadfishes occur worldwide in tropical to temperate waters. Most species are coastal, but some reside in freshwater and others occur on continental shelves to 250 m. All species are benthic, generally on sandy to mud bottoms, but some occur on coral reefs. Toadfishes are sluggish but voracious carnivores. Food consists of benthic invertebrates and fishes. Fertilized eggs are negatively buoyant and adhesive, and are guarded by males in most species. There are 69 species in 19 genera, and 4 species in 3 genera occur in the Gulf of Mexico. The family is divided into three subfamilies: Thalassophryninae have two hollow dorsal spines and one hollow opercular spine that serve as venom-injecting apparatuses for the venom glands, Porichthyinae generally have photophores on body but lack venom glands, and Batrachoidinae have three solid dorsal spines and solid opercular spines but lack venom glands and photophores. Only the latter two subfamilies occur in the Gulf of Mexico.

Key to the Species of the Gulf of Mexico
(Adapted from Collette 1978a; pers. com., May 3, 1995)

1a. Dorsal fin spines two; no subopercular spine; no axillary pore behind pectoral fin base; canine teeth and photophores present. . . . . *Porichthys plectrodon* p. 812

1b. Dorsal fin spines three; one or two subopercular spines; axillary pore behind pectoral fin base present or absent; canine teeth and photophores absent 2

2a. Discrete gland present on inner surface of upper membrane of pectoral fin; dorsal fin rays 23 to 27; anal fin rays 19 to 23 3

2b. Discrete gland absent on inner surface of upper membrane of pectoral fin; dorsal fin rays 30 to 32; anal fin rays 25 or 26. *Sanopus reticulatus* p. 813

3a. Ground color dark, with light crossbars or mottled pattern; pectoral fin with light crossbars composed of row of light spots; dorsal fin rays usually 24 or 25; pectoral fin rays usually 18 or 19. . . . . *Opsanus beta* p. 810

3b. Ground color light, with brown spots as large as eye on body and fins; pectoral fin with brown spots on light background; dorsal fin rays usually 26; pectoral fin rays usually 20 to 22. . . . . *Opsanus pardus* p. 811

Opsanus beta   (Goode and Bean 1880)
Gulf toadfish

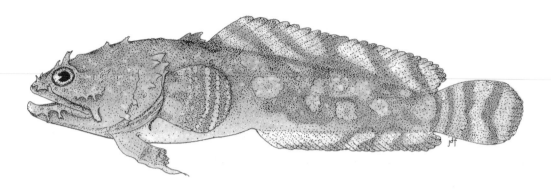

Opsanus beta is moderately compressed anteriorly and depressed posteriorly, with axillary pore behind pectoral fin base and gland on inner surface of upper membrane of pectoral fin. It is distinguished from the other species of the family by the following combination of characters. Head has tentacles over inner margin of eye; fleshy tabs along lower jaw; and blunt, flattened maxillary barbel. Lower jaw extends slightly beyond upper jaw, and mouth is moderately oblique. Jaws, vomer, and palatine have narrow bands of moderately blunt and moderate-sized teeth; canine teeth are lacking in jaws. Head length is 31% to 31.9%, head width is 26.7% to 27%, orbit diameter is 5.2% to 6.2%, interorbital width is 3.3% to 4.3%, snout to second dorsal fin is 41.3% to 45.1%, snout to anal fin origin is 54.2% to 56.3%, pectoral fin length is 22% to 22.3%, and pelvic fin length is 14.7% to 17.5% of SL. Operculum has two solid, sharp spines; suboperculum has single sharp spine; and all spines may be hidden in skin. Pectoral fin has 18 or 19 rays. First dorsal fin has three short, solid spines. Second dorsal fin has 24 or 25 rays. Anal fin has 19 to 23 rays. Body lacks scales and has three lateral lines. Color is brown to grayish brown, marbled and mottled with tan to white. Pale areas on body often form rosettes posteriorly. Dorsal and anal fins are diagonally barred, and pectoral fin has light-colored spots and blotches on dark background.

This species occurs in the western Atlantic from southeastern Florida, south of Cape Canaveral, to the Gulf of Mexico and the Bahamas in shallow coastal waters. It is most common in seagrass beds, bays, lagoons, and shallow coastal areas. Maximum known size is 300 mm TL.

REFERENCES: Schultz and Reid 1937; Böhlke and Chaplin 1968; Hoese and Moore 1977; C. R. Robins et al. 1986; Boschung 1992.

Opsanus pardus   (Goode and Bean 1880)
Leopard toadfish

Opsanus pardus is moderately compressed anteriorly and depressed posteriorly, with axillary pore behind pectoral fin base and gland on inner surface of upper pectoral fin membrane. It is distinguished from the other species of the family by the following combination of characters. Head has tentacles on inner margin of each eye; fleshy tabs along lower jaw; and blunt, flattened maxillary barbel. Lower jaw extends slightly beyond upper jaw, and mouth is moderately oblique. Jaws, vomer, and palatine have narrow bands of moderately blunt and moderate-sized teeth; canine teeth are lacking. Head length is 32.4%, head width is 30.5%, orbit diameter is 7.3%, interorbital width is 5.5%, snout to second dorsal fin origin is 47.4%, snout to anal fin origin is 59.6%, pectoral fin length is 25.4%, and pelvic fin length is 19.4% of SL. Operculum has two solid, sharp spines; suboperculum has single spine; and all spines may be hidden in skin. Pectoral fin has 20 to 22 rays. First dorsal fin has three short, solid spines. Second dorsal fin has 26 rays. Anal fin has 19 to 22 rays. Body lacks scales and has three lateral lines. Color is yellowish, buff to straw colored, with dark brown markings forming reticulations on body. Dorsal and anal fins have diagonal dark brown bars over light ground color. Pectoral and caudal fins have dark blotching on light ground color, but blotching seldom forms bars.

The leopard toadfish occurs in the western Atlantic in the Gulf of Mexico on the continental shelf over rocky bottoms. Maximum known size is 380 mm TL.

REFERENCES: Schultz and Reid 1937; Hastings et al. 1976; Hoese and Moore 1977; C. R. Robins et al. 1986; Boschung 1992.

Porichthys plectrodon   Jordan and Gilbert 1882
Atlantic midshipman

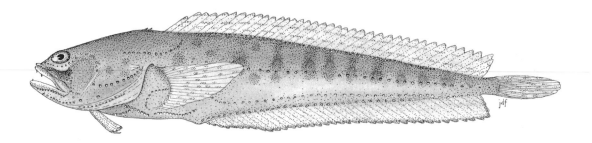

Porichthys plectrodon is moderately elongate and tapering and compressed posteriorly, with rows of photophores along sides and ventral aspect of head and body. It is distinguished from the other species of the family by the following combination of characters. Head is moderately depressed and lacks tentacles, fleshy tabs, and barbels. Lower jaw extends beyond upper jaw, and mouth is moderately oblique. Jaws extend posterior to eye. Teeth of upper jaw, vomer, and palatine are in single row. Palatine teeth number six to eight, are enlarged and directed forward, and some jaw teeth are caninelike. Teeth in lower jaw are in two rows anteriorly, with those of outer row enlarged and strongly hooked and those of inner row small. Gill rakers on first arch number 10 to 17. Operculum has single strong, solid spine. Suboperculum is poorly developed and lacks spine. Head length is 20.8% to 23.7%, head width is 13.1% to 16.7%, orbit diameter is 3.8% to 4%, interorbital width is 5.1% to 6%, snout to second dorsal fin origin is 29.3% to 33.6%, snout to anal fin origin is 38.1% to 42.1%, pectoral fin length is 21.5% to 24.3%, and pelvic fin length is 11.1% to 13.7% of SL. Pectoral fin has 17 to 18 rays and discrete gland between bases of uppermost rays. First dorsal fin has two short, solid spines. Second dorsal fin has 34 to 39 rays,

and anal fin has 31 to 35 rays. Body lacks scales and has four lateral lines. Lateral line pores have cirri. Photophores are present on head and body and are arranged in rows that follow lateral lines. Branchiostegal photophore series has forward-directed, U-shaped commissure comprising 35 to 47 photophores. Vertebrae number 43 to 47. Color is pale to dark, with small- to medium-sized brown to black spots in two rows on second dorsal fin and upper parts of head and body. Belly is light (golden in life). Pectoral fin has faint dark spots, and lower rays are slightly grayish. Anal fin has black margin. Caudal fin is dark at base, white medially, and progressively darker toward margin.

This species occurs in the western Atlantic from Cape Henry, Virginia, to northern South America, including the Gulf of Mexico, on the continental shelf to 256 m. It is generally found in less than 91 m on soft bottoms. Bioluminescence is thought to be used during spawning, but it might also enable this species to mimic ctenophores (Springer 1957).

REFERENCES: Lane 1967 (as *P. porosissimus*); Gilbert 1968 (as *P. porosissimus*); Hoese and Moore 1977 (as *P. porosissimus*); Uyeno et al. 1983; C. R. Robins et al. 1986; Cervigón 1991; Boschung 1992.

Sanopus reticulatus   Collette 1983

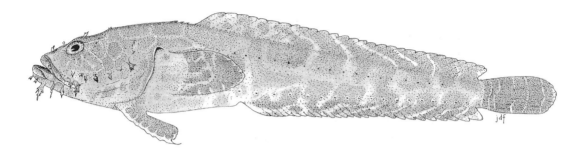

Sanopus reticulatus is relatively elongate and moderately depressed anteriorly, with branched chin barbels and axillary gland behind pectoral fin base. It is distinguished from the other species of the family by the following combination of characters. Head is covered with branched barbels, fleshy tabs, and cirri, except between eyes. Maxillary barbel is present and is deeply branched. Lower jaw extends slightly beyond upper jaw, and mouth is moderately oblique. Jaw teeth are molarlike and relatively large, and canine teeth are absent. Vomer and palatine have band of sharp, moderately sized, conical teeth. Premaxilla has 34 to 41 teeth, lower jaw has 18 to 19 teeth on each side, vomer has 8 to 10 teeth, and palatine has 9 to 14 teeth. Head length is 32.6% to 36.5%, head width is 24.5% to 30.3%, orbit diameter is 4% to 4.5%, interorbital distance is 6.1% to 7.7%, snout to second dorsal fin base is 40.3% to 41.9%, snout to anal fin origin is 58.7% to 59.2%, pectoral fin length is 16.2% to 18.3%, and pelvic fin length is 13.2% to 15.7% of TL. Operculum has two solid spines, suboperculum has single spine, and all spines may be hidden in skin. Pectoral fin has 19 or 20 rays and lacks discrete gland on medial surface of upper pectoral fin membrane. Axillary pore, leading to group of glands, is present behind pectoral fin base. First dorsal fin has three solid spines. Second dorsal fin has 31 to 32 rays. Anal fin has 25 or 26 rays. Body lacks scales and has upper and lower lateral lines, with 34 to 36 and 30 to 32 papillae respectively. Trunk vertebrae number 11, and tail vertebrae number 27 to 29. Color is brown, with light tan reticular pattern and dark brown blotches. Ventral sides of head and belly are yellowish white to white, with small light brown blotches. Fins are dark brown with light reticulations. Lower lateral line pores are white.

This toadfish occurs in the western Atlantic in the eastern Gulf of Mexico at Progreso, Yucatán. Only three specimens have been reported, all from the same locality. Maximum known size is 236 mm SL.

REFERENCE: Collette 1983.

LOPHIIFORMES

Lophiiformes consist of 16 families that are grouped into three suborders: Lophioidei (with Lophiidae in the Gulf), Antennarioidei (with Antennariidae in the Gulf), and Ogocephalioidei (with three superfamilies: Chaunacioidea, Ogocephalioidea, and Ceratioidea). Chaunacioidea and Ogocephalioidea each consist of a single family, Chaunaciidae and Ogcocephalidae, and both occur in the Gulf. Ceratioidea consists of 11 families, and 7 (Ceratiidae, Diceratiidae, Himantolophidae, Linophrynidae, Melanocetidae, Oneirodidae, and Thaumatichthyidae) occur in the Gulf.

Key to the Families of the Gulf of Mexico
(Adapted from Bertelsen 1951; Pietsch 1986a)

1a. Pelvic fin present 2
1b. Pelvic fin absent 5
2a. Head and trunk greatly depressed 3
2b. Head and trunk globose or slightly compressed 4
3a. Three or more free dorsal spines on top of head; scales lacking; mouth very large and bearing needlelike teeth .... Lophiidae p. 827
3b. One short dorsal spine (illicium) on top of head in cavity between eyes; scales on body forming bony armor; mouth small and bearing villiform teeth .... Ogcocephalidae p. 833
4a. First dorsal spine short and stubby, and associated with depression on snout; second and third dorsal spines not visible externally .... Chaunacidae p. 824
4b. First dorsal spine not short and stubby, and not associated with depression on snout; second and third dorsal spines on head well developed and covered with integument .... Antennariidae p. 815
5a. Illicium (first dorsal fin spine on head) well developed (females)... 6
5b. Illicium (first dorsal fin spine on head) absent or vestigial (males)... 12
6a. Dorsal fin rays 12 to 172 .... Melanocetidae p. 863
6b. Dorsal fin rays fewer than 11 7
7a. Two or three bulbous caruncles (modified dorsal fin spines) on dorsal midline anterior to second dorsal fin; mouth vertical to strongly oblique.............. Ceratiidae p. 849
7b. No bulbous caruncles (modified dorsal fin spines) on dorsal midline; mouth oblique to nearly horizonta 8
8a. Second dorsal spine on head well developed, with esca at tip............................. Diceratiidae p. 851

8b. Second dorsal spine on head embedded beneath integument
. . . . 9
9a. Skin naked 10
9b. Skin with spiny scales. 11
10a. Branchiostegal rays 4 or 5; dorsal fin rays 2 to 4; anal fin
rays 2 to 4 . . . . Linophrynidae p. 858
10b. Branchiostegal rays 6; dorsal fin rays 5 to 8; anal fin rays 4
to 7 . . . . Oneirodidae p. 867
11a. Dermal spines small and slender; premaxilla extending posteriorly beyond lower jaw . . . . . Thaumatichthyidae p. 870
11b. Dermal spines consisting, in part, of large bony plates
bearing medial spine; premaxilla not extending beyond
lower jaw. . . . . Himantolophidae p. 853
12a. Olfactory organs very small . . . . Ceratiidae p. 849
12b. Olfactory organs large 13
13a. Eye telescopic and directed anteriorly
. . . . Linophrynidae p. 858
13b. Eye not telescopic and directed laterally 14
14a. Anterior naris positioned anteriorly, near tip of snout . . . 15
14b. Anterior naris positioned laterally, on side of snout 16
15a. Head rounded, broader than it is deep; dorsal fin rays 5 or
6; anal fin rays 4 . . . . Diceratiidae p. 851
15b. Head tapering, not broader than it is deep; dorsal fin rays
5 to 8; anal fin rays 4 to 7 . . . . Oneirodidae p. 867
16a. Nasal area pigmented; median series of denticles connected
with fused denticles (denticular) on snout
. . . . Melanocetidae p. 863
16b. Nasal area unpigmented; no median series of denticles connected with fused denticles (denticular) on snout
. . . . Himantolophidae p. 853

ANTENNARIIDAE   Frogfishes

Frogfishes are short, globose, and slightly compressed, with a slender illicium, second and third dorsal spines generally erect and
free of second dorsal fin, and integument generally covered with
dermal spinules. They are distinguished from the other families
of the order by the following combination of characters. Snout
is moderately to strongly diagonally oriented. Mouth is terminal
to superior, and strongly oblique to vertical. Jaw teeth are villiform and arranged in two to four rows. Posterior tip of maxilla is
spatulate. Vomer and palatine bear teeth. Eye is lateral. Opercular bones are reduced. Branchiostegal rays number 6. Opercular

opening is restricted to small porelike opening located ventral to or posterior to pectoral fin base. Pectoral fin is limblike, with pectoral girdle radials forming limblike base of fin. Pectoral fin lobe is broadly connected to side of body but is not membranously connected to pelvic fin rays. Pectoral rays number 6 to 14. Spinous dorsal fin consists of three cephalic spines, with anteriormost one free and forming illicium bearing fleshy esca in most species. Illicium is usually naked. Illicial pterygiophore is not retractable. Second and third dorsal spines are generally widely separated from each other and from second dorsal fin. Second dorsal fin is long based and consists of 10 to 16 rays. Pelvic fin is thoracic and has one spine and 5 rays. Anal fin is long based and has 6 to 10 rays. Body is generally covered with dermal spinules (except in *Histrio histrio*) and cutaneous filaments or appendages. Vertebrae number 18 to 23. Coloration is extremely variable within species, and this variation enables these fishes to match their background in a variety of habitats.

Frogfishes occur worldwide in tropical waters, with exception of the Mediterranean Sea, between the surface and shoreline to 300 m. Most species live on the bottom, where they move by means of their pectoral and pelvic fins. Food consists of a large variety of mobile invertebrates and fishes, which are captured by aggressive mimicry. The frogfish remains motionless on the substrate and attracts prey by dangling the esca in front of the mouth. The esca resembles various invertebrates and fishes. The coloration and cutaneous filaments camouflage the frogfish. Eggs are spawned encapsulated within a nonadhesive, positively buoyant, mucoid mass. Some frogfishes, however, retain the egg masses on sides of the body. There are about 41 species in 12 genera, and 6 species in 2 genera occur in the Gulf of Mexico.

Key to the Species of the Gulf of Mexico
(Adapted from Pietsch and Grobecker 1987)

1a. Skin smooth, without dermal spinules
. . . . *Histrio histrio* p. 823
1b. Skin densely covered with close-set dermal spinules 2
2a. Illicium distinctly shorter than second cephalic dorsal spine; second cephalic dorsal spine membranously connected to third cephalic dorsal spine; third cephalic dorsal spine membranously connected to second dorsal fin
. . . . *Antennarius pauciradiatus* p. 820
2b. Illicium equal in length or longer than second cephalic dorsal spine; second cephalic dorsal spine membranously connected to head but not connected to third cephalic dorsal spine; third cephalic dorsal spine not connected to second dorsal fin 3
3a. Illicium equal in length to second cephalic dorsal spine. . . 4

3b. Illicium about twice as long as second cephalic dorsal spine
. . . . *Antennarius multiocellatus* p. 818

4a. Second cephalic dorsal spine connected to head, and membrane divided into naked dorsal and ventral portions by patch of dermal spinules; radial of illicium terminating well behind symphysis of upper jaw. 5

4b. Second cephalic dorsal spine connected to head, and membrane not divided into dorsal and ventral portions by patch of dermal spinules; radial of illicium extending anteriorly to or slightly beyond symphysis of upper jaw
. . . . *Antennarius striatus* p. 822

5a. Pectoral fin rays bifurcate; three ocelli on side of body, one below dorsal fin, one at midbody, and one on caudal fin
. . . . *Antennarius ocellatus* p. 819

5b. Pectoral fin rays simple; single ocellus on side of body below dorsal fin . . . . *Antennarius radiosus* p. 821

Antennarius multiocellatus (Valenciennes 1837)
Longlure frogfish

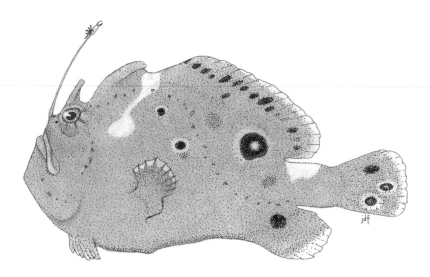

Antennarius multiocellatus is globose and slightly compressed, with skin covered with close-set, bifurcate dermal spinules and illicium about twice as long as second cephalic dorsal spine. It is distinguished from the other species of the family by the following combination of characters. Distal two-thirds of maxilla is naked and located beneath skin folds. Eye diameter is 4.6% to 7.3% and illicium is 21% to 31.8% of SL. Esca is broad, laterally compressed, and about 45% of illicial length, with numerous small appendages arising from base. Anterior end of illicial pterygiophore ends posterior to symphysis of upper jaw. Second cephalic dorsal spine is straight to slightly curved posteriorly, about 9.2% to 19.4% of SL, and connected to head by narrow membrane covered with dermal spinules, but membrane does not connect with third cephalic dorsal spine. Third cephalic dorsal spine is curved posteriorly and is about 16.8% to 28.2% of SL. Pectoral fin has 9 to 10 simple rays. Second dorsal fin has 11 to 13 rays, with up to 5 posteriormost bifurcate. Only posteriormost pelvic ray is bifurcate. Anal fin has 6 to 7 bifurcate rays. Caudal peduncle is present. Head and body are partially or totally covered with low, rounded, wartlike swellings. Vertebrae number 19. Color is light tan, yellow brown, or dark brown to black, with zero to nine darkly pigmented bars radiating from eye. Light-colored specimens have darker mottling on head, body, and fins; round spots on unpaired fins; and white saddles on shoulder and caudal peduncle. Dark spots and ocelli may be present on body, ranging in size from one-half to 2 times eye diameter. Dark-pigmented specimens have lighter-colored saddles on shoulders and caudal peduncle. Black specimens lack markings.

This species occurs in the Atlantic Ocean. In the western Atlantic it occurs from Bermuda, the Bahamas, and the Florida Keys to Brazil (13°S), including the Gulf of Mexico and the Caribbean Sea, between the surface and 66 m. Maximum known size is 113 mm SL.

REFERENCES: Longley and Hildebrand 1941; Schultz 1957; Böhlke and Chaplin 1968; C. R. Robins et al. 1986; Pietsch and Grobecker 1987; Cervigón 1991.

Antennarius ocellatus   (Bloch and Schneider 1801)
Ocellated frogfish

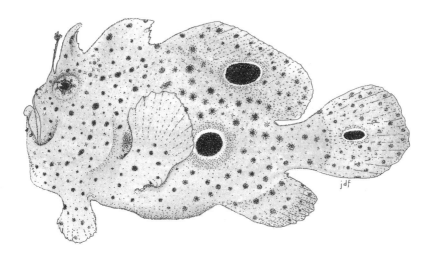

Antennarius ocellatus is globose and slightly compressed, with skin covered with close-set, bifurcate dermal spinules and illicium about as long as second cephalic dorsal spine. It is distinguished from the other species of the family by the following combination of characters. Distal one-fifth to one-fourth of maxilla is naked and located beneath skin folds. Eye diameter is 3.9% to 6.9% of SL. Illicium is 8.6% to 15% of SL and has dermal denticles along anterior margin. Esca consists of dense cluster of elongate, slender filaments and lacks eye spot. Anterior end of illicial pterygiophore ends posterior to symphysis of upper jaw. Second cephalic dorsal spine is curved posteriorly, about 9.5% to 16.5% of SL, and connected to head by membrane divided into dorsal and ventral portions by patch of dermal spinules. Membrane is nearly connected to third cephalic dorsal spine. Third cephalic dorsal spine is curved posteriorly and is 21.5% to 28% of SL. Pectoral fin has 11 or 12 bifurcate rays. Second dorsal fin has 12 or 13 bifurcate rays. All pelvic fin rays are bifurcate. Anal fin consists of 7 or 8 bi-furcate rays. Caudal peduncle is present. Vertebrae number 20. Color is beige, light brown, yellowish brown, brown, or gray to slightly pinkish, with three darkly pigmented ocelli, each surrounded by light ring. Ocelli occur at base of dorsal fin, at midbody, and on center of caudal fin. Head, chin, belly, and fins (or entire body) are marked with darkly pigmented spots. Illicium is usually banded, esca filaments are pigmented at base, and second and third cephalic dorsal spines may have eyelike spots. Eye is surrounded by zero to nine radiating bars.

This species occurs in the western Atlantic Ocean from North Carolina to Venezuela, including the eastern Gulf of Mexico, the Bahamas, and the continental coast of the Caribbean Sea. Depths range from the shoreline to 90 m and rarely to 150 m. Maximum known size is 320 mm SL.

REFERENCES: Schultz 1957; Böhlke and Chaplin 1968; Hastings et al. 1976; C. R. Robins et al. 1986; Pietsch and Grobecker 1987; Cervigón 1991; Boschung 1992.

Antennarius pauciradiatus Schultz 1957
Dwarfed frogfish

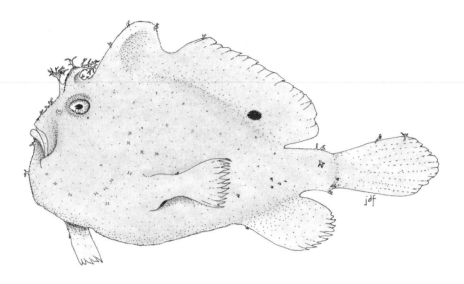

Antennarius pauciradiatus is globose and slightly compressed, with skin covered with close-set, bifurcate dermal spinules; illicium distinctly shorter than second cephalic dorsal spine; and pair of elongate, branched appendices on distal end of second cephalic dorsal spine. It is distinguished from the other species of the family by the following combination of characters. Distal two-thirds of maxilla is naked and located beneath skin folds. Eye diameter is 5.3% to 9.1% and illicium is 5.2% to 8.2% of SL. Esca is oval shaped, 5.9% to 7.2% of SL, and has numerous elongated filaments with slightly swollen tips along dorsal and ventral margin and one to three small eye spots posteriorly. Anterior end of illicial pterygiophore ends posterior to symphysis of upper jaw. Second cephalic dorsal spine is strongly curved posteriorly, about 10.3% to 13.2% of SL, and connected to head and to third cephalic dorsal spine by membrane. Membrane has appendages on margin; is off center to left, thus forming pocket for esca; and is covered with dermal spinules except anterodorsally. Third cephalic dorsal spine is strongly curved posteriorly, 24.5% to 31.7% of SL, and connected by membrane to second dorsal fin. Pectoral fin rays are simple and number 9 or 10. Second dorsal fin has 11 or 12 rays, with up to 3 posteriormost bifurcate. All pelvic fin rays are simple. Anal fin consists 7 or 8 bifurcate rays. Caudal peduncle is present. Vertebrae number 19. Color is pale gray or light beige to brown, with tiny dark spots and small spot on base of dorsal fin.

This species occurs in the tropical western Atlantic from Bermuda and the Atlantic coast of Florida to Belize and Colombia, including the Bahamas, the Dry Tortugas in the eastern Gulf of Mexico, and the Caribbean Sea. Depths of capture range from 6 to 73 m. Maximum known size is 40 mm SL.

REFERENCES: Longley and Hildebrand 1941 (as *Antennarius pleurophthalmus*); Schultz 1957; Böhlke and Chaplin 1968; C. R. Robins et al. 1986; Pietsch and Grobecker 1987; Cervigón 1991.

Antennarius radiosus   Garman 1896
Big-eye frogfish

Antennarius radiosus is globose and slightly compressed, with skin covered with close-set, bifurcate dermal spinules; illicium about as long as second cephalic dorsal spine; and single ocellar spot. It is distinguished from the other species of the family by the following combination of characters. Distal one-fifth to one-fourth of maxilla is naked and located beneath skin folds. Eye diameter is 7.4% to 11.4% and illicium is 14.6% to 19.4% of SL. Esca is simple and oval shaped, with numerous more or less parallel vertically aligned folds. Anterior end of illicial pterygiophore ends posterior to symphysis of upper jaw. Second cephalic dorsal spine is straight to slightly curved posteriorly, about 11.1% to 18.4% of SL, and connected to head by membrane divided into dorsal and ventral portions by patch of dermal spinules. Membrane is nearly connected to third cephalic dorsal spine. Third cephalic dorsal spine is more or less straight and is 17.7% to 25% of SL. Pectoral fin consists of 12 to 14 simple rays. Second dorsal fin has 12 or 13 bifurcate rays. All pelvic fin rays are bifurcate. Anal fin consists of 7 or 8 bifurcate rays. Caudal peduncle is present. Vertebrae number 20. Color is beige, light brown to grayish brown, with single darkly pigmented ocellus surrounded by light-colored ring at dorsal fin base. Illicium is usually lightly banded, body is occasionally mottled with dark lines, and median fins are occasionally lightly barred.

This species occurs in the Atlantic Ocean. In the western Atlantic it occurs from Long Island, New York, to the Gulf of Mexico, the Florida Keys, and the Greater Antilles between 20 and 275 m. Maximum known size is 117 mm SL in the western Atlantic.

REFERENCES: Longley and Hildebrand 1941; Schultz 1957; Hoese and Moore 1977; Shipp and Hopkins 1978; Uyeno et al. 1983; C. R. Robins et al. 1986; Pietsch and Grobecker 1987; Cervigón 1991; Boschung 1992.

Antennarius striatus (Shaw and Nodder 1794)
Striated frogfish

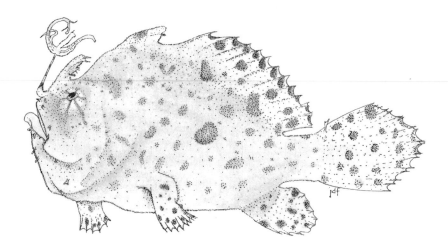

Antennarius striatus is globose and slightly compressed, with skin covered with close-set, bifurcate dermal spinules; illicium about as long as or longer than second cephalic dorsal spine; and body colored with numerous dark streaks or elongated blotches. It is distinguished from the other species of the family by the following combination of characters. Eye diameter is 3.5% to 7.4% and illicium is 13.6% to 22.7% of SL. Esca consists of two to seven elongate, wormlike appendages ranging from 4% to 27.8% of SL. Anterior end of illicial pterygiophore extends anterior to or slightly beyond symphysis of upper jaw. Second cephalic dorsal spine is more or less straight, 11.4% to 19% of SL, and connected to head by membrane. Membrane is not divided into dorsal and ventral naked portions and does not extend to third cephalic dorsal spine. Third cephalic dorsal spine is curved posteriorly and is 16.7% to 29.3% of SL. Pectoral fin consists of 9 to 12 simple rays. Second dorsal fin has 11 to 12 rays, with up to 4 posteriormost rays bifurcate. Anal fin rays number 6 or 7, with usually all bifurcate. Only posteriormost pelvic ray is bifurcate. Caudal peduncle is present. Vertebrae number 18 or 19. Color is beige, light yellow, orange, or dark yellowish brown to black. Lighter-colored specimens have 0 to 12 darkly pigmented streaks radiating from eye, and dark brown to black stripes or elongate blotches on body. Black-colored specimens have tips of pectoral rays white.

This species occurs in the Atlantic and Indo-Pacific Oceans. In the western Atlantic it occurs from New Jersey to Brazil, including Bermuda, the Bahamas, the Gulf of Mexico, and the Caribbean Sea. Depths range from the surface to 49 m. Maximum known size is 155 mm SL.

REFERENCES: Longley and Hildebrand 1941 (as *Antennarius scaber*); Baughman 1950b (as *A. nuttingii*); Böhlke and Chaplin 1968 (as *P. scaber*); Hoese and Moore 1977 (as *P. scaber*); Uyeno et al. 1983 (as *Phrynelox nuttingi* and *P. scaber*); C. R. Robins et al. 1986 (as *A. scaber*); Pietsch and Grobecker 1987; Boschung 1992.

Histrio histrio (Linnaeus 1758)
Sargassum fish

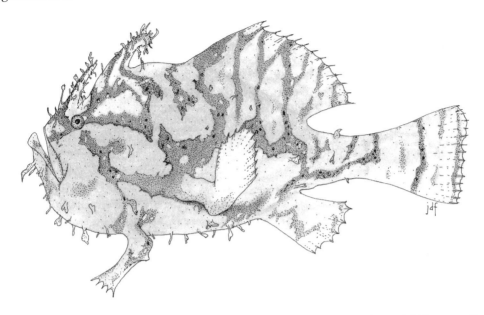

Histrio histrio is globose and moderately compressed, with two cutaneous cirri along midline between upper jaw and illicium, large pelvic fins, but without dermal spinules. It is distinguished from the other species of the family by the following combination of characters. Distal one-fifth to one-fourth of maxilla is located beneath skin folds. Eye diameter is 5% to 8.7% of SL. Illicium is less than one-half of length of second cephalic dorsal spine and about 4.5% to 9.3% of SL. Esca is an oval-shaped, tapering appendage, with numerous parallel folds and cluster of short, slender filaments arising from base. Anterior end of illicial pterygiophore ends posterior to symphysis of upper jaw. Second cephalic dorsal spine is narrow, straight to slightly curved posteriorly, 13.3% to 19.3% of SL, not connected to head by membrane, and posterior margin is covered with cutaneous papillae and appendages. Third cephalic dorsal spine is narrow, slightly curved posteriorly, 19.3% to 29.3% of SL, and connected to head by membrane covered with cutaneous papillae and appendages. Pectoral fin has 9 to 11 simple rays. Second dorsal fin has 11 to 13 rays, with posteriormost 2 or 3 bifurcate. All pelvic fin rays are simple. Anal fin rays number 6 to 8, with posteriormost 2 to 6 bifurcate. Caudal peduncle is present. Skin is covered with small, rounded, close-set papillae and numerous compressed appendages. Vertebrae number 18 or 19. Color is variable and changeable, from more or less plain grayish white to a pattern of streaks and mottling of brown, olive, and yellow, with small brown to black spots and irregular white lines. Pectoral and pelvic fins are occasionally edged in orange, cutaneous filaments are white, and dark bands or streaks radiate from eyes.

This species occurs in the Atlantic, Indian, and western Pacific Oceans. In the western Atlantic it occurs from the Gulf of Maine to Uruguay, including Bermuda, the Gulf of Mexico, the Bahamas, and the Caribbean Sea. Larvae and postlarvae up to 4 mm SL are pelagic between 50 and 600 m, and larger specimens occur at the surface associated with sargassum weed. Maximum known size is 141 mm SL.

REFERENCES: Longley and Hildebrand 1941 (as *Histrio gibba*); Schultz 1957; Hoese and Moore 1977; C. R. Robins et al. 1986; Pietsch and Grobecker 1987; Cervigón 1991; Boschung 1992.

CHAUNACIDAE   Gapers

Gapers are globose and slightly compressed, with a short, stubby illicium associated with a depression on the snout, a large cuboidal head, and no obvious second or third cephalic spines. They are distinguished from the other families of the order by the following combination of characters. Snout is moderately long and oblique. Mouth is superior and nearly vertical. Jaw, vomerine, and palatine teeth are villiform. Eye is dorsolaterally located and moderately large. Opercular bones are reduced, and opercular opening is restricted and located posterodorsal to opercular fin base. Gill filaments are absent on first branchial arch and are present on second through fourth arches. Gill rakers consist of clusters of small spines on pedicles. Branchiostegal rays number 6. Pectoral fin is limblike, with pectoral girdle radials forming limblike base of fin. Pectoral fin lobe is broadly connected to side of body, and pectoral fin rays are unbranched, membranously connected to side of body, and number 11 to 14. Pectoral fin rays are not membranously connected to pelvic fin rays. Spinous dorsal fin consists of three cephalic spines, with anteriormost free and located in U-shaped depression. Illicium bears fleshy esca. Illicial pterygiophore is retractable. Second and third cephalic dorsal spines are embedded in integument behind first. Second dorsal fin has long base and 10 to 12 rays. Pelvic fin is thoracic and consists of one spine and 4 unbranched rays. Anal fin has short base and 5 to 7 rays. Caudal peduncle is long and slender. Caudal fin has 8 rays. Body is covered with loose skin and small spinelike scales. Vertebrae number 19. Lateral line system is exposed and consists of canals on head and body, with spiny scales on each side.

Gapers occur in tropical to temperate seas worldwide. All species are benthic between 90 and 2,000 m. Food consists of benthic invertebrates and fishes that are caught by aggressive mimicry. Prey are attracted by means of the illicium and esca. There are 14 species in two genera, and 2 species in the same genus occur in the Gulf of Mexico.

Key to the Species of the Gulf of Mexico
(Adapted from Caruso 1989)

1a.   Illicial cavity dark brown to black, and strongly concave; esca bicolored, black on anterodorsal surface and translucent to white on posteroventral surface
. . . . *Chaunax pictus* p. 825
1b.   Illicial cavity pale, and flat to slightly concave; esca uniformly pale to dusky . . . . *Chaunax suttkusi* p. 826

Chaunax pictus   Lowe 1846

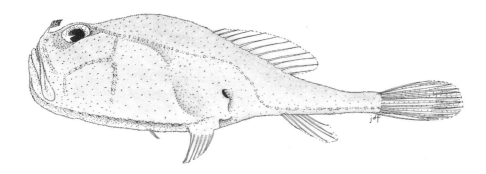

Chaunax pictus is balloon shaped and slightly compressed, with very loose, flaccid skin bearing closely spaced spinelike scales, and an esca consisting of short, fleshy cirri and fitting into a strongly concave cavity. It is distinguished from the other species of the family by the following combination of characters. Head is 39.8% to 48% of SL. Premaxilla is 16.2% to 20.5% of SL, and postmaxillary process lacks deep notch. Articular bone has relatively short anteroventral process. Illicium is 3.9% to 6.1% and pre-illicial length is 3.1% to 6.2% of SL. Distance between urogenital pores and end of hypural plate is 27.3% to 36.8%, between posterior end of second dorsal fin base and hypural plate is 17.4% to 19.1%, and between posterior end of anal fin base and hypural plate is 13.3% to 18.6% of SL. Pectoral fin rays number 12 to 14, and anal fin rays number 6 or 7. Lateral line neuromast counts are: AB = 10–13, CD = 6–7, EF = 5–8, FG = 3, GH = 12–14, AC = 6–8, BD = 2–3, DG = 3, and BI = 29–42. Color is pale tan or pinkish in preserved specimens. Illicial cavity is dark brown to black, illicium is pale, and esca is dark brown to black anterodorsally and translucent to white posteroventrally. Peritoneum is dusky. In life, color is light orange to rosy on flank, with fins and lips vermilion. Belly is nearly white suffused with flesh-colored or rosy blotches, and pelvic fin and anal fin are vermilion.

This species occurs in the Atlantic Ocean. In the western Atlantic it occurs from the Bahamas to Guatemala, including the eastern Gulf of Mexico and the Caribbean Sea, between 272 and 622 m. Maximum known size is about 280 mm TL.

REFERENCES: Böhlke and Chaplin 1968; Uyeno et al. 1983; Caruso and Pietsch 1986; M. M. Smith 1986b; Caruso 1989.

Chaunax suttkusi Caruso 1989

Chaunax suttkusi is balloon shaped and slightly compressed, with very loose, flaccid skin bearing closely spaced spinelike scales, and an esca consisting of short, fleshy cirri and fitting into a flat illicial cavity. It is distinguished from the other species of the family by the following combination of characters. Head is 38.4% to 45.4% of SL. Premaxilla is 16.2% to 20.6% of SL, and postmaxillary process lacks deep notch. Articular bone has relatively short anteroventral process. Illicium is 3.6% to 6.6% and pre-illicial length is 1.6% to 4.8% of SL. Premaxillary length is 16.2% to 20.6% of SL. Distance between urogenital pores and end of hypural plate is 28.2% to 37.7%, between posterior end of dorsal fin base and hypural plate is 14.8% to 21.7%, and between posterior end of anal fin base and hypural plate is 13.1% to 20.4% of SL. Pectoral fin rays number 10 to 13, and anal fin rays number 6 or 7. Lateral line neuromast counts are: $AB = 10-13$, $CD = 5-8$, $EF = 5-8$, $FG = 3-5$, $GH = 12-17$, $AC = 6-8$, $BD = 2-3$, $DG = 3-5$, and $BI = 29-42$. Color is pale tan to pinkish, with illicial cavity pale but surrounded by pigment, illicium pale, and esca pale to dark brown. In life, color is pale to rosy pink dorsally and on distal section of anal fin. Some specimens have bright yellow circular spots on dorsal side of body.

This species occurs in the Atlantic Ocean. In the western Atlantic it occurs from South Carolina to central Brazil, including the entire Gulf of Mexico and the Caribbean Sea, at 220 to 1,060 m and at temperatures between 6.1°C and 16.9°C. One specimen from Alabama was captured at 27 m.

REFERENCES: Caruso 1989; Boschung 1992.

LOPHIIDAE   Goosefishes

Goosefishes are moderately to greatly depressed and oval shaped, with a wide, superior mouth and a spinous dorsal fin divided into cephalic and postcephalic sections. They are distinguished from the other families of the order by the following combination of characters. Head is massive and has numerous bony spines. Jaws, vomer, and palatine bear long, slender, depressible teeth. Eye is moderate to small and is on dorsal surface of head. Opercular bones are reduced, and opercular opening is moderately restricted and extends below and behind, or below, behind, and in front of, pectoral fin base. Gill filaments are present on first three arches but are absent on fourth arch. Pectoral fin is limblike, with pectoral girdle radials forming limblike base of fin. Pectoral fin lobe is broadly connected to side of body, and pectoral rays are unbranched and terminate as fleshy tips. Pectoral fin rays are not membranously connected to pelvic fin rays. Spinous dorsal fin usually consists of three isolated cephalic spines (with first and second close to tip of snout) and one to three postcephalic spines. First cephalic spine is modified as angling device (illicium) and bears fleshy bait (esca). Second and third cephalic spines have tendrils along entire length. Postcephalic spines may be embedded. Second dorsal fin is long based, is located near caudal fin base, and has 8 to 12 rays. Pelvic fin is located on ventral surface of head anterior to pectoral fin base. Anal fin is long based and has 6 to 10 rays. Caudal peduncle is long and slender. Body is covered with thin, loose, scaleless skin bearing numerous prominent fleshy tendrils or cirri on lateral margin of head, lower jaw, and body.

Goosefishes occur worldwide from tropical to temperate seas. All species are benthic between the shoreline and 1,500 m. Food consists of a wide variety of invertebrates, fishes, and occasionally seabirds. Prey are attracted by means of the illicium and esca. Eggs and larvae are pelagic. There are 25 species in four genera, and 4 species in two genera occur in the Gulf of Mexico.

Key to the Species of the Gulf of Mexico

(Adapted from Caruso 1981, 1983, 1986)

1a. Frontal ridge (on either side of snout) smooth; opercular opening extending in front of pectoral fin base; articular bone of lower jaw with one spine before and one spine behind jaw articulation; sphenotic bone (behind eye) with one spine 2

1b. Frontal ridge (on either side of snout) with knobs, spines, or ridges; opercular opening not extending in front of pectoral fin base; articular bone of lower jaw with one spine before jaw articulation; sphenotic bone (behind eye) with two or three spines . . . . *Lophius gastrophysus* p. 832

2a. Spinous dorsal fin with three postcephalic spines . . . . *Lophiodes reticulatus* p. 831

2b. Spinous dorsal fin with two postcephalic spines 3

3a Esca with light, unpigmented bulb; illicium darkly pigmented . . . . *Lophiodes beroe* p. 829

3b. Esca with pigment progressively darker toward tip; illicium unpigmented . . . . *Lophiodes monodi* p. 830

Lophiodes beroe   Caruso 1981

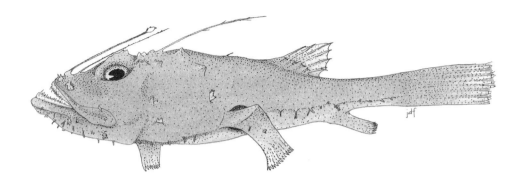

Lophiodes beroe is moderately depressed and oval shaped anteriorly, with two embedded postcephalic spines, a narrow snout, and well-developed fleshy tendrils on lateral surface of head and body. It is distinguished from the other species of the family by the following combination of characters. Snout is narrow, and supraorbital crest is not elevated. Interorbital area is moderately concave. Distance between sphenotic spines (behind eye) is usually greater than distance between posterior frontal spines (between eyes). Eye is relatively large. Teeth on alveolar process of premaxilla number 6 to 13 in outer row and are laterally slanted. Head length is 36.2% to 43.9% of SL, and head width is 52.3% to 63.2%, head depth is 63% to 68.1%, snout length is 52.9% to 60.3%, and snout width is 15.4% to 18.8% of head length. Articular bone of lower jaw has two spines, one anterior to and one posterior to articulation of jaw. Opercular opening extends below, behind, and in front of pectoral fin base. Quadrate has single lower spine, suboperculum has one spine, interoperculum has one or two spines,

and humeral spine is well developed. Pectoral fin rays number 18 to 21. Spinous dorsal fin has three cephalic and two embedded postcephalic spines. First cephalic spine (illicium) is 20.3% to 30.8%, second is 22.2% to 29.7%, and third is 28.5% to 39.3% of SL. Illicium is very dark distally, and esca is an unpigmented bulb with one apical cirrus and a variable number of basal cirri. First postcephalic spine is absent, and second and third postcephalic spines are embedded in integument. Second dorsal fin has 8 rays. Pelvic fin has one spine and 5 rays. Anal fin has 6 rays. Color varies from uniform light to dark brown or gray or mottled light and dark brown. Dorsal surface has small, circular, light-pigmented areas. Peritoneum is black.

This species occurs in the western Atlantic from south Florida, the northeastern Gulf of Mexico, and the Caribbean Sea at 347 to 860 m and at temperatures of 9°C to 11°C. Maximum known size is 234 mm SL.

REFERENCE: Caruso 1981.

Lophiodes monodi   (Le Danois 1971)

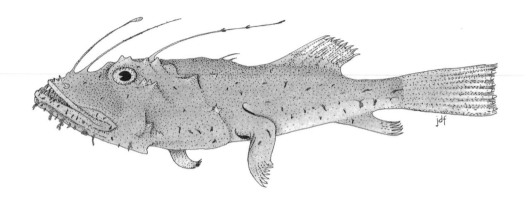

Lophiodes monodi is moderately depressed and oval shaped anteriorly, with postcephalic section of first dorsal fin reduced, a narrow snout, and well-developed fleshy tendrils on lateral surface of head and body. It is distinguished from the other species of the family by the following combination of characters. Snout is narrow, and supraorbital crest is not elevated. Interorbital area is moderately concave. Distance between sphenotic spines (behind eye) is slightly greater than distance between posterior frontal spines (between eyes). Eye is relatively large. Teeth on alveolar process of premaxilla number 6 to 17 in anterior row and are not laterally slanted. Head length is 35.8% to 41.8% of SL, and head width is 54.4% to 61.4%, head depth is 65.3% to 71%, snout length is 54.5% to 60.1%, and snout width is 16% to 19.4% of head length. Articular bone of lower jaw has two spines, one anterior to and one posterior to articulation of jaw. Opercular opening extends below, behind, and in front of pectoral fin base. Quadrate has single lower spine, suboperculum has one spine, interoperculum has one or two spines, and humeral spine is well developed.

Pectoral fin rays number 16 to 21. Spinous dorsal fin has three cephalic spines and two postcephalic spines. First cephalic spine (illicium) is 26% to 35.9%, second is 24.1% to 39.6%, and third is 33.7% to 48% of SL. Illicium is lightly pigmented and never darker than dorsal surface of body. Esca is a simple pigmented bulb, either round or flattened, and is darker dorsally than ventrally. First postcephalic spine is absent, second reaches base of second dorsal fin, and third is about one-half length of second or embedded. Pelvic fin has one spine and 5 rays. Anal fin has 6 rays. Color varies from light to dark on dorsal surface, occasionally with diffuse light spots or mottled brown spots. Ventral surface is light brown to gray and occasionally has small black spots. Peritoneum is black.

This species occurs in the western Atlantic Ocean from the Bahamas, Florida Keys, southern Gulf of Mexico, Caribbean Sea, and northern coast of South America to Suriname at 366 to 549 m. Maximum known size is 230 mm SL.

REFERENCES: Caruso 1981; Uyeno et al. 1983 (as *Lophiodes* sp.).

Lophiodes reticulatus   Caruso and Suttkus 1979

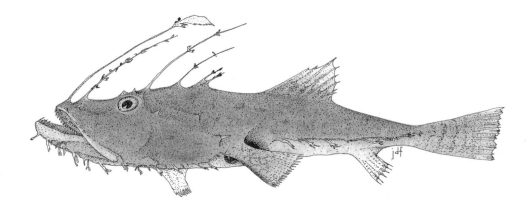

Lophiodes reticulatus is moderately depressed and oval shaped, with well-developed postcephalic dorsal spines and fleshy tendrils on lateral surface of head and body. It is distinguished from the other species of the family by the following combination of characters. Snout is moderately broad, and supraorbital crest is not elevated. Interorbital area is moderately concave. Distance between sphenotic spines (behind eye) is greater than distance between posterior frontal spines (between eyes). Eye is relatively large. Teeth on alveolar processes of premaxilla number 7 to 13 in outer row and are straight. Head length is 37.7% to 44.5% of SL, and head width is 54.9% to 61.1%, head depth is 62.2% to 70.9%, snout length is 54.2% to 65.7%, and snout width is 18% to 23.9% of head length. Articular bone of lower jaw has two spines, one anterior to and one posterior to articulation of jaws. Opercular opening extends below, behind, and in front of pectoral fin base. Quadrate has single lower spine, suboperculum has one spine, interoperculum has one or two spines, and humeral spine is well developed. Pectoral fin rays number 14 to 16. Spinous dorsal fin has three cephalic spines and three postcephalic spines. First cephalic spine (illicium) is 26.9% to 39.9%, second is 21.6% to 32.6%, and third is 22.7% to 44.7% of SL. Illicium is lightly pigmented, and esca is leaf shaped, with long cirri and dark, stalked, eyelike appendages. First postcephalic dorsal spine extends to base of second dorsal fin, and second and third postcephalic dorsal spines are short. All dorsal spines bear small, pale tendrils. Second dorsal fin has 8 rays. Pelvic fin has one spine and 5 rays. Anal fin has 6 rays. Color is light to dark brown, with darker reticulations on head, body, pectoral fin, and proximal section of second dorsal and caudal fins. Occasionally individuals are very pale except for faint reticulations on pectoral and caudal fins, and dark pigmentation on tendrils of fifth and sixth dorsal spines. Ventral surface is light tan to nearly white. Peritoneum is pale.

This species occurs in the western Atlantic Ocean from south Florida, the Florida Keys, the entire Gulf of Mexico, the Caribbean Sea, and the northern coast of South America to Suriname at 64 to 366 m and at temperatures of 12°C to 19°C. Maximum known size is about 250 mm SL.

REFERENCES: Caruso and Suttkus 1979; Caruso 1981; Uyeno et al. 1983; Ross and Caruso 1984; Cervigón 1991; Boschung 1992.

Lophius gastrophysus   Miranda Ribeiro 1915
Blackfin goosefish

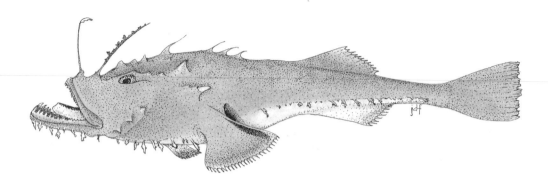

Lophius gastrophysus is strongly depressed and oval shaped anteriorly, with knobs, spines, or ridges on either side of snout, and postcephalic section of first dorsal fin reduced. It is distinguished from the other species of the family by the following combination of characters. Snout is relatively broad. Distance between sphenotic spines (behind eye) is greater than distance between frontal spines (between eyes). Eye is relatively small. Head length is 30.3% to 37.9% of SL, and head width is 48% to 58.9%, head depth is 68.3% to 78%, snout length is 54.2% to 59.3%, and snout width is 20.1% to 26.8% of head length. Articular bone of lower jaw has one spine anterior to articulation of jaw. Opercular opening extends below and behind pectoral fin base. Large parietal spines are present, quadrate has upper and lower spines, inner and outer sphenotic spines are present, suboperculum has one spine, interoperculum has one spine, and humeral spine is well developed and possesses smaller spines. Pectoral fin rays number 22 to 26. Spinous dor-

sal fin has three cephalic and three postcephalic spines. First cephalic spine (illicium) is 8.8% to 37.4%, second is 15.1% to 27.1%, and third is 5.7% to 16% of SL. Illicium is same color as dorsal body surface and lacks tendrils. Esca is a simple pennantlike flap. Postcephalic dorsal spines are short, slender, and without tendrils. Second dorsal fin has 9 or 10 rays. Pelvic fin has one spine and 5 rays. Anal fin has 8 or 9 rays. Vertebrae number 26 or 27. Color is uniform brown to dark gray. Ventral surface has fine reticulations in adult specimens. Small specimens are usually lighter in color. Peritoneum is light.

This species occurs in the western Atlantic Ocean from North Carolina to northern Argentina, including the northern Gulf of Mexico and the Caribbean Sea, at 183 to 662 m and at temperatures of 7°C to 22°C. Maximum known size is 460 mm SL.

REFERENCES: Caruso 1983; C. R. Robins et al. 1986; Boschung 1992.

OGCOCEPHALIDAE Batfishes

The batfishes are moderately to greatly flattened, with head and trunk forming subcircular to triangular-shaped disc and with a conspicuous cavity below snout containing short illicium and fleshy esca. They are distinguished from the other families of the order by the following combination of characters. Rostrum, formed by joined or fused scales at end of snout, is short and blunt to long and hornlike. Mouth is small to very small, inferior, and protrusible. Jaws and tongue, often vomer and palatine, bear bands of villiform teeth. Eye is moderately small to small and is located on dorsal or dorsolateral aspect of head. Opercular bones are narrow and elongated, and opercular opening is greatly restricted and located dorsomedial to pectoral fin base. Gill filaments are absent on first arch, present on second and third arches, and present or absent on anterior part of fourth arch. Pectoral fin is limblike, with pectoral girdle radials forming pedicle. Pectoral fin rays are unbranched and are not membranously connected to pelvic fin rays. Spinous dorsal fin consists of one cephalic spine (illicium) located in illicial cavity beneath rostrum. Illicium bears fleshy bait (esca), which envelops illicium and consists of single fleshy lobe or two bulbous lobes, occasionally with leaflike median section. The illicial pterygiophore is retractable. Second dorsal fin is located on tail. Pelvic fin is on ventral surface of head anterior to pectoral fin base. Anal fin is small and located distinctly posterior to anus. Body is covered with tubercles (conelike scales with single spine or occasionally several spines at apex) and/or bucklers (spinelike protuberances arranged in radiating pattern).

Batfishes occur worldwide in tropical to subtropical seas. All species are benthic between the shoreline and 1,000 m. The limblike pectoral and pelvic fins are used to "walk" over the bottom. Food consists of small invertebrates and fishes that are captured by means of aggressive mimicry. Prey are lured to within range of the mouth by projecting and retracting the esca-illicium apparatus. There are about 62 species in nine genera, and 9 species in four genera occur in the Gulf of Mexico.

Key to the Species of the Gulf of Mexico
(Adapted from Bradbury 1978, 1980)

1a. Ventral surface of body naked; pectoral fin lobe connected to tail by skin . . . . *Halieutichthys aculeatus* p. 836

1b. Ventral surface of body covered by modified scales (tubercles or bucklers); pectoral fin lobe free of tail 2

2a. Suboperculum with strong multifid spine; gills on second and third arches only . . . . *Dibranchus atlanticus* p. 835

2b. Suboperculum with weak spine or no spine; gills on second, third, and fourth arches 3

3a. Ventral surface of tail with small tubercles and two longitudinal rows of larger bucklers on each side of midline
. . . . *Zalieutes mcgintyi* p. 848
3b. Ventral surface of tail with small tubercles but with few if
any bucklers. 4
4a. Pectoral fin with 10 or 11 (occasionally with 12) rays . . . 5
4b. Pectoral fin with 12 to 15 (occasionally with 11) rays . . . 7
5a. Rostrum length 63% to 111% of head depth and 44% to
59% of length of disc margin
. . . . *Ogcocephalus corniger* p. 837
5b. Rostrum length 25% to 59% of head depth and 20% to
31% of length of disc margin 6
6a. Rostrum usually directed upward relative to long axis of
body; body surface rough with prominent bucklers, making contours craggy or broken; head depth 24% to 32% of
SL; mouth width 36% to 50% of head depth; distal ends
of pectoral fin rays with thickened fleshy pads on ventral
surfaces; pectoral fin membrane thick and opaque
. . . . *Ogcocephalus parvus* p. 846
6b. Rostrum usually horizontal or sloping downward relative
to long axis of body; body surface rough with prominent
bucklers, but not making contours craggy or broken; head
depth 20% to 23% of SL; mouth width 53% to 71% of
head depth; distal ends of pectoral fin rays without fleshy
pads; pectoral fin membrane thin and translucent
. . . . *Ogcocephalus declivirostris* p. 841
7a. Dorsal surface of disc without round dark spots, or if present, spots restricted to center of disc; pectoral fin without
spotted pattern, or if present, spots restricted to base of fin
. . . . *Ogcocephalus nasutus* p. 842
7b. Dorsal surface of disc and dorsal surface of pectoral fin
with round dark spots 8
8a. Mouth width less than 63% of head depth; interorbital
width 77% to 125% of jaw length; subopercular lateral
line scales 7 or 8 . . . . *Ogcocephalus cubifrons* p. 839
8b. Mouth width greater than 56% of head depth; interorbital
width 56% to 83% of jaw length; subopercular lateral line
scales 8 or more. . . . . . . *Ogcocephalus pantostictus* p. 844

Dibranchus atlanticus Peters 1876
Atlantic batfish

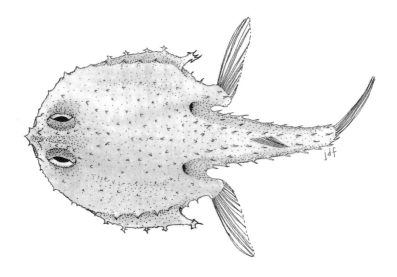

Dibranchus atlanticus is depressed and arch shaped anteriorly, with a strong multifid subopercular spine. It is distinguished from the other species of the family by the following combination of characters. Rostrum is wide based and upturned at oblique tip. Cranium rises slightly above disc, and head depth is 46.4% to 47.4% of length of disc margin. Width of cranium is 47.2% to 51.9% of length of disc margin. Iris lacks pupillary operculum on ventral margin. Interorbital space is flat, 32.9% to 37.2% of cranial width and 34.5% to 39.5% of head depth. Mouth width is 85.6% to 95.9% of head depth and 40.2% to 45.5% of length of disc margin. Jaw length is 53.1% to 58.6% of head depth. Teeth are conical, retrorse, villiform, and in bands in jaws, tongue, vomer, and palatine. Gill filaments occur on second and third gill arches. Gill rakers are pedicle-like, with small teeth at distal ends. Pectoral fin is a well-developed armlike pedicle, is well separated from body, and has 13 to 15 rays. Ventral surface of pectoral rays lacks fleshy pads. Illicial cavity is about as high as it is wide. Esca has two prominent lateral lobes and a single fleshy median lobe. Second dorsal fin has 6 or 7 rays. Pelvic fin is narrow based, slightly flared distally, and has fleshy pads at tips of rays. Anal fin has 4 rays. Body is covered with simple tubercles and tubercles with multiple spines at apex. Largest tubercles are on trunk. Lateral line is disjunct; trunk section is separate from lateral line on tail. Color is uniform reddish gray and slightly lighter ventrally in life, and uniform yellowish in preservative.

This species occurs in the Atlantic Ocean between 22 and 523 m. In the western Atlantic it occurs from Rhode Island to northeastern Brazil, including the Gulf of Mexico and the Lesser Antilles, generally between 360 and 500 m. Maximum known size is about 150 mm SL.

REFERENCES: Goode and Bean 1896; Longley and Hildebrand 1941; Hoese and Moore 1977; Uyeno et al. 1983; Cervigón 1991; Boschung 1992.

Halieutichthys aculeatus (Mitchill 1818)
Pancake batfish

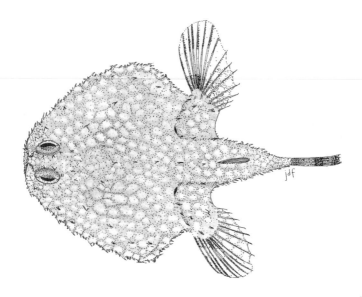

Halieutichthys aculeatus is extremely depressed and approximately circular in outline, with a nearly terminal mouth and pectoral fins broadly attached to disc and tail. It is distinguished from the other species of the family by the following combination of characters. Rostrum resembles wide-based shelf, does not extend beyond anterior margin of disc, and has slightly upturned tip with trifid spine. Cranium does not rise above disc, and head depth is 38.5% to 40.8% of length of disc margin. Width of cranium is 46.3% to 53.5% of length of disc margin. Iris has pupillary operculum on ventral margin. Interorbital space is strongly concave, 15.1% to 19.6% of cranial width, and 18.7% to 23.5% of head depth. Mouth width is 63.6% to 73.8% of head depth and 25.7% to 28.4% of length of disc margin. Jaw length is 34.7% to 38.9% of head depth. Teeth are conical, retrorse, villiform, and in bands in jaws, tongue, vomer, and palatine. Gills are found on second and third gill arches and on anterior part of fourth gill arch. Pectoral fin is well developed and fanlike, with pedicle covered by skin joining fin to tail. Pectoral fin rays number 16, and rays lack fleshy lobes. Illicial cavity is conical. Esca is a single, rather narrow and elongated lobe. Second dorsal fin has 4 or 5 rays. Pelvic fin is narrow based and moderately flared distally, with fleshy pads on distal section of rays. Anal fin has 4 rays. Body is covered with enlarged, irregular-shaped tubercles with pitted surfaces. Ventral surface is naked. Lateral line scales are continuous, with additional lateral line scales along ventral surface of tail. Color is tan to olive or yellowish gray with dark brown reticular pattern. Pectoral and caudal fins have broad, dark, diffuse crossbars.

This species occurs in the western Atlantic from North Carolina to northern South America, including the Gulf of Mexico, the Caribbean Sea, and the Bahamas, between 31 and 421 m. Maximum known size is 100 mm TL.

REFERENCES: Goode and Bean 1896; Böhlke and Chaplin 1968; Hoese and Moore 1977; Castro-Aguirre and Márquez-Espinoza 1981; Uyeno et al. 1983; C. R. Robins et al. 1986; Cervigón 1991; Boschung 1992.

Ogcocephalus corniger Bradbury 1980
Longnose batfish

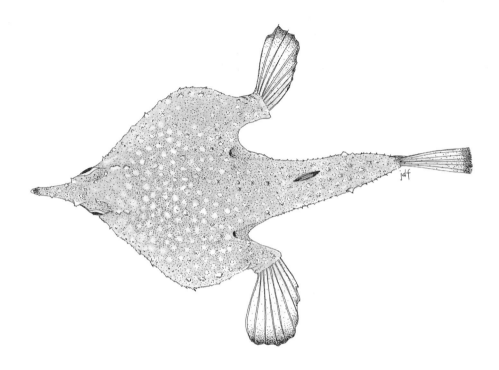

Ogcocephalus corniger is depressed and sub-triangular anteriorly, with a long rostrum and uniformly-distributed small pale spots on dorsal surface. It is distinguished from the other species of the family by the following combination of characters. Rostrum is wide based, slender distally, and 44% to 59% of length of disc margin. Cranium rises steeply above disc, and head depth is 53% to 63% of length of disc margin. Width of head is 29% to 35% of length of disc margin. Eye is 59% to 91% of head width. Iris has pupillary operculum on ventral margin. Interorbital space is flat to moderately convex, 40% to 59% of cranial width, and 22% to 33% of head depth. Mouth width is 50% to 67% of head depth and 27% to 39% of length of margin of disc. Jaw length is 39% to 46% of head depth. Teeth are conical, retrorse, villiform, and in bands in jaws, tongue, vomer, and palatine. Gills are found on second and third gill arches and on anterior part

of fourth gill arch. Gill rakers are oval plates and bear conical, villiform teeth. Pectoral fin has well-developed armlike pedicle, is well separated from body, and has 10 to 12 rays. Ventral surface of pectoral rays has fleshy pads. Illicial cavity is triangular and higher than it is wide. Esca has two prominent lateral lobes and a single fleshy median lobe. Second dorsal fin has 3 to 5 unbranched rays. Pelvic fin is narrow based, flared distally, and has fleshy pads on ventral sides of fin rays. Anal fin has 3 or 4 rays. Body is covered with close-set tubercles and bucklers. Lateral line scales extend in unbroken series from postorbital region to caudal fin and number 18 to 24, averaging 20.5. Vertebrae number 19. Color is dark brown to gray with small pale spots uniformly distributed on dorsal surface. Occasionally spots form reticular pattern. Pectoral fin is pale to dusky proximally, and has broad dark brown or black margin punctuated with white tips of rays and fleshy pads. Dorsal fin is dusky, and caudal fin is dark proximally, light medially, and black distally. Ventral surface is light.

This species occurs in the western Atlantic from Cape Lookout, North Carolina, to the Bahamas and the Greater Antilles, the northeastern Gulf of Mexico westward to Louisiana, and the southern Gulf of Mexico off Yucatán at 29 to 230 m. Maximum known size is 230 mm TL.

REFERENCES: Longley and Hildebrand 1941 (as *O. vespertilio*); Bradbury 1980; Castro-Aguirre and Márquez-Espinoza 1981; C. R. Robins et al. 1986; Boschung 1992.

Ogcocephalus cubifrons (Richardson 1836)
Polka-dot batfish

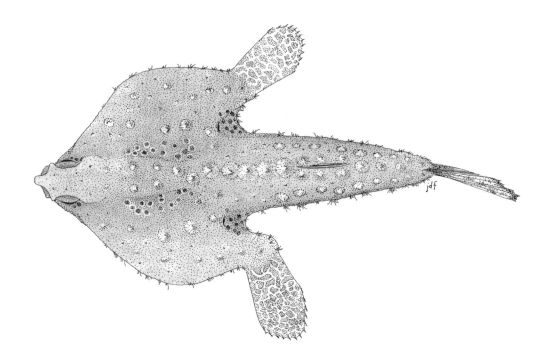

Ogcocephalus cubifrons is depressed and subtriangular anteriorly, with a variable rostrum and small dark spots on light-colored pectoral fins. It is distinguished from the other species of the family by the following combination of characters. Rostrum is long, upturned, and conical in small specimens, and small and knoblike in large specimens. Rostral length ranges from 16% to 56% of length of disc margin. Cranium rises steeply above disc, head depth is 46% to 59% of length of disc margin, and width of cranium is 28% to 39% of length of disc margin. Eye is 53% to 71% of cranium width. Iris has pupillary operculum on ventral margin. Interorbital space is slightly concave, 46% to 67% of cranium width, and 29% to 44% of head depth. Mouth width is 46% to 63% of head depth and 23% to 31% of length of disc margin. Jaw length is 31% to 40% of head depth. Teeth are conical, retrorse, villiform, and in bands in jaws, tongue, vomer, and palatine. Gill filaments occur on second and

third gill arches and on anterior part of fourth gill arch. Gill rakers are oval plates and bear conical, villiform teeth. Pectoral fin has well-developed armlike pedicle, is well separated from body, and has 11 to 14 rays. Fleshy pads occur on ventral surface of pectoral fin rays. Illicial cavity is small and subtriangular in small specimens and oval in large specimens. Esca has two prominent lateral lobes and a single fleshy median lobe. Second dorsal fin has 3 to 5 unbranched rays. Pelvic fin is narrow based and flared distally, with fleshy pads on ventral sides of fin rays. Anal fin has 3 or 4 rays. Body is covered with close-set tubercles and bucklers. Ventral surface of tail is covered with tubercles and short row or scattering of small bucklers. Lateral line scales extend from postorbital region to caudal fin and number 23 to 36, averaging 28.1. Vertebrae number 19 to 21. Color is light tan to dark brown or gray dorsally, with black spots on head, shoulder, lateral aspect of tail, pectoral fin, and usually on lateral margin of disc. Pectoral fin has broad dark brown to black border in small specimens. Caudal fin is dark proximally, light medially, and black distally, and generally has spots and blotches over length. Ventral surface, pelvic fin, and anal fin are pale.

This species occurs in the western Atlantic from Cape Lookout, North Carolina, to Yucatán, including the Bahamas and the northeast-ern Gulf of Mexico westward to Pensacola, Florida, between the shoreline and 68 m. Maximum known size is 230 mm SL.

REFERENCES: Longley and Hildebrand 1941; Böhlke and Chaplin 1968; Hastings et al. 1976 (all as *O. radiatus*); Bradbury 1980; C. R. Robins et al. 1986 (as *O. radiatus*); Boschung 1992.

Ogcocephalus declivirostris   Bradbury 1980
Slantbrow batfish

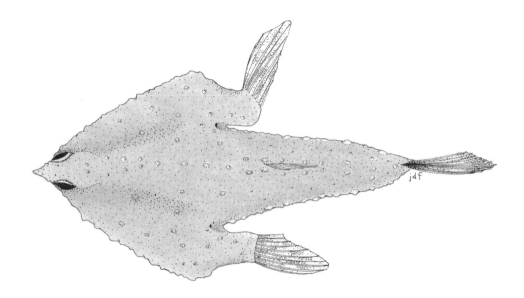

Ogcocephalus declivirostris is depressed and subtriangular anteriorly, with a relatively short rostrum sloping downward. It is distinguished from the other species of the family by the following combination of characters. Rostrum is rod shaped, with a narrow base, and length is 12% to 29% of length of disc margin. Cranium rises in gradual curve above disc, and head depth is 48% to 56% of length of disc margin. Width of cranium is 27% to 37% of length of disc margin. Eye is 63% to 71% of width of cranium. Iris has pupillary operculum on ventral margin. Interorbital space is concave, 29% to 48% of width of cranium, and 18% to 30% of head depth. Mouth width is 53% to 71% of head depth and 27% to 36% of length of disc margin. Jaw length is 37% to 48% of head depth. Teeth are conical, retrorse, villiform, and in bands in jaws, tongue, vomer, and palatine. Gill filaments occur on second and third gill arches and on anterior part of fourth gill arch. Gill rakers are oval plates and bear conical, villiform teeth. Pectoral fin has well-developed armlike pedicle, is well separated from body, and has 10 to 12 rays. Ventral surface of pectoral fin rays lacks fleshy pads. Illicial cavity is small, and oval to subtriangular shaped. Esca has two prominent lateral lobes and a single median lobe. Second dorsal fin has 3 to 5 unbranched rays. Pelvic fin is narrow based and flared distally, and fin ray tips lack fleshy pads. Anal fin has 3 or 4 rays. Body is covered with close-set tubercles and bucklers. Ventral surface of tail is covered with tubercles and short row or scattering of small bucklers. Lateral line scales extend in unbroken series from postorbital region to caudal fin and number 22 to 28, averaging 24.9. Vertebrae number 18 to 20. Color is gray to tan, with apices of bucklers paler than ground color. Head, shoulder, and side of tail occasionally have dull, rounded spots. Pectoral fin is dusky and occasionally darker toward tips. Second dorsal fin is dusky with some splotches, and caudal fin is dark basally, light medially, and black distally. Ventral surface, pelvic fin, and anal fin are light.

This species occurs in the western Atlantic from the northern and western Gulf of Mexico and the Straits of Florida (single specimen) at 3.5 to 180 m, and 388 m (single specimen). It is rare east of the Mississippi River. Maximum known size is 137 mm SL.

REFERENCES: Hoese and Moore 1977 (as *Ogcocephalus* sp.); Bradbury 1980; C. R. Robins et al. 1986; Boschung 1992.

Ogcocephalus nasutus   (Cuvier 1837)
Shortnose batfish

Ogcocephalus nasutus is depressed and subtriangular in shape anteriorly, with an extremely variable rostrum and uniform coloration dorsally. It is distinguished from the other species of the family by the following combination of characters. Rostrum is 18% to 53% of length of disc margin, varies from thick based and conical to slender and finger shaped, and is usually straight and either horizontal or upturned. Cranium rises steeply above disc, head depth is 46% to 59% of length of disc margin, and width of cranium is 25% to 40% of length of disc margin. Eye is 53% to 77% of width of cranium. Iris has pupillary operculum on ventral margin. Interorbital space is slightly concave to flat or slightly convex; width is 37% to 59% of width of cranium and 23% to 36% of head depth. Mouth width is 56% to 71% of head depth and 26% to 37% of length of disc margin. Jaw length is 40% to 48% of head depth. Teeth are conical, retrorse, villiform, and occur in bands in jaws, vomer, and palatine. Gill filaments occur on second and third gill arches and on anterior part of fourth gill arch. Gill rakers are oval plates and bear conical, villiform teeth. Pectoral fin has well-developed, armlike pedicle, is well separated from body and tail, and has 11 to 14 rays. Ventral surface of pectoral fin rays possesses fleshy pads. Illicial cavity is small, subtriangular, and higher than it is wide. Esca has two prominent lateral lobes and a single fleshy median lobe. Second dorsal fin has 2 to 5 rays. Pelvic fin is narrow based and flared distally, with fleshy pads on ventral surface of tips of rays. Anal fin has 3 or 4 unbranched rays. Body is covered with close-set tubercles and bucklers. Ventral surface of tail is covered with tubercles and short row or scattering of small bucklers. Lateral line scales extend in unbroken series from postorbital region over disc and on side of tail to caudal fin, and number 24 to 38, averaging 30.8. Vertebrae number 18 or 19. Color is tan or brown to dark brown, with roundish dark spots clustered in patch on either shoulder. Pectoral fin is pale dusky to nearly black. Second dorsal fin is pale to dark. Caudal fin is dark basally, light medially, and black distally. Ventral surface, pelvic fin, and anal fin are pale.

This species occurs in the western Atlantic from the northern Gulf of Mexico, southern Florida, the Bahamas, the Caribbean Sea, and the northern coast of South America to the mouth of the Amazon, from the shoreline to 275 m. Food consists of polychaetes, mollusks, crabs, fishes, and algae. Maximum known size is 380 mm TL.

REFERENCES: Cervigón 1966; Böhlke and Chaplin 1968; Randall 1968; Bradbury 1980; Uyeno et al. 1983; Robins et al. 1986; Cervigón 1991.

Ogcocephalus pantostictus Bradbury 1980
Spotted batfish

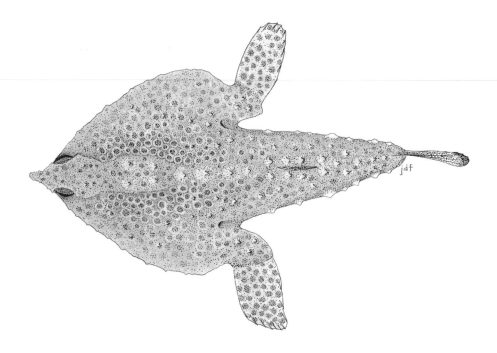

Ogcocephalus pantostictus is depressed and subtriangular in outline anteriorly, with a variable rostrum and dorsal surface covered with polka-dot pattern of dark spots. It is distinguished from the other species of the family by the following combination of characters. Rostrum is long and cone shaped in small specimens, and small and fingerlike in large specimens, with length varying from 16% to 39% of length of disc margin. Cranium rises steeply above disc, and head depth is 47% to 56% of length of disc margin. Width of cranium is 27% to 34% of length of disc margin. Eye is 56% to 71% of width of cranium. Iris has pupillary operculum on ventral margin. Interorbital space is slightly concave; width is 40% to 56% of width of cranium and 24% to 35% of head depth. Mouth width is 56% to 71% of head depth and 28% to 36% of length of disc margin. Jaw length is 37% to 48% of head depth. Teeth are conical, retrorse, villiform, and in bands in jaws, tongue, vomer, and palatine.

Gill filaments occur on second and third gill arches and on anterior part of fourth gill arch. Gill rakers are oval plates and bear conical, villiform teeth. Pectoral fin has well-developed armlike pedicle, is well separated from body, and has 11 to 14 unbranched rays. Ventral surface of pectoral fin rays possesses fleshy pads. Illicial cavity is subtriangular in small specimens and oval in large specimens. Esca has two prominent lateral lobes and a single fleshy median lobe. Second dorsal fin has 3 to 5 unbranched rays. Pelvic fin is narrow based and flared distally, with fleshy pads on ventral surface of rays. Body is covered with close-set tubercles and bucklers. Ventral surface of tail is covered with tubercles and short row or scattering of small bucklers. Lateral line scales extend in unbroken series from postorbital region to caudal fin and number 27 to 39, averaging 32.5. Vertebrae number 19 to 21. Color is gray or tan dorsally, with evenly spaced dark round spots on disc and tail. Markings are darkest on shoulder, side of tail, and axil of pectoral fin. Pectoral fin has same pattern as disc and tail. Dorsal fin is spotted, and caudal fin is dark basally, light medially, and black distally. Ventral surface and pelvic and anal fins are pale.

This species occurs in the western Atlantic in the northwestern Gulf of Mexico, from Mobile Bay, Alabama, to Tampico, Tamaulipas, between 9 and 31 m. Maximum known size is 310 mm TL.

REFERENCES: Hoese and Moore 1977 (as *O. radiatus*); Bradbury 1980; C. R. Robins et al. 1986; Boschung 1992.

Ogcocephalus parvus   Longley and Hildebrand 1940
Roughback batfish

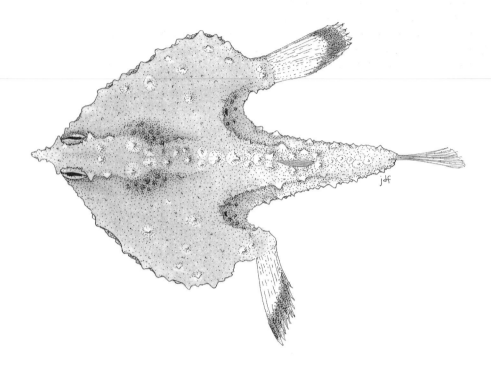

Ogcocephalus parvus is depressed and sub-triangular shaped anteriorly, with a short rostrum and a craggy or broken body contour. It is distinguished from the other species of the family by the following combination of characters. Rostrum is finger to cone shaped, and length ranges from 20% to 31% of length of disc margin. Cranium rises steeply above disc, and head depth is 50% to 63% of length of disc margin. Width of cranium is 28% to 39% of length of disc margin. Eye is 63% to 91% of width of cranium. Iris has pupillary operculum on ventral margin. Interorbital space is narrow and concave; width is 24% to 48% of width of cranium and 15% to 28% of head depth. Mouth width is 36% to 50% of head depth and 19% to 29% of length of disc margin. Jaw length is 29% to 36% of head depth. Teeth are conical, retrorse, villiform, and in bands in jaws, tongue, vomer, and palatine. Gill filaments occur on second and third gill arches and on anterior part of fourth gill arch. Gill rakers are oval plates and bear conical, villiform teeth. Pectoral fin has well-developed armlike pedicle, is well separated from body, and has 10 or 11 unbranched rays. Ventral surface of pectoral fin possesses fleshy pads. Illicial cavity is oval or subcircular. Esca has two prominent lateral lobes and a single fleshy median lobe. Second dorsal fin has 2 to 5 unbranched rays. Pelvic fin is narrow based and flared distally, with fleshy pads on ventral tips of rays. Anal fin has 3 or 4 rays. Body is covered with close-set tubercles and bucklers. Ventral surface of tail is covered with tubercles and short row or scattering of bucklers. Lateral line scales extend in unbroken series from postorbital region to caudal fin and number 15 to 19, averaging 17.2. Vertebrae number 18 to 20. Color is pale tan to brown dorsally, with irregular- to round-shaped dark brown spots, with or without whitish margins, on shoulder, head, and axil of pectoral fin, and occasionally on lateral side of tail. Pectoral fin is pale to white, with broad black margin punctuated by white tips of fin rays. Dorsal fin is colorless to slightly dusky. Caudal fin is colorless or banded. Ventral surface and pelvic and anal fins are creamy pale.

This species occurs in the western Atlantic from Cape Hatteras, North Carolina, to Recife, Brazil, including the eastern Gulf of Mexico and the Caribbean Sea, between 29 and 126 m. In the Gulf of Mexico it occurs east of Mobile Bay and off the northern coast of Yucatán. Maximum known size is 100 mm TL.

REFERENCES: Longley and Hildebrand 1940, 1941; Bradbury 1980; Uyeno et al. 1983; C. R. Robins et al. 1986; Boschung 1992.

Zalieutes mcgintyi (Fowler 1952)
Tricorn batfish

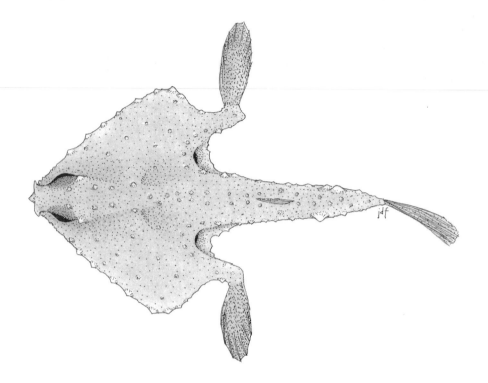

Zalieutes mcgintyi is depressed and triangular shaped anteriorly, with a short rostrum bearing prominent lateral horns. It is distinguished from the other species of the family by the following combination of characters. Rostrum is short and shelflike, projecting downward and bearing lateral projection that extends lateral to eye. Cranium rises moderately steeply from disc, and head depth is 40.1% to 46.1% of length of disc margin. Width of cranium is 46.8% to 50.8% of length of disc margin. Iris lacks pupillary operculum on ventral margin. Interorbital space is slightly convex, 16% to 21.7% of cranial width, and 19.5% to 23.4% of head depth. Mouth width is 54.8% to 63.6% of head depth and 23.7% to 25.4% of length of disc margin. Jaw length is 39.5% to 45.8% of head depth. Teeth are conical, retrorse, villiform, and occur in bands in jaws, tongue, vomer, and palatine. Gill filaments are present on second and third gill arches and on anterior part of fourth gill arch. Gill rakers are thin plates covered with minute teeth. Pectoral fin is a well-developed, armlike pedicle, is well separated from body, and has 10 to 12 rays. Ventral surface of pectoral fin lacks fleshy pads. Illicial cavity is small and triangular shaped. Esca consists of flared ventral section and leaflike dorsal section. Second dorsal fin has 4 or 5 rays. Pelvic fin is narrow based, slightly flared distally, and lacks fleshy pads. Anal fin has 4 rays. Body is covered with close-set tubercles and bucklers. Ventral surface of disc is covered with tubercles, and ventral surface of tail is covered with tubercles and two rows of bucklers. Lateral line scales are continuous and extend to caudal fin. Color is uniform pale brown to olive brown. Pectoral and caudal fins are pale and lack spots or bands. Base of dorsal fin is occasionally dusky.

This species occurs in the western Atlantic from Florida to northern South America, including the Gulf of Mexico and the Caribbean Sea, between 90 and 180 m. Maximum known size is 100 mm TL.

REFERENCES: Fowler 1952b; Uyeno et al. 1983; C. R. Robins et al. 1986; Boschung 1992.

CERATIIDAE Seadevils

Seadevils are extremely sexually dimorphic, with adult males parasitizing adult females. Females are elongate and somewhat compressed and are distinguished from females of other families of the order by the following combination of characters. Head is about 40% of SL, and greatest depth of body is at about 50% of SL. Mouth is large, vertical to strongly oblique, and does not extend past eye. Jaw teeth are slender, recurved, and depressible, with those of lower jaw longer and more numerous than those of upper jaw. Eye is small and subcutaneous. Opercular opening is circular, rather restricted in size, and located posterior to pectoral fin base. Branchiostegal rays number 6. Pectoral fin has relatively short pedicle and 14 to 17 rays. Illicium is short, emerges just posterior to eye, and protrudes on dorsal midline of trunk when pterygiophore is retracted. Esca is globular or pear shaped and is simple or has one or two distal filaments. Second cephalic spine bears gland and is sunk in skin posterior to illicium. Third and fourth, or third, fourth, and fifth cephalic spines are swollen to form globose caruncles bearing bioluminescent glands. Second dorsal fin is located on base of tail opposite anal fin and has 3 to 5 rays. Pelvic fin is absent. Anal fin has 3 to 5 rays. Caudal fin is expanded and fan shaped. Skin is covered with close-set dermal spines. Swim bladder is absent.

Free-living males are relatively small, elongate, and relatively slender, and lack illicium and esca. Snout has pair of large denticular teeth fused at base and articulating with illicial pterygiophore. Premaxilla is degenerate. Lower jaw has two pairs of denticular teeth. Eye is large, bowl shaped, and directed laterally. Olfactory organ is minute. Caruncles are absent. Skin is naked. Parasitic males have spiny skin and degenerate denticular teeth, eyes, and gut.

Seadevils are nearly worldwide between 100 and 4,000 m but are most common between 400 and 2,000 m. Females passively attract prey by means of their illicial apparatus. Food consists of fishes, cephalopods, and crustaceans. Males seek females by means of well-developed eyes, attach to females with denticular denticles, and become parasitic by means of fusion of tissue and blood vessels. Eggs are released in gelatinous veils, and larvae are epipelagic but sink as they develop. There are about four species in two genera, and one species occurs in the Gulf of Mexico.

Cryptosaras couesii Gill 1883

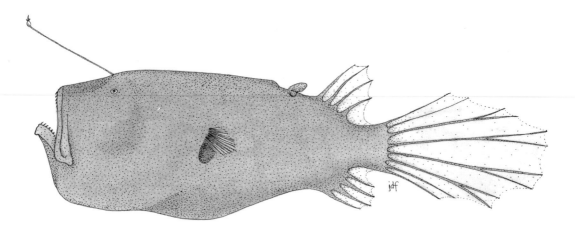

Females of *Cryptosaras couesii* are elongate and moderately compressed and are distinguished from females of the other species of the family by the following combination of characters. Teeth in lower jaw number 42 to 68, and teeth in vomer number 2 to 10. Illicium is very short and nearly fully enveloped by esca. Esca has single distal filament with one to several pairs of smaller filaments originating at base. Third, fourth, and fifth cephalic dorsal spines are swollen to form globose, club-shaped caruncles. Pectoral fin rays number 14 to 18, second dorsal fin has 4 or 5 rays, anal fin has 4 rays, and caudal fin rays number 8. Skin is covered with close-set spinules. Color is dark brown. Esca has H-shaped pigment patch at base of terminal filament. Males have two pairs of denticular teeth, with anterior pair considerably longer than posterior pair.

This species occurs nearly worldwide between 63°N and 43°S. In the western Atlantic it occurs from the mid-Atlantic United States to the mouth of the Amazon, including the Gulf of Mexico and the Lesser Antilles. It has been captured between 75 and 4,000 m and is most common between 500 and 1,250 m. Maximum known size for females is 440 mm SL, for free-living males is 10 to 11 mm SL, and for attached males is 73 mm TL.

REFERENCES: Bertelsen 1951; Uyeno et al. 1983; Pietsch 1986a,d.

DICERATIIDAE

These deep-sea anglers are thought to be extremely sexually dimorphic. Females are short and globose and are distinguished from females of the other families of the order by the following combination of characters. Body depth is about 50% of SL. Mouth is large, oblique, and extends posterior to eye. Jaw teeth are numerous, slender, recurved, and depressible. Vomerine teeth are present. Lower jaw has well-developed symphyseal spine extending slightly beyond upper jaw. Eye is small and subcutaneous. Opercular opening is oval, somewhat restricted in size, and located posteroventral to pectoral fin base. Branchiostegal rays number 6. Pectoral fin has relatively short pedicle and 13 to 16 rays. Illicium is slender and about one-fourth to one-third of SL. Esca is globular and bears filaments. Second cephalic spine is located close behind illicium and bears small esca with light organ. Second dorsal fin is located on base of tail opposite anal fin and has 5 to 7 rays. Pelvic fin is absent. Anal fin has 4 rays, and caudal fin has 8 or 9 rays. Skin is spinose.

Males are very small and have curved denticular teeth, small eyes, olfactory organs well separated from eyes, and chin covered with sharply pointed dermal spines (Bertelsen 1983). Males of at least one species are apparently free living.

These deep-sea anglerfishes occur in tropical to subtropical seas of the Atlantic and Indo-Pacific Oceans on the continental slope between 400 and 2,300 m. Apparently adults are associated with the bottom. Females attract prey by means of illicial apparatus. Food consists of fishes, coelenterates, crustaceans, polychaetes, gastropods, and sea urchins. Eggs are released in gelatinous veils, and larvae are epipelagic and sink as they develop. There are four species in two genera, and one species occurs in the Gulf of Mexico.

Phrynichthys wedli   Pietschmann 1926

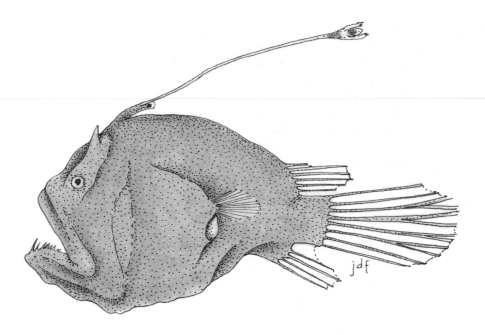

Females of *Phrynichthys wedli* are short and globose and are distinguished from females of the other species of the family by the following combination of characters. Distance between tip of snout and insertion of illicium is about 29% to 61% of SL. Jaw teeth are well developed and number 21 to 65 in upper jaw and 16 to 55 in lower jaw. Vomerine teeth number 7 to 15. Illicium is relatively long, greater than 83% to 225% of SL, and originates between sphenotic spines on head. Esca has low terminal papilla, posterior filamentous appendage, filamentous paired anterior and lateral appendages, and pore at posterior end of base. Illicial pterygiophore is short, does not extend to frontals, and is not exposed. Illicial trough is relatively shallow.

This species occurs in the Atlantic Ocean. In the western Atlantic it occurs in the Gulf of Mexico and the Caribbean Sea.

REFERENCES: Bertelsen 1951 (as *Paroneirodes wedli*), 1986d; Uwate 1979; Uyeno et al. 1983; Pietsch 1986c.

HIMANTOLOPHIDAE

These deep-sea anglerfishes are extremely sexually dimorphic, but males apparently do not attach to females. Females are very robust and deep bodied, with thick skin, snout and chin covered with papillae, and body covered to some degree with dermal spines. Females are distinguished from females of the other families within the order by the following combination of characters. Head is large and deep. Snout is very blunt, short, and nearly vertical in profile. Head has moderately large sphenotic spine above and behind eye. Eye is small. Mouth is large, moderately oblique, and extends to or beyond eye. Jaw teeth are slender, recurved, and flexible, with those of lower jaw larger than those of upper jaw. Branchiostegal rays number 6. Pectoral fin has rather short pedicle and 14 to 18 rays. Illicium is moderately long to long. Illicial pterygiophore is short and does not protrude on snout. Esca is pear shaped, without distinct demarcation from illicium, and bears spherical photophore and several appendages. Photophore has central lumen surrounded by tubular glands, both of which are filled with bacteria. All species have light-guiding distal appendage that arises from distal wall of photophore vestibule. Second dorsal fin is located just anterior to caudal peduncle and has 5 or 6 rays. Anal fin is located behind second dorsal fin origin and has 4 rays. Caudal fin has 9 rays. Vertebrae number 19.

Free-living males are rather robust and deep bodied shortly after metamorphosis but become rather slender with growth. Snout is narrow and pointed. Denticular teeth of upper jaw fuse to form upper denticular bone that attaches to premaxilla and maxilla, and denticular teeth of lower jaw fuse to form lower denticular bone that attaches to lower jaw. Nostril is laterally located and large.

These deep-sea anglerfishes occur worldwide in tropical to temperate seas at mesopelagic and bathypelagic depths. Females passively attract fish and cephalopod prey by means of their illicial apparatus. There are 18 species in a single genus, and 3 species occur in the Gulf of Mexico. Males are not known for many of these species.

Key to the Species of the Gulf of Mexico

(Adapted from Bertelsen and Krefft 1988)

1a. Posterior escal appendage present 2
1b. Posterior escal appendage absent
.... *Himantolophus cornifer* p. 855
2a. Proximal one-half of distal escal appendage undivided; no appendages on base of escal bulb; distal pair of appendages on illicial stem 1 to 2 times diameter of bulb below base of posterior escal appendage
.... *Himantolophus melanolophus* p. 857
2b. Distal escal appendage divided at base; 2 to 11 postero-lateral appendages on and below base of escal bulb; distal pair of appendages on illicial stem less than diameter of bulb below base of posterior escal appendage
.... *Himantolophus groenlandicus* p. 856

Himantolophus cornifer   Bertelsen and Krefft 1988

Females of *Himantolophus cornifer* are very robust and deep bodied, with distal appendage of esca bifurcated at or very near base. They are distinguished from females of the other species of the family by the following combination of characters. Illicium is 29% to 35% of SL. Escal bulb is 7.9% to 12% of SL and has light-guiding distal appendage but lacks anterior and posterior appendages. Appendages on illicial stem are also lacking. Each main branch of distal appendage of esca has posterior side branch near base. Length of dorsal appendage is 9% of SL in specimens 27 mm SL, 54% of SL in specimens 52 mm SL, and 72% of SL in specimens 90 mm SL. Length of posterior side branch of distal appendage is 4.3% of SL in specimens 27 mm SL and 30% of SL in specimens 52 to 90 mm SL. Pectoral fin has 16 to 18 rays, dorsal fin has 5 rays, and anal fin has 4 rays. Papilla on snout and chin are well developed. Dermal spines are sparsely distributed on body and pectoral fin of large specimens. Dermal spines also occur on illicial stem, on escal bulb, and on base of distal appendage. Color is black, with distal appendage of esca darkly pigmented. Anterior side of illicial stem, snout and chin, dorsal side of body to base of second dorsal fin, and side of caudal peduncle are white or lightly pigmented.

This species occurs in the tropical waters of the western and central Atlantic and western and central Pacific Oceans. In the western Atlantic it occurs in the Gulf of Mexico (single record). Maximum known size is 90 mm SL.

REFERENCE: Bertelsen and Krefft 1988.

Himantolophus groenlandicus   Reinhardt 1838

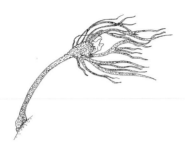

Females of *Himantolophus groenlandicus* are very robust and deep bodied, with the light-guiding appendage of the esca divided at the base. They are distinguished from females of the other species of the family by the following combination of characters. Illicium is 28% to 54% of SL. Escal bulb diameter is 4.8% to 11% of SL and has anterior, light-guiding distal and posterior appendages. Anterior appendage is 2.7% to 16% of SL in specimens less than 100 mm SL, and 16% to 42% of SL in larger specimens. Distal appendage of esca is 0.9% to 2.1% of SL in specimens less than 200 mm SL, and 4.2% of SL in larger specimens. Posterior appendage is undivided proximally and simple or divided into two to six branches distally. Base of bulb of esca has 2 to 11 posterolateral appendages that are more or less regularly ar-ranged in pairs and either simple or divided into two to nine branches. Pectoral fin has 14 to 18 rays, dorsal fin has 5 rays, and anal fin has 4 rays. Papillae on snout and chin are low and indistinct. Body is sparsely covered with dermal spines. Illicial stem, escal bulb, and append-ages are covered with dermal spines. Body is grayish brown, and fins are grayish brown with black tips. Escal appendages are pigmented ex-cept for tips, which are bright silvery.

This species occurs in the Atlantic Ocean and possibly in the western Indian Ocean be-tween 250 and 1,800 m. Food consists of cephalopods and fishes. Maximum known size is 365 mm SL.

REFERENCES: Uyeno et al. 1983; Bertelsen and Krefft 1988.

Himantolophus melanolophus   Bertelsen and Krefft 1988

The females of *Himantolophus melanolophus* are robust and deep bodied, with proximal part of light-guiding distal appendage of esca undivided and distal part bifurcated. They are distinguished from the females of the other species of the family by the following combination of characters. Illicium is 23% to 41% of SL. Escal bulb is 6.7% to 8.6% of SL and has light-guiding distal and posterior appendages but lacks anterior appendage. Proximal part of light-guiding distal appendage is undivided, but distal part is bifurcated. Posterior appendage is divided near base into pair of main branches, with each branch either simple or bifurcated once or twice. Esca has distal swelling surrounding distal appendage base that is more or less divided into four narrow lobes. Proximal parts of distal and posterior appendages are darkly pigmented. Illicial stem has five to seven appendages, including three or four at its base and a distally located posterolateral pair about 1 to 3 times diameter of bulb below posterior appendage. Pectoral fin has 15 to 17 rays, dorsal fin has 5 rays, and anal fin has 4 rays. Papillae on snout and chin are well developed in large specimens. Body is sparsely covered with dermal spines. Illicial stem and escal bulb have dermal spines. Color is dark with indistinct lightly pigmented spots on dorsal and ventral aspects of caudal peduncle. Caudal fin rays are pigmented.

This species occurs in the tropical Atlantic Ocean. In the western Atlantic it occurs off the east coast of Florida and in the eastern Gulf of Mexico between 350 and 550 m.

REFERENCE: Bertelsen and Krefft 1988.

LINOPHRYNIDAE

These deep-sea anglerfishes are extremely sexually dimorphic, with the males becoming parasitic on adult females. Females are short and moderately deep and are distinguished from females of the other families of the order by the following combination of characters. Head is large and broad. Mouth is nearly horizontal and extends beyond eye. Jaw teeth are small to large. Head has well-developed sphenotic spines located above and posterior to eye. Opercular opening is posterior to and below pectoral fin base. Branchiostegal rays number 4 or 5. Pectoral fin has relatively short pedicle and 13 to 19 rays. Illicium is short to moderate in length. Illicial pterygiophore is short and either concealed or slightly protruding near tip of snout. Esca is bullose and with or without appendages. Second dorsal fin is located at base of tail, opposite anal fin, and has 2 to 4 rays. Pelvic fin and girdle are absent. Anal fin has 2 to 4 rays. Caudal fin has 9 rays.

Free-living males have large, tubular, somewhat forward-directed eyes. Olfactory organ is large. Premaxilla and premaxillary teeth are present or absent. Denticles are relatively stout, and number three to six in upper and three to nine in lower denticular. Upper denticular bone does not articulate with pterygiophore of illicium. Skin is naked.

These deep-sea anglerfishes occur in the Atlantic, Indian, and eastern Pacific Oceans. Females passively attract prey by means of illicial apparatus. Eggs are released in gelatinous veils, and larvae are epipelagic but sink as they develop. There are 49 species in five genera, and 3 species in two genera occur in the Gulf of Mexico.

Key to the Species of the Gulf of Mexico
(Adapted from Bertelsen 1986e)

1a. Illicium present (females) 2
1b. Illicium absent (males) 4
2a. Hyoid barbel present; skin black 3
2b. Hyoid barbel absent; skin unpigmented
    . . . . *Halophryne mollis* p. 860
3a. Stem of hyoid barbel divided near base into three to five
    main branches, three of these unpaired, with one between
    anterior pair of bifurcated main branches; each side
    branch of barbel with number of transparent branched
    or unbranched filaments; length of barbel, excluding fila-
    ments, less than 60% of SL; length of distal appendage
    on esca 16% to 39% of SL in specimens greater than
    50 mm SL. . . . . *Linophryne densiramus* p. 862
3b. Stem of hyoid barbel divided near base into three to five
    main branches, three of these unpaired, with one between

anterior pair of bifurcated main branches; side branches of barbel without filaments; length of barbel 85% to 115% of SL; length of distal appendage on esca less than 7% of SL
. . . . *Linophryne brevibarbata* p. 861

4a. Skin dark pigmented; premaxillary and dentary teeth absent; denticular teeth well developed
. . . . *Linophryne* spp. p. 861

4b. Skin unpigmented; premaxillary and dentary teeth present; denticular teeth small . . . . *Halophryne mollis* p. 860

Halophryne mollis (Brauer 1902)

Females of *Halophryne mollis* are short and moderately deep, lack a branched hyoid barbel, and are distinguished from the females of the other species of the family by the following combination of characters. Head has well-developed frontal (over eyes) and sphenotic (behind eyes) spines. Teeth in jaws are relatively small and in more than one series. Preoperculum is angular and has compressed spine with three to five radiating cusps. Pectoral fin has 15 or 16 rays. Illicium is short, and illicial pterygiophore is not retractable. Esca is located on snout anterior to eye, is nearly globular, and has small posterior branched appendage. Second dorsal fin has 3 or 4 rays, anal fin has 3 or 4 rays, and caudal fin has 9 rays. Skin is unpigmented.

Free-living males retain premaxilla and premaxillary teeth. Upper and lower denticular teeth are small and do not meet anteriorly when jaws are closed. Skin is unpigmented except for lateral series of subdermal melanophores on each side of body.

This species occurs in the Atlantic, Indian, and eastern Pacific Oceans in tropical and subtropical seas. In the western Atlantic it occurs in the Gulf of Mexico and the Caribbean Sea. Maximum known size of females is 50 mm SL, of free-living males is 12 to 14 mm SL, and of parasitic males is 12 mm SL.

REFERENCES: Bertelsen 1951 (as *Edriolychnus schmidti*), 1986c.

Linophryne brevibarbata   Beebe 1932

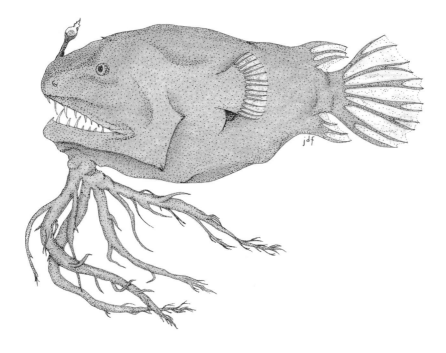

Females of *Linophryne brevibarbata* are short and moderately deep, with a branched hyoid barbel, and are distinguished from females of the other species of the family by the following combination of characters. Head has short, blunt frontal spines over eyes and well-developed sphenotic spines behind eyes. Teeth in jaws are strong, with longest 10% to 15% of SL, and in two or three series. Hyoid barbel is divided near base into three unpaired main branches and two bifurcated main branches, and ranges from 85% to 115% of SL. Anterior main branch has proximal pair of side branches. Anterior bifurcated branches bear series of side branches. Intermediary main branch is bifurcated and bifurcations are of nearly equal length. Posterior branch is simple. Each of three main unpaired branches has single series of simple side branches. All branches have one or several photophores near tip but lack filaments. Preoperculum is angular and has strong horizontal spine. Pectoral fin has 14 to 19 rays. Illicium is on snout and is short, 20% to 30% of SL. Illicial pterygiophore is concealed or slightly protruding. Esca is large and has single distal appendage of about 10% of SL, with short side branches. Second dorsal fin has 3 rays, anal fin has 3 rays, and caudal fin has 9 rays. Color is black.

Free-living males have short, blunt sphenotic spines that do not penetrate skin. Upper denticular bone has three to six denticles, and lower denticular bone has single median denticle and four to seven lateral denticles on each side. Premaxillae are reabsorbed. Skin is darkly pigmented.

This species occurs in the Atlantic, Indian, and eastern Pacific Oceans in tropical to subtropical seas. In the western Atlantic it occurs off Bermuda and in the Gulf of Mexico. Males are parasitic on mature females. Maximum known size for females is 220 to 230 mm SL, for free-living males is 16 mm SL, and for parasitic males is 29 mm SL.

REFERENCES: Bertelsen 1951 (as *L. arborifera*), 1980, 1982, 1986e.

Linophryne densiramus   Imai 1941

Females of *Linophryne densiramus* are short and moderately deep, with a branched hyoid barbel, and are distinguished from females of the other species of the family by the following combination of characters. Head spines, tooth patterns, body proportions, fin ray counts, and subdermal pigmentation are as in *L. brevibarbata*. Hyoid barbel is divided near base into five main branches and is less than 60% of SL. Anterior median branch is bifurcated, with proximal branch nearly as long as main stem and bearing posterior series of side branches. Anterior pair of main branches, on either side of main branch, are bifurcated nearly to base, with bifurcations of about equal length. One branch of each anterior pair of main branches bears number of side branches. Intermediary unpaired main branch is bifurcated, with bifurcations of about equal length, one bifurcation

with anteroventral series of side branches, and other bifurcation prolonged into one or more filamentous branches. Posterior main branch has series of five to eight side branches, with proximal branch longer than others. All barbel branches are distally divided into several filaments bearing photophores. Photophores are present in transparent tips and filamentous prolongations of barbel branches. Esca is large and has single distal appendage of about 16% to 39% of SL.

This species occurs in the western Atlantic and Pacific Oceans. In the western Atlantic it occurs off the southeastern coast of the United States and in the Gulf of Mexico. Males are parasitic on mature females. Maximum known size for females is 68 mm SL.

REFERENCES: Bertelsen 1980, 1982.

MELANOCETIDAE

These deep-sea anglerfishes are extremely sexually dimorphic, but males are not parasitic on adult females. Females of this family are short, deep, and globose and are distinguished from females of the other families of the order by the following combination of characters. Head is short, and mouth is large, nearly vertical, with cleft not extending past eye. Teeth in jaws are slender, recurved, and depressible, with those of lower jaw less numerous but slightly larger than those of upper jaw. Teeth in lower jaw number 32 to 142, and those of upper jaw number 29 to 178. Longest tooth of upper jaw is 6.9% to 25% of SL. Vomer has 0 to 12 teeth. Lower jaw has well-developed symphyseal spine. Eye is small and subcutaneous. Branchiostegal rays number 6. Suboperculum has strong anterior spine. Opercular opening is oval shaped, rather restricted in size, and located slightly posterior and ventral to pectoral fin base. Pectoral fin has relatively short pedicle and 15 to 23 rays. Illicium is slender and 23% to 61% of SL. Illicial pterygiophore is exposed anteriorly between eyes. Esca is bulbous, simple, usually with rounded or conical distal prolongation, and often with anterior and posterior crests. Second dorsal fin has 12 to 17 rays, anal fin has 3 to 5 rays, and caudal fin has 9 rays. Pelvic fin is absent, but pelvic girdle is present. Skin is scarcely covered with minute spines in some species.

Males lack jaw teeth but possess upper denticular bone with two or three semicircular series of strong recurved denticles fused with three to nine enlarged dermal denticles articulating with illicial pterygiophore. Lower denticular bone has 10 to 23 recurved denticles fused into median and two lateral groups. Eye is directed laterally and is elliptical. Olfactory organ is large. Dorsal fin rays number 12 to 16, anal fin rays number 4, and caudal fin rays number 9. Skin is naked or spinose.

These deep-sea anglerfishes occur worldwide in tropical to subtropical seas at mesopelagic or bathypelagic depths. There are five species in a single genus, and one or two species occur in the Gulf of Mexico.

Key to the Species of the Gulf of Mexico

(Adapted from Pietsch and Van Duzer 1980)

1a. Illicium and esca present (females) 2
1b. Illicium and esca absent (males) 3
2a. Anterior margin of vomer deeply concave; interorbital
width 9.1% to 17.8% of SL; lower jaw teeth 46 to 142;
escal bulb width 1.9% to 5.1% of SL
. . . . *Melanocetus murrayi* p. 866
2b. Anterior margin of vomer nearly straight; interorbital
width 13.5% to 28.6% of SL; lower jaw teeth 32 to 78;
escal bulb width 4.3% to 8.6% of SL
. . . . *Melanocetus johnsoni* p. 865
3a. Median series of denticles on snout 3 to 5; denticles in
lower denticular bone 10 to 13; pectoral fin rays 15 to 18
. . . . *Melanocetus murrayi* p. 866
3b. Median series of denticles on snout 8; denticles in lower
denticular bone 12 to 24; pectoral fin rays 17 to 21
. . . . *Melanocetus johnsoni* p. 865

Melanocetus johnsoni   Günther 1864

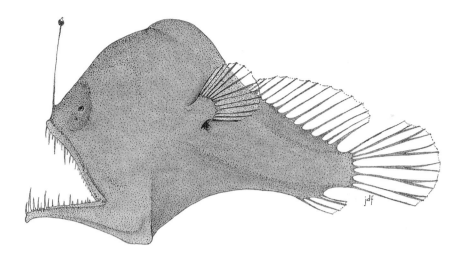

Females of *Melanocetus johnsoni* are short, deep, and globose and are distinguished from females of the other species of the family by the following combination of characters. Anterior margin of vomer is nearly straight. Lower jaw teeth number 32 to 78, and longest lower jaw tooth is 8.4% to 25% of SL. Width of pectoral fin lobe is 10.7% to 17.8% of SL. Illicium is 32.4% to 60.6% of SL. Escal bulb is slightly compressed (4.3% to 8.6% of SL) with low, rounded or conical distal prolongation nearly always pigmented to tip, and compressed posterior crest usually darkly pigmented and smaller, and compressed anterior crest occasionally present. Esca has posterior and (usually) anterior crests. Skin spines are minute and present over much of body. Pectoral fin has 17 to 23 rays. Second dorsal fin has 13 to 17 rays, and anal fin has 3 to 5 rays.

Males have posterior nostril contiguous with eye. Snout has median series of 8 denticles, and lower denticular bone has 12 to 24 denticles. Dorsal fin rays number 13 to 15, and pectoral fin rays number 17 to 21. Skin is either naked or has denticles.

This species occurs worldwide generally between 100 and 2,000 m. In the western Atlantic it occurs from Labrador to northern Argentina. It has been recorded once from the Gulf of Mexico and from the Caribbean Sea, but these records are questionable. Maximum known size of females is 120 mm SL and of males is 28 mm SL.

REFERENCES: Bertelsen 1951, 1986e; Pietsch and Van Duzer 1979; Uyeno et al. 1983; Pietsch 1986b.

Melanocetus murrayi   Günther 1887

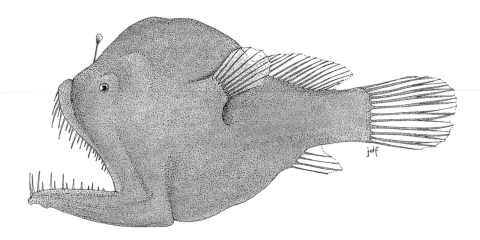

Females of *Melanocetus murrayi* are short, deep, and globose and are distinguished from females of the other species of the family by the following combination of characters. Anterior margin of vomer is deeply concave. Lower jaw teeth number 46 to 142, and longest lower jaw tooth is 7.7% to 16.7% of SL. Width of pectoral fin lobe is 6.1% to 8.9% of SL. Illicium is 23.1% to 32.2% of SL. Escal bulb is 1.9% to 5.1% of SL; is not compressed; has low, rounded distal prolongation unpigmented at tip; and has minute or no crests. Skin spines are minute and are restricted to caudal peduncle. Second dorsal fin has 12 to 14 rays, pectoral fin has 15 to 19 rays, and anal fin has 4 rays.

Males have posterior nostril contiguous with eye. Snout has median series of 3 to 5 denticles, and lower denticular has 10 to 13 denticles. Second dorsal fin rays number 12 to 14, and pectoral fin rays number 15 to 18. Skin is either naked or has few denticles.

This species occurs worldwide, generally between 1,000 and 2,500 m, and rarely above 800 m. In the western Atlantic it occurs from Cape Cod to the mouth of the Amazon, including the Gulf of Mexico and the Caribbean Sea. Maximum known size of females is 120 mm SL and of males is about 30 mm SL.

REFERENCES: Bertelsen 1951, 1986c; Pietsch and Van Duzer 1980.

ONEIRODIDAE

These deep-sea anglerfishes are extremely sexually dimorphic, although males of most species are not parasitic on mature females. Females are short and deep and are distinguished from females of the other families of the order by the following combination of characters. Body depth is 50% to 75% of SL. Head is moderate to large in size and globular. Mouth is large, horizontal to somewhat oblique, and occasionally extending beyond eye. Jaw teeth are slender, recurved, and depressible, with those of lower jaw considerably larger and more numerous than those of upper jaw. Eye is small and subcutaneous. Opercular opening is oval and located posterior to pectoral fin base. Branchiostegal rays number 6. Pectoral fin has relatively short pedicle and 14 to 30 rays. Illicium emerges between frontal bones just posterior to eyes. Escal bulb is variable in shape. Second cephalic dorsal spine is vestigial. Second dorsal fin is located on tail opposite anal fin and has 4 to 8 rays. Anal fin has 4 to 7 rays, and caudal fin has 8 or 9 rays. Pelvic fin is absent. Skin is naked. Swim bladder is absent.

Males lack dermal spines on snout and lack jaw teeth. Upper denticular bone does not articulate with anterior end of illicial pterygiophore. Upper and lower denticular teeth are generally fused at base. Eye is elliptical and is directed anteriorly. Olfactory organ is large. Skin is naked. Swim bladder is absent.

These deep-sea anglerfishes occur nearly worldwide between 300 and 3,000 m but are most common between 800 and 1,500 m. Larvae are epipelagic, and juveniles and adults are mesopelagic or bathypelagic. There are about 60 species in 16 genera, and 2 species in separate genera occur in the Gulf of Mexico.

Key to the Species of the Gulf of Mexico
(Adapted from Bertelsen 1951)

1a. Illicium and esca present (females) 2
1b. Illicium and esca absent (males) 3
2a. Caudal fin without black skin extending beyond base; anal rays four. . . . . *Oneirodes bradburyae* p. 869
2b. Caudal fin with black skin extending beyond base; anal rays generally five (rarely four)
. . . . *Dolopichthys pullatus* p. 868
3a. Caudal peduncle unpigmented; anal rays four
. . . . *Oneirodes bradburyae* p. 869
3b. Caudal peduncle pigmented; anal rays five (rarely four)
. . . . *Dolopichthys pullatus* p. 868

Dolopichthys pullatus   Regan and Trewavas 1932

Females of *Dolopichthys pullatus* are relatively long and slender, with a large mouth, a relatively long illicium, and well-developed sphenotic spines behind eyes. They are distinguished from females of the other species of the family by the following combination of characters. Snout is relatively long and acute. Two nares are located on each side of snout at end of short tube. Dorsal profile of head is straight to sphenotic spines. Mouth is terminal and extends past eye. Lower jaw has well-developed spine on symphysis, and angular bone terminates as small spine in some specimens. Lower jaw and quadrate bear spines, with spine on quadrate larger than spine on lower jaw. Teeth are slender, recurved, and increase in number with growth. Lower jaw teeth number 44 to about 600, numbering 85 or more in specimens between 18 and 25 mm SL, more than 150 in specimens between 25 and 70 mm SL, and 300 or more in specimens larger than 70 mm SL. Vomerine teeth number 4 to 14. Eye is small and located beneath skin, appearing through round, translucent area. Gill opening is oval shaped and located below and posterior to pectoral fin base. Head length is 35.3% to 45.2%, head depth is 33% to 47.1%, lower jaw length is 38.7% to 47.5%, premaxillary length is 25.9% to 34.2%, and illicium length is 26.4% to 42.4% of SL. Anterior end of illicial pterygiophore is exposed between frontal bones on snout. Esca consists of large basal bulb and long, tapering, sigmoid-shaped distal filament. Bulb bears small, rounded, anteriorly to anteroventrally directed papilla that is internally connected with distal filament. Thickened basal section of distal filament is darkly pigmented in specimens 84 mm SL and larger. Second dorsal fin rays number 5 to 7, anal fin rays number 4 to 6, and pectoral fin rays number 17 to 22. Skin is naked and covered with small, rounded papillae. Color is dark brown to black.

This species occurs worldwide between 34°N and 34°S at lower mesopelagic and bathypelagic depths. In the western Atlantic it occurs in the eastern Gulf of Mexico. Maximum known size is 115 mm SL.

REFERENCES: Bertelsen 1951; Pietsch 1971.

Oneirodes bradburyae Grey 1957

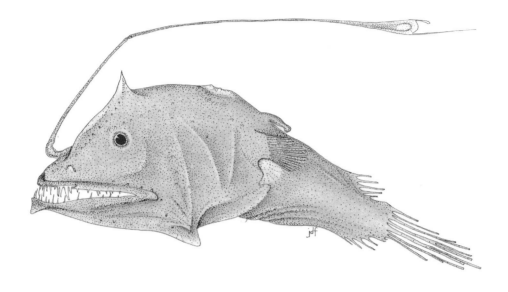

Females of *Oneirodes bradburyae* are short and deep and distinguished from females of the other species of the family by the following combination of characters. Snout is relatively short. Mouth is large and extends beyond eye. Lower jaw has symphyseal spine. Jaw teeth are slender and depressible, and are either short or long. Upper and lower jaws have about 28 teeth. Sphenotic spines are located behind eye. Double articular spines are located on posterior corner of lower jaw, with smaller one concealed in integument. Partially invaginated posterior appendage occurs on back above pectoral fin base. Pectoral lobe is relatively short and broad, and pectoral fin has 14 rays. Illicium is located on snout and is about 74% of SL. Pterygiophore of illicium is long, and its posterior end protrudes on back. Esca is compressed and transparent, with a large, black inner bullose photophore; a long filament arising from left side of distal end; a single short, club-tipped prolongation on right side; and short, delicate cluster of filaments centrally. Second dorsal fin has 5 rays, anal fin has 4 rays, and caudal fin has 9 rays. Skin is naked. Color is black. Males are unknown for this species.

This species occurs in the western Atlantic in the Gulf of Mexico at 1,426 m. It is known from a single specimen captured at 28°28′N and 92°40′W.

REFERENCES: Grey 1956; Pietsch 1974.

THAUMATICHTHYIDAE

These deep-sea anglerfishes are extremely sexually dimorphic, males are known for only a single species, and it is not known whether or not males are parasitic on females. Females are relatively elongate and depressed. Mouth is large, nearly horizontal, and extends to eye. Premaxilla overhangs and extends far beyond lower jaw. Anteriorly premaxillae are separated and only loosely connected by elastic membrane. Jaw teeth are long and hooked. Upper arm of operculum is divided into two or more branches. Sphenotic and articular spines are present or absent. Eye is moderate to small in size and subcutaneous. Opercular opening is oval and located below pectoral fin base. Pectoral fin has 14 to 16 rays. Illicium and illicial pterygiophore are short to long. Esca has one to three denticles and is located on head or in roof of mouth. Second dorsal fin is vestigial. Skin is naked or spiny.

Known males have premaxilla but lack premaxillary teeth. Upper denticular bone has four separate denticles arranged in two pairs above each other, with lower pair shorter and more strongly hooked than upper pair. Lower denticular bone has seven denticles fused at base and arranged into lower transverse series of four denticles and upper series of three denticles. Operculum is divided into 7 to 13 radiating rays.

These deep-sea anglerfishes occur in the tropical and subtropical waters of the Atlantic and Pacific Oceans. Some or all species are apparently benthic. Food consists of holothurians, copepods, crustaceans, and fishes. There are about six species in two genera, and a single species occurs in the Gulf of Mexico.

Thaumatichthys binghami   Parr 1927

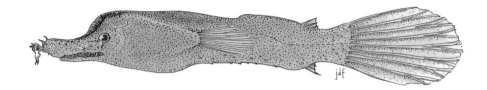

Females of *Thaumatichthys binghami* are elongate and depressed, with a broad head and spiny skin, and are distinguished from females of the other species of the family by the following combination of characters. Premaxilla is 23.5% to 27% of SL and has long, hooked teeth extending far beyond lower jaw and arranged in six overlapping, oblique longitudinal series; number of teeth increases with growth. Eye and olfactory papillae are close to angles of mouth and are about 11% to 13% of head length. Sphenotic, preopercular, and articular spines are absent. Pectoral fin rays number 14 or 15. Illicium and illicial pterygiophore are short, and illicium emerges anteriorly in roof of mouth from ventral side of membrane connecting premaxilla. Esca is located in mouth, is sessile, an has two or three pairs of lateral-pointed lobes, curved denticle, and single internal black bulb-shaped photophore. Second dorsal fin has 6 or 7 rays, anal fin has 4 rays, and caudal fin has 9 rays. Skin of lower part of head and entire body has numerous small spines. Color is dark brown to black.

Males are slender and have slender, pointed snout. Premaxilla is present but lacks teeth. Upper denticular bone articulates with premaxilla and has two bilateral, symmetrical pairs of denticles. Lower denticular bone has seven denticles in two bilateral series. Eye is circular and of moderate size. Olfactory organ is very large. Pectoral fin has 15 rays, second dorsal fin has 6 rays, anal fin has 4 rays, and caudal fin has 9 rays. Skin has numerous small spines and is dark brown.

This species occurs in the western Atlantic from the east coast of Florida to the Caribbean coast of South America, including the Gulf of Mexico and the Bahamas, at 1,270 to 4,032 m on or near the bottom. Larvae and juveniles are pelagic, with larvae occurring between 20 and 1,500 m and juveniles occurring between 1,000 and 1,750 m. Maximum known size is 53 mm SL.

REFERENCES: Parr 1927a; Bertelsen 1951 (as *Amacrodon binghami*); Bertelsen and Struhsaker 1977; Anderson et al. 1985.

MUGILIFORMES

Mugiliformes is a newly constituted order for a taxon that was formerly classified within the Perciformes. Recent studies suggest that it is either the sister group of Atherinomorpha and the Percomorpha or forms a taxon with several other orders that, in turn, constitute the sister group of the remainder of the Percomorpha. The order consists of a single family, and it occurs in the Gulf of Mexico.

MUGILIDAE Mullets

Mullets are moderately elongate and subcylindrical, with two widely separated dorsal fins and subabdominal pelvic fins. They are distinguished from the other families of fishes by the following combination of characters. Snout is short and slightly acute to blunt. Mouth is terminal and relatively short. Jaws bear small teeth or are toothless. Premaxilla is moderately protractile. Gill openings are wide and free of isthmus. There are four gill slits, and gill rakers are well developed. Upper gill rakers are modified into oral and branchial filter-feeding apparati. Pseudobranch, on medial surface of operculum, is well developed. Pectoral fin is located high on flank and is of moderate size. First dorsal fin originates near midlength of body and has four slender spines. Second dorsal fin is located over posterior one-fourth of body and is short based. Pelvic fin inserts posterior to pectoral fin base and consists of one spine and five branched rays. Anal fin is anterior to or under origin of second dorsal fin and is short based. Caudal fin is forked. Scales are cycloid or weakly ctenoid. Lateral line is lacking or weakly developed.

Mullets occur worldwide at tropical to temperate latitudes in coastal and brackish waters and in freshwater with access to the sea. Most species are pelagic, form schools, and feed in the water column on plankton and in the bottom on detritus. There are about 66 species in 17 genera, but most taxa are poorly known and defined. Seven species in 2 genera occur in the Gulf of Mexico, but several of these are poorly defined.

Key to the Species of the Gulf of Mexico

(Adapted from Jordan and Evermann 1896; Rivas 1980)

1a. Adipose eyelid absent; scales ctenoid
. . . . *Agonostomus monticola* p. 874

1b. Adipose eyelid present; scales cycloid 2

2a. Second dorsal fin and anal fin with only few scales over anterior rays; side of body with distinct longitudinal stripes
. . . . 3

2b. Second dorsal fin and anal fin densely covered with scales; side of body without distinct longitudinal stripes 4

3a. Lateral scale rows 31 to 36; pectoral fin longer than distance between dorsal fin bases; origin of second dorsal fin above origin of anal fin; posterior margin of caudal fin angular . . . . *Mugil liza* p. 879

3b. Lateral scale rows 37 to 43; pectoral fin shorter than distance between dorsal fin bases; origin of second dorsal fin posterior to origin of anal fin; posterior margin of caudal fin evenly concave . . . . *Mugil cephalus* p. 875

4a. Lateral scale rows 28 to 31; second dorsal fin with one spine and 7 rays; anal fin with three spines and 8 rays (two spines and 8 rays in juveniles) . . . . *Mugil gyrans* p. 878

4b. Lateral scale rows 32 to 40; second dorsal fin with one spine and 8 rays; anal fin with three spines and 8 or 9 rays (two spines and 9 or 10 rays in juveniles) 5

5a. Anal fin with three spines and 8 rays (two spines and 9 rays in juveniles); lateral scale rows 32 to 36 (usually 33 to 35); jaw teeth conspicuous (visible without magnification); first dorsal fin origin closer to caudal fin base than to tip of snout . . . . *Mugil trichodon* p. 880

5b. Anal fin with three spines and 9 rays (two spines and 10 rays in juveniles); lateral scale rows 35 to 40 (usually 36 to 39); teeth inconspicuous (usually not visible without magnification); first dorsal fin origin about midway between caudal fin base and tip of snout 6

6a. Lateral scale rows 35 to 38 (usually 36 or 37); more than 30 teeth on each side of upper and lower jaws; eye red in life . . . . *Mugil gaimardianus* p. 877

6b. Lateral scale rows 37 to 40 (usually 38 or 39); fewer than 30 teeth on each side of upper and lower jaws; eye not red in life . . . . *Mugil curema* p. 876

Agonostomus monticola (Bancroft 1834)
Mountain mullet

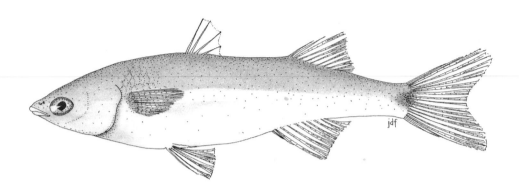

Agonostomus monticola is elongate and compressed posteriorly, with a rounded lower lip and ctenoid scales, and without adipose eyelids. It is distinguished from the other species of the family by the following combination of characters. Head is rather conical, and interorbital region is convex. Snout is blunt and as long as eye diameter. Both lips are rather thick in adults but thin in juveniles. Maxilla extends to anterior margin of eye and is covered when mouth is closed. Head is 23.5% to 26.3% and body depth is 22.2% to 23.5% of SL. First dorsal fin originates anterior to midlength of body. Second dorsal fin originates distinctly posterior to anal fin origin and has two weak spines and nine rays. Anal fin has two spines and nine rays. Lateral scale rows number 40 to 42. Color is brownish dorsally and silvery ventrally and on lower flank. Each scale has dark margin, and silvery band extends from pectoral fin base to caudal fin. Axil of pectoral fin is blackish. Caudal fin is yellowish, with dusky blotch at base.

This species occurs in the western Atlantic and eastern Pacific Oceans in inshore, brackish, and fresh waters with access to the sea. In the western Atlantic it occurs from North Carolina and the northern Gulf of Mexico to Venezuela, including the West Indies. It is rare in the northern Gulf of Mexico. Maximum known size is 30 cm TL.

REFERENCES: Jordan and Evermann 1896; Meek 1904; Suttkus 1956; Hoese and Moore 1977; Castro-Aguirre 1978; C. R. Robins et al. 1986; Boschung 1992.

Mugil cephalus Linnaeus 1758
Striped mullet

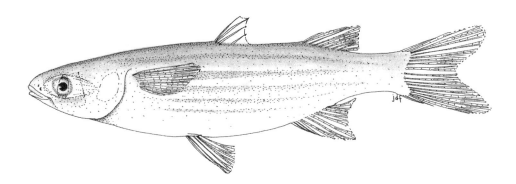

Mugil cephalus is subcylindrical and slightly compressed anteriorly, with adipose eyelids and a deeply forked caudal fin, and without dense covering of scales on second dorsal fin or anal fin. It is distinguished from the other species of the family by the following combination of characters. Snout is shorter than eye diameter. Mouth is moderately oblique, with lower jaw included in gape of upper jaw, and maxilla extending to anterior margin of eye and covered when mouth is closed. Lower lip has thin edge directed horizontally forward, and mandibular symphysis is notched. Jaw teeth are close-set and small. Interorbital region is nearly flat. Adipose eyelid covers eye except for elliptical area over pupil. Gill rakers number 24 to 26 on epibranch and 50 to 76 on lower limb. Head length is 25.4% to 27.7%, lower jaw length is 7%, interorbital width is 9.3% to 10.4%, body depth is 25.4% to 26%, predorsal length is 50.8% to 57.1%, and preanal length is 73% to 73.5% of SL. Pectoral fin has 14 to 18 rays and, when appressed, fails to reach dorsal fin origin. Second dorsal fin has one spine and 7 (rare) or 8 rays. Anal fin has three spines and 8 rays (juveniles have two spines and 9 rays). Lateral scale rows number 37 to 43, and predorsal scale rows number 23 to 26. Second dorsal fin and anal fin lack scales except for several along anterior margin of fins. Trunk vertebrae number 11 or 12, and tail vertebrae number 12 or 13. Color is grayish olive to grayish brown dorsally, silvery white on side, and pale yellow or white ventrally, with dark spot at center of each scale on upper one-half of body forming series of stripes.

This species occurs worldwide from tropical to warm temperate latitudes in coastal, brackish, and occasionally fresh waters. In the western Atlantic it occurs from Nova Scotia and Bermuda to Brazil, including the Gulf of Mexico. It is absent, however, in the Bahamas and throughout most of the West Indies. Typically this species is found near the surface in schools. Spawning occurs in the autumn far offshore. Food consists of planktonic organisms and detritus. Maximum known size is 91 cm TL.

REFERENCES: Jordan and Evermann 1896; Anderson 1958; Moore 1974; Hoese and Moore 1977; Martin and Drewry 1978; C. R. Robins et al. 1986; Boschung 1992.

Mugil curema Valenciennes 1836
White mullet

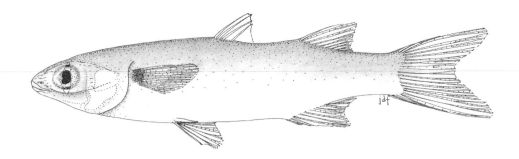

Mugil curema is subcylindrical and slightly compressed anteriorly, with adipose eyelids, densely scaled second dorsal fin and anal fin, and a moderately forked caudal fin. It is distinguished from the other species of the family by the following combination of characters. Snout is shorter than eye diameter. Mouth is moderately oblique, with lower jaw included in gape of upper jaw, and maxilla not extending to anterior margin of eye and only partially covered when mouth is closed. Lower lip has thin edge directed horizontally forward, and mandibular symphysis is notched. Adipose eyelid covers eye except for elliptical area over pupil. Primary jaw teeth are close-set, small, simple, and in single row. Vomer and palatine lack teeth. Gill rakers on first arch number about 65. Head length is 24.3% to 27.8%. Snout length is 16.7% to 23%, eye diameter is 23% to 31.7%, and interorbital width is 34.5% to 41.7% of head length. Pectoral fin has 15 to 18 rays and, when appressed, fails to reach first dorsal fin origin. Origin of first dorsal fin is equidistant between tip of snout and caudal fin base. Second dorsal fin has one spine and 7 to 9 rays. Anal fin has three spines and 9 rays (two spines and 10 rays in juveniles). Lateral scale rows number 37 to 40. Trunk vertebrae number 11 or 12, and tail vertebrae number 12 or 13. Color is bluish green or olive with bluish reflections dorsally and silvery ventrally and on side. Two bronze blotches often occur on each side of head, operculum is yellowish or golden, and caudal fin is yellowish at base.

This species occurs in the Atlantic and eastern Pacific Oceans at tropical to warm temperate latitudes in coastal, brackish, and occasionally fresh waters. In the western Atlantic it occurs from Massachusetts and Bermuda to Brazil, including the Gulf of Mexico and the Caribbean Sea. This species is absent from the northwestern Gulf of Mexico in the winter. Spawning occurs offshore during the spring. Maximum known size is 91 cm TL.

REFERENCES: Jordan and Evermann 1896; Gunter 1945; Anderson 1957; Böhlke and Chaplin 1968; Moore 1974; Hoese and Moore 1977; C. R. Robins et al. 1986; Boschung 1992; Cervigón 1993a,b.

Mugil gaimardianus   Desmarest 1831
Redeye mullet

Mugil gaimardianus is relatively robust, sub-cylindrical, and slightly compressed anteriorly, with adipose eyelids, second dorsal fin and anal fin densely covered with scales, and a moderately forked caudal fin. It is distinguished from the other species of the family by the following combination of characters. Snout is rather narrow and pointed, with upper and lower profiles about equally oblique. Upper lip is rather thick, and mandibular symphysis is notched. Maxilla extends to between posterior naris and anterior margin of eye. Jaw teeth are wide-set and inconspicuous (difficult to see without magnification). Adipose eyelid covers eye except for elliptical area over pupil. Interorbital region is nearly flat. Head length is 24.7% to 26.5% and body depth is 23.8% to 27.9% of SL. Appressed pectoral fin extends to first dorsal fin origin and has 16 or 17 rays. First dorsal fin origin is about equidistant between tip of snout and caudal fin base. Second dorsal fin has one spine and 8 rays. Anal fin has three spines and 9 rays (juveniles have two spines and 10 rays). Lateral scale rows number 35 to 38. Color is dark dorsally, with bluish reflections, and silvery ventrally and on side. Iris of eye is orange, pectoral fin has dusky blotch at base, second dorsal fin has dark tip, and caudal fin is pale with broad, dark margin.

This species occurs in the western Atlantic from the east coast of Florida, the Florida Keys, and Cuba to the northern coast of South America. It has not been positively identified from the Gulf of Mexico but probably occurs at least in the eastern Gulf. Maximum known size is 67 cm TL.

REFERENCES: Jordan and Evermann 1896; C. R. Robins et al. 1986; Cervigón 1993a,b.

Mugil gyrans (Jordan and Gilbert 1884)
Fantail mullet

Mugil gyrans is relatively slender, subcylindrical, and slightly compressed anteriorly, with adipose eyelids and second dorsal fin and anal fin densely covered with scales. It is distinguished from the other species of the family by the following combination of characters. Snout is about one-half of orbit diameter. Mouth is rather narrow, and symphysis of lower jaw forms acute angle. Teeth in jaws are in single row and are relatively well developed. Adipose eyelid covers eye except for elliptical area over pupil. Head is about 31% and body depth is about 27% of SL. Origin of first dorsal fin is closer to base of caudal fin than to tip of snout. Second dorsal fin has one spine and seven rays. Anal fin has three spines and eight rays. Lateral scale rows number 28 to 31. Color is green or bronze dorsally and silvery ventrally and on side. Pectoral fin has bluish-black spot at base.

This species occurs in the western North Atlantic from Bermuda and eastern Florida to Brazil, including the Gulf of Mexico. It is found along the coast in clear water. Maximum known size is 46 mm TL.

REFERENCES: Jordan and Evermann 1896; Rivas 1980; C. R. Robins et al. 1986.

Mugil liza Valenciennes 1836
Liza

Mugil liza is relatively slender, subcylindrical, and slightly compressed anteriorly, with adipose eyelids, second dorsal fin and anal fin almost free of scales, and a deeply forked caudal fin. It is distinguished from the other species of the family by the following combination of characters. Snout is broad and blunt, with upper profile almost straight and lower profile slightly rounded. Upper lip is rather thin, and symphysis of lower jaw is notched. Adipose eyelid covers eye except for elliptical area over pupil. Jaw teeth are very small. Head is 25% to 27% and body depth is 20.4% to 21.9% of SL. Appressed pectoral fin extends nearly to first dorsal fin origin and has 16 to 18 raya. First dorsal fin is closer to tip of snout than to caudal fin base. Second dorsal fin originates slightly behind anal fin origin and has one spine and 8 rays. Anal fin has three spines and 8 rays (juveniles have two spines and 9 rays). Lateral scale rows number 31 to 36. Posterior margin of caudal fin is angular rather than evenly convex. Color is dusky to bluish dorsally, and silvery ventrally and on lower flank. Pelvic fin is pale to faintly yellowish; other fins are dusky. Dusky streak runs along each scale row, forming horizontal stripes on body.

This species occurs in the western Atlantic Ocean from Bermuda and eastern Florida to Argentina, including the eastern Gulf of Mexico and the Bahamas. Maximum known size is 60 cm to possibly 91 cm TL.

REFERENCES: Jordan and Evermann 1896 (as *M. brasiliensis*); Böhlke and Chaplin 1968; Castro-Aguirre 1978; Rivas 1980; C. R. Robins et al. 1986; Cervigón 1993a,b.

Mugil trichodon Poey 1875

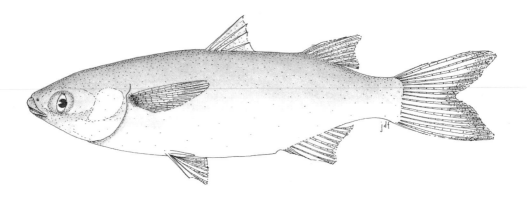

Mugil trichodon is subcylindrical and slightly compressed anteriorly, with adipose eyelids, scales densely covering second dorsal fin and anal fin, and a broadly forked caudal fin. It is distinguished from the other species of the family by the following combination of characters. Snout is rather narrow and pointed, with upper and lower profiles about equally oblique. Upper lip is relatively thick. Symphysis of lower jaw is notched. Adipose eyelid covers eye except for elliptical area over pupil. Jaw teeth are wide-set and relatively large. Head length is 23.8% to 29% and body is 26.2% to 29.6% of SL. Interorbital width is convex and about 40% of head length. Appressed pectoral fin reaches only about one-half distance to origin of first dorsal fin and has 16 rays. Origin of first dorsal fin is equidistant between tip of snout and caudal fin base. Second dorsal fin has one spine and 7 or 8 rays. Anal fin has three spines and 8 rays (juveniles have two spines and 9 rays). Lateral scale rows number 32 to 36. Color is dusky olive with bluish reflections dorsally, and silvery ventrally and on lower side. Anal and pelvic fins are pale or light yellow; other fins are dusky. Caudal fin has dusky margin. Pectoral fin has bluish spot at base.

This species occurs in the western Atlantic from Bermuda and Florida to central Brazil, including the eastern Gulf of Mexico. Maximum known size is 25 cm TL.

REFERENCES: Jordan and Evermann 1896; Böhlke and Chaplin 1968; Castro-Aguirre 1978; Rivas 1980; Cervigón 1993a,b.

ATHERINIFORMES

Atheriniformes, Beloniformes, and Cyprinodontiformes make up the Atherinomorpha. Recent studies suggest that the Atherinomorpha are the sister group of the Percomorpha or that they and several other orders make up a taxon that is the sister group to the remainder of the Percomorpha. The order consists of five or six families, and one of these occurs in the Gulf of Mexico.

ATHERINIDAE   Silversides

Silversides are slender, elongate, and moderately compressed posteriorly, with two moderately to widely separated dorsal fins and no lateral line on body. They are distinguished from the other families of the order by the following combination of characters. Snout is short and acute. Head length is equal to or greater than body depth. Mouth is terminal and small to moderate in size but does not extend beyond middle of pupil. Premaxilla is usually protractile. Teeth are small, weak, and present in jaws, and occasionally in vomer, palatine, pterygoid bones, and tongue. Anterior naris is typically small and located just posterior to fold of skin surrounding maxilla. Posterior naris is generally a small slit located just anterior to, or dorsal to, orbit. Eye is large and laterally located. Opercular opening is unrestricted, extends from upper margin of pectoral fin base to isthmus, and is free of isthmus. Gill rakers on first arch are few, short, and slender. Pectoral fin is on midflank and is narrow based. First dorsal fin is short based and has small, slender spines. Second dorsal fin has one slender spine, 1 unbranched ray, and a variable number of branched rays. Pelvic fin is usually abdominal and located midway between pectoral fin base and first dorsal fin origin, and has one slender spine and 5 rays. Anal fin is moderately long based and has one slender spine, 1 unbranched ray, and 11 to 16 branched rays. Caudal peduncle is long and moderately slender to slender. Caudal fin is emarginate to moderately deeply forked. Scales are cycloid and relatively large. Midlateral stripe runs from pectoral fin base to caudal fin base.

Silversides occur worldwide in tropical to temperate seas from near shore, including bays and estuaries, to the midcontinental shelf. Some species live permanently in either brackish water or freshwater. Most species aggregate into schools during daylight hours and feed on zooplankton. Many eggs are extruded at one time during spawning, and eggs have long chorionic filaments for attachment to floating and attached vegetation. There are about 165 species in 25 genera, and 7 species in 5 genera occur in the Gulf of Mexico.

Key to the Species of the Gulf of Mexico
(Adapted in part from Randall and Miller 1977)

1a. Jaws forming short beak; snout length greater than eye diameter. . . . . *Labidesthes sicculus* p. 885
1b. Jaws not forming short beak; snout length equal to or less than eye diameter. 2
2a. Anal fin with 8 to 13 soft rays 3
2b. Anal fin with 13 to 28 soft rays 4
3a. Inner posterior surface of lower jaw only slightly elevated; head width about 62% of head length
. . . . *Atherinomorus stipes* p. 883
3b. Inner posterior surface of lower jaw with distinct elevated bony prominence; head width about 55% of head length
. . . . *Hypoatherina harringtonensis* p. 884
4a. Four shallow glandlike depressions on dorsal surface of snout; scales with scalloped edges, rough to touch
. . . . *Membras martinica* p. 886
4b. No glandlike depressions on dorsal surface of head; scales with smooth edges, smooth to touch 5
5a. Horizontal distance between first dorsal fin origin and anal fin origin generally less than 7% of SL; posterior extension of swim bladder extending into urosome usually long and transparent or opaque 6
5b. Horizontal distance between first dorsal fin origin and anal fin origin usually greater than 7% of SL; posterior extension of swim bladder extending into urosome usually short and opaque (visible in freshly preserved or live specimens only) . . . . *Menidia peninsulae* p. 889
6a. Second dorsal fin rays usually 8; posterior extension of swim bladder extending into urosome long and opaque, with slightly blunt tip . . . . *Menidia clarkhubbsi* p. 888
6b. Second dorsal fin rays usually 9; posterior extension of swim bladder extending into urosome long and transparent, with smoothly rounded tip
. . . . *Menidia beryllina* p. 887

Atherinomorus stipes   (Müller and Troschel 1848)
Hardhead silverside

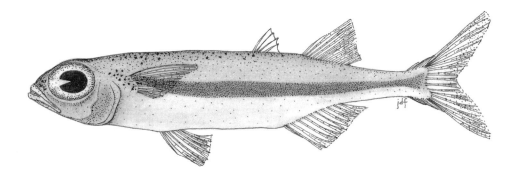

Atherinomorus stipes is moderately slender, elongate, and moderately compressed posteriorly, with a relatively broad head and a relatively short anal fin. It is distinguished from the other species of the family by the following combination of characters. Mouth is oblique, and lower jaw is equal to or extends slightly beyond upper jaw and has slight bony prominence on inner posterior surface. Jaw teeth are small and in narrow bands. Snout length is 5.4% to 6.7%, head length is 26.4% to 30.1%, head width is 15.6% to 16.6%, body depth is 20.1% to 20.3%, snout to first dorsal fin origin is 53.4% to 57.2%, horizontal distance between first dorsal fin origin and anal fin origin is 8.6% to 13.4%, snout to second dorsal fin origin is 70.2% to 75%, and snout to anal fin origin is 67% to 70.4% of SL. Pectoral fin extends beyond pelvic fin insertion and has 1 unbranched ray and 13 to 14 branched rays. First dorsal fin has four or six spines, and second dorsal fin has one spine and 8 to 10 rays. Anal fin has one spine, 11 or 13 rays, and a concave margin. Scales have crenate posterior margin, and lateral scale rows number 37 to 41. Color is greenish dorsally and pale ventrally, with silvery stripe about as broad as pupil and bordered by black stripe on midflank. Dusky pigment occurs on dorsum and reaches stripe. Caudal lobes are often black in large specimens.

This species occurs in the western Atlantic Ocean from southern Florida to Brazil, including the eastern and southern Gulf of Mexico, the Bahamas, and the Caribbean Sea, in coastal waters. Maximum known size is 100 mm TL.

REFERENCES: Longley and Hildebrand 1941 (as *Hepsetia stipes*); Böhlke and Chaplin 1968; Randall 1968; C. R. Robins et al. 1986; Cervigón 1991.

Hypoatherina harringtonensis   (Goode 1877)
Reef silverside

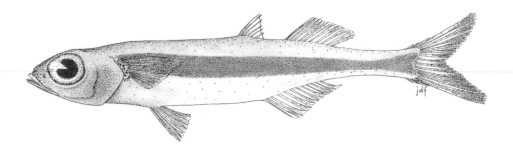

Hypoatherina harringtonensis is slender, elongate, and moderately compressed posteriorly, with a relatively narrow head and a relatively short anal fin. It is distinguished from the other species of the family by the following combination of characters. Mouth is oblique, and lower jaw is equal to or extends slightly beyond upper jaw and has markedly elevated bony structure on posterior inner surface. Jaw teeth are small, villiform, and arranged in narrow bands. Snout length is about 6%, head length is about 23%, head width is about 11%, body depth is about 14%, snout to first dorsal fin origin is about 53%, horizontal distance between first dorsal fin origin and anal fin origin is about 13%, snout to second dorsal fin origin is about 71%, and snout to anal fin origin is about 65% of SL. Pectoral fin extends to pelvic fin insertion and has 1 unbranched ray and 10 branched rays. First dorsal fin has five to seven spines, and second dorsal fin has one spine and 8 to 10 rays. Anal fin has one spine and 11 or 12 rays, and fin margin is straight. Lateral scale rows number 42 to 45. Color is greenish dorsally and silvery ventrally, with silvery stripe bordered by black stripe on side. Dusky pigment on dorsum fails to reach stripe, and distal tips of caudal fin lobes are dusky to black.

This species occurs in the western Atlantic around Bermuda, and from southern Florida, the Bahamas, and the West Indies to northern South America, including the southern Gulf of Mexico. It is pelagic in coastal waters and offshore waters, especially near drift lines. Maximum known size is 100 mm TL.

REFERENCES: Beebe and Tee-Van 1933; Böhlke and Chaplin 1968; Randall 1968; C. R. Robins et al. 1986; Cervigón 1991.

Labidesthes sicculus (Cope 1865)
Brook silverside

Labidesthes sicculus is slender, elongate, and moderately compressed, with beaklike jaws, long anal fin, and relatively small scales. It is distinguished from the other species of the family by the following combination of characters. Snout is conical and slightly depressed. Mouth is large and curved downward posteriorly, with upper jaw very protrusible and projecting slightly beyond lower jaw. Lower jaw extends almost to anterior margin of orbit. Jaw teeth are in narrow band anteriorly and in single row posteriorly. Teeth are small, conical, and slightly recurved. Snout length is 7.2% to 8.3%, head length is 20.5% to 23.5%, eye diameter is 4.7% to 5.3%, body depth is 13.8% to 15.3%, snout to first dorsal fin origin is 52.9% to 55%, and snout to anal fin origin is 51.6% to 53.6% of SL. Pectoral fin extends nearly to pelvic fin insertion and has 12 or 13 rays. First dorsal fin has three to six spines and second dorsal fin has one spine and 9 to 13 rays. Anal fin has one spine and 20 to 27 rays. Lateral scale rows number 65 to 90. In life, body is translucent, with straw-colored dorsal surface, scales slightly outlined by dark pigment, silvery stripe on flank, and ventral surface silver to pale straw. In preservative, body is pallid, with dark stripe on side tapering anteriorly, dorsal surface finely pigmented with melanophores, and straw-colored ventral surface. Maximum known size is 112 mm SL.

This species occurs in North America from the Great Lakes and St. Lawrence River to the southeastern seaboard and Gulf coast of the United States. It occurs in both standing and running water in a variety of habitats. This species is most frequently found in freshwater, but along the west coast of Florida it occurs in brackish water (Richard E. Matheson, pers. com. 1995)

REFERENCES: Jordan and Evermann 1896; Lee et al. 1980; Jenkins and Burkhead 1994.

Membras martinica (Valenciennes 1835)
Rough silverside

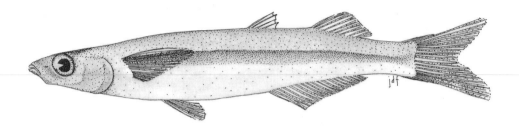

Membras martinica is slender, elongate, and moderately compressed posteriorly, with a spinous dorsal fin originating posterior to anus and a relatively long anal fin. It is distinguished from the other species of the family by the following combination of characters. Dorsal aspect of snout has anterior and posterior pair of glandlike depressions. Mouth is oblique, and lower jaw is equal to or extends slightly beyond upper jaw. Jaw teeth are small and villiform, and are arranged in narrow bands. Snout is 5.4% to 5.8%, head length is 21.5% to 22.5%, body depth is 17% to 18%, snout to first dorsal fin origin is 60.2% to 61.7%, horizontal distance from first dorsal fin origin to anal fin origin is 1% to 2.4%, snout to second dorsal fin origin is 74% to 76.1%, and snout to anal fin origin is 58.8% to 60.3% of SL. Pectoral fin extends beyond pelvic fin insertion and has 1 unbranched ray and 12 or 13 branched rays. First dorsal fin has four or five spines, and second dorsal fin has one spine and 7 or 8 rays. Anal fin has one spine and 14 to 21 rays and originates anterior to second dorsal fin origin. Scales have scalloped edges, and lateral line scales number about 43. Color is greenish dorsally and pale ventrally, with silvery stripe on side. Dusky pigment on dorsum extends to stripe.

This species occurs in the western Atlantic from New York to Mexico, including the Gulf of Mexico. It is common along shores and in more saline parts of bays and estuaries. Maximum known size is 125 mm TL.

REFERENCES: Hoese and Moore 1977; C. R. Robins et al. 1986; Boschung 1992.

Menidia beryllina (Cope 1867)
Inland silverside

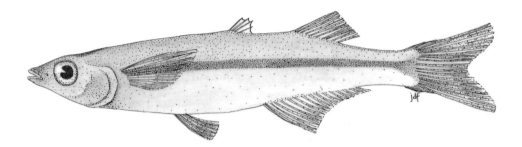

Menidia beryllina is slender, elongate, and moderately compressed, with a spinous dorsal fin originating anterior to anus and a relatively long anal fin. It is distinguished from the other species of the family by the following combination of characters. Mouth is oblique, and lower jaw is equal to or extends slightly beyond upper jaw. Posterior margin of premaxilla is rounded. Jaw teeth are small and arranged in two rows. Snout length is 4.1% to 8.8%, head length is 19.9% to 27.7%, body depth is 11% to 21.7%, snout to first dorsal fin origin is 43% to 57.6%, horizontal distance between first dorsal fin origin and anal fin origin is 1.2% to 7.2%, and snout to anal fin origin is 47.9% to 63.8% of SL. Pectoral fin extends beyond pelvic fin insertion and has one unbranched ray and 13 or 14 branched rays. First dorsal fin has four to six spines, and second dorsal fin has one spine and 8 to 10 (generally 9) rays. Anal fin has one spine and 15 to 19 rays, originates anterior to or ventral to last precaudal vertebra, and has a strongly curved margin. Lateral scale rows number 37 to 41, and predorsal scales number 16 to 22. Vertebrae number 35 to 42. Color is greenish dorsally and pale ventrally, with prominent silver stripe on side. Dusky pigment occurs on dorsum and reaches stripe.

This species occurs in the western Atlantic along the eastern seaboard of the United States from Massachusetts to Florida, along the northern Gulf of Mexico to Veracruz, and in fresh waters below the fall line over most of this range. It is abundant in shallow-water habitats from freshwater to coastal areas but is generally more abundant in freshwater than *M. peninsulae*. Maximum known size is 100 TL.

REFERENCES: M. S. Johnson 1975; Hoese and Moore 1977; Edwards et al. 1978; Lee et al. 1980; Chernoff et al. 1981; C. R. Robins et al. 1986; Boschung 1992.

Menidia clarkhubbsi   Echelle and Mosier 1982
Texas silverside

Menidia clarkhubbsi is slender, elongate, and moderately compressed posteriorly, with a spinous dorsal fin originating anterior to anus and a relatively long anal fin. It is distinguished from the other species of the family by the following combination of characters. Mouth is oblique, and lower jaw is equal to or extends slightly beyond upper jaw. Posterior margin of premaxilla is rounded. Jaw teeth are small and arranged in two rows. Snout length is 5.8% to 7.1%, head length is 24% to 27.6%, body depth is 16.9% to 18.9%, snout to first dorsal fin origin is 51% to 54.9%, horizontal distance between first dorsal fin origin and anal fin origin is 2.6% to 8.3%, snout to second dorsal fin origin is 66% to 70.4%, and snout to anal fin origin is 55.8% to 60.5% of SL. Pectoral fin extends beyond pelvic fin insertion and has one unbranched ray and 12 to 14 branched rays. First dorsal fin has four to six spines, and second dorsal fin has one spine and 7 to 9 (generally 8) rays. Anal fin has one spine and 16 to 18 rays, and originates below or posterior to last precaudal vertebra. Posterior end of body cavity ends above or posterior to anal fin origin. Lateral line scales number 38 to 40, and predorsal scales number 15 to 17. Swim bladder extends past insertion of fourth anal ray, and posterior extension is opaque and rather blunt (only evident in fresh or freshly preserved spec-imens). Color is greenish dorsally and pale ventrally, with prominent silver stripe along side. Dusky pigment occurs on dorsum and reaches lateral stripe.

This species occurs in the western Atlantic Ocean in the northern Gulf of Mexico; in a pond near Rockport, Texas; and in a pond near Galveston, Texas, and may occur along the northwestern coast of Florida (Richard E. Matheson, pers. com. 1995). This species is the result of hybridization between *M. beryllina* and *M. peninsulae*. All individuals are females that mate with males of one of their parent species. The sperm of the males stimulates development of the egg, but the chromosomes of the male do not conjugate with those of the egg. This type of reproduction is called *gynogenesis*. Because of the range of the parent species across the northern Gulf of Mexico, as well as its hybrid origin, it is likely that *M. clarkhubbsi* is not a species in the true sense. It is very likely that the populations at Rockport, Galveston, and along the Florida coast each had separate origins, and if this is the case, the populations do not form a natural group. This viewpoint is reinforced by the fact that the existence of *M. clarkhubbsi* depends solely on the existence of its parent species.

REFERENCE: Echelle and Mosier 1982.

Menidia peninsulae   (Goode and Bean 1879)
Tidewater silverside

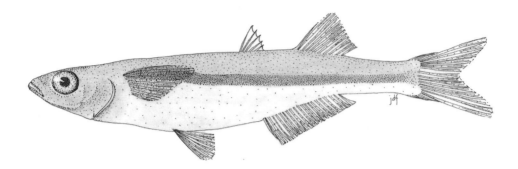

Menidia peninsulae is moderately slender, elongate, and moderately compressed, with a spinous dorsal fin originating anterior to anus and a relatively long anal fin. It is distinguished from the other species of the family by the following combination of characters. Mouth is oblique, and lower jaw is equal to or extends slightly beyond upper jaw. Posterior margin of premaxilla is rounded. Jaw teeth are small and are arranged in two rows. Snout length is 5.5% to 8.9%, head length is 22.2% to 36.2%, body depth is 15.7% to 38.1%, snout to first dorsal fin origin is 39.6% to 73.9%, horizontal distance between first dorsal fin origin and anal fin origin is 7% to 14%, snout to second dorsal fin origin is 66.9% to 71.8%, and snout to anal fin origin is 57.5% to 85% of SL. Pectoral fin extends beyond pelvic fin insertion and has one unbranched ray and 11 to 14 branched rays. First dorsal fin has four to six spines, and second dorsal fin has one spine and 7 to 12 (generally 9 or more) rays. Anal fin has 13 to 19 rays, originates ventral to or posterior to last precaudal vertebra, and has relatively straight margin. Posterior end of body cavity ends above or posterior to anal fin origin. Lateral scale rows number 34 to 43, and predorsal scales number 12 to 19. Vertebrae number 36 to 41. Color is greenish dorsally and pale ventrally, with prominent silver strip along side. Dusky pigment occurs on back and reaches stripe.

This species occurs in the western Atlantic from Daytona Beach along the Atlantic coast of Florida; from Horn Island, Mississippi; and from Galveston, Texas, to Tamiahua, Veracruz. It occurs along the coast, including bays and estuaries, but is absent along the Louisiana and east Texas coast. Maximum known size is less than 150 mm SL.

REFERENCES: M. S. Johnson 1975; Edwards et al. 1978; Chernoff et al. 1981; C. R. Robins et al. 1986; Boschung 1992.

CYPRINODONTIFORMES

Cyprinodontiformes are the sister group of the Beloniformes. The order consists of two suborders: Aplocheiloidei, with a single family (Aplocheilidae) that occurs in the Gulf of Mexico; and Cyprinodontoidei with seven families, three of which (Cyprinodontidae, Fundulidae, and Poeciliidae) occur in the Gulf.

Key to the Families of the Gulf of Mexico
(Adapted from Parenti 1981)

1a. Anterior naris surrounded by distinct tube of skin projecting anteriorly over upper jaw; covering of eye is continuous, at least in part, with skin of head
. . . . Aplocheilidae p. 890
1b. Anterior naris not tubular (except in one extralimital genus); covering of eye not continuous with skin of head
. . . . 2
2a. Pectoral fin high on flank; pelvic fin subthoracic or thoracic; males with anal fin modified into intromittent organ (gonopodium). Poeciliidae p. 919
2b. Pectoral fin low on flank; pelvic fin abdominal; anal fin of males not modified into intromittent organ 3
3a. Jaw teeth compressed and tricuspid
. . . . Cyprinodontidae p. 893
3b. Jaw teeth conical and unicuspid. . . . . Fundulidae p. 901

APLOCHEILIDAE   Rivulins

Rivulins are moderately slender to slender, and cylindrical to moderately compressed posteriorly, with a single posteriorly located dorsal fin and low-set pectoral fins. They are distinguished from the other families of the order by the following combination of characters. Snout is short to moderately long. Mouth is terminal to slightly superior and does not extend to anterior margin of eye. Premaxilla is protractile. Teeth are small, weak, and present in jaws, and occasionally in vomer and palatine. Anterior naris is surrounded by distinct tube of skin that projects anteriorly over upper jaw. Posterior naris is typically small and slitlike and located just anterior and dorsal to eye. Eye is moderate to large and laterally located. Skin covering eye is continuous, at least in part, with skin of head. Opercular opening is unrestricted and free of isthmus. Branchiostegal rays number 3 to 7. Gill rakers on first arch are few, rosettelike, and slender. Pectoral fin is narrow based and rounded posteriorly. Single dorsal fin is posteriorly located and generally has short base and rounded outline. Pelvic fin is abdominal and usually located short distance anterior to anal fin origin. Anal fin has moderately long base, generally longer than dorsal fin base, and has rounded margin. Caudal peduncle is moderately long and rather stout. Caudal fin is generally rounded, occasionally lyre shaped in males. Scales are cycloid and relatively large. Sensory pores on head are reduced to series of neuromasts. Sexes are often dimorphic and dichromic. Fins of males may be longer than those of females and pointed rather than rounded. Males are also larger and more colorful than females, and females often have ocellar spot on caudal peduncle.

Rivulins occur in the tropical and subtropical fresh and brackish waters of Africa, southeastern Asia, southern North America, and South America. Most species live near the surface in quiet waters. Some species of Africa and South America are annuals living in temporary ponds and ditches. These species undergo rapid development and spawn before the waters evaporate. The fertilized eggs undergo diapause until seasonal rains return water to the ponds and ditches. Most species are oviparous, but fertilization is internal. One species consists of individuals that are simultaneous hermaphrodites and practice self-fertilization. Many species are part of the aquarium trade because of their bright colors and hardy nature. There are about 310 species in 20 genera, and 1 species occurs in the Gulf of Mexico.

Rivulus marmoratus   Poey 1880
Mangrove rivulus

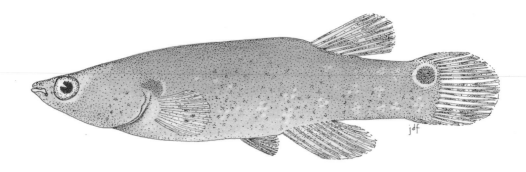

Rivulus marmoratus is slender, anteriorly cylindrical, and moderately compressed posteriorly, with a single posteriorly located dorsal fin and an ocellus on upper base of caudal fin in adults. It is distinguished from the other species of the family by the following combination of characters. Snout is short and moderately acute. Mouth is terminal, small, and moderately oblique. Upper lip is small. Premaxilla is protractile and has outer row of about 14 conical, curved teeth, with 3 enlarged, and inner narrow row of small teeth, with 3 enlarged. Lower jaw has 10 large teeth in outer row, and inner row of minute teeth. Eye is of moderate size and is set far forward. Gill rakers on lower limb of first arch number 9, including rudiments. Snout length is 5.4% to 7%, interorbital width is 11.5% to 15.9%, width of head is 19.9% to 23.4%, predorsal length is 73.8% to 77.3%, prepelvic length is 52.5% to 58.6%, and preanal length is 60.5% to 64.7% of SL. Pectoral fin has 12, dorsal fin has 8, pelvic fin has 6, and anal fin has 10 or 11 rays.

Lateral scale rows number 47 to 51, and predorsal scales number 34 to 39. Color is dark brown, with small dark spots dorsally and laterally, and slightly paler ventrally. Females have ocellus on posterodorsal angle of caudal peduncle. Pupil of ocellus is same color as dorsum and is surrounded by cream-colored iris. Males lack ocellus and have reddish orange cast on side and fins.

This species occurs in the western Atlantic Ocean from the eastern coast of Florida to Tampa Bay, Florida, in the Gulf of Mexico; the Bahamas; and the West Indies to Rio de Janeiro, Brazil. It frequents brackish water usually low in dissolved oxygen. Individuals of this species are simultaneous hermaphrodites that practice self-fertilization. Males occur but they are rare. Maximum known size is 50 mm TL.

REFERENCES: Harrington and Rivas 1958; Tabb and Manning 1961; Böhlke and Chaplin 1968; C. R. Robins et al. 1986; Gilbert 1992.

CYPRINODONTIDAE Pupfishes

Pupfishes are moderately long and robust to short and deep bodied, with a flat head, a single posteriorly located dorsal fin, and low-set pectoral fins. They are distinguished from the other families of the order by the following combination of characters. Snout is short and blunt. Mouth is terminal to slightly superior, with lower jaw extending slightly beyond upper jaw. Premaxilla is protractile. Jaw teeth are small to moderate, unicuspid to multicuspid (tricuspid in species of the Gulf of Mexico), and generally in single row. Anterior naris is not tubular, and posterior naris is slitlike and located anterodorsal to eye. Alveolar arm (posterior arm) of premaxilla is S-shaped. Dorsal processes of maxillae are expanded medially and nearly meet along midline, and lateral arms are greatly expanded. Lower jaw is expanded medially and is robust. Eye is moderately large and laterally located. Skin covering eye is not continuous with skin of head. Opercular opening is unrestricted and free of isthmus. Gill rakers are poorly developed. Pectoral fin is low on flank, narrow based, and round in outline. Single dorsal fin is rather short and originates slightly anterior to midbody or more posteriorly. Pelvic fin is abdominal but usually well anterior to anal fin origin, and is absent in two genera. Anal fin is moderately short based, generally located posterior to dorsal fin origin, and has rounded margin. Caudal peduncle is relatively long and moderately deep to deep. Caudal fin is truncate to moderately rounded. Scales are cycloid and relatively large, or occasionally absent. Lateral line is obsolete on body in most taxa. Sensory pores on head are reduced but not to neuromasts. Sexes are dimorphic and dichromic. Males often have more pointed fins and are more slender and more colorful than females. Females are larger than males.

Pupfishes occur in tropical to temperate fresh waters to coastal marine waters of the Mediterranean Anatolian region, North America, the Caribbean, and South America. Most species are found in shallow waters and feed near the surface. Many exploit ephemeral or rigorous habitats beyond the tolerances of other fishes. Species are oviparous, and fertilization is external. There are about 100 species in nine genera, and 4 species in 3 genera occur in the Gulf of Mexico.

Key to the Species of the Gulf of Mexico
(Adapted from Rosen 1973)

1a. Enlarged scale present above pectoral fin insertion
. . . . *Cyprinodon variegatus* p. 895
1b. No enlarged scale above pectoral fin insertion 2
2a. Dorsal fin rays 11 to 13; pectoral fin rays 16 to 18
. . . . *Floridichthys carpio* p. 897
2b. Dorsal fin rays 14 to 18; pectoral fin rays 14 to 17 3
3a. Principal caudal fin rays 17 to 21; anal fin rays 11 to 13;
first dorsal fin ray in adults represented by short, pungent
spine . . . . *Jordanella floridae* p. 899
3b. Principal caudal fin rays 12 to 16; anal fin rays 8 to 10;
first dorsal fin rays normally developed
. . . . *Jordanella pulchra* p. 900

Cyprinodon variegatus Lacepède 1803
Sheepshead minnow

Cyprinodon variegatus is relatively short, compressed, and deep bodied, with a short head and a blunt snout. It is distinguished from the other species of the family by the following combination of characters. Snout is moderately short, and dorsal profile of head is strongly oblique. Mouth is small and oblique. Jaw teeth are tricuspid and in single series. Eye diameter is greater than length of lower jaw, slightly less than interorbital width, and equal to snout length. Operculum is connected to shoulder girdle above base of pectoral fin. Gill rakers on first arch number 18 to 23. Branchiostegal rays number 5 or 6. In males, snout is 7.8% to 8.9%, head length is 28.6% to 31.6%, body depth is 42.5% to 44.9%, snout to dorsal fin origin is 50.7% to 53.8%, snout to anal fin origin is 65.8% to 69.4%, and caudal peduncle depth is 18.7% to 20.8% of SL. In females, snout length is 8.4% to 9.2%, head length is 29.2% to 30.5%, body depth is 41.1% to 47.2%, snout to dorsal fin origin is 50.6% to 53.8%, snout to anal fin origin is 66.4% to 68.8%, and caudal peduncle depth is 18.4% to 19.7% of SL. Pectoral fin is broadly rounded and has 14 to 17 rays. Dorsal fin originates midway between snout and caudal fin base and has 9 to 13 rays. Anal fin has 9 to 12 rays. Pelvic fin inserts slightly posterior to dorsal fin origin. Caudal fin is broadly rounded, has nearly straight posterior margin, and has a total of 28 or 29 rays and 14 to 16 principal rays. Lateral scale rows number 24 to 29. Scale above pectoral fin base (humeral) is large and elongate. Vertebrae number 25 to 27. Males are olivaceous, with steel blue or bluish green pigment from nape to dorsal fin, series of poorly defined dark bars on flank, and yellowish white to orange belly. Females are light olive, brown, brassy, or light orange dorsally, with usually 9 to 14 dark crossbars on flank alternating with 7 or 8 light crossbars. Lower side and belly are yellowish white. Dorsal fin is olive or dusky, with one or two ocelli on posterior rays.

This species occurs in the western North Atlantic from Cape Cod to Venezuela, including the Gulf of Mexico, the Florida Keys, the Bahamas, Cuba, and Jamaica, along the coast from freshwater to full seawater. In the Gulf of Mexico it occurs from the west coast of Florida to northeastern Mexico and the Yucatán Peninsula. It is most common in shallow water with submerged vegetation. Fecundity ranges up to 140 eggs, and females spawn a number of times during the spawning season. Spawning takes place over territories defended by the males. Maximum known size is 75 mm TL.

REFERENCES: Hobbs 1936; Gunter 1945; Tabb and Manning 1961; Böhlke and Chaplin 1968; Hoese and Moore 1977; C. R. Robins et al. 1986; Boschung 1992.

Floridichthys carpio (Günther 1866)
Goldspotted killifish

Floridichthys carpio is relatively short, compressed, and deep bodied, with a short head and a blunt snout. It is distinguished from the other species of the family by the following combination of characters. Snout is moderately short, and dorsal profile of head is oblique. Mouth is terminal, small, and moderately oblique. Lower jaw extends slightly beyond upper jaw. Jaw teeth are tricuspid and in single series. Eye diameter is slightly greater than lower jaw length, less than interorbital width, and slightly less than snout length. Gill rakers on first arch are rather short and stout and number 12. Operculum is connected to shoulder girdle above pectoral fin base. In males, snout length is 10% to 11.8%, head length is 31.1% to 38.5%, body depth is 34.9% to 43.8%, snout to dorsal fin origin is 54.6% to 58.3%, snout to anal

fin origin is 64.4% to 69.1%, and caudal peduncle depth is 19% to 21% of SL. In females, snout length is 7.8% to 12%, head length is 31.6% to 33.1%, body depth is 33.9% to 40.7%, snout to dorsal fin origin is 47.3% to 52.9%, snout to anal fin origin is 61.6% to 66.7%, and caudal peduncle depth is 15.8% to 21.5% of SL. Pectoral fin is broad and has 16 to 18 rays. Dorsal fin originates slightly anterior to mid-distance between snout and caudal fin base and has 11 or 12 rays. Pelvic fin insertion is slightly anterior to dorsal fin origin. Anal fin has 9 or 10 rays, and fin rays of males are considerably longer than those of females. Caudal fin is broadly rounded. Lateral scale rows number 23 to 25. Scale above pectoral fin base (humeral) is of normal size. Males are olive colored, with silvery side and 6 to 8 faint, narrow, and irregular bands on lower side. Dorsal, anal, and caudal fins are speckled with olive, forming radiating bands. Females are pale, with numerous blotches of light orange on side and light orange on dorsal and caudal fins.

This species occurs in the western North Atlantic from central-eastern Florida (Cape Canaveral) to Cape San Blas, Florida; in the eastern Gulf of Mexico; and along the Yucatán Peninsula. The Yucatán populations have been described as separate subspecies but may in fact represent a different species. This species is found along the shoreline, in saline tidal flats and creeks, and is less common in brackish water. It is associated with seagrass beds. Maximum known size is 65 mm TL.

REFERENCES: Hubbs 1936; Tabb and Manning 1961; Rosen 1973; Relyea 1983; C. R. Robins et al. 1986.

Jordanella floridae Goode and Bean 1879
Flagfish

Jordanella floridae is relatively short, moderately compressed, and deep bodied, with a moderately short head, first dorsal fin ray short and spinelike, and caudal fin rounded. It is distinguished from the other species of the family by the following combination of characters. Mouth is terminal, moderately small and oblique, with lower jaw projecting slightly beyond upper jaw. Jaw teeth are tricuspid, with middle cusp slightly longer than lateral cusps, and in single row. In males, head length is 30.3% to 32.6% and body depth is 41.7% to 46.5% of SL, and orbit length is 23.8% to 29.4%, snout length is 25.9% to 29.6%, and upper jaw length is 27.3% to 30.3% of head length. In females, head length is 30.3% to 31.8% and body depth is 40% to 43.5% of SL, and orbit length is 27% to 29.4%, snout length is 25% to 30.6%, and upper jaw length is 27% to 29.4% of head length. Pectoral fin is relatively long and has 14 to 16 rays. Dorsal fin originates slightly anterior to mid-distance between snout and caudal fin base and has 14 to 18 rays. Pelvic fin inserts anterior to end of dorsal fin base and has 6 rays. Anal fin has 11 to 13 rays. Caudal fin is slightly convex. Lateral scale rows number 25 to 27. Scale above pectoral fin base (humeral) is only slightly enlarged. Color is olivaceous and slightly darker dorsally than ventrally, with flank orange or brassy. Pigment is concentrated along distal margin of scales, forming irregular stripes. Dark vertical bar is located below eye, and large black spot is located on midflank below origin of dorsal fin. Males have well-developed horizontal stripes resulting from concentration of pigment on distal section of scales. Juveniles have small, black, ocellated spot near posterior margin of dorsal fin and four or five dark vertical bands or saddles along upper flank.

This species occurs in the western North Atlantic from the Florida Peninsula in fresh and brackish water. It is generally located in shallow water that is heavily vegetated. Maximum known size is 39 mm SL.

REFERENCES: Jordan and Evermann 1896; Hubbs 1936; Rosen 1973; Lee et al. 1980; Page and Burr 1991.

Jordanella pulchra   (Hubbs 1936)

Jordanella pulchra is relatively short, moderately compressed, and deep bodied, with a moderately short head, a blunt snout, and an elevated dorsal fin. It is distinguished from the other species of the family by the following combination of characters. Mouth is terminal, moderately small, and oblique. Lower jaw extends slightly beyond upper jaw. Jaw teeth are tricuspid, with middle cusp longer than lateral cusps, and in single row. In males, head length is 32.4% to 35.7% and body depth is 33.3% to 41.7% of SL, and orbit length is 28.6% to 37% and upper jaw length is 29.9% to 34.5% of head length. In females, head length is 31.3% to 35.7% and body depth is 35.7% to 42.6% of SL, and orbit length is 27.8% to 33.3% and upper jaw length is 28.6% to 31.3% of head length. Pectoral fin is relatively long and has 15 to 17 rays. Dorsal fin originates slightly anterior to mid-distance between snout and caudal fin base and has 15 to 17 rays. Pelvic fin inserts below dorsal fin insertion and has 6 to 8 rays. Anal fin has 8 to 10 rays. Caudal fin is truncate to slightly emarginate. Lateral scale rows number 22 to 24. Scale above pectoral fin base (humeral) is only slightly enlarged. Color of males is silvery, with several dark saddles and stripes on dorsum and side. Dark bars increase in number and become more obscure and reticular with growth. Dark cheek bar extends anteroventrally from eye, and dorsal, anal, and caudal fins are finely speckled with dark pigment. Color of females is silvery, with distinct dark bars on dorsum and side, and dark cheek bar extending anteroventrally from eye. Dorsal, anal, and caudal fins are coarsely speckled with dark pigment.

This species occurs in the western North Atlantic from the Yucatán Peninsula and nearby islands in fresh and brackish water as well as in full seawater.

REFERENCES: Hubbs 1936 (as *Garmanella pulchra*); Rosen 1973.

FUNDULIDAE Killifishes

Killifishes are slender to moderately stout, cylindrical anteriorly, and compressed posteriorly, with a pointed and drawn-out snout, a single posteriorly located dorsal fin, and low-set pectoral fins. They are distinguished from the other families of the order by the following combination of characters. Mouth is small and terminal to slightly superior, with lower jaw extending slightly beyond upper. Premaxilla is protractile. Teeth are small to moderate, conical, and arranged in single row or in outer row and inner narrow band. Anterior naris is porelike, and posterior naris is slitlike and located anterodorsal to eye. Alveolar arm (posterior arm) of premaxilla is S-shaped. Ventral arm of maxilla is anteriorly directed and often forms hook. Lower jaw is robust and expanded medially. Eye is moderately large and laterally located. Skin covering eye is not continuous with skin of head. Opercular opening is unrestricted and free of isthmus. Gill rakers are poorly developed. Pectoral fin is narrow based and round in outline. Dorsal fin is short and originates posterior to midlength. Pelvic fin is abdominal and usually well anterior to anal fin origin, but is absent in several freshwater species. Anal fin is moderately short based, generally located posterior to dorsal fin origin, and has round margin. Caudal peduncle is long and moderately deep. Caudal fin is truncated to broadly rounded. Scales are cycloid and relatively large. Lateral line is obsolete on body. Sensory pores on head are reduced but not to neuromasts. Sexes are dimorphic and dichromic. Males often have pointed fins and are more slender and more colorful than females. Females are larger than males.

Killifishes occur in tropical to temperate freshwater to coastal marine waters of North America southward to Yucatán, and in Bermuda and Cuba. Most species occupy shallow waters near shore. Many species have wide salinity and temperature tolerances. Fertilization is external, and development is oviparous. Generally eggs are benthic and adhesive and are often laid in plants or in other organisms. Eggs are extruded one at a time and have a thick chorionic membrane. There are about 48 species in five genera, and 12 species in three genera occur in the Gulf of Mexico.

Key to the Species of the Gulf of Mexico

(Adapted from Rosen 1973)

1a. Jaw teeth in single series 2
1b. Jaw teeth in more than one series 3
2a. Dark lateral band extending on flank from snout to tail; dorsal and anal fins of males with proximal and distal dark bars . . . . *Lucania goodei* p. 917
2b. No lateral band on flank; dorsal and anal fins of males without dark bars but with black spot on anterior base of dorsal fin . . . . *Lucania parva* p. 918
3a. Midlateral scale rows more than 30; mandibular sensory pores 3 to 10 4
3b. Midlateral scale rows fewer than 30; mandibular sensory pores lacking . . . . *Adinia xenica* p. 904
4a. Dorsal fin origin in males posterior to anal fin origin 5
4b. Dorsal fin origin in males directly above or anterior to anal fin origin 6
5a. Side of body with 12 to 30 round, scale-sized spots, often arranged in two rows above and below lateral line or occasionally fused into indistinct vertical bars; usually 16 scales around caudal peduncle . . . . *Fundulus jenkinsi* p. 911
5b. Side of body with 12 or fewer distinct vertical bars (males) or small, light, pearl-shaped spots scattered over side of body (females); usually 20 scales around caudal peduncle . . . . *Fundulus chrysotus* p. 906
6a. Least depth of caudal peduncle less than 13% of SL . . . . *Fundulus seminolis* p. 919
6b. Least depth of caudal peduncle usually greater than 13% of SL 7
7a. Snout pointed, length slightly less than 2 times eye diameter; postorbital head length 2 to 3 times orbit diameter . . . 8
7b. Snout round, length about 1 times eye diameter or less; postorbital head length 1 to 2 times orbit diameter 9
8a. Dorsal fin rays 11 to 16; midlateral scale rows 32 to 36; scales around circumference of body 26 to 32 . . . . *Fundulus majalis* p. 912
8b. Dorsal fin rays 9 to 11; midlateral scales rows 34 to 37; scales around circumference of body 32 to 36 . . . . *Fundulus persimilis* p. 914
9a. Adult females with unpigmented dorsal fin; females with well-developed fleshy pouch at anterior base of anal fin, pouch greater than 10% of depressed anal fin length . . . 10
9b. Adult females with ocellus or one or two black blotches on last few dorsal fin rays, remainder of dorsal fin unpigmented; females with small or no fleshy pouch at anterior base of anal fin, pouch less than 10% of depressed anal fin length 11

10a. Midlateral scale rows 31 to 38 . . . *Fundulus grandis* p. 908

10b. Midlateral scale rows 37 to 41

. . . . *Fundulus grandissimus* p. 910

11a. Females with numerous dark spots as large as pupil of eye, spots may be coalesced into longitudinal lines; vertical bars absent; dorsal fin rays 9 to 11

. . . . *Fundulus pulvereus* p. 915

11b. Females with numerous dark, narrow, vertical bars, but without dark spots; dorsal fin rays 10 to 12

. . . . *Fundulus confluentus* p. 907

Adinia xenica (Jordan and Gilbert 1882)
Diamond killifish

Adinia xenica is relatively short, compressed, and deep bodied, with a sharply pointed head and concave dorsal profile of head. It is distinguished from the other species of the family by the following combination of characters. Lower jaw extends slightly beyond upper jaw, and mouth is small, terminal, and nearly horizontal. Jaws have outer row of moderate-sized, slightly compressed, and daggerlike teeth and inner band of villiform teeth. Eye is relatively large, about twice length of lower jaw. Gill rakers on first arch number 14 or 15. Operculum is attached to shoulder girdle above base of pectoral fin. In males, snout length is 9.3% to 12.1%, head length is 35.6% to 38.6%, body depth is 44.8% to 47.1%, snout to dorsal fin origin is 58.1% to 61.3%, snout to anal fin ori-

gin is 66.6% to 72.9%, and caudal peduncle depth is 22.9% to 23.1% of SL. In females, snout length is 10.2% to 11.2%, head length is 32.6% to 34.6%, body depth is 38.1% to 39.9%, snout to dorsal fin origin is 61.2% to 63.1%, snout to anal fin origin is 68.2% to 73.4%, and caudal peduncle depth is 17.7% to 20.1% of SL. Pectoral fin is moderately broad and has 14 to 16 rays. Dorsal fin is high (extending to caudal fin base in males when depressed), strongly rounded, and has 9 or 10 rays. Anal fin originates slightly posterior to dorsal fin and has 11 or 12 rays. Caudal fin has slightly convex posterior margin. Scales are relatively large and number 24 to 26 in lateral series and 9 or 10 anterior to dorsal fin base. Males are dark green, with 8 dark bands on flank, often with pale centers; and dorsal, anal, and caudal fins are spotted. Females are greenish, with fewer and broader bands on flank; and dorsal, anal, and caudal fins are evenly pigmented by small melanophores.

This species occurs in the western North Atlantic along the northern Gulf of Mexico from Florida Bay to San Patricio County, Texas. It ranges from freshwater to hypersaline lagoons, estuaries, and mangrove swamps but is apparently most abundant at salinities between freshwater and full seawater. Maximum known size is 40 mm TL.

REFERENCES: Gunter 1945 (as *Adinia multifasciata*); Tabb and Manning 1961; Hastings and Yerger 1971; Rosen 1973; Hoese and Moore 1977; C. R. Robins et al. 1986; Boschung 1992.

Fundulus chrysotus   (Günther 1866)
Golden topminnow

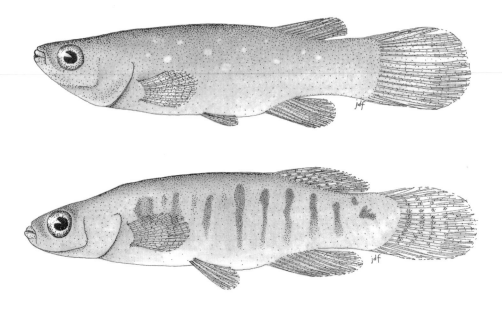

Fundulus chrysotus is relatively slender and moderately compressed, with a moderately short snout and a relatively slender caudal peduncle. It is distinguished from the other species of the family by the following combination of characters. Dorsal profile of head is straight, and snout is slightly shorter than diameter of eye. Mouth is small and slightly oblique, with lower jaw extending slightly beyond upper jaw. Jaw teeth consist of outer row of widely spaced, conical, recurved teeth, and inner narrow band of villiform teeth. Operculum is attached to shoulder girdle considerably above pectoral fin base. Gill rakers on first arch number 6 to 8. In males, snout length is 8.1% to 8.6%, head length is 25.5% to 29.2%, body depth is 23.7% to 28%, snout to dorsal fin origin is 71.7% to 71.9%, snout to anal fin origin is 65.5% to 68%, and caudal peduncle depth is 16.2% to 18% of SL. In females, snout length is 7.3% to 9%, head length is 27.4% to 29.2%, body depth is 24.6% to 27.5%, snout to dorsal fin origin is 70.6% to 74.3%, snout to anal fin origin is 68.8% to 72.6%, and caudal peduncle depth is 14.5% to 15.8% of SL. Pectoral fin has slightly narrow base and 14 or 15 rays.

Dorsal fin originates posterior to mid-distance between snout and caudal fin base and has 8 to 10 rays. Anal fin originates slightly anterior to dorsal fin origin and has 10 or 11 rays. Caudal fin has broadly rounded margin. Lateral line scales number 32 to 34. Males are olive brown, with dark streak along dorsal midline anterior to dorsal fin, 6 to 12 narrow dark brown vertical bars on flank, and diagonal dark brown bar on operculum. Fins are transparent except for small dark spots concentrically arranged on fin rays. Females are olive brown, slightly darker dorsally than ventrally, with dark streak mid-dorsally anterior to dorsal fin, pearl-colored spots scattered on side of body, and fins transparent.

This species occurs in fresh to brackish waters of North America from South Carolina to Tennessee and Missouri, southward to Florida and along the Gulf of Mexico to eastern Texas. It is commonly found in low-salinity water and has once been reported from 24.7%. Maximum known size is 50 mm SL.

REFERENCES: Brown 1956; Tabb and Manning 1961; Rosen 1973; Boschung 1992.

Fundulus confluentus Goode and Bean 1879
Marsh killifish

Fundulus confluentus is relatively slender and moderately compressed posteriorly, with a short, rounded snout and a moderately slender caudal peduncle. It is distinguished from the other species of the family by the following combination of characters. Snout is slightly oblique and about equal to eye diameter. Mouth is small and horizontal. Jaw teeth consist of outer row of conical, sharp-pointed teeth, and inner band of villiform teeth. Gill rakers on first arch are short and number five. Operculum is attached to shoulder girdle considerably above pectoral fin base. In males, snout length is 7.4% to 8.6%, head length is 30.6% to 34%, body depth is 22.1% to 27.8%, snout to dorsal fin origin is 62.2% to 69.2%, snout to anal fin origin is 64.2% to 71.6%, and caudal peduncle depth is 14.7% to 18.3% of SL. In females, snout length is 8.2% to 8.9%, head length is 30.1% to 32%, body depth is 22.7% to 24.1%, snout to dorsal fin origin is 67% to 71.4%, snout to anal fin origin is 66.6% to 73%, and caudal peduncle depth is 14.2% to 15.1% of SL. Pectoral fin is moderately narrow and has 14 to 17 rays. Dorsal fin originates posterior to mid-distance between snout and caudal fin base and has 10 or 11 rays. Anal fin originates below or slightly posterior to dorsal fin origin and has 9 or 10 rays. Caudal fin has slightly convex posterior margin and 24 to 29 rays. Lateral line scales number 36 to 40. Males are dark olive brown or dark green dorsally, with 14 to 18 silvery or white bars on flank, and belly is white, yellow, golden, or yellow-orange. Dorsal fin usually has distinct black ocellus near distal edge. Females are brown to olive dorsally, with poorly defined vertical bars on side, and belly is pale, dusky white, yellowish, or slightly greenish. Distinct ocellus is either present or absent on dorsal fin.

This species occurs in the western North Atlantic from Chesapeake Bay to southern Florida and from the northeastern Gulf of Mexico to Mississippi. Over this range it is found in grassy backwaters and brackish bays to freshwater but not along open beaches. Maximum known size is 75 mm TL.

REFERENCES: Tabb and Manning 1961; Rosen 1973; Hardy 1978; C. R. Robins et al. 1986; Boschung 1992.

Fundulus grandis Baird and Girard 1853
Gulf killifish

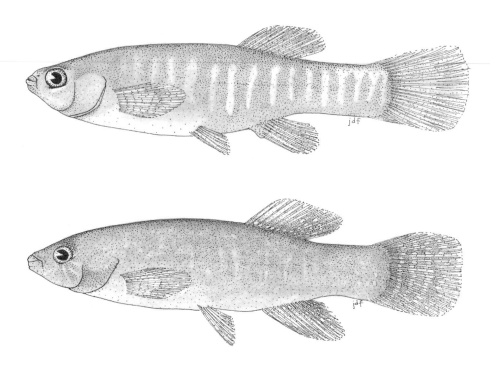

Fundulus grandis is relatively slender and moderately compressed posteriorly, with a short, rounded snout and a moderately stout caudal peduncle. It is distinguished from the other species of the family by the following combination of characters. Dorsal profile of head is straight to slightly convex. Snout is about equal to eye diameter. Mouth is small and nearly horizontal. Lower jaw extends slightly beyond upper jaw. Gill rakers on first arch are short and number 7 to 13. Operculum is attached to shoulder girdle considerably above pectoral fin base. In males, snout length is 9.2% to 10%, head length is 31.5% to 33.7%, body depth is 25% to 26.6%, snout to dorsal fin origin is 65.5% to 68.3%, snout to anal fin origin is 65.5% to 68.3%, and caudal peduncle depth is 14.7% to 16% of SL. In females, snout length is 9.5% to 10.2%, head length is 33.8% to 35.7%, body depth is 28.6% to 29.5%, snout to dorsal fin origin is 69.5% to 69.6%, snout to anal fin origin is 69.5% to 69.6%, and caudal peduncle depth is 16.2% to 18.1% of SL. Pectoral fin is narrow, bluntly pointed, and has 15 to 21 rays. Dorsal fin originates posterior to mid-length between snout and caudal fin base and has 10 to 14 rays. Anal fin originates slightly posterior to dorsal fin origin and has 10 or 11 rays. Caudal fin has straight to slightly convex posterior margin. Mandibular pores number 9 or 10 (rarely 11 or 12). Lateral scale rows number 31 to 38. Color is dark dorsally and pale yellowish white ventrally, with many pale spots, mottling, and inconspicuous bars on flank. In males, bars are obscure; dorsal, anal, and caudal fins are darkly pigmented and have small light spots; and rays of dorsal and anal fins are longer than in females.

This species occurs in the western North Atlantic from northeastern Florida to Key West, and the western coast of Florida and the northern Gulf to eastern Mexico (Laguna de Tamiahua, Veracruz) and Cuba. This species occurs near shore, generally in grassy bays, canals, and nearby freshwater. Maximum known size is 180 mm TL.

REFERENCES: Gunter 1945; Tabb and Manning 1961; Hoese and Moore 1977; Relyea 1983; C. R. Robins et al. 1986; Boschung 1992.

Fundulus grandissimus   Hubbs 1936

Fundulus grandissimus is moderately slender and moderately compressed posteriorly, with a long snout and a relatively large mouth. It is distinguished from the other species of the family by the following combination of characters. Dorsal profile of head is straight. Snout length is about 2 times eye diameter. Mouth is large and slightly oblique, and lower jaw is about one-half head length and anteriorly extends beyond upper jaw. Jaw teeth consist of outer row of relatively small, conical teeth and inner band of villiform teeth. Gill rakers on first arch number 8 to 11. Operculum is attached to shoulder considerably above pectoral fin base. Lower jaw length is 38.5% to 45.6% of head length. Head length is 33.9% to 37%, body depth is 21.7% to 28.6%, snout to dorsal fin origin is about 68% to 70%, snout to anal fin origin is 70% to 71%, and caudal peduncle depth is 14% to 15% of SL. Dorsal fin originates posterior to mid-distance between snout and caudal fin base and has 10 to 12 rays. Anal fin originates below, to slightly posterior to, dorsal fin origin and has 10 to 12 rays. Lateral scale rows number 36 to 42, and predorsal scales number 20 to 24. Mandibular pores number 12. Vertebrae number 36 to 38. Males are blue to olive, with light vertical streaks and light spots. Females are drab olive. Median fins of both sexes are blue with light spots.

This species occurs in the western North Atlantic in the Gulf of Mexico near Progreso, Sisal, and Río Lagartos, Yucatán, and from Chiquila, Quintana Roo, in the Caribbean Sea. Maximum known size is 131 mm SL for males and 179 mm SL for females.

REFERENCES: Hubbs 1936; Miller 1955; Rosen 1973; Relyea 1983.

Fundulus jenkinsi (Evermann 1892)
Saltmarsh topminnow

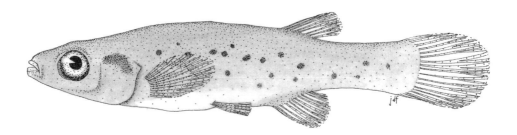

Fundulus jenkinsi is relatively slender and moderately compressed posteriorly, with a bluntly pointed snout and a moderately slender caudal peduncle. It is distinguished from the other species of the family by the following combination of characters. Dorsal profile of head is straight to slightly concave. Snout is about equal to eye diameter. Mouth is small and nearly horizontal. Jaw teeth consist of outer row of conical, sharp-pointed teeth and inner band of villiform teeth. Gill rakers on first arch are short and slender and number 10. Operculum is attached to shoulder girdle considerably above pectoral fin base. Snout length is 8.1% to 8.4%, head length is 29.6% to 30%, body depth is 21.8% to 22.6%, snout to dorsal fin origin is 69.3% to 72.8%, snout to anal fin origin is 68.6% to 69%, and caudal peduncle depth is 13.4% to 14.8% of SL. Pectoral fin is moderately narrow and has 15 or 16 rays. Dorsal fin origin is posterior to mid-distance between snout and caudal fin base and has 8 or 9 rays. Anal fin origin is slightly anterior to dorsal fin origin and has 11 to 13 rays. Lateral line scales number 34 to 36. Sexes are of similar shape and color. Body is pale yellow with minute dark specks along edges of scales, generally with 15 to 30 spots about same size as scales arranged in two rows on flank and a dark blotch on operculum.

This species occurs in the western North Atlantic in the northern Gulf of Mexico from the west coast of Florida to Texas. It is most common in brackish streams and bays from Louisiana to eastern Texas. Maximum known size is 65 mm TL.

REFERENCES: Jordan and Evermann 1896; Rosen 1973; Hoese and Moore 1977; C. R. Robins et al. 1986; Boschung 1992.

Fundulus majalis   (Walbaum 1792)
Striped killifish

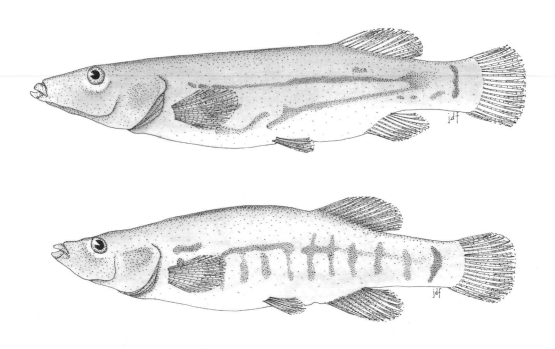

Fundulus majalis is moderately slender and moderately compressed posteriorly, with a long snout and a moderately stout caudal peduncle. It is distinguished from the other species of the family by the following combination of characters. Dorsal profile of head is straight to slightly concave. Snout length is about 2 to 3 times eye diameter. Mouth is small and nearly horizontal. Lower jaw extends beyond upper jaw. Jaws have outer row of conical, sharp-pointed teeth and inner band of villiform teeth. Gill rakers on first arch are short and number 6 to 10. Operculum is attached to should girdle considerably above pectoral fin base. In males, snout length is 9.6% to 10.6%, head length is 31% to 31.9%, body depth is 23.2% to 23.8%, snout to dorsal fin origin is 62.4% to 64.8%, snout to anal fin origin is 65.2% to 67.8%, and caudal peduncle depth is 13.2% to 14.6% of SL. In females, snout length is 11.2% to 12.7%, head length is 31.9% to 35.4%, body depth is 24.8% to 26.9%, snout to dorsal fin origin is 68.5% to 71.7%, snout to anal fin origin is 71.6% to 73.8%, and caudal peduncle depth is 13.3% to 14.5% of SL. Pectoral fin has 16 to 21 rays. Dorsal fin originates posterior to mid-distance from snout to caudal fin base and has 11 to 16 rays. Anal fin originates slightly posterior to dorsal fin origin and has 9 to 13 rays. Mandibular pores number 7 or 8. Lateral scale rows number 33 to 37. Males are olivaceous dorsally and bronze ventrally, with 10 to 15 narrow dark bars, narrower than interspace between bars, and dark blotch above pectoral fin base. Dorsal and anal fins are pigmented from base to about midlength, and anal fin is longer than in females. Females are olivaceous dorsally and laterally and white ventrally, with narrow black bars or longitudinal stripes on side. Dorsal and anal fins either lack pigment or are sparsely pigmented.

This species occurs in the western North Atlantic along the coast from New Hampshire to southeastern Florida (Lake Worth, Palm Beach County) and in the Gulf of Mexico from the west coast of Florida (Collier County) to Tampico, Mexico. An allopatric population occurs in the Florida Keys and Florida Bay, and it may represent a distinct species. This species is most abundant in bays, estuaries, and coastal marshes, although it also occurs along ocean beaches. Maximum known size is 180 mm TL.

REFERENCES: Hildebrand and Schroeder 1928; Gunter 1945 (as *F. similis*); Hoese and Moore 1977 (as *F. similis*); Relyea 1983; C. R. Robins et al. 1986; Boschung 1992.

Fundulus persimilis   Miller 1955
Yucatán killifish

Fundulus persimilis is moderately slender and moderately compressed posteriorly, with a long snout and relatively small dorsal and anal fins. It is distinguished from the other species of the family by the following combination of characters. Dorsal profile of head is straight to slightly concave. Snout length is about 2 times eye diameter. Mouth is small and nearly horizontal. Lower jaw extends slightly beyond upper jaw. Jaws have outer row of conical, sharp-pointed teeth and inner row of villiform teeth. Gill rakers on first arch are short and number 6 to 8. Operculum is attached to shoulder girdle considerably above pectoral fin base. Snout length is 33.3% to 38.5%, length of lower jaw is 27.4% to 30.3%, and caudal peduncle depth is 40% to 45.5% of head length. Head length is 31.3% to 33.9%, body depth is 22.2% to 26.7%, snout to dorsal fin origin is 66.7% to 71.4%, and snout to anal fin origin is 66.7% to 71.4% of SL. Dorsal fin originates posterior to mid-distance from snout to caudal fin base and has 9 to 11 rays. Anal fin originates below (females) or slightly posterior to (males) dorsal fin origin. Caudal fin has straight posterior margin and 16 to 18 principal rays. Lateral scale rows number 32 to 37. Vertebrae number 35 to 37. Males have 10 to 15 narrow vertical bars, with first above pectoral fin base and about one-half length of second, and interspace broader than bars. Females have 12 to 18 narrow bars of variable length, with first weak or obsolete. Males have more pigment on medial fins than females.

This species occurs in the western North Atlantic from the Yucatán Peninsula in shallow water in a tidal lagoon near the Río Lagartos. Maximum known size is 75 mm SL for males and 108 mm SL for females.

REFERENCES: Miller 1955; Rosen 1973; Relyea 1983.

Fundulus pulvereus   (Evermann 1892)
Bayou killifish

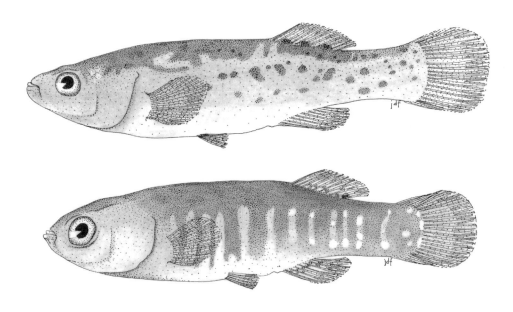

Fundulus pulvereus is relatively slender and moderately compressed posteriorly, with a short, round snout and a moderately slender caudal peduncle. It is distinguished from the other species of the family by the following combination of characters. Dorsal profile of head is slightly convex. Snout is equal to or slightly less than eye diameter. Mouth is small and horizontal. Jaws have outer row of conical, sharp-pointed teeth and inner band of villiform teeth. Gill rakers on first arch are short, moderately stout, and number 7. Operculum is attached to shoulder girdle considerably above pectoral fin base. In males, snout length is 7.8% to 10.5%, head length is 29.7% to 33%, body depth is 23.9% to 26.8%, snout to dorsal fin origin is 68.6% to 73.2%, snout to anal fin origin is 67.4% to 70.8%, and caudal peduncle depth is 13.6% to 16.1% of SL. In females, snout length is 7.2% to 9.7%, head length is 29.3% to 32.7%, body depth is 25.2% to 27.6%, snout to dorsal fin origin is 68.3% to 75.8%, snout to anal fin origin is 69.8% to 74.2%, and caudal peduncle depth is 14.1%

to 14.4% of SL. Pectoral fin has 18 or 19 rays. Dorsal fin originates posterior to mid-distance between snout and caudal fin base and has 9 or 11 rays. Anal fin originates below to slightly posterior to dorsal fin origin and has 9 or 10 rays. Lateral scale rows number 34 to 36. Males are olivaceous dorsally and yellowish ventrally, with 12 to 17 narrow dark bands alternating with light bands along flank. Dorsal fin often has dark spot on posteriormost rays. Females are olivaceous to brown dorsally and laterally, and yellowish white ventrally, with irregularly arranged dark spots along flank. Dorsal fin and other fins are lightly pigmented.

This species occurs in the western North Atlantic in the northern Gulf of Mexico from Alabama to Corpus Christi, Texas. It is most abundant in brackish bays and estuaries. Maximum known size is 75 mm TL.

REFERENCES: Jordan and Evermann 1896; Hoese and Moore 1977; Lee et al. 1980; C. R. Robins et al. 1986; Boschung 1992.

Fundulus seminolis   Girard 1859
Seminole killifish

Fundulus seminolis is slender and moderately compressed posteriorly, with a long snout and a long, slender caudal peduncle. It is distinguished from the other species of the family by the following combination of characters. Dorsal profile of head is straight to slightly convex. Snout length is about 2 to 3 times eye diameter. Mouth is small and nearly horizontal. Lower jaw extends beyond upper jaw. Jaw teeth are arranged in narrow bands, with those of outer row enlarged, conical, and recurved. Gill rakers on first arch are short stubs and number six or seven. Operculum is attached to shoulder girdle considerably above pectoral fin base. In males, snout length is 9.3% to 10.1%, head length is 25.7% to 28.7%, eye diameter is 4.7% to 5.8%, body depth is 19.2% to 22.3%, snout to dorsal fin origin is 48.9% to 53.4%, snout to anal fin origin is 55.4% to 61.6%, and caudal peduncle depth is 11.4% to 13.3% of SL. In females, snout length is 8.9% to 9.9%, head length is 26.8% to 28.7%, eye diameter is 5.3% to 6.6%, body depth is 19.4% to 22.1%, snout to dorsal fin origin is 52.9% to 55.47%, snout to anal fin origin is 59.7% to 63.2%, and caudal peduncle depth is 11% to 12.5% of SL. Pectoral fin has 19 or 20 rays. Dorsal fin origi-nates anterior to anal fin origin and has 13 to 20 rays. Anal fin originates slightly posterior to dorsal fin origin and has 10 to 15 rays. Lateral scale rows number 50 to 55. Males are olivaceous to brown dorsally and pale ventrally, with hatched pattern produced by concentration of pigment at angles of scales. Dorsal fin has narrow brown bands, caudal fin is pigmented with brown or olivaceous small spots, and other fins are clear. Females are similarly colored but have few or no spots at angles of scales, bands on dorsal fin, and spots on caudal fin.

This species occurs on peninsular Florida from the St. Johns River drainage on the Atlantic side and the New River, east of Apalachicola, on the Gulf side, to just south of the Everglades. It inhabits open areas of streams and lakes over sandy bottoms, and brackish water along the coast (Richard E. Matheson, pers. com. 1995). Maximum known size is 160 mm TL.

REFERENCES: Jordan and Evermann 1896; Rosen 1973; Lee et al. 1980; Page and Burr 1991.

Lucania goodei   Jordan 1880
Bluefin killifish

Lucania goodei is elliptical and elongate, with back distinctly elevated in front of dorsal fin, and caudal peduncle relatively deep and compressed. It is distinguished from the other species of the family by the following combination of characters. Head is flattened, and dorsal profile is slightly convex. Snout is slightly greater than one-half eye diameter. Mouth is small and horizontal. Lower jaw extends slightly beyond upper jaw. Jaw teeth are in two rows anteriorly and single row posteriorly, with those of outer row enlarged, conical, and recurved. Gill rakers on first arch are short and number five or six on lower limb. Operculum is attached to shoulder girdle considerably above pectoral fin base. Snout is 5.5% to 6.4%, head length is 27.3% to 30.2%, eye diameter is 8.3% to 9.3%, body depth is 22.4% to 25.7%, snout to dorsal fin origin is 54.2% to 57.7%, snout to anal fin origin is 58.8% to 62.5%, and caudal peduncle depth is 11.8% to 14.6% of SL. Pectoral fin is inserted low on flank and has 10 to 13 rays. Dorsal fin originates just posterior to mid-distance between snout and caudal fin base and has 8 to 10 rays. Anal fin originates at about midlength of dorsal fin base and has 8 to 10 rays. Caudal fin is truncate. Lateral line scales number 29 to 32. Color is olivaceous to brown dorsally, and tan on flank and ventral surface, with wide, zigzag, black stripe, about one scale height in width, from snout through eye to black spot on caudal peduncle. In males, dorsal and anal fins are bright iridescent blue with black band on bases and along margins.

This species occurs in eastern North America from coastal South Carolina to the tip of Florida, and along the western coast of Florida to the Choctawhatchee River drainage. It most frequently occurs in streams, rivers, and lakes, and other standing waters but also occurs along the coast in brackish water. Maximum known size is 42 mm SL.

REFERENCES: Jordan and Evermann 1896; Rosen 1973; Lee et al. 1980; Page and Burr 1991.

Lucania parva (Baird and Girard 1855)
Rainwater killifish

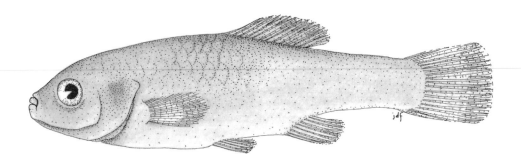

Lucania parva is moderately robust and moderately compressed posteriorly, with a blunt snout and a relatively narrow caudal peduncle. It is distinguished from the other species of the family by the following combination of characters. Head is flattened, and dorsal profile is straight. Snout is about one-half eye diameter. Mouth is small and oblique. Lower jaw extends slightly beyond upper jaw. Jaw teeth are uniserial and hooked. Gill rakers on first arch are short and number seven on lower limb. Operculum is attached to shoulder girdle considerably above pectoral fin base. Snout is 6.7% to 8.1%, head length is 27.5% to 29.8%, body depth is 26.9% to 31.6%, snout to dorsal fin origin is 52.8% to 57.4%, snout to anal fin origin is 63.5% to 65.7%, and caudal peduncle depth is 13.1% to 15.7% of SL. Pectoral fin inserts low on flank and has 10 to 15 rays. Dorsal fin originates just posterior to mid-distance between snout and caudal fin base and has 9 to 14 rays. Anal fin originates at about midlength of dorsal fin base and has 8 to 13 rays. Caudal fin has moderately convex posterior margin and 12 to 18 principal rays. Lateral line scales number 23 or 31. Vertebrae number 28. Color is pale green, olive, or brown dorsally, with small melanophores outlining scale pockets, more dense dorsally than ventrally. Belly is gray to silvery white. Males are more brightly colored than females.

This species occurs in the western North Atlantic from Cape Cod to the Florida Keys and from the eastern and northern Gulf of Mexico to the Río Panuco in Tamaulipas, Mexico. It is most common along the shoreline and in brackish bays and estuaries among aquatic vegetation. Maximum known size is 62 mm TL.

REFERENCES: Jordan and Evermann 1896; Gunter 1945; Hubbs and Miller 1965; Hoese and Moore 1977; Hardy 1978; Lee et al. 1980; C. R. Robins et al. 1986; Boschung 1992.

POECILIIDAE   Livebearers

Livebearers are cylindrical, slender to moderately slender, and moderately compressed posteriorly, with a flattened head, pectoral fins set high on flank, and anal fin of males modified into an intromittent organ. They are distinguished from the other families of the order by the following combination of characters. Snout is short and acute. Mouth is terminal to slightly superior, with lower jaw extending slightly beyond upper jaw, and jaws failing to reach anterior margin of eye. Premaxilla is protractile. Jaw teeth are small, in narrow bands, and either compressed, conical, cylindrical, or clublike. Anterior naris is not tubular, and posterior naris is located near anterior rim of orbit. Alveolar arm of premaxilla (posterior arm) has a distal extension and is S-shaped. Lower jaw is greatly expanded at anterior end. Eye is moderately large and laterally located. Opercular opening is unrestricted and free of isthmus. Gill rakers on first arch are poorly developed. Pectoral fin is located high on flank and is of moderate size. Single dorsal fin is posteriorly located and has short- to moderate-length base. Pelvic fin is subthoracic or thoracic and is modified in males of some species. Anal fin is of moderate size, with origin slightly anterior to dorsal fin origin and first two rays small and slender and lying near third ray. In males, third, fourth, and fifth rays are greatly enlarged, strengthened, and embellished with series of hooks, spines, and serrae near tip to form intromittent organ (gonopodium). Anal fin radials and anterior hemal spines are modified to form apparatus to support gonopodium. Caudal peduncle is moderately long and moderately slender to stout. Caudal fin margin is truncate to convex. Scales are cycloid and rather large. Sensory pores on head are reduced but not to neuromasts. Species are sexually dimorphic and dichromic. Males occasionally possess modified pectoral and pelvic fins and are more brightly colored than females. Females are larger and more robust than males.

Livebearers occur in fresh, brackish, or marine coastal waters of North America, Central America, and South America, including the Antilles and the Bahamas. They are one of the dominant groups of fishes in Central America. Most species live near the surface in protected habitats and feed on insects, other small invertebrates, and fishes. Fertilization is internal by means of the gonopodium of males, and development is ovoviviparous or viviparous, except for a single species. Females of some species can carry more than a single brood at one time (superfetation). Some species consist entirely of females resulting from hybridization of two species. These females mate with males of one of their parent species and produce all female progeny. There are about 293 species in 30 genera, and 7 species in 4 genera occur in the Gulf of Mexico.

Key to the Species of the Gulf of Mexico
(Adapted from Rosen 1973)

1a. Tip of pelvic fin of male swollen and/or elongate 2
1b. Pelvic fin of males like that of females or only slightly
   smaller 3
2a. Dorsal fin origin anterior to vertical from pelvic fin origin;
   dorsal fin rays 12 to 16 (rarely 11)
   . . . . *Poecilia latipinna* p. 927
2b. Dorsal fin origin posterior to vertical from pelvic fin origin;
   dorsal fin rays fewer than 9 to 11
   . . . .*Poecilia mexicana* p. 929
3a. Tip of ventral branch of middle elongate fin ray of male
   intromittent organ (first branched or fourth anal ray) ends
   with decurved hook; adult males about 15 mm SL; broad
   black band from snout to caudal fin base
   . . . . *Heterandria formosa* p. 926
3b. Tip of ventral branch of middle elongate fin ray of male
   intromittent organ (first branched or fourth anal ray)
   simple, not decurved; adult males greater than 15 mm SL;
   no black band on flank. 4
4a. Jaws greatly enlarged and elongated; inner jaw teeth larger
   than outer ones; lateral line scales more than 45
   . . . .*Belonesox belizanus* p. 921
4b. Jaws not greatly enlarged and elongated; inner jaw teeth
   smaller than outer ones; lateral line scales fewer than 45
   5
5a. Male intromittent organ bluntly rounded distally; distal
   spinose segments of anterior unbranched ray antrorse,
   long, 12 or 13 in number, and anterior segments extending
   forward to tip of fin, with their bases extending internally
   as fingerlike processes . . . . . *Gambusia rhizophorae* p. 925
5b. Male intromittent organ pointed; distal spinose segments of
   anterior unbranched ray short to moderate in length, about
   8 to 11 in number, and their tips falling short of or slightly
   exceeding tip of adjoining, more posterior ray 6
6a. Mean dorsal fin rays 7; rays 4a and 4p of gonopodium
   strongly bowed away from one another distally, maximum
   distance between them greater than segment width of rays
   4a or 4p; elbow on 4p slightly recurved and relatively
   broad based . . . . *Gambusia holbrooki* p. 924
6b. Mean dorsal fin rays 6; rays 4a and 4p of gonopodium
   weakly bowed away from one another distally, maximum
   distance between them less than segment width of rays 4a
   or 4p; elbow on 4p strongly recurved and relatively narrow
   based. . . . . *Gambusia affinis* p. 922

Belonesox belizanus Kner 1860
Pike killifish

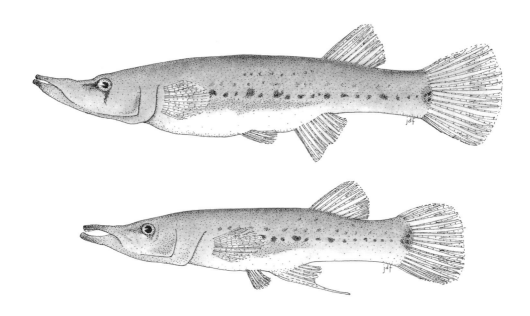

Belonesox belizanus is cylindrical, moderately slender, and moderately compressed posteriorly, with jaws greatly enlarged and anal fin origin anterior to dorsal fin origin. It is distinguished from the other species of the family by the following combination of characters. Snout is long and slightly convex. Mouth is slightly oblique, and lower jaw extends beyond upper jaw. Jaw teeth are caniniform, with outer series conical, recurved, and smaller than inner series. Operculum is attached to shoulder girdle above pectoral fin base. Snout length is 9.3% to 12.8%, interorbital width is 8% to 9.9%, head length is 34.2% to 40.4%, body depth is 19.3% to 24.8% in males and 13.9% to 21.7% in females, snout to dorsal fin origin is 72.5% to 74.4%, snout to anal fin origin is 62.1% to 67.3%, and caudal peduncle depth is 11.6% to 12.3% of SL. Pectoral fin is fanlike, has 14 or 15 rays (for Gulf of Mexico populations), and is unmodified in males. Dorsal fin has 8 or 9 rays, anal fin has 9 or 10 rays,

and caudal fin has 17 to 19 rays (for Gulf of Mexico populations). Gonopodium of mature males has elbow on ray 4a and poorly developed ray 5a. Scales are relatively small, and lateral rows number 52 to 63. Color is brownish olive dorsally and white ventrally, with longitudinal series of black dots and round black spot on caudal peduncle. Fins are transparent.

This species occurs in the western North Atlantic from the southern Gulf of Mexico to Nicaragua. In the Gulf of Mexico it occurs from the Río Antigua basin, from Veracruz to Yucatán, in freshwater to brackish water along the coast. It has been introduced into Florida; it has been captured in Tampa Bay and is common in the Everglades (Richard E. Matheson, pers. com. 1995). Maximum known size is 122 mm TL for males and 217 mm TL for females.

REFERENCES: Jordan and Evermann 1896; Hubbs 1936; Rosen and Bailey 1963; Lee et al. 1980.

Gambusia affinis   (Baird and Girard 1853)
Western mosquitofish

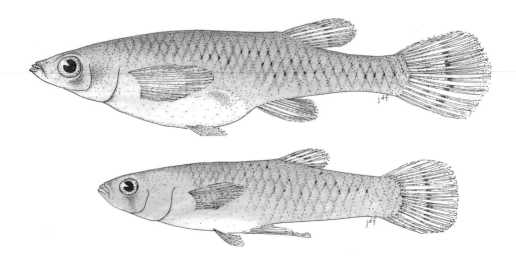

Gambusia affinis is moderately robust and moderately compressed posteriorly, with a depressed head and a relatively narrow caudal peduncle. It is distinguished from the other species of the family by the following combination of characters. Mouth is slightly oblique, and lower jaw extends slightly beyond upper jaw. Jaw teeth consist of outer row of large recurved teeth and several rows of smaller pointed teeth. Gill rakers on first arch number 5 to 12. In males, snout length is 7.4% to 8%, head length is 22.9% to 24.8%, body depth is 22.1% to 24.1%, snout to dorsal fin origin is 59.1% to 62.2%, snout to anal fin origin is 43.4% to 47.5%, and caudal peduncle depth is 14% to 15.3% of SL. In females, snout length is 7.7% to 9.2%, head length is 22.5% to 25.4%, body depth is 23.9% to 27.1%, snout to dorsal fin origin is 64.8% to 69.2%, snout to anal fin origin is 58.3% to 58.5%, and caudal peduncle depth is 13.3% to 15% of SL. Pectoral fin has 12 to 14 rays, and that of males is modified; fifth ray has distinct scalloped portion near its distal tip. Dorsal fin originates posterior to anal fin origin and has 5 to 10 ($\bar{x}$ = 6) rays. Anal fin of females originates about midway between snout and caudal fin base and has 8 to 11 rays.

Caudal fin is fanlike and has about 24 rays. Gonopodium is formed by enlarged third, fourth, and fifth anal rays, and is exaggeratedly drawn out at distal tip. Inner processes on segments of ray 3 preceding elbow are entire and lack spinelike projections, and spines near tip of ray are small and stout, with distal tips bifid. Ray 4a has bladelike elbow consisting of many segments coalesced along their anterior margins, and ray 4p has about 7 segments distal to serrae. Scales in lateral series number 29 to 32. Trunk vertebrae number 13 or 14, and tail vertebrae number 17 to 20. Color is light olive, olivaceous tan, dark greenish brown, silvery, yellowish silvery, or yellow dorsally and pale ventrally, with scale margins dusky and forming diamond-shaped pattern. Dorsal fin has two or three transverse rows of fine black dots. Females have gravid spot on body.

This species occurs in the western North Atlantic, in the Gulf of Mexico from west of Mobile Bay to Tampico, and in fresh waters of North America, from the Mississippi River drainage to the Pecos River and Rio Grande. It is found in quiet, slow-moving freshwater and in protected brackish and marine waters. Food consists of surface insects, insect larvae, and crustaceans. Fecundity ranges from 1 to over 300 fertilized eggs or embryos. It hybridizes with *G. holbrooki* along the Gulf coast from Alabama to Louisiana. Maximum known size is about 50 mm SL for males and about 80 mm SL for females.

REFERENCES: Darnell 1962; Rosen and Bailey 1963; Rosen 1973; Hoese and Moore 1977; Hardy 1978 (all included *G. holbrooki*); Black and Howell 1979; C. R. Robins et al. 1986; Rauchenberger 1989; Wooten and Lydeard 1990; Boschung 1992.

Gambusia holbrooki   Girard 1859
Eastern mosquitofish

Gambusia holbrooki is moderately robust and moderately compressed posteriorly, with a depressed head and a relatively narrow caudal peduncle. It is distinguished from the other species of the family by the following combination of characters. Head is depressed. Mouth is slightly oblique, and lower jaw extends slightly beyond upper jaw. Jaw teeth consist of outer row of large recurved teeth and several rows of smaller pointed teeth. Gill rakers on first arch number 5 to 12. In males, snout length is 7.7% to 9.8%, head length is 26% to 27.7%, body depth is 23.1% to 24.3, snout to dorsal fin origin is 60.6% to 68%, snout to anal fin origin is 47.1% to 52.2%, and caudal peduncle depth is 15.1% to 16.3% of SL. In females, snout length is 8.7% to 9.9%, head length is 23.8% to 26.2%, body depth is 22.8% to 26.7%, snout to dorsal fin origin is 61.5% to 69.4%, snout to anal fin origin is 56.1% to 61%, and caudal peduncle depth is 14% to 15% of SL. Pectoral fin has 12 to 14 rays, and those of males are modified; fifth ray has distinct scalloped portion near its distal tip. Dorsal fin originates posterior to anal fin origin and has 5 to 10 ($-x = 7$) rays. Anal fin of females originates about midway between snout and caudal fin base and has 8 to 11 rays. Caudal fin is fanlike and has about 24 rays. Gonopodium is formed by enlarged third, fourth, and fifth anal rays, and is exaggeratedly drawn out at distal tip. Inner processes on segments of ray 3 preceding elbow have spinelike projections, and spines near tip of ray are small and stout, with distal tips bifid. Ray 4a has bladelike elbow consisting of many segments coalesced along their anterior margins, and ray 4p has about seven segments distal to serrae. Scales in lateral series number 26 to 34. Trunk vertebrae number 13 or 14, and tail vertebrae number 17 to 20. Color is light olive, olivaceous tan, dark greenish brown, or silvery dorsally and yellowish ventrally. Scale margins are dusky on dorsum and side, with occasionally a thin, dark streak and bluish black or purple triangular bar below eye. Dorsal fin has two or three transverse rows of fine black dots. Females have gravid spot on body.

This species occurs in the western North Atlantic from coastal and freshwater of New Jersey to southern Florida and the northern Gulf of Mexico to Mobile Bay. Food consists of surface-living insects, insect larvae, and small crustaceans. Fecundity ranges from 1 to 315 fertilized eggs or embryos. Maximum known size is 52 mm SL for males and 80 mm SL for females. It hybridizes with *G. affinis* along the Gulf coast from Alabama to Louisiana.

REFERENCES: Hildebrand and Schroeder 1928; Rosen and Bailey 1963 (as *G. affinis*); Rosen 1973 (as *G. affinis*); Hoese and Moore 1977 (as *G. affinis*); Hardy 1978 (as *G. affinis*); Black and Howell 1979; C. R. Robins et al. 1986 (as *G. affinis*); Rauchenberger 1989; Wooten and Lydeard 1990.

Gambusia rhizophorae   Rivas 1969
Mangrove gambusia

Gambusia rhizophorae is moderately robust and moderately compressed posteriorly, with a depressed head and a relatively narrow caudal peduncle. It is distinguished from the other species of the family by the following combination of characters. Mouth is slightly oblique, and lower jaw extends slightly beyond upper jaw. Operculum is attached to shoulder girdle above pectoral fin base. Jaws have uniserial outer and inner rows of enlarged, depressible, recurved canines, separated by a row of small teeth. Teeth of outer row are larger than those of inner row. Gill rakers on first arch number 14 to 17. In males, snout length is 9.6% to 10.2%, head length is 27.8% to 29.1%, body depth is 26.8% to 27.7%, snout to dorsal fin origin is 64.6% to 67.9%, snout to anal fin origin is 53.4% to 56.9%, and caudal peduncle depth is 16% to 17.7% of SL. In females, snout length is 10.1% to 10.3%, head length is 28.4% to 29.6%, body depth is 29.6% to 34.2%, snout to dorsal fin origin is 68.3% to 73.4%, snout to anal fin origin is 58.4% to 65.5%, and caudal peduncle depth is 16.9% to 17.6% of SL. Pectoral fin has 13 to 15 rays, and those of males are modified; blade on ray 2 is thickened abruptly near its proximal end, and segments in area are anastomosed (fused). Dorsal fin originates posterior to anal fin origin and has 8 to 10 rays. Anal fin originates at about mid-length between snout and caudal fin base and has 11 rays. Caudal fin has 13 to 15 branched rays. Gonopodium is formed by enlarged third, fourth, and fifth anal rays. Second anal ray is thickened at base. Spines and inner processes on ray 3 are very elongate and straplike. Ray 4a has spatulate elbow, and ray 4p has one or two segments distal to serrae and serrae are transversely enlarged. Hooks on rays 4p and 5a are enlarged and scythelike. Ray 5 has prominent bump. Lateral scale rows number 28 to 30. Color is yellowish brown to brownish yellow dorsally and laterally, and yellow ventrally, with dark markings on scales of back and flank. Side of body has four to six longitudinal rows of dark spots overshadowing reticulate pattern. Suborbital bar is weak or absent. Dorsal fin has two or three rows of dark spots. Caudal fin has two or three rows of dark spots.

This species occurs in the western North Atlantic from southeastern Florida, the Florida Keys, and northwestern Cuba. It is found in estuaries associated with red mangroves. This species has not been reported from the Gulf of Mexico, but it is likely to occur in southwestern Florida. Maximum known size is 36 mm SL for males and 41 mm SL for females.

REFERENCES: Rivas 1969; C. R. Robins et al. 1986; Rauchenberger 1989.

Heterandria formosa Girard 1859
Least killifish

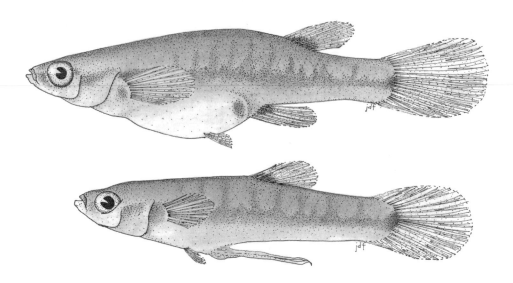

Heterandria formosa is moderately slender to moderately robust and moderately compressed posteriorly, with a slightly convex dorsal profile and a moderately narrow caudal peduncle. It is distinguished from the other species of the family by the following combination of characters. Snout is slightly blunt and much shorter than eye diameter. Mouth is strongly oblique and very small. Lower jaw extends beyond upper jaw. Jaws have outer row of relatively large, conical teeth and inner band, two teeth wide, of smaller teeth. Gill rakers on first arch number eight or nine. In males, snout length is 6% to 6.8%, head length is 25.6% to 27.2%, body depth is 27.2% to 29.1%, snout to dorsal fin origin is 58.3% to 59%, snout to anal fin origin is 43.6% to 45.6%, and caudal peduncle depth is 13.6% to 15.4% of SL. In females, snout length is 6% to 6.7%, head length is 21.8% to 27.3%, body depth is 22.6% to 31.4%, snout to dorsal fin origin is 65.9% to 66.7%, snout to anal fin origin is 58.7% to 62.5%, and caudal peduncle depth is 13.5% to 16.5% of SL. Pectoral fin has 10 to 12 rays, and that of males is not modified. Dorsal fin originates posterior to anal origin and has 6 or 7 rays. Anal fin has 6 or 9 rays. Caudal fin is fan shaped. Gonopodium is formed by en-

larged third, fourth, and fifth anal rays. Rays 3 and 5 extend to tip of membranous portion of gonopodium. Ray 3 has 5 to 10 rudimentary spinous processes distally. Ray 4a has distal hook consisting of one to three or more anky-losed elements projecting beyond membranous tip. Ray 4p has 7 to 10 subdistal serrae, and distal portion of ray 5 curves ventrally and anteriorly to meet terminal elements of ray 4. Lateral line scales number 28 to 30, and vertebrae number 31 to 33. Color is brownish olive dorsally and slightly lighter ventrally, with six to nine indistinct brownish black vertical bars on flank, a dark band running from mouth to caudal peduncle, and a black spot, the size of a single scale, on caudal peduncle. Dorsal and anal fins have dark spot at base.

This species occurs in the western North Atlantic along the coast from South Carolina to Florida and along the northern Gulf of Mexico to east Texas in fresh to brackish waters. Maximum known size is 14 mm SL for males and 24 mm SL for females.

REFERENCES: Tabb and Manning 1961; Rosen and Bailey 1963; Rosen 1973, 1979; Hanks and McCoid 1988; Boschung 1992.

Poecilia latipinna (Lesueur 1821)
Sailfin molly

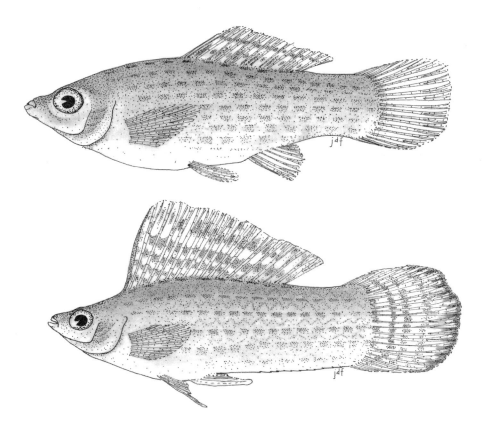

Poecilia latipinna is moderately robust, with a straight dorsal profile, a relatively long dorsal fin, and a moderately deep caudal peduncle. It is distinguished from the other species of the family by the following combination of characters. Snout is acute and short. Mouth is oblique and very small. Jaws have outer row of small, conical, recurved teeth and inner band of villiform teeth. Gill rakers on first arch number 22 to 27. In males, snout length is 8% to 9%, head length is 27.2% to 29.1%, body depth is 32.2% to 35%, snout to dorsal fin origin is 37.3% to 42.5%, snout to anal fin origin is 48.7% to 52.5%, and caudal peduncle depth is 23.2% to 27% of SL. In females, snout length is 8.9% to 10.2%, head length is 25.6% to 30.3%, body depth is 37.1% to 38.8%, snout to dorsal fin origin is 48.2% to 51.5%, snout to anal fin origin is 65.9% to 68.8%, and cau-

dal peduncle depth is 19.9% to 21.3% of SL. Pectoral fin is located slightly below midflank and has 14 or 15 rays. Dorsal fin originates anterior to pelvic fin insertion and has 11 to 16 rays. Pelvic fin of mature males has fleshy swelling on distal section of ray 1; long, fleshy extension of ray 2 and rays 1 and 2 are joined by dense connective tissue and separated from rays 3, 4, and 5 by notch. Anal fin originates under middle to posterior section of dorsal fin base and has 7 to 9 rays. Gonopodium is formed by enlarged third, fourth, and fifth anal fin rays. Third ray bears fleshy palp on ventral surface and short retrorse spines near tip. Ray 5a has small retrorse claw at tip and tough, membranous or bony hook projecting ventrally from tip of ray 3. Ray 5b extends to within two or three segments of ray 5a. Lateral scale rows number 26 to 30. Color is olive green to grayish brown, with cross-hatching on upper flank produced by dark pigment along posterior margin of scale pockets. Fins are transparent except for minute dark spots along fin rays and, to lesser extent, on fin membranes. In life, dorsal fin of males has orange margin.

This species occurs in the western North Atlantic from southeastern North Carolina to the Florida Keys and from southwestern Florida along the Gulf of Mexico to the base of the Yucatán Peninsula. It occurs from freshwater to full seawater and is abundant in tidal ditches and brackish canals. Maximum known size is 125 mm TL.

REFERENCES: Gunter 1945; Rosen and Bailey 1963; Rosen 1973; Hoese and Moore 1977; C. R. Robins et al. 1986; Boschung 1992.

Poecilia mexicana   Steindachner 1863
Shortfin molly

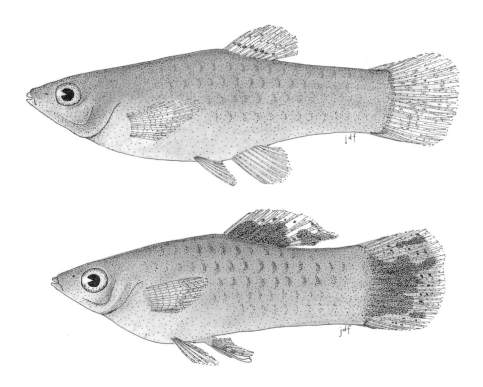

Poecilia mexicana is moderately robust, with a straight to slightly convex dorsal profile, a relatively short dorsal fin, and a relatively deep caudal peduncle. It is distinguished from the other species of the family by the following combination of characters. Snout is acute and of moderate length. Mouth is oblique and very small. Jaws have outer row of small, conical, recurved, unicuspid teeth and inner band of villiform teeth. Gill rakers on first arch number 21 to 26. In males, snout length is 7.1% to 8.9%, head length is 22.9% to 26.4%, body depth is 26.1% to 28.5%, snout to dorsal fin origin is 54.6% to 58.7%, snout to anal fin origin is 51.2% to 55.2%, and caudal peduncle depth is 17.6% to 18.4% of SL. In females, snout length is 7.5% to 8.4%, head length is 23.9% to 24.9%, body depth is 26.5% to 29.4%, snout to dorsal fin origin is 58.5% to 59.1%, snout to anal fin origin is 61.5% to 64.6%, and caudal peduncle depth is 16.6% to 18.1% of SL. Pectoral fin is located just below midflank and has 13 to 15 rays. Dorsal fin originates posterior to pelvic fin insertion and anterior to vent, and has 8 to 11 rays. Pelvic fin of mature males has fleshy swelling on distal section of ray 1; long, fleshy extension of ray 2 and rays 1 and 2 are joined by dense connective tissue and separated from rays 3, 4, and 5 by notch. Anal fin originates under anterior one-half of dorsal fin base and has 7 or 8 rays. Gonopodium in males is formed by enlarged third, fourth, and fifth anal fin rays. Third ray bears fleshy palp on ventral surface and short retrorse spines near tip. Ray 5a has small retrorse claw at tip, and tough, membranous or bony hook projects ventrally from tip of ray 3. Ray 5b extends to within two or three segments of ray 5a. Lateral scale rows number 28 to 30. Color is variable, light brownish green to light brownish gray dorsally and pale yellow ventrally. Upper flank has series of spots produced by pigment at rear of scale pockets. Males may have light vertical bars and dark blotches on side of body, and on dorsal and caudal fins. Fins of females are transparent.

This species occurs in the western North Atlantic from the western Gulf of Mexico, at the mouth of the Rio Grande, to Colombia and the southern islands of the West Indies. It occurs in freshwater to full seawater throughout its range. Maximum known size is 90 mm SL.

REFERENCE: Rosen 1973.

BELONIFORMES

This order consists of five families, and three (Belonidae, Exocoetidae, and Hemiramphidae) occur in the Gulf of Mexico.

Key to the Families of the Gulf of Mexico

1a. Upper jaw at least slightly elongate; upper and lower jaws with large teeth; scales on body small. . . . Belonidae p. 931
1b. Upper jaw not elongate; upper and lower jaws without large teeth; scales on body large 2
2a. Lower jaw elongate in juveniles and in most adults; premaxilla pointed anteriorly; pectoral fin short to moderately long . . . . Hemiramphidae p. 955
2b. Lower jaw not elongate in adults; premaxilla straight anteriorly; pectoral fin very long . . . . Exocoetidae p. 941

BELONIDAE   Needlefishes

The needlefishes are elongate, subcylindrical, or compressed, with both jaws greatly elongated into a beak bearing small to rather large teeth. They are distinguished from the other families of the order by the following combination of characters. Mouth is large, horizontal, and does not extend to anterior margin of eye. Jaw teeth are needlelike. Single nasal opening on each side of head is located dorsoanterior to eye, is not tubelike, and possesses protruding tentacle. Eye is moderately large and located laterally. Opercular opening is unrestricted, extends from above pectoral fin base to isthmus, and is free of isthmus. Gill rakers are present or absent on first arch. Pectoral fin is not enlarged, is located on upper flank, and has straight diagonal to strongly concave posterior margin. Single dorsal fin is posteriorly located, moderately long, and lacks fin spines. Pelvic fin is abdominal, lacks spines, and consists of one unbranched ray and five branched rays. Anal fin is posteriorly located and moderately long to long based, with anterior rays often greatly elongated, forming hooklike margin. Caudal peduncle is narrow, and caudal fin is weakly to strongly forked, often with lower lobe extending beyond upper lobe. Scales are small and cycloid. Lateral line is complete and runs along ventral margin of body, with branch running dorsal to pectoral fin base in many species. Swim bladder is present.

Needlefishes occur worldwide in tropical to temperate epipelagic waters. Some species, however, are present in fresh waters of

Central and South America, India, and Southeastern Asia. Most species occur from bays and estuaries to the outer continental shelf and feed near the surface on small schooling fishes that are captured by means of the prolonged jaws and sharp teeth. Eggs are demersal and bear sticky filaments that attach to floating and attached vegetation. Larvae are pelagic, and most pass through a "halfbeak" stage in which lower jaw is enlarged beyond upper jaw. There are 32 species in 10 genera, and 7 species in 4 genera occur in the Gulf of Mexico.

Key to the Species of the Gulf of Mexico
(Adapted from Collette 1978b; pers. com., May 3, 1995)

1a. Body laterally compressed; series of 12 to 14 vertical bars on flank; anal rays 24 to 28 . . . . *Ablennes hians* p. 934

1b. Body rounded or squarish in cross section; vertical bars absent; anal fin rays 12 to 23 2

2a. Caudal peduncle strongly depressed (least depth about one-half width) and with well-developed lateral keels; 7 to 14 gill rakers present. . . . . *Platybelone argalus* p. 935

2b. Caudal peduncle not strongly depressed (deeper than it is wide) and with small keel or no keel; gill rakers absent. . . 3

3a. Dorsal fin rays 12 to 17; no keels on caudal peduncle; caudal fin truncate; dorsal fin without expanded posterior lobe in juveniles or adults 4

3b. Dorsal fin rays 21 to 26; small, dark-pigmented keel on each side of caudal peduncle; caudal fin forked, with lower lobe longer than upper lobe; juveniles with expanded black posterior lobe in dorsal fin 6

4a. Posterior section of maxilla concealed under preorbital bone; distinct vertical bar at posterior margin of preoperculum; anal rays 12 to 15; predorsal scales 76 to 117 . . . . *Strongylura notata* p. 937

4b. Posterior section of maxilla not concealed under preorbital bone; vertical bar at posterior margin of preoperculum lacking; anal rays 16 to 20; predorsal scales 120 to 304 5

5a. Pigment behind eye usually extending to ventral margin of orbit; preorbital bone densely pigmented; predorsal scales 120 to 185; two gonads. . . . . . . *Strongylura timucu* p. 938

5b. Pigment behind eye not extending below middle of orbit; preorbital bone slightly pigmented; predorsal scales 213 to 304; one gonad . . . . *Strongylura marina* p. 936

6a. Anterior lobe of dorsal fin 9.4% to 18.5% of body length; anterior lobe of anal fin 12.5% to 18.2% of body length; pectoral fin 12% to 15.2% of body length; pelvic fin 9.4% to 13.7% of body length; dorsal fin rays usually 21 or 23 . . . . *Tylosurus crocodilus* p. 940

6b. Anterior lobe of dorsal fin 7.5% to 9.5% of body length;
anterior lobe of anal fin 8.5% to 10.3% of body length;
pectoral fin 8.1% to 12.5% of body length; pelvic fin 7.1%
to 10% of body length; dorsal fin rays usually 24
. . . . *Tylosurus acus* p. 959

Ablennes hians (Valenciennes 1846)
Flat needlefish

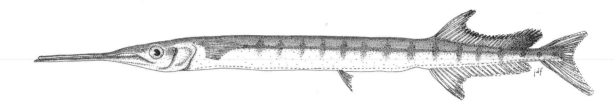

Ablennes hians is elongate and compressed in cross section, with lower jaw slightly longer than upper jaw, falcate pectoral fins, and dorsal and anal fins with high falcate anterior lobes. It is distinguished from the other species of the family by the following combination of characters. Jaw teeth are in bands, and are sharp pointed and small. Gill rakers are absent. Snout length is 33% to 35.9%, head depth is 5% to 6.2%, head width is 3.2% to 3.9%, orbit diameter is 3.2% to 4.2%, interorbital width is 2.8% to 3.2%, preopercular width is 3% to 3.1%, height of anterior dorsal fin lobe is 5.4% to 7%, height of anterior anal fin lobe is 7% to 9.1%, pectoral fin length is 6.9% to 8.6%, and pelvic fin length is 4.9% to 6.1% of body length. Pectoral fin has 13 to 15 rays. Dorsal fin has strongly emarginate margin and has 23 to 26 rays. Anal fin lacks prominent posterior lobe of dorsal fin and has 24 to 28 rays. Caudal peduncle lacks lateral keels. Caudal fin is strongly forked, with lower lobe much longer than upper lobe. Vertebrae number 93 to 97. Color is bluish green dorsally and silvery ventrally, with broad, dark blue stripe and about 12 to 14 prominent dark vertical bars on flank. Both juveniles and adults have elevated black lobe in posterior part of dorsal fin.

This species occurs worldwide in tropical and subtropical seas. In the western Atlantic it occurs from Massachusetts to Rio de Janeiro, Brazil, including the Gulf of Mexico, the Bahamas, and the Caribbean Sea. This species is most common offshore but occurs near shore in insular areas. Food consists of pelagic fishes. Eggs are about 3 mm in diameter. Maximum known size is 1,100 mm TL.

REFERENCES: Böhlke and Chaplin 1968; Collette and Parin 1970; Hoese and Moore 1977; Collette 1978b; Hardy 1978; Uyeno et al. 1983; C. R. Robins et al. 1986; Cervigón 1991; Boschung 1992.

Platybelone argalus (Lesueur 1821)
Keeltail needlefish

Platybelone argalus is elongate and pentagonal in cross section, with lower jaw extended considerably beyond upper jaw, a depressed caudal peduncle, and well-developed caudal keels. It is distinguished from the other species of the family by the following combination of characters. Lower jaw is about 20% longer than upper jaw. Jaw teeth are small and needlelike, and vomerine teeth are absent. Gill rakers are present. Snout length is 30.8% to 38.5%, head depth is 4.4% to 5.7%, head width is 3.9% to 5.4%, orbit diameter is 3.4% to 4.1%, interorbital width is 2.4% to 3.7%, preopercular width is 3.9% to 4.1%, height of anterior dorsal fin lobe is 6.3% to 7%, height of anterior anal fin lobe is 7.8% to 9.3%, pectoral fin length is 7.1% to 8.4%, and pelvic fin length is 5.9% to 6%. Pectoral fin has 10 to 13 rays. Dorsal fin has strongly concave margin and 12 to 15 rays. Anal fin is similar to dorsal fin but is longer and has 17 to 20 rays. Very broad keel is located on either side of caudal peduncle. Caudal fin is forked, and upper and lower lobes are about equal in length. Scales are relatively large, and predorsal scales number 101 to 137. Vertebrae number 62 to 76. Color is dark greenish dorsally and silvery ventrally, with narrow horizontal stripe running from operculum to caudal peduncle. Fins are transparent, and caudal peduncle keel is bluish black. Juveniles have greatly elongated lower jaw.

This species occurs worldwide in tropical and subtropical seas. The population in the western Atlantic is considered a distinct subspecies, *P. argalus argalus,* that occurs from North Carolina to Brazil, including the Gulf of Mexico, the Bahamas, and the Caribbean Sea. It is restricted to oceanic waters and seldom is found in shallow coastal waters. Maximum known size is 500 mm SL.

REFERENCES: Böhlke and Chaplin 1968; Randall 1968; Collette and Parin 1970, 1986; Hoese and Moore 1977; Collette 1978b; C. R. Robins et al. 1986; Cervigón 1991; Boschung 1992.

Strongylura marina (Walbaum 1792)
Atlantic needlefish

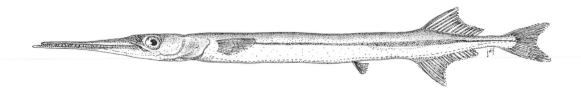

Strongylura marina is elongate and oval in cross section, with lower jaw slightly longer than upper jaw, and a compressed caudal peduncle that lacks keels. It is distinguished from the other species of the family by the following combination of characters. Jaw teeth are in bands and are sharply pointed, with innermost ones enlarged and caninelike. Gill rakers are absent. Snout length is 32.2% to 44.5%, head depth is 6.4% to 7.6%, head width is 4.5% to 5.4%, orbit diameter is 3.8% to 4.8%, interorbital width is 3.7% to 4.4%, preopercular width is 5.6% to 7.3%, height of anterior dorsal lobe is 6.4% to 11%, height of anterior anal fin lobe is 10.1% to 13.6%, pectoral fin length is 10.4% to 13.4%, and pelvic fin length is 5.3% to 6.3% of body length. Pectoral fin has 11 or 12 rays. Dorsal fin has strongly concave margin and 14 to 17 rays. Anal fin is similar to dorsal fin and has 16 to 20 rays. Caudal peduncle lacks lateral keels. Caudal fin is emarginate but not deeply forked, and lower lobe is slightly longer than upper lobe. Scales are relatively small, and predorsal scales number 213 to 304. Vertebrae number 69 to 77. Gonad is single. Color is bluish green dorsally and silvery ventrally, with dark blue stripe along flank and black pigment posterior to eye, usually not extending below middle of eye.

This species occurs in the western Atlantic from Massachusetts to Rio de Janeiro, including the Gulf of Mexico and the Caribbean coast of Mexico and Central America. It is most frequently found in coastal areas, estuaries, and lagoons. Food consists of small fishes. Spawning takes place in bays and estuaries, and occasionally in freshwater. Eggs are demersal and are attached to vegetation by tightly coiled filaments. Maximum known size is 781 mm SL.

REFERENCES: Gunter 1945; Hoese and Moore 1977; Collette 1978b; Hardy 1978; C. R. Robins et al. 1986; Cervigón 1991; Boschung 1992.

Strongylura notata (Poey 1860)
Redfin needlefish

Strongylura notata is elongate and oval in cross section, with lower jaw slightly longer than upper jaw, posterior section of maxilla concealed under preorbital bone, and a compressed caudal peduncle lacking lateral keels. It is distinguished from the other species of the family by the following combination of characters. Jaw teeth are in bands and are sharply pointed, with innermost ones enlarged and caninelike. Gill rakers are absent. Snout length is 38.2% to 42.6%, head depth is 8.8% to 9.8%, head width is 7.3% to 8%, orbit diameter is 5.3% to 5.5%, interorbital width is 6.4% to 8.9%, preopercular width is 7.3% to 8.3%, height of anterior dorsal fin lobe is 11.8% to 14%, height of anterior anal fin lobe is 14.5% to 15.4%, pectoral fin length is 14.7% to 16.8%, and pelvic fin length is 7.4% to 7.7% of body length. Pectoral fin is not falcate and has 11 or 12 rays. Dorsal fin has strongly concave margin and 12 to 15 fin rays. Anal fin is similar to dorsal fin and has 12 to 15 rays. Caudal fin is emarginate but not forked. Scales are relatively large, and predorsal scales number 76 to 117. Vertebrae number 53 to 61. Gonads are paired. Color is bluish green dorsally and silvery ventrally, with dorsal, caudal, and anal fins reddish or orangish and black bar on posterior margin of preoperculum.

This species occurs in the western Atlantic Ocean from the east coast of Florida and Bermuda to Central America, including the Gulf of Mexico, the Bahamas, and the Lesser Antilles. It is most common in inshore waters, including bays, estuaries, and occasionally freshwater. Maximum known size is 610 mm TL.

REFERENCES: Beebe and Tee-Van 1933; Hubbs 1936; Böhlke and Chaplin 1968; Randall 1968; Collette 1978b; C. R. Robins et al. 1986; Boschung 1992.

Strongylura timucu   (Walbaum 1792)
Timucu

Strongylura timucu is elongate and oval in cross section, with lower jaw slightly longer than upper jaw, and a compressed caudal peduncle lacking lateral keels. It is distinguished from the other species of the family by the following combination of characters. Jaw teeth are in bands and are sharply pointed, with inner teeth caninelike and larger than outer teeth. Gill rakers are absent. Snout length is 34.6% to 38.7%, head depth is 7% to 7.6%, head width is 5.3% to 5.9%, orbit diameter is 4.5% to 4.8%, interorbital width is 4.4% to 4.8%, preopercular width is 6.8% to 7.6%, height of anterior dorsal fin lobe is 10.3% to 11.9%, height of anterior anal fin lobe is 11.7% to 13.6%, pectoral fin length is 10.8% to 12.9%, and pelvic fin length is 5.8% to 6.7% of body length. Pectoral fin is not falcate and has 10 to 12 rays. Dorsal fin has strongly concave margin and 14 to 17 rays. Anal fin is similar to dorsal fin and has 16 to 20 rays. Caudal fin is emarginate but not deeply forked, and lower lobe is slightly longer than upper lobe. Scales are relatively large, and predorsal scales number 120 to 185. Vertebrae number 68 to 75. Gonads are paired. Color is bluish green dorsally and silvery ventrally, with black pigment behind eye usually extending to ventral margin of orbit, and preorbital bone densely pigmented.

This species occurs in the western Atlantic Ocean from the east coast of Florida to Rio de Janeiro, including the northeastern Gulf of Mexico westward to Pensacola, Florida, the Bahamas, and the Caribbean Sea. It is most common in coastal water, including estuaries and lagoons. Food consists of small pelagic fishes. Maximum known size is 418 mm SL.

REFERENCES: Böhlke and Chaplin 1968; Randall 1968; Collette 1978b; C. R. Robins et al. 1986; Cervigón 1991.

Tylosurus acus   (Lacepède 1803)
Agujon

Tylosurus acus is elongate and oval in cross section, with lower jaw slightly longer than upper jaw, and small, black lateral keel on caudal peduncle. It is distinguished from the other species of the family by the following combination of characters. Jaw teeth are in bands and are sharp pointed, with inner teeth enlarged and caninelike. Vomerine teeth are absent. Gill rakers are absent. Snout length is about 21.5%, head length is 31.7% to 32.8%, head width is 4.7% to 5.6%, eye diameter is 3.4%, height of anterior dorsal fin lobe is about 5.9%, height of anterior anal fin lobe is 6% to 6.2%, and body depth is 4.8% to 7.7% of SL. Pectoral fin has 13 or 14 rays. Dorsal fin has strongly concave margin and 22 to 26 rays. Anal fin is similar to dorsal fin and has 20 to 24 rays. Caudal fin is deeply forked, and lower lobe is much longer than upper lobe. Scales are very small, and predorsal scales number 325 to 389. Vertebrae number 90 to 95. Color is dark bluish dorsally and silvery white ventrally, with dark blue stripe along flank. Juveniles have dark elevated lobe in posterior part of dorsal fin.

The species occurs worldwide in tropical and subtropical seas. The western Atlantic population is a separate subspecies, *T. acus acus,* that occurs from Massachusetts and Bermuda to Rio de Janeiro, Brazil, including the entire Gulf of Mexico, the Bahamas, and the Caribbean Sea. This species occurs in both offshore and coastal waters, with young more common in inshore waters and adults more common in offshore waters. Food consists of small pelagic fishes. Spawning occurs offshore, and eggs are 3.2 to 4 mm in diameter. Maximum known size is 128.5 mm SL.

REFERENCES: Beebe and Tee-Van 1933; Böhlke and Chaplin 1968; Collette 1978b; Collette and Parin 1986; C. R. Robins et al. 1986; Cervigón 1991; Boschung 1992.

Tylosurus crocodilus   (Péron and Lesueur 1821)
Houndfish

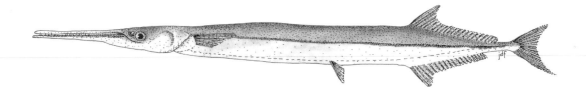

Tylosurus crocodilus is elongate and oval in cross section, with lower jaw slightly longer than upper jaw, and small black keel on caudal peduncle. It is distinguished from the other species of the family by the following combination of characters. Jaw teeth are in bands and are sharp pointed, with inner teeth enlarged and caninelike. Vomerine teeth are absent. Gill rakers are absent. Snout length is 18.3% to 18.6%, head length is 30.1% to 34.2%, head width is 7.4% to 7.7%, eye diameter is 2.8% to 4%, height of anterior dorsal fin lobe is 8.5% to 9.4%, height of anterior anal fin lobe is 8.4% to 10%, and body depth is 7.4% to 8.6% of SL. Pectoral fin has 13 to 15 rays. Dorsal fin has strongly concave margin and 21 to 23 rays. Anal fin is similar to dorsal fin and has 18 to 22 rays. Caudal fin is deeply forked, and lower lobe is much longer than upper lobe. Scales are very small, and predorsal scales number 240 to 290. Vertebrae number 79 to 84. Color is dark bluish green dorsally and silvery ventrally, with dark blue stripe along flank and with green scales and bones. Juveniles have teeth in both jaws directed anteriorly and have an elevated black lobe in posterior part of dorsal fin.

This species occurs worldwide in tropical and subtropical seas. The population in the western Atlantic represents a subspecies, *T. crocodilus crocodilus*, and it occurs from North Carolina to Salvador, Brazil, including the Gulf of Mexico, the Bahamas, and the Caribbean Sea. This species occurs in both offshore and coastal waters but is more common in coastal waters. Food consists of small pelagic fishes. Maximum known size is 101.3 mm SL.

REFERENCES: Beebe and Tee-Van 1933 (as *T. raphidoma*); Böhlke and Chaplin 1968; Randall 1968; Collette and Parin 1970; G. B. Smith et al. 1975; Hoese and Moore 1977; Collette 1978b; Castro-Aguirre and Márquez-Espinoza 1981; C. R. Robins et al. 1986; Boschung 1992.

EXOCOETIDAE Flyingfishes

Flyingfishes are elongate, subcylindrical to laterally compressed posteriorly, and usually flattened ventrally, with pectoral fins high on flank and greatly elongated. They are distinguished from the other families of the order by the following combination of characters. Snout is short and blunt. Mouth is short, terminal to slightly superior, with lower jaw extending slightly beyond upper jaw. Lower jaw is often elongated during some stage of development. Premaxilla is not protractile and has straight anterior margin. Jaw teeth are absent or small. Chin barbels or barbel occasionally occur during development. Single nasal opening on each side of head is located anterodorsal to eye and consists of a pit-like depression and protruding tentacle. Eye is large and laterally located. Opercular opening extends from dorsal margin of pectoral fin base to isthmus and is free of isthmus. Gill rakers are well developed and range from 17 to 33. Pectoral fin extends beyond dorsal fin origin and has 12 to 20 rays. Single dorsal fin is posteriorly placed, lacks spines, and has 9 to 16 rays. Pelvic fin is abdominal in position, consists of 1 unbranched ray and 5 branched rays, and ranges from moderately to extremely long. Anal fin is located under dorsal fin and consists of 7 to 15 rays. Caudal peduncle is moderately long and moderately slender. Caudal fin is deeply forked, with ventral lobe considerably longer than upper lobe. Scales are cycloid and large. Lateral line runs along ventral contour of body. Vertebrae number 35 to 52. Swim bladder extends into hemal canal.

Flyingfishes occur worldwide in tropical to subtropical epipelagic seas. They inhabit the surface zone and are capable of emerging from the water by means of their elongated lower caudal lobe and of gliding for considerable distances by means of their expanded pectoral fins. Food consists of zooplankton. Eggs are demersal but have sticky filaments that attach to floating and attached vegetation. Larvae are pelagic. There are about 52 species in seven or eight genera, and 12 species in six genera occur in the Gulf of Mexico.

Key to the Species of the Gulf of Mexico (to specimens greater than 100 mm SL)
(Adapted from Bruun 1935)

1a. Length of pelvic fin less than 21% of SL. 2
1b. Length of pelvic fin greater than 24% of SL 5
2a. Snout length greater than 9% of SL
. . . . *Fodiator acutus* p. 950
2b. Snout length less than 7% of SL. 3
3a. Pectoral fin less than 60% of SL
. . . . *Parexocoetus brachypterus* p. 953

Cheilopogon comatus (Mitchill 1815)
Clearwing flyingfish

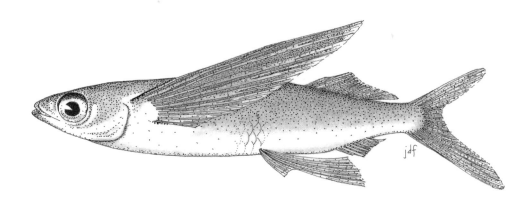

Cheilopogon comatus is robust, with a pointed snout, a low and transparent dorsal fin, and uniformly dusky pectoral fins. It is distinguished from the other species of the family by the following combination of characters. Snout is acute and slightly shorter than eye diameter. Mouth is oblique and extends to anterior margin of eye. Jaw teeth are tricuspid, with lateral cusps shorter than median cusp. Palatine teeth are weak and few in number. Gill rakers on first arch number 18 to 23. Snout length is 3.7% to 7%, head length is 23.7% to 27.6%, eye diameter is 7.8% to 9.9%, interorbital distance is 7.7% to 9.8%, body depth is 18.1% to 21.2%, snout to dorsal fin origin is 65.4% to 76.8%, snout to anal fin origin is 77.9% to 80.8%, snout to pelvic fin origin is 58.8% to 66.3%, pectoral fin length is 57.5% to 70.9%, and caudal peduncle depth is 6.8% to 8.1% of SL. Pectoral fin extends beyond midlength of dorsal fin base and has 12 to 16 rays, with first ray unbranched. Dorsal fin has 10 to 14 rays, and anal fin originates under sixth or seventh dorsal fin ray and has 8 or 9 rays. Scales above lateral line number 5 to 8, and predorsal scales number 22 to 30. Vertebrae number 40 to 43. Color is dark dorsally and silvery ventrally, with pectoral fin uniformly gray but slightly darker distally. Dorsal fin is transparent between lightly colored fin rays. Pelvic fin is gray and slightly darker along margin. Anal fin is transparent. Juveniles have single, long, flat, simple median barbel. Barbel length is equal to SL in specimens less than 100 mm SL.

This species occurs in the tropical western Atlantic Ocean from Florida to Brazil, including the Gulf of Mexico and the Caribbean Sea. It is not common in the western Gulf of Mexico, and it is usually found within 480 km of shore. Breeding season is between February and April in North Atlantic populations. Eggs are 1.33 mm in diameter and have filaments. Maximum known size is 243 mm SL.

REFERENCES: Bruun 1935; Staiger 1965; C. R. Robins et al. 1986.

Cheilopogon cyanopterus (Valenciennes 1847)
Margined flyingfish

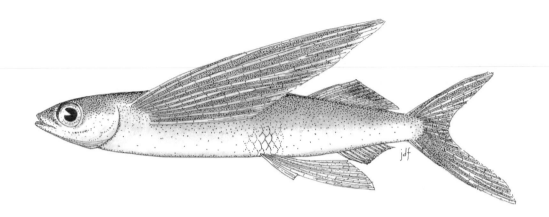

Cheilopogon cyanopterus is robust, with a moderately blunt snout, a low dorsal fin that is transparent anteriorly and dark posteriorly, and uniformly dark pectoral fins. It is distinguished from the other species of the family by the following combination of characters. Snout is moderately acute and shorter than eye diameter. Mouth is oblique and does not extend to anterior margin of eye. Jaw teeth are slightly curved and generally unicuspid but occasionally weakly tricuspid. Palatine teeth are present but variable in size and number. Gill rakers on first arch number 16 to 28. Snout length is 3% to 6.7%, head length is 22% to 27.4%, eye diameter is 4.9% to 8.5%, interorbital distance is 6% to 10.1%, body depth is 13.1% to 19.3%, snout to dorsal fin origin is 63.1% to 74.5%, snout to anal fin origin is 72% to 80.7%, snout to pelvic fin origin is 56% to 61%, pectoral fin length is 45.9% to 78.5%, and caudal peduncle depth is 6% to 84.4% of SL. Pectoral fin extends beyond midlength of dorsal fin base and has 12 to 16 rays. Dorsal fin has 11 to 14 rays, and anal fin originates under fifth to seventh dorsal fin rays and has 8 to 11 rays. Scales above lateral line number 6 to 9, and predorsal scales number 30 to 41. Vertebrae number 43 to 45. Color is dark dorsally and silvery ventrally, with pectoral fin bluish black, dorsal fin black posteriorly, and pelvic and anal fins transparent. Juveniles have paired mandibular barbels that are longer than SL, uniformly colored pectoral fin, and dorsal fin ranging from 9.4% to 34.2% of SL.

This species occurs in the tropical Atlantic Ocean. In the western Atlantic it occurs from New Jersey to Brazil, including the Gulf of Mexico and the Caribbean Sea. It is usually found within 640 km of the coast but is absent in inshore waters. Maximum known size is 333 mm SL.

REFERENCES: Bruun 1935; Staiger 1965; Bright and Cashman 1974; Hoese and Moore 1977; C. R. Robins et al. 1986; Cervigón 1991; Boschung 1992.

Cheilopogon exsiliens (Linnaeus 1771)
Bandwing flyingfish

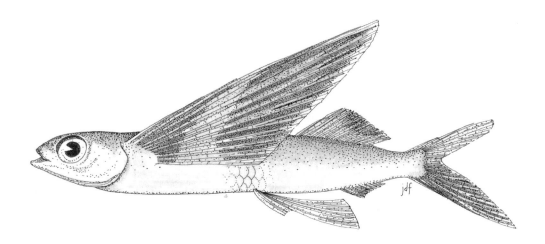

Cheilopogon exsiliens is robust, with a moderately blunt snout; a high, bicolored dorsal fin; banded pectoral fins; and a bicolored caudal fin. It is distinguished from the other species of the family by the following combination of characters. Snout is moderately acute and shorter than eye diameter. Mouth is oblique and does not reach anterior margin of eye. Jaw teeth are unicuspid, and palatine teeth are absent. Gill rakers on first arch number 16 to 26. Snout length is 3.7% to 6.4%, head length is 20.5% to 27.3%, eye diameter is 4% to 9.9%, interorbital width is 6.4% to 10.6%, body depth is 16.6% to 20.2%, snout to dorsal fin origin is 64.4% to 70.9%, snout to anal fin origin is 73.1% to 81.4%, snout to pelvic fin origin is 53.6% to 59.2%, pectoral fin length is 52.8% to 75%, and pelvic fin length is 33.4% to 49.7% of SL. Pectoral fin extends beyond midlength of dorsal fin base and has 13 to 16 rays. Dorsal fin is high (12.4% to 34.4% of SL) and has 13 to 15 rays. Anal fin originates under sixth to eighth dorsal fin rays and has 8 to 10 rays. Scales above lateral line number 5 to 8, and predorsal scales number 21 to 30. Vertebrae number 43 to 44. Color is dark dorsally and silvery ventrally. Dorsal fin is black at center. Pectoral fin is dark, with pale triangular crossband, broader posteriorly than anteriorly, and posterior edge of first rays are unpigmented or lightly pigmented. Pelvic and anal fins are unpigmented. Upper lobe of caudal fin is transparent, and lower lobe is black. Juveniles have pair of short, flaplike barbels and transparent or white upper caudal lobe.

This species occurs in the tropical western and central Atlantic. In the western Atlantic it occurs from Cape Cod and Bermuda to Brazil, including the Gulf of Mexico. It is uncommon in the western Gulf of Mexico. This species is oceanic but enters coastal areas in clear water, though it does not enter bays and estuaries. Maximum known size is 236 mm SL.

REFERENCES: Bruun 1935; Staiger 1965; C. R. Robins et al. 1986; Boschung 1992.

Cheilopogon furcatus   (Mitchill 1815)
Spotfin flyingfish

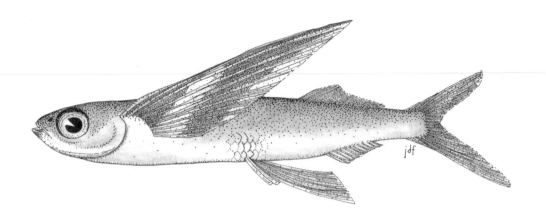

Cheilopogon furcatus is robust, with an acute snout, bicolored pectoral fins, and a dusky caudal fin. It is distinguished from the other species of the family by the following combination of characters. Snout is slightly blunt and shorter than eye diameter. Mouth is oblique and does not extend to anterior margin of eye. Jaw teeth are small and unicuspid. Palatine teeth are absent. Gill rakers on first arch number 16 to 24. Snout length is 2.3% to 8.5%, head length is 20.5% to 26.4%, eye diameter is 7.3% to 12.2%, interorbital width is 6.9% to 9.1%, body depth is 15.5% to 20.7%, snout to dorsal fin origin is 64.5% to 74.3%, snout to anal fin origin is 72.3% to 78.5%, snout to pelvic fin origin is 51.9% to 58.7%, pectoral fin length is 31.9% to 74.8%, pelvic fin origin is 32.8% to 58.2%, and caudal peduncle depth is 5.2% to 8.1% of SL. Pectoral fin extends beyond midlength of dorsal fin base and has 14 to 17 rays. First pectoral fin ray is greater than 38% of SL. Dorsal fin is low (9.5% to 19.5% of SL) and has 11 to 14 rays. Anal fin originates below anterior one-half of dorsal fin base and has 8 to 12 rays. Scales above lateral line number 6 to 9, and predorsal scales number 22 to 35. Vertebrae number 44 to 46. Color is dark dorsally and silvery ventrally. Dorsal fin is transparent, and pectoral fin is black with curved transparent central area, wider along front edge of fin than along posterior edge. Pelvic fin is dark edged, and caudal fin is darkly pigmented. Juveniles (up to 150 mm SL) have mandibular barbels greater than 16% of SL, low dorsal fin with uneven pigmentation, six vertical bars on body, and first pectoral fin ray longer than 38% of SL. Mandibular barbels consist of fleshy shaft gradually tapering to slender point, with black membrane extending length of shaft and tapering distally.

This species occurs in the tropical western and central Atlantic. In the western Atlantic it occurs from Massachusetts and Bermuda to the Gulf of Mexico and the Caribbean Sea. It is common in oceanic waters but enters bays and estuaries. Maximum known size is 293 mm SL.

REFERENCES: Beebe and Tee-Van 1933; Bruun 1935; Staiger 1965; Hoese and Moore 1977; C. R. Robins et al. 1986; Boschung 1992.

Cheilopogon melanurus   (Valenciennes 1847)
Atlantic flyingfish

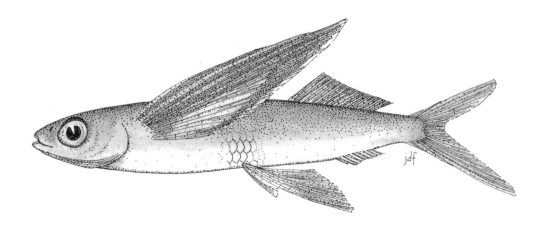

Cheilopogon melanurus is robust, with a transparent dorsal fin, bicolored pectoral fins, and a dusky caudal fin. It is distinguished from the other species of the family by the following combination of characters. Snout is acute and shorter than eye diameter. Mouth is oblique and does not extend to anterior margin of eye. Jaw teeth are very small and unicuspid. Palatine teeth are lacking. Gill rakers on first arch number 17 to 26. Snout length is 3.2% to 8.7%, head length is 20% to 27.1%, eye diameter is 6.3% to 11.5%, interorbital width is 7.1% to 8.8%, body depth is 16% to 20.3%, snout to dorsal fin origin is 65.3% to 71.7%, snout to anal fin origin is 75% to 80.1%, snout to pelvic fin origin is 51.8% to 56.9%, pectoral fin length is 39.3% to 77.8%, and caudal peduncle depth is 6.3% to 7.7% of SL. Pectoral fin extends beyond midlength of dorsal fin base and has 13 to 17 rays. Dorsal fin is low (7.8% to 23.8% of SL) and has 10 to 15 rays. Anal fin originates below midlength of dorsal fin base and has 8 to 12 rays. Scales above lateral line number 6 to 9, and predorsal scales number 22 to 35. Vertebrae number 42 to 46. Color is dark dorsally and silvery ventrally. Pectoral fin is dark, with pale crossband and lightly pigmented first ray. Crossband is wider posteriorly than anteriorly and does not extend to anterior margin. Anal fin is transparent, and caudal fin is darkly pigmented. Juveniles (less than 150 mm SL) have low (less than 20% of SL) and unevenly pigmented dorsal fin, short (less than 10% of SL) mandibular barbels, and short (less than 38% of SL) first pectoral fin ray, with first and second rays separated by distance equal to 1.7 times distance between second and third rays. Pectoral fin has two pigment spots along first ray, one spot at fin base, and one spot along distal edge posterior to transparent area.

This species occurs in the tropical to warm temperate Atlantic Ocean. In the western Atlantic it occurs from 42°N to 23°S, including the Gulf of Mexico and the Caribbean Sea. It is a coastal species generally found within 640 km of the shoreline, and it enters bays and estuaries. Eggs are 1.6 to 1.8 mm in diameter and have long tendrils.

REFERENCES: Bruun 1935; Staiger 1965; Hoese and Moore 1977; Castro-Aguirre and Márquez-Espinoza 1981 (all above as *C. heterurus*); C. R. Robins et al. 1986; Cervigón 1991; Boschung 1992.

Exocoetus obtusirostris   Günther 1866
Oceanic two-wing flyingfish

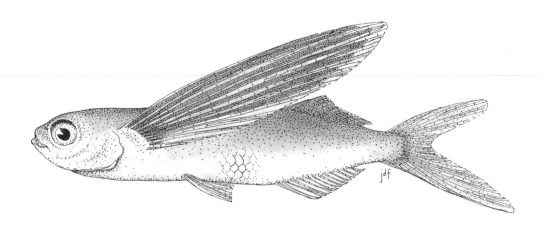

Exocoetus obtusirostris is moderately robust, with a blunt snout, very long pectoral fins, and an anteriorly located anal fin. It is distinguished from the other species of the family by the following combination of characters. Snout is shorter than eye diameter. Mouth is oblique and fails to reach anterior margin of eye; lower jaw extends slightly beyond upper jaw. Jaw and palatine teeth are absent. Gill rakers on first arch number 24 to 29. Snout length is 4.4% to 5.4%, head length is 23.5% to 26.6%, eye diameter is 6.6% to 8.3%, interdorsal width is 8% to 9.7%, body depth is 18.8% to 22.4%, snout to dorsal fin origin is 66% to 70%, snout to pelvic fin origin is 39.9% to 43.1%, snout to anal fin origin is 66.1% to 69.4%, pectoral fin length is 71.3% to 77.7%, and pelvic fin length is 12.3% to 14.8% of SL. Pectoral fin extends beyond dorsal fin base and has 16 or 17 rays. Dorsal fin is low (7.2% to 11.3 % of SL) and has 13 or 14 rays. Anal fin originates slightly anterior to dorsal fin origin and has 13 to 15 rays. Scales above lateral line number 7, and predorsal scales number 18 to 21. Vertebrae number 44. Color is iridescent blue dorsally and silvery ventrally, with fins grayish to transparent.

This species occurs in the tropical Atlantic and subtropical South Pacific. In the western Atlantic it occurs from New Jersey to southern Brazil, including the Gulf of Mexico and the Caribbean Sea. It is an oceanic species and is not frequently captured near shore. Eggs are pelagic and lack filaments. Maximum known size is 200 mm SL.

REFERENCES: Bruun 1935; Hoese and Moore 1977; Parin 1986; C. R. Robins et al. 1986; Cervigón 1991; Boschung 1992.

Exocoetus volitans   Linnaeus 1758
Tropical two-wing flyingfish

Exocoetus volitans is moderately robust, with a moderately blunt snout, very long pectoral fins, and an anteriorly located anal fin. It is distinguished from the other species of the family by the following combination of characters. Snout is shorter than eye diameter. Mouth is oblique and fails to reach anterior margin of eye; lower jaw extends slightly beyond upper jaw. Jaw and palatine teeth are absent. Gill rakers on first arch number 29 to 37. Snout length is 4.3% to 5.6%, head length is 24.9% to 27.1%, eye diameter is 6.2% to 6.8%, interorbital width is 7.9% to 8.6%, body depth is 16.8% to 19.4%, snout to dorsal fin origin is 64.7% to 68.4%, snout to pelvic fin origin is 41.9% to 44.1%, snout to anal fin origin is 66.9% to 69.5%, pectoral fin length is 73.2% to 77.1%, and pelvic fin length is 13.3% to 14.5% of SL. Pectoral fin extends to near caudal fin base and has 14 or 15 rays. Dorsal fin is low (9.1% to 11.1% of SL) and has 14 rays. Anal fin originates slightly posterior to dorsal fin origin and has 12 to 14 rays. Scales above lateral line number 6, and predorsal scales number 17 to 20. Vertebrae number 43 to 45. Color is dark dorsally and silvery ventrally. Pectoral and dorsal fins are uniform light gray. Pelvic and anal fins are transparent. Caudal fin is dark gray.

This species occurs worldwide in tropical seas. In the western Atlantic it occurs from northeastern Florida to southern Brazil, including the Gulf of Mexico and the Caribbean Sea. It is oceanic, rarely captured near shore, and it is not common in the western Gulf of Mexico. Maximum known size is 180 mm SL.

REFERENCES: Bruun 1935; Parin 1986; C. R. Robins et al. 1986.

Fodiator acutus   (Valenciennes 1847)

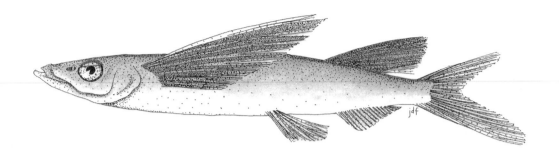

Fodiator acutus is robust and compressed posteriorly, with a long, acute snout and relatively short pelvic fins. It is distinguished from the other species of the family by the following combination of characters. Snout is longer than eye diameter. Mouth is of moderate size but does not extend to anterior margin of eye, and lower jaw extends slightly beyond upper jaw. Jaw teeth are small, conical, and in narrow bands. Gill rakers on first arch number about 29. Snout length is 9.1% to 10%, head length is 26.2% to 27.8%, eye diameter is 7.1% to 8%, interorbital width is 7.1% to 7.5%, body depth is 20.9% to 23.5%, snout to dorsal fin origin is 72.4% to 74.7%, snout to pelvic fin origin is 57.3% to 59.4%, snout to anal fin origin is 75% to 77.5%, pectoral fin length is 48.2% to 50.9%, and pelvic fin length is 14.6% to 16.7% of SL. Pectoral fin fails to reach origin of dorsal fin and has 14 to 16 rays, with first ray unbranched. Dorsal fin is elevated (longest rays reach 18.1% to 21.3% of SL) and has 10 or 11 rays. Anal fin originates behind dorsal fin origin and has 11 rays. Lower caudal fin lobe is only slightly longer than upper lobe. Scales above lateral line number 5, and predorsal scales number 21 to 24. Vertebrae number 38 or 39. Color is dark dorsally and silvery ventrally, with pectoral fin uniformly gray and pelvic and anal fins transparent. Dorsal fin is dusky and grades to black near tip, with distal margin transparent. Caudal fin is grayish, with membranes slightly darker than rays.

This species occurs in the tropical Atlantic and eastern Pacific. In the western Atlantic it occurs from Suriname, the West Indies, and in the western Gulf of Mexico at Isla de Lobos, near Veracruz. This is a coastal species. Maximum known size is 250 mm SL.

REFERENCES: Bruun 1935; Castro-Aguirre and Márquez-Espinoza 1981.

Hirundichthys affinis   (Günther 1866)
Fourwing flyingfish

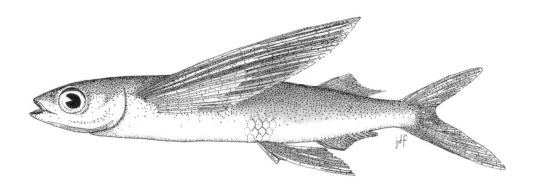

Hirundichthys affinis is relatively slender, with relatively long pelvic fins, and dorsal and anal fins similar in position and size. It is distinguished from the other species of the family by the following combination of characters. Snout is acute and shorter than eye diameter. Mouth is oblique and nearly reaches anterior margin of eye; lower jaw extends slightly beyond upper jaw. Jaw teeth are relatively large, conical, and unicuspid. Palatine teeth are absent. Gill rakers on first arch number 26 to 30. Snout length is 5.8% to 6.6%, head length is 23.3% to 24.6%, eye diameter is 6.7% to 7.5%, interdorsal width is 7.5% to 8.7%, body depth is 14.7% to 18.2%, snout to dorsal fin origin is 71.2% to 74.7%, snout to pelvic fin origin is 57.2% to 61.5%, snout to anal fin origin is 71.3% to 75.6%, pectoral fin length is 61.5% to 68.6%, and pelvic fin is 25.7% to 28.3% of SL. Pectoral fin extends beyond dorsal fin base and has 17 or 18 rays. Dorsal fin is low (longest ray ranges from 7.6% to 9.1% of SL) and has 11 or 12 rays. Anal fin originates slightly anterior to slightly posterior to dorsal fin origin and has 11 to 13 rays. Scales above lateral line number 5 to 7, and predorsal scales number 28 to 33. Color is dark dorsally and silvery ventrally. Dorsal fin is transparent. Pectoral fin is dusky, with transparent area near middle of fin.

This species occurs in the tropical Atlantic. In the western Atlantic it occurs from Virginia to northern Brazil, including the Gulf of Mexico and the Caribbean Sea. Maximum known size is 224 mm SL.

REFERENCES: Bruun 1935; Uyeno et al. 1983; Parin 1986; C. R. Robins et al. 1986; Cervigón 1991; Boschung 1992.

Hirundichthys rondeletii (Valenciennes 1847)
Blackwing flyingfish

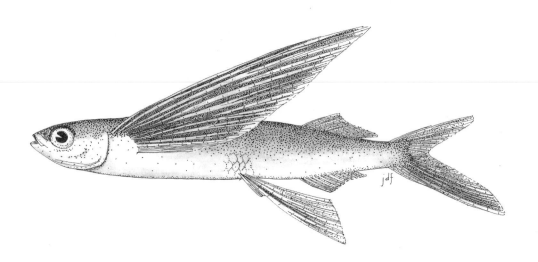

Hirundichthys rondeletii is relatively slender, with relatively long pelvic fins, and dorsal and anal fins similar in position and size. It is distinguished from the other species of the family by the following combination of characters. Snout is acute and shorter than eye diameter. Mouth is oblique and nearly reaches anterior margin of eye; lower jaw extends slightly beyond upper jaw. Jaw teeth are relatively large, conical, and unicuspid. Palatine teeth are absent. Gill rakers on first arch number 25 to 29. Snout length is 4.4% to 5.1%, head length is 20.6% to 21.5%, eye diameter is 6.4% to 7.2%, interorbital width is 7.7% to 9.1%, body depth is 13.3% to 14.9%, snout to dorsal fin origin is 71.2% to 73.8%, snout to pelvic fin origin is 58.1% to 61.6%, snout to anal fin origin is 72.6% to 75.3%, pectoral fin length is 72.2% to 76.3%, and pelvic fin length is 30.9% to 33.5% of SL. Pectoral fin extends beyond dorsal fin base and has 16 to 19 rays.

Dorsal fin is low (longest ray is 9.3% to 10.3% of SL) and has 11 or 12 rays. Anal fin originates below or slightly posterior to dorsal fin origin and has 11 to 13 rays. Scales above lateral line number 7, and predorsal scales number 27 to 30. Color is dark dorsally and silvery ventrally. Dorsal fin is dusky, and pectoral fin is bluish black with narrow transparent posterior margin. Juveniles have transparent dorsal fin with dark area near distal edge.

This species occurs worldwide in the tropical seas. In the western Atlantic it occurs from Massachusetts and Bermuda to southern Brazil, including the Gulf of Mexico and the Caribbean Sea. Eggs have numerous filaments. Maximum known size is 250 mm SL.

REFERENCES: Bruun 1935 (as *Danichthys rondeletii*); Hoese and Moore 1977; Parin 1986; C. R. Robins et al. 1986; Boschung 1992.

Parexocoetus brachypterus (Richardson 1846)
Sailfin flyingfish

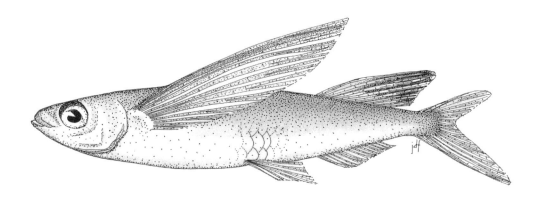

Parexocoetus brachypterus is relatively robust, with relatively short pectoral fins and a long dorsal fin. It is distinguished from the other species of the family by the following combination of characters. Snout is relatively blunt and slightly shorter than eye diameter. Mouth is slightly oblique and fails to reach anterior margin of eye. Jaw teeth are relatively large, conical, and unicuspid. Palatine teeth are minute. Gill rakers on first arch number 28 to 32. Snout length is 4.8% to 6.1%, head length is 22.8% to 24.2%, eye diameter is 7.4% to 8%, interorbital width is 7.2% to 7.6%, body depth is 16.9% to 19.9%, snout to dorsal fin origin is 68% to 71.1%, snout to pelvic fin origin is 52.3% to 55.4%, and snout to anal fin origin is 69.7% to 72.9% of SL. Pectoral fin extends to anal fin base and has 13 rays. Dorsal fin is high (longest rays are 22.8% to 25.4% of SL)

and has 12 or 13 rays. Anal fin originates under or slightly posterior to dorsal fin base and has 13 or 14 rays. Scales above lateral line number 5, and predorsal scales number 19 to 23. Vertebrae number 38 or 39. Color is dark dorsally and silvery ventrally. Dorsal fin is black posteriorly, pectoral fin is light gray, and caudal fin is light gray.

This species occurs worldwide in tropical seas. In the western Atlantic it occurs from northeastern Florida and the Bahamas to Brazil, including the Gulf of Mexico and the Caribbean Sea. It is oceanic and seldom is found closer than 640 km to shore.

REFERENCES: Bruun 1935; Hoese and Moore 1977; C. R. Robins et al. 1986; Cervigón 1991; Boschung 1992.

Prognichthys gibbifrons   (Valenciennes 1847)
Bluntnose flyingfish

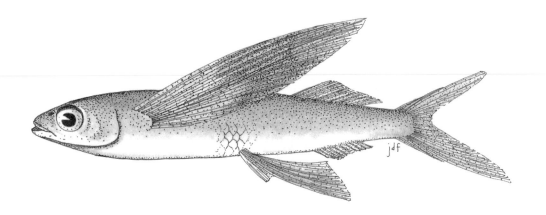

Prognichthys gibbifrons is relatively slender, with long pectoral and pelvic fins, and anal fin origin below midbase of dorsal fin base. It is distinguished from the other species of the family by the following combination of characters. Snout is slightly blunt and slightly shorter than eye diameter. Mouth is oblique and fails to reach anterior margin of eye. Jaw teeth are relatively large, conical, and unicuspid. Palatine teeth are present in juveniles but are absent in adults. Gill rakers on first arch number 21 to 27. Snout length is 4.7% to 5%, head length is 22.7% to 26.1%, eye diameter is 7.1% to 9.4%, interorbital width is 8.2% to 11.8%, body depth is 16.2% to 19.5%, snout to dorsal fin origin is 69.6% to 71.9%, snout to pelvic fin origin is 55.8% to 59.8%, snout to anal fin origin is 75.4% to 79.6%, pectoral fin length is 62.2% to 69.9%, and pelvic fin length is 29.3% to 39.9% of SL. Pectoral fin extends beyond anal fin base and has 17 to 19 rays, and

first 2 rays are unbranched. Dorsal fin is low (length of longest ray is 8.7% to 11.3% of SL) and has 12 or 13 rays. Anal fin originates at about midlength of dorsal fin base and has 9 or 10 rays. Scales above lateral line number 6 or 7, and predorsal scales number 20 to 24. Vertebrae number 42 or 43. Color is dark dorsally and silvery ventrally. Pectoral fin is dusky to about midlength and dark from midlength to tip. Dorsal fin is transparent. Dorsal fin of juveniles is dusky.

This species occurs in the western Atlantic from Massachusetts to Brazil, including the Gulf of Mexico and the Caribbean Sea. Adults are oceanic, and juveniles occur near shore. Maximum known size is 182 mm SL.

REFERENCES: Bruun 1835; Hoese and Moore 1977; C. R. Robins et al. 1986; Boschung 1992.

HEMIRAMPHIDAE Halfbeaks

Halfbeaks are elongate, nearly round anteriorly to laterally compressed posteriorly, with lower jaw extended into long beak in most species and pectoral fins short to moderately long. They are distinguished from the other families of the order by the following combination of characters. Snout is moderately long. Premaxilla is short and triangular in shape. Teeth in jaws are small, tricuspid or unicuspid, and in several rows. Lower jaw is elongate in juveniles of all genera and in adults of most species. Single nasal opening on each side of head is located anterior to eye and consists of a pitlike depression with protruding tentacle. Eye is large and laterally located. Opercular opening extends from dorsal margin of isthmus and is free of isthmus. Gill rakers are well developed on first and second arches in all but one genus and number 11 to 78 on first arch. Third pair of upper pharyngeal bones are fused into plate. Pectoral fin is high on flank and has 7 to 14 rays. Single dorsal fin is posteriorly located and has 8 to 25 rays and no spines. Pelvic fin is abdominal and consists of 1 unbranched and 5 branched rays. Anal fin has 8 to 25 rays and no spines. Caudal peduncle is of moderate length and is moderately slender. Caudal fin is emarginate to forked, with lower lobe slightly to greatly longer than upper lobe. Scales are cycloid and large. Swim bladder does not extend into hemal canal. Lateral line is complete and extends along ventral margin of body to tail, with branch to pectoral fin origin. Vertebrae number 37 to 73.

Halfbeaks occur worldwide in tropical to warm temperate epipelagic seas. Some species are restricted to freshwater in tropical areas. All species inhabit surface waters and are capable of leaping from the water. Food consists of algae, floating sea grasses, small crustaceans, and small fishes. Eggs are demersal, with adhesive filaments that attach to floating and anchored vegetation. Larvae are pelagic. There are about 85 species in 12 genera, and 7 species in 5 genera occur in the Gulf of Mexico.

Key to the Species of the Gulf of Mexico
(Adapted from Collette 1978c; pers. com., May 3, 1995)

1a. Lower jaw not greatly elongate. 2

1b. Lower jaw greatly elongate. 3

2a. Gill rakers on first arch 19 to 23; pectoral fin short, usually with 12 to 14 rays . . . . *Chriodorus atherinoides* p. 957

2b. Gill rakers on first arch 30 to 36; pectoral fin long (30% to 35% of SL), with 11 to 13 rays
. . . . *Oxyporhamphus micropterus* p. 963

3a. Dorsal fin rays 21 to 24; anal fin rays 20 to 24; pectoral fin very long (25% to 28% of SL), usually with 7 or 8 rays
. . . . *Euleptorhamphus velox* p. 958

3b. Dorsal fin rays 11 to 17; anal fin rays 10 to 18; pectoral fin short, with 9 to 13 rays 4

4a. Caudal fin deeply forked; scales absent on snout; preorbital ridge absent; anal fin rays usually 11 to 13. 5

4b. Caudal fin slightly forked; scales present on snout; pre-orbital ridge well developed; anal fin rays usually 14 to 18
. . . . 6

5a. Pectoral fin extending anterior to anterior margin of nasal pit when bent forward (length is 18.5% to 22.2% of SL); anal fin rays 10 or 13; gill rakers 31 to 37
. . . .*Hemiramphus balao* p. 959

5b. Pectoral fin not extending to anterior margin of nasal pit when bent forward (length is 15.6% to 18.9% of SL); anal fin rays 11 or 15; gill rakers 29 to 34
. . . . *Hemiramphus brasiliensis* p. 960

6a. Gill rakers on first arch 31 to 40 (usually 33 or more); gill rakers on second arch 20 to 30 (usually 25 or more); pectoral fin rays 10 or 13; preorbital length greater than 70% of orbital diameter . . . . *Hyporhamphus meeki* p. 961

6b. Gill rakers on first arch 26 to 35 (usually 32 or fewer); gill rakers on second arch 19 to 28 (usually 24 or fewer); pectoral fin rays 9 or 12; preorbital length less than 70% of orbit diameter . . . . *Hyporhamphus unifasciatus* p. 962

Chriodorus atherinoides   Goode and Bean 1882
Hardhead halfbeak

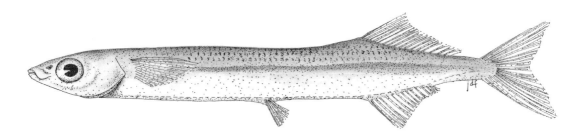

Chriodorus atherinoides is elongate and moderately compressed, with a short, rounded lower jaw; a rounded snout; and a symmetrical caudal fin. It is distinguished from the other species of the family by the following combination of characters. Jaw teeth are tricuspid and arranged in narrow bands. Gill rakers on first arch number 19 to 23. Snout is 6% to 6.7%, head length is 20.2% to 21.3%, head width is 8.3% to 9%, orbit diameter is 5.1% to 6.3%, interorbital width is 5.5% to 5.9%, height of anterior dorsal fin lobe is 9.4% to 12.6%, height of anterior anal fin lobe is 8% to 11.5%, pectoral fin length is 12.9% to 15.1%, and pelvic fin length is 9.3% to 10.2% of SL. Pectoral fin is relatively short and has 12 to 14 rays. Dorsal fin is emarginate and has 15 to 18 rays. Anal fin is similar to dorsal fin and has 15 to 17 rays. Caudal peduncle is slender. Caudal fin is moderately forked and has equally developed upper and lower lobes. Body and cheeks are covered with large deciduous scales. Lateral scale rows number 51 to 55, and vertebrae number 49 or 50. Color is translucent olive or tan dorsally, with dark spots on scales forming streaks, and silvery ventrally. Narrow lateral stripe runs from operculum to caudal peduncle and is widest under dorsal fin. Fins are transparent.

This species occurs in the western North Atlantic from the east coast of Florida to Belize, including the southern Gulf of Mexico, the Bahamas, and Cuba. It is a nearshore species and is occasionally present in freshwater. Food consists of algae. Maximum known size is 164 mm TL.

REFERENCES: Hubbs 1936; Böhlke and Chaplin 1968; C. R. Robins et al. 1986.

Euleptorhamphus velox   Poey 1868
Flying halfbeak

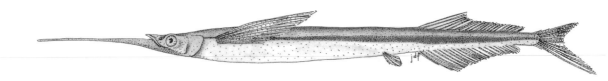

Euleptorhamphus velox is elongate and ribbonlike, with a very long, pointed lower jaw; very long pectoral fins; and a symmetrical caudal fin. It is distinguished from the other species of the family by the following combination of characters. Jaw teeth are arranged in bands and are very weak, with those of lower jaw tricuspid. Gill rakers on first arch number 26 to 35. Snout length is 4% to 6.7%, head length is 12.4% to 15.1%, head width is 3.4% to 4.4%, orbit diameter is 3.1% to 3.9%, interorbital width is 2.6% to 3.6%, height of anterior dorsal fin lobe is 6.8% to 11.8%, height of anterior anal fin lobe is 6.8% to 10.7% of SL. Pectoral fin length is 25% to 28%, and pelvic fin length is 3% to 3.7% of SL. Pectoral fin has 7 long rays and 1 short ray. Dorsal fin is relatively long based and has 21 to 24 rays. Anal fin originates posterior to dorsal fin origin and has 20 to 24 rays. Caudal peduncle is relatively slender and compressed. Caudal fin is moderately forked, with ventral lobe greatly exceeding dorsal lobe. Body and cheek are covered with moderately large cycloid scales. Vertebrae number 71 to 73. Color is olivaceous dorsally and silvery ventrally.

The flying halfbeak occurs in the tropical and subtropical Atlantic. In the western Atlantic it occurs from Rhode Island to Recife, Brazil, including Bermuda, the Caribbean Sea, and the Gulf of Mexico. It is an offshore species capable of leaping from the water and gliding for short distances. Maximum known size is 281 mm TL.

REFERENCES: Collette 1965; Bright and Cashman 1974; G. B. Smith et al. 1975; Hoese and Moore 1977; C. R. Robins et al. 1986; Cervigón 1991; Boschung 1992.

Hemiramphus balao Lesueur 1821
Balao

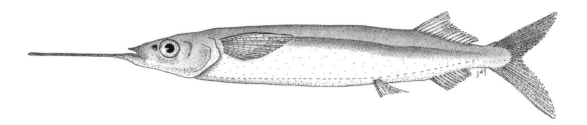

Hemiramphus balao is moderately elongate and moderately compressed, with an elongate, pointed lower jaw; relatively short pectoral fins; and a deeply forked asymmetrical caudal fin. It is distinguished from the other species of the family by the following combination of characters. Jaw teeth are arranged in bands and are weak and mostly tricuspid. Gill rakers on first arch number 31 to 37. Pectoral fin has 10 to 12 rays (usually 11). Dorsal fin is emarginate and has 11 to 15 rays. Pelvic fin extends to origin of dorsal fin. Anal fin originates posterior to dorsal fin origin and has 10 to 13 rays. Caudal peduncle is relatively stout. Caudal fin is deeply forked, with lower lobe extending beyond upper lobe. Body is covered with moderate-sized cycloid scales, but scales are absent on upper jaw and on dorsal and anal fins. Vertebrae number 54 to 56. Color is dark bluish dorsally and silvery ventrally. Moderately broad lateral stripe extends from operculum to caudal peduncle. Lower jaw is black, with fleshy red tip. Upper lobe of caudal fin is bluish violet, and lower lobe is bluish.

This species occurs in the tropical and subtropical Atlantic. In the western Atlantic it occurs from New York to southern Brazil, including the Gulf of Mexico, the Bahamas, and the Caribbean Sea. It is an inshore species often forming large schools. Food consists of small fishes and planktonic organisms. Maximum known size is 258 mm SL in the western Atlantic (B. B. Collette, pers. com., May 3, 1995).

REFERENCES: Collette 1965, 1978c; Böhlke and Chaplin 1968; Randall 1968; Hoese and Moore 1977; C. R. Robins et al. 1986; Cervigón 1991.

Hemiramphus brasiliensis (Linnaeus 1758)
Ballyhoo

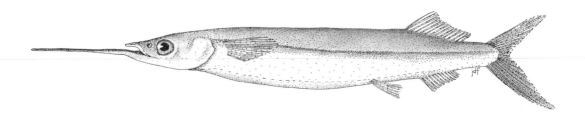

Hemiramphus brasiliensis is moderately elongate and moderately compressed, with an elongate, pointed lower jaw; relatively short pectoral fins; and a deeply forked and asymmetrical caudal fin. It is distinguished from the other species of the family by the following combination of characters. Jaw teeth are arranged in bands and are weak and mostly tricuspid. Gill rakers on first arch number 29 to 34. Pectoral fin has 10 to 12 rays. Dorsal fin is emarginate and has 12 to 15 rays. Pelvic fin extends to origin of dorsal fin. Anal fin originates posterior to dorsal fin origin and has 11 to 15 (usually 13) rays. Caudal peduncle is relatively stout. Caudal fin is deeply forked, with lower lobe considerably longer than upper lobe. Relatively large cycloid scales occur on body but are absent on upper jaw and on dorsal and anal fins. Vertebrae number 52 to 55. Color is dark bluish green dorsally and silvery white ventrally. Lower jaw is black, with fleshy red tip. Upper lobe of caudal fin is yellowish orange, and lower lobe is dusky.

This species occurs in the tropical and subtropical Atlantic. In the western Atlantic it occurs from Massachusetts to Rio de Janeiro, Brazil, including the Gulf of Mexico and the Caribbean Sea. It is an inshore species often forming large schools. Food consists of small fishes and sea grasses. Maximum known size is 290 mm SL (B. B. Collette, pers. com., May 3, 1995).

REFERENCES: Collette 1965, 1978c; Böhlke and Chaplin 1968; Hoese and Moore 1977; C. R. Robins et al. 1986; Cervigón 1991; Boschung 1992.

Hyporhamphus meeki   Banford and Collette 1993

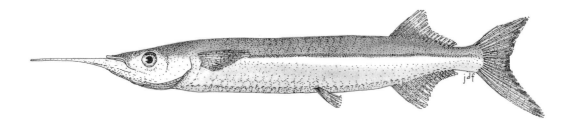

Hyporhamphus meeki is elongate, moderately compressed, and oval in cross section, with an elongated, beaklike lower jaw; preorbital ridge lateral to naris; and relatively short pectoral fins. It is distinguished from the other species of the family by the following combination of characters. Jaw teeth are arranged in bands and are weak, with those of upper jaw unicuspid and those of lower jaw tricuspid. Gill rakers on first arch number 31 to 40. Snout length is 7.9% to 8.5%, head length is 22.3% to 23.4%, head width is 6.7% to 7.4%, orbit diameter is 4.6% to 5.2%, interorbital width is 5.3% to 5.5%, height of anterior dorsal fin lobe is 8% to 9.1%, height of anterior anal fin lobe is 8.5% to 8.7%, pectoral fin length is 9.3% to 12.4%, and pelvic fin length is 7.9% to 9% of SL. Pectoral fin has 10 to 13 (usually 11 or 12) rays. Dorsal fin is emarginate and has 12 to 17 (usually 14 or 15) rays. Pelvic fin fails to reach origin of dorsal fin. Anal fin is similar in size and shape to dorsal fin and has 14 to 18 (usually 16) rays. Caudal peduncle is rather slender. Caudal fin is emarginate to slightly forked, with lower lobe extending beyond upper lobe. Body, upper jaw, and dorsal and anal fins are covered with cycloid scales. Color is greenish dorsally and silvery ventrally, with three narrow black lines running from head to dorsal fin origin. Tip of lower jaw and upper lobe of caudal fin are yellowish red.

This species occurs in the western Atlantic from New Brunswick to southern Florida, along the northern Gulf of Mexico to Galveston, Texas, and off Yucatán. Until recently this species was confused with *Hy. unifasciatus.* Maximum known size is 179 mm SL.

REFERENCES: Gunter 1945; Hoese and Moore 1977; C. R. Robins et al. 1986 (all above as *Hy. unifasciatus*); Boschung 1992 (as *Hy.* sp. cf. *unifasciatus*); Banford and Collette 1993.

Hyporhamphus unifasciatus (Ranzani 1842)
Halfbeak

Hyporhamphus unifasciatus is elongate, moderately compressed, and oval in cross section, with an elongated, beaklike lower jaw; preorbital ridge lateral to naris; and relatively short pectoral fins. It is distinguished from the other species of the family by the following combination of characters. Jaw teeth are in bands and are weak, with those of upper jaw unicuspid and those of lower jaw tricuspid. Gill rakers on first arch number 26 to 35. Snout length is 8.2% to 8.8%, head length is 21.9% to 22.7%, head width is 6.9% to 7.6%, orbit diameter is 5% to 5.8%, interorbital width is 5.5% to 6.1%, anterior dorsal fin lobe is 7.5% to 10.7%, anterior anal fin lobe is 6.9% to 11.9%, pectoral fin length is 11.6% to 13.6%, and pelvic fin length is 7.3% to 8.3% of SL. Pectoral fin has 9 to 12 (usually 10 or 11) rays. Dorsal fin is emarginate and has 13 or 16 rays. Pelvic fin fails to reach origin of dorsal fin. Anal fin is similar in shape and size to dorsal fin and has 14 to 18 rays. Caudal peduncle is moderately slender. Caudal fin is emarginate to slightly forked, with lower lobe extending beyond upper lobe. Body, upper jaw, and dorsal and anal fins are covered with cycloid scales. Color is greenish dorsally and silvery ventrally, with three narrow black lines running from head to origin of dorsal fin. Fleshy tip of lower jaw is yellowish red.

This species occurs in the western Atlantic from Bermuda and southern Florida to Uruguay, including the Gulf of Mexico off the west coast of Florida and off Veracruz, and the Caribbean Sea. It is an inshore schooling species that often enters estuaries. Food consists of floating algae, sea grasses, small invertebrates, and fishes. Maximum known size is 270 mm TL.

REFERENCES: Beebe and Tee-Van 1933; Böhlke and Chaplin 1968; Collette 1978c; Snelson 1983; C. R. Robins et al. 1986 (in part); Cervigón 1991.

Oxyporhamphus micropterus (Valenciennes 1847)
Smallwing flyingfish

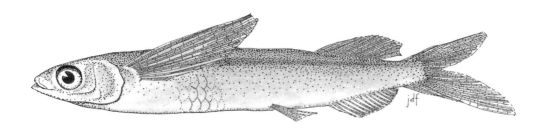

Oxyporhamphus micropterus is elongate, moderately compressed, and oval in cross section, with a short, rounded lower jaw; relatively long pectoral fins; and an asymmetrical caudal fin. It is distinguished from the other species of the family by the following combination of characters. Jaw teeth are in bands and are weak and uniserial in upper jaw. Gill rakers on first arch number 30 to 36. Snout length is about 4.4%, head length is about 18.3%, head width is about 9%, orbit diameter is about 5.3%, interorbital width is about 6.5%, anterior dorsal fin lobe is about 10.1%, anterior anal fin lobe is about 7.6%, pectoral fin length is about 32.3%, and pelvic fin length is about 12.4% of SL. Pectoral fin has 11 to 13 rays. Dorsal fin has 13 to 15 rays, and anal fin has 14 or 15 rays. Caudal peduncle is moderately narrow. Lower lobe of caudal fin extends beyond upper lobe. Body is covered with cycloid scales. Color is bluish green dorsally and silvery ventrally.

This species occurs in the western North Atlantic from northeastern Florida to northern South America, including the Gulf of Mexico and the Caribbean Sea. Maximum known size is 180 mm TL.

REFERENCES: Bruun 1935; Hoese and Moore 1977; C. R. Robins et al. 1986; Boschung 1992.

STEPHANOBERYCIFORMES

Stephanoberyciformes and the Beryciformes, Zeiformes, Gastero-steiformes, Syngnathiformes, Scorpaeniformes, Perciformes, Pleu-ronectiformes, and Tetraodontiformes make up the Percomorpha, the most derived of the ray-finned fishes. The Stephanoberyci-formes are the sister group to the remainder of the clade. Opin-ion varies as to the composition of the order (Johnson and Patter-son 1993; Moore 1993), but as interpreted herein, it consists of two superfamilies: Stephanoberycoidea, with three families in the Gulf (Gibberichthyidae, Melamphaidae, and Stephanoberycidae), and Cetomimoidea, with four families in the Gulf (Barbourisi-idae, Cetomimidae, Mirapinnidae, and Rondeletiidae).

Key to the Families of the Gulf of Mexico

(Adapted from Woods and Sonoda 1973; Paxton and Bray 1986)

1a. Pelvic fin absent . . . . Cetomimidae p. 984
1b. Pelvic fin present 2
2a. Fin spines absent 3
2b. Fin spines present. 5
3a. Pelvic fin jugular in position and with laterally projecting
    lobes . . . . Mirapinnidae p. 993
3b. Pelvic fin abdominal or subabdominal in position and
    without laterally projecting lobes 4
4a. Scales present; lateral line consists of tube pierced by small
    pores; red in life, white in preservative
    . . . . Barbourisiidae p. 982
4b. Scales absent; lateral line consists of series of vertical
    rows of papillae; color orange-brown in life, brown in
    preservative . . . . Rondeletiidae p. 995
5a. Pelvic spine absent 6
5b. Pelvic spine present . . . . Melamphaidae p. 967
6a. Dorsal fin with five or more spines
    . . . . Gibberichthyidae p. 965
6b. Dorsal fin with fewer than four spines
    . . . . Stephanoberycidae p. 980

GIBBERICHTHYIDAE

Gibberichthyids are moderately slender, nearly rectangular in lateral profile, and moderately compressed, with a very large head, subabdominal pelvic fins, and a slender and distally expanded caudal peduncle. They are distinguished from the other families of the order by the following combination of characters. Head is very cavernous, with spiny crests and skin bearing large pores. Snout is moderate in length and has concave to straight dorsal profile. Mouth is very large and slightly oblique. Eye is moderate to large. Jaw teeth are minute and in two or three irregular rows. Vomer and palatine lack teeth. Upper edge of maxilla bears single, reduced supramaxilla and fits under preorbital and anterior suborbital bones. Preoperculum has spines along anterior and posterior edges. Operculum has broad, flat, inconspicuous spine. Gill rakers on first arches are long and slender. Pectoral fin inserts low on flank. Up to seven strong, semi-isolated spines precede dorsal and anal fins. Rayed sections of dorsal and anal fins are posteriorly located. Caudal fin is forked and has six or seven upper and five to seven lower procurrent rays. Body is covered with small, deciduous cycloid scales. Lateral line scales are relatively large. Prejuveniles (kasidoron stage) possess long, elaborate, arborescent appendage attached to third pelvic fin ray. Adults lose pelvic appendage, but base of third pelvic ray is bowed and unsegmented where appendage was attached. Prejuveniles have relatively larger eyes and a shorter and more oblique snout than adults.

Gibberichthyids occur in the Atlantic, Indian, and western Pacific Oceans at bathypelagic depths. There are two species in a single genus, and one species occurs in the Gulf of Mexico.

Gibberichthys pumilus   Parr 1933

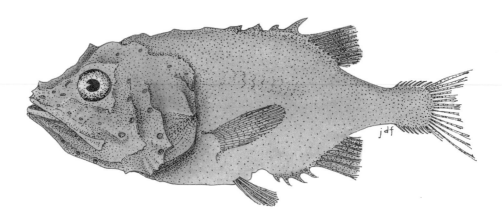

Gibberichthys pumilus is relatively slender bodied and moderately compressed, with relatively large scales. It is distinguished from the other species of the family by the following combination of characters. Snout does not protrude beyond maxillary symphysis. Gill rakers on first arch number 18 to 22. Pectoral fin has 13 to 15 rays. Dorsal fin consists of five or six semi-isolated spines and 13 to 15 rays. Anal fin has four or five semi-isolated spines and 7 to 9 rays. Pelvic fin has 1 spinous ray and 5 or 6 rays. Lateral line scales number 28. Vertebrae number 28 or 29. Color is black. Metamorphosis from the kasidoron stage to the juvenile stage occurs between 16 and 31 mm SL.

This species occurs in the western Atlantic Ocean from the east coast of Florida to northern South America, including the Gulf of Mexico, the Bahamas, and the Greater Antilles. Adults and juveniles are benthic to bathypelagic between 300 and 1,000 m. Prejuveniles are epipelagic in oceanic waters. Food consists of calanoid copepods for prejuveniles, and gammarid and hyperiid amphipods and calanoid and harpacticoid copepods for juveniles and adults. The pelvic appendage may mimic the nectostoma of siphonophores and thus reduce predation. Maximum known size is 92 mm SL, and maturity is reached at about 81 mm SL.

REFERENCES: Parr 1933; Grey 1959; C. R. Robins and de Sylva 1965 (as *Kasidoron edom*); C. R. Robins 1966 (as *K. edom*); Ebeling and Weed 1973; de Sylva and Eschmeyer 1977; Uyeno et al. 1983.

MELAMPHAIDAE

Melamphaids are oblong in lateral profile and subcylindrical, with a large head and a dorsal fin that is larger and more anteriorly located than anal fin. They are distinguished from the other families of the order by the following combination of characters. Head is cavernous and has well-developed sensory canals. Snout is very blunt, and mouth is large and oblique. Jaw teeth are minute and are arranged in single series or in bands. Eye is moderate to small in size. Pectoral fin is moderately large and is located on lower one-half of flank. Dorsal and anal fins have one to three weak spines. Pelvic fin is thoracic or subthoracic and consists of one spine and 6 to 8 rays. Caudal fin has three or four procurrent spines. Scales are thin, cycloid, usually deciduous, and occasionally rather large. Lateral line is vestigial, consisting of one or two pored scales behind shoulder girdle.

Melamphaids occur worldwide in tropical to temperate latitudes, although most species are limited to tropical waters. Half-grown juveniles and adults are mesopelagic to bathypelagic, and larvae and small juveniles are epipelagic. There are 33 species in 5 genera, and 11 species in 4 genera occur in the Gulf of Mexico.

Key to the Species of the Gulf of Mexico
(Adapted from Ebeling and Weed 1973; Ebeling 1986)

1a. Longitudinal scale rows fewer than 15; scales almost always lost, represented by large, shaggy, ill-defined scale pockets. 2
1b. Longitudinal scale rows 20 to 40; scales often lost but pockets well defined 3
2a. Gill rakers on first arch fewer than 26 . . . . *Scopelogadus mizolepis* p. 979
2b. Gill rakers on first arch 26 or more . . . . *Scopelogadus beanii* p. 978
3a. Bony ridges on top of head crestlike, with serrated margins; conspicuous medial spine on head anterior to eye (Fig. 152) 4
3b. Bony ridges on top of head not crestlike, margins more or less smooth; medial spine on head anterior to eye absent or inconspicuous. 6
4a. Eye diameter greater than 20% of head length . . . . *Poromitra megalops* p. 975
4b. Eye diameter less than 17% of head length 5
5a. Preoperculum with strong, retrorse spine on posteroventral angle about as long as anal fin base . . . . *Poromitra capito* p. 973

FIG 152

5b. Preoperculum with weak or no spine on posteroventral angle; if present, about one-half length of anal fin base . . . . *Poromitra crassiceps* p. 974

6a. Total spines and rays in dorsal fin fewer than 16; usually more than two cheek scales 7

6b. Total spines and rays in dorsal fin 17 or more; two cheek scales 8

7a. Gill rakers on first arch 19 to 25; horizontal distance between pectoral and pelvic fin insertions 5% or less of SL . . . . *Scopeloberyx robustus* p. 977

7b. Gill rakers on first arch 14 to 17; horizontal distance between pectoral and pelvic fin insertions 10% or more of SL. . . . . *Scopeloberyx opisthopterus* p. 976

8a. Gill rakers on first arch 16 or more 9

8b. Gill rakers on first arch 14 or 15 . . . . *Melamphaes typhlops* p. 972

9a. Head ridges expanded into flanges of reticulate bone; scales usually intact . . . . *Melamphaes eulepis* p. 969

9b. Head ridges not expanded into flanges of reticulate bone; scales usually missing 10

10a. Anal fin with one spine and 9 rays; dorsal fin with three spines and 16 rays . . . . *Melamphaes simus* p. 971

10b. Anal fin with one spine and 7 or 8 rays; dorsal fin with three spines and 14 or 15 (very rarely 16) rays . . . . *Melamphaes pumilus* p. 970

Melamphaes eulepis   Ebeling 1962

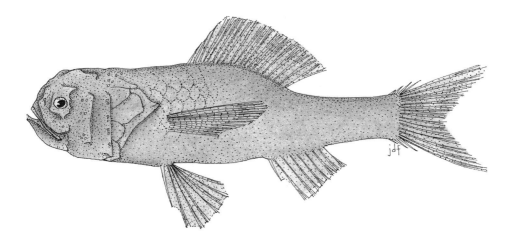

Melamphaes eulepis is oblong and subcylindrical, with expanded head ridges, a relatively long dorsal fin, and intact scales. It is distinguished from the other species of the family by the following combination of characters. Margins of the head ridges are wide and expanded. Internarial spine anterior to eye is indistinct. Teeth in jaws are arranged in bands, with widest part of band in upper jaw possessing six to eight rows of teeth and widest part of band in lower jaw possessing four to six rows. Gill rakers on first arch are moderately long and number 4 on epibranch and 14 or 15 on lower limb. Branchiostegal rays number 8. Supramaxilla is well developed. Head length is 37% to 40%, upper jaw is 17% to 19%, predorsal length is 42% to 45%, caudal peduncle length is 23% to 26%, and caudal peduncle depth is 10% to 11% of SL. Pectoral fin rays number 14 or 15.

Dorsal fin has three spines and 14 to 16 rays. Pelvic fin is located slightly behind pectoral fin base and has one spine and 7 or 8 rays. Anal fin has one spine and 8 rays. Scales are relatively thick and platelike. Scales from nape to caudal fin base number 34 to 36, and scales in diagonal series from anterior to dorsal fin origin to anterior to anal fin origin number 8. Cheek scales number 2. Head pores are small. Vertebrae number 29 or 30. Color is dark brown to blackish.

This species occurs in the Atlantic, Indian, and western Pacific Oceans below 200 m in tropical waters. In the western Atlantic it occurs in the Gulf of Mexico. Maximum known size is 38 to 46 mm SL.

REFERENCES: Ebeling 1962; Ebeling and Weed 1973.

Melamphaes pumilus   Ebeling 1962

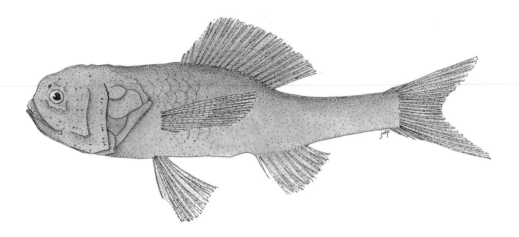

Melamphaes pumilus is oblong and subcylindrical, with a relatively smooth head and a relatively long dorsal fin. It is distinguished from the other species of the family by the following combination of characters. Margins of head ridges are thin and not expanded. Internarial spine anterior to eye is indistinct. Teeth in jaws are arranged in bands, with widest part of band in upper jaw possessing five to seven rows of teeth and widest part of band in lower jaw possessing three to five rows of teeth. Gill rakers on first arch are moderately long and number 3 or 4 on epibranch and 12 to 14 on lower limb. Branchiostegal rays number 8. Supramaxilla is well developed. Head length is 35% to 39%, upper jaw length is 16% to 18%, predorsal length is 41% to 46%, caudal peduncle length is 23% to 27%, and caudal peduncle depth is 9% to 10% of SL. Pectoral fin rays number 14 to 16. Dorsal fin has three spines and 14 to 16 rays. Pelvic fin is located slightly behind pectoral fin insertion and has one spine and 7 or 8 rays. Anal fin has one spine and 7 or 8 rays. Scales from nape to caudal fin base number 30 to 33, and scales in diagonal series from anterior to dorsal fin origin to anterior to anal fin origin number 8. Cheek scales number 2. Head pores are small. Vertebrae number 27 or 28. Color is dark brown to blackish.

This species occurs in the western and central Atlantic Ocean between 40°N and 10°N and west of 25°W to 30°W, including the Gulf of Mexico and the Caribbean Sea. Adults are generally found between 300 and 400 m and are rare above 100 m. Postlarvae and small juveniles are generally found between 50 and 100 m. Maximum known size is 25 mm SL.

REFERENCES: Ebeling 1962; Rass 1971; Ebeling and Weed 1973; Murdy et al. 1983.

Melamphaes simus   Ebeling 1962

Melamphaes simus is oblong and subcylindrical, with a relatively smooth head and a relatively long dorsal fin. It is distinguished from the other species of the family by the following combination of characters. Margins of head ridges are thin and not expanded. Internarial spine in front of eye is indistinct. Teeth in jaws are arranged in bands, with widest part of band in upper jaw possessing four to seven rows of teeth and widest part of band in lower jaw possessing three to five rows. Gill rakers on first arch are rather long and slender and number 3 or 4 on epibranch and 12 to 15 on lower limb. Branchiostegal rays number 8. Supramaxilla is well developed. Head length is 34% to 40%, upper jaw length is 15% to 18%, predorsal length is 41% to 45%, caudal peduncle length is 23% to 26%, and caudal peduncle depth is 9% to 12% of SL. Pectoral fin rays number 14 to 16. Dorsal fin has three spines and 15 to 17 rays. Pelvic fin is located slightly behind pectoral fin insertion and has one spine and 7 rays. Anal fin has one spine and 8 or 9 rays. Scales in lateral series number 32 to 36, and scales in diagonal series from anterior to dorsal fin origin to anterior to anal fin origin number 10 or 11. Cheek scales number 2. Head pores are small. Vertebrae number 28 to 30. Color is dark brown to blackish.

This species occurs in the Atlantic, Indian, and western and central Pacific Oceans. In the western Atlantic it occurs in the Gulf of Mexico and the Caribbean Sea. Adults are generally found below 100 or 200 m. Postlarvae and juveniles occur between 35 and 40 m. Maximum known size is 29 mm SL.

REFERENCES: Ebeling 1962; Rass 1971; Ebeling and Weed 1973; Murdy et al. 1983.

Melamphaes typhlops   (Lowe 1843)

Melamphaes typhlops is oblong, subcylindrical, and relatively large, with a smooth head and a moderately long dorsal fin. It is distinguished from the other species of the family by the following combination of characters. Margins of head ridges are not expanded, and spine is lacking in front of eye. Teeth in upper jaw are arranged in band six or seven teeth wide at greatest width and those in lower jaw are arranged in band four to seven teeth wide at greatest width. Gill rakers on first arch are very short and slender, with 3 or 4 on epibranch and 11 or 12 on lower limb. Supramaxilla is well developed. Head length is 33% to 36%, upper jaw length is 16% to 17%, predorsal length is 40% to 41%, caudal peduncle length is 21% to 25%, and caudal peduncle depth is 10% to 12% of SL. Pectoral fin has 14 to 16 rays. Dorsal fin has three slender spines and 14 or 15 rays. Pelvic fin inserts behind pectoral fin insertion and has one spine and 7 rays. Anal fin originates posterior to last dorsal fin ray and has one spine and 8 rays. Scales in lateral series from dorsal opercular margin to caudal fin base number 29 to 32, and scales in diagonal series from just anterior to dorsal fin to just anterior to anal fin number 8. Cheek scales number 2. Vertebrae number 25 to 27. Color is dark brown to black.

This species occurs in the Atlantic Ocean from tropical to warm temperate waters at mesopelagic to bathypelagic depths. In the western Atlantic it occurs from Bermuda and the eastern coast of the United States to the Gulf of Mexico. Adults are generally caught below 500 to 600 m, juveniles are found below 150 m, and postlarvae occur up to 50 m below the surface. Maximum known size is 100 mm SL.

REFERENCES: Grey 1959 (as *M. microps*); Ebeling 1962; Ebeling and Weed 1973; Murdy et al. 1983; Maul 1986c.

Poromitra capito   Goode and Bean 1883

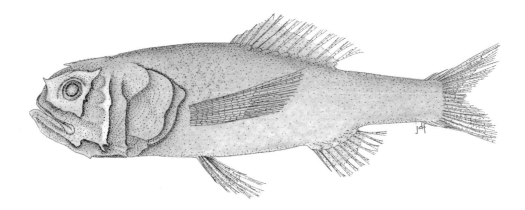

Poromitra capito is oblong and subcylindrical, with crestlike bony ridges on head, a medial spine between nares, and a relatively short dorsal fin. It is distinguished from the other species of the family by the following combination of characters. Serrated crests on head have relatively long, strong antrorse spines. Internarial spine is slightly recurved to hooklike. Preoperculum has 16 to 24 spines on horizontal margin, with one at corner largest. Jaw teeth are in single row. Gill rakers on first arch number 10 or 11 on epibranch and 22 to 24 on lower limb. Branchiostegal rays number 8. Head length is 39% to 43%, upper jaw length is 16% to 18%, eye diameter is 5% to 6%, predorsal length is 50% to 54%, and caudal peduncle length is 22% to 24% of SL. Pectoral fin has 13 or 14 rays. Dorsal fin has 3 spines and 11 or 12 rays. Pelvic fin inserts slightly anterior to pectoral fin insertion and has 1 spine and 7 rays. Anal fin originates under third- to fifth-from-last dorsal fin ray and has 1 spine and

8 or 9 rays. Scales are adherent and strongly sculptured, with widely spaced circuli. Horizontal scale rows from upper opercular margin to base of caudal fin number 25 to 36. Cheek scales number 3 or 4. Head pores are moderate to large and usually single. Vertebrae number 25 or 26. Color is dark brown to black.

This species occurs in the subtropical North Atlantic. In the western Atlantic it occurs from 40°N to 10°N, including the Gulf of Mexico and the Caribbean Sea. Adults are most common below 400 to 500 m, and postlarvae and juveniles are most common between 50 and 100 m and are generally deeper during the day than during the night. Spawning peaks off Bermuda during November and December. Maximum known size is 99 mm SL.

REFERENCES: Ebeling 1962; Rass 1971; Ebeling and Weed 1973; Maul 1986c; Keene et al. 1987.

Poromitra crassiceps   (Günther 1878)

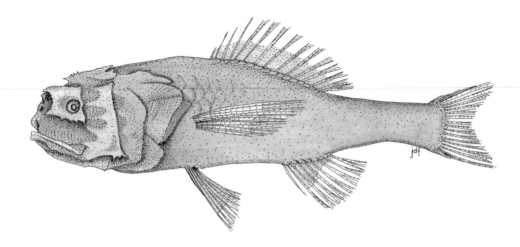

Poromitra crassiceps is oblong and subcylindrical, with crestlike ridges on head and a medial spine anterior to eyes. It is distinguished from the other species of the family by the following combination of characters. Serrated crests on top of head possess relatively short, weak antrorse spines. Internarial spine is straight and projects forward. Jaw teeth are in single row. Gill rakers on first arch number 8 to 12 on epibranch and 18 to 24 on lower limb. Head length is 34% to 43%, upper jaw length is 15% to 19%, eye length is 4% to 6%, body depth is 25% to 32%, predorsal length is 44% to 54%, and caudal peduncle length is 22% to 31% of SL. Pectoral fin has 13 to 15 rays. Dorsal fin has three slender spines and 11 to 14 rays. Pelvic fin inserts under pectoral fin insertion and has one spine and 7 rays. Anal fin originates under fifth- to eighth-from-last dorsal fin ray and has one spine and 8 to 11 rays. Scales on body are deciduous and weakly sculptured, with widely spaced circuli. Horizontal scale rows number 24 to 31. Head pores are moderate to large in size and generally simple. Vertebrae number 26 to 29. Color is dark brown to black.

This species occurs worldwide in tropical to temperate seas at mesopelagic to bathypelagic depths. In the western Atlantic it occurs from the eastern seaboard of North America to the Caribbean Sea, including the Gulf of Mexico. Adults mainly occur below 600 m, and juveniles and postlarvae are found in shallower water. Maximum known size is 156 mm SL.

REFERENCES: Ebeling 1962; Ebeling and Weed 1973; Murdy et al. 1983.

Poromitra megalops   (Lütken 1877)

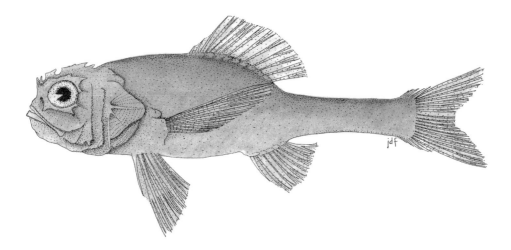

Poromitra megalops is oblong and subcylindrical, with crestlike bony ridges on head, a medial spine between nares, and a relatively short dorsal fin. It is distinguished from the other species of the family by the following combination of characters. Serrated crests on head have relatively short, weak antrorse spines. Internarial spine is straight and projects forward. Jaw teeth are in single series. Preoperculum has five to nine spines on horizontal margin. Gill rakers on first arch number 6 to 8 on epibranch and 15 to 20 on lower limb. Branchiostegal rays number 8. Head length is 30% to 38%, upper jaw length is 14% to 18%, eye diameter is 8% to 10%, predorsal length is 42% to 49%, body depth is 25% to 33%, caudal peduncle length is 30% to 37%, and caudal peduncle depth is 8% to 10% of SL. Pectoral fin has 13 to 15 rays. Dorsal fin has two or three spines and 10 to 12 rays. Pelvic fin inserts anterior to pectoral fin insertion and has one spine and 7 rays. Anal fin originates under about middle of dorsal fin base and has one spine and 8 to 10 rays. Scales on body are deciduous and weakly sculptured, with indistinct circuli. Horizontal scale rows number 25 to 29. Cheek scales number 3 or 4. Head pores are moderate to large and generally single. Vertebrae number 26 to 30. Color is dark brown to black.

This species occurs worldwide in tropical waters. In the western Atlantic it occurs off Bermuda and in the Gulf of Mexico and the Caribbean Sea. Adults are most common below 400 to 500 m, and postlarvae and juveniles are most common between 150 and 200 m. Maximum known size is 62 mm SL.

REFERENCES: Ebeling 1962, 1986; Rass 1971; Ebeling and Weed 1973; Murdy et al. 1983; Maul 1986c; Keene et al. 1987.

Scopeloberyx opisthopterus   (Parr 1933)

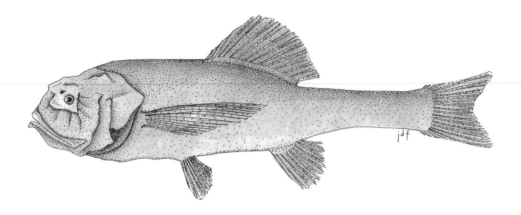

Scopeloberyx opisthopterus is oblong and sub-cylindrical, with a relatively smooth head, large head pores, and pelvic fins located relatively far behind pectoral fin insertions. It is distinguished from the other species of the family by the following combination of characters. Margins of head ridges are not serrate, and inter-narial spine is absent. Teeth in jaws are arranged in bands up to three to five tooth rows wide at greatest width. Gill rakers on first arch are long and narrow and number 2 to 4 on epibranch and 10 to 13 on lower limb. Supramaxilla is well developed. Head length is 30% to 36%, upper jaw length is 15% to 20%, eye diameter is 1.8% to 3.6%, body depth is 23% to 27%, predorsal length is 46% to 52%, horizontal distance between pectoral and pelvic fin insertions is 10% or more, caudal peduncle length is 25% to 30%, and caudal peduncle depth is 6% to 11% of SL. Pectoral fin has 12 to 15 rays. Dorsal fin has two or three spines and 11 or 12 rays. Pelvic fin has one spine and 7 or 8 rays. Anal fin originates under last or second-to-last dorsal fin ray and has one spine and 7 or 8 rays. Scales in lateral series from upper opercular margin to caudal fin base number 23 to 25, and cheek scales number 3 or 4. Vertebrae number 24 to 27. Color is dark brown to black.

This species occurs in the Atlantic, Indian, and eastern Pacific Oceans in tropical waters at mesopelagic and bathypelagic depths. In the western Atlantic it occurs off Bermuda and in the Gulf of Mexico. Adults generally occur below 500 to 600 m. Maximum known size is 37 mm SL.

REFERENCES: Parr 1933; Ebeling 1962, 1986; Ebeling and Weed 1973; Murdy et al. 1983; Maul 1986c; Keene et al. 1987.

Scopeloberyx robustus   (Günther 1887)

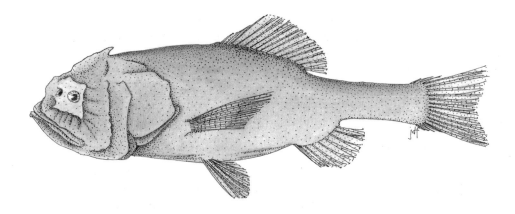

Scopeloberyx robustus is fusiform and sub-cylindrical, with a relatively smooth head, large head pores, and pelvic fins located close behind pectoral fin insertions. It is distinguished from the other species of the family by the following combination of characters. Margins of head ridges are not serrate, and internarial spine is absent. Jaw teeth are arranged in bands up to two to four teeth wide. Gill rakers on first arch are long and number 5 to 7 on epibranch and 15 to 19 on lower limb. Supramaxilla is well developed. Head length is 36% to 45%. upper jaw length is 19% to 24%, eye diameter is 2.1% to 4.4%, body depth is 24% to 31%, predorsal length is 45% to 55%, horizontal distance between pectoral and pelvic fin insertions is 5% or less, caudal peduncle length is 21% to 27%, and caudal peduncle depth is 8%

to 11% of SL. Pectoral fin has 12 to 14 rays. Dorsal fin has two or three spines and 10 to 13 rays. Pelvic fin has one spine and 7 or 8 rays. Anal fin originates under second- or third-to-last dorsal fin ray and has one spine and 7 or 8 rays. Scales in lateral series from upper opercular margin to caudal peduncle number 24 to 27, and cheek scales number 3 or 4. Vertebrae number 23 to 27. Color is dark brown to black.

This species occurs worldwide in tropical to temperate seas at mesopelagic and bathypelagic depths. In the western Atlantic it occurs from the eastern coast of North America to the Caribbean Sea, including the Gulf of Mexico. Maximum known size is 73 mm SL.

REFERENCES: Ebeling 1962, 1986; Ebeling and Weed 1973; Murdy et al. 1983.

Scopelogadus beanii   (Günther 1887)

Scopelogadus beanii is oblong and subcylindrical, with a relatively smooth and blunt head, a relatively short dorsal fin, and relatively large scales. It is distinguished from the other species of the family by the following combination of characters. Ridges on head are smooth, and internarial spine is absent. Jaw teeth are in single series. Gill rakers on first arch number 8 to 10 on epibranch and 18 to 22 on lower limb. Branchiostegal rays number 8. Head length is 32% to 38%, upper jaw length is 13% to 16%, body depth is 27% to 31%, caudal peduncle length is 33% to 38%, and caudal peduncle depth is 10% to 12% of SL. Pectoral fin has 14 to 16 rays. Dorsal fin has two spines and 10 or 11 rays. Pelvic fin inserts slightly anterior to pectoral fin insertion and has one spine and 7 rays. Anal fin originates under fifth- or sixth-from-last dorsal fin ray and has one spine and 7 to 9 rays. Scales are deciduous, and scale pockets are ill-defined. Horizontal scale rows from upper opercular margin to caudal fin base number 12 or less. Cheek scales are absent. Head pores are minute to moderate in size and generally single. Vertebrae number 25 to 27. Color is dark brown to black.

This species occurs in the Atlantic, southern Indian, and western Pacific Oceans. In the western Atlantic it occurs in the waters of the Gulf Stream and in the southern Gulf of Mexico. There is only a single record from the Gulf of Mexico. Adults are mesopelagic between 800 and 1,000 m, juveniles occur between 500 and 600 m, and postlarvae occur at about 150 m. Maximum known size is 122 mm SL.

REFERENCES: Ebeling 1962, 1986; Ebeling and Weed 1963, 1973.

Scopelogadus mizolepis   (Günther 1878)

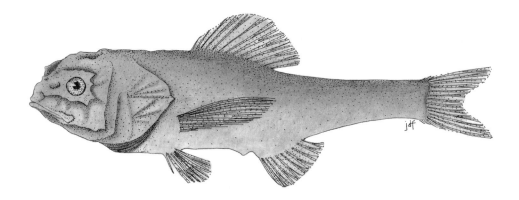

Scopelogadus mizolepis is oblong and sub-cylindrical, with a relatively smooth head, a relatively short dorsal fin, and relatively large scales. It is distinguished from the other species of the family by the following combination of characters. Ridges on head are smooth, and internarial spine is absent. Jaw teeth are in single series. Gill rakers on first arch number 6 to 8 on epibranch and 15 to 18 on lower limb. Branchiostegal rays number 8. Head length is 38% to 40%, upper jaw length is 12% to 16%, body depth is 23% to 27%. caudal peduncle length is 30% to 37%, and caudal peduncle depth is 10% to 12% of SL. Pectoral fin has 14 to 16 rays. Dorsal fin has two spines and 10 to 12 rays. Pelvic fin inserts slightly anterior to pectoral fin insertion and has one spine and 7 rays. Anal fin originates under fourth- to sixth-from-last dorsal fin ray and has one spine and

8 or 9 rays. Scales are deciduous, and scale pockets are ill defined. Horizontal scale rows from upper opercular margin to caudal fin base number 12 or less. Cheek scales are absent. Head pores are minute to moderate in size and generally single. Vertebrae number 24 to 26. Color is dark brown to black.

This species occurs worldwide in tropical to warm temperate seas. In the western Atlantic it occurs from the Caribbean Sea to 30°N, including the Gulf of Mexico. Adults are most common below 500 m, and postlarvae and juveniles are most common from 50 to 300 m. Maximum known size is 94 mm SL.

REFERENCES: Ebeling 1962; Rass 1971; Ebeling and Weed 1963, 1973; Uyeno et al. 1983; Keene et al. 1987.

STEPHANOBERYCIDAE

Stephanoberycids are oblong and subcylindrical, with a large head and similarly shaped and positioned dorsal and anal fins. They are distinguished from the other families of the order by the following combination of characters. Head has well-developed sensory canals and generally has well-developed serrated ridges. Snout is blunt, and mouth is large and horizontal to slightly oblique. Jaw teeth are minute, setiform, and arranged in wide bands. Eye is of moderate size. Pectoral fin is located at midflank and is of moderate size. Dorsal fin has zero to three weak spines preceding rays. Pelvic fin is subabdominal to abdominal in position and consists of 5 rays. Anal fin has one to three weak spines preceding rays. Caudal fin has 8 or 9 procurrent rays. Body is covered with small ctenoid scales (except for one genus) that have one to six large, sharp, outwardly directed spines. Lateral line is well developed, and lateral line scales have reduced ctenii.

Stephanoberycids occur in the tropical and subtropical seas of the Atlantic, Indian, and western Pacific Oceans at bathypelagic or abyssal depths. There are three species in separate genera, and one of these occurs in the Gulf of Mexico.

Stephanoberyx monae   Gill 1883

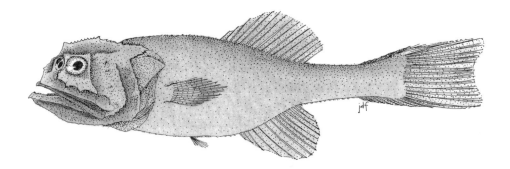

Stephanoberyx monae is spindle shaped, with relatively large dorsal and anal fins. It is distinguished from the other species in the family by the following combination of characters. Head is strongly convex and has prominent serrated ridges. Snout profile is blunt but does not extend beyond lower jaw. Single supramaxilla on dorsal margin of maxilla is triangular shaped and has two or more rows of spines along ventral edge. Gill rakers on first arch number 12 to 15 on epibranch and 25 to 27 on lower limb. Head length is 36%, length of upper jaw is 23% to 26%, postorbital length of head is 18% to 21%, and snout to pelvic fin origin is 40% to 44% of SL. Pectoral fin has 12 or 13 rays. Dorsal fin has one to three weak spines and 11 to 13 rays. Pelvic fin is subabdominal. Anal fin usually has one to three weak spines and 11 or 12 rays. Caudal fin has 9 to 11 procurrent rays above, and 8 to 11 procurrent rays below, caudal peduncle. Scales are small, rectangular or oval shaped, with six to eight moderate-sized spines on posterior field. Vertebrae number 31 to 33. Color is black.

This species occurs in the western Atlantic from the Gulf of Mexico and the Caribbean Sea at abyssal depths. Maximum known size is 81 mm SL.

REFERENCES: Rass 1971; Ebeling and Weed 1973.

BARBOURISIIDAE

Barbourisiids are moderately elongate and relatively stout bodied, with small eyes; a large, slightly compressed head; and abdominal pelvic fins. They are distinguished from the other families of the order by the following combination of characters. Snout is long and acute, and mouth is very large, terminal, and horizontal. Jaw teeth are minute and are arranged in bands. Vomer has round tooth patch, and palatine lacks teeth. Four free gill arches are present; moderate-sized slit is located behind last gill arch. Gill rakers on first arch are slender and relatively long. Pectoral fin is small and has strongly oblique base located on lower flank. Dorsal fin originates posterior to midlength and has convex margin. Pelvic fin is located on lower side of belly and is small. Anal fin is similar in shape but slightly shorter than dorsal fin and originates slightly posterior to it. Caudal peduncle is relatively narrow and relatively long. Caudal fin is moderately broad, with emarginate posterior margin. Head and body are covered with minute embedded scales, each bearing small, single, central spine. Lateral line consists of small round pores extending from upper opercular margin to caudal fin base. Vertebrae number 40 to 43. Swim bladder is present.

Barbourisiids occur worldwide at mesopelagic and bathypelagic depths. There is a single species in the family, and it occurs in the Gulf of Mexico.

Barbourisia rufa Parr 1945

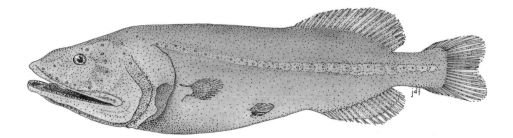

Barbourisia rufa is relatively stout bodied and slightly compressed, with small eyes, a large head, and posteriorly located dorsal and anal fins. It is distinguished from the other species of the order by the following combination of characters. Gill rakers on first arch number 5 or 6 on epibranch and 14 to 16 on lower limb. Head length is 32.9% to 35.6%, snout length is 11.2% to 11.7%, upper jaw length is 24% to 25.6%, lower jaw length is 23% to 28%, orbit diameter is 3.4% to 4%, interorbital width is 12.5%, snout to dorsal fin origin is 59.9% to 64%, length of dorsal fin base is 24% to 27%, snout to anal fin origin is 69% to 70.4%, and length of anal fin is 17.8% to 18% of SL. Pectoral fin has 13 or 14, dorsal fin has 19 to 22, pelvic fin has 6, and anal fin has 15 to 18 rays. Lateral line pores number 28 to 33. Color is bright red, with eye, operculum, and visceral cavity violet in life and unpigmented in preservative.

This species occurs worldwide at mesopelagic and bathypelagic depths. In the western Atlantic it occurs off the southeastern United States and in the northern Gulf of Mexico between 329 and 1,000 m. Maximum known size is 330 mm SL.

REFERENCES: Parr 1945; Struhsaker 1965; Rass 1971; Fitch 1979; Paxton and Bray 1986; Tolley et al. 1989.

CETOMIMIDAE Whalefishes

Whalefishes are moderately elongate to elongate, stout anteriorly, and compressed posteriorly, with minute eyes, a large cavernous head, and cavernous lateral lines. They are distinguished from the other families of the order by the following combination of characters. Snout is long and blunt to very acute. Mouth is very large, terminal to slightly inferior, and horizontal to slightly oblique. Jaw teeth are small, close-set to widely spaced, and conical to triangular in shape. Teeth generally occur in vomer and palatine. All teeth are depressible. Three or four free gill arches are present, depending on presence or absence of slit behind fourth arch. Gill rakers are modified club shaped or represented by toothed knobs, tooth plates, or gill teeth. Pectoral fin is small, is located on lower one-half of flank, and has 17 to 24 rays. Dorsal fin originates posterior to midlength, with first 4 or 5 rays short and occasionally embedded in integument. Pelvic fin is absent. Anal fin is similar in shape and opposition to dorsal fin. Caudal peduncle is moderately narrow and moderately long. Caudal fin has forked to slightly convex posterior margin. Lateral line on both head and body is usually well developed and consists of wide canals pierced by large pores in skin roofing canals. Skin is naked except for lateral line scales on trunk.

Whalefishes occur worldwide in tropical to temperate and south polar waters at bathypelagic depths. There are 20 species in nine genera, and at least 5 additional species remain to be described. There are 7 species in four genera in the Gulf of Mexico.

Key to the Species of the Gulf of Mexico

(Adapted from Harry 1952; Paxton 1989; pers. com., November 1996)

1a. Dorsal fin rays 29 to 37; anal fin rays 26 to 34; dorsal and anal fins set on peduncles higher than adjacent body; slit behind fourth gill arch very small and tubular
. . . . *Cetostoma regani* p. 989

1b. Dorsal fin rays and anal fin rays 12 to 23; dorsal and anal fin bases not set on peduncles higher than adjacent body; slit behind fourth gill arch either very long or absent 2

2a. Four free gill arches, slit behind ventral arm of fourth gill arch; gill tooth plates club shaped or domed; lateral line scales round to rectangular and flat, without dorsal and ventral projections . . . . *Ditropichthys storeri* p. 990

2b. Three free gill arches, no slit behind ventral arm of fourth gill arch; gill tooth plates contiguous or fused and flat; lateral line scales elongate and curved, with dorsal and ventral projections supporting lateral line canal. 3

3a. Jaw teeth in distinct longitudinal rows; all but new-formed teeth longer than 3 times basal tooth width; vomerine tooth patch flat and rectangular 4

3b. Jaw teeth in indistinct diagonal rows; all teeth shorter than 2 times basal tooth width; vomerine tooth patch domed and round to oval. 5

4a. Dorsal fin base 14.5% of SL; anal fin rays 18; caudal fin rays 14 . . . . *Gyrinomimus simplex* p. 992

4b. Dorsal fin base 17.6% to 24.9% of SL; anal fin rays 17; caudal fin rays 17 to 19 . . . . . *Gyrinomimus myersi* p. 991

5a. Cavernous tissue present at anus, anterior to dorsal fin, on posterior lateral line flaps, and either behind third and fourth gill arches or on caudal peduncle; posterior lateral line flaps moderate to large but not longer than 2 times pore diameter . . . . *Cetomimus teevani* p. 988

5b. Cavernous tissue restricted to anus, and occasionally anterior to dorsal fin and under anterior dorsal and anal fin rays; posterior lateral line flaps absent or very small (less than 50% of pore size). 6

6a. Cavernous tissue around anus, under anterior anal fin rays, and usually under anterior dorsal fin rays
. . . . *Cetomimus hempeli* p. 987

6b. Cavernous tissue limited to around anus and, occasionally, under anterior anal fin rays . . . . . . *Cetomimus gillii* p. 986

Cetomimus gillii   Goode and Bean 1895

Cetomimus gillii is elongate, slender, and compressed posteriorly, with a moderately large head, dorsal and anal fin bases not elevated, and posterior lateral line pores with moderate lappets or flaps. It is distinguished from the other species of the family by the following combination of characters. Dorsal profile of head is convex, and snout is acute. Jaw teeth are short, close-set, and in indistinct diagonal rows. Vomerine tooth patch is round and dome shaped. Palatine teeth are present. Ventral midline of gill arches has single, moderately long, broad, and slightly dumbbell-shaped tooth patch (copular tooth plate). Eye is very small and lacks lens. Three and one-half gill arches are present, with small filaments on fourth. First gill arch has tooth plates with small granular teeth. Pectoral fin has 16, dorsal fin has 16 to 19, and anal fin has 16 to 19 rays. Lateral line consists of broad tube pierced by 14 to 19 pores. Posterior pores have lappets or flaps covering about two-thirds of pore. Cavernous tissue is present around anus and on either side of first five anal fin rays. Color is blackish brown in preservative.

This species occurs in the western Atlantic, eastern Pacific, and Indian Oceans. In the western Atlantic it occurs off the mid-Atlantic states of the United States and from Bermuda to the Gulf of Mexico at mesopelagic and bathypelagic depths. In the Gulf of Mexico it has been captured between 900 and 1,300 m. Maximum known size is 70 mm SL.

REFERENCES: Goode and Bean 1895; Harry 1952; Paxton 1989; Tolley et al. 1989.

Cetomimus hempeli   Maul 1969

Cetomimus hempeli is elongate, slender, and compressed, with a moderately large head, dorsal and anal fin bases not elevated, and posterior lateral line pores with small flaps. It is distinguished from the other species of the family by the following combination of characters. Dorsal profile of head is convex, and snout is acute. Mouth is slightly oblique. Jaw teeth are arranged in several series and are short, pointed, and broad based. Vomerine teeth are in circular dome-shaped patch. Palatine teeth are arranged in two patches on each side. Anteriormost tooth patch on first gill arch is closer to anterior margin than to middle of copular tooth patch. Copular tooth patch is narrow. Head is 35.3%, snout is 13.5%, upper jaw length is 32.7%, interorbital width is 13.7%, snout to dorsal fin origin is 78.2%, dorsal fin base is 15.6%, anal fin base is 15.4%, and body depth is 17.9% of SL. Pectoral fin has 23, dorsal fin has 19, and anal fin has 18 rays. Lateral line consists of 20 pores, with posterior ones bearing flaps that cover less than 50% of pore. Small patch of cavernous tissue is present around anus, along first 3 or 4 dorsal fin rays, and along first 1 to 3 anal fin rays. Vertebrae number 49. Color is uniform brown, except abdominal area is blackish brown.

This species occurs in the tropical Atlantic Ocean. In the western Atlantic it occurs in the northeastern Gulf of Mexico.

References: Maul 1968; Tolley et al. 1989; John R. Paxton, pers. com., September and November 1996.

Cetomimus teevani   Harry 1952

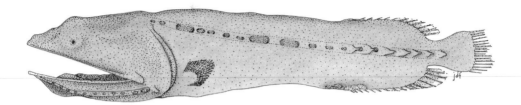

Cetomimus teevani is elongate, slender, and compressed posteriorly, with a moderately large head, dorsal and anal fin bases not elevated and relatively short, and posterior lateral line pores covered by long, narrow lappets. It is distinguished from the other species of the family by the following combination of characters. Dorsal profile of head is angular, resulting from bony projections above eye, and snout is acute. Jaw teeth are short and closely spaced in indistinct rows. Vomerine tooth patch is round and dome shaped. Palatine teeth are present. Ventral midline of gill arches has single moderately long, broad, dumbbell-shaped tooth patch. Eye is very small and lacks lens. First gill arch has tooth plates, with small granular teeth. Three free gill arches are present, with small filaments on fourth but no slit behind third arch. Head is 37.8%, snout length is 14.1%, upper jaw is 30.1%, interorbital width is 12.1%, snout to dorsal fin origin is 77.6%, dorsal fin base is 17.9%, snout to anal fin origin is 76.5%, and anal fin base is 18% of SL. Pectoral fin has 20, dorsal fin has 16, and anal fin has 17 rays. Lateral line consists of tube pierced by 18 pores, with last 7 possessing flaps on anterior margins. Patches of cavernous tissue are located around base of first dorsal fin ray, around anus, and around bases of first 4 anal fin rays, and on lateral line flaps. Vertebrae number 50. Color in preservative is uniform dark brown, with tips of fins light and inside of mouth brown.

This species occurs in the western Atlantic off Bermuda and in the Gulf of Mexico at bathypelagic depths. Maximum known size is 105 mm SL.

REFERENCES: Harry 1952; Paxton 1989.

Cetostoma regani Zugmayer 1914

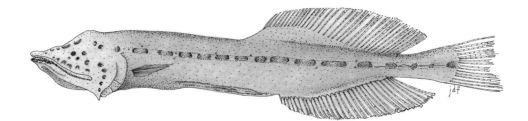

Cetostoma regani is elongate, slender, and compressed posteriorly, with a moderately long head, elevated and relatively long dorsal and anal fin bases, and numerous skin ridges along belly. It is distinguished from the other species of the family by the following combination of characters. Snout has slightly concave dorsal profile and is acute. Jaw teeth are small and are arranged in diagonal rows. Palatine teeth are present. Ventral midline of gill arches has three narrow tooth plates (copular tooth plates). Eye is minute and lacks lens. Four free gill arches are present, and slit behind fourth is restricted to tubular hole. First gill arch has 3 to 5 tooth plates on epibranch and 8 to 10 on lower limb. Head length is 22.3% to 31.4%, snout length is 7.9% to 12.5%, upper jaw length is 15.4% to 23.5%, lower jaw length is 15.9% to 24.7%, snout to dorsal fin origin is 50.5% to 60.1%, dorsal fin base length is 28.1% to 38.1%, snout to anal fin origin is 51.8% to 65.9%, and anal fin base length is 22.4% to 35.2% of SL. Pectoral fin has 20 or 21, dorsal fin has 29 to 37, and anal fin has 26 to 34 rays. Lateral line system on head consists of series of large canals with wide pores. Lateral line on trunk consists of tubes pierced by 16 to 18 pores, with posterior pores covered by flaps extending from anterior margin of pores. Lateral line scales are round, rectangular, or diamond shaped and number 15 to 17. Vertebrae number 48 to 53. Color in preservative is brown, with head light brown and mouth, gill cavities, and intestinal track light brown. In life, head is reddish brown, body is black, and fins are black with bright red margins.

This species occurs worldwide in tropical to warm temperate seas at mesopelagic and bathypelagic depths. In the western Atlantic it occurs from Florida to northern South America, including the Gulf of Mexico and the Caribbean Sea. Small specimens are found in shallower depths than large specimens and may make diurnal migrations of up to 600 m. In the Gulf of Mexico the largest specimens occur at the greatest depths. Food consists of euphausiid and decapod crustaceans. Maximum known size is 220 mm SL.

REFERENCES: Parr 1928, 1934; Paxton 1986, 1989; Tolley et al 1989.

Ditropichthys storeri   (Goode and Bean 1895)

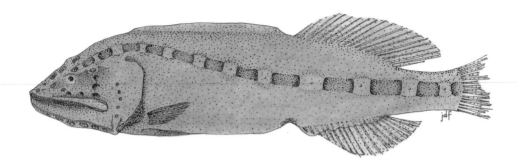

Ditropichthys storeri is moderately deep bodied and compressed posteriorly, with a relatively large head, a pair of thin dermal folds along abdomen, and anal fin lappets. It is distinguished from the other species of the family by the following combination of characters. Snout is straight in dorsal profile and moderately acute. Jaw teeth are very small and close-set in irregular diagonal rows. Vomerine tooth patch is elongate and oval shaped. Palatine bears villiform teeth. Ventral midline of gill arches has single moderately long and very broad tooth plate. Eye is very small and lacks lens. Four free gill arches are present; slit is present behind fourth gill arch. First gill arch has club-shaped gill rakers, with 3 or 4 on epibranch and 9 to 11 on lower limb. Head length is 29.1% to 34.9%, snout length is 9.4% to 14.4%, upper jaw length is 19.2% to 23.4%, lower jaw length is 19.8% to 23.3%, body depth is 20.9% to 26.6%, snout to dorsal fin origin is 63.2% to 68.7%, dorsal fin base length is 20.9% to 26.6%, snout to anal fin base is 62.4% to 70.7%, and anal fin base length is 15.1% to 19.8% of SL. Pectoral fin has 17 to 21, dorsal fin has 19 to 22, and anal fin has 15 to 18 rays. Lateral line system on head consists of shallow canals covered with skin pierced by pores. Lateral line on trunk consists of broad tube pierced by 11 to 14 pores without flaps or keels. Vertebrae number 38 to 41. Color in preservative is dark brown.

This species occurs worldwide in tropical to warm temperate seas at mesopelagic and bathypelagic depths. In the western Atlantic it occurs from New York to northern South America, including the Gulf of Mexico and the Caribbean Sea. In the Gulf of Mexico it has been captured between 800 and 2,150 m. Large specimens occur at the lower portion of the depth range, and small specimens occur at the upper portion of the depth range and may make diurnal migrations of up to 650 m. Maximum known size is 128 mm SL.

REFERENCES: Goode and Bean 1895; Parr 1934; Harry 1952; Murdy et al. 1983; Paxton 1989.

Gyrinomimus myersi Parr 1934

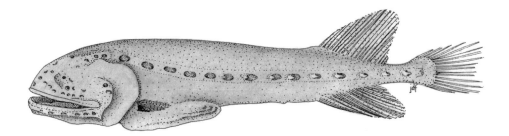

Gyrinomimus myersi is elongate, slender, and compressed posteriorly, with narrowly rectangular lateral line scales, cavernous tissue anterior to anal fin, and dorsal fin extending slightly beyond anal fin. It is distinguished from the other species of the family by the following combination of characters. Head is straight in dorsal profile, and snout is moderately acute. Jaw teeth are elongate, close-set, and in distinct longitudinal rows. Vomer has three transverse series of teeth forming triangle. Palatine has undulating series of teeth. Ventral midline of gill arches has single shield-shaped tooth plate (copular tooth plate). Eye is very small and lacks lens. First gill arch has solid, flat tooth plate covering most of lateral face of arch. Three free gill arches are present; slit is lacking behind fourth arch. Head length is 32% to 33%, snout length is 12.5%, upper jaw length is 29.3%, lower jaw length is 27.8%, interorbital width is 10.7%, body depth is 24% to 25.9%, snout to dorsal fin origin is 62% to 71.7%, dorsal fin base length is 17.6% to 24%, snout to anal fin origin is 70.5%, and anal fin base length is 15.7% to 23% of SL. Pectoral fin originates below posterior margin of operculum and has 16 to 19 rays. Dorsal fin has 17 rays, and anal fin has 17 rays. Trunk lateral line consists of broad tubes pierced by 14 or 15 pores, with pointed flap extending from anterior margin of pores. Flaps increase in size posteriorly until they completely cover pores on caudal peduncle. Cavernous tissue is present under pectoral fin, posterior to cleithrum, and around anus. Vertebrae number 47 to 56. Color is uniform brownish black in preservative.

This species occurs in the western Atlantic from the Gulf of Mexico and the Caribbean Sea at bathypelagic depths (1,280 m). Maximum known size is 66 mm SL. Recent information suggests that this species is a composite of two species (John R. Paxton, pers. com, November 1996).

REFERENCES: Parr 1934; Bigelow 1961 (as *G. parri*); Richardson and Garrick 1964 (in part as *G. parri*); Paxton 1989.

Gyrinomimus simplex Parr 1946

Gyrinomimus simplex is elongate, slender, and compressed posteriorly, with narrowly rectangular lateral line scales, cavernous tissue anterior to anal fin, and anal fin extending slightly beyond dorsal fin. It is distinguished from the other species of the family by the following combination of characters. Snout is convex in dorsal profile and moderately acute. Jaw teeth and vomerine teeth are elongate, close-set, and in distinct longitudinal rows. Palatine teeth are present. Ventral midline of gill arches has single shield-shaped tooth plate (copular tooth plate). First gill arch has solid, flat tooth plates covering most of lateral surfaces. Three free gill arches are present; slit behind fourth gill arch is lacking. Head length is 28%, snout length is 10.5%, upper jaw length is 26%, lower jaw length is 24%, body depth is 18%, snout to dorsal fin origin is 71%, dorsal fin base length is 14.5%, snout to anal fin origin is 72%, and anal fin base length is 15% of SL. Pectoral fin originates behind posterior margin of operculum and has 18 rays. Dorsal fin has 17 rays, and anal fin has 18 rays. Lateral line on trunk consists of broad tubes pierced by 16 round pores lacking flaps or keels. Lateral line scales are strap shaped or narrowly rectangular. Color is brownish black in preservative.

This species occurs in the western Atlantic from Bermuda and the Gulf of Mexico at bathypelagic depths (1,200 m). Maximum known size is 66 mm SL.

REFERENCES: Parr 1945; Bigelow 1961; Paxton 1989.

MIRAPINNIDAE

Mirapinnids are elongate, moderately stout bodied to very slender, and compressed posteriorly, with jugular pelvic fins and dorsal and anal fins located just anterior to caudal fin. They are distinguished from the other families of the order by the following combination of characters. Snout is short to very short, and blunt. Mouth is terminal to slightly superior, rather small and oblique. Maxilla extends to level of eye. Upper jaw is slightly protrusible. Single supramaxilla is located on dorsal margin of maxilla. Eye is relatively large and laterally located. Gill membranes are separate and free of isthmus. Pectoral fin is laterally located and fanlike. Dorsal fin is posteriorly located above similar-shaped anal fin. Pelvic fin is located anterior to pectoral fin base. Caudal fin has 19 principal rays. Body lacks scales but is covered with hairlike outgrowths of epidermis or minute papillae. In some taxa, skin of caudal fin is prolonged into ribbonlike streamer.

Mirapinnids occur in the Atlantic, Indian, and western Pacific Oceans at mesopelagic depths. There are five species in separate genera, and one species occurs in the Gulf of Mexico.

Eutaeniophorus festivus Bertelsen and Marshall 1956

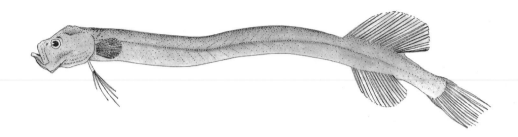

Eutaeniophorus festivus is elongate and moderately compressed, with fan-shaped dorsal and anal fins located near the caudal peduncle, and a caudal fin prolonged as a ribbon-shaped streamer. It is distinguished from the other species of the family by the following combination of characters. Snout is short. Mouth is terminal and strongly oblique. Teeth are very small and pointed, and are arranged in single row in premaxilla and in several rows in lower jaw. Gill rakers on first arch number two on epibranch and eight on lower limb. Branchiostegal rays number 8. Head length is 7.7% to 10%, body depth is 11.5% to 12.2%, dorsal fin base length is 21%, and anal fin base length is 19% of SL. Pectoral fin is fan shaped and has free muscular base and 23 fin rays. Dorsal fin originates two myomeres anterior to anal fin origin and has 16 to 20 fin rays. Pelvic fin has narrow muscular base and 4 or 5 fin rays. Anal fin has 15 to 18 fin rays. Caudal fin has truncate posterior margin but is extended as long (up to 2 to 3 times SL) streamer. Body is covered with microscopic papillae. Physoclistous swim bladder, with two rete, occurs in larvae only. Vertebrae number 47 to 55. Larvae are similar to adults but are more elongate. Color is purple in life and pale in preservative.

This species occurs worldwide in tropical seas between the surface and 200 m. It has been captured at least twice in the western Gulf of Mexico. Underwater observations from submersibles suggest that this species hovers vertically with head up in the water column. The caudal streamer may assist assuming this posture. Food consists of copepods. Maximum known size is 54 mm SL.

REFERENCES: Bertelsen and Marshall 1956, 1958; Bertelsen 1986c.

RONDELETIIDAE

Rondeletiids are moderately deep bodied and compressed, with a very large head, a moderately large mouth, and lateral line consisting of vertical series of pores. They are distinguished from the other families of the order by the following combination of characters. Snout is long, obtuse, and undulating in dorsal profile. Mouth is terminal and horizontal. Upper jaw extends to under eye. Jaw teeth are coarsely granular. Vomer and palatine lack teeth. Four free gill arches are present; slit occurs behind fourth gill arch. Gill rakers are numerous and long and slender. Branchiostegal rays number 7. Pectoral fin is small and is located on lower one-half of flank. Dorsal fin is rather short and located just anterior to caudal peduncle. Pelvic fin is small and located just above midline of belly. Anal fin is short and located opposite dorsal fin. Caudal peduncle is short and moderately deep. Caudal fin is small and slightly forked. Lateral line scales are absent.

Rondeletiids occur worldwide in tropical to warm temperate seas at mesopelagic and bathypelagic depths. There are two species in a single genus, and one species occurs in the Gulf of Mexico.

Rondeletia bicolor   Goode and Bean 1895

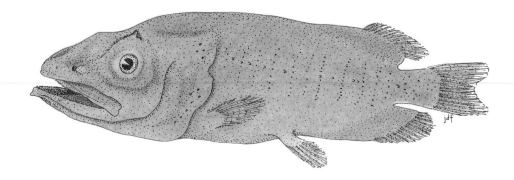

Rondeletia bicolor is moderately deep bodied and compressed, with a large head bearing a pair of large, bony protuberances over orbits. It is distinguished from the other species of the family by the following combination of characters. Gill rakers on first arch number 6 or 7 on epibranch and 17 to 19 on lower limb. Pectoral fin has 8 or 9, dorsal fin has 13 to 15, pelvic fin has 5 or 6, and anal fin has 12 to 14 rays. Color is purplish black with cherry-colored fin margins in life, and whitish in preservative.

This species occurs in the Atlantic, Pacific, and Indian Oceans at mesopelagic and bathypelagic depths. In the western Atlantic it occurs off Bermuda and in the Gulf of Mexico. Maximum known size is 87 mm SL.

REFERENCES: Goode and Bean 1895; Parr 1928; Harry 1952; Rofen 1959; Paxton 1989; Tolley et al. 1989.

BERYCIFORMES

Beryciformes are considered to be the sister group of the remainder of the Percomorpha, either exclusive of the Zeiformes (G. D. Johnson and Patterson 1993) or inclusive of the Zeiformes (Nelson 1994), as recognized herein. There are three suborders: Trachichthyoidei, with three families in the Gulf (Anoplogasteridae, Diretmidae, and Trachichthyidae); Berycoidei, with a single family in the Gulf (Berycidae); and Holocentroidei, with one family in the Gulf (Holocentridae).

Key to the Families of the Gulf of Mexico
(Adapted from Woods and Sonoda 1973)

1a. Pelvic fin spine absent . . . . Anoplogasteridae p. 997
1b. Pelvic fin spine present 2
2a. Dorsal and anal fins without spines; lateral line absent
    . . . . Diretmidae p. 999
2b. Dorsal and anal fins with spines; lateral line present 3
3a. Dorsal fin with 10 to 13 strong spines
    . . . . Holocentridae p. 1011
3b. Dorsal fin with 3 to 8 spines. 4
4a. Anal fin with 4 spines and 12 to 30 rays; maxilla with two
    supramaxillae. . . . . Berycidae p. 1008
4b. Anal fin with 2 or 3 spines and 8 to 12 rays; maxilla with
    one supramaxilla . . . . Trachichthyidae p. 1004

ANOPLOGASTERIDAE   Fangtooth

This family contains one species, and it occurs in the Gulf of Mexico.

Anoplogaster cornuta   (Valenciennes 1833)
Fangtooth

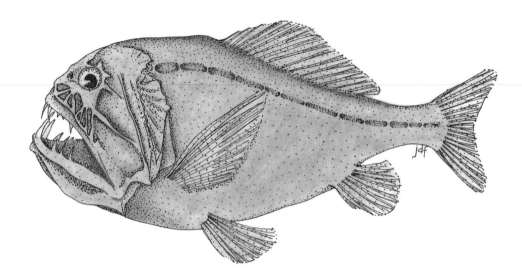

Anoplogaster cornuta is relatively deep bodied, robust anteriorly, and compressed posteriorly, with fanglike teeth in jaws, mucous cavities on head, and a slender caudal peduncle. It is distinguished from the other families of the order by the following combination of characters. Lateral profile of head is strongly convex. Mouth is oblique, and upper jaw is almost as long as head. Premaxilla has three fanglike teeth and lower jaw has four (with anteriormost largest), which fit into sockets of orbital cavity when mouth is closed. Teeth are present or absent in palatine. Single supramaxilla occurs on posterodorsal margin of maxilla. Bony ridges bearing small denticles arranged in rows occur on head. Gill rakers on first arch number 6 to 10 on epibranch, 1 in corner, and 7 to 11 on lower limb in juveniles, and consist of groups of one to three spinules in adults. Branchiostegal rays number 8 or 9. Head length is 33.5% to 39.8%, snout length is 10% to 12.9%, eye diameter is 5.9% to 9.8%, interorbital width is 10.7% to 15%, body depth is 44.6% to 56%, pectoral fin length is 23.7% to 27.7%, and pelvic fin length is 19% to 21.7% of SL. Pectoral fin has slightly oblique base and 14 or 15 rays. Dorsal fin is slightly convex and has 17 to 19 rays. Pelvic fin originates slightly posterior to pectoral fin insertion and has 1 unbranched ray and 6 branched rays. Anal fin is rounded, originates near insertion of dorsal fin, and has 8 or 9 rays. Caudal fin is emarginate and has 17 branched rays. Body and cheek are covered with small, thin, platelike scales that are embedded in skin. Lateral line is an open groove bridged by scales at irregular intervals. Swim bladder is gas filled in larvae but regressed and fat filled in adults. Vertebrae number 28. Color is uniform dark brown to black. Juveniles are slightly deeper bodied and have a more convex head, smaller jaw teeth, longer cephalic and preopercular spines, larger eyes, and a shorter caudal peduncle than adults.

This species occurs worldwide in tropical to temperate seas. In the western Atlantic it occurs from St. Georges Bank to the Falkland Islands, including the Gulf of Mexico and the Caribbean Sea, between 46 and 4,900 m. Food consists of crustaceans for juveniles and mostly fishes for adults. Maximum known size is 152 mm SL for adults.

REFERENCES: Woods and Sonoda 1973; Murdy et al. 1983; Uyeno et al. 1983; Hulley 1986e; Post 1986d.

DIRETMIDAE Spinyfins

The spinyfins are compressed and nearly circular to oval in lateral view, with a single supramaxilla and ventral scutes along ventral midline before and behind the anus. They are distinguished from the other families of the order by the following combination of characters. Bones of head are thin and delicate, with ridges and shallow intervening cavities. Mouth is very oblique, and premaxilla has long ascending process with cartilaginous projection that extends to between orbits. Jaw teeth are minute and arranged in bands that narrow to a single series posteriorly. Vomerine teeth are absent except in some large specimens, and palatine teeth are absent. Eye is very large, and interorbital region is very narrow. Preopercular angle is expanded ventrally and posteriorly beyond gill membranes to cover lower opercular bones. Medial wall of gill chamber bears aggregates of epidermal glands. Pectoral fin is short and located on lower one-half of flank. Dorsal and anal fins lack spines, and dorsal fin is about one-third longer than anal fin. Pelvic fin inserts below pectoral fin base and has one spine and 6 rays. Caudal fin is emarginate. Scales are ctenoid and shield shaped, with anterior end broader than posterior end, and occur on body and cheek. Lateral line is absent.

Spinyfins occur worldwide in tropical to temperate seas at mesopelagic depths. Food consists of zooplankton. There are three species in two genera, and all occur in the Gulf of Mexico.

Key to the Species of the Gulf of Mexico
(Adapted from Post and Quéro 1981; Post 1986c)

1a. Adult specimens 2
1b. Juvenile specimens 4
2a. Anus midway between pelvic fin and anal fin origin; ventral midline not keeled anterior to pelvic fin; three to six bony ridges on upper part of operculum. 3
2b. Anus immediately anterior to first anal fin ray or separated by only one or two scutes; ventral midline anterior to pelvic fin keeled and covered by scutes; more than 10 bony ridges on upper part of operculum
 . . . . *Diretmus argenteus* p. 1003
3a. Depressed pelvic fin extends to or beyond origin of anal fin; dorsal fin rays 26 to 29 (usually 27 or 28); gill rakers on first arch 16 to 20 (usually 18 or 19)
 . . . . *Diretmoides parini* p. 1001
3b. Depressed pelvic fin fails to reach origin of anal fin; dorsal fin rays 24 to 26 (usually 25); gill rakers on first arch 12 to 16 (usually 13 to 15)
 . . . . *Diretmoides pauciradiatus* p. 1002

4a. Preopercular process directed posteroventrally
.... *Diretmus argenteus* p. 1003
4b. Preopercular process directed anteroventrally. 5
5a. Large, brownish, horseshoe-shaped blotch on flank; no
spot on posterior section of anal fin
.... *Diretmoides parini* p. 1001
5b. Large, brownish blotch on flank not shaped like horseshoe;
brown spot on posterior section of anal fin
.... *Diretmoides pauciradiatus* p. 1002

Diretmoides parini   Post and Quéro 1981

Diretmoides parini is compressed and elliptical in lateral profile, with very large eyes, three to six bony ridges on operculum, and relatively long pelvic fins. It is distinguished from the other species of the family by the following combination of characters. Snout is blunt. Mouth is very oblique, and lower jaw extends beyond upper jaw as projecting knob. Jaw teeth are small, pointed, and arranged in double or triple rows. Teeth are lacking in vomer and palatine. Maxilla is broad posteriorly and extends to posterior margin of eye. Supramaxilla is large and triangular. Orbital bones form thin, bony flange along anterior and posterior margins of eye. Frontal bone has spiny ridges forming shallow cavities. Operculum is thin, with radiating ridges, but ridges are widely spaced on upper section and number three to six. Gill rakers on first arch are short and number 4 to 7 on epibranch and 10 to 13 on lower limb. Head length is 33.3% to 38.4%, orbit diameter is 13.3% to 18.7%, maxillary length is 22% to 24.9%, interorbital width is 4.3% to 7%, and body depth is 43.7% to 50.9% of SL. Pectoral fin has 17 to 20 rays. Dorsal fin has evenly convex margin and 26 to 29 rays. Anal fin is similar in shape to dorsal fin and has 20 to 23 rays. Scales are ctenoid. Vertebrae number 29 to 31, and prehaemal vertebrae number 13 or 14. Preanal scutes are larger than postanal scutes, and postanal scutes number 9 to 13. Color is silvery in small specimens and black in large specimens. Juvenile specimens have large, brownish, horseshoe-shaped blotch on flank.

This species occurs worldwide in tropical to temperate seas. In the western Atlantic it occurs in the Gulf of Mexico and the Caribbean Sea. Juveniles occur from the surface to 200 m, and adults are mesopelagic below 500 m. Maximum known size is 400 mm SL.

REFERENCES: Woods and Sonoda 1973; Post and Quéro 1981; Uyeno et al. 1983; Post 1986b,c.

Diretmoides pauciradiatus   (Woods 1973)

Diretmoides pauciradiatus is compressed and elliptical in lateral profile, with very large eyes, three to six bony ridges on operculum, and relatively short pelvic fins. It is distinguished from the other species of the family by the following combination of characters. Snout is blunt. Mouth is very oblique, and lower jaw extends beyond upper jaw as projecting knob. Jaw teeth are small, pointed, and arranged in double or triple rows. Maxilla is broad posteriorly and extends to posterior margin of eye. Orbital bones form thin, bony flange along anterior and posterior margins of eye. Frontal bone has spiny ridges forming shallow cavities. Operculum is thin, with radiating ridges. Gill rakers on first arch are short, and number 4 or 5 on epibranch and 7 to 10 on lower limb. Head length is 34% to 40%, orbit diameter is 12.6% to 17.3%, maxillary length is 22.4% to 28.6%, interorbital width is 5.1% to 10.5%, and body depth is 52.3% to 75.6% of SL. Pectoral fin has 16 to 19 rays. Dorsal fin has evenly convex margin and 24 to 26 rays. Anal fin is similar in shape to dorsal fin and has 18 to 21 rays. Vertebrae number 26 to 29, with 12 to 14 prehaemal vertebrae. Preanal scutes are larger than postanal scutes, and postanal scutes number 9 to 12. Color is silvery in small specimens and black in large specimens. Juveniles have large, brownish blotch on flank.

This species occurs worldwide in tropical to temperate seas. In the western Atlantic it occurs from the east coast of Florida to the southern and western Caribbean Sea and the Gulf of Mexico. Juveniles occur between the surface and 200 m, and adults occur to 600 m. Maximum known size is 370 mm SL.

REFERENCES: Woods and Sonoda 1973; Post and Quéro 1981; Uyeno et al. 1983; Post 1986b.

Diretmus argenteus Johnson 1864

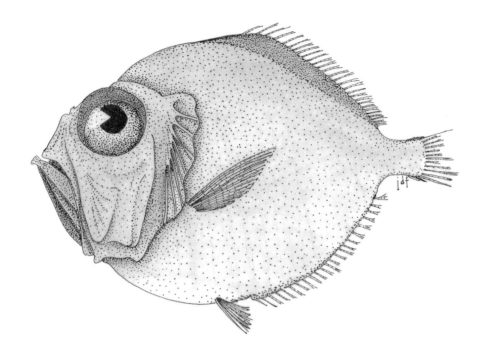

Diretmus argenteus is compressed and nearly circular in lateral view, with very large eyes, 7 to 20 striae on operculum, and anus contiguous with anal fin. It is distinguished from the other species of the family by the following combination of characters. Lower jaw extends beyond upper jaw as projecting knob. Jaw teeth are small, pointed, and arranged in several rows. Maxilla is broad posteriorly and extends below middle of pupil. Supramaxilla is large and triangular. Teeth are lacking on vomer and palatine. Orbital bones form thin flange on anterior and posterior margins of orbit. Bony projections on frontal bones are thin, striated, and have fine spines on margins. Gill rakers on first arch are of moderate length and number 17 to 24. Branchiostegal rays number 7 or 8. Operculum is entirely covered with radiating ridges. Head length is 34.4% to 48.2%, orbit diameter is 11.1% to 27%, interorbital width is 3.9%

to 8.4%, and body depth is 60.7% to 88.8% of SL. Pectoral fin is acutely pointed and has 18 or 19 rays. Dorsal fin has evenly convex margin and 25 to 29 rays. Anal fin is similar in shape to dorsal fin and has 18 to 24 rays. Preanal scutes are larger than postanal scutes. Vertebrae number 27 to 29, with 11 to 14 prehaemal vertebrae. Juveniles are deeper bodied than adults. Color is dark brown in preservative.

This species occurs worldwide in tropical to temperate seas. In the western Atlantic it occurs from Nova Scotia and Bermuda to the northern Gulf of Mexico and the Bahamas. Juveniles range from near the surface to 250 m, and adults occur from 300 to 1,000 m. Maximum known size is 125 mm SL.

REFERENCES: Woods and Sonoda 1973; Post and Quéro 1981; Murdy et al. 1983; Uyeno et al. 1983; Post 1986b,c.

TRACHICHTHYIDAE   Slimeheads

Slimeheads are moderately elongate to deep bodied and compressed, with large mucous cavities on head separated by very thin bony septa and covered with thin integument. They are distinguished from the other families of the order by the following combination of characters. Head is short and deep. Premaxilla has distinct spine at angle. Mouth is large and oblique. Teeth in jaws are small and arranged in bands. Most species have vomerine and palatine teeth. One supramaxilla is located on posterodorsal margin of maxilla. Posttemporal bone bears a posteriorly directed spine. Dorsal fin has three to eight striated spines and 10 to 19 rays. Anal fin is about one-half length of dorsal fin and has two or three spines and 8 to 12 rays. Pelvic fin is located under pectoral fin base and has one spine and 6 or 7 rays. Caudal fin generally has 4 to 7 procurrent spines. Body is covered with scales. Scales vary from thick and spiny to thin and cycloid. Series of scutes or enlarged scales is present along midline of abdomen.

Slimeheads occur worldwide in tropical to temperate seas near the bottom at depths of 100 to 1,000 m. There are about 33 species in seven genera, and 3 species in two genera occur in the Gulf of Mexico.

Key to the Species of the Gulf of Mexico
(Adapted from Maul 1986b)

1a. Dorsal fin spines seven or eight; spinous part of dorsal fin base not shorter than anal fin base
. . . . *Gephyroberyx darwini* p. 1005
1b. Dorsal fin spines four to seven; spinous part of dorsal fin base shorter than anal fin base 2
2a. Anal fin rays 9; scales rough and adherent
. . . . *Hoplostethus occidentalis* p. 1007
2b. Anal fin rays 10; scales smooth and deciduous
. . . . *Hoplostethus mediterraneus* p. 1006

Gephyroberyx darwini (Johnson 1866)

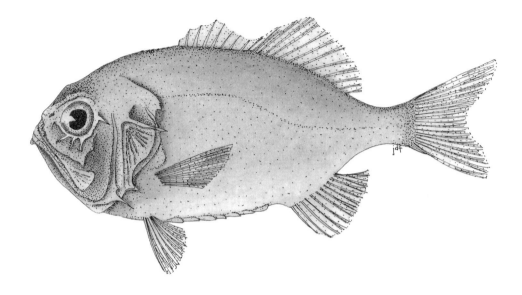

Gephyroberyx darwini is deep bodied, oval shaped, and compressed, with low ridges on head, and spinous section of dorsal fin longer than anal fin base. It is distinguished from the other species of the family by the following combination of characters. Dorsal profile is slightly rounded and snout is blunt. Bones of head are slightly cavernous, and skin covering depressions is relatively thick. Nasal bone has anterior rugose spine. Jaw teeth are arranged in band in upper jaw, with inner row larger than outer row. Teeth in lower jaw are arranged in band anteriorly and in two rows of hooked teeth posteriorly. Vomerine and palatine teeth are well developed. Gill rakers on first arch are long and slender and number 12 or 13. Preopercular spine is strong and triangular. Operculum has single strong spine and numerous radiating, denticulated striae. Posttemporal bone projection is rounded and does not form spine. Head length is 35.4% to 44.2%, snout length is 8.6% to 10.2%, eye diameter is 10.2% to 16.2%, interorbital width is 10.8% to 13%, body depth is 44.8% to 53%, pectoral fin length is 20.5% to 28.3%, and pelvic fin length is 20.7% to 24.4% of SL. Pectoral fin has oblique base and 13 to 15 rays. Dorsal fin has seven or eight rugose spines and 11 rays, with fourth spine longest. Anal fin has three spines and 11 rays. Body is covered with ctenoid scales. Lateral line scales are enlarged and separated from each other by one or two smaller scales without tubes. Abdomen has medial row of heavy scutes. Color is red on head and red to brownish red on back. Lower side is silvery gray to red. In preservative, specimens are dusky brown dorsally and pale silvery ventrally.

This species occurs in tropical to warm temperate waters of the Atlantic, Indian, and western Pacific Oceans. In the western Atlantic it occurs from Delaware Bay to Panama, including the northern Gulf of Mexico and the western Caribbean Sea, at 70 to 500 m on or near the bottom. Food consists of small shrimps and fishes. Maximum known size is 480 mm SL.

REFERENCES: Woods and Sonoda 1973; Murdy et al. 1983; Heemstra 1986e; Maul 1986b; Boschung 1992.

Hoplostethus mediterraneus   Cuvier 1829
Rough fish

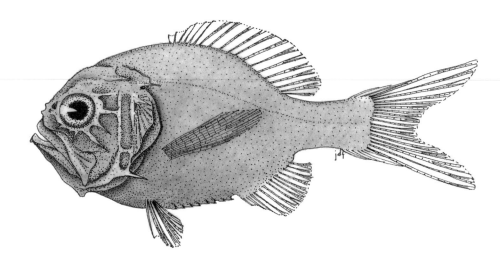

Hoplostethus mediterraneus is oval shaped, deep bodied, and compressed, with ridges on head, and spinous section of dorsal fin shorter than anal fin base. It is distinguished from the other species of the family by the following combination of characters. Bones of head are very rugose and have minute spines. Skin covering deep cavernous channels is thin and contains many pores. Nasal bone has short spine. Jaw teeth are arranged in bands, with inner teeth slightly larger than outer teeth. Vomer lacks teeth in adults. Palatine has narrow band of teeth. Preopercular spine is short, triangular, and extends to or just beyond opercular bones. Operculum has low denticulated ridge but no spine. Posttemporal bone has strong ridge and associated spine. Gill rakers on first arch are long, with minute teeth on inner edge, and number 23 to 26. Head length is 37% to 43%, snout length is 7% to 10.2%, eye diameter is 13.5% to 16.1%, interorbital width is 11.2% to 14.6%, body depth is 43.9% to 49%, pectoral fin length is 32.2% to 58.5%, and pelvic fin length is 19% to 25.2% of SL. Pectoral fin has strongly oblique base and 14 to 16 rays.

Dorsal fin has six rather weak striated spines and 13 rays. Anal fin has three increasingly longer spines and 10 rays. Caudal fin is forked. Body and cheek are covered with thin, deciduous scales that either are smooth or have minute spines. Lateral line scales are enlarged, very broad, and have low central spine. Abdomen has row of large scutes bearing strong spines. Color is pale pink dorsally, and flank and belly are blackish. Fins are bright red. Inside of mouth and branchial chamber is black.

This species occurs in tropical to warm temperate waters of the Atlantic, Indian, and western Pacific Oceans. In the western Atlantic it occurs from New Jersey to the Greater Antilles, including the Gulf of Mexico, at depths between 320 and 1,463 m. It is rare in the northern Gulf of Mexico. Food consists of crustaceans. Maximum known size is 186 mm SL in the western Atlantic but 300 mm SL elsewhere.

REFERENCES: Rass 1971; Woods and Sonoda 1973; Heemstra 1986e; Maul 1986b; Boschung 1992.

Hoplostethus occidentalis Woods 1973

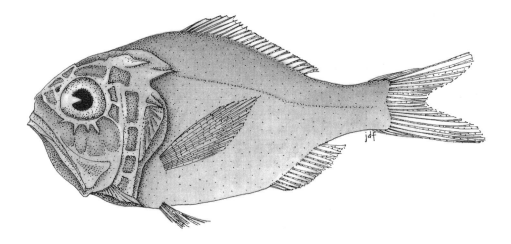

Hoplostethus occidentalis is oval shaped, deep bodied, and compressed, with high ridges on the head, and spinous section of dorsal fin shorter than anal fin base. It is distinguished from the other species of the family by the following combination of characters. Bones of head are very rugose and have minute spines. Skin covering deep cavernous channels is thin and contains many pores. Nasal bone has short spine. Jaw teeth are arranged in bands and are minute. Vomerine teeth are absent in adults. Palatine teeth are present. Preopercular spines are short, triangular, and extend to or just beyond opercular bones. Operculum has low denticulated ridge but no spine. Posttemporal bone has strong ridge and associated large spine. Gill rakers on first arch are long and number 18 to 22. Head length is 39.8% to 43%, snout length is 8.3% to 10.9%, eye diameter is 13% to 16.3%, interorbital width is 11.7% to 14.5%, body depth is 47.2% to 53.9%, pectoral fin length is 24.2% to 33.5%, and pelvic fin length is 19.3% to 27.4% of SL. Pectoral fin has strongly oblique base and 14 to 18 rays. Dorsal fin has four to seven rather weak striated spines and 12 to 14 rays. Anal fin has two or three increasingly longer spines and 8 to 10 rays. Body and cheek are covered with adherent scales possessing several rows of spinules. Lateral line scales are enlarged, more than 3 times broader in dorsoventral plane than in anteroposterior plane. Vertebrae number 26. Head and body are light grayish tan to yellowish or reddish tan, and back is darker in preserved specimens.

This species occurs in the western Atlantic from the east coast of Florida to the Guianas, including the northern Gulf of Mexico and the Caribbean Sea, between 124 and 549 m. Food consists of small shrimps. Maximum known size is 173 mm SL.

REFERENCES: Woods and Sonoda 1973; Uyeno et al. 1983; Boschung 1992.

BERYCIDAE   Alfonsinos

Alfonsinos are moderately deep bodied, compressed, and ovate in lateral profile, with a large eye and a dorsal fin without a notch. They are distinguished from the other families of the order by the following combination of characters. Mouth is oblique, and upper jaw extends to below middle of eye. Jaw teeth are small and in bands that narrow posteriorly. Teeth are present in vomer and in palatine. Two supramaxillae occur on posterodorsal margin of maxilla. Bones of head have low, finely serrated ridges and shallow intervening cavities. Preopercular angle is produced and serrate but lacks spines. Operculum has low ridges but no spines. Pectoral fin is located below midflank, has oblique base, and fails to reach anal fin origin. Dorsal fin originates at midlength or slightly anterior to midlength and has four to seven progressively longer spines. Pelvic fin is located slightly behind pectoral fin insertion and has one spine and 7 to 12 rays. Anal fin is equal to or longer than dorsal fin and has four spines and 12 to 30 rays. Caudal fin is deeply forked and has pointed lobes. Body, cheek, and upper part of operculum are covered with small, shield-shaped cycloid or ctenoid scales. Lateral line scales bear tubes and pores.

Alfonsinos occur worldwide in tropical to temperate seas between 200 and 600 m. There are about nine species in two genera, and one or two species in the same genus occur in the Gulf of Mexico.

Key to the Species of the Gulf of Mexico
(Adapted from Woods and Sonoda 1973)

1a. Eye diameter 14.4% to 17.2% and body depth 44.4% to 49.5% of SL; dorsal fin rays 16 to 18
. . . . *Beryx decadactylus* p. 1009
1b. Eye diameter 13.9% to 14.4% and body depth 36.3% to 40% of SL; dorsal fin rays 13 to 15
. . . . *Beryx splendens* p. 1010

Beryx decadactylus Cuvier 1829
Red bream

Beryx decadactylus is compressed and relatively deep bodied, with a relatively large eye and an anal fin that exceeds length of dorsal fin. It is distinguished from the other species of the family by the following combination of characters. Snout is broad and blunt, and head has rounded profile. Lower jaw extends slightly beyond upper jaw, and mouth is moderately oblique. Jaw teeth are small and in bands, with bands slightly broader and teeth slightly larger anteriorly. Vomer and palatine have tooth patches. Lachrymal bone has strong, curved spine directed laterally. Frontal bone has serrated ridge over eye. Anterior margin of preoperculum has widely spaced serrae on anterior margin and produced area with serrae on either side of angle of posterior margin. Operculum has flat spine, and interoperculum is serrate. Gill rakers on first arch are slender and long and number 22 to 24. Branchiostegal rays number 8. Head length is 32.8% to 37.2%, snout length is 6.7% to 8.3%, eye diameter is 14.4% to 17.2%, interorbital width is 8.1% to 9.9%, body depth is 44.4% to 49.5%, pectoral fin length is 28.1% to 31.7%, and pelvic fin length is 23% to 25.7% of SL. Pectoral fin has nearly horizontal base and 15 to 17 rays. Dorsal fin has three or four spines and 16 to 18 rays, with last spine longest and first ray filamentous. Pelvic fin inserts behind pectoral fin base and has one spine and 10 rays. Anal fin has four spines and 25 or 26 rays, with first ray longest. Caudal peduncle is relatively short between anal fin insertion and caudal fin base. Body, cheek, and opercular bones are covered with small ctenoid scales. Scales are bell shaped or shield shaped, flaring at anterior corners, and have parallel ridges forming spines along posterior margin. Lateral line is slightly arched anteriorly and extends to base of caudal fin. Vertebrae number 24. Top of head, iris, trunk, and fins are bright red. Side of head is white, anterior side of body is silvery, posterior side of body is yellowish, and breast is yellowish white. Red color disappears in preservative.

This species occurs worldwide in subtropical to temperate seas between 400 and 600 m. In the western Atlantic it occurs from Cuba to Maine. It has not been captured in the Gulf of Mexico, but it probably occurs there. Maximum known size is 365 mm SL.

REFERENCES: Woods and Sonoda 1973; Basakhin 1982; Heemstra 1986d; Maul 1986a.

Beryx splendens Lowe 1834
Alfonsino

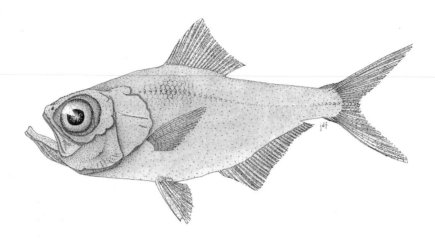

Beryx splendens is compressed and relatively slender, with a relatively small eye and an anal fin that exceeds length of dorsal fin. It is distinguished from the other species of the family by the following combination of characters. Snout is broad and blunt, and head has smoothly convex profile. Lower jaw extends slightly beyond upper jaw, and mouth is strongly oblique. Jaw teeth are minute and in bands that are broader anteriorly than posteriorly. Vomer and palatine have teeth that are slightly larger than jaw teeth. Gill rakers on first arch are slender and number 25 to 27. Branchiostegal rays number 8. Lachrymal bone has strong lateral spine, with tip directed posteriorly. Frontal bone has finely serrated ridge above eye. Preoperculum is produced and serrate at angle. Operculum has one spine extending width of bone and a small spine below it. Head length is 33.4% to 35.6%, snout length is 6.7% to 8.3%, eye diameter is 13.9% to 14.4%, interorbital width is 6.8% to 8.8%, body depth is 36.3% to 40%, pectoral fin length is 26.5% to 30.6%, and pelvic fin length is 21.6% to 27.6% of SL. Pectoral fin has nearly horizontal base and 17 or 18 rays.

Dorsal fin has four spines and 13 to 15 rays, with fourth ray longest. Pelvic fin inserts behind dorsal fin base and has one spine and 11 to 12 rays. Anal fin has four spines and 26 to 29 rays. Caudal peduncle is relatively short between anal fin insertion and caudal fin base. Caudal fin is deeply forked. Body, cheek, and opercular bones are covered with small ctenoid scales. Scales are bell shaped or shield shaped, flaring at anterior corners, and have ridges forming spines along middle part of posterior margin. Lateral line is slightly arched anteriorly and extends to caudal fin base. Color is bright red on dorsum and fins. Flank is pink on silvery background. Peritoneum is black.

This species occurs worldwide in tropical to temperate seas between 200 and 1,000 m. In the western Atlantic it occurs from the Gulf of Maine to southern Brazil, including the northern Gulf of Mexico. Maximum known size is 400 mm SL.

REFERENCES: Woods and Sonoda 1973; Heemstra 1986d; Maul 1986a.

HOLOCENTRIDAE Squirrelfishes

Squirrelfishes are moderately compressed and elongate to ovate in lateral profile, with two supramaxillae; an elongate, divided or notched dorsal fin possessing 10 to 13 spines and 11 to 18 rays; and a slender caudal peduncle. They are distinguished from the other families of the order by a combination of the following characters. Nasal organ is located in shallow, triangular cavity. Mouth is slightly oblique and moderately large. Teeth in jaws, vomer, and palatine are villiform and in bands. Bones of head are grooved and/or strongly ridged, and some external bones bear spines. Margins of operculum and subopercular bones have series of spinules. Pectoral fin has oblique base and is located on lower one-half of flank. Pelvic fin inserts slightly posterior to pectoral fin base and has 1 spine and 7 rays. Anal fin has 4 spines and 7 to 16 rays. Caudal fin is forked and has 17 branched rays. Scales occur on body and cheek and are smooth or ridged, with cteni along posterior margin. Lateral line is complete. Color is usually red.

Squirrelfishes occur worldwide in tropical to subtropical seas on coral reefs and rocky bottoms to about 200 m. Most species are nocturnal carnivores. There are about 65 species in eight genera, and 11 species in five genera occur in the Gulf of Mexico.

Key to the Species of the Gulf of Mexico
(Adapted from Woods and Sonoda 1973)

1a. Preoperculum sharply angled, with single spine much longer than it is broad; anal rays 7 to 10 2

1b. Preoperculum crescent-shaped, with no spine, short triangular projection, or two strong spines; anal rays 9 to 13
. . . . 8

2a. Last dorsal spine longer than penultimate spine and close to first fin ray; lower jaw extending beyond upper jaw and forming part of dorsal profile of head
. . . . *Holocentrus marinus* p. 1017

2b. Last dorsal spine shortest and separated from first fin ray; lower jaw equal to or shorter than upper jaw, not forming part of dorsal profile. 3

3a. Spiny and ray portions of dorsal fin continuous; anterior section of ray portion of dorsal fin and upper caudal fin lobe elongated 4

3b. Spiny and ray portions of dorsal fin almost or completely separated; ray portion of dorsal fin and upper caudal fin lobe not elongated 5

4a. Upper jaw 13.6% to 15.8% of SL; lower jaw 17.2% to 19.8% of SL; lateral line scales 46 to 51
. . . . *Holocentrus ascensionis* p. 1014

4b. Upper jaw 11.4% to 13.4% of SL; lower jaw 14.7% to 17.1% of SL; lateral line scales 50 to 57
.... *Holocentrus rufus* p. 1019

5a. Dorsal fin rays 13................................6

5b. Dorsal fin rays 12...............................7

6a. Pectoral fin rays 14; lateral line scales 37 to 40
.... *Holocentrus poco* p. 1018

6b. Pectoral fin rays 15; lateral line scales 40 to 44
.... *Holocentrus vexillarius* p. 1020

7a. Pectoral fin rays 13; nasal bone with spines, one projecting over posterior nostril opening; large black spot on anterior spinous portion of dorsal fin membrane
.... *Holocentrus coruscus* p. 1016

7b. Pectoral fin rays 14; nasal bone without spines; small black dash on distal part of spinous portion of dorsal fin membrane .... *Holocentrus bullisi* p. 1015

8a. Dorsal fin spines 11......... *Myripristis jacobus* p. 1021

8b. Dorsal fin spines 12 9

9a. No spines on suborbital bones; last dorsal spine longer than penultimate spine ... *Ostichthys trachypoma* p. 1022

9b. Long spines on suborbital bones; last dorsal spine longer or shorter than penultimate spine................. 10

10a. Suborbital spines slender, curved, in part antrorse; last dorsal spine shorter than penultimate spine; lateral line scales 32 to 36.............. *Plectrypops retrospinis* p. 1023

10b. Suborbital spines large, strong, directed posteriorly; last dorsal spine longer than penultimate spine; lateral line scales 28 to 30............. *Corniger spinosus* p. 1013

Corniger spinosus Agassiz 1829
Spinycheek soldierfish

Corniger spinosus is oblong and moderately deep bodied, with long spines on suborbital bone and one or two large spines on preoperculum. It is distinguished from the other species of the family by the following combination of characters. Mouth is slightly oblique and terminal, with lower jaw forming fleshy knob at symphysis, projecting slightly beyond upper jaw, and fitting into notch between lateral tooth plates of premaxilla. Teeth in jaws are short and either rounded or pointed, and form bands tapering posteriorly. Vomer has triangular tooth patch, and palatine has elongate tooth patch. Nasal bone has anteriorly directed spines, and suborbital bone has four or five marginal spines. Preoperculum has double serrated margin and one or two spines at margin extending beyond opercular margin. Operculum is spiny on surface and along margin. Gill rakers on first arch are short and number 18 to 20. Branchiostegal rays number 8. Head length is 38.5% to 41.3%, snout length is 7.6% to 9.5%, eye diameter is 11.7% to 14.3%, interorbital width is 5.4% to 6.5%, body depth is 42.4% to 49.7%, pectoral fin length is 24.2% to 28.6%, and pelvic fin length is 22.6% to 25.3% of SL. Pectoral fin has 16 or 17 rays. Dorsal fin is notched and consists of 12 strong spines, with last longer than next to last, and 13 or 14 rays. Anal fin has 4 spines, with first minute, and 9 to 12 rays. Scales are large, thick, and rectangular or square. Lateral line scales number 28 to 30, and vertebrae number 27. Color is bright red, with center of body scales pale or reflecting silvery. Spiny dorsal fin membranes are dark red, and soft dorsal fin rays are red and membranes are hyaline.

This species occurs in the western Atlantic from South Carolina to Brazil, including the northern Gulf of Mexico and the Greater Antilles, between 45 and 275 m. Maximum known size is 200 mm TL.

REFERENCES: Woods and Sonoda 1973; Haburay et al. 1974; Hastings and Bortone 1976; Uyeno et al. 1983; Boschung 1992.

Holocentrus ascensionis (Osbeck 1765)
Squirrelfish

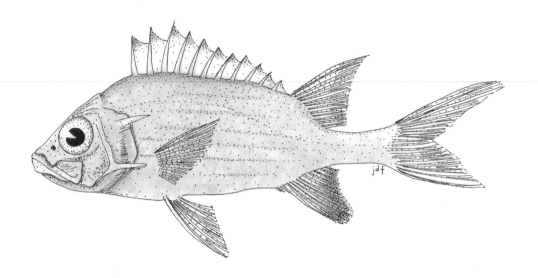

Holocentrus ascensionis is relatively slender and oblong, with a strong preopercular spine and a continuous dorsal fin in which the anterior part of the rayed section is greatly enlarged. It is distinguished from the other species of the family by the following combination of characters. Snout is acute, and upper jaw extends to posterior margin of pupil. Jaw teeth are arranged in bands that narrow posteriorly. Vomer and palatine have well-developed tooth patches. Preorbital margin is denticulated, with large anterior and posterior spines. Premaxilla has double denticulate margin and enlarged triangular spine at angle. Operculum is striated and serrate, and has 1 large, flat, triangular spine. Head length is 31.8% to 36.2%, snout length is 6.5% to 8.7%, eye diameter is 10.6% to 14.5%, interorbital width is 5.2% to 7.1%, upper jaw length is 13.6% to 15.8%, lower jaw length is 17.2% to 19.8%, body depth is 32.9% to 37.2%, pectoral fin length is 19% to 23.4%, and pelvic fin length is 26.9% to 33.9%

of SL. Pectoral fin has 15 to 17 rays. Dorsal fin has 11 spines, with last spine shortest, and 14 to 16 rays. Anal fin has 4 spines, with third spine very strong, and 10 rays. Scales are rectangular, with anterior corners slightly produced and rounded. Lateral line scales number 46 to 51. Vertebrae number 27. Color is dull red or pinkish or red-and-white striped or blotched. Spinous dorsal fin is largely clear with yellowish spots along margin.

This species occurs in the tropical to subtropical Atlantic Ocean. In the western Atlantic it occurs from North Carolina and Bermuda to Brazil, including the Gulf of Mexico, the Caribbean Sea, and the Bahamas, from 31 to 91 m. Maximum known size is 258 mm SL.

REFERENCES: Longley and Hildebrand 1941; Böhlke and Chaplin 1968; Randall 1968; Woods and Sonoda 1973; Hoese and Moore 1977; Uyeno et al. 1983; C. R. Robins et al. 1986; Boschung 1992.

Holocentrus bullisi Woods 1955
Deepwater squirrelfish

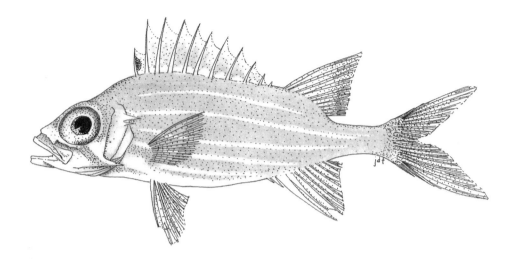

Holocentrus bullisi is ovate, relatively slender, and compressed, with a long preopercular spine and separate spinous and rayed sections of the dorsal fin. It is distinguished from the other species of the family by the following combination of characters. Snout is acute, with dorsal margin nearly straight. Mouth is of moderate length, maxilla extends to anterior one-half of pupil. Lachrymal bone has strong, recurved spine, and suborbital bone has two rows of spines. Jaw teeth are arranged in bands that narrow posteriorly. Tooth bands also occur on vomer and palatine. Preoperculum has long spine at corner extending beyond opercular membrane. Operculum has 2 flat, triangular spines diverging from single base, with upper one longer than lower one. Gill rakers on first arch number 16 or 17, including rudiments. Head length is 33.7% to 37.6%, snout length is 7.8% to 9.4%, eye diameter is 12.4% to 15.8%, interorbital width is 7.3% to 9.7%, upper jaw length is 13.7% to 16.3%, lower jaw length is 18% to 20.8%, body depth is 29.8% to 36.2%, pectoral fin length is 20% to 23.6%, and pelvic fin length is 22.2% to 25.2% of SL. Pectoral fin has 13 to 15 rays. Dorsal fin has 11 slender spines, with last shortest, and 11 or 12 rays, with third and fourth longest. Anal fin has 4 spines, with third longest and reaching or nearly reaching caudal fin base. Caudal fin is deeply forked, with lobes acute and about of equal length. Scales are rectangular, with sides nearly straight and corners slightly rounded. Lateral line scales number 39 to 43. Vertebrae number 27. Color is salmon red, with six narrow, horizontal white stripes bordered by narrow brown bands, and a broad yellow band along midflank. Lips, jaws, and breast are white. Dorsal fin is yellow, with shades of pink and a row of white spots along base and black spot between first and second spines.

This species occurs in the western Atlantic from North Carolina and Bermuda to the eastern and southern Gulf of Mexico, the Bahamas, and the Caribbean Sea between 33 and 110 m. Food consists of fishes. Maximum known size is 129 mm SL.

REFERENCES: Böhlke and Chaplin 1968; Randall 1968; Woods and Sonoda 1973; G. B. Smith et al. 1975 (all above as *Adioryx bullisi*); Uyeno et al. 1983 (as *Sargocentran bullisi*); C. R. Robins et al. 1986; Boschung 1992 (as *A. bullisi*).

Holocentrus coruscus (Poey 1860)
Reef squirrelfish

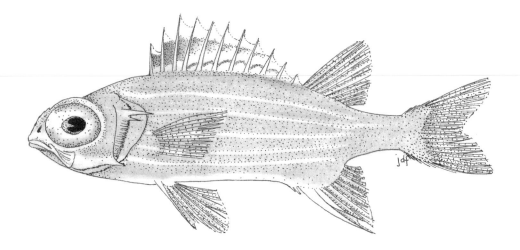

Holocentrus coruscus is ovate, relatively slender, and compressed, with a relatively short preopercular spine and separate spinous and rayed sections of the dorsal fin. It is distinguished from the other species of the family by the following combination of characters. Snout is acute, with dorsal profile rounded. Mouth is of moderate size, maxilla extends to about middle of pupil. Lachrymal bone has well-developed anterior spine, and suborbital bone has fine serrations along margin. Jaw teeth are arranged in bands that narrow posteriorly. Teeth are present on vomer and palatine. Gill rakers are short and number 15 to 18, including rudiments. Preopercular spine is short and broad. Operculum has 2 spines, with upper one larger than lower. Head length is 31.4% to 35.8%, snout length is 6.6% to 7.9%, eye diameter is 13.5% to 15.7%, interorbital width is 7.8% to 9.4%, upper jaw length is 13% to 15.7%, lower jaw length is 16.4% to 20.3%, body depth is 28% to 32.6%, pectoral fin length is 18.5% to 23.4%, and pelvic fin length is 21.2% to 24.6% of SL. Pectoral fin has 12 or 13 rays. Dorsal fin has 11 slender spines, with last shortest, and 11 to 13 rays, with fourth

longest. Anal fin has 4 spines, with third longest, and 8 rays. Caudal fin is deeply forked, with lobes rounded and of equal length. Scales are rectangular, with sides straight and anterior corners rounded. Lateral line scales number 39 to 44. Vertebrae number 27. Color is red on head, back, and bases of caudal rays, with narrow, pink to orange horizontal stripes on flank. Dorsal fin has large black blotch between first and second and between second and third spines, broad red stripe behind blotch, and white base and distal margin.

This species occurs in the western Atlantic from southern Florida to Panama, including the eastern Gulf of Mexico, the Bahamas, and the Caribbean Sea, over shallow reefs. Food consists of small shrimps and crabs. Maximum known size is 104 mm SL.

REFERENCES: Beebe and Tee-Van 1933 (as *H. tortugae*); Longley and Hildebrand 1941; Böhlke and Chaplin 1968; Randall 1968; Woods and Sonoda 1973 (all as *Adioryx coruscus*); C. R. Robins et al. 1986.

Holocentrus marinus   (Cuvier 1829)
Longjaw squirrelfish

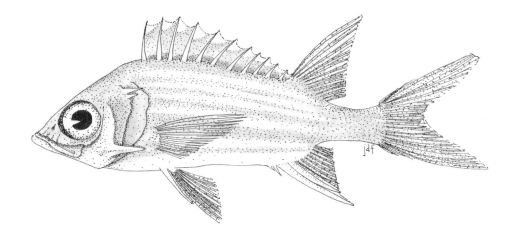

Holocentrus marinus is relatively slender and oblong, with lower jaw extending beyond upper jaw, a strong preopercular spine, and dorsal fin continuous but deeply notched. It is distinguished from the other species of the family by the following combination of characters. Snout is acute, and mouth is moderately large. Maxilla extends to center of pupil. Jaw teeth are in bands that are broader anteriorly than posteriorly. Vomer and palatine have tooth patches. Preorbital margin has posteriorly curved spines, with anteriormost enlarged. Preoperculum has serrated margins, with strong spine at corner. Operculum has 2 spines on upper margin, with upper one larger than lower one and directed slightly dorsally. Head length is 35% to 38%, snout length is 8% to 10.7%, eye diameter is 12.3% to 16.8%, interorbital width is 6.8% to 8.7%, upper jaw length is 14.3% to 17%, lower jaw length is 20.6% to 21%, body depth is 30.8% to 34.2%, pectoral fin length is 20.2% to 27.7%, and pelvic fin length is 18.1% to 23.4% of SL. Pectoral fin has 14 rays. Dorsal fin has 11 spines and 12 or 13 rays, with last spine much longer than penultimate spine and close to first ray. Anal fin has 4 spines, third of which is very strong and long, and 8 or 9 rays. Scales are square or rectangular, with anterior corners rounded and posterior margin bearing small, flat, triangular spines. Lateral line scales number 45 to 48. Vertebrae number 27. Color is red, with yellow and silver stripes, or head and tail are yellow and trunk is plain red. Operculum has yellow bar. Spinous dorsal fin is yellow with white spots at margin.

This species occurs in the western Atlantic from the Florida Keys and the Bahamas to Trinidad and Belize, including the western Gulf of Mexico. It is most common over patch reefs below 15 m. Maximum known size is 124 mm TL.

REFERENCES: Böhlke and Chaplin 1968; Randall 1968 (both as *Flammeo marianus*); Woods and Sonoda 1973; Dennis and Bright 1988.

Holocentrus poco (Woods 1965)
Saddle squirrelfish

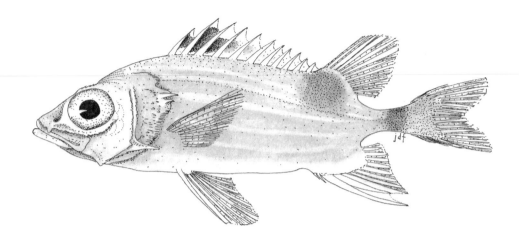

Holocentrus poco is ovate, moderately slender, and compressed, with an elongate preopercular spine and separated spinous and rayed sections of the dorsal fin. It is distinguished from the other species of the family by the following combination of characters. Snout is blunt, with dorsal profile slightly convex. Mouth is of moderate size, maxilla extends to middle of pupil. Lachrymal bone has prominent spine, and suborbital bone has serrae on margin. Jaw teeth are in bands that narrow posteriorly. Teeth are present on vomer and palatine. Gill rakers are short and number 18 to 20, including rudiments. Preopercular spine is as long as pupil diameter. Operculum has 2 spines along upper margin, with upper larger than lower. Head length is 37.2% to 37.4%, snout length is 8.4% to 8.9%, eye diameter is 14% to 14.5%, interorbital width is 5.9% to 6.7%, upper jaw length is 15.7% to 16.9%, lower jaw length is 20.3% to 20.7%, body depth is 34.1% to 35.4%, pectoral fin length is 24.4% to 26.2%, and pelvic fin length is 23.9% to 25.1% of SL. Pectoral fin has 13 or 14 rays. Dorsal fin has 11 moderately slender spines, with last short-est, and 13 rays. Anal fin has 4 spines, with third very strong and extending beyond caudal fin base, and 8 or 9 rays. Caudal fin is deeply forked and has rounded lobes of about equal length. Scales are rectangular to nearly square, with sides straight and anterior corners angular. Lateral line scales number 37 to 40. Vertebrae number 27. Color is uniform red, with black blotch on membrane between first 4 spines of dorsal fin and black saddle below rayed section of dorsal fin and on caudal peduncle.

This species occurs in the western Atlantic from the Gulf of Mexico, the Bahamas, and the Caribbean Sea between 37 and 137 m. In the western Gulf of Mexico it is known only from West Flower Gardens Reef. Maximum known size is 108 mm SL.

REFERENCES: Woods 1965; Böhlke and Chaplin 1968; Randall 1968; Woods and Sonoda 1973; Bright and Cashman 1974 (all above as *Adioryx poco*); Hoese and Moore 1977; C. R. Robins et al. 1986.

Holocentrus rufus (Walbaum 1792)
Longspine squirrelfish

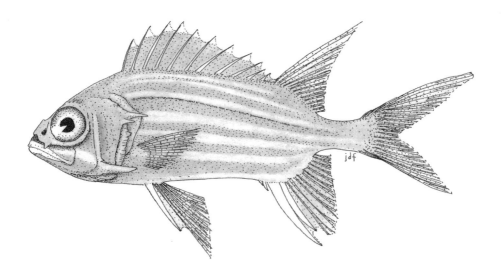

Holocentrus rufus is relatively slender and oblong, with a long preopercular spine and anterior part of rayed section of dorsal fin and dorsal lobe of caudal fin greatly elongated. It is distinguished from the other species of the family by the following combination of characters. Snout is sharply rounded. Mouth is slightly oblique and of moderate size, with maxilla extending to below center of pupil. Jaw teeth are in bands that narrow posteriorly. Vomer and palatine have well-developed tooth patches. Preorbital bone margin is serrate, with anterior spine enlarged. Premaxilla has double serrated margin and enlarged triangular spine at angle. Operculum has 1 large, flat, triangular spine. Gill rakers on first arch are of moderate length and number 24 to 26. Head length is 28.8% to 32.9%, snout length is 6.1% to 7.3%, eye diameter is 10.3% to 14%, interorbital width is 6.1% to 7.7%, upper jaw length is 11.4% to 13.4%, lower jaw length is 14.7% to 17.1%, body depth is 28.8% to 33%, pectoral fin length is 18.7% to 23.6%, and pelvic fin length is 25.1% to 33.5% of SL. Pectoral fin has 15 to 17 rays. Dorsal fin is continuous and has 11 spines and 14 to 16 rays, with last spine shortest. Anal fin has 4 spines and 9 to 11 rays. Scales are rectangular, with anterior corners slightly produced and rounded. Lateral line scales number 50 to 57. Vertebrae number 27. Color is bright red or red-and-white striped or blotched. Spinous dorsal fin has white spots along distal margin.

This species occurs in the western Atlantic from South Florida and Bermuda to northern South America, including the Gulf of Mexico, the Bahamas, and the Caribbean Sea, over shallow reefs. Maximum known size is 300 mm SL.

REFERENCES: Böhlke and Chaplin 1968; Randall 1968; Woods and Sonoda 1973; Bright and Cashman 1974; G. B. Smith et al. 1975; C. R. Robins et al. 1986; Boschung 1992.

Holocentrus vexillarius (Poey 1860)
Dusky squirrelfish

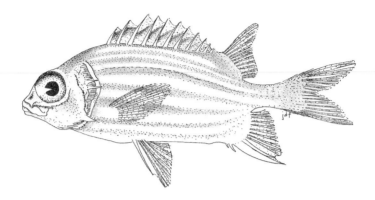

Holocentrus vexillarius is ovate, moderately slender, and compressed, with a moderately elongate preopercular spine and separate spinous and rayed sections of the dorsal fin. It is distinguished from the other species of the family by the following combination of characters. Snout is blunt and slightly acute, with dorsal profile convex. Mouth is relatively small, maxilla extends to middle of pupil. Lachrymal bone has large anterior spine projecting ventrally. Suborbital spines are minute. Jaw teeth are in bands that narrow posteriorly. Vomer and palatine have tooth patches. Gill rakers on first arch number 17 to 19, including rudiments. Preopercular spine extends beyond opercular margin. Operculum has 2 spines, and lower spine is larger than dorsal spine. Head length is 32.9% to 39.3%, snout length is 7.2% to 8.7%, eye diameter is 12.4% to 16.6%, interorbital width is 9.3% to 10.9%, upper jaw length is 11.5% to 13.5%, lower jaw length is 15.7% to 18.8%, body depth is 34.7% to 39.7%, pectoral fin length is 22.7% to 28.8%, and pelvic fin length is 20.6% to 26.6% of SL. Pectoral fin has 14 to 16 rays. Dorsal fin has 11 moderately strong spines, last of which is short-

est, and 12 to 14 rays. Anal fin has 4 spines, third of which is very stout and extends nearly to base of caudal fin, and 9 or 10 rays. Caudal fin is deeply forked, and upper and lower lobes are angular to rounded and about of equal length. Scales are rectangular, with dorsal and ventral margins slightly convex and anterior corners rounded. Lateral line scales number 40 to 44. Vertebrae number 27. Color is dusky red, with white horizontal stripes on scales. Dorsalmost stripe is edged with black. Breast and belly are silvery white. Dorsal fin is red, with dark red spots.

This species occurs in the western Atlantic from Florida to Panama and northern South America, including the Gulf of Mexico and the Caribbean Sea, over shallow reefs. Food consists of benthic invertebrates and fishes. Maximum known size is 139 mm SL.

REFERENCES: Longley and Hildebrand 1941; Randall 1968; Woods and Sonoda 1973 (as *Adioryx vexillarius*); Hoese and Moore 1977; Castro-Aguirre and Márquez-Espinoza 1981; C. R. Robins et al. 1986; Boschung 1992.

Myripristis jacobus Cuvier 1829
Blackbar soldierfish

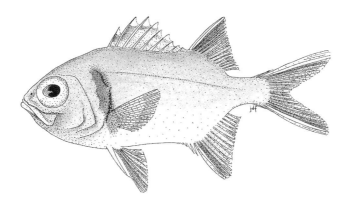

Myripristis jacobus is ovate, relatively deep bodied, and compressed, with bones on top of head smooth, a crescentic preopercular margin, and a short opercular spine. It is distinguished from the other species of the family by the following combination of characters. Snout is blunt and has a slightly convex dorsal margin. Mouth is relatively large, maxilla extends nearly to posterior margin of pupil. Lachrymal and suborbital bones have finely serrated margins. Jaw teeth are slightly larger near symphysis and are arranged in bands that narrow distally. Vomer and palatine have teeth. Gill rakers on first arch are moderately long and number 27 to 32. Preoperculum lacks spines. Operculum has single short but strong spine and serrated posterior margin. Head length is 33.8% to 37%, snout length is 6.9% to 8.4%, eye diameter is 14.2% to 17.7%, interorbital width is 7.3% to 9.2%, upper jaw length is 19.5% to 21%, body depth is 33.8% to 37%, pectoral fin length is 27.7% to 26.7%, and pelvic fin length is 21.1% to 24.9% of SL. Pectoral fin has 14 or 15 rays. Dorsal fin has 11 spines, with last longer than penultimate spine and very close to first ray, and 13 to 15 rays. Anal fin has 4 relatively short spines, with third about same length as fourth, and 12 or 13 rays. Caudal fin is deeply forked, with upper and lower lobes pointed and about of equal length. Scales are large, deeper than they are long, with anterior margins straight or with median rounded projection, anterior corners angular, and posterior margins evenly convex. Lateral line scales number 34 to 36. Vertebrae number 26. Color is red on upper one-half of head and body, paling to silvery ventrally, with red to brownish black bar posterior to operculum and on pectoral fin base. Spinous dorsal fin has red-and-white markings. Leading edges of rayed section of dorsal fin, pelvic fin, anal fin, and outer edge of caudal fin are white.

This species occurs in the tropical and subtropical Atlantic. In the western Atlantic it occurs from southern Florida to Brazil, including the Gulf of Mexico, the Bahamas, and the Caribbean Sea, on shallow reefs. In the western Gulf of Mexico it may be limited to the West Flower Gardens Reef. Maximum known size is 200 mm SL.

REFERENCES: Longley and Hildebrand 1941; Böhlke and Chaplin 1968; Woods and Sonoda 1973; Bright and Cashman 1974; G. B. Smith et al. 1975; Hoese and Moore 1977; Uyeno et al. 1983; C. R. Robins et al. 1986; Boschung 1992.

Ostichthys trachypoma   Günther 1859
Bigeye soldierfish

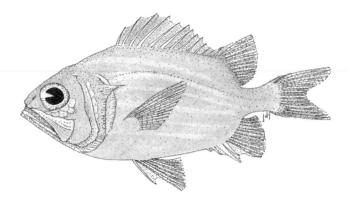

Ostichthys trachypoma is ovate, moderately deep bodied, and compressed, with bones on top of head rugose and spiny, a crescentic preopercular margin, and caudal peduncle slender and slightly expanded distally. It is distinguished from the other species of the family by the following combination of characters. Snout is blunt and has slightly convex dorsal margin. Mouth is large, maxilla extends beyond posterior margin of orbit. Lachrymal and suborbital bones have serrated margins. Jaw teeth are slightly enlarged and form knobs on either side of symphysis, with knobs of lower jaw fitting into groove in upper jaw. Vomer has small patch of teeth, and palatine has narrow bands of teeth. Gill rakers are of moderate length and number 25 to 35. Preoperculum has double serrated margin. Operculum has single strong spine extending from horizontal ridge. Head length is 38.7% to 42.2%, snout length is 6.5% to 7.7%, eye diameter is 13.7% to 17%, interorbital width is 6.6% to 9.2%, upper jaw length is 23.5% to 25.8%, body depth is 45.2% to 50%; pectoral fin length is 26.3%

to 29.9%, and pelvic fin length is 23% to 29.6% of SL. Pectoral fin has 14 to 16 rays. Dorsal fin has 12 strong spines, with last longer than penultimate spine, and 13 or 14 rays. Anal fin has 4 spines, with third spine slightly longer than fourth, and 10 to 12 rays. Caudal fin is deeply forked, with upper and lower lobes angular and of about equal length. Scales are large, with anterior margins straight, corners angular, and exposed portions rugose and ridged. Ridges form short, flattened spines on edge of scales. Lateral line scales number 29 or 30. Vertebrae number 26. Color is reddish, with indistinct horizontal bands along side. Dorsal fin membrane is dark red.

This species occurs in the western Atlantic from Long Island to Brazil, including the Gulf of Mexico and the Caribbean Sea, between 38 and 503 m near the bottom. Maximum known size is 190 mm SL.

REFERENCES: Randall 1968; Woods and Sonoda 1973; Uyeno et al. 1983; C. R. Robins et al. 1986; Boschung 1992.

Plectrypops retrospinis   (Guichenot 1853)
Cardinal soldierfish

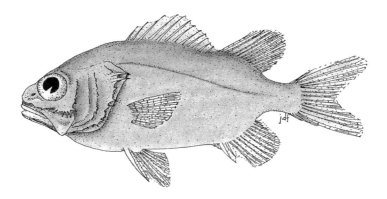

Plectrypops retrospinis is oval shaped, moderately deep bodied, and compressed, with external bones of head rugose and spiny, a crescentic preopercular margin, and well-developed suborbital spines. It is distinguished from the other species of the family by the following combination of characters. Snout is blunt, overhangs jaws, and has convex dorsal margin. Mouth is large, maxilla extends to posterior margin of orbit. Nasal bone extends anterior to premaxilla. Lachrymal bone has smooth margin, and suborbital bone has 3 large spines directed anteriorly and several directed downward and backward. Jaw teeth are larger on either side of symphysis. Lower jaw teeth form knob that fits into notch in upper jaw. Vomer has small patch of teeth, and palatine has narrow bands of teeth. Gill rakers are of moderate length and number 23 to 27, including rudiments. Preoperculum has double serrated margin. Operculum has 2, or occasionally 3, spines. Spines are short, heavy, and diverge from single base. Head length is 38.8% to 42.4%, snout length is 7.1% to 9%, eye diameter is 10.5% to 14.3%, interorbital width is 5.3% to 6.7%, upper jaw length is 22.4% to 23.8%, body depth is 40% to 48.1%, pectoral fin length is 24.5% to 27%, and pelvic fin length is 21.2% to 24.9% of SL. Pectoral fin has 16 to 18 rays. Dorsal fin has 12 moderately slender spines, with last very close to first ray but not longer than penultimate spine, and 13 or 14 rays. Anal fin has 4 spines, with third longest, and 10 to 12 rays. Caudal fin is deeply forked, with upper and lower lobes rounded. Scales have straight to slightly convex anterior margin and rounded anterior corners. Lateral line scales number 32 to 36. Vertebrae number 26. Color is bright red, including fins.

This species occurs in the western Atlantic from southern Florida and Bermuda to northern South America, including the Gulf of Mexico, the Bahamas, and the Caribbean Sea, between 2 and 26 m. It has been captured on the West Flower Gardens Reef in the western Gulf of Mexico. Maximum known size is 118 mm SL.

REFERENCES: Beebe and Tee-Van 1933; Böhlke and Chaplin 1968; Randall 1968; Woods and Sonoda 1973; Bright and Cashman 1974; Hoese and Moore 1977; C. R. Robins et al. 1986.

ZEIFORMES

Zeiformes are considered to be either the sister group of the Beryciformes and the Percomorpha (Johnson and Patterson 1993) or the sister group of the assemblage that includes Gasterosteiformes, Synbranchiformes, Scorpaeniformes, Perciformes, Pleuronectiformes, and Tetraodontiformes (Nelson 1994), as recognized herein. The order is divided into two suborders: Zeioidei, with four families in the Gulf (Grammicolepididae, Macrurocyttidae, Parazenidae, and Zeidae); and Caproidei, with one family in the Gulf (Caproidae). Johnson and Patterson (1993) place the Caproidei in the Perciformes.

Key to the Families of the Gulf of Mexico
(Adapted in part from Heemstra 1980; Smith and Heemstra 1986)

1a. Mouth very small, upper jaw about one-half eye diameter; scales vertically elongate . . . . . Grammicolepididae p. 1025

1b. Mouth moderate to large, upper jaw greater than one-half eye diameter; scales small or absent, not vertically elongated 2

2a. Body depth about equal to head length; anal spine weak or absent. 3

2b. Body depth distinctly greater than head length; anal fin with one to four spines. 4

3a. Two lateral lines along anterior section of trunk; pelvic fin with no spine and seven segmented rays . . . . Parazenidae p. 1030

3b. Single lateral line; pelvic fins with one stout spine and six segmented rays . . . . Macrurocyttidae p. 1028

4a. Bony scutes along ventral part of abdomen, or scutes absent; pelvic fin with one spine and six rays; dorsal and anal rays unbranched . . . . Zeidae p. 1032

4b. Bony scutes along ventral part of abdomen absent; pelvic fin with one spine and five rays; dorsal and anal rays branched. . . . . Caproidae p. 1035

GRAMMICOLEPIDIDAE   Diamond dories

The diamond dories are moderately deep bodied and compressed, with very small terminal mouths and vertically elongated scales. They are distinguished from the other families of the order by the following combination of characters. Mouth is strongly oblique and has very short, ridged maxilla. Jaw teeth are small, slender, and arranged in one or two rows. Vomer and palatine lack teeth. Supramaxilla is absent. Eye is moderate to large and laterally located. Three free gill arches are present; slit behind fourth gill arch is absent. Gill rakers are rudimentary. Branchiostegal rays number 7. Pectoral fin is short and has nearly vertical base. Dorsal fin is very long and has five to seven slender spines and 27 to 34 rays. Pelvic fin is thoracic, inserts below pectoral fin base, and consists of one spine and 6 rays. Anal fin is long and has two small spines and 27 to 35 rays. Caudal peduncle is long and slender. Caudal fin is small and has 13 principal rays. Body, including cheek, operculum, and suboperculum, is scaled. Bases of dorsal and anal fins possess row of thin bony bucklers, each bearing single spine. Lateral line is arched over pectoral fin base. Vertebrae number 37 to 46.

The diamond dories occur in the Atlantic and Pacific Oceans at tropical to subtropical latitudes near the bottom between 250 and 900 m. There are four species in three genera, and two species in separate genera occur in the Gulf of Mexico.

Key to the Species of the Gulf of Mexico
(Adapted from Karrer and Heemstra 1986)

1a. Total dorsal ray elements 32 to 35; no spiny scutes on body . . . . *Xenolepidichthys dalgleishi* p. 1027
1b. Total dorsal ray elements 39 to 41; spiny scutes present on side of body and caudal peduncle of young specimens (less than 24 mm SL). . . . *Grammicolepis brachiusculus* p. 1026

Grammicolepis brachiusculus Poey 1873
Thorny tinselfish

Grammicolepis brachiusculus is moderately to very deep bodied and compressed, with a very small terminal mouth and relatively long dorsal and anal fins. It is distinguished from the other species of the family by the following combination of characters. Gill rakers on first arch are rudimentary and number 1 or 2 on epibranch and 12 on lower limb. Head length is 26.3% to 31.3% of SL in prejuveniles and 22.7% to 23.8% of SL in adults; body depth is 62.5% to 71.4% of SL in prejuveniles and 43.5% to 50% of SL in adults. Pectoral fin has 14 or 15 rays, and dorsal fin has six or seven spines and 32 to 35 rays. Anal fin is preceded by two free spines and has 33 to 35 rays. In prejuveniles, anal fin origin is about opposite dorsal fin origin, but in adults, anal fin origin is distinctly posterior to dorsal fin origin. Prejuveniles have 29 to 34 spiny scutes at base of dorsal fin rays and 27 spiny scutes at base of anal fin rays, but adults lack these scutes. Lateral line is strongly arched anteriorly in prejuveniles but weakly arched anteriorly in adults. Metamorphosis from prejuvenile to juvenile stages occurs at about 25 to 30 cm SL. Color is silvery. Juveniles have irregular black blotches on body, five black bars on anal fin, and black spots on caudal fin.

This species occurs in the Atlantic and western Pacific Oceans at tropical to warm temperate latitudes on or near the bottom between 250 and 900 m. In the western Atlantic it occurs from Georges Bank to southern Florida and the Bahamas between 250 and 900 m. Maximum known size is 50 cm. SL.

REFERENCES: Myers 1937; Uyeno et al. 1983 (as *Daramatturus americanus*); Karrer and Heemstra 1986; Quéro 1986b; C. R. Robins et al. 1986 (as *Daramatturus americanus*).

Xenolepidichthys dalgleishi   Gilchrist 1922
Spotted tinselfish

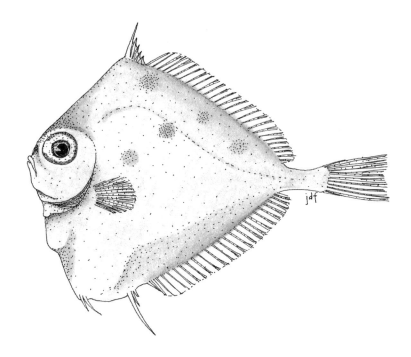

Xenolepidichthys dalgleishi is deep bodied and compressed, with a very small terminal mouth and relatively short dorsal and anal fins. It is distinguished from the other species of the family by the following combination of characters. Gill rakers are rudimentary. Head length is 27% to 34.5% and body depth is 83.8% to 125% of SL. Pectoral fin has 14 or 15 rays, dorsal fin has five spines and 27 to 30 rays, and anal fin has two free spines (first is very long) and 27 to 29 rays. Prejuveniles and adults have 29 spiny scutes at base of dorsal fin rays and 26 or 27 spiny scutes at base of anal fin rays. Vertebrae number 36 to 37. Color is silvery, with round black spots on body.

This species occurs in the Atlantic, Indian, and western Pacific Oceans at tropical to subtropical latitudes on or near the bottom between 660 and 880 m. In the western Atlantic it occurs from Virginia to northern South America, including the Gulf of Mexico and the Caribbean Sea. Maximum known size is 150 mm TL.

REFERENCES: Parr 1933 (as *Grammicolepis squamilineatus*); Myers 1937; Uyeno et al. 1983; Karrer and Heemstra 1986; C. R. Robins et al. 1986; Boschung 1992.

MACRUROCYTTIDAE

Macrurocyttids are moderately elongate, oval shaped, and compressed, with very large eyes and very long serrated pelvic spines. They are distinguished from the other families of the order by the following combination of characters. Mouth is moderately large, strongly oblique, and terminal to slightly superior. Upper jaw is very protrusible. Supramaxilla is absent. Three free gill arches are present, slit is lacking behind fourth gill arch. Branchiostegal rays number 7 or 8. Head length is slightly greater than body depth. Ventral surface of belly is flat or broadly rounded. Pectoral fin is small to moderate in size and located on lower one-half of flank. Dorsal fin is long and has six or seven stout spines and 25 to 29 rays. Pelvic fin inserts slightly posterior to pectoral fin base and consists of one spine and 5 or 6 rays. Anal fin has zero to two weak spines and 23 to 32 rays. Caudal peduncle is slender and rather short. Caudal fin is moderate to small and truncate, and has 11 principal rays. Body is covered with small ctenoid scales. Vertebrae number 25 to 27. Swim bladder is present.

Macrurocyttids occur in the Atlantic and Indo-West Pacific Oceans in tropical to subtropical latitudes at 300 to 600 m near the bottom. There are about four species in two or three genera, and one species occurs in the Gulf of Mexico.

Zenion hololepis (Goode and Bean 1896)

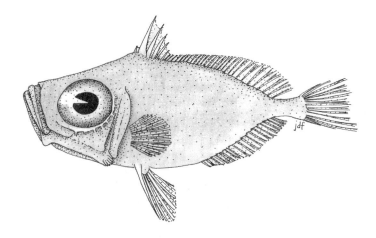

Zenion hololepis is moderately elongate, oval shaped, and compressed, with large eyes and a very long serrated pelvic fin spine. It is distinguished from the other species of the family by the following combination of characters. Gill rakers on first arch number 14 to 16 on lower limb. Head length is 33% to 37% and body depth is 33% to 40% of SL, and eye diameter is 47.6% to 52.6% of head length. Pectoral fin has 16 rays. Dorsal fin has six or seven spines, with second longest, and 25 to 28 rays. Anal fin has one spine and 23 to 28 rays. Small scales run along base of dorsal and anal fins. Vertebrae number 25 or 26. Color is reddish.

This species occurs in the Atlantic and Indian Oceans in tropical and subtropical waters at 300 to 400 m. In the western Atlantic it occurs in the eastern Gulf of Mexico and the Caribbean Sea.

REFERENCES: Goode and Bean 1896; Longley and Hildebrand 1941; Kotthaus 1970 (as *Z. longipinnis*); Heemstra 1980, 1986i.

PARAZENIDAE

Parazenids are moderately elongate, oval shaped, and compressed, with two lateral lines and dorsal and ventral profiles equally convex. They are distinguished from the other families of the order by the following combination of characters. Snout is moderately long, slightly concave, and acute. Mouth is of moderate size, slightly oblique, and upper jaw is extremely protractile. Maxilla extends to anterior edge of eye. Supramaxilla is absent. Jaw teeth are slender and conical. Vomer has teeth, but palatine lacks teeth. Branchiostegal rays number 7. Pectoral fin is small and inserts on lower one-half of flank. Dorsal fin is divided into anterior spinous, and posterior rayed, sections. Pelvic fin is thoracic and inserts distinctly behind pectoral fin base. Anal fin is similar in shape to rayed section of dorsal fin. Caudal peduncle is of moderate depth and length. Caudal fin is forked. Body is covered with ctenoid scales. Lateral lines originate above and below junction of operculum with body wall, diverge from origin, run parallel for most of length, and converge at level of insertion of rayed section of dorsal fin.

Parazenids occur in the Atlantic and western Pacific Oceans near the bottom between 146 and 512 m. One species is recognized, and it may occur in the Gulf of Mexico.

Parazen pacificus   Kamohara 1935

Parazen pacificus is moderately elongate, oval shaped, and compressed, with two lateral lines. It is distinguished by the following combination of characters. Teeth on premaxilla are slightly smaller than those of lower jaw and are arranged in single row anteriorly and in two rows posteriorly. Gill rakers on first arch number 1 or 2 on epibranch and 6 on lower limb. Head length is 37.2% to 39.4%, snout length is 14.9% to 16.1%, eye diameter is 12.3% to 13.3%, body depth is 34.2% to 39.4%, distance from snout to dorsal fin origin is 46.3% to 47.5%, distance from snout to anal fin origin is 58% to 62.3%, and depth of caudal peduncle is 11% to 12.2% of SL. Pectoral fin has 15 or 16 rays, and dorsal fin has eight slender spines and 27 to 30 rays. Pelvic fin has 7 rays, first of which is unbranched. Color is silvery, with margin of spinous section of dorsal fin black. Lateral scale rows from upper opercular margin to caudal fin base number about 90.

This species occurs in the western Atlantic off Cuba and in the western Pacific off Japan between 146 and 512 m. It has not been reported from the Gulf of Mexico, but it likely occurs there. The Caribbean and Japanese populations may represent separate species. Maximum known size is 118 mm SL.

REFERENCES: Mead 1957; Heemstra 1980.

ZEIDAE Dories

Dories are deep bodied and compressed, with a large mouth and generally with bony scutes on ventral aspect of abdomen. They are distinguished from the other families of the order by the following combination of characters. Snout is long and either convex or concave in dorsal profile. Mouth is terminal and moderately to strongly oblique. Supramaxilla is absent. Jaw teeth are minute, conical, and arranged in narrow bands, or occasionally small and canine in shape. Eye is large and laterally located. Three free gill arches are present, slit behind fourth gill arch is absent. Branchiostegal rays number 7. Pectoral fin is small and located at or below midflank. Dorsal fin has 7 to 10 stout spines and 25 to 37 rays. Pelvic fin is thoracic, has no or 1 spine and 6 to 10 rays, inserts below or anterior to pectoral fin base, and is very large. Anal fin has 1 to 4 spines and 20 to 39 rays. Dorsal and anal fin rays are unbranched. Caudal fin is of moderate size, slightly convex, and has 11 branched rays. Scales are small, rudimentary, or absent. Bony scutes on ventral midline are more or less developed. Vertebrae number 29 to 42.

Dories occur worldwide in tropical to warm temperate seas near the bottom between 100 and 300 m. There are 13 species in seven genera, and 2 species in separate genera occur in the Gulf of Mexico.

Key to the Species of the Gulf of Mexico
(Adapted from Heemstra 1980)

1a. Pelvic fin with no spine and 9 or 10 segmented rays; anal fin with one or two spines, 29 or 30 rays
.... *Cyttopsis roseus* p. 1033
1b. Pelvic fin with 6 or 7 rays (first is unsegmented and spinelike); anal fin with three spines, 24 to 26 rays
.... *Zenopsis conchifer* p. 1034

Cyttopsis roseus (Lowe 1843)
Red dory

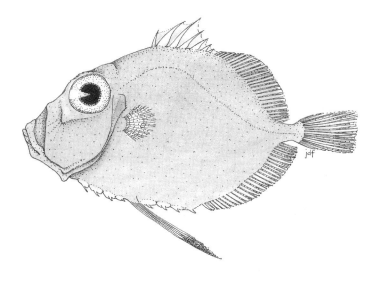

Cyttopsis roseus is deep bodied and compressed, with a large mouth; a row of low, bony ridges along bases of rayed dorsal fin and anal fin; and small, deciduous cycloid scales. It is distinguished from the other species of the family by the following combination of characters. Jaw teeth are villiform and granular and are arranged in bands. Vomer has similar teeth. Gill rakers are rudimentary and number 1 on epibranch and 8 to 10 on lower limb. Head length is 37% to 41.7%, body depth is 50% to 58.8%, distance between pelvic fin base origins is 10% to 13%, and caudal peduncle depth is 5.3% to 6.7% of SL. Eye diameter is 34.5% to 43.5% of head length. Pectoral fin has 13 or 14 rays. Dorsal fin has seven or eight spines and 28 to 30 rays. Pelvic fin has 9 or 10 segmented rays and no spine. Anal fin has one or two compressed spines and 28 to 30 rays. Caudal fin has 3 or 4 spiny, unsegmented, procurrent rays anterior to principal rays. Lateral scale rows number 73 to 84 between upper opercular margin and caudal fin base. Bony scutes are located along ventral midline from isthmus to anus. Color is uniform reddish.

This species occurs in the Atlantic, Indian, and western Pacific Oceans in tropical to warm temperate waters between 250 and 600 m. In the western Atlantic it occurs from southeastern United States to the Caribbean Sea, including the northern Gulf of Mexico. Food consists of pelagic crustaceans and fishes. Maximum known size is 300 mm SL.

REFERENCES: Heemstra 1980, 1986h; Uyeno et al. 1983; Quéro 1986a; C. R. Robins et al. 1986; Boschung 1992.

Zenopsis conchifer (Lowe 1852)
Buckler dory

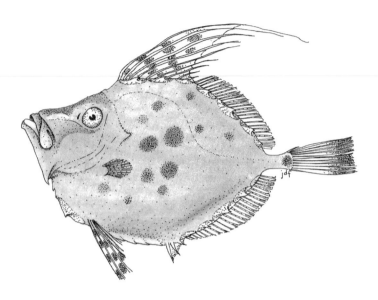

Zenopsis conchifer is deep bodied and compressed, with a large mouth and a row of bony bucklers along bases of dorsal and anal fins. It is distinguished from the other species of the family by the following combination of characters. Premaxilla has one row of mesially oriented canine teeth and three or four irregular series of relatively large canine teeth near symphysis. Lower jaw has two rows of small, curved, mesially oriented canine teeth. Vomer has three or four relatively large canine teeth. Head length is 35.7% to 41.7%, body depth is 50% to 66.7%, distance between pelvic fin origins is 3% to 4%, and caudal peduncle depth is 3.5% to 5% of SL. Eye diameter is 21.3% to 28.6% of head length. Pectoral fin has 12 rays. Dorsal fin has 9 or 10 spines and 25 to 27 rays. Pelvic fin has 6 or 7 rays, first of which is unbranched and unsegmented. Anal fin has 3 spines and 24 to 26 rays. Caudal fin has 1 unsegmented flexible ray anterior to principal rays but no procurrent spines. Scales are lacking. Series of bony bucklers with single spine are present along belly and along bases of dorsal and anal fins. Vertebrae number 35. Color is silvery, with 12 to 24 obscure dark spots. Young specimens have large black blotch behind operculum.

This species occurs in the Atlantic and Indian Oceans in tropical to warm temperate seas near the bottom between 90 and 400 m. In the western Atlantic it occurs from Nova Scotia to Argentina, including the Gulf of Mexico and the Caribbean Sea. Food consists of squids and small fishes. Maximum known size is 750 mm SL.

REFERENCES: Heemstra 1980, 1986h; Quéro 1986a; C. R. Robins et al. 1986; Boschung 1992.

CAPROIDAE   Boarfishes

Boarfishes are deep bodied and compressed, with a small, protrusible mouth and a well-developed occipital crest on head. They are distinguished from the other families of the order by the following combination of characters. Snout is short to moderately long, and obtuse to acute. Mouth is small or slightly superior. Jaw teeth are small and arranged in bands. Vomer and palatine lack teeth. Supramaxilla is absent. Eye is relatively large and laterally located. Three free gill arches are present, slit behind fourth gill arch is absent. Pectoral fin is of moderate to large size, with moderately to strongly oblique base. Dorsal fin is long, originates anterior to midlength, and has seven to nine strong spines and 25 to 30 branched rays. Pelvic fin is thoracic, inserts under or slightly posterior to pectoral fin base, and has one spine and 5 rays. Anal fin originates posterior to dorsal fin origin and has two or three short spines and 22 to 24 branched rays. Caudal fin is small and truncate to slightly convex. Body is covered with small ctenoid scales. Lateral line either is arched over pectoral fin or is straight. Vertebrae number 21 to 23.

Boarfishes occur worldwide, except for the eastern Pacific, in tropical to warm temperate waters near the bottom between 40 and 600 m. Juveniles live in midwater and school. Food consists of crustaceans. There are eight species in two genera, and two species in the same genus occur in the Gulf of Mexico.

Key to the Species of the Gulf of Mexico
(Adapted from Berry 1959)

1a. Dorsal fin spines 9 or 10; dorsal fin rays 26 to 30; anal fin rays 23 to 28; pectoral fin rays 12 to 14
.... *Antigonia combatia* p. 1037
1b. Dorsal fin spines 7 to 9; dorsal fin rays 31 to 37; anal fin rays 29 to 34; pectoral fin rays 13 to 15
.... *Antigonia capros* p. 1036

Antigonia capros Lowe 1843
Deepbody boarfish

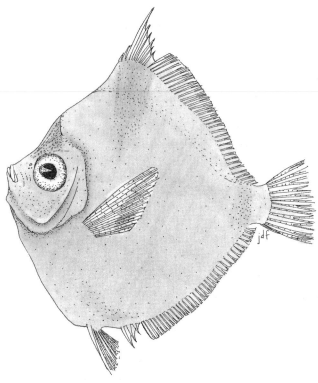

Antigonia capros is very deep bodied, compressed, and rhomboid shaped, with relatively long dorsal and anal fins. It is distinguished from the other species of the family by the following combination of characters. Snout is short and obtuse. Mouth is slightly superior and nearly vertical. Jaw teeth are small, conical, and in narrow band anteriorly and in single row posteriorly. Vomer and palatine lack teeth. Gill rakers on first arch are of moderate length and number 5 or 6 on epibranch and 13 to 16 on lower limb. Branchiostegal rays number 6. Head length is 33.9% to 42.3% (ratio decreases with increase in size), snout length is 8.8% to 11.7%, upper jaw length is 7.3% to 10.2%, eye diameter is 13.4% to 20.2%, and body depth is 98.3% to 136% (ratio decreases with increase in size) of SL. Pectoral fin has 13 to 15 rays. Dorsal fin has seven to nine spines, with third longest, and 31 to 37 rays. Anal fin has three spines, with first longest, and 29 to 34 rays. Caudal peduncle is deeper than it is long. Cau-

dal fin is subtruncate and has 12 principal rays. Body is completely covered with scales. Scales are ctenoid, with exposed section possessing elevated ridge bent posteriorly and denticulated along margin, and usually have ridges along base bearing one to four denticles. Scale rows from upper opercular margin to caudal fin base number 46 to 54. Color is orangish red, including fins, and slightly dusky on dorsal surface.

This species occurs in the tropical to warm temperate Atlantic, Indian, and western Pacific Oceans. In the western Atlantic it occurs from New Jersey to Brazil, including the Gulf of Mexico and the Caribbean Sea. Adults occur near the bottom between 64 and 385 m. Food consists of pelagic crustaceans. Maximum known size is 300 mm SL.

REFERENCES: Berry 1959; Uyeno et al. 1983; Quéro 1986c; C. R. Robins et al. 1986; Boschung 1992.

Antigonia combatia Berry and Rathjen 1958
Shortspine boarfish

Antigonia combatia is rhomboid shaped and compressed, with relatively short dorsal and anal fins. It is distinguished from the other species of the family by the following combination of characters. Snout is short and obtuse. Mouth is slightly superior and nearly vertical. Jaw teeth are small, conical, and arranged in narrow bands anteriorly and in single row posteriorly. Vomer and palatine lack teeth. Gill rakers on first arch are of moderate length and number 3 to 5 on epibranch and 14 to 16 on lower limb. Branchiostegal rays number 6. Head length is 34.2% to 43.4% (ratio decreases with increase in size), snout length is 9.9% to 12.5% (ratio decreases with increase in size), upper jaw is 8.1% to 11.1%, eye diameter is 13.2% to 20.4% (ratio decreases with increase in size), and body depth is 62.4% to 100% (ratio decreases with increase in size) of SL. Pectoral fin has 12 to 14 rays. Dorsal fin has 9 or 10 spines, with third longest, and 26 to 30 rays. Anal fin has 3 spines, with first longest, and 23 to 28 rays. Caudal peduncle is deeper than it is long. Caudal fin is subtruncate and has 12 principal rays. Body, including cheek and operculum, is covered with scales. Scales are ctenoid, with exposed section possessing elevated ridge bent posteriorly and denticulated along margin, and usually have ridges along base with one to four denticles. Scale rows from upper margin of operculum to base of caudal fin number 39 to 57. Color is reddish pink dorsally and silvery ventrally.

This species occurs in the western Atlantic from New Jersey to the mouth of the Amazon, including the Gulf of Mexico and the Caribbean Sea, at 68 to 594 m. Maximum known size is 118 mm SL.

REFERENCES: Berry and Rathjen 1959; Berry 1959; Uyeno et al. 1983; C. R. Robins et al. 1986; Boschung 1992.

GASTEROSTEIFORMES

Gasterosteiformes are considered to be members of the taxon Smegmamorpha that comprises the sister group of the assemblage that includes Dactylopteriformes, Scorpaeniformes, Perciformes, Pleuronectiformes, and Tetraodontiformes (Johnson and Patterson 1993) or, along with Synbranchiformes, the sister group of the Scorpaeniformes, Perciformes, Pleuronectiformes, and Tetraodontiformes (Nelson 1994), as accepted herein. The order is divided into two suborders, and one, Syngnathoidei, occurs in the Gulf. The suborder consists of eight families, and four of these occur in the Gulf.

Key to the Families of the Gulf of Mexico
(Adapted from Smith and Heemstra 1986)

1a. Body compressed and deep; scales with sharp ridges and spines; first dorsal fin with 5 to 8 spines, second greatly enlarged . . . . Centriscidae p. 1041
1b. Body elongated; scales without sharp ridges and spines; dorsal spines, if present, consisting of 8 to 12 isolated, short, and weak spines 2
2a. Pelvic fin absent; body encased in series of bony rings; gill openings restricted to small pores on dorsolateral part of head . . . . Syngnathidae p. 1047
2b. Pelvic fin present; body not encased in bony rings; gill openings not restricted 3
3a. Body compressed, with small scales; soft dorsal fin preceded by row of 8 to 12 isolated, weak spines; caudal fin rounded . . . . Aulostomidae p. 1038
3b. Body depressed, scales lacking (except juveniles have rows of hooked spinules); soft dorsal fin not preceded by isolated spines; caudal fin forked and with middle two rays fused and greatly elongated . . . . Fistulariidae p. 1044

AULOSTOMIDAE   Trumpetfishes

Trumpetfishes are slender, elongate, and compressed, with a fleshy barbel at tip of lower jaw and a series of isolated dorsal spines. They are distinguished from the other families of the order by the following combination of characters. Mouth is terminal and located at end of elongated, tubelike snout. Head is very compressed. Upper jaw lacks teeth, and lower jaw has minute teeth. Vomer has elongate band of small teeth. Four separate gill arches are present, slit is present behind fourth arch. Gill rakers are absent. Branchiostegal membranes are separate, free of isthmus, and branchiostegal rays number 4 or 5. Pectoral fin is small, has a nearly vertical base, and is located on lower flank. First dorsal fin consists of 8 to 13 isolated spines. Second dorsal fin is located just anterior to caudal peduncle. Pelvic fin is abdominal, is located just anterior to anus, and has 6 rays. Anal fin is located below second dorsal fin and is similar in size and shape. Caudal fin is rounded and has 10 branched rays. Body is covered with small ctenoid scales. Lateral line is well developed.

Trumpetfishes occur in the Atlantic and Indo-West Pacific Oceans in tropical to subtropical seas on or near coral reefs. There are three species in a single genus, and one species occurs in the Gulf of Mexico.

Aulostomus maculatus   Valenciennes 1837
Trumpetfish

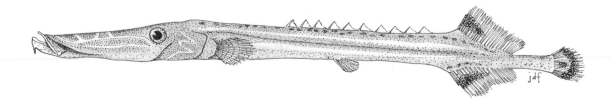

Aulostomus maculatus is slender, elongate, and compressed, with a fleshy barbel at the tip of the lower jaw and a series of isolated dorsal spines. It is distinguished from the other species of the family by the following combination of characters. First dorsal fin consists of 8 to 13 small, free spines and short, separate membranes. Second dorsal fin has 24 to 28 rays, and anal fin has 25 to 28 rays. Vertebrae number 59 to 61. Color is olive to pale red, with many black spots and whitish lines along head and side of body. Anterior rays of dorsal and anal fins have black bar near base, and caudal fin has one or two black spots.

This species occurs in the Atlantic Ocean. In the western Atlantic it occurs from south Florida and Bermuda to northern South America, including the Gulf of Mexico and the Bahamas. Large juveniles and adults occur in weedy areas and around reefs, where they swim with snout down. Food consists of crustaceans and fishes. Maximum known size is 91 cm SL.

REFERENCES: Fritzsche 1977; Hoese and Moore 1977; Böhlke and Chaplin 1968; C. R. Robins et al. 1986; Boschung 1992.

CENTRISCIDAE Snipefishes

Snipefishes are compressed and moderately deep bodied, with the snout produced into a long tube. They are distinguished from the other families of the order by the following combination of characters. Mouth is small, terminal, and located at end of snout. Jaw teeth are lacking. Eye is large, about one-half head length. Head is compressed. Four separate gill arches are present, slit is present behind fourth gill arch. Gill rakers are absent. Branchiostegal rays are free of isthmus. Pectoral fin is of moderate size, has oblique base, and is located slightly below midflank. First dorsal fin consists of five to eight spines, with second greatly enlarged. Second dorsal fin is located just anterior to caudal peduncle. Pelvic fin is abdominal. Anal fin is located below second dorsal fin and is of equal size or longer than second dorsal fin. Caudal fin is slightly concave, truncate, or slightly convex. Bony plates occur on flank above pectoral fin and/or along ventral midline. Body is covered with small scales bearing sharp ridges and spines. Lateral line is present or absent. Swim bladder is present.

Snipefishes occur worldwide in tropical to subtropical seas. Juveniles are pelagic, and adults are benthic or located close to the bottom in 50 to 150 m. There are 12 species in three genera, and 2 species in a single genus occur in the Gulf of Mexico.

Key to the Species of the Gulf of Mexico

(Adapted from T. A. Clarke 1984)

1a. Second dorsal fin spine shorter than snout length and, when depressed, reaching to caudal fin base
. . . . *Macroramphosus gracilis* p. 1042
1b. Second dorsal fin spine about equal to snout length and, when depressed, reaching to about midlength of caudal fin
. . . . *Macroramphosus scolopax* p. 1043

Macroramphosus gracilis (Lowe 1839)
Shortspine snipefish

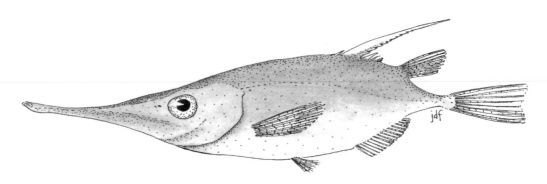

Macroramphosus gracilis is compressed, moderately deep bodied, and relatively elongate, with snout produced into long tube, body plates on flank, and relatively short second dorsal spine. It is distinguished from the other species of the family by the following combination of characters. Body depth is 22.4% to 24.9% ($\bar{x}$ = 23.2%), snout length is 34.5% to 37.8% ($\bar{x}$ = 36%), and second dorsal spine is 20.9% to 28.9% ($\bar{x}$ = 24.5%) of SL. Pectoral fin has 12 to 14 rays. First dorsal fin is separated from second dorsal fin and has six to eight spines. Second dorsal fin has 10 or 11 rays. Anal fin originates under first dorsal fin, has 17 to 19 rays, and base length is slightly more than twice as long as second dorsal fin base. Caudal fin has a slightly concave margin. Color is silvery in juveniles, with back darker. Adults are pinkish to reddish on upper side and silvery ventrally.

This species occurs worldwide in tropical seas. In the western Atlantic it occurs off Florida, the Bahamas, Cuba, and the northern Gulf of Mexico. In the Gulf of Mexico it has been captured off Alabama and Mississippi at 200 to 300 m.

REFERENCES: T. A. Clarke 1984; C. R. Robins et al. 1986; Boschung 1992.

Macroramphosus scolopax   (Linnaeus 1758)
Longspine snipefish

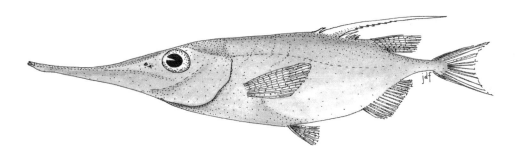

Macroramphosus scolopax is compressed, moderately deep bodied, and relatively elongate, with snout produced into long tube and with body plates on flanks above pectoral fins. It is distinguished from the other species of the family by the following combination of characters. Body depth is 24.7% to 27.3% ($\bar{x} = 26.3\%$), snout length is 32.8% to 35.9% ($\bar{x} = 34.3\%$), and second dorsal spine is 29.5% to 38.7% ($\bar{x} = 33.3\%$) of SL. Pectoral fin has 12 to 14 rays. First dorsal fin is separated from second by distinct gap and has five or six spines. Second dorsal fin has 10 or 11 rays. Anal fin originates under first dorsal fin base, has 16 to 18 rays, and base length is slightly more than twice as long as second dorsal fin base. Caudal fin is slightly concave.

Color is silvery in juveniles, with back bluish black. Adults are pinkish to reddish on upper side and silvery below.

This species occurs worldwide in tropical to warm temperate seas. In the western Atlantic it occurs from the Gulf of Maine to Argentina, including the Gulf of Mexico. Juveniles to about 100 mm SL live pelagically in oceanic waters. Adults live near the bottom at 50 to 350 m. Food consists of pelagic invertebrates, mainly copepods, for juveniles, and benthic fishes for adults. Maximum known size is 200 mm SL.

REFERENCES: T. A. Clarke 1984; Ehrich 1986; Heemstra 1986j; C. R. Robins et al. 1986; Boschung 1992.

FISTULARIIDAE   Cornetfishes

Cornetfishes are slender, elongate, and slightly depressed, with an extremely prolonged snout and a forked caudal fin. They are distinguished from the other families of the order by a combination of the following characters. Mouth is terminal and located at end of tubelike snout. Head is slightly depressed. Jaw teeth are small, and vomer lacks teeth. Four free gill arches are present, slit occurs behind fourth arch. Gill rakers are absent. Branchiostegal membranes are free of isthmus, and branchiostegal rays number 5. Pectoral fin is small, with vertical base located on lower one-half of flank. Spinous dorsal fin is lacking. Second dorsal fin is short based and located above anal fin base. Pelvic fin is abdominal and consists of 6 rays. Anal fin is similar in size and shape to second dorsal fin. Caudal fin has long filament extending from middle 2 rays. Lateral line is arched anteriorly and extends onto caudal filament. Body of juveniles is covered with rows of small hooked spinules. Adults either have hooked spinules or are naked. Row of elongate bony plates may be present in skin anterior to dorsal and anal fins.

The cornetfishes occur worldwide in tropical and subtropical seas and are usually associated with reefs. They are predators on small fishes. There are four species in a single genus, and two species occur in the Gulf of Mexico.

Key to the Species of the Gulf of Mexico
(Adapted from Fritzsche 1976)

1a.   Elongate bony plates embedded in skin along midline of back; ossifications in posterior section of lateral line with retrorse spine . . . . *Fistularia petimba* p. 1045

1b.   No elongate bony plates along midline of back; ossifications in posterior section of lateral line without retrorse spine. . . . . *Fistularia tabacaria* p. 1046

Fistularia petimba   Lacepède 1803
Red cornetfish

Fistularia petimba is slender, elongate, and slightly depressed, with an extremely prolonged snout and a forked caudal fin bearing a long filament. It is distinguished from the other species of the family by the following combination of characters. Upper, lower, and lateral ridges on snout are serrate in adults. Upper snout ridges are parallel. Preorbital and postorbital ridges are serrate. Posttemporal ridge has well-developed antrorse serrations. Interorbital region is narrow and smooth. Pectoral fin has 15 to 17 rays. Dorsal fin is subtriangular and has 14 to 16 rays. Anal fin is similar in size and shape to dorsal fin and has 14 or 15 rays. Caudal fin lobes are smaller than dorsal and anal fins. Skin is covered with spinules in juveniles and adults. Posterior ossifications of lateral line terminate in retrorse spine. Elongate bony plates are present along midline preceding anal fin and in front of and behind dorsal fin. Trunk vertebrae number 50, with first 4 fused, and tail vertebrae number 26. Color in life is red to orangish brown dorsally and silvery ventrally.

This species occurs in the Atlantic, Indian, and western and central Pacific Oceans in tropical coastal regions. It is usually found on soft bottoms at a depth greater than 10 m. In the western Atlantic it occurs from Massachusetts to central Brazil, including the Gulf of Mexico and the Caribbean Sea. Maximum known size is 150 cm TL.

REFERENCES: Fritzsche 1976; C. R. Robins et al. 1986; Boschung 1992.

Fistularia tabacaria Linnaeus 1758
Bluespotted cornetfish

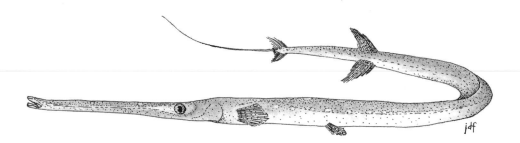

Fistularia tabacaria is slender, elongate, and slightly depressed, with an extremely prolonged snout and a forked tail bearing a long filament. It is distinguished from the other species of the family by the following combination of characters. Dorsal, lateral, and ventral ridges on snout are smooth in adults except for minute serrations on lateral snout ridges. Dorsal snout ridges are parallel. Postorbital ridge has slight serrations, and preorbital and posttemporal ridges are smooth. Interorbital width is 6% or less of snout length and is smoothly depressed. Pectoral fin has 15 or 16 rays. Dorsal fin is subtriangular, with pointed tip, and has 14 to 16 rays. Anal fin is similar in size and shape to dorsal fin and has 14 to 16 rays. Caudal fin lobes are equal in size to dorsal and anal fin lobes. Distance from operculum to pelvic fin origin is slightly less than 50% of distance between pelvic and anal fins. Body is naked in adults. Bony plates preceding dorsal and anal fins are absent. Trunk vertebrae number 53, with first 4 fused, and tail vertebrae number 34. Color is brown dorsally and lighter ventrally, with series of pale blue spots on snout and along back.

This species occurs in the Atlantic Ocean. In the western Atlantic it occurs from Nova Scotia and Bermuda to Brazil, including the Gulf of Mexico and the Caribbean Sea, to 200 m. It is generally associated with sea-grass beds and reefs. Maximum known size is 180 cm SL.

REFERENCES: Böhlke and Chaplin 1968; Fritzsche 1976; Hoese and Moore 1977; Uyeno et al. 1983; C. R. Robins et al. 1986; Boschung 1992.

SYNGNATHIDAE   Pipefishes

Pipefishes are slender and elongate, with a syringelike mouth and body encased in dermal plates arranged in series of rings. They are distinguished from the other families of the order by the following combination of characters. Mouth is small and located at end of a tubelike snout. Teeth are lacking. Four complete gill arches are present. Gill opening is reduced to pore in membrane above operculum. Gill filaments are lobate. Branchiostegal rays number 1 to 3. Spinous dorsal and anal fins are absent. Pelvic fin is absent. Pectoral fin is present or absent. Prehensile tail is present in seahorses and in some pipefishes but absent in most. Caudal fin is absent in some taxa.

Pipefishes occur worldwide in tropical to temperate latitudes. Most species are marine, but some occur in brackish water and a few occur in freshwater. Some of the marine species are oceanic and associated with pelagic filamentous algae, but most species live near shore in less than 50 m. Food consists of zooplankton that is captured by means of syringelike mouths. Fertilized eggs are carried by males on ventral surface or in well-defined brood pouches on the trunk and tail. There are about 215 species in 52 genera, and 17 species in 7 genera occur in the Gulf of Mexico.

Key to the Species of the Gulf of Mexico
(Adapted from Dawson 1982; Vari 1982)

1a. Caudal fin absent; tail coiled distally (prehensile); long axis of head angled 70% to 90% from axis of body 2
1b. Caudal fin present; tail usually straight (except in *Acentronura*); long axis of head and trunk usually parallel (except in *Acentronura*) 4
2a. Dorsal fin rays 10 to 13; pectoral fin rays 10 to 13 . . . . *Hippocampus zosterae* p. 1058
2b. Dorsal fin rays 16 to 20; pectoral fin rays 14 to 17 3
3a. Head and body pigmented with distinct dark spots of various sizes; snout length 41% to 49% of head length . . . . *Hippocampus reidi* p. 1057
3b. Head and body pigmented with blotches, streaks, or lines; snout length 33% to 46% of head length . . . . *Hippocampus erectus* p. 1056
4a. Inferior trunk and tail ridges interrupted near anal ring (Fig. 153) 5
4b. Inferior trunk and tail ridges confluent (Fig. 154) 9
5a. Tail coiled distally (prehensile); dorsal fin base elevated . . . . *Acentronura dendritica* p. 1050
5b. Tail not coiled; dorsal fin base not elevated 6

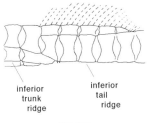

inferior trunk ridge   inferior tail ridge

FIG 153

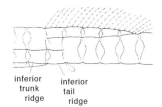

inferior trunk ridge   inferior tail ridge

FIG 154

6a. Caudal fin rays generally 9; pectoral fin rays 17 to 23; dorsal fin rays more than 30; brood pouch abdominal
.... *Microphis brachyurus* p. 1060

6b. Caudal fin rays generally 10; pectoral fin rays fewer than 16; dorsal fin rays fewer than 30; brood pouch caudal... 7

7a. Anal fin present; pectoral fin rays almost always 12 to 14
.... *Micrognathus ensenadae* p. 1059

7b. Anal fin absent; pectoral fin rays almost always 6 to 11
.... 8

8a. Pectoral fin rays 6 to 9; trunk rings 14 to 16 (from ring bearing pectoral fin base to ring bearing anus); tail rings 35 to 39 (from ring behind anus to penultimate ring)
.... *Anarchopterus criniger* p. 1051

8b. Pectoral fin rays 10 to 12; trunk rings 17 or 18 (from ring bearing pectoral fin base to ring bearing anus); tail rings 31 to 35 (from ring behind anus to penultimate ring)
.... *Anarchopterus tectus* p. 1052

9a. Supraopercular ridge, lateral snout ridge, and dermal flaps absent (Fig. 155); dorsal fin rays 28 to 49; 0.25 to 6.5 trunk rings under dorsal fin (subdorsal trunk rings)
.... 10

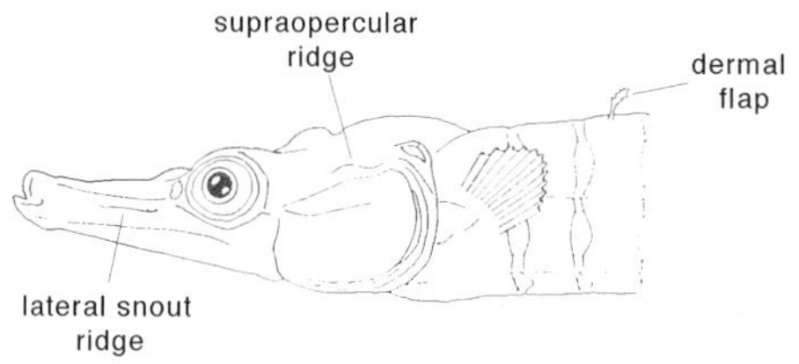

FIG 155

9b. Supraopercular ridge, lateral snout ridge, or dermal flaps present, at least in part; dorsal fin rays 19 to 27; 0 to 2.75 trunk rings under dorsal fin (subdorsal trunk rings).... 15

10a. Preorbital bone broad; length of pectoral fin base averages 77% of pectoral fin length ... *Syngnathus floridae* p. 1062

10b. Preorbital bone moderate to narrow; length of pectoral fin base averages 50% to 71% of pectoral fin length...... 11

11a. Trunk rings 18 to 24 (modally 19 or more) 12

11b. Trunk rings 14 to 19 (modally 18 or fewer) 13

12a. Trunk rings 22 to 24........ *Syngnathus springeri* p. 1066

12b. Trunk rings 18 to 21...... *Syngnathus louisianae* p. 1063

13a. Snout length 37% to 53% ($\bar{x}$ = 43%) of head length; snout depth 19% to 42% ($\bar{x}$ = 26%–36%) of snout length
.... 14

13b. Snout length 42% to 63% ($\bar{x}$ = 56%) of head length; snout depth 9.3% to 29% ($\bar{x}$ = 13%–15.9%) of snout length.................. *Syngnathus pelagicus* p. 1064

14a. Trunk rings 15 to 18 (modally 16); dorsal fin rays 25 to 37 (rarely 35 to 37); total rings under dorsal fin (subdorsal rings) 5.5 to 9.5 . . . . *Syngnathus scovelli* p.1065

14b. Trunk rings 17 to 19 (modally 18); dorsal fin rays 35 to 41 (modally 38); total rings under dorsal fin (subdorsal rings) 8.25 to 10 . . . . *Syngnathus affinis* p. 1061

15a. Snout length 40% to 59% ($\bar{x}$ = 50%–59%) of head length; snout depth 9.8% to 26% of snout length . . . . *Cosmocampus elucens* p. 1054

15b. Snout length 26% to 45% ($\bar{x}$ = 42%) of head length; snout depth 25% to 71% of snout length. 16

16a. Tail rings 31 to 35 (usually more than 31); pectoral fin rays 10 to 13 (modally 11) . . . .*Cosmocampus hildebrandi* p. 1055

16b. Tail rings 24 to 31 (usually fewer than 31); pectoral fin rays 11 to 15 (modally 13) . . . .*Cosmocampus albirostris* p. 1053

Acentronura dendritica   (Barbour 1905)
Pipehorse

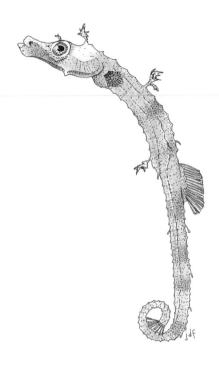

Acentronura dendritica is slender and elongate, with head bent slightly downward, dorsal fin elevated, and tail curled. It is distinguished from the other species of the family by the following combination of characters. Head length is about 13.9% of SL, snout length is about 32.3% of head length, and snout depth is about 33.3% of snout length. Body depth at anal ring is about 37%, and trunk depth is about 52.6% of SL. Pectoral fin has 12 to 15 rays. Dorsal fin originates between penultimate trunk ring and second tail ring and has 15 to 18 rays. Anal fin usually has 2 rays. Caudal fin has 9 or 10 rays. Trunk rings number 13 to 15, and tail rings number 50 to 55. Principal body ridges are prominent. Superior trunk and tail ridges are discontinuous near dorsal fin insertion. Inferior trunk ridge terminates at anal ring. Lateral trunk ridge is confluent with inferior tail ridge, and lateral tail ridge terminates below dorsal fin base. Dermal flaps range from simple to branched and are present on eye, head, and remainder of body. Brood pouch is located on 10 or 11 tail rings, and pouch plates are slightly enlarged. Color is light with dark blotches or uniformly dark.

This species occurs in the western Atlantic from New Brunswick to Brazil, including the Gulf of Mexico off the Mississippi River and the Bahamas. It has been captured in dredges in 15 m or less, and in plankton and neuston nets near the surface at night. This species is known from shallow water around islands and from oceanic waters off continental areas. Maximum known size is 81 mm SL, and males mature at about 47 mm SL.

REFERENCES: Dawson 1982 (as *Amphelikturus dendriticus*); C. R. Robins et al. 1986; Boschung 1992.

Anarchopterus criniger   (Bean and Dresel 1884)
Fringed pipefish

Anarchopterus criniger is slender and elongate, with inferior trunk ridge interrupted near anal ring, and anal fin absent. It is distinguished from the other species of the family by the following combination of characters. Head length is 7.7% to 12.2% of SL, snout length is 26.3% to 33.3% of head length, and snout depth is 55.6% to 66.7% of snout length. Body depth at anal ring is 27% to 43.4%, and trunk depth is 43.5% to 66.7% of head length. Pectoral fin has 6 to 9 rays. Dorsal fin originates between penultimate trunk ring and second tail ring, and has 15 to 19 rays. Caudal fin has 10 rays. Trunk rings number 14 to 16, and tail rings number 35 to 39. Superior trunk and tail ridges are discontinuous near insertion of dorsal fin. Lateral tail ridge ends below dorsal fin base. Lateral trunk ridge is confluent with inferior tail ridge near anal ring. Brood pouch is located below 13 to 20 tail rings, and pouch plates are slightly developed. Color is tan to brown, with three short whitish bars on each body ring, three black spots on upper trunk, and three pale streaks radiating from lower half of eye.

This species occurs in the western Atlantic from North Carolina to the east coast of Yucatán, including the Gulf of Mexico and the Bahamas, to 11 m. It is also found near the surface associated with *Sargassum*. Food consists of copepods, mysids, amphipods, and isopods. Maximum known size is 94 mm SL.

REFERENCES: Böhlke and Chaplin 1968; Hoese and Moore 1977 (all above as *Micrognathus crinigerus*); Dawson 1982; C. R. Robins et al. 1986 (as *M. criniger*); Boschung 1992.

Anarchopterus tectus (Dawson 1978)
Insular pipefish

Anarchopterus tectus is slender and elongate, with inferior trunk ridge interrupted near anal ring, and anal fin absent. It is distinguished from the other species of the family by the following combination of characters. Head length is 7.9% to 10.6% of SL, snout length is 27% to 32.3% of head length, and snout depth is 45.5% to 58.8% of snout length. Body depth at anal ring is 31.3% to 45.5%, and trunk depth is 37% to 55.6% of head length. Pectoral fin has 10 to 12 rays. Dorsal fin originates on trunk and has 18 to 21 rays. Caudal fin has 10 rays. Trunk rings number 17 or 18, and tail rings number 31 to 35. Bony body ridges are moderately developed. Superior trunk and tail ridges are discontinuous near insertion of dorsal fin. Inferior trunk ridge terminates at anal ring. Lateral tail ridge ends below dorsal fin base. Lateral trunk ridge is confluent with inferior tail ridge near anal ring. Brood pouch is located below 13 to 20 tail rings, and pouch plates are slightly developed. Color is light tan to brown, with mottling or diffuse bands.

This species occurs in the western Atlantic from the Bahamas and Florida Keys to northern South America, including the eastern Gulf of Mexico, to 26 m. It is known only from the Dry Tortugas in the Gulf of Mexico. Maximum known size is 114 mm SL.

REFERENCES: Longley and Hildebrand 1941 (as *Syngnathus jonesi*); Dawson 1982; C. R. Robins et al. 1986 (as *Micrognathus tectus*).

Cosmocampus albirostris (Kaup 1856)
Whitenose pipefish

Cosmocampus albirostris is slender and elongate, with a supraopercular ridge and a relatively short, deep snout. It is distinguished from the other species of the family by the following combination of characters. Head length is 9.5% to 13.9% of SL, snout length is 35.7% to 45.5% of head length, and snout depth is 25% to 38.5% of snout length. Depth at anal ring is 22.2% to 52.6%, and trunk depth is 32.3% to 66.7% of head length. Pectoral fin has 11 to 15 rays. Dorsal fin extends over 0 to 2 trunk rings and 3.5 to 5.75 tail rings, and has 21 to 25 rays. Anal fin has 2 to 4 rays, and caudal fin has 10 rays. Trunk rings number 16 to 18, and tail rings number 25 to 31. Principal body ridges are prominent. Superior trunk and tail ridges are discontinuous near dorsal fin insertion. Inferior trunk and tail ridges are continuous. Lateral trunk and tail ridges are discontinuous below dorsal fin base. Brood pouch is located below 12 to 20 tail rings. Pouch plates are well developed. Color is white to brownish. Snout is white or unpigmented, and occasionally body has irregular tan and dark brown bands.

This species occurs in the western Atlantic from Bermuda and South Carolina to northern South America, including the Gulf of Mexico and the Caribbean Sea, to 50 m. Maximum known size is 208 mm SL.

REFERENCES: Böhlke and Chaplin 1968 (as *Corythoichthys albirostris*); Dawson 1982; C. R. Robins et al. 1986; Boschung 1992.

Cosmocampus elucens   (Poey 1868)
Shortfin pipefish

Cosmocampus elucens is slender and elongate, with a supraopercular ridge and a long, slender snout. It is distinguished from the other species of the family by the following combination of characters. Head length is 11% to 15.4% of SL, snout length is 40% to 83.3% of head length, and snout depth is 10.8% to 25.6% of snout length. Depth at anal ring is 17.5% to 33.3%, and trunk depth is 23.8% to 35.7% of head length. Pectoral fin has 11 to 15 rays. Dorsal fin extends over 0 to 1.5 trunk rings and 3.5 to 5.25 tail rings, and has 19 to 25 rays. Caudal fin has 10 rays. Trunk rings number 15 to 18, and tail rings number 29 to 34. Principal body ridges are prominent. Superior trunk and tail ridges are discontinuous near dorsal fin insertion. Inferior trunk and tail ridges are continuous. Lateral trunk and tail ridges are discontinuous below dorsal fin base. Brood pouch is located below 12 to 20 tail rings, and pouch plates are well developed. Color is tan to greenish brown, with dorsum and side of body usually mottled.

This species occurs in the western Atlantic from New Jersey and Bermuda to northern Brazil, including the eastern Gulf of Mexico and the western Caribbean Sea. It has been reported from turtle-grass beds, coral reefs and estuaries, and from surface waters over 100 km from shore. Maximum known size is 164 mm SL.

REFERENCES: Beebe and Tee-Van 1933 (as *Syngnathus elucens*); Longley and Hildebrand 1941 (as *S. elucens* and *S. robertsi*); Dawson 1982; C. R. Robins et al. 1986 (as *S. elucens*); Boschung 1992.

Cosmocampus hildebrandi   (Herald 1965)
Dwarf pipefish

Cosmocampus hildebrandi is slender and elongate, with a supraopercular ridge and a moderately short snout. It is distinguished from the other species of the family by the following combination of characters. Head length is 9.1% to 14.3% of SL, snout length is 31.3% to 38.5% of head length, and snout depth is 27.8% to 45.5% of snout length. Body depth at anal ring is 31.3% to 40%, and trunk depth is 38.5% to 50% of head length. Pectoral fin has 10 to 13 rays. Dorsal fin extends over 0 to 1 trunk ring and 4 to 5.5 tail rings, and has 19 to 22 rays. Caudal fin has 10 rays. Trunk rings number 16 or 17, and tail rings number 31 to 35. Principal body ridges are prominent. Superior trunk and tail ridges are discontinuous near dorsal fin insertion. Inferior trunk and tail ridges are continuous. Lateral trunk and tail ridges are discontinuous below dorsal fin base. Brood pouch is located below 12 to 20 tail rings, and pouch plates are well developed. Color is red in life and light brown to tan in preservative.

This species occurs in the western Atlantic from North Carolina to southern Florida and in the northeastern Gulf of Mexico off Florida. It has been captured between 4 and 73 m over coral, rock, or sand. Maximum known size is 86 mm SL.

REFERENCES: Longley and Hildebrand 1941 (as *Syngnathus elucens,* in part); Herald 1965 (as *S. hildebrandi*); Dawson 1982; C. R. Robins et al. 1986 (as *S. hildebrandi*); Boschung 1992.

Hippocampus erectus Perry 1810
Lined seahorse

Hippocampus erectus is angular, with head distinctly demarcated and angled ventrally from trunk, and has a prehensile tail lacking a caudal fin. It is distinguished from the other species of the family by the following combination of characters. Snout is moderately long and lacks mid-dorsal snout ridge. Head is movable with respect to trunk along medial axis. Head length is 20% to 27%, body depth is 11% to 22% (females) and 16% to 24% (males), trunk length is 36% to 40% (females) and 33% to 43% (males), and tail length is 54% to 64% (females) and 57% to 67% (males) of TL. Snout length is 33% to 46%, orbital diameter is 12% to 18%, and postorbital head length is 38% to 49% of head length. Pectoral fin has 14 to 17, dorsal fin has 16 to 20, and anal fin has 3 or 4 rays. Trunk rings number 10 or 11, and tail rings number 33 to 38. Penultimate trunk ring is septangular or, rarely, novemangular. Ultimate trunk ring is septangular or, rarely, novemangular. Superior trunk and tail ridges are discontinuous and overlap along 2 or 3 rings under dorsal fin base. Lateral trunk ridge is confluent with inferior tail ridge. Inferior trunk ridge terminates at ultimate trunk ring. Median ventral trunk ridge ends at penultimate trunk ring. Brood pouch extends along 5 to 8 tail rings. Branched dermal flaps are variously developed. Color is light yellow to nearly black, usually with large, pale blotches and dark lines on neck and back.

This species occurs in the western Atlantic from Nova Scotia and Bermuda to Argentina, including the Gulf of Mexico, the Bahamas, and the Caribbean Sea, to 73 m. It is usually associated with vegetation. Food consists of copepods and amphipods. Maximum known size is 173 mm TL.

REFERENCES: Longley and Hildebrand 1941 (as *H. punctulatus*); Böhlke and Chaplin 1968; Hoese and Moore 1977; Vari 1982; C. R. Robins et al. 1986; Boschung 1992.

Hippocampus reidi   Ginsburg 1933
Longnose seahorse

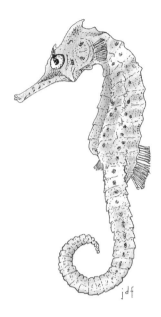

Hippocampus reidi is angular, with head distinctly demarcated and angled ventrally from trunk, and has a prehensile tail lacking a caudal fin. It is distinguished from the other species of the family by the following combination of characters. Snout is moderately long to long and lacks mid-dorsal snout ridge. Head is movable with respect to trunk along medial axis. Head length is 23% to 27%, body depth is 11% to 15% (females) and 13% to 17% (males), trunk length is 39% to 45% (females) and 35% to 41% (males), and tail length is 55% to 61% (females) and 59% to 65% (males) of TL. Snout length is 41% to 49%, orbit diameter is 13% to 18%, and postorbital head length is 35% to 41% of head length. Pectoral fin has 15 to 17, dorsal fin has 16 to 19, and anal fin has 3 or 4 rays. Trunk rings number 11, and tail rings number 33 to 37. Penultimate trunk ring is septangular or novemangular. Ultimate trunk ring is octangular. Superior trunk and tail ridges are discontinuous and overlap along 1 to 3 rings under dorsal fin base. Lateral trunk ridge is confluent with inferior tail ridge. Inferior trunk ridge terminates at ultimate trunk ring and median ventral trunk ridge terminates at penultimate trunk ring. Brood pouch extends over 5 to 7 tail rings. Dermal tabs are absent. Color is brownish, with evenly distributed dark brown spots. Occasionally specimens are dark brown without dark spots.

This species occurs in the western Atlantic from Cape Hatteras and Bermuda to Rio de Janeiro, including the eastern Gulf of Mexico, the Bahamas, and the Caribbean Sea, to 55 m. Maximum known size is 175 mm TL.

REFERENCES: Ginsburg 1933; Böhlke and Chaplin 1968; Vari 1982; Uyeno et al. 1983; C. R. Robins et al. 1986.

Hippocampus zosterae Jordan and Gilbert 1882
Dwarf seahorse

Hippocampus zosterae is angular, with head distinctly demarcated and angled ventrally from trunk, and has a prehensile tail without a caudal fin. It is distinguished from the other species of the family by the following combination of characters. Snout is relatively short and lacks mid-dorsal snout ridge. Head is movable with respect to trunk along medial axis. Head length is 19% to 25%, body depth is 12% to 19% (females) and 14% to 21% (males), trunk length is 37% to 47% (females) and 34% to 44% (males), and tail length is 53% to 63% (females) and 56% to 66% (males) of TL. Pectoral fin has 10 to 13, dorsal fin has 10 to 13, and anal fin has 3 or 4 rays. Trunk rings number 9 to 11, and tail rings number 28 to 34. Penultimate trunk ring is septangular or, rarely, octangular. Ultimate trunk ring is sexangular or octangular. Superior trunk and tail ridges are discontinuous and overlap on 0 to 2 rings under dorsal fin base. Lateral trunk ridge is confluent with inferior tail ridge. Inferior trunk ridge terminates at ultimate trunk ring, and median ventral trunk ridge terminates at penultimate trunk ring. Brood pouch extends along 5 to 7 tail rings. Dermal tabs are rarely present but, when present, are not numerous in adults. Color is usually uniform tan, with dorsal fin possessing submarginal stripe.

This species occurs in the western Atlantic from the east coast of Florida and Bermuda to the Bahamas and the Gulf of Mexico in shallow water. It is associated with grass flats and occasionally with floating vegetation. Food consists of crustaceans. Maximum known size is 42 mm TL.

REFERENCES: Böhlke and Chaplin 1968; Hoese and Moore 1977; Vari 1982; C. R. Robins et al. 1986; Boschung 1992.

Micrognathus ensenadae (Silvester 1915)
Harlequin pipefish

Micrognathus ensenadae is slender and elongate, with inferior trunk ridge interrupted near anal ring, and anal fin present. It is distinguished from the other species of the family by the following combination of characters. Head length is 8.8% to 13.2% of SL, snout length is 27% to 37% of head length, and snout depth is 34.5% to 58.8% of snout length. Body depth at anal ring is 26.3% to 45.5%, and trunk depth is 32.2% to 40% of head length. Pectoral fin has 12 to 14 rays. Dorsal fin extends over 0 to 1.25 trunk rings and 3.5 to 4.5 tail rings. Anal fin has 2 to 4 rays. Trunk rings number 17 or 18, and tail rings number 33 to 35. Superior trunk and tail ridges are discontinuous near dorsal fin insertion. Inferior trunk ridge ends at anal ring. Lateral tail ridge terminates below dorsal fin base. Lateral trunk ridge is confluent with inferior tail ridge near anal ring.

Brood pouch is below 10 to 17 tail rings, and pouch plates are not greatly enlarged. Color consists of bright yellow and dark purplish brown bands on side, most of which join medially to form rings.

This species occurs in the western Atlantic from the east coast of Florida and Bermuda to Brazil, including the southern Gulf of Mexico and the Bahamas, to 21 m. There is only a single record from the Gulf of Mexico, off Cayos Arcas on the Yucatán Peninsula. This species occurs over rocks, coral reefs, or coarse sand bottoms. Maximum known size is 146 mm SL.

REFERENCES: Böhlke and Chaplin 1968 (as *M. crinitus*, in part); Dawson 1982 (as *M. crinitus*, in part); C. R. Robins et al. 1986.

Microphis brachyurus (Bleeker 1853)
Opossum pipefish

Microphis brachyurus is slender and elongate, with an elongate, slender snout and a low mid-dorsal snout ridge. It is distinguished from the other species of the family by the following combination of characters. Head length is 14.9% to 21.7% of SL, snout length is 50% to 66.7% of head length, and snout depth is 7.6% to 14.7% of snout length. Body depth at anal ring is 11.6% to 20.8% of head length. Pectoral fin has 17 to 23 rays. Dorsal fin extends over 1.5 to 3.5 trunk rings and 4 to 7.25 tail rings, and has 40 to 47 rays. Anal fin has 4 rays, and caudal fin has 9 rays. Trunk rings number 18 to 20, and tail rings number 22 to 25. Principal body ridges are well developed and have single spine at each ring. Superior trunk and tail ridges are discontinuous near dorsal fin insertion. Inferior trunk ridge terminates at anal ring. Lateral tail ridge ends below dorsal fin base. Lateral trunk ridge is confluent with inferior tail ridge. Brood pouch originates below second or third trunk ring and extends to last trunk ring. Pouch plates are well developed. Color is tan to dark brown, and plain, mottled, or with indistinct dark stripe above lateral trunk ridge.

This species occurs in the western Atlantic, Indian, and western Pacific Oceans. The western Atlantic populations are considered a separate subspecies, *M. b. lineatus,* and occur from New Jersey to Brazil, including the Gulf of Mexico, the Bahamas, and the Caribbean Sea, in shallow water. In the Gulf of Mexico, it is most common off Mexico. Adults are also found in freshwater. Maximum known size is 194 mm SL.

REFERENCES: Böhlke and Chaplin 1968; Hoese and Moore 1977; Dawson 1982 (all above as *Oostethus lineatus*); C. R. Robins et al. 1986; Boschung 1992.

Syngnathus affinis Günther 1870
Texas pipefish

Syngnathus affinis is slender and elongate, with a relatively short, deep snout. It is distinguished from the other species of the family by the following combination of characters. Head length is 10% to 13.9% of SL, snout length is 38.5% to 47.6% of head length, and snout depth is 20% to 41.7% of snout length. Body depth at anal ring is 20% to 37%, and trunk depth is 27.7% to 47.6% of head length. Pectoral fin is 18.2% to 33.3% of head length and has 13 to 16 rays. Dorsal fin extends over 4 to 5.75 trunk rings and 3.5 to 5.5 tail rings, and has 35 to 41 rays. Anal fin has 2 to 4 rays, and caudal fin has 10 rays. Trunk rings number 17 to 19, and tail rings number 32 to 35. Principal body ridges are rather low. Superior trunk and tail ridges are discontinuous near dorsal fin insertion. Inferior trunk and tail ridges are continuous. Lateral trunk and tail ridges are discontinuous below dorsal fin base. Brood pouch is located under tail, and brood plates are present. Color ranges from white to dark brown.

This species occurs in the western Atlantic from the western Gulf of Mexico. In the Gulf it is known from Louisiana, Corpus Christi Bay, and the Laguna de Términos, Campeche. Maximum known size is 218 mm TL.

REFERENCES: Hoese and Moore 1977 (as *S. fuscus*); Dawson 1982; Robins et al. (as *S. fuscus*).

Syngnathus floridae (Jordan and Gilbert 1882)
Dusky pipefish

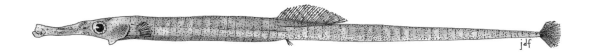

Syngnathus floridae is slender and elongate, with a relatively long snout and a broad pre-orbital bone. It is distinguished from the other species of the family by the following combination of characters. Head length is 12.7% to 18.9% of SL, snout length is 47.6% to 62.5% of head length, and snout depth is 9.6% to 20.8% of snout length. Body depth at anal ring is 10.5% to 31.3%, and trunk depth is 16.4% to 45.5% of head length. Pectoral fin has 12 to 16 rays. Dorsal fin extends over 0.25 to 3 trunk rings and 4 to 7 tail rings, and has 26 to 35 rays. Anal fin has 2 to 4 rays, and caudal fin has 10 rays. Trunk rings number 16 to 19, and tail rings number 29 to 39. Principal body ridges are rather low. Superior trunk and tail ridges are discontinuous near dorsal fin insertion. Inferior trunk and tail ridges are continuous. Lateral trunk and tail ridges are continuous be-low dorsal fin base. Brood pouch is located under tail, and brood plates and membranes are present. Color is white to brownish and variably mottled or blotched on dorsum and upper side, but markings do not form bands.

This species occurs in the western Atlantic from Chesapeake Bay and Bermuda to Panama, including the northern Gulf of Mexico, the Bahamas, and the western Caribbean Sea. It is most abundant in grass beds, both in coastal areas and estuaries. Food consists of microcrustaceans. Maximum known size is 258 mm SL.

REFERENCES: Longley and Hildebrand 1941; Gunter 1945 (as *S. mackayi*); Böhlke and Chaplin 1968; Hoese and Moore 1977; Dawson 1982; C. R. Robins et al. 1986; Boschung 1992.

Syngnathus louisianae   Günther 1870
Chain pipefish

Syngnathus louisianae is slender and elongate, with a long, slender snout and a chainlike row of marks on sides. It is distinguished from the other species of the family by the following combination of characters. Head length is 11.5% to 17.5% of SL, snout length is 52.6% to 66.7% of head length, and snout depth is 7.6% to 14.5% of snout length. Body depth at anal ring is 11% to 23.8%, and trunk depth is 11% to 29.4% of head length. Pectoral fin has 12 to 16 rays. Dorsal fin extends over 1.5 to 4 trunk rings and 3.75 to 6 tail rings, and has 29 to 42 rays. Anal fin has 2 to 4 rays, and caudal fin has 10 rays. Trunk rings number 19 to 21, and tail rings number 33 to 38. Principal body ridges are rather low. Superior trunk and tail ridges are discontinuous near dorsal fin insertion. Inferior trunk and tail ridges are continuous. Lateral trunk and tail ridges are discontinuous below dorsal fin base. Brood pouch is located below tail, and pouch plates and membranes are present. Color is white to light tan, with a row of diamond-shaped marks along lower side.

This species occurs in the western Atlantic from New Jersey to southern Florida and in the eastern Gulf of Mexico to 38 m. It is most common in aquatic vegetation, such as *Zostera* and *Thalassia*. It is commonly captured in estuaries and has been reported from freshwater. Food consists of amphipods, mysids, and small shrimps and, to a lesser extent, copepods, isopods, and ostracods. Maximum known size is 381 mm SL.

REFERENCES: Longley and Hildebrand 1941; Gunter 1945; Hoese and Moore 1977; Dawson 1982; C. R. Robins et al. 1986; Boschung 1992.

Syngnathus pelagicus Linnaeus 1758
Sargassum pipefish

Syngnathus pelagicus is slender and elongate, with a long, slender snout and a pale band or spot on each trunk ring. It is distinguished from the other species of the family by the following combination of characters. Head length is 12% to 18.2% of SL, snout length is 41.7% to 58.8% of head length, and snout depth is 12% to 29.4% of snout length. Body depth at anal ring is 12.5% to 32.3%, and trunk depth is 15.6% to 40% of head length. Pectoral fin is 12.3% to 22.2% of head length and has 12 to 16 rays. Dorsal fin extends over 1 to 3 trunk rings and 3.75 to 6.25 tail rings, and has 25 to 34 rays. Anal fin extends to middle of second tail ring and has 2 to 4 rays, and caudal fin has 10 rays. Trunk rings number 15 to 18, and tail rings number 30 to 34. Principal body ridges are rather low. Superior trunk and tail ridges are discontinuous near dorsal fin insertion. Inferior trunk and tail ridges are continuous. Lateral trunk and tail ridges are continuous below dorsal fin base. Brood pouch is located under tail, and pouch plates and membranes are present. Color is tan to brown, with brown stripe on snout and pale band or spot on trunk rings.

This species occurs in the western and central Atlantic from Nova Scotia to Colombia, including the Gulf of Mexico, the Bahamas, and the Caribbean Sea. It is most often captured in oceanic waters in floating sargassum weed. Maximum known size is 181 mm SL.

REFERENCES: Bigelow and Schroeder 1953b; Böhlke and Chaplin 1968; Hoese and Moore 1977; Dawson 1982; C. R. Robins et al. 1986; Boschung 1992.

Syngnathus scovelli   (Evermann and Kendall 1896)
Gulf pipefish

Syngnathus scovelli is slender and elongate, with a relatively short, deep snout. It is distinguished from the other species of the family by the following combination of characters. Head length is 11.2% to 15.9% of SL, snout length is 37% to 52.6% of head length, and snout depth is 18.5% to 41.7% of snout length. Body depth at anal ring is 17.9% to 40%, and trunk depth is 21.3% to 66.7% of head length. Pectoral fin is 13% to 27.8% of head length and has 11 to 17 rays. Dorsal fin extends over 1 to 5 trunk rings and 3.25 to 5.5 tail rings, and has 25 to 37 rays. Anal fin has 2 to 4 rays, and caudal fin has 10 rays. Trunk rings number 15 to 18, and tail rings number 28 to 34. Principal body ridges are rather low. Superior trunk and tail ridges are discontinuous near dorsal fin insertion. Inferior trunk and tail ridges are continuous. Lateral trunk and tail ridges are dis-continuous below dorsal fin base. Brood pouch is located under tail, and pouch plates and membranes are present. Color is light tan to dark olive brown, with markings of various shades of brown. Dorsum is usually lighter than side, and dorsum and side are often streaked with fine brown lines.

This species occurs in the western Atlantic from northeastern Florida to southern Brazil, including the Gulf of Mexico, to 6 m. It is commonly associated with algae and turtle grass (*Thalassia*) and is also found in *Spartina* marshes and in freshwater. Maximum known size is 183 mm SL.

REFERENCES: Gunter 1945; Hoese and Moore 1977; Dawson 1982; C. R. Robins et al. 1986; Boschung 1992.

Syngnathus springeri   Herald 1942
Bull pipefish

Syngnathus springeri is slender and elongate, with a moderately long snout and a relatively high number of trunk rings. It is distinguished from the other species of the family by the following combination of characters. Head length is 10.5% to 13.2% of SL, snout length is 50% to 58.8% of head length, and snout depth is 8.5% to 23.8% of snout length. Body depth at anal ring is 12.7% to 32.3%, and trunk depth is 15.6% to 45.5% of head length. Pectoral fin is 12.6% to 23.8% of head length and has 12 to 14 rays. Dorsal fin extends over 3 to 4.75 trunk rings and 3.5 to 5 tail rings, and has 32 to 38 rays. Anal fin has 2 to 4 rays, and caudal fin has 10 rays. Trunk rings number 22 to 24, and tail rings number 34 to 37 rings. Superior trunk and tail ridges are discontinuous near dorsal fin insertion. Inferior trunk and tail ridges are continuous. Lateral trunk and tail ridges are discontinuous below dorsal fin base. Brood pouch is located below tail, and pouch plates and membranes are present. Color is pale with broad dark saddles or bands on trunk and tail.

This species occurs in the western Atlantic from Massachusetts to the Florida Keys, and in the Bahamas and the eastern Gulf of Mexico. It is most common between 18 and 128 m, is found up to 185 km offshore, and occurs throughout the water column. Maximum known size is 355 mm SL.

REFERENCES: Herald 1942; Böhlke and Chaplin 1968; Dawson 1982; C. R. Robins et al. 1986; Boschung 1992.

GLOSSARY

(Irregular plural form of noun is in parentheses following singular term.)

Abdominal: refers to position, such as placement of pelvic fins, below abdomen just anterior to vent or anus.

Abdominal keel: a sawtoothlike margin along midline of belly formed by scutelike scales.

Adipose eyelid: transparent to translucent tissue covering anterior and posterior sections of eye and leaving elliptical depression over pupil of some fishes.

Adipose fin: transparent to translucent fleshy lobe along dorsal midline of caudal peduncle resembling small fin but without obvious fin rays.

Alar thorns: clawlike thorns of males of Rajidae arranged in rows just medial to lateral extremes of the disc.

Ammocoete: larval stage of Petromyzontidae that lacks functional eyes and adult specializations of mouth, branchial chamber, and median fins.

Ampullar pore: orifice on skin leading to jelly-filled canal and ampulla housing electric sensory cells; found on dorsal and ventral surfaces in chondrichthyans and bony fishes with electric reception.

Anadromous: type of life history in which organism moves from marine waters to ascend freshwater streams to spawn. Young migrate from freshwater to marine waters to complete development.

Anal fin: median, unpaired fin located on midventral surface anterior to caudal fin.

Anterior nasal flap: flexible fold of integument along inner margin of naris or nostril that partially covers same.

Antrorse: pointing or oriented anteriorly.

Anus: external opening of intestine.

Aphaktic space: area along margin of pupil of eye that allows light to strike retina without passing through lens (typical of deepsea teleosts).

Aplacental: development of embryo and later ontogenetic stages in the uterus or oviducts of the mother in which the mother provides nutrients by means other than by a placenta.

Arcuate: arched or bowed in shape.

Attenuate: to taper to a point.

Axil: posterior extreme of fin base.

Axillary scale: enlarged and often elongated scale(s) at posterior base of pectoral or pelvic fins in some fishes (Clupeiformes).

Barbel: fleshy, tentacle-like protuberance located on head and sensitive to tactile and/or chemical stimuli.

Basibranch: median skeletal element of gill arch (branchial) skeleton, located behind tongue.

Basihyal: median skeletal element of hyoid arch that forms tongue.

Bathypelagic: pelagic realm between 1,000 and 4,000 m.

Benthic: refers to the substrate area or to organisms that live on the substrate in the marine habitat.

Benthopelagic: refers to the area or to organisms that live just above the benthic habitat.

Bicuspid: refers to tooth with two cusps or points.

Bifurcate: divided into two parts.

Bilobate: divided into two lobes.

Bioluminescence: production of light by means of chemical reaction.

Biserial: arranged in two rows or series.

Branchial: refers to gill region.

Branchial arch: gill arch, skeletal structure bearing gill filaments.

Branchiostegal ray: raylike skeletal elements articulating with hyoid bar (ceratohyal) and opercular elements and supporting branchiostegal membrane.

Buckler: enlarged or fused thorn (elasmo-branchs), or bony plate, located in dermis at base of fins on belly (teleost fishes).

Canine: large, conical, pointed tooth.

Caniniform: canine shaped; referring to pointed teeth that are larger than other teeth in mouth.

Cardiform: refers to short, fine, pointed teeth arranged in patch.

Caudal peduncle: portion of the body between end of anal fin and base of caudal fin.

Cephalic lobe: finlike structure on either side of head formed by anterior section of pectoral fins and lateral components of rostral cartilage (Rhinopteridae and Mobulidae).

Ceratobranch: paired skeletal elements of branchial skeleton articulating with hypobranch and epibranch, and bearing gill filaments and gill rakers.

Ceratotrichia: fin supports of chondrichthyan fishes that are unpaired, unsegmented (hairlike), and very close together.

Cheek: surface of head between eye and anterior margin of preoperculum in actinopterygian fishes.

Chromatophore: pigment cell in epidermis that is responsible for much of the color in fishes.

Circulus (circuli): bony ridge on cycloid and ctenoid scales.

Clasper: male intromittent organ developed from metapterygial and radial cartilages of pelvic girdle; found in chondrichthyan fishes.

Cloaca: depression that contains anus and urogenital openings of chondrichthyans.

Commissure: bundle of nerve fibers connecting two distinct areas of brain or spinal cord.

Compressed: laterally flattened.

Confluent: joined together.

Ctenoid scale: thin and flexible to slightly thickened and inflexible scale bearing small spines (ctenii) on posterior surface.

Cusp: pointed, distal, exposed portion of tooth.

Cusplet: minor cusp of tooth, shorter than cusp.

Cycloid scale: thin, flexible scale with a smooth posterior surface.

Deciduous: loosely attached and easily lost; refers to scales.

Demersal: refers to substrate area or to organisms that live on the substrate.

Dentary: dermal skeletal element bearing most of teeth in lower jaw of actinopterygian fishes.

Denticle: scale consisting of inner pulp cavity, middle dentine or bony layer, and outer enameliod layer that does not grow after formation and is found in elasmobranch fishes.

Depressed: dorsoventrally flattened.

Diapause: phase of arrested embryonic development.

Diastema: gap in teeth of upper jaw into which canine tooth of lower jaw fits.

Dioecious: refers to individuals that possess either functional male or functional female sex organs.

Diphycercal: refers to caudal fin in which vertebral column extends straight to tip, with equally developed upper (epichordal) and lower (hypochordal) lobes.

Disc: flattened surface formed by lateral expansion and confluence of integument of head and pectoral fins; typical of torpediniforms, pristiforms, rhinobatoids, rajoids, and myiolobatiforms (batoid fishes).

Distal: refers to region of structure away from region of attachment.

Dorsal blade: keel-like structure medially located on dorsal surface anterior to dorsal fin and formed by dorsal fin radials; occurs in Sternoptychidae.

Edentate: without teeth.

Elver: immature stage of eels, after the glass eel stage, in which individual acquires pigment of adult.

Engybenthic: refers to organisms that hover above the bottom of the deep sea.

Epibranch: paired upper element of branchial skeleton articulating with ceratobranch and pharyngobranch, and bearing gill filaments and gill rakers.

Epihyal: upper element of hyoid skeleton.

Epipelagic: upper region of water column, generally between surface and 200 m.

Esca: terminal element of fishing apparatus (illicium) in Lophiiformes.

Falcate: sickle shaped, referring to shape of fin.

Fecundity: reproductive potential, usually expressed in number of mature eggs or ova.

Filamentous: threadlike.

Fin ray: supporting structure of the fin membrane that is bilaterally paired, segmented, and often branched (Actinopterygii).

Fin spine: supporting structure of the fin membrane that is unpaired, unsegmented, and unbranched, usually stiff and sharp pointed.

FL/Fork length: linear length from tip of snout to center of caudal fin.

Fossa: depression or pit.

Frontal clasper: long slender projection on top of head in male chimaeriforms that generally has disc-shaped tip bearing short thorns.

Gill filaments: threadlike, fleshy parts of gills that function in the exchange of gases, electrolytes, and metabolic wastes between the fish and the environment.

Gill plates: projections on inner surface of gill slits forming mesh for filtering small organisms suspended in water (Mobulidae).

Gill raker: bony projection along anterior margin of gill arch, varying from low protuberance to fingerlike or lathlike extension.

Gular plate: median (or paired) skeletal element(s) located between dentary elements of lower jaw (Elopiformes).

Gynogenesis: type of development in which there is no conjugation of sperm and egg chromosomes; egg initiates develop with mechanical stimulation of sperm.

Heterocercal: caudal fin in which the vertebral column is bent upward and extends into the dorsal lobe of the fin, resulting in a tail that is asymmetrical, with dorsal lobe longer than ventral lobe (most Euselachii and Acipenseriformes).

Homocercal: caudal fin in which the vertebral column is bent upward but is truncated and does not extend into either lobe of tail fin, resulting in a tail that is externally symmetrical or nearly symmetrical.

Hyaline: translucent, amorphous connective tissue between pectoral radials and rostral cartilages in skates.

Hyoid barbel: conical fleshy structure located medially under the chin.

Hypobranch: paired element of branchial skeleton articulating with basibranch and ceratobranch and often bearing gill rakers.

Hypocercal: caudal fin in which vertebral column is bent downward into ventral lobe of fin (Squatinidae).

Ichthyocide: poison used to capture fishes, especially used for secretive taxa unavailable by other methods.

Illicium: part of fishing apparatus bearing esca and derived from dorsal fin ray (Lophiiformes).

Imbricate: overlapping; refers to scales in which anterior scale partially overlaps contiguous posterior scale.

Inferior mouth: refers to mouth located below anteriormost part of head.

Infracaudal gland: luminous gland above caudal peduncle.

Infraorbital: refers to area above orbit.

Inquiline: organism that lives within body cavity of another organism.

Insertion: site of attachment, as in attachment of fin to body of fish.

Isthmus: ventral part of body connecting trunk with lower part of head and separating right and left gill chambers.

Labial: referring to lips.

Labial fold: fold above and/or below lips.

Lachrymal bone: anteriormost of the circumorbital dermal bones that surround or partially surround orbits.

Lamella(e): gill filaments.

Lanceolate: narrow and tapering to a point; lance shaped.

Lateral keel: longitudinal ridge along lateral aspect of caudal peduncle.

Lateral line: series of tubes or canals in integument partially communicating with surface and containing sensory cells that respond to low frequency sounds. It usually consists of network of branching canals on head and single tube along trunk.

Lateral line scales: scales on trunk over lateral line that are perforated by lateral line tubules.

Lepidotrichia: segmented and laterally paired fin ray of actinopterygian fishes.

Leptocephalus (leptocephali; adj. = leptocephalous): transparent, ribbonlike, pelagic larvae of Elopiformes, Anguilliformes, Albuliformes, and Notacanthiformes.

Lower limb: refers to gill arch segment below epibranch that consists of ceratobranch and hypobranch.

Lozenge shaped: in the shape of a rectangle or rhomboid.

Maxilla: posterior of two dermal, tooth-bearing bones of upper jaw in actinopterygian fishes. It lacks teeth and is located medial to premaxilla in derived teleost fishes.

Mental: refers to area under the chin.

Mesopelagic: pelagic realm between 200 and 1,000 m.

Molariform: molar shaped; refers to teeth that are stout, blunt or rounded, and designed for crushing hard-bodied invertebrates.

Monoecious: refers to individuals that possess functional male and functional female sex organs.

Monophyletic: refers to a group (two or more species) that includes all the descendants (species) of a common ancestor.

Monotypic: single form; a taxon consisting of a single species.

Nape: region on dorsal surface of body behind head.

Naris: nostril opening, usually partially or totally divided into incurrent and excurrent openings.

Nasal curtain: inner extension of anterior nasal flap that partially covers naris and is connected to isthmus between nares; found in Rajidae and Myliobatiformes.

Neurocranium: cartilaginous or bony skeleton surrounding brain and supporting sensory organs of head.

Nictitating eyelid: movable membrane along anteroventral corner of eye in some elasmobranchs.

Nonmonophyletic: refers to a group (two or more species) that does not include all of the descendants (species) of a common ancestor.

Nonocclusible: refers to teeth of upper and lower jaws that are not capable of fitting together to enable the mouth to close.

Nuchal: refers to nape, or region behind head on dorsal surface.

Obtuse: broadly rounded or angled.

Occlusible: refers to teeth of upper and lower jaws that are capable of fitting together, enabling the mouth to close.

Ocellus (ocelli): circular to oval pigment pattern consisting of central dark pigment surrounded by ring of light pigment and usually with outer ring of dark pigment; also called "eyespot."

Oophagy: type of internal development in which embryo is nourished by fertilized and unfertilized eggs.

Opercular fold: Superficial covering of gills formed by integument and cartilaginous supports (Chimaeriformes).

Operculum (opercula): dermal bone covering much of gill cavity.

Oral disc: concave region around oral opening bearing horny teeth in lampreys (Petromyzontidae).

Oral plate: band or patch of tough connective tissue bearing horny teeth that is located anterior and posterior to oral opening in Petromyzontidae.

Origin: anterior end of fin base.

Oronasal groove: depression connecting excurrent naris to mouth; typical of some elasmobranchs.

Oronasal pit: depression anterolateral to mouth and dorsal to nasal curtain; found in some Rajidae and Torpediniformes.

Oviparous: external development of embryos—either fertilized egg is not retained by mother or fertilization of egg takes place in the water column.

Ovoviviparous: internal development of embryos and later ontogenetic stages—fertilized egg is retained by mother.

Paedomorphic: retention of juvenile characters into adult stage of life.

Palatine: anteriormost dermal bone of upper section of mandibular or first arch that often bears teeth.

Papilla (papillae): small fleshy projection.

Pelagic: refers to organisms that live suspended in the water column.

Peritoneum: membrane lining abdominal cavity and covering viscera.

Photophore: organ in epidermis that emits light produced either by bacteria or by chemical luciferin-luciferase reaction.

Phylogeny: a hypothesis of evolutionary relationships within a putative monophyletic group of organisms based on the shared possession of derived character states.

Physostomous: refers to swim bladder that is connected to gastrointestinal tract by pneumatic duct.

Pineal organ: small glandular outgrowth on dorsal surface of diencephalon of brain thought to be sensitive to light.

Placenta: connection between mother and embryo in oviduct or uterus that furnishes nutrients from mother to embryo; in fishes it is formed by the yolk sac.

Placque: Bony covering of lateral line scale (Paralepididae)

Postabdominal spine: spine formed by extension of cleithrum; present in some Sternoptychidae.

Postcleithrum (postcleithra): dermal bone of pectoral girdle that articulates with cleithrum and extends posterior to cleithrum.

Postorbital organ: light organ located behind orbit.

Posttemporal spine: spine located at distal tip of posttemporal bone of pectoral girdle.

Preanal ridge: narrow elevated area preceding anal fin produced by skeletal support of fin; typical of elasmobranchs.

Precaudal pit: transverse to semicircular groove preceding dorsal lobe of heterocercal caudal fin of some elasmobranchs.

Predorsal plate: dermal bone on dorsal surface of body behind cranium and anterior to dorsal fin (Ariidae).

Prehaemal vertebra(e): trunk vertebrae, vertebrae for which the transverse processes do not meet ventrally to form hemal arch.

Premaxilla (premaxillae): anterior of two dermal bones that form tooth-bearing upper jaw in actinopterygian fishes.

Prenarial groove: narrow depression running medial to naris along anterior margin of blade of head in some hammerhead sharks (Sphyrnidae).

Preoperculum (preopercula): dermal bone that precedes operculum and articulates with hyomandibula.

Preorbital organ: light organ that precedes orbit.

Prepelvic claspers: small appendages that are retractable within slits located just anterior to pelvic fin base in mature male chimaeriforms.

Procurrent: refers to rays or spines that precede caudal fin rays.

Protandric hermaphrodite: individual that changes sex and is a functional male before changing into a functional female.

Protrusible: condition in which upper jaw or both jaws are projected forward to form tube or scooplike cutting surface.

Pseudobranch: small, gill filament–like organ, located on the medial aspect of opercular bones, that supplies oxygen to retina of eye.

Pterygoid: bone of upper section of hyoid

arch that articulates with palatine and metapterygoid.

Pyloric caeca (caecae): diverticulum of junction of stomach and intestine that is either simple or greatly branched.

Quincunx: an arrangement of five objects (teeth) in which one is located at each of four corners and one is located in the middle; adjacent teeth are offset from each other by diameter of base of tooth (Torpediniformes, Pristiformes, Rajiformes, and Myliobatiformes).

Radial: cartilaginous or bony skeletal element supporting base of fin in Actinopterygii or supporting base and much of the fin surface in cartilaginous fishes (Chondrichthyes).

Rete mirabile (retia mirabilia): capillary bed in which arterial capillaries run parallel and in opposite direction to venous capillaries; also called "wonder net."

Retrorse: pointing or oriented posteriorly.

Rostral fins: anterior extensions of pectoral fins and rostral cartilage forming fleshy lobes extending anteriorly on each side of head (Mobulidae).

Rostrum: projecting snout or beak anterior to eyes in some ray-finned fishes (Actinopterygii) or projecting anterior part of neurocranium in cartilaginous fishes (Chondrichthyes).

Scapula, scapular: refers to region of trunk over shoulder girdle.

Scute: modified bony scale that bears keel, ridges, or spines.

Serrate: referring to surface or margin bearing sawlike spines or notches.

Sexually dichromic: refers to different sexes of a species having different color patterns.

Sexually dimorphic: refers to different sexes of a species differing in shape.

Simple: single, not branched.

SL/Standard length: linear length from tip of snout to end of caudal peduncle.

Sole/sole reflecting organ: greatly flattened ventral surface between the isthmus and anus that supposedly reflects light downward (Opisthoproctidae: *Opisthoproctus*).

Spine: sharp projection or modified fin ray

(lepidotrichium) that is unsegmented, unbranched, and usually stiff and pointed.

Spiracle: opening into branchial cavity behind eye representing space between jaws and second, or hyoid, arch.

Subconical: refers to structure that is less than conical.

Subcylindrical: refers to structure that is less than cylindrical.

Suborbital: refers to area beneath eye.

Suborbital gland: light organ located beneath orbit.

Subrostral lobe: anterior extension of pectoral fins and rostral cartilage projecting anterior to head above mouth (Myliobatidae, Rhinopteridae).

Subterminal notch: indentation below terminal lobe of heterocercal caudal fin.

Subthoracic: refers to position posterior to pectoral fin base and anterior to vent, such as for pelvic fins.

Superior mouth: refers to a mouth located above anteriormost part of head.

Supracaudal gland: light organ located on dorsal aspect of caudal peduncle.

Supramaxilla (supramaxillae): dermal bone located on dorsal surface of maxilla, usually near distal section of maxilla.

Supraorbital: refers to area above orbit.

Symphysis: junction or line of junction between two bones.

Terminal mouth: refers to a mouth located at the anteriormost part of the head.

Thoracic: refers to position below pectoral fin base, such as for pelvic fin base.

Thorn: enlarged denticle or placoid scale of elasmobranchs.

Thornlet: enlarged denticle or placoid scale of elasmobranchs that is smaller than a thorn.

TL/Total length: linear length from tip of snout to tip of caudal fin.

Tooth plate: teeth consisting of pavementlike surfaces capable of crushing hard-shelled organisms (Myliobatidae, Rhinopteridae, Chimaeriformes).

Transverse curtain: fold of integument attached to roof of mouth behind upper jaw.

Tubular eye: eye located in tubular-shaped orbit, with retina, or light-sensitive region, located at end of tube. This type of eye concentrates light on retina.

Tympanum (tympana): ossified plate covering lateral line scale (Paralepididae).

Vexillifer: pelagic larval form that possesses a highly modified, deciduous first dorsal fin ray, or vexillum (Ophidiiformes: Carapidae).

Vexillum: highly modified first dorsal fin ray of pelagic larvae (Ophidiiformes: Carapidae).

Villiform: shaped like a small bristle; refers to teeth that are filament-like and arranged in bands.

Viviparous: internal development in which the mother provides nutrients to the embryo.

Vomer: median skeletal structure at front of palate that often bears teeth.

Weberian apparatus: complex of modified vertebrae and ligaments between the inner ear and the swim bladder (Ostariophysi: Siluriformes)

Key to Abbreviations

AC: ventral row photophores above anal fin

Ant: antorbital photophore

AOa: anterior anal photophore

Aop: posterior anal photophore

BR: photophores on branchiostegal rays

Ce: cervical photophore

Dn: dorsonasal photophore

IP: ventral row photophores of prepectoral series

IV: ventral row photophores of prepelvic series

OA: lateral row photophores

OP: photophores on operculum

ORB: photophore(s) near eye

OV: lateral row photophores of prepelvic series

PLO: suprapectoral photophore

PO: thoracic photophore

Po: postorbital photophores

Pol: posterolateral photophore

Prc: precaudal photophore

PV: ventral row photophores from pectoral to pelvic fin

PVO: subpectoral photophore

SAO: supra-anal photophore

SO: photophores on symphysis

So: suborbital photophores

Suo: supraorbital photophore

VAL: lateral row photophores of postpelvic series

VAV: ventral row photophores of postpelvic series

VLO: supraventral photophore

Vn: ventronasal photophore

VO: ventral photophore

REFERENCES

Title abbreviations and full publication information for frequently cited works are listed below.

FN-EAM = Fishes of the North-eastern Atlantic and the Mediterranean, ed. P. J. P. Whitehead, M. L. Bauchot, J. C. Hureau, J. Nielsen, and E. Tortonese. 3 vols. Vol. 1, 1984: 1–510; Vol. 2, 1986: 511–1008; Vol. 3, 1986: 1009–1473. Paris: UNESCO.

FWNA = Fishes of the western North Atlantic, 9 vols. New Haven: Sears Found. Mar. Res., Mem. 1.

Vol. 1, Lancelets, cyclostomes, sharks, ed. John Tee-Van et al. 1948.

Vol. 2, Sawfishes, guitarfishes, skates and rays, and chimaeroids, John Tee-Van et al. 1953.

Vol. 3, Soft-rayed bony fishes, Acipenseroidei, Lepisostei, Isospondyli (part) Elopoidea, Clupeoidea, Salmonoidea, ed. H. B. Bigelow et al. 1963.

Vol. 4, Soft-rayed bony fishes, Isospondyli (part) Argentinoidea, Stomiatoidea, Esocoidea, Bathylaconoidea, Gigantiroidei, ed. H. B. Bigelow et al. 1964.

Vol. 5, Iniomi, Lyomeri, ed. G. W. Mead et al. 1966.

Vol. 6, Heteromi, Cyprinodontoidei, Berycomorphi, Xenoberyces, Anacanthini (part) Macrouridae, ed. D. M. Cohen et al. 1973.

Vol. 7, Iniomi (Myctophiformes), ed. R. H. Gibbs, Jr., et al. 1977.

Vol. 8, Gasterosteiformes, Syngnathoidei, ed. J. E. Böhlke et al. 1982.

Vol. 9 (in 2 vols.), ed. B. B. Collette et al. Vol. 1, Anguilliformes and Saccopharyngiformes; Vol. 2, Leptocephalis. 1989.

SSF = Smith's sea fishes, ed. M. M. Smith and P. C. Heemstra. 1986. New York: Springer-Verlag, 1047 pp.

Ahlstrom, E. H., H. G. Moser, and C. M. Cohen. 1984. Argentinoidei: development and relationships. *In:* Ontogeny and systematics of fishes, ed. H. G. Moser et al. Special Publ. No. 1, Amer. Soc. Ichthyol. Herpet. Lawrence (KS): Allen Press, pp. 155–169.

Anderson, M. E., R. E. Crabtree, H. J. Carter, K. J. Sulak, and M. D. Richardson. 1985. Distribution of demersal fishes of the Caribbean Sea found below 2,000 meters. Bull. Mar. Sci. 37: 794–807.

Anderson, W. W. 1957. Early development, spawning, growth and occurrence of the silver mullet (*Mugil curema*) along the south Atlantic coast of the United States. U.S. Fish Wildl. Serv. Fish. Bull. 57: 397–414.

Anderson, W. W. 1958. Larval development, growth and spawning of striped mullet (*Mugil cephalus*) along the south Atlantic coast of the United States. U.S. Fish Wildl. Serv. Fish. Bull. 58: 501–519.

Anderson, W. W., J. W. Gehringer, and F. H. Berry. 1966. Family Synodontidae. *In:* FWNA 5: 30–102.

Applegate, S., L. Espinosa, L. B. Menchaca, and F. Sotelo. 1979. Tiburones mexicanos. Mexico City: Subsecretaría de Educación e Investigación Tecnológicas, Dirección General de Ciencia y Tecnología del Mar, 146 pp.

Badcock, J. 1984a. Gonostomatidae. *In:* FN-EAM 1: 284–301.

Badcock, J. 1984b. Sternoptychidae. *In:* FN-EAM 1: 302–317.

Badcock, J. 1984c. Photichthyidae. *In:* FN-EAM 1: 318–324.

Badcock, J., and R. C. Baird. 1980. Remarks on systematics, development, and distribution of the hatchetfish genus *Sternoptyx* (Pisces, Stomiatoidei). U.S. Fish Wildl. Serv. Fish. Bull. 77: 803–820.

Backus, R. H., S. Springer, and E. L. Arnold, Jr. 1956. A contribution to the natural history of the white tip shark, *Pterolamiops longimanus* (Poey). Deep-Sea Res. 3: 178–188.

Baird, R. C. 1971. The systematics, distribution, and zoogeography of the marine hatchetfishes (family Sternoptychidae). Bull. Mus. Comp. Zool. 142: 1–128.

Baird, R. C. 1986. Genera *Argyropelecus*, *Polyipnus* and *Sternoptyx*. In: SSF: 255–259.

Banford, H. M., and B. B. Collette. 1993. *Hyporhamphus meeki*, a new species of halfbeak (Teleostei: Hemiramphidae) from the Atlantic and gulf coasts of the United States. Proc. Biol. Soc. Wash. 106: 369–384.

Barnett, M. A., and R. H. Gibbs, Jr. 1968. Four new stomiatoid fishes of the genus *Bathophilus*, with a revised key to the species of *Bathophilus*. Copeia: 826–832.

Basakhin, S. V. 1982. Systematics and distribution of the family Berycidae (Osteichthyes) in the World Ocean. J. Ichthyol. 22(6): 1–20.

Bass, A. J., J. D. D'Aubrey, and N. Kistnasamy. 1973. Sharks of the east coast of southern Africa. 1. The genus *Carcharhinus* (Carcharhinidae). Invest. Rep. Oceanogr. Res. Inst. (Durban) 33: 168 pp.

Baughman, J. L. 1943a. Notes on sawfish, *Pristis perotteti* Müller and Henle, not previously reported from the waters of the United States. Copeia: 43–48.

Baughman, J. L. 1943b. Note on the Texas occurrence of a shark not previously known from the waters of the United States. Copeia: 189.

Baughman, J. L. 1950a. Random notes on Texas fishes. Part I. Texas J. Sci. 2: 117–138.

Baughman, J. L. 1950b. Random notes on Texas fishes. Part II. Texas J. Sci. 2: 242–263.

Baughman, J. L. 1955. The oviparity of the whale shark, *Rhineodon typus*, with records of this and other fishes in Texas waters. Copeia: 54–55.

Baughman, J. L., and S. Springer. 1950. Biological and economic notes on the sharks of the Gulf of Mexico, with especial reference to those of Texas, and with a key to their identification. Amer. Midl. Nat. 44: 96–152.

Beebe, W., and J. Tee-Van. 1933. Field book of the shore fishes of Bermuda and the West Indies. New York: G. P. Putnam's Sons.

Bekker, V. E., Y. N. Shcherbachev, and V. M. Chuvasov. 1975. [Deep-sea pelagic fishes of the Caribbean Sea, Gulf of Mexico and Puerto Rican Trench] (in Russian). Trudy Inst. Okeanol. 100: 289–336.

Belianina, T. N. 1980. Codlets (Bregmacerotidae, Osteichthyes) of the Caribbean Sea and Gulf of Mexico. J. Ichthyol. 20(1): 138–141.

Belianina, T. N. 1981. The larvae of some rare mesopelagic fishes from the Caribbean and the Gulf of Mexico. J. Ichthyol. 21(1): 82–95.

Berry, F. H. 1959. Boarfishes of the genus *Antigonia* of the western Atlantic. Bull. Fla. State Mus. Biol. Sci. 4: 205–250.

Berry, F. H., and W. F. Rathjen. 1959. A new species of the boarfish genus *Antigonia* from the western Atlantic. Quart. J. Fla. Acad. Sci. 21: 255–258.

Berry, F. H., and C. R. Robins. 1967. *Macristiella perlucens,* a new clupeiform fish from the Gulf of Mexico. Copeia: 46–50.

Bertelsen, E. 1951. The ceratioid fishes, ontogeny, taxonomy, distribution and biology. Dana Rep. 39: 1–276.

Bertelsen, E. 1958. The argentinoid fish *Xenophthalmichthys danae.* Dana Rep. 45: 1–10.

Bertelsen, E. 1980. Notes on Linophrynidae V. A revision of the deepsea anglerfish (Ceratioidei) of the *Linophryne arborifera* group. Steenstrupia 6: 29–70.

Bertelsen, E. 1982. Notes on Linophrynidae VIII. A review of the genus *Linophryne,* with new records and descriptions of two species. Steenstrupia 8: 49–104.

Bertelsen, E. 1983. First records of metamorphosed males of the families Diceratiidae and Centrophrynidae (Pisces: Ceratioidei). Steenstrupia 8: 309–315.

Bertelsen, E. 1986a. Mirapinnidae. *In:* FN-EAM 2: 521.

Bertelsen, E. 1986b. Eutaeniophoridae. *In:* FN-EAM 2: 522–523.

Bertelsen, E. 1986c. Melanocetidae. *In:* FN-EAM 2: 1376–1377.

Bertelsen, E. 1986d. Diceratiidae. *In:* FN-EAM 2: 1381–1382.

Bertelsen, E. 1986e. Linophrynidae. *In:* FN-EAM 2: 1408–1414.

Bertelsen, E. 1986f. Family Mirapinnidae. *In:* SSF: 406–407.

Bertelsen, E., and G. Krefft. 1988. The ceratioid family Himantolophidae (Pisces, Lophiiformes). Steenstrupia 14(2): 9–89.

Bertelsen, E., G. Krefft, and N. B. Marshall. 1976. The fishes of the family Notosudidae. Dana Rep. 86: 1–114.

Bertelsen, E., and N. B. Marshall. 1956. The Mirapinnatoidei: a new order of teleost fishes. Dana Rep. 42: 1–34.

Bertelsen, E., and N. B. Marshall. 1958. Notes on Mirapinnati (an addendum to Dana Rep. No. 42). A change of name and further records. Dana Rep. 42: 9–10.

Bertelsen, E., and P. J. Struhsaker. 1977. The ceratioid fishes of the genus *Thaumatichthys:* osteology, relationships, distribution and biology. Galathea Rep. 14: 7–40.

Bigelow, H. B. 1961. A new species of the cetomimid genus *Gyrinomimus* from the Gulf of Mexico. Breviora 145: 1–2.

Bigelow, H. B., and Schroeder. 1940. Sharks of the genus *Mustelus* in the western Atlantic. Proc. Boston Soc. Nat. Sci. 41: 417–438.

Bigelow, H. B., and W. C. Schroeder. 1944. New sharks from the western North Atlantic. Proc. New England Zool. Club 23: 21–36.

Bigelow, H. B., and W. C. Schroeder. 1948a. Lancelets, cyclostomes and sharks. *In:* FWNA 1: 1–547.

Bigelow, H. B., and W. C. Schroeder. 1948b. New genera and species of batoid fishes. J. Mar. Res. 7: 543–566.

Bigelow, H. B., and W. C. Schroeder. 1950. New and little known cartilaginous fishes from the Atlantic. Bull. Mus. Comp. Zool. 103: 385–406.

Bigelow, H. B., and W. C. Schroeder. 1951a. A new genus and species of anacantobatid skate from the Gulf of Mexico. J. Wash. Acad. Sci. 41: 110–113.

Bigelow, H. B., and W. C. Schroeder. 1951b. Three new skates and a new chimaeroid fish from the Gulf of Mexico. J. Wash. Acad. Sci. 41: 383–392.

Bigelow, H. B., and W. C. Schroeder. 1952. A new species of the cyclostome genus *Paramyxine* from the Gulf of Mexico. Breviora 8: 1–10.

Bigelow, H. B., and W. C. Schroeder. 1953a. Sawfishes, guitarfishes, skates and rays, and chimaeroids. *In:* FWNA 2: 1–588.

Bigelow, H. B., and W. C. Schroeder. 1953b. Fishes of the Gulf of Maine. U.S. Fish Wildl. Serv. Fish. Bull. 53: 1–577.

Bigelow, H. B., and W. C. Schroeder. 1954a. A new family, a new genus and two new species of batoid fishes from the Gulf of Mexico. Breviora 24: 1–16.

Bigelow, H. B., and W. C. Schroeder. 1954b.

Deep water elasmobranchs and chimaeroids from the northwestern Atlantic slope. Bull. Mus. Comp. Zool. 112: 37–87.

Bigelow, H. B., and W. C. Schroeder. 1957. A study of the sharks of the suborder Squaloidea. Bull. Mus. Comp. Zool. 117: 1–150.

Bigelow, H. B., and W. C. Schroeder. 1958. Four new rajids from the Gulf of Mexico. Bull. Mus. Comp. Zool. 119: 201–233.

Bigelow, H. B., and W. C. Schroeder. 1962. New and little known batoid fishes from the western Atlantic. Bull. Mus. Comp. Zool. 128: 162–244.

Bigelow, H. B., and W. C. Schroeder. 1965. Further account of batoid fishes from the western Atlantic. Bull. Mus. Comp. Zool. 132: 446–477.

Bigelow, H. B., and W. C. Schroeder. 1968a. New records of two geographically restricted species of western Atlantic skates, *Breviraja yucatanensis* and *Dactylobatus armatus*. Copeia: 630–631.

Bigelow, H. B., and W. C. Schroeder. 1968b. Additional notes on batoid fishes from the western North Atlantic. Breviora 281: 1–23.

Bigelow, H. B., W. C. Schroeder, and S. Springer. 1953. New and little known sharks from the Atlantic and from the Gulf of Mexico. Bull. Mus. Comp. Zool. 109: 213–276.

Bigelow, H. B., W. C. Schroeder, and S. Springer. 1955. Three new shark records from the Gulf of Mexico. Breviora 49: 1–12.

Black, D. A., and W. H. Howell. 1979. The North American mosquitofish, *Gambusia affinis*: a unique case in sex chromosome evolution. Copeia: 509–513.

Böhlke, E., J. E. McCosker, and J. E. Böhlke. 1989. Family Muraenidae. *In*: FWNA 9: 104–206.

Böhlke, J. E. 1955. A new genus and species of ophichthid eels from the Bahamas. Notulae Naturae 282: 1–7.

Böhlke, J. E. 1956. A small collection of new eels from western Puerto Rico. Notulae Naturae 289: 1–13.

Böhlke, J. E. 1960. A new ophichthid eel of the genus *Pseudomyrophis* from the Gulf of Mexico. Notulae Naturae 329: 1–8.

Böhlke, J. E. 1967. The descriptions of three new eels from the tropical West Atlantic. Proc. Acad. Nat. Sci. Philadelphia 118: 91–108.

Böhlke, J. E., and E. Böhlke. 1976. The chestnut moray, *Enchelycore carychroa,* a new species from the West Atlantic. Proc. Acad. Nat. Sci. Philadelphia 127: 137–146.

Böhlke, J. E., and E. Böhlke. 1980. The identity of the moray *Gymnothorax conspersus* Poey, and description of *G. kolpos,* n. sp., from the western Atlantic. Proc. Acad. Nat. Sci. Philadelphia 132: 218–227.

Böhlke, J. E., and J. H. Caruso. 1980. *Ophichthus rex*: a new giant snake eel from the Gulf of Mexico (Anguilliformes, Ophichthidae). Proc. Acad. Nat. Sci. Philadelphia 132: 239–244.

Böhlke, J. E., and C. C. G. Chaplin. 1968. Fishes of the Bahamas and adjacent waters. Wynnewood: Livingston Publ. Co., 771 pp.

Böhlke, J. E., and D. G. Smith. 1968. A new xenocongrid eel from the Bahamas, with notes on other species in the family. Proc. Acad. Nat. Sci. Philadelphia 120: 25–43.

Boeseman, M. 1984. Hexanchidae. *In*: FNEAM 1: 72–75.

Bond, G. W., Jr., and K. A. Tighe. 1974. A diagnostic character for rapid identification of lightly pigmented species of the genus *Cyclothone* (Gonostomatidae) in the North Atlantic. Copeia: 272–275.

Bonfil S, R., D. de Anda F., and R. Mena A. 1990. Shark fisheries in Mexico: the case of Yucatan as an example. *In*: Elasmobranchs as living resources: advances in the biology, ecology, systematics, and the status of the fisheries, ed. H. L. Pratt, Jr., et al. NOAA Tech. Rep. NMFS 90: 427–441.

Boschung, H. T. 1992. Catalog of freshwater and marine fishes of Alabama. Tuscaloosa: Univ. Alabama, 266 pp.

Bowen, B. W., and J. C. Avise. 1990. Genetic structure of Atlantic and Gulf of Mexico populations of sea bass, menhaden, and sturgeon: influence of zoogeographic factors and life-history patterns. Mar. Biol. 107: 371–381.

Bradbury, M. G. 1967. The genera of batfishes (family Ogcocephalidae). Copeia: 399–422.

Bradbury, M. G. 1978. Ogcocephalidae. *In*: FAO species identification sheets for fishing purposes, Western Central Atlantic (Fishing area 31), ed. W. Fischer. Rome: FAO.

Bradbury, M. G. 1980. A revision of the fish genus *Ogcocephalus* with descriptions of new species from the western Atlantic Ocean (Ogcocephalidae: Lophiiformes). Proc. Calif. Acad. Sci. 42: 229–285.

Branstetter, S. 1981. Biological notes on the sharks of the north central Gulf of Mexico. Contrib. Mar. Sci. 24: 13–34.

Branstetter, S. 1982. Problems associated with the identification and separation of the spinner shark, *Carcharhinus brevipinna*, and the black tip shark, *Carcharhinus limbatus*. Copeia: 461–465.

Branstetter, S. 1984. Carcharhinidae. *In*: FN-EAM 1: 102–114.

Branstetter, S. 1987a. Age and growth validation of newborn sharks held in laboratory aquaria, with comments on the life history of the Atlantic sharpnose shark, *Rhizoprionodon terraenovae*. Copeia: 291–300.

Branstetter, S. 1987b. Age and growth and reproductive biology of the silky shark, *Carcharhinus falciformis*, and the scalloped hammerhead, *Sphyrna lewini*, from the northwestern Gulf of Mexico. Environ. Biol. Fish. 19: 161–173.

Branstetter, S., and J. D. McEachran. 1983. A first record of the bigeye thresher, *Alopias superciliosus*, the blue shark, *Prionace glauca*, and the pelagic stingray, *Dasyatis violacea*, from the Gulf of Mexico. Northeast Gulf Sci. 6: 59–61.

Branstetter, S., and J. D. McEachran. 1986a. A first record of *Odontaspis noronhai* (Lamniformes: Odontaspididae) for the western North Atlantic, with notes on two uncommon sharks from the Gulf of Mexico. Northeast Gulf Sci. 8: 153–160.

Branstetter, S., and J. D. McEachran. 1986b.

Age and growth of four carcharhinid sharks common to the Gulf of Mexico. *In*: Indo-Pacific fish biology: proceedings of the Second International Conference on Indo-Pacific Fishes, ed. T. Uyeno et al. Tokyo: Ichthyol. Soc. Japan, pp. 361–371.

Branstetter, S., J. A. Musick, and J. A. Colvocoresses. 1987. A comparison of the age and growth of the tiger shark, *Galeocerdo cuvieri*, from off Virginia and from the northwestern Gulf of Mexico. U.S. Nat. Mar. Fish. Serv. Fish. Bull. 85: 269–279.

Branstetter, S., and R. L. Shipp. 1980. Occurrence of the finetooth shark, *Carcharhinus isodon*, off Dauphin Island, Alabama. U.S. Nat. Mar. Fish. Serv. Fish. Bull. 78: 177–179.

Branstetter, S., and R. Stiles. 1987. Age and growth of the bull shark, *Carcharhinus leucas*, from the northern Gulf of Mexico. Environ. Biol. Fish. 20(3): 169–181.

Breder, C. 1927. Scientific results of the first oceanographic expedition of the 'Pawnee': Fishes. Bull. Bingham Oceanogr. Coll. 1: 1–90.

Bright, T., and C. W. Cashman. 1974. Fishes. *In*: Biota of the West Flower Garden Bank, ed. T. J. Bright and W. E. Pequegnat. Houston: Gulf Publ. Co., pp. 340–409.

Bright, T., and W. E. Pequegnat. 1969. Deep-sea hatchetfishes of the Gulf of Mexico. Quart. J. Fla. Acad. Sci. 32: 26–36.

Brockmann, F. W. 1975. An observation on mating behavior of the southern stingray. Copeia: 784–785.

Brown, J. L. 1956. Distinguishing characters of the cyprinodont fishes *Fundulus cingulatus* and *Fundulus chrysotus*. Copeia: 251–255.

Bruun, A. F. 1935. Flying-fishes (Exocoetidae) of the Atlantic, systematic and biological studies. Dana Rep. 6: 1–106.

Bullis, H. R., Jr. 1967. Depth segregation and distribution of sex-maturity groups in the marbled catshark, *Galeus arae*. *In*: Sharks, skates and rays, ed. P. W. Gilbert et al. Baltimore: Johns Hopkins Press, pp. 141–148.

Bullis, H. R., Jr., and P. Struhsaker. 1961. Life history notes on the roughtail stingray,

Dasyatis centroura (Mitchill). Copeia: 232–234.

Bullis, H. R., Jr., and J. R. Thompson. 1965. Collections by the exploratory fishing vessels *Oregon, Silver Bay, Combat,* and *Pelican* made during 1956 to 1960 in southwestern North Atlantic. U.S. Fish. Wildl. Serv. Spec. Sci. Rep. Fish. 510: 1–130.

Burgess, G. H., and S. Branstetter. 1985. Status of *Neoscopelus* (Neoscopelidae) in the Gulf of Mexico with distributional notes on *Caulolatilus chrysops* (Branchiostegidae) and *Etelis oculatus* (Lutjanidae). Northeast Gulf Sci. 7: 157–162.

Carlander, K. D. 1969. Handbook of freshwater fishery biology. Ames: Iowa State Univ. Press, 752 pp.

Carter, H. J., and D. M. Cohen. 1985. *Monomitopus magnus,* a new species of deep-sea fish (Ophidiidae) from the western North Atlantic. Bull. Mar. Sci. 36: 86–95.

Carter, H. J., and K. J. Sulak. 1984. A new species and a review of the deep-sea fish genus *Porogadus* (Ophidiidae) from the western North Atlantic. Bull. Mar. Sci. 34: 358–379.

Caruso, J. H. 1981. The systematics and distribution of the lophiid anglerfishes. Part 1, A revision of the genus *Lophiodes* with the description of two new species. Copeia: 522–549.

Caruso, J. H. 1983. The systematics and distribution of the lophiid anglerfishes. Part 2, Revisions of the genera *Lophiomus* and *Lophius.* Copeia: 11–30.

Caruso, J. H. 1986. Family No. 101. Lophiidae. *In:* SSF: 363–366.

Caruso, J. H. 1989. Systematics and distribution of the Atlantic chaunacid anglerfishes (Pisces: Lophiiformes). Copeia: 153–165.

Caruso, J. H., and T. W. Pietsch. 1986. Chaunacidae. *In:* FN-EAM 3: 1369–1370.

Caruso, J. H., and R. D. Suttkus. 1979. A new species of lophiid anglerfish from the western North Atlantic. Bull. Mar. Sci. 29: 491–496.

Casterlin, M. E., and W. W. Reynolds. 1979. Diel activity patterns of the smooth dogfish

shark, *Mustelus canis.* Bull. Mar. Sci. 29: 440–442.

Castle, P. H. J. 1960. Two eels of the genus *Synaphobranchus* from the Gulf of Mexico. Fieldiana Zool. 39: 387–398.

Castle, P. H. J. 1964. Deep-sea eels: family Synaphobranchidae. Galathea Rep. 7: 29–42.

Castle, P. H. J. 1986. Family No. 46. Synaphobranchidae. *In:* SSF: 188–190.

Castro, J. I. 1983. The sharks of North American waters. College Station: Texas A&M Univ. Press, 180 pp.

Castro, J. I. 1993a. The shark nursery of Bulls Bay, South Carolina, with a review of the shark nurseries of the southeastern coast of the United States. Environ. Biol. Fish. 36: 37–48.

Castro, J. I. 1993b. The biology of the finetooth shark, *Carcharhinus isodon.* Environ. Biol. Fish. 36: 219–232.

Castro, J. I., and J. P. Wourms. 1993. Reproduction, placentation, and embryonic development of the Atlantic sharpnose shark, *Rhizoprionodon terraenovae.* J. Morph. 218: 257–280.

Castro-Aguirre, J. L. 1978. Catálogo sistemático de los peces marinos que penetran a las aguas continentales de México, con aspectos zoogeográficos y ecológicos. Mexico: Depto. de Pesca, Dirección General del Instituto Nacional de Pesca, Serie Científ. No. 19: 1–298.

Castro-Aguirre, J. L., and F. García-Domínguez. 1985. Sobre la presencia de *Isistius brasiliensis* (Quoy y Gaimard) (Squaliformes: Squalidae: Dalatiinae) en el Golfo de México. Con un elenco sistemático de las especies mexicanas pertenecientes al superorden Squalomorphii. Anal. Escuela Nac. Cien. Biol. 32: 91–108.

Castro-Aguirre, J. L., and A. Márquez-Espinoza. 1981. Contribución al conocimiento de la ictiofauna de la Isla de Lobos y zonas adyacentes, Veracruz, México. Mexico: Depto. de Pesca, Dirección General del Instituto Nacional de Pesca, Serie Científ. No. 22: 1–85.

Cervigón, M. F. 1966. Los peces marinos de Venezuela. Monografía no. 11, 2 vols. Caracas: Fundación La Salle de Ciencias Naturales, 951 pp.

Cervigón, F. 1991. Los peces marinos de Venezuela. 2d ed. Vol. 1: 1–432. Caracas: Fundación Científica Los Roques.

Cervigón, M. F. 1993a. Sharks, batoid fishes and bony fishes. *In:* Field guide to the commercial marine and brackish-water resources of the northern coast of South America, ed. K. Carpenter, W. Fischer, and L. Garibaldi. Rome: M. Kautenberger-Longo, FAO.

Cervigón, F. 1993b. Los peces marinos de Venezuela. 2d ed. Vol. 2: 1–498. Caracas: Fundación Científica Los Roques.

Chernoff, B., J. V. Conner, and C. F. Bryan. 1981. Systematics of the *Menidia beryllina* complex (Pisces: Atherinidae) from the Gulf of Mexico and its tributaries. Copeia: 319–336.

Christmas, J. Y., and G. Gunter. 1960. Distribution of menhaden, genus *Brevoortia*, in the Gulf of Mexico. Trans. Amer. Fish. Soc. 89: 338–343.

Clark, E., and K. von Schmidt. 1965. Sharks of the central gulf coast of Florida. Bull. Mar. Sci. 15: 13–83.

Clarke, M. R., and J. D. Stevens. 1974. Cephalopods, blue sharks and migration. J. Mar. Biol. Assoc. U. K. 54: 949–957.

Clarke, T. A. 1971. The ecology of the scalloped hammerhead, *Sphyrna lewini*, in Hawaii. Pac. Sci. 25: 133–144.

Clarke, T. A. 1984. Diet and morphological variation in snipefishes, presently recognized as *Macrorhamphosus scolopax*, from southeast Australia: evidence for two sexually dimorphic species. Copeia: 595–608.

Cohen, D. M. 1958a. Revision of the fishes of the sub-family Argentininae. Bull. Fla. St. Mus. Biol. Sci. 3: 93–172.

Cohen, D. M. 1958b. *Nansenia candida*, a new species of argentinid fish from the North Pacific, with notes on other species of *Nansenia*. Stanford Ichthyol. Bull. 7: 52–57.

Cohen, D. M. 1961. A new genus and species of deepwater ophidioid fish from Gulf of Mexico. Copeia: 288–292.

Cohen, D. M. 1964a. Suborder Argentinoidea. *In:* FWNA 4: 1–70.

Cohen, D. M. 1964b. A review of the ophidioid fish genus *Luciobrotula* with the description of a new species from the western North Atlantic. Bull. Mar. Sci. Gulf Carib. 14: 387–398.

Cohen, D. M. 1974. A review of the pelagic ophidioid fish genus *Brotulotaenia* with descriptions of two new species. Zool. J. Linn. Soc. 55: 119–149.

Cohen, D. M. 1984a. Argentinidae. *In:* FN-EAM 1: 386–391.

Cohen, D. M. 1984b. Bathylagidae. *In:* FN-EAM 1: 392–394.

Cohen, D. M. 1984c. Opisthoproctidae. *In:* FN-EAM 1: 395–398.

Cohen, D. M. 1986a. Melanonidae. *In:* FN-EAM 2: 724.

Cohen, D. M. 1986b. Family No. 61. Argentinidae. *In:* SSF: 215–216.

Cohen, D. M. 1986c. Family No. 62. Bathylagidae. *In:* SSF: 216.

Cohen, D. M. 1986d. Family No. 91. Melanonidae. *In:* SSF: 328–329.

Cohen, D. M. 1986e. Family No. 98. Bythitidae. *In:* SSF: 354–356.

Cohen, D. M. 1987. Notes on the bythitid fish genus *Saccogaster* with a new species from the Gulf of Mexico. Nat. Hist. Mus. L. A. Co., Contrib. in Sci. 385: 1–4.

Cohen, D. M., and S. P. Atsaides. 1969. Additions to a revision of argentine fishes. U.S. Fish Wildl. Serv. Fish. Bull. 68: 13–36.

Cohen, D. M., T. Inada, T. Iwamoto, and N. Scialabba. 1990. Gadiform fishes of the world (Order Gadiformes): An annotated and illustrated catalogue of cods, hakes, grenadiers and other gadiform fishes known to date. FAO Species Catalogue, Rome, Fisheries Synopsis 125(10): 1–442.

Cohen, D. M., and J. G. Nielsen. 1972. A review of the viviparous ophidioid fishes of the genus *Saccogaster*. Proc. Biol. Soc. Wash. 85: 445–469.

Cohen, D. M., and J. G. Nielsen. 1978. Guide to the identification of the genera of the fish order Ophidiiformes, with a tentative classification to the order. NOAA Tech. Rep., NMFS Circ. 417: 1–72.

Cohen, D. M., and J. L. Russo. 1979. Variation in the fourbeard rockling, *Enchelyopus cimbrius,* a North Atlantic gadid fish, with comments on the genera of rocklings. U.S. Nat. Mar. Fish. Serv. Fish. Bull. 77: 91–104.

Collette, B. B. 1965. *Hemirhamphidae* (Pisces: Synentognathi) from tropical West Africa. Atlantide Rep. 8: 217–235.

Collette, B. B. 1978a. Batrachoididae. *In:* FAO species identification sheets for fishery purposes, Western Central Atlantic (Fishing area 31), ed. W. Fischer. Rome: FAO.

Collette, B. B. 1978b. Belonidae. *In:* FAO species identification sheets for fishery purposes, Western Central Atlantic (Fishing area 31), ed. W. Fischer. Rome: FAO.

Collette, B. B. 1978c. Hemiramphidae. *In:* FAO species identification sheets for fishery purposes, Western Central Atlantic (Fishing area 31), ed. W. Fischer. Rome: FAO.

Collette, B. B. 1983. Two new species of coral toadfishes, family Batrachoididae, genus *Sanopus,* from Yucatan, Mexico, and Belize. Proc. Biol. Soc. Wash. 96: 719–724.

Collette, B. B., and N. V. Parin. 1970. Needlefishes (Belonidae) of the eastern Atlantic Ocean. Atlantide Rep. 11: 7–60.

Collette, B. B., and N. V. Parin. 1986. Belonidae. *In:* FN-EAM 2: 604–609.

Compagno, L. J. V. 1984. Sharks of the world. *In:* FAO Species Catalogue. Vol. 4, Sharks of the world. An annotated and illustrated catalogue of shark species known to date. FAO Fisheries Synopsis 125(4, parts 1 and 2): 1–655.

Compagno, L. J. V., M. Stehmann, and D. A. Ebert. 1990. *Rhinochimaera africana,* a new longnose chimaera from southern Africa, with comments on the systematics and distribution of the genus *Rhinochimaera* Garman, 1901 (Chimaeriformes,

Rhinochimaeridae). S. Afr. J. Mar. Sci. 9: 201–222.

Courtenay, W. R., Jr. 1971. Sexual dimorphism of the sound producing mechanism of the striped cusk-eel, *Rissola marginata* (Pisces: Ophidiidae). Copeia: 259–268.

Crabtree, R. E. 1983. Confirmation of the validity of *Coryphaenoides alateralis* as distinct from *Coryphaenoides thelestomus* based on new captures from the North Atlantic. Copeia: 1083–1088.

Crabtree, R. E., K. J. Sulak, and J. A. Musick. 1985. Biology and distribution of species of *Polyacanthonotus* (Pisces: Notacanthiformes) in the western North Atlantic. Bull. Mar. Sci. 36: 235–248.

Dahlberg, M. D. 1970. Atlantic and Gulf of Mexico menhadens, genus *Brevoortia* (Pisces: Clupeidae). Bull. Fla. St. Mus. Biol. Sci. 15: 91–162.

Daiber, F. C., and R. A. Booth. 1960. Notes on the biology of the butterfly rays, *Gymnura altavela* and *Gymnura micrura.* Copeia: 137–139.

D'Ancona, U., and G. Cavinato. 1965. The fishes of the family Bregmacerotidae. Dana Rep. 64: 1–92.

Darnell, R. M. 1962. Fishes of the Río Tamesí and related coastal lagoons in east-central Mexico. Publ. Inst. Mar. Sci. 8: 299–365.

Dawson, C. E. 1966. *Gunterichthys longipenis,* a new genus and species of ophidioid fish from the northern Gulf of Mexico. Proc. Biol. Soc. Wash. 79: 205–214.

Dawson, C. E. 1971a. Supplemental observations on *Gunterichthys longipenis,* a northern Gulf of Mexico brotulid fish. Copeia: 164–167.

Dawson, C. E. 1971b. Records of the pearlfish, *Carapus bermudensis,* in the northern Gulf of Mexico and of a new host species. Copeia: 730–731.

Dawson, C. E. 1982. Family Syngnathidae. *In:* FWNA 8: 1–172.

Dennis, G. D., and T. J. Bright. 1988. New records of fishes in the northwestern Gulf of Mexico, with notes on some rare species. Northeast Gulf Sci. 10: 1–18.

de Sylva, D. P., and W. N. Eschmeyer. 1977. Systematics and biology of the deep-sea fish family Gibberichthyidae, a senior synonym of the family Kasidoroidae. Proc. Calif. Acad. Sci., Ser. 4, 41: 215–231.

Ditty, J. G., E. D. Houde, and R. F. Shaw. 1994. Egg and larval development of Spanish sardine, *Sardinella aurita* (family Clupeidae), with a synopsis of characters to identify clupeid larvae from the northern Gulf of Mexico. Bull. Mar. Sci. 54: 367–380.

Dodrill, J. W., and R. G. Gilmore. 1979. First North American continental record of the longfin mako (*Isurus paucus* Guitart Manday). Fla. Sci. 42: 52–58.

Ebeling, A. W. 1962. Melamphaidae I. Systematics and geography of the species in the bathypelagic fish genus *Melamphaes* Günther. Dana Rep. 58: 1–164.

Ebeling, A. W. 1986. Family No. 133. Melamphaidae. *In:* SSF: 427–431.

Ebeling, A. W., and W. H. Weed, III. 1963. Melamphaidae III. Systematics and distribution of the species in the bathypelagic fish genus *Scopelogadus* Vaillant. Dana Rep. 60: 1–58.

Ebeling, A. W., and W. H. Weed, III. 1973. Order Xenoberyces (Stephanoberyciformes). *In:* FWNA 6: 397–478.

Echelle, A. A., and D. T. Mosier. 1982. *Menidia clarkhubbsi*, n. sp. (Pisces: Atherinidae) an all female species. Copeia: 533–540.

Edwards, R. J., E. Marsh, and F. B. Stevens. 1978. The utility of the air bladder position in determining specific relationships in the atherinid genus *Menidia*. Contrib. Mar. Sci. 21: 1–7.

Ege, V. 1939. A revision of the genus *Anguilla* Shaw: a systematic, phylogenetic and geographical study. Dana Rep. 16: 256 pp.

Ehrich, S. 1986. Macroramphosidae. *In:* FN-EAM 2: 627.

Eldred, B. 1967. Larval bonefish, *Albula vulpes* (Linnaeus, 1758), (Albulidae) in Florida and adjacent waters. Fla. Bd. Cons. Mar. Lab. Leaflet Ser. 4, 1(3): 1–4.

Eldred, B., and G. Lyons. 1966. Larval ladyfish, *Elops saurus* Linnaeus, 1766, (Elopidae) in Florida and adjacent waters. Fla. Bd. Cons. Mar. Lab. Leaflet Ser. 4, 1(2): 1–6.

Fernholm, B., and C. L. Hubbs, 1981. Western Atlantic hagfish of the genus *Eptatretus* (Myxinidae) with description of two new species. U.S. Nat. Mar. Fish. Serv. Fish. Bull. 79: 69–83.

Fink, W. L. 1985. Phylogenetic interrelationships of the stomiid fishes (Teleostei: Stomiiformes). Misc. Publ. Mus. Zool. Univ. Mich. 171: 1–127.

Fitch, J. E. 1964. The ribbonfishes (family Trachipteridae) of the eastern Pacific Ocean, with a description of a new species. Calif. Fish Game 50: 228–240.

Fitch, J. E. 1979. The velvet whalefish, *Barbourisia rufa,* added to California's marine fauna, with notes on otoliths of whalefishes and possible related genera. Bull. S. Calif. Acad. Sci. 78: 61–67.

Fitz, E. S., and F. C. Daiber. 1963. An introduction to the biology of *Raja eglanteria* and *Raja erincaea* as they occur in Delaware Bay. Bull. Bingham Oceanogr. Coll. 18: 69–97.

Fowler, H. W. 1952a. Description of a new cusk (*Otophidium grayi*) from the east coast of Florida. Notulae Naturae 204: 1–4.

Fowler, H. W. 1952b. Fishes from deep water off southern Florida. Notulae Naturae 246: 1–16.

Fritzsche, R. A. 1976. A review of the cornetfishes, genus *Fistularia* (Fistulariidae), with a discussion of intrageneric relationships and zoogeography. Bull. Mar. Sci. 26: 196–204.

Fritzsche, R. A. 1977. Aulostomidae. *In:* FAO species identification sheets for fishery purposes, Western Central Atlantic (Fishing area 31), ed. W. Fischer. Rome: FAO.

Fritzsche, R. A. 1978. Development of fishes of the mid-Atlantic Bight: an atlas of egg, larval, and juvenile stages. Vol. 5, Chaetodontidae through Ophidiidae. U.S. Fish Wildl. Serv., Biol. Serv. Program 5: 323–324.

Garrick, J. A. F. 1967. A broad view of *Car-*

charhinus species, their systematics and distribution. *In:* Sharks, skates and rays, ed. P. W. Gilbert et al. Baltimore: Johns Hopkins Press, pp. 85–91.

Garrick, J. A. F. 1982. Sharks of the genus *Carcharhinus.* NOAA Tech. Rep. NMFS Circ. 445: 194 pp.

Garrick, J. A. F., R. H. Backus, and R. H. Gibbs. 1964. *Carcharhinus floridanus,* the silky shark, a synonym of *C. falciformis.* Copeia: 369–375.

Garrick, J. A. F., and L. P. Schultz. 1963. A guide to the kinds of potentially dangerous sharks. *In:* Sharks and survival, ed. P. W. Gilbert et al. Boston: D. C. Heath, pp. 3–60.

Garrick, J. A. F., and S. Springer. 1964. *Isistius plutodus,* a new squaloid shark from the Gulf of Mexico. Copeia: 678–682.

Gartner, J. V., Jr. 1991. Life histories of three species of lanternfishes (Pisces: Myctophidae) from the eastern Gulf of Mexico. Mar. Biol. 111: 21–27.

Gartner, J. V., Jr. 1993. Patterns of reproduction in the dominant lanternfish species (Pisces: Myctophidae) of the eastern Gulf of Mexico, with a review of reproduction among tropical-subtropical Myctophidae. Bull. Mar. Sci. 52: 721–750.

Gartner, J. V., Jr., W. J. Conley, and T. J. Hopkins. 1989. Escapement by fishes from midwater trawls: a case study using lanternfishes (Pisces: Myctophidae). U.S. Nat. Mar. Fish. Serv. Fish. Bull. 87: 213–222.

Gartner, J. V., Jr., T. L. Hopkins, R. C. Baird, and D. M. Milliken. 1987. The lanternfishes (Pisces: Myctophidae) of the eastern Gulf of Mexico. U.S. Nat. Mar. Fish. Serv. Fish. Bull. 85: 81–98.

Geistdoerfer, P. 1986. Macrouridae. *In:* FN-EAM 2: 644–676.

Gibbs, R. H., Jr. 1964a. Family Astronesthidae. *In:* FWNA 4: 311–350.

Gibbs, R. H., Jr. 1964b. Family Idiacanthidae. *In:* FWNA 4: 512–522.

Gibbs, R. H., Jr. 1969. Taxonomy, sexual dimorphism, vertical distribution and evolutionary zoogeography of the bathypelagic fish genus *Stomias* (Family Stomiatidae). Smithsonian Contrib. Zool. 31: 1–25.

Gibbs, R. H., Jr. 1984a. Astronesthidae. *In:* FN-EAM 1: 325–335.

Gibbs, R. H., Jr. 1984b. Chauliodontidae. *In:* FN-EAM 1: 336–337.

Gibbs, R. H., Jr. 1984c. Stomiidae. *In:* FN-EAM 1: 338–340.

Gibbs, R. H., Jr. 1984d. Melanostomiidae. *In:* FN-EAM 1: 341–365.

Gibbs, R. H., Jr. 1984e. Malacosteidae. *In:* FN-EAM 1: 366–370.

Gibbs, R. H., Jr. 1984f. Idiacanthidae. *In:* FN-EAM 1: 371–372.

Gibbs, R. H., Jr. 1986a. Family No. 68. Chauliodontidae. *In:* SSF: 230.

Gibbs, R. H., Jr. 1986b. Family No. 69. Astronesthidae. *In:* SSF: 231–234.

Gibbs, R. H., Jr. 1986c. Family No. 70. Idiacanthidae. *In:* SSF: 234–235.

Gibbs, R. H., Jr. 1986d. Family No. 72. Melanostomiidae. *In:* SSF: 236–243.

Gibbs, R. H., Jr., T. A. Clark, and J. R. Gomon. 1983. Taxonomy and distribution of the stomioid fish genus *Eustomias* (Melanostomiidae). Part 1, Subgenus *Nominostomias.* Smithsonian Contrib. Zool. 380: 1–139.

Gibbs, R. H., Jr., and N. J. Wilimowsky. 1966. Family Alepisauridae. *In:* FWNA 5: 482–497.

Gilbert, C. R. 1967. A revision of the hammerhead sharks (Family Sphyrnidae). Proc. U.S. Nat. Mus. 119(3539): 88 pp.

Gilbert, C. R. 1968. Western Atlantic batrachoidid fishes of the genus *Porichthys,* including three new species. Bull. Mar. Sci. 18: 671–730.

Gilbert, C. R. 1992. Rare and endangered biota of Florida. Vol. 2, Fishes. Gainesville: Univ. Fla. Press.

Gilmore, R. G. 1983. Observations on the embryos of the longfin mako, *Isurus paucus,* and the bigeye thresher, *Alopias superciliosus.* Copeia: 375–382.

Gilmore, R. G., J. W. Dodrill, and P. A. Linley. 1983. Reproduction and embryonic development of the sand tiger shark, *Odon-*

taspis taurus (Rafinesque). U.S. Fish Wildl. Serv. Fish. Bull. 81: 201–225.

Ginsburg, I. 1933. Descriptions of five new species of seahorses. J. Wash. Acad. Sci. 23: 560–563.

Ginsburg, I. 1951. The eels of the northern Gulf Coast of the United States and some related species. Texas J. Sci. 3: 431–485.

Ginsburg, I. 1954. Four new fishes and one little known species from the east coast of the United States including the Gulf of Mexico. J. Wash. Acad. Sci. 44: 256–264.

Goin, C. J., and D. S. Erdman. 1951. The crested oarfish, *Lophotus lacepedei,* from Florida, first record for the western North Atlantic. Copeia: 285–288.

Gomon, J. R., and R. H. Gibbs, Jr. 1985. Taxonomy and distribution of the stomioid fish genus *Eustomias* (Melanostomiidae). Part 2, *Biradiostomias,* new subgenus. Smithsonian Contrib. Zool. 409: 1–58.

Goode, G. B., and T. H. Bean. 1895. On Cetomimidae and Rondeletiidae, two new families of bathyhial fishes from the north-western Atlantic. Scientific results of explo-rations by the U.S. Fish Commission steamer "Albatross." No. 28. Proc. U.S. Nat. Mus. 17(1012): 451–454.

Goode, G. B., and T. H. Bean. 1896. Oceanic ichthyology, a treatise on the deep-sea and pelagic fishes of the world based chiefly upon the collections made by the steamers Blake, Albatross, and Fish Hawk in the northwestern Atlantic, with an atlas con-taining 417 figures. Spec. Bull. U.S. Nat. Mus. 2: Text, 553 pp.; Atlas, 123 pls.

Goodyear, R. H., and R. H. Gibbs, Jr. 1970. Ergebnisse der Forschungereisen des FFS "Walther Herwig" nach Südamerika. 10, Systematics and zoogeography of stomia-toid fishes of the *Astronesthes cyaneus* spe-cies group (Family Astronesthidae) with descriptions of three new species. Arch. FischWiss. 20: 107–131.

Goodyear, R. H., and R. H. Gibbs, Jr. 1986. Family No. 71. Malacosteidae. *In:* SSF: 235–236.

Grey, M. 1956. The distribution of fishes found below 2,000 meters. Fieldiana Zool. 36: 73–337.

Grey, M. 1958. Descriptions of abyssal ben-thic fishes from the Gulf of Mexico. Fiel-diana Zool. 39: 149–183.

Grey, M. 1959. Deep sea fishes from the Gulf of Mexico, with the description of a new species. Fieldiana Zool. 39: 323–346.

Grey, M. 1964. Gonostomatidae. *In:* FWNA 4: 78–240.

Gruber, S. H., and L. V. J. Compagno. 1983. Taxonomic status and biology of the big-eye thresher *Alopias superciliosus.* U.S. Nat. Mar. Fish. Serv. Fish. Bull. 79: 617–640.

Gudger, E. W. 1941. Food and feeding habits of the whale shark, *Rhineodon typus.* J. Elisha Mitchell Sci. Soc. 57: 57–72.

Guitart Manday, D. 1966. Nuevo nombre para una especie de tiburón del género *Isurus* (Elasmobranchii: Isuridae) de aguas cunanas. Poeyana, Ser. A., 1966(15): 9 pp.

Guitart Manday, D. 1975. Las pesquerías pelágico-oceánicas de corto radio de acción en la región noroccidental de Cuba. Ser. Oceanol. Acad. Cienc. Cuba 31: 26 pp.

Gunter, G. 1945. Studies on marine fishes of Texas. Publ. Inst. Mar. Sci. 1: 1–190.

Günther, A. 1878. Preliminary notices of deep-sea fishes collected during the voyage of the HMS "Challenger." Ann. Mag. Nat. Hist., Ser. 5, 2: 17–28.

Haburay, K., R. W. Hastings, D. DeVries, and J. Massey. 1974. Tropical marine fishes from Pensacola, Florida. Fla. Sci. 37: 105–109.

Haedrich, R. L., and P. T. Polloni. 1974. Rarely seen fishes captured in Hudson submarine canyon. J. Fish. Res. Bd. Canada 31: 231–234.

Hanks, B., and M. J. McCoid. 1988. First record of the least killifish, *Heterandria formosa* (Pisces: Poeciliidae), in Texas. Texas J. Sci. 40: 447–448.

Hardy, J. D. 1978. Development of fishes of the mid-Atlantic Bight: an atlas of egg, lar-val and juvenile stages. Vol. 2, Anguillidae through Syngnathidae. U.S. Fish Wildl. Serv., Biol. Serv. Program 2: 1–458.

Harold, A. S. 1994. A taxonomic revision of the sternoptychid genus *Polyipnus* (Teleostei: Stomiiformes) with an analysis of phylogenetic relationships. Bull. Mar. Sci. 54: 428–534.

Harrington, R. W., Jr., and L. R. Rivas. 1958. The discovery in Florida of the cyprinodont fish, *Rivulus marmoratus*, with a redescription and ecological notes. Copeia: 125–130.

Harry, R. R. 1952. Deep-sea fishes of the Bermuda oceanographic expeditions. Families Cetomimidae and Rondeletiidae. N. Y. Zool. Soc. 37: 55–72.

Hastings, P. A., and S. A. Bortone. 1976. Additional notes on tropical marine fishes in the northern Gulf of Mexico. Fla. Sci. 2: 123–125.

Hastings, R. W., L. H. Ogren, and M. T. Mabry. 1976. Observations on the fauna associated with offshore platforms in the northeastern Gulf of Mexico. U.S. Nat. Mar. Fish. Serv. Fish. Bull. 74: 387–402.

Hastings, R. W., and R. W. Yerger. 1971. Ecology and life history of the diamond killifish, *Adinia xenica* (Jordan and Gilbert). Amer. Midl. Nat. 86: 276–291.

Heemstra, P. C. 1980. A revision of the zeid fishes (Zeiformes: Zeidae) of South Africa. Ichthyol. Bull. J. L. B. Smith Inst. Ichthyol. (Grahamstown) 41: 1–18.

Heemstra, P. C. 1986a. Family No. 117. Lampridae. *In*: SSF: 398.

Heemstra, P. C. 1986b. Family No. 121. Lophotidae. *In*: SSF: 402–403.

Heemstra, P. C. 1986c. Family No. 122. Regalecidae. *In*: SSF: 403.

Heemstra, P. C. 1986d. Family No. 126. Berycidae. *In*: SSF: 409–410.

Heemstra, P. C. 1986e. Family No. 127. Trachichthyidae. *In*: SSF: 410–413.

Heemstra, P. C. 1986f. Family No. 133a. Stephanoberycidae. *In*: SSF: 431–432.

Heemstra, P. C. 1986g. Family No. 134. Polymixiidae. *In*: SSF: 432.

Heemstra, P. C. 1986h. Family No. 138. Zeidae. *In*: SSF: 435–438.

Heemstra, P. C. 1986i. Family No. 144. Zeniontidae. *In*: SSF: 441.

Heemstra, P. C. 1986j. Family No. 147. Macroramphosidae. *In*: SSF: 459–461.

Heemstra, P. C., and S. X. Kannemeyer. 1986. Family No. 119. Trachipteridae. *In*: SSF: 399–402.

Heemstra, P. C., and M. M. Smith. 1986. Family No. 85. Alepisauridae. *In*: SSF: 280–281.

Hensley, D. A. 1991. *Myxine mcmillanae*, a new species of hagfish (Myxinidae) from Puerto Rico and the U.S. Virgin Islands. Copeia: 1040–1043.

Herald, E. S. 1942. Three new pipefishes from the Atlantic coast of North America, with a key to the Atlantic American species. Stanford Ichthyol. Bull. 2: 125–134.

Herald, E. S. 1965. Studies on the Atlantic pipefishes, with description of new species. Proc. Calif. Acad. Sci., Ser. 4, 32: 363–375.

Hildebrand, S. F. 1963a. Family Elopidae. *In*: FWNA 3: 111–131.

Hildebrand, S. F. 1963b. Family Albulidae. *In*: FWNA 3: 132–147.

Hildebrand, S. F. 1963c. Family Engraulidae. *In*: FWNA 3: 152–249.

Hildebrand, S. F. 1963d. Family Clupeidae. *In*: FWNA 3: 257–454.

Hildebrand, S. F., and L. E. Cable. 1938. Further notes on the development and life history of some teleosts at Beaufort, N.C. Bull. U.S. Bur. Fish. 48: 505–642.

Hildebrand, S. F., and W. C. Schroeder. 1928. Fishes of Chesapeake Bay. Bull. U.S. Bur. Fish. 43: 336 pp.

Hoese. H. D. 1962. Sharks and rays of Virginia's seaside bays. Chesapeake Sci. 3: 166–172.

Hoese, H. D., and R. H. Moore. 1958. Notes on the life history of the bonnetnose shark, *Sphyrna tiburo*. Texas J. Sci. 10: 69–72.

Hoese, H. D., and R. H. Moore. 1977. Fishes of the Gulf of Mexico: Texas, Louisiana and adjacent waters. College Station: Texas A&M Univ. Press, 327 pp.

Hoffman, W., T. H. Fritts, and R. P. Reynolds. 1981. Whale sharks associated with fish schools off south Texas. Northeast Gulf Sci. 5: 55–57.

Houde, E. Q. 1984. Bregmacerotidae: Development and relationships. *In:* Ontogeny and systematics of fishes, ed. H. G. Moser et al. Spec. Publ. No. 1, Amer. Soc. Ichthyol. Herpet. Lawrence (KS): Allen Press, pp. 300–308.

Howell, W. H., and W. H. Krueger. 1987. Family Sternoptychidae, marine hatchetfishes and related species. *In:* Biology of midwater fishes of the Bermuda ocean acre, ed. R. H. Gibbs and W. H. Krueger. Smithsonian Contrib. Zool. 452: 32–50.

Howell Rivero, L. 1935. The family Ateleopidae and its West Indian form. Mem. Soc. Cubana Hist. Nat. 9: 91–106.

Howes, G. J. 1991. Biogeography of gadoid fishes. J. Biogeog. 18: 595–622.

Hubbs, C. L. 1936. Fishes of the Yucatan Peninsula. Carnegie Inst. Wash. Publ. 457(17): 157–287.

Hubbs, C. L. 1944. Species of the circumtropical fish genus *Brotula*. Copeia: 162–178.

Hubbs, C. L., and R. R. Miller. 1965. Studies of cyprinodont fishes. Contrib. 22, Variation in *Lucania parva*, its establishment in western United States, and description of a new species from an interior basin in Coahuila, Mexico. Misc. Publ. Mus. Zool. Univ. Mich. 127: 1–104.

Huff, J. A. 1975. Life history of Gulf of Mexico sturgeon, *Acipenser oxyrhinchus desoti*, in Suwannee River, Florida. Fla. Mar. Res. Publ. 16: 1–32.

Hulley, P. A. 1972. The family Gurgesiellidae (Chondrichthyes, Batoidei) with reference to *Pseudoraja atlantica* Bigelow and Schroeder. Copeia: 356–359.

Hulley, P. A. 1973. Interrelationships within Anacanthobatidae (Chondrichthyes, Batoidei) with a description of the lectotype of *Anacanthobatis marmoratus* Von Bonde and Swart, 1923. Ann. South African Mus. 62: 131–158.

Hulley, P. A. 1984a. Neoscopelidae. *In:* FN-EAM 1: 426–428.

Hulley, P. A. 1984b. Myctophidae. *In:* FN-EAM 1: 429–483.

Hulley, P. A. 1986a. Family No. 70. Idiacanthidae. *In:* SSF: 234–235.

Hulley, P. A. 1986b. Family No. 86. Myctophidae. *In:* SSF: 282–321.

Hulley, P. A. 1986c. Family No. 87. Neoscopelidae. *In:* SSF: 321–322.

Hulley, P. A. 1986d. Family No. 123. Stylephoridae. *In:* SSF: 404.

Hulley, P. A. 1986e. Family No. 131. Anoplogasteridae. *In:* SSF: 415.

Hureau, J.-C. 1986. Polymixiidae. *In:* FN-EAM 2: 738–739.

Inada, T. 1981. Studies on the merluccid fishes. Bull. Far Seas Fish. Res. Lab. 16: 1–72.

Iwamoto, T. 1966. The macrourid fish *Cetonurus globiceps* in the Gulf of Mexico. Copeia: 439–442.

Iwamoto, T. 1970. The R/V "Pillsbury" deep-sea biological expeditions to the Gulf of Guinea, 1964–65. Contrib. 19, Macrourid fishes of the Gulf of Guinea. Studies in Tropical Oceanogr. 4(2): 316–431.

Iwamoto, T. 1974. *Nezumia (Kuronezumia) bubonis*, a new subgenus and species of grenadier (Macrouridae: Pisces) from Hawaii and the western North Atlantic. Proc. Calif. Acad. Sci. 39: 507–516.

Iwamoto, T. 1986. Family No. 93. Macrouridae. *In:* SSF: 300–341.

Iwamoto, T., and Y. I. Sazonov. 1994. Revision of the genus *Kumba* (Pisces, Gadiformes, Macrouridae), with the description of three new species. Proc. Calif. Acad. Sci. 48: 221–237.

Jacob, B. A., and J. D. McEachran. 1994. Status of two species of skates, *Raja (Diptutus) teevani* and *R. (D.) floridana* (Chondrichthyes: Rajoidei), from the western North Atlantic. Copeia: 433–445.

Jenkins, R. E., and N. M. Burkhead. 1994. Freshwater fishes of Virginia. Bethesda: Amer. Fish. Soc., 1079 pp.

Johnson, G. D., and C. Patterson. 1993. Percomorph phylogeny: A survey of acanthomorphs and a new proposal. Bull. Mar. Sci. 52: 554–626.

Johnson, M. S. 1975. Biochemical systematics

of the atherinid genus *Menidia.* Copeia: 662–691.

Johnson, R. K. 1970. A new species of *Diplophos* (Salmoniformes: Gonostomatidae) from the western Pacific. Copeia: 437–443.

Johnson, R. K. 1974a. A revision of the alepisauroid family Scopelarchidae (Pisces: Myctophiformes). Fieldiana Zool. 66: 1–249.

Johnson, R. K. 1974b. Five new species and a new genus of alepisauroid fishes of the Scopelarchidae (Pisces: Myctophiformes). Copeia: 449–457.

Johnson, R. K. 1974c. A *Macristium* larva from the Gulf of Mexico with additional evidence for the synonymy of *Macristium* with *Bathysaurus* (Myctophiformes: Bathysauridae). Copeia: 973–977.

Johnson, R. K. 1982. Fishes of the families Evermannellidae and Scopelarchidae: systematics, morphology, interrelationships and zoogeography. Fieldiana Zool., n.s., 12: 1–252.

Johnson, R. K. 1984a. Scopelarchidae. *In:* FN-EAM 1: 484–488.

Johnson, R. K. 1984b. Evermannellidae. *In:* FN-EAM 1: 489–493.

Johnson, R. K. 1986a. Family No. 77. Scopelarchidae. *In:* SSF: 265–267.

Johnson, R. K. 1986b. Family No. 80. Giganturidae. *In:* SSF: 273–274.

Johnson, R. K. 1986c. Family No. 83. Evermannellidae. *In:* SSF: 278–280.

Johnson, R. K., and L. U. Berman. 1986. Stylephoridae. *In:* FN-EAM 2: 736–737.

Johnson, R. K., and E. Bertelsen. 1991. The fishes of the family Giganturidae: systematics, development, distribution and aspects of biology. Dana Rep. 91: 1–45.

Jones. E. C. 1971. *Isistius brasiliensis,* a squaloid shark, the probable cause of crater wounds on fishes and cetaceans. U.S. Fish Wildl. Serv. Fish. Bull. 69: 791–798.

Jones, P. H., F. D. Martin, and J. D. Hardy. 1978a. Development of fishes of the mid-Atlantic Bight. Vol. 1., Acipenseridae through Ictaluridae. U.S. Fish and Wildl. Serv., Biol. Serv. Program 1: 1–366.

Jordan, D. S., and B. T. Evermann. 1896. The fishes of North and Middle America: a descriptive catalogue of the species of fish-like vertebrates found in the waters of North America, north of the Isthmus of Panama. Bull. U.S. Nat. Mus. 47(1): 1–1240.

Joung, S. J., C. T. Chen, E. Clark, S. Uchida, W. Y. P. Huang. 1996. The whale shark, *Rhincodon typus,* is a livebearer: 300 embryos found in one 'megamama supreme.' Environ. Biol. Fish. 46: 219–223.

Kanazawa, R. H. 1957. A new species of eel, *Coloconger meadi,* and new records for the ateleopid, *Ijimaia antillarum* Howell Rivero, both from the Gulf of Mexico. Copeia: 234–235.

Kanazawa, R. H. 1958. A revision of the eels of the genus *Conger* with descriptions of four new species. Proc. U.S. Nat. Mus. 108: 219–267.

Kanazawa, R. H. 1961. *Paraconger,* a new genus with three new species of eels (family Congridae). Proc. U.S. Nat. Mus. 113: 1–14.

Kanazawa, R. H. 1963. Two new species of ophichthid eels from the western Atlantic. Proc. Biol. Soc. Wash. 76: 281–288.

Karnella, C. 1973. The systematic status of *Merluccius* in the tropical western Atlantic Ocean, including the Gulf of Mexico. U.S. Fish Wildl. Serv. Fish. Bull. 71: 83–91.

Karrer, C., and P. C. Heemstra. 1986. Family No. 140. Grammicolepidae. *In:* SSF: 440–441.

Keene, M. J., R. H. Gibbs, and W. H. Krueger. 1987. Biology of midwater fishes of the Bermuda ocean acre, Family Melamphaidae. Smithsonian Contrib. Zool. 452: 169–185.

Koefoed, E. 1927. Fishes of the sea-bottom. Rep. Sci. Res. "Michael Sars" North Atlantic Deep-Sea Exped., 1910, 4: 1–147.

Kotlyar, A. N. 1984. Systematics and the distribution of fishes of the family Polymixiidae (Polymixioidei, Beryciformes). J. Ichthyol. 24(6): 1–20.

Kotthaus, A. 1970. Fische des Indischen Ozeans, Ergebnisse der ichthyologischen

Untersuchungen während der Expedition des Forschungsschilles "Meteor" in den Indischen Ozean 1964 bis mai 1965. A. Systematischer Teil, VI Anacanthini (2), Berycomorphi, Zeomorphi. "Meteor" Fosch. -Ergebnisse Reihe D (5): 53–70.

Krefft, G. 1968. Knorpelfische (Chondrichthyes) aus dem tropischen Ostatlantik. Atlantide Rep. 10: 33–76.

Krefft, G. 1980. Results of the research cruises of FRV "Walther Herwig" to South America. 53, Sharks from the pelagic trawl catches obtained during Atlantic transects, including some specimens from other cruises. Arch. FischWiss. 30: 1–16.

Krefft, G. 1984. Notosudidae. In: FN-EAM 1: 421–425.

Krefft, G. 1986. Family No. 78. Notosudidae. In: SSF: 268–270.

Krueger, W. H., and R. H. Gibbs, Jr. 1966. Growth, change and sexual dimorphism in the stomiatoid fish Echiostoma barbartum. Copeia: 43–49.

Lane, E. D. 1967. A study of the Atlantic midshipmen, Porichthys porosissimus, in the vicinity of Port Aransas, Texas. Contrib. Mar. Sci. 12: 1–53.

Lane, E. D., and K. W. Stewart. 1968. A revision of the genus Hoplunnis Kaup (Apodes, Muraenesocidae), with a description of a new species. Contrib. Mar. Sci. 13: 51–64.

Lee, D. S., C. R. Gilbert, C. H. Hocutt, R. E. Jenkins, D. E. McAllister, and J. R. Stauffer, Jr. 1980. Atlas of North American freshwater fishes. North Carolina Biol. Sur. #1980–12: 1–854.

Leiby, M. M. 1989. Family Ophichthidae Leptocephali. In: FWNA 9(2): 764–897.

Leiby, M. M., and R. W. Yerger. 1980. The genus Bascanichthys (Pisces: Ophichthidae) in the Gulf of Mexico. Copeia: 402–408.

Longley, W. H., and S. F. Hildebrand. 1940. New genera and species of fishes from Tortugas, Florida. Carnegie Inst. Wash. Publ. 517: 223–285.

Longley, W. H., and S. F. Hildebrand. 1941. Systematic catalogue of the fishes of Tortugas, Florida, with observations on color, habits, and local distribution. Carnegie Inst. Wash. Publ. 535: 1–331.

Markle, D. F. 1978. Taxonomy and distribution of Rouleina attrita and Rouleina maderensis (Pisces: Alepocephalidae). U.S. Nat. Mar. Fish. Serv. Fish. Bull. 76: 79–87.

Markle, D. F. 1980. A new species and review of the deep-sea fish genus Asquamiceps (Salmoniformes, Alepocephalidae). Bull. Mar. Sci. 30: 45–53.

Markle, D. F. 1986. Family No. 64. Alepocephalidae. In: SSF: 218–223.

Markle, D. F., and N. R. Merrett. 1980. The abyssal alepocephalid, Rinoctes nasutus (Pisces: Salmoniformes), a redescription and an evaluation of its systematic position. J. Zool. Lond. 190: 225–239.

Markle, D. F., and J. E. Olney. 1980. A description of the vexillifer larvae of Pyramodon ventralis and Snyderidia canina (Pisces, Carapidae) with comments on classification. Pac. Sci. 34: 173–180.

Markle, D. F., and J. E. Olney. 1990. Systematics of the pearlfishes (Pisces: Carapidae). Bull. Mar. Sci. 47: 269–410.

Markle, D. F., and J.-C. Quéro. 1984. Alepocephalidae. In: FN-EAM 1: 228–253.

Marshall, N. B. 1966. Family Scopelosauridae. In: FWNA 5: 194–204.

Marshall, N. B. 1973. Family Macrouridae. In: FWNA 6: 496–537, 581–600, 610–623, 650–665.

Marshall, N. B., and T. Iwamoto. 1973. Genera Coelorhynchus, Coryphaenoides, Hymenocephalus and Nezumia. In: FWNA 6: 538–563, 565–580, 601–612, 614–649.

Martin, D. M. 1984. Distribution and ecology of the Synaphobranchidae of the Gulf of Mexico. Gulf Res. Rep. 7: 311–324.

Martin, F. D., and G. E. Drewry. 1978. Development of fishes of the Mid-Atlantic Bight: an atlas of egg, larval and juvenile stages. Vol. 6, Stromateidae through Ogcocephalidae. U.S. Fish and Wildl. Serv., Biol. Serv. Program 6: 1–416.

Matsui, T., and R. H. Rosenblatt. 1986.

Family No. 65. Platytroctidae. *In:* SSF: 223–225.

Matsui, T., and R. H. Rosenblatt. 1987. Review of the deep-sea fish family Platytroctidae (Pisces: Salmoniformes). Bull. Scripps Inst. Oceanogr. 26: 1–159.

Maul, G. E. 1955. Five species of rare sharks new for Madeira including two new to science. Notulae Naturae 279: 1–13.

Maul, G. E. 1986a. Berycidae. *In:* FN-EAM 2: 740–742.

Maul, G. E. 1986b. Trachichthidae. *In:* FN-EAM 2: 749–752.

Maul. G. E. 1986c. Melamphaidae. *In:* FN-EAM 2: 756–765.

Maul, G. E. 1986d. Stephanoberycidae. *In:* FN-EAM 2: 766–767.

Maul, G. E. 1986e. Family No. 84. Omosudidae. *In:* SSF: 280.

McCleave, J. D., and M. J. Miller. 1994. Spawning of *Conger oceanicus* and *Conger triporiceps* (Congridae) in the Sargasso Sea and subsequent distribution of leptocephali. Environ. Biol. Fish. 39: 339–355.

McCosker, J. E., and J. E. Böhlke. 1984. A review of the snake-eel genera *Gordiichthys* and *Ethadophis,* with descriptions of new species and comments on related Atlantic bascanichthyins. Proc. Acad. Nat. Sci. Philadelphia 136: 32–44.

McCosker, J. E., E. B. Böhlke, and J. E. Böhlke. 1989. Family Ophichthidae. *In:* FWNA 9(1): 254–412.

McDowell, S. B. 1973. Order Heteromi (Notacathiformes). *In:* FWNA 6: 1–228.

McEachran, J. D. 1970. Egg capsules and reproductive biology of the skate *Raja garmani* (Pisces: Rajidae). Copeia: 197–199.

McEachran, J. D. 1977. Variation in *Raja garmani* and the status of *Raja lentiginosa* (Pisces: Rajidae). Bull. Mar. Sci. 27: 423–439.

McEachran, J. D. 1984. Anatomical investigations of the New Zealand skates, *Bathyraja asperula* and *B. spinifera,* with an evaluation of their classification within Rajoidei (Chondrichthyes, Rajiformes). Copeia: 45–58.

McEachran, J. D., and S. Branstetter. 1984. Squalidae. *In:* FN-EAM 1: 128–147.

McEachran, J. D., and C. Capapé. 1984a. Dasyatidae. *In:* FN-EAM 1: 197–202.

McEachran, J. D., and C. Capapé. 1984b. Gymnuridae. *In:* FN-EAM 1: 203–204.

McEachran, J. D., and L. V. J. Compagno. 1979. A further description of *Gurgesiella furvescens,* with comments on the interrelationships of Gurgesiellidae and Pseudorajidae (Pisces, Rajoidei). Bull. Mar. Sci. 29: 530–553.

McEachran, J. D., and L. J. V. Compagno. 1982. Interrelationships of and within *Breviraja* based on anatomical structures (Pisces, Rajoidei). Bull. Mar. Sci. 32: 399–425.

McEachran, J. D., and R. E. Matheson, Jr. 1985. Polychormatism and polymorphism in *Breviraja spinosa* (Elasmobranchii, Rajiformes), with description of three new species. Copeia: 1035–1052.

McEachran, J. D., and J. A. Musick. 1975. Distribution and relative abundance of seven species of skates (Pisces: Rajidae) which occur between Nova Scotia and Cape Hatteras. U.S. Nat. Mar. Fish. Serv. Fish. Bull. 73: 110–136.

McEachran, J. D., and B. Seret. 1987. Allocation of the name *Sphyrina tudes* (Valenciennes, 1822) and status of the nominal species *Sphyrina couardi* Cadenat, 1951 (Chondrichthyes, Sphyrnidae). Cybium 11: 39–46.

Mead, G. W. 1957. An Atlantic record of the zeoid fish *Parazen pacificus.* Copeia: 235–237.

Mead. G. W. 1958. A new species of iniomous fish. J. Wash. Acad. Sci. 48: 188–191.

Mead. G. W. 1959. Three new species of archibenthic iniomous fishes from the western North Atlantic. J. Wash. Acad. Sci. 48: 362–372.

Mead, G. W. 1966a. Family Aulopidae. *In:* FWNA 5: 19–29.

Mead, G. W. 1966b. Family Bathysauridae. *In:* FWNA 5: 103–113.

Mead, G. W. 1966c. Family Bathypteroidae. *In:* FWNA 5: 114–146.

Mead, G. W. 1966d. Family Ipnopidae. *In:* FWNA 5: 147–161.

Mead, G. W. 1966e. Family Chlorophalmidae. *In:* FWNA 5: 162–189.

Mead, G. W., and J. E. Böhlke. 1953. *Leptoderma springeri,* a new alepocephalid fish from the Gulf of Mexico. Texas J. Sci. 5: 265–267.

Medved, R. J., and J. A. Marshall. 1981. Feeding behavior and biology of young sandbar sharks, *Carcharhinus plumbeus* (Pisces, Carcharhinidae), in Chincoteague Bay, Virginia. U.S. Nat. Mar. Fish. Serv. Fish. Bull. 79: 441–447.

Medved, R. J., and J. A. Marshall. 1983. Short-term movements of young sandbar sharks, *Carcharhinus plumbeus* (Pisces, Carcharhindae). Bull. Mar. Sci. 33: 87–93.

Meek, S. E. 1904. The fresh-water fishes of Mexico north of the Isthmus of Tehuantepec. Field Mus., Zool., Ser. 5: 1–252.

Melendez, R. C., and D. F. Markle. 1997. Phylogeny and zoogeography of *Laemonema* and *Guttigadus.* Bull. Mar. Sci. In press.

Merrett, N. G., and N. B. Marshall. 1981. Observations on the ecology of deep-sea bottom fishes collected off northwest Africa (08°–27°N). Prog. Oceanogr. 9: 185–244.

Merrett, N. R. 1973. A new shark of the genus *Squalus* (Squalidae: Squaloidea) from the equatorial western Indian Ocean; with notes on *Squalus blainvillei.* J. Zool. Lond. 171: 93–110.

Merrett, N. R. 1980. *Bathytyphlops sewelli* (Pisces, Chlorophthalmidae): a senior synonym of *B. azorensis,* from the eastern North Atlantic with notes on its biology. J. Linn. Soc. Zool. 68: 99–109.

Miller, R. R. 1955. An annotated list of the American cypronodont fishes of the genus *Fundulus,* with the description of *Fundulus persimilis.* Occ. Pap. Mus. Zool. Univ. Mich. 568: 1–27.

Miller, R. R. 1963. Genus *Dorosoma. In:* FWNA 3: 443–451.

Milliken, D. M., and E. D. Houde. 1984. A new species of Bregmacerotidae (Pisces), *Bregmaceros cantori,* from the western Atlantic Ocean. Bull. Mar. Sci. 35: 11–19.

Moore, J. A. 1993. Phylogeny of the Trachichthyiformes (Teleostei: Percomorpha). Bull. Mar. Sci. 52: 114–136.

Moore, R. H. 1974. General ecology, distribution and relative abundance of *Mugil cephalus* and *Mugil curema* on the south Texas coast. Contrib. Mar. Sci. 18: 241–255.

Moore, R. H. 1975. New records of three marine fish from Texas waters with notes on some additional species. Texas J. Sci. 26: 155–163.

Morrow, J. E. 1961. Taxonomy of the deep-sea fishes of the genus *Chauliodus.* Bull. Mus. Comp. Zool. 125: 249–294.

Morrow, J. E. 1964a. Family Chauliodontidae. *In:* FWNA 4: 274–289.

Morrow, J. E. 1964b. Family Stomiatidae. *In:* FWNA 4: 290–310.

Morrow, J. E. 1964c. Family Malacosteidae. *In:* FWNA 4: 523–549.

Morrow, J. E., and R. H. Gibbs, Jr. 1964. Family Melanostomiatidae. *In:* FWNA 4: 351–510. [Genera *Melanostomias* and *Eustomias* by R. H. Gibbs, Jr.; remainder by J. E. Morrow.]

Mukhacheva, V. A. 1964. [The composition of species of the genus *Cyclothone* in the Pacific Ocean] (in Russian). Trudy Inst. Okeanol. 73: 98–135.

Mukhacheva, V. A. 1980a. Geographical variability of *Cyclothone acclinidens* and the taxonomic status of *Cyclothone pseudoacclinidens* (Gonostomatidae). J. Ichthyol. 20(3): 134–136.

Mukhacheva, V. A. 1980b. A review of the genus *Ichthyococcus* Bonaparte (Photichthyidae). J. Ichthyol. 20(6): 1–14.

Murdy, E. O., R. E. Matheson, Jr., J. D. Fechhelm, and M. J. McCoid. 1983. Midwater fishes of the Gulf of Mexico collected from the R/V *Alaminos.* Texas J. Sci. 35: 109–127.

Musick, J. A., and J. D. McEachran. 1969. The squaloid shark *Echinorhinchus brucus* off Virginia. Copeia: 205–206.

Myers, G. S. 1937. The deep-sea zeomorph

fishes of the family Grammicolepidae. Proc. U.S. Nat. Mus. 84: 145–156.

Myrberg, A. A., and S. H. Gruber. 1974. The behavior of the bonnethead shark, *Sphyrna tiburo*. Copeia: 358–374.

Nafpaktitis, B. G. 1966. Two new fishes of the myctophid genus *Diaphus* from the Atlantic Ocean. Bull. Mus. Comp. Zool. 133: 401–424.

Nafpaktitis, B. G. 1968. Taxonomy and distribution of the lanternfishes, genera *Lobianchia* and *Diaphus,* in the North Atlantic. Dana Rep. 73: 1–131.

Nafpaktitis, B. G. 1973. A review of the lanternfishes (family Myctophidae) described by Å. Vedel Tåning. Dana Rep. 83: 1–46.

Nafpaktitis, B. G. 1974. A new record and a new species of lanternfish, genus *Diaphus* (family Myctophidae) from the North Atlantic Ocean. Contrib. Sci., L. A. Co. Mus. Nat. Hist. 254: 1–6.

Nafpaktitis, B. G. 1977. Family Neoscopelidae. *In:* FWNA 7: 1–12.

Nafpaktitis, B. G., R. H. Backus, J. E. Craddock, R. L. Haedrich, B. H. Robinson, and C. Karnella. 1977. Family Myctophidae. *In:* FWNA 7: 13–265.

Nafpaktitis, B. G., and J. R. Paxton. 1968. A review of the lanternfish genus *Lampadena* with a description of a new species. Contrib. Sci., L. A. Co. Mus. Nat. Hist. 138: 1–29.

Nelson, G. J., and M. N. Rothman. 1973. The species of gizzard shads (Dorosomatinae) with particular reference to the Indo-Pacific region. Bull. Amer. Mus. Nat. Hist. 150: 131–206.

Nelson, J. S. 1994. Fishes of the world. 3d ed. New York: John Wiley and Sons, 600 pp.

Nichols, J. T., and C. M. Breder. 1922. *Otophidion welshi,* a new cusk eel, with notes on two others from the Gulf of Mexico. Proc. Wash. Acad. Sci. 35: 13–16.

Nielsen. J. G. 1965. On the genera *Acanthonus* and *Typhlonus* (Pisces, Brotulidae). Galathea Rep. 8: 33–47.

Nielsen, J. G. 1966. Synopsis of the Ipnopidae (Pisces: Iniomi) with description of two new abyssal species. Galathea Rep. 8: 49–75.

Nielsen, J. G. 1969. Systematics and biology of the Aphyonidae (Pisces, Ophidioidea). Galathea Rep. 10: 7–90.

Nielsen, J. G. 1986a. Bythitidae. *In:* FN-EAM 3: 1153–1157.

Nielsen, J. G. 1986b. Ophidiidae. *In:* FN-EAM 3: 1158–1166.

Nielsen, J. G. 1986c. Aphyonidae. *In:* FN-EAM 3: 1167–1171.

Nielsen, J. G. 1986d. Family No. 99. Aphyonidae. *In:* SSF: 356–357.

Nielsen, J. G., and D. M. Cohen. 1986. Family No. 96. Ophidiidae. *In:* SSF: 345–350.

Nielsen, J. G., and M. E. Retzer. 1994. Two new bathyl *Neobythites* spp. from the Caribbean Sea (Pisces: Ophidiidae). Copeia: 992–995.

Nielsen, J. G., and D. G. Smith. 1978. The eel family Nemichthyidae. Dana Report 88: 1–71.

Notabartolo-di-Sciara, G. 1987a. Natural history of the rays of the genus *Mobula* in the Gulf of California. Fish. Bull. 86: 45–66.

Notabartolo-di-Sciara, G. 1987b. A revisionary study of the genus *Mobula* (Chondrichthyes, Mobulidae), with the description of a new species. Zool. J. Linnean Soc., Lond., 91: 1–91.

Notabartolo-di-Sciara, G., and E. V. Hillyer. 1989. Mobulid rays off eastern Venezuela (Chondrichthyes, Mobulidae). Copeia: 607–614.

Nybelin, O. 1957. Deep-sea bottomfishes. Rep. Swed. Deep-sea Exped. Contrib. 2, Zool. 20: 247–345.

Ogren, L. H., and H. A. Brusher. 1977. The distribution and abundance of fishes caught with a trawl in the St. Andrew Bay System, Florida. Northeast Gulf Sci. 1: 83–105.

Olney, J. E., and D. F. Markle. 1979. Description and occurrence of vexillifer larvae of *Echiodon* (Pisces: Carapidae) in the western North Atlantic and notes on other carapid vexillifers. Bull. Mar. Sci. 29: 365–379.

Page, L. M., and B. M. Burr. 1991. A field

guide to freshwater fishes of North America north of Mexico. Boston: Houghton Mifflin, 432 pp.

Palmer, G. 1961. The dealfishes (Trachipteridae) of the Mediterranean and south-east Altantic. Bull. Brit. Mus. Nat. Hist. Zool. 7: 335–351.

Palmer, G. 1986a. Lampridae. *In:* FN-EAM 2: 725–726.

Palmer, G. 1986b. Regalecidae. *In:* FN-EAM 2: 727–728.

Palmer, G. 1986c. Trachipteridae. *In:* FN-EAM 2: 729–732.

Palmer, G. 1986d. Lophotidae. *In:* FN-EAM 2: 734–735.

Palmer, G., and H. A. Oelschlager. 1976. Use of the name *Lampris guttatus* (Brünnich, 1788) in preference to *Lampris regius* (Bonnaterre, 1788) for the opah. Copeia: 366–367.

Parenti, L. R. 1981. A phylogenetic and biogeographic analysis of cyprinodontiform fishes (Teleostei, Atherinomorpha). Bull. Amer. Mus. Nat. Hist. 168: 335–557.

Parin, N. V. 1986. Exocoetidae. *In:* FN-EAM 2: 612–619.

Parin, N. V., and S. G. Kobyliansky. 1996. Diagnosis and distribution of fifteen species recognized in genus *Maurolicus* Cocco (Sternoptychidae, Stomiiformes) with a key to their identification. Cybium 20: 185–195.

Parin, N. V., and N. S. Novikova. 1974. [Taxonomy of viperfishes (Chauliodontidae, Osteichthyes) and their distribution in the world oceans] (in Russian). Trudy. Inst. Okeanol. 96: 255–315.

Parr, A. E. 1927a. Scientific results of the Third Oceanographic Expedition of the Pawnee, 1927, Ceratiodea. Bull. Bingham Oceanogr. Coll. 3(1): 1–34.

Parr, A. E. 1927b. The stomiatoid fishes of the suborder Gymnophotodermi (Astronesthidae, Melanostomiatidae, Idiacanthidae), with a complete review of the species. Bull. Bingham Oceanogr. Coll. 3(2): 1–123.

Parr, A. E. 1928. Deep-sea fishes of the order

Iniomi from the waters around the Bahama and Bermuda islands. Bull. Bingham Oceanogr. Coll. 3(3): 1–193.

Parr, A. E. 1933. Deepsea Berycomorphi and Percomorphi from the waters around the Bahama and Bermuda islands. Bull. Bingham Oceanogr. Coll. 3(6): 1–51.

Parr, A. E. 1934. Report on experimental use of a triangular trawl for bathypelagic collecting, with an account of the fishes obtained and a revision of the family Cetomimidae. Bull. Bingham Oceanogr. Coll. 4(6): 1–59.

Parr, A. E. 1945. Barbourisidae, a new family of deep sea fishes. Copeia: 127–129.

Parr, A. E. 1946a. The Macrouridae of the western North Atlantic and Central American seas. Bull. Bingham Oceanogr. Coll. 10: 1–99.

Parr, A. E. 1946b. A new species of *Gyrinomimus* from the Gulf of Mexico. Copeia: 115–117.

Parr, A. E. 1946c. On taxonomic questions related to the classification of *Barbourisia*, the Cetomimida and the Iniomi. Copeia: 260–267.

Parr, A. E. 1952a. Revision of the genus *Talismania* with description of a new species from the Gulf of Mexico. J. Wash. Acad. Sci. 42: 268–271.

Parr, A. E. 1952b. Revision of the species currently referred to *Alepocephalus, Halisauriceps, Bathytroctes* and *Bajacalifornia* with introduction of two new genera. Bull. Mus. Comp. Zool. 107: 255–269.

Parr, A. E. 1960. The fishes of the family Searsidae. Dana Rep. 51: 1–109.

Parsons, G. R. 1983. The reproductive biology of the Atlantic sharpnose shark, *Rhizoprionodon terraenovae* Richardson. U.S. Nat. Mar. Fish. Serv. Fish. Bull. 81: 61–73.

Parsons, G. R., and S. I. Candelini. 1986. Observation on the reproductive biology of the marbled catshark, *Galeus arae antillensis.* Northeast Gulf Sci. 8: 149–150.

Paulin, C. D. 1989. Review of the morid genera *Gadella, Physiculus,* and *Salilota*

(Teleostei: Gadiformes) with descriptions of seven new species. N. Z. J. Zool. 16: 93–133.

Paxton. J. R. 1986. Family Cetomimidae. *In:* FN-EAM 2: 524–525.

Paxton, J. R. 1989. Synopsis of the whale-fishes (family Cetomimidae) with descriptions of four new genera. Rec. Aust. Mus. 41: 135–206.

Paxton, J. R., and D. J. Bray. 1986. Order Cetomimiformes. *In:* SSF: 433–434.

Pietsch, T. W. 1971. Ergebnisse der Forschungsreisen des FFS "Walther Herwig" nach Südamerika. 19, Systematics and distribution of ceratioid fishes of the genus *Dolopichthys* (Family Oneirodidae), with the description of a new species. Arch. FischWiss. 23: 1028.

Pietsch, T. W. 1974. Osteology and relationships of ceratioid anglerfishes of the family Oneirodidae, with a review of the genus *Oneirodes* Lütken. Nat. Hist. Mus. L. A. Co. Sci. Bull. 18: 1–113.

Pietsch, T. W. 1986a. Order Lophiiformes. *In:* SSF: 361–363.

Pietsch, T. W. 1986b. Family No. 105. Ceratiidae. *In:* SSF: 373–375.

Pietsch, T. W. 1986c. Family No. 107. Melanocetidae. *In:* SSF: 375–376.

Pietsch, T. W. 1986d. Systematics and distribution of bathypelagic anglerfishes of the family Ceratiidae (Order: Lophiiformes). Copeia: 479–493.

Pietsch, T. W. 1986e. Family No. 109. Diceratidae. *In:* SSF: 376–377.

Pietsch, T. W., and J. Van Duzer. 1980. Systematics and distribution of ceratioid anglerfishes of the family Melanocetidae with the description of a new species from the eastern North Pacific Ocean. U.S. Nat. Mar. Fish. Serv. Fish. Bull. 78: 59–87.

Pietsch, T. W., and D. B. Grobecker. 1987. Frogfishes of the world: systematics, zoogeography, and behavioral ecology. Stanford Univ. Press, 460 pp.

Platania, S. P., and S. W. Ross. 1980. *Arius felis* (Linnaeus), Hardhead catfish. *In:* Atlas of North American freshwater fishes, p. 368, ed. D. S. Lee, C. R. Gilbert, C. H.

Hocutt, R. E. Jenkins, D. E. McAllister, and J. R. Stauffer. Raleigh: North Carolina State Museum of Natural History, 854 pp.

Post, A. 1969. Ergebnisse der Forschungsreisen des FFS "Walther Herwig" nach Südamerica. 7, *Pontosudis quadrimaculata* spec. nov. (Osteichthyes, Iniomi, Paralepididae). Arch. FischWiss. 20: 10–14.

Post, A. 1984a. Alepisauridae. *In:* FN-EAM 1: 494–495.

Post, A. 1984b. Omosudidae. *In:* FN-EAM 1: 496–497.

Post, A. 1984c. Paralepididae. *In:* FN-EAM 1: 498–508.

Post, A. 1986a. Family No. 81: Paralepididae. *In:* SSF: 274–278.

Post, A. 1986b. Family No. 130. Diretmidae. *In:* SSF: 414–415.

Post, A. 1986c. Diretmidae. *In:* FN-EAM 2: 743–746.

Post, A. 1986d. Anoplogasteridae. *In:* FN-EAM 2: 767–779.

Post, A., and J.-C. Quéro. 1981. Revision des Diretmidae (Pisces, Trachichthyoidei) de l'Atlantique avec description d'un nouveau genre et d'une nouvelle espece. Cybium 5: 33–60.

Pratt, H. L., Jr. 1979. Reproduction in the blue shark, *Prionace glauca.* U.S. Nat. Mar. Fish. Serv. Fish. Bull. 77: 445–470.

Pratt, H. L., Jr., and J. G. Casey. 1983. Age and growth of the shortfin mako, *Isurus oxyrinchus,* using four methods. Can. J. Fish. Aquat. Sci. 40: 1944–1957.

Pratt, H. L., Jr., J. G. Casey, and R. B. Conklin. 1982. Observations on large white sharks, *Carcharodon carcharias,* off Long Island, New York. U.S. Nat. Mar. Fish. Serv. Fish. Bull. 80: 153–157.

Quéro, J.-C. 1984a. Odontaspidae. *In:* FN-EAM 1: 78–81.

Quéro, J.-C. 1984b. Lamnidae. *In:* FN-EAM 1: 83–88.

Quéro, J.-C. 1984c. Cetorhinidae. *In:* FN-EAM 1: 89–90.

Quéro, J.-C. 1984d. Alopidae. *In:* FN-EAM 1: 91–92.

Quéro, J.-C. 1984e. Ginglymostomatidae. *In:* FN-EAM 1: 93–94.

Quéro, J.-C. 1984f. Scyliorhinidae. *In:* FN-EAM 1: 95–100.

Quéro, J.-C. 1984g. Sphyrnidae. *In:* FN-EAM 1: 122–125.

Quéro, J.-C. 1986a. Zeidae. *In:* FN-EAM 2: 769–772.

Quéro, J.-C. 1986b. Grammicolepididae. *In:* FN-EAM 2: 773–774.

Quéro, J.-C. 1986c. Caproidae. *In:* FN-EAM 2: 777–779.

Quéro, J.-C., T. Matsui, R. H. Rosenblatt, and Y. I. Sazonov. 1984. Searsidae. *In:* FN-EAM 1: 257–267.

Randall, J. E. 1968. Caribbean reef fishes. Jersey City: T. F. H. Publ., 318 pp.

Randall, J. E., and R. R. Miller. 1977. Atherinidae. *In:* FAO species identification sheets for fishery purposes, Western Central Atlantic (Fishing area 31), ed. W. Fischer. Rome: FAO.

Raschi, W., J. A. Musick, and L. J. V. Compagno. 1982. *Hypoprion bigelowi,* a synonym of *Carcharhinus signatus* (Pisces: Carcharhinidae), with a description of ontogenetic heterodonty in this species and notes on its natural history. Copeia: 102–109.

Rass, T. S. 1971. Synopsis on the investigations and resources of the Caribbean Sea and adjacent regions. Paris: UNESCO, pp. 510–518.

Rauchenberger, M. 1989. Systematics and biogeography of the genus *Gambusia* (Cyprinodontiformes: Poeciliiae). Amer. Mus. Novitates 2951: 1–74.

Regan, C. T., and E. Trewavas. 1929. The fishes of the families Astronesthidae and Chauliodontidae. Danish "Dana" Expedition 1920–1922. Ocean Rep. 5: 1–39.

Regan, C. T., and E. Trewavas. 1930. The fishes of the families Stomiatidae and Melacosteidae. Danish "Dana" Expedition 1920–1922. Ocean Rep. 6: 1–143.

Relyea, K. 1983. A systematic study of two species complexes of the genus *Fundulus* (Pisces: Cyprinodontidae). Bull. Fla. St. Mus. Biol. Sci. 29: 1–64.

Retzer, M. E. 1990. New records and range extensions of twelve species of fishes in the Gulf of Mexico. Northeast Gulf Sci. 11: 137–142.

Retzer, M. E. 1991. Life history of four species of cusk-eels (Ophidiidae: Ophidiiformes) from the northern Gulf of Mexico. Copeia: 703–710.

Richards, W. J. 1969. Elopid leptocephali from Angolan waters. Copeia: 515–518.

Richardson, L. R., and J. A. F. Garrick. 1964. A new species of *Gyrinomimus* (Pisces, Cetomimidae) from New Zealand. Copeia: 523–525.

Rivas, L. R. 1963. Genus *Harengula. In:* FWNA 3: 386–396.

Rivas, L. R. 1969. A revision of the poeciliid fishes of the *Gambusia punctata* species group, with descriptions of two new species. Copeia: 778–795.

Rivas, L. R. 1980. Synopsis of knowledge on the taxonomy, biology, distribution, and fishery of the Gulf of Mexico mullets (Pisces: Mugilidae). *In:* Workshop for potential fishery resources of the northern Gulf of Mexico, ed. M. Flandorfer and L. Skupien. Mississippi-Alabama Sea Grand Consortium MASGP-80–012: 35–53.

Robins, C. H. 1971. The comparative morphology of the synaphobranchid eels of the Straits of Florida. Proc. Acad. Nat. Sci. Philadelphia 123: 153–204.

Robins, C. H., and D. M. Martin. 1976. *Haptenchelys texis. In:* New genera and species of dysommine and synaphobranchine eels (Synaphobranchidae) with an analysis of the Dysomminae, by C. H. Robins and C. R. Robins, p. 267.

Robins, C. H., and C. R. Robins. 1976. New genera and species of dysommine and synaphobranchine eels (Synaphobranchidae) with an analysis of the Dysomminae. Proc. Acad. Nat. Sci. Philadelphia 127: 249–280.

Robins, C. H., and C. R. Robins. 1989. Family Synophobranchidae. *In:* FWNA 9(1): 207–253.

Robins, C. R. 1957. Effects of storms on the shallow-water fish faunas of southern Florida, with new records of fishes from

Florida. Bull. Mar. Sci. Gulf Carib. 7: 266–275.

Robins, C. R. 1959. Studies on fishes of the family Ophidiidae. Part 3, A new species of *Lepophidium* from Barbados. Breviora 104: 1–7.

Robins, C. R. 1960. Studies on fishes of the family Ophidiidae. V. *Lepophidium pheromystax*, a new Atlantic species allied to *Lepophidium jeannae* Fowler. Bull. Mar. Sci. Gulf Carib. 10: 83–95.

Robins, C. R. 1966. Additional comments on the structure and relationships of the mirapinniform fish, Family Kasidaroidae. Bull. Mar. Sci. 16: 696–701.

Robins, C. R. 1986. The status of the ophidiid fishes *Ophidium brevibarbe* Cuvier, *Ophidium graellsi* Poey, and *Leptophidium profundorum* Gill. Proc. Biol. Soc. Wash. 99: 384–387.

Robins, C. R. 1989. Phylogenetic relationships of anguilliform fishes. *In:* FWNA 9(1): 9–23.

Robins, C. R., and D. P. de Sylva. 1965. The Kasidoroidae, a new family of mirapinniform fishes from the western Atlantic ocean. Bull. Mar. Sci. Gulf Carib. 15: 187–201.

Robins, C. R., and J. Nielsen. 1970. *Synderidia bothrops,* a new tropical amphi-American species (Pisces, Carapidae). Stud. Trop. Oceanogr. 4: 285–293.

Robins, C. R., G. C. Ray, J. Douglass, and R. Freund. 1986. A field guide to Atlantic coast fishes of North America. (The Peterson Field Guide Series, 32.) Boston: Houghton Mifflin, 324 pp.

Robinson, M. C. 1969. Elasmobranch records and range extensions for the Texas Gulf coast. Texas J. Sci. 21: 235–236.

Rofen, R. R. 1959. The whale-fishes: families Cetomimidae, Barourisiidae and Rondeletiidae (order Cetunculi). Results from the Danish deep-sea expedition round the world, 1950–52. Galathea Rep. 1: 255–260.

Rofen, R. R. 1963. Diagnoses of new genera and species of alepisauroid fishes of the family Paralepididae. Aquatica 2: 1–7.

Rofen, R. R. 1966. Family Paralepididae. *In:* FWNA 5: 205–459.

Rofen, R. R. 1966b. Family Omosudidae. *In:* FWNA 5: 462–481.

Rofen, R. R. 1966c. Family Evermannellidae. *In:* FWNA 5: 511–565.

Rofen, R. R. 1966d. Family Scopelarchidae. *In:* FWNA 5: 566–602.

Rohr, B. A., and E. J. Gutherz. 1977. Biology of offshore hake, *Merluccius albidus,* in the Gulf of Mexico. U.S. Nat. Mar. Fish. Serv. Fish. Bull. 75: 147–158.

Rosen, D. E. 1973. Suborder Cyprinodontoidei. *In:* FWNA 6: 229–262.

Rosen, D. E. 1979. Fishes of the uplands and intermontane basins of Guatemala: revisionary studies and comparative biogeography. Bull. Amer. Mus. Nat. Hist. 162: 267–376.

Rosen, D. E., and R. M. Bailey. 1963. The poeciliid fishes (Cyprinodontiformes), their structure, zoogeography, and systematics. Bull. Amer. Mus. Nat. Hist. 126: 1–176.

Rosenblatt, R. H., and G. D. Johnson. 1976. Anatomical considerations of pectoral swimming in the opah, *Lampris guttatus.* Copeia: 367–370.

Ross, S. W., and J. H. Caruso. 1984. First record of *Lophiodes* from the United States Atlantic coast. Northeast Gulf Sci. 7: 117–118.

Roule, L. 1922. Sur un genre de Poisson abyssal japonais très rare, nouvellement retrouvé dans l'Ocean Nord-Africain. Comptes Rendus Acad. Sci. Paris 174: 640–642.

Sadowsky, V., A. F. de Amorim, and C. A. Anfelli. 1984. Second occurrence of *Odontaspis noronhai* (Maul, 1955). São Paulo: B. Inst. Pesca 11: 69–79.

Sadowsky, V., and P. Soares Moreira. 1981. Occurrence of *Squalus cubensis* Rivero, 1936, in the western South Atlantic Ocean, and incidence of its parasitic isopod *Lironecta splendida* sp. nov. Stud. Neotrop. Fauna Environ. 16(1981): 137–150.

Sage, M., R. G. Jackson, W. L. Klesch, and V. L. de Vlaming. 1972. Growth and seasonal distribution of the elasmobranch,

Dasyatis sabina. Contrib. Mar. Sci. 16: 71–74.

Saksena, V. P., and W. J. Richards. 1986. A new species of gadiform fish, *Bregmaceros houdei,* from the western Atlantic. Bull. Mar. Sci. 38: 285–292.

Sazonov, Y. I., and T. Iwamoto. 1992. Grenadiers (Pisces, Gadiformes) of the Nazca and Sala y Gomez ridges, southeastern Pacific. Proc. Calif. Acad. Sci. 48: 27–95.

Sazonov, Y. I., and M. Miya. 1996. First record of the platytroctid fish *Mentodus facilis* (Salmoniformes: Alepocephaloidea) from Japanese waters. Ichthyol. Res. 43: 87–89.

Sazonov, Y. I, and Y. N. Shcherbachev. 1985. Preliminary review of grenadiers of the *Cetonurus* group (Gadiformes, Macrouridae). Part 2, The genus *Cetonurus* Günther: taxonomic characters of the group. J. Ichthyol. 25: 12–27.

Schaefer, S., R. K. Johnson, and J. Babcock. 1986a. Family No. 73. Photichthyidae. *In:* SSF: 243–247.

Schaefer, S., R. K. Johnson, and J. Babcock. 1986b. Family No. 74. Gonostomaitidae. *In:* SSF: 247–253.

Schmid, T. H., L. M. Ehrhart, and F. F. Snelson, Jr. 1988. Notes on the occurrence of rays (Elasmobranchii, Batoidea) in the Indian River Lagoon system, Florida. Fla. Sci. 51: 121–128.

Schroeder, W. C. 1955. Report on the results of exploratory otter trawling along the continental shelf between Nova Scotia and Virginia during the summers of 1952 and 1953. Papers in Marine Biology and Oceanography. London: Pergamon Press, pp. 358–372.

Schultz, L. P. 1957. The frogfishes of the family Antennariidae. Proc. U.S. Nat. Mus. 107(3383): 47–105.

Schultz, L. P. 1964. Family Sternoptchidae. *In:* FWNA 4: 241–273.

Schultz, L. P., and E. D. Reid. 1937. The American Atlantic toadfishes of the genus *Opsanus.* Copeia: 211–212.

Schwartz, F. J. 1990. Mass migratory congregations and movement of several species of cownose rays, genus *Rhinoptera:* a worldwide review. J. Elisha Mitchell Sci. Soc. 106: 10–13.

Schwartz, F. J., and G. H. Burgess. 1975. Sharks of North Carolina and adjacent waters. Inf. Ser. N. C. Dep. Nat. Econ. Resour., Div. Mar. Fish., 1975: 57 pp.

Schwartz, F. J., and M. D. Dahlberg. 1978. Biology and ecology of the Atlantic stingray, *Dasyatis sabina* (Pisces: Dasyatidae), in North Carolina and Georgia. Northeast Gulf Sci. 2: 1–23.

Scott, W. B., and M. G. Scott. 1988. Atlantic fishes of Canada. Toronto: Univ. Toronto Press, 731 pp.

Scott, W. B., and S. N. Tibbo. 1968. An occurrence of the pelagic stingray, *Dasyatis violacea,* in the northwestern Atlantic. J. Fish. Res. Bd. Canada 25: 1075–1076.

Seigel, J. A. 1978. Revision of the dalatiid shark genus *Squaliolus:* anatomy, systematics, ecology. Copeia: 602–614.

Seigel, J. A., T. W. Pietsch, B. H. Robison, and T. Abe. 1977. *Squaliolus sarmenti* and *S. alii,* synonyms of the dwarf deepsea shark, *Squaliolus laticaudus.* Copeia: 788–791.

Shcherbachev, Y. N. 1980. Preliminary review of the Indian Ocean species of the Chlorophthalmidae (Myctophiformes, Osteichthyes). *In:* Fishes of the open ocean, ed. N. V. Parin. Moscow: Acad. Sci. Inst. Oceanol., pp. 47–67.

Shcherbachev, Y. N., and T. Iwamoto. 1995. Indian Ocean grenadiers of the subgenus *Coryphaenodes,* genus *Coryphaenoides* (Macrouridae, Gadiformes, Pisces). Proc. Calif. Acad. Sci. 48: 285–314.

Shcherbachev, Y. N., Y. I. Sazonov, and T. Iwamoto. 1992. Synopsis of the grenadier genus *Kuronezumia* (Pisces: Gadiformes: Macrouridae), with descriptions of a new species. Proc. Calif. Acad. Sci. 48: 97–108.

Shipp, R. L., and T. S. Hopkins. 1978. Physical and biological observations of the northern rim of the DeSoto Canyon made from a research submersible. Northeast Gulf Sci. 2: 113–121.

Shirai, S. Squalean phylogeny, a new framework of "Squaloid" sharks and related taxa. Sapporo: Hokkaido Press, 151 pp.

Shirai, S., and H. Tachikawa. 1993. Taxonomic resolution of the *Etmopterus pusillus* species group (Elasmobranchii, Etmopteridae), with description of *E. bigelowi*, n. sp. Copeia: 483–495.

Shores, D. L. 1969. Postlarval *Sudis* (Pisces: Paralepididae) in the Atlantic Ocean. Breviora 334: 1–14.

Smith, C. L., and J. C. Tyler. 1969. Observations on the commensal relationships of the western Atlantic pearlfish, *Carapus bermudensis*, and holothurians. Copeia: 206–208.

Smith, D. G. 1989a. Family Anguillidae. *In:* FWNA 9(1): 25–47.

Smith, D. G. 1989b. Family Moringuidae. *In:* FWNA 9(1): 55–71.

Smith, D. G. 1989c. Family Clopsidae. *In:* FWNA 9(1): 72–97.

Smith, D. G. 1989d. Family Colocongridae. *In:* FWNA 9(1): 413–419.

Smith, D. G. 1989e. Family Nemichthyidae. *In:* FWNA 9(1): 441–459.

Smith, D. G. 1989f. Family Congridae. *In:* FWNA 9(1): 460–567.

Smith, D. G. 1989g. Family Nettastomatidae. *In:* FWNA 9(1): 568–612.

Smith, D. G. 1989h. Family Synaphobranchidae: Leptocephali. *In:* FWNA 9(2): 682–698.

Smith, D. G. 1989i. Family Moringuidae: Leptocephali. *In:* FWNA 9(2): 699–703.

Smith, D. G. 1989j. Family Nettastomatidae: Leptocephali. *In:* FWNA 9(2): 704–722.

Smith, D. G. 1989k. Family Congridae: Leptocephali. *In:* FWNA 9(2): 723–763.

Smith, D. G. 1989l. Family Anguillidae: Leptocephali. *In:* FWNA 9(2): 898–899.

Smith, D. G. 1989m. Family Muraenidae: Leptocephali. *In:* FWNA 9(2): 900–916.

Smith, D. G. 1989n. Family Nemichthyidae: Leptocephali. *In:* FWNA 9(2): 925–932.

Smith, D. G. 1989o. Family Clopsidae: Leptocephali. *In:* FWNA 9(2): 933–942.

Smith, D. G., J. E. Böhlke, and P. H. J. Castle. 1981. A revision of the nettastomatid eel genera *Nettastoma* and *Nettenchelys* (Pisces: Anguilliformes), with description of six new species. Proc. Biol. Soc. Wash. 94: 535–560.

Smith, D. G., and P. H. J. Castle. 1972. The eel genus *Neoconger* Girard: systematics, osteology, and life history. Bull. Mar. Sci. 22: 196–249.

Smith, D. G., and P. H. J. Castle. 1982. Larvae of the nettastomatid eels: systematics and distribution. Dana Rep. 90: 44 pp.

Smith, D. G., K. E. Hartel, and J. E. Craddock. 1991. Larval development, relationships, and distribution of *Manducus maderensis*, with comments on the transformation of *M. greyae* (Pisces: Stomiiformes). Breviora 491: 1–17.

Smith, D. G., and R. H. Kanazawa. 1977. Eight new species and a new genus of congrid eels from the western North Atlantic with redescription of *Ariosoma analis*, *Hildebrandia guppyi*, and *Rhechias vicinalis*. Bull. Mar. Sci. 27: 530–543.

Smith, D. G., and R. H. Kanazawa. 1989. *Xenomystax congroides*. *In:* FWNA 9(1): 563–567.

Smith, D. G., and J. G. Nielsen. 1989. Nemichthyidae. *In:* FWNA 9(1): 441–459.

Smith, G. B., H. M. Austin, S. A. Bortone, R. W. Hastings, and L. H. Ogren. 1975. Fishes of the Florida Middle Ground with comments on ecology and zoogeography. Fla. Mar. Res. Publ. 9: 1–14.

Smith, H. M., and L. Radcliffe. 1913. *In:* Descriptions of seven new genera and thirty-one new species of fishes of the families Brotulidae and Carapidae from the Philippine Islands and the Dutch East Indies, ed. L. Radcliffe. Proc. U.S. Nat. Mus. 44: 135–176, pls. 7–17.

Smith, J. W., and J. V. Merriner. 1985. Food habits and feeding behavior of the cownose ray, *Rhinoptera bonasus*, in lower Chesapeake Bay. Estuaries 8: 305–310.

Smith, J. W., and J. V. Merriner. 1986. Observations on the reproductive biology of the cownose ray, *Rhinoptera bonasus*, in Chesapeake Bay. U.S. Nat. Mar. Fish. Serv. Fish. Bull. 84: 871–877.

Smith, J. W., and J. V. Merriner. 1987. Age

and growth, movements and distribution of the cownose ray, *Rhinoptera bonasus,* in Chesapeake Bay. Estuaries 10: 153–164.

Smith, M. M. 1986a. Family No. 92. Bregmacerotidae. *In:* SSF: 329–330.

Smith, M. M. 1986b. Family No. 103. Chaunacidae. *In:* SSF: 369–370.

Smith, M. M. 1986c. Family No. 124. Ateleopodidae. *In:* SSF: 404–406.

Smith, M. M., and P. C. Heemstra. 1986. Smith's sea fishes. New York: Springer-Verlag, 1047 pp.

Snelson, F. F., Jr. 1983. Ichthyofauna of the northern part of the Indian River Lagoon system, Florida. Fla. Sci. 46(3/4): 187–206.

Snelson, F. F., Jr., T. J. Mulligan, and S. E. Williams. 1984. Food habits, occurrence, and population structure of the bull shark, *Carcharhinus leucas,* in a Florida coastal lagoon. Bull. Mar. Sci. 34: 71–80.

Snelson, F. F., Jr., and S. E. Williams. 1981. Notes on the occurrence, distribution and biology of elasmobranch fishes in the Indian River Lagoon system, Florida. Estuaries 4: 110–120.

Snelson, F. F., Jr., S. E. Williams-Hooper, and T. H. Schmid. 1988. Reproduction and ecology of the Atlantic stingray, *Dasyatis sabina,* in Florida coastal lagoons. Copeia: 729–739.

Snelson, F. F., Jr., S. E. Williams-Hooper, and T. H. Schmid. 1989. Biology of the bluntnose stingray, *Dasyatis sayi,* in Florida coastal lagoons. Bull. Mar. Sci. 45: 15–25.

Springer, S. 1938. Notes on sharks of Florida. Proc. Fla. Acad. Sci. 3: 9–41.

Springer, S. 1939. Two new Atlantic species of dog sharks, with a key to the species of *Mustelus.* Proc. U.S. Nat. Mus. 86(3058): 461–468.

Springer, S. 1948. Oviphagous embryos of the sand shark, *Carcharias taurus.* Copeia: 153–157.

Springer, S. 1950a. A revision of North American sharks allied to the genus *Carcharhinus.* Amer. Mus. Novit. 1451: 13 pp.

Springer, S. 1950b. Natural history notes on the lemon shark, *Negaprion brevirostris.* Texas J. Sci. 1950: 349–359.

Springer, S. 1960. Natural history of the sandbar shark, *Eulamia milberti.* U.S. Fish Wildl. Serv. Fish. Bull. 61: 1–38.

Springer, S. 1963. Field observations on large sharks of the Florida-Caribbean region. *In:* Sharks and survival, ed. P. W. Gilbert et al. Boston: D. C. Heath, pp. 93–113.

Springer, S. 1966. A review of the western Atlantic cat sharks, Scyliorhinidae, with descriptions of a new genus and five new species. U.S. Fish Wildl. Serv. Fish. Bull. 65: 581–624.

Springer, S. 1967. Social organization of shark populations. *In:* Sharks, skates and rays, ed. P. W. Gilbert et al. Baltimore: Johns Hopkins Press, pp. 149–174.

Springer, S. 1979. A revision of the catsharks, Family Scyliorhinidae. NOAA Tech Rep. NMFS Circ. 422: 97 pp.

Springer, S., and H. T. Bullis. 1956. Collections made by the *Oregon* in the Gulf of Mexico. U.S. Fish Wildl. Serv. Spec. Sci. Rep. Fish. 196: 1–134.

Springer, S., and G. H. Burgess. 1985. Two new dwarf dogsharks (*Etmopterus,* Squalidae), found off the Caribbean coast of Colombia. Copeia: 584–591.

Springer, S., and P. W. Gilbert. 1976. The basking shark, *Cetorhinus maximus,* from Florida and California, with comments on its biology and systematics. Copeia: 41–54.

Springer, S., and V. Sadowsky. 1970. Subspecies of the western Atlantic cat shark, *Scyliorhinus retifer.* Proc. Biol. Soc. Wash. 83(7): 83–98.

Springer, S., and J. R. Thompson. 1957. Night sharks, *Hypoprion,* from the Gulf of Mexico and the Straits of Florida. Copeia: 160.

Springer, S., and R. A. Waller. 1969. *Hexanchus vitulus,* a new sixgill shark from the Bahamas. Bull. Mar. Sci. 19: 159–174.

Springer, V. G. 1957. Mysterious midshipman. Texas Game Fish (November): 6–7.

Springer, V. G. 1964. A revision of the carcharhinid shark genera *Scoliodon, Loxodon,* and *Rhizoprionodon.* Proc. U.S. Nat. Mus. 115(3493): 559–632.

Staiger, J. C. 1965. Atlantic flyingfishes of

the genus *Cypselurus*, with descriptions of the juveniles. Bull. Mar. Sci. 15: 672–725.

Stehmann, M., and D. L. Bürkel. 1984a. Torpedinidae. *In:* FN-EAM 1: 159–162.

Stehmann, M., and D. L. Bürkel. 1984b. Chimaeridae. *In:* FN-EAM 1: 212–215.

Stehmann, M., and D. L. Bürkel. 1984c. Rhinochimaeridae. *In:* FN-EAM 1: 216–218.

Stillwell, C., and J. G. Casey. 1976. Observations on the bigeye thresher shark, *Alopias superciliosus*, in the western North Atlantic. U.S. Nat. Mar. Fish. Serv. Fish. Bull. 74: 221–225.

Strasburg, D. W. 1963. The diet and dentition of *Isistius brasiliensis*, with remarks on tooth replacement in other sharks. Copeia: 33–40.

Struhsaker, P. 1965. The whalefish *Barourisia rufa* (Cetunculi) from waters off southeastern United states. Copeia: 376–377.

Struhsaker, P. 1969. Observations on the biology and distribution of the thorny stingray, *Dasyatis centroura* (Pisces: Dasyatidae). Bull. Mar. Sci. 19: 456–481.

Suarez, S. S. 1975. The reproductive biology of *Ogilbia cayorum*, a viviparous brotulid fish. Bull. Mar. Sci. 25: 143–173.

Sulak, K. J. 1974. Morphological and ecological observations on Atlantic ipnopid fishes of the genus *Bathytphlops*. Copeia: 570–573.

Sulak, K. J. 1977. The systematics and biology of *Bathypterois* (Pisces, Chlorophthalmidae) with a revised classification of benthic myctophiform fishes. Galathea Rep. 14: 49–108.

Sulak, K. J. 1984a. Aulopidae. *In:* FN-EAM 1: 403–404.

Sulak, K. J. 1984b. Synodontidae. *In:* FN-EAM 1: 405–411.

Sulak, K. J. 1984c. Chlorophthamidae. *In:* FN-EAM 1: 412–420.

Sulak, K. J. 1986a. Halosauridae. *In:* FN-EAM 2: 593–598.

Sulak, K. J. 1986b. Notacanthidae. *In:* FN-EAM 2: 599–603.

Sulak, K. J. 1986c. Family No. 52. Notacanthidae. *In:* SSF: 195–196.

Sulak, K. J. 1986d. Family No. 53. Halosauridae. *In:* SSF: 196–197.

Sulak, K. J. 1986e. Family No. 76. Chlorophthalmidae. *In:* SSF: 261–265.

Sulak, K. J., R. E. Crabtree, and J.-C. Hureau. 1984. Provisional review of the genus *Polyacanthonotus* (Pisces: Notacanthidae) with descriptions of a new species, *Polyacanthonotus merretti*. Cybium 8(4): 57–68.

Suttkus, R. D. 1956. First record of the mountain mullet, *Agonostomus monticola* (Bancroft), in Louisiana. Proc. Louisiana Acad. Sci. 19: 43–46.

Suttkus, R. D. 1963. Family Lepisosteidae. *In:* FWNA 3: 68–88.

Sutton, T. T., and T. L. Hopkins. 1996. Species composition, abundance, and vertical distribution of the stomiid (Pisces: Stomiiformes) fish assemblage of the Gulf of Mexico. Bull. Mar. Sci. 59: 530–542.

Sutton, T. T., and T. L. Hopkins. In press. Trophic ecology of the stomiid (Pisces: Stomiidae) assemblage of the eastern Gulf of Mexico: strategies, selectivity and impact of a top mesopelagic predator group. Mar. Biol. In press.

Svetovidov, A. N. 1962. Gadiformes. *In:* Fauna of the U.S.S.R., Fishes. Jerusalem: Nat. Sci. Found. by Israel Prog. Sci. Trans. 9(4): 1–304.

Tabb, D., and R. B. Manning. 1961. A checklist of the flora and fauna of northern Florida Bay and adjacent brackish waters of the Florida mainland collected during the period July 1957 through September 1960. Bull. Mar. Sci. Gulf Carib. 11: 552–649.

Taylor, W. R. 1978. Ariidae. *In:* FAO species identification sheets for fishery purposes: Western Central Atlantic (Fishing area 31), ed. W. Fischer. Rome: FAO.

Tesch, F. W. 1977. The eel. Biology and management of anguillid eels. London: Chapman & Hall, 434 pp.

Thorson, T. B. 1971. Movement of bull sharks, *Carcharhinus leucas*, between Caribbean Sea and Lake Nicaragua demonstrated by tagging. Copeia: 336–338.

Thorson, T. B. 1976. The status of the Lake Nicaragua shark: an update appraisal. *In:* Investigation of the ichthyofauna of Nicaraguan lakes, ed. T. B. Thorson. Lincoln: Univ. Nebraska Press, pp. 561–174.

Thorson, T. B. 1983. Observations on the morphology, ecology, and life history of the euryhaline stingray, *Dasyatis guttata* (Bloch & Schneider 1801). Acta Biologica Venezuelica 11: 95–125.

Tighe, K. A. 1989a. Family Serrivomeridae. *In:* FWNA 9(2): 613–627.

Tighe, K. A. 1989b. Family Serrivomeridae: Leptocephali. *In:* FWNA 9(2): 921–924.

Tolley, S. G., and E. B. Peebles. 1987. Occurrence of *Guntherichthys longipenis* (Osteichthyes: Bythitidae) in a southwest Florida estuary. Northeast Gulf Sci. 9: 43–45.

Tricas, T. C. 1979. Relationship of the blue shark, *Prionace glauca*, and its prey species near Santa Catalina Island, California. U.S. Nat. Mar. Fish. Serv. Fish. Bull. 77: 175–182.

Tringali, M. D., and R. R. Wilson, Jr. 1993. Differences in haplotype frequencies of mtDNA of the Spanish sardine *Sardinella aurita* between specimens from the eastern Gulf of Mexico and southern Brazil. Fish. Null. 91: 362–370.

Trott, L. B. 1981. A general review of the pearlfishes (Pisces: Carapidae). Bull. Mar. Sci. 31: 623–629.

Trunov, T. A. 1982. Species of the family Regalecidae (Lampridiformes) from the southeastern Atlantic. J. Ichthyol. 22(1): 1–6.

Tyler, J. C., C. R. Robins, C. L. Smith, and R. G. Gilmore. 1992. Deepwater populations of the western Atlantic pearlfish *Carapus bermudensis* (Ophidiiformes: Carapidae). Bull. Mar. Sci. 51: 218–223.

Uwate, K. B. 1979. Revision of the anglerfish Diceratiidae with descriptions of two new species. Copeia: 129–144.

Uyeno, T., K. Matsuura, and E. Fugii. 1983. Fishes trawled off Surinam and French Guiana. Tokyo: Japan Marine Fishery Resource Research Center.

Vari, R. P. 1982. Subfamily Hippocampinae. *In:* FWNA 8: 173–189.

Vergara, R. 1978. Merluccidae. *In:* FAO species identification sheets for fishery purposes. Western Central Atlantic (Fishing area 31), ed. W. Fischer. Rome: FAO.

Vladykov, V. D. 1955. A comparison of Atlantic sea sturgeon with a new subspecies from the Gulf of Mexico. J. Fish. Res. Bd. Canada 12: 754–761.

Vladykov, V. D., and J. R. Greeley. 1963. Order Acipenseroidei. *In:* FWNA 3: 24–60.

Vladykov, V. D., and E. Kott. 1980. First record of the lamprey, *Petromyzon marinus* L., in the Gulf of Mexico. Northeast Gulf Sci. 4: 49–50.

Wade, R. A. 1962. The biology of the tarpon, *Megalops atlanticus*, and the ox-eye, *Megalops cyprinoides*, with emphasis on larval development. Bull. Mar. Sci. Gulf Carib. 12: 545–622.

Walthers, V. 1961. A contribution to the biology of the Giganturidae with description of a new genus and species. Bull. Mus. Comp. Zool. 125: 297–319.

Walthers, V. 1964. Order Giganturoidei. *In:* FWNA 4: 566–577.

Weitzman, S. H. 1986. Order Stomiiformes. Introduction. *In:* SSF: 227–229.

Wenner, C. A. 1973. Occurrence of American eels, *Anguilla rostrata*, in waters overlying the eastern North American continental shelf. J. Fish. Res. Bd. Canada 30: 1752–1755.

Wenner, C. A. 1976. Aspects of the biology and morphology of the snake eel, *Pisodonophis cruentifer* (Pisces, Ophichthidae). J. Fish. Res. Bd. Canada 33: 656–665.

Wenner, C. A. 1984. Notes on the ophidioid fish *Dicrolene intronigra* from the middle Atlantic continental slope of the United States. Copeia: 538–541.

Whitehead, P. J. P. 1962. The species of *Elops* (Pisces: Elopidae). Ann. Mag. Nat. Hist., Ser. 13, 5: 321–329.

Whitehead, P. J. P. 1985. Clupeoid fishes of the world (Suborder Clupeoidei): An annotated and illustrated catalogue of the herrings, sardines, pilchards, sprats, shads, anchovies and wolf-herrings. Part I: Chirocentridae, Clupeidae and Pristigasteridae, ed. W. Fischer. FAO Fisheries Synopsis 125(1): 1–303.

Whitehead, P. J. P., G. J. Nelson, and T. Wongratana. 1988. Clupeoid fishes of the world (Suborder Clupeoidei): An annotated and illustrated catalogue of the herrings, sardines, pilchards, sprats, shads, anchovies and wolf-herrings. Part II: Engraulididae, ed. W. Fischer. FAO Fisheries Synopsis 125(2): 305–579.

Wiley, E. O. 1976. The phylogeny and biogeography of fossil and recent gars (Actinopterygii: Lepisosteidae). Misc. Publ. Univ. Kansas Mus. Nat. Hist. 64: 1–111.

Williams, J. T. 1983. Synopsis of the pearlfish subfamily Pyramodontinae (Pisces: Carapidae). Bull. Mar. Sci. 33: 846–854.

Williams, J. T., and R. L. Shipp. 1980. Observations on fishes previously unrecorded or rarely encountered in the northeastern Gulf of Mexico. Northeast Gulf Sci. 4: 17–27.

Williams, J. T., and R. L. Shipp. 1982. A new species of the genus *Echiodon* (Pisces: Carapidae) from the eastern Gulf of Mexico. Copeia: 845–851.

Wilson, P. C., and J. S. Beckett. 1970. Atlantic Ocean distribution of the pelagic stingray, *Dasyatis violacea*. Copeia: 696–707.

Wilson, R. R., Jr., and P. D. Alberdi, Jr. 1991. An electrophoric study of Spanish sardine suggests a single predominant species in the eastern Gulf of Mexico, *Sardinella aurita*. Can. J. Fish. Aquat. Sci. 48: 792–798.

Wolfson. F. H. 1983. Records of seven juvenile whale shark, *Rhiniodon typus*. J. Fish. Biol. 22: 647–655.

Wolfson, F. H. 1986. Occurrence of the whale shark, *Rhincodon typus,* Smith. *In:* Indo-Pacific Fish Biology, Proceedings of the Second International Conference on Indo-Pacific Fishes, ed. T. Uyeno et al. Tokyo: Ichthyological Soc. Japan, pp. 208–226.

Woods, L. P. 1965. A new squirrelfish, *Adioryx poco*, of the family Holocentridae from the Bahama Islands. Notulae Naturae 337: 1–5.

Woods, L. P., and P. M. Sonoda. 1973. Order Berycomorphi (Beryciformes). *In:* FWNA 6: 263–395.

Wooley, C. M. 1985. Evaluation of morphometric characters used in taxonomic separation of Gulf of Mexico sturgeon, *Acipenser oxyrhynchus desotoi. In:* North American sturgeon, Developments in the environmental biology of fishes, ed. F. Binkowski and S. I. Daroshov. Netherlands: Junk Publ. 6: 97–103.

Wooley, C. M., and E. J. Crateau. 1985. Movement, microhabitat, exploitation, and management of Gulf of Mexico sturgeon, Apalachicola River, Florida. N. Amer. J. Fish. Mgmt. 5: 590–605.

Wooten, C. M., and C. Lydeard. 1990. Allozyme variation in a natural contact zone between *Gambusia affinis* and *Gambusia holbrooki*. Biochem. Syst. Evol. 18: 169–173.

INDEX OF SCIENTIFIC NAMES